A HISTORY OF THE CATHOLIC CHURCH IN THE PACIFIC NORTHWEST

1743-1983

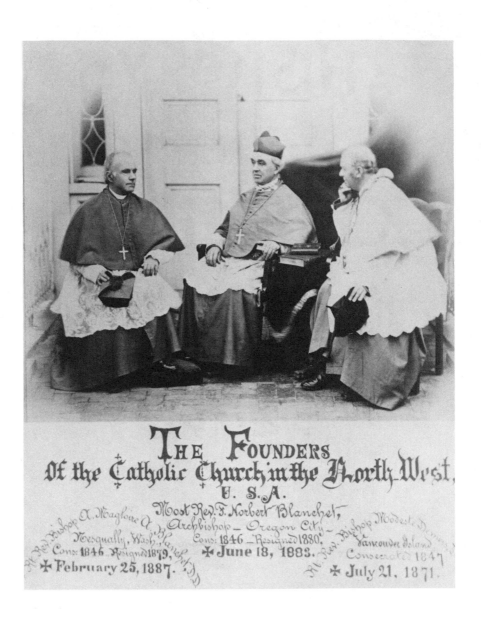

THE FOUNDERS
Of the Catholic Church in the North-West,
U. S. A.

Most Rev. F. Norbert Blanchet,
Archbishop — Oregon City,
Cons. 1846 — Resigned 1880,
✠ June 18, 1883.

Rt. Rev. Bishop A. Magloire A. Blanchet,
Nesqually, Wash.,
Cons. 1846 Resigned 1879,
✠ February 25, 1887.

Rt. Rev. Bishop Modeste Demers,
Vancouver Island,
Consecrated 1847,
✠ July 21, 1871.

A HISTORY OF
THE CATHOLIC CHURCH
IN THE PACIFIC NORTHWEST

1743-1983

WILFRED P. SCHOENBERG, S.J.

The Pastoral Press
Washington, DC

ISBN: 0-912405-25-2

The Pastoral Press
225 Sheridan Street, N.W.
Washington, D.C. 20011
(202) 723-5800

The Pastoral Press is the publications division of the National Association of Pastoral Musicians, a membership organization of musicians and clergy dedicated to fostering the art of musical liturgy.

Printed in the United States of America.

Dedicated to Mary,
the Immaculate Conception.
Patroness of America
"Our tainted nature's solitary boast."
Wordsworth

CONTENTS

ACKNOWLEDGMENTS

The history of the Catholic Church in the Pacific Northwest is presented for the first time in this volume. Compiling it has been my undeserved pleasure, made possible by the trust and generosity of almost countless others, among whom are the archbishops and bishops of this, the Twelfth Region, the publishers, and my own superiors.

Before performing the blessed rite of acknowledging my indebtedness by name, I would first like to state that it has been my intention in the present volume to call attention to published sources wherever possible. In the course of some thirty years, I have examined original records in every diocesan archive and most archives of religious orders in the Northwest. My references, however, reveal the existence and availability of reliable published sources with the cherished hope that others, making use of them, will be inspired to extend the perimeters of existing publications to innumerable volumes, erudite and pleasure giving, for the edification of our Catholics and the instruction of everyone who knows us.

Having got this off my chest, I now turn to the pleasant task of singling out those who deserve to be remembered in the present volume. First, there are the archbishops and bishops: Archbishop Cornelius Power of Portland in Oregon and Archbishop Raymond Hunthausen in Seattle; Bishops Thomas Connolly of Baker, William Skylstad of Yakima, Thomas Murphy of Great Falls, Laurence Welch of Spokane, Sylvester Treinen of Boise, and Auxiliary Bishops Paul Waldschmidt and Kenneth Steiner of Portland, all of whom have contributed to the cost of publication. Others who have contributed to the cost of publication are Mr. and Mrs. William Harmsen of Tucson and Mr. William Sherman of Portland. The use of my time for this project has been made possible by the generosity of my Provincial Superior, Father Thomas Royce, of Father John Kelley, Province Treasurer, Father Frank Costello, my Rector, and his assistant, Father Patrick Ford.

Obviously I owe everyone whose works I cite an expression of thanks. But the archivists and others who made records available deserve a special word. First among these are Father Clifford Carroll, Oregon Province Archivist at Gonzaga University, his successor Father Neill Meany, and his assistant, Brother Edward Jennings. Father Meany has generously provided my text with his maps. Three others among my Jesuit colleagues should be mentioned: Brother Robert Calouri, the Provincial's secretary (now deceased), Brother Michael Bennett, and Father Leo Kaufmann, a critical reader who has corrected galleys and offered other valuable, if sometimes surprising, suggestions. Another indefatigable reader was Monsignor John Doogan of Seattle, who knows more history of that archdiocese than anyone else, save God, at least so I think. Finally, Father Patrick Stewart of Tacoma, who was the appointed, very patient reader, the *peritus* whose approval was graciously granted.

The following are among the innumerable administrators or professionals who made my research forays in other depositories pleasant and profitable: Mary Ryan, Secretary to Bishop Waldschmidt; Mary Grant, Archivist, Portland Chancery Archives; Sister M. Anselma, Sisters of Providence Archives, Spokane; Father Martin Pollard, O.S.B., Mount Angel Archives; Father Dale McFarlane, Chancery Archives, Great Falls; Mary Ann Davis, Secretary to Bishop Connolly at Baker; Connie Flaherty Erickson, Chancery Archivist at Helena; Assistant Chancellor and Archivist, Father Donald Espen at Seattle, and his assistant Chris Bauer, who performed many kind services; Sister Rita Bergamini, Sisters of Providence Archives, Seattle; Sister Ann Herold, Sisters of the Holy Names Archives at Marylhurst and her successor, Sister Carolyn Ann Gimpl; Margaret Vocana of the *Catholic Sentinel*; Edward O'Meara, columnist and critic, Portland; Father Edward Kowrach and his assistant Father Theodore Bradley, Chancery Archives, Spokane; Father Gregory Moys, Chancellor, Portland; Father Joseph Browne, C.S.C., Librarian, and Father Barry Martin, C.S.C., University of Portland; Father John Scott, O.S.B., Archivist, St. Martin's Abbey; Joseph McKay, St. Paul (Oregon) Historical Society; Rose Coventry, Chancery Archives in Boise; Sister Brigitta Matt, Sisters of St. Dominic Archives, Spokane; Sister Jean Dorcy, O.P., well-known artist, Seattle; Mrs. Viola Weis of Uniontown, the compiler of Uniontown's stormy history; Polly and Bill Nordeen of Sandpoint, and Mrs. Dorothea Townsend of Spokane.

Special thanks also to my faithful typist, Charis Sherman Howser of Spokane, who managed to keep her perky little head on her shoulders despite the meticulous demands of this book and other duties occasioned by her husband and six lively children.

We all owe the publishers everlasting gratitude, especially Father Virgil Funk for his courage in undertaking so great a burden, and the editor, the irrepressible and sweet tempered Daniel Brendan Connors, whose expertise far exceeds his youthful exuberance. Others are Nancy Chvatal, Director of the western office in Portland; Lani Williams, Director of Marketing; and William Kalvin and all the people at Delmas Typesetting in Ann Arbor, Michigan.

My regrets, if I have failed by inadvertence to mention others deserving of it.

Wilfred P. Schoenberg
Gonzaga University

1

SOME PRELIMINARIES:
EARLY CATHOLIC INFLUENCES
1743–1847

The Catholic Church in the Pacific Northwest comprises two archdioceses, six dioceses and approximately six hundred parishes.[1] The total Catholic population in 1981 was exactly 939,931 souls. Located in what is regarded as "the most unchurched area" in the United States, it covers four states, Washington, Oregon, Idaho, and Montana, totalling 435,571 square miles, which is equal to the size of Italy, France, England and Ireland combined. In this vast area of wilderness, mountains, high plateaus and sea coast more extended than even sprawling California, Catholics represent only 11.3% of the population, exactly half of the national average.[2] This reveals the kind of uphill battle that Catholics have always experienced in an otherwise hospitable environment.

EARLY RESIDENTS: INDIANS

When Catholics first arrived, the area was thinly populated by its native residents, who had occupied it, at least in part, for something like ten thousand years. There were, in general, three categories of Indians: those who occupied the coastlands, sometimes generically referred to as "Canoe Indians," because of their common method of transportation; those who lived on the broad plateau between the lofty Cascades on the west and the rugged Rocky Mountains on the east, sometimes called "Pony Indians" to distinguish them from the Indians on the coastlands; and finally the Indians east of the Rockies on the high plains, also "Pony Indians" because of their common method of transportation.[3]

These Indians, estimated in 1846 to number something like fifty to seventy-five thousand in what is now the four northwestern states, spoke many different languages, none of which had been reduced to writing.[4] They practiced a great variety of customs and held numerous views about God and immortality, few, if any of them similar to the views of Christians.[5] References to "the Great Spirit" in later Indian history were largely the product of the Indians' exposure to non-Indian influences, which first appeared in the Northwest in the form of commerce. Merchants, sometimes crafty and crude, arrived by land from the East, then by ships from the Southwest, and finally, more effectively, by land again over the dusty trails of the mid-continent.

THE LA VERENDRYE EXPEDITION

There is some obscurity about those who came first. A Canadian Jesuit, Father Claude Coquard, assigned to visit the trading posts of the West to administer the sacraments, accompanied the two sons of the Chevalier La Verendrye, Pierre and Francois, on their historic voyage of 1742. Somewhere enroute Coquard parted from the expedition, because, it was said, some intrigue "prompted by jealousy forced him to leave."[6] The two adventurous Canadians, accompanied only by "two other Frenchmen," pressed on, arriving on New Year's Day, 1743, in the Belt Mountains near present Helena, Montana, from which they could see "the Shining Mountains," the Rockies.[7]

"In the course of the following year (1742)," says the Oblate Father Morice, church historian for western Canada, "took place that famous voyage which culminated in the [younger] Chevalier and his brother Francois de Lavréndrye discovering the Rocky Mountains, a spur of which they eventually partially climbed, after having faced numberless perils among hordes of uncouth savages (January, 1743). The explorers must have reached a point in the southwestern corner of what is now Montana."[8]

The latter is calculated speculation and probably accurate. Reuben Thwaites, another of western America's distinguished historians, simply states that after discovering the Rocky Mountains, Pierre and Francois "proceeded farther west for seven days before returning to Fort La Rein," near present Winnipeg, Canada.[9]

Though their stay was brief, it is not unlikely that the sons of La Verendrye and their two French companions left traces of their religion in Montana. "Seven days" farther west had brought them, very probably, to the Mission Valley, the *Sinielman*, the gathering place of the plateau tribes, where there was in residence at approximately this time, a chief, who was also reputed to be a mystic. "Shining Shirt" possessed a talisman of great power, a piece of metal inscribed with a cross. He predicted that "men with fair skin, dressed in long black skirts would come who would teach them the truth.... These Black Robes would teach people religion, would give them new homes and would make laws for their behavior."[10]

Each person can interpret what actually took place, for the records concerning this period are skimpy. But it is probable, I think, that the presence of four Catholics in western Montana in 1743 was duly noted by many Indians, who were groping for clearer concepts about the Great Spirit. Some Christian influence certainly had touched them. Thus it seems reasonable to conclude that the La Verendrye Expedition of 1742–1743 marked the beginning of the Catholic Church in the Northwest.

SPANISH EXPEDITIONS ALONG THE NORTHWEST COAST

Three decades later other Christian influences began to appear, superficially at first, along the shores of the Pacific. Spanish explorers, often motivated by a fierce urge to baptize the Indians, as much as by the desire to protect Spain's interests in the north Pacific, conducted a series of sea expeditions, which gave them, prescinding from the rights of the aborigines, the first and most binding claim to the region. There is a certain irony in all of this. The hard realities of geopolitics, combined with Spain's own mistakes, later compelled Spain to withdraw, leaving behind a Catholic nomenclature of landmarks, which was mostly destroyed by later explorers. But Spain is having the last word. The northwest church has become in recent years heavily populated with Catholics from old Mexico, the descendants of the Spanish colonials, who have returned in a sense, to claim their own.

In the sixteenth century, the Pacific Ocean was regarded as a Spanish lake. Only Spain had charts of parts of it and these were kept as well guarded as the bee keeps its honey; they had been gathered in the same way, a small portion at a time. But Spain, over-extended in its exploration and weakened by the expulsion of the Moriscoes, had lost much of its vitality by the seventeenth century when English ships began to challenge its monopoly in the Pacific. In the following century, both England and Russia were threatening rivals, mostly for the possession of the northwest coast where ports were needed to control the sea lanes to the Orient and where the currently popular fur trade was flourishing. To block the advance of Russia, which was moving south from Alaska, Spain was suddenly aroused in the latter half of the eighteenth century, and sent men in ships to explore the northwest coast to strengthen its own title to it. Among these men were Catholic chaplains, who brought with them not only their own Catholic traditions, but the sacraments, especially the Mass. Though these were nebulous, almost ethereaal beginnings, like the smoke of holy incense, one should regard them with the Christian's sense of values, as a presence that transcended political claims and monetary considerations.

The first of these eighteenth-century voyages was undertaken in 1774, two years before the founding of San Francisco. The northwest coast was undiscovered as yet. Antonio Bucareli.[11] Mexican Viceroy acting for Spain with characteristic vigor and determination, dispatched Juan Perez as commander of the brig *Santiago* from San Blas on January 25, with instructions to proceed as far north as 60° degrees and take possession of the country wherever possible.[12] Two Franciscan priests, Father Juan Crespi and Father Thomas de la Perra, accompanied the expedition as chaplains.

"*Santiago* sailed out of the [Monterey] harbor on Saturday, June 11. On the next day, Sunday, both Fathers celebrated Holy Mass and did so every Sunday but two throughout the voyage."[13] Thus as the brig moved cautiously north off the coast of Oregon and Washington, Mass was offered for the first time in these waters. "Fr. Perra during his Mass preached sermons. Holy Mass was also offered up by both Fathers on Principal feast days whenever the sea was sufficiently calm. Every evening the whole crew and their officers would recite the Rosary of the Blessed Virgin and other prayers together with the Fathers....As further evidence of the piety of the commander and his men, it may be noted that Holy Communion was received several times."[14]

When the vessel reached "forty-five degrees and thirty-five minutes latitude," on the high seas about due west of present Portland, Oregon, "the weather began to grow cold, but nothing extraordinary happened, except that one sailor, who had suffered from malignant fever, received the last Sacraments."[15] Thus, on this first voyage of exploration of the northwest coast, the customary practices of Catholicism appeared—the Mass, the preaching of the Gospel, the recitation of the rosary, and the administration of the sacraments.

Perez sailed northward until he first sighted land off the present coast of British Columbia, at 53°, 53' latitude. On the following day he named a cliff-like point "Santa Marguerite," honoring an old custom of Spaniards in the southwest of giving saints' names to landmarks.[16] On his return journey, on August 8, Perez found an anchorage which he named San Lorenze at approximately 49° 30', just north of the present American border. "When he finally dropped anchor in Monterey, California in late August, he had achieved the distinction of having discovered a portion of the Oregon and Washington Coast, the two great islands that make up the coast of British Columbia and also of giving the first description of the Northwestern natives."[17]

FIRST EUROPEANS SET FOOT
ON THIS NORTHWEST COAST

The success of his expedition prompted another, which Bucareli dispatched from San Blas on March 16, 1775. On this journey Bruno de Heceta [Ezeta], Lieutenant in the royal navy, was placed in command of the *Santiago*, and Perez was assigned to his command as sailing master. Accompanying the *Santiago* as her consort was the schooner *Sonora*, with Juan Francisco de la Bodega y Cuadra in charge. Aboard the two vessels were Franciscan Fathers Miguel de la Campa and Benito Sierra as chaplains.[18] The expedition reached Monterey in late May. "From thence they sailed northward to the present Point Grenville [Washington State] in latitude 47° 20', to the north of which Isla de Delores, or Destruction Island, was discovered and named [on July 13.]"[19]

"Early in the morning of the next day, Captain Bruno Ezeta, Fr. Benito Sierra, Surgeon Davalos, Cristobal the second pilot, and a few sailors landed and raised a cross on shore. *They were the first Europeans who set foot on this northwest coast.* . . . Before seven o'clock all returned to the frigate."[20]

Cuadra in the *Sonora*, anchored a few miles further north, sent a party of seven men ashore for wood and water. They had no sooner beached their boat, however, than they were attacked by natives. Two of the sailors leaped into the sea and were drowned, while the others were killed and their bodies torn to pieces. Succor was impossible. Seven Catholic men had died on the shores of Washington a year before the War of American Independence.

During a storm at sea, Heceta's two vessels became separated. Cuadra continued his course north, making further discoveries and additional speeches "of formal possession" in Alaska, while Heceta, with most of his crew in sick bay, turned southward to seek help. The winds were favorable, but when the *Santiago* passed the 46° latitude, Heceta tarried long enough to peer into the coastal fogs, hoping to discover evidence of the legendary straits that were presumed to be somewhere in the vicinity.[21] He paused briefly at sea between the capes of the Columbia River and concluded, from the currents and the eddies, that the place was "the mouth of some great river, or of some passage to another sea."[22] Short of men and denied any attempt of a landing by the fall of darkness, Heceta remained offshore until the next morning when heavier fogs obstructed his vision. He was unable to make his way back into what he called the "Ensenoda de Hezeta," the mouth of a river on which he bestowed the title of St. Roc.[23]

Cuadra rejoined Heceta on October 7 at Monterey whence both vessels sailed for San Blas, where they arrived on November 20.

Thus the whole extent of the northwest coast, from the northern California border to Alaska, was discovered and formally declared in favor of Spain by Perez, Heceta, and Cuadra in 1774–1775. "They gave to Spain whatever credit and territorial claims may be founded on the act of first discovery."[24]

In the following year orders were issued from Spain to fit out another expedition to continue the explorations on the northwest coast. Execution of these orders was delayed for three years, partly because the viceroy had ordered two new ships to serve on the expedition and partly because of the expulsion of the Jesuits from Spanish territories several years earlier.

This requires some explanation. First, the Jesuits were expelled by Charles III for political reasons "concealed in the royal bosom."[25] They conducted sixteen prosperous missions in lower California, which they were directed by His Catholic Majesty to hold until they were replaced by the Franciscans from Mexico.[26] This not only required a year's time, but reduced the number of Franciscans available for other missions of the crown, including chaplaincies on vessels crossing the sea. It was commonly understood that Spanish sailors did not embark on ships without chaplains, for their chances of perishing at sea, until a cure for scurvy was discovered by Cook, was one out of three.[27]

THE ARTEAGA EXPEDITION OF 1779

Thus Bucareli's energetic efforts to comply with orders sent from Spain were frustrated, not only by delays in the construction of a ship at San Blas, but also by his inability to provide chaplains. Nonetheless, by 1779 he had got his act together, dispatched two frigates, the *La Princesa* built in San Blas and the *La Favorita* purchased in Peru, under the command of Ignacio Arteaga to the northwest coast.[28] Departing from port on February 11, the two ships bore northward at a spanking pace, crossing latitude 54° by late April. Having entered Alaskan waters a few days later, the vessels entered Becareli Sound, named for the viceroy, of course, and remained there until July 15, compiling the best survey of that remote region ever made. Here, too, on May 13 they erected a cross and celebrated a solemn Mass, about which Bancroft commented with his characteristic pose of superiority, "to the accompaniment of music and artillery, the waving of flags and impressive salvos of musketry, the royal banner of Castille was unfurled to the breeze, while the ignorant natives gazed stolidly at this insanity of civilization."[29]

There were three priests present for the Mass, Franciscans Juan Garcia Riobo and Matias de Santa Catarina y Noriega, chaplains on the *Princesa*, and Father Cristobal Diaz, a secular priest from Peru, the first secular priest in the Northwest, chaplain on the *Favorita*.[30]

When the Arteaga expedition returned to San Blas in November the viceroy was dead.[31] Before his death he had declared himself highly pleased with the results of the voyage, feeling that "Spain's rights to all the northern country were at last secure, and that no further discoveries in a northerly direction would be required."[32] The vessels' crews learned, also, that Spain had declared war on England and that English ships had penetrated the frigid waters of the north.[33] Thus Spain's security was short-lived. Within the decade encroachments by English, American, and even French vessels forced Spain to face the challenge again by sending other expeditions and by establishing a fortified port at Nootka Sound on the ocean-side of Vancouver Island. Soon swarms of other ships, mostly English and American, some carrying Portuguese flags, invaded north-coast waters in the interest of trading for furs. Spanish policy, uncertain, vacillating, and timid, frightened off no one, unless it be themselves.

THE FIRST CATHOLIC SETTLEMENT AT NEAH BAY

In the spring of 1790, Captain Francisco Elisa was placed in charge of a small fleet of three ships, including the *Concepcion*, commanded by himself.[34] Lieutenant Salvador Fidalgo was captain of the *San Carlos*, and Alferez Manuel Quimper captain of the *Princesa Royal [Real]*, a sloop that had been captured from the British.[35]

Since the latter was instrumental in the founding of the first settlement on the American northwest coast, an explicitly *Catholic* settlement, I would like to include a description of it. The *Princesa Royal* was forty-three feet long on the keel and sixteen feet on the beam. It drew eight feet of water aft and seven and onehalf feet forward. Sloop-rigged, it bore a sixty-five ton burden and carried four one-pound cannons and eight swivel guns.[36]

The voyage north to Nootka Sound was uneventful. The less speedy *Princesa Royal* arrived two days after the others, on April 7. On May 4, Fidelgo and his men were ordered to proceed to Alaska to make additional explorations and on May 31 Quimper was dispatched to explore the Straits of Juan de Fuca. For several weeks the *Princesa Royal* darted in and out along the shores of the strait, arriving at last at a bay near the entrance on Sunday, August 1. In his formal report to officials in Spain, Quimper described what followed:

> Aug. 1. Day dawned with cloudy weather and a light wind from the W. At 6 [a.m.] I sent the longboat and one of the canoes with the pilot and second pilot to draw up the plan of the bay. At 1 they returned. At 2 I took

possession of it with all ceremonies which the instructions prescribe, had a cross planted close to the river, and the bottle buried at the foot of a large pine behind the cross. The pine bears NNE (of the compass) with the most northerly part of the island. At 3 I returned three salutes of musketry having been fired on shore, under my orders. The sloop answered with twenty-one shots. I bestowed on the bay the name of Nuñez Gaona.[37]

With this report Quimper included the specific details "of taking possession," a curious document, presented here in part because of its professedly religious nature.

In the name of the Most Holy Trinity, Father, Son and Holy Ghost, three persons and one true God, the first maker and creator of all things and without whom nothing good can be done, commenced or preserved, and because the good beginning of anything must be in and by God, it is therefore advisable to commence it for His glory and honor. In His most holy name may it be known to all those to whom the present testimonial, instrument or letter of possession comes, that today, Sunday, August 1, 1790, this sloop the *Princesa Real*, of the very illustrious and pious Catholic Señor Don Carlos IV....

In sign of possession, laying hand on his sword which he carried in his belt, he cut with it trees, branches and grass and moved stones and walked over fields and the beach without contradiction from anyone, asking those present to be witnesses to it and me, Esteban Banales, the clerk appointed by the command of this expedition to make a testimony of it in public form. Then immediately taking the large cross on their shoulders, the men of the vessel, being arranged in martial order, with their muskets and other arms, they carried this in procession, chanting a litany with all responding. The procession being concluded, the commander placed the cross and erected a pile of stones at the foot of it as a memorial and sign of possession of all these seas and lands and their districts, continuous and contiguous and named the bay Nuñez Goana in honor of a respected real admiral of the Spanish navy. As soon as the cross was planted, they adored it a second time and all begged and supplicated our Lord, Jesus Christ, to be pleased, as this would be for his holy service for the exalting and augmentation of the Faith, and for the sowing of the Holy Evangel among these barbarous nations who up to the present have turned away from the true knowledge and doctrine. The ceremony being over, the commander for a more perpetual sign of memorial and possession, had a tree stripped on which a cross was made and placed on it the following inscription: 'Sanisimo nombre de Nuestro Senor Jesu Cristo' with these four initials 'INRI'. At the foot of the cross he put Carolus IV Rex Hisperiarum. In order, this was signed by the commander and the witnesses, First Pilot Don Gonzalo de Haro and Pilot Don Juan Carrasco and I, the clerk appointed by the said commander.[38]

Characteristically this ceremony ignored the presence or rights of the Indians. There were at that time, says one authority, about two thousand Makahs, who called their bay "Nisina."[39] They were shirt-tail relatives of the Nootkas, who numbered about six thousand, and both tribes were friendly to the whites, despite American reports to the contrary.

On this first occasion, however solemn, the Spaniards remained only three days at Puerto Nuñez Gaona, which is now called Neah Bay. On August 4, Quimper sailed off under cloudy skies, and returned to Monterey.[40]

For two years nothing more' was done. Then on March 23, 1792, Lieutenant Salvador Fidalgo left San Blas in the *Princesa* and proceeded directly to Puerto Nuñez Gaona [Neah Bay] with instructions to build a fort there, as one of several in Spain's line of defense. Since the vessel was loaded with livestock, cows, pigs, sheep, and goats, as well as chickens, it was not a pleasant voyage. On May 29, the *Princesa* cast anchor in the bay. Fidalgo, employing his men to advantage, quickly built a shed on shore, cleared trees and built a house for a bakery and oven, then a blacksmith shop, and finally barracks for the staff. In the weeks that followed, six guns were mounted, pens and corrals were assembled for the livestock, fruit trees were set out and several large gardens were planted in what was regarded as uncommonly rich soil.[41]

The records say nothing about horses, which the conquistadores loved almost as much as their wives, proof, if any is required, that the Spaniards had no intention of invading the interior of the northwest, at least until their coastlines had been made secure. Nor do the records mention a chapel or a chaplain, a rather extraordinary oversight in view of the common practice. Chaplains had lived at Nootka, between voyages, serving the Indians as well as the Spaniards. Many of the former became Catholics, indeed since then the Nootkas have been regarded as a Catholic tribe.

Some of the Makhas, too, were converted, implying the presence of a priest and a special place of worship. The Spaniards, whatever their faults and sins, would not have had it otherwise.

AMERICAN EXPLORER, CAPTAIN ROBERT GRAY

Meanwhile, a Yankee ship called the *Columbia*, its skipper young, impetuous Captain Robert Gray, who was sometimes given to fits of anger, had entered the water that Spain claimed, mostly for the sake of trading with the Indians. On May 11 of that year, when the *Princesa*, plowing north through the waves, was already off the coast of Oregon,

Gray entered the St. Roc River [first discovered and named by Heceta], sailed serenely up its course far enough to obtain fresh water and "view the country." It took him three days to find the channel again for making his exit. Then he turned north again, under full sail on the high seas, to find other villages of Indians for trade. Though he scarcely realized the importance of his discovery, he gave a new name to the river, which still bears it. He called it "the Columbia's," the possessive form suggesting that he was thinking of his country as well as his ship.[42]

This daring adventure into the strange, unknown interior, oddly revealed to the world by the English explorer, George Vancouver, proved to be America's best claim to the northwest after the Spanish abandoned it.

On Gray's ship there was a youthful officer, named John Boit, who was a brother-in-law of one of its owners. Boit kept a log in which he made the following entry: "There was a small good harbour situate [sic] about 5 leagues from Cape Flattery within the Straits of Juan de Fuca, the Spaniards had erected a cross upon the beach, and had about 10 houses and several good gardens."[43]

No doubt Boit also took note of the six guns pointed not toward the forests, where the natives lived, but toward the shore, whence Spain's traditional rivals, the English, would have to come, passing the huge log cross on the beach, as they did so. Boit also knew that Gray had used *his* guns on the Indians, killing many of them and earning for the Americans the contemptuous title of "the Bostons."[44]

Boit did not know, nor did any of the residents of Nuñez Gaona know, how soon this village would be abandoned. In less than a year Cuadra at Nootka Sound gave Fidelgo order to desert it and return to Monterey.[45] When the *Princesa* departed, it carried what remnants it could, even some of the Catholic Indians, leaving behind indisputable evidence of their settlers' earlier intention to remain. Fire-baked bricks, probably used in the construction of ovens, were found there many years later.[46]

The significance of Neah Bay has been overlooked ever since. It was the first settlement of Europeans in the American Northwest. It was also the first Catholic "mission." Perhaps one has to use this expression in the broadest sense, for documents are lacking to support it. Nevertheless there seems to be no doubt that Nuñez Gaona, a Spanish village on American soil, was also a Catholic one. If there seems to be a strange conspiracy of silence about these roots of Christianity in our region, it is a Catholic oversight as well as another's. This is probably due to Anglo-Saxon America's failure to understand and accept, until recent years, Spain's contributions to our culture.

Alas for Spain! England succeeded in bluffing her until she departed in shame. In March 1795 Spain ceded Nootka Sound to the English, which in effect put an end to Spanish voyages on the northwest coast.[47]

THE LEWIS AND CLARK EXPEDITION

There was one flaw in Spain's claims to the Northwest: all of her explorations had been conducted by sea. Only two nations could readily penetrate the unknown continent south of the 49th latitude, that is by land, to establish claims to the Northwest. These were the United States and England, the latter via Canada. The United States was not the first to act because the immense interior of the continent, known only as Louisiana, belonged to France. But in 1803, President Jefferson concluded secret negotiations for its purchase, and a United States Army expedition, commanded by Captain Meriwether Lewis and Lieutenant James Rogers Clark, encamped on the Upper Missouri already poised to strike west. They departed finally for the Northwest in the spring of 1805.[48] Their journey of discovery, one of the greatest in history, brought them literally to the shores of Oregon and back to St. Louis the following year.

Neither Lewis nor Clark were Catholics, but a fair portion of their twenty-nine men were, including the interpreter, Jean Baptiste Charbonneau, who brought with him one of his three wives.[49] This was Sacajawea who became renowned as the principal guide and interpreter of the expedition.[50]

It is most unlikely that Charbonneau or his Catholic companions celebrated anything like a Catholic service during their journey. On the contrary, it is highly probable that they manifested their familiarity with the diety only by using profanity. Despite this the Catholic presence spoke for itself, however unworthy. The church is made of sinners, and sinners there were with Captain Lewis. So was the church.

THE FUR COMPANIES

All of these early Catholic beginnings, if one could call them that, were short lived. There now appeared in southwestern Montana another source of Catholicism that provided not only passing influences but the presence of the church over a long period of time. By the beginning of the nineteenth century the fur trade had penetrated most of the interior of the north and western Canada and Alaska. The largest and most powerful of the fur trading organizations were based in Canada. Two of these were the Hudson's Bay Company, an old corporation chartered in 1670 by the King of England himself, and the Northwest Company, its principal rival.[51] In both there were several levels of status, the more educated upper middle class men, often called factors or traders, occupying top rank. Many of these men were of Scottish descent and Presbyterian in religion. Working under them were assistants, mostly of Scottish descent, destined to become factors when new posts were established or when older men retired or were killed, as sometimes happened.

At the bottom of the corporate ladder were the gutsy boatmen, the *voyageurs*, who transported the furs overland in large canoes. Most of these men were Canadian Catholics, some of part Indian descent. Others were full blooded Indians of the Iroquois tribe. Also Catholics, were descendants of the Indians who had tortured and killed Jesuit missionaries in the seventeenth century in what is now New York state or in eastern Canada.

There were also some American fur companies, the most important of which was John Jacob Astor's Pacific Fur Company. This company founded Astoria on the Oregon coast, at the mouth of the Columbia River, and surrendered it during the War of 1812 to the British, who renamed it Fort George. Many of Astor's men were Canadians, lured from the other companies, and some of these, too, were Catholics, at least in name, if not always in practice.

It may be assumed, I think, that most of the *voyageurs* were hearty souls with deep Catholic convictions, but of loose morals, partly due to the wild environment in which they lived most of the year. But there were exceptions, especially among the Iroquois Indians. One of these was Ignace La Mousse who settled with other Iroquois among the Flathead Indians in southwestern Montana. The exact date of his arrival is given by Archbishop Francis Norbert Blanchet. "In the year 1812," he wrote, "twenty-four Catholic Iroquois Indians from Canada deserted from the expedition organized by Captain Hunt in 1811, and took up their abode among the Flathead nation where they intermarried and raised numerous families."[52] It will be remembered that this region of the Flatheads was, according to Morice, the western terminus of the La Verendrye expedition.

Ignace La Mousse, often referred to as "Old Ignace," to distinguish him from his worthy son "Young Ignace," was as devout in his religion as some of the *voyageurs* were lax. He converted many Flatheads, taught them prayers, and conducted a regular prayer service for many years, before he was able to persuade his adopted tribesmen to seek Blackrobes in the East.

FIRST REQUEST FOR PRIESTS

This required a considerable amount of time. Meanwhile there was at least one early request for priests that is almost as mysterious as the unknown wilderness from which it came. In the *Annals of the Association for the Propagation of the Faith* for both Lyons and Paris in 1823, there appeared a quotation from a letter by an unknown woman somewhere on the Columbia River in Oregon. It had been sent, it is said, to Bishop Dubourg of New Orleans. Translated from French the account reads as follows:

> Last year Monsignor [Bishop Dubourg] received a letter from an English woman who was more than a thousand leagues from St. Louis, on the Columbia River near the Pacific Coast. She implored him to send a priest. There are in that region nearly fifteen hundred Catholics and five hundred Protestants who are entirely deprived of religious services. This establishment [the Association] is growing, but alas! there is nobody to send.[53]

Despite its content of obvious errors, for example the estimated number of Catholics in the region, there is no reason to believe the letter was a hoax. But who was the woman of mystery? No copy of the letter exists in this country or another, and one can only speculate about her in an idle way. We know, however, that the letter did not produce results, for there were no available priests to send from midAmerica or France.

The mystery letter had been sent, apparently, in 1821, a critical year in the history of the fur companies, upon which the permanent beginnings of the church would depend. During that year, certain complications having been resolved by two deaths within a brief period, the Hudson's Bay Company and the Northwest Company were able to merge, forming one corporation under the name of the older institution.[54]

DR. JOHN McLOUGHLIN

The Hudson's Bay Company came into formal possession of the Oregon fur trade when its top executive, Governor George Simpson arrived at Fort George in 1824. Accompanying him was the newly appointed Chief Factor of the Oregon post, Dr. John McLoughlin, a Canadian of Irish-Scottish descent, who had been baptized as a Catholic but was reared in the Episcopal Church by a maternal grandfather.

Politically, Oregon in 1824 was a kind of no-man's-land, without a government. Spain formally had withdrawn its claim to lands north of California in 1818 and during that same fateful year the United States and England, both contenders for the control of western America, formed an agreement of "Joint Occupancy," in other words a treaty of retaining the *status quo* without prejudice, for all the territory between the

Rockies and the Pacific from California to Alaska.[55] Two governments meant no government at all. This political vacuum was more or less occupied by the Hudson's Bay Company as a political force as well as a commercial one, by the presence of its Chief Factor, McLoughlin, who became the *de facto* ruler of the Oregon Country. His authority was supreme, and until his forced retirement from the Company over twenty years later, there was peace and almost perfect order in the entire region of Oregon.

When McLoughlin disembarked from the Governor's canoe at Fort George on that happy day, he was in the prime of life, in his thirty-eighth year. Tall and muscular, he stood straight as an oar, spoke in a loud tone of voice without waste of words, and glanced about with an air of authority that nobody was tempted to test. Though he had a French accent when he spoke English everything else about him was Gaelic, his strong will moderated by the in-born benevolence of a gentleman, his undertone of excitement when he talked, his spirit of adventure and romance, which had attracted him to the fur trade in the first place.

Born in the parish of La Riviere du Loup in the Province of Quebec on October 19, 1784, he was the first son and second child of an Irish farmer, John McLoughlin, and Angelique, nee Fraser, daughter of a French mother and a Scottish father.[56] Thus young John's maternal grandfather was Scottish, also a gentlemen of means and an Episcopalian.

John lived with his grandfather who made no effort to conceal his desires that his grandson would become a physician. But a maternal uncle, Alexander Fraser, who was connected with the Northwest Fur Company, tried to persuade him to join the company for adventure and wealth in the intriguing forests of the west. At fourteen years of age, a strange time for a boy to give up his illusions about romance in the wilderness, he decided to follow his grandfather's suggestion. He went to Quebec to pursue his medical studies with Dr. James Fisher.[57] After four and one half years under the tutorship of this medic, he applied to the Lieutenant Governor of the province, Robert Shore, for a license to practice. His application was accompanied by the following recommendation of Dr. Fisher: "John McLoughlin, a Canadian, lived with me as an apprentice and student in medicine, surgery and pharmacy for four years and six months, during which he behaved honestly. He possesses talents and I sincerely believe him a good subject to the British government."[58] There it is, his docility to government was equally important with his knowledge of anatomy. McLoughlin at the callous age of nineteen, received his license to practice medicine and surgery on May 3, 1803. He put out his shingle in the already ancient city of Quebec.

He did not remain in Quebec long. Through the influence of his uncle he was appointed physician and surgeon in the service of the Northwest Company and he was stationed in various western parts, where he displayed administrative as well as medical talent. At one of these ports he married the widow of Alexander McKay of the ill-fated Astor expedition who was killed by Indians when the *Tonquin* was blown up in 1811.[59]

McLoughlin was his own man and he made his own decisions. One of the first of these was to re-establish Fort George on a new site, some eighty miles inland where he could more easily control the company's trade throughout the interior. Thus he established the Hudson's Bay Company post, headquarters for the region of all Oregon, on the north bank of the Columbia River, just about its confluence with the Willamette, gaining ready access by river to most of what is now the Pacific Northwest.[60] He called his new headquarters Fort Vancouver.

FORT VANCOUVER

The new fort was as elaborate and as civilized as a rare genius could make it. Orchards were planted, sheep imported from Europe, cattle ranches established. Gardens were cultivated, as were fields of wheat and oats. The chief factor's table, set with English porcelain, and provided with the best of French wines, would have given pleasure to a prince. The chief factor himself was attended with deference due a powerful lord. Upon him was bestowed the honorable epithet of "White Headed Eagle," recognition of his supremacy, as the eagle was regarded as supreme among the birds.

Under McLoughlin, Fort Vancouver was a haven of peace for all who came there, even the competitors of his company. Nathaniel Wyeth, one of the latter arrived at the fort in 1834. "He requested us to consider his house our home," he wrote, regarding his reception by the chief factor. He "provided a separate room for our use, a servant to wait upon us and furnished us with every convenience which we could possibly wish for. I shall never cease to feel grateful to him for his disinterested kindness to the poor, houseless and travel-worn strangers."[61] As will appear, this kindness to strangers proved to be his undoing, with disastrous results for the whole Northwest.

But McLoughlin was as zealous for the word of God as he was generous. Blanchet in his memoirs noted McLoughlin's early services to the church:

It is but just to make special mention of the important services which Dr. John McLoughlin—though not a Catholic—has rendered to the French Canadians and their families during the fourteen years he was Governor at

Fort Vancouver. He it was who read to them the prayers on Sunday. Besides the English school kept for the children of the bourgeois, he had a separate one maintained at his own expense, in which prayers and catechism were taught in French to the Catholic women and children on Sundays and week days by his order. He also encouraged the chant of the canticles, in which he was assisted by his wife and daughter, who took much pleasure in this exercise. He visited and examined his school once a week, which was already formed of several good scholars, who soon learned to read French and become a great help to the priest. He, it was, who saved the Catholics of the Fort and their children from the dangers of perversion.[62]

History contains many ironies. The first classes of Catholic doctrine in the Northwest were not taught by priests or nuns, but by an Iroquois Indian whose ancestors had killed priests, by a practicing Episcopalian, technically a "fallen-away Catholic, and by his Indian wife and daughter.

McLoughlin's humane conduct soon came into conflict with company policies, which favored profit as its priority. Profit came from the fur bearing animals, so company policy, to prevent settlement that would drive away the animals, required its employees, especially the more adventurous *voyageurs*, to sign up for service for a given number of years and then to return to Montreal at the end of their engagement, lest they be tempted to settle where trappers still gathered pelts from their trap lines. Company policy also discouraged the presence of other settlers, for example by restricting credit for company resources, like plows, seeds, cattle, and so on. But McLoughlin's higher priorities soon became apparent to company officials in London, where a compromise, presumably advantageous to British interests, gradually began to take shape. Contemporary British speculation, based on claims acquired by the exploration and now renowned maps of Captain Vancouver, assumed that the Treaty of Joint Occupancy of 1818, and renewed in 1828, would soon be terminated with the British getting the lion's share, everything north of the Columbia River or approximately the 45° degrees latitude. While McLoughlin's unauthorized practice of encouraging settlement, especially American settlement, created tensions on international levels, the Hudson's Bay Company chose to take advantage of it by strengthening the British claim north of 45°, for example by forcing British subjects to remain north of the Columbia.

FIRST CATHOLIC SETTLERS
IN THE WILLAMETTE VALLEY

About this time three Catholic Canadians formerly employed by *American* fur companies, settled north of the Columbia, near Fort Vancouver. Blanchet gives the details:

There remained in the country three Canadians, remnants of the old expeditions of Hunt and Astor, viz. Etienne Lucier one of the former, and Joseph Gervais and Louis Labonte of the latter.[64] Etienne Lucier, being tired of a wandering life, began in 1829 to cultivate the land near Fort Vancouver, and getting dissatisfied with his first choice, left it in 1830, and removing to the Willamette Valley, settled a few miles above Champoeg, then called by the Canadians 'Campement de Sable.' Following his example, the two others followed him in 1831 and settled some distance south of him, one on the right, and the other on the left side of the river. Some old servants of the Hudson's Bay Company, being discharged from further service, went over to them and increased their number. The good and generous Dr. McLoughlin encouraged the colony and helped it all in his power.[65]

This first permanent settlement of Catholics in the northwest had neither a church nor a priest. But developments, that had taken place in Canada some years earlier brought hope, as they were reported, to the settlers of the Willamette, who were eager for "religion" in their old age.

In 1818 the bishop of Quebec, in response to Catholic settlers in the Red River country in western Canada, sent two missionaries to live among them.[66] These were Abbe Joseph Norbert Provencher, who was appointed Vicar General, and Abbe Severe Dumoulin, his assistant. Provencher fixed his residence at what is now St. Boniface, Manitoba. Four years later he was consecrated as a bishop with the title of Bishop of Juliopolis *in partibus*, in fact Auxiliary of the Bishop of Quebec and Vicar Apostolic for the District of the Northwest, which included, in a rather vague way, northwestern America.[67] Thus in 1822, there was a bishop in Manitoba who had ecclesiastical jurisdiction over all of the region of Oregon.

This was progress, but not without confusion. The plain truth is that the Oregon Country was claimed by the United States also, and it was generally believed that Ecclesiastical jurisdiction depended upon the Bishop of Upper and Lower Louisiana from 1818, and the Bishop of St. Louis from 1826.[68] Bishop Rosati at St. Louis had so many scattered flocks to shepherd that it is unlikely he gave much thought to the little one in Oregon until much later, when news of it was borne to him. The point was largely moot anyhow. What suffered most was history because records about it were few and fuzzy.

But change was beginning to take shape. McLoughlin's presence alone was a reminder of better times, since he had openly begun to favor Catholics and the Catholic Church in his policies and appointments. His sister, a nun in Quebec, was egging him on, with prayers and appropriate exhortations, and the chief factor, scarcely without being aware of it, "turned Catholic," as his enemies later charged, an inexcusable offense for which no revenge was too severe.

PAMBRUM AT FORT WALLA WALLA

About this time, in 1826, James Douglas, McLoughlin's assistant who was both Presbyterian and kindly disposed toward Catholics, arrived at Fort Vancouver with a young Canadian clerk. The latter, Pierre Chrysologue Pambrum, was accompanied by his Indian wife, Kitty, and children, all of whom were devout Catholics. Governor Simpson described him in his secret "Character Book," a kind of *vade mecum* which Simpson kept at all times and in which he confided his inner thoughts, usually degrading, about the people he met. About Pambrun, who was subject number seventy in the nasty little book, Simpson wrote:

> A Canadian about 45 years of age—17 years in the Service.—An active, steady dapper little fellow, is anxious to be useful but is wanting in judgment and deficient in Education:—full of 'pluck', has a very good opinion of himself and is quite a 'Petit Maitre'. Does not manage the business of his Post well, owing more to a want of discretion & foresight than to indifference or inattention: would drink I am of opinion if not under restraint.—Cannot look to an interest in the business.—Stationed in the Columbia.[69]

McLoughlin, who was also ridiculed in the little book, judged Pambrun otherwise, and despite Pambrun's status as a French Canadian, and Catholic to boot, assigned him "to Fort Walla Walla as the chief clerk in charge of the post."[70] This was in March, 1832. Like McLoughlin, Pambrun soon became a dedicated teacher of Catholic doctrine, not only for his own children and staff members, but also for the Walla Walla and Nez Perce Indians who frequented the fort.

Later, when discussion about the Indians' famous delegation to St. Louis for priests became popular, Pambrun's teaching of the Nez Perce is cited as proof that the delegation was composed of Indians of that tribe.[71] Unfortunately for those who proposed this hypothesis, the Indians made their first journey in 1831, a year before Pambrun arrived at Walla Walla.[72] It must be admitted, however, that a number of Nez Perce Indians lived among the Flatheads, where Old Ignace had been prayer leader for a long time.

THE FLATHEADS' FIRST APPEAL FOR BLACKROBES

Old Ignace had finally convinced the Council to send for priests. In the spring of 1831, apparently, the general assembly adopted the proposal of Old Ignace and four braves volunteered to undertake the journey to the far country of the white men to seek Blackrobes for their people.[73] These four successfully, but painfully, reached St. Louis in the early part of

October. The privations of their journey had left them so ill that two of them soon died, both having been baptized. Their baptismal names were Narcisse and Paul, as shown by the records of the parish where they were buried, the one on October 31 and the other on November 17.[74] The other two left for their homes in the mountains but were never heard from again.[75] Probably murdered by the Sioux or the Blackfeet, they disappeared without leaving a trace, like an arrow shot into the sky.

Bishop Rosati of St. Louis informed the readers of the *Annals of the Association of the Propagation of the Faith* about the noble object of the Indians' journey under date of December 31, 1831.

> Some three months ago four Indians who live across the Rocky Mountains near the Columbia River (Clark's Fork of the Columbia) arrived at St. Louis. After visiting General Clark who, in his celebrated travels, has visited their country and has been well treated by them, they came to see our church and appeared to be exceedingly well pleased with it. Unfortunately there was no one who understood their language. Some time afterwards two of them fell dangerously ill....

> Two of our priests visited them and the poor Indians seemed delighted with their visit. They made the Sign of the Cross and other signs which appeared to have some relation to baptism. The sacrament was administered to them; they gave expression of satisfaction. A little cross was presented to them. They took it with eagerness, kissed it frequently, and it could be taken from them only after death.[76]

PROTESTANT RESPONSE

The arrival of these Indians in St. Louis bore curious fruit. The incident was given headline publicity in the Protestant press, which erroneously asserted that the four travel-worn Indians had come from the west seeking the white man's Book of Heaven [the Bible], and that having fallen into the hands of the Romanists, had been subjected to the errors of Catholics, and had finally left, to return to their people, with empty arms. Reports like this aroused such fervent enthusiasm that not one, but several, Protestant mission expeditions were soon dispatched to the West "to bring to the heathens the Book of Heaven."

The first of these was that of the Methodist elder, Jason Lee and his nephew Daniel Lee, who arrived at Fort Vancouver in September 1834, with three lay companions. They had visited the Flatheads enroute, but departed soon, explaining later that they had in mind a larger field of opportunity. There is reason to believe, however, that the Flatheads rejected them since they did not wear black robes, they did not practice celibacy, and did not carry crucifixes.[77] At the fort they were warmly welcomed by McLoughlin. In his diary under date of September 29, 1834, Jason Lee wrote that his missionaries were being treated with utmost politeness, attention, and liberality.[78] At McLoughlin's invitation, Lee preached at the fort. The chief factor also persuaded the Lees to locate their mission west of the Cascades. There were white settlers in the Willamette Valley already, so the Methodists selected a vast tract on the south bank of the river, adjacent to forests of fir and oak.[79] In one year they spent forty-two thousand pre-Civil War dollars there, making little progress as they did, partly because the Indians failed to respond. The Methodists soon conceded "that the adults were comparatively hopeless,"[80] so they turned their attention to a school for children, but this, too, failed in its purpose. "Very few of the Indians came under the influence of their labor," reported their bishop, Dr. Stephen Olin. "The missionaries were, in fact, mostly engaged in secular affairs—concerned in claims to huge tracts of land...." With unabashed indignation, Olin accused the missionaries of being "transformed into land sharks and horse jockeys."[81]

The French Canadians in the valley, now numbering about twenty-six families, accepted the Lees respectfully and requested them to perform certain religious services, like marrying them. Many, perhaps most of these Canadians, had taken Indian wives without benefit of clergy or ceremony, the so-called "fur trade" marriages, so they turned to the Methodists to supply what was lacking. Later, this too, would become cause for a bitter conflict on the frontier.[82]

WILLAMETTE SETTLERS' APPEAL FOR PRIESTS

During the same year that the Methodists arrived, the Canadians posted their first letter of appeal to Bishop Provencher at Red River, requesting priests for their spiritual care. Dated July 3, 1834, the letter required several months of overland travel before it reached the bishop, who took prudent measures, like consulting his own superior, the bishop of Quebec. This required more time during which the former *voyageurs* became impatient, and they dispatched a second request for priests on February 23, 1835.

Bishop Provencher, meanwhile, responded to both letters in June, 1835. He sent his reply with the Hudson's Bay Company brigade, in care of Dr. McLoughlin, including at the same time a letter addressed to the latter, composed two days earlier.

Both letters are enclosed here, not as much for their content as for their historical precedence. They are the first letters of their kind in the Northwest Church. The second letter may be classified as the first "Pastoral Letter" of a bishop to his flock in the region of Oregon.

To Dr. J. McLaughlin.

SIR: I have received last winter and this spring a petition from certain free families settled on the Willamette river, requesting that Missionaries be sent to instruct their children and themselves. My intention is to do all I can to grant them their request as soon as possible; I have no priest disposable at Red river, but I am going this year to Europe, and I will endeavor to procure those free people and the Indians afterwards the means of knowing God. I send together with this letter an answer to the petition which I have received; I request you to deliver it to them; I add some catechisms which might be useful to those people, if there is any one among them that can read. Those people say they are protected by you. Please induce them to do their best, and to deserve, by a good behavior, to derive benefit from the favor they implore.

I have the honor to be, sir,
Your most humble servant,
J.N., Bishop of Juliopolis
Red river, June 6, 1835

To all the families settled on the river Willamette and other Catholic persons beyond the Rocky Mountains, greeting:

I have received, most beloved brethren, your two petitions, the one dated 3d July, 1834, and the other 23d February, 1835. Both call for Missionaries to instruct your children and yourselves. Such a request from persons deprived of all religious attendance could not fail to touch my heart, and if it were in my power, I would send you some this very year. But I have no priests disposable at Red river: they must be obtained from Canada or elsewhere, which requires time. I will make it my business in a journey which I am going to make this year in Canada and in Europe. If I succeed in my efforts, I will soon send you some help.

My intention is not to procure the knowledge of God to you and your children only, but also to the numerous Indian tribes among which you live. I exhort you meanwhile to deserve by a good behavior that God may bless my undertaking. Raise your children the best way you can. Teach them what you know of religion. But remember, my dear brethren, that the proper means of procuring to your children and your wives some notion of God and of the religion which you profess is to give them good example by a life moderate and exempt from the great disorders which exist among many of the christians beyond the mountains. What idea do you give of God and of the holy religion you profess to the Indians, especially, who see in you, who are calling yourselves the servants of that great God, disorders which equal and perhaps surpass their own? You thereby prejudice them against a holy religion which you violate. When this same religion, which condemns all crime, shall be preached to them, the Indians will object [to] the wicked conduct of those who profess it as a pretext not to embrace it. On receiving this letter which apprizes you that probably you will soon receive the priests who you seem to call for earnestly, renounce then at once sin; begin to live a life more conformable to your belief, in order that, when the Missionaries will arrive among you, they will find you disposed to avail yourselves of the instructions and other religious assistance which they shall bring you. I wish God may touch your hearts and change them. My greatest consolation would be to learn hereafter that as soon as this letter was read to you, you began to pay a little more attention to the great affair of your salvation.

Given at St. Bonifacius of Red river, on the 8th day of June, 1835.

J.N., Bishop of Juliopolis[83]

When the retired *voyageurs* received this fatherly, if somewhat sober message from the church they had left behind, they composed a third dispatch containing expressions of gratitude. They announced they were building a church to "Receive oure kind father, in for some of us stands in greate Neade of your Assistance as quick as possible."[84] They informed the bishop that they had fifty-seven children in the settlement, who were "Learning very fast which makes us very eager for Youre assistance." They signed their rustic report "Willammett Settlers," and with their names also, if they knew how to write them.

By this time the bishop had clarified, in his own mind at least, the question of canonical jurisdiction or faculties. He had appealed to the Holy See for an indult, stating specifically what boundaries served as limits to the jurisdiction of the Bishop of Juliopolis. Under the date of February 28, 1836, Pope Pius VIII provided this indult which expressly assigned to him the territory "comprised between the Rocky Mountains on the east, the Pacific Ocean on the west, the Russian possessions on the north, and the territory of the United States on the south."[85] The indult, however, also granted authority for the Canadian missionaries "to use their powers, when needed in Russian possessions, as well as in that part of the American territory which borders on their missions."

ANOTHER FLATHEAD DELEGATION

As yet no one really knew what territory belonged to the bishop of Juliopolis, because the status of American Sovereignty "on the south" had not yet been resolved. As for the Flathead Indians in the Bitteroot Valley, the question of canonical jurisdiction was about as foreign to them as the Emperor of China. They merely wanted Blackrobes. Their mission to St. Louis had not yet produced results, so in the spring of 1835 they prepared another.

There had been rumors in the valley that year that Christian missionaries were enroute. Flathead leaders sometimes expressed the hope that the four braves who had not returned were serving as guides to the newcomers, and one of the chiefs, Insula, known also as Little Chief and Great Warrior, volunteered to meet them. Accompanied by several other Flatheads, Insula mounted his horse and traveled to the southeast, toward the Green River Rendezvous where Indians of many tribes gathered and where the wagon trains of the fur companies met them.[86] Attacked on the journey by hostiles, Insula and his warriors fought their way through without injury, and arrived expectantly at the Rendezvous where thousands of Indians had already gathered. To their great disappointment their missing braves were not there, nor were there any Blackrobes.

The rumored missionaries, however, had come. These were the Reverend Samuel Parker, a Presbyterian, and Dr. Marcus Whitman, a missionary doctor on his first trip west.[87] Having assembled the Indians, Parker introduced himself and Whitman as envoys sent to establish missions in their midst. Some of the Nez Perce who were present were quite pleased with this and, during a conference between them and the missionaries, it was determined that Parker should continue his tour of exploration" and that Whitman should return to the east to gather other missionaries for the Flathead and Nez Perce nations."

But Insula and his little band were not satisfied with the appearances of Parker and Whitman. They did not have black gowns. And like the Lees, who had come to the Bitteroot, they too married, and they did not have the crucifix and the great prayer, the Mass. From all this, Insula concluded they were not the Blackrobes that Old Ignace had described, and he would have nothing further to do with them. With his warriors, he mounted his horse again and hurried back to the Bitteroot with the bad news.[88]

Thus it was by the spring of 1836, when Dr. Whitman returning with a strong group of missionaries representing the Protestant American Mission Board of Boston, including two bitter opponents of all Catholics, the Reverend Henry Spalding and William H. Gray, and when an Episcopalian missionary, the Reverend Henry Beaver, with his high strung wife Jane, were on a British ship bearing north to Fort Vancouver, there were no priests for the settlers of the Willamette, nor Blackrobes for the Flatheads of the Bitteroot. After nearly one hundred years of Catholic presence, there still were no resident priests. Sometimes it seemed, Catholic priests were the last to arrive. At least this is the way it appeared to settlers in the Northwest. Looking at the bright side, however, it must be admitted that by autumn of 1836, there were growing numbers of those who took comfort in this melancholy fact.

BEAVER'S DIFFERENCES WITH McLOUGHLIN

Among these was the Reverend Beaver. Beaver's arrival at Fort Vancouver, long anticipated by the chief factor, who was determined to snub him, marked the opening of hostilities between the Catholics and the Protestants. The Reverend Parker, it is true, had already scandalized some pious Indians by plucking a wooden cross off a grave, breaking it into bits and casting it aside.[89] News of this alleged desecration of the cross had shocked many Indians of the interior and Parker's mission, otherwise favorable, had been doomed to failure. But at Fort Vancouver the conflict involved two Episcopalians, one of whom, Dr. McLoughlin, was openly Catholic in his preferences.

Deeply disappointed that priests had not yet come and vexed by his inability to change the situation, McLoughlin deliberately overlooked Beaver's need and expectancy of a church and separate quarters. Beaver, an autocratic person of the old school, smugly complacent in his superior position as a clergyman, and deeply humiliated by the chief factor's indifference, took the offensive. Using his pulpit he publicly demanded that McLoughlin regularize his "fur trade" marriage by submitting to a formal marriage ceremony in his presence. McLoughlin, with his Marguerite, arranged for a civil ceremony instead, in the presence of his assistant, James Douglas.[90]

There was also much disagreement over the supervision of the school. Beaver loftily disregarded the chief factor's orders that the children, mostly Catholic, be sent to McLoughlin for instructions in religion. Beaver sent scathing reports to the Hudson's Bay Company in London, and before McLoughlin sailed to London to defend himself and his policy of giving aid to American missionaries, the two men came to blows.[91] During his absence, Douglas dismissed Beaver, who really pleased no one, not even his wife, and shipped him off to England, where he continued to carry on his battle against McLoughlin and his Catholics.[92]

DEATH OF OLD IGNACE

This was in 1838. By this time a third delegation of Flatheads had taken the dangerous trail to St. Louis to secure Blackrobes. This expedition of four Indians, two Flatheads and two Nez Perce, was led by Old Ignace, who had made the journey safely, with his two young sons, during the previous autumn.[93] Before their departure, W.H. Gray, the mechanic with the Whitman party, disenchanted with his role in that noble enterprise, arrived in the Bitteroot Valley to consider its potential as a mission of his own.[94] He requested Old Ignace's permission to accompany the Indians to St. Louis. Ignace consented, though Gray was an unwelcome guest. The group of six set out in a somber mood, some of them, perhaps, sensing that they would never return.

But all went well until they reached Ash Hollow on the North Platte River in Nebraska. There, because of Gray's interference, they were attacked by a large band of bloodthirsty Sioux, who killed Ignace and his Indian warriers, after Gray erroneously declared them to be "Snakes," the bitter enemies of the Sioux.[95] There is no explanation for Gray's perfidious behavior and no defense for it. It simply happened and five men died. Thus it was that the third delegation of the Flatheads, like the first, ended in disaster. Nine Indians had given their lives in their quest for Blackrobes.

THE FIRST CHURCH IN OREGON

The French Canadians had not been idle. They completed their log church, its exact whereabouts presently unknown, and posted another report to the bishop, dated March 8, 1837, in which they expressed their growing impatience, their "Great Angstitty [anxiety] for youre Arrival."[96] The church, McLoughlin told them, was on the wrong site, and the chief factor soon arranged for its removal to another, with or without the settlers' approval. This building was seventy by thirty feet, "rebuilt on a large prairie, its present beautiful site," on the eastern side of the river "on the road to Champoeg."[97] The settlers added "a bedend" to it, meaning a room for living quarters, which measured twelve by thirty feet. There in the stage of near completion this first Catholic Church in Oregon awaited the arrival of the priest. The big question, taller than its steeple, was like grievous weight on everyone's mind: would the priests ever come and if so, when?

2

THE FIRST RESIDENT MISSIONARIES

1838–1841

Two priests from Canada came first. Their names were Francis Norbert Blanchet and Modeste Demers. Their passage to Oregon, finally provided by the Hudson's Bay Company, was a complicated matter that required something like an international treaty before it could be approved.

There were compelling reasons for this. To the bitter end—that is until 1846 when the 49th parallel was confirmed as the boundary between the United States and Canada—the Hudson's Bay Company actually believed that the boundary would run along the midstream of the Columbia, far south of 49°. Hence, the Company was most unwilling to provide passage for priests to serve former *voyageurs* living in territory destined to be American. If this were not reason enough, the Reverend Herbert Beaver was. Beaver, still smarting from McLoughlin's assault, relentlessly opposed the Company's concession to any "Roman priests," not only for political, but especially for religious reasons. The Company was British and Episcopalian in character, if anything, hence it was very properly identified with traditional British upper class religion. Bishop Joseph Signay of Quebec, who had requested passage for the priests in one of the canoes to Oregon, was not only Romanist, but he was also one of those quaint French ecclesiastics.[1] How very un-British.

On the other hand, Governor Simpson of the Company could not overlook the advantages of having two Canadian priests in the disputed region. French colonies north of the Columbia would counter-balance growing American interest in occupying this land. The presence of Catholic missionaries, the Company had learned, tended to pacify most Indians. Priests brought peace and order in their wake, and the company could do well to have them as allies in the event of trouble.

For Simpson it was a perplexing problem. On the one hand there was much opposition to the priests. "No need of priests," Reverend Beaver kept saying. "I suffice here, and the Methodists in the Willamette Valley."[2] As for the Methodist ministers, Blanchet later observed, "they were visiting the French settlers, and succeeded in bringing some of them to their Sunday meetings, baptized some women and performed marriages."[3]

The bishop's second request for passage for his two priests was agreed upon, but Simpson withdrew the permission almost as soon as he had granted it.[4] The bishop was persistent. After all, in the twenty-eight forts which the Hudson's Bay Company controlled, the majority of people were Catholics. Though they occupied positions of minor importance, they were essential to the success of the Company. They were like soldiers on whom the generals depended for victory.

Simpson had second and third thoughts. At last, having placed the matter before the Committee in London, he replied favorably to the bishop, insisting however, on one important reservation. "The priests," he wrote, "would be given passage provided that he [the bishop] would establish the Mission on the banks of the Cowlitz river, or the Cowlitz Portage, falling into the Columbia from the Northward, and given his assurance that the missionaries would not locate themselves on the south side of the Columbia river, but would form their establishment where the Company's representatives might point out as the most eligible situation on the north side. . . ."[5]

To this the bishop readily consented. It was like fencing with God, but there appeared to be no better way to get priests into Oregon. It seems unlikely the bishop realized that, by the terms of his agreement with Simpson, the priests he sent could not establish their residence among the people who had been appealing for them. Simpson, however was gratified, and he informed Signay "that if the [two] priests would be ready at Lachine to embark for the interior about the 25th of April, a passage would be afforded them."[6]

Doubtlessly Signay and his auxiliary Provencher were pleased to hear this. Concessions by the church, even in the New World, were often required. One might call it expedience, another prudence. The fact is, for Signay and the French Canadians in Oregon, alternatives to Simpson's offer were almost unthinkable. Without passage by the Hudson Bay Company's brigade from Lachine to Fort Vancouver, or by the Company's ships from London to Fort Vancouver, the priests would have to attempt the journey alone, or find an American fur company to provide them safe passage. One could take, for example, the American Fur

Company's overland brigade from Westport, near St. Louis, across the Oregon Trail as far as the Green River Rendezvous in Wyoming for something like fifteen hundred dollars in cold U.S. cash, round trip, starting in May. Really, this was no bargain either. But fur traders and trappers did not risk their lives lightly.

Simpson's offer, all things considered, was the best to be had, but time would expose its weakness. In the long run it proved to be very costly to the church.

FRANCIS NORBERT BLANCHET

Having arranged for the passage of two priests, Signay now engaged in correspondence with Provencher of Red River regarding the two subjects to be sent. Signay proposed an experienced missionary, the Abbe Francis Blanchet, whose life heretofore seems to have been a preparation for an assignment just like this.[7] Francis, or Francois as he was known then, had been born on September 3, 1795, into an old French Canadian family which had given many sons and daughters to the church. His parents, Pierre and Rosalie, modest farmers in the parish of Sainte-Pierre, Riviere du Sud, Lower Canada, named their son after the Apostle of the Indies, a popular Jesuit with the French, though he was a Basque. This seems to have had little influence with young Francois, who regarded the Jesuits, later when he was Archbishop in Oregon, with unfriendly eyes. When he was confirmed he added "Norbert" to his name, which now became officially Francis Xavier Norbert Blanchet, a longer than average title, which seems to have been a weakness of other Blanchets.

In 1810, with his younger brother Magloire, Francis was sent to the Minor Seminary in Quebec by his parents. Both were teenagers. Francis won some pompous Latin award that indicated nothing more than his dedication to writing Latin. This did not enhance the size of his body, which was smaller than average, nor his rather stubborn and unyielding disposition, but it would stand him in good stead when he became a bishop.

After three years in a major seminary, Francis was ordained in the priesthood. For a year following he was assigned to the cathedral in Quebec, where the bishop could keep a paternal eye on him; he was twenty-four years old then, shy and sometimes emotional, and his education in the seminary had left room for improvement, especially in matters where experience made a difference. The new priest apparently made great strides, and when the bishop-elect of New Brunswick,

Bernard Mac Eachern, appealed to Quebec for a French speaking priest for the Acadians of that area, he was appointed to go. In October 1820 he set out for the ancient mission of St. Antoine of Richibucto, New Brunswick, actually a wilderness containing many Acadians, who spoke French, a few Irish who spoke only English, and scattered Micmac Indians, some of whom spoke a little of either.

From the Irish the new Abbé learned English, and from the Indians he learned Micmac. He spent seven harsh and dedicated years in this mission, attending his flock by birch canoe or horseback in the summer and by skating on the river or by dog sled in the winters. Nothing he would experience in Oregon would exceed the hardships of his first pastorage in New Brunswick. On the other hand, almost everything he experienced in the latter prepared him well for his life's principal task, which lay ahead of him.

In the spring of 1827, Abbé Blanchet was assigned to a new parish, called St. Joseph de Soulange, which was in Cedars in the Diocese of Montreal. The village of Cedars was a bustling frontier rendezvous for boats going up and down the St. Lawrence, something like Westport at the jump-off point on the Oregon Trail in the United States. Here Blanchet became familiar with *voyageurs*, trappers and other adventurers, who often sat beside his fire and regaled him with tales of the rich harvest of the furs, gathered in trade with Indians of the west. He spent nearly eleven years at Cedars. Like some of the *voyageurs*, he was becoming a legend. If somewhat autocratic, even rigoristic like many French Canadian priests of his time, he was also capable of an easy rapport with the rustics of his village. Blanchet was neither proud nor vain. He never forgot his own humble origins. At Cedars, a long way from the pomp and splendor of liturgical happenings in the cathedrals of Quebec or Montreal, his personality took the shape it would always be, for better or worse.

BLANCHET'S ASSIGNMENT TO OREGON

One could be a less observant bishop than Signay, and still see the obvious regarding a choice of a priest for Oregon. Francis Blanchet was the ideal candidate. The bishop, no doubt, keenly regretted his loss at Cedars, but felt much consolation in making his decision, for there seemed to be no anxieties connected with it.

Governor Simpson had formally approved passage of priests on February 17, 1838. As soon as the bishop in Quebec received Simpson's letter, he "immediately," says Blanchet, gave charge of the Mission of

Oregon to himself as vicar general and appointed as his assistant, Modeste Demers, a young adventurous priest only twenty-six years of age, already in residence on the frontier at Red River.[8]

Demers had been ordained during the previous year, on February 7, 1837. When he was sent to Red River, which God knows was remote enough for most people, he was delighted. He worried, though, about his chances of getting farther west. He was afraid the bishop would forget him, as sometimes happened, and leave him at Red River. His fears were groundless, of course. He would soon have worries of a different nature.

After Signay had made his decision, he formalized it by dispatching to the two priests, on the same day, two sets of instructions, the longer one containing twenty-one detailed and sometimes petty directives.[9] The shorter form appears here as Blanchet included it in his *Historical Sketches:*

Instructions given to Very Rev. F.N. Blanchet and Rev. M. Demers, appointed Missionaries for that part of the Diocese of Quebec which is situated between the Pacific Ocean and the Rocky Mountains.
April 17th, 1838.

My Rev. Fathers.
You must consider as the first object of your Mission to withdraw from barbarity and the disorders which it produces, the Indians scattered in that country.

Your second object is, to tender your services to the wicked Christians who have adopted there the vices of Indians, and live in licentiousness and the forgetfulness of their duties.

Persuaded that the preaching of the Gospel is the surest means of obtaining these happy results, you will lose no opportunity of inculcating its principles and maxims, either in your private conversations or public instructions.

In order to make yourselves sooner useful to the natives of the country where you are sent, you will apply yourselves, as soon as you arrive, to the study of the Indian languages, and will endeavor to reduce them to regular principles, so as to be able to publish a grammar after some years of residence there.

You will prepare for baptism, with all possible expedition, the infidel women who live in concubinage with Christians, in order to substitute lawful marriages for these irregular unions.

You will take a particular care of the Christian education of children, establishing for that purpose schools and catechism classes in all the villages which you will have the occasion to visit.

In all the places remarkable either for their position or the passage of the voyagers, or the gathering of Indians, you will plant crosses, so as to take possession of those various places in the name of the Catholic religion. * * *

Given at Quebec on the 17th of April, 1838.
Joseph Signay,
Bishop of Quebec[10]

THE CATHOLIC SETTLERS IN OREGON

The bishop of Quebec, one gathers from this, did not have a very high opinion of the first Catholic settlers in Oregon, nor of their Indian neighbors. Sometimes that which appears to be tolerably acceptable in a distant and forlorn colony looks very wicked to the bishop, sitting in his chancery, surrounded by paintings and statues of the saints. The bishop, however, had reason to express, in private at least, his reservations about the behavior of the notorious *voyageurs* and especially the freemen.

Blanchet and Demers would travel with them, sharing the same canoes, companions and meals, for something like seven months. After that they would live among the freemen, the retired *voyageurs* who were in bad repute, "as generally a shiftless element who had saved nothing and did not care to return to the towns where they would have to work again. By the vicious habits into which they lapsed in their vagrant life, they earned the contempt of both Indians and whites, and they were a source of much trouble to the traders."[11]

If this was the bishop's view of his wandering subjects, one side of the coin, there was another side, a view of the *voyageurs* in action, the adventurous men with whom the two priests would travel. Fifty years ago, a respected historian presented a fair assessment of their good qualities:

The voyageurs were light hearted and good natured. Their respect for superiors often amounted to real affection, and they commonly addressed each other as brother or cousin. They sang constantly, and yelled lustily as their boats shot the rapids. The strongest men were given the posts of bowmen and steersmen and were paid higher wages, for the safety of the boats in dangerous water depended largely on their skill. They were capable of incredible endurance. For six months at a stretch, in their voyages across the country, they rowed or carried loads at the portages from dawn till nightfall, with two twenty minutes intervals for breakfast and dinner. Four hours was often their allowance for sleep, when it was possible and desirable to go on after dark. At the portages, each man took two bales, 180 pounds, on his back. With the load partly supported by a strap across his forehead, he could trot along for miles. The food of the boatmen was mostly meat. In the West they had no bread or vegetables. Each man was allowed eight pounds of meat a day and ten pounds if there was bone in it. It might be buffalo, deer or horse. In the fall months, the ration was often two geese or four ducks, and it was sometimes an equivalent amount of fish. In wet weather or at a long portage, a glass of rum was issued. At Christmas and New Year, flour was provided for cakes and puddings, and each man received half a pint of rum. They called this a *regale*, or royal privilege. The voyageurs wore capots made of blankets, over striped cotton shirts, leather or cloth trousers, moccasins, hats or fur caps and belts of variegated worsted, from which were suspended knives and smoking bags.[12]

So the Catholics forming the first parish in Oregon had their good qualities as well as bad and the two priests would be stuck with both.

When Blanchet left Montreal he was in his forty-third year, as strong and nimble in action as a veteran boatman and as toughminded as an experienced diplomat. He was a very pious priest, not in a sentimental way, and he shunned as softness anything less than absolute dedication to duty as he saw it. Sometimes he was despotic, like his brother Magloire, who followed him into the priesthood and who was often as rigid as a little Napoleon. Later even a hard-headed Demers could not stand up to the older Blanchet, nor could anyone else except McLoughlin, who, simply stated, was even more despotic. Among his own colleagues, Francis Blanchet was known as a man who got things done, a do-or-die macho man, who was also intelligent enough to pursue the right objectives.

Modeste Demers was almost fourteen years Blanchet's junior. He had already manifested his knack for learning Indian dialects while he was assigned to the mission in Red River. Unlike Blanchet, Demers was regarded as quite genial, a youthful, almost boyish kind of priest who could adapt to almost anything, even the stark loneliness of his missionary journeys in Oregon. He was the perfect complement to Blanchet, who usually took himself, and others, too seriously.

A point should be made here: These two priests should be regarded as the early founders of the church in the Northwest. Soon others would join them, but for several awesome years, they were the only priests in that foresaken wilderness, which then included most of western Canada.

THE PASSAGE TO OREGON

In a brief account contained in his *Historical Sketches*, Blanchet presented the basic facts of the journey:

> Accompanied by chief trader Hargrave, Vicar General F.N. Blanchet embarked in one of the light bark canoes carrying the express of the Hudson Bay Company, leaving Montreal on Thursday, May 3rd, 1838, reaching Fort Vancouver on the 24th of the following November. The journey from Lachine to Red River (2,100 miles) was made in canoes, with occasional portages, in thirty-three days. The journey from Red River to the Rocky Mountains (2,025 miles) occupied eighty-four days, including detentions. The river route was made in eleven light barges and the land trip—occupying five days—was made on horseback. Horses were also used in making the tedious trip across the Rocky Mountains, from Jaspar's House to Boat encampment or Big Bend on the Columbia river. This trip occupied nine days, a band of seventy-two horses being provided for the use of the company. It took six days to make the

ascent on the Eastern slope, and three days to descend to the plains on the Pacific side, but the missionaries were well repaid for the toils they underwent in the grandeur of the scenery that surrounded them at every step. The remainder of the journey, from Big Bend to Fort Vancouver (about 1,200 miles) was made in light boats down the Columbia river.[13]

According to this summary the total length of Blanchet's journey was five thousand, three hundred and twenty-five miles, the customary route of the fur trade brigade, and it lasted for a total of one hundred and ninety-six days, including off-days for prolonged stopovers. At first sight this estimate of distance appears to be exaggerated. But one should understand that the rivers and lakes, which comprised most of the route, zigzagged north and south in fretful sequences, adding literally hundreds of miles to the course that the crow could fly. In spite of this, and the long delays at major points, the brigades made much better time than that gained by the overland parties on the Oregon trail.[14]

More explicit details about Blanchet's journey are not wanting. His arrival, for example, at St. Boniface or Red River, coincided with his introduction to his assistant, who met him on the banks of the river. He remained with Bishop Provencher at St. Boniface for thirty-five days, observing during that time the departure of the caravan for the buffalo hunt. Eight or nine hundred wagons, drawn by oxen or shagnappe ponies, assembled in this caravan and departed across the plains in a great cloud of dust.[15]

St. Boniface then was the gateway to the Canadian West, similar to Omaha in the United States at a later date. It was the crossroads for travel in all directions. There were two schools there, each on opposite sides of the river. One of these, supported mostly by the Hudson's Bay Company, was like an Episcopalian mission school with Indian students from all over the West, selected by Governor Simpson and sent there in the interests of the Company. One of its distinguished students was Garry, a promising young Spokane Indian who was registered in the Red River school in 1825, when he was fourteen years old.[16] Garry, later a Chief of the Spokanes, returned to his own land in 1830 and for some years taught a modified form of Christianity which certainly was not Episcopalian.[17]

Garry had left Red River before Blanchet arrived there, but in the Catholic mission school at St. Boniface, across the river from the Episcopal school, there was another young man in his eighteenth year, the son of a Hudson's Bay Company trapper in Garry's tribal lands. Marcel Isidore Bernier had been born at Spokane House, near present Spokane, on November 10, 1819.[18] His parents, French Canadian and devout Catholics, sent him to school at St. Boniface in 1830, the year

Garry left Red River. Blanchet doubtlessly met Marcel at St. Boniface, for the lad was an acquaintance of Demers, who used him later, as a guide on his missionary journeys.[19]

DEPARTURE FROM ST. BONIFACE

The boat brigade, with Blanchet and Demers both aboard, clad modestly in their black soutanes or cassocks, departed in a burst of song from St. Boniface on July 10.[20] The most difficult part of the journey lay ahead—the ascent of the Rockies, passage through these lofty barriers, then a precarious descent to the headwaters of the Columbia River on the slopes beyond. During this period, which required almost three months, Blanchet was able to offer Mass on the crest of the Rockies, at approximately three in the morning of October 10th.[21] Profoundly moved by the majesty of nature around him he consecrated "to their Creator these mountains and abrupt peaks whose prodigious heights ascend toward heaven to celebrate the praise of the Almighty."[22] Blanchet also noted that he and his assistant had baptized one hundred and twenty-two people on the eastern slope of the Rockies and fifty-three on the western.[23]

ARRIVAL IN OREGON

Having reached the drainage of the Columbia, the two priests were now officially in the territory assigned to them. "Being at the foot of the most lofty mountain," the vicar general wrote ecstatically, "the two missionaries began to tread beneath their feet the long desired land of Oregon; that portion of the vineyard alloted them for cultivation. Filled with joy they retired a short distance from the place where the caravans were resting on the bosom of the beautiful prairie, and there fell on their knees, embraced the soil, took possession of it, dedicated and consecrated their persons, soul and body, to whatever God would be pleased to require of them for the glory of His holy Name, the propagation of His kingdom and the fulfillment of His will."[24]

No doubt Blanchet in this great moment of fervor meant all these words; nonetheless his human weakness remained, and there would be times later when one could question how willing he was to do everything required "for the glory of His holy Name."

On the evening of Saturday, October 13th, the travelers reached Big Bend, that point on the Columbia where they took, again, to the boats.[25] They were all overjoyed, until they found there only two boats instead of the four they expected. The captain of the expedition decided to split the

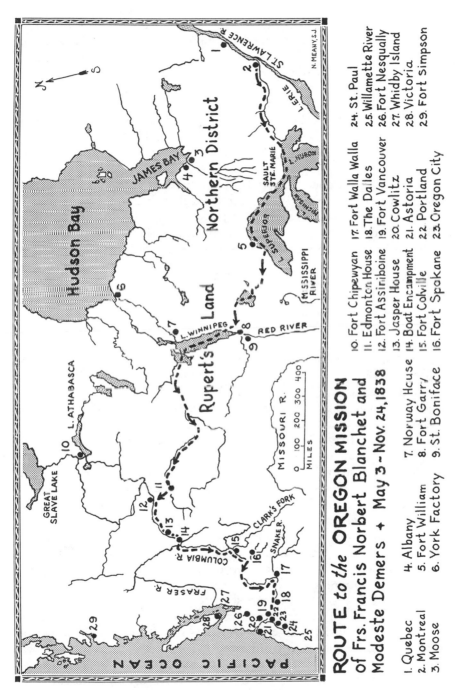

ROUTE to the OREGON MISSION
of Frs. Francis Norbert Blanchet and
Modeste Demers • May 3 – Nov. 24, 1838

N. MEANY, S.J

1. Quebec
2. Montreal
3. Moose
4. Albany
5. Fort William
6. York Factory
7. Norway House
8. Fort Garry
9. St. Boniface
10. Fort Chipewyan
11. Edmonton House
12. Fort Assiniboine
13. Jasper House
14. Boat Encampment
15. Fort Colville
16. Fort Spokane
17. Fort Walla Walla
18. The Dalles
19. Fort Vancouver
20. Cowlitz
21. Astoria
22. Portland
23. Oregon City
24. St. Paul
25. Willamette River
26. Fort Nesqually
27. Whidby Island
28. Victoria
29. Fort Simpson

group, one third remaining at Big Bend until a boat was returned for them. The priests were assigned to the party that would leave on the morrow.

"The following day (Oct. 14, 1838) being Sunday, it was on that day that the holy sacrifice of the Mass was offered for the first time in Oregon at Big Bend on the banks of the dangerous and perilous Columbia. At this great act of religion, performed by Rev. M. Demers, the two missionaries being much moved, consecrated themselves to the Queen of Angels, imploring her special protection for the rest of the voyage."[26]

There was some poetic propriety in the choice of the celebrant that day. Big Bend was deep in the heart of present British Columbia, more than five hundred miles north of the 49th parallel, which became the northern extremity of "Oregon." Later, when the territory was divided for ecclesiastic purposes, it was Demers who became bishop of the northern half; that is British Columbia. Thus, this so called "first Mass in Oregon" accurately described, given certain limitations of time and place, was celebrated by the priest who became its first bishop.[27]

Blanchet's many "dedications" seem to have paid off, for the two boats in which the priests were passengers successfully negotiated the most difficult rapids on the Columbia between Big Bend and House of the Lakes, a distance of one hundred and sixty-five miles. Having arrived at House of the Lakes, the priests pitched their tent, as usual, and announced a week of Masses, prayer, classes in catechism and "evening exercises," meaning more prayers. One of the boats in which they had come was quickly unloaded and sent north to bring the rest of the party waiting at Big Bend. The week passed, and the missing boat, expected hourly, did not appear. "A gloomy presentiment began to sieze the hearts of all."[28] At last, on October 24th, at the conclusion of Mass, a boat appeared afar off, half-broken, coming in mourning and without the usual joyful chant of the *voyageurs*. The rowers were hardly able to move their oars. When the boat approached shore, all ran to greet it. "At the sight of so few men, women, and children, a heart-rending spectacle took place; an indescribable scene of desolation and shedding of tears began; cries and piercing lamentations were long heard and echoed by the neighboring mountains. For alas! the boat had capsized and out of twenty-six souls, twelve had perished."[24]

Only a few bodies were recovered. These were brought down and given Christian burial, and wooden crosses were blessed and placed over their graves. There was no time for more tears. The expedition was already over one week behind time. Autumn was in the air, even at lower elevations. Nights in the tents were cold and mornings too chilly for comfort. No longer were there swarms of mosquitoes, which had been the curse of the earlier months. Food was getting scarce and an express canoe had been sent forward to Fort Colville to fetch additional supplies. On November 3, the brigade was ready again to embark.

FIRST MASS IN SPOKANE DIOCESE

When it reached Fort Colville three days later news of the coming of the priests had spread like lightning, said Blanchet, and the chiefs of five nations with their people had gathered at the Fort to await them.[30] As the boats drew near shore the Indians crowded around, each one eager to touch the hands of the long expected priests. A building was assigned and there for four days the priests offered Mass and taught the simple truths of Christianity.

Fort Colville, it should be noted, was located in the present state of Washington, and in the present diocese of Spokane.[31] It was here, then, strictly speaking, the first Masses in the Northwest were offered in the Latin language, by diocesan priests from eastern Canada, who wore plain, but complete vestments in accordance with the rubrics of the Tridentine Mass.

After leaving Fort Colville, where the church in our Northwest first became visible as such, the two priests made only two other brief stops, the first at Fort Okanogan, at the mouth of the Okanogan River, and the second at Fort Walla Walla, at that time at Wallula, where Pierre Pambrun warmly welcomed them on Sunday morning November 18. This was a happy beginning. A sour note, however appeared during the visit.

Pambrun, it seems, sent his children to Dr. Whitman's school at the mission called Waiilatpu, "Place of the Rye Grass," which was a few miles from the fort. Whitman, hearing of the rumored coming of Blanchet and Demers, expressed his displeasure and forbade the Indians of the vicinity to meet the priests. Despite the interference, understandable in the context of the times, the Indians flocked to Fort Walla Walla. "During the twenty-four hours they remained at this post," Blanchet wrote, speaking of himself and Demers in the third person, "they had three baptisms, celebrated one Mass and were visited by the Walla Walla and Cayuse Indians, who having heard by the [fur trade] express of the coming of the priests, notwithstanding the contrary orders of the Head of the Waiilatpu mission. Holy Mass was celebrated before the Indians, who assisted at it struck with amazement."[32]

On a subsequent visit by Demers, a young chief brought his child to be baptized by the priest. Pambrun served as the child's godfather, which gained for him the animosity of Dr. Whitman. "Since that time," Blanchet added ominously, "the young chief and his band always preferred the priests' religion to that of the minister."[33]

Thus it happened that at Waiilatpu many Protestant noses were out of joint. But many Catholic noses were out of joint, too, because the missionaries had not arrived at Fort Vancouver as scheduled. The Willamette settlers had all gathered at the fort to welcome the priests, perhaps to be seen also, but after nearly a week of waiting most had gone back to their farms, leaving three of their number to serve as a ceremonial committee. These were Joseph Gervais, Stephen Lucier, and Peter Beleque.

AT FORT VANCOUVER

The brigade left Fort Walla Walla on November 19 and reached Fort Vancouver on the following Saturday, November 24, after a week of slow, torturous descent of the Columbia. News of their imminent arrival preceded them, hence the sight of the in-coming flotilla, with banners waving and oars flashing in the dull gray waters of the river, was missed by no one. The entire populace had rushed to the river bank to catch a glimpse of the priests in their cassocks, as well as to greet old friends and to hear news from Montreal. In the absence of Dr. McLoughlin, who had not yet returned from Europe, James Douglas, acting Chief Factor, was the first to welcome the priests and to conduct them to the fort, where the flag was flying in honor of their arrival. Douglas ushered them into apartments prepared for them, appointed a servant to wait on them, and in every way manifested his hospitality and his delight at their arrival."[34]

It would be impossible to relate what Blanchet expected to find at the fort, since that is one of the few subjects he did not write about. He doubtlessly knew about the Reverend Beaver, and his recent discharge by Douglas himself. In view of this, the general cordiality of the Episcopalians in the fort toward Catholic priests is worthy of some comment. The expenses for the passage of Blanchet and Demers from Canada to Fort Vancouver had been paid by the Company. Now it was becoming clear that as far as the acting chief factor was concerned, the priests could make the fort their home as long as they liked, indefinitely, that they were free to come and go with the brigades at no cost, and that the Company, a British one to boot, would contribute a regular sum to their support.

As the sequel will show, neither the contributions of John McLoughlin nor those of James Douglas went unrecognized. There is a parish church in Oregon City today named St. John's, in honor of McLoughlin's patron saint, and a cathedral in Seattle named St. James in honor of Douglas' patron. Thus the kindness of these men for God's priests has given them earthly immortalness that neither could have suspected.[35]

Since the fort was the first western home of the missionaries, it would not be inappropriate to describe it as it appeared to be about this time, "the emporium of trade from Kamchatka to California." The Reverend C.G. Nicolay, an Episcopal clergyman, who visited the fort in 1843, has left one of the best descriptions of its attractions and activities:

> The fort is in shape a parallelogram, about 250 yards long by 150 broad, enclosed by a sort of wooden wall, made of pickets or large beams firmly fixed in the ground, and loosely fitted together, 25 feet high, and strongly secured on the inside by buttresses; the area is cultivated and surrounded by houses and offices, the governor's residence being in the center; there is a chapel and school. The officers of the Company dine together in the common hall, the governor presiding; but it has been remarked that the absence of their wives and the females of the establishment from the table does not contribute to the refinement of manners. There is also a public 'bachelor' hall' where after dinner the time is passed in conversation and smoking, but the latter is said to be declining as a habit. The hospitality of Fort Vancouver and its governor has been highly praised, especially by American writers, it should seem not without good reasons; and the general feeling of regret at leaving the society it affords speaks much in praise of the officers of the Company, not less than the good cheer of the governor.
>
> Beyond the fort are large granaries and storehouses; and before it, on the bank of the river, is the village in which the servants of the company reside; in all, the residents may be seven hundred. In the village is a hospital.
>
> Attached to Fort Vancouver is a magnificent farm of more than 3,000 acres; sawmills cutting many hundred thousand feet per annum; grist mills, and every other requisite for commerce and agriculture. Vessels of 14 feet draught can come abreast of the wharf at low water (says Lieutenant Wilkes),[36] and at the store of the Company every necessary can be supplied as cheap as in the United States; this, however, must be taken with considerable limitation, and refers probably to the English goods in particular. From hence the Company carries on a lucrative trade with California, the Sandwich Islands, and the Russian settlements, besides its exports to England.[37]

Nicolay was impressed by everything: the approach "which gives the stranger a high idea of its prosperity and importance; the thickly peopled village, the highly cultivated fields, the absence of all guards and defenses...." The magnificent scenery was not overlooked as Nicolay made special note of two snow covered mountain peaks, Mount Hood and Mount St. Helens.

While Blanchet admired the scenery, he had not come to convert it. He had come, he told his people, to convert them to God. For this purpose, a mission would begin that very night. There would be Mass each morning and prayers and sermons most of the day, and the mission would last as long as necessary. It actually lasted, according to Blanchet himself, four months and twenty days, which ought to be in the *Guiness Book of Records.*[38]

On Sunday, November 25, 1838, Blanchet offered Mass, making it as solemn high as possible. In the afternoon Vespers were chanted also. Many among his congregation wept, with joy we hope, though the sermons were long, tedious, and sometimes threatening. Blanchet described their content when he listed the immediate duties "of the missionaries."

"They were to warn their flock against the dangers of seduction, to destroy the false impression already received, to enlighten and confirm the faith of the wavering and deceived consciences, to bring back to the practice of religion and virtue all who had forsaken them for long years, or who, raised in infidelity, had never known nor practiced any of them. They were to teach the men their duties, the women and children their prayers and catechism, to baptize them, bless their unions, and establish good order and holiness of life everywhere.[39]

All this, he concluded, was "not effected by enchantment." The missionaries had to travel far and often and "to undergo much pain to enlighten the ignorant, to recall wavering consciences and bring back to the fold the lost sheep." This was tough talk and it characterized the man who said it.

Blanchet and Demers soon made a census of Catholics. They concluded there were seventy-six Catholics at the fort, "Canadian and Iroquois," men, women, and children. Most of the adults had contracted only "fur trade" marriages, so the priests lost no time in "separating them" until their marriages could be properly blessed.

Meanwhile everyone prayed and sang hymns. Like many French Canadians those at the fort loved to sing, and Blanchet provided for them an endless number of hymns, all in French, and all with an almost endless number of verses. For many hours each day the men formed one choir, the women another, and together they sang alternate verses with so much pleasure and gusto that the Indians in the village on the river wandered in to see and hear such beguiling music. On one occasion, one hundred and forty Indians, "who did not remain insensible to these chants," joined the assembly for the long evening prayers.[40]

Demers, it will be recalled, had a special talent for learning Indian languages. Blanchet assigned him to work with the Chinooks, who comprised most of those living in the village, a remnant, Demers noted, of a numerous tribe that inhabited the banks of the Columbia from the fort to the Pacific Ocean. In 1830 many had been carried to their graves, the victims "of the disastrous malady known by the name of fever-and-ague" or smallpox, "which God sent these Indians on account of their abominable lives."[41] Their language, says Demers, was almost unlearnable. For this reason early traders had developed a kind of hodgepodge dialect of English, French, and Indian words, numbering not over six hundred, called the "Chinook Jargon." Demers mastered this simple jargon in several weeks and thus was able to communicate without an interpreter with everyone in the village and in villages up and down the river.

COWLITZ MISSION AND THE WILLAMETTE

On two occasions, while the mission was still in progress, the vicar general departed for a time to visit the freemen and their families in their settlements, leaving Demers at the fort to keep up the barrage of sermons for renewal. Blanchet first went to Cowlitz Prairie, the place north of Fort Vancouver that had been recommended by Simpson. He left Vancouver on December 12, in a canoe paddled by four Indians. He arrived at the Cowlitz settlement, where there were four Canadian Catholic families, on Sunday, December 16.[42] On the same day he offered Mass in the home of Simon Plamondon, an indestructible but very attractive old patriarch who eventually outlived at least four wives, one of them the niece of Blanchet himself.[43]

Blanchet's principal purpose in making this journey was the establishment of a permanent mission, the first in what is now the state of Washington. Having selected six hundred and forty acres, one square mile of clear prairie land, he left his hired man, Augustine Rochon, whom he had brought from Canada, in charge of squaring timbers for a house and barns, and making rails for fences. On his departure on December 20, he appointed [Francois] Fagnant, "one of the farmers" as catechist, to teach the women and children their prayers and catechism until the missionary's next visit.[44]

Blanchet was back at the fort for Christmas. He had little to offer about the first Christmas in the wilderness. "Christmas Day," he wrote, "which in 1838 came on Tuesday, and being observed as a general holiday by the Company, the men had a chance to celebrate it. There were two low Masses at midnight in the room of the priests at which some assisted. . . . The music which accompanied the Gregorian chant at Mass, and that of the hymns at vespers in place of the anthems after the psalms, rendered the office of Christmas more solemn than usual; so that all returned home well pleased and contented."[45]

THE WILLAMETTE MISSION

On January 3, 1839, the vicar general embarked for the Willamette Valley. Two large canoes supervised by Stephen Lucier and Peter Beleque had come for him. About three in the afternoon, wearing a cloak over his cassock, Blanchet stepped gingerly into a canoe and settled down for the journey. It was Thursday. On Saturday about ten in the morning, the canoes reached the *Campement de Sable,* or Champoeg. Horses were ready for the rest of the journey and the men rode the last four miles, "horseback," Blanchet going to the log church, stopping here and there enroute to visit families. Wide-eyed, half-breed children, seeing for the first time a black robe about whom they had been lectured for months past, lost the use of their tongues or hid in the barn.

Blanchet announced the beginning of the mission as of that very evening, January 5, and took possession of his quarters in the rear of the church, the "bedend" that had been thoughtfully provided. "The following day, January 6th, being Sunday and the Epiphany of Our Lord, the church was blessed under the patronage of St. Paul, after which was celebrated the first Mass ever said in the valley, in the presence of all the Canadians, their wives and children ... the pastoral letter of the bishop who had heard their voice and sent them priests was read; the commandments of God and the Church were published, as well as the rules to be observed during the mission; and all terminated with reflections and advices which were very touching on both sides. All went home happy and willing to obey the church, even in regard to separation from their wives until their unions could be blessed."[46]

This separation of families "until their unions could be blessed" appeared to be quite proper to the vicar general and none of the Catholics objected to it. There were loud objections to it, however, from the Methodists who had already performed marriages for these people, usually at their own request. Until then, the Reverend Beaver had been the priests' principal opposition. Now the Methodists, whose numbers were increasing, became hostile. There were Methodists at The Dalles, too, east of the Cascades, where Dr. Whitman and the Reverend Spalding had missions. Blanchet's action in this matter irritated them all. Instead of cooperation between Catholics and Protestants, who were surrounded by thousands of non-Christian Indians, there was a deepening polarity, a gradually more shrill struggle of words in which both sides participated. While it is true there had been sectarian tensions on the frontier from the very beginning, it is also true that Blanchet's rather precipitous and public denial of the validity of the freemens' marriages ticked off a new kind of friction that developed into a very real persecution of the church.

Blanchet, happily, was ignorant of all of this until later. He preached hell and damnation with enthusiasm all during the mission, which lasted three weeks. His flock, in their first but not last fervor, responded generously, faithfully keeping a schedule that would kill off modern seminarians. The day began with Mass at six and a sermon after which there were prayers and "instructions intermixed with the singing of hymns, until 12 a.m. noon, and from 1 to 4 p.m."[47] Evening exercises began after the men had time to attend to their chores. "At dusk," the determined pastor wrote, "took place the evening prayer, the reading of pious books and singing of French hymns; after which some boys were taught to read French and serve at Mass." The women and children lived in tents for the duration of this survival campaign, and the men bunked where they could, most of them in the hall of the "bedend." The weather, fortunately, was very mild, "similar to the month of May in Canada." The fruits of the mission, all agreed, were most gratifying. Twenty-five Indian women were baptized "in excellent dispositions," and their unions with their husbands were blessed. Forty-seven other baptisms, mostly of children, were performed, including two who died, at which no one should be surprised, considering the demands of the mission for people unaccustomed to restraint. The two were the first to be buried in the new cemetery.[48]

There is little to suggest, in Blanchet's report, that he was worn out after three weeks of this kind of rigorous labor. He merely states that "taking the fourth and last week of his mission to rest a little, the vicar general went and took possession of a tract of ground of 640 acres for the mission and went around the whole establishment to visit the settlers." He also attended to a few other details: he had a communion rail built and installed in the church; he had a cross fixed on the gable; he selected an acre of ground for a cemetery, had it fenced and blessed it, "with a high cross in the Center." He blessed a wooden cross for each family and made sure that the hymns were properly memorized and sung at Mass, as well as at home. "Having given them five Sundays, the vicar general started on Monday, February 5th, and reached Vancouver on Tuesday, where he remained at work til March 14th."[49] The bishop, it would appear, had not sent the Canadians a human being; he had sent them a nineteenth century iron robot, programed to preach and bless crosses and holy water.

BACK TO COWLITZ—THE CATHOLIC LADDER

Blanchet's safari into the Willamette Valley had not been made in defiance of the bishop's agreement with Simpson. While the vicar general had conducted services at St. Paul, he had not, as yet at least, established a residence, and though he yearned to make St. Paul his permanent home, he respected the Hudson's Bay Company's directive to reside north of the Columbia. For the time being Cowlitz Prairie, which had a large Company farm, would be adequate for a permanent mission residence. The farm settlement was on the west side of the river, in a prairie six miles long and two wide, bounded on the east by the river and on the west by endless forests. Its soil was rich and fertile. Grass, fishing, and game were in abundance.[50] The four Canadian farmers there, including Plamondon, had been discharged from the Company's employment after long years of service.

On March 16, 1839, the vicar general arrived again at Cowlitz, this time primed and ready to give a mission. He found Augustine Rochon, "the servant of the mission," busy with his axe. He had cut six thousand fence rails and had squared the timbers for the house and barn. All that was lacking now was a team of oxen to drag these hewn logs to the building site. Blanchet moved in with Plamondon, who also provided a large room for services. There he began again with stern homilies on hell and damnation, long prayers, singing, and daily Mass.

The news of his presence at Cowlitz caused numerous delegations of Indians to come from even remote distances to see and hear the Black Robe. Among these delegations was one led by Chief Tsla-lakum, whose tribe inhabited Whidby Island in Puget Sound, one hundred and fifty miles distant from Cowlitz. They had first traveled by canoe for two days, then three days on foot, and they reached Cowlitz "with bleeding feet, famished and broken down." Their object was to see the Black Robe and to hear him speak of the Great Spirit. They could remain only a few days, so Blanchet was confronted with the age old problem of how to teach these complete strangers the prayers and simple truths of Christianity within a brief time.

His patron, St. Francis Xavier, had converted his lessons into songs, which the children of India quickly learned; then the adults learned from them. Father Peter DeSmet, who would soon appear on the northwest scene, placed the children in a certain order, like a chain, and then he taught each one a single phrase. When one child repeated his phrase after the other, an entire prayer was formed, and then other prayers, and then the most important elements of Christianity. Again the parents could learn from the children.

Blanchet had no children from Puget Sound to teach songs or prayers. His great difficulty, he said, was to give the Indians an idea of religion so plain and simple as to command their attention and which they could retain in their minds and carry back with them to their tribes.

In looking for a plan [he] imagined that by representing on a square stick, the forty centuries before Christ by 40 marks; the thirty-three years of our Lord by 33 points, followed by a cross; and the eighteen centuries and thirty nine years since, by 18 marks and 39 points, would pretty well answer his purpose, in giving him a chance to show the beginning of the world, the creation, the fall of angels, of Adam; the promise of a Savior, the time of His birth, and His death upon the cross, as well as the mission of the apostles. The plan was a great success. After eight days' explanation, the chief and his companions became masters of the subject; and, having learned to make the sign of the cross and to sing one or two hymns in the Chinook jargon, they started for home well satisfied, with a square rule thus marked, which they called *Sahale stick* (stick from above). That plan was afterwards changed from a rule to a large chart containing the great epochs of the world, such as the Deluge, the Tower of Babel, the ten commandments of God, the twelve apostles, the seven sacraments and precepts of the Church; these being useful to enable the missionary to teach the Indians and whites. It was called "The Catholic Ladder."[51]

In this simple way the first and best visual aid for missionaries was invented by Blanchet at Easter time, 1839, during his mission on the Cowlitz.

It was an immediate and howling success. So universally was the Catholic Ladder used by missionaries throughout the Northwest that it was commonly understood that the custodian "of the ladder" in each village was the catechist, in charge of the village liturgy in the absence of the priests.

Blanchet's later ladders, like DeSmet's and others who produced them, were unabashedly sectarian. Protestants were pictured as leaving the narrow path to heaven and falling head first into the vivid and unmistakable flames of hell. Stung to action by this gratuitous judgment of men, the loyal and now enraged wife of the Reverend Henry Spalding, produced a "Protestant Ladder" that provided tit for tat: the Catholic bishops, their mitres holding fast, and the black robes with faces like demons, were plunging headlong into the Protestant version of hell, as uninviting as the Catholic one.[52]

DEMERS AT FORT NISQUALLY

But all of this was a sign of the times. Neither the bishops nor black robes felt compelled to change their lives because of Mrs. Spalding's aid-to-theology, and Blanchet, for one, went about his business as usual. His mission on the Cowlitz did not end until May. On April 5 he noted that the prairies were blooming with wild flowers and strawberries. Two days later the grass was six inches high. These bucolic observations, however, were interrupted by a report on April 8 that a Methodist minister, the Reverend David Leslie, was on his way to Nisqually, a hundred miles north, to establish a Methodist mission among the Indians there.[53] This was ghastly news, of course, and Blanchet quickly summoned Demers from Vancouver, and sent him to Nisqually posthaste, where he arrived on April 21, "drenched with cold and continuous rain."[54]

The Hudson's Bay Company had a major fort at Nisqually, and also a considerable agricultural enterprise, both under the supervision of Mr. William Kitson, whose wife Helene was the daughter of one of the frontier's most colorful traders, Finian McDonald, or "Red Hair."[55] Kitson, described by Governor Simpson "as a short dapper little fellow with a very limited education, knew how his bread was buttered." A subject of McLoughlin and very familiar with the Company's current policies, he welcomed Demers with a cordialness reserved for top brass. Demers was given the run of the fort for the mission, which he lost no time in organizing. A problem soon developed, however. So many Indians attended the services, beginning with Mass at five in the morning, that Kitson feared for the safety of the fort and on one occasion, inadvertently pushed one of the Indians in a rough and rude manner. Only the sudden appearance of Demers put an end to the threatened riot. After that Demers conducted his Mass, prayers, songs and long sermons outside the fort, where Helene Kitson faithfully joined members from an estimated twenty-two different tribes. The mission lasted ten days, and when it was over Helene was one of thirteen who came forward and requested baptism. This was a great triumph, of course, like the conversion of a queen, and when Demers finally rejoined Blanchet at Cowlitz, both gloated over the confusion of Brother Wilson, whom Leslie had left in charge of the Methodist mission. Wilson, they alleged, had become despondent "at being witness to all he had seen."

Blanchet left orders with Rochon to complete the house at Cowlitz. Then he and Demers, enjoying more than their customary degree of righteousness, left by canoe for Vancouver. As the four Indians softly dipped their paddles, speeding them downriver, there was only one flaw to their contentment: Demers had a severe cold, which he had acquired at Nisqually. It was a small price to pay for such glorious success, but it kept him feeling miserable for several weeks.

CONTROVERSIES WITH THE METHODISTS

By this time April had passed and May, a beautiful month in the Willamette Valley, was passing quickly. The two priests had returned to

St. Paul, Demers to nurse his cold, after he had decided that he was good for nothing else, and Blanchet to tilt with his Methodist neighbors. The latter had finally revealed to him their wrath and indignation because he had re-baptized and re-married a number of persons already baptized or married by them. Making matters worse a number of Catholics, on demand from Blanchet, had withdrawn from the Methodist temperance society and prayer meetings conducted by the brethren.[56] The Reverend Leslie, determined to be revenged, says Blanchet, got up a revival, which the Catholics boycotted. Finally the Methodists complained to Acting Governor James Douglas that the priests were using undue influence "in order to keep the lambs of the flock out of the clutches of the Wesleyan wolves," Blanchet growled, using a mixed metaphor, which no one in the heat of battle noticed.

Douglas responded that the matter was none of his business, so the frustrated Methodists circulated throughout the valley copies of the "awful disclosures" of *Maria Monk*, an obscene book about Montreal convent life that had been completely discredited by Canadian Protestants years before. Now it was the settlers' turn to become indignant "at this vile artifice, hypocrisy, and ingratitude of the Methodist ministers whose lives they had been the means of saving but a short month before." It appears that an Indian had stolen some wheat, and having been discovered, was beaten so badly that his tribe threatened to massacre everyone at the Methodist mission. Leslie appealed to the Canadians to save them, which the Canadians gladly did.[57]

DEMERS ON THE UPPER COLUMBIA

While spring planting and the war of words occupied the Catholics in the Willamette, their priests were making plans for the summer months. The fur brigade had arrived at Vancouver on June 6.[58] When it departed again for the east on June 22, Demers went with it as far as Walla Walla. This flotilla consisted of nine barges manned by fifty-seven men under the command of Chief Factor Peter Ogden and Samuel Black. Arriving at Walla Walla, Demers procured an Indian to take him to Colville, where he eventually arrived, eight days behind schedule because of the treacherous behavior of his guide. At Colville he preached a mission lasting thirty-three days, then moved to Fort Okanogan, where he preached another mission of eight days. He found the location of this fort "forbidding and sterile," but he wrote: "For all that the population there is eager for the word of God. I had the pleasure of meeting there a Christian by the name of Robillard, who had taught the prayers to the natives. That unsuspected help spared me many difficulties."[59]

Having completed his mission at Okanogan, Demers returned to Walla Walla, where he preached another, lasting two weeks. Pambrun, like Robillard, was his catechist and interpreter, when necessary.

There is something very satisfying in the memory of men like Pambrun and Robillard. During the early formation of the church in old Oregon, they casually slipped into the roles of quasi-deacons, without formalities, simply because they were needed, for lack of priests, and because they wanted to share the religion they themselves valued. These were the French Canadians. Later the Irish, retired soldiers from the Indian Wars would occupy the same roles.

BLANCHET RETURNS TO THE COWLITZ

While Demers was "saving the souls of the redskins" on the plateau, Blanchet traveled to the Cowlitz, reaching that place on July 20.[60] He found Rochon recovering from stab wounds inflicted by an Indian who had sold him a horse, then tried to take it back again.[60] Rochon had completed the exterior of a log house, thirty feet by twenty and Blanchet offered Mass within it on the following day, and dedicated it under the patronage of St. Francis Xavier. Blanchet found also a barn, sixty feet by thirty, roofed and ready for a crop of six bushels of wheat and nine bushels of peas, quite enough for pea soup in the foreseeable future. Twenty-four acres of land had been fenced and fifteen more plowed for crops to be sown in the fall.

In August, Blanchet left Cowlitz for Nisqually, still anxious about the activities of Brother Wilson. He need not have worried. Wilson, a former "sailor boy" seems to have been as harmless as a garter snake, and almost as quiet. One suspects that if Blanchet had extended a hand of friendship Wilson would have accepted it gladly, and with enormous relief. Blanchet preached another mission at Nisqually, starting with Mass at five in the morning and Mr. Kitson served as his interpreter. As the days passed, Indians began to arrive in canoes until there were three hundred of them, one of them being Tsa-lakum, who still had his sahale stick.

Thus, the summer of 1839 passed for these two priests, who often regretted their inability to be everywhere at once, to respond to the needs of Indians who clamored for them but sometimes lost interest and returned to their old ways. As yet there had been no crisis and the future looked promising. The vicar general had unlimited credit at the Fort Vancouver store where he and Demers could buy what they required. No one, so far, had pressed for payment and the day of reckoning was a long way off.

THE FLATHEADS' FINAL DELEGATION TO ST. LOUIS

Neither priest could know that during this very summer the final act in another drama involving the Northwest church was slowly beginning. In the camps of the Flatheads on the Bitteroot, all hopes for the return of Old Ignace and his four companions had given way to despair. Like their brothers who had gone seven summers before, the five braves had vanished, leaving no trace whatever of how they had perished. After seven winters the Flatheads had no black robes of their own, though they knew there were black robes from Canada in the country beyond the mountains where the sun set in the sky. They must try again and this time they would succeed.

Two of the Iroquois, adopted by the Flatheads, showed themselves willing to undertake the task. These were Peter Gaucher, sometimes called "Left-hand Peter," and Young Ignace, the son of Old Ignace, who had been to St. Louis with his father. Leaving the Bitteroot Valley in the summer of 1839, they joined a Hudson's Bay Company brigade that floated down the Yellowstone River to the Missouri and on to St. Louis. In passing St. Joseph's Mission at Council Bluffs, they stopped to visit the blackrobes there, among whom was Father Peter DeSmet, a Flemish Jesuit attached to the Missouri mission.[61]

The two Indians from the Far West created a greater sensation than if President Martin Van Buren himself had walked through the door. DeSmet was ecstatic and he spent hours with them speaking in French which both Indians could understand, and questioning them about all particulars related to their nation. He offered to accompany them to their homes and composed for them a letter to his superiors in St. Louis, whence the Iroquois were determined to go. They arrived safely in St. Louis and met the Jesuits at the University, who doubtlessly remembered Young Ignace, and Bishop Rosati, who assured them that a priest would be sent in the following spring. Young Ignace remained for the winter at the Jesuit Novitiate at Florissant, so that he could serve as a guide to the Blackrobe. Peter Gaucher, however, accompanied by a Nez Perce, started for the Bitteroot Valley in late October, to bring the good news that the Blackrobe would come in the spring.

That winter was one of the coldest on record. Undismayed, Peter and his companion, with cold arctic winds and early blizzards blinding their way, urged their horses forward, warmed and sustained only by the thoughts of the good news they carried. Their journey was one of the most terrible in the annals of the West. Exhausted, starved, and almost frozen, the Nez Perce died on the trail, the last of ten Indians who gave their lives for the cause, but, Peter Gaucher pressed on. Finally in the early spring of 1840, when the Bitteroot was swollen with melting snow, Peter, skin and bones, but still alive, suddenly appeared in the Flathead camp at Eight Mile Creek.[62] Before taking food or rest he announced to the startled assembly that the Blackrobe, led by Young Ignace, was surely coming. He would arrive at the rendezvous on the Green River when the Long Knives came to trade for hides.[63]

WILLAMETTE MISSION APPROVED

Blanchet and Demers, meanwhile, had not been idle. On September 14, 1839, the Feast of the Holy Cross, Blanchet had blessed and planted a huge cross at the mission on the Cowlitz. He returned to Vancouver about the same time that Young Ignace and Peter Gaucher, crossing the continent, reached St. Louis. Demers joined Blanchet on October 1. The joy they shared at being together again was soon confirmed by a letter of James Douglas, who wrote as follows:

Fort Vancouver, Oct. 9th, 1839
My dear Sir: I am directed to inform you that the governor and committee have no further objection to the establishment of a Roman Catholic mission in the Willamette; and you are therefore at liberty to take any means you may consider necessary towards the promotion of that object. I remain, my dear Sir,
Yours very truly,
James Douglas[64]

Dr. John McLoughlin, of course, had wrung this concession out of the company in London. He himself, it was rumored, was expected daily by express boat from Canada.

Before he arrived, however, the two priests moved their frugal possessions out of their quarters at the fort, Blanchet taking his to St. Paul, which now became his official residence, and Demers moving his to the Cowlitz mission, to which Blanchet assigned him. Each had recently received a new bell for his church, one of them eighty pounds and the other fifty, so their canoes rested heavily in the water and their navigation required a longer time than usual. Blanchet had scarcely arrived at St. Paul when McLoughlin appeared on October 18. Full of concern for the vicar general and eager to visit all of the settlers in their homes, the White Headed Eagle combined his business with pleasure: he took mental note of everything he saw. He, too, was planning retirement. He has taken up a personal land claim in 1829, at the site of the falls on the Willamette, including an island in the river at the crest of the falls.[65] In the same year he had begun the erection of a sawmill at the falls, and several years later he had a mill race blasted out of the rocks at the head of the island.[66] What all this indicated, besides his eye for business, was his intention to retire in this area, rather than in eastern Canada, and more specifically in what all regarded as future American territory. His was one of the most valuable land claims in Oregon. He could not foresee how it would be stolen from him in part because of his conversion to Catholicism, nor could he foresee, as he galloped from one settler's home to another, the richest and most powerful man in Oregon, how he would die penniless and prematurely old, a broken man, betrayed by those he had befriended.

Nor could Blanchet foresee his future. He built a tower for his eighty pound bell and two days before Christmas he blessed it, as though it were a person with a voice of its own. Demers, too, had erected a tower for his bell. On Christmas night, 1839, the prolonged ringing of both bells called the faithful to Midnight Mass to commemorate the Coming of the Christ Child. Christmas carols, for the first time, filled the churches, and the countryside beyond. In all of old Oregon, men were at peace with one another.

3

PETER DeSMET AND THE JESUITS
1841–1843

Unlike Blanchet and Demers, Peter John DeSmet, born and raised in Belgium, was a naturalized American citizen.[1] He was perhaps excessively proud of this status, which tells something about his flamboyant personality.[2] In truth DeSmet was an incurable romantic and his love affair with his adopted country was exceeded only by another love, the American Indians. For him there was no such thing as a "bad" Indian, and he seems to have had some fixed impression that all the Indians on the continent were ready and willing for conversion. All they lacked, he often said, were priests to baptize them. He had left his home in Termonde, Belgium, without his father's knowledge or permission, to go to America to become a Jesuit. This was in 1821, when DeSmet was twenty in years, a strong robust youth, short in stature, with puffy eyelids, a plump chin, and long, flowing brown hair.[3] Though his heart was as tender as a mother's, he had the courage of a bear hunter. He was absolutely fearless—one feature of his character that saved his life, perhaps many times. He was very pious, also, and he tended to discover miracles behind every bush.

In America, appropriately, he made his novitiate in a log building at Florissant, Missouri, a kind of French settlement for retired frontiersmen, like the Willamette's French prairie. The Missouri Mission, then, was subject to the Jesuits province of Maryland. There were others like him at Florissant, great-hearted young men who were preparing to become missionaries to the Indians and scattered whites of mid-America. In due course DeSmet was ordained to the priesthood, but he seems to have become confused. After a brief time he left the Jesuit Order and returned to Europe.[4] A few years of reflection and rest restored his spirits. He was readmitted to the Order by the general, Father John Roothaan in Rome, and was assigned again to the Indian missions of America, for which his love had never wavered.

DESMET'S FIRST VOYAGE WEST

When Young Ignace appeared at his door he was overjoyed. The prospects of a voyage to the Far West, to meet and baptize countless hundreds of already godly Indians, stirred him so deeply that he could think of nothing else. His promise to Ignace, that he would come to the Bitteroot, was a premature one for, as yet at least, he had not the slightest evidence that his superior would assign him rather than another. But it was characteristic of his affinity with optimism and his own kind of sixth sense for divining his future prospects.

As it turned out he was eventually appointed to this task, for which he had so earnestly entreated, despite the misgivings of Roothaan in Rome and the hesitation of the mission superior in St. Louis. He left Westport for the great beyond on April 30, 1840, sitting astride his horse like one of Napoleon's chaplains, eager to cover the distance to the rendezvous, lest he arrive too late and miss the Flatheads. At his side was Young Ignace, a Jesuit at heart, destined to serve God in another way, which was as noble as his father's.

There was no need for DeSmet to be impatient. He was with the American Fur Company brigade of some thirty members, who were as anxious as he to reach the rendezvous, to trade for the best skins. The prairie grass for their mounts was plentiful; this was three years before the Great Emigration of 1843 when thousands of horses and cattle stripped the pasturage. Most of the Indians were at peace and no other obstacles, save sheer space, lay in their paths. They surpassed this in just two months, arriving at the rendezvous at the end of June.

Ten Flathead warriors were there to greet the Blackrobe. "Our meeting," DeSmet wrote, "was not that of strangers, but of friends. They were like children who, after a long absence, run to meet their father. I wept for joy in embracing them, and with tears in their eyes they welcomed me with tender words, with childlike simplicity."[5]

GREAT MASS OF THE PRAIRIE

July 5 was a Sunday that year. On that day DeSmet offered Mass at the rendezvous, on a stone altar, on which he had first placed wild flowers gathered on the green meadows. "I preached in French and English to the American and Canadian hunters, and then through an interpreter addressed the Flatheads and Snakes. The Canadians sang some hymns in French and Latin while the Indians chanted in their own tongue. The service was truly catholic. The place where the Holy Sacrifice was offered has since been called by the trappers the prairie of the Holy Sacrifice'."[6]

DeSmet, unlike Blanchet, preached mostly sweetness-and-light, the goodness of God rather than his judgments. Thus, it came to happen that the Indians and mountain men of the wilderness soon learned to love DeSmet almost fanatically. For Blanchet they had more respect than love.

After the Great Mass of the Prairie, DeSmet and his honor guard broke camp and traveled north to the main Flathead camp at Pierre's Hole, at the foot of the Three Tetons. They arrived here on July 12. DeSmet was unprepared for what he saw, an encampment of over sixteen hundred Indians, Flatheads, Nez Perces, and Pend d'Oreilles, some of whom had come eight hundred miles to see him. DeSmet was escorted to the tepee of the great chief called Big Face, who welcomed him in the most solemn manner possible. "Our hearts rejoice," he said, "for today the Great Spirit has granted our petition."

For several days DeSmet preached and taught the eager Indians the customary Christian prayers. He baptized over three hundred of them and promised others that he would baptize them also when they were prepared. Then the Indians broke camp again and moved north, their long column of horses stirring up clouds of dust that extended for miles.

On July 22 they reached the continental divide, the watershed that separates the flow of water to the Missouri from the tributaries of the Columbia. The Indians pitched camp there, in the cool mountain meadows, their tepees placed among the willows along the tiny streams, which criss-crossed the high plateau. There they rested their horses. After the long climb, DeSmet, full of vigor yet, spent the day of rest by exploring a mountain peak above them. For five hours he climbed, crossing snow fields and clambering over huge crag-like cliffs, until he reached a flat rock from which he could see in all directions, into endless space. Profoundly moved by the grandeur, he prayed. Before he left this lofty crowsnest, he scratched the following into the soft sandstone:

Sanctus Ignatius Patronus Montium.
Die Julii 23, 1840[7]

He also composed a little poem:

Salut Roche Majestueuse!
Futur asile de bonheur,
Des ses Tresors le Divin Coeur
T'ouvre aujourd 'hui la source hereuse.[8]

The next morning DeSmet offered a Mass of Thanksgiving at the foot of the mountain. The Indians moved north again, into what is now Montana, into the Beaverhead—Jefferson River Valley, where on the banks of the river, DeSmet offered Mass again, for the first time in that remote part of the world.[9] There near the three forks of the Missouri he hurriedly scribbled a letter to Blanchet, about whom he had been briefed before he left St. Louis. "Mr. Bruette" he wrote, "who is so kind as to carry my letter to Fort Colville, just ready to start, gives me but a few minutes to write."

Part of this letter ran as follows:

Very Reverend Sir:

Your Reverence will be glad to learn that Mgr. Rosati, Bishop of St. Louis, in concert with my provincial Superior of the Society of Jesus in Missouri and in compliance with the desire often repeated of the Flatheads, Pend' Oreilles, and a great number of Nez Perces, has sent me to the Rocky Mountains to visit these missions. I have found the first two in the best desirable disposition, well resolved to stand by the true children of Jesus Christ. The few weeks I had the happiness to pass among them have been the happiest of my life and give me firm hope, with the grace of God, to see soon in this country, so long forsaken, the fervor of the first Christians. Since I am among them I have three, four and five instructions daily. They cannot be tired, all come to my lodge at the first ringing of the bell. They are anxious to lose none of my words relating to these instructions on these heavenly subjects, and if I had the strength to speak to them they would listen to me whole days and nights. I have baptized about two hundred of their little children and I expect to baptize in a short time one hundred and fifty adults.[10]

DeSmet concluded this report by stating, "I will return to St. Louis before the winter, and will be back next spring with a caravan of missionaries, who are already preparing themselves."[11]

This letter was dispatched to Blanchet on August 10, 1840. Some weeks would pass before it reached its destination. During those weeks, with his back to the setting sun, DeSmet pursued his journey to St. Louis by the way of the Yellowstone and Missouri, with a single companion. This was Jean Baptiste Velder, a Belgian of Ghent, who had spent fourteen years trapping beaver in the mountains. On December 31, 1840, DeSmet was back again "in the kindly shelter of St. Louis University, having left it for his first journey to the Rocky Mountains nine months before."[12]

ASTORIA AND WHIDBY ISLAND

For some months Blanchet did not hear about DeSmet's presence in the west. In May, while the Jesuit was still crossing the plains, he sent Demers to Astoria at the mouth of the Columbia to preach a mission to the Chinooks. Demers, having arrived at Astoria on May 21, pitched his tent and looked about for Indians to fill it.[13] He found, instead, the Reverend Daniel Lee. Precisely at this time the ship *Lausanne,* chartered by the Methodists, crossed the treacherous bar on the Columbia and entered the harbor. Lee, said Blanchet tartly, left Demers "a clear stage, being in a hurry, no doubt, to visit the ship in order to have the first choice for a wife among the young misses."[14]

Demers, who could not have cared less, walked through the Chinook camp, tinkling a little bell in one hand and carrying the indispensable Catholic Ladder in the other. He succeeded in gathering a congregation, to whom he preached for three weeks before returning to the Cowlitz to supervise the erection of the new church.[15]

The vicar general had been at the Cowlitz until recently. He had departed rather unexpectedly, to see Kitson at Nisqually, who had become very ill. He also took the occasion to visit Whidby Island where he offered Mass on May 31, 1840, for four hundred Indians, among whom was faithful Tsla-lakum, the *"Sokwamish"* Indian with the Ladder.[16] With the help of his Indians he raised a wooden cross twenty-four feet long, which was still on the island in 1841 when Lieutenant Charles Wilkes, an American explorer, visited it and named it Cross Island.[17] Like other missionaries, Blanchet directed his neophytes to prostrate themselves before the cross and venerate it as the sign of our salvation and to sing many hymns, which the Indians enjoyed most of all. Blanchet baptized one hundred and twenty-two children that day, a ceremony which lasted four hours despite the oppressive heat, which made the children irritable. Blanchet simply reported, "The children were scared and crying, and soon all retired."[18]

Blanchet himself soon retired, all the way to the Cowlitz where he was able to share two happy days with Demers, before the latter had to leave to join the fur brigade on its summer voyage to Walla Walla and Colville.

DEMERS IN THE NORTH

Demers was in Colville during that late, hot summer when he first heard rumors that other Blackrobes were somewhere in the Rocky Mountains, teaching the Indians about the Great Spirit. One can guess his thoughts regarding this, when he wrote a letter on August 6, 1840, to the mysterious priests, "Catholic Missionaries with the Flatheads." He was not the kind to feel threatened by an unknown, unseen laborer in his own vineyard.

Said Demers, "Though I have not as yet the pleasure of knowing your names, I eagerly take the opportunity which is presented to send you news of the two poor missionaries of the Columbia, knowing that I am writing to Catholic priests, ministers of our holy religion, who have generously come to sacrifice themselves for the salvation of the savages. With what joy and contentment have I learned of your arrival among the Flatheads!"[19]

It should be noted that this letter to DeSmet was written only four days before DeSmet wrote to Blanchet. Both letters, of course, reached their destiny, without benefit of stamps or any such trappings of civilization.

EFFORTS TO OBTAIN NEW MISSIONARIES

Blanchet during this period had been writing letters of his own, to superiors in Canada. Quite reasonably, we think he was urging the bishop to send additional priests "for the harvest was great and the laborers few." The bishop agreed with the proposals, but felt helpless before the great bureaucracy that controlled the methods of transportation from Montreal to Fort Vancouver.

Signay had appealed to Governor Simpson, who replied in a manner that was most unsatisfactory. "I have read Your Lordship's letter," Simpson wrote, "before the Governor and Committee and...I am instructed to say that the Governor and the Committee do not feel disposed to facilitate the extension of the Roman Catholic missions on the river Columbia until they receive further information in reference to the progress that has been made by Rev. Blanchet and his colleagues in that quarter."[20]

No one had to suggest to Signay that the Honorable Company was stalling. Thus, His Lordship sought other avenues for his missionaries to follow. He contacted a local Jesuit in Montreal, Father Chazelle, inquiring of him if it were possible to send a Jesuit "of American origin," to Oregon. Then, after he heard of DeSmet's presence in the mountains, he wrote to Bishop Rosati in St. Louis, to learn about other routes to the west, in particular about DeSmet's route. He had two priests to send to Oregon he said, but the Hudson's Bay Company, which had accorded transportation for Blanchet and Demers, was not disposed to grant the same favor to other missionaries.[21]

Bishop Rosati, in Europe for his *ad limina* visit with the pope, had left a Jesuit, Father Peter Verhaegen, now superior of the Missouri Vice Province, in charge of his diocese. Verhaegen responded to Bishop Signay's request for information by providing some particulars about the overland route with the American Fur Company, which cost $800 per person, one way. He reminded Signay that DeSmet had not as yet returned from the mountains and he did not expect him until the following spring, but he assumed that thus far, at least, he was safe and busily engaged in Oregon.[22] At this point Verhaegen added a postscript,

"I have unsealed my letter to tell you my lord, that Father DeSmet has just returned from the mountains. Everything appears favorable to our project. It is, therefore, very probable, not to say certain, that some of the eFathers will leave here in the month of March. The good Father did not see the reverend gentlemen [Blanchet and Demers], but he wrote to them."

JESUITS LEAVE TO START A MISSION

The next day was New Year's, 1841. DeSmet, bubbling with enthusiasm, took no time to rest. He was already at work, making plans for the spring expedition "to the mountains" apparently oblivious to the fact that several hurdles had to be overcome before he would be allowed to return to his Flatheads. Like most dreamers he gave little attention to practical considerations, such as available men and money. There were, at that time, only twenty-four priests in the entire Vice Province of Missouri, including DeSmet. These Jesuits were scattered throughout the huge Mississippi basin. As for the cost, the eight hundred dollars per person quoted by Verhaegen to Signay covered only transportation to Wyoming, less than half the distance to Oregon, though, it must be admitted, additional mileage with the Indians cost very little more. Greater costs, however, would be incurred once the missionaries arrived at their destination. Plows, tools, seed, farm animals, nails, and other supplies would have to be purchased from the Hudson's Bay Company, which did not take Hail Mary's in exchange.

While DeSmet's superior conducted official consultations on the subject and corresponded with the general in Rome, DeSmet, as optimistic as Pollyanna, went begging from city to city, gathering what he could, including the jewelry and other trinkets of nice young ladies who were enchanted by his account of the holiness of his Indians. In his net, so to speak, he caught one Jesuit, Father Nicolas Point, an irascible Frenchman, who had been rector at Grand Coteau. Fortunately for the proposed mission, he had been removed by Verhaegen, though it must be admitted this unexpected turn of events did not prove to be an unmixed blessing. Point, it was reported, had been unable to control a community made up of French and American born Jesuits.[23] This was bad enough, but deadly epidemics of yellow fever that ravaged students and faculty of the college added to everyone's woes, especially the rector's. Verhaegen decided to remove him in the spring of 1840 and Point left Grand Choteau for St. Louis on July 21, 1840. "Ever after Father Point suffered periods of melancholy during which he berated himself, wholly unnecessarily, for his failure at Grand Coteau."[24]

Point was an excellent, but untrained artist. He could not bear to think of missing an opportunity like traveling with DeSmet to paint the exotic Indians. Thus he insisted that he be appointed to accompany DeSmet on his second voyage to the mountains. Verhaegen, apparently, welcomed the opportunity to appease the former rector. It was the Peter Principle: kick him upstairs.

Several times Verhaegen got cold feet, and was ready to call it off, but DeSmet's enthusiasm overcame Verhaegen's prudence, and six Jesuits, three priests and three brothers, finally gathered at Westport to organize their own wagon train to the west. Included among the priests were Peter DeSmet, superior of the new mission, Nicolas Point, and Gregory Mengarini, a young Italian fresh from Rome, selected by the Jesuit general himself. There were three brothers, Joseph Specht, an Alsatian, aged 32, known as a "tinner;" William Claessens, a Belgian, who looked like a French maitre'd; and Charles Huet, another Belgian, aged 35, said to be a carpenter.

To lead the wagon train DeSmet hired Thomas Fitzpatrick, a noted trail guide, who had conducted Marcus Whitman and his party across the plains in 1836. Fitzpatrick, also called "Broken Hand" by the Indians, was Irish born, but not conspicuously religious.[25] John Gray and Jim Baker, noted hunters and trappers, were employed to supply the party with game enroute. Finally, there were five teamsters and a young Englishman who was called "Romaine." His task was not given.

THE JOURNEY ACROSS THE PLAINS

In the early morning of May 10, 1841, Fitzpatrick barked his orders and the wagon train moved into single file. The three priests sat nervously on horses, all as grave in appearance as generals before a battle. The brothers were on carts and wagons. "The wagons started off in single file, the four carts and one small wagon of the missionaries; next eight wagons drawn by mules and horses, and lastly five wagons drawn by seventeen yolk of oxen."[26] With the morning sun on their backs the train moved steadily into the west where the almost empty prairies stretched for over a thousand miles.

At the Kaw River in Kansas the Jesuit train was joined by another, led by John Bidwell, fifty people added to the smaller group for protection against hostile Indians. Later another small group joined them, bringing the total to seventy-seven people in twenty wagons, "the first immigrant train to California."[27]

The journey had begun badly, some horses and mules were lost, and as it progressed the Jesuits fared no better. Mengarini was thrown from his horse six times, and Point, almost as often. Once DeSmet at full gallop was pitched over the horse's head. But no one was injured and DeSmet interpreted this as miraculous. On June 2, a solemn meeting was convened to discuss the Jesuits' wagons, which were in the lead and were going too fast. The complaint was well-taken, but DeSmet, keenly aware of the train's frequent delays, worried about his promise to meet the Flathead vanguard at the rendezvous in Wyoming about the first of July.

DeSmet's apprehensions were justified. The Indians had kept their appointment, but after sixteen days of waiting, when their food supplies were depleted, they departed for the mountains to hunt, leaving three of their number to await the coming of the Blackrobes. When the wagon train reached the rendezvous, a month late, the three Flatheads were still there. DeSmet sent John Gray, the hunter, to find the other Flatheads to direct them to meet him at Fort Hall, which was west and north of the rendezvous. The wagon train then creaked slowly forward, passing through Wyoming into Idaho. At Soda Springs, one hundred miles west of the present Wyoming border, another meeting was held in the late afternoon of August 10. Bidwell announced that he and his companions would turn south at this point, into Utah, then through the deserts of Nevada to California. The Jesuits would turn north to Fort Hall, and the third group decided to continue west to Fort Boise and beyond. DeSmet with his three Indians left that same evening for Fort Hall, to be there before the other Flatheads arrived.

On August 15, the Feast of the Assumption, the Jesuits and Indians were reunited. There were whoops of joy by the Indians, polite introductions, and incessant battles with swarms of mosquitoes, which tormented everyone day and night. There was also a shortage of food, and pemmican purchased at the Fort soon disappeared. From this time until they reached Montana, the travelers lived on fresh trout.

On August 30, they joined the main band of the Flatheads, who were hunting buffalo in the upper Beaverhead Valley. They were greeted with much affection. Long meetings, which the Indians especially liked, were conducted to determine the best place for the first mission. The Flatheads urged that it be placed in the Bitteroot Valley, where most of them wintered each year, and the Jesuits agreed to consider it. Then they began the last stage of their journey—several times over wretched trails that had never known the passage of wagons. Finally the Jesuits with their guides reached Hell Gate or "Gates of Hell," so designated because the treacherous Blackfeet often lurked behind the narrow defile in the rocks. For two days the Jesuits camped beyond it, where Missoula lies today, while they undertook several scouting sorties to confirm the Indians' recommendations. Having completed this, they selected a site in the broad, fertile valley, on the land the Indians had suggested. For the last time they loaded their creaking carts and turned south about forty miles and pitched their tents near the banks of the river, with its cool, sweet water. They had arrived at last, September 24, 1841, the Feast of Our Lady of Mercy.

ST. MARY'S MISSION

It was evening time. The Indians sent them buffalo meat for their dinner. The next morning they attended Mass, then began the arduous task of building a mission residence with the materials at hand. They called this mission St. Mary's. DeSmet, like Blanchet, raised a huge cross hewn from pine logs, and then he lined up his Flathead friends and persuaded them all, from the Chief to the youngest child, to come forward to embrace the symbol of their salvation. One by one they kissed the cross and on their knees swore a great oath to die a thousand deaths rather than abandon their religion. This was regarded as a good mission practice, a sample of the harshness of the times, and though many Indians did not have the slightest idea of what they were doing, most were duly impressed with their new obligations and some even lived and died by them.

The first St. Mary's residence, thrown up in a hurry, was built of logs with one door and several small windows two feet by one, covered with buckskin. "A church was soon built, of similar rude materials, fields were plowed for spring planting, and rails were split for fencing. While the brothers labored at these tasks, the fathers conducted classes in catechism and singing. Mengarini organized a band with instruments brought from St. Louis, a clarinet, a flute, two accordions, a tambourine, picolo, cymbols and base drums."[28] Point, directed by DeSmet to design a model mission like the Jesuit Reductions of Paraguay, laid out one on paper, but this was never realized. Point preferred to paint Indians, which he did whenever he was not engaged in other duties. By lamplight at night, when other activities were finished, Mengarini studied the Flathead language, becoming so adept in it that he was able to publish a dictionary and grammar for the use of other missionaries. He also gathered as much information as possible about the Flatheads and their neighbors for future publications.[29]

DeSmet, meanwhile, had left St. Mary's on October 28, escorted by ten Flathead warriors. He first visited the Kalispel Indians who lived in the mountains north and west of the Flatheads, but spoke the same tongue. When he reached the Kalispel camp, he was amazed to learn that all members of the tribe knew the Christian prayers. The Kalispels, long before his arrival, had sent one young member of the tribe, who had an excellent memory, to learn the prayers from the Flatheads. Then he taught the Kalispels. DeSmet baptized all of the children of this tribe and promised to send a missionary as soon as possible.

This was a general pattern of DeSmet's missionary tours. In the course of the months, and years, that followed, he visited tribes of Indians all over the interior of the Northwest, taught them prayers, baptized the children, and promised them missionaries, more missionaries than he could ever provide.

DeSmet's principal objective in this journey during the autumn of 1841, was Fort Colville where he purchased supplies for the mission: oats, wheat and potatoes for planting.[30] He also purchased other seeds and cows for the farm. As a gift to the mission the Fort's chief factor added supplies that were unknown to DeSmet until he returned to St. Mary's, "a number of delicacies such as sugar, coffee, tea, chocolate, butter, crackers, flour, poultry and so forth."[31]

DeSmet arrived at St. Mary's on December 8, 1841, the Feast of the Immaculate Conception. He had been absent forty-two days, had baptized one hundred and ninety people, and had preached the gospel to over two thousand Indians.

On Christmas Day, DeSmet administered baptism to one hundred and fifty adults and performed thirty-two marriages. He had begun his day by offering Mass at seven in the morning. At five in the afternoon he was still in the chapel. "The next day," he wrote to Verhaegen, "I sang a solemn High Mass in Thanksgiving for the favors God had showered upon His people. Between six and seven hundred converts, counting the children baptized the previous year, assembled in the heart of the wilds, where until now the name of God was unknown."[32]

ON THE LOWER COLUMBIA

Blanchet and Demers during the latter part of 1841, enjoyed no triumphs like these. They had labored, not in vain, with tribes heretofore not evangelized, like the Clackamas Indians, whose allegiance was being challenged by Brother Alvin Waller of the Methodist mission. Waller produced a Protestant Ladder to prove his claims, but Blanchet, somewhat righteously, asserted that the Indians regarded his Ladder as superior to Waller's.

Demers had lost his good friend, the chief clerk at Fort Walla Walla, in May.[34] Pierre Pambrun, who had served the church long and well, died in the prime of life, when everyone least expected it. An expert horseman, he had mounted his horse that day, carelessly perhaps, then had fallen, with his leg caught in the stirrup. The frightened horse dragged him some distance, and when Dr. Whitman, summoned from his mission, arrived to save him from his injuries, it was too late.

Another friend, William Kitson from Nisqually, died at Vancouver after a long illness, during which he requested and received baptism. His funeral conducted by Blanchet at the fort a few days after Christmas 1841, was apparently, a rather cheerful affair because Kitson had "died happy."[35] Certainly he had much to gain by death, since, he, too, had served God well by performing the duties of a catechist, even before he became a Catholic.

By this time Blanchet's letter to DeSmet had reached him at St. Mary's in the mountains. The vicar general, still struggling to establish the church in his vast territory, in which DeSmet now estimated the population at two hundred thousand souls, had not received help from Canada.[36] Having been informed of the presence of six Jesuits at St. Mary's, he quite naturally felt strongly compelled to appeal for the help of at least two. After assuring DeSmet of his own interest in the prosperity of the Jesuit mission, he went on to urge his own case:

> Judge then, Sir, how great are our labors and how much it would advance our mutual interest, were you to send hither one of your Rev. Fathers, with one of the three lay-brothers. In my opinion, it is on this spot that we must seek to establish our holy religion. It is here that we should have a college, convent, and schools. It is here that one day a successor of the Apostles will come from some part of the world to settle, and provide for the spiritual necessities of this vast region, which, moreover, promises such an abundant harvest.—Here is the field of battle, where we must in the first place gain the victory. It is here that we must establish a beautiful mission. From the lower stations the Missionaries and Rev. Fathers could go forth in all directions to supply the distant stations, and announce the word of God to the infidels still plunged in darkness and the shadows of death. If your plans should not permit you to change the place of your establishment, at least take into consideration the need in which we stand of a Rev. Father and of a lay-brother to succor us in our necessities.[37]

Not content with this, he persuaded Dr. McLoughlin to appeal to DeSmet also. McLoughlin extended a cordial invitation to the Jesuits to come to Vancouver, then added:

> I am fully convinced that the most effectual mode to diffuse the doctrines of the Roman Catholic Church in this part of the world is by establishing it on a good foundation in the Willamette and Cowlitz among the settlers—as the Indians will join themselves in what they see done by the whites. . . . . But if one of you with one or two lay brothers could come to assist Messrs. Blanchet and Demers til their reinforcements came from Canada, it would be an immense benefit to religion.[38]

It is not likely that DeSmet missed the point Blanchet was making: he wanted the Jesuits to move their western headquarters to the Willamette and to establish a college at or near St. Paul. Dazzled, perhaps, by the vistas that now lay open, DeSmet gradually yielded to Blanchet's proposals. This was later, in June 1842, when the founding members of the church met at St. Paul, on Blanchet's turf. This is where they should have been, but it was distinctly disadvantageous to DeSmet, the romantic dreamer, who could no more see a hole in a doughnut than he could make one.

Blanchet, meanwhile, had got caught in the ugly game of politics and had not come off unscathed. He did not seek a share in what happened, indeed he had been drafted against his will; nonetheless he was sharply criticized by those who had tried to use him and had something to gain by condemning him.

The basic problem was an old one: after twenty-two years of "Joint Occupancy" the Sovereignty of Oregon was still hanging in the balance. As the number of Americans increased there was growing concern among them for direct action by Congress to resolve the ambivalence and to provide more secure titles for their land claims. In 1840, a number of Americans addressed a formal petition to Congress to extend the American civil institutions over all of Oregon, but this was in violation of the treaty with England and nothing came of it.

On February 15, 1841, Ewing Young, a prosperous cattleman in the Willamette Valley, died without leaving a will or heirs. A meeting was called to settle the disposition of his estate. At this meeting a motion was made to establish a committee for drafting laws to form a provisional government. When another meeting was held to elect officers and committee members, Blanchet was appointed chairman, contrary to his wishes. He understood, as everyone else did, that he had been selected by the American majority to gain the support of the Canadians, many of whom had been identified with the Hudson's Bay Company and were still attached to the Canadian government, which protected them.

The committee was directed to report back to the people on June 1, 1841. When that day arrived, Blanchet admitted that he had not called the committee into session. He presented a perfectly legitimate reason. "Commador Wilkes," as he called him, was not due at St. Paul until June 7, and Blanchet wanted to consult him as a representative of the United States government before steps were taken toward provisional government. This explanation did not please the Americans, whose sly plot to use him had failed. They accused him of blocking their efforts to establish a provisional *American* government.

For this Blanchet has been harshly treated by partisan historians who regarded him as anti-American and pro-British, unforgivable offenses in the context of the conflict for sovereignty.

There is some obscurity about Blanchet's actions. He was doubtlessly pro-Canadian, no one could criticize him for that. He was also deeply grateful to McLoughlin personally, if not to McLoughlin's company, to which he was in debt. As for the settlers, he had a divided loyalty. Most of his own people were Canadians. Almost all of the Americans were non-Catholics, many of them openly antagonistic toward him.

But one key point in this matter has been overlooked: Blanchet's explicit unwillingness to take one side rather than another. He made it clear that he regarded the movement toward provisional government as premature, and Lieutenant Wilkes, when he was consulted by Blanchet, fully agreed, expressing as his view "that the country was too young." Finally, there was Blanchet's own concern for prudence. "In a word, let all comprehend," he wrote later, speaking of Demers and himself in the third persons, "that the two Catholic missionaries understood too well the delicacy of their position in this new and unsettled country to commit such imprudent blunders."[39]

This dispute and Blanchet's alleged disgrace following it were not soon forgotten, but only a handful of Americans were privy to it. Had Blanchet's unpopularity with the Americans received wider coverage in the American press, it is most unlikely that his nomination to be Oregon's first bishop would have got past the American hierarchy, who were mostly Irish and cheerfully anti-British.

But in 1841 this was still irrelevant. Blanchet's more immediate problem was the appeasement of the Americans, who, being a two-to-one majority, could have had their way anyhow, if they really wanted it. It is very likely that by mid-June they realized Blanchet was right. They were not ready for provisional government. But, they had found a goat in the vicar general and they cynically continued to treat him like one.

DESMET GOES TO VANCOUVER

The winter of 1841–1842 had been a bitter one in the mountains. It had snowed for three months without interruption, and even seasoned Indians had succumbed to snow-blindness and had to be rescued from the drifts. The old chief, Big Face, died that winter and he was buried, wrapped in the flag he had waved every Sunday to announce the Lord's Day.[40]

In the lower Columbia rain fell incessantly. When Lent came it was difficult for Blanchet and Demers to get around because of floods and winds. They were delayed in their journeys to other villages and each arrived at his own mission later than expected, barely in time for the Holy Week ceremonies.

Both priests had recently completed new houses at their missions and Demers was trying desperately to complete the church at the Cowlitz, which had been begun two years earlier.[41] They were both physically burned out now, though they did not realize it, and they needed replacements, which were on the way. But it would be many months before they could arrive.

Blanchet yearned for an opportunity to discuss problems with the Jesuits. DeSmet had promised to come sometime, but "sometime" as the months passed, appeared to be so vague it provided no great pleasure to which he could look forward. The time would come when Blanchet wanted to kick out of his diocese all members of religious orders, including the Jesuits, but now, as he drove himself relentlessly from village to village, he wanted Jesuits more than anything else.

DeSmet, preoccupied with his own adventures, was in no hurry to come, at least not until supplies at St. Mary's had been replenished. He had established two sodalities, one for men and one for women, and Victor, prefect of the former, had been selected to succeed Big Face as chief. DeSmet, with Mengarini's help, now turned to preparing all of the adult Christians for Holy Communion, and this occupied his attention for several weeks. Meanwhile, provisions at the mission ran short and DeSmet made preparations, at last, to travel to Vancouver.

He left St. Mary's on April 13, intending to preach to all the tribes on his route. Accompanied by Indians as guides and interpreters, he visited the Kalispels first, then the Kootenais, baptizing the children, the sick, and the old wherever he went. Departing from his usual trail down the Clark Fork River, he crossed the Bitteroot mountains and arrived among the Coeur d'Alenes, who had been eager to receive a Blackrobe since the Flatheads had begun to brag about them.

DeSmet was very much impressed by the Coeur d'Alenes and the uncommonly beautiful country they occupied, "a fertile, lovely valley, stretching westward hundreds of miles. Clusters of dark pines and cedars emerged from the green plain, in the center of which lay a lake well stocked with fish. A river ran through the valley and to the north, east and south snow-capped mountains pierced the clouds."[40] This was his description of Coeur d'Alene Lake, the Spokane Valley and the Spokane River.

Two days after his arrival among the Coeur d'Alenes, DeSmet, torn with regret, took his leave. He promised to send them a missionary soon. "Never has a visit to the Indians given me so much consolation," he said, "and nowhere have I seen such unmistakable proof of true conversion."[43]

The lands of the Spokanes were only a day's ride to the west, along the river DeSmet had admired. The Indians here were scattered, living in three bands many miles from one another, so DeSmet seems to have passed through their country without observing his usual procedures. He had intended, from this point, to continue south, through the country of the Palouse Indians, but the trails were flooded everywhere and his guides persuaded him to turn north instead to Fort Colville where, it was hoped, they could procure boats to go down the Columbia.

There were no boats available at Fort Colville. While the Indians made one, DeSmet visited the Kettle and Okanogan tribes, who received him eagerly. Young and old came running to the missionary. "Had we but a few more priests and the means of getting farming implements for the Indians," he said, "all mountain tribes would soon be Catholics."[44]

This was nonsense, of course. With all the farm implements in the world the Indians would not have been completely converted, nor would they have wanted to use the implements. The Indians were not farmers, and most never would be.

At the fort, DeSmet employed what he called *porteurs*, experienced men to steer his new boat down the raging river. All was ready on May 30 and while the crew sang lustily they pushed off from the bank of the river and drifted rapidly into the current, which had become swift and cold from the melting snows. At one point where the passage appeared to be difficult, DeSmet asked to be put ashore, so that he could walk along the river until the danger was past. This was unlike DeSmet, to be afraid, but his sudden decision probably saved his life.

The boat was caught in the rapids. DeSmet saw the river white with foam, the prow rising in the air, then suddenly disappearing into the abyss. Over the roar of the waters he heard one man shout: "We are lost!" Five men, sucked into the deep whirlpools, went down and never surfaced again. But the Indians survived. When the boat reached calm waters, it was recovered. DeSmet's baggage was lost. The survivors, badly shaken by the tragedy, gradually rallied, then continued their voyage down the river, more cautiously than before. They arrived at Vancouver on June 8.

Modeste Demers was there to greet DeSmet. Together they traveled to St. Paul, where DeSmet spent eight days with the two priests, sharing experiences and discussing, in an informal manner, the needs of the church in the Northwest. On Sunday, DeSmet sang a high Mass and preached in the church. Blanchet showed him the Catholic Ladder. "That plan," DeSmet exclaimed with characteristic magnanimity, "will be adopted by the missions of the whole world."[45]

THE FIRST OREGON COUNCIL

When the three priests had taken their rest and felt renewed, they returned to Fort Vancouver, Demers and DeSmet together and Blanchet "soon" after. There, as favored guests of McLoughlin, they settled down "to deliberate on the interests of the great mission of the Pacific Coast." As vicar general, Blanchet presided over the discussions, during which two premises were readily, perhaps too readily, agreed upon. Catholicism, they said, would penetrate into the eastern mountains from lower Oregon, and secondly, therefore, there was great and immediate need to establish the base of operations in the Willamette Valley. In practice, it was agreed, the missionaries from Quebec would continue to concentrate on coastal missions, west of the Cascades, and the Jesuits would take charge of missions east of the Cascades.

Specifically the following procedures would be undertaken: "the missions to be attended [by Blanchet] were those of Chinook Point, Vancouver, Cascades, Clakamus, Willamette Fall and the Sound, whose tribes were so famished for heavenly things; witness their running after the *black-gown* in 1840 and 1841, and their repeated calls for priests ever since."[46] Another mission, New Caledonia [British Columbia] should be occupied at once, "since it was threatened to be visited by Presbyterians at Walla Walla." Demers, cheerfully accepting this burden, agreed to prepare himself to spend the winter in New Caledonia. Finally, DeSmet, presuming on the approval of his superior, consented to return at once to St. Louis, then travel to Belgium to seek additional workers, materials, and money. It was also understood that DeSmet would consider the establishment of Jesuit headquarters on the Willamette and, as soon as feasible, a college for boys. Somewhat reserved regarding this proposal, DeSmet quickly supported Blanchet's suggestion that they request the Holy See for a bishop.

So these were the decisions, obviously all initiated by Blanchet. It would be difficult to determine which of the three priests had drawn the most arduous assignment: isolation for a long cold winter in New Caledonia, begging in Europe, or shepherd to thousands of noisy, scattered sheep. In a sense, each got what he deserved, a task for which he was most suited.

DeSmet, after a careful survey of the situation, finally decided to accept the request made by Blanchet and McLoughlin to establish a Jesuit residence on the Willamette, to serve as a base of supplies for all Jesuit missions of the interior. For McLoughlin, it must be admitted, this was a good stroke of business, because this would practically guarantee that supplies for all the Jesuit's activities in the Northwest would be purchased through the Hudson's Bay Company. The Jesuits charged what they bought and payment was made through Father George Jenkins, treasurer for the English Province, directly to the Company in London, a more secure arrangement than Blanchet's.[47] Blanchet, too, was delighted with DeSmet's confirmation of his own ambitious plans. They parted with mutual expressions of esteem and respect.

DeSmet and Demers departed together for Walla Walla, on barges of the Hudson's Bay Company. Blanchet wrote to Rosati in St. Louis, "Mr. Demers and myself have finally had the consolation of seeing Reverend Father DeSmet.... I cannot but wish to see in the Columbia [Valley] an increase in the number of priests of the Society of Jesus." To his own bishop, Signay in Quebec, he wrote, "I rejoice to see that this country is going to fall in regard to spirituals under the learned and enlightened direction of the Jesuits."[48]

Blanchet alas! had simply fallen under the spell of DeSmet. He would live long enough to eat these ill-chosen words. This would not be DeSmet's fault, nor the Jesuits. The vicar general himself would have to be more consistent, either for or against the Jesuits, but not both.

At Walla Walla Demers and DeSmet parted, the one eventually leaving via fur brigade for the north and the unknown in New Caledonia; the other on horseback, with additional horses loaded with provisions and clothes, for St. Mary's. DeSmet also had cattle, thirty-one head that he had purchased for fifteen dollars each, not so great a bargain as one might imagine, and a considerable handicap, like traveling in an old western cattle drive from Abilene to the railhead.[49] He arrived at St. Mary's on July 27, 1842.

Father Point was away with many of the Flatheads on their summer hunting expedition. DeSmet appointed Mengarini as acting superior of the Rocky Mountain Mission, then sought out the Indians on the Madison River. Having found them, he ordered Point, upon the return of the hunting expedition, to go with Brother Huet to establish a mission for the Coeur d'Alenes. Then he departed with an escort of ten Indians for St. Louis, to prepare for his longer journey to Europe, where he would learn that they wanted to make him the bishop of all Oregon.[50]

McLOUGHLIN BECOMES A CATHOLIC

The vicar general spent the summer hurrying from one Indian camp to another, spending interval periods at St. Paul and Vancouver, where the people complained loudly about his neglect of them, and at St. Francis Xavier's on the Cowlitz, where the absence of Demers was noted and respectfully criticized. For Blanchet that summer was like a never-ending marathon. But it was over at last. His people at St. Paul were gathering in the harvest, and he could smell the tangy spice of their gardens. On Saturday, September 17, he had been at St. Paul for a week. On that day two young priests arrived from Canada. Blanchet was overjoyed.[51]

The two new priests were Antoine Langlois[52] and John Baptiste Zacharie Bolduc,[53] who had been over a year on their journey to Oregon. They had left Boston on August 10, 1841, doubled Cape Horn on December 4 and crossed the bar on the Columbia on September 12.

On Sunday, following their arrival, September 18, a high Mass was celebrated with deacon and sub-deacon, for the first time in Oregon. This was followed with the singing of the *Te Deum*, which was about as much spiritual fireworks as the vicar general could provide. After that it was time to go to work. Leaving St. Paul to the care of Bolduc, Blanchet and Langlois, who was a very pious priest, traveled back to Vancouver where for three weeks they provided spiritual instructions for the women and children. On Sunday, October 30, before a large congregation, "seven ladies of the fort and two women of the village," were allowed to make their First Communion "for the first time in Vancouver."[54]

"After this," Blanchet said, implying immense relief, "Langlois was sent to St. Paul and Bolduc to the Cowlitz to attend to these missions." Blanchet remained at Vancouver, where on November 18, 1842, Dr. John McLoughlin, practically speaking the lord and master of all of Oregon, formally returned to the Catholic Church. At the hands of the vicar general the White Headed Eagle made his profession of faith and had his marriage blessed. Following this, during the four weeks of Advent, he lived on his claim at Willamette Falls, fasting every day to prepare for his First Communion. He also supervised surveyors in measuring blocks and lots, so that he could offer some for sale.

For Midnight Mass on Christmas, the little chapel at the fort was crowded with whites and Indians. It had been decorated lavishly and numerous lamps had been placed "for brilliant illumination", enough for a pope with weak eyes. "Christmas hymns sung in French and Chinook jargon stirred the souls of all, as well as the holy functions around the Altar."[55] At the proper time, McLoughlin made his First Communion "at the head of 38 communicants." For the Indians of Oregon this was the conversion of their king, but for the Methodists it was the crack of doom.

A certain coldness had developed between the latter and McLoughlin ever since he had refused to take their side in a dispute with Catholics. He had said it was none of his business, but he was partial to Catholics in his day-to-day decisions. When the "great reinforcement" arrived in the ship *Lausanne* in 1840, at least one Methodist appeared to be willing to defraud McLoughlin of his land claim and another, Felix Hathaway, started a building on McLoughlin's island.[56] McLoughlin protested and Hathaway ceased building, but five days after McLoughlin became a Catholic, Hathaway deeded the island to the Oregon Milling Company, most of the members of which belonged to the Methodist Mission. Hathaway had jumped McLoughlin's claim.[57] Later the island was "conveyed" to Governor George Abernethy, who conveyed his "rights" to W.P. Bryant, the first territorial Chief Justice of Oregon, including Oregon City.

Meanwhile, Brother Waller retained legal council and laid claim to the rest of McLoughlin's land. To avoid trouble, McLoughlin bought up Waller's pretended claim for five hundred dollars. As O'Hara noted in his history of this sordid affair, "Apparently the trouble was definitely settled; in reality it had just begun."[58]

These people who were defrauding McLoughlin were American immigrants, whose settlement in Oregon was made possible, in great part, by their adversary McLoughlin, who had extended over them his personal protection, saving them from hostile Indians and famine. He cared for their sick, furnished them with supplies and food and clothing and often with shelter, and provided them with seed grain for the spring, all this at his own loss, contrary to the express orders of his Company, and in spite of the calumnies which Americans in the region were already spreading about him.

The frontier brought out the best in men and the worst in men, and this was as true of the Catholics as it was of the Methodists or any other group.

"WHITMAN SAVED OREGON"

Far to the east in the mountains, the Flatheads were in no hurry to leave their hunting grounds since it was not easy to slip by the Blackfeet to get there. Once they were among the buffalo they remained until the early frosts of autumn appeared on the late flowers in the mountain meadows. Father Nicolas Point, their chaplain, so to speak, spent most of his time painting them in their pursuits, but he was getting anxious to return to St. Mary's to prepare for his new assignment. Winter in these mountains was unpredictable. If another came like the previous year, Point would encounter grave difficulties in crossing the two mountain ranges between St. Mary's and Coeur d'Alene territory.

By early October, Point returned to St. Mary's, where he prepared to undertake his new task. Precisely, as directed by DeSmet, he was to take with him Brother Huet, the jack-of-all-trades and countryman of DeSmet's, select a suitable site for a mission and get this under roof as soon as possible. He left St. Mary's with Huet and Indian guides before snow fell in the valley. Traveling north at first, taking the trail along the

Bitteroot to Hell Gate, he turned west and followed the Clark Fork River until it meandered north near present St. Regis, then crossed Lookout Pass into what is now Idaho. His final obstacle was the Coeur d'Alene mountain range, more formidable than the Rockies, with its numerous crossings through icy rivers and streams, and endless miles over fallen trees and other forest debris.

While Point and his companions toiled along this tiresome trail, burdened with tools, clothing, food, altar supplies and other ingredients of an incipient mission, Dr. Marcus Whitman of the renowned Protestant mission at Waiilatpu, was racing in the other direction, also by horse, "to save Oregon" it was said, for the Americans, because of an alleged British and Catholic conspiracy to take over for Canada. This was as fictitious as *Alice in Wonderland.* The facts were these: The American Board of Protestant Missions (the A.B.C.F.M.), which sponsored three missions in the plateau area south and west of the Coeur d'Alenes, had dispatched orders from Boston for the closure and proper disposal of two of these missions, and for the recall of the Reverend Henry Spalding and two others, including W.H. Gray.[59] Whitman had been ordered to join his colleagues at Tshimikain Mission, which served the Lower Spokanes. After a lengthy conference at Whitman's mission at Waiilatpu, the missionaries directed Whitman to leave at once for Boston to persuade the Board to reverse its decision.[60]

Whitman's famous journey began on October 3, 1842. In eleven days he covered more than five hundred miles to Fort Hall, from which he took the old Spanish Trail to Taos, New Mexico, a grave mistake, and then the Santa Fe Trail to the east.[61] He did not arrive in Boston until the following year on March 30, by which time DeSmet had already been in St. Louis for over five months.[62] Nor had DeSmet been idle. He had prepared his first book for the press and had toured most of the large cities of the country, including New Orleans, Boston, Louisville, Cincinnati, Baltimore, Washington, Philadelphia, and New York.[63] He had collected five thousand precious dollars, with which he was able to outfit a party of three new recruits for Oregon, Father Peter DeVos, formerly novice master at Florissant, Father Adrian Hoecken, and Brother Michael McGean. In April 1843, DeSmet himself escorted these three Jesuits to Westport, where they joined a wagon train for the west. In the same train was Peter Burnett, who later became the first governor of California, and Marcus Whitman, returning to Oregon after gaining a reprieve for his mission from the American Board.[64] "Two papal priests and their lay helpers are along," Whitman reported to his confreres in the east, "and DeSmet has gone back [to St. Louis] in order to go to Europe and bring others by ship."[65]

Four "others by ship" had already arrived from Europe, just before DeSmet embarked at New York for Ireland. An appeal for volunteers for the Oregon Missions, circulated by the general to Jesuit provinces in Europe, had brought four new recruits, Fathers Joseph Joset, a Swiss, Peter Zerbinatti, a Neapolitan, Tiberius Soderini, a Roman, and Brother Vincent Magri, a Maltese. They were promptly sent to Havre, where they embarked for New Orleans on March 20, 1843. They arrived in St. Louis on May 18, somewhat behind schedule, for their ship had been stalled at sea. Because the season was too far advanced for their journey to the mountains, they were directed by DeSmet to remain in St. Louis until the following spring. Subsequently DeSmet informed Joset by letter that he would meet them all at the Green River Rendezvous in late June 1844, a rather presumptuous commitment but perfectly in keeping with DeSmet's carefree style of government.

So the Whitmans were gradually being surrounded by "Romanist priests." They felt threatened. "Romanism," Mrs. Whitman had written a few months earlier, "stalks abroad on our right hand and on our left, and with daring effrontery, boasts that she is to prevail and possess the land. I ask, must it be so? The zeal and energy of her priests are without parallel, and many, both white men and Indians, wander after the beasts. Two are in the country below us and two are above in the mountains."[66]

SACRED HEART MISSION

Of the two priests "in the mountains," one of them, with Brother Huet at his side, finally reached his destination, the Coeur d'Alenes' principal camp, on Friday, November 4, 1842.[67] It was the first Friday in the month, the day on which Catholics all over the world, even in a wilderness, give special honor or devotion to the Sacred Heart of Jesus.[68] Father Point dismounted from his horse, fell upon his knees and devoutly dedicated his mission to the Sacred Heart, the name which it bears to this very day.[69]

It was a pious beginning but Point was under no illusions, despite DeSmet's eulogy about the "peerless Coeur d'Alenes." Some of these Indians had a bad reputation among the fur traders, who refused to settle near them. It was a case, perhaps, of the pot calling the kettle black, for the same Coeur d'Alenes had little respect for the fur traders, whom they regarded as being uncommonly stingy. Point found it impossible to find an interpreter, for no whites had bothered to learn the language. The tribe, numbering about five hundred at this time, lived along several rivers and a large lake, which bore the tribal name. On the north bank of one of these rivers, later called "St. Joseph" by the Jesuits, Point selected a site for a permanent mission, where Huet remained to construct first a log house for a dwelling and then other buildings.[70] Point spent the winter with the main body of the tribe at their fish camp on the lake, preaching as best he could, and sketching when no one would listen to him.[71] In the spring he returned to the mission on the river and assisted in the construction of the first church, a long, low hut of logs and moss. He called this mission "St. Joseph," which has confused historians ever since.[73]

PROGRESS IN OREGON

By this time Blanchet had become accustomed to the presence of young priests whom he could order about, and he was shifting them around like checkers on a board. There was no special pattern; Langlois and Bolduc were on the move most of the time. The latter was at the Cowlitz mission when Chief Factor James Douglas invited him to accompany his expedition of twenty-two men to found Victoria on the south end of Vancouver Island.[73] Since Blanchet consented to this, Bolduc left the Cowlitz on March 7, 1843. The members of the expedition first rode by horse to Nisqually, where the Company boat, called the *Beaver*, awaited them. On March 14, a week after the journey began, the one score and four men landed at Victoria. On the following Sunday, March 19, Bolduc celebrated Mass for his companions and twelve hundred Indians, and baptized one hundred and two children.

Having enjoyed these triumphs, he purchased a large canoe and crossed the bay to Whidby Island, where he found the large cross Blanchet had raised in 1840. Pitching his tent there, he preached several times a day for eight days and baptized another group of children numbering one hundred and seventy-three. The Indians were so happy to have him that they built him a house, measuring twenty-eight by twenty-five feet, says Blanchet. The feelings were mutual, for Bolduc, as soon as he returned to the Cowlitz, requested to be assigned to Whidby Island.[74] In effect he was telling the vicar general that he preferred work with the Indians on the island to work with the whites at the Cowlitz mission.

But Blanchet, for the moment, had other plans. He had gone to Willamette Falls in mid-March to buy a lot "for a chapel for the Indians," he said, little realizing that whites would soon take over the town. He paid $225 for the lot, then sat down to add up what he called "items" to send to the bishop in Canada.[75] From 1838 to March, 1843, he estimated, the missionaries in the lower Columbia had performed "2,666 baptisms, 148 marriages and 86 burials." It would appear from this that there were many more Catholic children than adults, which was due, Blanchet explained, to the many deaths of older, more vulnerable Indians from white man's diseases.

Demers, meanwhile, was still in New Caledonia with his faithful guide, Marcel Bernier, the young man born at Spokane House and schooled at St. Boniface in Canada. Marcell had served Blanchet and Demers in their missionary safaris since his return from school in 1842.

On Holy Thursday 1843, Demers suddenly reappeared at Fort Vancouver, gaunt, greatly fatigued, and nine months older. He recovered sufficiently from his incredible hardships to preach on Easter Sunday, then joined Bolduc in his preparations for an assault on Whidby Island. The two, having convinced Blanchet of the advantages, gathered their supplies and left for Nisqually on May 10, "with 2 men," says Blanchet, "and 11 horses, 7 of them with packages."[76]

Their departure left the field to Langlois, who finally completed the church at the Cowlitz for Mass on Pentecost Sunday, June 4, and to the vicar general, who either discovered recently a source of "biscuits," or the effect of biscuits when he presented them to Indians. His journal for several weeks following contains some refreshing accounts of his victories over the hearts of his neophytes, using these cookies for bait.

This is the "other side" of the vicar general. Usually quite dour, especially as he grew older, he impressed one more by his harshness than by his geniality. It is true he sometimes spoke of his affectionate reunions with Modeste Demers, but history accords him a more stormy relationship with his priests, and his somber sermons provided evidence of his aloofness from most people. But cookies for his Indians reveals a more human response to others and one should remember this when learning about Blanchet's later history.

The mission for Whidby Island flopped, "for reasons too long to explain here," Blanchet said, and both Demers and Bolduc were back in the lower Columbia during the summer. Blanchet was relieved. He had made up his mind by now that he should open his proposed college as soon as possible. He called it a college, which meant nothing more prestigious than a school where boys, aged six to twelve, could learn to read and write in both French and English.

"The 17th of October," he wrote triumphantly, "was a day of great rejoicing at St. Paul, on account of the solemn blessing of St. Joseph's College, after a Mass chanted by the vicar general before a large congregation. On that day, there entered as boarders, 30 boys, sons of the farmers, save one Indian boy, the son of a chief. Father Langlois was the director; Mr. King principal and teacher of English, and Mr. Bilodeau, assistant, and teacher of French. Several rods east of the college was seen, in way of erection, a building 60 by 30 ft., for the Sisters expected to arrive with Father DeSmet."[77]

If the vicar general had the gift of prophecy, he might have mourned instead. His school building would soon be empty, his parish of St. Paul decimated, and his church in Oregon so deeply in debt that it would be many years before the debts were liquidated.[78]

4

AN ARCHBISHOP FOR OREGON

1843–1847

The selection of a bishop for Oregon proved to be more complex than anyone expected. For two years in fact, there was so much agitation about this and related matters, like jurisdiction, that one would imagine the Congress of Vienna was still in session and bishops, instead of statesmen, were creating a new kingdom in the West. In the minds of the bishops who were involved, there were many unanswered questions yet, such as the boundaries of their dioceses.

According to Blanchet, in a letter to his bishop, Signay of Quebec, the principal subject discussed between him and DeSmet at their meeting in June 1842 was the ecclesiastical organization of Oregon Territory and its erection into a diocese. To interest the American prelates in this project and to secure aid for the proposed diocese, it was said, were the chief reasons that prompted DeSmet to return to St. Louis in 1842.[1]

But long before this Blanchet had recommended that Bishop Provencher of Red River be transferred to Oregon. Since he was auxiliary to Signay, no formalities from Rome would have been required for his change of residence. Signay could decide it, but Signay hesitated.

Provencher himself was not much interested in Blanchet's proposal. "You know," he wrote Blanchet, "that the bishop of Quebec hopes to be relieved of your mission. I do not know how the project progresses." Then he added sarcastically, "Who would want it?"[2]

Signay still had many doubts about the extent of his jurisdiction. On December 2, 1842, he wrote to Rosati in St. Louis, "A portion of the territory in question is in dispute between the government of the United States and Great Britain as regards temporalities. I should like to know if your Grace have [sic] any reliable data to determine the limits of your jurisdiction on that side. All I know is that my diocese extends to the Pacific Ocean and comprises all the territory, north of California, which has not been aggregated to any dioceses of the United States."[3]

No one doubted that action should be taken, for the advantages of an independent vicariate or diocese were obvious. Perhaps the greatest would be the presence in Oregon of the prelate who possessed final jurisdiction. St. Louis was over two thousand miles distant and Quebec was even farther. It required one year for Blanchet to send a letter to his bishop and to receive a response.

Signay's solution for this was a half measure. Indeed, almost anything was acceptable if it took him off the hook. Writing to Blanchet he said, "I have planned to ask the Holy See that the territory of the Columbia be placed under the care either of the bishop of St. Louis, who is nearer, or the bishop of Nicopolis (Msgr. Rouchouze) who is still better placed."[4]

Signay was not joking. He regarded "Msgr. Rouchouze," the vicar apostolic of the Vicariate of East Oceania, as "better placed," than himself or Rosati, since the most recent route from Canada to the Columbia was via South America and the Sandwich Islands.[5]

Obviously, Signay was trying to pass the buck, but it should be remembered that he had under his care all of western Canada "as well as the Russian possessions which are more than 2000 miles distant from me."[6]

From the beginning, Blanchet had been demanding money as well as additional priests, but the bishop of Quebec, whose local needs were before his very eyes, quite naturally relegated Blanchet's appeals to his file of "hopeful" or "maybe" to be implemented when he had a surplus of either men or money.

Blanchet could not live with this. In desperation he turned to St. Louis and the Jesuits for help. Later he admitted to his bishop, "I have let myself be carried away by the plan to obtain as soon as possible an independent bishop for the territory of the Columbia, on the model of dioceses established in the States, where even the poorest bishops have been successful in obtaining abundant help from all countries and have made rapid progress."[7]

Signay was not offended, indeed he accepted "the plan" with alacrity. "I have found it so much to my liking that I wrote at once to the Bishop of St. Louis so as to take up with him the steps of carrying it out. In his absence I received a response from Bishop Kenrick, his coadjutor, to whom the proposition was agreeable. It will be submitted to the bishops of the United States when they assemble at Baltimore next month."[8]

At this point everyone admitted that an independent bishop should be appointed. A bishop in Oregon dependent directly on the Holy See would eliminate a third party in what concerned local demands. Though Rome was farther away than Quebec, less time was required to correspond directly with Rome than through Quebec's bishop.

While all consented to this, there was no common agreement on who should be bishop. Signay, prompted by Blanchet, proposed the name of DeSmet. Writing to Rosati he raised premature questions like the name of the new *diocese* and the place of residence of the new bishop. "I have omitted to say to your Grace when speaking of the choice of a bishop for Oregon Territory that Mr. Blanchet, who might be considered in this connection, earnestly begs to be passed over. I only wish the rules of the Society of Jesus will put no obstacle in the way of Father DeSmet's acceptance of this dignity."[9]

Bishop Peter Kenrick, only recently appointed coadjutor to Rosati, responded at some length, saying that neither DeSmet nor any other Jesuit should be selected.[10] Although his reasoning was legitimate, since Jesuits by rule are not candidates to be bishops, one suspects Kenrick's motives. Peter Kenrick, like his brother Francis, who was also a bishop, seemed to have very belligerent attitudes towards Jesuits, partly because of their special status under the pope. "I ought to clip your wings," Kenrick once said to the provincial of the Missouri province.[11] He was very defensive about Jesuit influence in St. Louis and contemptuously regarded Jesuits "as a band apart." It was not likely, as far as Kenrick was concerned, that any Jesuit would be elevated to the episcopacy, even in distant, unwanted Oregon.

THE TERNA FOR BISHOP

But the Fifth Provincial Council of Baltimore disagreed with him. Assembled in May, 1843, it recommended to the Holy See the erection of a vicariate-apostolic west of the Rocky Mountains, and notwithstanding the well-known unwillingness of Jesuits to accept bishoprics, forwarded to Rome the names of three Jesuits whom they nominated for the position of vicar apostolic. Presented in the order of preference, this terna was as follows: "Father Pierre DeSmet, of the Society of Jesus, Father Nicolas Point, of the same Society, and Father Pierre Verheyden, of the same Society."[12]

Kenrick, swallowing his disappointment, dispatched a perky letter to Signay, who, I think was also disappointed. The fathers of the Council, he wrote, recommended the erection of a vicariate instead of a diocese because of the differences between the two governments with regard to Oregon. The fathers also favored a Jesuit to be the bishop because they felt that a Jesuit bishop, especially DeSmet, would more likely succeed, since he would have the resources of his Order to support him.[13]

Signay did not hesitate to acquiesce in these decisions, with mixed feelings, no doubt. The prospect of no longer being responsible for

Oregon was a most pleasant one, but he had led Blanchet to believe that he, not DeSmet, would be appointed bishop. Signay and his brother bishop in Canada, it appears, favored the appointment of a Canadian. The American bishops, on the other hand, made no bones about it: they wanted an American, even a Jesuit, if necessary.

Their *terna* of names, which listed Point as a second choice, revealed their lack of real knowledge about the candidates. Point, for example, would have been a disaster for any administrative post. He was moody, subject to fits of anger and as unpredictable as most artists. While Blanchet had his faults, he was a much better choice than Point. Even DeSmet was too emotionally involved in his Indians, and while he was a good administrator for pioneering, a good provider, and an inspiring superior, he would haved pined away at a desk in a stuffy chancery.

The Council's choice of DeSmet, according to Kenrick, depended largely on the concept that he would succeed because of Jesuit support, implying, it seems, that the choice of a non-Jesuit as bishop would be less desirable, because he would lack the support of the Jesuits. The fathers of the Council need not have worried about this, for subsequent events demonstrated that Jesuits, and other religious orders, provided great and indispensable support for the new bishop when he was finally appointed.

When the Council's *terna* reached the Jesuit General in Rome, Father John Roothaan, he submitted to the Holy See a forthright declaration, insisting that no Jesuit should be appointed and that the Society of Jesus should not be required to make an exception to its rule for this case. Roothaan also urged that a *diocese*, rather than a vicariate, be established, as Signay had proposed. Time proved that the general and the bishop of Quebec were right.

As for DeSmet's nomination, Roothaan's assistant, Father John Grassi who had lived in America, strongly opposed it on the grounds that he was not a suitable candidate. He gave as his opinion that Blanchet was a better choice, though it is doubtful he knew much about Blanchet. Thus he was saying something about DeSmet that others failed to see.

Blanchet, informed again of his prospects by Signay, showed much opposition to the proposal. He had decided that a priest from Canada should be appointed, consecrated there, and dispatched to Oregon forthwith, to save money and time. He urged this, adding that it would require only several months for a new bishop to become acquainted with missionary conditions. Since no one took this advice seriously, Blanchet changed his tune. He pressed again for DeSmet's appointment, then added a startling revelation to his bishop, "I am not far from becoming a member of this holy society [the Jesuits] with my confrers, so as better to secure unity in action in the spiritual government of all the missions."[14]

DESMET IN EUROPE

While these tedious negotiations dragged on, DeSmet was preaching in the pulpits of Catholic Europe, about his devout Indians who required only money and missionaries to transform them into living saints. Good Christians had a choice—they could go themselves to the mission and he would gladly see to their transportation, or they could give of their wealth. There were not many dukes or duchesses who opted for the former, but many there were who opened their purses, or emptied their dainty caskets of jewelry, when DeSmet called on them and pleaded the cause of the Indians. In effect he was holding up Catholic Europe without a gun. His weapon, tears for the Indians, was much more effective.

In his sweep though Europe, more like a glamorous African explorer than a beggar, he gathered a shipload of miscellaneous supplies, like books, candlesticks, or stones for grinding wheat. He also collected six Sisters of Notre Dame de Namur in his entourage and five more Jesuits, not to mention thirty thousand dollars in cold cash, enough in those frugal times to put an archdiocese in Siberia on its feet.[15] Satisfied with his gleanings, he chartered a brig called *The Indefatigable* and requested its captain to prepare for a voyage around the world to Oregon[16].

THE NEW VICARIATE

At this same time, on December 1, 1843, Pope Gregory XVI issued three briefs, which were forwarded to the bishop of Quebec: the first provided for the erection of the territory of Oregon into a vicariate apostolic, embracing "all the territory between the Mexican province of California on the south, and the Russian province of Alaska on the north," extending "from the Pacific Ocean to the Rocky Mountains;"[17] the second named Francis Norbert Blanchet, bishop of Philadelphia *in partibus infidelium* [in Asia Minor]; and the third placed the new vicariate under the care of the bishop. The Council of Baltimore in this decision of the Holy See, had shared a victory with Roothaan, the one had requested a vicariate, instead of a diocese, and the other had objected to the appointment of DeSmet. When Kenrick received the news, he was delighted. He wrote to Signay, expressing "great satisfaction on the promotion of M. Bachelet" [sic] whose merit he knew "perfectly well through the relations [or writings] of Father DeSmet."[18]

Buried in the wilds of Oregon, Blanchet did not learn about his appointment for nearly a year. In March, 1844, almost four months after the briefs had been dispatched to Quebec, he wrote again to Signay to protest his appointment, noting that during autumn of the previous year a vast influx of Americans in the lower Columbia made it advisable that an American bishop be assigned.[19]

During the following month of April, Signay had an opportunity, at last, to forward the briefs to Blanchet by the Hudson's Bay Company brigade. He enclosed his personal congratulations, or condolences, depending on one's point of view, and laid the blame for Blanchet's promotion on DeSmet. "If I deserve any blame...the good Father deserves much more, for he has worked harder than myself to have [this dignity] conferred on you. As he is on the ground, you can show your resentment over it at your convenience."[20]

VOYAGE OF THE INDEFATIGABLE

Signay would have been startled to know that when he wrote this, DeSmet was not "on the ground." With his Jesuits and nuns, he had boarded the *Indefatigable* on December 12, 1843, less than two weeks after the papal briefs were issued. But the winds failed to stir the brig, which remained in the estuary of the Schelde for weeks, while its passengers were learning Italian and English.[21] The lessons in Italian were therapeutic in nature, one supposes, for there were no Italians where the boat was going. On board, however, there were several who were learning English, which proved to be one of the hardships of their missionary vocation. The superior of the sisters was Sister Loyola and the names of her five subjects were as follows: Sisters Marie Cornelie, Mary Catherine, Mary Aloysia, Norbertine and Mary Albine. Sister Loyola kept a journal.[22] The five Jesuits with DeSmet were Fathers John Nobili, Michael Accolti, Anthony Ravalli and Louis Vercruysse, and Brother Francis Huysbrecht. Unfortunately, none of these kept a journal though DeSmet made up for their neglect. Day and night he was scratching out letters and other "relations" which became the substance of his many books.

The *Indefatigable* finally navigated the Schelde and passed into the North Sea on January 9, 1844. Cape Horn was rounded on March 20, and on July 28, after many terrifying storms had been encountered, the coast of Oregon came into view. On July 31, the feast of St. Ignatius Loyola, a circumstance not lost on DeSmet, the perilous bar of the Columbia was safely crossed, though the captain, without maps or charts, had guided his ship through the wrong channel, and all were saved only when a huge wave heaved the ship over the shallow sands. Having survived by the last of countless miracles, according to DeSmet, the *Indefatigable* cast anchor, at length, off the banks of Astoria.

On the next day, the six sisters went ashore to visit the home of James Birnie, whose broad, pleasant face, with its double chins, gave him the appearance of a jovial English inn-keeper. Birnie, renowned for his hospitality, which was usually associated with much dancing, gave the sisters a royal welcome and introduced them to his many daughters. These were the first sisters to set foot in the northwest.

DeSmet, meanwhile, impatient to return to Vancouver, persuaded several Indians to take him there in a dugout canoe. He paddled away while the more cumbersome *Indefatigable* proceeded cautiously up the river to the fort, where it arrived five days later. Assembled to greet the new missionaries, were DeSmet, Dr. John McLoughlin and his wife, and many others, including the bespectacled Dr. Forbes Barclay, the company surgeon who had married Marie, daughter of the late Pierre Pambrun of Fort Walla Walla. When the sisters stepped primly ashore, there was a flutter of excitement as the Indians and whites saw for the first time the lady black gowns.

For nine days the weary travelers rested in the placid confines of the fort as guests of the McLoughlins. News of their arrival was dispatched to Blanchet at St. Paul and Blanchet left at once for Vancouver, making the trip in a single day.

The vicar general at this time, still unaware of his appointment as bishop, manifested signs of fatigue and self-deprecation. One of his priests, Antoine Langlois, had been bitterly critical of him, and of almost everything else, and Demers complained to Quebec that the conduct of Langlois was "disgraceful" and that the vicar general was such in name only. "He had to keep silence to keep peace." Demers added that he did not admire either "the conduct of Langlois or the patience of Blanchet."[24]

Langlois had spent most of the summer in the mountains with the Jesuits presumably discussing with one or another his spiritual problems and his desire to enter the Jesuit Order. Blanchet complained that he returned "much worn out by a journey of 42 days on horseback. His feet were much swollen."[25] Mengarini was with him, for both had heard rumors that DeSmet was due to arrive soon by sea.

On August 14, with Blanchet serving as escort, DeSmet's missionaries embarked again in a flotilla of four large canoes and one small sloop, which slowly proceeded down the Columbia to the mouth of the Willamette, then navigated past an island in the Willamette delta and up the broad river, heavily forested on either side. When dusk fell they camped on the bank of the river at the present site of Portland. Mosquitoes tormented them all night and the next morning Blanchet offered the Mass of the Assumption of Mary and all received Holy Communion. Two days after the voyage ended. The flotilla arrived at St. Paul at eleven in the morning, August 17, 1844.

When the six sisters hopped ashore this time, it was with firm determined steps. They were now engaged in founding the first convent school in Oregon. They were undertaking, without trumpets or fanfare, the very foundations of parochial education in the Northwest, and if no one else realized the solemnity of the moment, Sister Loyola and her five nuns certainly did.

ST. PAUL BECOMES A CATHOLIC CENTER

The new missionaries were dispatched at once to the church, some miles distant, the sisters on a horse drawn cart and the Jesuits with Blanchet on horseback. There a *Te Deum* was sung, to thank God for their safe deliverance from the perils of the sea. "The Church," Loyola wrote in her journal for August 17, "is not a bad resemblance of Bethlehem."[26] This was a rather tactless judgment about the place of worship which the French Canadians regarded as very dear, perhaps an instance of European snobbishness. It indicated, at least, that neither Loyola nor her nuns were prepared to accept needless primitive conditions, not in their convent and not anywhere else.

As for a new church, a raised cross had been pointed out to the recent arrivals, with an explanation that this was the site of a brick church to be built in the next, or the following year, 1846.[27]

The Sisters' convent was not completed yet, mostly because Blanchet had no certain knowledge of their arrival. The sisters, like the Jesuits, were given temporary housing in St. Joseph's College nearby, and all returned to the nuisance of learning English, while Blanchet and DeSmet rode horses around the neighborhood in search of property for the Jesuits' new motherhouse. The Methodists had decided to abandon their mission on the Willamette and they offered to sell it to DeSmet for a price that was never made public. But DeSmet rejected the offer, "reporting that it was entirely destitute of wood and arable land." This was not an accurate description of a farm worth a quarter of a million dollars even then.[28]

DeSmet selected, instead, a section of land near St. Paul. "Monseigneur Blanchet," he wrote to Father Roothaan on August 29, 1844, "has given me a fine piece of land, an English square mile in extent."[29] DeSmet was almost ecstatic about it, perhaps because there was a small lake on the land, which he promptly named "St. Ignatius." "I hesitated not a moment in selecting this spot for the mother mission of St. Francis Xavier," he wrote, adding many sentimental remarks about his own novitiate on the Missouri, then a prayer "that here also might be formed a station, whence the torch of faith would diffuse its cheering light among the benighted tribes of this immense territory."[30]

Such extravagant phrases were not uncommon in DeSmet's writings, but seldom were they applied with such abandon to a project which was a failure from the very beginning. Consider the title of the property, for example. Blanchet, unintentionally, had given what he did not own, so the Jesuits' title, until it was corrected some years later, was really worthless. DeSmet's dream of novitiate here never materialized. For many years to come, the Jesuits, having learned that a "Motherhouse" on the Willamette was as useless to them as a castle on the Rhine, complained to the general about it and demanded that it be sold.

But DeSmet understood none of this, and when he ordered the construction of a two-story brick house, measuring forty-five by thirty-five feet, containing fifteen rooms and almost as many fireplaces, he seemed to have no misgivings whatever about its future. He happily summoned Father Peter DeVos from the Coeur d'Alene in Idaho to direct the new foundation and prepared to leave for the month to establish another mission. DeVos, it will be recalled, had been novice master in Missouri, so he knew more than a smattering of English. Indeed as things turned out, he became very influential with the whites in Oregon, who regarded him with respect because of his command of the language.

DeVos was supposed to teach everyone English, but DeSmet, before his departure, at Blanchet's insistence, assigned his Jesuits to many tasks not altogether conducive to study. Father Ravalli, a skilled doctor of medicine, visited the lodges of Indians throughout the region, treating them for a mysterious malady that had struck every family. Father Vercruysse was assigned to the care of the French Canadians at Grand Prairie, where he supervised the building of the Church of St. Louis. Father Nobili was sent to Fort Vancouver to work with the whites at the fort and the Indians in the village. DeVos, in addition to serving as chaplain for the sisters, undertook the care of the Catholics at Oregon City where many American immigrants of 1843 and 1844 had established their homes.

On Thursday, October 3, DeSmet, Mengarini and the Canadian called Peter Biledot, probably the former teacher at St. Joseph's College, left the Willamette by canoe for Vancouver.[31] At the fort, DeSmet spent a great deal of money for supplies for St. Mary's, then gathered what he had purchased and his two companions and embarked by boat for Walla Walla. As soon as he arrived there, he bought some horses and mules, most of them to carry Mengarini, Biledot, and the supplies to St. Mary's. With others he departed for the mission, called St. Michael's, on the Pend Oreille River.

Mengarini and Biledot, while passing through the Coeur d'Alene Mountains, encountered heavy early snowfalls that cost the lives of most of his horses. These were overburdened anyhow with buhrstones that

Ravalli had brought from Europe.[32] Both men survived the ordeal and arrived eventually at St. Mary's with most of the baggage intact.

DeSmet, meanwhile, trotted north from Walla Walla to join Hoecken, preoccupied, no doubt, with thoughts of St. Mary's mission, which attracted him like a lodestone whenever he was free. He seems to have forgotten Father Joset and the three other Jesuits expecting him at the Green River rendezvous. He knew, of course, that it would be useless to go there or to try to find them in the wilderness. At the moment, ironically, as he plodded along, Joset, Zerbinatti, and Magri had already arrived at St. Mary's, no thanks to DeSmet.[33]

They arrived on Monday, October 7, their faces tanned by the sun and wind, their bodies lean and strong like cowboys, and their spirits as cheerful as the day they left St. Louis. Their arrival was almost, if not entirely, miraculous.

JOSET'S OVERLAND JOURNEY

With his companions, Joset had spent the winter of 1843–1844 in St. Louis, where they studied English and taught catechism to the children. A petite man, more French than Swiss, with a wide face like a full moon, and a larger than normal sized nose, Joset peered through small, sharp eyes, neither blinking nor displaying hesitation, indicative, I think, of his whole personality. He was entirely positive as he was fearless, an innocent young priest who was as guileless as a boy. He was also considered very impractical. As one of his colleagues said, he could get lost in his own room with a road map.

With Father Zerbinatti, who was riding to his death, and Brother Magri, he left St. Louis for Westport on April 23, 1844 and departed for the West over the well-beaten immigrant trail with a wagin train. In the course of the journey, "which advanced only at a snail's pace," Joset had occasions to use "the little English" he learned at St. Louis. He conducted four funeral services for those who had perished, non-Catholics as well as Catholics, which reveals the kind of popularity he enjoyed with the members of the wagon train.

At the Green River rendezvous there was no DeSmet to greet them; DeSmet, in fact, was sailing up the California coast about that time. Perhaps, Joset said to his companions, DeSmet would meet them at Fort Hall. The Jesuits agreed to go to Fort Hall. Joset tried to hire a guide, without success, so they set forth alone, with the sun to guide them.

Now this is something sublime to contemplate: three Jesuits with a wagon and several horses, unable for the most part to speak English, in the middle of a vast unknown continent, and confronted with hostile

Indians, going forth innocently without maps or guides and precious little food, seeking a place called St. Mary's, somewhere in the mountains. Only a man like Joset could survive a situation like this and live to tell about it.

So the three men, lonely miniatures on the wide horizon, traveled west, following the afternoon sun. In early evening each day, Joset rode in advance of the others to select a campsite. Thus, on September 8, the Feast of the Nativity of the Virgin Mary, he was a mile or two ahead when he observed a single man in the distance. As the stranger approached on his horse, Joset could see that his hair was long and black like an Indian's, but he wore clothes like a white man. "Great was my joy," Joset wrote later, "when I heard him return my *bon jour*." The stranger spoke French. Was he Canadian? No, he answered, he was Iroquois. "Do you know St. Mary's?" Joset asked. "I have just come from there."

The stranger was Young Ignace, son of Old Ignace, who had brought his two sons, Ignace and Francois to St.Louis for solemn baptism in 1836, eight years before. There is no record to explain how or why Young Ignace had come alone, more than five hundred miles from St. Mary's and through enemy territory. But he was there when he was needed, as happened again and again when the missionaries found themselves in desperate straits.

The three Jesuits with Ignace arrived safely at St.Mary's, still fasting for the reception of the Eucharist. First they sang a *Te Deum* in the mission church, then Joset said Mass. Joset wrote the epilogue of the journey, "Thanks to the kindly care of Providence, in which we had all placed our hope, this last stage of our journey, which in everybody's opinion was the most perilous of all, was not only the most successful, but even the pleasantest."[34]

All three of these Jesuits lived and died in the wilderness. Zerbinatti drowned in the Bitterroot River in less than a year, the first missionary to die in the Northwest. Magri lived until his sixtieth year and died in the odor of sanctity. And Joset? Joset lived for a long time, until the twentieth century, having earned before he gave up the ghost, an edifying reputation as "the Apostle of the Coeur d'Alenes."[35]

THE PAPAL BRIEF APPOINTING BLANCHET ARRIVES IN OREGON

At St. Paul on the Willamette, meanwhile, the sisters finally completed their convent, called St. Mary's, and moved in on October 19. On the following day, Father DeVos, superior of the Jesuits, offered the first Mass in the sisters' chapel, doubtlessly the most elegant in the entire Northwest. The sisters were happy with their convent even though the roof leaked. The Jesuits were busy completing their own home, and Langlois, the devil's advocate for Blanchet, was far away at the Cowlitz. Blanchet had begun to think that his admissions of his own defects had prevented him from being appointed bishop.

"I am already old," he lamented in a last minute plea to be overlooked, "my powers diminish; I am slow at business and it is only by close application that I arrive at a knowledge of anything; I have a treacherous memory; my vigor is gone; I do not know English; I have never had a time to study due to the demands of the ministry where I have always been busy."[36]

For months, Blanchet had been depressed and tempted to self pity. "I am blamed at all times," he wailed, "at all times I am taken to task; I am at fault, lacking."[37]

But in early November 1844, he was suddenly transformed. The fur brigade arrived early that year, and with it there came a packet of documents from the bishop of Quebec. In retrospect, Blanchet described this event and its aftermath very casually:

"On November 4th," he wrote in his memoirs, "two Briefs arrived, dated Rome, Dec. 1st. 1843; one erecting the mission of Oregon into a Vicariate Apostolic, and the other appointing the vicar general, F.N. Blanchet, to the position, with the title of *Philadelphia*, which, on representation to Rome from Quebec, was changed to that of *Drasa*, on May 7th, 1844. The addresses of his letters from Canada betraying his case, felicitations were tendered to the vicar general, but he refused them for several days. His consultation being answered, it was useless to refuse, so he gave his consent on the 8th [of November], and made a resolution to go to Canada to receive his episcopal consecration from the archbishop of Quebec and hence to go and visit Rome."[38]

Signay had some fatherly advice to offer. Perhaps, he said, in letters that accompanied the Roman documents, his lordship could be consecrated in California or the Sandwich Islands. If the latter, his lordship should have an appointment, for the bishop was often absent, visiting his many islands. Above all, his lordship should take warning. Bishop Rouchouze, to whose vicariate Signay had suggested the addition of Oregon, had left France nearly eighteen months ago in a chartered ship, his destination the Sandwich Islands. But he had never arrived.

Signay was right, Bishop Rouchouze had left St. Malo in December 1842 in a chartered brig of 128 tons, called *Marie Joseph* with its captain named O'Sullivan and a crew of twelve. On board, volunteers for the missions, were six priests, one sub-deacon, seven lay brothers, ten sisters, and a native boy called Evarist. Subsequent investigation showed that the brig had dropped anchor near the island of St. Catherine off the west coast of Brazil on February 11, 1843. The bodies of a young sister and Evarist, who had died at sea, were carried ashore and buried. The *Marie Joseph* set sail and was never heard from again.[39] Its loss confirmed the sometimes wild tales of DeSmet and other missionaries who revealed their experiences. DeSmet, it was sometimes said, drew a long bow, but the unknown fate of the *Marie Joseph*, long remembered in the mission annals of the West, gave the appearance of credibility at least, to his many accounts of "miracles" on land and sea.

By the time that Blanchet was reconciled to accepting his new role, he had been transformed from a meek, little lamb, into a determined shepherd. He soon composed his first pastoral letter to the whole vicariate, giving orders that it was to be read at all Masses on the first Sunday after its reception. He dated it November 22, 1844.[40] He also appointed DeVos as administrator of the vicariate in his absence and took passage on December 5, on the bark *Columbia*, bound for Canada via England. By this time he knew that he was in charge and he seldom, if ever, let anyone forget it.

ST. MICHAEL'S MISSION AND
ST. IGNATIUS MISSION

Before the bishop-elect departed for Canada, he compiled a report on the state of the vicariate, which appeared as follows: "Mission Stations: Cowlitz by Rev. A. Langlois, Fort Vancouver by Father Nobili, Oregon City by Father Accolti, St. Paul by Vicar General Demers, St. Joseph's College by Father Bolduc, and the Sisters by Father DeVos. According to the best calculation, the Indian population at that time numbered 110,000, of which 6,000 were Christians; about half of them being at the Rocky Mountains and the remainder in the lower part of Oregon.[42] The White Catholic population was about 1,000, of which 600 were in the Willamette Valley, 100 at Vancouver, 100 at Cowlitz and the rest in the various trading posts. The Jesuit Fathers had four missions at the Rocky Mountains in [1844], viz: St. Mary, St. Joseph, St. Peter and St. Michael; the Coeur d'Alene was one of them."[43]

As noted above, the Coeur d'Alene mission, located at this time on the St. Joe River, was called St. Joseph. St. Mary's, too, was an existing mission when Blanchet listed it. But there is reason to believe that in November 1844, the other two missions, St. Peter and St. Michael, existed mostly in the prodigious imagination of Peter DeSmet. DeSmet had *plans* for them, as he had plans for many other missions, but as yet neither could boast of anything more than a name.

"I gave the name of St. Paul to the Skoyelpi nation," DeSmet wrote in one of his letters, "and placed under the care of St. Peter the tribe inhabiting the shores of the great Columbia lakes, whither Father Hoeken [sic] is about to repair to continue instructing and baptizing adults."[44]

So far as DeSmet was concerned, this constituted the existence of a "mission" and Blanchet never doubted it. The fact is Hoecken never arrived at St. Peter's, mostly because DeSmet changed his mind and left him where he was.

Hoecken was building St. Michael's Mission on the Pend O'reille River, when DeSmet returned to the Kalispels from the motherhouse on the Willamette.[45] Hoecken was a sturdy Hollander, in his fortieth year, just nine years younger than Blanchet, who complained of being too old. He had come from a family that had given seven of its members to the church, all of whom persevered and brought great honor to their parents.

DeSmet arrived on November 6, 1844, fetching with him a small quantity of supplies for St. Michael's. He was welcomed into camp "with the ringing of bells and the discharge of musketry."[46] There was little for him to see, only a few temporary buildings had been thrown together, and he left soon for the Coeur d'Alene mission, four days by horseback, to help the priest there settle some squabbles among the Indians. He had decided to spend the winter at St. Mary's across the mountains, but the early snowstorm which had blocked Mengarini's path had closed the pass entirely. He returned to St. Michael's to arrange for transportation up the river as far as Horse Plains, whence he expected to travel by horse into the Bitteroot Valley. In this he was frustrated, also, by ice on the river, and he was forced to join Hoecken and the Kalispels in their winter camp, some distance upriver from St. Michael's, probably near the present Albeni Falls, Idaho. There in makeshift hutches of poles, fir boughs, and bark mats, they celebrated Christmas, 1844, with a discharge of guns at midnight and a choir of three hundred voices singing Christmas carols.[48] On that day, in this rustic *House of Prayer*, many adults in the tribe were baptized and at benediction fifty couples renewed their marriage vows.

Winter lasted longer than usual that year, but DeSmet, with customary eclat, managed to arrive at St. Mary's by Easter. He shared in what he regarded as "the conquest of many souls for God," without being accused of clerical triumphantalism, then returned to St. Michael's again. That was DeSmet's way of doing things, mostly by traveling here and there on a horse, and there were some in the Missouri vice-province who thought of him as a cowboy missionary.

Hoecken, who had selected this first site of the Kalispel mission, now wanted to change it. Spring floods wiped out what little progress they had made, so Hoecken, with DeSmet and several chiefs, explored the east bank of the river for another site.

"We found a vast and beautiful prairie," DeSmet reported, "three miles in extent, surrounded by cedar and pine, in the neighborhood of the cavern of New Manresa and its quarries, and a fall of water more than 200 feet, presenting every advantage for the erection of mills. I felled the first tree, and after having taken all necessary measures to expedite the work, I departed for Walla Walla...."[49]

The proximity of the "New Manresa," reminiscent of the cave in Spain where St. Ignatius Loyola composed his famous *Spiritual Exercise,* doubtlessly inspired DeSmet to change the mission's name. He called it St. Ignatius. One should keep an eye on this mission. Sooner or later it would become the Indians' *Maria Laach* of the Rocky Mountains.[50]

THE CONSECRATION OF BISHOP BLANCHET

While DeSmet trotted about on his horse, the bishop-elect was on a small boat at sea, a very tiring ordeal that lasted six months. The *Columbia,* after doubling Cape Horn on March 5, 1845, sailed into the stormy Atlantic, but did not make port in England until May 22. Blanchet remained in London for ten days, during which he addressed a long, almost obsequious letter to Roothaan, pleading for more Jesuits to staff his vicariate. He wanted twelve priests, he wrote. "It would be very serviceable if some among them knew English," to occupy several very important Indian posts "before Protestant missionaries come and sow error." These posts were as follows:

"1st New Caledonia situated to the north of the Columbia river, 300 leagues from Fort Vancouver, towards the sources of the Frazer River. The Indians of the country have received the faith, have had their children baptized and beg earnestly for a priest. 2nd Puget Bay [Sound], which is to the west of the above mentioned Caledonia and on the Pacific Seaboard. There also the Indians have received the faith, have had their children baptized and cry aloud for missionaries. Four would be needed in New Caledonia, two in Puget Bay, one on Vancouver Island, two on Queen Charlotte Island, which is very populous and as large as England. 3rd Walla Walla, 80 leagues from Fort Vancouver on the Columbia, and also a very important post. The Protestant ministers who are some distance away are taking away from us such Indians as have received the faith. If to all this you add to the establishment of Lake St. Ignatius [St. Paul's], a college, the serving of three posts or settlements of American farmers, the charge of the parish of St. Paul, of the convent of the same place, and also of Fort Vancouver and of St. Francis Xavier at Cowlitz, you will have some small idea how pressing it is to increase the number of missionaries in my vicariate."[51]

Early in June, Blanchet was on his way again. Embarking at Liverpool, he crossed the Atlantic, reaching Boston on June 19 and Montreal five days later.[52] He went to Quebec where he hoped to be consecrated by Archbishop Signay, but found him away on a visitation of his diocese. Thus, he returned to Montreal and requested Bishop Ignatius Bourget of that see to perform the administration of the sacrament. On July 11, *Le Canadien* of Quebec announced that the bishop-elect would be consecrated in Montreal on Saturday, July 25, along with Charles Prince, bishop-elect coadjutor of Montreal. "Accordingly on that date there took place at St. James Cathedral in Montreal one of the most impressive ceremonies ever witnessed in that city. The church was filled with an immense crowd which was thrilled by the inspiring spectacle of the consecration of two bishops. There were present besides the two bishops-elect, five others [bishops]... not less than 143 priests and 57 ecclesiasties. The Most Reverend Ignatius Bourget, Bishop of Montreal, was the consecrator, Blanchet was assisted by Bishop Gaulin of Kingston and his coadjutor, Bishop Phelan; Prince by Bishop Turgeon and Power [of Toronto]."[53]

Oregon finally had its first bishop, but he would never arrive there as the "Titular Bishop of Drasa," a mere vicar apostolic. In one of the most amazing decisions in the history of the church, Gregory XVI created an archdiocese in the Oregon wilderness and appointed Francis Norbert Blanchet, for a brief time Titular Bishop of Drasa, as the archbishop of Oregon City, a mere village, the second only archbishop in the entire United States—Baltimore being first and Kenrick's St. Louis, the third.[54] This action was taken before Blanchet returned to Oregon, but not without his complicity, nay, his stubborn insistence, if the truth were known.

The account of all of this, little known at the time, makes for fascinating reading, especially in view of Blanchet's inexperience in the tangled politics of Rome. He had come a long way, indeed, from being the diffident pastor of St. Paul, afraid, as Demers said, to speak out.

After his consecration, Blanchet remained in Canada for a month and a half, visiting relatives and renewing old acquaintances. He left Montreal for Boston on August 12, and sailed for Liverpool whence he went to London, then across the channel to Paris. In Paris he paused to reflect on plans for his vicariate. He decided then that he needed "some assistant bishops," a preposterous pretension when you think about it, but an innocent one. He also needed, he told himself, a chartered ship full of missionaries and supplies, and a ton of money to pay for it all.[55] He was in distressing circumstances financially, almost penniless and up to his ears in debt. He was gradually learning that as Bishop of Drasa, like other missionary bishops, he had to use a tin cup for begging more often than a crozier for solemn celebrations.

While he was still in Paris, seeking funds to pay his bills and to gather others for the vicariate, Demers in a letter dated October 8, 1845, dispatched to him a progress report on events in Oregon. In this Demers noted the following:

> Father Nobili had left in June with the Brigade of the North for New Caledonia, Father DeSmet visited lower Columbia at the end of June, Father DeVos had the care of Oregon City and Fort Vancouver, and Father Accolti was chaplain of the Sisters at St. Paul. The priest house was finished at Oregon City, and the church much advanced. The church built by Father Vercruisse [sic] at La Grand Prairie was soon to be blessed and opened for divine service. Father Ravalli had left for the Rocky Mountains. Sixty thousand bricks had been burnt for the new church at St. Paul. St. Joseph's College, containing 28 boarders, being too small, had been enlarged with a second story by its principal, Father Bolduc. The good religious of Notre Dame de Namur were overburdened with occupations in the care and teaching of 42 little girls, and a chapel, measuring 80 by 30 feet was in course of construction for them.[56]

Demers added later that Dr. McLoughlin was preparing to leave the Hudson's Bay Company and retire to Oregon City. "I was forgetting," he also wrote, "to say a word or two about the political state of the country. A provisory government had been established, Mr. George Abernethy is governor, the Hudson Bay Co. joins in with the provisory government; Vancouver, Cowlitz and Nisqually form a district of which Chief Factor Douglas is the judge in chief."[57]

THE NEW ST. JAMES CHURCH

Somewhere lost in the report was a small item: "Chief Factor Douglas having desired the erection of a Catholic Church, one was put up and shingled." The church here built in 1845, on land provided by Douglas, was called St. James, the patron saint of Douglas, who, it will be recalled, was a devout "Church of England man." This appears, no doubt, to be a trifling matter, but it was a highly significant point later, completely overlooked in the St. James Mission Land Case, involving one square mile of present Vancouver, Washington.[58]

BLANCHET'S MEMORIALE

Blanchet did not reveal where in Europe he received this dispatch from Demers. He was busy, basking, like DeSmet before him, in the sunshine of familiarity with kings and queens, who responded generously to his supplications. The possession of money gave him confidence, and when he arrived at Rome, where he spent four months, he was ready for anything, even a pious confrontation with some wise old cardinals.

In Rome, he presented to the Sacred Congregation of Propaganda his now famous *Memoriale,* his proposal for Oregon, comprising some sixty pages of statistics, exhortations, and unsought advice.[59]

This memoriale, says Garraghan, more amused than shocked by Blanchet's boldness, "embodied a rather startling plan, in view of the mere handful of Catholics in the territory, for the erection of the vicariate into an archdiocese with seven suffragan sees dependent thereon."[60] In other words, Blanchet, falsely interpreting the history of the missions in California, attributing their downfall to a lack of bishops, proposed the canonical establishment of eight dioceses in a wilderness with sixteen priests and by his own estimate only six thousand Catholics. As yet, there was not a single city, there were no roads, no postal service, not even a sovereign government.

At the moment, in fact, there was general feeling in the United States that war with England over the Oregon boundary was inevitable. During the political campaign for president in 1844, Democratic candidate James K. Polk ran on the slogan "Fifty-four Forty or Fight," indicating his party's position that America claimed the entire west coast from the California border to Alaska.[61] England claimed everything north of the Columbia to Alaska. On April 27, 1846, Congress adopted a resolution abrogating the Treaty of Joint Occupation and this was forwarded to London on the following day. The feisty Americans were ready for battle, but the British foreign secretary, Lord George Hamilton-Gordon, 4th Earl of Aberdeen, in June 1846, proposed a new treaty making the 49th parallel the boundary to the sea, reserving free navigation for her ships and protecting the property and rights of the Hudson's Bay Company. The United States Senate ratified this treaty on June 18. The political sovereignty of Oregon was finally determined after twenty-eight years of procrastination by both governments.

Bishop Blanchet was aware of all of this by reports from America. In his *Memoriale,* however, he was more concerned with church politics. In its second part he speculated about the future of religion in the Northwest and offered his plan to secure its success. He stressed the relationship that should exist between the bishop and his priests, and in this context he demanded the restriction of the privileges of religious communities in

Oregon. "The problem of rights and jurisdiction of bishops over regulars [Order priests] in their dioceses was a matter which gave him much concern and of which he heard 'incessant talk' in Rome. Perhaps this accounts for a change in his attitude toward the Jesuits, to whom he had given a whole-hearted welcome a short time before."[62]

In practice, Blanchet listed three requests with regard to religious:

2) In all that concerns the exercise of the external ministry all authority without distinction over the missionaries, secular and regular, as to the administration of temporal goods in the diocese confided to my care, of such sort that to carry out the orders of the Holy See, the regulars may not have recourse to an authority foreign to the mission.
3) The power to suspend the formation of the religious novitiate until the time when there will be formed the nucleus of a native secular clergy, sufficient to support and sustain the action of the bishop.
4) That these two powers (Nos. 2 and 3) will be equally accorded to the bishops or vicars apostolic of the province.[63]

These demands, proposed in open disagreement with centuries of church history, would have in effect abolished religious orders in the Northwest, a happening that Blanchet might have embraced but obviously not one in the interests of the Holy See or the church.

Blanchet faced a long, painful struggle in his determination to keep an almost absolute control over the religious priests of his diocese. He would never succeed because in most disputes with religious, Rome ruled in favor of the Orders.[67]

THE ARCHDIOCESE OF OREGON CITY

In accordance with the *Memoriale,* considerably modified, Gregory XVI by a brief dated July 24, 1846, created the archiepiscopal see of Oregon City and the dioceses of Walla Walla and Vancouver Island, together with five districts that were to become dioceses in the foreseeable future: Nesqually, Fort Hall, Colville, Princess Charlotte, and New Caledonia. Of these, Vancouver Island, Princess Charlotte, and part of Colville were now in British Territory. At the same time, with the creation of the new dioceses, Blanchet was appointed to Oregon City, his companion Modeste Demers to Vancouver Island, to which was added the administration of the districts in British territory. Blanchet's brother, Father Magliore Blanchet, a canon in Montreal, was appointed to the see of Walla Walla, together with the administration of the districts in American territory. Thus, within six weeks of the settlement of the boundary question, an extensive hierarchy was provided to fill a void, which still lacked a visible government and for the most part, people.

The archbishop learned of his elevation when he returned to Paris. His principal objective, now, was to find a ship he could charter and to gather his recruits for the mission. While the latter was simple enough, he encountered many obstacles with the former, and there were times when the delays, totalling nearly six months, appeared to be caused by the devil himself.

He received news from Oregon. The church at Oregon City, dedicated to St. John, was blessed and opened for divine service on Septuagesima Sunday, February 8, 1846. This was Oregon's "Cathedral" now, a rather pompous title for a modest frame church. Perhaps it should have been called a pro-cathedral, but no one seems to have thought about it and everyone in Oregon City grabbed a little personal glory by being identified with *the cathedral*.

What pleased the archbishop more was the completion of his church at St. Paul. The cornerstone for this was blessed by the vicar general, soon bishop-elect Demers, on May 24, 1846. On November 1 of the same year, the church was dedicated and opened for divine service. Blanchet proudly described it: "It was the first brick building ever erected in the country, measuring 100 feet by 45, with wings or chapels of 20 feet; its belfry showing the sign of our redemption 84 feet from the ground."[65]

Especially gratifying were reports of conversions at Oregon City by Father DeVos. Several prominent people had entered the church and crowds of Protestants attended services to hear either DeVos or Accolti preach. The latter, who loved to fill the church with song, had a booming voice and an ever pleasant round face like a monsignor's, and the manners and gestures of an Italian count.

But not all the news from home was good. Demers, who had taken the bishop-elect at his word to erect substantial churches and residences without anxiety about cost, had run up a debt that was "more the less, enormous, frightening—150,000 francs or almost."[66]

"First I will speak to you of Father DeSmet," he wrote. "Do not be astonished if I tell you that the good Father has made his voyage in Europe like a man who had never been in this country or who had no idea of its needs. He has failed to bring the most necessary things; of those which cannot be bought here except for a high price, he has brought nothing. As for books, which Father Langlois asked, I doubt if he has brought a single one, it is the same with many other articles. Besides the Jesuits are dissatisfied they did not come here to establish schools but to found missions for the Indians. Following advice given to the Father General by Father DeSmet he has ordered that they form an establishment in the Willamette Valley, which will be a mother mission, a central place which can furnish the needs of the missions of the mountains. But the Willamette is not any more central for the mountains than Kingston is for Rimouski. You know already what distances there are and how many of the voyages are not only difficult but dangerous. The Fathers here feel keenly the mistake in calculation and the inconvenience of being stationed at Willamette but they can do nothing..... "[67]

Actually, Demers was mostly concerned about money and he admitted that what he feared most was that his lordship would not bring home enough of it to pay the debts.[68]

JESUIT PROBLEMS

Fortunately, Demers, who was beginning to lose his grip, did not know how many problems the Jesuits faced. At French Prairie, for example, there were rumblings about Father Vercruysse, a very gloomy man like some ancient prophets, who was preaching too much hell and damnation in the church of St. Louis. The French Canadians were beginning to rebel. In particular they did not like his sermons on temperance, for these left little room for social drinking, not to mention the *regale*, to which old *voyageurs* had become accustomed. Through McLoughlin's influence the sale of liquor in the valley had been controlled, but with his impending departure from the company, two Irishmen had built a still and were producing enough cheap booze to demoralize many of the Catholics in Oregon.

In the north DeSmet had established another mission, with visible evidence of its existence. "I left Kettle Falls August 4th," he wrote, giving an account of his activities in late 1845, "accompanied by several of the nation of the Crees to examine the lands they have selected for the site of a village.[69] The ground is rich and well situated for all agricultural purposes. Several buildings were commercial; I gave the name of St. Francis Regis to this new station, where a great number of mixed race and beaver hunters have resolved to settle, with their families."[70]

DeSmet was almost at the end of his rope, for the time being at least. Father Point, in one of his occasional snits, had insisted, again, that he be transferred to another mission, preferably in South America. He had got South America in his head, and decided he wanted to go there. His letter to Roothaan, composed and sent off two years earlier had brought, as yet, no response, so Point was hard to live with. Joset, who could live with anybody, even a dog with fleas, took his place at St. Joseph's Mission on the river, with orders to move the place. This was in November 1845.[71]

Nothing had gone right. The basic problem was the mission's location. The site, very attractive in autumn, when Point had selected it, was flooded in the spring. Roads and fields became impassable bogs and mosquitoes swarmed over the sloughs created by high water. Brother Huet, plagued by these pests, was forced to take to his bed "with a fever." Because of these conditions, endured annually, the mission lacked food. The Jesuits there, like their Indian friends, were often reduced to living on moss and roots.

So, DeSmet, finally aware of true conditions, directed Joset to seek a new location. With Brother Huet, who was much relieved to escape the mosquitoes and floods, Joset set about this task in the spring of 1846, selecting at last, a knoll surrounded by flat alluvial lands, on the Coeur d'Alene River ten miles above the lake.[72] Huet began again. He quickly assembled a "bark chapel," then a "bark barn," then three log cabins. Finally a field for wheat, oats, and potatoes were fenced in and the new mission by the summer of 1846, was in operation.

At. St. Ignatius Mission on the Pend Oreille River, similar problems confronted Adrian Hoecken. The mission's first crops were flooded in the spring of 1845. The potato fields were ruined and only enough wheat and barley were saved for seeding the following year. In 1846 more than one hundred acres were sown, and again high water reduced most of them to a marsh, in which the animals sank knee-deep in mud. Even the deer, on which the Kalispels depended for meat, seemed to have abandoned the area and the missionaries with the Indians were forced to eat "pine-moss cooked with a little *gamache,* a meal of which no begger would care to taste."[73]

Only St. Mary's showed progress. "Through the persistent efforts of Father Ravalli, the two Brothers and a French-Canadian [Biledot], a miniature milling plant, the first grist mill in Montana, was constructed," Palladino wrote, "where in the tiny burhstones, made to run by water power, were turning out excellent flour.....''[74] The mission needed a sawmill. Ravalli arrived in the summer of 1845 and with the help of Biledot constructed a primitive mill using the rims of wagon wheels. On the same day that Zerbinatti drowned, September 15, Ravalli successfully tested his mill, which like the flour mill, was the first in all of Montana.[75]

Both of these mills were regarded as great triumphs, and perhaps they were in the long run. The one provided lumber for St. Mary's, the other flour for making communion hosts for all of the missions of the interior, neither of which were historically earthshaking.[76] But in the end, they were giant strides toward civilization in an area more vast in size than all of western Europe. While the Jesuits at St. Mary's recognized these accomplishments, they felt no sense of elation, for they already knew that St. Mary's was under attack by some of the Indians. Maybe Zerbinatti was the lucky one. For the rest, no one could say how long St. Mary's would survive.

DeSmet dropped by in the summer of 1846. He was determined to convert the Blackfeet, traditional enemies of the Flatheads, who lived in jeopardy as long as the Blackfeet were not Christian. On August 16, taking Nicolas Point with him, he left St. Mary's for Blackfeet country, enroute to St. Louis, where he had been summoned.[77] His course was long and dangerous, but, as usual, he lived to write books about it. Point, too, survived, and like DeSmet, he composed his memoirs for print, but more than a century went by before they were published.

DeSmet left Point at Fort Lewis on the upper Missouri where he spent the winter of 1846–1847 painting Indians and teaching children. He lived in a room at the fort, a post of the American Fur Company, which placed another room at his disposal for use as a classroom. Here, in the first school in eastern Montana, Point taught the Blackfeet. When he left the fort for St. Louis and his new assignment in Canada, on May 21, 1847, he carried with him sixty-seven new portraits of Indians and a large number of other drawings, and his baptismal book which contained the records of 651 baptisms at the fort.[78] Whatever else one might say about Nicolas Point, he never enjoyed an idle moment.

There is an epilogue about the troubles of the Jesuits, perhaps the saddest of all. DeSmet was transferred from the Rocky Mountain Missions to a desk job in St. Louis. Of the three Jesuit priests who founded the mission in 1841, DeSmet, Point, and Mengarini, only Mengarini was left after five brief years, and his days were numbered. Joset was appointed superior and that, too, became a "trouble."

BLANCHET'S RETURN

The new archbishop in Europe continued to experience many difficulties in finding a ship to take him and his recruits for the mission to Oregon. For the time it took, many months, a ship could have been built for him, especially a small bark like the one he finally chartered at Brest.[79] There was much coming and going of missionaries while the vessel was being readied for its long voyage. At last, on February 2, 1847, "in the presence of a religious crowd," said the archbishop, he blessed the ship and gave it a name, *L'Etoile du Matin*, "The Evening Star."[80]

As soon as the weather was favorable all went aboard. But the following day, February 11, the sea was dead calm again, and all returned to shore. They waited eleven more days, then *The Evening Star* put out to sea. "The religious colony she carried," Blanchet wrote, "was composed of 22 persons, including the archbishop, viz: 7 Sisters of Notre Dame de Namur; the three Jesuit Fathers, Goetz, Gazzoli and Menetrey, and three [Jesuit] lay brothers; 5 secular priests, LeBas, McCormick, Deleneau, Pretot, and Veyret; 2 deacons, B. Delorme and J.F. Jayol and a cleric, T.

Mesplie.[81] The apartment of the sisters was very good; a long saloon and a long table was common to all. An Altar had been fixed at the after part of the ship, whereon holy Masses were daily celebrated...."[82]

On August 17 the bark landed at the mouth of the Willamette and on the nineteenth the missionaries left for St. Paul. This they reached on Saturday, August 26, very late at night, when the sweet-spicy scent of the harvest in the fields, contrasting with the salty smells of the ocean, reminded them of villages at home. They were all young, on the threshold of a new, difficult life. Some would live it, some would not.[83]

The archbishop did not accompany them. He went directly to Oregon City, celebrated Mass "at the Cathedral" and reached Champoeg the following day. "From thence," he added, "accompanied by a large concourse of Catholics and Protestants, he entered the church at St. Paul, vested with episcopal robes, mozette, mitre and crozier." The bishop-elect, he said, had been two years and seven months absent.[84]

One senses in Blanchet's report an undertone of exaltation, still felt three decades later, when he wrote it. No longer the underdog, he had found a new faith in himself and his future. This faith would soon be tried severely, by the cruel events which were about to inundate him.

5

STORM CLOUDS OVER OREGON

1847–1849

The archbishop's younger brother Augustin was as strong willed as a mule, like the archbishop himself, and sometimes he was more determined than either. He was only two years junior to the archbishop in terms of time, and like the latter had been born on the family farm near the village of St. Pierre, Riviere du Sud. Canada.[1] With Francois, he had gone to the seminary and he was ordained on June 3, 1821, when he was only twenty-three years old. After serving in various pastoral capacities, he was appointed canon in the cathedral at Montreal, a very long distance from Oregon and Francois, who sometimes insisted that Augustin be appointed bishop rather than himself.

If Augustin owed his nomination as bishop to his brother, he was at least as worthy as Francois and probably better instructed in the politics of the Canadian church. A very handsome man, even in middle age, he looked the part of a prosperous French bourgeois, with firm lips like a self-made merchant, deep, expressive eyes and a receding hairline, presumably caused by his excessive use of the brain. As the elder Blanchet grew older, there was a kind of patriarchal air about him, but Augustin continued to appear aggressive, as though he had a chip on his shoulder, which he expected someone to knock off.

His full name was Augustin Magliore Alexandre Blanchet in the French form, which he liked to use, but he usually went by "A.M.A. Blanchet" in contrast to "F.X.N. Blanchet" the archbishop. There has always been some confusion about the two brothers, and this was made even more mysterious by the appearance on the scene of other Blanchets, who were not related to them.

Augustin was consecrated by Bishop Bourget in St. James Cathedral in Montreal on September 27, 1846. There is evidence to believe that he was quite happy about this and expected to find, when he finally arrived in

Oregon, a diocese that had everything except priests and a cathedral. He remained in Canada until the following spring, using his time to promote his diocese and to make final arrangements for his journey.

THE OBLATES OF MARY IMMACULATE

The lack of priests was his first problem. He had appealed to the bishops of eastern Canada and to the Superior General of the Oblates of Mary Immaculate in Marseilles for volunteer for his diocese.[2] Through the influence of the Oblate superior in Canada, Father Joseph Guignes, he was able to obtain five Oblates, one priest, three scholastics, and one brother.

Writing to an unknown bishop, he was almost ecstatic (strange disposition for him): "Yesterday's post brought me such consolation that I am almost overcome. The bishop of Marseilles announced to me that the Oblates had embarked February 1 from Havre for New York and would await my orders.[3] The bishop of Montreal who wrote me January 14 was most favorable toward Oregon. The administration has today given to Father [John Baptist Abraham] Brouillet, a curé of Acadia, permission to follow me . . . I asked at least one secular priest—prudent, virtuous, of some experience. I asked at least two Oblates. I asked 1000 or 1200 louis. I shall have all of that and perhaps more!"[4]

OFF TO OREGON

Accompanied by Brouillet and two students for the priesthood, Bishop Blanchet left Montreal on March 23, 1847, for St. Louis, where he expected to meet the Oblates.[5] He kept a daily journal of his entire journey to Walla Walla and beyond, and this has proved to be more revealing about his rigid personality than any of his letters to other bishops or to Rome.[6] The journal begins with his departure on a stagecoach, which tipped over enroute, injuring to some small extent his right arm. From Albany, New York to Buffalo the party traveled by train, which was delayed by heavy snows. In Buffalo, they took the stagecoach to Erie and Blanchet made his first of many petty remarks about America and its people, "One finds cities everywhere, more or less spread out," he wrote on March 29. "In Canada they are called *villages*."

Blanchet arrived in Pittsburgh on Holy Saturday, April 3, and was able to celebrate Easter Mass with great solemnity despite his sore arm, which the deacon had to hold up when the celebrant incensed the altar. His Lordship was shocked because vespers were not chanted in the cathedral and he noted, with undisguised scorn, "What is more, without any scruple, they move about the streets during the time there is some divine service in the cathedral."[8]

From Pittsburgh to St. Louis, about four hundred miles, the missionaries traveled by river boat. The bishop found his American companions on the boat "polished and engaging" but he could not approve "of their manner of raising their legs as high as their heads when they are sitting down."[9] He added that one could always recognize Americans by this mannerism.

After passing through Cincinnati and Louisville, where he had visited with bishops, he noted their comments on religious orders. They thought, he wrote, that the best way to train young men was by religious orders, but not the way to train the secular clergy. "The Jesuits know better than others how to gain the affection of young students and to attract them to the Society. The Bishops of Pittsburgh and Louisville think this way and the latter says the Jesuits have taken 40 or 50 of his best subjects."[10]

In the years to come these words would bear bitter fruit. Like his brother the archbishop, Augustin Blanchet would not get along with religious orders, and one can see from the advice he was getting, why he did not. The archbishop, it will be recalled, had been deeply concerned about the exemptions of religious and in his *Memoriale* he had done his best to have them abolished as religious for his diocese. It was inevitable that disputes would arise, often because of misunderstandings, but more often because of differences of viewpoint between the two bishops and religious superiors, especially of the Jesuits and the Oblates. In addition to exemption and the alleged influence of Jesuits over young candidates for the priesthood, there was a common complaint about the ownership of land. This became a source of friction between several bishops and religious orders for the next century and longer, with fault at times on both sides.

One can be sure that Augustin Blanchet had already made up his mind about his Oblates when he arrived at St. Louis on April 15. The next day the Oblates arrived, also by boat, and for the first time he had an opportunity to assess their strengths and weaknesses. He left no record of this, but he was probably wrong. The Jesuits at the university in St. Louis had invited the Oblates to remain with them until their departure with Blanchet. They accepted the invitation eagerly, and while Blanchet's party were guests of the bishop, the Oblates joined the Jesuits, with whom they shared a cordial relationship. At the cathedral, Blanchet noted, "a very sorry state of affairs existed," these Americans simply were "not accustomed to have ceremonies such as those in Canada."[11]

The superior of the Oblates was Father Pascal Ricard, formerly

superior of Notre Dame de Lumieres, the Oblate seminary. He was a
gentle, sensitive Frenchman, known mostly for his chronic sickness,
which kept him frequently in bed. The sea voyage from Le Havre seems
to have restored his precarious health. As for his strength of will, he was
more than a match with Augustin Blanchet, as the latter soon learned.
The three scholastics were in the pink of condition; each one, filled with
zeal and God's love, was an excellent missionary. These were Eugene
Casimir Chirouse and George Blanchet, both twenty-six years in age,
and Charles Pandosy, who was twenty-three. The lay brother was
Celestin Verney.[12]

On April 26, all but Brouillet embarked on a river boat and started the
ascent of the Missouri. Blanchet grumbled about the cost, especially for
his two heavy freight wagons, which he had acquired in St. Louis. He had
other observations to offer, "We have the opportunity to practice
patience and charity on these American boats because the servants are
far from polite—there is nothing very surprising in this."[13] By May 1,
they arrived at Kansas Landing [Kansas City] where, four days later,
Brouillet met them, having purchased on his way from St. Louis, sixteen
oxen, two cows and five horses. The weather was wet, the ground rain-
soaked, and the skies gloomy.

THE OREGON TRAIL

For the next week there was much coming and going. The bishop
complained that while he loaded the wagons, others stood around and
cleaned their rifles. He was referring, of course, to the teamsters whom
he had employed for the journey. On Sunday, May 9, he finally found a
guide whom he trusted, a certain Joseph Huneau, and on the following
Thursday, the combined train of twenty-six wagons and forty-nine men
lumbered into line and headed west.

Blanchet's day by day entries in his journal continue to reveal his own
attitudes more than the raw wilderness around him. On Friday, June 11,
for example, he states that this being the Feast of the Sacred Heart, he
dedicated again his diocese in honor of the Sacred Heart, disclosing his
own deep piety toward a personal Jesus. At Fort Laramie, which the
wagon train reached on June 26, he wrote censoriously, "The Sioux men
there are not dressed in a decent manner."[15] It is not difficult to reconcile
this righteousness with his piety: The French Canadian clergy of the
period had been greatly influenced by French Jansenism of the previous
century.[16]

At the end of the first week in August, the wagon train was as far as
Fort Hall on the Snake River, where Blanchet, alarmed by the slow pace
endured so far, decided to go ahead on horseback with Ricard, Brother

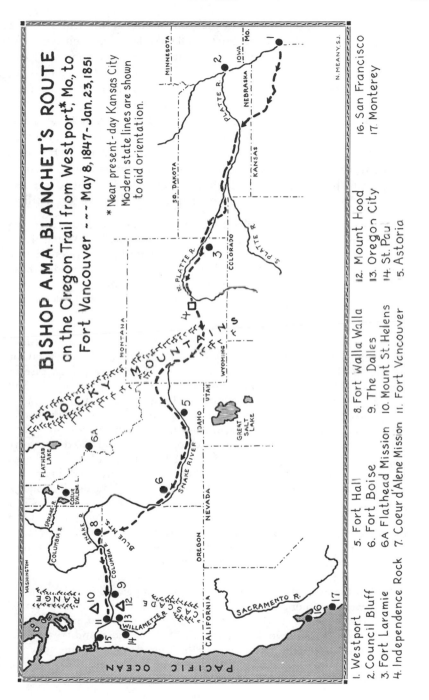

BISHOP A.M.A. BLANCHET'S ROUTE
on the Oregon Trail from Westport,* Mo., to
Fort Vancouver ~~ May 8, 1847 - Jan. 23, 1851

* Near present-day Kansas City
Modern state lines are shown
to aid orientation.

N. MEANY, S.J.

1. Westport
2. Council Bluff
3. Fort Laramie
4. Independence Rock
5. Fort Hall
6. Fort Boise
6A. Flathead Mission
7. Coeur d'Alene Mission
8. Fort Walla Walla
9. The Dalles
10. Mount St. Helens
11. Fort Vancouver
12. Mount Hood
13. Oregon City
14. St. Paul
15. Astoria
16. San Francisco
17. Monterey

Blanchet and Mr. Rousseau.[17] They left on August 4, riding about thirty-five miles a day, and reached Fort Walla Walla on September 5. The bishop was astonished by what he found, not a frontier city, as he expected, not even a small town, but only a lonely fur trading post. This forlorn and uncouth fortress, which could not even be imagined in Rome, was the seat of his new diocese called Walla Walla.

Mr. William McBean, who had succeeded Pambrun as Chief Factor, was also a Catholic, and treated the new bishop with great attention and respect.[18] He provided temporary housing at the fort while the bishop and Ricard toured the area, seeking sites for missions. Shortly after his arrival, the bishop, in a letter to Bishop Turgeon of Toronto, composed a classic description of a do-it-yourself trip across the Oregon Trail:

> If there is any priest who wishes to come here by the same route, there are several things he should have in order not to find himself in my embarrassing situation. If he is alone and without baggage, the best plan would be for him to procure at Westport or elsewhere a good guide, accustomed to these trips, to purchase a pack-horse (they call them prairie horses), and then to join a caravan because of the danger there would be in traveling alone or in small numbers, especially in passing through the lands of the Pawnees and the Sioux. If he has baggage, it will be necessary to purchase a wagon at St. Louis and to buy some oxen, five or six years old, not too fat; if the load does not weigh more than 1200 to 1500 pounds, three pair will be sufficient for the wagon but it is necessary to have one or two extra pair in case of accidents, which are likely to happen. The provisions are sea biscuits and flour; one pound a day ought to be sufficient for each person. It is essential to have plenty of meat, bacon and salted or chipped beef, three fourths pound of bacon each day is enough for each; also, tea, coffee, sugar, rice, etc., etc. A milk cow is of great service. My best oxen cost me $40 and $50 the pair; my wagons $80 each, my horses from $25 to $30. Although I had purchased twelve pair of oxen, I had trouble making the trip; many are dead or have been abandoned, unable to walk farther. The cause of the death of such a great number of animals this year has been lack of food. The number of wagons to come and go will be over a thousand. The early emigrants had pasturage for their stock but the later arrivals found nothing or almost nothing for theirs to feed on. Father Brouillet tells me that from Fort Hall to Walla Walla there were no less than a hundred wagons abandoned on the road because there were no more beasts to pull them. My wagons are still usable but the oxen are so worn with fatigue, hunger and thirst that it was necessary to leave along the way some of the supplies carried from St. Louis, such as the plow, etc. . . . My expenses for the trip exceeded my estimate. I had planned that they would be about £500 at the most; and they almost doubled this amount. Farewell then, to the hope of beginning the episcopal establishment with the money subscribed by Quebec and Montreal; one must live while awaiting such help as may come from France.[19]

One finds in this no bitterness but a certain lack of humor which appeared to be wanting in both bishops Blanchet. There are also indications of Augustin's more practical bent, as contrasted with his brother, who seems to have been given to more pious observations, like DeSmet.

Whatever their dispositions, neither of the Blanchets were prepared for what followed. Augustin Blanchet, still at the fort, met Dr. Marcus Whitman there on September 23. Whitman on his way from The Dalles to Waiilatpu, his own mission, stopped at the fort to meet the new bishop, mostly to manifest his resentment because of the Catholic presence in the valley. The Doctor expressed himself in abusive language, shouting excitedly that he would like to take his own blood and smear it on the Catholic ladder "to show the persecution of Protestants by Catholics." He became calm gradually, however, as Blanchet offered him words of friendship, and the two parted in amicable spirits.[20] For the bishop, this shattering confrontation was an entirely new experience. For the Doctor it was the beginning of the end.

The Doctor, understandably, had been over-wrought, and was not acting like his usual self, for whatever his faults, he was not a boorish man. From the beginning, his mission had not succeeded as he had hoped, and though he had accumulated great wealth in land and livestock, he felt professionally frustrated. Most of his Indians had abandoned him and at that very moment some were spreading discontent by harangues and meetings. The winter of 1846-1847 had been one of the most severe on record. Indian cattle and horses froze to death. Many of the Cayuses and Walla Wallas were attacked by measles and dysentery, and not a few of them, unaccustomed to these diseases, quickly died.[21] Whitman with his simple remedies, did what he could for them, but when his cures failed, he was accused of poisoning them as a means of acquiring more of their land. In keeping with Indian custom, medicine men who failed to cure their patients, were themselves doomed.

During the summer of 1847, a well-known Canadian artist, Paul Kane, visited Whitman at his mission and warned him that his life was in danger. Dr. McLoughlin, too, had sent him reports of threats on his life. By this time the White Headed Eagle was no longer the uncrowned king of Oregon and his power was felt no longer by many Indians of the Interior. They had been outraged by the increasing numbers of whites, who were arriving from the East and taking Indian land for their cattle ranches. Their pent-up anger was certain to explode and either Whitman's or Spalding's missions were the likeliest places for it.

Whitman had talked vaguely about leaving. He put it off until the following spring. He would retire there, he said, and settle somewhere in the Willamette Valley, or in the fertile rolling hills west of the Willamette, toward the setting sun and the western sea.

THE FIRST ORDINATION

The Oblates, meanwhile, having consulted many friendly Indians in the area, proposed that they locate their own mission in the Yakima Territory far to the west of Walla Walla. Piopiomosmos, Chief of the Walla Wallas, who was also called "Yellow Serpent," offered Father Ricard a piece of land near the mouth of the Yakima River on the Columbia.[22] Ricard discussed the proposal with Bishop Blanchet and subsequently sent Father Joset a memorandum regarding it:

> Arriving at Ft. Walla Walla each sought to establish himself—Bp. settled among the Cayuse—gave us the right bank of the Columbia—sought to settle among the Walla Walla at mouth of the Yakima river. The chief of the Walla Walla gave me before witnesses the lands I asked for our mission and these lands were given to me *nommement*. Bp. was present at this negotiation and said nothing—but after everything was over, took me aside and said—I would wish you to give me a written *acte* in which you declare that it is not to you but to the Mission, i.e., to the Bishop that this land has been given. Answered that I saw no necessity. Bp. answered it was to provide for the contingence of our being driven from the country. Answered, we are becoming American citizens & cannot see who would drive us out. Bp. answered that, expulsion apart, if I made a will in favor of one of our congregation, he might *apostatize*. Answer, we ought not to presume such a misfortune. Bp. returns to case of expulsion—answer, are becoming Amer. citizens—will take out a deed (& *record* it) for a square mile so that if any bishop chases us out, I can reimburse myself for expenses by selling the land. The Bp. gives me a copy of the famous memoir. This opened my eyes. I saw what religious could expect. Told Bp. that if we put up churches and residences at our expense, they would belong to us. Bp. and Vicar General examined and Bp. approved, said he saw nothing in it that was not just.[23]

If Ricard required a warning of events to come, he had received it. This came on December 4, 1847, scarcely three months after his arrival, in the form of a property dispute, a rather odd encounter in view of the millions of empty acres all around the disputants. But the bishop had reasons to be wary. He had passed recently through eastern America, where lay trustees or priests held title to church property and used their control of it to blackmail or bully bishops. If this were not bad enough, American courts, reflecting the consensus of the American people, tended to favor trustees or priests in contentious court cases. Ricard, it is true, was properly alerted to the complexities of holding title to real estate, but so was the bishop.

Anxious yet, and worried about the Oblates' future relations with the bishop, Ricard sent Brother Blanchet on a voyage of exploration along the Columbia as far as Fort Vancouver, and up the Willamette to Oregon City. There the brother was warmly welcomed by the archbishop, who had returned recently from Europe.

The archbishop, Brother Blanchet learned, was much preoccupied with liturgical celebrations, filling the gap, as it were, because of the absence of a bishop for the preceding years. He had first presented Dr. John McLoughlin with the honors bestowed upon him by the pope. Gregory the Sixteenth had created McLoughlin a Knight of the Order of St. Gregory the Great, which not only revealed the Catholic position regarding McLoughlin's religious status, but said something significant to the Catholics themselves. The pope's recognition of the former Chief Factor elevated the dignity of all.[24] It was no longer proper to think of the Oregon church as a primitive, uncouth mission. Its people had an archbishop, and one among them, a long, long way from Rome, had been honored by Christ's vicar himself.

The archbishop hastened to and fro, administering the sacrament of confirmation on most Sundays, in one church or another. He made elaborate preparations for his first ordination at St. Paul for Sunday September 19, a day on which the Canadian farmers could take time from their harvest. In the church crowded to the rafters, he ordained to the priesthood Father John Jayol, in the first ceremony of its kind in the Oregon Country.

Bishop-elect Demers had not as yet been consecrated. He seemed to be in no hurry, indeed, he was a little bewildered by it all and wondered how he could administer an unknown diocese without priests or money. He had begun preparations for his consecration, accepting at last the bare necessity of having only one bishop as consecrator in the event Augustin Blanchet did not arrive on time. The date for his ceremony was set for November 30, the feast of the Apostle St. Andrew.[25] Though St. John's in Oregon City was regarded as a "cathedral," the archbishop chose St. Paul for the occasion. Meanwhile, on October 31, the archbishop performed his second ordination at St. Paul. He ordained to the priesthood Father Bartholomew Delorme, a chubby, good-natured, young French man with bushy hair and eyes that easily filled with laughter. He looked like some noble character out of Dickens, the compassionate benefactor of Oliver Twist, perhaps. For many years he served in Willamette Valley churches, after the college of St. Joseph was closed, when most people ran off to California.

Brother Blanchet had long gone when the ceremony of consecration for Demers was finally performed, sixteen months after he was appointed by the pope. November 30 was a Tuesday that year, 1847. As the archbishop noted, this "put the crown to all the previous festivities and rejoicings of the faithful, by the episcopal consecration which the bishop-elect of Vancouver Island received in the church of St. Paul on that day, at the hands of the Archbishop, in presence of a numerous clergy and a very large number of the faithful."

One can not find fault with the prelate's enthusiasm, but the consecration of Bishop Demers was certainly less solemn than this passage indicates. The "numerous clergy" could not have been more than a baker's dozen, scarcely enough for a May Day procession, and instead of three ordaining bishops, as was customary in the church, there was only one. Bishop Augustin Blanchet had not arranged for his presence, which, as things turned out, was a misfortune for him.[26] As for "the very large number of the faithful," mentioned by the archbishop, one presumes that three hundred would suffice, and there may be reasonable doubts about that. After all, what one regarded as a "crowd" in Oregon was a far cry from the crowds in Montreal and St. Louis, and even Toussaint Mesplie, the youngest of the clerics, knew that.

THE WHITMAN MASSACRE

Brother Blanchet returned to Walla Walla from the lower Columbia on October 4, just in time to welcome the other members of the wagon train who had arrived on the previous day. Under the direction of Ricard, the Oblates soon departed to occupy the land offered them by Yellow Serpent, leaving the bishop with only one priest, Father Brouillet, who was also vicar general of the diocese.

The site on the Yakima River, suitable, even convenient for the Indians, proved to be less desirable to the missionaries, when they began to build their mission. Wood for construction was three to four miles distant, requiring cartage under primitive conditions. The land was not suitable for cultivation, so it was obvious that a new site would have to be found sooner or later. Nonetheless, the Oblates built their first mission there, a rude home and church at best, and they dedicated it to St. Rose on the Yakima. Later it was known as St. Rose on the Simcoe.[27]

Brouillet chose the Cayuse tribe for his special care. On November 27, 1847, after a long delay occasioned by Young Chief's absence, he opened St. Anne's Mission in an old house provided by the chief, near the Umatilla River, about twenty-five miles from the Whitman Mission at Waiilatpu.[28] This was only three days before Demers was consecrated at St. Paul.

It was also only two days before Dr. Whitman, his wife and eight others were murdered by the Cayuse Indians. Brouillet, the first outsider to appear on the ghastly scene, described it in detail for military officials, who were investigating charges that Catholic priests had instigated the massacre. It will be noted that Brouillet's account appears in the form of a defense of the priests. Later Brouillet himself extended his remarks to comprise a booklet, which became the most famous of all Catholic publications in the early Northwest.

Brouillet's letter to Colonel Cornelius Gilliam appears in part as follows:

On Saturday, November 27th, I left the Fort, in company with the bishop and his secretary, for our mission on the Umatilla, twenty-five miles from Dr. Whitman's. We had scarcely arrived in the evening, when, on going to see a sick person, I learned that Dr. Whitman and Mr. Spalding were en route for my mission, Dr. Whitman having been called to attend to the sick. The next day, being Sunday, we were visited by Dr. Whitman, who remained but a few minutes at the house, and appeared to be much agitated. Being invited to dine, he refused, saying that he feared it would be too late, as he had twenty-five miles to go, and wished to reach home before night. On parting, he entreated me not to fail to visit him when I would pass by his mission, which I very cordially promised to do. On Monday, 29th, Mr. Spalding took supper with us, and appeared quite gay. During the conversation he happened to say that the Doctor was unquiet, that the Indians were displeased with him on account of the sickness, and that even he had been informed that the murderer (an Indian) intended to kill him. But he seemed not to believe this, and suspected as little as we did what was taking place at the mission of the Doctor.

Before leaving Fort Walla Walla it had been decided that after visiting the sick people of my mission on the Umatilla, I should go and visit those of Tilokaikt's camp, for the purpose of baptizing the infants and such dying adults as might desire this favor; and the Doctor and Mr. Spalding having informed me that there were many sick persons at their mission, I was confirmed in this resolution, and made preparations to go as soon as possible.

After having finished baptizing the infants and dying adults of my mission, I left on Tuesday, the 30th of November, late in the afternoon, for Tilokaikt's camp, where I arrived between seven and eight o'clock in the evening. It is impossible to conceive my surprise and consternation, when, upon my arrival, I learned that the Indians the day before had massacred the Doctor and his wife, with the greater part of the Americans at the mission. I passed the night without scarcely closing my eyes.

Early the next morning I baptized three sick children, two of whom died soon after, and then hastened to the scene of death to offer to the widows and orphans, all the assistance in my power. I found five or six women and over thirty children in a situation deplorable beyond description. Some had just lost their husbands, and the others their fathers, whom they had seen massacred before their eyes, and were expecting every moment to share the same fate. The sight of those persons caused me to shed tears, which, however, I was obliged to conceal, for I was the greater part of the day in the presence of the murderers, and closely watched by them, and if I had shown too marked an interest in behalf of the sufferers, it would only have endangered their lives and mine; these, therefore, entreated me to be upon my guard. After the first few words that could be exchanged under the circumstances, I inquired after the victims, and was told that they were yet unburied. Joseph Stanfield, a Frenchman, who was in the service of Dr. Whitman, and had been spared by the Indians, was engaged in washing the corpses, but, being alone, he was unable to bury them. I resolved to go and assist him, so as to render to those unfortunate victims the last service in my power to offer them. What a sight did I then behold! Ten dead bodies lying here and there; covered with blood, and bearing the marks of the most atrocious cruelty, some pierced with balls, others more or less gashed by the hatchet. Dr. Whitman had received three gashes on the face. Three others had their skulls crushed so that their brains were oozing out.

It was on the 29th of November, between two and three o'clock in the afternoon, while all the people at the Doctor's house were busy, that the Indians, with their arms concealed beneath their blankets, introduced themselves successively into the yard, and in an instant executed their horrible butchery. Three or four men (Americans) only were able to escape.

The ravages which the sickness had made in their midst, together with the conviction which a half-breed, named Joseph Lewis, had succeeded in fixing upon their minds, that Doctor Whitman has poisoned them, were the only motives I could discover which could have prompted them to this act of murder. This half-breed had imagined a conversation between Doctor Whitman, his wife, and Mr. Spalding, in which he made them say that it was necessary to hasten the death of the Indians in order to get possession of their horses and lands. 'If you do not kill the Doctor,' said he, you will all be dead in the spring.'

I assure you, sir, that during the time I was occupied in burying the victims of this disaster, I was far from feeling safe, being obliged to go here and there gathering up dead bodies, in the midst of assassins, whose hands were still stained with blood, and who, by their manners, their countenances, and the arms which they still carried, sufficiently announced that their thirst for blood was yet unsatisfied. Assuming as composed a manner as possible, I cast more than one glance aside and behind at the knives, pistols, and guns, in order to assure myself whether there were not some of them directed toward me.

The bodies were all deposited in a common grave, which had been dug the day previous by Joseph Stanfield; and before leaving I saw that they were covered with earth. But I have since learned that the grave, not having been soon enough enclosed, had been molested by the wolves, and that some of the corpses had been devoured by them.

Having buried the dead, I hastened to prepare for my return to my mission in order to acquaint Mr. Spalding of the danger which threatened him; because on Monday evening, when he supped with us, he said that it was his intention to return to Doctor Whitman's on the following Wednesday or Thursday; and I wished to meet him in time to give him a chance to escape.

This I repeated several times to the unfortunate widows of the slain, and expressed to them my desire of being able to save Mr. Spalding. Before leaving the women and children, I spoke to the son of Tilokaikt, who seemed to be acting in the place of his father, asking him to promise me that they should not be hurt, and that he would take care of them. 'Say to them,' said he, 'that they need fear nothing; they shall be taken care of and well treated.' I then left them, after saying what I could to encourage them, although I was not myself entirely exempt from fear on their account.

On leaving the Doctor's house I perceived that the son of Tilokaikt followed, in company with my interpreter, who himself was an Indian, his friend and his relative by his wife. I did not think that he had the intention of coming far with us; I believed that he was merely coming to the river to point out some new place for crossing, and that he would afterwards return. But when, after crossing the river, he still continued going on with us, I began strongly to fear for Mr. Spalding. I knew that the Indians were angry with all Americans, and more enraged against Mr. Spalding than any other. But what could I do in such a circumstance? I saw no remedy; I could not tell the Indian to go back, because he would have suspected something, and it would have been worse; I could not start ahead of him, because he had a much better horse than mine. I resolved, then, to leave all in the hands of Providence. Fortunately, a few minutes after crossing the river, the interpreter asked Tilokaikt's son for a smoke. They prepared the calumet, but when the moment came for lighting it there was nothing to make fire. 'You have a pistol,' said the interpreter, 'fire it, and we will light.' Accordingly, without stopping, he fired his pistol, reloaded it, and fired it again. He then commenced smoking with the interpreter, without thinking of reloading his pistol. A few minutes after, while they were thus engaged in smoking, I saw Mr. Spalding come galloping towards me. In a moment he was at my side, taking me by the hand, and asking for news. 'Have you been to the Doctor's?' he inquired. 'Yes,' I replied. 'What news?' 'Sad news.' 'Is any person dead?' 'Yes, sir.' 'Who is dead? Is it one of the Doctor's children?' (He had left two of them very sick.) 'No,' I replied. 'Who, then, is dead?' I hesitated to tell him. 'Wait a moment,' said I, 'I cannot tell you now.' While Mr. Spalding was asking me those different questions, I had spoken to my interpreter, telling him to entreat the Indians, in my name, not to kill Mr. Spalding; which I begged of him as a special favor, and hoped that he would not refuse it to me. I was waiting for his answer, and did not wish to relate the disaster to Mr. Spalding before getting it, for fear that he might, by his manner, discover to the Indian what I had told him; for the least motion like flight would have cost him his life, and probably expose mine also. The son of Tilokaikt, after hesitating some moments, replied that he could not take it upon himself to save Mr. Spalding, but that he would go back and consult the other Indians; and so he started back immediately to his camp, I then availed myself of his absence to satisfy the anxiety of Mr. Spalding. I related to him what has passed. 'The Doctor is dead,' said I; 'the Indians have killed him, together with his wife and eight other Americans, on Monday last, the 29th, and I have buried them before leaving today.' 'The Indians have killed the Doctor?' cried Mr. Spalding; 'they will kill me also, if I go to the camp!' 'I fear it very much,' said I. 'What, then, shall I do?' 'I know not; I have told you what has happened; decide now for yourself what you had best do; I have no advice to give you in regard to that.' 'Why has that Indian started back?' he inquired. 'I begged him to spare your life,' said I, 'and he answered me that he could not take it upon himself to do so, but that he would go and take the advice of the other Indians about it; that is the reason why he started back.' Mr. Spalding seemed frightened and discouraged. 'Is it possible! Is it possible!' he repeated several times; 'they will certainly kill me;' and he was unable to come to any decision. 'But what could have prompted the Indians to this?' he inquired. 'I know not,' said I; 'but be quick to take a decision; you have not time to lose. If the Indians should resolve not to spare your life, they will be here very soon, as we are only about three miles from their camp.' 'But where shall I go?' 'I know not; you know the country better than I; all I know is, that the Indians say the order to kill Americans has been sent in all directions.' Mr. Spalding then resolved to fly. He asked me if I was willing to take charge of some loose horses that he was driving before him. I told him that I could not, for fear of becoming suspicious to the Indians. I told him, however, that if the interpreter was willing to take them under his charge at his own risk, he was perfectly at liberty to do so. To this the interpreter agreed.

I gave Mr. Spalding what provisions I had left, and hastened to take leave of him, wishing him, with all my heart, a happy escape, and promising to pray for him. In quitting him I was so much terrified at the thought of the danger with which he was threatened, that I trembled in every limb, and could scarcely hold myself upon my horse. I left him with my interpreter, to whom he again put many questions, and who pointed out to him a by-road which he would be able to follow with most safety. I thought he advised him to go to The Dalles, but I am not certain. Mr. Spalding still continued to ask new questions; and hesitating to leave, the interpreter advised him to hasten his flight, and he left him a moment before he had decided to quit the road. The interpreter had not left Mr. Spalding more than twenty minutes when he saw three armed Cayuses, riding hastily towards him who were in pursuit of Mr. Spalding. Upon coming up to the interpreter, they seemed much displeased that I had warned Mr. Spalding of their intentions, and thereby furnished him with an opportunity to escape. 'The priest ought to have attended to his own business, and not to have interfered with ours,' they said, in an angry tone, and started immediately in pursuit of him. And they must inevitably have overtaken him, had not the approaching darkness of the night and a heavy fog that happened to fall down prevented them from discovering his trail, and forced them to return.[30]

Spalding reached his own mission at Lapwai after six days, more dead than alive.[31] Terrified by his experiences, as well as by the threat of a violent death at the hands of his Indians, he dispatched an obsequious letter to Bishop Blanchet on December 10, 1847. "My object in writing," he said to the bishop,

> is principally to give information, through you, to the Cayuses that it is our wish to have peace; that we do not wish the Americans to come from below to avenge the wrong; we hope the Cayuses and the Americans will be on friendly terms; that Americans will no more come in their country unless they wish it. As soon as these men return, I hope, if alive, to send them to the Governor to prevent Americans from coming up to molest the Cayuses for what is done.... [32]

At Waiilatpu the carnage continued. "You are acquainted, sir, with the event which followed," Brouillet wrote; "the murder of two sick men, who were brutally torn from their beds and had their throats cut, the murder of a young American when returning from the mill; the good fortune of the other Americans at the mill who owed their escape to a single Indian (Tintinmitsi) when the others wished to kill them; the violation of three young girls, the letter of Mr. Spalding which occasioned the assembling of the chiefs at the Catholic mission, and their asking for peace; the arrival of Mr. Ogden and the delivery of the captives."[33]

Peter Skene Ogden, also known as "Uncle Pete," was with James Douglas, who had succeeded Dr. McLoughlin, at Fort Vancouver. As soon as news of the massacre reached Vancouver, Ogden without delay, started upriver with a quantity of goods in a boat with sixteen paddlers. The journey took twelve days and Ogden arrived at Fort Walla Walla on December 19. The Cayuse chiefs, as Brouillet had noted, gathered at the Catholic mission at Umatilla and Bishop Blanchet prepared a petition to Governor Abernethy, which the five chiefs signed, asking for a peace conference and offering to give up their prisoners. The bishop included a letter of his own urging the same course. The conference at Umatilla had just adjourned when news reached the chiefs that Ogden had arrived at Walla Walla. Ogden requested Blanchet and the chiefs to attend a council at the fort.[34]

At the Council, the Indians consented to the surrender of all of the captives, including Spalding and others at Lapwai. The Hudson's Bay Company from its own resources paid the ransom, which consisted of sixty-two blankets, sixty-three cotton shirts, twelve company guns, six hundred rounds of ammunition, thirty-seven pounds of tobacco, and twelve flints.[35] Ogden could not get away until January 2, 1848, for it was necessary to wait for Spalding from Lapwai. This delay of ten days was a period of great tension because Ogden and the bishop expected at any moment news of an avenging army of American volunteers.[36] Fortunately, no serious complications arose.

In the midst of the crisis, Blanchet decided to ordain his two Oblate candidates for the priesthood. Summoned to Walla Walla, Chirouse and Pandosy were ordained to the sub-diaconate and diaconate in seven days, and Blanchet made plans for the final step, ordination to the priesthood, on January 2, the eighth day. Ogden was anxious to leave with his ransomed people as soon as Spalding came in, which was on January 1. He agreed, however, to wait until noon on the following day, allowing Blanchet time for ordination before departure.

Thus the first ordination to the priesthood in the present state of Washington, took place on the morning of January 2, 1848, in the bishop's one room frontier shack at Walla Walla. The place was so poorly equipped that it was necessary to borrow a white night shirt from McBean of the fort, to serve as an alb.[37] While the ceremony progressed, the boats were made ready for bringing the sixty-two captives to safety.[38]

At two in the afternoon, the boats shoved off with Spalding in the middle boat, surrounded by guards. They were scarcely gone when a band of fifty Cayuse warriors rode up to the fort in a cloud of dust and demanded that Spalding be released to them. They now realized they had let him get away too soon.[39] With Ogden was the bishop and Ricard. Another member of the party was John Mix Stanley, a noted artist who helped care for the children in the perilous six day flight downstream to Vancouver.

No sooner had Spalding reached a place of safety than he began to demand vengeance on the Indians. All buildings at Waiilatpu, except the grist mill, were burned by the Indians shortly after the rescue, and wolves dug up the bodies of the victims.[40] A volunteer army was equipped and dispatched under Colonel Gilliam before Ogden and Bishop Blanchet had time to present their letters to the governor, requesting peace. The so-called Cayuse Indian War, the first of its kind in the Northwest, had begun despite the offer of the five Cayuse chiefs to negotiate a just peace.

At this point, Spalding, possibly deranged by his harrowing experiences of the previous weeks, began a campaign of vilification of the Catholic priests that did not end until he himself died in 1874.[41]

Writing about himself in the third person Brouillet, very calmly in the circumstances, referred to Spalding's version of the massacre:

A certain gentleman, moved on by religious fanaticism, and ashamed of owing his life and that of his family and friends to some priests, began to insinuate false suspicious about the true causes of the disaster, proceeded, by degrees, to make more open accusations, and finally declared publicly that the Bishop of Walla Walla and his clergy were the first cause and the great movers of all the evil. That gentleman is the Rev. H.H. Spalding, whose life had been saved from the Indians by a priest, at the peril of his own.

His first insinuations were so malicious, and their meaning so well understood, that Colonel Gilliam and his troops, about starting for the purpose of chastising the murderers at Wailatpu, said publicly that the priests, missionaries of the Cayuses, were deserving death, and they would shoot or hang the first one of them they should meet.[42]

Fortunately for Brouillet, who certainly did not want to be hanged, Gilliam learned the truth "and from that moment to his death he did not cease to be one of [the priests'] best and most sincere friends."

Despite overwhelming evidence to the contrary, Spalding's slanderous accusations against the priests were generally accepted as true by certain uneducated groups of Protestants.[43] These accusations can be reduced to two: that the Catholic missionaries did consciously and deliberately cause the massacre of the thirteen Americans at Waiilatpu, by manipulating the Indians, and secondly, that Bishop Blanchet was grossly remiss in protecting the three white girls of the mission from sexual abuse by the Indians.

The first charge is so ridiculous that no scholar, Protestant or Catholic, takes it seriously.[44] The second is more difficult to defend, because the bishop, who was greatly outnumbered and threatened with death, actually was not harmed. The probabilities are, had he interfered with the Indians who took the girls by force, that he, too, would have been killed. Since there were thirteen corpses at the mission, his lordship had little reason to think otherwise. A dead bishop, Blanchet doubtlessly reasoned, would have been less useful for the protection of the girls than a live one, so he did what he could and left the rest to God. Some have since said that it was not enough.[45] In more recent years, however, when emotions have yielded to reason, there is a common consensus that Blanchet had done all that was possible.

THE CAYUSE WAR

In the Diocese of Walla Walla at the time of the massacre, there were three groups of Catholic missionaries at work, the bishop with his contingent of diocesan clerics, including Brouillet, in and around Fort

Walla Walla, the Oblates to the west in Yakima territory, and the Jesuits in the mountains some two hundred and fifty miles or more distant. There were three Presbyterian missions in the interior, those at Waiilatpu and Lapwai and a third at Tshimikain for the Spokanes. All three of these missions had to be abandoned at once because of hostile Indians seeking vengeance. The ministers in these missions, Archbishop Blanchet noted, "became jealous in seeing the Jesuit Fathers safe and quiet among the Indians of the Rocky Mountains."[46] The war against the Cayuse Indians did not directly affect them.

The Oblates, too, continued their work with the Yakimas, unmolested for a brief period. In late December, while they were still building their residence at St. Rose, a Yakima chief, called Aourrhai, who lived at a distance of several days travel, visited them to request a missionary for his people. Brother Blanchet accompanied him on his return to his home to survey the situation. Finding it favorable, he sent for Brother Verney, who arrived in a week to help him. The two brothers then began construction of the second Oblate mission chapel on the banks of Mnassatas Creek, dedicating it to the Immaculate Conception.[47]

The two new priests, Chirouse and Pandosy, returned to St. Rose after their ordination and resumed their labors for the Yakimas. Father Brouillet, also, after the departure of the captives, returned to St. Anne's on the Umatilla, but it soon became evident to him that mission work there was impossible as long as the Indians and whites were at war. The first so-called battle in this odd kind of war, in which scarcely anyone got scratched, took place on February 19, 1848. On the following day, Brouillet left for Fort Walla Walla. The Indians were so displeased with his departure that they plundered his house and set it on fire.[48]

The Bishop of Walla Walla, meanwhile, traveled by boat to St. Paul in the company of Father Ricard, who had been invited by the Jesuits to rest at their mission on the Willamette.[49] At St. Paul, Ricard met with both Francis N. Blanchet and Demers, who suggested that the Oblates establish missions in their dioceses. Ricard expressed the desire to do so, but he had certain reservations about the autonomy of the Oblates in matters concerning money. As a result of their conversations, he composed and dispatched a letter to all three bishops, containing seven propositions, one of which evoked certain objection. This involved support of the Oblate missions by the Propagation of the Faith.[50]

A week later Ricard could get no response from the bishops. He continued to press for some decision regarding the basic point of their differences: Who would support the Oblate missions, the Propagation of Faith or the bishops? If the former, how much autonomy would the Oblates enjoy?

At the Jesuit missions on the Willamette, Ricard pondered these questions and waited in vain for a response. Were the truth known, it was very difficult for the bishops to reply. Ricard doubtlessly regarded his query as a simple one, but the bishops, dependent upon the Propagation of the Faith, which allocated money either through them or higher superiors in Europe, were largely responsible for the use of those funds, and they could not provide a single answer to a complex question.

There were other problems for the archbishop. At Oregon City some of the American settlers, aroused by the wild charges of Spalding, were threatening to burn down the Catholic church, and the archbishop was informed that threats had been made for burning all the Catholic buildings in the valley. But wiser heads prevailed. No harm was done and Catholics were free to come and go as they pleased.[51]

Bishop Demers was still in St. Paul. With the help of his friends he was attempting to organize his own diocese, for which he had not a single priest. The archbishop had been counting his own priests and those of his lordship, the Bishop of Walla Walla, with something less than smug complacency. There is nothing to suggest that he offered Demers any of the priests he had, though he spoke of them frequently "as a large number of clergymen."

"By the arrivals from France and Canada," he wrote later, "the ecclesiastical Province of Oregon City possessed in the fall of 1847, 3 bishops, 14 Jesuit Fathers, 4 Oblate Fathers of M.I., 13 secular priests, including a deacon ordained in 1849, and a cleric, T. Mesplie, ordained in May, 1850; 13 Sisters and 2 houses of education."[52] One gathers from this that the archbishop was given to counting his chickens before they were hatched.

THE FIRST PROVINCIAL COUNCIL

It was not often that three bishops were found in the same parish in early Oregon. The archbishop regarded this as an unexpected opportunity for calling a formal meeting for discussing the needs of the various dioceses. This may have appeared rather ironic to Demers, whose needs required no discussion; he already knew them: priests and money. But the elder Blanchet wanted a council. "The three bishops availing themselves of the chance of their reunion at St. Paul," he wrote, "with a large number of clergymen, [held] the first provincial Council of Oregon City, in that church, on Feb. 28 and 29th, and March 1st. in which regulations for discipline, and 16 decrees were made which received later on the approbation of the Holy See."[53]

This was Leap Year, of course, so the bishops had an extra day to determine which should be Holy Days of Obligation and which days of fasting and abstinence. They got carried away, it appears, at least by contemporary standards. The fast days they decided, should be all the days of Lent, Sunday excepted, the three Ember days four times a year, all Fridays in Advent, and the vigils of the feasts of Pentecost, Saints Peter and Paul, the Assumption of the Blessed Virgin Mary, All Saints, and Christmas. The days "of obligation" were as follows: The Nativity of Our Lord, the Circumcision, the Epiphany, the Annunciation of the Blessed Virgin Mary, the Ascension of Our Lord, Corpus Christi, Saints Peter and Paul, All Saints, the Assumption of the Blessed Virgin Mary, and the Immaculate Conception.[54] No special talent is required to recognize in all of this the French Canadian influence. The American Catholics would have to be patient. American customs would be adopted eventually, no thanks to either of the Blanchets.

Worthy of note are decrees nine to eleven inclusive: these direct the fostering of devotion and liturgical functions to honor the Blessed Sacrament, the Sacred Heart of Jesus and "the Immaculate Virgin Mary."[55] All were, and still are, traditional Catholic practices that the church has encouraged for centuries.

In the Council, not all was sweetness and light. The three bishops shared a common anxiety about the recruitment of priests to carry on the work of their dioceses. They faced a cruel dilemma. While they depended upon the services of religious orders, they feared the orders' influence especially in attracting young men to their novitiates. Demers at the Council proposed the opening of as many novitiates as possible on the condition that the Orders "import their novices from Europe rather than accept secular priests which the Oregon bishops had procured at great expense."[56]

On March 1, the three bishops signed the decrees of the Council and Father Bolduc, secretary, sent them off to Rome in flawless Latin. Pope Pius IX "benignly" approved of them and they were printed in 1855 on the S.J. McCormick Press in Portland, with the Roman Calendar for the annual liturgy.[57] This was heady stuff for a little archdiocese in the wilderness. No doubt the archbishop of St. Louis, who was elevated to his position a year after Blanchet, took note of it, and for only a moment, perhaps, had some doubts about the primitive quality of the church in the Far West.

Blanchet himself had no time for vain glory, for his diocese was on the threshold of collapse. There was no evidence of this, of course, when the Council adjourned on the first of March. On March 12, Demers left Fort

Vancouver, with the spring fur express, for the east and north, on his way to Canada and Europe to raise funds and to find missionaries for his diocese.

In the midst of countless rumors about battles and burned villages, Brouillet and all of the Oblates on the Yakima mission left Fort Walla Walla on the following day, March 13, going down-river to Fort Vancouver and eventually to St. Paul. Since Ricard had come to St. Paul earlier, the Oblates were reunited, unharmed, and not the least intimidated by the hostiles. They wanted to return to their mission and soon did, despite the objections of the provisional army.

The archbishop wanted at least some of them to establish a new mission "in the district of Nesqually," which at that time was still under his jurisdiction. Ricard agreed and in May, 1848, he undertook an exploratory journey into the Puget Sound area, seeking a suitable site for that region for a kind of motherhouse, a center of operations for the Oblates. Having found what he wanted on Budd's Inlet, on a promontory henceforth known as Priest's Point, he paid sixty dollars for "a large section of land the possession of which was authorized by law, full and entire, on the condition that part of it be cleared and cultivated within six months time."[58] The Oblates took possession of the land on June 14, 1848, naming it at that time "St. Joseph of Newmarket."[59]

Ricard, now on the best of terms with the two Blanchets, was delighted with his choice, regarding it as the likely site of a vast city in the near future. He was only partly right and by the time his predictions were fulfilled, he was at odds again with the bishop.

This was Augustin Blanchet, still Bishop of Walla Walla, when Ricard established the mission on Priest's Point. Augustin was at St. Paul when Ricard left for Puget Sound. He had pontificated at St. Paul on Easter Sunday, April 23, that year, and in other ways assisted his brother the archbishop while he awaited favorable news from the war zone. Finally, on June 4, bored with inactivity, he departed for his mission on the Umatilla River. At the Dalles, however, a government agent, representing the Superintendent of Indian Affairs, denied him passage any further, so he settled down in that village, which had a prosperous Methodist mission. Blanchet established his own mission, called St. Peter's.[60] It is not unlikely that this choice of a patron was for the benefit of the Methodists, since both of the Blanchets were still living in their cozy little world of Catholicism, incapable really of broader vision.

The summer of 1848 passed slowly, almost ominously. The Cayuse War dragged on indecisively, with most of the Indians scattered in the mountains, and the soldiers unpaid or not paid at all. Word finally arrived at St. Paul that the vessel *Vancouver* bearing the annual provisions for the Catholic missions of Oregon, had gone down at the mouth of the Columbia and all was lost.[62] Father Auguste Veyret, who had worked among the Puget Sound Indians before the Oblates took over, wanted to become a Jesuit. And the Oblates in Yakima country got orders from the military to cease and desist in their mission activities while the war prevailed, but that they could "work in their gardens." In July, despite this, they started a third mission at a place called Aleshecas, in the valley of the Simcoe. They called this mission St. Joseph.[63] During the same month, Chirouse trotted his horse, not a very good one, up toward the headwaters of the Yakima River and at a place called Camp of the Lake, he baptized seventeen Yakimas, including the two sons of the wily Chief Kamiakin.[64]

The Jesuits, who regarded themselves exempt from military restrictions, because their missions were outside the war zone, soon found themselves unpleasantly involved. The Oregon Territorial Legislature had passed a law forbidding delivery of all firearms and ammunition to the Indians. Father Joset, DeSmet's successor as superior of the Jesuits, usually a mild tempered man with predispositions "of anything goes," came roaring out of his mountains like a she-bear defending her cubs. In one of his very rare sorties to a white man's town or settlement, he traveled all the way to Oregon City to demand a change in the law to permit his Indians to have firearms and ammunition. The Catholic Indians, he said, had been peaceably disposed and loyal to the provisional government. They needed firearms for their livelihood, and especially for protecting themselves against the Blackfeet.

One of the legislators was impressed by Joset's appeal and promised to have the law repealed. At this point, the annual shipment of arms for all of the Jesuit missions of the north arrived at Vancouver. This included one thousand and eighty pounds of powder, fifteen hundred pounds of balls, three hundred pounds of buckshot, and thirty-six guns.[65] Joset, expecting the law to be repealed, directed Accolti to send the shipment north. But at The Dalles, a certain Lieutenant Rodgers, influenced by Spalding's slander and no longer subject to Colonel Gilliam, who had been killed in a gun accident, intercepted the shipment.[66] He falsely accused the Jesuits of intending the use of this ammunition for the extermination of Protestants, and his calumnies were given wide credibility by the gullible people who formed a majority in Oregon.

What disposition was made of the munitions is not known, but because of Rodgers' preposterous allegations and anti-Catholic feeling in general, a petition for the expulsion of all of the Catholic clergy in Oregon was introduced into the territorial legislature in December, 1848.[67] This was finally rejected by a two thirds vote, meaning that one out of three, presumably educated men, had voted in favor of it.

Meanwhile, there were other diversions. On August 14, 1848, Congress passed an act to establish the territorial government of Oregon, which contained a proviso that title to land not exceeding 640 acres then occupied as a mission station for the Indians, was to be confirmed and established in the name of the respective religious group occupying it. According to this, title to certain mission properties, for example St. Francis Xavier on the Cowlitz, St. Paul on the Willamette and St. James at Vancouver, were confirmed and established in the name of the Catholic bishop.[68] All this appeared to be so obvious that no one suspected what and how many dragon teeth had been sown. Time would reveal them, too late to save St. James Mission, which became a most celebrated case in law. Needless to say, the Methodists enjoyed a more favorable status, because they were of American origin and their relationship with England's Honorable Hudson's Bay Company was, if anything, not cordial. There will be more about this later, much more, but the implications were always the same: the Catholics, somehow, were like gypsies or Jews, not quite American. For all of that, the Indians were not regarded as Americans either, so one can discern the lack of objectivity in the judgments about all of them, the Indians, the Jews, the gypsies, and the Catholics.

As noted above, it had been a depressing summer. There were flashes of hope in the progress of autumn, when the farmers of the Willamette were gathering their crops. In September, the Sisters of Notre Dame de Namur opened their second school in Oregon City, and in October two new priests arrived via the Oregon Trail. The latter were Honore Lempfrit, an Oblate, who was sent during the following year to Victoria in Bishop Demers diocese, and Louis Joseph Lionet, a diocesan priests from France.[69]

The archbishop sent Lionet to establish a mission at Astoria. Lionet, however, having a mind of his own, chose instead a site on the north side of the Columbia and built a mission that he called Stella Maris, Star of the Sea. Although he labored diligently, he enjoyed only indifferent success. He soon returned to France, leaving behind as the most tangible trace of his presence here, a well-worn pocket note book of twenty-eight pages, in which he had written from time to time, a dictionary of the Chinook jargon.[70]

As the final event in the dismal year, the archbishop, on December 21, 1848, moved his residence from St. Paul, to which he had become greatly attached, to Oregon City, where he lacked even a house. The rectory had been turned over to the Sisters, so he lived for a month "at Mr. McKinley's" then rented a house "from Mr. Pomeroy for the rest of the winter."[71] When the end of the year arrived, he was relieved to see it, but the new year would be as bad, perhaps worse.

THE CALIFORNIA GOLD RUSH

Meanwhile, in the autumn of 1848, Father Brouillet landed in San Francisco.[72] The fame of the gold fields had spread far and wide and the thought naturally suggested itself to him that there would be many Catholics among the miners, to whose generosity he might appeal for help to relieve the heavily debt-burdened diocese. Brouillet landed on schedule, but did not proceed to the diggings because of the spiritual destitution of the inhabitants of the town. On all sides was the greedy crowd, pouring in from every clime, mostly Catholic in background at least, and in dire need of spiritual sustenance. Murders occurred almost twice daily. The victims required burial and the perpetrators, if apprehended, counseling and the last rites on the gallows.

Brouillet was overwhelmed. A few months later, Father Langlois joined him, Langlois a Canadian priest, was on his way to Canada to enter the Society of Jesus, a pleasant prospect to him but disloyalty, perhaps even betrayal in the eyes of the two Blanchets. Although DeSmet had established a Jesuit novitiate on the Willamette it had never served as one, so Langlois was advised to go to Canada to undergo the usual probation for Jesuit membership. In San Francisco, however, Brouillet appealed to him for assistance. The field was vast and the cause urgent. The would-be novice did not consider himself free to interrupt his journey without the approval of those whom he regarded as his Jesuit superiors. He submitted his case, therefore, to Father Michael Accolti, the superior of the Jesuit residence on the Willamette. Accolti directed him to assist Brouillet in San Francisco and leave the future in God's hands.

With this, Langlois was content. With the vicar general of the Walla Walla diocese he founded the first church for English speaking Catholics in San Francisco. Brouillet offered the first Mass in this church on June 17, 1849, "the third Sunday after Pentacost [sic]." They named the church St. Francis Xavier.[73]

In Oregon, the news of the gold rush, at least, got the archbishop's critics off his back. People in St. Paul and Oregon City talked of little else, and the disputes between Catholics and Protestants were soon forgotten. At St. Paul, French Prairie, and Vancouver, especially, many plans were being hatched for a mass exodus to the gold fields. On March 19, 1849, a large "brigade," as the archbishop called them, with Father Delorme as their chaplain, left Oregon for California, with much shouting and boasting about fortunes they would find. Many of them found death instead, for shortly after their arrival in California, "a burning fever decimated them." Forty persons died during the epidemic, including "twenty heads of families, thirteen single men and boys, four women and some children." Father Delorme, exhausted with fatigue in caring for the sick, also came down with the fever, but survived.[74]

By June, St. Paul was almost deserted and St. Joseph's College, the apple of the archbishop's eye, had to be closed for lack of students. The Jesuits, too, wanted to leave Oregon, and their mission system in the north was almost a shambles. The Jesuit general, Father Roothaan, attributed many of the problems to poor Joset, but the causes of the general malaise were deeper than that, and Joset was just the scapegoat.

MORE JESUIT TROUBLES

First, there was Father Nobili. He had gone into New Caledonia [British Columbia] two years earlier and established St. Joseph's mission on Lake Okanogan, where Father Anthony Goetz joined him. Goetz, a difficult kind of person with whom Nobili was incompatible, remained for about one year, during which Nobili penetrated the far reaches of the continent, baptizing Indians almost as far north as the Alaskan border. "I instructed, baptized and gave other sacraments to thirteen or fourteen hundred Indians, including about five hundred children carried off by the measles," Nobili wrote later.[75] He endured incredible hardships. Both Jesuits, in broken health, returned to the Rocky Mountain Mission in 1849. Nobili was sent to St. Francis Xavier's on the Willamette to recuperate. There was no one to replace him or Goetz in New Caledonia and St. Joseph's Mission disappeared from the earth.

At St. Francis Xavier's was Father Michael Accolti, the Jesuit with the inventive mind, a genial churchman who liked to hear himself sing. In February of 1848, Accolti, no longer needed at Oregon City, was appointed by the archbishop to develop St. Patrick's mission, a vast churchless area west of the Willamette and south of Oregon City. This was the Mission of the Yamhill, settled mostly by Irish emigrants. There is nothing to indicate that Accolti disappointed his Irish parishioners, but he had larger prospects on his mind. He was like a dog with a bone. California, he was convinced, was the larger scene for his labors, thousands of Catholics without priests, who could appreciate his talents, as sunny as their climate. Determined to go there, he first appealed to Father General who said "No," then he nagged poor Joset, the general mission superior.

Joset, two years earlier, had built a log mission called St. Paul's near Kettle Falls on the Columbia, where Ravalli had started a mission before he was recalled.[76] He finally sent Father Peter DeVos to live there, as its first resident priest. DeVos was practically killing himself, trying to cover an area as large as Ireland.[77] It seemed to be such a waste of a man who had converted many prominent white people in the lower Columbia.

Forty miles to the south of DeVos, was St. Francis Regis, the mission DeSmet had founded for the Cree Indians. When news of gold in California reached this settlement, the Crees went south, like the birds, leaving Father Vercruysse without a flock. He packed his belongings on a horse and rode over the Flowery Trail to St. Ignatius on the Pend Oreille, while those unfavorably disposed to Catholics, burned down the whole settlement.

At St. Ignatius, it was feast or famine. In most years the mission's crops were flooded out by the late spring rampage of the river that, ironically, flowed out of Lake Roothaan, the beautiful Alpine-like body of ice cold water, discovered and named by DeSmet for the Jesuit general.[78] The superior at St. Ignatius was still Father Adrian Hoecken, who had no response for the Indians' totally relevant question: Do you want us to stay here and die?

The most highly publicized of all the missions was St. Mary's among the Flatheads. This was in the deepest trouble of all. Under almost constant siege by the Blackfeet, deserted by the young braves who had lost faith in its "medicine," and left helpless by the grand old chiefs and elders who had all died, the mission had become a fragile shelter for the Jesuits. Mengarini was still there, with Ravalli and the brothers. Their gardens were mischievously trampled, their nights disturbed by shooting and war whoops, even their religious services were interrupted by militants in the church. who shouted at them in defiance.[79]

Only the Coeur d'Alene mission on its new site was prospering, a lonely beacon in a dark, threatening sky. Joset, who directed it, as well as the Rocky Mountain Mission bore the weaknesses of his virtues: he was so agreeable that stronger men like Accolti manipulated him, even against his better judgement.

THE JESUITS' MISSION IN CALIFORNIA

With the Jesuits there was a question of priorities. They had come to the Northwest to serve the Indians, and men like Joset insisted that they should remain with the Indians. Problems such as the lack of priests in California belonged to the bishops, not to Jesuits. Accolti held other views. He had never worked among the Indians. He had urged Jesuit concentration on the lower Columbia where he envisioned a vast population. When, on the contrary, Oregon's population vanished during the gold rush, Accolti's faith in Oregon vanished with them.

The Jesuit Willamette farm on which Accolti depended to pay off Jesuit debts, was now practically worthless.[80] Like the archbishop, he looked to the gold mines for the money he needed. Francis Blanchet owed a fortune, something like fiftythousand pre-Civil War dollars, and his support had melted away. He had welcomed Brouillet's proposal to seek funds in the gold fields though he tended to regard Langlois' departure as a personal rejection.

Accolti now proposed the bizarre scheme of going to California with two brothers who would dig enough gold to pay off the Jesuits' debts while he preached and administered the sacraments. The idea appealed to Joset, who doubtlessly saw in it some benefit for the Indians. However, he continued to stall until Accolti came up with another plan.

When Nobili arrived at the Willamette, almost dead, Accolti had the cause for which he had been searching. He would take the dying Nobili to California to recover from his illness, a journey of mercy, and who could improve on that?

There is an almost humorous element in all this: Joset had been replaced as superior of the missions by Accolti, but the general's letter of appointment did not arrive for over one year. Thus, when Accolti and Nobili boarded a ship for San Francisco on October 30, 1849, Accolti was actually superior of the missions, a great misfortune in his eyes when he learned of it, because he had to return to Oregon.[81]

Nobili had a scruple, which only the general could, and eventually did dispel, but Accolti felt no such qualms when the two landed in San Francisco on December 9, 1849. Langlois welcomed them warmly and recommended that Nobili be assigned to Mission Santa Clara, a neglected and run-down church in the valley, sixty miles to the south. Docile like most sick people, Nobili agreed to take the task of restoring the mission, and there he labored until his premature death in 1856, establishing in 1851 the college which became Santa Clara University in 1912.[82]

The archbishop had not entirely approved of Accolti's southern safari. Perhaps he distrusted Accolti as Bishop Demers did.[83] He wanted more Jesuits and he kept writing a stream of correspondence to Roothaan, urging him to send enough of them to establish a new college. One infers from this that his Grace had either not yet comprehended the extent of the disaster taking place in his diocese, or that he expected his wayfaring gold diggers to return to Oregon when they finally became rich.

THE ARCHBISHOP'S DISPUTE WITH THE OBLATES

At this particular time he was more concerned about the Oblates. It will be recalled that during the early months following his triumphant return to Oregon, that he ordained his first priest, John F. Jayol. This created a special bond between the two, so one can understand the archbishop's anguish when Jayol in 1849, requested His Grace's permission to join the Oblates. Blanchet did not respond directly to the request, but ordered Jayol to make a retreat to examine his vocation. After his retreat, Jayol repeated his request, then the archbishop informed him that this was denied and he was to return to Oregon City immediately.[85] Jayol refused. He entered the Novitiate of the Oblates and later pronounced his vows.

The sequence is rather sordid, but one can understand the frustration and disappointment of the archbishop, who had lost, in a sense, his first son. In a fit of anger he ordered Jayol to return under penalty of interdict and "absolute and total suspension *ipso facto* reserved to the archbishop himself."[86] When at last the dispute was referred to Rome, the Holy See supported Jayol and the Oblates and demanded an explanation from Blanchet for his arbitrary conduct toward his priests. This was not, alas, the end of Blanchet's quarrels with his priests and his scoldings from Rome. Strong willed and dictatorial to the end, he never accepted correction gracefully. He had long since forgotten what it was like to be the underdog.

THE EXECUTION OF THE CAYUSE INDIANS

With another new year, the mid-century mark, conditions in Oregon did not improve. The archbishop, seemingly no wiser for all the controversies he experienced, soon found himself involved in another sad enough to make even angels weep.

The government had finally suppressed the rebellion of the Cayuse Indians, despite numerous desertions of soldiers who disappeared in the California gold fields. Proper authorities demanded the extradition of the murderers of the Whitmans and others. The Cayuse chiefs responded, not once, but many times, that the ten Indians involved in these murders were dead, but this satisfied no one and the American government continued to harass the chiefs. The chiefs at last found five men who consented to go down to Oregon City, not as guilty men, but to meet with the whites and to convince them that the murderers were all dead. Sent by their chiefs to convey this message, they all expected to return home.

They arrived in the early spring. They were instantly clapped into jail, charged with murder, and kept as prisoners. A sham trial, which deceived no one, was conducted in Oregon City, and on May 27, 1850, all having been declared guilty, were sentenced to be hanged. On hearing their sentence, they asked to see priests and for baptism in the Catholic Church. The archbishop himself went to see them without delay and continued to go twice a day to teach them in preparation for baptism.[87]

On the eve of their execution, June 2, the old chief Kilo Kite and his four companions made a solemn statement before witnesses. The first Indian declared that he had been opposed to the massacre, but his two sons had taken part and both were dead. The second Indian stated that he had been absent during the massacre. The third said he saw the dead, but did not participate, and he was sorry. The fourth and fifth Indians stated that they were innocent and were dying for nothing. All testified that the priests had not counseled the Indians to commit the crime. The priests, too, were innocent.

On the following day, the prisoners attended Mass, after which they were baptized and confirmed. The execution, the archbishop wrote, took place at two in the afternoon "before an immense crowd." Then he added, "The archbishop, assisted by Rev. F. Veyret, now a Jesuit, accompanied them to the scaffold, where the prayers for the dying were recited. Touching words of encouragement were addressed to them on the moment of being swung into the air: 'Onward, onward to heaven children; into Thy hands, O Lord Jesus! I commend my spirit.' They were then swung into eternity."[88]

THE DIOCESE OF NESQUALLY

After the execution of these innocent Indians, a ray of sunshine appeared. A brief of Pope Pius IX, bearing the date of May 31, 1850, created the district of Nesqually into a diocese, and transferred Bishop A.M.A. Blanchet of Walla Walla to this new see. The diocese of Walla Walla, contrary to statements often made, was not suppressed by this brief.[89] The administration of Walla Walla, as well as the districts of Colville and Fort Hall, was placed under the care of the archbishop of Oregon City.[90]

Montana, east of the Rockies, was not included in this new ecclesiastical structure. On July 19, 1850, Pius IX erected the Vicariate Apostolic of Kansas and the Rocky Mountains, which included eastern Montana. At the same time, Father John Baptist Miege, a Jesuit, was appointed its first vicar apostolic as titular bishop of Messemia.[91] There were no missions in eastern Montana, then, and it would be almost a decade, DeSmet's heroic efforts to the contrary, before resident priests would be found there. These intervening years would be sad ones, not only for the Jesuits but also for the archbishop, whose jurisdiction bordered on that of Bishop Miege.

ST. MARY'S MISSION CLOSED

Another catastrophe was the closing of St. Mary's among the Flatheads. As a mission, only St. Paul in Oregon was comparable to it. Lauded by DeSmet in his writings and supported by people all over Europe, it had become symbolic of the Indians' conversion to Christianity. On November 9, 1850, the deed was done: The Jesuits moved out, having sold the improvements on the land to an entrepreneur, a certain Major John Owens, who used them for the mercenary business of fur trading. Ravalli took refuge among the Coeur d'Alenes. Mengarini, his health shattered, soon arrived at Santa Clara, where he joined Nobili and exclaimed in the depths of his anguish that never again did he want to see an Indian.

The closing of St. Mary's left many doubts in the minds of those who had made the decision. Had Jesuits run from danger? Vercruysse, who had been forced to abandon his own post, was especially critical. "Our Fathers in China have more to fear from the sword of the Mandarin," he cried, "still they stand firm."[92]

In Rome there was the devil to pay. Father Roothaan, especially, was bewildered, for he had just received a letter from Joset informing him that the Flatheads were "never better." To another Jesuit, Joset had written, "Father Nobili eulogizes St. Mary's in the highest terms. He puts it above every other mission and in all respects."[92] Perhaps it was Joset who had misled the general on the true state of affairs.[94] As usual, he got most of the blame. Nonetheless he had cause to rejoice: his Coeur d'Alene Mission had acquired the genius of Ravalli, just when they needed it. Ravalli could now design and supervise construction of the new church— his great masterpiece.

THE OREGON LAND CASE

While the Jesuits were trying to cope with these painful eventualities, the church's most notable convert was faring even worse. Dr. John McLoughlin, with his back against the wall, was being subjected to systematic robbery of all of his cherished property by the very ones he had befriended.

"The conspiracy against McLoughlin assumed definite form in 1849, when Samuel Thurston was elected Territorial Delegate to Congress from Oregon through the efforts of the Mission Party."[95] At that time, settlers in Oregon were most interested in congressional legislation that would confirm title to their lands. Thurston, in the interests of those who elected him, manipulated this legislation to strip McLoughlin of the ownership of his section of land at Oregon City. In other words, the Oregon Donation Land Bill was framed in such a way as to secure title to the settlers' land, with one explicit exception, McLoughlin's Oregon City Claim, which was put at the disposal of the Territorial Legislature for the establishment of a university. In effect, the bill, by an act of Congress, confiscated all of McLoughlin's land.[96]

As soon as it was generally known that Thurston was resorting to lies, calumnies and distortions of history to deprive McLoughlin of his claim, a public meeting of protest was held in Oregon City and a resolution was drafted and passed, requesting Congress to exclude Section II of the bill, that part which denied McLoughlin's title. In recognition of McLoughlin's services, the resolution declared that he "merits the gratitude of the multitudes of persons in Oregon for the timely and long continued assistance rendered by him in the settlement of the territory."[97]

Thurston's bill became law before this resolution reached Washington, and further efforts of those who favored the venerable doctor were useless. The Mission Party, meanwhile, held a meeting in Salem, their peculiar stronghold, and passed resolutions upholding the action of Thurston and confirming the calumnies against McLoughlin and the Hudson's Bay Company. These people in Salem were the men whom McLoughlin had fed, clothed and housed, when they arrived penniless at the end of the Oregon Trail. "He had cared for their families and nursed their sick. He had loaned them thousands of dollars which they never returned. He had saved them from the cruelty of the Indians."[98]

Thus it happened, that the Father of Oregon, the Great White Headed Eagle, became impoverished in his old age. His lands were confiscated. His life savings, expended on improvements, vanished like his land claim. His own home was taken from him though "he was indeed suffered to occupy the house simply because no one had any interest in evicting him. It was no longer his."[99]

At this time, he was persuaded to sit for a photographer who made of his features a daguerreotype, which is still extant.[100] This presents him as a sad, old man, whose spirit of self-confidence has turned to bitterness. His flowing white hair, parted in the middle, frames his face, which is hard and cold. His deep, almost fierce eyes, like an eagle's widely spread under bushy eyebrows, stare off in the distance, seeing only phantoms, perhaps, and beneath his prominent, wellformed nose, his lips turned down, adding to his melancholy appearance. He wears a high collar and black coat, which contrast sharply with his hair and pallid skin. Despite these many marks of gloom and depression, his strong, dominating character still emerges, as defiant in these years of slow dying as in his youth when he left home to become a doctor.

Like his appearance, his somber words reflect the wintry blight on his declining years. "I founded this settlement," he said, speaking of Oregon City, "and prevented a war between the United States and Great Britain, and for doing this peaceably and quietly, I was treated by the British in such a manner that from selfrespect I resigned my situation in the Hudson's Bay Company's service, by which I sacrificed $12,000 per annum, and the 'Oregon Land Bill' shows the treatment I received from the Americans."[101]

In this manner the prophets were oppressed. The church in the Northwest was not being denied the same fate.

6

THE SISTERS COME TO STAY
1850–1859

When the bishop of the newly established diocese of Nesqually occupied his residence in Vancouver on October 27, 1850, the fur trading fort was still there. This was not, however, its finest hour. No longer the seat of government for the Northwest, the old fort had become a motley collection of weathered log and frame buildings selectively scattered up the slope of the mud-covered hill. It was surrounded by pickets, which formed a quadrangle approximately one mile long.[1]

Below this bastion of frontier commerce, the broad sweep of the Columbia's gray waters, placid on a windless day, stretched like a long inlet protected from the sea. Along its shore, wild blackberry vines tumbled in profusion, and east of the pickets, within a rail fence, fat cattle grazed in grass up to their bellies. North and west of the pickets was the sprawling village of Vancouver, consisting of St. James Church, a few log houses and shacks, seemingly thrown like dice in a heedless pattern. Beyond them were the rolling hills, heavily forested with douglas fir trees, presenting to the sight a natural barrier for the settlement, but hiding from view the mountains to the north. From vantage points upriver, on a clear day, one could see the mantle of snow covering Mount St. Helen's, which peaked conspicuously along the Cascades some fifty miles beyond the fort. Across the river, to the south, was another majestic peak of the Cascades, Mount Hood. One could see this, too, on clear days from any one of the "plains" of Vancouver, even the upper levels still buried in trees.

The river in its course was fickle. It turned sharply north some few miles west of Vancouver and beyond its bend, the Willamette, flowing in the same direction, glided silently into the mainstream with so little commotion that one could scarcely notice it. The banks of the Willamette were heavily wooded also, and hills rose above the trees, especially in the western sky, like an unyielding barricade to the winds from the ocean. The fir trees in crowded array along the river and up the lofty heights were very dark, and in these coastal regions where skies were often the color of slate, they appeared to be darker still, almost like the Black Forest.

A village had begun to develop along the Willamette. First called 'Stump Town" because its early settlers had left so many stumps, painting them white to be more easily avoided, this village acquired the name "Portland" at the flip of a coin.[2] Most of these first residents abandoned it for the gold fields of California, but others came eventually to take their places, and Portland survived.

The population of Vancouver, as well as the fort's, had also been decimated by the gold rush.[3] When Augustin Blanchet arrived there was an unexpressed spirit of gloom over the place, which gave him little comfort for the series of misadventures that had befallen him. First there had been the shock of finding his "episcopal city" but a rude wilderness, a trading post without even the suggestion of a cross or church. Then there was the bloody Whitman massacre, for which he had been blamed. This was followed by the war that had exiled him from his diocese, and now it was a new diocese consisting of ghost towns.

His Lordship had another cross to bear—malaria, to which he had succumbed somehow, verily a great nuisance when it flared up, as it had during the summer.[4] Its fevers had delayed his arrival in Vancouver.

Unlike the fort's, this was Blanchet's finest hour. For despite the grim realities surrounding him, he moved into the frame house near his pro-Cathedral of St. James and earnestly took up the task of organizing a diocese.

ST. JAMES PRO-CATHEDRAL

The pro-cathedral, at this time, was scarcely four years old. It had replaced a "chapel" or old store within the pickets, a structure that had served for divine worship for both Catholics and Protestants from the time of the arrival of the priests.[5] It had been called the "Old Roman Catholic Church" on early maps, a significant clue regarding the common judgment concerning it, but the Honorable Hudson's Bay Company considered it a loan and reserved the right to use it for Episcopal services, though Governor Simpson complained that it was "unworthy of the establishment."[6]

Understandably, the priests insisted on acquiring another church that would be located outside the stockade. The Company offered them the use of a tract of land north and east of the fort for this purpose. The site, it was reported, was selected by Dr. McLoughlin and James Douglas.[7] The priests desired to purchase the land but the Company's officers refused to sell it. It was agreed, however, that the missionaries could fence it off, a compromise that carried with it little more than appearances.[8]

Construction on the church was probably begun in the autumn of 1845. The large timbers were cut within a quarter of a mile of the building site and the lumber came from the Company mills. The furnishings, no doubt, were provided by the Catholics.

Dr. John Hussey describes what followed:

> The church was opened and blessed by Father DeVos, S.J., on May 31, 1846. After delivering a 'most impressive and solemn discourse' to a congregation of about 150 persons, Father DeVos dedicated the structure 'under the auspices of the Holy name of Mary and the patronage of the Apostle, St. James the Greater.' In making the dedication, the priest specifically stated that the church had been 'founded and built by Mister James Douglas.'
>
> The non-Catholic officers of the Company, most of whom attended the dedication ceremonies, treated the naming of the church somewhat as a joke. When one of them was asked, some years later, why the chapel was called 'St. James the Greater,' he replied, 'pshaw don't you know, why after James Douglas of course who built it.'
>
> The new church was 81 or 83 feet long, 36 feet wide, and 20 feet high. Inside, a gallery, 12 feet wide, extended across the width of the building. According to a newspaper account of the time, accommodations were provided for about 500 persons. The roof was shingled.
>
> Although the priests were permitted to use the structure without charge, the Hudson's Bay Company considered that it owned both the church building and the adjoining dwelling intended as a residence for the missionary fathers.[9] The two structures were listed in the inventory of Company property made in 1846-1847. And, for a time during 1850, when the priests seem to have been on one of their periodic absences from Vancouver, the firm's officers appear to have rented a part of the church to the Quartermaster's Department of the United States Army. Certain witnesses later testified, on the contrary, that the church was never used for anything but religious services."[10]

Unlike the church, the bishop's house was within the stockade. It, too, had been built by the Company for the use of the priests, about the same time as the church. This was a dwelling that measured 50 x 30 feet and was lined and ceiled. "[It] had two exterior doors, one in the center of the south wall and the other in the middle of the north wall. It was weather-boarded and covered with a shingled, hip roof. There was a chimney, seemingly of stone, on the west wall of the structure. The windows were of the casement or 'French' type."[11]

This, then, was the Bishop's House that Blanchet occupied on that singular autumn day in 1850. For the Nesqually diocese, it was the first chancery, if so elegant a word can be applied to an unpainted frontier structure. But it represented a beginning, which always has to come before the middle and the end.

Progress, apparently, was slow for it was several months before Blanchet could reserve the Blessed Sacrament in the church. On January 23, 1851, he wrote, "The Blessed Sacrament is placed in the tabernacle for the first time since the foundation of the mission at Vancouver. The Tabernacle is lined only with white cotton, while we wait to get some silk."[12]

This entry in the bishop's diary had deeper implications than its brevity indicates. The reservation of the Sacrament required the presence of a priest, or the bishop, so one can assume, given the fewness of his priests, that the bishop himself had determined to spend most of his time in Vancouver. This had a stabilizing effect on his diocese, which had nowhere to go but up. In other words, Augustin Blanchet, former Canon of the Cathedral, was starting again from scratch, and his diocese, overrun by missionaries for twelve years, needed a specific office where business was usual.

THE ARCHBISHOP GOES TO MEXICO

The Archbishop of Oregon City, meanwhile, found himself and his archdiocese in worse condition than this. Indeed, were the truth known, the archdiocese was at the bottom of a pit, in debt up to the archbishop's ears, and every effort he made to get out of debt proved to be useless. He decided, finally, after much vacillation, to go to Mexico to seek help. Having summoned Father Brouillet from San Francisco, where, it was reported, he had raised twenty-five thousand dollars for building a church there, the archbishop appointed him his vicar general in his absence and then sailed south hopefully, into the warm spring breezes.[13]

This was during March 1851. He returned on August 16 "with a successful collection of money, sacred vessels, pictures and sacerdotal vestments."[14] There was some pious deception about the "success" of this expedition, for there is evidence to believe that the archdiocese still owed as much money as before.

Both Blanchets had appealed to the Bishop of Quebec for his help, and a general collection had been taken to bail out the two missionaries, but these aids to solvency were too little and too late, like taking aspirin for a brain tumor.

Most mysterious about all this was the failure of the two bishops to appeal to their colleagues in the United States. DeSmet had always found them generous. There appears to be no doubt whatever that had the archbishop gone to the Catholics of Philadelphia, Baltimore, and New Orleans, to take but several examples, he would have collected all of the money he needed to pay his debts.

One suspects that both Blanchets suffered from a kind of inferiority complex about Americans, the bishops in particular. Since most of the latter were from Ireland, vocal, independent men with social graces that enabled them to feel comfortable in any company, they appeared to have, as prelates, characteristics lacking in the Blanchets. There was an old expression in eastern America: "Nothing counts west of Chicago" (NCWC), an opinion of long standing with some of the bishops of America. Perhaps it was easier for a priest like DeSmet to appeal for help in eastern America than for the bishops of the West.[15]

Whatever the case, the church in the Northwest languished for six miserable years, from 1850 to 1856. After St. Joseph's College was terminated, the Jesuits closed their mission of St. Francis Xavier on the Willamette.[16] The sisters of Notre Dame de Namur, forced by the same circumstances, abandoned their school in St. Paul in March 1852.[17] Because of the infamous Oregon Donation Land Act of 1849, which deprived McLoughlin of his claim, no land could be sold in Oregon City and this town rapidly declined. Thus by 1853, the Sisters were forced to close their one remaining school in the Northwest. They packed their belongings and sailed off to California where the people had gone. Their departure was a terrible blow, because the archdiocese was bereft at once of all of its sisters and all of its educational institutions.[18]

THE FIRST SISTERS OF PROVIDENCE

An encouraging development now occurred. Bishop Augustin Blanchet, lacking nearly everything a diocese required, had returned to Canada to appeal for help. On April 2, 1852, at the request of Bishop Bourget of Montreal, he presided over the profession of vows of two Sisters of Providence,[19] and taking this opportunity to expose the poverty of his diocese, he requested the assembled sisters to share the work of the Northwest church. Five sisters of the many who volunteered, were assigned to the new mission. Their superior was Sister M. Laroque. They left Montreal on October 18, traveling via New York by boat to the Isthmus of Panama, thence to San Francisco, which they reached on November 17, 1852.[20] When they finally arrived at Oregon City on December 1, they found a ghost town. Only a few diehards had remained when the populace vanished.

The sisters panicked. They decided to return to California to await orders. Departing in lamentable haste on February 1, 1853, they arrived in San Francisco, paused there only a brief time, then departed again for Chile, where they founded a House of Providence and remained.[21]

Their presence in Oregon had been like two month's of summer sunshine, their departure like the emptiness of the lonely gray skies of winter. One cannot blame the sisters for their decision, the demands were great elsewhere. But the bishops were profoundly disappointed. One can appreciate their reasons for harboring distrust for religious orders. Abandoned by all but a few, including a handful of Oblates and Jesuits who were faithful to the Indians, they were tormented with honest doubts regarding their continued relationship with the orders on the same terms as the past.

It was now clear to them that the financial difficulties of the archdiocese were the least of all. O'Hara summed it up, "The schools had all been closed; all the religious, both men and women, had left the diocese; the clergy diminished from 19 to 7; the missions that were once flourishing were now unattended; work among the Indians was paralyzed; bigotry and prejudice were spreading apace, and the seat of the diocese, Oregon City, declining from day to day."[22]

THE OBLATES

One point should be noted, however. At this time, the archbishop was the administrator of the diocese of Walla Walla and the districts of Colville and Fort Hall, where the Oblates and the Jesuits were still engaged in mission work.

The Jesuits had but three missions left, none of them destined to survive where they were: St. Paul on the Columbia, St. Ignatius on the Pend Oreille, and Sacred Heart among the Coeur d'Alenes. The latter, despite its isolation, was the focal point of Jesuit activity in the interior.[23]

The Oblates covered less territory but they occupied more missions, six in number: St. Rose, the first one in terms of chronology; Immaculate Conception Mission on Mnassatas Creek, near present Ellensburg;[24] St.

Joseph's of Newmarket, where the superior lived; and St. Joseph's on the Simcoe, at Aleshecas. In addition to these there were temporary missions at "Moksee," Holy Cross Mission in the lower Attanum Valley and most important of all, St. Joseph's on Attanum Creek near present Yakima.[25]

The Attanum Creek Mission, at first occupied during the summer months only, was founded by Pandosy and a new Oblate recruit, Father Louis D'Herbomez, who later became the first bishop in the interior of British Columbia. On April 3, 1852, these two Oblates established themselves in a crude hut, which was more immediate to the Cascades and more accessible to the Yakimas in their summer activities. "Little by little," the Oblate historian reports, "the mission progressed in a material way. In order to win over the natives from their nomadic life and make them a settled community, the fathers taught them the cultivation of the soil. Soon beautiful fields of wheat, corn, and apple orchards made their appearance."[26]

About this time, there was a renowned visitor who subsequently published an American classic called *Canoe and Saddle*. Theodore Winther was a New Englander who, like Francis Parkman, enjoyed visiting remote and exotic places and describing these for America's more sophisticated readers. "A strange and unlovely spot for religion to have chosen for its home and influence," Winther wrote about St. Joseph's. "It needed all the transfiguring power of sunset to make the desolate scene endurable; only ardent hermits would banish themselves to such a hermitage. The missionary spirit of the military religious discipline must be very positive which sends men to such unattractive heathen as these, to a field of labor far away from any contact with civilization where no exalting result of converted multitudes can be hoped for.... The mission was a hut-like structure of adobe clay plastered upon a frame of sticks. It stood near the stony bed of the Atinam [sic]. The sun was setting as we came down into the valley, that moment abandoned by the sunlight. My Indians launched forward to pay their friendly greetings to the priests. But I observed them quickly pause, walk their horses, and noiselessly dismount. As I drew near a sound of reverend voices met me—vespers at this station of the wilderness. Three souls worshipping in the rude chapel attached to the house. It was rude indeed—a cell of clay—but the sense of the Divine Presence was there, not less than in many a dim old cathedral far away.... Vespers ended, the missionaries coming forth from their services, welcomed me with quiet cordiality. Visits from men not savages were rare to them as are angels' visits to worldings. In winter they resided at a station on the Yakima [St. Rose] in the plains eastward.

Atinam was their summer abode when copper colored lambs of their flock were in the woods, plucking berries in the dells, catching crickets on the slopes."[27]

In 1852, Archbishop Blanchet requested the Oblates to reestablish St. Anne's on the Umatilla, which had been closed and burned during the Cayuse War. Chirouse was sent to take charge. The fickleness of the Indians in this area and their deep attachment to ancient superstitions were great obstacles for Chirouse. But his greatest problem was the fallout of the Whitman Massacre, which had left deep scars and two opposing factions, one Catholic and the other Presbyterian. Chirouse, a holy priest, who resembled the Cure d'Ars, never faltered in his efforts to unite the Indians in a common Christianity. By 1855, when war broke out again on the plateau, he had succeeded so well that St. Anne's had become a respected and peaceful mission.[28]

CONTROVERSIES WITHIN

About this time there appeared on the scene a young Irish priest, whose brother was the Archbishop of Cashel on the old sod.[29] Father James Croke was an uncommonly able priest and a very zealous one also. He seemed to harbor, however, certain antipathies toward Jesuits, which did not surface until a few years later when he became vicar general in San Francisco.[30] This appears to be irrelevant but one suspects when all is known, that Father Croke, like many other ecclesiastics, was not so much anti-Jesuit as anti-religious orders, which were exempt from the bishop. This had already been touched upon in the case of the Blanchets.

The archbishop, involved in frequent disputes with his priests, both diocesan and religious, "found himself under accusation to Pope Pius IX from his own men."[31] In his response to Roman authorities, he ignored his own priests and was especially defensive about the religious priests whom he suspected, unjustly as the sequel showed, of reporting him to Rome. In his effort to discover the alleged informers, he dispatched sharp rebukes to superiors of both the Oblates and the Jesuits. For some reason it was generally believed that the religious were to blame and when the archbishop and his brother attended the First Plenary Council of Baltimore in 1852, both of them were absolved by the fathers of the Council of any guilt of charges brought against them "by certain religious societies in their dioceses."[32]

This was not enough however, for the archbishop. He continued to pursue the matter, demanding acquittal in a lengthly letter to Pius IX, listing the charges against himself and his brother as follows: "extending extremely harsh treatment of the diocesan clergy and above all of the religious clergy, obstructing the priestly ministry, contributing to a less fruitful missionary apostolate, being the archenemies of the Oblate Fathers, and accusing his priests of more interest in agriculture than in the care of souls."[33] The archbishop disavowed every charge.

Ricard was the Oblate superior. In a spirited reply to the archbishop, he denied that the Oblates had communicated any information except to their own superiors. Giving tit for tat, he reminded the archbishop that "everybody knows, and Your Grace ought not ignore the fact, that everyone knows that the secular clergy of Oregon addressed complaints to Rome more than a year and a half ago; and that in a collective letter mention was made of antipathy against the regulars."[34] He then reviewed past difficulties between the Oblates and the bishops, and reminded Blanchet that the archbishop had undercut these rights by attempting to gain privileges contrary to law.

Father Michael Accolti, the Jesuit superior, was almost as indignant as Ricard about the archbishop's allegations. He responded with less asperity, however, partly because he possessed a delicate awareness of how his bread was buttered, and partly because he did not care much anymore. He had made up his mind that sooner, rather than later, he was going to California where his heart had remained. Instead of engaging in an open rupture with the archbishop, he summoned three of his Jesuits to the Willamette and then assigned them to the California mission. These were Peter DeVos, Anthony Goetz who had been with Nobili in New Caledonia, and young Francis Veyret, who had become a Jesuit following his ordination by the archbishop.[35] The loss of these three priests doubtlessly spoke more eloquently to Blanchet than Ricard's fiesty attack.

In Rome, His Eminence, Allesandro Cardinal Barnabo was Prefect of Propaganda, under whose jurisdiction these missionary dioceses operated. Barnabo more than once urged the two bishops to conduct themselves in a more kindly manner and to treat their priests with more understanding and compassion. Both responded with letters that might be called obsequious. The dispute, however, raged on. At one point, the archbishop informed Barnabo, "The Jesuits and the Oblate Fathers cannot help me."[36] He accused both orders of neglecting Indians, adding tartly that the government could take better care of them. He asked Barnabo to send another order to replace both groups of missionaries and when this was denied him, he found it difficult to understand.

NEW DIOCESAN BOUNDARIES

At the Baltimore Council, where Archbishop Blanchet seems to have enjoyed considerable support from his brother bishops, he submitted a request for changes in the boundaries of the diocese of Oregon City and Nesqually. In addition to the urgent need to equalize, more or less, the two dioceses in terms of area, there were now compelling political reasons for change. The small settlement of Seattle had come into being. Whites living here and elsewhere north of the Columbia and south of Canada, petitioned Congress to create a new territory, independent of Oregon to be called the Territory of Columbia. The boundaries suggested were the Columbia River, the forty-ninth parallel and the Pacific Ocean. On November 4, 1852, the Oregon legislature also adopted a memorial asking for the division. Oregon's delegate in Congress, Joseph Lane, pressed for passage of the bill, which was presented to the House on February 8, 1853. When it was proposed that the name be changed from Columbia to Washington, Lane agreed. There were no further opposition, and the bill passed the Senate on March 2, 1853. It was signed by President Millary Fillmore two days before he left office.[37]

Upon the recommendation of the Council then, Pius IX promulgated the apostolic brief *Per Similes Nostros* on July 29, 1853. In accordance with this, the Diocese of Walla Walla was formally suppressed and the Columbia River and the forty-sixth parallel became the dividing line between the Archdiocese of Oregon City and the Diocese of Nesqually from the Pacific Ocean to the Rocky Mountains.[38] This decree placed all of the northwest Jesuits, except those on the Willamette, and all Oblates, except Chirouse at St. Anne's on the Umatilla, under the Nesqually Diocese, with Augustin Blanchet as their bishop. If anything, the position of the religious was less secure than before.

CHURCHES IN PORTLAND AND WESTERN OREGON, FATHER CROKE

But what about Father Croke? During these melancholy years beginning with 1851, he was the ubiquitous apostle of western Oregon, traveling incessantly by horse, serving the scattered white Catholics from Portland to Jacksonville. In the autumn of his first year, he was assigned by the archbishop to gather funds for a church in Portland. He raised about six hundred dollars forthwith, a tidy sum, then purchased a half block of land at Fifth and Couch from old Captain J.H. Couch himself. While the church was under construction, he first offered Mass for his new flock in a private home and later in the sacristy at the end of the church. At last, on Christmas eve, at midnight, he celebrated the first Mass in the new edifice, as they say when speaking of churches, but the interior of it was so rough and incomplete that it looked more like Bethlehem than a pro-cathedral, which it eventually became.

Two months later, after much sawing of boards and pounding of nails, Father Croke decided to have his church dedicated. There were no pews yet, rough benches served as well, and the interior lacked many final touches, but the archbishop, assisted by Fathers Croke and Brouillet, presided over the customary scenario with pomp and splendor on February 22, 1852. Dedications were like baptismal ceremonies: names were given and sponsors were recognized. So the name of Mary, the Immaculate Conception, was bestowed on the pastor's frame box, a very popular designation, just two years before Pope Pius IX pronounced the dogma of the Immaculate Conception.

If by this time Croke was happy with the church, his people were not. They said it had been built in the wrong place. They said the site was too remote. The road to it was a mere trail through the woods, blocked by fallen trees over which those going to church had to make their journey.[39] After a meeting (even then some people thought meetings solved everything), four lots were secured from Benjamin Stark at Third and Stark Streets, closer to the center of town, and the church was moved there at a cost of five hundred dollars. "We completed the work, thank God, without the slightest accident and our church now stands on its new site as perfect and as strong as if it were built there." Thus, the pastor reported to the archbishop. The money for it had already been paid but the parish owed the contractor another eighty dollars for enlarging the sacristy, and this, too, would be paid at once. This indicates what kind of charming fund raiser the pastor really was. He was also prompt in sending the archbishop his reports, which he signed: "Your Lordship's very humble and obedient servant, James Croke." Surely this was most gratifying to the aging prelate, whose current correspondence with the Oblates bristled with contention.

Father Brouillet, of course, belonged to the Nesqually diocese across the river. His grace would have given an arm to get him for the archdiocese. He had another young priest, Toussaint Mesplie, whom he had ordained in 1850. Before ordination, Mesplie spent a few months in Astoria with the Chinook Indians, and the soldiers at the fort there, an experience that left its mark.[40] For the rest of his life he had a special predilection for soldiers. When he was a priest, the archbishop assigned him to The Dalles, where he remained, with serene content for some years. With Mesplie, the archdiocese now had four priests on whom Blanchet could depend: Croke in Portland, Delorme at St. Paul, McCormick at Astoria and Mesplie at The Dalles. Blanchet himself served Oregon City. With Chirouse on the Umatilla, this totalled six, a frail little troop to engage in combat with the devil, the flesh, and the world.

While the whites trickled in slowly from the east, taking up land in what was left of the Willamette Valley, then in the meadows and valleys along the coast, the archbishop gave his first attention to the care of Indians, perhaps because the whites had deserted him for gold, leaving him to bear the debt alone. Mesplie at The Dalles also gave a priority of time and interest to the Indian tribes of his region. "Thence he evangelized," says his biographer, "and attended to the spiritual needs of the Wascos, Wisrams, Fair Valley Indians, Tininos, Deschoutes, Dog River and other confederated tribes who were later brought together at the Warm Spring Reservation." Less frequently he visited other Indians: "Meanwhile he periodically visited the Yaquimas, the Kliquitates, the Cayuse, the Wallulas and Walla Wallas."

What Mesplie was doing for the scattered Indians, Croke was doing for the scattered whites south of Portland and west of the Willamette. One gets saddle sore just reading about his long safaris into the unknown forests and lost, remote valleys of western Oregon, seeking Catholics who had not seen a priest for years. In his reports to the archbishop, he noted that he met no Catholic in Salem, a Protestant settlement, except "Mr. Dubois"; there was an O'Reilly at Rogue River, a Mr. Sheehy, a lawyer at Scottsburgh, "Albany built on a large plain, supported by a very extensive country" was expected to become a post of some importance. Croke called upon the town's proprietors to get more lots. "The Messrs. Menteith, two brothers," were very liberally disposed, and offered two lots for a church in the very center of town, but only on condition that the church be erected next spring."

Croke found another "old O'Reilly" on his claim fourteen miles south of Marysville. He offered Mass in O'Reilly's home, feeling sorry for him because as a Catholic, he was treated like an outcast by his neighbors, "who held him in abhorrence."[41]

When he reached "Kouse Bay, Lower Umqua," he was heartily tired, as was his horse. Most Catholics he met were Catholics in name only and prospects for the future were very gloomy. He had visited the home of Jesse Applegate, one of the founders of Oregon, and Mrs. Applegate, in the absence of her husband, had been very hospitable. Some twenty eight miles beyond was Winchester, consisting of a few houses and a store belonging to General Lane's son-in-law. Beyond Winchester was "The Canyon," a narrow passage twelve miles long, temporarily closed because of a small-time Indian war, during which thirteen whites had been killed and others had fled to Jacksonville for safety. Rumor stated that there were six hundred Indian warriors involved. Since he regarded it as imprudent to challenge a force so vast, Croke rode his weary horse to Scottsburg instead, then took the steamer *Washington* "to Koose or Coose or Coos river." Who cares? Nobody did then. They called the town there Empire City, a very grandiose designation for a few shacks. The inhabitants received him kindly and gave him four lots on Third Street for a church.

He finally reached Jacksonville in September, after Indian vanity had been saved and the war over, thanks to the superior muskets of the whites. He preached a mission in the Court House to an assemblage of miners, packers, storekeepers, and gamblers.[42] He did not mention ladies of the street, but no doubt there were a few of them too, because in mining towns, diversions like a good sermon were rare indeed.

Croke finally reached the Willamette, where he had to trade in his horse, which was almost worn out. He expected to spend a few days of rest with Father Mengarini at the Jesuit residence before returning to Portland, but there is no evidence whether he arrived there or not.

This was a typical missionary journey for the 1850's. More noteworthy than the hardships, which were *de rigueur* in those Spartan times, were the paucity and indifference of the Catholics for whom the pioneer priests endured much with no visible rewards and precious little appreciation. Small wonder that the priests preferred to work with the Indians and the landless soldiers, who sometimes shot at one another.

NEW SITE FOR ST. IGNATIUS MISSION

By the spring of 1854, the Jesuits at St. Ignatius Mission on the Pend Oreille River had reached the nadir of frustration. On the verge of starvation themselves, they had no food to offer the Indians who had trusted them and built their homes near the mission. Even the poor, dumb animals of the mission were starving.[43]

At this point a loyal and pious chief, Alexander by name, offered to show the fathers another site beyond the mountain to the east. This was the plateau rendezvous, he said, where the tribes of the interior bartered, raced their horses and played stick games. It was common ground to all the tribes, in a valley covered with grass and crossed by creeks of cold water that never dried up. Fish, game, and berries were plentiful there, and the high, snow-capped mountains on the east protected the valley from the chilling winds off the Rockies. Alexander guided Father Joseph Menetrey and Brother McGean to the rendezvous in the summer of 1854. The two Jesuits, having whole-heartily agreed with their guide, lost no time in conveying their impressions to Father Hoecken, the mission's superior. After several councils with Indians, the Jesuits decided to move at once. Hoecken sold the mission cattle for two thousand dollars. The mission's accumulated possessions, many of which had been sent by DeSmet, were collected and packed, and the long journey up the river was begun, with the Indians leading the way and the Jesuits following. The emigrants reached the rendezvous on September 24, 1854, the official date of the founding of St. Ignatius Mission in Montana.

Under Hoecken's direction, pioneering began anew. A log hut, which still stands, was hastily built for the missionaries. Tipis were thrown together, provisions were quickly gathered. Before the end of that year, eighty-two Indians had been baptized, a chapel, two houses, a carpenter and blacksmith shop were erected and word spread far and near that the Blackrobes had arrived to live at the rendezvous.

CALIFORNIA MISSION ESTABLISHED

During this happy time for the Kalispels, another event was taking place in faraway Rome, a decision made that would have a profound effect on them and their missionaries for many years to come. The *de facto* establishment of the California Mission by Oregon Jesuits, without the approval of Rome, was finally recognized by Father General and given a canonical approbation that permitted poor Father Nobili to die in peace.[44] By way of confirmation, Roothaan united both the California and Rocky Mountain missions under one superior and placed what was now one mission in western American under the care of the Turin Province of Italy.[45] Roothaan also appointed Father Nicholas Congiato as the first superior of the new province-in-the-making.

For the Rocky Mountain Missions this was a disaster. Congiato was a good priest and an able administrator, but he knew very little about the Indian missions and from his behavior one would judge that the cared even less about them. He lived in San Francisco, serving a dual role, as rector of the college there as well as superior of the mission. When Jesuits arrived in San Francisco, attached to the Indian missions by the writings of Father DeSmet, they were assigned, instead, to college work in San Francisco or Santa Clara, while the Jesuits in the north were left to whistle "Yankee Doodle." A day of reckoning would come but it was seven years distant, a week of years during which Accolti's cool indifference to the northern missions turned to neglect and eventually to no interest at all.

GOVERNOR ISAAC STEVENS

The so-called Rogue River War, reported by Father Croke, was the beginning of a trend. Other Indian wars followed, mostly for the same reasons, the invasion of the whites, especially miners, and the threatened deprivation of their land. The new Territorial Governor of Washington, Isaac Ingalls Stevens, an honor graduate of West Point, received two other presidential assignments as part of his office: Superintendent of Indian Affairs, and the director of a survey for a northern railroad to the Pacific.

His first concern was for the Indians, especially those in western Montana who still had much to fear from the Blackfeet. Thus, Stevens began his work as peacemaker for the Indians at a great council at Fort Benton with the chiefs of the Piegans, the Bloods, and the Blackfeet.[46] The Indians were persuaded to consider Stevens' peace proposals, and another great council was scheduled for two years following.

The Indians were now at peace with one another. But as Stevens pursued his schedule of peace councils with them, their anger was turned against the whites. Not even the priests could pacify all of them.

On May 29, 1855, a council of eight tribes was held at Walla Walla. Present as non participants were two of the priests, Oblate Pandosy and Jesuit Menetrey, both in attendance at the insistence of the governor, who used them for his own ends.[47] On July 16, another council of Montana tribes was held at Hell Gate and this time Hoecken was present. The Hell Gate Treaty was a giveaway for the Indians, who accepted it grudgingly, only because they were offered no other options. By this time, the entire plateau buzzed in a subtle, almost silent manner, with the Indians' anger and desire for revenge. The Yakima Chiefs went among all the other tribes formenting discontent.[48] The non-Indians, on the other hand, basked in complacency, assuming quite foolishly that all was well because some of the chiefs had placed an "x" beside their names, partly to gain time for organizing opposition.

At The Dalles, St. Peter's Mission church and rectory had burned down in late February and all of the mission records were destroyed.[49] Understandably, Father Mesplie was occupied throughout the spring in replacing the buildings but he took time to keep the American military authorities posted on the plans of hostile Indians, especially the Cayuse and Yakimas. The Oblates, too, notified the government of impending dangers, but these warnings went unheeded.[50] There were other signs of danger, for example, occasional "massacres" of travelers and small wagon trains by young disgruntled Indians. In the summer of 1855, Qualchan, a nephew of Kamiakin, a prominent Yakima chief, encountered a group of six white men on the Yakima River and killed them all.[51] Still there was no official interference. In fact, action was not taken until a government bureaucrat, Indian agent A.J. Bolen, was murdered on September 20, 1855.[52] This homicide, a direct challenge to the authority of the government, could not be overlooked. Accordingly, a party of fifty soldiers under the command of Major George Haller, was dispatched into the Yakima country to apprehend those who were suspected of murdering Bolen and the other white men.

OBLATE MISSIONS CLOSED

Two days later, without knowledge of Bolen's death or the avenging soldiers, Father Pandosy left his mission and went to Olympia to inform Acting Governor C.H. Mason of Kamiakin's efforts to unite all Indians against the encroaching whites.[53] He was in Olympia when news of Bolen's death was received.

Ricard reported these events to his superior in France:

Finally fifty soldiers of the regular army have come into the Yakima Country to arrest several individuals who have killed some Americans. Every day new proofs of a vast plot are seen, at the head of which appears to be Kamiakin. It will be nothing less than bringing everything under fire and sword. The government is proceeding with its investigations. Very probably, after the inquiry, some of the culprits will be hung in order to intimidate the others. But the savages seem resolved to maintain the struggle to the death, convinced that the treaties of the government for the purchase of their lands are nothing but frauds.[54]

The position of the Oblates was now an awkward one. Dedicated to keeping the peace and given freedom of action by the hostiles, they were suspected by the whites of aiding and abetting insurrection. To some they appeared to be double agents, advisors to the Indians for the sake of peace, and informers to the government for the protection of the whites.

Convinced of the Oblates' treason, many of the settlers in Olympia demanded that they should be hung. Ricard wrote to Mason on October 12 to protest the injustice of these unwarranted allegations, citing the services that the Oblates had rendered the government, and requesting a public vindication of the patriotism of the Oblates. When Mason declined to provide this, he prepared the way for the violent attacks on the Oblates which followed.

Despite the risks involved, the four Oblates, Pandosy, and Paul Durieu among the Yakimas, and Chirouse and Richard among the Cayuse, remained at their posts as long as possible. On October 12 Ricard sent orders for Pandosy and Durieu to leave their mission of St. Joseph on the Attanum, and to proceed to Fort Vancouver via The Dalles. If they received these orders, they decided, for reasons not known, to remain at the mission.

Meanwhile at The Dalles, Father Mesplie was using his influence to keep the Wascos and other near-by tribes from entering the conflict. According to his biographer, "[he] kept thousands of Indians from the warpath; he pacified large numbers among the chiefs who had commenced hostilities; and by keeping the military authorities informed of the plots of hostile tribes, he saved not only The Dalles City from destruction, but also many lives of those whom the government employed as a defense of the valuable interests in that region."[55]

Unfortunately, the government forces under Haller were not doing as well. Underestimating the strength of their foe, they were driven from the Yakima country. Major Gabriel Raines was placed in command of a superior force consisting of volunteers who entered the Yakima Valley on October 30, reaching St. Joseph's Mission on the Attanum on November 13. The hostile Indians had fled, taking Pandosy and Durieu with them. They had plundered the mission, by this time a more pretentious establishment than Theodore Winther had found two years earlier. The recently erected log church of considerable size, despite its cross on top, and its obvious use for divine worship, appeared to some soldiers to be the fortress of the enemy. Hence when they discovered a half keg of gunpowder buried in the orchard, their worst suspicions were confirmed. Like noisy mobs of bullies found on every frontier, they burned to the ground every building on the premises within the very hour.

The Oblates had buried the powder to keep it from falling into the hands of the hostiles.[56] Responsible army officials expressed regrets, but no one was punished and no one offered to rebuild the mission.

Likewise, no one knew where Pandosy and Durieu had gone. Father Chirouse, still clinging to his post on the Umatilla, wrote to Ricard on November 18, "Rumor had it that Father Pandosy has been killed. Several people confirm it.....For fifteen days I have not slept, shall I be able to sleep any better tonight!"[57]

The answer was "No." Some of the volunteer soldiers rode off to the mission of the Immaculate Conception on Mnassatas Creek, where they plundered the buildings and clothed themselves in the Mass vestments. Thus attired, they set fire to the buildings and danced crazily around them until nothing was left but ashes.[58]

After this, four hundred volunteers set off for St. Anne's on the Umatilla. Meeting a large force of Cayuse Indians, they were cut to pieces and retreated in disorder. The Cayuses, exhilarated by their victory over the whites, looted and sacked the entire neighborhood including St. Anne's. After they had pillaged the mission, they burned it down again, the second time within seven years. Fortunately, Chirouse and Richard were absent from the mission when this last madness took place; the Indians were in no mood to spare them.

There is some obscurity about the ordeal of the other two Oblates, Pandosy and Durieu. One has reason to believe that they left their mission willingly, as prisoners of the Indians, to escape the fury of the American volunteers. For some days they had traveled in a northeasterly direction, subsisting on roots and berries. They were either released then or escaped from their captors.[59] Eventually they found refuge "at Colville" meaning the Jesuits' St. Paul Mission on the Columbia, where the ever-present Joset was on hand to welcome them and to give them the comfort they deserved.

Pandosy, a feisty little Gallican, who in later years was always seen wearing a long droopy beard, was determined to return to Yakima. A letter arrived from Governor Stevens, however, informing him that neither he nor Durieu were to enter Yakima territory as long as the war lasted. Pandosy, bitterly disappointed, characterized the governor as "a new Pilate," an allusion that scarcely applied. He laid plans to circumvent the governor's orders, but these failed and he was forced to spend more time at St. Paul, teaching a handful of Indians there the benefits of European church music.

In the following spring, 1856, he was invited by Colonel George Wright, commander of a new force of American troops, to serve in his command as an interpreter and chaplain. Pandosy eagerly accepted the position, riding on horseback sixty to seventy miles a day to join Wright's army. There followed for Pandosy a period of relative tranquility "in the midst of this dreadful turmoil," the war.[60] The officers and men manifested the greatest respect toward him, for they realized that largely due to his influence and efforts, many Indians remained neutral and others made a quick peace. The soldiers saluted him when he passed, the officers regarded him as an equal, the army surgeon gave him medicines for the Indians.[61]

When peace was restored in the autumn of 1856, Chirouse, Durieu and Richard, having given up all hope of accomplishing any good in their former missions, moved what they had left to St. Joseph's mission near Olympia, but Pandosy went back to the Yakimas. He was now the only Oblate left on the plateau and his life was not an easy one. Governor Stevens, writing in March, 1857, noted that "the hostile Yakimas retain the herder they captured as a secretary. They have likewise seized and whipped the Catholic missionary, Father Pandosy."[62]

This was bad enough, but a change in army personnel brought into the area prejudiced soldiers who treated him as badly as the Indians did. Thus, he was insulted and menaced by the Indians and threatened by the soldiers who said they would shoot him. For his own safety he had to leave the Yakimas again, to take refuge with the Jesuits at Sacred Heart Mission.

From St. Joseph's near Olympia, Chirouse made one last visit to St. Anne's on the Umatilla. "Often I cannot hold back my tears at the sight of the rocks still red with blood of the victims of the carnage. If by chance one sees a building still standing, it is filled with wounded or furious people who have lost all."[63]

He returned to Olympia, to the motherhouse, to share in the work of his brother Oblates among the Puget Sound Indians. He never saw the ashes of St. Anne's again, but from these ashes another mission was built, and another. There was no holding back the hand of God.

OBLATE HEADQUARTERS MOVED TO CANADA

On September 25, 1855, the archbishop departed for an extended begging tour of South America to secure money for liquidating the debts of the Oregon Church.[64] Fortified with a discreet letter of authorization from the Prefect of the Congregation of Propaganda, he traversed the largely Catholic dominions of Peru, Bolivia, and others, including Chile, where he was most successful of all. In Chile, he published, in Spanish, a pamphlet providing a sketch of the Oregon church, with all its vicissitudes, and an appeal for funds to save his diocese.[65] The fact that he was successful in raising the money he needed, in countries poorer than those in Europe or North America, speaks eloquently about the Catholics of South America. Their sacrifices for the pioneer church of Oregon must never be forgotten.

The archbishop returned in triumph to Oregon City on December 17, 1857, after the Yakima Indian War had been terminated. Peace reigned again on the plateau. That was the good news. But the bad news was disheartening: the new superior of the Oblates, indicating the course of the future, had moved the headquarters of the Oblates from Olympia to Esquimault on Vancouver Island, British Territory.

Louis D'Herbomez had replaced Ricard as acting superior in June 1857.[66] Ricard's health, never robust, had begun to fail noticeably and the superior general recalled him to France.[67] Almost immediately upon taking office, D'Herbomez decided to move his motherhouse to Vancouver Island, which was within the jurisdiction of Bishop Demers and to gradually move his subjects from the Diocese of Nesqually into that of Vancouver.

In a letter to de Mazenod, D'Herbomez gave one of the reasons for his decision:

> Time is pressing, the English already have a bishopric there; minsiters are spreading everywhere, and they know as well as we do, how to choose the best places for the success of their purpose. The news of the gold mines is more and more encouraging; the miners are already on the spot by the thousands. This spring they will be counted by the tens of thousands. Among them are, and there are more yet to come, a great number of Canadians, half-breeds, Irish, French, Mexicans, Spaniards, Italians, who are all Catholic. It is true they are not all very fervent, but they desire to have missionaries, and they are grieved not to see any priests. Bishop Demers has only two priests.[68]

This sounds like the gold rush to California, but there was one significant difference: the Oblates were leaving the Nesqually Diocese because of disagreements with the bishop.[69] Augustin Blanchet, despite his coldness toward the Oblates, wanted them to take over the care of other Indian reservations besides Tulalip, where Chirouse, in September of 1857, had established the first mission on Ebey Slough, near Priest's Point.[70] D'Herbomez, having approved of this, assigned two other Oblates to assist Chirouse—Father Durieu and Brother Celestine Verney.

"We have some difficulty with Bishop Blanchet relative to the reservations of Indian tribes," D'Herbomez reported to de Mazenod. "I have written him that we can only take that of the Snohomish where Fathers Chirouse and Durieu are now."[71] This was not enough for Augustin Blanchet, nor for his brother the archbishop, who accused the Oblates of being in Olympia for ten years without establishing one new mission for Indian or white. "The good fathers," he wrote to Cardinal Barnabe, "have lived and live together independent of the Bishops."[72]

D'Herbomez was not intimidated. He felt convinced there was no future for the Oblates in the Oregon missions. "Experience has proved only too clearly," he wrote, basing his remarks on about eight years of experience, "that all the good we can hope to do among the Indians of the Oregon and Washington Territories can be reduced to this—to care for the Indians who are still benevolent towards us (and their number decreases every day), to baptize the children, the sick and the agonizing. It is therefore morally certain that more good can be done among the Indians of the North....."[73] They were more numerous. They were more industrious. They were anxious to have Blackrobes among them.

The exodus of the Oblates was a slow process. Only two left for Canada in 1857--D'Herbomez and Richard. Jayol was in charge of St. Joseph's at Olympia. Pandosy was ordered to close St. Rose, the first of the Oblates' missions, and to begin a new mission on Lake Okanogan in Canada. The Yakima mission was closed also, and D'Herbomez gave an account of it in his annual report to the general:

> This mission was abandoned by the missionaries on March 28, 1859, on the order of the Superior of the Missions of Oregon, dated March 13, 1859. This mission has no more than 160 Baptisms since its foundation, more children than adults.....This mission was abandoned because, for the moment, our ministry has practically no usefulness, because of the threat of war which everyone thinks will soon re-commence, because the friendly Indians are soon to be placed on reservations that the government has assigned to them.....We have left because we are not regarded by the Americans as agents who will, by their ministry, keep the tribes in submission, and dispose them to accept all whims of government. We are well aware that all the American employees, civil and military, detest us cordially and conduct themselves towards us in the most indifferent and frigid manner.[74]

At St. Joseph's Mission near Olympia, Jayol was alone at the beginning of the year 1860, when another Oblate was assigned to assist him.[75] Both of these priests, however, were soon summoned to Canada and St. Joseph's Mission was turned over to Bishop Blanchet. Thus, when the

year 1861 dawned, only two Oblates were left in the Nesqually Diocese—
Chirouse and Durieu at Tulalip. They, too, would soon join their
brothers in Canada.

EARLY SCHOOLS

The loss of the Oblates was a terrible blow from which the Nesqually
Diocese did not recover during the lifetime of Bishop Augustin Blanchet.

But His Lordship still had his vicar general, the highly esteemed John
Baptist Brouillet, who did not hesitate to talk back to the bishop when
need arose.

At Vancouver, Brouillet opened an academy for boys. Classes were
begun on November 3, 1856, under the stern tutelage of a laymen whose
first name, being unimportant then, has not come down to us. He was
simply known as Mr. Kinsela to his diminutive scholars, who learned
mostly the basic essentials, plus a heavy dose of Christian Doctrine.[76]

During this same year, Father Adrian Hoecken opened a boys' school at
St. Ignatius Mission. Hoecken placed too much trust in the government's
promises in the great peace conference at Hell Gate. The Flatheads had
been guaranteed funds for a school. They were to receive school
teachers, a blacksmith, a carpenter, and other skilled laborers to teach the
boys and provide the temporal needs of the tribe. "The Fathers and
brothers at the Mission were instructed to carry out, in the name of the
Government, this part of the agreement. They did so cheerfully, and
continued to do the same for a long time; but theirs was only the privilege
of doing the work, whilst remuneration seemed to be entirely lost sight
of, or stranded on the way."[77]

"We have done and shall continue to do all in our power for the
government officers," wrote Hoecken to DeSmet. "Our brothers assist
the Indians, and teach them how to cultivate the ground; our blacksmith
works for them; he repairs their guns, their knives, and their axes; the
carpenter renders them great assistance in constructing their houses, by
making the doors and windows; in a work, all we have and all we are is
sacrificed to their welfare. Still, our poor Mission has never received a
farthing from the Government."[78]

Since the funds promised for the school never arrived, Hoecken was
forced to close it after one year. It would be eight long years before the
mission was able to support a small school, at its own expense, and many
years after that before the government or the tribe provided the living
expenses for the Indian boys in residence at the school. But a precedent

had been set. Hoecken's school of 1856 was really the Jesuits' first in the Northwest, the predecessor of many distinguished institutions that followed.[79]

Although the Yakima Indian War was technically over, there was much unrest among the Indians of the lower Columbia, which created an ongoing crisis for the missions in the Rocky Mountains. The northern Indians, sympathizing with their southern neighbors, found common cause with them and discovered their own grievances with the whites for violations of treaties. "I fear a general uprising among the Indians toward the commencement of spring," Father Ravalli wrote in 1856.[80]

Father Congiato of San Francisco, the mission superior who succeeded Accolti, finally visited St. Ignatius during that same summer. Writing about Hoecken, he said, "he does the work of several men and has succeeded in uniting together three nations under his spiritual jurisdiction."[81] Hoecken's influence, he could have added, was so great that, despite the agitation of other tribes during this period of Indian wars, his three tribes remained at peace.[82]

Instead of wars and rumors of wars, Congiato found tranquility and progress at this new St. Ignatius Mission. "We must first mention," Palladino noted, "the erection of a flour mill, the stones or buhrs being quarried from native rock, the same hands that cut the stones making the tools to cut them with. Together with the flour mill, a whip saw mill was also constructed, the power for both plants being obtained from a stream close by, through a race over one thousand feet long and five feet wide, made, bottom and sides, of hewn tamarack timbers."[83]

Hoecken had already learned; it was easier to build mills than to conduct a school.

MOTHER JOSEPH

But mission schools for girls would soon appear. These depended upon the coming of the sisters, God bless them, sisters who would arrive and remain. There was only one Mother Joseph to lead them, a perky little lady with big peasant's hands that could do anything, sew linens, cook, do carpentry work, or write long letters. Like the Blanchets, she was born in eastern Canada of French related parents, Joseph and Francoise Pariseau. Born on April 16, 1823, the third child of her devoutly Catholic parents, in the village of Saint Elzear, she was christened on the following day under the patronage of one of the saints called Esther. So she was Esther Pariseau, a clever and determined, petite child, who loved nothing more than helping her father in his carriage shop.

When Esther was twenty, her father brought her to Montreal to Mother Emmelie Gamelin, who had recently founded a religious congregation under the direction of Bishop Bourget himself. The good bishop somewhat carried away by long titles, named the congregation, "Daughters of Charity, Servants of the Poor," but they soon came to be known quite simply as the Sisters of Providence. It was the day after Christmas, 1843, and the convent was the *Providence Asile* or asylum for poor old ladies on St. Catherine Street.

When the door of the *asile* opened to Esther and her father, they stepped briskly over the threshold. Joseph Pariseau addressed Mother Gamelin. "Madame," he said, "I bring you my daughter Esther, who wishes to dedicate herself to the religious life. She is twenty years old, and for some time she had prayed with her family for enlightenment. Her mother and I have talked about her future with her as well as with Monsieur le Curé. It is a great sacrifice for me to part with Esther, but if you will accept her into your company, you will find her able to give you valuable assistance. She has had what education her mother and I could give her at home and at school. She can read and write and figure accurately. She can cook and sew and spin and do all manner of housework well. She has learned carpentry from me and can handle tools as well as I can. Moreover, she can plan and supervise the work of others, and I assure you, Madame, she will some day make a very good superior."[86]

"Esther is healthy and strong," her father continued. "She has been eager to serve God in Providence ever since Monseigneur [Bishop] Bourget visited us and appealed for helpers."

"And you, Monsieur Pariseau," asked Mother Gamelin, "are you quite willing to give up your daughter?"   "Certainly, Madame," came the prompt reply. "This is our Christmas gift to the Divine Child."[87]

Esther's name in religion was Sister Joseph. She was present at the *Asile* when Bishop Augustin Blanchet made his first appeal for sisters in 1852, and she had been one of the first to volunteer to go to Oregon. But the Council had decided against her, saying she was too much needed as bursar in Montreal. Five others were chosen and she, Sister Joseph, had provided all their needs for their journey.

The bishop's misadventure with the sisters this first time, had left him a little touchy on the subject of the foundation in Chile. But the needs of his diocese had humbled him, and now in the autumn of 1856 he was knocking once again on the doors of the convent and asking for another group of sisters for the Northwest. Mother Gamelin had died prematurely and the new superior, Mother Caron, who had succeeded her, understandably received the bishop warily, putting him off at least for the present.[88]

ENTER THE JEWISH CONVERT FATHER LOUIS ROSSI

At this point the bishop acquired an eloquent surrogate. Father Louis Rossi, an Italian Jew, convert to Catholicism and former member of the Passionist Order, had met Blanchet in Belgium and volunteered to serve in his diocese.[89] He joined Blanchet, whom he always called "Monsignor," in London following which the two clerics sailed on the *Anglo Saxon* to Quebec. Blanchet remained in Quebec "to say a last goodbye to his old parents," then rejoined Rossi in Montreal within a fortnight.

"He nursed the hope," Rossi wrote, "of introducing the Sisters of Charity [of Providence] to his diocese; he had already tried, but unfortunately his expenditure of time and money was unsuccessful. Since that time, lots of objections have been made to him and to his plans. He has had lots of difficulties and has suffered because of prejudices, so much so that one day he said to me, 'I don't know how to succeed in this, Your Reverence. See whether you can't do something to help.' The difficulties came from two areas, from the nuns and the clergy....I shall say that God blessed my efforts. We got the sisters."[90]

Mother Caron called for volunteers and this time Sister Joseph was chosen, with four others, and when she was appointed superior of the new foundation, Bishop Bourget gave her a new name: Sister Joseph of the Sacred Heart.[91]

In addition to Mother Joseph, those assigned to the new mission were as follows: Sister Praxedes of Providence, Sister Blandine of the Holy Angels, only eighteen years old, and two postulants, Sister Adelaide Theriault and Sister Mary Ellen Norton.[92]

Determined to avoid the loss of his sisters a second time, His Lordship himself, with Father Rossi as his cherished assistant, escorted them to Vancouver. The five nuns clad in secular garb, left their convent and joined the bishop and Rossi as they boarded "a steamer" to cross the river, at nine in the morning of November 3, 1856. Their departure had been delayed some weeks, because of the bishop's recent illness. Rossi, too, had spent eleven days in the hospital "due to his renewed colic attacks."

He, and Mother Joseph also, left detailed accounts of their journey to Oregon, the one with countless long-winded but fascinating asides, like descriptions of ships at which he often poked fun, and the other with words as spare as her belongings. This is Mother Joseph's description of the first stage of their adventure:

Very soon the bell tower of Providence, our happy home, was lost to view. We went to the ferry, and on the Saint Lambert, where we took the train to Rouse's Point. From thence we went by boat over the calm and placid waters of Lake Champlain and the Hudson River. The moon was bright and gave evidence of a fair day to come. The peaceful trip offered no inducement to sleep.[93]

This passage, it seems, reveals as much about Mother Joseph as about her journey. Orderly, practical, and forthright, these were her more obvious characteristics as she embarked on her career as a superior and missionary. But she was also a mystic. Behind her plain features, her small dark eyes, like two raisins in a pudding, her large nose and wide mouth, she cherished her own dreams. Impulsive at times, but very practical, she personified something mysterious beyond her appearance, some mystique reflected in her accomplishments and her prayers with God.

With her companions she was in New York City for the election of James Buchanan, fifteenth president of the United States, and predecessor of Abraham Lincoln.[94] The steamer on which she had passage, the S.S. Illinois, was delayed until November 6, so that news of the election could be carried to the west coast. But the cruise, once the vessel was on the high seas, was a swift one. The missionaries were in Jamaica on November 13, and four days late they docked in Aspinwall, the Atlantic port for the isthmus.[95] The trip to Panama by narrow gage railroad required only five hours, a vast improvement over the mule-back journey made by the sisters only four years earlier. From Panama they sailed to San Francisco, where the Sisters of Mercy presented them with an accordion, and a few days later they sailed to Oregon in a sturdy ship called Brother Jonathan. This part of their voyage was uncommonly stormy; even the bishop was alarmed at times by the violence of the raging sea.[96]

ARRIVAL OF THE SISTERS OF PROVIDENCE

Finally, at three in the afternoon on the Feast of the Immaculate Conception, the bishop with the five sisters happily disembarked from the Brother Jonathan. There was no pier, so the travelers stepped shakily from their larger vessel to a smaller one, which served as a makeshift wharf. Near the landing a few people had gathered to greet them. One of these, a distinguished looking cleric, middle-aged with long white hair reaching his high clerical collar, came forward and knelt to kiss the hand of the bishop. This was the vicar general, Father Brouillet. Introductions were exchanged and the little group moved up the hill toward the mission church, when the bell in the steeple began to ring.

"We had to walk about a mile," Rossi reported, "before coming to the bishop's palace. The road which led there wasn't made to be walked on in dainty ankle boots; we sank in to the knees, and it wasn't always easy to get out of those unexpected ruts. When we reached a little wooden ramshackle house, I asked Mr. Brouillet—the vicar general who had accompanied me thus far—what that shanty was. 'It's the bishop's palace,' he replied.

"The bishop's palace!!! Three ten-feet-square rooms and a passage twenty feet long by five wide made up the ground floor. To the left of this passage was a kink of an alcove through which you went to the school, the church and the kitchen. It also led to the loft."[97]

Brouillet was busy explaining to His Lordship why a house for the sisters had not been prepared.[98] The bishop was displeased and sharp words were exchanged. Brouillet then informed the bishop there was no other place in town for the sisters, except an open shed that provided little or no protection. In the midst of this discussion, the sisters' baggage arrived and was piled high, awaiting its final disposal.

"Bring in the baggage," the bishop finally said, "the sisters will remain here tonight."

The loft, an unfinished attic measuring twenty-five by twelve feet, was a catchall domestic warehouse without amenities of any kind. It had one partition, which allowed space for Rossi also. The larger portion, tidied up as only sisters can do it, was the first residence of the sisters who had come six thousand miles to occupy it.

The old church was being renovated, Brouillet had said, but a sisters' convent would be begun at once. His Lordship had great plans for the nuns; they should care for the bishop's house and the church, and they should establish a school, a hospital and a mission for the poor Indians. There were only five of them? His Lordship thought that was quite enough.

They moved, at last, into their new home on February 25, 1857. The annals of the convent record the event:

On Ash Wednesday, February 22 [sic], we took possession of our new convent—a small wooden building 16' x 24' with four windows and a glasspaneled door. A stairway led to the attic which served as our dormitory. A partition walled off a small room which we fitted up temporarily as a chapel. With a few boards, Sister Joseph built a suitable altar; from a candle box she made a gem-like little tabernacle, painted and decorated with gold ornament with the best material she could afford for a tabernacle veil.

Our kind bishop said the first Mass and for our comfort reserved the Most Blessed Sacrament there.[99]

Three weeks later, while the sisters were preparing to open a school, a stranger knocked on the convent door, presented a three-year-old child called Emily Lake, then quickly disappeared, never to be seen again.[100] It has sometimes been reported that little Emily of an unknown origin was "the first pupil of the first Catholic school in the Northwest." Neither Adrian Hoecken at St. Ignatius, nor the mysterious Mr. Kinsela would agree with this. It must be admitted, however, that Emily's arrival and the opening of the sisters academy for seven little girls on April 15, 1857, were events of great moment in the history of the Northwest Church. Certainly as the term parochial schools came to be understood, Providence Academy in Vancouver holds the unique honor of being the first in the Diocese of Nesqually.[101]

What is more important is that Providence of Vancouver gradually evolved into all that the bishop asked and more. When, for example, in May 1857, an old man of eighty-five years, feeble and penniless knocked on the convent door and asked the sisters to take him in, Mother Joseph made room for him in the frugal quarters they occupied. A bed by the kitchen stove, his food, and gentle love for him in his loneliness—all these the sisters gave him, setting a precedent for their future hospitals and homes for senior citizens. Above all, the convent became a motherhouse from which other foundations, all over the Northwest, were established, many of them within the lifetime of Mother Joseph, the indomitable superior with a heart bigger than her head.

WAR WITH THE
COEUR D'ALENES, PALOUSES AND SPOKANES[102]

It has been said that the Coeur d'Alenes were the most Catholic tribe on the plateau. Despite this recommendation, Father Congiato in 1857, decided that this mission should be closed. This was "a paper decision" a verdict based upon statistics that could be used to confirm the *status quo,* a big lie, or anything else. No one could dispute Congiato's position, however, for it was true that the fervor of the Coeur d'Alenes had cooled and attendance at Mass and the sacraments had declined. This was doubtlessly due to misunderstandings between the tribe and the priest in charge, the much admired Ravalli, who was so busy with buildings and sick patients that he tended to neglect the needs of the common people who make up the majority of those deplorable statistics.

Joset tried to convince Congiato that the Coeur d'Alenes were lacking proper direction, not piety and he rallied support of others to save the mission. He was right of course, but even Joset whose voice evoked a loyal response whenever he called the Indians to church, could not dampen the new spirit that had entered into the warriors of the tribe and had rendered them less docile, even resentful toward the priests. In the spring of 1858, inspired by the militant Yakimas, who sometimes coaxed and sometimes jeered them, the young braves frequently attended war rallies of other tribes and gradually became so involved with the excited Spokanes and Palouses that they regarded war with the whites as inevitable. Joset's reminder that nothing is gained but everything is lost by war fell on deaf ears. No one knew better than Joset that the plateau in May 1848 was a powder keg about to explode, and that his Catholic Coeur d'Alenes were deeply involved.

At that time there were only three missions still operating in the interior—St. Ignatius, St. Paul on the Columbia, and Sacred Heart for the Coeur d'Alenes. All three were conducted by the Jesuits, seven priests and six brothers, a brave little band at peace with their Indians, who alas! were turning over in their hearts the many unjust grievances they had received at the hands of other whites. In times like this, well-placed rumors become "facts" for injured people. Thus it happened that when rumors reached the Coeur d'Alenes that their lands would be taken from them and that an army would come to subdue them, they no longer doubted. They sang their war chants and clothed themselves in the regalia of the battle.

An opportunity to confront the troops of the whites presented itself that very month. In mid-May, 1858, a detachment of soldiers under Colonel Edward Steptoe, who were marching north from Fort Walla Walla with peaceful intent and lacking even adequate ammunition to protect themselves, was challenged by a large coalition of Indians, mostly Coeur d'Alenes, Spokanes, and Palouses. The two forces met in the rolling, grassy hills south of present Rosalia, Washington on Sunday, May 16. A number of older chiefs, half-hearted in their desire for peace, accompanied the younger braves. An anxious Joset, who had raced to the battlefront determined to prevent the war, had wrung from them a willingness to parley. Steptoe foolishly failed to cooperate.

On the following day, the battle began in earnest, as usual under controversial conditions—some saying the Indians fired the first shot, some saying the soldiers did. Heavily outnumbered, Steptoe's troops eventually gained control of the highest hill where they prepared, as the evening sun went down, for a last ditch battle on the morrow. There was no hope of winning it. Torture and death appeared to be certain.

What occurred at this point is shrouded in secrecy, with all the knowledgeable witnesses in their graves. One fact is simple enough: Steptoe's troops, having decently buried the dead and lashed the injured on horses, discovered a perfectly safe exit through the enemies' lines and slipped away into the night. When the Indians rushed the hill at midnight, in a surprise attack, they found their prisoners had fled.

It is unlikely, I think, that the soldiers escaped without the help of some Indians. One can only speculate, for Joset, the probable instrument of the soldiers' flight, protected those Indians to whom, presumably, he appealed. His lips were sealed until he died. So the mantle of mystery fell over the Steptoe battlefield. The frustrated and angry Indians, after this tainted victory over an inferior force of whites, prepared for other battles, which proved to be their destruction. During the summer of the same year, a punitive force under Colonel George Wright wreaked terrible vengeance upon all. Indians were hanged. The Spokanes' power was broken forever when their horses were killed and their winter food caches destroyed. The Coeur d'Alenes, in an agony of shame and uncertainty, withdrew to their own lands to lament their dead and await punishment.

Joset, having failed to prevent the war, and faced with the accusation of some whites that he had acted treacherously against the United States, became so depressed that he lost confidence in the tribe's leadership. He agreed with Congiato. The mission should be abandoned.

Fortunately, others did not agree. Colonel Wright, for example, regarded the proposal as an invitation to disaster for the entire plateau. Lieutenant John Mullan, engaged in making his road, but wise in the politics of Indians, dispatched a touching request to Congiato to keep the mission open:

> I trust, therefore, father, you will not abandon these poor children of the wilds to themselves, but on the contrary, since they have been willing to trace their steps, rather let them be confirmed in their present good intentions, to set to work to build themselves up again, to forget the errors of the past and live only in the brightness of the future.[103]

The immediate problem was how to save the Coeur d'Alenes from the kind of punishment other tribes had received. Joset hurried off to Vancouver to plead their cause at the fort. He found General Newman Clarke, the commandant, sympathetic but determined to impose conditions that were hard if not unreasonable. Clarke authorized Joset and Congiato, who had spent this summer of 1858 in the Northwest, to bear his proposals to the Indians.[104]

The two priests trotted their horses into every camp on the reservation, to present the government's terms of peace and to convince the Indians they should accept them. At first, they met with much unexpected resistance. Kamiakin, still living among the Coeur d'Alenes, fostered the Indians' strong desire for revenge, and the young warriors began to chant war songs again and to pick up their coup sticks. Gradually, however, the priests persuaded them that they had no hope of victory and the Coeur d'Alenes, laying down their arms, met with Wright on September 17, 1858, in the cabin residence of the missionaries. Crowded in the small rooms, they heard and accepted the terms spoken by Wright, then signed the papers Wright laid before them making an "X" if they could not sign their names. Later, in a display of Christian forgiveness and good will, they accompanied Wright and his detachment of soldiers thirteen miles downstream, to ferry them across the Coeur d'Alene River in their canoes and scows.[105]

This was not the end of the episode. In September, two days before the peace treaty was signed, Father Peter DeSmet sailed from New York with General William Harney, the new commander of the recently established "military department of Oregon and Washington," with headquarters at Vancouver. Technically, DeSmet was Harney's chaplain, but the general had arranged for his services to help him pacify the tribes of the Northwest in a spirit of compassion rather than fear. The two men reached their destination in late October.

Soon after, on October 29, DeSmet left by boat for Walla Walla, where he met the Coeur d'Alene hostages held by Colonel Wright,[106] Securing their release, he returned to the Coeur d'Alene mission with them, arriving on November 21. His mere presence was like a tonic for the Indians, who flocked to his side from every corner of the plateau. During the entire winter and spring of 1859, he visited all the interior tribes to convince them of the futility of war. He was so successful that never again did these tribes take up arms in a war against the whites.

On April 16, 1859, accompanied by nine chiefs, each one delegated by his respective tribe, DeSmet left the mountains for Vancouver,[107] After many hardships, they arrived at the fort and were ushered into the presence of General Harney. There the Indians offered their peace, which was graciously accepted by the general. Long speeches were doubtlessly made, since most Indian chiefs love to hear themselves talk. Then the general loaded down each chief with gifts. An essential part of the ritual was then performed: the Indians were given the five-dollar tour of the military establishments to impress them with the irresistible power of the whites. They had really traveled five hundred miles for this and the army made sure that each got his money's worth. After this formality, and "at the expense of the army, the chiefs were [then] granted a tour of several weeks through the Oregon coastal towns, with presents for all."[108]

DeSmet wrote, "the poor Indians can make nothing or very little" out of the industrial establishments, steam engines, printing shops, and the like. But they were vastly impressed with the chained wretches in the prison cells at Portland. They asked many questions about prisons and chains.[109]

In the solicitous care of their shepherd, the chiefs, like sheep, returned to their homes in June. The wars were formally over and it was business as usual for members of the struggling church in the Northwest.

CHURCHES IN ROSEBURG AND JACKSONVILLE

The archbishop, during this period, not being directly involved in the troubles east of the mountains, found time to make history in the small towns of his archdiocese. In the autumn of 1858, while DeSmet and Harney were sailing north to Vancouver, he rode his horse to Roseburg, where he established a mission called St. Stephen the Martyr. He baptized twenty-five persons and confirmed eight in a vacant Masonic Hall, which had been hastily adapted for the purpose.[110] On October 21, he made his first visit to Jacksonville and approved plans for a church to be erected there under the patronage of St. Joseph. Construction on this was begun on November 8, 1858, which was, in truth, the beginning of a mother church. In the years that followed, sixteen missions, most of which became parishes, were founded from the Jacksonville church.

Unlike the archbishop, Father Congiato was still in the mood to close missions. Since his proposal to abandon Sacred Heart Mission had backfired, he decided to close St. Paul's on the Columbia instead. In late October 1858, the last of the Jesuits there, Father Louis Vercruysse, whose sermons bore vivid testimony on the realities of hell, packed his meager belongings on the back of a horse and clopped cheerlessly through the prolific Colville Valley. He passed the old Chewelah Mission, which had been burned in contempt by settlers, and then trotted disconsolately to Sacred Heart Mission bearing his own thoughts, which could not have been happy ones.[111] St. Paul's, he had been told, would be closed only temporarily, like St. Mary's. But St Mary's had been sold eight years before. Now there were only two missions left and only God knew whether or not they would survive.

ST. MARY'S ACADEMY, PORTLAND

On February 14, 1859, when Oregon became by law a state of the union, its largest city had an estimated population of 2874 persons. This was Portland, on the west bank of the Willamette. On the southwest edge of town, at the corner of Fourth and Mill Streets, there was an unfinished frame house, two stories in height in the middle section, with small one storied wings, seventeen by seventeen feet on either side. Four high pillars supported the front facade, and between them were three sets of rails on each floor, forming porches, one above the other, somewhat suggestion of an old southern mansion. This was called Lownsdale House after its former owner, Daniel H. Lownsdale, one of the former part-owners of the Portland townsite.

Lownsdale House in its current state, offered few attractions except to vagrants who sometimes pried boards loose and found a night's shelter from Portland's heavy rains. When Archbishop Blanchet first examined it, with an eye to its use as a convent school, he was more impressed by the site than by its building. Despite the decrepit condition of the latter, he bought it, tongue in cheek, for he had neither teachers nor children to occupy it.

But he cherished hopes for both. His old friend, Bishop Bourget in Montreal, had founded three congregations of sisters, first the Sisters of Charity of Providence, then the Sisters of the Holy Names of Jesus and Mary, and finally the Sisters of St. Anne. While he, the archbishop, was away in South America gathering funds to pay the church's debts, his brother Augustin had persuaded Bourget to send five of the Sisters of Providence to the Nesqually Diocese. Then Bishop Demers had obtained three Sisters of St. Anne for the Diocese of Vancouver Island.[112] The archbishop concluded now, quite reasonably, that it was his turn. He would go to Montreal to claim his share and those would be teachers, for that was the specific purpose of Bourget's second congregation. With the sisters the Lownsdale House would do for a school. A paint job, some patching here and there, and furnishings, of course, would make the place attractive; the sisters would do the rest.

His Grace returned to Canada to arrange for the sisters, fully confident that Bishop Bourget would respond to his request. Nor was he disappointed. Thus it happened that with the support of the local bishop and her Council, the Superior General of the Congregation assigned twelve Sisters of the Holy Names to the new convent in Portland.[113]

ARRIVAL OF THE SISTERS OF THE HOLY NAMES

September 15, 1859, the day of departure for the twelve, finally came. At three in the morning, Bishop Bourget began the celebration of Mass in the Motherhouse at Longueuil. A hurried breakfast followed. Then two hours later the missionary party assembled at St. Lambert, the railroad station, to entrain for New York. Among the sisters were the following: Sister Mary Alphonse, the superior of the new convent, Sister Mary of Mercy, Sister Mary Margaret, Sister Mary of the Visitation, Sister Mary

Francis Xavier, Sister Mary of Calvary, Sister Mary Febronia, Sister Mary Florentine, Sister Mary Perpetua, Sister Mary Arsenius, Sister Mary Julia, and Sister Mary Agatha.[114] With these, to see them off at the dock in New York, were Mother Theresa of Jesus, the Superior General, and Mother Veronica of the Crucifix. This comprised fourteen. There were four more sisters, however, Sisters Agness and Prudent, who were Sisters of Providence destined to supplement the pioneers at Vancouver, and Sisters Mary of Bon Secours and Mary Providence, Sisters of St. Anne, who were new recruits for Victoria. Sixteen sisters to the Northwest! It was like an invasion, enough to make believers of all the heretics in Oregon.

With the sisters were five clerics, the archbishop himself, more complacent than usual, the indispensable Father Brouillet, and three new priests for the archdiocese, Fathers J.F. Malo, Andre Poulin, and L. Piette, the latter to serve as chaplain for the new school.[115]

At New York, when the cannon was fired and the anchor raised on the vessel called *Star of the West*, the Superior General with Mother Veronica waved the missionaries off. The ship's band played the "Star Spangled Banner" then slowly left her moorage and coasted serenely out of the harbor into the Atlantic.

On board was General Winfield Scott, of Mexican War fame, and his staff. Several times daily the general sent tropical fruits and other delicacies to the sisters, and whenever possible he engaged them in conversation, which seemed to give him comfort. Scott had an only daughter who wanted to be a nun. In vain he endeavored to thwart her hopes by sending her abroad, but at last, realizing that he was destroying her happiness, he permitted her to enter the convent. But one day soon he was called upon to follow his daughter's coffin to the grave, while he wept bitter tears. He could never be the same. All sisters were like his daughter. They gave him an opportunity to make amends.

Whenever the *Star of the West* put into port, gun salutes were sounded to acknowledge the presence of the general, and when the missionaries arrived at Asinwall, the general invited them to share his private car across the Isthmus. At Panama *The Golden Age* awaited them and they embarked when the general did, on October 7. At San Francisco they transferred to *The Northern*, bound for Fort Vancouver, where their vessel cast anchor on October 21. Another volley greeted the general, but the missionaries were greeted by Mother Joseph, who stood firmly on shore when small boats brought the newcomers to her side. There was much jubilation as old friends met, then Mass in the "Cathedral" celebrated by the archbishop. Finally the twelve Sisters of the Holy Names departed for Portland, some four hours distant by the ship that had brought them north.

Portland's citizens crowded the dock to see General Scott, while the canon boomed and bands played. Unseen in the October fog was the little procession to Lownsdale House on the edge of the woods. Unheralded, unobserved, the sisters took possession of their dilapidated convent and began on that very night, October 21, 1859, the renovations required for the opening of school on November 6.[116]

Dedicated to the Immaculate Conception, but called St. Mary's, this was not the first Catholic school in Oregon, nor the largest, but it would become, in the course of time, one of the most celebrated. On June 25, 1925, the whole world would hear about it when the United States Supreme Court rendered its decision in the Oregon Anti-Parochial School Case. By then St. Mary's Academy was in its heyday, known far and wide for its graduates trained in the genteel tradition of the sisters. But it occupied the same site to which twelve determined nuns had quietly marched when the guns were booming and the bands were playing to honor the soldier who had adopted every one of them.

7

A DECADE OF EXPANSION
1859–1869

The Northwest, which had suffered for over a century as the victim of international rivalry, began to emerge as a Land of Promise as soon as fascination with the California gold fields vanished. Even during the gold rush, the lumber industry in the Northwest flourished. One observer noted that "at the end of 1853 there were fourteen new sawmills at work around Puget Sound, and as many more on the banks of the Columbia, making lumber for the California market."[1] The discovery of gold in the upper Columbia region and the Fraser River Valley in 1857 brought a hundred thousand miners into the Northwest, while a great depression in the United States during the same year brought many thousands more who were seeking free land and a new start in life. The miners came and left for new gold fields in Idaho and Montana while the refugees of the depression remained. In 1850 the population of all of Oregon Territory was 13,294. Ten years later, in 1860, the settled population of the Northwest, divided into the State of Oregon and the Territory of Washington, was 64,059.[2]

Meanwhile, the Mullan Road, a wagon trail of 624 miles into the interior, uniting the headwaters of the Missouri with Wallula on the Columbia, was completed in 1862 at a bargain cost of $230,000[3] This primitive road bed opened a vast wilderness as large as France, and confirmed the Indians' anxieties regarding the loss of their lands. A survey for a transcontinental railroad north of the forty-fifth parallel had been completed also, though its construction was delayed by the war between the states.

The Indians, for whom the Jesuits had come in 1841, had got lost in bureaucratic shuffling in the nation's capital, but there were hopeful signs among the Jesuits that a renaissance of their own missions was about to appear. The Indian War of 1858 which had drawn the Jesuit superior, Nicholas Congiato, into the conflict, prompted him to entertain second thoughts about the missions' future. He finally accepted De-Smet's conclusion, that there would be no security for the Flatheads and Kalispels, who remained loyal to the missionaries in the late war, until the Blackfeet were converted to Christianity.

THE FIRST BLACKFEET MISSION

Thus, it happened that in the autumn of 1859, Congiato directed Father Adrian Hoecken at St. Ignatius Mission to leave with Brother Vincent Magri for the country of the Blackfeet, to establish a new mission. This was the first to be founded by the Jesuits in ten lean years.[4]

Hoecken selected a site on the Teton River near present Choteau, Montana, and, with Magri's help, built three log cabins, which looked like hovels, to provide winter quarters and a haven to study the Blackfeet language. The two Jesuits spent a miserable five months, deciding at last that the site had been ill chosen. On March 13, 1860, they moved to another, on the banks of the Sun River. There they built two more log cabins, hovels like the first, and settled down again to study the Blackfeet language. As spring passed into summer, Hoecken learned more than verbs and nouns: the Sun River Mission, like the one on the Teton, was misplaced. Blackfeet war parties frequented the area and threatened the missionaries. This was bad enough, but the most compelling argument for moving again was the remoteness of the site from the Blackfeet people. In August, 1860, Hoecken and Magri packed up what they still possessed—their axes, frying pans, bedding, and altar supplies—and moved back to St. Ignatius over the mountains to the west. The first Blackfeet Mission had been a dismal failure, but it served in a lofty manner as the chemistry that helped to produce a rebirth of the missions east of the Cascades.

FATHER LOUIS ROSSI AND PUGET SOUND

When Rossi arrived at Vancouver in 1856, he knew two languages well—his native Italian and French. He knew little or no English, so his first assignment was to learn this language from Brouillet's school teacher in Vancouver. "I placed myself," he wrote, "under the tutelage of the schoolmaster, who was a stern task-master.[5] He treated me very harshly, without any consideration for my age, without any deference to my disposition, and without paying attention to the difficulties of the language. He would often get angry when I was reading and mis-pronouncing words."[6]

Having learned enough to preach in this formidable tongue, he was permitted to travel for business or pleasure before being assigned to the mission of Puget Sound. He crossed the river to Portland "on a little runt of a screw-steamer called *The Eagle*, which was also a cockleshell of a boat." This, he said, had three successive owners, each having retired in wealth, because the cost of passage was an exorbitant, "15 francs [$3.00] for this short trip." He was directed by Bishop Blanchet to accompany him to the Cowlitz Mission to gather testimony on marriage cases. Even then the principal penance for priests was a marriage case. The heavy perfume of the spring flowers, which abounded near the mission, distracted him "from hearing crowds of witnesses testifying about the contested marriage." When all had been said, he left on a horse, "dating from the time of Noah," for Olympia "to dock after our business with the Oblates." There he had the consolation of baptizing seventeen Indians, "to whom I gave the names of my Brussels friends." He returned to Cowlitz on the ancient horse, then to Vancouver in a boat in which one of the oarsmen was so drunk he fell out and had to be assisted back in the boat at the risk of the lives of everyone. "This wretched man swore, jumped around and kicked up a row for the remaining hour of the trip."[7]

These and similar adventures prepared Rossi for the work to which Blanchet now assigned him. As Rossi noted, the bishop had divided the Nesqually diocese into four districts: "The Mountains, administered by the Jesuits;[8] Columbia, kept by the bishop for himself and the vicar general; Cowlitz, served *pro tempore* by an Oblate, and Puget Sound or Puget Strait."[9] The latter required someone who could speak English, hence Rossi's "brutal" language lessons, and appointment in November, 1857. On a good horse, presented by an American lady in Portland, and wearing a wide brimmed hat, with baggage consisting of "half a buffalo skin and a blue, woolen blanket rolled up behind the saddle for use as a bed, if the need arose, and saddle bags, one hanging on each side of my mount," he plunged north from the Cowlitz, his destination the capital of Washington Territory. He finally arrived in Olympia in pouring rain, soaked to the skin, his foppish hat dripping rivulets of water and his horse worn out from struggling through bogs up to his belly. He found three to four hundred inhabitants there and two churches, one Catholic and one Methodist, both unfinished.

"So it was to this mission that he [the bishop] sent me," wrote Rossi, "making me a priest to the Whites and vicar to the Indians, while the Oblates were priests to the Indians and vicars to the Whites. I must say, however, that they had sometimes more work as my vicars than I had as their priest."[10]

Rossi made a survey of his parish. He found the Oblate mission "an hour to go from Olympia, a little less by water," an unpretentious mission, in truth, but "perfectly suited for their goals." Port Gamble had a lumber mill that employed five to six hundred people, and he counted there "nine ships of considerable tonnage...one of them laden with 1,000,000 feet of sawn timber."[11] Seattle was a small village "but it bids fair to become very important because of fertile land and dense forests that surround it."

There were only two churches in Rossi's parish, one at Olympia and one at Fort Steilacoom. Rossi chose the latter for his first residence because there were more Catholics here than elsewhere, "about sixty faithful, soldiers as well as civilians." One observer noted that nearly one-half of the officers and a large majority of the soldiers at Fort Steilacoom were Catholics.[12] Most were Irish, of course, an unexpected bounty for which Rossi was totally grateful. Where to find Catholics? he once asked himself. "As far as the Irish were concerned, it wasn't difficult: they would recognize a priest even if he was dressed as a soldier; and as soon as they see one, they greet him by touching the rim of their hats or their caps."[13]

Rossi finally returned to Olympia to complete the church there, a chapel "which measured forty feet by twenty-five...too small to hold the people who did come." He was suffering from rheumatism, which was difficult to bear in the wet coastal climate. Much more serious were the ever-increasing stomach pains, caused in part by poor food and lodging and the fatigues of travel.[14] He had scarcely arrived in Olympia when he was summoned to Fort Steilacoom to assist at an execution. A Nisqually Chief, Leschi by name, had been convicted by alleged perjured testimony and he was sentenced to hang.

NISQUALLY CHIEF LESCHI

Before Rossi had arrived in the north littoral region of Washington, there had occurred a series of Indian disturbances sometimes called "wars," and in Seattle's case, "a siege." A few heads were cut off, literally, and Indian war canoes occupied Port Gamble, scaring the whites half to death.[15] These bloody hijinks were symptoms of the Indians' diehard frustrations, to which the settlers' response was force. A navy battleship called the *Decatur* entered the fray and plopped a few shells where the Indians were said to be hiding, and from Fort Steilacoom, Lieutenant Colonel Silas Casey, the commanding officer, trotted his army troops from one crisis to another. Like his soldiers, he tended to favor the

Indians in their struggle for survival, but the unreasonable fears of the settlers demanded action of the military. Casey and his Irish soldiers sometimes found themselves in opposition to the whites, whom they were sent to protect.

Thus it was with Chief Leschi, who had participated in the "war." To prevent his execution, Casey's men kidnapped the Sheriff and his assistants, following which there was an awful uproar.[16] The settlers finally had their way, but Casey refused them the use of the fort for the execution. They set up their gallows a mile from its barricades.[17]

Rossi rode his horse from Olympia, through the snow, to assist Leschi, who was not a Catholic because he had taken many wives. This was regarded with appropriate disparagement, even by the missionaries who had become accustomed to looking the other way from some of their neophytes' indiscretions. Chirouse, too, came to the prison where they had the hapless Leschi chained. He succeeded in converting him after he renounced all of his wives, save one. The poor fellow had nothing to lose. He would never see any of them again anyhow.

"He was hanged," said Rossi, "and he underwent his punishment with heroic courage. In his last moment he cried out, 'I pardon everyone!' and that is truly Christian. But, unfortunately, he added one exception which distressed me a lot. It was the only witness who had given evidence against him and who, as everyone knew, had never told the truth in his whole life."[18]

ROSSI'S DEPARTURE

Rossi was in his forty-first year when Leschi died. Despite increasingly bad health, he continued to make the rounds of his scattered parish. In August 1858, he visited Seattle and purchased two lots for a church there, but he remained only a brief spell, because he could find no Catholics in the village.[19] In May, 1859, he was in Port Townsend which, he decided, should replace Fort Steilacoom as his permanent residence.

"It was time for me to start building a church in Port Townsend," he wrote later. "I had already collected 5000 francs [$1,000] for it, not enough, but quite a lot when you realize that this village hadn't more than two hundred inhabitants, and hardly fifteen of them were Catholics."[20]

One of these, especially, was an excellent Catholic. "May God bless Doctor Patrick O'Brien," Rossi exclaimed. O'Brien provided the first hundred dollars for the church, and his professional care of the priest was exceeded only by his devotion to God. On May 30, 1859, a contract for the construction of the church was signed by Rossi, P.M. O'Brien [the doctor], J. McKissock, William Johnson, and Charles Center. "The church was built," Rossi continued, "a nice little church that I called *Star of The Sea* because it was situated about one hundred yards from the shore, because it was the first building one saw on entering Puget Sound from the Pacific Ocean and finally, because I had promised the Holy Virgin—the beautiful Star of the Sea I loved to invoke—that I'd give this name to the first church I built in these parts."[21]

O'Brien was the resident doctor in the naval hospital at Port Townsend. According to Rossi, this was little more than a shed where sailors served as nurses. Rossi was confined there for some months, undergoing several operations on his stomach, which had become so violently painful that Rossi was unable to travel. He reported at length to the bishop who came to realize the situation and advised Rossi to return to Steilacoom and remain there until his health improved. Rossi had other ideas. He had been advised by the doctor to return to Europe. Certainly Fort Steilacoom was the last place he wanted for a residence, because "the regimental major" there, "not even a Christian," upset him so much that his stomach pains increased.

This man was Sergeant William Archbold, a native of Kilkenny, Ireland, who put on certain airs "and thought himself important enough to be able to judge the bishop and the priests." Rossi detested him. "When he wasn't busy at his work," Rossi growled, "you'd see him at home seated in an armchair, the *Lives of the Saints* in his hand, his spectacles perched on his nose as if he were in deep contemplation before the throne of the Lord."[22]

But Archbold took advantage of the soldiers, that was the rub. When they needed money to tide them over—they received pay only four times annually—Archbold cheerfully loaned them what they needed "at fifty or sixty per cent interest rate." Archbold was one Irish Catholic who did not tip his hat to the priest.

The bishop at length came to understand that he could not keep Rossi in his diocese. He gave Rossi what he had, his blessing and letters of introduction. Rossi then went to Portland, where he awaited a ship to take him to Europe, via San Francisco. He had reserved passage on the *Northerner*, which did not arrive when due. A fortnight later, on January 7, 1860, the *Columbia* brought the bad news that the *Northerner* had gone down with all on board, including fifty passengers. With his stomach pains and his frugal baggage, Rossi boarded the *Columbia* on the same day and sailed away into the January gloom.

ADRIAN CROQUET IN OREGON

By this time a new Indian missionary, a holy man to watch, appeared in Oregon. His name was Adrian Croquet, pronounced "Crockett" by the local rustics.[23] Like DeSmet, he was from Belgium, but unlike this compatriot, he was a diocesan priest, educated at the University of Louvain for the Archdiocese of Mechlin. Born at Braine-l'Alleud, March 12, 1818, three years after the battle of Waterloo, which was fought in the fields near his parents' home, he entered an illustrious Catholic family that gave many sons and daughters to the church, including one cardinal, the incomparable Francois Mercier. Spurning opportunities for ecclesiastical advancement, he served as a country curate in his own village, where poverty occasioned by the destruction of war provided him with an opportunity to serve the poor. It is said that "more than once did he, even in the heart of winter, return home shoeless and stockingless, seeking to conceal his bare feet by covering them as well as he could with his humble, priestly robes."[24]

When the time came for Croquet to be advanced to a higher pastorate, to which his learning and zeal entitled him, he heard of the appeal for priests made through the Rector of the recently founded American College at Louvain by the Bishops of the United States. He offered himself. After some months spent in the study of English, he set sail from Ostend for New York, via London and Liverpool, in August 1859. On the nineteenth of September, his ship docked in New York, where Archbishop Blanchet awaited him. "In the company of the archbishop, five priests and seven Religious [he] sailed for Panama, from there to San Francisco, and thence to Oregon, arriving in Oregon City on the twenty-first of October 1859."[25]

During the first year in America, Croquet resided with the archbishop, leaving Oregon City whenever possible, in the company of Father Mesplie on visits to the Indian missions.

"I have just returned from an apostolic expedition," he wrote to his colleague, Father J.T. Fierens in Belgium, whom he was trying to lure to Oregon,

> that I made with Father Mesplie among several Indian tribes dwelling along the banks of the Columbia River and in the neighborhood of Mount Hood. We were everywhere most affectionately received, the chiefs honoring us by offering the calumet. Willy nilly we had to try the aroma of their tobacco, making ourselves perfectly at home with them. A certain number among them have already been regenerated in the waters of Baptism. On this very trip we baptized about a hundred. Two of these were very old men, whose

good dispositions deeply touched and edified us. One especially was admirable; for in the very words of the holy man Job, he said: "I feel that my body is about to return to the dust whence it came; for the earth is my mother, and the worms are my brothers and sisters." Many adults need only to have a priest for a short while to instruct them and prepare them for holy Baptism. They are all willing enough to become Christians.

We are now on the eve of visiting other tribes toward the southeast, near the coast of the Pacific Ocean. It is probably there that I shall have my permanent place of residence. I learned that there are seven thousand Indians in the district. The flock to be evangelized is, as you see, not a small one....

These Indians are confined to two reservations from thirty to forty miles apart. But, besides these two reservations, there are three more in the diocese, each of which has in round numbers, three thousand Indians.[26]

Croquet added that "Monsignor Blanchet and his brother, the Bishop of Nesqually, have just established at Fort Vancouver, Washington Territory, an asylum for the orphaned children of these parts."[27] He also requested that his old schoolmates at the American College may not forget to pray "for my poor Umpquas, Killimocks, etc."

By this time, Croquet had become deeply attached to the Indians and wanted nothing more. The archbishop assigned him to the Grand Ronde Reservation in Yamhill country, west of present Sheridan, Oregon. On October 11, 1860, he dispatched a very long letter to his associates at the American College, relating the details of his activities, with an eye to persuade some of them to join him in Oregon.

This letter appears here in part:

Last spring, owing to the absence of the Vicar General, Monsignor Brouillet, I spent a month at Fort Vancouver, in the home of Bishop Blanchet. April 20, I took leave of His Lordship and of the excellent Religious who conduct there a hospital, a boarding school, a day school, and an orphan asylum, with some forty inmates. My objective point on leaving Fort Vancouver was The Dalles, where I was to meet Father Mesplie, the Rector of that mission. Together we were to undertake an apostolic tour among the Indians of the Warm Spring Reservation. The first part of the voyage was made by steamer, on the Columbia River, which I ascended as far as the little city of The Dalles. Skirting the Cascades, I admired these steep, snow-capped mountains, whose base was bright with variegated flowers of spring; and the peaked rocks that looked like the impregnable walls of some mighty cities hidden behind them. I reached The Dalles at sunset, and found Father Mesplie at home. Reports that came from the Indians apprised us that they were about to leave the Reservation and that, in all likelihood, we should find but a few Redmen there. The fishing season, just begun, had already partly scattered them, and still more so, it was rumored, the alarm spread among them by the fear of the 'Snakes,' their neighbors.[28] Arrows coming from these dangerous foes had been found in the camps of the Reservation Indians, who retaliated in kind, as may be supposed. We, therefore, agreed upon the safest plan, that of visiting the wigwams we knew we should find along the banks of the Columbia, in the direction of the Deschutes River. We started on Monday, 23rd of April, and having traveled eighteen miles, we reached a place called Wanouawe. We arrived there very opportunely to bestow the consolations of the Christian religion on a sick woman, a Catholic, and to administer holy Baptism to her child. Having gone the following morning to an Indian camp three miles to the west, we baptized twenty-two children. The same day, continuing our route towards The Dalles, we baptized, at about seven miles from that city, nine children and a very old man who seemed to be entirely forsaken by everybody, but who manifested the noblest sentiments and who was perfectly resigned to his fate. We reached our home late the same evening. The next day, April 25, we crossed the Columbia, to visit Wisram, nine miles from The Dalles, where we again conferred Holy Baptism, on fourteen Indian children. The 26th, Father Mesplie left for the Warm Spring Reservation with the Chief of the Wasthos, whom we had met at our last encampment, and who told us that we should find many Indians there. It was agreed that I should stay over Sunday at The Dalles to hold divine service, after which I should overtake my colleague. I left, therefore, on the 29th with an Indian whom Father Mesplie had sent to be my guide. I spent the night at Tygh, thirty miles from The Dalles, with a Canadian named Charbonneau. Being still a novice in the horsemanship's art, I felt somewhat tired after having covered that distance in somewhat less than half a day. The next day I progressed only twenty miles, and stopped at Wapinitia, where two families of Canadian half breeds live isolated on an immense plain, near the lands of the Indian Reserve. My guide showed no disposition to stop in order to visit these families. He went on towards Warm Spring, leaving me to do the best I could. It would have been folly to risk making the rest of the journey—some thirty miles—alone. To my great regret, I was forced to there await Father Mesplie's return. However, the days which I spent with these good people were not wasted. They had several children sufficiently advanced in years to be instructed. I kept myself engaged by teaching them the catechism. On May 2, Father Mesplie arrived from the Reserve, where he had regenerated forty-nine children in the holy waters of Baptism. On the following day, after hearing confessions, we gave Holy Communion, during the Mass which we celebrated, to several members of the families whose guests we were. On our way home we had again the satisfaction at Tygh of conferring the grace of Baptism on an Indian centenarian as well as on a child of Mr. Charbonneau, by whom we were once more hospitably entertained. We reached The Dalles May 4, in the evening. We have every reason to be pleased with the way the different Indian tribes received us and met our advances. The Waskos, whom Father Mesplie had visited before, welcomed him with enthusiasm, and they made earnest entreaties to secure a resident missionary. Among their number—which reaches the three-thousand mark—there are some few who profess the Catholic Faith; many others would, in a very short time, be adequately prepared to be baptized if a priest could reside there to instruct them.[29]

After becoming engaged in other adventures, including visits to Fort Hoskins, Corvallis, and an Indian village on the Siletz River where the two priests baptized eighteen children, Croquet returned to his own mission.

"The Indians of the Grandronde have their missionary now," he wrote, "for I am again in their midst, to make my home with them henceforth."

Croquet believed in the law of residence, so he remained in his isolated reservation at all time, unless he was called for the sake of Indians to travel elsewhere. Hidden away among the fir trees and banks of Scotch broom, he gradually assembled a modest frame home, the kind of habitat only the poorest of settlers occupied, and then two churches. On December 29, 1862, he wrote about his Indians at Grand Ronde, "they have now a 45 x 20 church, which his Grace the Archbishop blessed early last October, dedicating it to St. Michael the Archangel. It is my second church: the other, under the patronage of St. Patrick is situated eighteen miles from there, among the white settlers.[30] I go there on the first Sunday of every month. Monsignor assigned a third station to me, which I am to visit from time to time.[31] There is no church in the place yet; but there is some talk of building one next spring, if the necessary funds can be raised."[32]

Much attention has been given at this point to Father Croquet, not only because he has been much neglected in our local history, but also because he was generally regarded by his contemporaries as an authentic saint. "The Saint of Oregon," his fellow priests often called him, and even Archbishop Blanchet, who tended to be critical of his priests, found only perfection in everything Croquet did. In 1862, when Louvain's Father Adolph Vermeersch arrived in Oregon, he wrote to Father De Neue in Belgium: "In a few days we intend to pay a visit to Father Croquet. The wonders that are told of that man would make you think that you are listening to the story of an anchorite and a penitent of ancient Thebais."[33]

"It was a rare good fortune," another priest wrote, "to meet 'the Saint of Oregon' when important business would cause him to call upon his archbishop. And the news of his presence in Portland would hurry

together at the archbishop's residence the priests of the whole neighborhood: they all wished to be edified by his modesty, piety and learning."[34]

"His piety was simply admirable," his biographer wrote, "especially in
regard to the Blessed Sacrament. In the most accurate and devout
manner did he say Holy Mass, whenever his unavoidable and wearisome
rides on horseback did not deprive him of an opportunity. In the church,
with the Divine Prisoner of Our Tabernacles, more than in his modest
residence, did he make his home; if he could be found nowhere else when
he was in Portland on a visit to his hospitable Archbishop, one had but to
seek him in the church. He used to read his breviary on his knees and his
private devotions took up a considerable part of his time. From repeated
observations I learned that he was in the habit of making at least one
hour's meditation every afternoon—in the church if possible."[35]

THE ARRIVAL OF NEW PRIESTS

It is not surprising then, that his appeals to priests in the American
College at Louvain got results. In addition to Father Vermeersch and
Fierens, there were two others who arrived within a brief period—
Leopold Dieleman and Aegidius Junger, who was destined to succeed
Augustin Blanchet as Bishop of Nesqually.[36]

The arrival of Vermeersch provided the archbishop with the opportunity he had long sought: The reestablishment of St. Anne's Mission
among the Umatillas. Thus the archbishop, expressing his predilection
for the Indians, assigned the young priest to eastern Oregon. On
November 1, 1865, Vermeersch selected a new site for the mission on the
south bank of the Umatilla River "presently indicated by a lone pine tree."
There he built a new church and residence, which he occupied for the
eight years following, when he was succeeded by Father Bertrand Orth,
another future bishop.[37]

Neither the archbishop nor his brother the Bishop of Nesqually had
been neglecting the recruitment of priests in Canada and Europe. Both
had caught some big fish in their nets, including one nephew, Father
Francis X. Blanchet, who chose to serve in the archdiocese. The
archbishop had appointed Fierens to be the first resident pastor of St.
Joseph's Church in Jacksonville, where he arrived on December 5, 1861.[38]
He lived in the United States Hotel, a respectable, if not as elegant a
residence as suggested by the honorific title, and later in the sacristy of
the church. When he was transferred to Portland, where he became
identified with the development and growth of the parish there, the

archbishop's nephew was sent to Jacksonville to replace him, and there he remained for twenty-five years as pastor of St. Joseph's, becoming a legend in the historic traditions of that isolated town. No one could accuse the archbishop of nepotism, for despite its charms, Jacksonville was strictly the backwater of the archdiocese. Until the next gold rush, into Idaho this time, most of the action was going on near Portland and Oregon City. Even Croquet on his Indian reservation was closer to the center of things than Francis X. Blanchet.

NEW SCHOOLS

These were the 1860's. The two groups of sisters were expanding like mercantile establishments in frontier towns. On April 23, 1860, two Sisters of the Holy Names opened a school at Oregon City in a house near the church. This was a one-story cottage with three rooms, one of which was a kitchen.[39] Six pupils reported for class the first day, occupying another room most of the day, permitting the sisters to use only the third for a convent. In the following year on February 1, four Sisters of the Holy Names opened a school at St. Paul, in the building vacated by the Sisters of Notre Dame du Namur when they left for California. On August 26, two other Sisters of the Holy Names opened the first parochial school in Portland at Third and Stark, in the parish of the Immaculate Conception. Boys, it should be noted, were accepted as students here while St. Mary's Academy continued to serve girls only.[40]

Meanwhile, the sisters at St. Mary's acquired some star boarders. On August 16, 1862, the archbishop, finally convinced that Portland, not Oregon City, was the metropolis of the future, moved his residence from one to the other, where the church of the Immaculate Conception became his pro-cathedral. He lived in a little house near the sisters' academy and ate his meals with his priests and guests at the academy. Taking care to keep everything kosher, he informed Rome of the change, requesting approval to retain the name of the Archdiocese of Oregon City to avoid confusion with the Diocese of Portland in Maine. In November 1863, Rome approved his proposal without comment.[41]

Across the Columbia River, the Sisters of Providence had gained some star boarders also. Mother Joseph, as Croquet had reported in his letter to Louvain, had opened orphanages for both boys and girls. On October 21, 1862, she purchased a new site in Vancouver for an academy, and on the following day, picking up steam as it were, she signed a three-year contract with the territorial government of Washington to care for "insane people" for eight dollars a week per patient. No one gets rich on that, but it must be admitted the mentally ill were better off with the sisters than with anyone else. For reasons difficult to accept, the government terminated these arrangements in 1866, and moved their patients to Monticello.[42]

The loss of these patients was no calamity, for the sisters were so overworked that they were forced to spend whole nights without sleep in order to make ends meet. Mother Joseph reported to Montreal regarding their manifold activities at this time:

> We were nine professed Sisters and two Novices employed here. We divide among us the care of the sacristy, our small Cathedral, the Bishopric, the college, our boarding school for girls and day pupils, an orphanage for boys, another for girls, and a little hospital. Apart from all this, we visit the sick in their homes. The entire establishment is composed of about one hundred persons occupying six separate houses, five of which are built on a two-acre lot of ground. The sixth house is located about four acres distant and is occupied by the orphan boys. All the persons of the establishment, with the exception of the last mentioned, are fed from the same kitchen managed by a poor little novice with two orphan girls to help her, and these latter must have time off for their school. . . . [43]

It was difficult for Mother Joseph to conceal the special affection she had "for the orphan boys." She had acquired a house for them "a former hotel, 45 x 24 feet" in which there was a good kitchen. The bishop had donated $200 for lumber to make over the building "from cellar to attic" but since this was not sufficient, an officer at the Fort "of high rank" made up the difference of cost and a group of Canadians provided volunteer labor. Mother Joseph was learning that everybody loved *orphan boys*. She soon had forty of them ensconced in the new home, which she named St. Vincent. The boys, she said, wore "nice little costumes on Sundays; they have their place in the church pews behind the orphan girls who also dress in uniform." Only one problem appeared. Strangers still took St. Vincent's for a hotel and periodically invaded the place looking for a room. Mother Joseph had a fence put up, not to keep the boys in, but the strangers out.[44]

THE OBLATES AT TULALIP

Father Chirouse was still around, though most of the Oblates had gone by now to develop their missions in British Columbia. By the end of 1860, only Chirouse and Durieu were left. D'Herbomez, the Oblate superior, had turned over St. Joseph's Mission near Olympia to Bishop Blanchet and the two Oblates had moved to the Tulalip Reservation where they hastily erected a little shanty to serve as a church, a school, and residence.

Father Rossi, before his departure, had visited them there and described what he saw:

The new settlement had only one hut, made from tree bark, a few planks and wisps of straw. The inside was in keeping with the outside. A few stools, a table, and a newly-invented fireplace. That was the furniture and the comfort in this abode.... A new eight by six feet holes served as bedrooms. Each one of these contained a kind of box—seven by three feet and six inches high—in which there was a bag of straw, the same kind of pillow, and a few woolen blankets.[45]

Chirouse called this St. Francis Xavier of the Snohomish, calling attention, perhaps, to the language of the people there.[46] Some months later, he requested formal governmental approval to build a permanent mission. Michael Simmons, the Territorial Indian Agent for Puget Sound, recommended this petition to the region's Superintendent of Indian Affairs and the desired permission was granted. Chirouse then supervised the construction of larger buildings, planted extensive gardens and organized a boy's band. The latter became famous. With Chirouse directing its troop of dusky players, it presented concerts in villages and camps everywhere, taking, on each occasion, an opportunity to pass the hat for the support of the school.[47] By 1860, two hundred Indians had settled near the mission and fifteen pupils were in attendance in the school, which means, I suppose, that everyone played in the band.[48]

During that same year, Simmons came to Tulalip to hold a conference with the tribes. Before leaving, he appointed Chirouse as the provisional reservation agent,[49] and gave him every possible mark of approval for serving Indians on other Puget Sound Reservations, the Swinomish, Lummi, Muckleshoots, and Fort Madison. Simmons also recommended that Chirouse be formally appointed a salaried teacher to the Indians of the Tulalip Reservation.

This recommendation was accepted and on January 1, 1861, the Oblate school was opened under government auspices. In his first annual report as teacher, Chirouse stated that the school had twenty-five pupils, twenty boys and five girls. After giving an account of a typical school day, he complained bluntly about the school's meager resources, the stingy appropriations allotted for the upkeep and care of the children and of the consequent need for using his own funds to feed, clothe, and educate the students. "As yet," he added sarcastically, "there is no [government] schoolhouse on the reservation. I am obliged to use for this purpose the lodges of the Indians or a wretched loghouse...."[50] The number of scholars he could accommodate was small and there was no hope of increasing it until boarding facilities were provided "to keep the children separated from their parents."

According to the Treaty of Point Elliott in 1855, the government had promised that "within a year" an agricultural and industrial school to accommodate one thousand students would be available to the tribes free of charge. Medical supplies and facilities were also promised. But nothing had been forthcoming. The lone teacher provided was a low-salaried Catholic priest who had to use his frugal income to support the students.

The laments of Chirouse finally bore fruit. In 1863 the Indian Bureau authorized the construction of a dormitory and a house for the teacher. The Chirouse report for 1864 reflected these improvements.

"Thirty seven pupils," he wrote, "have attended school with an average attendance of twenty-nine.... I am very happy to give you my thanks for the very comfortable dwelling you have provided for us, and also for the new building you are erecting for the female department. In accordance with the arrangement made with Mr. Hale, the Superintendent, and yourself, I took the necessary steps to secure the services of two Sisters of Charity[51] for this reservation. I am happy to say I succeeded; the sisters are now ready to come as soon as their house is finished."[52]

Because of lack of funds, which were being squandered on bullets and cannon balls for the Civil War, the school for girls built at Tulalip was not put into use until 1868. Two Sisters of Providence arrived that year and Chirouse in his report provided cautious comments about their success. "The children who are in charge of the sisters are progressing favorably and though being about a month at school, they are giving evident signs of reform both in cleanliness and general deportment."[53]

Indian Agent Henry C. Hale, demonstrating that not all bureaucrats were prejudiced, was lavish in his praise of both schools. "They [the Oblates and the Sisters of Providence] are doing a great and good work, and will meet their reward in the future by seeing their scholars grow up to be good men and women. Too much cannot be said in praise of this good work."[54]

For the Oblates not all was school routine or band concerts. As priests, their first concern was the care of souls in mission churches, three of which were constructed in a seven year period. In 1861, Chirouse acquired two of these churches. The first called St. Joachim's, was built in an old Lummi village on the shores of Bellingham Bay by the first Catholic Lummi chief, whose name was David Crocket.[55] The second church, called St. Peter's, was built for the Suquamish Indians near "Old Men House" on the Fort Madison Reservation. Chief Jacob was the principal promoter of this church and Chief Seattle attended it in his old age.[56]

By August 1868, when the Sisters of Providence arrived, Chirouse had erected another church on Fidalgo Island, on the Swinomish Reservation. Apparently this was called St. Paul's[57] This served the needs of the Indians, but eventually whites from La Conner attended Mass there, until they had their own church in 1872.[58] When the Swinomish church was first completed, the register of the Oblate Fathers for the Puget Sound area showed a total of 3,811 baptisms since their arrival twenty years earlier. This success was due, in part, to the inherent peaceful dispositions of the Puget Sound Indians, but one cannot overlook the influence of Chirouse and his confreres. Chirouse especially was the great teacher and father of these people, who reckoned their time for many years after his departure by "before Father Chirouse came" and "after Father Chirouse came."[59]

GIORDA: SECOND FOUNDER OF THE JESUIT MISSIONS

Among the Jesuits now there was another DeSmet. His name was Joseph Giorda. Born to wealth and nobility near Turin, Italy on March 19, 1823, he entered the Jesuit Order in his twenty-third year. He came to America in 1858 and after three years of preparation in St. Louis, he arrived at the Coeur d'Alene Mission, already a mature, prudent man with a young man's heart. It must be admitted that he had trouble with the English language, which he spoke like an untutored immigrant, but he was otherwise a brilliant thinker and a deeply spiritual priest. Shorter than most, olive complexioned and handsome in features, like a papal diplomat, he won everybody with his kindness and other-worldly simplicity.

His arrival marked the beginning of a new era for the Jesuit missions. In 1861, the Jesuits had only two missions left, St. Ignatius and Sacred Heart, and these were staffed by a scant thirteen men who were discouraged and overworked. White men, seeking gold, had begun to penetrate the interior, bringing with picks and shovels their booze and dice and camp followers, not to mention the lawless hangers-on who robbed stages and murdered the defenseless. What is now Idaho and Montana were drawn into such criminal violence that only determined vigilantes could restore order by wholesale executions and these required several years.

Giorda was first assigned to reestablish St. Peter's Mission among the Blackfeet. Thus, in the autumn of 1861, he set out for Blackfeet country with two Jesuit companions, bringing on the backs of their horses and in one wagon the essentials for a winter at Fort Benton on the Missouri.[60] One of his companions was Father Imoda, who had shared the hardships of the first Blackfeet missions with Hoecken. Imoda was younger in age by six years, but he knew the country well and had studied the Blackfeet dialect for some months. It was doubtlessly Imoda who had persuaded Congiato, the Jesuit superior, to make another attempt in establishing the Blackfeet mission.

The Jesuits spent the winter learning the language and seeking a site for their new mission. At last they found what they wanted, on the Missouri River near present Ulm, and on February 12, 1862, they took possession of it, their third site for St. Peter's Mission. While his companions were felling cottonwood trees to provide shelter, Giorda inspected the premises more carefully. He explored the shoreline by walking on the ice of the river, which bore his weight until he moved out where the current was strong beneath him. The ice gave way and Giorda fell through as far as his arms and there he was suspended, shouting for help, in imminent danger of being pulled under to his destruction. An Indian who pitched his tepee near the river, heard his shouts and skillfully dragged him to safety with his lariat.[61]

Realizing that, after God, he owed his life to this Indian, Giorda there and then made a solemn vow to devote himself for the rest of his life to the salvation of these Indians, should his superiors approve of it. Thus he was confirmed in his vocation as an Indian missionary and, in the struggle that lay ahead, he favored support of the Indian missions whenever there was a reasonable choice.

St. Peter's needed his energy and influence. Beset on all sides with dangers, especially from prowling warriors from Canada, the Jesuits suffered much from poverty. Their cabins with low ceilings and bare earthen floors, warmed by open fireplaces that filled the rooms with smoke on damp days, provided little comfort in the bitterly cold winters and hot dry summers. They lacked medicine, food, and even decent clothing, and when their conventional cotton or woolen underclothes wore out, they were forced to use others made of buckskin that became so lousy in winter that they put them outside at night to freeze out the lice. When, thanks to some kind benefactors, they were provided better clothes, Indians lurked about eager to steal them. On one occasion, Giorda was captured by a small group of hostiles and was stripped to the skin in weather that was forty degrees below zero.[62] Yet, the Jesuits remained, with more than modest success in converting the Blackfeet.[63]

Meanwhile, on January 21, 1862, Giorda was appointed by Father Peter Beckx, the Jesuit General, to replace Congiato as superior of the Rocky Mountain Mission. As soon as possible, the new superior departed for California to claim his Jesuits who had been diverted to teaching there. He was able to jar loose a few, including Father Ravalli, who had been pressed into service as Novice Master at Santa Clara. Giorda was a patient man, as gentle as a dove, but henceforth, Jesuits assigned to the Rocky Mountain Mission arrived at their destination or he knew the reasons why not. No longer was there a practice of what contemporary Jesuits called "hi-jacking," and the Rocky Mountain Mission soon began to prosper.

In the spring of 1862, Giorda assigned two more Jesuits to the Blackfeet mission—Father Joseph Menetrey and Brother D'Agnostino—making it clear to all where he had lost his heart. He strengthened existing missions and very gradually reopened others. Ironically, because of the formation of towns for whites occasioned in part by the gold rush, his early years as superior were occupied with the beginnings of non-Indian parishes, mostly in Montana.

During this same period, two secular priests were establishing the church for whites in southern Idaho. These were Fathers Mesplie and Poulin, both of whom were attached to the archdiocese. It will be recalled that nine years prior to this, when the Walla Walla Diocese was suppressed, the territory of the Archdiocese of Oregon City and the Diocese of Nesqually were redefined.[64] Separated by the forty-sixth parallel, each extended from the Pacific Ocean to the Rocky Mountains. Thus, western Montana and northern Idaho belonged to Nesqually and the southern portion of Idaho to Oregon City. Discovery of gold in the latter now prompted the archbishop to assign two of his priests to that area.

GOLD RUSH CHURCHES IN IDAHO

Like many of his predecessors at the altar, Father Croke had departed for California, the archbishop's "very humble and obedient servant" to the end.[65] He had served the Northwest well, before he was recalled to San Francisco for higher things. Others took his place in western Oregon, priests like Francis X. Blanchet, J.F. Fierens, Adrian Croquet, and Andre Poulin.

The latter was assigned to build a church in Marysville, now called Corvallis, Oregon, and he started his fund drive right at home by taking one hundred dollars from the amused archbishop. After several months he had collected another twelve hundred dollars and sundry other gifts, such as one cow, some wheat, and a plow, and he began construction at last on a frame church. This was completed and dedicated by the archbishop in honor of St. Mary on February 18, 1861.[66]

The loss of Father Croke was costly. Not only was he the most successful beggar in the archdiocese, but he was needed rather desperately to build pioneer churches in Idaho which, like Montana, was swarming with miners.[67]

Mining had begun in southern Idaho in the spring of 1862 when a group of twelve prospectors from Auburn, Oregon, wandered into the mountains east of Oregon and discovered gold in what became the Boise Basin. Attacked by Indians who killed their leader,[68] they retreated to Walla Walla to organize a larger party, fifty-four in number, and returned to the Basin in October. With the arrival of other prospectors, many of whom were of Irish origin, the settlement was given the name of New Dublin.[69] By this time the "secret" of gold in Idaho and neighboring Montana was known by every prospector from Mexico to British Columbia.

Father Mesplie, who had worked with both Indians and whites for ten years, seemed to be the logical priest to send to the diggings to build churches and to shrive and bury the Irish Catholics when occasion required it. He had built two churches at The Dalles, one to replace the church that burned down, and another larger one to accommodate a growing parish. This last one, measuring thirty by seventy feet, and located on the corner of Lincoln and Third Streets, was completed in 1861 when Mesplie was not only the pastor of The Dalles, with two Indian reservations in his care, but also the administrator of St. Patrick's Church in Walla Walla.[70] He had started St. Patrick's from scratch. It will be recalled that he enjoyed a happy rapport with soldiers on the frontier, so at Walla Walla he appealed to the Catholics at the fort to help him with his task. A certain Michael Kenny and others responded generously, assembling under the priest's directions a rude chapel consisting of poles stuck in the ground, roofed over with shakes. This chapel had no flooring, and only one log bench for the use of the ladies. When Father Mesplie offered the first Mass, there were present only two soldiers and a half dozen Indian women, but by the end of that year, 1859, St. Patrick's Mission consisted of seventy-five adults and fifty-four children.

Mesplie, despite his many labors, had put on middle-age weight. When he left The Dalles for his new assignment in Idaho, he was almost forty years old. Someone described him as "short and stout with keen black eyes and cropped hair."[71] His heavy eyelids drooped sleepily, giving his face a puffy look. His long black clerical coat scarcely concealed his amply covered bones, and his short arms and stubby hands, one of which often clutched a walking stick, made him appear shorter than he was. A genial man, he was a general favorite despite his inability to preach in the king's English. His greatest problem, however, was impatience. He was one of those hyperactive persons who put into immediate execution whatever occurs to their minds and he expected results as soon as he acted.

Father Andre Poulin, pastor of Corvallis, was just the opposite. He was orderly and patient, a keeper of accounts and a follow-up clerk in the wake of Mesplie's turmoil. Together they made a great team.

The archbishop appointed Mesplie first. On June 13, 1863, he directed Mesplie to proceed to the Boise Basin and establish there whatever churches that would be proper. Mesplie arrived at the Basin and was astounded to find the population of the district to be between ten and fifteen thousand, many of whom were Irish, recently removed from the exhausted mines of California and Nevada. In September, the archbishop dispatched Father Poulin to assist him. What followed is rather bewildering, by reason of the tornado-like activities of the two priests. Here is a verbatim report:

> With Father Poulin, [Mesplie] at once began soliciting funds for building churches in four towns. Idaho City, the largest of the four communities, received earliest attention, and St. Joseph's church (20' x 75') was ready for services in November, 1863. At the dedication services on November 15 'Father Mesplie delivered an earnest and—but for a difficulty in articulating plainly in English—a very impressive discourse....' St. Thomas' Church (20' x 40') at Placerville was dedicated December 20, 1863; and St. Dominic's Church (20' x 40') at Centerville, December 25, 1863. Though services had begun in Pioneerville in 1863, it was not until September 25, 1864, that the Church of St. Francis there was dedicated; a remodeled building bought in the summer of 1864. Before providing for this house of worship Father Mesplie preached a mission there January 1 to 3. 'Sometime after the arrival of Father Poulin in September, 1863, the two priests visited the newly laid out settlement of Boise City, a settlement growing up about the Fort which had been built by the Army in 1863 to provide protection from the Indians for the gold rushers to the Basin. The town was just beginning, but accidentally they met the John O'Farrell family, whose cabin became the chapel for the first Mass in Boise City. Father Poulin became the resident

pastor of Idaho City, while Father Mesplie residing at Placerville, attended mostly to the other churches in the Basin, occasionally visiting Boise City. Services on Christmas day, 1863, were held at Centerville, Placerville,and Idaho City. On April 23, 1864, Father Mesplie's services were announced for Placerville, Centerville, and Pioneerville, on succeeding Sundays at 10:30.

In 1864, gold was discovered in Owyhee County across the Snake River to the southward. The first miners in Owyhee came from Placerville, a town in which there were relatively few Catholics. In 1865, they discovered the rich Poorman mine and Silver City began. Father Mesplie visited the new community from time to time, holding services in makeshift buildings. It was not until 1868 that Father Poulin bought the Methodist Church there and remodeled it for a Catholic Church which he placed under the patronage of St. Andrew.[72]

FIRST SISTERS IN IDAHO

The pace took its toll. First Mesplie, then Poulin had to return to Portland to recuperate, the latter taking the opportunity to persuade the Sisters of the Holy Names to open a school in Idaho City.

The sisters were most willing, but they had recently opened a school in Salem and were short of teachers. On August 17, 1863, three of them had arrived in Salem and had moved into a two story building that formerly had been a Masonic Hall. This was dedicated as Sacred Heart Academy on August 22, 1863, and the pastor, Father Dieleman, one of Croquet's acquisitions from Louvain, threw enough holy water on the building to put out a fire. He was quoted as saying, "The devil that day had danced his last polka in the building." There was not much love lost between the Catholics and the Masons.

On September 7, the academy was formally opened for eighty students, which must have surprised everybody, since Salem was regarded as a solidly Protestant town and did not as yet have a completed Catholic church.

The sisters eventually relented under pressures from Mesplie and Poulin, and on December 13, 1867, three of them, accompanied by Father F.P. Cazeau, left Portland for Idaho City, which they reached on December 21. On January 13, 1868, they opened St. Mary's Academy, which was the first Catholic school in Idaho.[73] The occasion was generally regarded as one of many signs that the Territory of Idaho was ready for a bishop. While it must be acknowledged that the territory was far more advanced than the Oregon wilderness in 1843, when Blanchet was appointed vicar apostolic, the American bishops, especially the

Blanchets, should have recognized the nature of the territory's population in the 1860's. Here today, gone tomorrow best describes the gold seekers who represented the greater portion of Idaho's people.

SEARCH FOR A BISHOP OF IDAHO

The fact is, a bishop was being selected for Idaho at this very time. The names of three Jesuits had been submitted to the Sacred Congregation of the Propaganda by Archbishop Kenrick of St. Louis. In a letter of February 10, 1866 to Archbishop Odin of New Orleans, Kenrick revealed that he had requested the Sacred Congregation to erect the territories of Idaho and Montana into a vicariate apostolic. He submitted the names of DeSmet, Giorda, and Grassi as suitable incumbents for the proposed vicariate. "The two last [Giorda and Grassi] are known to me only through Father DeSmet. They are already engaged in the Indian Mission of these two territories."[74]

DeSmet, having learned that his name was on the *terna*, wrote to the general: "If my name appears in the list of Monseigneur of St. Louis, as the Reverend Father Provincial assures me it does, I take it that it is done with the idea of filling up the list, on which ordinarily three names are entered. In sincere conviction of my lack of virtue and talents for such a task and believing that your paternity will be consulted in so important an affair, I consider myself perfectly safe against such a danger."[75]

The mystery in all of this is the intervention of the Archbishop of St. Louis in business that primarily concerned the Archbishop of Oregon City. Kenrick, usually at odds with the Jesuits, was able to rise above this in recommending Jesuits for the hierarchy; but his reservations about the appointment of a Canadian priest for Oregon in the first place seem to have survived these twenty-three years, during which there was little rapport between the Blanchets and other American prelates. As noted above, Blanchet's appeal to non-Americans for help in his financial crises indicated his standoffishness toward American bishops, and Kenrick's correspondence with Odin, rather than Blanchet, seemingly indicated his lack of confidence in the Blanchets, whose jurisdiction was involved in the Idaho matter.

FURTHER DEVELOPMENTS EAST OF THE CASCADES

Giorda and Grassi, meanwhile, were entirely in ignorance of the proposal to make one of them bishop. Both probably would have enjoyed the thought of being summoned to the hierarchy as a huge joke, for neither entertained the slightest suspicion of being worthy of it.

Not to be outdone by the two zealous diocesan priests in southern Idaho, Mesplie and Poulin, Giorda was dashing about Montana on horseback, seeking those who needed spiritual or temporal succor. In March 1863, he offered the first Mass in the Deer Lodge area. He assigned Brother Claessens, one of Montana's first Jesuits, the task of building a church for whites at Hell Gate, near present Missoula. Completed in the summer of 1863 and called St. Michael's, this was the first Catholic Church for whites in Montana. On October 31 Giorda made his first visit to Alder Gulch, a roaring mining camp later known as Virginia City. He celebrated the first Mass there on the following morning, the Feast of All Saints, and remained in the area nearly a month. In late autumn he sent Joset to re-open St. Paul's Mission near Kettle Falls, and Father Joseph Menetrey to take up his residence at the Immaculate Conception Church for whites near Colville.[76]

Giorda's trouble with English was like Mesplie's, but unlike Mesplie, he spoke four or five other languages very well. One of these was Blackfeet. His predilection for the Blackfeet people had not blinded him to the risks he and his brother Jesuits were taking by living on the Missouri. He had selected another site for a mission, the fourth St. Peter's, less vulnerable in these dangerous times when the Indians, quite reasonably I think, were becoming restless with the heavy influx of the whites. He sent two Jesuits to this location at Bird Tail Rock, near present Cascade, to build another mission there in the event of open hostilities.

MONTANA'S FIRST SISTERS

Prodded now by Father Urban Grassi, the new superior at St. Ignatius, Giorda began to negotiate with Mother Joseph in Vancouver to obtain sisters for a hospital and school at St. Ignatius. The proposal doubtlessly intrigued Mother Joseph, but the demands being made upon her and her very limited supply of sisters delayed action for some time. On November 25, 1863, the Sisters of Providence had opened an academy at Steilacoom in the Puget Sound region, where the white population had increased rapidly since the settlement of Seattle in 1851. Then, on February 18, 1864, another group of Providence sisters had established St. Vincent's Academy at Walla Walla at the request of Father Brouillet, Mesplie's successor, to whom the sisters would refuse nothing. St. Vincent's was a two-story frame building on Fifth and Poplar Streets, erected by Brouillet at the cost of seven thousand dollars. The sisters enrolled eighty boys and girls on the first day, as had happened also at Sacred Heart

Academy in Salem. In Walla Walla this relatively high attendance merely indicated how far the Catholics had come since St. Patrick's Church was opened less than five years earlier.

Giorda's appeals eventually bore fruit. Mother Joseph agreed to send four sisters, who came directly from the Motherhouse in Montreal, arriving at Vancouver on July 11, 1864. The names of these adventurous sisters, the first in Montana, were as follows: Sister Mary of the Infant Jesus, Superior, Sister Mary Edward, Sister Remi, and Sister Paul Miki, who was regarded as "very delicate."[77]

In September, Giorda and Father Gazzoli met the sisters at Walla Walla, where they had arrived by river boat. By the seventeenth of that month, all preparations for the journey to St. Ignatius had been completed. Giorda made the sign of the cross and set out, leading the way. In the entourage were Giorda, Gazzoli, and Father Francis Kuppens, a greenhorn Jesuit enroute to the missions, all riding horses, then the four sisters also on horseback, seated sideways like the modest ladies of those gentle times, and finally a large prairie schooner heavily loaded with baggage and supplies, driven by two Irishmen who were doubtlessly embarrassed by such holy company.

The sisters soon became accustomed to this kind of travel. Giorda was the personification of gallantry, and even the two Irishmen acted like perfect gentlemen, as they say, and the voyage went very well, except that one sister got kicked by a horse that was no respecter of persons. And Gazzoli's horse got away when he was alone, and he had to walk two days to the Coeur d'Alene Mission without anything to eat. Everybody, even Gazzoli, finally arrived at the mission landing dock on the river,[78] where the Indians had lined up to greet the "Lady Black Robes." After a brief rest, Giorda and Kuppens departed with the sisters for the tiresome trip over the mountains. On October 15, they reached Frenchtown and on the following day celebrated their arrival in Montana by having Mass in the small log church called St. Louis, just completed there by Brother Claessens.[79] On the next day, October 17, after a month on the trail, Giorda led the five new missionaries into the Indian village at St. Ignatius and introduced them to the Jesuits there and to the Indians, who showed them every mark of hospitality.

Giorda did not tarry long. With his bacon, beans, and flour in one saddle bag, portable Mass kit and clothes in the other, and young Father Kuppens in tow, he trotted off to the diggings at Silver Creek in the Helena area, some three days to the east. On October 30, Kuppens offered Mass for the whites, Giorda for the Indians. Kuppens remained there and built a church of hewn logs down by the creek. The first Mass in this was celebrated on Easter Sunday, 1865. Unfortunately, this small church was used for less than two years, because the miners departed when the gold gave out, and the logs were dismantled and sawed up for firewood.

EARLY CHURCHES FOR WHITES

Down in Oregon, Father Dieleman finally completed his church at Salem. This was dedicated under the title of St. John by Archbishop Blanchet on April 10, 1864.[80] If His Grace was pleased with the pastor's unique accomplishment, a thriving parish with a church and school in a citadel of Masonic power, he showed it in a strange manner, for he transferred poor Dieleman to Canyon City, Oregon, a gold rush town about two miles from present John Day. There he had to start over. In July he started construction on the church for Canyon City, called St. Andrew's, and he celebrated the first Mass in it in November. It was completed on December 20 at a total cost, down to the penny, of $2,201.67. Dieleman was able to enjoy St. Andrew's for only ten months before he was transferred again, this time to The Dalles. Such was the fate of the pioneer priests. They labored and spun and seldom reaped. At least this was true of many of them, though occasionally one appeared who prospered in more than spiritual ways.

CHARLES VARY AND PREFONTAINE AT STEILACOOM

Such a one was Father Francis X. Prefontaine, usually recognized as the founder of the church in Seattle. Prefontaine was another French Canadian, born in the same year, 1838, that Blanchet and Demers established the church in Oregon, in the same little town below Montreal where the Sisters of the Holy Names had their motherhouse.[81] Ordained by Archbishop Bourget on November 20, 1863, he volunteered for mission work in the Diocese of Nesqually. He arrived here in February 1864. One month later he was assigned to Steilacoom, where there was a sisters' school already, and a resident priest, successor to Father Rossi. His name was Father Charles Vary.

Vary was not the aristocratic type. He was born in Longueuil near Montreal about three years earlier than Prefontaine. It has been said that he earned his way through school by working in lumber yards, but he was not physically a strong man or "a joiner" like Prefontaine. Ascetic looking, slim and rigidly disciplined, he presented the appearance of a pious, perhaps too solemn schoolmaster, who regarded life as a very serious matter indeed; just the opposite of Prefontaine about whom it was said that he even enjoyed the sport of bear hunting.[82] One cannot imagine Charles Vary hunting bears.

At first delighted with his new assistant, Vary directed Prefontaine to care for the whites on Puget Sound outside the immediate vicinity of Steilacoom. Hence he had charge of the Olympic peninsula, the islands of the sound and the mainland as far as British Columbia.

Sadlier's Catholic Directory for 1865 described the territory covered by the two priests as follows:

Steilacoom, Immaculate Conception: Rev. C. Vary; Rev. F.X. Prefontaine.

Cowlitz, St. Francis Xavier's
Olympia, St. Michael's
Seattle
Port Townsend
Whitby Island
Port Madison, Port Gamble
Whatcom[83]

In other words, the Steilacoom parish covered all of Rossi's former parish, the area currently occupied by the vast majority of the people in the State of Washington.

Prefontaine needed no one to tell him on which side his bread was buttered. He began his apostolate by writing to the bishop to demand an increased in salary from $150 a year to $200, and he threatened to return to Canada if he did not receive the additional fifty dollars.[84] Blanchet was shocked. He replied that it was not possible to augment the priests' income then and he begged Prefontaine not to give the people an occasion to think that priests were more interested in their own well-being than in the good of religion.

It soon became obvious that Vary and Prefontaine, who was a loner, could not get along together, so Blanchet sent Prefontaine to Port Townsend, where he became the second resident priest, accountable for the entire region of Puget Sound. What Chirouse was doing for the Indians north and west of Seattle, Prefontaine now was doing for the whites south and east of Port Townsend, Seattle included.[85]

THE CHURCH IN SEATTLE

Prefontaine was not the first priest in Seattle. This honor should be awarded to Bishop Demers who visited the one-year old settlement in

August, 1852, enroute to Vancouver Island. He conducted the first formal religious service in Seattle's history in Yesler's new cook-house on what is now the site of Pioneer Square. Arthur Denny, one of the settlers, prepared an altar for Mass, which was celebrated on Sunday morning, August 22. Everyone in the village attended the Mass, during which His Lordship preached on the subject of charity.[86]

There is something refreshing in this vignette in Seattle's bawdy history, particularly in view of the indifferent years that followed, during which the Catholic Church, always on the defensive, enjoyed little or no acceptance by the establishment.

Demers, of course, had his own diocese to administer, and there was no one to follow up on his happy beginnings until Rossi came, and then Prefontaine. The latter as tough in body and spirit as a *voyageur*, used as little of his time as possible in Port Townsend, buzzing about instead, "anywhere and everywhere," as one of his contemporaries observed.[87] One of his experiences during this period deserves recognition, I think, for it provides some insight on the hardships of the itinerant missionary in western Washington:

> One afternoon in the fall of 1866 two Indians knocked at my door. To judge from their conversation, which I did not understand very well, it was a sick call at Whatcom. I hurriedly packed my valise, fastened the door and took my place in their canoe. The day was far from pleasant, the sky cloudy, the sea heavy and a sharp wind blew from the Straits. Suddenly we found ourselves in the power of the swells, and our canoe was cast on a small, deserted island. For three days the weather kept us prisoners. A few biscuits formed our only provisions. We resorted to clam digging; but even our clams we had to eat raw on account of the absence of matches; which in my haste I had forgotten. Our beds were of the most rudimentary kind, and with a drizzling rain and without covering the mornings found me thoroughly chilled. But greater than my desire for food and my sensation of cold was my anxiety about the dying man.
>
> Finally the weather relented and we arrived without further mishap at Whatcom, a small mining and lumber station. You may judge of my surprise when I was informed that my presence was required not for funeral purposes, but for a marriage ceremony!
>
> Men in those days were many in camps like Whatcom; but white women were scarce; and thus it happened that many wooed for this one woman's hand. In those days it was Hobson's choice as far as the selection of a wife was concerned; but a woman had her difficulties in choosing a husband out of the many. Bloodshed was not rarely the consequence of such choice.
>
> The girl had not even made up her mind regarding her favorite, but finally followed my advice and chose the one she liked the best.

The ceremony over, we settled down to a substantial wedding meal. General good feeling and harmony seemed to prevail. Suddenly two bullets crashed through the window, one passing rather dangerously close to my head, and put an end to the feast. It was evidently the revenge of the jilted lover. The would-be assassin was never discovered.

On my return trip the canoe was again driven ashore at Kellogg's Point on Whitby Island, and only with great difficulty, including a long tramp, I reached Port Townsend two days later.[88]

SCHOOLS IN VANCOUVER AND WALLA WALLA

While Prefontaine raced back and forth over his broad territory, other churches, missions, and schools were popping up all over the Northwest in the great surge of the 1860's. Two new schools for boys appeared within a short period. The first, in the latter part of 1864, was Holy Angels College, established by Bishop Blanchet in Vancouver. Its teachers were provided by the local clergy, some of them attached to the cathedral and since all became famous for one reason or another, they are listed herewith: The director or principal was Father Aegidius Junger; the prefect for the boys and assistant to the director was Father Paul Mans, who brought grief to the heart of his bishop by becoming a Jesuit; Louis St. Onge was listed as "teacher" and J.B. Boulet as "lay teacher."[89] Actually, Boulet's status was a bit more interesting, he was an ex-seminarian, fed up with study and taking a break to ponder his future.

The other school was in Walla Walla. Called St. Joseph's College, it was founded on July 10, 1865, by Father Brouillet whose zeal knew no bounds. In its first year there were forty boys in attendance; most of them were in their early teens, taught by a devoted layman named H.H. Lamarche, a kind of Mr. Chips, who remained with successive groups of boys like them for fifteen hectic years.[90]

About the same time, Brouillet replaced Mesplie's rude-hut-church with a second one, also called St. Patrick's. This was dedicated on August 20, 1865. Its fate was so extraordinary that some mention of it should be made. In 1870, just five years after it was completed, it was judged to be too small for its need. So, the contractor cut off the sanctuary, the head as it were, and added a long section to the nave before attaching it again. Perhaps that was a mistake. Twelve years later the church was too small again.

THE THOMAS FRANCIS MEAGHER AFFAIR

This pattern of growth was reflected in the political development of the entire Northwest. In January 1863, an effort was made to establish

Washington Territory as a state. This failed and the net result was that Idaho Territory was organized consisting of the present states of Idaho, Montana, and Wyoming, more than three hundred thousand square miles.[91] But in March 1864, Montana Territory was created, and four years later Wyoming was detached from Idaho. Thus Idaho was reduced to its present form, about eighty-five thousand square miles.

Idaho's first territorial legislature convened on December 7, 1863, at Lewiston, which had become a center for supplies for the mining activities in the mountains to the east. Lewiston, like Walla Walla then, had become a population center of the interior with some twelve hundred souls sadly in need of a priest, but none as yet was available.

The Northwest in this respect was not unlike the rest of the United States, which experienced a Catholic growth between 1840 and 1860 far greater than the general population.[92] This was common knowledge held by Catholics for they experienced the shortage of priests in their cities and towns almost everywhere. In July 1865, General Thomas Francis Meagher, a surviving hero of the Civil War, enroute to Montana to assume the office of acting governor, visited Archbishop John Ireland and Bishop Thomas Grace in St. Paul to discuss this problem as it was related to the church in Montana.[93] Seemingly well informed, he laid open to both prelates his proposal for providing priests. Ireland wrote about it some years later:

> [General Meagher] had several conversations with Bishop Grace and myself about his plans for the spread of the Holy church in Montana. It was, he repeatedly said, his wish to colonize the territory with Catholics—drawing principally from Irishmen in Ireland and Irishmen in America with whom naturally his influence was potent. He would at once take steps to secure priests and would write to All Hallows' College in Dublin to engage there ten students for whom tuition he would make himself responsible. He would furthermore, he added, take steps to have a Bishop in Montana. Bishop Grace told him that the mode of procedure to have Montana erected to a Diocese was to put himself in communication with the Bishop of St. Louis, under whose Metropolitan jurisdiction the greater portion of Montana then lay. With those purposes of General Meagher I was quite conversant, having heard him time and again and having encouraged him very much to go forward and become the great founder of the Church in Montana.

> When the Bishops met in the Second Plenary Council of Baltimore—this I heard from Bishop Grace on his return from the Council, and again and again at latter dates—the Archbishop of St. Louis stated that he had letters from General Meagher and Mrs. Meagher earnestly requesting the appointment of a Bishop for Montana. The Archbishop was himself quite

willing to accede to the request of General and Mrs. Meagher, and on the strength of their request urged upon the Council the erection of Montana into a vicariate apostolic. The Council decided in favor of the project, and recommended Very Rev. A. Ravoux, of St. Paul, for the new vicariate apostolic. The action of the Council, both as to the erection of the vicariate and the nomination of Father Ravoux was ratified in Rome ... while of course the official act was that of the Council of Baltimore, it was the act of General Meagher that brought the attention of the Council to Montana, and induced the Council to erect it into a vicariate. The situation of the Church in Montana at the time was such that there was nothing in it to justify the erection of the vicariate, but, as Bishop Grace said on his return from Baltimore, confidence was put on the promises and representations of General Meagher, and with those promises before them the bishops of the Council decided that they could do what otherwise conditions in the territory would not have justified.[94]

Father Augustine Ravoux, a veteran missionary among the Sioux Indians, was formally named Titular Bishop of Limyra and Vicar Apostolic of Montana on March 3, 1868.[95] On the same day, Pope Pius IX established the Vicariate of Idaho and appointed Father Louis Lootens of Sonoma, California as the titular Bishop of Castabella and the first vicar apostolic.[96]

Ravoux, according to Archbishop Ireland, "received his letters of appointment and kept them under consideration for several months. I was charged by him to explain matters to Cardinal Simeoni—his reasons being based entirely on his health why he asked to be released."[97] Thus, Ravoux never became a bishop, and the Vicariate of Montana was temporarily attached to the Vicariate of Nebraska.

General Meagher did not live to see these historic events. On July 1, 1867, he took passage on the Missouri river boat *G.A. Thompson* and mysteriously disappeared during the night. He was never seen again. Charges of murder and suicide were bandied about but no evidence for either has ever been presented.[98]

Had Meagher lived, the history of Montana doubtlessly would have been very different. But he had left the scene, his plans bore no tangible fruit, and most of Montana remained as spiritually desolate as it had always been.

ST. PETER'S MISSION CLOSED AGAIN

In his brief tenure as acting governor, Meagher had become a warm friend of the Jesuits. Giorda, especially, was dear to the governor, whose territorial capitol was Virginia City, where Giorda served as local pastor whenever he was able. Meagher was an eloquent orator, another Irish William Jennings Byan, who could gather a crowd at the snap of his fingers. He consented to deliver a benefit lecture for Giorda's All Saints Church in Virginia City. He spoke on the work of the church in spreading the true faith. "Behold," he exclaimed suddenly in the midst of his discourse, "there is here in our midst a man of God, a priest, a missionary, a man distinguished for his knowledge of science, known in Europe as a profound master of philosophy and theology, a man universally esteemed and beloved by all . . . he had given up the brightest prospects of doing great things at home to come to the Rocky Mountains, to come here to Virginia City to build a house of God for the faithful of Christ. Yes, that noble, heroic missionary is our own dear Father Giorda."[99]

Thunderous applause, says Palladino, followed these words of the speaker, who might have been delivering the nomination speech for the Democratic convention instead of a church benefit lecture. Doubtlessly through Meagher's influence, Giorda, over his many objections, was elected to be the first chaplain for Montana's Territorial Legislature.[100]

Giorda was in Virginia City for Easter that year.[101] A messenger arrived at this time to inform him that the mission herder at St. Peter's, John Fitzgerald by name, had been murdered by the Blackfeet. Ten head of the mission cattle had been killed as well. Angry Indians were seeking vengeance on the Jesuits for giving shelter to a squawman who had incurred their displeasure.[102]

Giorda left as soon as possible for St. Peter's, arriving there on April 26. When details regarding recent events had been communicated to him, he wept. What about the mission at Bird Tail Rock? He was informed that it was almost ready for occupation.

"He told us in the evening," says Father Kuppens, "that we would move in the morning with all our belongings. We had a short but impressive exhortation in the chapel; and in the morning bade goodbye to St. Peter's on the Missouri. Father Giorda as a last act, visited the place of his rescue from the waters; and this third mission was abandoned.

"During our short journey to the new place we saw several parties of Indians and Whites on the war path, and it was evident that whiskey had set their brains afire. We occupied the Mission houses [at Bird Tail Rock] only one night. The four Fathers said Mass in a new chapel and on a new altar; and all felt confident that the new Mission, on its fourth and last location, had found a permanent home."[103]

After a frugal breakfast, Giorda announced his decision. The new mission would be closed. The risks were too great for the few men on whom the church in Montana depended. They would close the new St.

Peter's and return again when peace was restored.[104] Obedient, even when they felt guilty of abandoning the Blackfeet, the four Jesuits packed their horses and wagons and set forth with their superior over the Mullan Road for St. Ignatius Mission, in the serene, high grassy meadows of the Mission Valley.

ST. MARY'S MISSION RESTORED

By this time, Giorda was physically and emotionally exhausted, and he requested the Jesuit General in Rome to relieve him of his duties as superior. Father Beckx, reluctant to lose Giorda in this capacity, appointed Father Grassi as an interim vice-superior of the Rocky Mountain Mission, with the intention of appointing Giorda when he recovered. In the late summer of 1866, therefore, Giorda, performing his last act as superior, reestablished St. Mary's Mission and persuaded Grassi to assign him to St. Mary's with two assistants, Ravalli and Brother Claessens. Had he waved a gun he could not have got more, for all three were the cream of the crop and they all deserved these golden years in Montana's banana belt, rebuilding Montana's first mission. At St. Mary's they were secure. The Flatheads were respectful now, if not loving. The forsaken Blackfeet, occupied by their own wars, left them in peace. But the Jesuits had to start over, on a site only a short distance from the original mission.

They built their new church, which still stands, while they lived in an Indian's old cabin. On Sunday, October 28, this church was ready for dedication. Father Giorda, feeling more buoyant than he had felt in recent years, offered the first Mass in it, which was attended by many Indians and a few whites, including old Major John Owens, who had paid $250 for the buildings of the first St. Mary's.[105] Owens now regarded the priests warily, as competitors for the Indians' loyalty.

In the course of time, Claessens erected a log home for the three Jesuits, built shops and corrals, and fenced in suitable pastures for cattle and horses. Giorda acquired farm animals and gradually life at St. Mary's took on the appearance it had known sixteen years before.

Grassi continued to live at St. Ignatius Mission, while he directed the destinies of the Jesuits in three other missions—Sacred Heart, St. Paul's on the Columbia, and old St. Mary's—and Jesuits in white parishes at Colville, Virginia City, and Helena. In the latter were Kuppens and Jerome D'Aste, both occupied with building the first church in Helena proper, on land provided by General Meagher.[106]

Imoda, too, resided at Helena when he was the itinerant missionary, covering the Missouri Basin in Montana. Whenever possible he visited

Bird Tail Rock, where a courageous friend of the Jesuits guarded the mission's property. This was Thomas Moran "whose loyal and faithful stewardship proved deserving of all praise."[107]

FATHER DERYCKERE AT DEER LODGE

It should be noted here, perhaps, that during this same year the first resident diocesan priest arrived in Montana and established a parish for whites in Deer Lodge.[108] This was Father Remigius DeRyckere, a newly ordained Belgian priest, who had made his theological studies at the American College in Louvain for the Nesqually Diocese. For some time Giorda had urged Bishop Blanchet to assign one of his priests to Deer Lodge, where he had baptized eighteen children and adults on St. Joseph's Day, 1864.[109] DeRyckere came to the Northwest in 1865, just after his twenty-eighth birthday, and he was assigned to western Montana during the following summer. He was an excellent choice for a most difficult mission. Sturdy and zealous, he covered regularly on horseback an area larger than his native country.

"The difficulties and hardships of Father DeRyckere's early mission life," wrote Palladino who knew him well, "far from being easy to recount, can hardly be imagined, except by the few knowing ones whose own personal experience enables them to visualize them. Horseback rides of 40, 60, 90 and more miles over dangerous and at times almost impassable trails, in the dead of winter and through deep snows, or under the scorching rays of the sun in summer, were weekly occurrences in the discharge of his missionary duties, accidents in the mining camps were frequent, and no less frequent were broils and shooting scrapes, and the good Samaritan had to be in the saddle whole days, and even nights, to reach the patients in time for the last comforts of religion."[110]

In October 1866, when Giorda was restoring St. Mary's, DeRyckere commenced construction of a church on Main Street in Deer Lodge, between Fourth and Fifth, and by the feast of the Immaculate Conception on December 8, the hewn log structure was ready for use. DeRyckere dedicated the church on that day in honor of Mary's Immaculate Conception. In the rear of this church was his residence, a cell so modest that no monk could be ashamed of it. He was undoubtedly very happy there, for he never asked the bishop to change him. "By the condition of things," Palladino added, "the Deer Lodge Mission had the honor and privilege of becoming the mother-Mission, wherefrom, as from a parent stock, sprang several offshoots or dependencies."[111]

One of these was the Butte church. Another was Helmsville, then

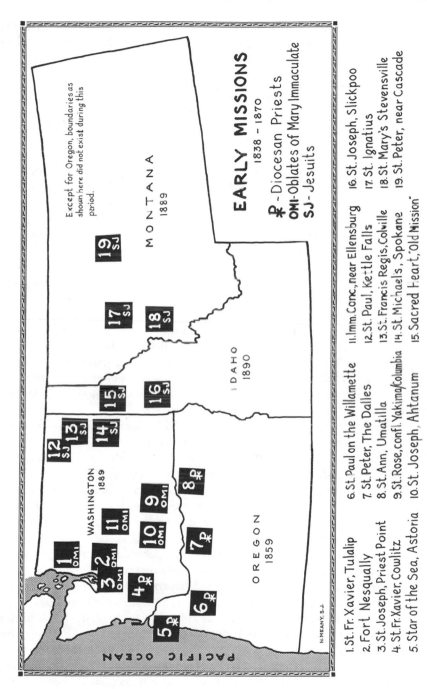

EARLY MISSIONS
1838 – 1870

P - Diocesan Priests
OMI - Oblates of Mary Immaculate
SJ - Jesuits

Except for Oregon, boundaries as shown here did not exist during this period.

MONTANA 1889

IDAHO 1890

WASHINGTON 1889

OREGON 1859

PACIFIC OCEAN

N. MEANY, S.J.

1. St. Fr. Xavier, Tulalip
2. Fort Nesqually
3. St. Joseph, Priest Point
4. St. Fr. Xavier, Cowlitz
5. Star of the Sea, Astoria

6. St. Paul on the Willamette
7. St. Peter, The Dalles
8. St. Ann, Umatilla
9. St. Rose, confl. Yakima/Columbia
10. St. Joseph, Ahtanum

11. Imm. Conc., near Ellensburg
12. St. Paul, Kettle Falls
13. St. Francis Regis, Colville
14. St. Michael's, Spokane
15. Sacred Heart, "Old Mission"

16. St. Joseph, Slickpoo
17. St. Ignatius
18. St. Mary's, Stevensville
19. St. Peter, near Cascade

Phillipsburg, Granite, and Anaconda. The Founder of these churches, Remigius DeRyckere, has long since been forgotten, but each, nonetheless, is a monument to his faith and zeal.

FATHER JOSEPH CATALDO

Among recent Jesuit arrivals in the Northwest was a precocious young priest who had already been declared dead, kicked out of two countries because of his Jesuit affiliation, and practically kidnapped by his brother Jesuits at Santa Clara. This was Father Joseph Cataldo, a Sicilian of only twenty-nine years, a brilliant scholar who was destined to become a superior of the Jesuits for the longest period in northwest history. Born on March 17, 1837, near Palermo, he entered the Jesuit Order at the age of seventeen.[112] He was sent home, however, as an incurable consumptive. His determination, or fate, produced a change in the judgment of the Jesuits who accepted him again and eventually sent him to America to become a missionary to the Indians. Detained at Santa Clara to complete his studies, he soon found himself teaching theology, instead of merely studying it. His protests, heard all the way to Rome, secured his release and he happily traveled to the Rocky Mountain Mission, Sacred Heart in Idaho, doomed to die within six months, according to the medical savants in California. He lived longer than these funereal prophets, much longer indeed, and while their names have long since been forgotten, his appears in at least one post office, a lengthy avenue in Spokane, and an elegant dining hall on the Gonzaga University campus.

Cataldo had been introduced to mission life, incidentals like riding a horse and eating salt pork and beans for breakfast by an open fire, by Father Giorda. In October 1865, Giorda met Cataldo at Walla Walla, a triumphant occasion on which the former had come to claim his prize, wrested from the powerful and influential at Santa Clara. Together the two priests rode their horses to the mission, becoming such intimate brothers during these brief days that not even the finality of death could lessen their love for one another.

Enroute to the mission, the two priests had passed through the lands of the Spokane Indians where no Catholic missionary as yet resided. Four years earlier, Giorda and Caruana had baptized a few Spokanes when they visited their fish camp by the falls on the river; and two years after this Caruana had built a little temporary shack of sorts on the lands of the Upper Spokanes, where he remained a brief time to teach them the Christian religion.

Cataldo felt drawn to these people. He wanted to be their priest. But when he had completed his initial training as a missionary, Giorda, who shared his views, was no longer superior. Grassi, a more practical man than Giorda, had doubts about priorities in this case. Prescinding from the great need there was for a resident priest in Seattle, a prominent new settlement on the coast, which was not really Grassi's concern, there were urgent demands for missionaries for the Yakima Indians, many of whom were already Catholic, and the Nez Perce, who had been sending appeals for Blackrobes since the days of DeSmet. Both were large and important tribes, four or five times larger than the Spokanes. The Yakimas had been deprived of a resident priest since the Oblates had left them.

THE SPOKANE MISSION

But Cataldo was a persistent priest, as well as a stubborn one. He finally wrung from Grassi permission to visit the Spokanes for at least a few weeks. Thus it happened that with Father Paschal Tosi as his companion (another recently arrived Jesuit), and an Indian guide, Cataldo followed the Mullan Road into the Spokane Plateau. The three men forded the river near the place where St. Joseph's Orphanage was built later, on land purchased by Cataldo from the railroad. Their guide led them to a basaltic eminence on the north side of the river, and as they ascended it, he extended his hand and said, "Az-a-gham." Look and see. They came and looked for the first time on the majestic Spokane Falls.[113]

They first visited a Coeur d'Alene camp below the falls, staying a few days among the Catholic Indians to serve their spiritual needs. Some Upper Spokanes appeared then and requested that the Blackrobes come to their camp to teach them. Their chief, Peone, whose name has been identified with the fertile prairie northeast of Spokane, urged Cataldo to remain with them, but Grassi had given both priests orders to return to the Coeur d'Alene Mission before snowfall.

When Cataldo returned to the mission he pleaded the cause of the Spokanes so earnestly that in a few days he was allowed to go back to them for the winter. By late November, with an Indian boy for his only companion, he was in the saddle again, enroute to Peone Prairie. He was warmly received, but when he proposed building a log church, Peone and his people were strangely opposed. Cataldo soon learned that Garry, now head chief of the Spokanes, disapproved of Catholic missionaries. He was away on the hunt and it was not likely that he would tolerate the construction of a Catholic mission. Cataldo, not easily balked, and a very determined man, as I have noted, persuaded the Indians to allow him to build a temporary church, agreeing to destroy it when Garry returned, if he disapproved.

Taking an axe, Cataldo led the way. At first the Indians merely watched him chop down suitable pine trees, then they joined the priest in his labors. With their assistance, Cataldo put together his crude mission hut, unpeeled logs with a mud roof, the first of its kind in the region of the Spokanes.[114] He called it St. Michael's. On December 8, 1866, he offered Mass in this humble abode, and here he taught the Indians catechism twice daily, baptizing them as they were prepared for the sacrament. By Christmas time, the little church, eighteen by twenty feet, was too small for his congregation. And by February 2, 1867, one hundred Upper Spokanes had become Catholics and sixty-seven of these had already received their First Communion.

When spring came and the pussy willows appeared along the banks of the creek, a messenger arrived from the Coeur d'Alene Mission. Father Caruana, the messenger said, wanted Cataldo to return to the mission at once. Despite the noisy objections of the Indians, Cataldo prepared to leave. Should he burn down their church as he had agreed. No, they responded grimly, Garry should let sleeping dogs lie or take the consequences.

Late snows had blocked the mountain passes that year, but Cataldo eventually arrived at the mission, where orders to report to St. Ignatius, in Montana awaited him. These proved to be a mistake, which only shows how, even in those days before the telephone, directions got mixed up and people wasted precious time getting things straight. But Cataldo met Grassi who had, at this point, only one priority: a priest for Lewiston, Idaho, and for the Nez Perce Indians. Bishop Blanchet was almost insufferable in his demands. He insisted that a Jesuit be sent to Lewiston forthwith, for it was the *de facto* capitol of Idaho. Unlike most frontier towns, it was already wealthy. It was estimated that a hundred million dollars in silver and gold had passed through the town in a ten year period, an amount close to a billion dollars today.[115] Violence produced by Henry Plummer and other road agents, before they were hanged, gave the city a bad name, but the majority of its citizens were law abiding and wanted a church, any kind of church at all.

Under the bishop's pressure, Grassi agreed to send a Jesuit to Lewiston. He had no one to spare, he explained to the bishop, but he would recall someone, perhaps Father Cataldo, from another mission. This, of course, would require some time.

Blanchet, at least, was now off the hook where Lewiston was concerned. The Jesuits would take it. He still needed a priest for the Yakimas. The archbishop, his brother, had no one to give him, nor the Jesuits, nor the Oblates. The Yakimas had been abandoned since Mesplie had left for the Boise Basin.

ROSEBURG, OREGON

The archbishop had recently acquired another gem, like Brouillet and Croquet. This was a Belgian priest also, Father Alphonsus Glorieux, aged twenty-three, a good organizer who was endowed with both generosity and common sense. The archbishop assigned him to the new parish in Roseburg almost as soon as he got off the boat from San Francisco.

The elder Blanchet was partial to Roseburg, perhaps because of his friendship for Governor Joseph Lane, whose frontier empire, called Mount Lane, covered considerable land about ten miles distant from the city. On August 22, 1866, Blanchet himself purchased from one Aaron Rose, "for the sum of 400 [Dollars], block 26 of the City of Roseburg," for a church.

The Lanes were not Catholics, in fact the governor had been a prominent member of the Masonic Lodge. Their admiration for Blanchet, however, prompted them to make inquiries about Catholicism and in October, 1867, before Glorieux arrived to develop a parish, the archbishop received into the church the governor and his two adult sons, and a prominent local lawyer, Colonel T'Vault by name.[116]

When Glorieux appeared on the scene a few weeks later, he purchased "an old building" that had served as a blacksmith shop, moved it onto the parish property and converted it into a church and a residence.[117] He dedicated this to St. Stephen the First Martyr.[118]

There is an interesting sequence to all of this. At the first commencement at St. Mary's Academy in Portland, there were two graduates, both non-Catholics. One was Amanda Mann, who later married Governor Lane's son Lafayette. Their son, Arthur, born in 1872, was ordained to the priesthood on August 5, 1895, at the age of twenty-three. He was the first native Oregonian to be raised to the priesthood.[119] In this there is some irony, in view of the presence in Oregon of the so-called born-Catholics, especially in Catholic settlements like St. Paul and French Prairie, where there was strong pro-Catholic influence. The first native born priest, a very distinguished cleric who also became a monsignor, was the product of a convert family in remote Roseburg.[120]

THE NEW YAKIMA MISSION

But in 1867, all this was conjecture. Augustin Blanchet still wrestled with "the Yakima problem" and he finally resolved it by ordaining a French Canadian candidate for the priesthood, who had found his way to Vancouver. Louis Napoleon St. Onge, a strong, young Hercules, born on April 14, 1842, possessed a straightforward Yankee-like face, partly concealed by a bushy beard, which gave him the appearance of one of the

Smith Brothers, the doctors who dispensed cough drops. In Vancouver, apparently in a less-than-formal manner, he studied for the priesthood and served as a volunteer coworker with Mother Joseph, who was engaged in the embellishment of the cathedral.[121] Another volunteer for Mother Joseph was John Baptiste Boulet, mentioned above as a teacher in Holy Angels College.

Father St. Onge was willing to restore the mission of the Yakimas. In September 1867, a few weeks before Cataldo arrived in Lewiston, before Glorieux arrived in Roseburg, and Prefontaine arrived in Seattle, St. Onge traveled from Vancouver over Satus Pass to the site of the Attanum Creek mission of St. Joseph, bringing with him "a chapel chest, carpenters' tools, shoemaking tools and nine dollars."[122] Arriving at his destination, he quickly assembled a temporary hut for a dwelling, then built a log cabin sixteen by twenty-four feet for a church and permanent residence. He learned the Yakima language, then gathered his scattered flock and preached to them as the Oblate Fathers had done. He brought much comfort to them, especially to the elders who had been Christian for nearly two decades.

He soon realized that he needed assistance. Returning to Vancouver in March 1868, he persuaded young Boulet, who was still debating with himself whether to receive Holy Orders or not, to accompany him back to Attanum Creek. When they departed from Vancouver, up the north bank of the Columbia, then over the pass, they carried in their baggage mission supplies and "forty or fifty fruit trees and a small printing press."[123] The trees became one of Yakima Valley's first orchards. The printing press, the earliest mission press in Washington, was used for a three year period for producing small booklets in the Yakima language, which were distributed to the Indians. No copy of these has been known to survive.

PREFONTAINE IN SEATTLE

Meanwhile, Chief Seattle died.[124] The town that bore his name, on the shores of Elliott Bay, had neither a resident priest nor a Catholic church, though it was becoming obvious that it would replace Fort Steilacoom as the center of Puget Sound's population. Seattle was, of course, Prefontaine's mission. He finally arrived there in the autumn of 1867, still under-paid because the bishop had never yielded on that touchy matter of a higher salary. The settlement had six hundred inhabitants, less than half the number in Lewiston, and of these, Prefontaine could find only ten who admitted to being Catholics. He decided to remain, nonetheless, rented a small cabin at Third and Jefferson for six dollars a month, and converted two of its rooms into a chapel. He built the altar himself and installed six pews. One would have been sufficient, for his first congregation on November 24, 1867, consisted of two ladies.[125]

The small number did not dishearten him. With the encouragement of his new friends, "he purchased four lots on the south side of Mill Street (on Washington between Third and Fourth Avenues) for the sum of two hundred dollars during the fall of 1868. There he cleared stumps and underbrush with his own hands during the following winter."[126]

About this time, his biographer continues, Bishop Blanchet appeared to investigate what this autocratic and sometimes vexing priest was doing. He commended Prefontaine for his efforts but refused him permission to build a church on the land, because, he said, "Seattle as a mission center was a lost cause."[127] Prefontaine was forced to admit that his congregation had grown but little, to only thirty souls, men women and children, but he begged so earnestly for approval that not even the stern Bishop could refuse him. Prefontaine, Blanchet finally allowed, could build a church provided he incurred no debt.

Father William Metz, his most ardent admirer, described Prefontaine's efforts to provide this church:

> A small church fair, at which everybody helped, gave Father Prefontaine the first substantial aid towards the erection of his little sanctuary, 20 x 50 feet in size. In order to remain within the limited financial means at his disposal, he personally performed all the work required. He was the superintending architect, carpenter, painter and decorator. He rose early, and after saying Mass and partaking of a self-prepared breakfast he donned the required artisan's apron. The little church was begun in the summer of 1869 and finished in the autumn of 1870.[128]

Father Vary, by this time, had been replaced at Fort Steilacoom by another Belgian priest with the name of John Baptist Brondel. Brondel lived at the Church of the Immaculate Conception, covering the lower Sound area from this base without much contact or friction with Prefontaine. He was a much sturdier man than Vary who, after seven years on the mission, had become "a burned-out priest," somewhat disillusioned and eager to join a religious order where he could find peace and companionship. He decided to return to Canada to join the Jesuits, a decision that endeared neither him nor the Jesuits to the bishop, who had more than enough of this priests going over the wall for something else. On February 1, 1868, Vary entered the Jesuit Novitiate at Sault-au-Recollect where "he was surprised to find that religious life was both sweet and easy in comparison with his missionary apostolate in the west."[129]

LEWISTON AND THE NEZ PERCE MISSION

It is quite probable that Father Vary did not meet any of the twenty-seven Jesuits in the Northwest in 1867. Distance and communication then were greater obstacles than we experience; Jesuits were confined in the eastern portion of the church's far flung vineyard, and there is no record that he ever visited them. Father Grassi had his own fields to plow, none of them narrow, and though his own special responsibility, St. Ignatius, required all of his attention, he seldom passed up an opportunity to visit his Jesuits in their remote missions.

He had decided to send Cataldo with Brother Carfagno, the missions' best cook-carpenter, to Lewiston in October 1867. Deeply concerned about the Nez Perce Indians, especially, he had directed Cataldo to give them a certain priority of attention, which was, perhaps, stretching the bishop's demands just a little.

After their arrival in Lewiston in Late October, the two Jesuits proceeded to Lapwai, the seat of the tribal and government bureaucracy, presumably to establish a small day school for Indian children.[130] Opposition to their presence appeared at once and they were politely informed by the Indian agent, one James O'Neil, that under no circumstances would they be allowed to teach in a school. They returned to Lewiston to await results of their own protests, and here in the winter of 1867, urged by the importunate residents of the town, they built the first church for whites in northern Idaho. Constructed on land acquired in 1865 by Father Charles Richards, who had traveled all the way from Cowlitz Prairie for this purpose,[131] this "first religious building in Lewiston was a small Catholic Church north of the Hahn plumbing building on the same block.... A larger church was built where Hahn's building stands, a few years later."[132]

This first church, then, dedicated like subsequent churches in this parish to St. Stanislaus Kostka, was located approximately on Fifth and C. It was only eighteen by twenty feet in size, an obvious miscalculation by Cataldo, but its smallness was not remedied for nineteen years.[133]

Cataldo had not given up on the Nez Perce Indians. Using Lewiston as his base of operations, he visited Indian camps that sought his attentions and instructed their people as best he could under the circumstances. He kept the bishop informed on his progress, or lack of it, and welcomed His Lordship's vicar general, Father Brouillet, when he arrived in Lewiston in January 1868, to press for action on the Lapwai school. Several conferences followed with a new Indian agent, Dr. Newell, who vacillated timidly between the demands of the priests and the objections of hostile Indians. Finally, Cataldo received approval for building a mission church at a place called Arrow on the Clearwater River. With the help of three unemployed miners, he and Carfagno soon completed a log cabin, the first of several on the Nez Perce reservation.

In March of 1869, Cataldo received a request to attend a dying woman, Mrs. Ryan, in one of the mining camps called Oro Fino. Parting from Brother Magri, who had replaced Carfagno as his companion, he hastened by horse to the camp where he administered the last rites to the dying woman. It was Holy Thursday. In spite of warnings that the trail home was too icy for travel, he set forth, expecting to be in Lewiston for Holy Week and Easter services. His mount, however, slipped and fell, causing the rider to break his leg, leaving him helpless and abandoned by the rascal horse.

Providentially, Indian hunters found him. After appropriate alarms had been sounded, Cataldo was eventually taken to the home of two kind Presbyterians in Oro Fino. For forty days he was gently cared for by these generous Christians. News, meanwhile, had come that Brother Magri was ill and alone. Cataldo insisted on leaving the home of his hosts, though he was still convalescing, and he was able to join a pack train Lewiston bound. He arrived just in time to give the last sacraments to Magri, one of the founders of the Rocky Mountain Mission, who had come west with DeSmet. This holy brother died on June 18, 1869, in his sixtieth year of life. Cataldo piously took his remains to Walla Walla to bury them in consecrated ground.[134]

THE COLVILLE MISSION

By this time Giorda was reinstated as the General Superior of the Rocky Mountain Mission. He recalled Cataldo to the Coeur d'Alene Mission with instructions to visit Lewiston and the Nez Perce when occasion allowed. Grassi, too, had received a new status. With Brother Campopiano as his assistant, he built a new church for the Spokane Indians to replace the log shack with its mud roof that Cataldo had thrown together in 1866.[135] Giorda then assigned Grassi to establish a new mission for Indians of the upper Columbia River region in north central Washington. St. Paul's was still there, attended by the indefatigable Joset. But this was far from adequate for the several thousand Indians in the area.

After an abortive attempt to establish a mission fifteen miles downriver from St. Paul's, Grassi finally chose another site halfway between St. Paul's and the Church of the Immaculate Conception for whites in the Colville Valley. There, on October 3, 1869, he performed the first baptism. He purchased forty acres of land from a French Canadian by the name of Francis Lagourtre and built several log cabins, placing them under the special care of St. Francis Regis, patron of the earlier mission near Chewelah at the southern end of the valley.[136] Four years later Grassi moved the mission again, about one half mile west, where it remained for many long years, on a lofty eminence overlooking a prolific green valley surrounded by heavily forested mountains and watered by a fresh meandering river noted for the size of its trout.[137]

BISHOP LOUIS LOOTENS

Louis Aloysius Lootens, born in Bruges, Belgium on March 17, 1827, ten years to the day before Joseph Cataldo, was ordained to the priesthood in Paris by Bishop Demers on June 14, 1851.[138] He had volunteered for Vancouver Island, and here he landed, after a perilous crossing on August 29, 1852. His first appointment was the pastoral care of the miners in the Caribou and Fraser River country of British Columbia. This was an almost impenetrable mountain region, containing for the most part wild bears, and a few men, only rugged individualists, the toughest of the miners and sometimes the most violent.

Lootens, with his long arms and large hands and his tall, muscular-looking body, was regarded as a healthy specimen, strong enough to cope with the hardships of his mission. Since his student days, however, he had suffered from a chronic gastric ailment, which weakened his body, especially when his diet consisted of unpalatable foods of Indians and the course foods of the miners. After nine years of strenuous activity in the mountains, and lack of more refined foods, his health was broken and his spirit sorely tired. He requested his bishop to allow him to transfer to a diocese in California where he could recover his health. Demers consented and, in 1861, he became chaplain in an orphanage, then pastor of St. Patrick's Church, Sonoma, California. He built a new church at Petaluma, enlarged the academy of San Raphael, and made numerous friends who were attracted by his learning and piety.[139]

By this time, he acquired the appearance of a refined American cleric, with his hair trimmed short, his steady, gentle eyes behind his rimless glasses, his firm mouth and chin suggesting his ability to govern, and his tall, well-proportioned body, which moved gracefully, like that of a member of the aristocracy. When he was appointed Vicar Apostolic for the Vicariate of Idaho in 1868, he made no fuss about it, neither protesting it nor embracing it. He calmly made arrangements for his consecration, which took place on August 9, 1868, in the cathedral in San Francisco. Archbishop Joseph Alemany was the consecrating prelate. He was assisted by Bishop Eugene O'Connell of Grass Valley and Bishop Francis Mora of Monterey. Lootens remained in California until after the new year, 1869, giving his four diocesan priests in southern Idaho a chance to get used to the idea of having a bishop within a day's ride in the saddle.

Father Alex Archambault, another young French Canadian priest, whose cousin Sister Mary Euphemie happened to be one of the pioneer Holy Names Sisters, volunteered to accompany Bishop Lootens to his new vicariate. Archambault was also younger and more energetic, perhaps impulsive besides. He was a genial companion, however, when the bishop, traveling by boat to Wallula, then stagecoach to Boise City, arrived at the latter on February 15, 1869. Mesplie was in Boise to met them, and from Mesplie His Lordship heard the bad news about his vicariate. This is what he learned:

> In [all of] Idaho there were five churches for the white people and two for the Indians. For the whites there were the churches of St. Joseph at Idaho City, St. Dominic at Centerville, St. Andrew at Silver City, St. Francis at Pioneerville, St. Stanislaus at Lewiston; and in [western] Montana, churches at Frenchtown and Hell Gate attended by the Jesuit Fathers as missions, and Deer Lodge where Father Remigius DeRyckere was the first pastor. The Indian Missions in Idaho were at Arrow for the Nez Perces, and Sacred Heart for the Coeur d'Alenes; in Montana, St. Ignatius for the Pend d'Oreilles, and St. Mary's for the Flatheads. The churches in the south were attended by Father Mesplie, Poulin, Coll and Perret.[140] Boise City had no church. Mass had first been said there in the fall of 1863 in the home of Mr. John O'Farrell and continued to be said there regularly for about four years.[141]

The bishops and Father Archambault spent Sunday, February 14, with Mesplie in Boise then took Monday's stage to Idaho City where they were welcomed by Perret, Poulin, and Coll and the four Sisters of the Holy Names at St. Mary's Academy. It was time for the bishop to make his decisions. He chose to make his residence at Granite Creek where his pro-cathedral was a modest frame church, unpainted like many in the West, resting on a small hill that sometimes was buried in the snow.[142]

Several families in Granite Creek were Catholic, and Irish to boot. Numbers meant little. The entire population of the town was only 299.

This was suggestive of current conditions in Idaho. "In 1869 according to the 1870 official United States census, the entire Idaho population was 20,560 including 10,618 White, 4,274 Chinese, 5,600 Indians and 68 Negroes. Boise City, the metropolis, in that year boasted of a population of 995; Idaho City had 889; Centerville, 474; Pioneerville, 477; and Placerville, 318. In 1869, the Boise Basin has a population a little less than 2,500, instead of the 20,000 it had in 1863."[143]

The gold rush that had begun in 1863 had vanished by 1870, leaving ghost towns throughout the territory. The years 1870–1880 were the most difficult in Idaho history. The great depression following the Civil War brought countless thousands of settlers into Oregon and Washington, especially along the coast where the climate was milder, but Idaho and Montana were left in desolation.

Within a brief time, Bishop Lootens had almost nothing, no personal possessions, three impoverished priests, a few missions supplied by the Jesuits, and a debt of $4,000 which he could not pay. His future looked hopeless.

And thus it happened that by 1870 all of the Territory of Idaho and half of Montana, almost half in extent of the entire Northwest, was in desperate circumstances. The bishop, looking over the vast area of mountains and deserts, plateaus and fertile valleys, could see a thriving church someday, but only God knew when that would be. For the present, there were a few scattered ghost towns and mostly empty churches.

The archbishop in Portland was not very sympathetic. Nor the bishop in Vancouver. They had not been responsible for the tragic mistake of establishing the Vicariate of Idaho. They would not pay off the debt of $4,000. They did not know it yet, but they, too, would soon have more to worry about than the alleged insubordination of their own priests. Augustin Blanchet would soon lose the title to some of his choice church lands, and both of them would lose some of their cherished Indian missions in the catastrophic Peace Policy of the United States President, Ulysses Grant.

8

THE LAST OF THE BLANCHET YEARS

1869–1879

On the eighteenth of July in 1869, Archbishop Blanchet observed the fiftieth anniversary of his ordination to the priesthood. Before the Pontifical Mass celebrated by him, assisted by his brother, the bishop of Nesqually, the Catholic Library and Christian Doctrine Society of Portland presented an appropriate address:

> The event of this day, they said, reminds us of the fact that during the present year our Holy Father, Pius the Ninth, has likewise had the good fortune of celebrating the jubilee of the fiftieth anniversary of his ordination to the priesthood. As your Grace will leave in a short time to attend the approaching General Council, we take this occasion to say that our hearts and our prayers will be with you in your far distant journey. We pray that you may have a safe and pleasant voyage to the Holy See of St. Peter.... [1]

The members of the Society also gave the archbishop a purse of $160 to be presented to the Holy Father, and his Grace responded with kind words and beseeched their prayers for a safe journey. In October, he addressed a pastoral on the Infallibility of the Church to the Catholics of his own diocese, most of whom had no idea about its meaning, and surely no suspicion that it would soon affect their lives. The archbishop was a strong advocate of Papal Infallibility, which made him in this sense a bosom friend of the Jesuits. The latter, it was said, had invented the machine "Infallibility" and were running it all over the world. Both Blanchets hopped into this mythical conveyance and so did Bishop Demers.

The archbishop, enroute to the Council, traveled from San Francisco to New York by rail.[2] In New York he embarked for Europe with Bishop John Ireland, later the provocative Archbishop of St. Paul, who shared Blanchet's darker side, his aversion to religious orders. Demers, too, went to the Council, but the younger Blanchet, still plagued with malaria, remained home. It was fortunate that he did so; he might have returned to find his cathedral in other hands.[3]

At the Council, neither the elder Blanchet nor Demers had much to say. Both, like the other fathers of the Council, kept a nervous eye on developments in Prussia, where rumblings and, later, troop movements of the Franco-Prussian War were causing such a disturbance that the prelates in the Vatican were distracted from the business at hand. Garibaldi's Black Shirts, too, were threatening. All of Europe was in political turmoil.

In September, about six months after the Council had begun, Blanchet obtained an audience with Pius IX, to make the presentation of the Librarian Society's purse and an address of loyalty to the Holy Father.

"On this occasion," a correspondent reported, "the archbishop presented the address spoken of, together with a speech he had prepared to be delivered in Council upon the same subject, but renounced his right to deliver, with other prelates, in order to stop discussion. We are informed that the address of the archbishop was a beautiful profession of faith and that of the clergy and laity of his diocese on the shores of Oregon...."[4]

Not content with all of this, the archbishop then wrote a very lengthy letter to the faithful back home, concluding this rather pompously: "Given at the Flaminian gates of Rome, July 31, 1870." He sent instructions with it that it was to be read in all of the pulpits of the diocese. Thus on October 30, his "Pastoral letter concerning the First two Dogmatic Constitutions of the Oecumenical Vatican Council," was read from all of the pulpits in Oregon, delaying, no doubt, the Sunday brunches of a considerable portion of the Catholic population.[5]

Bishop Demers returned home before Blanchet, arriving in Portland on the steamship *California* in late October. He was accompanied by his secretary, a popular young Belgian priest whose name was Charles Seghers.[6] The archbishop did not return until December 17, on the same ship, the *California,* which made frequent runs between San Francisco, Portland, and sometimes Sitka.[7] His Grace, it was said by those who greeted him at the dock at eleven in the morning, appeared to be young and lively, and one parishioner from the Cathedral noted that "he could still run up and down the steps." Demers, unfortunately, in the last year of his life, did not look as well. Nor did Augustin Blanchet, whose face was creased with deep wrinkles, and his dark eyes tired looking and almost cadaverous from sleepless nights.

For almost two years now he had been engaged in bitter struggles— one to save his land and the other to cope with problems on the Yakima reservation. Both of these historic confrontations were still threats to his diocese, and neither could be satisfactorily resolved. Perhaps this is why Augustin Blanchet, unlike his brother the archbishop, seemed to grow more crotchety with age.

A SURVEY 1870

The Northwest now enjoyed the presence of three congregations of sisters: The Sisters of Providence, the Sisters of the Holy Names, and the Sisters of Charity of Leavenworth. There were only two orders of men, the Jesuits and the Oblates, and the latter, only two in number, would soon leave for Canada.

Including Bishop Demers of Vancouver Island and Bishop D'Herbomez of the interior of British Columbia, there were five bishops. Only three, however, were in the Northwest of the United States and two of these were on the ragged edge of exhaustion because of overwork or old age.[8]

The archdiocese in 1870 was comprised "of at least 30,000 Catholics,"[9] twenty-three priests, twenty two churches, sixty-eight sisters, nine academies for girls and one college for boys, four parochial schools for boys, two parochial schools for girls, an orphanage, and a hospital.[10] Directly under the archbishop were two Indian reservations, Grande Ronde, with Father Croquet and a sister's school, and Umatilla, with Father Vermeersch who directed another small school.

While these statistics, bare bones of the church's structure, reflected its remarkable growth in the Northwest, no one had to remind the bishops of one grim fact: the population of the Northwest was increasing far more rapidly than the number of priests. This point should be regarded as significant for, later, when the cheerless subject of the "unchurched Northwest" is discussed, it will merit special consideration as a contributing cause.

The three pioneer bishops, about this time, posed for an official portrait, each in his half-acre of episcopal robes, the archbishop seated in the middle, wearing his purple biretta, his younger brother seated on the archbishop's right, holding his biretta like a sack lunch, and Demers on the left. All three had lost most of their hair, though the archbishop's medieval hat concealed part of the fact. All three struck historic poses, staring off into space, rather beatific looking, but perfectly conscious of the historic nature of their actions.

At the beginning of 1870, the archbishop was in his seventy-fifth year. Augustin Blanchet and Demers were younger by two years and fourteen years respectively, but Demers, the youngest, would be the first to die.[11] Demers was the most gentle, the most patient of the three. It is quite possible the lives of the others were extended somewhat because they were less inhibited in scolding their subjects.

THE CATHOLIC SENTINEL

In March 1870, while the archbishop was still in Rome attending the Council, he received the first copy of *The Catholic Sentinel* by post. This had appeared on February 5, 1870, in Portland. Its introduction, as he tactfully admitted, was a great surprise to his Grace, who nonetheless approved it and expressed "many warm wishes for its success and long life." This first Catholic paper in the Northwest was published by two lay men, H.L. Herman and J.F. Atkinson, a printer, who distributed an earlier prospectus announcing their intention to undertake this publication "in consequence of the kind of encouragement and promised support of the Very Rev. J.F. Fierens, Vicar General and Administrator of the Archdiocese."[12]

While the timing of the first issue coincided with the absence of the archbishop, there seems to have been no ulterior reason for this, and the paper was acclaimed from the beginning not only by the archbishop but also by the bishops of the other dioceses, for which local reporting had been arranged.

H.L. Herman was a greengrocer, as indicated by advertisements that appeared in each issue of the paper. His establishment, located on Washington and Third Streets in Portland, carried a full stock of fresh vegetables and fruit imported by ship, of course, from salubrious farms to the south or in Hawaii. Carrots, for example, even in mid-winter, were five cents a pound, and one could buy a dozen heads of cauliflower for one dollar and fifty cents. Herman at first served as editor of the paper but in the course of time he yielded this position to S.J. McCormick, one of the first mayors of Portland and pioneer merchant on Front Street.

McCormick's business was established in 1851. It described itself as an "Importer and Dealer in Books, Stationary, Toys, Music, Newspapers," and at certain seasons of the year as "Santa Claus Headquarters."[13] Next to McCormick's on Front Street at number 105, was Hack's Photograph Gallery, which advertised its services as follows: "If you want a natural picture go to Hack's Gallery and sit for it. But if you want a handsome one send somebody else to sit for it." One can judge from this that the Northwest's first Catholic paper did not take itself too seriously.

S.J. McCormick has been remembered more for his publications than for his editorship. Even before the appearances of the *Sentinel*, he had established a press that produced, among other imprints, a number of Catholic documents or apologetics, items like Brouillet's classic work on the Whitman Massacre.[14]

It is clear in retrospect at least, that the founding of a Catholic newspaper at this time, mostly accomplished by several Catholic lay men, was a turning point in the history of the church in the Northwest. One could say that it was a milestone, indicating the church's arrival at a certain maturity. More than this, I think, was the new sense of identity it provided for Catholics who were scattered sparsely throughout the four states and territories, representing, probably, less than ten per cent of the population. The paper unified these Catholics and motivated them to become more aggressive in seeking and defending their rights.

From the beginning, the bishops recognized the basic role of *The Catholic Sentinel* and provided letters of approval, which were printed regularly to encourage subscriptions. On February 13, 1874, the Northwest bishops finally formalized their commitment to it by adopting it as the official organ of the archdiocese and diocese. It has been published ever since, a faithful witness to the church, recording its happenings week by week, becoming one of its principal sources of history.

THE SISTERS OF CHARITY OF LEAVENWORTH

Among the statistics brought forward by the *The Catholic Sentinel*, was one that was passed over without comment. This was the reference to *three* congregations of sisters in the Northwest. The third group, hitherto unmentioned, was a home-grown order in America, the Sisters of Charity of Leavenworth, who arrived in Montana in the following way:

During the summer of 1869, Van Gorp, who had succeeded Kuppens in Helena, made many earnest appeals to Father DeSmet in St. Louis for sisters to staff a hospital and a school for whites. At St. Ignatius Mission these facilities for Indians had long since been provided and Van Gorp, who had come to prefer his work in white settlements rather than the Indian missions, was determined that Helena would have them also. DeSmet, under this barrage of importunities, yielded, then sought to keep his promise, while Van Gorp purchased land for the sisters along the east side of Ewing Street. This, unfortunately, overlooked a famous old tree, the pine tree on which the vigilantes hanged their victims.

It so happened one day, while DeSmet walked along the streets of St. Louis, that he met an old Jesuit friend , John Baptist Miege, Bishop of Leavenworth, who was enroute to the Vatican Council. Miege owed DeSmet many a favor, so DeSmet's request for sisters, made then and there on the street, was favorably received. Miege referred DeSmet to the community in Leavenworth, the Sisters of Charity by whom he was regarded as the founder. "Tell the Mother I am willing the Sisters should go, if they can be spared."[15]

DeSmet lost no time. Having solicited sufficient funds from wealthy ladies to defray the cost of the sisters' passage, he took the first train to Leavenworth and sought an interview with the Council of the Sisters of Charity. The sisters, too, were obliged to DeSmet, so five members of the community were hastily assigned to Montana and that was that.

The chosen ones were as follows: Sister Julia, appointed superior of the gallant little group; Sister Bertha, Sister Loretto, Sister Mary, and Sister Regina. At DeSmet's request, the five were assembled in the parlor for approval, and soon the sisters were entrained and speeding to their destination.

They left Leavenworth on the Feast of St. Michael, September 29, 1869 and reached Helena on October 10.[16] It was late in the evening and their arrival was unexpected. Van Gorp, at some distance from his residence, was informed that five sisters had passed by in the stagecoach, bound for Helena. He raced home to beat the coach, arriving just before it did, and quickly made arrangements for the sisters' care in the homes of three parishioners.[17] Several days later the Jesuits moved out of their quarters, an old shanty that had been occupied formerly by the *Gazette* printing establishment, and the sisters moved in, making it their home until the new academy was built. Some of the sisters, meanwhile, went out to solicit contributions for their new home, traveling throughout the territory, "their appeals meeting everywhere with a response hearty and substantial from the miners."[18]

The long frame structure of moderate dimensions began to loom up on what came to be called Academy Hill. It was ready for occupancy by late December. On January 3, 1870, St. Vincent's Academy, the first institution of its kind for the whites in Montana, was opened for the reception of pupils, both boarders and day scholars. The old *Gazette* shanty was converted for the third time, into classrooms for boys, and was designated piously as the St. Aloysius Institute.

The new academy was cozy and comfortable, but the sisters had one vexing problem: when they looked out of their convent windows they saw the hanging tree. In full sight from the convent, only three hundred yards away, there arose that grim, solitary tree with a stout limb projecting from the trunk almost horizontally, ten to twelve feet above the ground.[19] A casual glance at it one morning by one of the sisters produced the shock of her tender young life, because the tree that night had borne grisly fruit: a human body could be seen dangling from the ugly branch. On another morning, only a few weeks later, the tree had become more prolific, for two human forms were hanging from the same limb.

This was on April 30, 1870. The two men charged with holding up, robbing and *"almost* murdering" a neighboring rancher were condemned and informed of their impending doom.[20] One of the two asked for a priest, but both Father Imoda and Van Gorp were out of town performing missionary duties. Imoda was expected to return at any moment, so the leaders who were presiding over the execution suspended proceedings awaiting his arrival. A large crowd gathered. The hours dragged by, but no Father Imoda appeared. Finally, the leaders decided to wait no longer. As the two wretches, placed in a cart, were brought to the baneful tree, Imoda dashed up, overtaking the mournful cortege only at the last moment. He climbed into the wagon and administered conditional baptism and absolution as best he could, then stood by his new convert until the last moment. Later he recorded the name of the "good thief" as Peter Arthur L. Compton, which has an aristocratic ring to it, perhaps that of a son of a Boston brahmin. We are told, "that the other robber felt no need of any priestly service."

The sisters' Helena schools were only beginning. On November 1, of this same year, three more Sisters of Charity opened St. John the Baptist Hospital in Helena in a one and a one-half story cottage, which was made to last for fourteen years.[21] On October 9, 1872, they opened a second hospital called St. Joseph's, in Deer Lodge, in a log building that lasted only one year. It was replaced by a new frame hospital in 1873.[22] Three years later the sisters opened another hospital in Virginia City. Having remodeled the old court house as best they could, they named it St. Mary's and moved in, their fingers crossed, for even then the future looked bleak. Unlike the other hospitals, St. Mary's did not survive. After the miners abandoned Virginia City it was closed, and the sisters went elsewhere.[23]

The presence of these sisters and others in Montana produced a remarkable awareness of certain delicate Christian values, like reverence and gentleness. For the church, especially in Montana, these were the subtle needs of the hour; feminine characteristics also demonstrated the church's civilizing influence. Only God could measure fully the results from the apostolate of the sisters, as angels of mercy, as confidantes for the troubled and gentle, devoted teachers for the children.

THE ST. JAMES MISSION LAND CASE

The existence of *The Catholic Sentinel* as a means of defense was timely, for the melancholy events alluded to in the last chapter were already in the making. The first of these dismal misfortunes, involving the loss of a substantial portion of the church's land, specifically the title to 640 acres claimed by St. James Mission in what is now downtown Vancouver, Washington, had its origins in the relationship of the church to the

Hudson's Bay Company, and in counter claims by three contending parties—the widow and family of Amos Short, deceased, Clark County of Washington Territory, and the United States War Department.

In May, 1853, three years after becoming the Bishop of Nesqually, Augustin Blanchet filed a claim on the mission's land, but no action on his request was taken, because the license of the Hudson's Bay Company to conduct business, in accordance with the Canadian Boundary Treaty of 1846, had not yet expired.[24] Upon the expiration of the time clause in 1859, the Commissioner of the United States Land Office confirmed the St. James Mission claim, which was based on an Act of Congress, August 14, 1848. Washington's territorial governor, Isaac Stevens, then objected to the St. James Mission title on behalf of the military base at Vancouver, the town of Vancouver, and the heirs of Amos Short. There followed a flurry of reports and correspondence which extended the dispute for ten years without definitive court decisions or appeasement of the military.

Since this became the most celebrated legal case of its kind, the position of the church as filed with the Surveyor General of Washington Territory is presented here at some length:

STATEMENT OF FACTS

This claim is founded upon a proviso in the first section of the act of Congress, entitled 'An Act to establish the Territorial Government of Oregon,' approved August 14, 1848. The language of the proviso is: 'that the title of the land, not exceeding six hundred and forty acres, now occupied as Missionary Stations among the Indian tribes in said territory, together with the improvements thereon, be confirmed and established in the several religious societies to which said Missionary Stations respectively belong.'

The claim is made under the following circumstances:

In August, 1848, the Hudson's Bay Company, *a British Fur Trading Association,* had its headquarters at Fort Vancouver, in that part of Oregon now known as Washington Territory. Its establishment at that place was an *Indian trading post* in an *Indian country,* and in the *midst of Indians.* The Klikatat nation, among which it existed, did not then number less than 300 to 500 Indians, besides the numerous Indian visitors who were constantly coming from all parts of the country for trading and other purposes. Some years before not less than 2,000 Indians had been seen at one time at Vancouver. No white settlement had yet been allowed in the vicinity of the post, and for miles around, every effort in that line had been thwarted by the company. The post was intended mainly for Indian trade and was occupied mainly by Indians. Only a few dozens of whites, officers and servants, were there, all engaged in Indian trade, and all married to Indian women, not one of them having the liberty to marry a white woman.

Alongside of the Hudson's Bay Company's establishment, a few hundred yards of its enclosures or pickets, was a small Church building occupied by a

Catholic Missionary priest, as a place of public Catholic worship and religious instruction, open to the whole population of the place and vicinity, which population consisted of the 300 or 500 Klikatat Indians, in whose country the Church edifice was situated, of the Indians who in large numbers were in the habit of visiting the place several times a year for trading and religious purposes, and of the few whites who were attached to the company's trading post.

The Church edifice had been dedicated and consecrated to divine worship two years previous under the name of St. James, and had been constantly and exclusively used for that purpose until August, 1848, and from that date until the present day it has never been turned to any other purpose.

Public religious service was performed in the Church regularly every Sunday, and religious instruction given every Sunday and frequently on week days to large numbers of Indians, who almost exclusively composed the population of the place. The priests in charge of the Station used to visit them in their lodges, to administer to them the rites of the Church, to teach them in their native tongue and the 'jargon' of the country, to unite them in marriage, to baptize large numbers of adults and children, to console them in sickness and to give them Christian burial. The few whites attached to the service of the Hudson's Bay Company were not excluded from the same privileges, which were extended *indiscriminately* to all.

The same Missionary labors had been carried on at Vancouver, from the 24th of November, 1838, to the 14th of August, 1848, without any interruption. Before the dedication of the Church edifice in May, 1846, they were performed in an old stone house inside the fort, furnished by the Hudson's Bay Company for that purpose, and in an old house outside of the fort purchased by the head of the Oregon Mission for the same purpose, and also in the Indian camps. These labors had been even more extensive in the former years, as the number of Indians was much larger.

Every circumstance shows that from the first establishment of the Oregon Mission in 1838 up to 1848, and from 1848 to the present time, it has been the uninterrupted intention and will of its head to have a permanent Station at Vancouver. When that Vancouver Station was commenced, it was commenced with the positive intention that it should be continued indefinitely.

The Church edifice and the ground which it occupies, were a free gift of the Hudson's Bay Company or of its Chief Factor to the Church.

The priest in charge belonged to the Oregon Catholic Mission. He depended on that Mission exclusively, and was independent of the Hudson's Bay Company, as well as of any other individual. The head of the Oregon Mission appointed to that Station whomsoever he chose, and changed him whenever he pleased, without being obliged to render account to anybody.

Neither the head of the Oregon Mission nor the priest in charge of the Station had any engagement, oral or written, with the company, or any one else in regard to the spiritual attendance of that Station. Whatever attendance was there, it was spontaneous on the part of either. It was optional with them. They could attend or not, whenever they chose; no one had any right to interfere, and in fact no one ever did interfere in any way since the dedication of the Church to the present day. The priests were at home at the Church, and have been always considered so by the Hudson's Bay Company.

The current expenses of the Church, consisting of repairs, church furniture and vestments, altar wine, bread, lights, &c., were at the charge of the Oregon Mission. The priest in charge was also *supported* by the same Mission and *aided* by the Hudson's Bay Company, which *spontaneously* granted him his board and lodging free.

Such being the state of things at the St. James Mission Station at Vancouver, when the act of Congress mentioned above, was passed on the 14th of August, 1848, the Bishop of the diocese of Nesqually, in which that Station is situated, claims for it, under that act, 640 acres of land, holding that all the requisites to constitute a Missionary Station among the Indian tribes, have been fulfilled at that Station.

Three opponents arise against him, viz: the 'military authorities,' the 'citizens of Vancouver,' and the 'widow and heirs of A.M. Short,' and assert that the Mission Station of St. James cannot enjoy the favor granted by the act to all Missionary Stations—1st. Because the priests in charge of the Station were not Missionaries, but Chaplains of the Hudson's Bay Company. 2d. Because the Station is on lands formerly claimed by the Hudson's Bay Company as 'possessory rights,' which the United States Government was obliged to 'protect.'[25]

This statement of fact speaks for itself. The position of the church had been confirmed by the actual occupation of its land, except for a brief time in 1850, when the priests seem to have been absent for an interlude, during which a Hudson's Bay Company clerk rented a small log house on the disputed property to the Quartermaster's Department of the United State Army, giving the appearance of company ownership on this and other church occupied buildings.[26]

If the army did occupy the building, its tenure was brief, for on October 27, 1850, as noted above, Bishop Blanchet took up his residence at Fort Vancouver, and continued to occupy it for many years thereafter. The little church, then, was openly regarded as "the cathedral," a distinction it held until it was replaced in the same city.

"Meanwhile," as the best of Fort Vancouver's historians observes,

... the position of the Church at Vancouver had been greatly strengthened. From September 21, 1852, to May 20, 1855, the military post at Fort Vancouver was under the command of the famous frontiersman, Lieutenant Colonel Benjamin L.E. Bonneville, a Frenchman by birth who was confirmed in the Catholic faith at Vancouver on March 30, 1854. A great friendship grew up between Colonel Bonneville and Father J.B.A. Brouillet, the 'snuffy, cherry, good-hearted little padre' resident at the St. James Cathedral. Under Bonneville's protection and with his encouragement, the improvements of the church were greatly extended. About five acres of land were enclosed, an orchard was planted, and a house was built for the Bishop. It was even rumored that it was Bonneville who suggested to the priests that they file a mission claim under the act of 1848.

In subsequent years, with the approval of the military authorities, additional buildings were erected. These included a large two-story frame structure for the College of the Holy Angels, other school buildings, and a hospital for the indigent and sick.[27]

By this time the claims of Widow Short and the County were disposed of as untenable, but the claim of the United States Army continued to be asserted with more thunder, it seems, than open-minded fairness. The commander of the post had got a prize, and he was loath to let it go. The mission could well afford to wait, though Blanchet continued to press for further clearance on the title. Time passed by quietly . Witnesses in the dispute died. There were changes in the administration of departments. No one at the mission, least of all the bishop, expected what followed.

Suddenly, in November 1869, the commanding officer of Fort Vancouver dispatched to the bishop, the priests, and sisters an order he had received to expel all occupants of the mission within sixty days.[28] Blanchet immediately protested to the authorities concerned, pointing out the injustice of taking away the mission's lands, which had been formally ceded to them by law. At the same time he offered to vacate the lands in question on the payment of a reasonable sum to compensate for the loss entailed. A commission composed of officers of the War Department was appointed to investigate the bishop's claim: their report was in his favor. Weeks passed by without further action. Suddenly again, on March 4, 1870, the bishop received an arbitrary order to vacate the mission lands. This appeared as follows:

Headquarters, March 3, 1870—In compliance with instructions received from Adjutant General U.S.A. and Headquarters' Department of the Columbia, Portland, Oregon, ninety (90) days from today will be the time

allowed for the pretended Catholic Mission of St. James to remove from the
military reserve of Fort Vancouver.

By Command of Br't Brig. General Blake

E.G. Forse

1st Lieut. and Adjutant, 1st Cavalry and Post.[29]

A harsh and rigid military order like this might be expected from the
commander of an occupation army, not a public servant of American
citizens. It was outrageous, of course, but coming from such a high
source, it appeared to be final and irrevocable. However, the bishop, the
priests, and sisters had nowhere to go. Mother Joseph, with more
foresight than the others, perhaps, and fully aware of the controversial
legality of the mission's land deed, had purchased land elsewhere in
Vancouver for such an emergency, but so far no convent had been built
on this land to accommodate the sisters.[30] Thus, the sisters' position, like
the bishop's, was desperate.

Not unlike pious Catholics everywhere, they "stormed heaven" with
their prayers, making earnest petitions "to God, to the Blessed Virgin, to
St. Joseph, and to all the saints," which must have been quite a large
number even then.[31] In keeping with the old adage that God helps those
who help themselves, Blanchet dispatched an indignant telegram to the
War Department, a procedure apparently not expected by the army's
impersonal puppets in Vancouver. To the utmost surprise of everyone,
especially the bishop's lawyer's, who had decided that the mission's goose
was cooked, the bishop received a response to his protest barely four
hours later. This read: "Order for removal has been suspended by
Secretary Belknap."[32]

This was, alas!, not the end of the deplorable affair. While the bishop
enjoyed peaceful possession of the mission's land for the next decade or
more, his successor would be confronted with more violent action by the
United States Army, which ordinarily protects people from oppression.
This, the last round of the prolonged match between David and Goliath,
would be taken by Goliath and the church would be denied its title to land
now worth a college endowment. An account of this must be left to the
next chapter.

THE YAKIMA MISSION

But the church's battles were not all lost. There were men like
Croquet, Chirouse, and Cataldo who seemed to lead charmed lives far
from the bustling settlements, quietly teaching and baptizing Indians,
ignoring the bureaucrats from Washington, and winning the respect of
all except those who would exterminate their neophytes.

Another of these men was St. Onge at the Yakima mission. He had built up the mission with the help of his ex-seminarian, J.B. Boulet, until its glory rivaled the good old days when the Oblates were there. Time, however, began to take its toll. St. Onge, fatigued by his labors, requested the bishop for a change and Boulet decided to return to the seminary to seek ordination. At the request of Augustin Blanchet, Cataldo visited the mission during April 1870. He came to inspect the place with the prospect of Jesuits replacing St. Onge.

His report to Giorda was favorable and Father Joseph Caruana was appointed in October of this same year to take up his residence at St. Joseph's Mission to serve as an understudy of St. Onge.[33] Except for the Willamette farm fiasco, the Jesuits had not been involved heretofore in anything so far west as Yakima. The decision to be there was an omen; the Jesuits would soon be in Seattle, and there were those who would regard this as the enlargement of a plague.

Caruana proved to be a good learner. He soon was able to speak the Yakima language, which was entirely different from the Kalispel, and became so familiar with the territory that St. Onge trusted him completely.

During the spring of 1871, St. Onge supervised the construction of a new mission building, which was dedicated by Bishop Blanchet on July 15, 1871.[34] After the ceremony, St. Onge formally turned over the mission to the Jesuits, in the person of Caruana, and departed for a new field of labor in faraway New York State.[35]

His Lordship the bishop had always been very touchy about the Yakimas. Perhaps it was his nagging concern for the Indians, for whom he had come originally from Canada. The Yakimas, he understood very well, controlled central Washington, a vast area that showed great promise for agricultural development. This fact was not lost on the bishop who had come from a farming community.

GRANT'S PEACE POLICY

But a more serious threat had arisen. The Yakimas were by and large a Catholic tribe, converted in the early period by the Oblates. Despite this a new government policy had designated the Yakima reservation as an exclusively Methodist domain and an aggressive Methodist minister, who called himself "Father Wilbur," had taken control of the government's structure for ruling the Indians, using his influence to destroy the Catholic Church on the reservation. This new government policy, held in such contempt by Catholic missionaries, has often been called Grant's Peace Policy. Like the St. James Mission case, but on a much broader scale, this became a celebrated controversy that left in its wake the destruction of many Catholic missions and the denial of the most basic American right of freedom of religion for over ninety thousand Catholic Indians.[36]

The policy had not evolved overnight. During the several preceding decades a bitter anti-Catholic campaign had been waged. Identified with the new nationalism, this spread throughout eastern America emanating mostly from certain Protestant seminaries and brought west in the hearts and baggage of some of the seminary graduates. This was one element. Another concerned the administration of the Indian reservation system.

Catholic missionaries found themselves confronted with serious obstacles in their relationship with the United States government. There had been an ongoing crisis for years. Sectarian quarrels on various reservations added to the confusion occasioned by frequent changes in government policy, kept many of the tribes in turmoil, and cost taxpayers tons of money to keep frontier forts open and thousands of soldiers in the West. Many Indian agents were political appointees, often greedy men who, far from the restraints of Washington, exercised a crafty, ruthless art in robbing the Indians. The Episcopal Bishop Henry B. Whipple described some of them from his own experience: "They are often men without any fitness, sometimes a disgrace to a Christian nation; whiskey sellers, barroom loungers, debauchers, selected to guide a heathen people."[37] Bishop O'Connor of Omaha also spoke fearlessly about the heartless and inventive rapacity of Indian Agents and Palladino dedicated some pages of his text to accounts of their dishonesty.[38] While there were some good agents, these were greatly outnumbered by the bad.

Catholic opposition to government policy ran deeper than this problem of personnel. Officially, Congress, influenced by the Christian fundamentalists, favored both the sequestering of Indians on reservations to protect them and a "Christian education to civilize them." In practice, however, the reservations imprisoned the Indians, often with wicked caretakers, and impoverished them by selecting the poorest land for reservations. Isolated and denied proper education, the Indians were cut off from potential growth with the rest of the nation. White settlers, free to take advantage of them, without restraints of the law, gradually invaded the reservations and robbed the Indians of what few resources they had left.

President Grant was not the first to conceive the idea of using missionaries to keep the Indians under control. General William t. Sherman had used DeSmet in an almost cynical manner. DeSmet, he said, "has always been noted for his strict fidelity to the interests of our

Government, for indefatigable industry and an enthusiastic love for the Indians under his charge."[39] In 1866, Sherman told Grant: "We must act with vindictive earnestness against the Sioux, even to their extermination, men, women and children."[40] But the government did not exterminate the Sioux. They sent DeSmet in 1867 to make a treaty with them, partly to save money. Sitting Bull, who had sworn to kill the first white he saw, accepted DeSmet and made peace through him with the Americans, without a shot being fired or a dollar spent. Singlehanded, DeSmet had accomplished what the entire United States Army could not do. Well and good, he was a hero as long as he was "noted for his strict fidelity to the interests of our Government."

In 1870, it was estimated by government officials that "more than $1,000,000 had been spent for every Indian killed in warfare."[41] Yet the government, very often at the partial expense of the missionaries, cheated Indians, allocated frugal budgets, sent venal agents to rob them, and decried the missionaries who were trying to protect their rights.

By 1867, Grant openly suggested the use of these same missionaries to keep peace with the Indians and he recommended to Congress that certain reservations be turned over to the Quakers, "the peaceful people" who were expected to reduce friction between the Indians and government.[42] In making this proposal, Grant did not reveal that he intended to place some reservations under Army officers, who were to be mustered out of service. But Congress blocked his plan, for its own selfish reasons. Then Grant, unable to persuade Congress to adopt yet other measures to maintain peace on the reservations, announced a new policy. By this he sought to use *all* missionaries by allocating reservations to specific religious groups, giving each group the restricted right to nominate its own government agent for its reservation.

The allocation, according to the president's plan, was to be determined by reasonable principles, for example, priorities were to be allowed for the first arrivals, or the sect which the majority of Indians on a reservation favored. According to these norms, the Catholics had a clear right to forty nominations.

Archbishop Blanchet hailed the president's action with joyful approval. "This wise plan," he wrote happily to Washington, "will put an end to the sufferings of the poor Catholic Indian missions."[43] In another letter he said, "Hoping that the time of reformation has arrived, and that the new system proposed by our excellent President is not a mere show of vain words..." he then entered his request for the three reservations in the archdiocese: Grande Ronde, Warm Springs, and Umatilla.

The euphoria of the New Year soon passed. On January 3, 1871, DeSmet, the only Catholic representative, attended a meeting of missionaries called by the president to allocate the reservations. What followed shocked the bewildered old Jesuit, who left Washington sick at heart, doomed to die soon, a broken man. Of the forty nominations expected, the Catholics received seven reservations.[44] All other tribes, including the Blackfeet and the Yakimas, to whom the Catholics had a clear right according to the terms of the Policy, were turned over to Protestant agents, in many cases ministers who used their government positions to exclude the Catholic religion.[45] When Indians on those reservations rebelled, they were shot by American soldiers.[46]

A Catholic journalist protested. "If it be true," he wrote, "that the Indians are condemned to annihilation, should they not at least be allowed to choose the faith in which they wish to die? Baptized and instructed as Catholics, the Indians have been divided between the various denominations, and the missionaries, who collected money in Europe for evangelizing these poor savages, are expelled from the missions they founded."[47]

"We hope and pray that justice will be done," DeSmet said mournfully; but not content with praying, he spent the last months of his life writing letters of protest to General E.I. Parker, Commissioner of Indian Affairs, who owed his success with the Sioux to DeSmet. He also wrote frequently to the Secretary of the Interior. Neither of these men had the decency to respond to the priest who had done more than any other white man for the Indians of America.[48] On May 23, 1873, the Feast of the Ascension, DeSmet gave up his soul to God. He was not the first victim of Grant's Peace Policy, nor the last. But he was the only one who was labeled with ironic injustice, "a Judas Goat," for assisting his country in making peace with the Indians.[49]

"FATHER WILBUR"[50]

The government agency for the Catholic Yakimas, several hundred in number, was located in an abandoned army fort called Fort Simcoe, which, in its heyday, had been one of the army's most elegant and attractive posts. It was located in a warm, placid valley east of the Cascades, north of The Dalles, Oregon by four days with a good horse.

From The Dalles James H. Wilbur had come in 1860, uninvited seeking an opportunity to preach a new religion to the Yakimas. Wilbur was a Methodist minister. He requested the local agent to be appointed to the position of government instructor and received the job, which provided him with a salary.[51]

His services, however, proved to be unacceptable to the agent, B.F.

Kendall, who dismissed him, saying: "I was forced to remove a preacher of the Gospel from the post he occupied not because he was a preacher but for reasons too numerous to assign in a personal communication."[52] During the weeks that followed, Wilbur's influential friends attacked Kendall so bitterly, accusing him "of being influenced by a Catholic priest at Olympia," that he was forced to publish his reasons for taking the action he did.

> Occasionally presents were made to these boys from the annuity goods by the superintendent of teaching to secure their constant attendance at the school, he said.
>
> In accordance with my view of duty, I removed several employees from positions on the reservation, among those removed was the Rev. James H. Wilbur, superintendent of teaching. He had on a former occasion taken sides with Agent Lansdale in defying the authority of the superintendent when attempting the discharge of his duty. He had usurped the authority of the agent and seemed determined that no employee should be allowed to continue on the reservation who entertained religious sentiments differing from those professed by himself.
>
> He had induced the agent, without consulting the superintendent, to discharge some of the more worthy of the employees and to fill their places with his own wife and nephew. He had preferred charges to Supt. Geary (Kendall's predecessor), against the physician, not through the agent but direct. After the same had been examined by the superintendent and shown to his satisfaction to be unfounded, he renewed the charges in a letter to a gentleman upon whom rumor had conferred the appointment as superintendent of Indian Affairs.
>
> He made it his frequent business to write to officials and citizens not connected with the service inviting them to interfere to further his own selfish schemes, some of which communication has come into my hands.[53]

In other words, Wilbur replaced other employees with his wife and relatives without authority; he dipped into government property, which he used as bribes for school and church attendance; he tried to keep off the reservation any employees who did not agree with his own religious views; and he interfered in other ways in the administration of the agency.

But such was his determination and influence that he obtained the dismissal of Kendall as superintendent and got himself appointed to this position by President Lincoln himself. He returned in triumph to take charge of Fort Simcoe. When Grant's Peace Policy was announced, he grasped at it eagerly, using appropriate slogans to justify his views. With renewed zeal, he now encountered the Catholics head on, openly using his position as government agent to use government property to either punish Catholic Indians or to persuade them to change their religion.

Wilbur's biographer presents the minister's justification for this conduct:

> One of the Catholic Yakimas was irate at finding a fellow Catholic attending Wilbur's service and called him to task.
> 'Well, I needed a horse,' the friend answered. Some time later the horse was seen tied outside the Methodist chapel and an explanation demanded. 'My wagon needed fixing,' the owner said sheepishly, 'but when that's done I'll be a good Catholic again.'
> Wilbur had always seen his role at the agency as a dual one—missionary and agent. To him the two were complementary. He freely admitted that his dual role gave him an advantage, but he said it worked both ways. 'I think when a man has a commission from the President and when he is recognized as having communion with the Father of Spirits it gives him additional power in the management of the agency,' he said in testifying before the Indian commissioners.[54]

According to government policy, Wilbur could forbid Catholic proselytizing on the reservation. He went further, however, and sought to keep Catholic Indians from crossing the reservation line to attend Mass.[55] He complained to Washington about the influence of Catholic missionaries:

> They succeed in drawing off a few Indians and instructing them that marriages solemnized, baptisms administered and religious instruction given them by the agent are invalid. It seems the object of those in charge to keep the Indians in a feverish and dissatisfied state. This teaching is doing the Indians an injury and keeping them from settling on the reserve.[56]

During this period, obviously, the Catholic missionaries were not passive to "Father Wilbur's" aberrations. St. Onge openly defied him, as did the Jesuits later. The Catholic press, for example, *The Catholic Sentinel* in Portland, maintained a constant barrage of protests, accusing the Grant administration of dishonesty and of favoring the Methodist church, to which Grant belonged. These protests placed the Methodists on the defensive, especially in the matter of the Yakima reservation. Even the Methodists had to admit that the Catholics were the first missionaries to the Yakimas, but they justified their position by presenting a most ridiculous claim. They had a right to the Yakima reservation, they said, because "they had held themselves in readiness to go there since 1833."[57]

For the most part the Catholic Indians refused to join "Father Wilbur's" church. Father Urban Grassi, who covered most of Central Washington on horseback during this critical period, provided the Catholic press with an example of the Indians' fidelity:

A Methodist minister, who for some time had labored to turn Ignace, the Chief of the Yakimas, from his faith, asked him one day how much he would want for changing to Protestantism.[58]

"A big price," the chief answered him.

"Two hundred dollars?"

"More than that."

"Then how much? Five hundred, six hundred dollars?"

"Oh, more than that!"

"Indeed! State your price."

"The price of my soul."[59]

DEATH OF BISHOP DEMERS

On July 28, 1871, at approximately three in the morning, Modeste Demers died as unobtrusively as he had lived.[60] An uncommonly kind and understanding bishop, he had won the respect, even the affection, of his priests who rightly regarded his passing as the end of a heroic era. His burial three days later, attended with liturgical splendor reserved for prelates, left his brother bishops in the limbo of their own fleeting mortality, a status not overlooked by any one of them.

Eventually, on March 23, 1873, Demers' secretary, Charles John Seghers, was appointed bishop to take his place. Seghers, like DeSmet and Croquet, had been born and nursed in Belgium. He had volunteered for service in Vancouver Island, becoming what might be called an overqualified missionary, a circumstance noted not only by Demers, but by the other bishops of the region. He was consecrated in St. Andrew's Cathedral in Victoria by Archbishop Blanchet on June 29, 1873. Co-consecrators were Bishop Blanchet and D'Herbomez, so all the action was kept in the neighborhood.

Seghers was so thin then that one got the impression he was also tall, though he was only average in height. He wore rimless eye glasses which gave his small, oval-shaped face the appearance of a vigilant and underpaid schoolmaster. His firm lips, forming an even gash above his narrow chin and long neck, revealed his stubbornness, which eventually proved his undoing. Despite this residual tenaciousness, he was conspicuously gentle. He was also naive, a kind of incurable romantic like DeSmet, who saw nothing but good in others. Thus he got along very well with everyone, so well that Pius IX soon began to hear about him, but too well for his own good. Seghers was regarded as a very holy man. Like a St. Francis Xavier, he was obsessed with the salvation of his people, the good shepherd who cheerfully gave his life for his sheep.[61]

Meanwhile, the priests and sisters in the four northwest states were occupied, too, with the salvation of souls, expanding the frontier of the church as time and money permitted. The *Catholic Sentinel* presented accounts of it all, usually on the second and third pages amidst the advertisements, because the editor ordinarily dedicated the first page to speeches and the troubled politics in Europe.

NEW CHURCHES

In that period of time between the first issue of the *Sentinel* and Chief Joseph's War in 1877, twenty-one churches were built, either to replace others or as first churches in their own vicinity. In addition to St. Joseph's Mission church on Attanum Creek, built by Father St. Onge, as already noted, St. Patrick's Church in Boise City was assembled by Father Mesplie with the help of the soldiers from Boise City.[62] This church burned to the ground three weeks after dedication, on January 12, 1871, leaving a debt on it of two thousand dollars. In spite of the debt, plans for rebuilding the church were made at once, though it was five years before they were realized.[63]

In less time, Father Vermeersch built a new church for the Umatilla Indians. Brouillet offered the first Mass in this on February 25, 1871.[64] Exactly a month later, the ubiquitous Father Dieleman was in Baker City, where he celebrated public Mass on Easter Sunday, April 9, 1871. By October he had completed the first church in Baker City, located on the corner of Church and First Streets. This was dedicated in honor of St. Francis de Sales on October 19, 1871.[65] Another mission church called St. Peter's was built by Father Chirouse and his Indians at Port Madison on Puget Sound. This appears to have been the second church on the site, which was later preempted by the military. At that time, St. Peter's was dismantled. Doors, windows, and lumber were carried across Agate Pass in a rowboat by a Cherokee Indian and reassembled near the Indian cemetery at Suquamish.[66]

North of Vancouver, Washington, two new churches were established—one at Cathlamet, built by Father Richards of Cowlitz Prairie and dedicated in October, 1871 in honor of St. Charles Borromeo, and the other built by Father Halde just eight miles west of Vancouver. This was dedicated on November 5, 1871, in honor of St. John the Evangelist.[67] In Central Washington, Grassi made his first visit to the Simpesquensi Tribe on the Wenatchee River in the summer of 1872. Subsequently, in December 1873, he built the first church for these Indians eleven miles west of Wenatchee near present Cashmere. He named this mission St. Francis Xavier.[68]

In September of 1872, Father Richards was in Kalama, where he celebrated the first Mass in the upper story of Shelenger's Block. A church completed there in the following year was blessed in honor of St. Charles.[69] Father Prefontaine, meanwhile, donned a carpenter's apron and, with his own hands, built Sacred Heart Church for whites at La Connor, Washington. Bishop Blanchet blessed this on July 8, 1873.[70]

In 1874, there were three new churches: the first one dedicated was on September 8, at Slickpoo, Idaho, built for the Nez Perce Indians with money collected from whites in Lewiston, Indians on the Coeur d'Alene reservation, and Chinese miners in the Coeur d'Alene mining district.[71] The second church was Mary Star of the Sea in Astoria, built by Father Patrick Gibney on land purchased by thirty-six soldiers, Battery C, Second United States Artillery, stationed at Fort Stevens. This was dedicated by Archbishop Blanchet on October 11, 1874.[72] The third was St. Anthony's Church at Nesqually, Washington, built on a three hundred foot plateau despite opposition from the local Indian agent, who refused the Indians even the use of a wagon. Under Father Charles Richards' direction, the Indians carried all the lumber to the site on their backs.[73]

During the next two years, the log church at Deer Lodge, Montana was replaced with a stone structure and the frame church in Helena was replaced with a magnificent brick edifice, which cost thirty-eight thousand dollars. Blessed under the patronage of "The Sacred Hearts of Jesus and Mary," this became Montana's first cathedral in 1884.[74] In the same period, 1875-1876, seven first time churches were built: at Gervais, Oregon, begun in 1872, dedicated to Saints Gervase and Protase on June 13, 1875;[75] on the Puyallup reservation, St. John the Baptist mission church, dedicated by Bishop Blanchet on August 22, 1875;[76] at Verboort, Oregon, St. Francis Xavier Church, built for the use of six Catholic families who had migrated to Oregon to found a Catholic colony. Its first pastor was Father William Verboort, for whom the settlement was named.[77] Near Yakima City, [at Union Gap], a chapel in the Sisters' academy served as a temporary church for whites. Here Mass was offered for the first time on November 13, 1875, by Father John Raiberti, an elderly Jesuit who looked so frail people called him a ghost.[78]

At McMinnville in Oregon, the first St. James Church was built by Father J. Dols. This was dedicated by Archbishop Blanchet on June 20, 1876.[79] Then several months later, on October 8, Father Richards offered the first Mass in St. Rose of Lima Church, which had been built at Frenchtown, a settlement comprising some two hundred Catholics a few miles west of Walla Walla.[80]

Finally, in the autumn of 1876, there were two more new Catholic churches to serve the needs of the growing archdiocese, one in East

Portland and the other in Montana. The Portland church, called St. Francis of Assisi, was dedicated by Archbishop Blanchet on September 24. His Grace was assisted by Father Louis Verhaag, the parish's first pastor, who later merited the lasting gratitude of church historians: he produced a precious little periodical called *Reminiscences and Current Topics of the Ecclesiastical Province of Oregon,* a magazine of sorts but also a rare and priceless source of history.[81] The East Portland church was demolished by a hurricane in January 1880, a most unlikely fate for anything in the Northwest, least of all for a church.[82]

The last of these many temples of God was St. Joseph's, erected in Canton, Montana. It was dedicated on October 22, 1876, a small church in a vast area, bearing witness to the faith of the handful of people who produced it.[83]

These were recently-built churches, each one representing countless heartaches and frustrations. The soldier's role in their construction surfaces over and over, manifesting not only the faith and generosity of these men of arms, many of whom were of Irish and German extraction, but also their sense of priorities. These were the enlisted men mostly, not their officers who, generally speaking, were not well disposed toward the progress of the church. This was one difference on the frontier between the upper social classes of America and Catholic immigrants.

THE NEW SCHOOLS

One expects the construction of churches. What is surprising, perhaps, is the preoccupation of American Catholics, even in the mendicant church of the Northwest, with schools. This fact was immediately recognized by Protestant mission groups, who became somewhat paranoid about the number and influence of Catholic education on America's frontiers.

"The growth of Roman Catholicism," one later-day historian remarked, "was just as much an incentive for the establishment of Protestant schools and colleges in the West as for the erection of Protestant churches. The educational activities of the Catholics in the West were a challenge to Protestantism. The schools in the West conducted by Catholics, mainly primary schools and academies, were numerous. The children of Protestant parents frequently attended them either because there were no other schools available or because of their excellence.... Sinister motives were frequently attributed to these laudable efforts in behalf of education. The teachers were referred to as 'Jesuits', and no doubt many of them did belong to the order that has concerned itself especially with education."[85]

No doubt the author of this passage would be surprised to learn that the Jesuits themselves, during the early years, produced only one mission school, St. Ignatius, founded in 1856. The first college was St. Joseph's at St. Paul on the Willamette, a short-lived institution that accepted its demise when Oregon was abandoned in the gold rush. This, like two other early colleges, was conducted by the diocesan clergy under the stern surveillance of the bishops. Holy Angels College in Vancouver, established in 1856, also survived in one form or another until 1911, when it gave up the ghost, allegedly because of the popularity of the Jesuits' Gonzaga, which was founded much later.

ST. MICHAEL'S COLLEGE

St. Michael's College in Portland, which opened exactly one month after the death of Bishop Demers, on August 28, 1871, eventually suffered the same fate as its predecessors: it perished for lack of students. In this respect it was similar, also, to scores of small Protestant colleges that popped up all over the West, in part to meet the challenge of Catholic schools. More than sixty students appeared at St. Michael's for registration on the first day. Subsequently, they wandered curiously about the frame building that had been thrown together on Fourth Street between Mill and Montgomery in three hectic months.

The success of the school's early beginnings, indeed its very existence, was due to the energetic Father Fierens, pastor of the cathedral and vicar general with the title of "Very Reverend." Father A.J. Glorieux was the first principal and Father John Heinrich, recently ordained, was his assistant. The *Sentinel* had announced that classes would be conducted "in Primary, Intermediate and Higher Courses," but said nothing about the transfer of "Orphan boys" from the care of the sisters at St. Mary's to the new college.[87]

Nor did the *Sentinel* comment on one of the principal reasons for the college's presence. Perhaps no one expressed this, but it undoubtedly played an important part in the decisionmaking process that assigned two of only sixteen priests in the whole archdiocese to a small college for boys. This part involved, of course, the fostering of vocations to the secular priesthood. This had always been one of the priorities of both the Blanchets, who had long since learned how the Jesuits had attracted candidates to their order. St. Michael's, in this respect, served its purpose, for one of its first students was precocious little Edward O'Dea, the future third Bishop of Nesqually.

In other respects, St. Michael's soon rivaled the older college, Holy Angels. According to contemporary accounts, it boasted of "a brass band, telegraph apparatus, physical laboratory and a printing office."[88] Its students also published a paper called *The Archangel*, which enjoyed a circulation of about five hundred.

The *Sentinel* now carried substantial advertisements for California's Santa Clara College, calling attention to its courses in geology and assaying, also for St. Michael's in Portland and Holy Angels, as well as for St. Mary's, which was the proper finishing school for well-to-do young ladies. All of these schools gave notice "of strict discipline," but only St. Michael's excluded all visitors during school hours, because their presence, the principal noted, disturbed the concentration of the college's very studious scholars.

During this period 1871–1876, eight other Catholic schools appeared. These were as follows:

In 1871, exact date unknown, William McBean, former trader at Walla Walla, opened a school for Catholic children at Frenchtown, four years before the church was completed.[89]

At St. Francis Regis Mission on the Colville reservation, four Sisters of Providence from Vancouver, having traveled by boat, stagecoach, and wagon, opened a school called Providence of the Sacred Heart on September 26, 1873. This was an elementary school for Indian girls.[90]

The Sisters of Providence from Vancouver opened another school in March 1874, at Missoula, Montana. Initially this was to provide for orphan children. Later it was established as Sacred Heart Academy.[91]

ST. MICHAEL'S MISSION AT GRANDE RONDE

On April 17, 1874, three Sisters of the Holy Names from Portland, arrived at Father Croquet's mission, St. Michael's at Grande Ronde, to open a school. They were greeted with a thirteen gun salute from the soldiers of the nearby fort, and a cavalcade of Indians, some of whom bade them welcome with eloquent speeches in Indian.[92] The fireworks were gratifying, no doubt, but the revelations that followed soon left the sisters disheartened. Though they were called "Clooch men le pretre," which means in Chinook "women priests," they learned that they were taken for granted by all except Father Croquet, who was so wrapped in prayer he scarcely knew they were there. They had brought with them, as gifts from their sisters in Portland, a harmonium and four artificial rose bushes. They would cheerfully have traded all of these for a stove. Croquet had three rooms adjoining the church, but these were filled with mice, who were so bold they built their nests in his straw mattress. The sisters' "house," a frame 26 x 44, boasted of an exact half dozen chairs, bedsteads, and a cupboard as bare as bones. That was all.[93] Despite this, they were expected to have their school ready by June 1 and to accommodate what turned out to be fifty-two resident students.[94]

Several months after these heroic souls opened their school, the pastor, Patrick Gibney, started a parish school in Astoria on September 2, 1874. Unable to obtain sisters for teaching, he persuaded Miss Nancy O'Brien to serve until sisters could be provided.[95] There is no record on how long O'Brien survived, but the Holy Names Sisters did not make it to Astoria for twenty-two more years. This was ironic, too, since Astoria was the first permanent white settlement in the Northwest, and the first to enjoy the presence of Catholic sisters.[96]

SISTERS AT BAKER CITY

Four sisters of the Holy Names left Portland on April 23, 1875, to establish an academy in Baker City. These were Sisters Mary Justina, Mary Loecadia, and Mary Stephan. Their travel schedule is worthy of note: First train to Celilo on the Columbia, steamboat to Umatilla. This they boarded at 3:30 a.m. on Sunday and arrived at 5:00 p.m. on April 25. They remained in a hotel, where they received a gift of $24.00. On April 26, they left by stagecoach at 7:00 a.m. for Weston, where they registered in another hotel at 5:00 p.m. On April 27, in Blue Mountains their stagecoach became stuck in mud at 6:00 p.m. and they were ordered out by two rude men who brought them in a wagon to another stagecoach beyond. At 10:00 p.m. they reached a stage station where they "rested" until breakfast at 4:00 a.m. The stagecoach left at 5:00 a.m. and arrived in Baker City at 8:00 p.m. where Father DeRoo greeted them warmly.[97] He was especially delighted to have them in his parish, partly because he was able to take his meals at the convent, gratis.

In Baker City, the sisters rented a temporary shelter while they raised funds and contracted for a new convent near the church. Awaiting completion of the latter, they opened their temporary home for classes. Only four girls applied for admission because of a wave of anti-nun prejudice occasioned by the circulation of Maria Monk's notorious book.[98] However, by the time that the new convent academy was completed, the storm had spent itself. The sisters inaugurated the new school called Notre Dame Academy on August 23, only four months after leaving Portland. In their first class they had twenty-three students, about one for each problem they faced, most of them with the name of Father DeRoo.

THE SISTERS OF PROVIDENCE

These were very difficult times for the sisters. When they started schools or academies, they had no contracts or agreements. They seldom received a decent salary, if anything at all, and they were often taken advantage of by thoughtless pastors, who expected them to perform many duties in the parish without support or recognition.

When three Sisters of Providence left Vancouver for Yakima City by stagecoach, they experienced a six-day voyage similar to that which the Holy Names Sisters endured some months earlier. They departed from Vancouver on November 6, 1875, to open the first school for whites in the present diocese of Yakima. Sixteen days later they accepted their first students, nine in number, for St. Joseph's Academy. In May, 1877, a new frame school was built for them, for two hundred dollars, an almost ludicrous amount which removes all doubt about the elegance of the edifice.[99]

Finally, on September 12, 1876, three other Sisters of Providence from Vancouver arrived at Cowlitz Prairie to establish Our Lady of Lourdes Academy.[100] Classes there were begun on November 13 for the girls and on November 27 for the boys. The use of the district school was offered to the Sisters who accepted it happily and by the end of the first year they counted a total of sixty students. Unfortunately this school was closed prematurely because of the frequent absences of the local priest who left the sisters without daily Mass.

MOTHER JOSEPH'S NEW CONVENT

Poverty, also, had played a part in the sisters' decision to cut back on some of their widely-spread activities. The fact is, the Sisters of Providence at this time were deep in debt, and the demands being made upon them seemed to increase by leaps and bounds. Mother Joseph had determined, finally, to build the long hoped-for convent on their new land, which was not subject to litigation. There was no money for it, but Mother Caron, the Superior General of the Congregation who had come from Montreal to visit her sisters, approved of the proposal and urged Mother Joseph to proceed.[101] She pointed out the inadequacy of the present collection of buildings and the threat that the sisters faced from "the disputed land." The local sisters needed little encouragement; what they needed was money.

On June 9, 1873, his Lordship the Bishop, with Father Junger of the cathedral, Mother Caron, Mother Joseph, and a group of other sisters, accompanied by "the larger orphan boys," formed a procession to the site selected for the new "central building" as it was called, and Mother Caron turned over the first shovelfuls of earth. "The orphan boys continued the shoveling" and Mother Caron said, "Sisters, fear nothing! Go ahead with confidence!"[102]

Some of the sisters had been begging money "in the mines of Idaho" and they had on hand eleven thousand, four hundred dollars. This was less than one-fourth of what was required, so sisters were dispatched in all directions to gather what crumbs of gold and silver they could find. They traveled to Chile, to Peru, to Canada, to California, and elsewhere, grossing twelve thousand dollars in all, four thousand of it from the people of Chile.[103]

While some of the sisters were out begging, others moved into the new convent on September 7, 1874, and on the following day, attended the first Mass there in the parlor, which was made to serve as a chapel for many years.[104] At this point, Mother Joseph listed the number of people "in the Providence of the Holy Angels:" 39 Professed Religious, 6 Aspirants to the religious life, 5 Tertiary Sisters, 3 Aged men, 2 Aged women, 30 Orphan boys, 36 Orphan girls, 43 Day pupils, 33 Collegians, 105 Patients and 1 Employee." No mention is made of the number of dogs and cats in the convent's menagerie.

ST. VINCENT'S HOSPITAL, PORTLAND

Despite her heavy burden of management of this diverse collection of mankind, Mother Joseph gave time and thought to the needs of the Catholics across the river in Portland. The entire Archdiocese of Oregon City did not have a Catholic hospital, a not-so-small detail of which Mother was reminded when her sisters made an occasional trip by rowboat to visit the Holy Names Sisters at St. Mary's. In July of 1874, during construction of the "Central building" in Vancouver, she was pleased to receive two offers of land for the use of a hospital in Portland, one on the east side made by the renowned frontiersman Ben Holladay, and the other on the west side made by Portland's energetic St. Vincent de Paul Society.[106] The west side property, located on Twelfth and Marshall Streets, carried with it a cash offer of one thousand dollars.

It is not likely that Mother Joseph hesitated for long in making her decision to accept the proposal made by the St. Vincent de Paul Society. One thousand dollars in cash looked pretty good when you hovered on the brink of bankruptcy. Construction on the new hospital, designed to accommodate seventy-five beds, was begun in August of the same year. On May 10 of the following year, 1875, four sisters from Vancouver took up residence in the almost completed building to prepare for its inauguration, and on July 19 Archbishop Blanchet formally dedicated it in honor of St. Vincent de Paul.[107] Portland now had its first Catholic hospital, a most gratifying acquisition for his Grace, who at the ripe old age of seventy-nine, was looking his own last confinement squarely in the eye.

SISTERS OF PROVIDENCE IN SEATTLE

For the sisters, the experience of opening a new hospital was exhilarating. It had all worked out so well that, when Mother Joseph was contacted by Father Prefontaine in Seattle about taking over the County Poor Farm, she was immediately interested.

Prefontaine tended to take himself too seriously and he seemed to resent the presence of another priest in his territory. He certainly did not want an assistant, but, despite this, the bishop in 1876 appointed Father Emil Kauten to help him.[108] Seattle at this time had less than 4,500 people, but there were missions attached to it as part of the parish. Prefontaine did not like the bishop's decision.

The presence of another priest, however, allowed him an opportunity to return to his home in Canada for the first time since he came to Washington. It also provided him with time to visit the Exposition in Philadelphia, which had captured his fancy.[109]

Upon his return in December, he entered into negotiations with the County Commissioners regarding the care of public invalids by the Sisters of Providence. A favorable agreement was reached and, on May 2, 1877, two Sisters of Providence, Sisters Blandine and Peter Claver, arrived in Seattle to take charge of the County's farm.[110]

During the following year, 1877, Prefontaine was instrumental again in aiding the sisters to acquire land for a hospital. There is some doubt about the nature of this land's previous use, "an old soap factory," says Father Metz, and "the former Moss residence" according to the sisters. Perhaps it was both. All agree that this half-block of land was at fifth and Madison Streets and that the building upon it was converted into a primitive hospital, which they called on the advice of others, Providence Hospital.[111] Thus, says Father Metz in conclusion, "the remodeled soap factory was the insignificant beginning of the present Providence Hospital."[112]

In Portland, the archbishop's awareness of his own decline was shared by Bishop Lootens, whose Vicariate of Idaho had drifted from bad to worse. The *Catholic Sentinel*, in November 1874, reported that "Catholic families are fast leaving Boise Basin. St. Joseph's Academy has thus far lost ten children this year. Our Catholic children in school will not exceed twenty-five in number this year. The congregation attendance at Idaho City on Sunday was about forty, twenty at Pioneer City, three at

Centerville, and where His Lordship lives at Granite Creek, there are not more than forty in attendance."[113]

The bishop had next to nothing and could not pay the church's debt. The archbishop continued to complain about this, without however, lifting a hand to help him.[114]

FATHER MESPLIE ARMY CHAPLAIN

Bishop Lootens had another source of headaches. This was Father Mesplie, the hyperactive pastor of Boise who had got into his head that he must be an army chaplain. Mesplie had kept diaries for twenty years, and these contained very valuable material regarding the history of Indian people as well as of the church. In 1871, when the rectory in Idaho City burned down, all of the diaries burned up with it. Mesplie was heartbroken and lamented to his friend Thomas Donaldson: "Zey is all gone, all burned up! My love's my life's labor! All, All, All! But, oh why?"[115]

The experience left him desolate and he yearned for distractions—something to keep him busy, or a new position that would allow him to move about. Encouraged by the commandant of the local fort in Boise, he applied for an appointment as chaplain of the base.[116] Subsequently, Bishop Lootens sent him to Washington to lobby for the return of the Fort Hall Indian reservation to the Catholics, and while there, he did a little lobbying of his own. Through influential friends, like General Philip Sheridan, whom he had known on the West Coast, he received his appointment on August 17, 1872. His salary was $1,500 a year.[117] He expected to be assigned to Fort Boise, but was ordered to proceed to Camp Harney in Oregon, instead. This deprived the vicariate of his services for a time, leaving the bishop with only two diocesan priests for the entire territory.

While Mesplie enjoyed the glamor of his new status, he did not neglect to help the Indian people wherever he was assigned. The government recognized this, and used his services to pacify Indians when required. Thus, he was free to move about the various reservations, where he preached to the Indians and baptized hundreds, especially the dying adults and children.

In June 1874, Mesplie was back in Boise as chaplain at the fort. He used this as a base for visiting Fort Hall Indians and settlements of the whites, preaching and baptizing all over southern Idaho. This was all to the good, but his habitual carelessness in keeping records became a matter of grave concern to his bishop. Archbishop Blanchet had opposed his appointment as a chaplain for this very reason. "I declare," he said when his approval was requested, "that you are too easy-going to be competent for that office [chaplain]."[118] This lack of accountability proved, in the end, to be his downfall, for, as we shall see later, he barely escaped a long rest in the penitentiary. The archbishop made no effort to conceal his differences with Mesplie and one suspects that when Mesplie became entangled with the law, he merely said, "I told you so."

RESIGNATION OF BISHOP LOOTENS

Bishop Lootens, meanwhile, confided in Mesplie. On March 10, 1874, he wrote to him to say that he would submit his resignation to the Holy See "within a few days."[119] He kept his word, but Rome was slow in responding. Shattered in health, forlorn, and penniless, he left Idaho on October 25, 1875, and returned to seek lodging with his old friends in Victoria, in the Diocese of Vancouver Island, where he had begun his priestly labors. And there he retired, living in a little cottage by the sea, his companion a Japanese servant whom he afterwards converted. Eleven years later, in 1886, the bishops of the Province of Oregon agreed to give him a small pension. The Vicariate of Idaho, for example, contributed the frugal amount of $120 a year.[120]

During his retirement, Lootens composed a book in French on Gregorian music. He played the organ in a mission church and directed the choir. He spent much time fishing on the banks of the Cowichan River, a distinguished and learned senior citizen, biding his time till death.

These were not happy years. Time had taken its toll and Lootens now presented the spectacle of a disillusioned and tired old man with heavy jowls and a nose that flared out, as though it detected a foul smell in the air. Wisps of white hair appeared above his rimless glasses, through which his soft, gentle eyes peered warily, suspicious of the intentions of others. Gone was the bejeweled pectoral cross of 1871 and in its place was a simple, cheap cross, which dangled from its thin gold chain, above the wide episcopal sash enveloping his large body. Thus he waited for years, like old men everywhere, growing heavy with flesh, uncertain about the future.[121]

Rome finally accepted his resignation on July 16, 1876. At the same time, Archbishop Blanchet was appointed administrator of the Vicariate of Idaho. In a letter to the clergy, dated August 22, 1876, His Grace informed the faithful of the archdiocese of his new responsibilities. It is not likely that he viewed them with favor, for in all of Idaho and western Montana the total population of Catholic whites was given as 800. The entire area had only three secular priests, ten Jesuits, twelve churches and one convent.[122] It is quite likely that the debt of $4,000 was still there, awaiting the archbishop's honest payment.[123]

FATHER ALEX ARCHAMBAULT

One of Looten's pioneer priests was Alex Archambault, who had come into the vicariate with his lordship in 1869. Archambault, like Poulin, as noted above, was totally different from the flamboyant Mesplie. He was a steady, orderly worker, like a beaver, as compared to an elk. He was also buried under debts and, on January 2, 1877, as he informed the archbishop, he had to sell his horse to make a mortgage payment on the church.[124] Three months later, he was still crying, "poor man," to the archbishop, who seemed to be deaf to his pleas. In December, he reported, a new priest had come to Idaho City, uninvited, and he was giving scandal "to many people" by frequenting the saloon.

Archambault, whose French Canadian origins resembled those of the archbishop, was scandalized also. A very spiritual priest, as his assignment required, he proposed to organize "a group of Priests under the Sacred Heart, to go out alone in this vast territory to work for God." Each year, he added, "they should make a retreat together with the Jesuits."[125] From these comments, one learns something very intimate about Father Archambault, who by this time, December 1877, had the spiritual care of all of southern Idaho.[126]

The archbishop, during the previous July, had dispatched a letter of apology to the Catholics of Idaho, admitting he had done very little for the vicariate.[127] He promised to send another priest, then unabashedly gave orders for a special collection to be taken at all the Idaho churches to reduce their debts. Archambault, though he was still recovering from diphtheria, spent two months traveling through the wilderness to read the archbishop's letter at each lonely little church. There is no record regarding the results of these efforts. As for the promises made, another priest did not arrive to help him until 1879, when he was broken in health and unable to beat himself, like a tired horse, any longer. He left Idaho the following year, when the dark clouds of monetary depression were beginning to break.[128]

THE BUREAU OF CATHOLIC INDIAN MISSIONS

Meanwhile, the arbitrary decisions of the Washington bureaucrats began to bear unexpected fruit: Catholic prelates and others were forced to unite in their efforts to correct the injustices occasioned by the presidents's policy. The net result was the establishment of the Bureau of Catholic Indian Missions, which evolved in this manner:

Archbishop Blanchet, like DeSmet, had taken the initiative in making protests to Washington. He had demanded the return of Catholic reservations to Catholic control, in particular the Klamath in Oregon and the Fort Hall reservation in Idaho. Gradually, he came to realize that nothing could be accomplished in Washington without an intermediary who could serve formally as an on-the-ground lobbyist. Subsequently and frequently, he called the attention of other bishops to the need for a Washington agent "to promote the cause of Catholic Indian missions on government reservations."[129]

Father Mesplie, who had spent some months in the nation's capital as the representative of Bishop Lootens, recommended that Father Brouillet of the Nesqually Diocese be appointed to this task. Others had preceded Brouillet on a temporary basis; unlike them, however, he was designated "as a permanent participant in the affairs of the Catholic Indian Missions, work for which he was well qualified by ability and experience."[130] Brouillet accepted the commission and was given Archbishop Blanchet's power of attorney "but without any of the parties *intending* that the assignment was to be permanent."[131] This sounded like double talk, but the important consequence is that Brouillet went to Washington at the end of 1872 and became identified with what eventually became the Bureau.[132]

Brouillet's loss to the diocese of Nesqually was like the loss of Mesplie to Idaho. So far, however, the northwest dioceses had not been deprived of any of its priests by death. This favorable record was broken when a young man of the archdiocese, the first secular priest to die in the Northwest, unexpectedly, and for no known reason, died in September 1873. His name was Julian DeCraene, aged thirty, and like most young people who die, he "showed great promise."[133]

Two other intimate friends of the Blanchet's soon followed DeCraene in death. The first of these was old Judge Joseph Petrain of Vancouver, one of the star witnesses for the Church in the St. James Mission Land Case.[134] Apparently he had begun his services with the Hudson's Bay Company as a baker when he arrived in Vancouver on November 4, 1837. He was the first to welcome Blanchet and Demers when they arrived in 1838, and in the course of the years he became a highly respected citizen and a judge. His friendship for the priests never lessened. His death was a great loss of a different kind. Because he could not testify at the future trials in the land case, the testimony of deeply prejudiced witnesses was accepted by the court, determining ultimately the outcome of the case.

A new young priest from Belgium, Father Peter Hylebos, was resident at the Cowlitz church when an old Indian died. This was Kisskaxe, one of the faithful interpreters for the pioneer priests. The *Sentinel's* obituary is presented here in full because it contains many details of general interest, details that appear nowhere else but are very useful for disclosing Indian characteristics of that age:

DEATH OF THE OLDEST INDIAN ON THE COAST
Cowlitz Prairie, W.T., Dec. 20th, 1875

The oldest Indian on this Coast died at Cowlitz Prairie, W.T., last week, at the age of 114 years. His Christian name was Simon, and he was a Christian only three years. In his youth he used to be called Kisskaxe. He was one of the greatest Chiefs of the Cowlitz tribe, and was renowned for his prudence and warlike courage. Twenty years ago, when making an enrollment of his subjects, he stood at the head of 936 warriors, to-day he leaves a tribe of only five families to mourn his loss. Small-pox and whiskey did the work here as elsewhere.

In early days when Bishop Demers was evangelizing this part of the country, old Kisskaxe was his interpreter, and always proved himself to be a friend and a help to the priests. For reasons unknown Kisskaxe refused the saving waters of Baptism up to three years ago, when he was also married in the Catholic Church.

He never touched a drop of liquor but twice in his long lifetime, and that was when he was taken down with the fever and ague somewhere along the Columbia River. Not long ago he was heard to address in the following manner a white man who was addicted to evil intimacy with king alcohol: 'You Boston-man, you kill Indians, you kill yourself. An Indian drinks and has no boots, no pants, no coat, no hat, no nothing, no wife, no children, no gun. You Boston-man, you die and you have no clothes around you in your coffin; your head, your feet, and your body, but no clothes. You go down in the coffin, down in the grave, and your feet knock the coffin flox! flox! because no clothes, because you drink.

As an honor, the Indians who arrive to a very old age, get their name changed and so Kisskaxe became Tghemals. Shortly before dying he received the last sacraments, repeated several times all his prayers in the Indian dialect which he had learned when interpreter and had taught to his tribe over thirty-five years ago, when believing but not professing the Catholic faith. Finally, with all the fervor of a dying Christian, he recommended himself to the Blessed Virgin, and her Son, sang the beautiful hymn: 'Oias Skukum maika,' etc., laid down his head and died.

When laid in the coffin, he was dressed in a suit of the finest black cloth, imported by the Hudson Bay Company, which he had bought some thirty years ago, and which he used to show to his brethren of the forest as the reward of temperance. R.I.P.
Yours Devotedly,
P.F.H.[135]

So death, like California in the early days, was taking its toll. British Columbia, too, had taken its share—the incomparable Oblates, leaving only a corporal's guard to placate the crusty old bishop, who could not make up his mind about them. But now the time had come, said the

Oblate superior in British Columbia, for the remaining Oblates to leave the Nesqually Diocese for Canada.

FATHER CHIROUSE AND THE OBLATES

The transition had been in the making for several years. Chirouse with Father Richards and two brothers, had kept the Tulalip Mission functioning from its inception in 1861. Its school had become a model for Indian schools elsewhere, and Chirouse himself had become a kind of legend, not only among Catholic missionaries, but elsewhere, particularly in Washington. He had been, of course, the United States Indian agent, theoretically supported by the government, but as noted above, he had used his meager salary for keeping his school open.

Father Chirouse saw no advantage whatever in Grant's Peace Policy. He wrote from Tulalip to Brouillet in Washington on March 22, 1876: "Why do they not understand at Washington that Grant's Indian policy is and shall always be a necessary cause of war and injustice among the sects, and a drawback in the civilization of the Indians, and why do they not select good and honest military men and let them have the control and let the Indians free in their religion?"[136]

Chirouse had ample reason to complain, for, in 1874, those reservations outside the Tulalip Agency, and to which he and Richards had been ministering, were turned over to the Presbyterians and Methodists. The official government report itself stated that "There have never been Protestant missions nor regular Protestant teaching of any kind among the Indians of the Puget Sound or vicinity."[137]

There were Protestants, and many of them, who appreciated the work of the Catholic missionaries and one of them described his visit to the Tulalip Mission:

Attending sick calls in a parish the size of Ireland is no child's play. When one of the Fathers in the month of April or May attends a call by the Columbia lakes, or in some place more remote, he carries with him a few pounds of potatoes and plants three or four in each place where he may hope to find a dinner in harvest when he returns on the path of duty. Fishhooks and lines are very useful to these men; they are often compelled to fish for a dinner, and find it or fast. When they return to the mission, it is not to rest, but to work, picking potatoes, cooking, ploughing; they are the only men I ever saw who could enjoy the pleasure produced by working eighteen hours a day. Their influence over the Indian tribes is not at all surprising. I attended Mass on the 2nd of November, All Soul's Day ... The Indians on their knees prayed with the priest for the souls of the dead. Mass over, the whole tribe, male and female, followed the priest to the graveyard ... they marched all around the graves singing the litanies. I did not understand a word of their language but it electrified me. I followed the procession to see the sport, and to laugh at the performance, but when I saw the crowd of savage men halt before the Cross in the wilderness, and kneel to pray, I took off my hat, and knelt down with them and prayed in earnest; and I can tell you that praying in earnest was something new to me and beautiful. It was a solemn scene. They returned in silence to the village, the chief leading, and followed by the priest and the procession. At night, the Indian village was a picture of domestic peace—no whiskey, no noise, or rudeness. There was good humor smiling on their faces, and there was the laugh that was musical because it was the echo of mirth.[138]

After five years of service as an agent of the Indian Bureau, Chirouse tendered his resignation because, he said, "of the failure of the Indian Bureau to provide an adequate number of employees on the reservation had made his work equivalent to that of two or three men . . . and he had also been meeting opposition lately from 'bad Freemasons' who were desirous of having him removed from his position."[139]

There was a long delay before his successor was named. It was not until July 14, 1876, that his resignation was filed with the Secretary of the Interior by Charles Ewing, the Catholic Commissioner of Indian Missions, who recommended Major Edmund Mallet as the new agent. Three months later, on October 11, 1876, Mallet, having been approved for the post, arrived at Tulalip to replace Chirouse.

The first inkling of the Oblates final departure from the Diocese of Nesqually was a letter written by Chirouse to Brouillet, dated August 29, 1877, and containing the following: "I inform you that His Lordship, Right Reverend D'Herbomez has concluded to recall all of us from Tulalip very soon." Chirouse, reluctant to leave, wanted Brouillet to intervene.[140] On December 6, 1877, Mallet, a firm supporter of the Oblates, was replaced by a new agent, Alfred Marion, who made it known in a subtle manner, that he would not be unhappy to see the Oblates leave. Seven months after Marion arrived, on February 28, 1878, he formally notified Brouillet that the Oblates had received official orders from D'Herbomez to retire to British Columbia. "Father Chirouse told me today that it was definitely settled he would have to leave Tulalip. . . ."[141]

Chirouse and Richards were not the only ones saddened by their impending departure. There were many protests and petitions from the Indians, and a great amount of correspondence flying back and forth between Washington and Tulalip. But in the end D'Herbomez, now somewhat on the defensive, had his way. "On August 15, 1878, having settled their accounts with the government and resigned the charge of the contract school, the last of the little band of Oblate pioneers who had undertaken to teach the truths of Catholicism to the tribes of the North

West Coast of the United States, passed from the diocese of Nesqually to that of New Westminster."[142]

D'Herbomez, in his report to Rome, tried to clear the air. "We desired to make our reasons to our Very Reverend Father Superior General and he has found them good and has approved them. Since then we have had a long correspondence with Bishop A.M. Blanchet on this subject; His Excellency has finally consented, asking me to give him six months so that he can take measures to replace our personnel; we have given him more than twelve months and we have left him on the best of terms."[143]

JESUIT PROGRESS

If the Jesuits, contrary to the infallible opinions of some savants, had not created a system of schools in the Northwest, it was only a matter of time before they would. There were, of course, compelling reasons for their failure to plow this promising field, the greatest of which was lack of men. At this time there were about forty-three Jesuits; twenty-three priests and twenty brothers, to serve all of eastern and central Washington, northern Idaho, and western Montana.

Two Jesuits especially were dashing about central Washington's mountains, deserts, and potholes, like Pinkerton men looking for horse thieves, searching out bands of wandering Indians and occasionally finding Catholic settlers on homestead land, the first citizens of many future towns. These two were Joseph Caruana and Urban Grassi, both of whom now called the Yakima mission home. Another soon joined them, Aloysius Parodi, who was a very saintly Italian Jesuit, conspicuous for learning and prayer, but almost helpless in the practical order. Father John Raiberti, mentioned above, appeared also. Whence he came, no one knows, some said from the grave because of his bony, almost fleshless appearance.[144]

In northeastern Washington, Father Tosi had moved St. Francis Regis Mission again, and started construction on a new church, for which the Indians wanted new statues. They gathered a fund consisting of the following: "$125 in coins, 4 horses, 1 cow, 1 buffalo robe, 1 blanket and a few pieces of calico."[145] This provided enough statues for a baroque church.

At St. Ignatius Mission in Montana, the Jesuits' only school was flourishing. It was mostly a trade school where Indians were taught practical skills such as making saddles or rounding up cattle. Gardening, the Father learned, was regarded "as women's work" and the Indian boys could not be persuaded to undertake it. They would have starved first.

Father Giorda had brought the sisters an organ. There was something else he wanted for the mission, a printing press, not only to be used for teaching the boys this messy art, but also for the production of grammars, dictionaries, bibles, and prayer books in the Indian languages for the use of missionaries and Indians. Thus Father Alexander Diomedi, a recent volunteer from Europe, was directed to remain at Woodstock College in Maryland, where there was a major Jesuit press, to learn whatever was required. Diomedi completed his apprenticeship, then entrained for St. Louis, where he purchased a large press for $591.81 from the St. Louis Type Foundry and Paper Warehouse. This was on September 10, 1874.[146] This piece of machinery, the most important Catholic mission press in the western United States, was shipped via Helena to St. Ignatius Mission at the incredible cost of $415.21.[117]

The press arrived in January 1875. It was soon installed in the long, frame school called "The Shops," and Diomedi's dusky little apprentices were instructed in setting up type. The first imprint in twenty-two pages was a letter in Latin of the General in Rome, Father Peter Beckx, addressed "to the Fathers and Brothers of the Society of Jesus." The second was in the Kalispel Indian language, an exotic book of 140 pages called *Smiimii Lu Tel Kaimintis Kolinzutin, Narratives From the Holy Scripture,* St Ignatius, 1876. This first book for the public from the St. Ignatius Press, a translation of scripture stories, should be recognized as evidence that Catholics, contrary to the allegations of some, favored the use of Holy Scriptures by all, including the uneducated.

The greatest work from the press required three years to set in type and print, 1877-1879. This was the monumental dictionary in Kalispel and English, encompassing three volumes and a total of 1,156 pages, printed from manuscripts by Giorda, Joseph Bandini, Gregory Mengarini, Joseph Guidi, and Leopold Van Gorp.[148] The existence of this philological masterpiece is illustrative of the brilliant Indian language work produced by the Jesuit missionaries. The Oblates, too, produced several items, the Blanchets and St. Onge several others, but the major works, hundreds in number, flowed from the minds and pens of the Jesuits.[149]

GOVERNMENT BOONDOGGLING

If the bureaucrats in Washington knew about the remarkable language work of these men, they mostly ignored them while they spent large amounts of tax money in other ways for preserving the Indian tongues.[150] There was, at times, in Washington, superficial approval of Catholic missionaries, usually in words of dubious value, designed to placate the emerging Catholic press. Within the brief span of five years, the government, with chilly indifference about results for any but political advantages, changed the boundaries of four reservations, radically affecting Catholic missionaries in the Northwest. The boundaries of two of these, the Colville and the Coeur d'Alene, were shifted as much as thirty miles, leaving the missions far behind.[151] It should be noted that both reservations had been allocated to Catholics by the iniquitous Policy of Grant. Thus, the missionaries at St. Francis Regis, a relatively new mission, found themselves more than six miles from the reservation where the Indians lived.

The Coeur d'Alene Mission experienced special problems: The Indians refused to leave their magnificent historic church on Joset's knoll. Father Diomedi, now relieved of his meticulous assignment at St. Ignatius, finding persuasion or arguments useless, finally moved the mission's statues and furnishings to a new site within the boundaries of the new reservation.[152] The Indians soon followed, dragging their feet, drawn only by their love of their old statues, some of which had been carved by Father Ravalli.

On April 15, 1874, the boundaries of the Blackfeet reservation were also changed. This left St. Peter's Mission at Bird Tail Rock, recently reopened by Father Imoda, sixty miles south of the border.

NEZ PERCE WAR

Perhaps the most tragic of all the tampering with reservation land was that of the Nez Perce, where Jesuits had been able, at last, to provide a permanent mission church and a resident priest, Father Anthony Morvillo.[153] Youthful Nex Perce Warriors, inflamed with the currently fashionable religious doctrine of "The Dreamers" or "The Drummers" demanded certain reforms, over which the government vacillated, unable to act on principle, but only under political pressure. As a last resort, General O.O. Howard, commonly referred to as "the Bible General" because he had a long white Old Testament beard and often quoted scripture, called for a "peace meeting" to be held at Fort Lapwai in May 1877. Cataldo was asked to attend and open the meetings with "prayer talk" in the language of the Nez Perce.

While the meetings convened in the sweltering May weather, Nez Perce militants were busy in their tepees making plans for war. The last meeting ended on a false note of optimism. The American brass returned to their cozy quarters at Vancouver, and Nez Perce runners hurried off in all directions of the plateau to seek allies for their final stand against the whites.

The Cayuse and Umatilla Indians were not disposed to join the hostiles.[154] Most of these were Catholic. Even on the Nez Perce reservation the Catholics refused to join the malcontents, many of whom were Dreamers or Drummers. Umatilla Indians had a new missionary, Father Louis Conrardy, who had replaced Father Bertram Orth some seventeen months earlier.[155] Conrardy, another Belgian, one-time missionary in India, had volunteered for the Indian missions of the Northwest when he read the works of Peter DeSmet. A whirlwind of energy, he was soon covering most of eastern Oregon on horseback, teaching whites as well as Indians, with whom he was particularly popular. He readily became a close friend of Cataldo, on whom the restriction of the war within limited parameters now depended.

On June 16, 1877, Giorda, the general superior, conducted a meeting of Jesuits at the old mission in Idaho. Cataldo was present. Discussion at the moment centered around the cost and source of funds for a new school at Sacred Heart Mission, DeSmet, to be conducted by the Sisters of Providence.[156] A messenger arrived with two urgent pieces of mail. The first, from Father Peter Beckx in Rome, appointed Cataldo as the new general superior, replacing Giorda. The second letter, also addressed to Cataldo, informed him that some of Chief Joseph's Nez Perce had killed whites in a race-inspired dispute. The Nez Perce, formerly America's most loyal and cooperative tribe, was, in fact, now at war with the United States.

Cataldo in his forty-first year, was also in his prime. He took control of the situation at once, announcing peace on the plateau as his first priority. All Jesuits were directed to work for peace by persuading the tribes to shun any and all contacts with the hostiles. This placed the Jesuits in a very difficult position for the second time within a generation.[157] They appeared to be taking sides with the whites, though it was obvious that the war had been occasioned by the injustices of bureaucrats in a predominantly white nation. On the other hand, it was obvious to most that the Indians had everything to lose and nothing to gain by war.

The Nez Perce War ended as abruptly as it had begun, in the autumn of that same year. After a brilliant retreat and several costly battles, Chief Joseph and his warriors were forced to surrender, within a relatively short distance of Canada, their goal in their long flight from the Idaho reservation. When the smoke of the last battle had blown away in the crisp autumn breezes besides the Bear Paw Mountains, one point was clear: the war was swiftly over because the Nez Perce had not been able to gain the allies they expected. The influence of the Jesuits had saved the day for the American troops, who had to enforce the unjust orders of their government.

Cataldo took the ambivalence of his position in stride. There was no perfect order here. When asked by the Nez Perce on which side he stood, he had replied, "Neither." He was there, he said, on God's business. And God's business sometimes demanded more than favoritism, even when justice was violated.

THE CHANGE OF THE GUARD

The two Blanchets had watched the results of the war with more than ordinary interest. So, too, had Bishop James O'Connor from Omaha, Vicar Apostolic of Nebraska, who still held jurisdiction over eastern Montana. O'Connor had arrived in Helena on June 8, 1877, late in the evening, still anxious about the threatened crop failure back home because of a plague of grasshoppers.[158] On the succeeding Sunday, June 10, he confirmed 145 persons, among them several gray-haired old men. A week later, when Joseph's War was in progress, he confirmed another 45 persons in Father Menetrey's little church in Missouri Valley. Eager to visit the renowned St. Ignatius Mission, His Lordship then crossed over to western Montana via stagecoach, and accepted the hospitality of the Jesuits there for a brief period, which coincided with the arrival of Joseph's warriors in the Bitter Root Valley. The proximity of Joseph added spice to the wine of his visit, like the thrill of an attack on a wagon train. His Lordship dispatched a lengthy telegram to the *New York Herald* to reassure the republic concerning the safety of their western territory.[159] This was most gratifying to the readers of the *Herald,* for the farther away from battle one stood, the more dangerous it appeared. The *Herald's* crosstown rival, the *Times,* had not heard from Bishop O'Connor. This was a misfortune, for the editor of the *Times* printed such silly balderdash as the following: "It shocks all our finer feelings to be compelled to say that so far [Chief] Joseph has fiendishly refused to be exterminated."[160] In this respect, the noble Nez Perce were like Nebraska's grasshoppers.

After O'Connor left St. Ignatius, he returned to eastern Montana via stagecoach, "churned all about," as he reported amiably. On August 15, 1877, he dedicated the first church in Laurin, Montana, indeed one of the first churches in that half of the state. This was called St. Mary of the Assumption.[161] He returned to Omaha, with his scalp intact, and delivered a lecture on his adventures.

O'Connor was one of those *Irish* bishops, whom the Blanchets tended to avoid. The eastern United States had many of them and they seemed to perpetuate their control of the American church by nominating other Irish priests for the available bishoprics. In California there were many Irish priests, some of them quite critical of the Jesuits, but in the

Northwest there were none. Most of the priests were from Belgium or eastern Canada so it was not likely that the archbishop would get an Irish bishop to succeed him.

On February 14, 1878, the pope died. His death had been expected, so the Vatican was prepared more, rather than less, for the Papal conclave to choose his successor. Thus it happened that Pope Leo XIII was elected only six days later, on February 20. F.N. Blanchet's familiarity with Pio Nono was no longer useful to him.

Local Catholic news at this time was preoccupied with the never-ending safaris of the Bishop of Vancouver Island to strange, unheard of places in the remote part of his diocese, hidden bays on the island, and faraway Eskimo or Aleut villages in Alaska. Seghers was almost never in Victoria taking his refreshments at tea time with other former residents of Europe. He seemed to be everywhere else at once and a friendly correspondent at the *Sentinel* devoted a considerable portion of each edition to his Lordship's geographical and apostolic exploits. Augustin Blanchet seems to have disappeared from the scene and the Nesqually Diocese was seldom mentioned anymore.

In August there was a great fuss made over the laying of the cornerstone of the new cathedral in Portland.[162] Father Fierens, who was celebrating his silver jubilee as a priest about the same time, left nothing to chance in organizing the greatest Catholic demonstration in Oregon history for this event. The archbishop presided. Father Gibney preached and everybody marched around with banners to the tunes of St. Michael's College band. On occasions like this, the old archbishop visited the orphan children and distributed candy.

The archbishop moved about with a noticeable limp. Nobody expected him to lope about like a beardless youth, but there was growing concern about the venerable old prelate when he could no longer get about the diocese. Nor was anyone surprised when a unique pastoral letter, concerning himself, appeared in the *Sentinel*.[163]

Archbishop Blanchet's Retirement

"To the Clergy of the Archdiocese of Oregon and Vicariate of Idaho," it began. "Venerable Brethren:

From the time it has pleased God to send us, in June 1871, an affliction which impaired our right leg, and rendered somewhat difficult the visitations of the remote missions of our Archdiocese, we have often thought of retiring from our position. Our affliction increasing with our years we gave at last our resignation in a reunion of the Bishops of our Province, in July,

1876, and sent it to Rome. But the Holy Father advised us rather to ask a coadjutor, which we did, expecting the matter would be brought to an end in a short time when contrary to our expectations it has taken nearly three years to have it settled.

Having disposed of the problem of "our leg" the archbishop continued:

We have therefore much joy in announcing to you that the important affair of the Episcopal succession in this Archdiocese is at last settled. The Most Rev. Charles John Seghers, heretofore Bishop of Vancouver Island, and now Archbishop of Emesa, *in partibus*, has received the Apostolic Letters whereby he is appointed our coadjutor, with the right of succession. Notwithstanding his attachment to his diocese, where he enjoyed the love of his diocesans, he considered that it was his duty to bow down in submission to the order of the Holy See, and you will be pleased to learn that his obedience is complete.

But as, at the time of our meeting, there still remained many things to be settled before his leaving, and our beloved coadjutor expressed his desire to obtain ample time for the settlement of all the affairs of the diocese of Vancouver Island previous to his final departure, we have willingly acceded to a request so just, and so reasonable. So that our excellent co-adjutor is not expected soon, but will not come until after the feast of Pentecost, or the first of June. And as we expect to receive from Rome by that time a full discharge of all our official business, he will then assume the administration of the Archdiocese. . . .

The archbishop dated this pastoral, after expressing his gratitude to God for his blessings, on April 14, 1879.

There seems to be some mystery about all this, for the fact of the matter is that Pope Leo had appointed Seghers on December 10, 1878, six months earlier. Whatever the cause of delay in making the matter public, Seghers was in no hurry to leave Victoria. He arrived in Portland finally, on July 1, 1879.[164] He was met at the wharf by a large delegation of citizens "and when he disembarked, a carriage drawn by four white horses waited to receive him. A great procession marched with him to the church where Archbishop Blanchet, assisted by Father Orth, welcomed his coadjutor with these words: "My Lord Archbishop Coadjutor: This day of your reception in this cathedral as my coadjutor and future successor is the happiest day of my life. . . . " There is no doubt that the archbishop's words came from his heart. He was old and he was weary.

In the following week, Seghers left Portland for a prolonged visitation of the missions and churches of Idaho.

Augustin Blanchet, meanwhile, also submitted his resignation to the Holy See in June 1879, just before Seghers' arrival in Portland. His request was accepted but he was appointed administrator of the Nesqually Diocese, pending the appointment of his successor. On

September 4, the *Sentinel* reported that "as administrator of the Diocese," he had visited Steilacoom on August 13. John B. Boulet, a priest now, was there to greet him. "It was a source of pride for the venerable Prelate to see his first church in Olympia built in 1870, completed and now rendered too small," the *Sentinel* said. "He visited the new church erected this year."

One week later, the editor of the *Sentinel* declared war on the *New York Freeman's Journal*. First in bold print it ran a lengthy quotation from the *Journal:*

> The Catholic Sentinel of Oregon says it has *reliable information* that the Very Rev. A.E. Junger has been made coadjutor of the Venerable Bishop Blanchet of Nesqually. The *Sentinel* has 'relied' on some one that ran without a message. Had the *Sentinel* informed itself at the hands of the venerable Bishop of Nesqually, in place of ludicrous attempts elsewhere, it might have learned that the venerable Bishop Blanchet, broken by so many years of labor, had beseeched the Holy See to accept his resignation of his See; and that his prayer was granted. The Very Rev. A.E. Junger, hitherto Vicar-General, has been made—not as the *Sentinel* puts it *Coadjutor*—but *Bishop of Nesqually.*[165]

So far, the journalistic scorn of the *Freeman's Journal.*

For some unknown reason, there was bad blood between these two Catholic papers, one at each end of the continent. The *Sentinel* staff was deeply offended by this pointless criticism and in the course of two columns, cleaned the *Journal's* old clock. "No *official* information of the nomination of Father Junger to the See of Nesqualy [sic] either as bishop or as coadjutor to Bishop Blanchet has yet been received from Rome," the *Sentinel* stated categorically, adding at some length, that its staff had *telephone* connections with both the archbishop and the bishop, and was better informed than the *Journal* could possibly be.

It was, as they say, a storm in a teacup. But the mystery of the Vatican's appointment was finally put to rest when Aegidius Junger was consecrated in Vancouver, Washington, as the second Bishop of Nesqually on August 28, 1879. The ordaining prelate was Archbishop Blanchet assisted by his brother the bishop and Father Fierens of Portland.[166] There seemed to be something ominous by the suddenness and simplicity of it all—like a shotgun wedding. Time demonstrated however, that Aegidius Junger was an excellent choice for bishop. His consecration proved to be another milestone in the history of the church in the Northwest.

9

MONTANA'S FIRST BISHOP
1879–1885

The new Archbishop of Emesa was as restless as a trapper. He had just concluded two years of unbroken travel to the villages of southwestern Alaska and the Aleutians, then to the rugged coast of Vancouver Island, and finally to the interior of Alaska—all of them voyages that would nearly kill an ordinary man, or at least retire him so that he could publish his adventures and brag about them the rest of his life.[1] If Seghers thought of them at all, it was only by way of reflection on the commitments he had made to return some day.

SEGHERS' TOUR OF INSPECTION

On July 11, 1879, briefly after his arrival in Portland, he was on the trail again. He left considerable comforts of home in Portland for "an inspection tour" of the Vicariate of Idaho, which included all of Idaho and western Montana.

The elder Blanchet had encouraged Seghers to undertake this task. "I am glad to have a coadjutor," he remarked drily one day. "I'm going to throw all my miseries on his shoulders. He can have my troubles." The Vicariate of Idaho, which he had never visited, was undoubtedly his principal misery. With a kind of lofty detachment, like a general smartly throwing a brave soldier into battle, he dispatched Seghers into the wilderness, then provided the itinerary he had worked out for him for the readers of the *Catholic Sentinel*.[2]

Seghers was happy to be off. Aboard a steamer, he proceeded up the Columbia River to The Dalles, a voyage of less than a day, unfortunately, for it was the most restful part of the five thousand miles of travel he faced. He was welcomed at river's edge by the pastor, Father Louis Gaudon, and a parish committee, who had buggies at hand to convey the reverend gentlemen to St. Peter's church, less than a mile distant in the busy little town. The archbishop conducted evening services, which prompted the surprised admission by the press that "he speaks English very well." Being a Roman bishop, no doubt, he was expected to speak with a heavy foreign accent.

On the following morning, Seghers offered Mass in the church, paid a courtesy visit to the Sisters of the Holy Names in their academy, then left for the east via river boat, accompanied by Fathers Joseph Cataldo and Louis Conrardy. This was the beginning of a delightful friendship of the three clerics, whose lives henceforth would be profoundly affected by their association. At Umatilla landing, Conrardy left the party to return to his mission for gathering the chiefs and other Indian celebrities. He would join the archbishop later. The boat with its holy burden chugged on to Lewiston, where it arrived on Sunday, July 13. At this point, Seghers' hectic, almost nightmarish, adventure really began.

After appropriate festivities in Lewiston's miniature St. Stanislaus Church, the archbishop traveled by buggy some twenty-five miles east, up the Clearwater River to St. Joseph Mission at Slickpoo, where Father Morvillo was gathering his renowned dictionary in Nez Perce. Conrardy, with his Umatilla escort, appeared and shared the prelate's attention with the Nez Perce, like happy puppies. They all left together on horses for the Coeur d'Alene mission, with the noisy and extroverted Conrardy at the head of the Umatillas. As the procession moved into the mountain country, it grew in size. It found its way, eventually, into Palouse City, where old Father Joset met the archbishop with a carriage from the mission. After morning services at Palouse City on July 19, Seghers arrived early in the afternoon at DeSmet, where Tosi and Gazzoli and another crowd of curious Indians in feathers and porcupine roaches, extended the visitors a raucous welcome then knelt for the archbishop's blessing.

On Sunday, July 10, Seghers confirmed forty-eight children during a solemn pontifical Mass. The eyes of the Indians were upon him every moment, so enthralled were they by the splendor of his person and vestments, the likes of which they had never seen before. The next day, the procession with the addition of Seltis, Head Chief, and other Coeur d'Alenes, proceeded to Spokane Bridge where Chief Stellame and a few Spokane Indians joined it for the torturous passage over the Mullan Road. There were now seventy-five horses in the caravan. At the old Sacred Heart Mission on Joset's knoll, all of the horses and their mounts were refreshed by a night of rest. Then the procession took up again for a trek of six continuous days, to Frenchtown in western Montana.

On July 28, the party halted, six miles south of their goal. Another procession of one hundred Catholics in wagons and buggies, and on horseback, had come to meet them. Their leader was T. J. Demers, nephew of the deceased Bishop Demers, Seghers' predecessor in the See of Vancouver Island. A three-piece band contributed its renditions to the noise and confusion, a balloon ascension was made, and other performances consistent with the majesty of the occasion were presented, more for the sake of the townspeople than for the weary archbishop.

At St. Ignatius Mission, the archbishop's arrival was marked with the most impressive of all receptions. Two hundred Indians in full regalia of eagle feather headdresses and beaded buckskin, greeted his stagecoach some six miles from the mission. Brandishing their muskets and shouting joyfully, they took their places on either side as guards of honor. Then they galloped forward, showing off as it were, while the coach rattled along beside them, threatening to fall apart at every bump of the road. They paused momentarily when they reached the hilltop, whence one could look down into Mission Valley, with the mission and Indian village below, like toys against the vast backdrop of the eastern mountains still capped with snow on that warm day in July. Then Father Giorda appeared, only sixteen years older than Seghers, but worn out and near the end of his life. The Sisters of Providence were there also, primly proper in their buggy. The procession wound slowly down the grade. About five hundred yards from the mission church, it stopped again to be greeted by eleven hundred Indians in their Sunday best, forming two lines and shouting a great hurrah as the coach rattled slowly along between them. When the archbishop reached the church, they all followed him as he entered it, in two lines, the men on one side and the women on the other. Seghers conducted a Benediction service and responded to his people with words of encouragement.[3]

On Sunday, August 3, in the presence of fourteen hundred Indians who crowded into every inch of space in the old wooden church, and assisted by Father Conrardy and six Jesuits, His Grace celebrated another Pontifical Solemn Mass, during which he confirmed 104 persons, some of them well advanced in years.[4] To each he presented a religious medal and to all an exhortation in simple language to live Christian lives. Four days later, at sunset, he blessed the cornerstone of the new church at the Jocko Agency. He visited the sisters' school and hospital and spoke kind words to them, and charmed everyone with his simplicity and compassion.

On August 11, he left for Missoula, where there was as yet no church.[5] Mass was offered regularly by Father Menetrey in the chapel of St. Patrick's Hospital. Seghers visited the Sisters of Providence there, praising them for their hospital and academy in Missoula, and then left by coach for old St. Mary's Mission near Stevensville, fifty miles to the south. The Flathead Indians, prompted by Menetrey and Father Jerome D'Aste, presented another festive demonstration on his arrival, after which he graciously praised them. He was beginning to feel like the pastor who had praised his housekeeper's apple pies, and was never again served another kind of dessert.

Seghers was forty years old and much closer to death than he realized.[6] He took everything in stride with remarkable serenity. Father Cataldo in later years, described his conduct when he was on tour:

> For weeks and months at a time, I have traveled with him, mostly on horseback; we slept out in the open, sometimes on the prairies, sometimes on the mountains; and I can say that he always edified me. I admired his zeal for the salvation of souls not less than the sanctity of his own life. He was punctual in all his daily spiritual exercises, even when on horseback. He was always ready to preach to any kind of an audience—Indians or whites, the ignorant or the intelligent.
>
> When we camped out, sometimes for six or seven days or more, he always wanted to share the chores; cut or carry wood, make the fire, draw water from the brook, or even cook. And it was not easy to turn him from his purpose; he would say that since he shared the meal he should share the toil. He would never permit us to put any extra bedding on the rug that served as his couch; if blankets sufficed for the others, he said, they were sufficient for him too, and he would camp and sleep in the same way as the others.
>
> When there was an opportunity of doing any apostolic work, he would always hasten to select the most difficult for himself. He visited the Indian huts, baptized the children, and encouraged and consoled the sick, especially the deserted old people. Whenever he foresaw that we were to pass near dwellings without being able to stop, he would start off in advance, do whatever spiritual good he could, and be ready to rejoin the rest of us as soon as we came up.
>
> His preaching was always clear and spirited, and perfectly adapted to the mind of his audience. Hearing him speak to Indians or to whites, to children or to adults, one might suppose oneself to be hearing a different orator in each case.
>
> His conversation was friendly, good-humored, and spiritual; he made it a point always to do good to those with whom he conversed.
>
> More than any others he loved his Indian missions; so much so, in fact, that certain white persons complained at times that he showed too great a preference for these miserable people. But he only replied smiling: 'These poor Indians have more need of help because they have not the knowledge that white people have.' When he became Archbishop of Oregon, he made it a point every year to visit each one of the Indian missions under his jurisdiction.[7]

Though he loved his Indians more, Seghers now turned his attention to the white Catholics of Montana and Idaho. Ironically, the whites were more scattered than the Indians and they outnumbered the Catholic Indians in the vicariate by a scant three hundred and fifty.[8]

In mid-August, accompanied by Cataldo, who was as travel-prone as himself, Seghers boarded the stage from Missoula to Deer Lodge, meeting at the half-way mark enroute, Father DeRyckere, the only secular priest in all of western Montana. At Deer Lodge on August 24, the archbishop conducted the Sunday services in the Immaculate Conception Church, then sat in conference for some hours with Father Palladino, the Jesuit pastor in Helena, who took the sacred precincts of Montana a bit too seriously. Palladino, supported by his Jesuit colleagues, proposed that Montana, all of it, east and west, bu united at once in one vicariate with its own vicar apostolic. This, he urged, should be only a *brief* prelude to the formation of an independent diocese. Seghers agreed with this audacious plan, with some conviction, it is supposed, for he took up the matter with the Holy See as soon as opportunity presented itself.[9]

This was on Sunday. On Tuesday, Seghers, with DeRyckere, arrived in Butte, "6,000 feet nearer to heaven than Victoria." Some forty carriages of Catholics had gone to greet His Grace on his arrival and escort him to the yet untitled frame church that DeRyckere had built three years earlier. The archbishop playfully invited his hosts to select the title for their church. Most were Irish, so there was little difference of opinion. On Sunday, August 31, Seghers dedicated their modest edifice in honor of St. Patrick.

For all its attractions, Butte was not regarded as a "beautiful city." Thus only a very unaffected man could be carried away by what he saw there. Seghers was that kind of man.

"A lovely valley," he wrote, "beyond which, as a dark blue background, rise to the South lofty peaks; a high hill standing by itself in bold relief to the West giving its name to the city, the first Canadian miners having christened it 'la butte'; and to the [east] the highest ridge of the Rocky Mountains rises in its grandeur, about three miles from Butte, dividing the waters of the Pacific from the waters of the Atlantic."[11]

The large number of Catholics in Butte kept Seghers occupied for a week, then he departed to inspect other frontier towns. Any place with at least eight people and half as many dogs was regarded as a town and Seghers visited them all: Phillipsburg, Pioneer, Blackfoot City, Vestel, Silver City—not much then and ghost towns now.

Then on to Helena, where Palladino still prevailed in the warm glow of the magnificent brick church he had built—the largest in all of Montana, which is to say, the largest in an area as big as Germany. It would be the cathedral, he predicted, and Helena, the city of the future, would have its own bishop and a Jesuit college. Palladino made no bones about it; he looked with disfavor on his superior's priorities. He regarded Cataldo's preoccupation with Indians in Idaho and eastern Washington as untimely. Van Gorp, unfortunately, agreed with him, but it is not likely that Seghers was taken in. His priority, kept to himself, was still Alaska.

Eschewing Blanchet's proposed route to Boise City via Utah, and more or less intrigued by the comments of T. J. Demers, who had freighted goods in the Salmon River area, Seghers decided to take the more formidable route south through central Idaho.

"No priest," he wrote, "had ever penetrated into the heart of the Salmon River Country; and that fact was an all sufficient reason to make me arrive at the conclusion of traversing that newly discovered portion of Idaho, no matter at what expense, chiefly with a view of acquiring accurate knowledge of it, various conflicting reports having only succeeded in giving doubts to my mind as to the presumed wealth and bright future of the country."[12]

This is Seghers the explorer speaking, revealing an adventurous spirit that could not be intimidated. He had been on the Yukon River twenty years before the gold rush. Were the mountains of Idaho more hostile than the empty spaces of Alaska? He soon learned that they were.

SEGHERS IN CENTRAL AND SOUTHERN IDAHO

On October 2, he entered Salmon City, where an estimated twenty Catholics lived, twice as many as Prefontaine found in Seattle when he founded the church there. Seghers offered Mass for them on the following day, the first Mass in the town's twelve years of existence. Salmon City was in high country and so was Challis where Seghers next appeared. He had traveled to Challis with four companions and the route was dangerous.

> There are two parts of the Challis trail that appear particularly dangerous; one, rounding a lofty rock at a place about two hundred feet above the level of the river, where my horse at every step made stones and earth roll down an incline almost perpendicular; the other passing over the bluffs which overhung the river and where one misstep would be, for both horse and rider, inevitable death.[13]

Seghers surveyed the features of Challis and described it as "a settlement near Round Valley, strewn with stones and shells, and absolutely deserted except along the river banks." Several days later he departed "in a fruit wagon" for Bonanza, forty miles west of Challis.

> The road to Bonanza leaves the succession of valleys and canyons through which the Salmon River flows, and strikes out west into what may be called a very sea of mountains. About half way a kind-hearted Irishman made me share his tent for that night, which I passed very comfortably.
>
> At Salmon City, when writing a letter on the hotel keeper's desk, I was mistaken for a bookkeeper by a miner, who paid me $1 for two meals, and whom I thanked with a grateful smile; at Challis I was taken for a 'bilk' and a

'bogus' Bishop—and by a Catholic, at that! But here, half way between
Challis and Bonanza I was mistaken for a gambler! Such is the fate that
awaits clergymen when they pioneer through new countries![15]

The travelers, having survived a snowstorm while crossing a mountain
pass 9,000 feet high, arrived at Bonanza on October 15, at six in the
evening. The town had a population of five or six hundred, of whom a
hundred were Catholics. No priest or minister had ever set foot in this
town, said the local paper, "we acknowledge a pleasant visit."

Boise City was next on Seghers' itinerary. After vainly seeking means
of going there by a preferred route, he was forced to travel first to
Banner, then to Idaho City. He left on October 21 with a trader, who
procured both a saddle horse and a pack horse for him. Three miners
joined the party.

> ...we were all mounted and had three pack horses. We made a few miles
> before sunset, spent a comfortable night, and discovered next morning to
> our dismay that two horses were gone. The day of Wednesday was spent in
> searching in vain for the runaways, and on Thursday morning we left, two
> of the party having to make the trip on foot. It was about noon that we found
> ourselves upon the highest divide, 10,000 feet above the ocean, having had
> to lead our horses by the bridle, and to make the ascent with wearied step
> and panting for breath. There we found three pretty little lakes half frozen
> over, and fifteen inches of snow; but nothing is more beautiful than, from
> those elevated summits, to look down upon six or seven ranges of
> mountains on each side. The descent was made in the same fashion as the
> ascent, and we sat down to lunch on a piece of dry bread and a drink of water.
> We camped at the head of a beautiful valley which runs 60 miles to Wood
> River; and from our camping place we descried the rugged and variously
> shaped peaks of the Sawtooth Range, well deserving of its name, which, at a
> rough estimate, or rather guess, we pronounced at least 15,000 feet above
> the level of the sea.
>
> The next morning I was startled from a deep sleep by something I saw
> crawling on all fours, getting near to the smoldering ashes of our fires of the
> previous evening, turning over one of the logs, and warming itself, at the
> same time shaking a presumed paw, as if finding that fire too hot. Whilst,
> before being altogether conscious of where I was, I expected every moment
> to hear a growl, I saw to my satisfaction the supposed bear erect himself on
> his feet and turn into our packer![16]

In passages like this, Seghers resembled DeSmet, his countryman now
dead and almost forgotten. DeSmet, it was sometimes said, drew a long
bow and the Jesuit General once accused him of writing poetry. Seghers
was more restrained, though some of his writings, like the above, could
be attributed to DeSmet without most readers recognizing the deception.

Time was running out. Seghers had reached Banner on Sunday, October 16, too late to offer Mass for the few Catholics there. He had promised an old friend, Father John Baptist Brondel of the Nesqually Diocese, who had been appointed to be his successor, the third bishop of Vancouver Island, that he would preside over his consecration ceremonies in mid-December. Only the month of November remained, so he had to hasten his progress. He made a brief visit to the churches in the Boise Basin, then arrived before schedule at Baker City in eastern Oregon, on November 21.

Father Peter DeRoo, another Belgian priest, was pastor in Baker City at that time. An energetic, scholarly priest, he directed their spiritual and educational activities of an estimated seven hundred Catholics in his parish. The apple of his eye was St. Joseph's College, begun in a frame building in January of that same year. DeRoo himself served on its staff, assisting two lay teachers—John Donnelly and Jacob Constantine.[17] Notre Dame Academy, conducted by the Sisters of The Holy Names, was in its fourth year, precariously situated and a great worry to the pastor, who was over-anxious about its success. When the archbishop pontificated at Mass on Sunday, November 23, St. Francis de Sales Church was packed and overflowing. Besides administering confirmation, he preached at great length on the subject of Catholic education and the obligation of parents to send their children to Catholic schools when possible. These remarks served the special interests of the pastor, but they also reflected the views of the archbishop. No doubt, Seghers' words were convincing and very correct, but the results were disappointing. Neither the academy nor the college survived, for lack of support.

DeRoo pleaded with the archbishop for his influence in getting brothers to teach at St. Joseph's. Seghers agreed and subsequently obtained two members of the Viatorian Order from Canada, Father J. B. Manseau and Brother Aime Champoux.[18] Four more brothers from Canada joined them and they changed the name of the school to Viatorian School for Boys.[19]

These were not Baker City's finest years. Worse would appear before the church came into its own and Peter DeRoo would not be there to see it.

When Seghers returned to Portland in early December,[20] he found an ailing archbishop who was still saddled with the ultimate responsibility, the *ordinarius loci*, holding top jurisdiction over the archdiocese and vicariate. If the situation depressed Seghers, he was too humble to show it. There was something enigmatic about it: the young archbishop, Belgian born, but presently at ease with everyone, zealous energetic, and so open to others that he was almost naive, as contrasted with the decrepit, old archbishop, French Canadian and still locked in his own provincialism, in his eighty-sixth year, more than twice the age of his coadjutor. He had less than three years to live, which would surprise no one. The only element of surprise concerned the younger man, who would outlive his older colleague by only three years. Perhaps this is why Seghers was burning the candle at both ends. His love of God was consuming him.

The cagey old archbishop loved God, too, but in a different manner. He was in no hurry to die, nor for that matter to change roles with his coadjutor. But he wrote often to Rome, requesting that he be relieved of high office. No longer was it enough that younger shoulders carried his miseries.

BISHOP JOHN BRONDEL

John Baptist Brondel had been born on February 23, 1842, at Bruges, a quaint old Flemish City in West Flanders.[21] He was the youngest of five boys in a family of seven children, whose parents were Charles Joseph and Isabella Becquet Brondel. His father followed the business of chair manufacturer and both of his parents were intensely religious people who prepared their children well for a Christian life.

John received his primary instruction from the Xaverian Brothers. He was a docile student, perhaps too serious for his companions, but otherwise good-natured and responsive to affection. When he was ten he entered the College of St. Louis where he spent ten years studying the classics and nursing his desire to become a missionary. One day an older brother brought home a book of DeSmet's writings, which John read by the paternal fireside, being greatly aroused by what he was reading. He soon made up his mind, and when he graduated from St. Louis College he announced that he was going to the American College at Louvain to become a missionary to the Indians of the Northwest. In his twentieth year, in 1861, John entered the American college. He was allowed to be ordained three years later, by way of exception, but he chose to remain longer at the college to prepare himself better for the missions and to learn the English language.[22]

In September 1866, Brondel left Bruges for America. After a tedious journey by way of England and the Isthmus of Panama, he arrived at the bishop's residence, Fort Vancouver, on October 31. He spent ten months in Vancouver, teaching in Holy Angels College, assisting the bishop at the cathedral, and praying for an assignment to the Indian missions, for which he had been prepared. Finally, he was given his opportunity. In 1867 he was assigned to Steilacoom on Puget Sound, where he learned that the missions were not quite as romantic as DeSmet described them.

He wrote about his disappointment to his former superior at the American College:

Ten miles north of Steilacoom, at the mouth of the Puyallup, and ten miles to the south, on the banks of Nesqually are the Indian reserves bearing these names. There are scattered about, throughout the country, sixty families of white farmers. Twenty of these—the nearest living five miles from my residence—are Catholics. By dint of hard labor they eke out a poor but honest living. At Steilacoom itself but three families, of the forty making up the population, are of the Faith. A mile and a half from the town I have a few church members among the soldiers of the United States Fort established there. My church looms up in the middle of the woods. Connected with it there is no presbytery; but I rejoice in having a convent near by. Its community of three Sisters takes care of a few orphans and teaches the children of the town and of the surrounding country. On the first Sunday following my arrival, after three ringings of the church-bell, I celebrated Mass for a congregation—filling one half of the seats—of fifty people. Accustomed as I had been to seeing crowded churches, I said to myself: 'Was it worth my while to leave all that was dearest to me on earth, to bury myself in these solitudes, to expose myself to all sorts of dangers, for the sake of a handful of God's adorers who call for my ministrations?' When later I was brought face to face, not only with the indifference of many, but also with the scorn and hatred of not a few; when I came to apprehend the want of even the necessaries of life, I mused: 'What good is there in staying here, since, with the exception of three sisters and a few children under their care, scarcely any one approaches the Sacraments?'[23]

Eventually the young priest discovered his own answers and succeeded so well as a missionary that he attracted the attention of the archbishop in Portland. For eleven years he labored. He offered the first Mass in Tacoma on October 26, 1873, in the home of a Catholic woman who was the only member of the congregation.[24] Later he was pastor of Walla Walla for one year. He offered the first Mass in Colfax on March 21, 1878, in the home of the M. Sextons, and in Uniontown, a settlement of German Catholics, he built the first St. Boniface Church in the spring of 1879.[25]

Brondel was in his prime by now, and a logical choice as bishop to replace his compatriot Charles Seghers as Bishop of Vancouver Island. Seghers doubtlessly had much to say about this appointment, and Seghers offered to consecrate Brondel, if such was his pleasure. Thus it happened that he was consecrated by Archbishop Seghers in St. Andrew's Cathedral on December 14, 1879. The co-consecrator was Bishop Lootens, and D'Herbomez and Bishop Junger, with several priests from the Nesqually Diocese, attended the ceremony. Miss Kelley's performance at the organ, we are told, was perfectly angelic.[26]

In his younger years, the new bishop had been as slender as a sapling; but as time passed, he gradually picked up weight until, like Bishop Junger, he acquired several chins too many and a girth of such proportions that he preferred wide church aisles to narrow ones, lest he bump against the pews. His bland, round face beneath his receding hairline, resembled that of a prosperous burgher rather than a prelate, but what he lacked in the common characteristics of leaner bishops, he compensated for with spirit. He was very touchy, they say, about his episcopal dignity, but not above carrying his own valise, trudging afoot, sometimes for long distances.[27] This endeared him to his priests especially, for there was no virtue honored more by honest frontier clergymen than the practice of humility.

CONTINUATION OF THE INSPECTION TOUR

Seghers regarded the consecration ceremonies as a brief interruption of his official survey begun in July. As soon as possible, he left Victoria to resume his journey in the northern cities of Oregon. Before the end of January 1880, he visited The Dalles again, then Pendleton and Umatilla, where his carriage horses, frightened by volleys from the Indians' guns, ran away with him.[28] Astoria was next, then McMinnville and Grande Ronde, where Adrian Croquet was in debt and living in "a miserable barn of a building."[29] Mr. P. Sinnott, Indian agent at Grande Ronde and trusted friend of the Catholic missionaries, sent a carriage to McMinnville to fetch the archbishop and his baggage. Croquet's "house" had only two pieces of furniture in it, a table and a broken chair—these and a straw mattress on the floor for a bed. He had no blankets.[30] Once he had made a vow "to the Blessed Virgin" not to go to bed before midnight, but in fact he spent most nights "saying my beads, and meditate, and I find it also the best time to read scriptures."[31]

Ordinarily he looked like a scarecrow, dressed in clothes cast off by others. At this time, he was depressed as well. The Holy Names Sisters at his mission would be recalled soon to the motherhouse, "after six years of all sorts of trials and difficulties," leaving the missionary wounded in heart and bewildered in mind. He was tempted to return to Belgium, "to seek there a little rest and peace among my old friends and relatives. That is perhaps a want of courage, but I feel that I am not made of iron. May God's holy will be done."[32]

The sisters, when they were there, provided food for the priests, so it is likely that the archbishop had substantial, if not epicurean meals. Among the priests of Oregon it was well known that Croquet, when he lived alone, had his meals in a little bowl, a small measure of wheat flour mixed with water. If something better was served to him, he never realized it, for he was completely indifferent to food. Except on Saturdays. On Saturdays, like Fridays, he refused to eat meat, even when there was nothing else to be had. This was another expression of piety in honor of the Mother of God.

There is something sacred in this little vignette of two holy clerics in the rustic shack "which leaned in the wind," one sitting on a broken chair, the other, perhaps, on a straw mattress, explaining the reasons for his debt, the construction of the convent that would soon be cold and empty. Two very spiritual men, one called "the Saint of Oregon" by his brother priests, who were not likely to be mistaken, and the other"the Apostle of Alaska," by all who knew him. It was reminiscent of the meeting of Francis Blanchet and DeSmet in 1842, when each knelt at the other's feet begging for his blessing.

Seghers remained at Grande Ronde for several days, then left for French Prarie where Father Vermeersch had just completed the new "Gothic-style" St. Louis Church, one of those almost ubiquitous nineteenth century fakes, made in ninety days or less out of local lumber and generous coatings of white paint.[33] This church had more to recommend it. The remains of the storied Madame Marie Dorion, guide and heroine in Washington Irving's *Astoria*, were buried beneath it. On Sunday, April 18, 1880, Archbishop Seghers, at the end of a procession, said to have been "one third of a mile long," followed it into the church, blessed it generously, despite its flimsy construction,and then preached to its goggling congregation twice on the same day, at Mass and at Vespers.

SEGHERS IN SOUTHEASTERN OREGON

There were other parishes included in the archbishop's inspection tour, too many to mention. He crossed back and forth, from La Grande to Jacksonville, using every available kind of conveyance and walking when he had nothing else. He was especially eager to visit the Lake Country, a sparsely settled region, where Irish sheepherders tended their flocks. He wanted to see for himself whether or not *schools* might be established there.

Leaving Canyon City on Saturday, July 3, he began his trip with a wagon ride of seventy-five miles, made in one day. The road led upward to the summit of mountains, crossed a totally arid plateau and descended into a region which was so cold in winter that even native animals froze to death. In the area were millions of crickets, with which the ground was covered. Leaping in masses, like clouds of some foreign and hideous insects, they were crushed by the wagon wheels and their pulverized remains devoured by the voracious survivors.

On Monday, July 5, Seghers left Camp Harney on horseback for Sage Hen, a ranch on the banks of the Sage Hen Creek, where he met Mr. J. Wheeler.[34] With Wheeler he was to cross the desert,

> . . . a desert with never a house, with almost no water, with no trees except an occasional stunted juniper; with nothing but sand, salt, and sage tufts. A peculiarity of this desert is the extreme dryness of the wind; it hardens the lips and parches the mouth to such an extent that one speaks with difficulty and can barely swallow food.[35]

The two men began their crossing on July 6, at noon. Six hours by horse brought them to the valley of Warm Springs, where they spent a sleepless night fighting swarms of mosquitoes. They rode forty-five miles on the next day, without water, through Buzzard Canyon, well named for the ugly birds that devoured rotting flesh wherever they found it. On July 8, they made their way cautiously through Warner Valley, a lost wilderness of lakes and treacherous marshy terrain, sometimes referred to as "the pot-holes." Finally, on July 9, the two men crossed over a mountain pass, just "a little below the snow line," and entered the Surprise Valley in California. Seghers had the grim satisfaction of knowing that he had penetrated and survived Oregon's most dreaded wastelands. He had found there no people to baptize or teach, no congregation to inspire. This does not seem to have bothered him. He had inspected the last frontier of his territory.

AT LAKEVIEW

But there were countless settlements that still beckoned to him, isolated little hamlets without churches or clergy, some hostile to Catholics but all sharing in his solicitude.

There is a touching account about his journey to one of these. The time was July 14, a few days after his passage through the desert. The scenario began about twelve miles west of Lakeview. A Catholic officer from Fort Klamath, directing a supply train with thirty men in the detachment, overtook the Archbishop of Emesa.

"We came across a tall, erect and slender man, dressed in dark clothes and carrying on his back a bundle of clothing and provisions. He was on foot. I stopped and asked the man his name and destination. He replied that his name was Seghers and that he was bound for Lakeview. I asked him if he might be related to the great Archbishop Seghers of Portland.

He answered that he was the man himself. Myself and men were greatly edified on meeting this great apostle and I insisted that he should occupy one of the ambulances of our train. He refused. Finally I persuaded him to take one of our horses, which he did. The Archbishop was a splendid horseman. In Lakeview he remained with us several days, where we had daily services."[36]

THE SECRET SOCIETY OF THE KNIGHT COMMANDERS OF THE SUN

The daily services were motivated in part by the presence in Lakeview of an anti-Catholic organization called "The Secret Society of the Night Commanders of the Sun." Judged by their title, these frightened zealots were no match for Seghers, who chided them for their secrecy, and tried to lure their leader, called "The Grand Master" out of his law office for a debate. "Whoever dislikes the Catholic Church," Seghers scolded, "let him meet us on fair grounds, in broad day light with open argument."[37]

Better known as "The Knights of the Sun," they had singled out Catholic schools as the object of their hatred, and this was precisely where Seghers was most vulnerable. When Bishop of Vancouver Island, he had come to the conclusion that the only solution to the mediocrity [or worse] of Catholicism in the Northwest, was the *school*. Accustomed to the ancient Catholic traditions of his home in Belgium, he was shocked by the indifference of Catholics in his mission, and he was determined to correct the situation by stressing the need for schools.

The Catholic press supported him, going perhaps too far by finding fault with the public schools, which were at that time the pride and joy of most Protestants. The *Catholic Sentinel* of Portland was especially defensive of Seghers' position and no issue appeared during this period without a lengthy polemic on this sensitive subject. Resentment of Catholic criticism of public schools was nationwide, though most of the battles, unlike the Know Nothing era, were fought on the local level. "The Knights of the Sun" for example, existed in Oregon; their counterparts in Kentucky were called "The Elephants."

The movement seems to have enjoyed little influence, at least in the Northwest. Catholics threatened to boycott candidates for election if they were involved in any manner whatsoever in "The Knights of the Sun," and that was enough in those simple days of small town politics to give the *coup de grace* to the organization. The bitterness, however, survived, and it was still there in 1922, when, by an ironic turn of events, many Oregonians attempted to give the same *coupe de grace* to the Catholic schools.[38]

SEGHERS RETURNS TO PORTLAND

It was late November when Seghers returned to Portland. He had visited all but one of the churches in the archdiocese and vicariate.[39] He had met every priest and most of the sisters. He was ready now to make plans for the future.

For a friend he summarized his recent adventures:

> My tour lasted sixteen months (from July, 1879, to the end of November, 1880). Altogether I traveled a distance of about 5000 miles. I confirmed 800 people. I traveled by steamboat, railway, coach, cart, sled, foot, and handcar. I have been at an altitude of 9000 feet. Once an accident to the coach hurled me into the snow; I have been thrown from a horse onto rocks; once, riding without a saddle I was thrown into water. I spent many a night on the bare ground; sometimes, tormented by mosquitoes, I did not close my eyes all night. I have said Mass in churches, chapels, ruined hovels, schoolhouses, hotels, and once in the Odd Fellows' Lodge.... I have visited sections of the country where a bishop had never set foot, and where the people had never seen a bishop; I have been with wild Indians; I have preached missions lasting several days. Once I spoke to the people of a little village where there was not a single Catholic. Crossing the desert, I have traveled forty-five miles without finding water.... And here I am, as full of life as ever.[40]

ARCHBISHOP BLANCHET RETIRES

The archbishop undoubtedly was pleased with his coadjutor. He had moved into St. Vincent's Hospital where the sisters cared for him like "a walking saint" about to leave for heaven. He finally received his permission from Rome to retire, on January 25, 1881, and he set about the composition of his "Farewell Pastoral" in a garrulous mood and still addicted to the editorial "we." For some inexplicable reason his letter was not published until March 3, 1881, nearly three months after Leo XIII actually accepted his resignation.

"When we announced to you," the venerable old archbishop wrote, "by letter of April 14, 1875, the appointment of Most Rev. Charles John Seghers as our Coadjutor Archbishop with right of succession, we expected to receive soon our discharge, demanded as early in 1876, and to pass the administration of the Arch-Diocese [sic] to our worthy successor; but our repeated supplication from the burden of episcopal administration did not receive a favorable answer.

"It was only on the 12th day of December 1880 that the Holy Father condescended to grant our petition.... Never forget your old and affectionate spiritual father; forgive him his faults and failings; pray for him that his sins may be pardoned and forgotten when he shall be called to render an account of his stewardship."[41]

Francis Blanchet had been a faithful priest for sixty-two years when he wrote this. He had come to Oregon forty-three years before. He had been a bishop for thirty-six years and for one year less the head of an ecclesiastical province, which was one of the first in the United States, second only to Baltimore itself. Now his companion, Bishop Demers, was gone, his younger brother the Bishop of Nesqually, replaced. He was the last of the three to lay down his crozier. They had all been French Canadians, deeply influenced by the spirituality of their youth, and they were never required to change. As bishops they had created their own French Canadian church in the Northwest, somewhat out of touch with the American church at large. Now a profound change was taking place. The three bishops in their former sees were all *Belgians.* They had a different spirit that expressed itself in style. They were more American, in a sense, than the Irish bishops in the East. An entirely new era, indeed, had already begun.

THE FIRST BENEDICTINE SISTERS

Archbishop Blanchet had retired in March. Seghers, of course, succeeded as *Ordinarius Loci.* In keeping with his gentle, sensitive nature, he continued to consult Blanchet, partly to keep him informed on current developments. One subject in particular still occupied the thoughts of the old archbishop, for in his last months of administration, he had begun the process that finally produced results after his resignation. This concerned the replacement of the Sisters of the Holy Names at Grande Ronde with others who were willing to take the school.

Initially prodded by Seghers, who had promised Croquet that he would find sisters for St. Michael's Mission, Blanchet had taken up the matter with Father Brouillet in Washington. Brouillet suggested an appeal to Abbot Alexius Edelbrock of St.John's Abbey in Collegeville, Minnesota. Urged by both Blanchet and Brouillet, the Abbot then persuaded Mother Scholastica, prioress of St. Benedict's down the road from Collegeville, to provide three sisters. That was the way things got done in the nineteenth century: one had to know somebody who knew somebody who knew somebody else.

In due course, on April 4, 1881, Mother Scholastica and three Benedictine Sisters arrived in Portland, at one in the morning. Seghers had supplied two hacks to convey them to St. Vincent's Hospital where both Blanchet and Brouillet awaited them. They were treated like visiting royalty, a point not lost on Mother Scholastica, who succumbed at once to everyone's charm. Five days later, under the solicitous care of Brouillet and the protection of Mother Scholastica, the sisters arrived at Grande Ronde. Seghers showed up to help them get their school under way.

Mother Scholastica was much impressed. So was Seghers. He had got what he asked for so far; he would try his luck in seeking more. (Give some people an inch and they will take a yard.) He asked Mother Scholastica not only to use her influence with Abbot Edelbrock to establish a monastery in Oregon, but also to send more sisters for a new school at the Umatilla mission, where Conrardy was already entertaining second thoughts about remaining there.[42]

Seghers and Brouillet escorted Mother Scholastica to Umatilla. She was still enthusiastic, declaring Umatilla to be "the most beautiful and fertile country I have ever seen."[43] One detects in this an echo of Conrardy's sentiments, which he, too, expressed when requested to do so, with less sincerity, perhaps, than Mother Scholastica.[44] On the following day the latter wrote to the Abbot, urging him to comply with Segher's request for a monastery in Oregon.

When she returned to Minnesota, she was prepared to choose sisters for the proposed new school at Umatilla.

BISHOP AEGIDIUS JUNGER

His Excellency, Bishop Junger, probably heard, more than once, this quaint bit of medieval cynicism about bishops: "When you become a bishop you never hear the truth again and you never eat a bad meal." Bishops were often reminded of this, in good humor of course, at tasteless banquets that followed the consecration ceremonies. It was an attempt, presumably, to remind new bishops about their fallibility.

For Bishop Junger, no such reminder was required. He was the epitome of simplicity, a populist bishop with a special love and understanding of children. Mild mannered, almost diffident, he was just the opposite of his predecessor, Augustin Blanchet, who never let anyone forget who was boss.

In his physical appearance, Junger was said to resemble the great Irish emancipator, Daniel O'Connel. In the course of time, however, for lack of exercise or because of those fine meals bishops allegedly received, his Lordship's appearance changed. His bulk increased considerably, giving him additional characteristics—unlike Bishop Blanchet—the appearance of a jolly baker.

Bishop Junger, I think, was no genius at administration, nor an energetic peripatetic like Seghers, but he performed his office well, with common sense and humility. He was a comfortable bishop and a popular one, without being the subject of lavish praise or more than ordinary attention.

In retrospect, it appears that Junger's greatest limitation was his lack of political expertise. He was very much unlike the Irish bishops in this respect, and because of it, at least in part, Catholics in his diocese have been at a disadvantage ever since. Washington became a state during Junger's tenure, and Washington's constitution was adopted with little or no Catholic participation.[45] Somebody in the bishop's office in Vancouver was asleep at the controls of the diocese, and it is quite probable that this was the bishop himself. What we needed then was an Archbishop Seghers, but there was only one of him, and he had been in his grave for three years when the convention was held.

Meanwhile, Junger traveled leisurely about Washington Territory, his diocese. He had been consecrated in October 1879. On November 23 of that year, he dedicated St. Leo's, the first church in Tacoma. Measuring forty by twenty-four feet, this had been built by a young priest in the diocese, who would become a kind of permanent fixture, a long-lived local character like Prefontaine in Seattle. Father Peter Hylebos, another import from Belgium, had the distinction of being the last resident pastor of Steilacoom and the founder of the Church in Tacoma.[46] In the capacity of the latter, he exercised great influence in this area of Junger's diocese, at Olympia, for example, and other neighboring missions.

In January of 1880, the heaviest snowfalls in decades buried the Puget Sound area, causing the collapse of some roofs on mission churches.[47] Over in Walla Walla, the banana belt of the Northwest, Father Thomas Duffy presided at the opening of St. Mary's Hospital on January 27, 1880. The Sisters of Providence conducted this new establishment along with their academy.[48] Duffy, one of several Irish priests recently acquired by the church in the Northwest, occupied the hearts of all, including the Jesuits, who named their favorite horse in his honor. Had he been older he might have been made bishop, instead of one of those Belgians, but again, he died too soon.[49] He enjoyed a special rapport with his bishop. Junger apparently enjoyed Walla Walla, for he spent more than three weeks there in the lovely month of May. Duffy dispatched some news about His Lordship's activities to the *Catholic Sentinel:*

> When Bishop Junger concludes his labors here he will set out to visit that portion of his Diocese which extends from Walla Walla to Fort Colville, a distance of 210 miles and which contains the flourishing missions of Colfax, Big Lake [Sprague Lake], Spokan [sic], Uniontown and Pomeroy. During the past four years thousands of settlers poured into this region and there are Catholics enough there at present to occupy the time and energy of three or four missionaries.[50]

The charms of the Walla Walla Valley with its early garden produce like fresh asparagus, detained the bishop longer than expected. He finally departed for the north "on the 10th ultimate" leaving behind him the flesh pots of another Egypt, just when the famous Walla Walla onions were beginning to mature.[51]

CATALDO VERSUS CAPTAIN WILKINSON

The town of Spokane Falls in 1880 had an estimated 350 people, about one-tenth of those in Seattle. The village of Sprague had not emerged yet, though it was the principal watering place for freighters out of Walla Walla. It soon became the main stopping place for stages also, and in June, 1880, a Mr. Edwin Dane, who was a railroad timekeeper with his ear to the ground, erected the first frame building there, a hotel on Railroad Avenue. Junger was impressed by what followed. It was rumored that the railroad, the Northern Pacific, would make Sprague a division point because of several large springs of water that could be channeled into the trains' boilers by the force of gravity.[52]

In Spokane Falls, however, the Jesuit mission superior disagreed with Junger's preference for Sprague. Cataldo's predilection for Spokane Indians seems to have left him gazing through tinted spectacles that excluded from view any place but the new town by the falls.

Cataldo had been reassessing the state of the Indian missions ten years after Grant's nefarious Peace Policy. He had come to a conclusion similar to that of Seghers: schools were the only solution to the disturbing problems on the reservations. Perhaps the hullaballoo created by the Catholic press had helped to shape his thinking. More likely, recent events on the reservations had forced him to plan a viable program to resolve certain injustices that now appeared on some of the reservations. It was another case of the coyotes getting the lambs.

On February 25, 1880, a Methodist school called Training School of Indian Youth, was established on four acres of ground belonging to the Congregationalists' Pacific University at Forest Grove, Oregon.[53] Subsidized by the United States Indian Department, this school was directed by Captain Melville C. Wilkinson, an officer of the United States Army who was dedicated to the establishment of a school similar to Carlisle in Pennsylvania, but conducted under Methodist auspices. Wilkinson, alas did not recruit his students on Methodist reservations only, but invaded Catholic reservations with the approval of the government, searching out the brighter students for his school, where efforts were made to change their religion. In other words, the Wilkinson plan was as simple as it was bold: If Methodists were restricted in religious activity on certain reservations allocated by the Policy, then the Methodists could bring the promising youth of those reservations to a central school where they could be indoctrinated. The Spokane Indians and the Umatillas became Wilkinson's favorite targets.

During the summer of 1880, Cataldo realized that some radical changes had to be made to cope with Wilkinson's challenge. There were four Indian schools under Cataldo's supervision: St. Ignatius in Montana opened in 1856; St. Peter's in Montana, opened in 1874; Sacred Heart near present DeSmet, Idaho, opened in 1878; and St. Francis Regis near Colville, also opened in 1878.[54] All of these were resident schools. Cataldo had no illusions about their stability; any one of them could be wiped out in minutes for their existence hung by mere threads.

Cataldo's first response to Wilkinson was a day school for the Spokanes. During the summer of 1880, he directed Brother Carfagno to build a schoolhouse at St. Michael's, on the old site near the Treaty Tree.[55] This school, subsequently listed by the Indian Office in the Department of the Interior, was completed in the late autumn of 1880, and was opened with an enrollment of twenty-five children, several of whom were whites.[56]

Cataldo's long range plan, however, was more complex. He decided to establish other resident schools for Indian children on other reservations *not* allocated to Catholics, and one central college in Spokane Falls where brighter graduates of all Catholic related schools could acquire a Carlisle-type education under Jesuit supervision. To implement this, he sent Father Canestrelli to Spokane Falls to either file for homestead property on the river or to purchase property from the Northern Pacific Railway.[57]

At the same time, Archbishop Seghers, aroused by the cunning of Captain Wilkinson, followed a different course. He applied pressure to the bureaucrats in Washington: "It is with no little regret," he wrote,

> that I bring to your notice a practice that causes among the Catholics of this State a feeling of sadness and indignation. I refer to the permission given to Captain Wilkinson to take to his school a number of Catholic children of the Umatilla reservation. The school of Captain Wilkinson is professedly a Methodist institution and it grieves me to see the Indian Department favor and countenance an act which is, at best, but one of sectarian bigotry.... Such intemperate zeal will necessarily lead to trouble, and if trouble ensues, we will hold the department which permits it responsible.[58]

The recent Indian Wars, the Sioux against Custer in 1876, and the Nez Perce War of Joseph, were still fresh in the minds of the American public, who regarded them as a threat to *Manifest Destiny*, the country's most infallible panacea. Thus Seghers' veiled reference to "trouble" evoked an immediate response with the almost immovable bureaucrats. "[Wilkinson's school] seems to have been well started on a splendid site and by a man well qualified for such a humanistic undertaking," a Pacific University historian noted, "but through political means removal was secured."[59]

"Removal of Wilkinson" actually was secured, post haste. Much to his chagrin, he was forced out of his position and Forest Grove ceased to be a threat. By this time, however, the Peace Policy was little more than a slogan. It had never served its purpose and it met its demise with the regrets of no one.[60]

GONZAGA COLLEGE LAND

The fate of Wilkinson resolved some problems but created others. Cataldo was left with his grand design. The proposed new college could no longer be regarded as a link in a chain of schools. Nevertheless, there was need for it, in a modified form perhaps, and Cataldo was more determined than ever to have it. Canestrelli had been unable to find land, neither by grant nor purchase, so Cataldo, with eyes on the whites pouring into the area, made hasty plans to go there before his last opportunity faded away.

That winter of 1880–1881 was one of the coldest on record. Cataldo spent January and February at St. Ignatius Mission, literally cooling his heels and anxious to be away. It was spring before he could make the journey, but he arrived at last and learned to his dismay that the land he sought had been acquired by Colonel Jenkins, an old settler.

In the company of John Sims, the Colville Indian Agent, he then went land hunting, finding in due time a one-half section tract, 320 acres on the north bank of the Spokane River, where Gonzaga University stands today. He found another site north of town, several miles south of the Treaty Tree where St. Michael's Mission lay, on land that legally belonged to Chief Peone. The Chief had informed Cataldo that he would sell *his* land soon, so the mission would have to be relocated. Both half sections of the new land had belonged to the Northern Pacific Railroad.

Having found what he wanted, Cataldo assigned Father Giorda, on whom he could always depend, to remain in Spokane and to secure title to the half section on the river. After much fuss and feathers, Giorda succeeded in purchasing this for $2.60 an acre.[61]

While these negotiations were dragging on, Cataldo himself purchased three lots from James Glover, the so-called "Father of Spokane" whose gamble on the approximate position of the railroad's right of way had paid him off very handsomely.[62] These lots at Main and Bernard, on the east end of the business section of town contained an old carpenter shop, which Cataldo converted into a church, dedicating it in honor of St. Joseph the carpenter. He himself served as the first pastor of this primitive church, which began with a congregation of five people. On Christmas Day 1881, Father Van Gorp offered Mass in St. Joseph's for twelve people, but on the same day, at St Michael's Mission, three hundred Indians attended Mass and received Holy Eucharist.

Both Seghers and Junger viewed Cataldo's activities with approval. At this time, Cataldo as superior directed the destinies of some forty-three Jesuits in the Northwest, almost twice as many as all other priests in the region. Seghers was not above casting an acquisitive eye on Cataldo's men and he never ceased to pester Cataldo for more and more Jesuits for the vicariate in particular, for care of whites as well as the Indians. There never were enough priests available, and priorities were not well defined. So both bishops began to think again about prospects of getting priests from other religious orders.

THE BENEDICTINES OF MOUNT ANGEL

Since the Oblates had departed, the only order of priests left in the Northwest were the Jesuits. The Franciscans had concentrated on the Southwest where their American roots lay. The Benedictines at Collegeville had never responded to Archbishop Seghers' invitation to come to Oregon. Nor did Mother Scholastica. The blizzards of Minnesota, perhaps, had buried both.

The Benedictines, unlike the Jesuits, lacked a single superior with whom the bishops could correspond. They were *monastic,* collectively attached to different monasteries and subject to different abbots, independent of each other and dependent upon the decision of monastery chapters for sending monks to new locations. One should not be surprised, then, by the complexity of Benedictine foundations, which sometimes were accomplished only by one stepping on the toes of other monks.[63]

Thus it happened that in the course of 1881 not one but two monasteries became involved in seeking prospects for western foundations—St. John's, already invited by Seghers, but slow to respond, and a Swiss monastery at Engelbert, whose monks wandered into Oregon on their own tour of inspection to find a site for their proposed monastery.

The latter appeared first, and since they eventually founded the Northwest's first and most distinguished Abbey, Mount Angel, it is appropriate that their earlier beginnings be presented.

In 1873, when religious suppression appeared to be imminent in Switzerland, Abbot Anselm Villiger of the Monastery of Engelberg, appointed two fathers to go to America to search for a new Engelberg. Fathers Frowin Conrad and Adelhelm Odermatt traveled first to St. Meinrad's Monastery in Indiana, then to the town of Conception in Missouri where a new monastery was already under construction, awaiting the arrival of monks from Switzerland. By April 15, 1881, this Conception monastery was so firmly established that it was formally designated as an independent abbey.[64]

At this time, its monks were required to decide whether they wanted to transfer their vow of stability to the new abbey or to return to Engelberg. Thus Adelhelm, with a companion, Father Nicholas Frei, and the abbot's blessing, set out for the west of America, in search of an appropriate site for a new monastery. Their prolonged journey brought them to Colorado, California, and finally Oregon.[65] They arrived in Portland on August 1, 1881, and were welcomed by Seghers, who suggested that they investigate the Rogue River Valley and Jacksonville in southwest Oregon.[66] The two Benedictines, already enchanted by what they saw and heard from Seghers, hurried off to this fancied Eden, where the nephew of the old archbishop was still pastor.

The following item from the *Catholic Sentinel* provides evidence of their presence there and their zeal in seeking what their abbot had instructed them to find:

> Fathers Adelhelm Odermatt and Nicholas Frei, formerly of Switzerland, more recently of Conception, Mo., have spent five weeks in Jackson County on a tour of observation. It is rumored they are favorably impressed with our Belle valley and its people, climate and prospective resources, and according to report, it appears they found a fair outlook for building a monastery of their Ancient Order, generous people being willing to devote liberally toward the project.[67]

FILLMORE, MOUNT ANGEL

Meanwhile in a small German settlement called Fillmore, the Catholic people under the guidance and inspiration of Mathias Butsch had built a new frame church. Butsch, a very handsome fellow with a well-trimmed beard along and below his chin, earnest blue eyes and heavy black wavy hair, like a romantic opera singer, owned the local saw mill and provided all the lumber for this church. When it was completed, Archbishop Seghers was requested to come and bless it. Of course Seghers complied with this pious request and on August 21, 1881, he was at Fillmore for the dedication.[68]

After the ceremony, Butsch suggested that Seghers should ascend the nearby flat "butte," which was more like a high mesa about four hundred feet above the valley. There are several accounts about *how* the archbishop got there, but it seems certain that he did. From the top he looked over the valley, with its prosperous fields and the mountains beyond them. What his thoughts were one can only guess, but it is not unlikely he realized this was the ideal place for a monastery.[69]

About this time, on September 19, President Garfield died. He had been shot by an assassin on July 2, and for some weeks there was talk of little else. Adelhelm and Nicholas returned from Jacksonville when the nation was mourning. They visited the archbishop who asked them to preside over church services at Fillmore during the weekend, the feast of the Holy Rosary.[70] The church was dedicated as St. Mary's, he said, and the people would appreciate having priests on her feast day. Odermatt agreed to go.

As Seghers doubtlessly anticipated, Butsch invited them also to ascend "the butte" to take a look at the countryside. When they did, Odermatt was ecstatic. Indeed! This was the site for which he had searched so long. Its view, its fertile land, the devout German families scattered in their cozy homes over the heavily fruited plains below made it the most desirable place in all of America for the new Engelberg.

ABBOT ALEXIUS EDELBROCK FROM ST. JOHNS

Seghers was a man of action and he was growing impatient with the Benedictines. He had appealed to two groups without results so far, but perhaps with a little pressure he could get both of them to establish monasteries in Oregon—one in the north and one in the south. On October 1, 1881, probably the day after Adelhelm and Frei returned from Jacksonville, he wrote to the Abbot of St. John's to apprise him of the present situation:

> There are two Benedictine Fathers of the Swiss branch of your illustrious Order looking for a suitable place in the Diocese where to locate a mission. They will soon request me to give my views, and I candidly acknowledge I am very anxious to consult you before coming to any agreement with them. An early answer will oblige Yours Truly.... [71]

When Edelbrock received this letter, he almost had old-fashioned apoplexy. He immediately summoned a chapter of his community, which voted to accept Seghers' invitation to consult with him—they could scarcely have voted for less and even to establish a monastery in Oregon "provided such arrangements could be effected as would give mutual satisfaction." The Abbot himself decided to make the journey. He directed Father Edward Ginther to accompany him. If it appeared that a monastery could be founded, Ginther would remain to begin it.

In mid-November, Edelbrock had not yet arrived in Portland. The archbishop and two monks from Engelberg met in consultation on November 16. If they were to settle in Oregon, Seghers wanted to know, what place pleased them most? Where would they like to make a foundation? The two answered at once: "Fillmore and Sublimity." The archbishop had been prepared for this. "I could also give you Gervais," he said. This was an extra bonus, its meaning not lost on either of the Benedictines.

The final decision had to be postponed until after the archbishop conferred with the abbot from St. John's. Meanwhile, Frei went south to learn English and to take a second look at a possible monastery site at St. Inez, and Odermatt moved to Gervais, to assume the pastoral care of this and its two missions, Fillmore and Sublimity.

When Edelbrock finally arrived in Portland on December 4, 1881, he was suffering from "a bad cold" (there were no good ones). His bronchia pained him much and he did not feel like living, much less parleying with an archbishop who was so hospitable that one became indebted to him. He remained in bed all day Monday, December 5, and then, on Tuesday, in a mood as black as Good Friday, he left for McMinnville, where he spent the night with the local pastor. This was Father J. S. White, a Canadian, who seems to have formed some very negative views of his own about Oregon. The longer Edelbrock talked to White, the more dejected he became. According to White, only five towns in the whole diocese could support a priest, and these had pastors already. Other than in Portland, where the debt was very oppressive, there was not another brick church "in this puffed up state."[72] "There were not Catholic schools anywhere, and they could not be supported if they were built.... Eastern Oregon is almost void of people."[73] "This Father White," Edelbrock added, "is an able and honest man and he gave us a great deal of valuable information."

The two monks should have gone home at this point, but Edelbrock wanted to see the worst. They went on through the pouring ran to Grande Ronde. Later, reporting to the prior at St. John's on the alleged hazards to health in so unhealthy a climate, he complained that "a dozen other diseases are now active in the state." Then he got down to real business:

> It has rained every day we were here, in fact, it has rained here almost daily since the *beginning of September*. ... Everything is wet. The roads are such as I have never seen in my life and in coming from Sheridan to this glorious place by train, 14 miles, I made an act of contrition. It is damp and disagreeable, and no one will affirm, I trust, that such weather is healthy.... Besides being wet and damp it is also *cold*. During the short time I have been here I have felt cold more than I would in Minn. for 5 months.[74]

Oh well, nothing's perfect. The Most Reverend Abbot was just suffering from a *bad* cold. His companion, Father Ginther, maintained his silence, but his views, according to the ruffled abbot, differed basically from those of Mother Scholastica. The sisters were being starved, and worse, cheated—that was it—by Brouillet who was "a fraud and a cheat."[75]

The sisters, he declared, "cannot remain in this agency [Grande Ronde] because their pay is insufficient . . . even Rev. J. B. Brouillet's contracts won't be worth a continental, and if the Indians want schools they will have to pay for them as the White folks. It is therefore doubtful if the sisters will be here after January 1882."

After visiting Umatilla, which pleased him even less, he had further remarks for posterity, ending them all with "and I really cannot understand why Msgr. Seghers wants the Benedictines here."[76]

With Ginther beside him, Edelbrock stealthily departed from Portland on December 14, without discussing additional complaints with Seghers. So far as the diocese was concerned, the abbot's visit was a disaster, for not only did he depart in a snit, he took Mother Scholastica's nuns with him. They were recalled from Grande Ronde in early January 1882.

Edelbrock seems to have experienced some regret for his hasty flight from Portland. He wrote to Seghers at length from San Francisco on December 18, in a vain attempt to provide alibis for his less than generous attitudes. "We are not prepared to take an Indian mission," he said, referring to Umatilla,

> and according to statements of two of your Fathers there is as yet no mission in eastern Oregon that could support a priest and there is no hope of a Catholic population coming into eastern Oregon before the completion of the Northern Pacific R.R. In Western Oregon you have some Benedictines and some of the clergy are not over-pleased that regulars [religious orders] should take away the best Missions. . . . Your clergy told us they could attend to the spiritual wants of the people, and all they expected of religious was the establishment of a college. But where to establish a college in the West?[77]

There would be no people and, judging from the way Edelbrock reasoned, there never would be any people.

At least the archbishop knew where he stood. He was free now to deal with the Swiss Benedictines and to obtain through them replacements for sisters who had left Grande Ronde.

It would be presumptuous to say that Adelhelm Odermatt relished the results of his rival's visit. He was aware of Edelbrock's displeasure and childish behavior. His explanation for it was simple enough, too simple in fact, but it placed his attitudes toward his rival in perspective. The Abbot of St. John's, he said, "heard that we had settled down (where he wanted to be)—and left in a huff because, as he told Fr. Nicholaus [Frei] we had taken the best away from him. That was true in Oregon—but not in California—to which state he cleverly and immediately repaired in order to take St. Inez from us to repay us for the trick in Oregon. If he steals St. Inez from us, he will have gotten away with the best."[78]

This is not the end of the melancholy saga of Abbot Edelbrock, because correspondence continued to flow back and forth between Minnesota and Oregon, nothing coming of it all. The archbishop himself looked into the St. Inez proposal, consulting in due time with the Archbishop of San Francisco and the Bishop of Monterey.[79] The latter informed him that the Benedictines would not be welcome in California "because there are so many Irish there and they don't care for the regulars at all."[80] Father Frei returned to join his colleague at Gervais, better instructed in the wicked ways of the world than in English, and the two Benedictines settled down to plan the realization of the new Engelberg.

On Sunday May 7, 1882, Seghers joined them in a meeting with parishioners at Gervais, to discuss the buildilng of a school. A favorable decision was quickly arrived at. In two days the parishioners, joined by their Protestant neighbors, raised $2,000 in cash. Adelhelm himself begged for money and land, and was given two lots for a convent. The archbishop thought Adelhelm should leave for Switzerland to seek recruits and final authority to establish the monastery. Leaving Frei in charge, he sailed at midnight, May 11, for San Francisco. He was off to Europe to request Abbot Villiger's approval for the Oregon foundation, to obtain sisters for Gervais, Umatilla, and Grande Ronde, and to recruit priests and brothers.[81]

Adelhelm reached Engelberg on June 17, obtained the permission he requested and several recruits. "On the way back across America, he recruited Mother Bernardine Wachter, O.S.B., whom he had known in Missouri, and several other Benedictine Sisters who had come to America from the convents of Maria Rickenbach and St. Andrew (Sarnen) near Engelberg. On October 28 he arrived back at Portland with twenty-seven companions, including the sisters, three priests, one lay brother, and some student candidates.

"The monks moved into the rectory at Gervais, where they stayed until the summer of 1884."[82] St. Scholastica's Convent was nearly completed and the sisters were able to occupy it on October 30. Three days later, on December 2, 1882, three of the sisters, those from Sarnen, left for Grande Ronde, where they became the mission's third team of school teachers in eight years.

BENEDICTINE SISTERS FROM SARNEN AT GRANDE RONDE

Mother M. Johanna Zumstein, the superior of this frail contingent of missionaries from Switzerland, was a very proper looking nun who called a spade a spade and nothing else. With firm views about most things and the ability to express them well, she could stare down the bishop, if necessary, though very respectfully, and one suspects that if called upon she could control a penitentiary of convicts as well as any warden. Fortunately she left a detailed, and very shrewd narrative about this adventure and others. Even the "Saint of Oregon" merited her subtle but unmistakable scorn when she thought he deserved it.

There was for example, Croquet's horse. "His Grace, the Archbishop had procured for the good pastor a very nice white horse," she wrote with a touch of tartness in her account. "One morning when Father Croquet went to the stable to feed her, he found in place of his pretty white mare a shabby looking bay. What did he do? Nothing, but feed the new horse, saying 'I thought I had a white horse.' Some Indian, who liked the gentle animal, had played the trick of exchanging it. He knew well enough that no prosecution would follow."[83]

Mother Johanna described the appearance of the mission as it was when she arrived:

> The house which for the present was to be our home was an old, illshapen frame structure, patched with additions as necessity may have required. The poorest part was the boys' dormitory, a low unceilinged attic over the classrooms. One room upstairs was used as a chapel, in which Holy Mass was celebrated on weekdays, as the only worshipers were the inmates of the mission house.
>
> About 500 feet from the house stood a new church of ordinary size, with the addition of some rooms for the priest. The church was used for Sunday services.[84]

Archbishop Seghers paid the nuns an unexpected visit. No one had to remind him about the difficulties for refined women like these at St. Michael's Mission. He planned a reward for them, if they persevered until his turn from Rome. "Just trust in me," he told the superior. I will take care of you like a father and will give you a good place in my diocese."[85]

"November came and with its cold breath chilled the air," Mother Johanna said, "but an unexpected message chilled our very blood. What news did it bring?" Seghers would not return as Oregon's archbishop.

CROQUET'S VICES

One wonders about the Indians' reactions to all of this coming and going of missionaries. Fortunately they were accustomed to the arrivals and departures of bureaucrats from Washington. But poor old Croquet had begun to feel like a leper, a poor one to boot, who could not provide food enough for the sisters. He knew what the problem was. He gave everything to the Indians. He could not bear to turn an Indian down when he was asked for something, and it must be admitted that many took advantage of him, telling falsehoods, for example, to get his food or his candles.[86] Seghers did not approve of all of this, but, unlike his predecessor, he bailed out the poor old priest now and then and Croquet's brother priests kept him supplied in clothes. But most of these he gave away.

Croquet's liberality with his and others' earthly goods actually pleased Seghers, who gave prodigiously of himself the way Croquet gave of his possessions. He had determined in May, 1882 to make another inspection tour of the missions. Since the missions were in good hands, and there was nothing seriously amiss in them, one concludes that he had an uncontrollable itch to be back among the Indians partly for the glamor and partly for encouraging the missionaries. He left Portland in early June and, following official visits at Lewiston and Lapwai, he arrived at DeSmet.

Two days earlier, on June 10, Father Gregory Gazzoli had died at DeSmet and there was much mourning, especially by Giorda with whom Gazzoli had a very intimate and holy relationship. The deceased had been ill for some time. He had been unable to speak or hear another's voice. He was only in his sixty-ninth year, but he had become feeble and required much care. The archbishop himself presided over the funeral Mass, which was appropriate, since Gazzoli's brother was a cardinal.

Cataldo, too, grieved over Gazzoli, who had been the perfect Jesuit, a humble, self-effacing missionary, whose most remarkable accomplishment was daily routine service for nearly forty years. Cataldo was much preoccupied at this time with the relocation of St. Michael's Mission near Spokane Falls. This had always been his pet mission, the first he had established. On the second half-section of land, more lately purchased from the Northern Pacific Railroad,[87] the new mission was being assembled by Brother Carfagno, in a small, pine clad valley about half way between the Treaty Tree and the assembly grounds of the Upper Spokanes.[88] This log house and separate chapel comprised the third St. Michael's mission, not counting the first bark shelter devised by Father Caruana.

The new mission would serve as Cataldo's headquarters, at least until he got that college built, and from here he soon sallied forth on weekends to St. Joseph's Church in the town, some eight miles by horse and the balance by boat, across the river. While all this appeared to be normal for Cataldo, something he expected to be doing for the next decade, there was considerable action in some quarters to make him a bishop, and that would, of course, change everything. This bishop matter was deadly serious and it came about in the following manner.

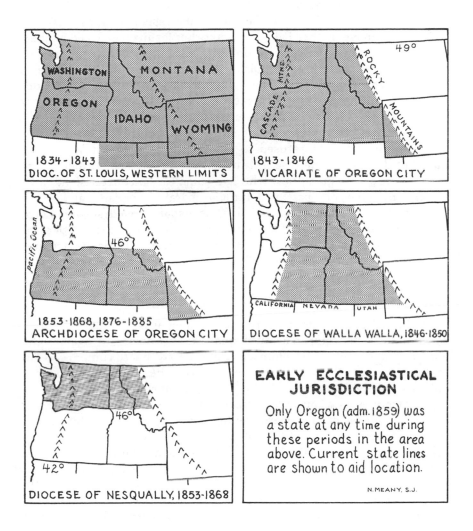

1834–1843
DIOC. OF ST. LOUIS, WESTERN LIMITS

1843–1846
VICARIATE OF OREGON CITY

1853–1868, 1876–1885
ARCHDIOCESE OF OREGON CITY

DIOCESE OF WALLA WALLA, 1846–1850

DIOCESE OF NESQUALLY, 1853–1868

EARLY ECCLESIASTICAL JURISDICTION

Only Oregon (adm. 1859) was a state at any time during these periods in the area above. Current state lines are shown to aid location.

N. MEANY, S.J.

THE VICARIATE OF MONTANA

There were two vast areas in the Northwest without resident bishops: the Vicariate of Idaho, which had been vacant since the resignation of Lootens, and Montana, which was presently split and administered by bishops of other sees—Seghers of Oregon City for the western portion and O'Connor of the Vicariate of Nebraska for the eastern.[89] One lived in

Portland, the other in Omaha, fifteen hundred miles apart and both of them hundreds of miles from their Montana responsibilities.

As noted above, Father Palladino and other Jesuits had urged Seghers to use his influence in Rome to obtain a bishop for Montana. Seghers agreed, but at this time Archbishop Blanchet was still in charge of Oregon City. Motivated by Seghers, Blanchet with Junger and Brondel, the bishops of the Province of Oregon, submitted to Rome a request for a vicariate to be coterminus with the Civil Territory of Montana. At the same time they recommended that a Jesuit be appointed Vicar Apostolic.

But Jesuit superiors refused to permit this and on April 2, 1880, Blanchet dispatched the first *terna* of names for the appointment: John Joseph Leroy, a Belgian priest who had come to Vancouver Island; John Fierens, the energetic pastor of the Cathedral in Portland; and Joseph Cataldo, the unwilling Jesuit. Rome, as usual, moved slowly. Leroy became ill. Blanchet retired. Seghers was archbishop. Brondel, leaving for Rome for his *ad limina* visit in 1882, was authorized by Seghers to urge the matter of Montana with Cardinal Simeoni, Prefect of Propaganda.[90]

LAST YEARS OF FATHER MESPLIE

At this time a certain mischievous element was introduced. Father Toussaint Mesplie, still an army chaplain at Fort Boise, still overweight, pompous, and ready to take himself too seriously, heard rumors one day that he was going to be appointed bishop, the successor to Bishop Lootens, for the Vicariate of Idaho. Credence in rumors like this, which crop up frequently when a see is vacant, is always foolish, but sometimes the victim, whose desires overcome his common sense, puts his faith in them and then there is the devil to pay. So it was with Mesplie: he believed the rumors, which persisted, until one day he received a bogus letter confirming them. Mesplie was overjoyed. Losing no time to lay hold of so great an honor, he immediately placed an order for the episcopal robes with a supply house, where the management, unaware of a prelate's recent appointment, contacted Seghers. Soon the awful truth was known. Someone, preying on Mesplie's gullibility, had made a fool of him.

It would be needless to add that Sehgers disapproved of the prank, and felt compassion for poor Mesplie. But Mesplie, in his deep humiliation, turned to his Indian friends and his soldiers who became his only comfort in the darker years that lay ahead.

About this time, Mesplie received a long letter of advice from his old friend, Bishop Lootens in Victoria. Lootens had been accused of taking "certain things" with him when he left Idaho. "Is not a man always master of his own property?" he asked Mesplie indignantly. In the outpourings of his heart he revealed the poverty into which he had fallen: "Truth to tell, even one-hundreth part of that sum [$10.00] would at times serve to relieve me from embarrassment, and if I had only the half of your pay, I should consider myself as a high salaried official. In that case I should no longer have to be my own cook. . . .

"You speak of my coming to Boise as though that place were on the other side of the street. I thank you all the same for the invitation, which I know to be sincere, but my recollections of that whole country are not attractive enough to make me hope to ever revisit it, though there are people there I should be extremely happy to meet."[92]

Mesplie still had his fine walking stick, which added dignity to his strolls, and his position as chaplain, with its annual stipend of $1,500. This was little enough for a priest who had given over thirty years of his life to the church in the Northwest. He had yearned for a leave of absence to return to France, which he had not seen for thirty-six years. Now, in his spirit of depression occasioned by his humiliation, he requested it. On October 10, 1882, the *Boise Statesman* announced that his leave of absence had been granted.

The venerable missionary would visit the home of his father for an extended time, after which, it was said, he would return to the Boise barracks.

Mesplie's leave had expired on January 1, 1883. When he returned in July, he was charged with absence without leave and with duplicating warrants for his salary, collecting more money than he was entitled to. His explanation that he kept poor records did not appease the court. On January 15, 1884, he was tried by courtmartial and dismissed from the service. Only a hue and cry from his friends kept him from going to prison.

Some of his friends felt that the government had used this means of silencing him, for he was very outspoken in his criticism of government conduct toward the Indians.[93] Their appeals for a new trial went unheard, and President Chester Arthur himself confirmed the court martial. It was impossible to carry the case further.[94]

Disillusioned in the army he had loved, and crushed in spirit, Toussaint Mesplie, in his sixtieth year, retired to Grass Valley, California, where he spent his remaining life. When he died in 1895, he was buried in an unmarked grave, unsung and forgotten, a great missionary and pioneer, who gave twenty-three years of volunteer service to the army before he was commissioned. He had built churches, baptized hundreds, counseled and comforted thousands. All that was left when he died was his walking stick.[95]

GIORDA'S DEATH

Meanwhile, the struggle between Cardinal Simeoni and the Jesuit general in Rome continued to rage. Simeoni wanted Cataldo to be vicar apostolic of Montana and Peter Beckx, the general, was equally determined that *no Jesuit*, but especially not Cataldo, be appointed. When Leroy died, Simeoni decided to appoint Cataldo anyway, and Beckx took his parting shot. He informed Simeoni that if Cataldo were appointed, the Jesuits would have to abandon their missions in Washington and Idaho to concentrate on Montana.[96] Simeoni had no response to this. Seghers and Junger then made another proposal: transfer Bishop Brondel to Montana, and appoint Father John Jonckau of Vancouver Island, as Brondel's successor. This at least got Cataldo off the hook.

Father Joseph Giorda was Cataldo's confidante as Gazzoli had been Giorda's. Neither he nor Cataldo shared in the correspondence about bishops on so lofty a level, and it is unlikely that either one was aware of the enormous gamble Beckx had taken with the missions of Washington and Idaho. Giorda in August of that very year was in residence at DeSmet in Idaho. He also was in fact dying, and on August 7, Father Joseph Caruana, the local superior, informed the editor of the *Catholic Sentinel* that Giorda had died "in my arms last Friday evening at half-past six o'clock after a painful illness of 55 days."[97]

One less Jesuit of Giorda's rank had many repercussions. For example, Cataldo's plans for the Spokane College were affected by it. If the manpower situation was as tight as Beckx implied, there would be no college for years to come.

But when the New Year arrived, the breaks began to appear. On January 1, 1883, for example, Conrardy at Umatilla was able to open his school, the culmination of years of struggle. Father Brouillet had induced the Sisters of Mercy in Philadelphia to provide four sisters, and paid their fare to Pendleton.[98] The sisters and the principal of the new school, Father C. A. Delatte were federal employees, and their salaries were paid by the government. This appeared to be too good to be true.

The Benedictines, also, were making progress. On January 6, 1883, with the full approval of the archbishop, Fillmore was designated as a duly canonical parish, and Benedictine Fathers Bede and Barnabas were placed in charge. Adelhelm had not given up on the so-called butte for his monastery site. He had been buying up farm land at the base, as well as the land on the summit, with borrowed money. "From 1882 to 1888," it was reported, "he purchased at about $25.00 an acre, parcels of land amounting to 1800 acres."[99] There was one other improvement Adelhelm sought: the change of the town's name to Mount Angel. Fillmore had been bestowed upon it by the railroad, which had no objections to the Benedictine proposal. So Fillmore became Mount Angel and Adelhelm was one step closer to his dream of the new Engelberg.[100]

The archbishop, too, was closer to achieving his goals when, at last, on March 5, 1883, the Vatican announced the erection of the Vicariate Apostolic of Montana, comprising all the territory of the future state. For the present, jurisdiction remained with the archbishop of Oregon City, but a few weeks later this, too, was changed. By letters of April 17, 1883, Brondel was appointed to be the "Apostolic Administrator of the Vicariate of Montana," retaining his title and authority as Bishop of Vancouver Island. John J. Jonckau was appointed coadjutor bishop to Brondel for Vancouver Island, to be consecrated and constituted Bishop of Vancouver Island when Brondel was formally appointed bishop in Montana. Brondel was to reside in Montana, but his choice of residence was left to him. His immediate task was to create the required conditions for a diocese, of which he would be appointed the first bishop.[101]

THE DEATH OF ARCHBISHOP BLANCHET

In Portland, Seghers was very gratified that things were working out as he had hoped. He was anxious to go to the missions again and he offered to accompany Brondel as far as Idaho to introduce him to the Indians of the mountains. But the condition of the old archbishop was so critical Seghers was not sure he could leave. Francis Blanchet had offered his last Mass on March 29, 1883. Some weeks later, on April 22, Seghers sent word to the pastor at St. Paul to prepare a brick burial vault. The old man received Viaticum on his knees, then struggled back into bed, where his life was gradually ebbing away. He could linger for months, but the business of the archdiocese had to go on. Seghers decided to make a quick trip with Brondel.

They left for the missions on May 16, stopping at leisure to visit the Indians of Idaho still under Seghers' administration. At Spokane Falls, the two parted, Seghers to return to Portland via Pendleton and Heppner, Brondel to meet with Cataldo and his Jesuit advisors. When Seghers arrived home he was greeted with the news that the old archbishop had died. At 5:50 in the evening of Monday, June 18, 1883, the pioneer priest in the Northwest quietly breathed his last. Seghers had arrived twenty-four hours too late. Much was made of his passing. Reporters declared his death to be the end of an era; actually the new era had begun long before, when Seghers had appeared on the scene. Seghers had buried Demers, and succeeded him in the see of Vancouver Island. It was appropriate now that he bury Blanchet, whom he succeeded in Oregon. There were long ceremonies in the cathedral. After they were over, the dead prelate was buried in the brick vault at St. Paul. His death had really changed nothing.

BRONDEL IN MONTANA

The Northern Pacific Railroad was completed that summer from west to east and for the first time the whistle of the locomotive was heard in Helena. Father Palladino, who would be Brondel's principal assistant for many years to come, piously remarked that it was not less important that "the Rt. Rev. Administrator" also arrived that summer. Bishop Brondel had received the papal bulls of his appointment at Butte on July 2, and this was interpreted by the visionaries as an omen of great moment. July 2, it was pointed out, was the feast of Mary's Visitation on which the holy gospel was read as follows: *"Maria abiit in montana cum festinatione."*[102]

While some may have regarded this as a good omen, there were others in Rome who interpreted it differently. Vatican protocol is very exacting. It seems that by its standards, Brondel had been premature in his visit to Montana since he did not have the papal bull of his appointment *in his possession* when he entered the vicariate. This oversight was duly noted at the Vatican and His Eminence Cardinal Simeoni was reported to have admonished the bishop. Using the same gospel text he said: *"Administrator Montanensis abiit in Montana cum festinatione."*[103] Palladino taking note of the animadversion was quick to defend the bishop: "Any and all irregularities that might have attended the innocent oversight were soon remedied by the Holy See."[104] This pedantic fuss over a technicality was put to rest by these carefully selected words and the business of the vicariate was promoted as before.

Having prudently investigated all possible sites in Montana for the location of his see, His Lordship, somewhat influenced by the Jesuits there, chose Helena. The Jesuits, who had been the first and only priests in Helena, had acquired a considerable amount of property for their activities, including a school. They offered to withdraw and turn over to the bishop all these property rights. His Lordship seized the offer cheerfully, clearing the way for an early erection of the diocese. The property, says Palladino, was first conveyed to Brondel by Cataldo in terms that the bishop regarded as inaccurate or as unfair to the Jesuit Order, so a new contract was drawn up at a later date. This read in part as follows:

> The party of the first part (that is J. B. Brondel) gives to Jos. M. Cataldo, S.J., the party of the second part, the right, possession and deed of all property of the white Mission in Missoula, with all future improvements, to

be henceforth the property of the Society of Jesus, in consideration of the property of the Society of Jesus in Helena, Montana, which by this agreement is deeded to the said Right Reverend J. B. Brondel, Bishop of Helena, the part of the first part. [105]

This agreement was absolutely satisfactory with the bishop, but at least one of his successors used it as an occasion for a celebrated dispute.[106]

Due no doubt to Palladino's knowledge of Montana and his instant contacts with Catholics throughout the territory, Brondel was able to submit to the Vatican plans for a well-organized diocese before the end of the year. Acting on this with almost unprecedented haste, Pope Leo XIII, by appropriate bulls, established the Diocese of Helena and appointed Brondel its first bishop. Later Brondel made a formal announcement of these proceedings in the *Catholic Sentinel:*

> By Apostolic Letters, dated Rome, the seventh of March, 1884, the Vicariate of Montana was erected into a Diocese, whose episcopal see was established at Helena; the church of the Sacred Hearts [sic] was raised to the rank of a Cathedral and the Apostolic Administrator was appointed the first Bishop of Montana.[107]

THE CHEYENNE AND CROW MISSION

South of Helena and east of the Great Divide were the ancestral tribal grounds of two great Indian nations, the Cheyennes and the Crows. Both tribes had been involved in the spectacular victory over General Custer, whom they called "Yellow Hair," and many of them had been punished cruelly for what was regarded as the virtue of patriotism. The Cheyennes, who had a nickname too—"The Race of Sorrows—had suffered incredibly in their treaties with the United States. After the Custer War, they were forced to live in Oklahoma for a time, then they were moved to Fort Keough near Miles City, where a sympathetic listener became their surrogate with the bishop. At that time, 1882, the Cheyennes were allowed to return to their own reservation—mostly to starve, for the buffalo had been killed off.

But their surrogate, whose name was George Yoakum, did not allow the bishop to forget them. The bishop was James O'Connor of Nebraska, and he urged the Jesuits at Helena to send a priest to the Cheyennes. Father Peter Barcelo, a mild mannered, very delicate, Mexican Jesuit, was dispatched to reconnoiter and to do whatever he could for these forsaken and battered people.[108]

Barcelo had already visited the Crows in the late summer of 1880, and he had baptized one hundred and fourteen children in their camps.[109]

These people were unlike the Cheyennes. DeSmet had described them as "tall and handsome." They were more rugged in spirit, less gentle and trusting, hence they had suffered much less than the Cheyennes. Overly impressed yet by what they regarded as the exotic color of the white man, the Crows tended to disregard Barcelo as unimportant. He was smaller than they were and he had dark skin like themselves, two strikes against him.

Barcelo made his first visit to the Cheyennes in July 1883, during the week following Brondel's arrival at Butte. He remained several months, but in the end was ordered to return to the Crows, with whom he felt inadequate and unwanted.

THE URSULINES ARRIVE

George Yoakum did not give up on the Cheyennes. He urged Brondel to help and Brondel appealed to his brother bishops in the east. This cry for help brought a response no one expected: Mother Amadeus from an Ursuline convent in Toledo, Ohio, with a little band of other Ursulines, arrived in Miles City on January 17, 1884. They were prepared to open a school in Miles City, and some of them had come to rescue the Cheyennes from their ignorance and poverty.

The church in Miles City, dedicated to the Sacred Heart, had been built just three years earlier under the direction of the army chaplain at Fort Keough.[110] This was Father E. W. J. Lindesmith, also from Ohio, a tall, angular priest who was sometimes seen wearing a coonskin cap, like Daniel Boone. Lindesmith took the Ursulines under his care, along with the soldiers at the fort, and when early spring permitted travel, he arranged for army ambulances to transport three of the nuns, accompanied by Mother Amadeus, to the Cheyenne mission. They left Miles City on March 29, 1884, and arrived at their destination, more dead than alive, four days later. Seven miles from the mission the nuns were met by Father Joseph Eyler, a diocesan priest from the Cleveland Diocese,, who had arrived already at the mission.

Father Eyler had acquired by purchase a log cabin with a low, mud roof, consisting of three rooms, each of which had only outside entrances. The first compartment on one end, 16 x 22 feet, was assigned to the Ursulines for a convent and chapel. The middle compartment was designated as a school, and the last as the rectory. Because of the mission's utter poverty, it was dedicated by the bishop to St. Joseph Labre, a very poor French vagabond, who had recently been canonized.[111]

White settlers in the area did not approve of Father Eyler or his mission. In fact, they did not approve of the Indians, whose land they had taken. They wanted the Indians to disappear somehow, and the months that followed were filled with hate, terror, and violence. Eyler's health broke and he had to leave. Two other diocesan priests successively replaced him for brief periods, then in September 1884, Father Peter Barcelo returned. It was like returning to a battle zone where hope was left behind.

THE NEW BISHOP OF VANCOUVER ISLAND

The grand design of Archbishop Seghers had succeeded thus far. He had encountered only one obstacle and that was, in the opinion of His Grace, the obstinacy of Father Jonckau, the bishop-elect of Vancouver Island. The deplorable fact was simply this: Father Jonckau refused to be bishop. Seghers argued, coaxed, wheedled, and threatened, but Jonckau stood his ground. He was too old, he said. He was too sick. And if that was not enough, he was "too small and insignificant in stature," and if the Cardinal Prefect did not believe this, he would go to Rome and show himself.

It must be admitted that there was nothing attractive about the see of Vancouver Island. It included, at this time, all of Alaska, sometimes referred to as "Seward's Icebox," but, unlike most ice boxes, it appeared to be empty. Only God knew what was in it, although Seghers himself had a peek or two at some few parts of it. Most of the time he probably did not know what he was looking at, because he tended to miss the forests while he was inspecting the trees.

His embarrassment about Jonckau's balkiness was expressed, mostly, in trying to change Jonckau's mind, while church officials in the Vatican began to look elsewhere. The Third Plenary Council of Baltimore was in the planning stages and Pope Leo XIII had requested American archbishops to present themselves in Rome for special meetings to prepare the *schema* for it. Seghers' visit would give all concerned an opportunity to discuss the Jonckau matter and resolve it with some alternative.

FIRST SYNOD IN THE NORTHWEST

Before departing from Portland, Seghers summoned a council of his own, the first Archdiocesan synod in the history of the Northwest. On Wednesday, September 12, 1883, the archbishop convoked this meeting of his priests in Portland and presided over its sessions for two days. According to custom, decrees in Latin, reflecting the decisions of the priests in sessions, were assembled and promulgated. There were local regulations involving such subjects as mixed marriages, parochial education, required dress for the clergy, and so on. In other words, synods were mini-councils conducted locally, and this first one in the Northwest was no different from others, except that it was the first.[112]

On the following Sunday, September 16, Seghers bade farewell to the cathedral parishioners at the 10:30 Mass, then traveled by buggy to south Portland to bless the cornerstone of the new church there, called St. Lawrence.[113] The pastor of this new parish was Father Bertram Orth, a German priest, who had been ordained at Brussels, Belgium in 1872. The cornerstone ceremony, very exciting for the parishioners, was old hat for Seghers, who performed it graciously as always. It never occurred to him, I am sure, that this would be his last official act in the Archdiocese of Oregon City. On the next day, he left by train eastbound for New York, enroute to Rome. He was accompanied by Father Peter Hylebos, pastor of New Tacoma, who served as his secretary on this journey to Europe, and nine boys from Oregon whom Seghers was taking to Montreal to begin their studies for the priesthood.

SEGHERS IN ROME

The archbishop and Hylebos sailed from New York on the *City of Chicago* on October 5, 1883. After a calm voyage, they disembarked at Liverpool, then spent a few weeks in England and Belgium before arriving in Rome. The first meeting of the archbishop was on November 13 at the College of Propaganda. Exactly one month later their sessions at the Vatican were completed, undoubtedly with a great sigh of relief. The prelates had an audience with the Pope on December 17, after which most left for America.

But Seghers remained. There was this business about a bishop for Vancouver Island. He had already sat in conference with Cardinal Simeoni and Archbishop Domenico Jacobini, Secretary of Propaganda.[114] They had been shocked when he proposed a new solution to the dilemma: they could transfer him to Vancouver Island. It would be easy, he said, to get someone for Oregon City, so he could resign Oregon City and go back to Vancouver Island. The Roman prelates regarded Seghers with disbelief. One of them pointed out the consequence of this proposal, but Seghers remained firm. He would take Vancouver Island on one condition only: the Pope's approval and blessing.

What followed has few precedents in church history, so it is appropriate that many details be presented. First Seghers confirmed his offer by letter to Cardinal Simeoni:

Belgian College, Rue du Quirinal,
November 19, 1883.
To His Eminence Cardinal Simeoni,
Prefect of the Sacred Congregation of the Propaganda.

Your Eminence knows that from 1863 to 1879 I worked in the missions of
the Diocese of Vancouver Island and in the Territory of Alaska or Russian
America. In the latter year, as Your Eminence also knows, I was elevated to
the post of coadjutor to the Archbishop of Oregon City with the right of
succession. I would never have given my consent to this transfer had I not
known that in doing the will of the Sovereign Pontiff I was accomplishing
the will of God.

Now, because of the transfer of Bishop Brondel from the Diocese of
Vancouver Island to the Apostolic Vicariate of Montana, and because of the
illness of Reverend Father Jonckau who has been his administrator, the
Church of Vancouver Island is bereft, to the great detriment of religion,
especially in the Territory of Alaska, which is now abandoned by all.

Therefore, considering on the one hand that it will not be easy to find a
bishop fitted for the Diocese of Vancouver Island who will also take charge
of Alaska; and believing, on the other hand, that the appointment of another
archbishop for Oregon City would not present any great difficulty; and
moved, moreover, by the love which I have always had for Vancouver Island,
I beg of Your Eminence, as a grace and a favor, that the Holy See may grant
me the liberty of resigning the metropolitan church of Oregon City, and
returning to the Diocese of Vancouver Island.

This is not an unprecedented thing in the Church. St. Lievin, who is said to
have been Archbishop of Dublin, in Ireland, left his episcopal see for Belgium
where he worked for the conversion of the barbarious tribes near Ghent, my
native city, which today honors him as its patron. St. Boniface, too, gave up
the Archbishopric of Mayence, and leaving Lullius in his place, went to
convert the Frisians.

If Your Eminence looks with favor upon my request and judges it worthy
of being presented to the Sovereign Pontiff, and if Bishop Brondel is released
from the Diocese of Vancouver Island, then I humbly and earnestly ask that
the matter may be decided as soon as possible, so that while I am still in
Europe I may procure priests and funds and vestments and all things
necessary for the Alaskan missions.

Your Eminence's humble servant in Jesus Christ,
Charles John Seghers,
Archbishop of Oregon City.[115]

After the other archbishops had left Rome, Seghers was summoned to
the private apartment of the Pope. Leo questioned him carefully. Seghers
explained his proposal, giving reasons. "When I left Vancouver Island to
become Archbishop of Oregon," he said, "I did so, though with the

greatest of regret, yet willingly, because I knew that as I had been named by the Holy See, I was doing God's will in doing the will of the Pope. Now I am seeking to know the Pope's will, because only if I see my plan approved and blessed by him shall I believe that I am doing the holy will of God."

The Pope was profoundly moved. Several times the archbishop noticed that his eyes were moist, his lips pressed together to control his emotion. Then, with simple finality, unable to say more lest he break into tears, he said, "I approve."

On that very day, March 7, 1884, Seghers was designated the bishop of Vancouver Island.

MUSICAL CHAIRS

History, they say, is stranger than fiction. The mysterious chain of events taking place in the northwest church in the 1880's seems to confirm this. First, Francis Blanchet and Modeste Demers the pioneer priests in the Northwest, became bishops, the one in Oregon, the other on Vancouver Island. When Bishop Lootens resigned, Blanchet became bishop over Idaho and western Montana, also, and when Demers died, Charles Seghers succeeded him as Bishop of Vancouver Island. When Blanchet retired, Seghers then succeeded him as Archbishop of Oregon City and bishop over Idaho and western Montana. John Brondel, meanwhile, succeeded Seghers, first on Vancouver Island, then as bishop over Montana. Finally, Seghers succeeded Brondel as Bishop of Vancouver Island. All of this occurred in a space of less than five years.

In this same period, it should be noted, Seghers was, at one time or another, bishop of an area presently comprising eight dioceses, four of which are among the largest in extent in the American church: Anchorage, Fairbanks, Helena, and Great Falls-Billings.[116]

His return to Vancouver Island was confirmed by his formal appointment on March 7, 1884. When the bull was issued, he was still in Europe busily engaged in the many details of his succession in Oregon City and Idaho, and in raising funds for the missions attached to his diocese.

The railroad had arrived in Idaho and Seghers, like others familiar with the church there, believed that it was time for the appointment of a vicar apostolic. Seghers' candidate for the position was Alphonse Joseph Glorieux, another Belgian, who had worked under his nose as the principal of St. Michael's College in Portland.[117] Glorieux had impressed Seghers as well as the suffragan bishops of the province, especially with his no-nonsense attitude with his youthful subjects. Idaho had only two secular priests at this time. Glorieux could handle that also. He would assemble priests and get things moving the way he had assembled a faculty and organized a new college.

The appointment was made in Rome on October 7, 1884 and word of it was received "by telegraphic news" in Portland on the same evening. Though his appointed field was a desolate wilderness, Glorieux, just forty years old at the time, was very gratified with his appointment, regarding it as a great honor, and he dispatched an effusive letter to Pope Leo, which revealed a spiritual man, if one somewhat overeager.[118]

When the announcement was made, Glorieux had a real problem, but he did not as yet know about it. The Third Council of Baltimore, scheduled to open on November 9, was only a few weeks distant. As the days passed by, and no papal bulls of his appointment arrived in Portland, there was considerable discussion regarding his status at the Council. If the bulls did not arrive on time, was he or was he not, an *ex officio* member of the Council, like Seghers, Brondel, and Junger, the other active bishops of the Northwest?

Seghers' position, too, was unusual. As the newly assigned bishop of Vancouver Island, he did not represent as such an American diocese under Baltimore. Nothing was made of this, however, because he was still regarded as the Archbishop of Oregon City. No other had been assigned to replace him.

THE THIRD PLENARY COUNCIL OF BALTIMORE

As a religious superior, Father Cataldo was entitled to take his place as a member of the Council. Like the northwest bishops, he made his plans for the journey in due time. He had hoped to be able to use the opportunity to go to Europe to seek volunteers for the mission, which had lost another of its pillars in October when Father Ravalli died.[119] Not many of the original members of the mission were left. Old Father Joset, now in his seventy-fifth year, was still going strong. The mission needed more Josets, but the new Vicar General in Rome, Anton Anderledy, did not approve of Cataldo's proposal to tour Europe.[120]

Seghers left Europe on September 25, with ample time to arrive in Baltimore to finalize the Council's *schema* with the other archbishops.

By this time, officials in Rome had been contacted concerning the right of Bishop Elect Glorieux to participate as a voting member of the Council.[121] Rome's reply was in the affirmative, so Glorieux, like Bishop Elect Maes of Covington, Kentucky, who was in the same situation, was allowed to take his place.

November 9, the opening day, was marked by a dazzling splendor that only the Roman church could provide. Early in the morning, twenty-five thousand people, Catholic and Protestant alike, began to gather in the neighborhood of the cathedral, to see the free show, and some of them, no doubt, to tremble at the growing power of Romanism in America. At nine-thirty in the morning, the Fathers of the Council began to vest in the archbishop's residence. After chanting the *Veni Creator*, they formed a procession to the cathedral, passing through the mostly respectful crowd, which according to the press, threatened the safety of one another, "but no one, despite the squeezing, was injured."

At the head of the procession, after the cross-bearer, walked the students of the seminary, then the members of the regular and secular clergy, then the choir; after that the theologians of the council, vested in chasuble, and the superiors of religious orders, in cope; then rectors of the seminaries, prelates, and mitered abbots; finally, sixty bishops and thirteen archbishops in cope, with miter and crosier. Archbishop Gibbons brought up the rear with his secretary and his chancellor.

They advanced slowly, majestically; observers were struck with their dignity of bearing—some of them bent beneath the weight of years and apostolic labors, others younger, bringing to mind the rich harvest they would glean for the Church. They had come from all parts of America, even from beyond the Rocky Mountains, from New Mexico, from California; all, in Catholic unity, had but one heart, one soul.[122]

The Council closed on December 7, with as much pageantry as when it opened, but with considerably fewer expectations and more church politics.[123] Seghers and Junger had taken the opportunity to badger religious superiors for priests for their missions. Not succeeding with others, they descended on poor Cataldo, insisting that he go to Europe to gather recruits among the Jesuits. Cataldo replied that the general had already refused him permission to do this. Seghers, especially, was persistent. He urged Cataldo to try again. Finally, he made a proposal that the general could not turn down: Cataldo, he said, with the approval of the other bishops, was needed to assist ailing Bishop Junger to make his *ad limina* visit in Rome. To this request the Jesuit vicar general responded favorably.

Thus it happened that during December 1884, in the pious company of Bishop Junger and Abbot Frowin of Conception Abbey in Missouri, Cataldo embarked for Antwerp. At the time no one recognized the significance of this event, but during the years that followed, it became increasingly evident that this was the journey that saved the Jesuits' Rocky Mountain Mission and produced a unique kind of faculty for Gonzaga College, assuring it, too, of survival.

THE DEROO AFFAIR

Meanwhile, Seghers, still technically Archbishop of Oregon City, had to cope with the Father Peter DeRoo affair in Baker City. DeRoo, it seems, had got carried away in his struggle for total control of his parish.

He had not been getting along with the Sisters of the Holy Names, who conducted their academy independently of him. He insisted that the sisters' school was parochial and subject to the pastor of the parish. To secure the support of the Council, he drafted a petition to this august body, and secured it with the signatures, some of them forged, of seventeen priests of the archdiocese.[124] He also sent copies of the petition to archbishops in the Council.

Actually, DeRoo's petition was like a fly on the paper, brushed away by prelates who had more than passing experience in such matters. But for Seghers, it was an occasion not only of embarrassment but of anxiety, for it concerned a principle involving the basic relationship of religious women and pastors in the church's parishes. No one, least of all Seghers, denied the nature of parochial schools subject to the pastor. But Notre Dame Academy in Baker, like other academies conducted by the sisters, was not a *parochial* school, and that made a substantial difference to which Seghers was committed.

The grand climax to this sorry affair, sordid only because of DeRoo's forgeries, occurred on December 9, 1884. The convent at Baker City was surprised to receive a visit of the archbishop's secretary from Portland. With Father Louis Metayer were two Sisters of the Holy Names, Sisters Mary of the Assumption and Mary Isidore. Metayer summoned the Baker City Sisters to the parlor where they met the visitors who were already crying. In a trembling voice the priest handed a letter to the superior: "I am delegated by His Grace," he said, "Bishop C. J. Seghers, and of the Mother House, to execute this deliberation therein, formal order for recall today or tomorrow. Two sisters are to remain here to close up the convent."[125]

The pupils were assembled and the superior, scarcely holding back her tears, tremulously announced that the school would be closed and the sisters recalled to Portland. No other explanation was given. All of the sisters and the pupils were crying now. One would imagine they had been condemned to be shot.

The sisters, heart-sick and filled with fatigue, packed all night. On the following day, December 10, they sent their trunks to the depot, then all five of the sisters, for the convent was closed, gathered at the depot to await the 1:30 train. People of the town joined them, weeping and inconsolable. "What will happen to us?" they wailed. The editor of the *Baker City Democrat* was there and wanted an interview, but no one responded. When the train departed, the people were still on the platform, among them the ten boarding students who had nowhere to go.[126]

DeRoo, of course, was stunned. He truly loved the sisters and admired their work, but his apologies and explanations were useless. The archbishop was determined, and the sisters, I suspect, were delighted with this notorious precedent asserting their independence from bossy pastors. News about it, at least, soon spread throughout the country and Canada, not by DeRoo, you may be sure, nor by the prelates, who had more ponderous matters to discuss.

SEGHERS' DEPARTURE

After more than three months of fund raising and lecturing in eastern America, Seghers returned to Portland on March 24, 1885. He had been absent for eighteen months. His successor in Oregon had been appointed on February 1, over six weeks earlier, and it was appropriate that Seghers say his goodbyes and get out of town before the new archbishop arrived. On Sunday night, March 29, Seghers addressed a sad, dejected flock in the cathedral. It was his farewell sermon. Then he imparted the apostolic blessing over his people and departed in a stream of tears. The saddest of all were his orphans, for they were the cherished portion of his flock.

On Tuesday, two days later, he boarded the *George E. Starr* for Victoria.[127] On his mind, apparently more than any other subject, was his promise to a sparse handful of Indians at Nulato on the distant Yukon River. He had told them that he would return. Now he would have an opportunity to keep his promise. It had all worked out the way he wanted it. But he was rushing to his death. He would never again cast his eyes on Nulato.

ARCHBISHOP WILLIAM GROSS

The new archbishop was a Redemptorist, a member of a congregation of priests that had come to America from Europe at a relatively recent date.[128] His name was William H. Gross and he was already a bishop, having been the Bishop of Savannah, Georgia for twelve years. Like Seghers, he was, first of all, a man of God, not an ambitious or career man. He looked very meek and his prison-like pallor gave him the appearance of an innocent but abused defendant in a spy trial. Slender and graceful in his gait, he made the episcopal cassock so much a part of him that it was hard to imagine what he looked like without it. He wore no glasses, though he was a bookish man and loved to discourse on the theology of St. Thomas Aquinas.

Gross was a native of Baltimore, having been born there on June 12, 1837, grandson of an Irish patriot who had been exiled in 1798.[129] In the streets of Baltimore he passed from childhood to young manhood. He was a bosom buddy of James Gibbons, who became Archbishop of that city, and cardinal. Gross joined the Redemptorists in 1857 and was ordained to the priesthood on March 12, 1863, with nineteen other young men, by Archbishop Patrick Kenrick. This was during the Civil War, in the same year as the Battle of Gettysburg.[130] When Gross was appointed to the See of Savannah, probably through the influence of Gibbons, he was superior of the Redemptorists in Boston. The sheltered life in a religious cloister appealed to him. After Boston nothing would ever be the same again.

10

NEW CHURCHES AND SCHOOLS

1885–1888

In Portland that winter, a wandering cow was killed by one of the city's streetcars. This occasioned more gossip than damage and demonstrated for the benefit of the city fathers the need for a new ordinance concerning the detention of local cows.

More disturbing, of course, was news about cattle in the Yakima Valley. Yakima cows were dying of black leg, an exotic kind of affliction, and some of the ranchers there were beginning to panic.

In eastern Oregon there were complaints about the price of hay. It was too low for the growers, but too high for the cattlemen. Father DeRoo had gone into the cattle business, without much success, however, for his market was far from Baker City and the Powder River, where his cattle grew fat and lazy.

If all this news about cows rendered serious people melancholy, the reports from western Canada were even more disturbing. Louis Riel, an aroused Metis patriot who had once taught for the Jesuits at St. Peter's Mission, was leading an Indian rebellion against the crown.[1] Hostilities had begun on March 2,1885. Riel, they say, was a fanatic. He and his ill-equipped revolutionaries were soon suppressed by the Dominion Government, and Riel was hanged.[2] The disclosure of all of this, especially the hanging, was shocking to American sensibilities, because a more righteous attitude toward Indians had begun to influence easterners, who no longer had something to gain by depriving Indians of their rights.

Some of the people in Montana, unfortunately, did not share their fellow Americans' new concern for the Indians. Local ranchers cherished their cows but hated the Cheyennes. They also hated George Yoakum for defending the Cheyennes and they wasted no love on Father Peter Barcelo at St. Joseph Labre's Mission, where this Jesuit mystic agonized daily over his "Race of Sorrows." One evening while Yoakum and Father

Barcelo conferred together in the primitive hut called "the rectory," in the light of a flickering kerosene lamp, several masked men appeared and brutally beat up Yoakum while Barcelo stood helplessly aside. They took Yoakum away at gun point, threatening to hang him as they departed.[3] The outrage shattered poor Barcelo's delicate health, which had already been undermined by his hardships on the Cheyenne Mission. He had to return to Helena, leaving the Ursulines once again without a priest or Mass.

At Grande Ronde in Oregon, it was just the opposite: Father Croquet remained and the sisters left him again. The three new Benedictine Sisters, who had been there eighteen months or less, departed with regrets and empty stomachs. Unfortunately, they had to leave or starve. They could not live on the bark of the fir trees or on the scotch broom plants, both of which abounded in the area.

BENEDICTINE SISTERS AT UNIONTOWN

Mother M Johanna Zumotein was still the superior of the sisters and her subjects were Sister M. Magdalen Suter and Sister M. Rosalia Rubli. They moved from the Grande Ronde to Uniontown in Washington Territory where there was a surplus of food and no shortage of German-speaking Catholics.

Bishop Junger had asked for them. He had told them that if they would found a convent in his diocese, they would have their choice of four locations, Tacoma, Sprague, Pomeroy, or Uniontown. He added that if they chose the latter, he would throw into the bargain one of the pioneer Benedictines, Father Nicholas Frei, who would serve as their chaplain and establish a parish.[4]

Toward the end of November 29, 1884, they reached Uniontown. Mother Johanna described their reception in a letter:

> Early on Friday morning, we started for Uniontown and were landed at the home of Mr. M. Schultheis, a home indeed for all of us. We were royally treated there. The kindness and attention of the good lady Schultheis especially can never be forgotten.
>
> We stayed for Sunday services in order to meet more Catholics, who were living scattered on their farms. Sunday morning, team after team was seen on the way to church. We Sisters were warmly welcomed by the good people. Their unfeigned friendliness and sincere intentions made us feel quite at home among them.
>
> They agreed to build a house according to instructions, but emphasized that nothing could be done before the following summer, since the season was far advanced. Nothing definite was enacted....[5]

At this point, Father Frei, who was as generous as he was ubiquitous, vacated his rectory and turned it over to the sisters. In the spring, the men of the parish began work on the convent. Frei laid the cornerstone of the 45 by 50 foot frame structure in August and, on December 3, 1885, the sisters moved in.[6] They called it St. Andrew's after the motherhouse in Sarnen, Switzerland. They intended, of course, to open an academy, and Sister M. Rosalia, who could speak English very well, passed the territory's teacher examination with flying colors. Thus she was able to teach children in the district school at a salary of forty dollars a month, almost enough to support the convent.[7]

Out at Mount Angel, while Grover Cleveland was being sworn in as the twenty-second president of the United States, the monks were planting their spring crops. Under the supervision of Adelhelm Odermatt, now called "the prior," they had built a temporary three-story frame monastery on the side of the bluff, near the present site of the abbey shops.[8] It was understood that the top of the bluff was reserved for the permanent monastery, to be built when the community had money and time for it. Meanwhile, as Odermatt explained to the Catholics in the valley, the monks were closer to their fields and St. Mary's Church.

There was some uneasiness about the nuns who had been left behind at Gervais. They had recently completed their spacious new convent in Gervais, presuming that the monks would remain there. It was becoming clear, however, that a Benedictine school would be established soon, for boys of course, and this would be like driving a nail in the coffin at Gervais. So the sisters really had little choice. In the spring of 1885, they opened their own school for girls at Mount Angel. Meanwhile, they retained St. Scholastica's Convent in Gervais, expecting the worst, but hoping for a miracle, the nature of which they could not decide upon.

About this time, two of the Northwest's Irish priests died, both of them within a fortnight. This produced a Carpathian gloom in two chanceries and as many parishes. Father Peter Mackin expired in Portland on February 4, 1885, and Father Thomas Duffy, the venerated pastor of Walla Walla, followed him into the Great Beyond eleven days later. Duffy's demise was very sudden, at the somewhat tender age of forty-three. He dropped dead while visiting San Francisco, fulfilling the adage adopted from Naples: See San Francisco and die. His funeral, the largest in the history of Walla Walla up to this point, attracted over two hundred carriages, forming a procession to the cemetery four times the length of most covered wagon trains.[9]

CONSECRATION OF BISHOP GLORIEUX

The new bishop of Idaho had not returned to the West Coast. His reason for the delay was simple enough: he could not be consecrated as a bishop because the documents from Rome had not arrived. He awaited them anxiously at Baltimore while he toured the environs seeking funds for his mission. The papal briefs, dated at Rome on February 27, 1885, finally arrived on April 6, a mere 182 days after he was informed of his appointment.[10]

Glorieux had first appealed to Seghers to serve as his consecrating prelate, but His Grace, ignorant of the arrival of the proper documents, was somewhere in the country promoting his own mission as if salvation depended upon it. Thus on April 19, in the Cathedral at Baltimore, Alphonse Glorieux was consecrated Titular Bishop of Apollomia and Second Vicar Apostolic of Idaho by Archbishop Gibbons.[11] The co-consecrators were Archbishop Gross and Bishop Camillus Maes of Covington, who had been consecrated on January 25, 1885, though his appointment was made about the same time as Bishop Glorieux's.

ARRIVAL IN PORTLAND

Accompanied by Archbishop Gross, Glorieux returned at last to Portland. There was, of course, much holy excitement in the city in anticipation of the advent of the new archbishop, not to mention the return of their local priest as a bishop. The two celebrities were expected on Saturday, May 23. Arrangements were then made for fifteen representative of the various societies, including two priests, Verhaag and Gibney, to meet the prelates at The Dalles in a chartered river boat. Accordingly, the duly appointed and highly energized ladies and gentlemen arrived in The Dalles the previous night and sought lodgings in the city while the boat awaited them at the dock.

At precisely 5:30 in the morning of May 23, the Union Pacific train bearing Gross and Glorieux steamed into The Dalles, where the committee gave it a sleepy welcome. The prelates were respectfully summoned and greeted with appropriate remarks, then all, fully awake by this time, processed to the church for Mass. At 8:00 a.m., they all marched back to the boat, where everybody made at least one speech of welcome, while it churned down the Columbia into the morning mists drifting along the mountains.

In late afternoon, the boat docked briefly at Vancouver. Other ecclesiastical dignitaries clambered aboard. About seven in the evening, the proper time for a reception according to the *Sentinel*, all arrived in Portland where St. Michael's College band and an immense crowd had gathered to produce a noisy welcome. Again they marched to the church, for some of them the second time that day, and passed under a great arch bearing the legend, "Welcome to Our Western Land," and into the cathedral where endless speeches of welcome were presented far into the night. The entire affair, as solemn as organized enthusiasm could make it, was a grim reminder to both bishops that henceforth they would be victims of the good will of their people.

GLORIEUX OCCUPIES HIS VICARIATE

For two weeks the newly consecrated Bishop of Appolomia was busy in Portland, settling his affairs at St. Michael's College and saying his goodbyes. Then he left for Boise, via Kuna, Idaho, the nearest railroad station, where he disembarked from the dusty train on Friday, the Feast of the Sacred Heart, June 12, 1885. Father Francis Hartlieb, one of his two diocesan priests in the whole vicariate, pastor of St. John's in Boise, met him at the station with a primitive conveyance, a two-seated farm wagon driven by faithful John Farrell, whose home served as a church while another was being built. It was John, too, who had donated the block of land for the church in Boise, so he should be regarded as something more than a patron, perhaps something like an archangel.

When Bishop Glorieux looked about him, there was no arch, or band, or cheering crowd. Just two men and a wagon in the hot sun. It was twenty miles from Kuna to Boise, all sagebrush and desert. As the horses clopped along, pulling the wagon through dust up to the hubs of the wheels, great clouds filled the still air, which was pungent with the odor of sage and crackling dry like the Gobi.[31]

On his arrival in Boise, a typical western town with almost as many horses and dogs as people, the bishop found as his "cathedral" a small, wooden chapel, without embellishment of any kind, or even a graceful form to recommend it, on the southeast corner of Ninth and Bannock Streets, facing the latter. Attached to the rear of this structure, like an afterthought, was an unsightly addition of four rooms, which the pastor used as a rectory. It was no place for a bishop. Glorieux sought temporary rooms in a boarding house, a respectable residence belonging to Mrs. James Flanagan.[14]

There were twenty Catholic families in Boise and the church was built to accommodate one hundred and twenty. The average Sunday collection was nine dollars in the winter, five in the summer. Fortunately, the bishop brought with him a little nest egg presented by friends, $2,650.00 which he deposited in the bank, pending decisions to build churches and a bishop's house.[15] The Boise Catholics, mostly of Irish origin, were characteristically generous. Confirming the old dictum that "the Germans give to the church and the Irish to the priest," they purchased for $100 a grandiose throne that appeared to be as out of place in the shanty-like church as a diamond pendant around the cook's neck.

Soon after the bishop's arrival, some details were provided by one of the priests:

> The coldness of the reception I received at His Lordship's hands considerably awed me. He was not at all given to demonstrations, very stern with himself and stern with others, he was, nevertheless, of extreme simplicity of life and manners. To illustrate, one day on leaving the house I saw His Lordship come down the street swinging a slop pail, which he had bought at one of the stores on the main street, three blocks away. The sight drew from me an involuntary smile, which the Bishop perceived. He remarked carelessly: "I have been shopping, Father." Had I permitted it, he would have fetched the firewood from the shed, made kindling, etc. I used to do that for him when I was in Boise; but whenever I would go on the mission, and I was gone often from two to five weeks, he would thus wait upon himself. He was a model pioneer Bishop, just the man to lay the foundations of a new diocese in a country with no past, but with a bright future looming up in the far distance. Absolutely disinterested as far as the material was concerned, he was content with the poorest food, the poorest clothing, for himself, but wanted the best that his means allowed him to procure for the church.
>
> When he came to Boise in 1885, after the Council of Baltimore, he found not only poverty, but church conditions that would scarcely have met with the approval of either canonist or liturgist....
>
> ...No wonder then that in the pompously so-called Cathedral there were neither wax-candles for the altar nor vegetable oil for the sanctuary lamp and that the Mass wine used was manufactured from Boise grapes by an honest non-Catholic resident, who guaranteed its purity. The candles we used were the stearic wax candles in great demand by miners....
>
> Kerosene oil-lamps did duty as sanctuary lamps and the Mass-wine which we bought at the rate of 75 cents the demijohn, was fetched from up town by one of the altar-boys. It was hardly a temptation for them; for the wine was tarter than a sour apple.[16]

When he was in Boise, the bishop took his principal meal with Father Hartlieb at a place called "The Spanish Restaurant," where a card good for twenty-one meals was purchased for $4.00. Breakfast and lunch were taken at the rectory in back of the church, in the form of a light repast, usually bread and cheese. With dinners at nineteen cents each and other meals more simple than a sheepherder's snack, it was not likely that the

Vicar Apostolic of Idaho would gain weight. He remained, in fact, as thin as a pole, tall and graceful, like a learned professor who lives on Greek verbs and nouns.

TOUR OF THE VICARIATE

He lost no time in making the tour of his territory—not a simple matter even in 1885, when most of it was made by stagecoach. He prepared in due time a Directory for the Vicariate in 1885, a document as sparse as his poverty in everything else.[17]

1. Boise, St. John's Church, Rt. Rev. A. J. Glorieux, D.D., Pastor.
Mission: Our Lady of Tears, Silver City
Stations: Caldwell, Emmettsville, Weiser, Payette, Mountain Home[18]

2. Granite Creek, St. Thomas Church, Rev. Francis Hartlieb, Pastor.
Missions: St. Joseph's Church, Idaho City; St. Dominic's Church, Centerville; St. Francis de Sales Church, Pioneer
Stations: Quartzburg, Garden Valley, Jerusalem

3. Haily, St. Charles Church, Rev. E. M. Nattini, Pastor
Mission: St. Peter's Church, Shoshone
Stations: Bellevue, Bullion, Broadford, Custer, Rocky Bar, Atlanta, Glenns Ferry, Pocatello, Montpelier, Dempsey, McCammon, Eagle Rock, Blackfoot, Rexburg and St. Anthony

4. DeSmet, Sacred Heart Church, Rev. J. M. Cataldo, S.J. Pastor.
Stations: Murray, Mullan, Wallace, Fort Sherman, Coeur d'Alene

5. Lewiston, St. Stanislaus Church, Rev. Alexander Diomedi, S.J. Pastor
Stations: Moscow, Genesee

6. Lapwai, St. Joseph's Church, Rev. A. Morvillo, S.J. Pastor and the Rev. G. Gazzoli, S.J.[19]
Stations: Keuterville, Mount Idaho, Salmon Mines.

This was the vicariate—one bishop, two secular priests, four Jesuits, and eight nuns.[20] Of the territory's sixty thousand inhabitants in 1885, only thirty-five hundred were Catholics. That was about six percent of the total population and no improvement over the census of 1870.[21] Now there were fifteen churches and chapels, the best of which was the old Sacred Heart Mission Church begun by Ravallli in 1849 and used only on special occasions. All the others were like the cathedral: frame buildings, most of them unpainted, aging ungracefully in the wintry snows of some places, or in the baking desert suns of others.

Mostly the bishop needed new churches in the more promising settlements, additional priests, and a bishop's house. When Father Emmanuel Nattini, a former Jesuit who had volunteered for service in Idaho in 1880, had to retire after seven years of heroic service and debilitating labors, the bishop was so short-handed that he sought a dispensation from the Holy See for ordaining Cyril Van der Donckt nineteen months before he reached the canonically required age of twenty-four.[22] Thus Van der Donckt, ordained to the priesthood on June 24, 1887, was the first priest ordained specifically for Idaho and the second priest incardinated in the Vicariate. The first incardinated priest was Father Hartlieb.[23]

The episcopal residence, not a "bishop's palace" by any stretch of the imagination, was finally erected in the spring and summer of 1886 with funds contributed by the Propagation of the Faith in Rome.[24] This was a two-story brick edifice at 317 North 9th Street, containing office and living space for the bishop and Father Hartlieb, and two extra bedrooms for guests. There was no kitchen or dining room, so the gourmet dinners at the Spanish Restaurant, nineteen cents each, continued to be His Lordship's fare. The total cost of the episcopal residence was $2,914.00 for the eight rooms it contained, approximately one percent of the cost of some rectories four generations later. Like the bishop, the house expressed a no-frills message to the people, though it appeared to be almost palatial to Father Hartlieb when he moved in during September 1886.

LEWISTON, IDAHO

By this time Father Diomedi had completed the new church in Lewiston on the corner of Fifth and D Streets.[25] This was an edifice with some style, a frame church like most, and painted white with a dark trim. It boasted front doors with an honest canopy design above, similar decorative canopies over the windows on either side, and a simple "rose" window in the gable space above all three. Surrounded by a picket fence and garnished with ornamental trees, it could have been an architectural gem even in a more sophisticated city.[26]

To the left of the church was "a St. Aloysius Academy," Lewiston's parochial school, which had been opened by three Sisters of St. Francis of

New Castle, Minnesota, in September 1884. This was a two-story frame building dominated by a row of tall Lombardy poplar trees which appeared to have been there for years. This served as both school and convent, at least until the sisters were recalled to their motherhouse in August 1887.[27]

Lewiston, like many other small towns or cities in the Northwest, faced an almost unsolvable dilemma: the small number of Catholics buried under a vast majority of indifferent so-called Christians. The "unchurched" areas of the Northwest, as noted above, were unchurched from the beginning, because most of the people who settled there were not interested in formal religion. Without a sudden influx of practicing Christians, it was a situation well nigh impossible to change. It was difficult, then, for the bishops or Mother Superiors of teaching orders to assign personnel for churches and schools where there was relatively little response. And because there was a shortage of personnel, it was difficult for things to change.

Thus Lewiston's tiny first church lasted for years, its second church was not much larger, and its school of not more than thirty students could not justify the presence of the sisters who were needed desperately elsewhere.

By way of contrast, the three Indian missions in northern Idaho, representing less than one-third of the Catholic population in the territory (one thousand out of three and one-half thousand), accounted for most of the Catholic baptisms, marriages, and reception of the other sacraments.[28] One seeks in vain for the ultimate reasons for this dramatic disproportion. How does one explain, for example, the report of approximately eight thousand recipients of the Eucharist at DeSmet in 1885, and only 312 at Lewiston in the white parish in the same year?

While no exact parallel existed in Oregon and Washington, there were distressing similarities. In Catholic colonies like Uniontown in Washington and Verboort, St. Paul, and Mount Angel in Oregon, traditional Catholic devotion to duty and the sacraments prevailed, even during this early period, but in larger cities where Catholics represented only a small minority, participation in church activities was more than proportionately less. Only in Spokane was this phenomenon reversed. In the beginning, Spokane Falls, as it was called until 1889, was no different from Seattle or Lewiston.[29]

The subject of the unchurched will appear again and again in the history of the Northwest, for it was, and still is, the most striking characteristic of Northwest Christianity. It is also its most dismal failure. In this, unfortunately, the Catholic Church shares, if not the blame, at least in the consequences.

TWO NEW CATHEDRALS

If this trend was already apparent to the hierarchy in the summer of 1885, no one commented on it. Two of the bishops, Gross in Oregon and Junger in Washington, were awaiting the completion of their new cathedrals. One suspects that Gross was not particularly happy about his, for he did not like the site on which it was being built. It also appeared that Father Fierens, pastor of Portland's cathedral parish, was engaged in a race with Junger, in the spirit of competition as for the Glory of God. Whatever the cause, the race for completion was neck and neck until August 15, 1885, when the cathedral in Portland was dedicated in honor of the Immaculate Conception.

Described as being "pointed Gothic of the fourteenth century, one hundred and fifty-feet long, sixty-nine feet wide and two hundred feet from the floor to the top of the spire," this cathedral cost well over a hundred thousand dollars, which put the parish in debt until it was time to build another. Actually, the site had been ill chosen. At Third and Stark, where the old frame church had stood, there was no room for expansion and the area, cluttered with sundry commercial blocks, soon disintegrated in appearance and succumbed to noisy traffic.

The dedication ceremony was conducted by Archbishop Gross, whose procession into the church was timed at exactly ten in the morning while three bells pealed forth, filling the Saturday morning downtown streets with reminders that the Catholics were up to something again.[30] Two thousand people, it was said, attended the blessings, which lasted only forty-five minutes. After that, the archbishop celebrated a pontifical Mass and preached, as was customary, for at least one hour. When the almost three-hour ritual was concluded, most of the participants felt like going to bed to recover.

VANCOUVER CATHEDRAL

Across the river at Vancouver, the new cathedral was not ready for dedication, but construction was sufficiently advanced for its first use. Accordingly, Father Schram offered the first Mass in it on Sunday, August 16, 1885, which was the day after Portland's conventional dedication. "After the gospel," the *Sentinel* reported, "Father McGuckin, O.M.I., ascended the pulpit and for nearly an hour held that vast concourse of people spell-bound by his eloquence."[31]

This brick church, very large by contemporary standards, was designed by Donald McKay, and construction by contractors from Portland had begun in May of 1884. It was finally dedicated in honor of St. James and St. Augustine on Sunday, November 1, 1885. It rained so heavily that day that Bishop Junger, who presided, could not conduct the blessings outside, but Archbishop Gross made up for this slight omission by preaching for ninety minutes.[32] Bishop Blanchet, who had followed news of the construction of the building with pardonable pride, was unable to attend. No doubt he was missed by a few, but memories are short. The old prelate had retired six years earlier, and he was now in his eighty-eighth year, an age when most old people are remembered only on their birthdays.[33]

Even the absence of the ever-popular Seghers went unnoticed. When he finally returned to Victoria on April 1, 1885, he found the old rectory there in the last stage of decline. Six days later, at a meeting of prominent members of the laity, it was decided to replace the rectory with a new one to cost $20,000.[34] Construction of this three story-brick residence was the least of Seghers' worries, for he had two other priorities in mind, a return to Alaska and the provision of an adequate college in his diocese. In Portland, he had carped so much on Catholic education that he was now identified with the group in the church who opposed the presence of Catholics in public schools. To staff his St. Louis College he needed teachers. Precisely at this point the superior of the Viatorian school in Baker City offered to abandon Oregon for Victoria. Father Manseau had become disillusioned with DeRoo in Baker City, especially after the academy's ill-starred closure, but his principal reason for deciding to leave Oregon, I think, was money, or the lack of it. By the spring of 1885, the situation had become so disheartening that even raw, windy, and soggy Victoria looked good. When it came down to the nitty-gritty, however, Manseau and his colleagues could not come to an agreement with Seghers and they remained in Oregon until they were recalled to eastern Canada. "The Bishop is a Belgian," Manseau grumbled, because Victoria had not panned out, "and when he gets an opinion in his head it stays there."[35]

SISTERS OF ST. FRANCIS

The Viatorians left Baker City in September, 1885. Before their departure, on August 24, a new group of sisters arrived to reopen Notre Dame Academy, which had been closed following the DeRoo fiasco with the Holy Names Sisters. There were four Sisters of the Third Order of St. Francis from Glen Riddle, Pennsylvania, the first of their congregation to live in the Northwest. The name of the school was changed again to St. Francis Academy, which served notice to the students that a new spirit was about to prevail.[36] The presence of the nuns was a tribute to DeRoo's ingenuity and to his deep conviction that all Catholic children should be in Catholic schools.

Of some interest here is the apparent serenity, which for a brief time seemed to linger in the parish. There was no open conflict between the pastor and the sisters, as there had been in the past. Not all was well, however, for a faction of the parishioners continued to agitate behind the scenes, among themselves, but not without the knowledge of the deeply sensitive pastor, who kept hoping that the trouble would just go away. But it did not go away. Sooner or later DeRoo would have to face it.

CATALDO'S NEW JESUITS

As Manseau had observed, when Seghers got an idea in his head, no one could change it. This would prove to be his undoing. He had got Alaska in his head and he was determined to return there to establish missions along the Yukon River. He had badgered Cataldo and other religious superiors for priests to accompany him, and when Cataldo, yielding at last to his entreaties, agreed to assign one priest for the Alaska mission, Seghers had responded with cavalier loftiness: "It would be unwise to leave *one* priest by himself in Alaska; and as my desire is to locate *two* in the interior and then to continue my trip to parts unknown, I beg you to arrange matters so that two Fathers of the Society with one or more brothers may accompany me."[37] Now that he was promised one Jesuit, he wanted four.

Cataldo in fact had returned from to Europe in late summer of this same year with a whole troop of Jesuits, producing "the jump which saved the Rocky Mountain Mission." Among his recruits was the future first bishop of Alaska, Raphael Crimont, and five future presidents of Gonzaga College. Three of these recruits arrived in New York in September 1885. These were Fathers James Rebmann and Herman Schuler and one scholastic, Balthasar Feusi.

Rebmann, in his thirty-third year, had been born at Speyer on the Rhine, the son of Elizabeth whose husband had gone to America shortly after her son's birth. He was never heard from again. Cataldo assigned Rebmann to Frederick, Maryland, to complete his studies as a Jesuit, an occasion of sacrifice for the mission, which needed him desperately.

Cataldo had lost his favored subject in January. This was Louis Ruellan, a young French priest who became the first resident pastor of Spokane Falls in April 1884. In September, Ruellan had started "a collection" to build a new church replacement for the shanty on Main Avenue, to be called Our Lady of Lourdes in fulfillment of a vow he had made. This was the beginning of the present cathedral parish in Spokane.[38] Ruellan killed himself with work. Lacking even a horse most of the time, he walked for long hours each day, seeking fallen-away Catholics in his primitive parish, which was settled so sparsely that people kept chickens and cows even in the middle of town. Every home was like a farm. In January 1885, nearly dead from exhaustion, he paused to make his retreat, but he died from pneumonia scarcely after he had begun.[39]

Another of Cataldo's favorites was Grassi, who was back in the saddle, covering some six or seven thousand square miles of wilderness in north central Washington. "Father Wilbur," formerly the kingpin of the Yakima reservation, was no longer there.[40] He owned valuable real estate in several towns, but it was widely believed he was in Washington D.C., lobbying on behalf of the Methodist church for the return of the Yakima Reservation to the Methodists. Due to the lapse of Grant's Peace Policy, Wilbur no longer controlled the fate of the tribe, and Catholic missionaries now had free access to the reservation. Grassi, who was attached to the Yakima mission, labored among the Indians in the more difficult terrain to the north, and other Jesuits, like Father Aloysius Parodi, arrived to help Caruana with the Yakimas and the southern portion of Central Washington.

Beyond the reservation borders there were a number of growing settlements. The largest of these was Yakima City, called Union Gap today. Father Caruana from the mission built a frame church about a mile west of the town, intending its use for both Indians of the reservation and Catholics in the town. He offered the first Mass in this church on the feast of St. Joseph, March 19, 1884.[41] Unhappy with this arrangement, certain whites, angry because they had to share the church with the Indians, built another church in Yakima City, but contrary to their expectations, they could not get a priest to occupy it. They soon abandoned the place.

Two years later, the railroad people, as often happened on the frontier, changed everything by placing their station at North Yakima, four miles distant from Yakima City. The clever settlers hurriedly relocated their homes and businesses. Soon the older town was almost abandoned, and the new pastor of the church, Father Victor Garrand, who had been a missionary in Syria and Egypt, decided to accept the railroad's offer of free land, and to move the church there. At this point, the die-hards, irate members of the parish, still stung by their failure to force their will on others, threatened to burn the church if Garrand attempted to move it. But Garrand felt he had no other choice if he was to serve the convenience of the majority. He dismantled the building, moved it, and reassembled it on the new site without incident. Garrand then blessed it and offered the first Mass in it on December 8, 1886.[42]

Meanwhile, other Jesuits were building churches in other settlements, with fewer conflicts, but also with less money. Father Aloysius Folchi acquired an old log building, formerly a trading post, for a church in Chewelah, Washington Territory, about one mile south of the first St. Francis Regis Mission.[43] This was in January 1885. In the summer of the following year, he built a new frame church on land donated by James Monaghan, an early self-styled capitalist, who, like John Farrell in Boise, keeps turning up in the church's local history. Folchi spent one thousand dollars completing this church and he dedicated it in honor of St. Mary of the Rosary.[44]

In present Ellensburg, Washington, Father Aloysius Parodi built another church, which he called St. Andrew's.[45] This was northwest of the Yakima country in a beautiful valley that was already renowned for its horses and cattle. Parodi, like Croquet in Oregon, was like a saint, a holy man of prayer. He was also impractical. He eventually became a missionary in Alaska, where he lost his mind completely.[46] Before this, however, he covered enormous distances, driving his one horse buggy out to the lonely homes of ranchers scattered throughout half of the central plateau.

Grassi needed help. On October 4, 1885, Stephen DeRouge, the son of a French count, was ordained to the priesthood by Bishop Brondel in Helena. This was the first ceremony of its kind in Montana.[47] DeRouge was one of Cataldo's recent recruits, an aloof, aristocratic young man with a stubborn streak and an inherited characteristic toward baldness. He began his missionary career eleven days after he was ordained. Departing from St. Francis Regis Mission on the back of a horse on October 15, 1885, he rode into the west, over the mountains and down the Okanogan Valley to a place near Ellisford, where he built a home and completed a small chapel of hewed logs.[48] Since he was French, he called the place Our Lady of Lourdes. Both Indians and whites attended his chapel and later, after he provided it, his little school.

Time proved that this site was badly chosen for a central mission, and particularly for a school, which he regarded as equally important with the church. In May of 1886, DeRouge rode north along the Okanogan River to a valley from which Omak Creek flowed. In this small valley was a log hut, really a miserable hovel scarcely decent enough for animals. He purchased it from the Indians and gave it the name of St. Mary's. It became in time a mission of great renown.

ST. PETER'S MISSION FOR THE BLACKFEET

The Jesuits had reopened St. Peter's Mission near Bird Tail Rock in the spring of 1874. In that same year, it will be remembered, the boundaries of the Blackfeet Reservation were moved sixty miles north, leaving the mission high and dry as it were, far from the Blackfeet people. Thus it was converted into a school for boys.

In 1884, Father Joseph Damiani was superior. He used to say that a mission without sisters was no mission at all, and for some months he had been negotiating with Mother Amadeus for a staff of Ursulines to open a school for girls. Amadeus was a kind of "Lady Father DeSmet" who buzzed hither and yon, wherever duty summoned and duty was mostly the romantic call of the Indians. She finally appeared at St. Peter's on October 30, 1884, with two nuns under her wing.[49] Joined later by two others, they occupied four log cabins which had to serve as school and convent for seven crowded years.

Bishop Brondel paid St. Peter's a formal visit. Since arriving at Helena, he had heard endless discussions about St. Peter's, especially by Father Imoda, who had never lost faith in its usefulness. Imoda was a practical joker, too, so His Lordship may have had mixed ideas about the mission before he arrived there on Saturday evening in late July, 1885.

The bishop's companion, "C.F." described for the readers of the *Catholic Sentinel* the events of the following day, which gave the bishop much food for thought.

> The following Sunday was quite an eventful day in the history of the Mission. For the first time a Catholic bishop was to officiate with crosier and mitre in administering the Sacrament of Confirmation and giving the white veil of the order of Ursuline nuns to the young lady novices, who had been in retreat for several days previous in preparation for this important epoch in their lives. At an early hour crowds of people from the vicinity of the Mission, Fort Shaw, Sun River, and other places, began to congregate around the premises, and at 10 o'clock a procession was formed at the Fathers' residence to escort His Lordship to the Church. The little white and Indian girls, all dressed in white and carrying a beautiful banner, on which was a picture of the Blessed Virgin, led the procession. The white and Indians boys, also carrying a banner, came next followed by the Sisters, and several hundred people, principally half breeds, who all marched two deep in perfect order to the Church. Here the procession opened out in single file, and all knelt down to receive the Bishop's blessing as he passed through, accompanied by four priests and altar boys in their surplices, and entered the Church by the front door. High Mass was celebrated by Rev. Father Genna, S.J., the choir rendering Dermont's Royal Mass, in good style. At the end of the Mass His Lordship confirmed sixteen persons, having first given them a beautiful instruction on the efficacy of this great sacrament. Speaking first in French and then in English....

Under the superintendency of Father Genna, who speaks the Blackfoot language fluently and Sister Gertrude, their accomplished teacher, the following programme was successfully carried out:

PROGRAMME

Indian Music..........
....Medley
Hymn to our Lady............. ..."Our Ranainir Rsim Mania"
Prayers.......................Blackfoot language
Hymn........................ ..."St. Joseph, Arsi Rinna"
English, Reading and Spelling.........................
Arithmetic...
Indian Play...................."Medicine"
Hymn......................... ..."Kimmis Arsi Mania"
Indian Catechism.....................................
Indian song and English recitation....................
Distribution of Premiums

All the children acquitted themselves remarkably well, considering the short time they had been under instruction, and their rapid improvement, while reflecting much credit upon the painstaking efforts of their teachers, shows that, with proper treatment, these children as a rule have great aptitude for learning. It is a few months since these good Sisters opened their schools at the mission, and if one may judge by what they have already accomplished, it is safe to predict that in a few years they will have one of the most flourishing schools in the Territory at St. Peter's. At the conclusion of the programme one of the Indian boys stepped up, making his bow, to the Bishop, read the following address in the Blackfeet language:

'Mmax Si Kinnou, Kanaetahamitakeop Kaxksinaukoxsi Ksistoa Kinnon KultaKinnon Ke Montana SiKepistsisu Kasimiks Wmaxsinna, Nistoa Rita Kumimmoxpinnau, Kistoa ennaKai Kistoa Kinnon Ke Nistoa Ku-Kosiks Kukkinnau axsi auuaxK KsaxKumKi stsiki Spuxsis.'

Of which one of the little Indian girls read the following literal translation.

'Our great and noble Chief. We are all glad to see you. Our father of our souls and of Montana, blackrobes Great Chief! We love you because you are our Father and we are your children. Give us your blessing now for this world and also for heaven.'[50]

It is not likely that His Lordship would have witnessed a better performance in any school for whites in his diocese. That was the paradox. The mission schools excelled when the children were young and impressionable. But often, when the Indian children reached adolescence, they became restless and reticent, even uncomfortable in the presence of whites. The boys especially had no taste for competing with whites. Thus they sometimes left others with the impression that they were inferior. This was far from the truth, but it would be many years before the true situation was generally understood.

MORE SCHOOLS AND HOSPITALS

While Cataldo struggled to get his college in Spokane Falls off the ground, Archbishop Gross was trying to save his St. Michael's College from the scrap heap. Alphonse Glorieux had been more than a principal there, and when he departed for higher things, the institution, lacking its cohesive force, began to fall apart. The archbishop in his native Baltimore had been a pupil in St. Peter's school conducted by the Brothers of Christian Schools, sometimes called the Christian Brothers. Though he had a great affection for them and was disposed to invite them to take over St. Michael's, he first contacted the Franciscans in California. He offered them the administration of St. Michael's College. Their response is unrecorded, but since they did not arrive in Portland after a decent interval, Gross appealed to the Christian Brothers in San Francisco. They responded favorably.

Three brothers arrived in Portland on January 25, 1886, and found a dilapidated old school with living quarters that were scarcely inhabitable.[51] They pitched in, nonetheless, and soon won the respect of the boys, who were so impressed by their dedication that they bought the principal a "new razor outfit" as a present. The superior, Brother Adalrick, meanwhile, died from overwork and illness. He had lasted only two months.[52]

By this time, schools were in demand everywhere and the so-called teaching orders, especially the sisters, were swamped with requests for teaching staffs. Even the small country parishes like Sprague and Pomeroy in Washington Territory, neither of which had been in existence for as much as ten years, insisted on having parochial schools, since it was commonly asserted that the public schools were "godless."[53]

In Sprague, the first resident pastor, Father A. Meuwese, arrived near the end of 1885. He immediately proposed to his people that a parish school should be established. The people responded enthusiastically, so Meuwese appealed to the Superior of the Sisters of Providence at Vancouver. Mother John, the superior then, had no one to send. Then the pastor appealed to another Congregation of Sisters, who said they would come. The parish lost no time in erecting a three-story frame building, but when it was ready Meuwese was informed, very casually, that there were no sisters after all. Then, quite suddenly, on December 18, 1886, when all looked as black as ink, he received a telegram from Mother John, saying that the Sisters of Providence would accept the school. Ten days later three sisters left Vancouver for Sprague. They were joined by two others and, on January 3, 1887, St. Joseph's Academy in Sprague was opened with twelve pupils. By the end of the year, it had a hundred.[54]

In Pomeroy, the first resident pastor was Father Peter Poaps, who built the town's first church in 1878. It was called Holy Rosary. Infected with parochial school fever and unable to obtain sisters, Poaps employed a lay teacher in his parish school in September 1886. After the first year, he was able to import Benedictine Sisters from Uniontown.[55]

The Uniontown Convent was flourishing, according to Father Adelhelm from Mount Angel. Adelhelm in February, 1886, joined his Benedictine colleague, Nicholas Frei, for the dedication of the new convent. The ceremony, after much discussion, was finally set for Sunday, February 10, for the convenience of all. But Father Frei was suddenly called away to aid a dying Catholic, and his buggy got bogged down in mud, for the rains were very heavy that week. Adelhelm presided over the blessings and dedication, with strings of well trained and scrubbed-up altar boys. "The new convent of St. Andrew's," he reported to the *Sentinel*, "is now the finest school in the county and perhaps the finest in eastern Washington Territory." Then he added as a discreet after-thought, "Outside of Walla Walla."[56] He was getting ready to open a college at Mount Angel. He certainly did not want a quarrel with the pastor of Walla Walla.

THE CHURCH IN SEATTLE

In Bishop Junger's diocese, the two most "Catholic" towns were Walla Walla and Vancouver. Tacoma showed promise. Father Hylebos, a dynamo of energy, had become one of the local patriarchs with immense civic influence. But the real future of the church in Washington lay in Seattle and Spokane. In Seattle, especially, growth was regrettably slow, mostly due, I think, to the idiosyncrasies of Father Prefontaine. This highly individualistic priest, with an almost chronic aversion for other clerics, finally got rid of his assistant, Father Kauten, but the bishop appointed another, a Belgian whose name was Father Emmanuel Demanez. Demanez, not easily intimidated by Prefontaine's sour opposition, was assigned to serve in a double capacity, as chaplain in Providence Hospital and as assistant in the parish. There were now about 42,000 people in Seattle proper, more than enough for two parishes, so Demanez in 1884, took the initiative to consult with Bishop Junger on the advisability of erecting a new parish in the city and of buying land for a cemetery.[57]

Prefontaine was indignant. He accused Demanez of attempting to advance himself, and he refused to cooperate with either Demanez or the bishop, despite his orders to the contrary.[58] The bishop felt obliged to drop the matter. When Demanez then proposed that he use the chapel of the hospital for the people of the future parish, the bishop refused, because of Prefontaine's resistance. At Demanez' insistence, however, the bishop allowed him to buy land for a cemetery. When he was unable to pay for it, Prefontaine "sneered at him and ridiculed his inability to pay."[59]

A competitor, alas, brought out the worst of Prefontaine. This pioneer priest in Seattle had many redeeming qualities. He was very dedicated to his own parish and church, so dedicated in fact, that he would allow no one to touch either. His civic consciousness, his interest in his fellow citizens, and his cooperation with them indicated that in this respect at least, he was a man ahead of his times. He was regarded as very popular in Seattle, a situation he shrewdly recognized and used to his advantage. To his credit, certainly, was his zeal for Catholic education. He had been instrumental in bringing the Sisters of the Holy Names to Seattle in 1880, and they had responded not only be establishing Holy Names Academy at Second and Seneca, but by befriending him for the rest of his life.[60]

It is proper to say, I think, that the greatest influence in Catholic education in Seattle during this early period, and for many years to come, was this academy of the sisters. It would take the Jesuits, whom Prefontaine also invited to Seattle, many years to acquire similar influence.[61] Prefontaine, who had helped to produce this academy, no doubt preferred it that way.

SPOKANE FALLS

When Father Ruellan went to his unexpected but well-earned rest, another Jesuit, equally remarkable for his talents, was assigned to take his place as pastor of the struggling church in Spokane Falls. Aloysius Jacquet, a Belgian of only thirty innocent years in 1884, was especially adept at gathering other people's money for good causes. Now that he was charged with completing Ruellan's dream church, Our Lady of Lourdes, he took up his task by appealing to everyone he met for the required money. He had long since learned that soldiers were generous donors to religion. For some, perhaps, it was their way to counterbalance the excesses they enjoyed in frontier posts. There were two forts among the settlements Jacquet visited, Fort Sherman at Coeur d'Alene and Fort Spokane on the Spokane River near its confluence with the Columbia. Jacquet called at each regularly, his collection basket extended conspicuously for the convenience of everyone. With the help of these soldiers, Jacquet soon gathered all the required funds for the new church.

Designed by an architect by the name of Frank Johnson, whom Jacquet met at Fort Spokane, the church was begun in the spring of 1885. It was nearly completed by April 30 of the following year when Mother Joseph of Vancouver, accompanied by Sister Joseph Arimathea, arrived at Spokane Falls on the Northern Pacific. They gazed north over the straggling homes here and there, unimpressed by what they saw. The tall lone steeple of the new church, 98 feet above the ground, caught their eye. There was no rectory nearby. The Jesuit Fathers, they learned, lived in a frame house across the river, where the new Gonzaga College, almost completed, faced the churning waters, higher than normal for the spring runoff.

Mother Joseph had come to establish a hospital. With characteristic haste, she rented a "temporary" building the same day, called it Sacred Heart Hospital, then announced her intention of buying property for a permanent building. For this she selected a site two blocks from the church, on the north side of Trent at Browne Street, with access to the river on the north.

The church was completed in June and Father Rebmann, the newly appointed president of Gonzaga College, arrived from Maryland during the same month, on the feast of Sts. Peter and Paul. "The building of the college was just finished, but not furnished," he wrote in his Reminiscences later. "In the room which was given to me was a straw sack, the only furniture, on the floor, without bed stead, table or chair. Sitting on that straw sack I wrote my first letters to Dittonhall and to my mother. My knees were my desk. An empty lime barrel, which I found in the yard and cleaned, served as washstand the following morning. In the evening we had Benediction. An old tin tomato can served as censer fastened to some picture wire, and a small sardine can as incense boat."[62]

The significance of this passage is not so much the poverty described by Rebmann, as the celebration of Benediction under these conditions. No one could doubt what the new president's priorities would be. If it came to push and shove, as sooner or later it would, Gonzaga would remain deeply Catholic, with all that this implied.

On July 2, 1886, the cornerstone of the new hospital was laid by Bishop Junger, who was assisted by the acquisitive pastor, Father Jacquet. His Lordship remained in town for several days because the dedication of the new church was scheduled for July 4. He had a room at the new college, not much better than Rebmann's, but like the latter, he preferred it to the old frame residence on the property, which was full of bedbugs. Old Father Joset, now living at Spokane Falls, was not so squeamish. He roomed in the old house and sallied forth periodically, driving his buckboard out to St. Michael's Mission where he took care of the Indians. He was seventy-six, already past the three-score years and ten that most people only hoped for, but he risked his life on every trip he made by driving through the stumps and over the rocks at a breakneck speed, like Ben Hur in the Roman Circus.

The dedication of Our Lady of Lourdes Church, which was regarded as one of the most elegant brick churches in the Northwest, was described in detail in the *Catholic Sentinel:*

> The Altar and sanctuary on Sunday presented a most beautiful aspect. The work of decorating them had been undertaken by some pious ladies of the parish. . . . At 10 A.M. the Bishop, preceded by the Cross and acolytes and accompanied by the attendant clergy, left the sacristy and marched to the front of the new church, whence he passed around it, sprinkling the walls with Holy Water. Having reached the main entrance again he entered the church and blessed the interior in the same manner. When the doors were opened the immense multitude standing in waiting without was admitted and filled every available place.

There followed "the dedicatory sermon" which was delivered by the bishop, and "was listened to with breathless silence." On occasions like this, His Lordship sometimes played his violin. In full pontifical robes, seated on his episcopal throne, he accompanied the choir in rendering portions of the Mass. The narrator failed to mention this extra attraction, so it is unlikely that the violin was heard on this occasion. Even without it, the ceremony was the grandest ever witnessed in the perky little city by the falls.

DEPARTURE FOR ALASKA

Two priests who assisted the bishop in this very solemn happening were in Spokane Falls, not by chance, but because they were preparing to leave for Alaska with Archbishop Seghers. They we Fathers Paschal Tosi, a tall Italian with the prickly disposition of a tax collector, and Aloysius Robaut, a chunky, short Frenchman who could get along with anybody. Seghers, who knew both, had personally approved of their selection by Cataldo. A third man for the expedition, chosen by Seghers over the stern objections of Cataldo, was a layman by the name of Frank Fuller, a handyman currently working at St. Michael's Mission.[63] Once a candidate to be a Jesuit brother, he had been rejected before noviceship, but he still referred to himself as "Brother Fuller."

In a letter to the *Catholic Sentinel* dated July 12, 1886, Seghers announced details of his journey. The party would leave Victoria on July 13, 1886, aboard the steamer *Ancon* bound for Juneau. From Juneau they would proceed to Haines, and with the help of porters, cross the Chilkoot Pass on the Alaskan Canadian border. Then they would drop down into the Yukon River drainage via Lake Lindeman.[64] It all sounded so simple. They would be in Nulato in autumn.

Tosi could not bear the sight of Fuller. Nevertheless, with Robaut and Fuller, he departed from Spokane Falls for the rendezvous with the archbishop on July 5, the Monday following the dedication of the church. When the three men reached Victoria, Tosi knew already that the expedition was doomed, and before sailing on the *Ancon* he sent a desperate plea to Cataldo to send reinforcements. Unlike Seghers, who regarded Fuller with a certain bizarre affection, Tosi was convinced that they were entering the wilderness with a madman. Robaut on this point, at least, agreed with Tosi, though he usually sided with Seghers in the ever-increasing number of disputes.

NEW MONTANA CHURCHES

It was time for school to start again in Baker City. The summer had been quiet, but bits of routine local information had been gathered for the *Sentinel* and presented with the usual many columns of speeches by bishops and commentaries on politics in Ireland. Among the reports of note were the following: In Helena Father Imoda had been found dead, and he was buried in the cemetery there in an army-issue, iron coffin.[65] In Billings a church finally had been built to replace the rented quarters of the Gazette Publishing Company,[66] and in Three Forks, Bishop Brondel blessed a new chapel built by Father Joseph Guidi.[67]

The latter, an olive skinned, diminutive Italian like Cataldo but more playful in disposition, had come to Montana in 1872. His younger brother, Monsignor John Guidi, later Archbishop and Apostolic Delegate to the Philippines, had attracted the attention of American bishops when the Pope selected him that very summer to bear the zucchetto to his Eminence Cardinal Gibbons.[68] Joseph Guidi, the Jesuit missionary, accompanied his distinguished brother on visits to Helena and St. Ignatius, where the Monsignor purchased two ornate saddles made by the Indian boys.

Joseph Guidi was not present when Bishop Brondel dedicated Our Lady of the Most Holy Rosary Church—the first in Bozeman. He had started to build this church, then another young priest, the first to be ordained in Montana for the Helena Diocese, was assigned to the care of Bozeman. This was Father Cyril Pauwelyn.[69] Pauwelyn completed the church and offered the first Mass in it on May 2, 1886.

OCCUPATIONAL HAZARDS

By this time DeRoo was in the news again. On September 2, 1886, overcome at last by the struggle with those who opposed him, he composed the following letter to the archbishop:

My Lord:
   I shall never forget the Christians and pious behavior of many Catholics and the friendly dispositions of non-Catholic people of Baker City. I regret, however, that my labor and my sacrifices are not appreciated by, nor useful to, some members of my congregation. In hopes that the latter may, for their eternal welfare, avail themselves of the ministry of another priest, I herewith respectfully tender my resignation of the rectorship of St. Francis De Sales'
Mission in Baker City....
P. De Roo, Mis. Pr.[70]

The archbishop on September 4, accepted this, saying, "you labored hard in Baker City and adorned the congregation with good schools."

That was the rub, the good schools. DeRoo left Baker City for Pendleton, where he became that town's first resident pastor on September 4, 1886. He brought with him his obsession for good schools, and with his encouragement the Sisters of Mercy from the Umatilla Mission opened an academy on Pendleton's east side on October 30.[71]

This event, too, was attended with controversy. It had been alleged that Father Conrardy had forced the Sisters of Mercy off the reservation. One of these sisters rose to Conrardy's defense:

Convent of Mercy, Pendleton, Oregon, November 30, 1886 Editor of the Sentinel:
   A friend having called my attention to an article in Saturday's Oregonian in which it was said that 'Rev. L.L. Conrardy broke up the Indian school on the reservation and the Sisters of Mercy left the place,' I write to say that such was not the case. The Rev. Father did not break up the school. It was mainly through his exertions that the school was first started, and he never failed to show his appreciation of work done. On 30th of October, the Sisters employed there sent their resignation to the Agent Coffey and on the 2d of Nov. they left the reservation.... Sister Mary Ignatius[72]

The archbishop needed no defense of Father Conrardy. He had toured eastern Oregon with him, making plans for the future of the church. He seemed to favor Pendleton and when DeRoo sponsored a fund drive to complete St. Mary's church, he presented his gold-headed cane for auction to help the cause. The academy of the sisters in Pendleton was not going well. It was like the early years of the academy in Baker City all over again—not many students, not enough money, and too much indifference.[73] At the end of the year, the sisters were forced to leave.

DeRoo would not give up. He persuaded the Franciscan Sisters in Baker City to send two of their number to Pendleton. Three more sisters from Pennsylvania soon joined them. The academy was renamed in honor of St. Joseph, and the pastor's battle for Catholic education went on as before.[74]

THE ALASKAN MISSION FIASCO

On August 31, 1886, Charles Seghers, encamped with the two Jesuits and Fuller, near the mouth of the Salmon River, composed a lengthy report of his adventures to Father Jonckau, his vicar general in Victoria.[75]

"The voyage" he said, "was not attended by any remarkable incidents." The Indians at the base of the Chilkoot Pass "had charged $13.00 per 100 pounds of packing, but also guide fees," bringing the total he owed to $303.00, which was about all he had. He was entering "the Yukon Country" almost penniless. They had reached the summit of the pass at last and peered down through the fog into the wilderness basin covered with rivers, lakes, and forests. Also bears. The bear tracks were everywhere. They saw one swimming on a lake, thinking at first it was a snag. Brother Fuller shot and "the bear drifted into camp."

"This is not a bear story," Seghers added, "but a bare fact; and proof of it is that after giving a good deal of the meat to others [miners] our last meal on the flesh of that bear took place the tenth day after he had been killed."

The letter ended with more specific details:

> August 27th, we had our first snowstorm and camped at the head of Lake Labarge, which is 40 miles long, and was crossed by us on Saturday August 28th. Finally, starting again on Monday, which was yesterday, we made 65 miles in eight hours, traveling not unfrequently at the rate of 12 miles in hour.... I cannot find another chance to write to you until next year, Adieu!

It was characteristic of Seghers to either overlook or conceal the unpleasant, even threatening, crises that were happening every day. He had barely recognized the fact that he was entering the vast unknown with three companions and without possible contact with the outside world "until next year," without money or adequate supplies. He failed entirely to mention that their guide had disappeared in a mysterious manner. The guide was a taciturn French Canadian by the name of Antoine Provost, an unhappy derelict for whom Fuller had an immediate dislike. The spirit of unanimity in the expedition had long since broken down, mostly because of Fuller, whose actions had become menacing. Not a day passed but some incident occurred revealing Fuller's dangerous disposition.

In retrospect at least, the Jesuits thought Seghers knew more about Provost's disappearance than he revealed.[77] Fuller, on the brink of mental collapse, defiantly insisted that Provost had returned to Juneau. As for the Jesuits, they suspected that Fuller had killed him and concealed the body. Thus matters went from bad to worse, while the archbishop pretended not to see anything at all.

On September 7, the expedition reached Harper's Place, a trading post on the Yukon where the Stewart River enters the larger stream. All four men were in a state of extreme mental and physical fatigue. For weeks they had battled the elements, transported baggage in leaky do-it-yourself boats across wind-swept lakes, endured long portages, and suffered the frustration of primitive trails, leaving them finally with frayed nerves and exhausted bodies. All this had been bad enough but worse were the anxieties about Fuller and the almost constant bickering, especially by Tosi, who openly criticized the archbishop for his obvious ineptness. Even good natured Robaut had come to detest Fuller, and the archbishop, while not in a state of panic, recognized Fuller's aberrations and the two Jesuits' unwillingness to remain in his company.

At Harper's Place, he proposed alternatives for subsequent action and decided, after some discussions, to leave on the following morning for Nulato, where he would establish a mission and spend the winter.[77] The two Jesuits were directed to remain at Harper's to serve the spiritual needs of miners who wintered there.[78]

On September 8, 1886, the archbishop, with Fuller as his only companion, departed by boat from Harper's. Carefully guarded among his frugal belongings were a Bible and a Russian dictionary.[79] These were symbolic of his great and lofty enterprise, not only the conversion of the native people of Alaska, but their education as well. The archbishop was a pathetic figure sitting in that boat, bundled in his coats and boots, for the morning was frosty. His patience and his humility had been tested almost beyond endurance, but he had borne it with the meekness of a lamb going to slaughter.

In the weeks that followed, both Tosi and Robaut dispatched long accounts of their voyage to Father Cataldo.[80] Their news was ominous: the expedition so far had been a disaster. The archbishop was alone in the wilderness with a madman. The future for all looked bleak.

Robaut had composed his letter on Sunday, November 28. The archbishop was already dead. Early that very morning he had been shot through the heart by Fuller. Ironically he was less than one day's travel by dogsled from Nulato, his long sought goal.

THE SEQUEL

Fuller had no remorse for his deed. He gladly accompanied an Indian to Nulato, leaving the body where it had fallen. While others went upriver to obtain the body, he gained the confidence of the fur company agent, Mr.Frederickson, who turned over to him the archbishop's belongings, including his Bible, Russian dictionary,and diaries. Fuller was cunning enough to go through the diaries, but all adverse references to himself had been written in French, and he left them undisturbed.

On December 10, 1886, a little caravan of three sleds left for St. Michael on the lower Yukon. Fuller was in the first with a miner. Two Indians were in the second. In the third, guarded by two faithful Indians, was the coffin enclosing the remains of the archbishop. On arriving at St. Michael, Fuller presented himself to Henry Neuman, the agent of the Alaska Commercial Company. "I have brought the Archbishop Seghers," he said. Neuman, looking around, asked, "Where is he?" "He is in the sled. I killed him," was Fuller's answer. Then showing the startled agent the letter of introduction which he was carrying, he declared that he had killed Seghers in self-defense.[81]

Until arrangements could be made to transfer the coffin to Victoria, the archbishop's body was placed in a zinc coffin and laid first in the old Greek church of St. Michael, but as this church was to be demolished that spring, the coffin was taken to the historic fort, where it remained until July, 1887.[82]

Meanwhile, in May, 1887, Tosi and Robaut left Harper's Place and sailed down the river, picking up, as they got closer to Nulato, rumors, and finally confirmation, of the archbishop's death. They hurried on to St. Michael, where Tosi took passage on the steamer *Dora* to bring the news of the tragedy to superiors, and get instructions regarding the future of the church in northern Alaska. When the *Dora* touched at Unalaska,they found in the harbor a United States Government cutter, the famous *Bear* whose Captain was Michael Healy, brother of the Bishop of Portland, Maine, who had been impressed by Seghers at the Council of Baltimore. Healy also had a brother who was the President of Georgetown University.

As a government official, Healy was asked to arrest Fuller and bring him to Sitka for trial. Accordingly the *Bear* went to St. Michael. Healy, with a detachment of officers and four sailors, went ashore and arrested the accused man in his tent.[83]

He did not have the authority however, to take the remains of the archbishop aboard the cutter, so Robaut, the last of five men who had entered Alaska together, made arrangements for the burial.[84] He described what followed:

> The only way left me then was to bury temporarily the remains of the Archbishop at St. Michael's. As soon, therefore, as I received this answer from Captain Healy, I made arrangements for burial. I chose a corner of the Russian graveyard about two hundred yards from the post, on a bluff overlooking the sea, as being the driest place. After the grave had been dug, six white men, who happened to be at St. Michael's, carried the coffin to the cemetery. Among those who accompanied the sorrowful procession were two Presbyterian ministers. On arriving at the grave, I recited the prayers for the dead over the remains of the Archbishop, and blessed the grave. Mr. Romanoff made, at my suggestion, a large cross to be put over the grave, which will be surrounded by a fence. On the cross will be inscribed in Roman characters his Lordship's name and titles.[85]

After these dolorous duties had been performed, Robaut returned to the interior of Alaska to keep faith with the people for whom the archbishop had given his life. Whether they wanted it or not, the northwest Jesuits were now stuck with the Alaska Mission.

ST. FRANCIS XAVIER MISSION, MONTANA

Cataldo's ambitious mission school program was beginning to take shape. In 1885, he had applied to the United States Commissioner of Indian Affairs for permission to open three mission schools: one for the Gros Ventres and Assiniboines on the Fort Belknap Reservation in north central Montana; another for the Crow Indians in south eastern Montana; and a third for the Blackfeet on the reservation proper to replace St. Peter's. Formal permission was granted. Two of the projected schools were opened during the year 1887, the third Holy Family Mission for the Blackfeet in 1890.

The first two were produced almost simultaneously over a period of several years. St. Francis Xavier Mission, for the Crow Indians, for example, had been identified for some years with the Cheyenne mission. Peter Barcelo had visited the Crows often, and DeSmet before him. It was Father Peter Paul Prando, however, who founded the first permanent mission among them, and built their first school.

There was something appropriate in this for Prando's personality suited the humor-loving Crows in an uncommonly exacting manner. He was irrepressible, witty, and quick at repartee, which the Crows admired. He was a most delightful life of-the-party type, who had been very successful already on the Blackfeet reservation.

PRANDO'S ADVENTURES WITH THE BLACKFEET

It will be recalled that the Blackfeet reservation boundaries had been changed and that the reservation was given to the Methodists, as had the Yakima reservation, despite obvious Catholic right to it according to the terms of Grant's Peace Policy. When Prando was assigned to St. Peter's Mission, he openly challenged the policy. He made his first safari into the forbidden land in May 1881, spending six months visiting Catholic Indians, baptizing their children, and performing marriages. Before leaving he built a crude hut on the off-reservation side of Birch Creek, acquiring by this means a base from which he could sally forth, on the reservation and off, like an outlaw sought by the sheriff. Waggish to the degree of sauciness, and absolutely fearless, he soon had the agent Major John Young standing on his head with bewilderment and anxiety.

Young was no match for Prando. He could think of only one solution to his dilemma: he ordered Prando off the reservation. With a saucy retort, Prando obeyed, taking with him to his hut on Birch Creek an army of Indians—displaced persons who personified in their mournful appearance the very depths of injustice.

To make a long, fascinating story short, because of government pressures brought to bear, Prando was removed and assigned to St. Ignatius Mission, where he was surrounded by enough restraints to cool off. He used the year for composing some of his priceless manuscripts on the Blackfeet language and for printing a rare mission press item in Blackfeet.[86]

WITH THE CROWS

Then he was assigned to work with the Crows. He made his first excursion among them with Barcelo in 1883. For the three years following, while he was attached to St. Joseph Labre's Mission, he traveled on horseback over all parts of the Crow Reservation with nothing more than a blanket and a portable altar to supply his needs. He slept in the Indian lodges and ate what the Indians had to eat, which was often "a piece of bread for breakfast and supper and nothing for dinner." Referring to himself in the third person, he wrote that "he was riding hard, sometimes eating wild cherries, and he was sometimes regaling himself with a piece of dog without salt or bread, thinking only of going ahead in evangelizing the poor, rough [Indians]."[87]

In late January, 1887, equipped with a large tent and two smaller ones, and accompanied by Father Peter Bandini, who was adventurous and tough like himself, and a friend by the name of Eddie Dillon, Prando arrived at the Custer station, ready to establish a permanent mission for the Crows. With Grassi during the previous summer, he had selected the site for it on Rotten Grass Creek south of present Hardin, Montana. The snow was too deep for travel, so the three men spent several weeks in a hotel in Custer, impatiently awaiting a Chinook. On February 18, they left the hotel by wagon, and finally reached their destination three days later. Having cleared the snow still on the ground, they set up a tent, built a fire and got warm again for the first time since they had left Custer.

Thus it was over forty years after the Crow Indians had requested DeSmet for a mission that Prando was able to respond. He and his companions, during the spring and summer, put together a frame building two and one-half stories high measuring sixty by forty feet on the ground. This was the first St. Francis Xavier Mission school and convent. By September 1, it was completed, but school was delayed because the Ursulines were five hundred miles away and had no money to make the journey. Finally, after acquiring enough money, the sisters made the journey by train and stagecoach and entered the country of the Crows in the midst of a tumultuous intertribal war. Some of the warriors, having noted the arrival of the Lady Blackrobes, declared an armistice, escorted the sisters to the mission, then resumed the war.[88]

Prando, who was called "Iron Eyes" by the Indians because of his metal rimmed glasses, became the great guru of the Crows. He learned their language perfectly and remained faithful and dedicated to them for many long years.

ST. PAUL'S MISSION, MONTANA

Meanwhile, another legendary missionary was engaged in producing a similar mission for the Gros Ventres and Assiniboines. Father Frederick Eberschweiler, a meek and lovable Rhinelander of some forty-six very active years, was generally known as a holy man. But even holy men behave like the rest of us sometimes. When he was pastor of the Immaculate Conception Church at Fort Benton, which had been built by Father Imoda in 1878, he became irritable because his parishioners mispronounced his name. "Ebberschweeler," he would correct them, saying each syllable distinctly, then he gave up and told them to call him "Father Evanston." For this reason, perhaps, he did not like Fort Benton and he was very happy when Cataldo assigned him to the formidable task of building a mission and school on the Fort Belknap reservation.

Eberschweiler arrived at Fort Belknap near present Harlem, Montana, on November 11, 1885, with orders from Cataldo to throw together a building, any kind of building, before the end of the year. This was intended, one presumes, to impress the government with Catholic determination to start a mission in that part of Montana before permission was withdrawn.

At least one attempt to build a mission in this area had ended in disaster. Years before, Father Philip Rappagliosi, scion of a noble Italian family, had died mysteriously in a rough cabin on the Milk River.[89] Rumors indicated that he had been murdered, which could not have been as bad as the probable way he had died. There is evidence to believe he had starved to death, slowly and painfully.

Going directly to the government agent at Fort Belknap, Eberschweiler presented evidence of his permission to establish a mission. The agent, one dour and reticent individual called Major Lincoln, who had the reputation of being bitterly anti-Catholic, did not object. Eberschweiler then contacted an old friend of the Jesuits, Thomas O'Hanlon. O'Hanlon helped him select a temporary site on the Milk River, and secured the aid of several Indians to help him build a log house. By December 7, 1885, the new establishment was ready and Eberschweiler moved in. On the following day, December 8, he offered the first Mass in it. Present were O'Hanlon with one of his employees, the only Catholics in the entire area, and a few curious Indians.

In the weeks and months that followed, Eberschweiler, accompanied by Cyprian Mott, who had served as DeSmet's guide, scrambled about the countryside, searching for a permanent mission site. At last on May 2, 1886, he found what he wanted, about forty miles southeast, on People's Creek at the foot of the Little Rocky Mountains, not far from the battlefield of the Bear Paw Mountains, where Chief Joseph had surrendered. To Eberschweiler the lonely site was almost as attractive as the Garden of Eden.

Having acquired title to the property through the instrumentality of Senator Vest from Missouri, who had praised Catholic missionaries in the United States Senate, Eberschweiler sought lumber for the new mission in Fort Benton, two hundred miles distant. He returned home empty-handed, however, because a current "Indian War" in that district rendered shipment impossible. Finally he persuaded a local frontiersman to build three log cabins, one for a church and priest's residence, twenty-five by seventy-five feet in size, and the others for a convent and school. The cornerstone for the church was laid on September 15, 1886. O'Hanlon provided lumber for floors, sash and roofs, and all was ready in early September 1887. At that time Eberschweiler with two Ursulines, Mother Francis and Sister Martha, left St. Peter's Mission with a party of Indians bound for Fort Belknap. On September 13, after some of the local children had been gathered by the nuns, the journey to the new mission, called St. Paul's, got under way. For forty miles the wagons and buckboards moved slowly across the grassy plains, skirting the Bear Paws on the south. An untoward accident occurred when a buckboard overturned in the ditch, and the caravan reached the mission at one in the morning. This was September 14, 1887, the official date for the founding of St. Paul's Mission School, which in the course of time developed into the major educational resource within an area as large as some small states.

DEATH OF THE PIONEERS

These agreeable productions appeared in Montana while more melancholy events were transpiring in Vancouver on the Columbia. First of all, the venerable old bishop, Augustin Blanchet, died on February 25, 1887, at the age of ninety. He was the last of the three pioneer bishops to go, and his passing from this world marked another milestone, not only in the history of the church but in the history of the state. Almost all of the old timers of his generation were gone, including his brother the archbishop, Dr. John McLoughlin, the Chief Factor at the fort, and old Judge Petrain, who had welcomed the first priests when they docked at Vancouver.[90] Dr. Forbes Barclay, the post physician, had been gone fourteen years,[91] and Father Brouillet, Blanchet's able vicar general, had died three years earlier, the victim of a blizzard in the Dakotas.[92] James Douglas, also Chief Factor from whom the church at Vancouver was named, had died ten years earlier in 1877. Joseph Gervais and Etienne Lucier, the early French Canadian settlers who had appealed to Canada for priests, had been dead for years, the one in 1861 and the other in 1853 at the relatively youthful age of sixty years. And William McBean was dead, the faithful clerk at Fort Walla Walla, who had come to the aid of both Blanchet and Brouillet at the time of the Whitman Massacre. Peter Skene Ogden, "Uncle Pete" to the Indians, was also gone these many years.[93]

Most of the early Jesuits, too, were gone. DeSmet, of course and Michael Accolti, the first member of California's Chamber of Commerce.[94] Peter DeVos had died early, mostly of exhaustion, only three years after John Nobili who founded Santa Clara College with death knocking at his door.[95] Mengarini, Spechts, and Magri, all companions of DeSmet in 1841, were gone.[96] Ravalli, Giorda, Gazzoli and Huybrechts, all gone.[97]

Three of the early Jesuits were still living. Old Father Joset in his seventy-eighth year was still kicking around the mission and Brother Claessen and Adrien Hoecken were both living in retirement, the former at Santa Clara and the latter at Milwaukee.[98]

Among the deceased bishop's early associates, two prominent old men were still clinging to life like withered leaves hanging precariously on a barren, wintry tree. These were Simon Plamondon, a handsome old romanticist, even at eighty-seven years, who had outlived his many wives, one of whom was the niece of the bishop.[99] Simon had settled at Cowlitz and it was in his home that Francis Norbert Blanchet had offered Mass on December 16, 1838. The other survivor was Marcel Bernier, known as the first white child born in the Northwest, near Spokane House on the banks of the Spokane River on November 10, 1819. He had served as Blanchet's guide and helpmate for many years, a respected pioneer whose roots had stuck deep in the gravel of Spokane until they were transplanted into the clay at Cowlitz Prairie.[100]

When one reflects on the absence of all of these early pioneers, potential witnesses in any land dispute, an ominous threat begins to appear on the horizon. The old bishop was dead and in his tomb. What better time was there to renew the battle for the church's claim to the St. James Mission Land. The case had been in limbo long enough; conditions now favored the government.

ST. JAMES MISSION CLAIM CONTINUED

Obviously the point was not overlooked by the United States Army, for on April 9, 1887, just forty days after the remains of the old bishop were placed beneath the floor of the sanctuary of St. James Cathedral in Vancouver, an army officer appeared at Holy Angels College with a guard to forcibly evict the teachers and students from their building. Lieutenant Richard Zeatman, U.S.A., summarily announced that all had ten minutes to leave the building under threat of imprisonment. To inquiries he replied in a rude manner that the priests were in defiance of the law, therefore they must vacate at once or be arrested.[101]

A new battle over the church's valued land in Vancouver, awarded by Congressional action and by at least two courts, was now underway, and most of the church's proof of its title was buried in Catholic cemeteries throughout the Northwest. Thus the timing alone revealed the astuteness of the adversary.

Thomas M. Anderson, Commandant of Fort Vancouver in 1887, published twenty years later an article entitled, "The Vancouver Reservation Case."[102] From the content of this, one deduces his considerable bias in favor of the government as well as the government's witnesses, at least one of whom was a notorious bigot.[103] On the other hand, one cannot overlook his ill-mannered method of ridiculing the witnesses that the church could still call upon. A portion of his article appeared as follows:

After the lapse of thirty-nine years, the spell was at last broken by the Post Commander ejecting the teachers and pupils of the so-called Holy Angels College, tearing down the fences around its enclosure, and taking possession of Heaven's half-acre itself. This trespass on the mission grounds left its representatives no alternative but to ask for an injunction from the courts. To secure this they had to bring suit, and in so doing had to set forth in detail their title to the property.

The suit was brought under the title of: 'The corporation of the Roman Catholic Bishop of Nesqually vs. John Gibbon, Thomas M. Anderson and Richard Zeatman.' These defendants, representing the government, were the Department Commander and the Commandant and Quartermaster of the Post of Vancouver Barracks.

First came an order restraining the military authorities from exercising control over that part of the reservation in dispute and giving twenty days in which to show cause why this injunction should not be made perpetual. Accordingly the Department and Post Commander went to Olympia to show cause why. There they met the United States District Attorney, who had been instructed to intervene in behalf of the United States. Then the church filed a complaint, or bill in equity.

The complaint recited at length the decisions and counter-decision of the Surveyors-General, the Attorney-General, the commissioners and secretaries, and finally set forth that they had to bring suit in equity because the Secretary of the Interior had made a mistake in law; that he was right in his decisions as to questions of fact which induced him to offer them a patent for a half-acre, but wrong in not extending his ruling to the whole 640 acres. Therefore, they claimed that the court was bound by the decision of the Secretary as to facts and also bound to correct his erroneous decision as to the law. Here was a brilliant piece of legal *leger-de-main*, worthy of the talents of lawyers and churchmen. . . .

At the spring session of the court, held at Vancouver in April 1887, the answer to the respondents was filed and the law points argued in demurrer before Judge Allyn. At this hearing all the points of the complainant's demurrers were overruled, the injunction dissolved as to all except the ground upon which the church stood. Testimony was ordered to be taken before a commissioner and then submitted for consideration at the next session of the court.

It now became evident that the crucial question was this: Were the priests at the Hudson Bay post of Vancouver acting as missionaries to the Indians on August 14, 1848?

To meet this question, the writer hunted up dozens of old settlers and wrote scores of letters. Out of the whole number there were comparatively few who had personal knowledge of facts transpiring prior to August, 1848; nevertheless, when the time came, both the church and the military had mustered quite a number of witnesses.

The leading witnesses for the church were a Father Joset, an old Jesuit priest who succeeded Father DeSmet in his mission in the Coeur d'Alene country; Joseph St. Germain and Marcel Bernier, old Canadian-French trappers and couriers-du-bois; August Rochon, a servant of the priests Blanchet and Demers when they came here in 1838; Mary Petrain, a wife of one of the old Hudson Bay Company's servants; Mary Prouix, the first woman married in the church; and, finally, one Francis A. Chamberlain, an employee of the Hudson Bay Company, the only one who testified in favor of the mission. They were a queer-looking lot, antiquated and awkward, soiled, snuffy and redolent with a rather too pungent odor of sanctity. Their talk and manners recalled the traditions of a buried past. If they had all floated down the Columbia in a canoe, with red blankets around them, it would have seemed natural and proper.

The leading witnesses for the defense were John Stensgair and Napoleon McGillvray, old Hudson Bay Company servants; William H. Gray, the historian of Oregon and an early pioneer; William H. Dillon, Peter W. Crawford and Silas D. Maxon, Charles J. Bird and John J. Smith, county officials and surveyors; Louisa Carter and Sarah J. Anderson, women who came out as early as the Whitman massacre; and, finally, General Rufus Ingalls and Mr. Lloyd Brooke, who represented the Quartermaster's Department. These witnesses were also advanced in years, but they looked like people who had 'kept up with the procession.'

The first set of witnesses swore that the mission people were entirely independent of the Hudson Bay Company and intent solely on the saving of souls. The government witnesses testified that the priests were paid and willing servants of the company, and that it was the trappers who converted the Indian women, and that the church here was not a mission but a congregation. The trial also brought to light the fact that the record of the first injunction suit against the post authorities had been cut out of the first record book of the county court and the book itself thrown in the river; but it was recovered, water-stained and mutilated. The testimony of the old witnesses was, apart from its legal value, very interesting. It recalled the feudal ways of the old Hudson Bay barons; the contrasted savagery and gentleness of the Indians; the wild ways of the pioneers; the zeal of the priests; the earnestness of the Protestant missionaries.

One of the questions at issue was: What was a mission? The answer revealed, by a strange sidelight, the difference in the motives and methods of the Catholic and Protestant missionaries. To the first a mission meant a cross raised in the shadow of the woods, the baptism of savages, the saving of souls. To the latter, mission work meant Christianizing by civilizing. A mission was to be an object lesson in industry, sobriety and prayer. Their purpose was really the same; they only differed in their methods.

The case came up for trial before the district court at Vancouver at the spring term of 1888. It was argued by District Attorney W. H. White for the government representatives and by Whalley, Bronaugh and Northrup, counsel for the church. It was decided by Judge Allyn in favor of the defendants. Appeal was then taken to the Supreme Court of the Territory of Washington, and it came up for hearing in January, 1889. After full argument the court decided that the plaintiff had legal remedies for all wrongs complained of and should not have brought suit in equity; that, properly speaking, it was only open to them to bring an action of ejectment; that the matter was a judicial question and not dependent on decisions of ministerial officers.

As to the interpretation of the words of the statute, 'Occupied by a religious society as a mission station among the Indian tribes,' the court held that 'occupied' meant possession, domain, absolute control. The court held that the Hudson Bay Company held such occupancy and domain, and not the church; that the present claimant claimed as the representative of the Bishop of Quebec and that the Bishop of Quebec was not the original grantee; that the American missionary societies were incorporated companies; that the Catholic church was not, as a church, a legally incorporated body under our laws at the time of the grant; that the law was passed to reward American pioneers and not the subjects of another government, which, at the time the Mission of St. James was established, was maintaining an adverse claim of sovereignty. The court also noted the fact that the United States then, by purchase, extinguished the rights of the Hudson Bay Company and all other British subjects (for £1,200,000) and concluded by giving the decree for the defendants.

A motion for a rehearing was granted, but before the case was re-argued Washington was admitted as a State. The included territory became a judicial district, and in July, 1890, the case was presented and argued *de novo* before District Judge Hanford. He reserved his decision, but on the third of November gave it in favor of the defendant. His opinion was based on a clear and exhaustive analysis of the case. It is for the most part too technical for general interest. He noted the fact that the church took no measures to establish its claim until after the military reservation had been declared, and for that reason the claim of the defendants was superior in equity to that of the plaintiff.[103]

Counsel for the plaintiff, the Diocese, appealed to the Supreme Court. The showdown here would not occur for seven years. Classes in Holy Angels College, meanwhile, were conducted in P. O. Keane's building, which was formerly occupied by the public school.

TWO NEW COLLEGES IN THE NORTHWEST

One would imagine that with two Catholic colleges in the Northwest, both of them struggling for bare existence, and a third recently closed for lack of students, there would be little interest in the establishment of others. Holy Angels in Vancouver in rented quarters, and St. Michael's in Portland under new management, were not prospering, while expansive illustrated advertisements for Notre Dame in Indiana and Santa Clara in California, regularly placed in the *Catholic Sentinel*, promoted the attractions of successful colleges elsewhere.

In Spokane Falls, fifteen affluent citizens had subscribed the parsimonious sum of $2,650 "to aid J. M. Cataldo in constructing a college building or rather one wing of a building to be used as a college under supervision similar to Santa Clara College in California. The wing or building now proposed to be erected to be of brick or stone and in size not less than forty feet wide by eighty feet long and three stories high."[104]

What the fifteen spirited citizens proposed was a brick building or wing with ninety-six hundred square feet. If purchased with the purse they offered, this could have been produced at a cost of something less than thirty cents a square foot. There were some holy Jesuits in the vicinity at this time, but none of them, I think, capable of performing this kind of miracle.

The Jesuits did not qualify for the proffered grant on other grounds: the school had not opened, as demanded, in the autumn of 1882. As already noted above, the Gonzaga building was not completed until the summer of 1886, at which time there were neither furnishings nor faculty. Assigned as first president, Father James Rebmann was committed to assembling both, out of thin air as it were, by waving a wand.

At Mount Angel in Oregon, the Benedictines, too, had their hearts set on the opening of a college. One of the monks especially, Barnabas Held, a gifted but restless young priest, favored the project as did others who were familiar with the success of Abbey schools elsewhere. In 1883, when the monastery at Mount Angel received recognition by the State of Oregon as a formal corporation, Barnabas Held, with Fathers Adelhelm and Anselm Wachter, were the incorporating officers.[105] The articles of incorporation specified educational work as an objective of the corporation, so state officials applied discrete pressure on the monks to conduct a school.

Accordingly, the Benedictines built a two-story frame structure measuring thirty by thirty-five feet, not exactly what the Spokane Falls' citizens would have recommended, but an adequate one with the essential requirement of being ready for business. In the summer of 1887 the monks issued a prospectus for "Mount Angel College," which offered both classical and commercial courses to boarding and day students for a five-month term. The fees were $90.00 and $50.00 respectively, indicating that board and room were eight dollars a month.[106] Fortunately the monks raised most of their own food, or their boarders, at that price, would have devoured them out of house and home.

The director of the college was Barnabas Held. He welcomed fifteen students on the opening day, Tuesday, September 6, 1887. The first of these to register was Frank Coleman of St. Paul, Oregon. During its first year, the total number of students was "about fifty," but during the following year, due to the remarkably persuasive powers of the director, not to mention his energetic administration, the number of students was 130, enough to inspire the monks to erect another college building.

At Gonzaga in Spokane Falls, the projected opening date was September 15, 1887, and some little boys arrived even before that. They entertained themselves by riding the school's two horses, Dick and Duffy, the latter named for the late pastor of Walla Walla. Not unlike Barnabas Held, Rebmann, in appearance, except that he wore glasses, had been kept on pins and needles because Bishop Brondel was making so much noise about a proposed Jesuit college in Helena, and Bishop Junger, who should have raised his voice in favor of Spokane, seemed to have lost it altogether. Junger could not make up his mind whether the Jesuits should locate a college in Spokane at all; he favored Sprague, or thought he did. Brondel, on the other hand, secured the unanimous approval of his clergy, seven secular priests and six Jesuits in his Second Diocesan Synod, for locating the proposed school in Helena; and if this were not enough, a petition to Cataldo, containing the signatures of sixty-three prominent citizens of Montana, urged the same objective. Attached to the petition was a cash offer of $25,000, only five thousand less than the Gonzaga building had cost and probably ten times the cost of Mount Angel College. As late as July of that summer, Cataldo polled the opinions of his official advisors and other Jesuits, getting in return mostly unrealistic suggestions such as opening both colleges and abandoning parishes in Missoula and Yakima.[107] On the latter, within a year or two, would hang the fate of a college in Seattle.

Throughout these tense proceedings, Rebmann showed himself to be greatly concerned about the fate of Gonzaga and the consequences of the elaborate prospectus he had mailed out already announcing the formal opening of the school. He had known from the beginning that there was opposition to Gonzaga, not only from the Montana Jesuits, some of whom favored greater concentration of manpower on working with whites, but also from the Indian missionaries who feared, with reason, the growing preoccupation with education. Rebmann continued to urge postponement of the Helena college decision, but he might have saved his breath. When the showdown came, Cataldo backed Gonzaga and scraped together a faculty, which finally assembled by September 17.

This was a Saturday, but the school bell rang anyhow. Days of the week made little difference since regulations required all students to be in residence. The cost was $250 for a ten month term, including board, room, tuition, and laundry. Text books and music lessons were extra. On the first day there were only seven students, the oldest of whom was Charles Dowd, aged seventeen years. By the end of the first year only twenty students had been in attendance, all of them Catholics, but two boys were expelled during the year, leaving a maximum attendance of only eighteen students at any one time.

There were now four Catholic colleges in the Northwest, none of them comparable to the excellent Sisters' academies like Providence in Vancouver or St. Mary's in Portland. Only Gonzaga among the colleges had a permanent building, but its eighteen students scarcely constituted a roaring operation. The sisters had, in those times, a notable advantage: they were committed to education or nursing, or both, but not to the routine management of church affairs as were the clergy. At that time, most priests received a general education, excellent by contemporary standards, but not designed for a specialty like teaching. The sisters and teaching brothers, on the other hand, despite the brevity of their formal education, had the advantage of specialized preparation, as well as a certain continuance in their work. The priests were often transferred from one position to another: for example, from parish work to the classroom. In due time all this was corrected, but for the early decades it was nip and tuck in the boys' colleges in the Northwest. This is undoubtedly one reason, too, why their survival rate was poor.

FIRST CARDINAL IN THE NORTHWEST

In October of that same year, Archbishop Gross received the pallium, the lamb's wool symbolic of his office, from Leo XIII. It was conferred on him by his old friend, Cardinal Gibbons, who was the first Prince of the Church to visit the Northwest.

Gibbons left Baltimore in the latter part of September, 1887, accompanied by Dr. Chapelle.[108] Enroute west, he stopped at Chicago, Milwaukee, and St. Paul, where he was received royally in festive receptions at each stop. On October 5, he reached Helena, whence he traveled to Spokane. At Bonneville on the Columbia, he left the train and embarked on the steamer *R. R. Thompson*, which arrived in several hours at Fort Vancouver. The commanding officer, Lieutenant Thomas Anderson, met him. "Your Eminence," the officer said, "It was customary in ancient times when a prince of the realm travelled for governors of cities to release some prisoners in honor of his visit. As you are a Prince of the Church, I propose to release some men confined here." At that time he summoned six private soldiers from the prison in the fort and said, "Soldiers consider yourself free in honor of Cardinal Gibbons."[109]

When the prelate's party reached Portland, a vast crowd awaited it. A parade was formed quickly. Religious societies, policemen mounted on horses, Conrardy with his colorfully-clad Indians, and the clergy all marched down First Street to the Cathedral. Bishop Junger pontificated at the Mass. Father Bertram Orth, soon to become a bishop, preached the occasional sermon.[110] The Cardinal's presence, "in scarlet brocade and royal ermine," represented something more than his personal friendship with Archbishop Gross. He was also the emissary of the Pope. Suddenly, as it were, the pomp and splendor of the papal court could be seen and felt in Portland, where Catholics were still regarded by many as ignorant aliens who somehow sneaked in.

THE FIRST SEMINARY

In the Archdiocese of Oregon City, a very close bond began to develop between the archbishop and the Benedictines. This eventually led to the archbishop's request that the monks conduct a minor and major seminary at Mount Angel, a very bold step at the time, which received the immediate approbation of the prior and his chapter. Characteristically, Odermatt lost no time in getting things under way. Father Dominic Waedenschwyler, was appointed as the first rector. Students in the college who were candidates for the monastic life or the priesthood were singled out and placed in a separate program.[111]

"Already a number of bright intelligent and pious youths," the archbishop announced, "have of their own accord begged to be set apart with those who will aspire to the holy priesthood . . . with deepest respect we most cordially invite their Lordships, the Bishops of the Pacific slopes also to send to Mt. Angel Seminary, young aspirants to the honors of the altar."[112]

By March 21, Feast of St. Benedict, the new seminary dedicated to St. Anselm, was in existence. "The rules and regulations of the Sulpicians at St. Charles Seminary at Baltimore were chosen and enforced. The archbishop stressed the Sulpician [classical] exemplar while noting the Benedictine tradition."[113] Five students were enrolled, four of whom survived for the following year when they were joined by nineteen candidates for minor seminary.

During the first decade, St. Anselm had eight different rectors and never more than thirty students at one time, seemingly a frail beginning. It was not numbers that mattered. The very existence of the seminary was another milestone for the church in the Northwest. It soon produced a profound influence in the lives of many, not only of the seminarians, but also of countless others to whom the seminary reached out through its alumni, the priests who occupied parishes and missions all over the West.

As more parishes developed, there was a critical need for these priests. In the year 1887, for example, there were two new parish churches in

Portland alone, the Immaculate Heart parish dedicated by Archbishop Gross on June 5, and St. Joseph's parish for German-speaking people, dedicated on September 21.[114] In Ashland, Oregon, too, a new church had been built by Father Fabian Noel.[115] In the Helena Diocese, Bishop Brondel blessed another church at Billings.[116] At Olympia in Washington, the Sisters of Providence opened another hospital, called St. Peter's, which would require, sooner or later, a resident chaplain.[117]

There had always been a shortage of priests. Perhaps there would always be one. The most obvious solutions were good Catholic colleges and seminaries, but these, too, required priests who were not available. No one knew this better than Archbishop Gross, who had been religious superior for the Redemptorists in Boston before he was consecrated bishop. Thus he supported the Benedictines' seminary at Mount Angel. For reasons that are not clear, however, it appears that he did not give equal support to St. Michael's College, which languished, despite heroic efforts of the Brothers.

Eastern Oregon had kept the archbishop busy. It was like southern Idaho. The demands for priests there kept increasing but the few scattered Catholics scarcely justified the presence of resident priests in most of the small towns. Father Conrardy, for example, in addition to his care of the Umatilla mission, covered the pioneer settlements of three counties, Morrow, Wheeler, and Gilliam, a superhuman feat that required some change.

FATHER LOUIS CONRARDY

Conrardy had been hinting for years that he wanted to leave Oregon for Molokai.[118] His bishop had known this as did Father Cataldo, who was his spiritual director. Conrardy seems to have been convinced that Gross wanted to replace him on the mission with the Jesuits. In 1887, he wrote to Damien: "I've been here among the Indians for thirteen years. Do you want me my dear fellow countryman? I can still work at least twenty years. My Bishop has confided this mission to the Jesuits. If I don't come to Molokai I must join the Jesuits in order to stay here."[119]

While it is conceivable that Gross wanted Conrardy to leave the Umatilla mission to concentrate on developing the church for whites in eastern Oregon, it is most unlikely that anyone suggested he become a Jesuit. At this time Conrardy was forty-six years old.[120] He had already spent several years (1871–1874) in India as a missionary, and he was generally characterized as high-handed, impatient, and irascible. He was a loner—certainly not a suitable candidate for a religious order. Cataldo knew him well and regarded him with much affection. But there is not the slightest likelihood that Cataldo would have advised him to apply for the Society, or would have accepted him if he had applied.

On the other hand, in his relations with the Indians, Conrardy was one of the most successful missionaries on record. Like Adrien Croquet, he was absolutely selfless. The Indians called him "Himtuken" the Bearded One, because he wore a heavy black beard as a mark of distinction, a leader among Indians who were beardless. "He was a good man and we Indians loved him," said an old lady, who still remembered him with respect after an absence of seventy-two years. He spoke their language fluently and according to numerous legends about him "he worked many cures for them."[121]

As for the Jesuit take-over of the Umatilla Mission, it should be noted that Cataldo was very reluctant to consider it because of the shortage of Jesuits. But Archbishop Gross literally begged him to take it. Cataldo had scraped together all the men he could spare for his pet project, Gonzaga College, but he yielded, at last, to the archbishop's plea and agreed to take Umatilla. He knew as well as Gross did that Conrardy had already given his heart to the lepers. Damien wrote to him, "Come in God's Name," and this was all he needed. With the archbishop's blessing, he sailed for Molokai, arriving there on May 15, 1888, ready to begin a new career, which proved to be more stormy than the last.[122]

THE JESUITS AT UMATILLA

Father Urban Grassi at this time was still attached to the missions in central Washington, integrating his activities with Victor Garrand, the superior in Yakima, Aloysius Parodi, a missionary at large, and Stephen DeRouge, the French count's son who had laid the foundations of the church for north central Washington at Omak. DeRouge was scheduled to return to France to complete his studies as a Jesuit. This would require adjustments by other Jesuits and a temporary gap in the ranks.

Grassi, meanwhile, with the help of his Indian people, built another church near Lake Chelan at Manson, on land donated by the famous Chief Wapato. When it was completed in the early spring of 1888, he blessed this "house of prayer" under the title of St. John the Baptist.

Grassi was now in his fifty-eighth year,[123] scarcely ready for the bone-yard. but worn out with labors and living on the trail where he seldom had even a roof over his head. In spite of all of this, Cataldo assigned him to replace Conrardy at the Umatilla mission. Thus Grassi, who arrived at the mission in May 1888, became the first Jesuit administrator of the mission begun by Augustin Blanchet forty-one years earlier, on the eve of the Whitman Massacre.

SPOKANE'S PAROCHIAL SCHOOLS

The archbishop was undoubtedly pleased, but Bishop Junger, who had lost another priest, was not. Junger had become greatly attached to Gonzaga in the way that Gross had taken to Mount Angel. He visited the school on special occasions, mingled with the boys like an indulgent father, and praised the Jesuits for the obvious progress they were making. Gonzaga had become "another Santa Clara," drawing students from as far away as San Francisco, Portland, and Vancouver, as well as from Seattle, and His Lordship found nothing in this that was alarming.

In Spokane Falls, a new two-story brick parochial school had been built next to Our Lady of Lourdes church, with a picket fence around it to keep out the town's countless dogs. On July 25, 1888, three Sisters of the Holy Names from Portland arrived to staff the school. They were met at the railroad depot by Father Rebmann, who drove them to the church in his new buggy, pulled by Fanny, his horse, and accompanied by Caro, his dog. Several weeks later, the following item appeared in the local paper: "The Main Street School opens for girls on August 27th and for boys on August 28th but boys under twelve only will be admitted."[124]

When school finally convened on the dates prescribed, the sisters were almost buried under the children who responded. Three hundred applied for admission, and an appeal was hurriedly dispatched to Portland for reinforcements. This was only four brief years after Spokane's first pastor had lamented to his family: "This morning I said Mass in my poor little miserable cabin which is the Spokane Church. For fifteen days now I have been alone." And again: "Since that time I have been in Spokane, spending my mornings in my room and my afternoons in town visiting very indifferent Catholics, 40 or 60 [in number] for whom I say Mass each Sunday...."[125]

ST. GEORGE'S INDUSTRIAL SCHOOL

Unlike Tacoma, where Father Hylebos was still alone, holding the fort "against all the powerful forces of evil," Spokane Falls now had a parish, a college, a hospital, and a parochial school. Hylebos was well aware of it. He was particularly concerned about the Indian children in his own area, and after some well expressed pleas for help, he acquired in the name of the Catholic Indian Bureau a one hundred and forty acre tract seven miles north of Tacoma for a mission school. During August of 1888, he built a three story frame structure on the property, and on October 19, four Sisters of St. Francis from Glen Riddle arrived to open the new institution, which was called St. George's Industrial School.[126] The first superior was Sister Jerome, who obtained government subsidies for fifty children for three years only.

An account of St. George's was provided by a contemporary:

A week after the arrival of the Sisters, October 26th, the first children were brought to school to receive with the rudiments of a secular education also the germs of true christianity, for He who is the 'Alpha and Omega' should not be ignored in the training of the child. Right Rev. Bishop Yunger [sic] he who by his fatherly kindness will always hold a warm place in the hearts of both clergy and people of Washington, appointed Rev. Father Chas. DeDecker as Superintendent of the Indian Industrial school Sept. 25th, 1888. Rev. Chas. DeDecker who was born in St. Nicolas in Belgium, made his first studies in his native place and, after finishing his theological course in the American College of Louvain, was ordained a priest in Ghent June 19th, 1886. He came to Nesqually diocese in the same year and remained in Vancouver attending missions and helping in the Cathedral until his appointment to the Indian mission in 1888. Ever since the Rev. Father has remained in charge of the Indian Industrial School whilst Father Hylebos was superintending the construction of the building, which required his constant attention. Father DeDecker remained at Tacoma until Father Hylebos' return, November 5th, 1888. On the feast of Our Lady Help of Christians, May 25th, 1889, Bishop Yunger visited the school for the first time and blessed the chapel and class room.

On June 30th, 1889, a second contract was granted by the government, but it had been reduced from 50 to 25 pupils to be obtained exclusively from the Puyallip consolidated Agency. About the end of 1889, through a spirit not friendly to Catholic Indian schools the contract was entirely abolished, for they alleged that the Agency school on the Puyallip Reservation had ample accommodations for all the Indians. This was a great blow aimed at the destruction of the Catholic school, but 'He that dwelleth in Heaven' laughs at the efforts of those who stand up against the Lord, and against his Christ trying to break their bonds asunder and to cast away their yoke.' Next to Divine Providence, thanks to Mother Catherine Drexel, foundress of the Sisters of the Blessed Sacrament who devote themselves exclusively to the education of Negro and Indian children, and other benefactors, the mission has flourished without the government aid. During the two first years, the expenses of the school amounted to $6,325, not including the cost of the land. The government paid only $4,099 of that amount.

Towards the end of September 1890, a new building 62 x 16 feet, one story high, was erected. It contains a laundry, a small room for strangers and a bakery with an additional shed containing the bake oven. In August 1892, a woodshed 60 x 18 feet was built. In September 1893, a 400 pound steel bell was placed in the little belfry which ornaments the top of the roof.

Gradually the land is cleared of the heavy timber, about twenty acres being now under cultivation and two acres in orchard.[127]

The existence of this school demonstrated a need, like the Indian resident schools Cataldo had been promoting in Idaho and Montana. It bore witness to the concern of the church for Indian children at a time and in a place where no one seemed to care.[128]

But there was something anachronistic about St. George's: it was too little too late. The Indians along the coast by this time had little or no tribal identity. With rare exceptions, their collective existence in or near population centers of the West had ceased to be, at least temporarily. During this very decade, in fact, the Indian population of the United States reached its lowest point in history.[129]

While the government had been partly to blame for this, it did precious little to change the trend toward extinction of the Indian. Grant's Peace Policy on the reservations had yielded a policy of secularization. The official religion now was secularism and the niggardly subsidies provided for Indian children in schools like St. Ignatius Mission were gradually being withdrawn. The 1890's would bring disaster; the 1900's death.

But life went on. Churches for Indians and whites multiplied, indicating by visible structures the advent of the New Order. It seemed strange now to speak about "pioneer Catholics." These were third generation Catholics in the contemporary Northwest, many of them as coldly indifferent as some of the first. But there were others who built churches, eight more of them in 1888. These were: at Old Mission near Cashmere, built in February for the Wenatchee Indians; St. Urban's church at Napavine, a German settlement;[130] at Enumclaw, Sacred Heart Church, completed in June; St. James Church at Bonners Ferry, constructed of tamarack logs, a mission church for the Kootenai Indians; at Lewistown, Montana, St. Leo's church dedicated by Bishop Brondel on September 23; Immaculate Conception at Roslyn completed in October; at Anaconda, a splendid brick church costing $12,000, dedicated on November 25 in honor of St. Paul; and at Medical Lake, St. Ann's church, built by Father William Dwyer.

There was a time for everything and this was the time for building churches and schools. It was a deceptively serene time and the Catholics of the Northwest, preoccupied with the problems of growth, were not vigilant. They were not ready for the subtle assault on the church already in the making, nor for the more blatantly open attacks in the not-distant future.

11

SISTERS OF ST. MARY OF OREGON

1886–1895

In Sublimity, Oregon, in the prolific Willamette Valley, beneath the gnarled old oak trees and surrounded by a frontier rail fence, there stood an ugly two story frame building that bore the name, locally, of the United Brethren College. There was a short belfry for a bell in the front of the building and a chimney at the back. By the front gate a lone fir tree grew, straight and tall, like a totem guarding the hearth of a powerful clan.

But the powerful clan had departed for lack of students. Thus it happened that a group of pious ladies took over the building and changed its name to the Maria Zell Convent. A Benedictine priest, Father Werner Ruttiman, with the explicit directive of Archbishop Gross, had gathered these pious ladies, who wanted to live in common like nuns, in this cold, damp, schoolhouse at the edge of the dark forest. This was the humble beginnings of Maria Zell, the convent of an almost anonymous founder that eventually evolved into the prestigious Congregation of the Sisters of St. Mary of Oregon. This was the first of its kind in the history of the Northwest. [1]

THE ORIGIN OF THESE MYSTERIOUS SISTERS

Among the mysteries of the early Northwest church was the origin of the ten pious ladies who occupied Maria Zell. This is a romantic account of very brave women who endured many hardships before they found peace in Oregon, far from the little settlement of their birth.

The scenario begins in a forlorn, schismatic colony of former Catholics in Rush Lake, Minnesota in 1866. The leader of the colony was Father Joseph Albrecht, an eccentric guru who had already experienced marriage, membership in the Society of the Precious Blood, and a pastorship in a parish in Ohio.[2] Described as a "well built man, tall and erect with a bright countenance," he had, as well, a generous streak of rigid stubbornness.

"This determination of will together with a fanatic hatred of anything savoring of vanity, worldliness, or self-indulgence brought him into conflict with church authorities." He preached most of the time on two subjects—dancing and feminine vanity—excoriating both with blistering disapproval. These were the ultimate sins, the cause of all the others. One afternoon, after a morning diatribe of this sort, several young ladies returned for services, attired in all their finery, perhaps to bait him. He calmly walked to the pulpit, read an appropriate text from the Bible, then took a long hickory rod and drove them out of the church.[3] For this he was reprimanded by Archbishop Purcell. Refusing to accept correction, he planned to withdraw from his parish in Himelsgarten to a place where he would have his own way without interference. Seven hundred acres of land were acquired at Rush Lake. His followers, including "religious brothers and sisters of the Society of the Precious Blood as well as laymen," then traveled to Rush Lake where a life of rigor and penance under a despotic priest began again.

Many efforts were made to reconcile the groups with the church, but Albrecht prevailed. No other priest was allowed to see his flock, who were trapped in a cult-like prison not unfamiliar to Americans today. Four times Bishop Thomas Grace of St. Paul tried in vain to recall Albrecht to obedience, and finally, on November 23, 1871, he formally excommunicated him. This brought a few to their senses. Some fifteen families defied Albrecht and returned to the church. The remainder, however, refused to capitulate. They refused to leave Albrecht, and their lives of grim servility continued as before.

In the early spring of 1884, Albrecht had premonitions of his death. Then in April, he died.

By his followers, Albrecht was venerated as a saint. His body was placed in a metal coffin and buried beneath the altar of the church. His will disclosed that he had left all "his" property to the church, to be administered by three trustees. Quarrels and disputes followed. More left the colony, but most remained. They faced an insurmountable problem now: they had no priest. To resolve this, they finally determined to move again, to Jordan, Oregon, where they hoped to find an understanding bishop. They sold what they had, then broke into the church secretly at night and removed Albrecht's body. They concealed it in large crates of vegetables, which they smuggled into an immigrant train.[5] Then they took passage on the same train for Oregon where they made another attempt to establish themselves as an independent schismatic church. But the magnetic influence of their founder was not with them.[6] They had no Mass, no devotions, no sermons to make plausible their eccentric behavior.

Some women now began to have doubts, They sent a young man, formerly a member of the Society of Precious Blood, to carry a letter written by the oldest of the young woman to Mount Angel, where they hoped to get help.[7] Father Werner Ruttiman responded to their appeal.

The three trustees in charge of the colony approved Werner's suggestion that Archbishop Gross come for Confirmation. Gross arrived at Jordan on July 31, 1885. He informed the people, as they gathered together, that certain procedures must be observed before they could be reconciled into the church. He described these and the trustees objected. Some of the people sided with them. Then the archbishop said, "All who are willing to do what I request and follow me, stand up." Ten girls stood up. Their fathers protested. "Sit down!" they hissed. But the girls, determined to do what God wanted them to do, remained standing.

"After the confirmation ceremonies he [the archbishop] visited the sisters and told them that they were not religious in the eyes of the church even though they wore the Religious Habit." They had not been canonically examined and invested by ecclesiastical authority. "You will be my Sisters and help me in my work," the archbishop said.

Since these young ladies were persecuted by their parents, the archbishop sent them to Gervais to the Benedictine Convent where they remained from June until August 1886. The Benedictines wanted them to join their order, but the archbishop said no. He had other plans. He proposed two places, one at Milwaukie [Oregon], the other at Sublimity, an abandoned "college" building that had become a roost for pigeons. They chose Sublimity and arrived there on August 15, 1886. They called this new convent Maria Zell, which was the name of a shrine in Europe. They adopted Benedictine habits at first and their first spiritual director was Father Werner.

Thus the strange saga ended on a note of joy for those who had responded to the call of the archbishop. As for those left behind, nothing mattered anymore. All they had was the shrine of Father Albrecht conspicuously placed in a wooden vault above the ground in the Jordan Cemetery. His magic was gone. They left him and drifted away into the new settlements of western Oregon. In 1897, a priest arrived—Father Joseph Bucholzer was the new pastor of Jordan. One evening when he was ringing the Angelus bell, he saw flames leaping in the cemetery. The shrine was mysteriously burning, and there was no way to save it. After it was all over, the priest gathered the charred bones of the misguided prophet, Joseph Albrecht, and placed them in the wet earth.

THE NEW CONGREGATION

In March of 1887, only six months after they had come together in the schoolhouse, His Grace the Archbishop permitted five of the sisters to make their first religious profession. Maria Zell had become, indeed, a convent.

Father Ruttiman's involvement had not been altogether altruistic. Like other pastors of rural parishes he was trying to provide sisters to teach in a parochial school, plans of which had lurked for some time in his pragmatic mind. In October 1888, satisfied that Sister Mary Johanna, a member of the original group, was ready to teach, he opened what was known as Marion County's first parochial school in a simple frame building, also in Sublimity, and almost as ugly as the convent. This was unpainted, like the latter, and surrounded by the dark fir trees, which looked, on rainy days, almost as black as the nuns' habits. This primitive shelter, comprised of one room equipped with two long tables and benches, and later a bell presented by friends in the East, was filled on opening day with twenty solemn but noisy students, both large and small [8]

Assisting Sister Mary Johanna was Sister Francis DeSales, a Franciscan from Milwaukee. Thus it happened that this pioneer parochial school was the modest achievement of the combined activities of a Maria Zell sister, a Franciscan sister, a Benedictine priest, and a Redemptorist archbishop. [9]

The number of students soon became forty-seven. [10] It is not likely that any of them, assembled at the long tables, gave much thought to the significance of their presence. Nor could they know how far Sister Mary Johanna and her colleagues were destined to go. But a number of providential happenings were already shaping the future of Maria Zell. The first of these was the orphanage for boys on which Archbishop Gross had set his heart.

Until this time, the Sisters of the Holy Names had cared for the orphans of Portland and the Sisters of Providence for those in Vancouver. But as the population of these two cities became greater, there were more orphans, and more of their care was required.

THE ORPHANAGE AT BEAVERTON

In early February 1889, His Grace preached to the prisoners in the state penitentiary at Salem. In the afternoon of the same day, he gave a lecture to the patients in the state mental hospital. [11] He was especially pleased to be there, he said, and he could not conceal his happiness about recent developments for his new orphanage for boys. During the previous month, Father Henry Drees, a member of the Congregation of Precious

Blood, had arrived at Portland at the archbishop's request. While Gross was engaged in other duties[12] Drees made a survey of available land in the immediate area. He selected a site near Beaverton, a village west of Portland, and purchased there a tract for "St. Mary's Boy's Home." The archbishop visited this site two days before his sojourn to Salem. Having inspected the property, he gave it his hearty approval. Arrangements were made at once for the land to be cleared and for the construction of the buildings.

In June 1889, while the archbishop was in Europe, the cornerstone of St. Mary's Home was properly blessed and placed in the presence of five hundred people who felt attracted to the poor orphans. Drees was replaced in August by Father Alphonse Grussi from Beloit, Kansas, also a Father of the Precious Blood, and a few weeks later, on Thanksgiving Day, November 27, the new St. Mary's was dedicated. A number of boys by this time were already in residence.

In 1891, Grussi, too, was recalled by his superior. The archbishop turned to the Maria Zell Sisters for help, and then a great leap forward was taken: on March 18, 1891, three sisters from Sublimity took charge of St. Mary's.[13]

Not far from Beaverton was Verboort. The pastor of this all-Catholic settlement wanted sisters, also, and the archbishop turned again to the Maria Zell convent. Four sisters from Sublimity responded to the appeal and, in January 1891, opened another parochial school at Verboort.

It was now evident to the sisters that Beaverton was the logical site for their Novitiate, and, on June 27, 1891, four novices, three postulants, and five aspirants moved from Sublimity to St. Mary's.[14] On January 28, 1894, Archbishop Gross dedicated the new motherhouse at St. Mary's and a few years later in a special General Chapter the sisters adopted a new name for their congregation. Henceforth, they would be known as the Sisters of St. Mary of Oregon.[15]

From Beaverton the sisters expanded their activities to other parishes and dioceses, so that within two decades they counted their membership at one hundred and forty sisters, who supervised two academies and twelve parochial schools. On May 1, 1934, they acquired the status of a Pontifical Institute when Pope Pius XI placed his final approval and confirmation upon its constitution. Thus the Sisters of St. Mary of Oregon became the first congregation founded in the Pacific Northwest to be elevated to that status of a Pontifical Institute.[16]

THE FIRST DOMINICAN SISTERS

During this period of Maria Zell's growth, a gratifying number of other religious groups arrived in the Northwest, mostly to staff schools, orphanages, and hospitals. Among these were the Dominicans.

Perhaps it should be pointed out that there are many branches of Dominicans. One should not be surprised by this, for the Dominicans, like the Benedictines and the Franciscans, too, are united by a common rule rather than by one common superior. Thus the Dominican Sisters, like the Benedictines, came to the Northwest from different mother convents elsewhere.

Over the years, eight separate congregations of Dominican Sisters arrived, mostly to teach. The first was directed by Mother Mary Thomasina, who responded to an appeal of Bishop Junger. Having departed from St. Dominic's Convent in Jersey City, she arrived in Pomeroy, Washington on August 24, 1888, accompanied by two other meek little nuns who were undoubtedly surprised to find so sleepy a settlement as Pomeroy, where the most exciting event all week was a runaway horse. The three sisters took over Holy Rosary school on October 29.[18]

The first student to register was Nellie Ryan. Nellie was so awestruck by the sisters in their ivory white gowns, or as they said in those days, "holy habits," that she decided to request one. She became the first western postulant of the new foundation. When a novitiate was formally established at Pomeroy, through the intervention of Bishop Junger, in April 1890, Nellie was the first novice admitted to the novitiate; and with her on April 9 was another young lady whose name was Mary Finn.

The Pomeroy convent, by decree of the Mother General of the Dominican Order, was now regarded as an independent convent. Like the Beaverton sisters, the Dominicans were ready for anything, and anything was possible.

No one had to tell Mother M. Thomasina that Pomeroy was not going to become a roaring metropolis, so she looked around and decided, finally, to file for incorporation papers in Seattle. This was on August 5, 1892.[19] A year later, she sent two sisters from Pomeroy to conduct a parochial school in St. Patrick's parish in Tacoma, which was too poor to provide a building; so the sisters conducted their classes in church. They supported themselves by taking up a collection, in person, at Mass on the first Sunday of each month.[20] This was intolerable, of course, and Mother M. Thomasina resolved the problem by moving the Dominican mother-house and novitiate to Tacoma.[21] From these unexpected beginnings came many distinguished institutions, not the least of which were Marymount and Aquinas Academy in Tacoma.

THE SISTERS OF THE GOOD SHEPHERD

The next group to arrive were the Good Shepherd Sisters who came to Helena on February 11, 1889, when Montana was still a territory and widely regarded as a very wicked one. No doubt the services and dedications of these sisters were sorely needed. They were so successful in the guidance of Helena's wayward girls, and the protection of the virtue of others, that Bishop Junger urged the Superior in St. Paul to send a contingent of their congregation to Seattle. Five sisters arrived on July 29, 1890, and occupied as a temporary home the residence of Mrs. Levi Foss on Thirteenth Street. Here on July 21 they opened St. Euphrasia's home. Six weeks later, on September 15, they moved to Judge Green's home at 413 Ninth Avenue, which they had purchased for $15,000.[22] At this time they cared for twelve orphans and five older girls.

A similar group of sisters called Sisters of Charity of the Refuge, Good Shepherd, from Ottawa, Canada, established the Good Shepherd Home at Park Place near Oregon City in 1891. Confronted with many unforseen difficulties, however, this community asked to be received into the Congregation of the Sisters of the Good Shepherd. This required more red tape than moving City Hall, but eventually, on March 19, 1902, the union was effected and the community was attached to the St. Paul Province. Mother Mary of St. Rose of Lima, known more simply as Mother Rose, or "Rosy," was appointed the first superior. Her arrival in May, 1902, with a small group of sisters from St. Paul, marked the beginning of the Sisters of the Good Shepherd's work in Oregon.[23]

Three years later, in 1905, another contingent of these sisters arrived in Spokane.[24] It seems that Spokane also had some misguided young ladies who needed the restraints and counseling of a sisters' refuge. Spokane's mayor, Francis Boyd by name, encouraged the Bishop of Nesqually to send for sisters. Father Charles Mackin, who was really at the bottom of it all, appealed to St. Paul and six sisters came, bag and baggage, and rented a temporary home on the bank of the river near Mission Avenue bridge. Father Mackin offered Mass there, then made the rounds of his many friends to secure money for a permanent residence. From one, Mr. Charles Sweeney, who regarded himself as a capitalist, he received a forty acre tract on North Lidgerwood, where the Northtown Shopping Center is now. On December 28, 1906, a new spacious brick building was ready for the sisters and their twenty mostly unwilling "guests," and Michael Shea, another friend of Mackin's, who wore a fashionable mustache and owned the Spokane Cab Company, sent a large cab drawn by four horses to move them all. It was in some ways like a sleigh ride party, but there were no boys to escort the girls.[25]

THE SISTERS OF THE HOLY CROSS

Meanwhile, in the Vicariate of Idaho, Bishop Glorieux was anxious, as were the other northwest bishops, to expedite the directives of the Third Plenary Council of Baltimore regarding parochial schools. The only parochial school in the vicariate was at Lewiston, and even this was in a precarious state.[26] Since Glorieux expected Boise, the capitol of the state, to be designated as the seat of his forthcoming diocese, he was determined to establish here a parochial school and hospital. He first turned to the Sisters of the Holy Cross in South Bend, Indiana, because these sisters had successful schools in Ogden and Salt Lake City, Utah— "Mormon Country" like southern Idaho.[27]

The Holy Cross Sisters, like the others, were deluged with requests, but the superior accepted Glorieux's plea for help and promised the bishop that several sisters would arrive before September 1889.

During the summer of that year, Glorieux made his northern visitation. On August 6, Father Van der Heyden in Boise received a letter from Father Peter Poaps, Chaplain at Sacred Heart Hospital in Spokane, advising him that the bishop was gravely ill with typhoid fever and would be a patient for an indefinite period in the hospital. Van der Heyden was not to forward the bishop's mail, but was to open it and attend to all matters of administration to the best of his ability.[28]

During the bishop's absence, Van der Heyden welcomed to Boise five Sisters of the Holy Cross, who arrived on August 24, 1889. Their coming had not been expected so soon, hence there was no residence prepared for them, and at two in the morning, half-asleep and half-dead from their long train ride, they were deposited at the home of J.H. Hawley, who gave them shelter until they could find a home of their own.

What followed is described by Father Bradley:

> During the previous summer (1888) Bishop Glorieux had St. Patrick's Hall erected on Bannock Street, next to St. John's Church, at a cost of $600.00. Father Van der Heyden and the Sisters used this as a temporary school. On September 9, 1889, the academy opened in this hall with two Sisters on the teaching staff. The three-room convent, much too small for a community of five, was abandoned two weeks after the opening of school. In the meantime the Sisters rented the O.P. Johnson residence, facing Jefferson Street with State Street to the north and between 12th and 13th Streets, and transferred classes thither on September 20, 1889. In March 1890, the Superior General, Mother Augusta, visited the academy, and during her visitation bought from E. Boll the block of property bounded by Jefferson and State Streets between 3rd and 4th Streets. This property had belonged to Father T. Mesplie when he was chaplain at Fort Boise (1872–1880). The

Sisters rented from O.P. Johnson a suitable private residence on Jefferson Street and 4th Street. On September 20, 1890, this became St. Teresa's Academy, a boarding and day school.[29]

When the academy was firmly established, the sisters undertook the development of a hospital. Ground for this was broken in April, 1893. On July 6 of the same year, the first stone was laid. The current depression then delayed construction, but the sisters' Motherhouse in Indiana came to the rescue by advancing sufficient funds for completion. Named St. Alphonsus in honor of the bishop, the hospital was dedicated by Glorieux on November 11, 1897.[30]

Eventually St. Teresa's became a girls-only academy, but some of the sisters objected to this, quite properly, I think, because Idaho's boys required a Catholic education as much as the girls did. In 1900, St. Joseph's School for Boys was opened in old St. Patrick's Hall. Sister Lucy was the principal and among her first pupils was John Regan who died for his country in World War I. In 1905, the hall was moved to make way for the new cathedral, and the boys went with it.[31]

THREE VOYAGES TO EUROPE

While Bishop Glorieux was convalescing from his encounter with typhoid bacillus in Spokane, two of the other northwest bishops were traveling to Rome to make their required *ad limina* visits. These were Archbishop Gross and Bishop Brondel.

Gross left Portland on April 29, 1889. On the previous night, his clergy celebrated his departure with a party at the archbishop's residence, not, however, without the consent of Gross. One cannot doubt that the party was properly discreet, especially with His Grace present, but sufficient hilarity was generated by the refreshments for a prolonged songfest, during which, according to reports, songs were presented in "English, German, French, Dutch, Flemish [sic], Latin, Italian and Chinook Indian."[32] The Chinook performance came last. It was presented, of course, by Father Croquet, who was the special pet of all the clergy from the archbishop on down.

Also, according to reports, a generous purse was offered to the archbishop by the lay people of the archdiocese, demonstrating their regard for their archbishop, despite his seeming aloofness and reserved academic demeanor. The presentation of purses to bishops when they departed on job-related junkets to Rome was a common custom in those days, partly because prelates lacked sufficient means to travel without this gratuity.

Some weeks later, Father Adrian Croquet also went to Europe. It seems that this was brought about by the insistence of his relatives in Belgium, and by a desire on his own part to visit the sanctuary at Lourdes. He left Oregon in early July, 1889. From the steamer *Belgenland* of the Red Star Line, he wrote to his nephew Bishop Mercier that he would land at Antwerp and it was his intention of going on to Lourdes, hopeful that the bishop would accompany him.[33]

The bishop, despite Croquet's protests, provided transportation from Antwerp to the grotto in a first class compartment in the railway carriage. Others in the compartment, much to their chagrin, were required to share his devotions during the entire voyage. "What do you say to another rosary?" he would say to them when they had completed the last one. After they arrived at Lourdes, Mercier lost track of him and learned later that he had spent most of his time at the shrine hearing confessions.[34]

Father Peter DeRoo, by this time subdued or less inclined to be bossy with the local nuns, was in Europe also, to celebrate in his home town of Waterdyke, Belgium, the twenty-fifth anniversary of his ordination. He made use of the occasion by conducting research for his renowned book, *History of America Before Columbus*, which eventually appeared in two volumes.[35]

While his colleagues were thus engaged, Bishop Junger, the only prelate in the Northwest who remained in his diocese, had time to ponder his own problems. The St. James Mission I and Case, which was still in the courts, occupied a high place among these. The original mission church, really the pro-cathedral of the diocese, mysteriously burned to the ground at midnight on June 21, 1889. Two hours later, another fire destroyed many of Vancouver's buildings and though no one doubted that arson was committed in all cases, no charges or arrests were made.[36]

Bishop Junger had taken note of Father DeRouge's return from his Jesuit tertianship in France.[37] This was an occasion of some relief to His Excellency, for the missions in central Washington had suffered from DeRouge's one year absence. Father Aloysius Parodi had substituted for him by making several prolonged journeys along the Columbia and Okanogan Valleys. The Okanogans had a language of their own and though they understood Kalispel and Chinook, they were very fussy about being instructed in their own tongue. Parodi knew only enough of this to hear confessions. For preaching he had at his disposal twenty-eight sermons composed by Grassi in Okanogan, and Parodi used them, much to the delight of the Indians. But he soon ran out of these and preached the next sermon in Chinook. The chief hastily interrupted him, saying "away with that language! We talk that language transacting business and trading with white people. We never speak Chinook in Church."[38] Parodi then requested a half-breed, Pion by name, to translate Giorda's catechism into Okanogan. This kept Pion busy all day. The next day, Chief Antoine asked Parodi to translate a letter into the Okanogan language and the priest had to admit that he could not do this. When Antoine complained to Pion, the latter expressed great surprise. "Yesterday," he exclaimed, "I taught him the language from morning to night."[39]

Antoine was informed that a priest could not attend the mission for Christmas.[40] So he went to town and purchased a huge clock, which he brought back to the tribe. He laid it out in the log chapel, then covered the logs with calico. After the Indians of the camp had supper on that Christmas Eve, they entered the chapel and sat around the clock. When the clock showed that it was midnight, they arose, marched around the clock, then knelt down and recited all the prayers they knew and sang all their hymns.[41]

There is something strangely perverse about that Christmas Eve. The Okanogans had no priest and celebrated Christmas with a new clock. At St. Francis Regis mission, for the Colvilles, however, there were several priests and brothers, because the Indians had flocked to this mission from all parts of the reservation. But alas, just before midnight, while the Okanogans guarded their clock, the vast log church of St. Regis burned to the ground with all its contents, including the precious statues the Indians had purchased for it. Three years had been required for the construction of this church, and it vanished in a few hours, while the Indians gazed upon it in silent wonder.[42]

But De Rouge was back and he took up his residence again at St. Mary's near Omak in October 1889. Here he remained until his death in 1916. During these twenty-seven years, with the help of Mother Drexel and his own relatives in France, he built up one of the most successful missions in the history of the Northwest. Under his care, St. Mary's became the cultural center of all of the Indians in a vast area in north central Washington. And from this base De Rouge struck out in all directions, establishing missions for both Indians and whites. Thus his influence would be felt for generations to come.

WASHINGTON'S NEW CONSTITUTION

There was during this year, 1889, one sour note, which was not recognized at first, perhaps because no one knew the entire melody. This was the new state constitution for Washington, a document that was hammered out by a delegation of citizens to exist eternally in its first form. It was from the beginning as resistant to change or tolerance as a slab of marble. It was then and still is the most secular document of its kind in the entire United States. One cannot say that it was anti-Catholic, or even anti-religion. It simply excluded all relationships between the sovereignty of Washington and religion under any name. Except for its preamble, it is as godless as a vacuum and in the course of time it has proved to be an insurmountable obstacle for Catholics and others to share in certain legitimate services of state government.

No one can judge the motives of the delegates at this state constitutional convention. One can say however, that this document would haunt Catholics for generations to come. All efforts to change it would be futile. "After all," people said, "it is the state constitution."

The question naturally arises: how was this done? Were there no Catholics aware of the impending disaster? Had they known about it, could they have altered matters? An account of the convention follows, and in this one can find some answers.

For more than a decade some of the citizens of Washington Territory had been seeking Congressional approval for statehood. Oregon had been a state since 1859, more than thirty years, while Washington, Idaho, and Montana waited enviously for politicians to take action. Finally, on February 22, 1889, the 157th anniversary of George Washington's birthday,[43] Congress passed the Enabling Act, which was designed "to provide for the division of Dakota into two States and to enable the people of North Dakota, South Dakota, Montana, and Washington to form constitutions and State governments, and to be admitted into the Union on an equal footing with the original States, and to make donations of public lands to such states."[44]

Nothing was said about Idaho, which had shown so much promise during the 1860's that some speculators, prematurely to be sure, gambled on its being called to the lofty pinnacle of statehood before the others.[45] But Idaho had defaulted. Its population in the 1880 census was only 32,610 compared, for example to Washington's 75,116. By political standards, a small population representing fewer voters was the ultimate in rejection.

The provisions of the Enabling Act were clear. The governors of Washington and Montana were enjoined to issue proclamations calling for elections of delegates and assemblies to be endured at the seats of territorial government. After new state constitutions had been approved locally, they could be submitted to Congress for approval. State governments could be formed and final action taken.

On July 4, 1889, seventy-five duly elected delegates convened at Olympia in Washington Territory to form the new government. Having declared that, on behalf of the people, they adopted the Constitution of the United States, the delegates then proceeded to form a state constitution that expected to be "Republican in form, and make no distinction in civil or political rights on account of race or color ... perfect toleration of religious sentiment, the title of unappropriated public land was to be recognized as in the United States, the debts of the Territory were to be assumed by the State, public schools must be maintained and kept free from sectarian control."[46]

Of the seventy-five delegates, forty-three were members of the Republican party, twenty-one were Democrats and three were independents. They came originally from all sections of the United States and there were a number from foreign countries; five from Scotland, three from Germany, two from Ireland, and two from Canada. Only one had been born in the Territory. "There were twenty-one lawyers, thirteen farmers, six merchants, six doctors, five bankers, four cattlemen, three teachers, two real estate dealers, two editors, two hop growers, two loggers, two lumbermen, one minister, one surveyor, one fisherman and one mining engineer."[47]

Now this presents the spectacle of some very nice people, even if there was only one man of the cloth, compared with twenty-one barristers. There were no women delegates. There were no Indians or blacks. Almost all of the members were Protestants in religion, at least nominally, and there is reason to believe that most of these cherished very definite reservations regarding the church's place in public life.[48]

The proceedings of the sessions that followed contain few if any allusions to religion. Delegates simply reported that in their discussions they had been much influenced by the constitutions of other states, especially by those of Oregon, California, and Wisconsin. "We, the people of the State of Washington," they wrote in their Preamble, "grateful to the Supreme Ruler of the Universe for our liberties, do ordain this Constitution."

For fifty days they labored. Then, on August 22, seventy-one of the seventy-five delegates signed the document they had just completed.[49] In this form, the expression of the will of the majority, it was dispatched to Washington, D.C., for approval. Passed upon by Congress, it was then submitted to President Benjamin Harrison, who issued a proclamation admitting Washington into the Union, November 11, 1889. The State of Montana was admitted on the same day.

These are the plain facts of the case. For the whys and wherefores, we must speculate.

The mishap was, I think, contrived, at least in part. In the United States generally, the 1880's were a period of deep evangelical feeling, of emerging social awareness. It was also a period of compulsive support for public schools. Most Americans cultivated a profound sense of pride in their public schools, which had no equals in the contemporary world. Any criticism of them was regarded as criticism of America itself. Even the choice to not use the public schools, for example by the adoption of a parochial school system, was interpreted to be an attack on the American Way.[50]

It will be remembered that Archbishop Charles Seghers, unduly influenced by his Belgian one-religion-only beginnings, frequently attacked the public school system as pagan and unsuitable for Catholic children. The Third Plenary Council of Baltimore had passed a decree directing every American parish to have its own parochial school. To this seemingly stubborn zeal of Catholics for producing their own "Better-than-thine" schools, the Protestants overreacted, choosing to sacrifice completely their own religious influence in the nation's schools rather than risk a Catholic takeover. It was during this period precisely when the new, rigid interpretation "of separation of Church and State" became fashionable even among some Catholics.[51] It was also during this period that the beginnings of total secularization can be found. America henceforth would show a split personality in public, committed to a Christian God but allowed to express this commitment rarely, only in harmless ways, like chaplains opening Congress with a prayer.

There was another aspect of frontier society that should not be overlooked: the influence of so-called fraternal lodges. As I have noted earlier, the Northwest, perhaps more than most sections of the country, was churchless in its origins. Frequently lodge membership, especially lodges like the Masonic Order, the Odd Fellows, and others of a "secret" nature, were substituted for membership in a parish or church, sometimes even by Catholics. One cannot help but be amazed, in reviewing the funeral customs of the period for example, by the high percentage of burials from lodges. The Masonic Lodge was especially influential in the Pacific Northwest during the last several decades of the nineteenth century and early decades of the twentieth, and it is no secret that many members of the Masonic Order were implacably opposed to parochial schools. This hostility appeared in a highly organized form later when certain Masons joined forces with the Ku Klux Klan and others to outlaw parochial schools altogether.

The Oregon School Bill of the 1920's had its origins in the collective confusion of the nineteenth century. So did Washington State's Constitution. In a secluded, unchallenged manner, it was simply hammered out by people who were determined to keep the state strictly secular lest worse befall it. If they went too far, as they undoubtedly did, they were

merely expressing the national trend. It was not the best of times for
Catholics or any other dissenters who denied the absolute state.

Perhaps the Catholics were as much to blame for the misadventure as
anybody. Most Catholics in the Northwest at this time had come from
one of three sources: French Canada, Ireland, or Germany. The French
Canadians had settled largely in Oregon, where, as a lower middle class
people, they turned to farming, eschewing politics for personal, rather
than for ideological reasons. The Irish as a group had come next, first to
America during the Potato Famine, and then to the West as members of
the United States Army and as railroad workers. Like the Irish elsewhere,
they were politically active, but more concerned with what was going on
in Dublin than in Olympia, Washington or Salem, Oregon. Their enemy
was the English, there war was for Irish independence. They had no
quarrel with American Protestants, indeed many of them waved flags
whenever the crowds gathered to prove they were as American as
anyone.

German Catholics who came later to settle on the land were often
fugitives from Bismarck's ruthless *Kulturkamp*, which had destroyed their
religious freedom.[52] They had seen enough of Church-State politics and
wanted nothing more than to be left alone. As far as they were
concerned, paying for their own parochial schools was a small price for
their freedom.

But where were the Catholic bishops? Junger of Nesqually, a Belgian
and a very good missionary bishop, seems to have missed entirely the
significance of what was taking place at Olympia between July 4 and
August 22, 1889. Like the other bishops—Gross in Oregon, Brondel in
Montana and Glorieux in Idaho—Junger was preoccupied with survival
in this interval of enormous growth. New parishes were taking form on
all sides. Junger, too, was suffering from chronic sickness. Glorieux was
recovering from typhoid that summer and Gross and Brondel were in
Europe. Gross did not return until December 10, when the constitution
had already been adopted. Brondel, after leaving Rome, made a pilgrimage to the Holy Land, and did not return to Helena until the
following year.

When all was said and done, it is highly improbable that Catholics, had
they taken action, could have influenced the legislation. Representing
less than ten percent of the total population, and an even smaller
percentage in the professional classes, they had no political clout
whatever. Undoubtedly they realized this and went about their own
business, totally oblivious to the nature of the disaster taking place. Time
alone would reveal it.

WARFARE AT UNIONTOWN

No history, apparently, is complete without the revelation of inner conflicts of disputes among those who share the same vision, but see it differently. In the history of the Northwest, there were several notorious feuds between factions of Catholics. The first, involving all levels of the church—laity, religious, priests, and prelates—was so bitter that those who participated in it carefully guarded its particulars as something too secret, too shameful to bear the light of day. Thus for nearly a hundred years there was a kind of conspiracy of silence about it, while younger generations of Catholics speculated about the causes and consequences, knowing only that something dreadful had happened.

Another dispute, which will appear later, involved for the most part only priests and their bishops, but like the first, it ended up in Rome, where heads were clearer and more experienced with the wiles of human nature. In a sense, in both cases, the good guys won in the end but the raging battles were so painful that they seared the souls of the most dauntless and left scars that crippled for life. Thus no one won, everyone lost, including the innocent bystanders who were exposed to public scandal.

It will be recalled that when the Benedictine Sisters from Sarnen, Switzerland, established a convent school in Uniontown, Washington, the bishop had promised them a chaplain. Father Nicholas Frei, one of the pioneer Benedictines with Father Adelhelm Odermatt, filled this position well. Frei organized St. Boniface parish, served the sisters faithfully at the convent, and traveled throughout the broad Palouse country seeking Catholics and bringing them the sacraments. In 1886, he purchased a seven acre tract for a church in Colfax, one of his missions, and prepared the way for the development of a new parish there.[53] The hardships he endured in the care of so vast an area undermined his health, which had never been robust, so the bishop assigned him to Colfax and appointed a new volunteer priest from Germany.

This was Father Anthony Joehren, who had been ordained at the age of twenty-five, just one year before he arrived on April 13, 1887, which was Good Friday in that unfortunate year. Though still a very young priest, he wore a huge, scraggly black beard, like some of the older Jewish rabbis. He also wore his biretta, whenever occasion allowed, and in portraits of the period he held his right hand over his heart in the approved manner for clerics. All these were ominous signs of rigidity and Teutonic dictatorial propensities.

The Sisters at St. Andrew's Convent were undoubtedly uneasy about the new pastor. No one, it seemed to them, could really replace Father

Nicholas, who had been most considerate of their needs and grateful for their help. But they were now stuck with Joehren. They did not have long to wait for the first of many donnybrooks. "From the very first [he] objected to the Sisters teaching in the public schools," one of the sisters cautiously observed later, manifesting, in her gentle reference to the past, amazing restraint. "When the new term opened in September, he gave strict orders that all the Catholic children should attend the convent school. Objections arose among the people, and sad to say, pastor, people and the little struggling community suffered intensely for many years under the grave misunderstandings which arose."[54]

The sisters and the people of the parish complied, though some of the latter, as the sister reported, did not approve. It was Father Joehren's turf, so to speak; they were all anxious to respect it, but they did not have to agree with its master.

Mother M. Johanna, as thin-lipped and straight-backed as a German baroness, the very personification of efficiency and propriety, now had to cope with a pastor who was becoming more unpredictable every day. She kept a journal that is precise enough to please a board of directors, and this was published at last, revealing not only the acrimonious nature of her diplomacy with the pastor, but her determination to hold her own against a Prussian juggernaut.[55]

In this journal, Mother Johanna presents a brief comment about the Sister's passing association with a school in Pomeroy. "After some deliberations we decided to accede to his [the pastor's] wishes," Mother Johanna wrote. "On August 13, 1887, Sister M. Rosalia and Sister M. Ida were appointed to open a parochial school. There was no building suitable for the purpose and the church had to be used as a temporary classroom. The sisters lived in a small house rented for them.... Some peculiar difficulties made it advisable for the Sisters not to resume their charge at Pomeroy."[56]

BEGINNINGS OF TROUBLE AT PALOUSE CITY

Mother Johanna provides the background for a prolonged confrontation at Palouse City; this ended up in civil court.

> Besides Uniontown, our Pastor, Rev. Father Anthony Joehren had one mission to attend, Palouse City.
> There were but few Catholics belonging to that mission and there was no church. Fev. Father Joehren held services for them about once a month in a private residence. He took great interest in this mission and was induced by some local parties to provide a Sisters' school for them; business advantages seem to have been the main underlying motive for this step. The Rev. Father

entered into their views, however, and urged us strongly to purchase property at Palouse and to establish a school. He selected the location himself on top of a hill north of town. The property was a tract comprising 10 lots. A small one and a-half story farmhouse was the only building on the place. As for water, we would have needed the staff of Moses; for although a well was sunk, it never furnished a sufficient quantity of the needed liquid. The purchase price amounted to $1000.

On the opposite hill, south of town, we were offered better location gratis, but Father Joehren insisted that we keep his selection. The latter might have been suitable for a home, but not for a school. Moreover the distance from town was too great and the hill too steep. In October, 1889, the two untiring missionaries, Sister M. Rosalia and Sister M. Ida were sent to Palouse City to open a school. The enrollment for the first day was only 11 pupils; that was about all our small house could accommodate for the time being. Gradually, however, the number of our school children increased, most of them being non-Catholics. Religious services were held regularly on the first Sunday of every month. On the remaining Sundays the Sisters had either to travel 36 miles to Uniontown by train or do without Holy Mass and the Sacraments. They felt this bereavement deeply and had to take turns on the mission to attend so that everyone had an opportunity. In 1891 a small frame church was built near the school, with an addition of two rooms for a priest to live in.

The following year Rev. Father Fintan Becker was given charge of the mission by the bishop. This was of great benefit to the Sisters, too good however to last long, as the saying goes. In less than two years the Rev. Father left again; the meagre salary which the few Catholics could afford to give him being insufficient to support him.

In spite of unfavorable conditions, Rev. Father Joehren entertained great hopes for our mission in Palouse. He made us put up a school house at our own expense, in the summer of 1892. By fall one room was finished and used for the school. The rest remained incomplete. [57]

By this time the convent at Uniontown had become crowded. St. Andrew's was a motherhouse for the formation of novices, as well as an academy and residence for the sisters. Additions had been made, but the pastor had got it into his head that the novitiate and motherhouse should be moved "to a more secluded place." The sisters yielded on this point, as they always had, and requested Abbot Frowin from Conception, Missouri, to advise them. Joehren himself undertook the task of finding a new location, which was really none of his business, and he accompanied the Abbot to Cottonwood, Idaho, high on Camas Prairie, to examine a tract of land that a devout Catholic farmer, John Uhlencott by name, had offered the sisters as a gift. The Abbot was pleased with the site, where St. Gertrude's Convent now stands, but there were no railroad facilities and the roads were bad, so the proposal was rejected.

ENTER FATHER JAMES FREI

On the sixteenth of October 1891, another priest entered the scene. James Frei, nephew of Nicholas, was a devoted friend of the sisters. His niece, Sister M. Benediction, had left the Convent in Sarnen to serve in Uniontown, and with the approval of his own bishop, he also came to America with the intention of entering a monastery to be a monk.[58] He stopped in Uniontown, enroute to Mount Angel, to visit his niece. In need of a rest, he accepted the sisters' invitation to remain there for a few weeks.

So far all was well. Mother Johanna continues her narrative:

> Rev. Anthony Joehren was very favorably impressed by Father Frei and conceived a high esteem for him. He voiced his earnest desire that Rev. Fr. Frei should consent to become our chaplain, and first broached the matter to him, trying to bring him to accept the position. Fr. Joehren also urged the Sister Superior to put in her own request, saying: 'Try your best to keep Fr. Frei; he is a pious, a learned and experienced priest.' According to the wish of the Pastor, the Superior then proposed to the Rev. guest to take up his abode with us permanently as our chaplain. Our petition, for what has been said, was entirely according to the mind of our Rev. Pastor. Rev. Father Frei hesitated; but in the hope of being able to help our Community, he finally yielded and decided to stay. The necessary faculties from the Rt. Rev. Bishop had already been procured for the new chaplain by Fr. Joehren. He could begin work at once. The Rev. Pastor of Uniontown requested the chaplain to teach the Catechism in the Sisters' school and also to preach occasionally. The request was readily granted.
>
> The people were much pleased with the preaching of Fr. Frei and especially the children took well to his catechetical instructions. Father Frei stayed strictly at home, was careful not to meddle with any affairs of the parish. He abstained from visiting the people and declined their invitations unless accompanied by the Reverent Pastor. In the spring of 1892, we had a small dwelling house erected for our chaplain, a short distance from the Convent. Towards fall he had a severe attack of sciatica, which held him on the sicklist for many weeks.
>
> As mentioned before, Rev. Father Anthony Joehren had been active to find a suitable place for the translocation of our motherhouse, but had failed to find one to his taste. Now he laid the task on our Rev. chaplain who, on the advice of Fr. Joehren, visited several places, but did not meet with what he wanted.[59]

As time passed, the pastor felt threatened by his more talented colleague. In the summer of 1892, his friendly attitude toward Frei and the sisters rapidly declined. When he spoke of the sisters he soon began to use language unbecoming a priest, and began to spread slanderous reports against them. They were entirely ignorant of the causes for all of this and at their request Frei went to Joehren to inquire into the reasons for his dissatisfaction. He informed Joehren that the sisters were ready to do all in their power "to set things right." Joehren replied angrily, saying that the sisters "do nothing for the Church, they are lazy and idle, and the whole congregation is against them. The people cannot see why there should be so many of them when only a few are needed for a school."[60]

Frei answered that under the circumstances the best thing for the sisters to do would be to look for another location. "For no Religious Community would think of staying in a place to mortify and provoke the priest."

Joehren then said, "Let them go wherever they please: the sooner the better."

The pastor's remarks were not only utterly silly, they were damaging as well. Two factions now formed in the parish, those for Joehren, subsequently recognized as the Uniontown group, and those for the sisters and Father Frei, subsequently known as the Colton group. The former, unfortunately, were blind to Joehren's defects, partly because his opponents belonged to Colton.

THE THREATENING RIVAL COLTON

Colton was a rival townsite and there had been bad blood between its promoters and those of Uniontown from the very beginning. It has been alleged, among other things, that Colton "stole" Uniontown's only doctor and hotel, an unforgivable felony in those competitive days, when a successful townsite created instant millionaires for those who owned it.

The Catholics of Colton wanted their own church. Since Colton was only three miles distant from Uniontown, this was viewed with some apprehension by the faithful in Uniontown, but the local paper seemed to regard it as a sign of progress. "Colton will have a Catholic church by fall," it announced. "The Becker Brothers and others are taking hold of the matter and it is to cost $3,000."[61] In the same paper other marks of progress were noted: that "lumber was on the ground for a Methodist Church to cost $2,500," and "The Colton city dads [sic] are advertising for bids to build a jail."

The pastor of Uniontown required no reminders about progress in Colton. What he did need, rather desperately, was an addition to St. Boniface. "If you help me now," he said to the Catholics of Colton, "I will later help you build a church for yourselves." Colton did help, and Mother Johanna relates what followed:

Several Catholic families had meanwhile settled in the place and on May 12, 1889, the bishop was again petitioned to allow the erection of a church. He gave his hearty approval and encouragement to the project. Preparations were made and steps were taken, and in June of 1890 the contract was let to

Mr. H. Schaaf and work commenced at once for the building of a small frame structure which was located on the hill south of the Colton flour mill. On June 12, 1892, the Catholic congregation of Uniontown voted to build a new church at that place. The Coltonites did not fancy the idea, since they now had a church of their own. It was now for them to decide to either help build the new church in Uniontown, or with the sanction of the bishop to form an independent congregation. They were to hand in their decision by January 1, 1893. They opined for the latter course, and were taxed $1,000 for the privilege.

They next sent a petition to the bishop to appoint Father Frei as their Pastor; the bishop acceded to their wish and made the appointment. The interior of the church was still incomplete, and steps were taken at once to finish and provide it with altar and pews. On the feast of Easter, April 2, 1893, Father Frei held the first services in the Colton church, which he continued henceforth with the exception of the first Sunday of each month, when he had to minister in Palouse, which mission had previously been turned over to him. The Colton congregation felt happy over their zealous Pastor. The Messrs, Becker took him to and fro by team for the Sunday services.[62]

So Colton had a church, a pastor, and a debt to Uniontown of one thousand dollars. It was all very proper. Father Joehren had insisted on a formal promissory note, dated May 2, 1893, and signed by Father Frei and six members of the new parish.[63] The new church was called St. Gall's in honor of a saint who had lived in Switzerland, not Germany. This, too, sounded like a sour note to some, because the sisters had come from Switzerland.

None of this should have been surprising, since the sisters had decided to accept an invitation offered by Colton Catholics to move their school there.[64] But they still resided in Uniontown while their new convent was being built, with stone provided by Michael Schultheis.

This was a time of an uneasy truce, when it was generally understood that peace would fall with the departure of the nuns. Then, suddenly, without warning or expectation, Joehren closed the sisters' school. He simply stalked into the classrooms and ordered the children to leave.[65] Not even the superior had been informed. The sisters, nearly paralyzed with fright, took refuge in their convent. The following Sunday, Joehren got up into the pulpit of St. Boniface and announced that hereafter Catholics were forbidden to send children to the sisters' school "under the penalty of being refused the sacraments."

This was the last straw. The lines were now clearly drawn: Uniontown versus Colton. Some members of St. Boniface parish went to Mass on Sundays in St. Gall's Church in Colton, and some members of St. Gall's Church attended Mass in St. Boniface. They were not on speaking terms, of course, but sometimes when buggies passed one another, going in opposite directions, the drivers would use their whips to beat their adversary's horses.[66] None of this was conducive to the union of hearts and wills appropriate in the lives of Christians.

By this time, matters were out of hand. Mother Johanna held a promissory note signed by Joehren for five hundred dollars, with the Palouse Church as collateral. She turned the note over to Father Frei, who called Joehren into court for non-payment. In other words he sued Joehren in civil court.[67] But Joehren had no money, he had spent all, and more, on the foundations of the new church, for which the Colton Catholics owed one thousand dollars. Joehren had been unable to complete the church because the previous year was a disaster for farmers.[68] It had rained so much in the summer they could not gather in their crops. A great national depression had also reduced the supply of money available, and Joehren could not pay on the note.[69]

So the sheriff of Whitman County, John Luthrum by name, announced a public auction for the sale of the Palouse church. This looked like a sacrilege but Luthrum meant business. On the 29th day of September 1894, at the hour of two in the afternoon and on the steps of the courthouse in Colfax, he sold the church to the highest bidders.[70] And who were these? They were Michael Schultheis of Colton and William Codd of Colfax, acting for Nicholas Frei and Father Barnabas Held of Spokane. They bought St. Anthony church and presented it to the Palouse congregation.

FATHER FREI IS SUSPENDED BY THE BISHOP

The lawsuit against Joehren had been filed on June 28, 1894. About six weeks later Father Frei received a letter from Bishop Junger "announcing that Father Frei was hereby deposed from his office as Pastor [of Colton] and chaplain and was not allowed to perform any priestly functions in his diocese...."[71] And the reasons? None were given. "The Catholics of Colton," Mother Johanna reported,

> were in great distress when they heard the sad news. For two consecutive Sundays no services were held in the Colton church.
> Soon after, the Bishop appointed Rev. Father Barnabas Held of Spokane to attend the place. Being already in charge of Sacred Heart Hospital, as chaplain, the Rev. Father found it nigh impossible to assume additional duties. The bishop then allowed Rev. Father J. Burri of Genesee to attend Colton, while Father Frei ministered in his place in Genesee, in the diocese of Boise. The people were greatly impressed by Father Frei's capable administration. The Right Reverend Bishop Glorieux of Boise offered him to join his diocese. But Father Frei declined, saying, 'I will not abandon the Sisters. Besides, I have done nothing wrong and will not, by departing, convey the

idea that I had to go. God will in his own good time restore what belongs to me.' He frequently made his trip to and from Genesee on foot. The congregation of Colton did not forget their good Pastor, however. On his namesday, July 25, they presented him with a buggy. We Sisters bought him a nice bay horse, 'Fannie' from Mr. H. Streibich.[72]

THE SISTERS MOVE TO COLTON

The sisters left Uniontown when their new convent in Colton was ready.

It was a depressing matter, for we had grown fond of Uniontown and hated to leave it. But we were braced to the sacrifice by many sad incidents which had occurred during the last year of our stay. The little children even had learned to show disrespect to their formerly loved so much Catechist, Father Frei. The Sisters who had taught and loved those children shared no better. Petty annoyances were occasionally carried on against us in the dark of the night.

On the 27th of November we left Uniontown for our new convent at Colton. Some farmers from Colton helped us to move our belongings. Our Community numbered at that time 23 professed Sisters and 5 Novices. Our 13 boarders came along with us. The day school was also being taught in the new building.

The faculties had not yet been restored to Father Frei. On December 11 the bishop sent a young priest as Pastor of Colton, the Rev. Father H. Frencken. Everybody was glad to get a priest, but they felt sad to see him take the place of Father Frei. Colton had no parsonage, and we had to find headquarters for the priest in our house. Father Frei retired into a small room of an outbuilding with the chickens as his nearest neighbors. He was greatly comforted in his severe trials by the dedicated kindness of the Rev. Father J. Burri of Genesee and F. Hartleib of Moscow, who often visited him and tried their best to lighten his burden.[73]

Father Frei, meanwhile, had appealed to the Apostolic Delegate, Archbishop Francesco Satolli, and had petitioned him for an investigation of his cause. At the same time George Bauer, a clerk of the Colton church trustees submitted a report in support of Frei's petition.

His Excellency ordered an investigation, and appointed Very Reverend Louis Schram, V.G. of Vancouver, and Rev. L. Justes of Ellensburg to conduct it.

The two appointees arrived on January 27, 1895, and held session in Colton on the two following days. All who were concerned in the matter, were placed under oath and their statements were recorded. On January 21, the investigation continued at Uniontown in the same manner and form, but the results of the proceedings were not made known. The investigators left on January 24. They sent their report to Msgr. L. Satolli in February.[74]

ST. BONIFACE SUES ST. GALL'S

It was now time for the treasurer of St. Boniface, Father Joehren's front man, to collect on Colton's promissory note. Mr. Henry Michels probably felt a certain complacency in undertaking this godly parish duty when he filed as plaintiff in the suit in January 1895.[75] Whether Colton Catholics had the money to pay or not was moot. They simply refused to do so because Father Frei had been deposed as their pastor.

The defense, of course, employed attorneys, "Hanna, McCloskey and Ettinger," who responded to the allegations of the plaintiff with twelve statements, mostly humbug, covering three legal size pages. To this the plaintiff replied, tartly, that "defense arguments one to twelve were sham, frivolous, redundant, argumentative and irrelevant." That about covered it. The trial was set for Monday, October 7, 1895.[76]

THE DEPARTURE OF FATHER JOEHREN

At last the terrible ordeal of the Sisters and Father Frei was coming to an end. On May 13, 1895, Bishop Junger dispatched a letter to Frei. In this Junger fully restored Frei as pastor and chaplain to the sisters, acknowledging at the same time that "he had been imposed upon regarding the case and he protested that from now on he would be a lifelong friend."[77] Actually His Lordship lived only seven months longer, but he did his best to make amends to Father Frei. Anthony Joehren did not fare so well. He was severely reprimanded. He left Uniontown and the Northwest forever, a wiser, humbled man, who nonetheless expressed the hope that the sisters would someday establish a new convent near his Wisconsin parish.[78]

There is an interesting sequel to all of this, an unexpected revelation from the past that illustrates a terrible lesson: violence begets violence. St. Boniface parish had been in turmoil for a decade. Peace did not descend upon it when Anthony Joehren departed. The new pastor, a man of peace, was confronted with controversy also, as if the so-called pious Catholics of the settlement could not clear the bone from their throats. More about this will appear later.

THE JESUITS AND THE BISHOP OF NESQUALLY

In Spokane, Father Mackin had been pastor of the parish. Tall and rosy Irish in complexion, with long white hair flowing like a mane almost to his shoulders, he was a very attractive priest in a benevolent, despotic manner.[79] He was the kind of cleric who enjoyed lawn socials and he was as much at home in the parlors of the wealthy as he was in the kitchens of the poor. Much concerned about Spokane's orphans, he appealed to the Franciscan Sisters in Glen Riddle, Pennsylvania, for sisters to start an orphanage in Spokane, and he appealed to the Jesuit superior, Father Cataldo, for land to put it on.

Father Rebmann, the first president of Gonzaga College, shared Mackin's interests in the orphans, but in most respects the two men were not compatible. Many tensions gradually arose between them, creating a non-confidence attitude of the Gonzaga community toward Rebmann. Thus he was relieved as president on January 10, 1890 and Mackin succeeded him.

The change came as a shock to many, especially to Rebmann, who spent the next three weeks offering tearful goodbyes to his bewildered friends who could not understand why he was being assigned to St. Ignatius Mission in Montana.

Mackin, too, was bewildered. He decided to make a retreat at Sacred Heart Mission in Idaho, but enroute at Oaksdale, he found the snow so deep he had to turn back. A short time later, old Father Joset joined him in Spokane. He arrived on March 5, on a stretcher, more dead than alive. After a serious fall at DeSmet, Joset was injured so badly that no hope was held for his recovery. Although he was eighty years old, he recovered, and lived for ten more years to brag about it. And brag he did, in a loud voice, which comes naturally for old people who are hard of hearing.

GRASSI'S DEATH

Instead of Joset, who was almost indestructible, it was Father Grassi who died. He had taken Conrardy's place on the Umatilla mission with characteristic gusto.[80] He found the Umatilla school closed, because of the Indian agent's high-handed dealings, and the sisters were gone. The first Jesuit in eastern Oregon, he began his work by moving the church to a site about one-half mile eastward. Then he turned his attention to building a new school.

About five years earlier, in 1885, a certain Francis Anthony Drexel, a famous banker in Philadelphia, went to bed for the last time and died, leaving to his two daughters, Katherine and Elizabeth, a fortune totalling, it was said, $15,000,000. Katherine, at the suggestion of Pope Leo XIII, became a nun, the foundress of the Sisters of the Blessed Sacrament. Through the Catholic Indian Bureau she and her sister channelled some of the income of their inheritance into the Indian missions of the Northwest. Through the Bureau, then, Grassi received $6,000 from Mother Drexel for his St. Joseph's Mission School.[81] Grassi then begged Mother General of the Franciscan Sisters of Glen Riddle to send four sisters to help him.

Mother General, bless her, dispatched to Umatilla four of the sisters, who opened their school on March 10, 1890. Thirteen apprehensive pupils appeared on the first day. Eleven days later on March 21, Grassi died. The cause of his death was said to be pneumonia, but the more elementary fact of overwork undoubtedly accounted for it. On the previous day, a telegram had been sent to Gonzaga calling for a priest to assist the dying man. Father Folchi set out at once for Umatilla. With Folchi at his side Grassi breathed his last. He was buried beneath the mission church, with his boots still on.

SISTERS OF ST. FRANCIS

During the same summer, Mackin in Spokane received a favorable reply from Mother General in Glen Riddle. The first sisters arrived in Spokane on August 22, 1890, to establish St. Joseph's Orphanage. Their building, on a large plot of gravel near the river some seven blocks from Gonzaga, was almost completed when they came, and occupied on October 4. The fairy godmother, or principal benefactress of the orphans was Mrs. James Monaghan, whose husband was another local "capitalist" on Mackin's list. Though a wealthy woman with a multi-storied mansion to maintain, Mrs. Monaghan refused to have servants, saying that she could do the housework herself and give the money she saved to the orphanage.[82]

Even this was not always enough. One of the fathers at Gonzaga, it was said, reported to the president that the Franciscan Sisters had no money for food for the orphans. The president inquired about the money on hand at the college.

"About two hundred dollars. It is all we have."

"Give it to the sisters," the president said. "God will provide."[83]
God did provide or Gonzaga would have ceased to be.

FATHER WILLIAM DWYER AND THE BIG BEND MISSION

Among the early diocesan priests in eastern Washington was Father William Dwyer, a gentle, sensitive priest who labored faithfully as a missionary or "circuit rider" over a vast territory containing so few Catholics and so many jackrabbits that no one bothered to count either.[84] Dwyer, first generation Irish, was twenty-five years old when he was ordained to the priesthood by Bishop Frederick Baraga, the most renowned Indian missionary in that part of America, and the first bishop of Marquette.[85] For twenty-four years Dwyer served in the Marquette Diocese. Then, for reasons of health, he came west to work in the Nesqually Diocese.

In 1888, Bishop Junger appointed him to the care of "Sacred Heart Mission of the Big Bend," which included all of the Catholics north of Sprague and Harrington, stretching from Cheney on the east to Waterville and the Columbia River on the west. This was an area about 125 miles in length and in some places 75 miles in width, almost ten thousand square miles in that extent. If this were not enough, Bishop Glorieux of Boise requested Dwyer, an old man by contemporary standards, to serve as pastor for the Coeur d'Alene mining district in northern Idaho, including Wallace and Mullan.[86]

"When Father Dwyer came to these missions there were few communities of any size ... Cheney, Medical Lake, Davenport, Wilbur, and the army post of Fort Spokane. In the rest of the area the settlers were widely scattered."[87] The mission owned only two pieces of property, land deeded to the church on February 2, 1881, by Medical Lake pioneer Andrew Lefevre, and a small wooden church at Cheney, called St. Rose of Lima. This was begun by Father Giorda on September 10, 1881, on a lot purchased from the Northern Pacific Railroad.[88] Father Aloysius Jacquet from Gonzaga completed it two years later. There was no rectory, no barn for Dwyer's horse, and not much money.

Old Andrew Lefevre was the Macaenas. He built a huge brick house with fourteen rooms and five fireplaces near the railroad depot and invited Father Dwyer to occupy one of the rooms. The priest, undoubtedly bewildered by the bigness and emptiness of his mission, gratefully accepted the offer and made his home in Medical Lake, where there was no church till the following year, 1889. With the help of Lefevre, Dwyer built it and called it St. Ann.[89]

One can only imagine the rest, the long days on horseback beneath the relentless sun, the lonely hours in local trains, crossing the drab plateau of scab rock and scattered farms, the depressing task of organizing small congregations of Catholics who had not seen a priest for decades, the weariness and pain in a sick old man. Dwyer survived it until October 1896, when he retired, worn out and ill.[90] In May 1910, he became a patient in Sacred Heart Hospital in Spokane. He died there, five months later, on November 28, aged seventy years, forgotten by almost all except the sisters who nursed him, as poor and helpless as when he entered the world. His fate was not unlike many of the church's pioneers.

12

THE IRISH ARE COMING

1890–1895

Spokane at this time, was enjoying a boom. During the previous summer, which was hot and dry, both Seattle and Spokane had extensive fires that were called "disasters," but in reality had burned up most of the worthless pioneer shacks in both cities.[1] Seattle, which had not yet emerged as the Northwest's principal city, was rebuilding slowly and with considerable anxiety. Spokane, on the other hand, because of recent discoveries of the greatest silver mines in America some fifty miles east, was experiencing unprecedented prosperity. New parishes were required as the population increased.[2] The Jesuits were still in charge, a situation that Father Cataldo deplored. He had entreated Bishop Junger for sometime to take over the principal church, Our Lady of Lourdes, a flourishing on-the-other-side-of-the-river parish with more than three hundred children in its school.[3]

In the early part of 1890, after Mackin had been installed as president of the college, Junger agreed to meet Cataldo at Gonzaga to resolve Spokane's problems.

The Jesuits had purchased a large section of Fairmount Cemetery for a Catholic burial ground. They had also established St. Ignatius Prep, under Mr. Thomas Purcell,[4] for older boys whom the sisters in the parochial school could not accommodate. Under Father Van Gorp they built a new church called St. Joseph's, on the north side. Thus they found themselves committed to the care of three churches, two elementary schools and a college, and a cemetery for Catholics only, in addition to St. Michael's mission north of town and the rural missions for whites in all of Pend Oreille and Stevens Counties.

DIOCESAN PRIESTS COME TO SPOKANE

On Thursday, May 1, 1890, Father Emil Kauten, a diocesan priest from Seattle, arrived at Gonzaga with the news that he had been appointed by his Lordship as the new pastor of Our Lady of Lourdes parish. Kauten was accompanied by Father Meweuse, pastor of Sprague. The bishop arrived on Monday and visited the boys in the college, giving them a holiday, for which they cheered him lustily, as though he had just endowed them all with eternal life.[5]

Cataldo was away until the evening of May 15. The bishop blessed the new St. Joseph's Church that morning without him. Kauten celebrated the Mass *coram episcopo*, the Gonzaga choir rendered Battman's Mass in F, and Van Gorp preached to the congregation of two hundred. That evening Cataldo returned, more willing to give the bishop certain Jesuit properties than the bishop was to receive them.

On Friday morning, May 16, 1890, the bishop and the Jesuit Superior confronted one another. They came to terms without blows or threats of any kind and these were recorded in the college diary as follows.

> The City of Spokane Falls has been divided into 4 sections destined to become 4 different parishes. The river is the division line east and west. Howard street is the division line north and south. The bishop will take charge of 3 parishes: the fourth one will be left to the Society: But, until the Bishop is able to send another priest to help Fr. Kautens the newly appointed Pastor, we will remain in charge of the actual old parish whilst Fr. Kautens will attend himself to St. Joseph's Church on the North Side. Father Cataldo, in the name of the Society, dispossessed himself in favor of the Bishop of all the different Church properties which of late we had acquired with our own money, namely, 1) the place where the actual St. Joseph Church is built; (the building created at our own expense will also be the property of the bishop.) 2) a site in Cannon's addition lately purchased; 3) a site [blank]; 4) the site of the church of 'Our Lady of Lourdes' and of the parochial schools with the buildings. The only place therefore reserved to us is the site on which St. Ignatius school is built: and this we are free to sell when we deem it most convenient. The Bishop signed this agreement with his own hand, being over glad of the conditions in which he was taking possession of this new parish.[6]

It should be noted at this point, I think, that Father Cataldo was much relieved by what had occurred and the bishop went back to his so-called palace with more on his mind than his dinner.

MORE SISTERS, HOSPITALS AND SCHOOLS

During that summer of 1890, two other new congregations of sisters arrived in the Northwest, both of them destined to play important roles in the church's history of Washington's west coast. On August 14, two Sisters of St. Joseph of Peace detrained at Bellingham Bay.[7] They had come from New Jersey, from one extremity of the continent to another, to establish St. Joseph's General Hospital. Construction on this hospital on Fairhaven Hill, which suggests a cemetery more than a hospital site, was begun in September and four months later, on January 9, 1891, dedication ceremonies were celebrated. In attendance were two old friends, Father Hylebos from Tacoma, already a local celebrity, and Father John Baptist Boulet from Tulalip. The latter, growing old gracefully, was now using his spare time in hand-setting type for printing a quaint little magazine called "The Youth's Companion."[8]

Boulet, it will be recalled, had taken the place of Chirouse at Tulalip when the Oblate was recalled to Canada. That was twelve years ago, almost to the day.[9] Boulet had inherited a wilderness, but with it came the spirit of Chirouse. He built the first church in Bellingham (called "Sehome" then) in 1889 and offered the first Mass in it on August 22. Bishop Junger dedicated it on June 23, 1890, in honor of the Assumption in the presence of eight hundred people, an incredible audience for that part of the world.[10]

By that time, Boulet had built another church called St. Mary's, at Edison, a settlement near Anacortes. Patrick Smith had donated the land for this, Boulet designed it, and fourteen other people helped him put it all together.[11] Two years later, Boulet built a third church at Sumas and he called this one St. Ann.[12] Far from running out of steam, he opened a parochial school at Bellingham, in a small two-room house near Whatcom Creek, then sweet-talked two Sisters of St. Joseph of Peace into taking charge of it.[13]

Meanwhile, he had been visiting the little town of Ferndale at regular intervals, offering Mass each time in the home of B.N. McDonough, a Dublin Irishman, who had come to the Lummi Reservation after the Civil War and opened a trading post. The McDonoughs instructed the Indians there in the Catechism and reserved a room in their home for a chapel. In 1893, Boulet with his friends, built St. Joseph's Church and three years later the bishop made it a parish and appointed Boulet its first pastor.[14] Later, when the church was moved and rededicated, a special train from

New Whatcom brought three hundred and fifty people to witness the ceremony. They were friends of Boulet's, obviously so fond of him that they followed him wherever he went.

One cannot say that Boulet took advantage of them. Rather, he tried gently to please them all. While he gave instructions in the faith or entertained guests in his modest rectory in Ferndale, he composed his type for printing another mini-magazine for his friends. He called it *Good Tidings A Monthly Periodical Devoted to Giving Valuable Religious Information on Catholic Faith and Practice, and Well Adapted for Sunday Reading. Especially in Sections of the Country Seldom Visited by a Priest.* On his little press, he also printed Blanchet's *Historical Sketches* and Brouillet's *Authentic Account of the Murder of Dr. Whitman,* all of which speaks eloquently about his dedication to the interests of his people. [15] He was like Father Adrian Croquet, even in appearance, the holy man of Whatcom County.

ANOTHER VARIETY OF DOMINICANS

The second group of sisters who arrived in the summer of 1890 were Dominicans. Eventually they were referred to as the Congregation of the Holy Cross. [16] On August 30, Sister Mary Anselm Weber and six companions from Newburgh, New York, alighted at Aberdeen, a bustling lumber town, and looked around for a place to open a hospital. They succeeded in finding a small frame house on Second and H Streets, where they admitted their first patient on September 22. In the following year, they completed construction of a frame building at Fifth and G Streets, "the largest and best building on Gray's Harbor," named it St. Joseph's and moved in with their patients. They also built a school, which they called St. Mary's.

The pastor in Aberdeen was Father Deichmann, a kind of roust-about priest who could be counted on wherever he was sent. He had been appointed only three years earlier as a missionary in charge of southwestern Washington with headquarters at Aberdeen. He packed all of his personal goods and all of the mission supplies and put them on the steamer called *Telephone* (a very odd name for a ship), then took the train to his new home. While the ship was docked at Astoria, it caught fire and was completely destroyed with all of its contents. [17]

Poor Deichmann started over. On October 14, 1888, he called a meeting of the Catholics in Aberdeen to discuss ways and means for building a church. Plans were made and the church was built. Bishop Junger dedicated it on September 15, 1889, under the titles of Sts. Aegidius and Mary. [18] Three months later, on Christmas Day, it burned to the ground. It was the second time, in little more than a year, that all of

Deichmann's personal effects and the church's goods were destroyed. There was no insurance and nothing was saved. But the plucky priest did not give up. With the support of his people, he built another church, which still carried the scent of new wood when Sister Mary Anselm and her Dominicans arrived.

SISTERS OF PROVIDENCE NEW FOUNDATIONS

One must not suppose that while these more lately arrived congregations of sisters were getting settled that the pioneer congregations were resting on their laurels. Quite the contrary. The Sisters of Providence, for example, between 1888 and 1895 completed eight major projects. In February, 1888, they established St. Francis Xavier's School for Indians at Yakima. This functioned successfully until 1896 when it was forced to close by the withdrawal of government support.[19]

On March 10, 1889, the Sisters opened up the first permanent St. Patrick's Hospital in Missoula. This replaced the temporary hospital established in a private home on approximately the same site.[20] On June 3, 1890, Sister Mary Conrad and Sister Mary Nazareth, arrived at Port Townsend where they opened the first St. John's Hospital in a small house in back of the present hospital. A permanent St. John's was built and dedicated on August 5, 1891.[21] On July 1 a year later, two other Sisters of Providence arrived at Wallace, Idaho. There they followed the common pattern: they opened a temporary hospital, called "Providence" on December 18, 1891. This was followed with a permanent Providence Hospital, which was completed on July 22, 1892.[22]

Another hospital, called St. Elizabeth's, was opened in Yakima in a rented house at Naches and Yakima Avenue. Construction of a new building at Fourth and E streets was begun at once and the new St. Elizabeth's was occupied on August 23, 1892.[23] In Great Falls, five Sisters of Providence opened Columbus Hospital in a frame house that was located on three lots they had bought for $2600. They admitted their first patient the same day, September 23, 1892. On January 6, 1894, the second Columbus Hospital on Third Avenue and Sixteenth was occupied and during the same year a school of nursing was established.[24]

This is getting monotonous, but for the sake of the record I should include two more items. The first concerns St. Ignatius Hospital in Colfax. During 1892, the people of the towns of Palouse, Pullman, and Colfax, realizing the need for a Sisters' hospital somewhere in the district, asked Father Anton Joehren of Uniontown, the nearest priest, to help them secure the Sisters of Providence. On March 17, 1892, Joehren discussed the matter with Bishop Junger at Vancouver, and subsequently the sisters agreed to examine the three towns and select one. Colfax offered a tract of land, five thousand dollars in cash and free water in perpetuam, if the sisters would choose that town. This was an offer hard to refuse, so the sisters arrived. The sisters were Barnaby, Perpetua, and Jeanne of Jesus, each one prepared to nurse the sick. With them came Father Peter Kearns. St. Ignatius Hospital received its first patients on May 2, 1892.[25]

Finally, there was Portland. Old St. Vincent's Hospital had long since ceased to be adequate, despite its many new wings and additions. On July 14, 1895, Archbishop Gross presided over the dedication of a new St. Vincent's, which perched high on a hill west of the old city, a dark red brick edifice, like a military barracks guarding a moutain pass. Five days later the patients were transferred from the old frame hospital to the new, with some grumbling no doubt, and a few minor accidents. For the sisters, however, the progress occasioned by the new hospital would soon overwhelm them.[26]

SISTERS OF THE HOLY NAMES

While the Providence Sisters were producing hospitals like rabbits out of a hat, the Holy Names Sisters were building schools. Between 1859 and 1891, these sisters conducted schools in the following cities: Portland, Oregon City, St. Paul, Salem, The Dalles, Jacksonville, Idaho City, St. Michael's Mission in Oregon, Astoria, Baker City, Seattle, and Spokane. At each school a carefully composed journal was kept, providing for observers today an intimate glimpse into the busy lives of the sisters—their hardships, their little triumphs and joys—above all, their fortitude,[27] Included here are a few sample selections from these diaries.

[St. Mary's Academy, Portland] June 10, 1887
The scholastic year closes with the following statistics: pupils at the boarding school, 48; orphanage, 55; at day school, 410; total 513, of which 130 were taken gratis, and 209 partly so; 40 made their First Communion, 40 were confirmed, 7 were baptized, 74 took music, 27 took drawing and painting.[28]

[St. Mary's Academy, Portland] June 1, 1888
St. Flavia's Relics Enshrined. Sister Mary Delores having sent the wax work and robes of St. Flavia by Mother General, the installation of our dear little saint in our chapel took place this afternoon. The ceremony was performed by our Most Reverent Archbishop, assisted by the Reverend Fathers Beck of Eugene City, O'Dea of the city, Verhaag of East Portland and Rauw, our chaplain. She was carried into the chapel by the Misses J. O'Connor, C.

McGuinn, H.E. Edwards, and B. Hill.... The history of our little saint in brief, as far as we could learn is this: Flavia is her own name and not an imposed one. She was a young Roman girl who was put to death for the faith at the tender age of twelve years. Her body and the bodies of St. Jovian, St. Severin, and St. Victoria were brought from Rome by Most Reverent Archbishop Blanchet, who in 1845, descended to the catacombs himself several times and obtained the bodies of these four martyrs for his vicariate. [sic] On his return trip to Oregon where he arrived August 27, 1847, an altar had been erected on the after part of the ship, whereon Masses were said every day over the holy relics. [29]

[St. Paul's Academy, St. Paul] July 27, 1888

The orphanage in connection with St. Mary's Academy in Portland, which for years has been under the direction of the Sisters of the Holy Names of Jesus and Mary, has just been vacated and the remaining orphans transferred to our Mission of St. Paul, here to remain permanently. [30]

[St. Mary's Academy, Portland] April 21, 1889

The cornerstone of the new St. Mary's was laid today by His Grace, Most Reverend William H. Gross, C.SsR., D.D., assisted by the Reverend Fathers J. Rauw, chaplain, E.J. O'Dea of the Cathedral, B. Orth, rector of St. Lawrence, P.F. Gibney, rector of St. Patrick's, L. Verhaag rector of St. Francis East Portland, and G.B. Van Lin, rector of the Church of the Sacred Heart of Mary, Albina. Several hundred persons witnessed the ceremonies, which was not prolonged owing to the inclemency of the weather for rain was coming down in torrents. [31]

[Holy Names Academy, Seattle] August 1, 1890

Purchase In accordance with the desire of our Superior General, Mother Mary Baptist, we purchase a piece of land on which to build our future boarding school when circumstances will necessitate the change. The new property which is timber land we purchased from Mr. A. O'Meara for $15,000 cash. There are 27 2/3 acres. This tract is about five miles from the center of the city and beautifully situated on the shores of Puget Sound. We call it Villa Rosa in honor of our venerated Foundress, Mother Mary Rose. [32]

[Holy Names Academy, Spokane] July 29, 1891

Removal At last the welcome day has dawned upon us to move from the unhealthy surroundings of Main Street to our pleasant home, Academy of the Holy Names in Sinto Addition to the city of Spokane. However the convent school is retained on Main Street and will henceforth be a day school only. An effort was made by the Germans under the leadership of Reverend B[arnabas] H[eld], O.S.B., to establish a German English school on Fifth Street under the care of the Benedictine Sisters from Uniontown, Washington. [33]

[St. Mary's Academy, The Dalles] September 2, 1891

About 1:00 p.m. a terrible fire broke out and raged uncontrolled until evening. Nearly half of the town was destroyed, every building being swept from eighteen blocks, covering an area of thirty acres. For hours the flames soared above the tallest poplars, and every moment brought them nearer to the convent. The more prudent among the Sisters donned their best and prepared to move out, but when the fire was only two blocks away Divine Providence turned the course of the wind and all danger to us was happily averted. Even when the danger seemed imminent, it was touching to see the confidence the people placed in the Sisters. Many brought their valuables to the convent although it was much nearer to the burning district than their own residences.[34]

THE COMING OF THE IRISH: O'DEA AND O'REILLY

By this time, more priests of Irish descent were beginning to appear on the scene. Eddie O'Dea, everybody's pet at St. Michael's College and student for a brief time at St. Ignatius College in San Francisco, entered the seminary in Montreal and was ordained for the archdiocese on December 23, 1882.[36] Eddie had been born in Dorchester, near Boston, twenty-six years before, the son of Edward and Ellen Kelly O'Dea.[37] This, of course, qualified him to be a "Boston Irish" the highest of all pedigrees and, in the eyes of some, the best recommendation for advancement in the church. He was regarded as a great catch by the priests of the archdiocese and by others as the personification of the benefits of conducting a diocesan college.

In addition to pastoral work in Oregon, Father O'Dea served as the archbishop's secretary from 1882 to 1892. During this period, on June 29, 1890, the archbishop ordained another promising Irish lad in St. Mary's Cathedral. This was Charles Joseph O'Reilly, who, like O'Dea, was destined to become a bishop.

O'Reilly had been born at St. John in New Brunswick on January 4, 1862, the third of six children of Peter O'Reilly and Brigid [sic] nee Walsh, both natives of St. John.[38] The parents of both, however, had come from Ireland, so their children, especially their third, were characterized by features plainly from the old sod. Charles, for his legacy, possessed shining black hair, black eyebrows and eyes, a long thin neck and general good looks that equipped him for a career on the stage. His melodious Irish voice and keen interest in studies, not to mention his piety, indicated that he would someday be a priest, perhaps a bishop, so his parents sent him to St. Joseph's University at Memramcook when he was only sixteen. This university was conducted by the Fathers of the Holy Cross, who awarded O'Reilly a Master of Arts degree. This seems to have precipitated a major decision in the family, for immediately after Charles' graduation, they all moved to Portland, Oregon.

In Portland, at the callous age of twenty-one, Charles secured the position of principal of St. Michael's College, which occupied him from 1883 to 1887. During these four years, I suspect, he was struggling with "a vocation," a call to the priesthood that had been there all along. Whatever the case, he finally gave in and entered the Grand Seminary at Montreal for the Archdiocese of Oregon City.

After ordination, he was assigned to the pastorship of Oswego and Tegardville (Tigard) and adjoining missions. He built two churches in four years, a tribute to his parishioners as much as to himself, but the archbishop was very impressed by him. He placed O'Reilly in charge of a city parish, Portland's unfinished church of the Immaculate Heart of Mary, which had a large debt. His Grace also appointed him the editor of the *Catholic Sentinel*. [39]

In both positions, O'Reilly enjoyed an unusual amount of exposure for a young priest. He soon attracted the favorable attention of other bishops, not to mention his own, and his fellow priests, who liked to make predictions, were saying that he was "episcopabilis," and that the Pope had his eye on him. No one, however, expected him to become the bishop of a diocese that had fewer Catholics than a large parish.

As editor, O'Reilly was required to study his territory and his readership, and this provided him with the broader vision that served him well. Unfortunately, not all bishops in the Northwest enjoyed a similar opportunity. This accounted, in part at least, for a kind of parochialism that tainted the history of some dioceses in later years. O'Reilly would be the first bishop of Baker City, the toughest possible assignment for any Oregon priest. He was as well prepared for it as anyone could be.

THE DEATHS OF THREE PIONEERS

While Oregon rejoiced in her new priests, with their youthful holy zest burning like candles at both ends, three of the Northwest's early apostles passed to their well-earned rewards. Two of them were the first priests ordained in Washington, the Oblates Pandosy and Chirouse. [40]

Father Charles Pandosy died first, on February 6, 1891, at Penticton, British Columbia. His body was brought back to the northern Okanogan Mission whither he had gone after leaving the American Northwest, and there it was buried on the shores of the lake near Kelowna. All trace of his grave has been lost. [41]

Father Chirouse lived little more than a year longer. In December of

1891, he had suffered a stroke and was confined at St. Mary's Hospital in New Westminster, British Columbia, until his death on May 28, 1892. He was buried on the banks of the Fraser River.

Another great loss to the church was Stephen McCormick, the zealous layman who had assisted in the brith of the *Catholic Sentinel* and was its editor from 1874 to 1880, one of its greatest periods. [42] McCormick was also the publisher of early Catholic apologetical works like Brouillet's *Authentic Account of the Murder of Dr. Whitman and Other Missionaries.* He had left Portland to become editor of *The Monitor,* the Archdiocese of San Francisco's prestigious weekly. Born in Dublin on December 26, 1829, one of twelve children, he came honestly by his streak of piety from his godly parents. Until the day of his death in San Franciso on August 12, 1891, he attended Mass every day and devoutly recited the rosary.

THE NEW ST. IGNATIUS CHURCH

At St. Ignatius, Montana, Father Rebmann regarded himself as an exile for reasons he did not understand. But he held no grudge against anyone. Characteristically, once he became acquainted he was happy wherever he lived. Like other priests then, he had succumbed to the itch for building, the most common affliction in the church at that time. In the spring of 1891, when Archbishop Gross was looking for an excuse to move his cathedral, Rebmann was supervising the construction of a new mission church, destined after completion to be the largest in Montana. More than one million bricks were formed and baked on the ground for this stupendous undertaking, which commanded the attention of everyone in the valley.

St. Ignatius was in its heyday. Its renowned trade school, the first in Montana, operated shops in leather work, printing, carpentry, and other skills. Humming with cheerful toil, it was more prosperous than any other mission activity before or since, partly because of the support of its farm lands and partly because of modest government subsidies that allowed the mission to employ laymen to direct the students. In addition to the shops, there were three other schools at the mission, one for boys, who were taught by the Jesuits, one for older girls conducted by the Sisters of Providence, and a more recently established kindergarten, the apple of Rebmann's eye, opened on April 2, 1890, by the Ursulines. Priests from St. Ignatius supplied the spiritual needs of Catholics for the vast surrounding area, including little towns like Polson and Horse Plains, where a new church had been erected the previous year. [43]

Rebmann's monument required two years to complete, then several more years for Brother Joseph Carignano, the Jesuit who served alternately as cook and artist, to execute on its walls the fifty-eight murals, which soon attracted so much admiration that St. Ignatius became one of Montana's showplaces.[44] Carignano had been drafted by Rebmann, as a kind of concession by the superior, Father Cataldo. Whenever the Jesuits put up a new church, they urged Cataldo to assign Carignano to be their cook, so that he could paint murals in their churches, too. Carignano, it was said, was not the best cook in the mission; that distinction was borne proudly by another Italian brother, Achilles Carfagno, who was also an accomplished carpenter. It was obvious then, that when the Jesuits sought Carignano's services, they were placing the beauty of God's house above their stomachs. That is the way it should have been.

JESUITS AT YAKIMA

Over in Yakima, there was a French Jesuit in charge, Father Victor Garrand, who had been a missionary in Syria. It is no secret that Frenchmen like to eat well, so Garrand had a fine orchard, grape vines and a garden behind the rectory, which he called his "little paradise."[45] He also had Carfagno, the best cook, who built a small barn, a stable, and a carpenter's shop on the premises, when he was not engaged in the kitchen making omelets.

Garrand had three priests with him, a frail little band to wrest from the devil all the villages and settlements of Central Washington. There was Adrian Sweere, a Hollander who had devoted his early years to the Osage mission, a square-jawed, good natured fellow who was never in a hurry. Another was John Raiberti whose origins were somewhat mysterious. Raiberti was not much help especially on the windy plateau because in any breeze he would have blown away. The Indians called him "the ghost" since he was only skin and bones.

The newest member of the Yakima community was Augustine Laure, who claimed the distinction of being the first Jesuit to work in Seattle. Laure's virtue was proved beyond doubt by the fact that he persevered in living with Prefontaine for the whole of Lent in 1890. There is some mystery here too, insofar as Prefontaine is concerned, for on previous occasions, when the bishop had sent a young priest, James Cunningham by name, to live with him, Prefontaine assigned him a room placed inconveniently between the kitchen and the dining room, so that he would get discouraged and go away. This is also what he did to Laure. But Laure remained, to spy out the land, as it were, for the Jesuits who were eager to start a school in Seattle.

BEGINNINGS OF SEATTLE COLLEGE

Father Leopold Van Gorp, who was the Jesuits' treasurer, a tall thin man with a heavy shock of white hair, had also visited Seattle for the purpose of buying land. Dispatched by Cataldo a year after Seattle's great fire, which relieved the city of many ugly shacks and unsafe jerry-built structures, Van Gorp purchased eight lots along Madison and Broadway for $18,000. He made a down payment then and there, and provided the balance when the deed was delivered in February 1891.

At approximately this time, Prefontaine's own school project was taking shape, in the form of a two-story-with-attic brick building at Sixth and Spring, a nicely proportioned edifice with an elaborate brick design around the top of the walls. Capped with a gable roof, which confirmed its contemporary appearance as "a college," it was called St. Francis Hall. It contained two large classrooms, each with eight elongated windows, and a large auditorium on the second floor. Anticipating the completion of St. Francis Hall, and having persuaded the Holy Names Sisters to provide teachers, Prefontaine opened his school in the basement of Our Lady of Good Hope Church. [46] But he soon realized that he was over his head in an activity about which he knew very little. For once in his life, he appealed to the bishop for help.

There is no doubt that Bishop Junger knew and approved of the Jesuits's acquisition of land in Seattle. On April 11, 1891, he composed a letter to Cataldo requesting that the Jesuits take over "an already established boys' school," meaning St. Francis Hall. He added that the building for the school was for sale (Prefontaine himself owned it) and he wanted the Jesuits to start a third parish in Seattle. Junger was hopeful that Cataldo could comply with this request, for he had often visited Gonzaga College in Spokane and was very fond of it.

The closest Jesuit superior to Seattle was Garrand, whose abode was only one hundred miles distant, a little more by railway, a small matter in current practice. Theoretically, Seattle was part of his baliwick, so there was nothing unusual about Cataldo's orders to take over St. Francis Hall and start a new parish there.

Taking Sweere with him and leaving the ecstatic, over-zealous Laure in charge of Yakima, he entrained for Seattle. He arrived there on September 27, 1891. Two weeks earlier, on the feast of the Holy Name of Mary, Junger had formally established the new parish under the title of the Immaculate Conception. Thus, when Garrand and Sweere made their appearance, they were presented with an existing school in somebody else's building, located in the wrong parish, and a parish without anything but people, most of whom were regarded as poor.

Garrand was forty-four, a slightly balding French intellectual with a knack like Cecil B. DeMille's for processions, flowery novenas, and other spectacular altar celebrations. When he preached he sometimes wept and his people wept with him. They were very much attached to Garrand who worked too hard for his own good.

The two Jesuits lived in a rented house. They leased St. Francis Hall for a stiff $2,250 a year. Fortunately, the sisters consented to remain, and in that school year (1891–1892) they had 135 students, both boys and girls. The Jesuits' relations with Prefontaine were amicable, despite their oft repeated reminder that they must hasten to build their own school because the rent on St. Francis Hall was too high. Intended for the ears of their own parishioners, this subtle revelation of Prefontaine's greed undoubtedly reached Prefontaine, but there is no record of his objections. Like many capitalists, who make money on their investments, he was probably proud of the amount he received.

About this time, the Great Depression of 1893 struck Seattle. In Spokane, because of the discovery of the fabulous silver mines in the Coeur d'Alenes, the Jesuits at Gonzaga were scarcely aware of the hardships elsewhere. But Seattle was hard hit, and Garrand's efforts to raise money, even by borrowing, ended in failure. Through his family connections, Father Sweere was able finally to negotiate a loan in Amsterdam. Hence Garrand formally incorporated the School of the Immaculate Conception on June 30, 1893, then boldly started construction on a building on the Broadway property. What became Seattle College's first building slowly took shape in ponderous blocks of granite, which still stand.[47]

This building was blessed and dedicated on December 8, 1894. Four stories high, including a basement where the Jesuits lived, it served not only as a school, but as the parish church, which was located on the second floor and was entered by a long ramp from Madison. The church was two stories, "a chamber of worship that had three resplendent altars with enough statues for a cathedral and a sanctuary large enough to accommodate the oversized bishop, three priests and at least twenty-four altar boys."[48] As time progressed, it became the scene of such pageantry that even Hollywood would have been envious.

MORE ABOUT THE BENEDICTINES

The Benedictines, understandably, do not forget that they are the oldest order in the church. They have patiently endured for over fourteen centuries; stability therefore, is their hallmark. Their activities revolve around their abbey, a civilized kind of fortress that serves not only as a motherhouse for the monks, but also as a shrine of learning and culture for the entire area in which it is carefully guarded.

In 1890, Mount Angel was not as yet an independent abbey, for it was still attached to the mother abbey in Engelberg. It was called a priory and under its prior, Father Adelhelm Odermatt, a certain freedom of action was enjoyed, allowing the prior, for example, to make decisions in the use of local monks. Among these at Mount Angel were two, especially, who preferred to be in a parish or in some urban activity: Father Nicholas Frei, who pops up here and there in unexpected places; and Father Barnabas Held, the popular-as-Pied-Piper schoolmaster at Mount Angel College.

The bishops, hard pressed for zealous priests, were happy to use available Benedictines, particularly when specialized needs required them. The Benedictines, for instance, spoke German well. Certainly German speaking priests answered a specialized need, and Archbishop Gross, who came from a quasi-German background, did not overlook their potential usefulness in German colonies such as Mount Angel, to take but one example.[49] Nor were they overlooked by Bishop Junger whose diocese included the Palouse wheat country south of Spokane, settled mostly by Germans, many of them Catholics.

Gross was deeply concerned about the Germans in Portland. He invited his brother Redemptorists, whose origins were mostly German, to establish a parish in Portland, and on July 5, 1890, four priests and two brothers established St. Alphonsus Residence.[50] Among the priests were Father Charles Sigle and Father Mark Gross, a brother of the Archbishop. For reasons never given, Sigle and his colleagues changed their minds about Portland in March 1891.[51] They decided to abandon St. Alphonsus and to transfer their activities to Seattle where Bishop Junger had proposed their take-over of Sacred Heart parish and the Catholic cemetery. They assumed control of the Seattle parish on May 27, 1891.[52]

In the following year, Father William Lindner, a Redemptorist from Seattle, celebrated the first Mass in Everett, a lumber town thirty miles north. Everett lacked a church, so Lindner made use of the old public school on Broadway for this historic liturgy. Sometime in 1892, another Redemptorist, Father J.B. Cronin, selected a site for a church in the Riverside district and there a temporary frame church dedicated to Our Lady of Perpetual Help was begun in September.[53] Thus the Redemptorists were solidly established in the Puget Sound area by 1892.

But the problem of the Germans in Portland remained. Sometime in 1890, two Benedictines, Father E. Bolls and Father Nockter Meader, established for them a little chapel called St. Michael's. As a spiritual resort for the Germans, this did not last long because the neighborhood was settled by Italians, the latest wave of American immigrants. It came to be known as "Little Italy."[54] The more stolid Germans, unaccustomed to retreat in any form, but greatly outnumbered by the noisy, disorderly Italians, fled to St. Joseph's Church at Northwest Fifteenth and Couch Street.[55] This was declared a German national church and everybody was happy, especially the members of the St. Joseph Society, which had collected funds for the building.

Meanwhile, there was Tacoma. On July 16, 1891, Father William Evermann, a Benedictine from St. John's Abbey, Collegeville, arrived to arrange for a Benedictine parish in that city, heretofore under the singular care of Father Hylebos at St. Leo's. Bishop Junger, pleased with the addition of his staff, assigned Evermann to the little frame church of Our Lady of the Holy Rosary, and there, three days later, the first Mass was offered by him.[56] Junger dedicated this church on August 8 with ceremonies appropriate for the occasion.

Father Held in Spokane had not fared so well. First he purchased an abandoned sectarian church and moved it to a lot on Fifth and Bernard, where he renovated it and named it Sacred Heart.[57] The he bought a surplus public school and moved it next to the church. The two buildings, a second-hand church and a recycled school, were dedicated on November 21, 1891. Benedictine Sisters from Uniontown, as noted by the Holy Names Sisters in their *Chronicles*, assisted Father Held in teaching the boys, mostly of German origin. A dynamo of energy with the wheels always turning in his head, Held was not content with this. He rounded up the homeless boys he could find and made provision for them also, only God knows how.

Soon Father Held and his brother Benedictines had something more to evoke their tears. On May 3, 1892, the priory room at Mount Angel caught fire. "The building was quickly engulfed in flames. Everyone carried or threw out whatever he could. Meanwhile, monks, students, and lay people used bucket brigades and hoses to try to save the college building. They were successful, but the priory, chapel, seminary wing, and shops were smoking ruins. Only the college building and two other small buildings were still standing. The monks moved into these three buildings and began to try to rebuild their devastated priory."[58]

The Benedictines at St. John's Abbey in Collegeville soon learned about the disaster. Though little was being said, they had not given up the idea of a foundation in the Northwest, despite the unhappy venture lugubriously reported by Abbot Alexius Edelbrock ten years earlier. Mount Angel's fire renewed interest at St. John's. On August 14, 1892, Father Wolfgang Steinkagler, of the Holy Rosary parish in Tacoma, was requested by the abbot to locate a suitable monastery site somewhere in Washington. Steinkagler carefully examined the area between Seattle and Tacoma during the early part of 1893, but found all available land selling at a price too high for his purse. After a visit to Chehalis, where he met the sexton of the church there, a certain Mr. John Ferry, he purchased under Ferry's influence 160 acres of land at twenty-five dollars an acre. This land was located twenty miles west of Chehalis near a sawmill town called Dryad.[59] While this quarter-section had many charms, especially for milk cows who liked grass, it proved to be unsuitable for a college. Steinkagler's chagrin was the abbey's loss, $26,500 to be exact, but the land, too remote even for Carthusians, was theirs to enjoy. They had, at least, a stake in the West.

ST. MARTIN'S COLLEGE

Meanwhile, the new abbot of St. John's did not give up. His name was Abbot Bernard Locnikar. A relatively young-looking man, who bore the appearance of a dedicated engineering student, with his mouth set firmly and his dark, serious eyes gazing into the future, he seemed to be thinking of the great bridges he would build. Instead, he had visions of another abbey "in the evergreen state," which he had personally visited when Holy Rosary parish was organized.[60]

He returned to the Northwest two years later when another site four miles from Olympia became available. This was a tract of heavily timbered land at Woodland, later called Lacey. A Mr. A.H. Chambers of Olympia, dedicated friend of the Benedictines, had uncovered the availability of a nearly a section of land here at a price the Benedictines could afford. On September 22, 1893, Abbot Bernard first inspected the Dryad property, and expressed himself well pleased with it. He then visited Father Charles Claessens, pastor of Olympia, who earnestly hoped that the new Benedictine monastery and college would be located near Olympia. Abbot Bernard accompanied Chambers and Claessens to the Woodland site. The abbot climbed a hill through the thick brush, and having reached the top, paused for a moment, surveying the countryside with his dark eyes. "Right here my college will stand," he said. He ordered Father William Eversmann, pastor of Holy Rosary in Tacoma, to sell the Dryad property and to purchase the Woodland tract.

Chambers offered to help. He formed an organization to raise the funds, proposing to this group of Olympia businessmen that they take the Dryad property in exchange and buy the Woodland property for the Benedictines. Because of the current depression, however, they raised only $1,600, which they turned over to Father William.[61] Through their influence, the Woodland property was then put up for auction by the

State Land Commission for a minimum of ten dollars an acre. The auction was scheduled for the steps of the County Courthouse in Olympia.

When news about this circulated in the area, an anti-Catholic group known as the A.P.A., similar to the K.K.K. in their ideology and methods, made plans to attend the auction and outbid the Catholics.[62] On the day appointed, the crowd gathered. Then the auctioneer announced that the sale would strictly be for cash, and bidding began. Only the Benedictines had cash at hand, so they acquired on the spot title to 570 acres at ten dollars an acre.

About November 1, Father William left for Minnesota to confer with the abbot regarding the development of the college monastery. He found Abbot Bernard on his death bed. Locnikar died on November 7, 1894, and was succeeded as Abbot by Peter Engel, who had a bushy black beard. As soon as Abbot Peter's election was confirmed by Rome, as required, he gave approval for the construction of "St. Martin's," the name his predecessor had selected before his death.[63] On March 2, 1895, Father Demetrius Jueneman, assistant pastor of St. Boniface church in east Minneapolis, received orders from the new abbot to proceed to Tacoma at once and to make immediate preparations for the erection of a college building, which was to be ready to receive students in September of the same year. Father Demetrius, who looked more like a contemplative monk than an entrepreneur, arrived in Tacoma on March 13. Father William, meanwhile, had engaged Mr. Joseph McCabe of Tacoma as architect.

"The plan provided for a structure 50 x 100 feet with four floors. The walls for the first story were to be of brick, and the superstructure of wood. The first floor provided for a kitchen, two dining rooms, a furnace room and a lavatory. The second [entered by a different ground level porch], provided for a parlor, a chapel, several private rooms for the faculty. The third floor was devoted to study halls and class rooms and the fourth floor to dormitories, trunk rooms and quarters for the prefects."[64]

Construction was begun on April 12, 1895. By early August the building was nearly completed and by the end of the same month, a prospectus announcing St. Martin's College was distributed to friends and interested persons. The opening date was set for September 11. Three days earlier, the staff arrived from St. John's in Collegeville, rested and expectant. There is always a special tang in the air for pioneers, and members of the college faculty were aware of it when they gathered for the first time. They were Father Oswald Baran, Prior and Director;

Fathers Wolfgang Steinkagler, Demetrius Jueneman and Benedict Schmidt. Assisting them were "Brothers William, Francis and Herman."[65]

When the opening day of school arrived, only one student appeared, Angus McDonald, Father Wolfgang's altar boy from Shelton. For several months Angus was the only student. By the end of the year however, the enrollment was "about one dozen." Like Gonzaga College in Spokane, St. Martin's early beginnings were bleak enough to dampen the spirits of even Pollyanna.

THE ARRIVAL OF THE DOMINICAN PRIESTS

For Archbishop Gross, these were not the happiest years. His health, never robust, was rapidly declining, although his zeal continued to burn as before. Dispensing with a secretary, he wrote most of his correspondence himself, writing hastily in a large hand that covered a page with a few lines. As a young priest traveling in the missions of the south, he was noted for his fire and brimstone sermons. Now he had mellowed. He spoke often about his concern for Portland's Germans, many of whom had fallen away from the church, and about St. Thomas Aquinas, the brilliant Dominican theologian.

In September of 1885, he had invited the Dominicans to come to Portland, but the provincial was ill at the time, and nothing came of it.[66] Several years later, on April 12, 1893, Gross renewed his request and offered the Domincans property for a church in east Portland. This was land given to Archbishop Blanchet by Ben Holladay on March 3, 1873. After Holladay died, the Oregon Real Estate Company gained control of his tract and sold lots "for fine homes." The Blanchet property was Lot Number 119, located between Northeast 10th and Northeast 11th and between Multnomah and Wasco Streets.

In July 1893, the Dominican provincial, Father Pius Murphy, arrived in Portland and occupied Lot Number 119. When he started to build a church on it, there was a great fuss in the neighborhood, much to his surprise, and he was shown a phrase in the property covenant, which His Grace had failed to notice. "No churches, schools or saloons," it said, could be built on Lot Number 119. The matter was resolved when the developers traded two lots, Numbers 68 and 69[67] for Number 119, which now had piles of dirt and abandoned excavations. The neighboring kids called it "Murphy's Hole."

Undismayed, Murphy built his church on his new land, and on January 28, 1894, the archbishop dedicated it with cheerful dispatch under the title of Holy Rosary. At first this was a "conventional church," without a parish, but later, in 1909, a parish was attached to it and Holy Rosary was designated as a Dominican priory, the first in the Northwest.[68]

THE BISHOP'S HOUSE

Meanwhile, Archbishop Gross moved into the Bishop's House. If this appears to be nothing of moment, I should add that the Bishop's House was a spectacular architectural achievement, which still stands. It had been built in 1879, to serve as a chancery and archbishop's residence, but William Gross, in the simplicity of his heart, refused to leave his modest dwelling on Third and Oak Streets. He was finally persuaded to occupy the place in April, 1893.[69]

It was built on Stark Street next to the Cathedral, which was sixty-nine feet wide, allowing only twenty-seven feet for the width of the new edifice.[70] It was three stories in height, with the Chancery occupying the first floor, and living quarters above for the archbishop and his staff. Each floor was seventeen feet high. Long narrow leaded windows, five on the second floor and three on the third, one of these like cathedral window, embellished the brick surface, and two massive fireplaces provided a homey touch, strangely out of place above the busy thorough-fare. "Bishop's House" appeared on the crown of the building in indestructible letters that are still there. Like St. Patrick's Church in northwest Portland, it has become a national landmark.[71]

Archbishop Gross lived there for only one year. The principal reason for this brevity of residence was the crisis at the cathedral, which had become for His Grace a cause of much concern. The fact is Gross had never liked the cathedral's location on a busy downtown street, which was rapidly deteriorating into a commercial slum.

For a long time he had been stalling, seeking an acceptable excuse to move it. But he knew a storm of protest would follow. It had been built by the ever popular Father Fierens, at a cost of a hundred thousand dollars, which is like a million today, and the debt on it had just been paid off.[72]

Taking the bull by the horns, the archbishop announced through the *Oregonian* that "it was the intention of the Catholic Church at some future time to build its great cathedral and possibly to sell the present property on Third Street."[73] This appears to have been presented by His Grace with tongue in check, for he had already purchased land for the proposed cathedral two days earlier, October 29, 1891. This was in northwest Portland at Fifteenth and Davis. Gross paid Louis Fleischer $66,000 for it and waited for something else to happen.

THE DIOCESE OF BOISE

Meanwhile, there was the Vicariate of Idaho, still regarded as a "mission," lacking the cherished independence of an established diocese. Glorieux had taken up the matter of diocesan status with Rome, and

Gross as metropolitan of the Province of Oregon had done what he could
to secure Rome's approbation for it.

The Holy Father finally acted. On April 23, 1893, Pope Leo XIII raised
the vicariate to the privileged category of a diocese and appointed Bishop
Glorieux as the first Bishop of Boise.[74] At this time the diocese had
approximately seven thousand Catholics, hardly enough for one of
Father Garrand's better productions. It had sixteen priests besides the
bishop, but including six Jesuits, and it counted twenty-seven churches
and chapels. Some of these, built twenty-five years earlier, were ready to
collapse from the weight of heavy snow or the debris of pack rats.
Glorieux was delighted, of course, with diocesan recognition. He had
been agitating for it for two years since his recovery from typhoid, and he
took time off from moving the lawn and trimming his shrubs to make a
formal decision regarding his cathedral. He announced his decision a year
later. It would be St. John's of Boise, he reported, which is what everyone
expected all along. After all, this is where he had planted all his
evergreens and rose bushes.

Photographs of this period show him to be somewhat more formal, like
a French count posing for the portrait that will be hung with those of his
ancestors. His features are sharp and thin, almost pinched. His lips are
pressed firmly together, his chin juts determinedly forward and his dark,
tired eyes peer beneath heavy brows into the void. He was a tireless
shepherd, ever-watchful of his small flock and kindly disposed to his few
priests. For these reasons, perhaps, he was spared the trials and
tribulations of his brother bishops.

ADRIAN CROQUET IS MADE A MONSIGNOR

For the archbishop and his priests, there was an occasional celebration.
One of these, the last in the old cathedral, was the investiture of Grande
Ronde's Indian missionary as the first monsignor in the western United
States.

During the rainy weather in January 1894, Gross had moved his
residence from the Bishop's House to St. Joseph's, the German parish,
where he lived simply with Father James Rauw.[75] From here, early in
February, he wrote to Father DeRoo, then pastor at Verboort, to draw up
a petition to the Holy Father to appoint Croquet in his golden jubilee year
a member of the Holy Roman Court. DeRoo, elated with the opportunity
to use his talent for classical Latin, prepared the document, dating it "die
10 Februarii 1894."[76] On April 18, Cardinal Rampolla responded favorably in the name of the Holy Father.

It was intended that Croquet should know nothing about this until the anniversary in September, but in some way whispers of it reached his ear and he immediately raised such a hullaballoo that the archbishop feared he would refuse the honor altogether, whereupon DeRoo resorted to a strategem that overcame his friend's unholy scruples. Writing to Croquet, he suggested that even "if you do not deserve the honor, you should, at least, be obedient to the Pope, and moreover you might consider the bestowal of the Roman purple as a daily admonition to be thenceforth a better man than you have been before."[77]

This argument, almost as a fallacious as a "white" lie, achieved its purpose and Croquet agreed to appear on the appointed day. All preparations were made under the supervision of the archbishop himself. On Thursday morning, September 20, 1894, the great event was celebrated in the cathedral on Third and Stark. The papal document was read in the presence of the new monsignor, Archbishop Gross, Bishops Brondel and Junger, twenty-five priests,[78] and a large number of lay people, a congregation large enough for the funeral of a bishop. Croquet was then taken into the sacristy to be vested in his new robes, which His Grace had provided, and when he returned, Mass was offered. Bishop Brondel preached an almost interminable sermon, which was like a mini-history of the church.

A reception was held that afternoon with Father Edward O'Dea as toastmaster. Many toasts were offered, and many words of praise and congratulations, all of which proved to be more painful than pleasant for poor old Croquet.

And poor old Croquet was persuaded to tell at least one story on himself. Once when he was tired and weary, he said:

> He lay down by the roadside to rest for the night, leaving his horse to graze and rest also. The next morning he awoke, and, having placed the saddle on his faithful old 'plug' he had gone but a short distance when he noticed a pretty young colt following. He immediately turned back to the nearest house and told the sedate but astonished farmer to take back his colt, adding, 'I don't mean—I didn't at all mean to take it.' The farmer soon understood the situation, and, with much argument and persuasion, explained to him that the animal he rode was the mother of the colt, and that to his worldly wealth the colt had been added during the night.[79]

On the following day, despite everyone's pleas that he remain in Portland, Croquet went back to his mission. He took the train to McMinnville, then rode his horse twenty-eight miles to Grande Ronde. He carried his monsignor's purple robes with him, but he refused to wear them, saying this "his purple soutane would be worn out by the moths rather than by himself." But the archbishop, using pious strategy, persuaded him to don the robes now and then for the benefit of others.

All this, of course, was the occasion for many playful remarks by members of the clergy. One point, however, was clear: "The Saint of Oregon" was an inspiration to all. His deeply spiritual life, hidden away on a remote Indian reservation, provided the priests with a model and enriched the church in the entire Northwest. Insofar as we can judge, his penance and prayers brought as many to God's blessings in the flourishing parishes for whites as they did for the Indians at St. Michael's Mission.[80]

THE NEW PRO-CATHEDRAL

Meanwhile, in June 1894, the Willamette River went on a rampage, flooding part of the downtown area, including the cathedral. This provided Gross with the excuse he needed: less than three months later he signed a contract for the erection of a three story frame building one hundred by one hundred feet, on the new land at Fifteenth and Davis. This temporary church, a very poor substitute for the much admired "Gothic" cathedral downtown, was completed in sixty days, which is about what it was worth. The upper floor was designed to accommodate a school for boys, the two lower floors a pro-cathedral. The archbishop offered the first Mass in this new St. Mary's on December 16, 1894, at the cold, lonely hour of six in the morning. The site of the old cathedral was summarily sold. In sixty days, the resplendent, but not very old house of God was hurriedly demolished, as though it were a pox on the landscape. With the rubble went the injured pride of Portland's Catholics. Across the Columbia the cathedral of the Diocese of Nesqually was still standing, grander than ever, and almost a mockery to the envious Catholics beyond the broad river.

His Grace had done what he had to do, rather sooner than later. He felt hurt by the failure of some who should have understood why the cathedral site had to be changed. But during the summer, he went about his blessings and dedications as though nothing had happened. After dedicating the new St. Vincent's Hospital, he laid the cornerstone for the Magdalen Home north of Oregon City.[81] On August 5, he ordained Arthur Lane, grandson of Governor Joseph Lane. A priest at the precocious age of twenty-three, Arthur was Oregon's first native son to be ordained. He was baptized by Blanchet, confirmed by Seghers, and raised to the priesthood by Gross.[82]

In mid-August, the archbishop was at Lyons, Oregon to inspect the new St. Patrick's Church, and a few days later he blessed the new "St. Mary's Parochial School and College" at Fifteenth and Davis. This, for a time, replaced St. Michael's College, then it also passed into oblivion, unnoticed and lamented by only a few, though it had served the church well.[83]

OTHER SCHOOLS COMPARED

Although St. Michael's would be missed, there remained six other boys' "colleges" in the Northwest, including Holy Angels in Vancouver, which had become St. James Academy in July 1879, when the Brothers of Christian Schools arrived to take it over from the diocesan clergy.[84] Gonzaga in Spokane had awarded its first bachelor of arts degrees on June 28, 1894. The other four schools were Mount Angel, St. Martin's near Olympia, the School of the Immaculate Conception in Seattle, or "Seattle College" as it soon became known, and St. Aloysius Select School for Boys in Helena, another "college" only in the contemporary sense.[85] Four of the six, it will be observed, were in the Nesqually Diocese, and all but two schools, Seattle's and Helena's, had resident students. Holy Angels College dropped its boarding students in 1909, surviving only two years longer, a victim, it was sometimes said, of Gonzaga's success.[86] Helena's school also soon fell by the wayside and a large tract of land in Prickly Pear Valley, which the Jesuits had purchased for a future Catholic university, was presented to the Sisters of Charity of Leavenworth for the new St. Joseph's orphanage.[87] Obviously the Jesuits had given up on Helena, but not on Seattle. Seattle College, in the largest urban center of the state, languished painfully for the next forty years, barely surviving for lack of students and support. Yet the Jesuits clung to it desperately, struggling against odds in a hostile environment, but surrounded by loyal Catholics, until better days arrived.

There is somewhere in these regrettable failures an explanation for the success of the schools that prospered. Gonzaga and Santa Clara in California, have often been regarded as similar. Both were pioneers in their respective areas, Santa Clara in the 1850's and Gonzaga in the 1880's. Both were resident schools with a high percentage of Jesuit teachers. Both were identified with Jesuit formation, such as programs for scholastics. Both were in small population areas and both had very grave problems of financing until after World War II. Both became universities in 1912.

In the Spokane area alone, there were three Protestant colleges that were begun in high hopes, but each failed within a few brief years and left few traces behind. The Presbyterians' Whitworth College was founded in Tacoma and moved to Spokane in 1915 because failure in Tacoma was imminent. In Spokane, Whitworth has survived because of formal church support. Several other Protestant colleges established in the Northwest, mostly in the early years, have prospered. Among these are Willamette in Salem, Whitman in Walla Walla, and Pacific in Forest Grove. In the history of each of these colleges, one can find elements similar to those at Gonzaga and St. Martin's.

Meanwhile, colleges in the larger urban areas encountered almost insurmountable obstacles, such as those at Seattle College. Even the great University of San Francisco, founded almost as early as Santa Clara, had very difficult beginnings and, as late as 1919, the entire western Jesuit Province was called upon to save it from bankruptcy. [88]

In the passage of time, other norms of success for our northwest Catholic colleges became current and some of the older schools that had survived joined others in Vallhalla or wherever dead colleges go. With the new order, however, other church related problems arose. What, for example, was the extent of the local bishop's jurisdiction over these state chartered universities? What restrictions by bishops were Catholics, lay or clerical, required to observe in the establishment of new schools (for instance in Seattle, with reference to the long-standing objections of the local ordinaries to separate Jesuit faculties for Seattle University and Seattle Prep, both of which had developed from Seattle College)? Questions like these did not arise in 1895 when Bishop Junger regarded himself as a kind of benevolent paterfamilias of the four colleges in his diocese. But events even then were shaping the future, and the actions and personalities of the bishops, especially the successors of Junger and Brondel, would have far more influence on it than anyone could forsee.

BISHOP JUNGER'S LAST YEARS

The last years of Junger's life were not altogether pleasant. While not everything had gone awry, there were enough loose nuts and bolts in the machinery of his diocese to require occasional tinkering and sometimes a set of new parts.

First, but certainly not the most momentous problem, was the recent laxity that had crept into parish benefits and picnics. Heavens! Dances were being conducted by Catholics! And "on picnics or excursions beer or liquours were sold." His Lordship was highly distressed and he noted these aberrations "with deep sorrow." They were, indeed, violations of the decrees of the Third Plenary Council of Baltimore, Tit[ulus] IX, Cap V, No. 290 and 291. In a circular "to the Rev[d] Clergy Secular and regular of the Diocese of Nesqually" his Lordship directed the pastors of all churches to read the decrees of the Council in their pulpits and to explain them. The circular also included a reminder that a special collection was to be taken "for the African Missions, as ordered by the Holy Father."

Since most formal religious ceremonies end up with a collection, the circular was widely regarded as both orthodox and authentic.

The St. James Mission Case was argued before the Supreme Court by attorneys for both the plaintiff and defendants on the dates scheduled, April ninth and tenth in 1895. The decision of the Court was withheld until May sixth.[89] Contrary to all expectations, the Court awarded the disputed section of land to the United States Government, and it was formally added to the military reservation at Fort Vancouver. Once again, the mighty forces of war, designed to protect the people who were taxed to support them, consumed the bread of the church, its children, even its orphans, whose care depended upon this land.

It was not like Bishop Junger to be bitter or to complain about a setback like this. In thirty-one years of his life in Vancouver, no one had ever heard a disparaging word from him. Now when he knew death was near (for his health had been precarious for a year), he simply placed the land case behind him and gazed into an uncertain future.

The fact was he had Bright's disease. Mother Joseph at Vancouver had persuaded him to occupy the apartments of the late Bishop Blanchet at St. Joseph's Hospital. He had failed miserably, but was still determined to carry on. Less than two weeks before Christmas 1895, he had visited the Academy of the Holy Names Sisters in Seattle. He "gave Benediction of the Blessed Sacrament and spent some time in the community entertaining us in his kind fatherly manner."[90] Then he returned to Vancouver on December 14

Mother Joseph, deeply concerned about his condition, saw to it that every care was lavished upon him. Then, on December 26, with no time to summon Dr. Wall or Father Louis Schram, the Vicar General, but with Mother Joseph at his side, Bishop Junger died.[91] "He knew not the policy of duplicity nor the diplomacy of deceit," it was said of him. "He was as unbending as the church itself in upholding the rigid tenets of truth."[92]

This appraisal of his Lordship was also a commentary on the contemporary Diocese of Nesqually.

PRINCESS ANGELINE

As the last descendant of Chief Seattle, for whom the City on Puget Sound was named, Angeline (generally called *Princess* Angeline) was famous all over the world and countless thousands of her photographs had been sold. She was a familiar sight on the streets, bent and wrinkled

like a centenarian, with a red handkerchief over her head and a gaudy
shawl about her shoulders, limping slowly and painfully with the aid of a
cane. Sometimes one could see her sitting on the sidewalk, devoutly
reciting her beads, oblivious to the noisy traffic around her.

"I am a Catholic and I have a crucifix and a rosary," she would reply
when asked, and reaching up on the shelf where she kept her treasures
she would proudly produce both. Gazing lovingly on the crucifix, she
would say simply, "This is my friend."

She had lived fourscore and more years but never had been farther
from Seattle than Olympia, where the governor lived, just sixty miles
distant. She had gone there with her father to protest the use of his name
for the city, because he believed, as many other Indians did, that after
death your bones would turn over in your grave if your name was said
aloud. The old chief, Angeline used to say in Chinook, greatly feared that
he would have no rest, but would forever be turning over in his grave.[93]

The people of Seattle were kind to Angeline, though they regarded her
as a rare curiosity, to be shown off like an exotic fish in a bowl. They were
very sad to learn of her death on May 28, 1896. With Father Prefontaine,
her old friend, they planned a grand funeral that would have done justice
to a queen mother. The church of Our Lady of Good Hope as
magnificently decorated and the catafalque, on which the canoe-shaped
coffin rested, was draped in billows of black cloth. The funeral Mass was
as impressive as the old priest could make it. Then all that was mortal of
Princess Angeline was carried to her grave, to find rest.

Prefontaine, too, had begun to show his age. He was overweight, a tall,
heavy-set old man with hair as white as bleached cotton. The years had
been kind to him. He had a whole division of friends and an army of
associates who took pride in their being recognized by him. He was a
cherished local celebrity, a remnant of the past when Seattle was a
village. He knew its beginnings. He had been there over thirty-two years,
most of its existence, and he sometimes thought that he deserved to be a
monsignor like Adrian Croquet.

A MORE MATURE CHURCH

The church in these thirty-two years had become very complex. It was
rapidly changing into a highly structured institution, which many of the
pioneer Catholics deplored. There were the good old days when everyone
knew everyone else in the parish. Nowadays new parishes with their
churches and schools were springing up everywhere, like mushrooms
after a moist night, and one woke up to find himself cut off from his old
parish and friends, and in a new parish, with a new church to build. The

orders of sisters with their convents, hospitals, and academies were increasing so rapidly that even bishops lost count of them.

As for priests, the Oblates had come and gone. They would return some day, but for the present they were engaged in frontier missionary work in Canada. The diocesan priests, the Jesuits, Redemptorists, and Benedictines were here to stay. The Dominicans had recently joined them; the Franciscans, Servites, Trappists, and others would come later.

Most important was the church's new sense of direction, determined in part by the Council of Baltimore. Each diocese had become an identifiable entity, with its own benign prospects as well as with its own unique problems. In the 1890's, though, an enormous growth preoccupied all of the bishops. These prelates succeeded in creating a spirit of unity, based upon their own personal authority. Theirs was no frontier, distant command over priests, as heretofore—an uneasy domination of a scattered clergy who were almost incommunicado because of space, and independent as bears in the mountains. The bishops could talk less now about their authority and could exercise it more; that is, as quickly as the trains or mail arrived.

Now it was not so much "the northwest church," as it was the Archdiocese of Oregon City, the Diocese of Nesqually, or Helena. Roots had been struck and each tree as it developed had its own form, largely created by the priorities of the bishop. Events were now taking place that would produce new dioceses and given each the shape it would have for decades to come.

The new awareness of power and diocesan unity would not lessen the tension between bishops and religious orders, though usually in the disputes that arose, the conduct of both sides was characterized by accommodation for the good of the church. Disputes between bishops and individual priests were inevitable, because times had changed. Some of the "old guard" would find it difficult to accept the new order of things. This was not unlike the controversies of a later period, incited by changes of the Second Vatican Council. Archbishop Gross' successor would bear the greatest burden of these individual disputes and the Jesuits would lose most through the bishops' new awareness of their "jurisdiction," a concept that was misunderstood as often as not. But all this was a sign of growing pains that appeared first in the 1890's and finally yielded to an Old World maturity six decades later.

13

GROWING PAINS

1896–1905

As metropolitan of the province, Archbishop Gross presided over formalities for selecting Bishop Junger's successor. Everything at Vancouver was under control. On January 22, 1896, Father Louis Schram, as Administrator of the Nesqually diocese, sent to all the priests of the diocese "a circular letter" to inform them of the forthcoming meeting of the bishops: "The Most Rev. Archbishop W.H. Gross, D.D. has called together the Bishops of the Ecclesiastical Province of Oregon. The meeting is to take place February 26th prox.

"All priests who desire to communicate with His Grace in regard to the choice of a successor to the lamented Bishop Junger are assured that their letters will be considered strictly confidential. No anonymous letters however will be noticed or read."[1]

This matter of selecting a bishop was beginning to appear as something very solemn indeed. Not equally important was the following notice included in Schram's circular:

> Please permit me to call your attention that all collections ordered in this Diocese have still to be made.... Do not forget that the collection for the African Missions, ordered by Our Holy Father, Leo XIII was to have been taken already.

This sounded like Bishop Junger's voice from the grave.

BISHOP EDWARD O'DEA

According to well-founded rumors, the first terna considered by the bishops recommended the following, in the order of preference, as Junger's successor: Father Peter Yorke of San Francisco, an Irish firebrand, who had exposed the errors of the A.P.A. in California, Father Hylebos of Tacoma, and youthful Father O'Dea of Portland.[2] The older priests, especially the old guard in the Puget Sound area, composed of Prefontaine, Hylebos, and Maniouloux of Port Townsend, regarded O'Dea as "the young boy" who had been ordained only thirteen years. They preferred an older man, and when O'Dea was finally appointed, undoubtedly through the influence of Archbishop Gross and Cardinal Gibbons, they found it difficult to conceal their disappointment.

News of O'Dea's selection as the third Bishop of Nesqually leaked out on July 7, 1896, and the Sisters of St. Mary's Academy were among the first to hear about it. They were elated, of course, because "little Eddie" had been one of their most promising pupils before he entered St. Michael's college. Official notice from Father Schram was two weeks in coming. Under the date of July 23, 1896, the Administrator dispatched the following from St. James Cathedral:

> By letters dated Rome, June 13th, 1896, signed by the Cardinal Prefect of Propaganda and sealed with the seal of His Holiness Leo XIII, Rev. Edward O'Dea has been appointed successor to our lamented Bishop Aegidius Junger, for this Diocese of Nesqually.
>
> The Consecration will take place at Vancouver, Washington, on Tuesday, the 8th of September at 10 o'clock A.M., and you are cordially invited to assist.[3]

MOTHER JOSEPH

Father O'Dea was, so to speak, the first home-grown bishop in the Northwest. He had been a favorite of the archbishop for some time, so no one, except the old guard, was surprised to learn of his elevation to the hierarchy. He had been also a favorite of many others, including Mother Joseph, who regarded him as a kind of adopted son. She knew the O'Dea family well and often visited them in their home when she was in Portland on business for St. Vincent Hospital. It was Eddie who accompanied Mother Joseph on her inspection tours on dark evenings when the new hospital was being built. He carried the lantern and held it where she could examine the foundations and later the walls and stair wells after the workers had gone home. He had first confided to her that he wanted to be a priest and she had been pleased and happy about it. Now, as his consecration approached, she herself prepared his bishop's robes and embroidered the slippers he would wear.

In her basement workshop, Mother Joseph formed many statues of saints, especially of St. Joseph, for which she had a mold, and the Infant Jesus, a favorite in the convent. Most of her saints were cast in wax, but for some, like the Infant Jesus, she added real hair shorn from some of the heads of the orphan boys. One of the latter was Johnnie Steffan, whose head produced golden curls. When Johnnie was six years old, Mother Joseph cut them for the life-sized wax figure of Saint Lucien in the cathedral. Johnnie, she said, had been a girl long enough, and she tried to comfort his sister who cried when his hair was cut.

Because the number of orphans had increased, it was necessary for the sisters to beg for more support. They traveled in pairs to district places, but near at hand, across the street at Fort Vancouver, the soldiers, as always, were the most generous donors. A regulation had been passed, prohibiting solicitors from entering the military reserve. However, the commandant had issued strict orders that this did not apply to the sisters. "The Sisters of Providence are exempted," he decreed, "and it is my intention that they will always be well treated here." This officer also instructed his men to assist the sisters whenever they required help.[4] From this one can see that the Colonel and his men had their hearts in the right places, even if there were misunderstandings elsewhere.

CONSECRATION OF BISHOP O'DEA

O'Dea was finally consecrated as the Third Bishop of Nesqually on September 8, 1896. The ceremony took place in the cathedral in Vancouver, with Archbishop Gross presiding as Consecrator, assisted by Bishop John Nicholas Lemmons of Victoria and Bishop Alphonse Glorieux of Boise, former principal at St. Michael's College. Ironically, O'Dea's cathedral now was far superior to the huge wooden crate they used in Portland, where the brothers teaching in St. Mary's school lived in congested cubbyholes over the sacristy, like rabbits in pens.

If Nesqually's former bishop had suggested the appearance of a prosperous Flemish burgher, O'Dea in his early years as a prelate looked more like an Irish barrister. Official photographs present him as one young enough to take himself too seriously. His handsome well-proportioned head, with bland features, stood erect in a lordly manner above his longer than average neck. This gave him a wax bust-like appearance, like one of Mother Joseph's statues. He was already partly bald, a misfortune for which he compensated by growing furry tufts of hair over his ears. His eyes seem to contain the mysterious sadness of his race, and his mouth turned down at the corners in a pouting expression. O'Dea was not a harsh man, nor was he especially learned, like Junger. But he was quick and witty, the kind of prelate priests invited to serve their after dinner speeches with the coffee and cream. As he grew older, he became somewhat absent-minded and he acquired little idiosyncrasies of speech, using "I might almost say" frequently, even at the beginning of sermons: "In the name of the Father and the Son and I might almost say, of the Holy Ghost."

Religious orders had nothing to fear from O'Dea. He had served under Gross, a Redemptorist, and he seems to have come under very little influence of some bishops of the East, who shared a common apprehension about religious priests. If anything, O'Dea, like Junger, was too easy on his priests, and it was sometimes said that his successor had been selected to restore order where O'Dea had let matters slide.

One must not think, however, that O'Dea was a pushover. He had learned from Mother Joseph to inspect the work he was paying for, including that of priests. His customary kindness to them, for example, was not to be confused with his resolution to remain in charge.

As far as he was concerned, the Supreme Court decision notwithstanding, the St. James Mission Case was far from closed. He was determined to have his day in court to seek redress from Congress. The Methodist claim at The Dalles, lost on a technicality, was restored to them, and Congress had reimbursed them for the loss of only a portion of it for military purposes.[5] Similarly the Presbyterians had been paid for their land at Waiilatpu, from which they had been forced to leave during the Cayuse Indian War. O'Dea then, did not regard is as unreasonable that the Diocese of Nesqually be reimbursed for its losses in Vancouver.

Opposition to the Congressional bill for St. James was remarkably strong, indicating that more was involved than the claim itself. The chief opponents to it were two congressmen, blue-eyed, Swedish-born John Lind of Minnesota and southerner Charles Lafayette of Georgia. At last, on March 3, 1905, in the last moments of the final session of the 58th Congress, the opposition was routed, a favorable bill was passed and immediately signed. In accordance with this, the Diocese of Nesqually was paid $25,000 for the loss of its buildings on the Saint James Mission Claim.[6] Thus ended, by token compromise at least, a struggle that lasted nearly fifty years. It demonstrated, among other things, that the church was here to stay, and that like the indestructible corporations, it could afford to fight to the bitter end.

O'Dea's persistence, and success, in this matter won for him new respect from his flock, especially from the Germans, who often accused the Irish of being too verbose and "quarrelsome." But here was one who could be more stubborn than the Germans. After all by overcoming prejudice in Congress, he had won a lawsuit after the Supreme Court had decided against his case. He was a bishop they could support.

FATHER BARNABAS HELD

One of O'Dea's most immediate problems was the boundless zeal of Father Barnabas Held. Barnabas was a rare genius, in some ways, like an engine out of control. But, in truth, he performed in an excellent manner in whatever he undertook. He was a gifted musician, which was one reason why the abbey in Engelberg was loath to see him leave. But he seemed to flit about like a butterfly, from one project to another, committed to do good for everyone. He had been co-pastor of the Benedictines' first parish at Fillmore, later called Mount Angel, and he had been the first director of Mount Angel College. Yet he remained a capitulary of the Monastery in Engelberg. In Spokane, he had developed his school for Germans, his orphanage, and Sacred Heart Parish in a former Protestant church, as noted previously. He was up to his ears in the Uniontown-Colton dispute with his friend Father James Frei. At the same time he was visiting German farmers in the Big Bend Country west of Spokane, where he started construction on a church at Edwall.[7]

In October, 1897, he built a "technical college" on the south side of Spokane, near Thirteenth and Bernard.[8] After all of his boarders, as they were called, had moved in, and everything was in readiness for the opening, the college burned to the ground. It was a total loss. There was only twenty-five hundred dollars of insurance to pay for what he owed.

Another friend of Held was Father Louis Verhaag, currently pastor of St. Francis Church in Baker City, and formerly editor of the *Catholic Sentinel*. In February of that very year, Verhaag had begun to publish a monthly magazine containing memoirs and notes on the early church history of the Northwest. He introduced his first issue under the title of "Reminiscences of the Ecclesiastical Province of Oregon" and charged for subscriptions as follows: $1.00 per year Strictly in Advance."[9] A later issue called attention to the loss of Father Held's college:

> We are sorry to learn that the Technical College of Father Held, O.S.B. at Spokane was destroyed by fire Oct. 10th. Knowing Father Held, whose name is characteristic of his work, we have no doubt that his indomitable energy will not suffer to let the grass grow over the ruins of his burned college.[10]

Unfortunately, the grass or weeds grew over the ruins, because Held was unable to rebuild it. His health had been poor. A lung ailment was at the bottom of it and doctors advised him to seek a milder climate. He moved to Nada, Texas. Here, at last, he settled down as pastor of the parish, but still a monk attached to the monastery in Engelberg. He celebrated his golden jubilee in Nada, then died there and was buried in the local cemetery.

After his departure from Spokane, all of his projects collapsed. In 1901, the church was closed and in 1903 it was dismantled, its lumber and bell being used for the construction of the first St. Ann's Church on Spokane's east side. So little remained at Fifth and Bernard that within a score of years all traces of Held's little German empire had disappeared.

But nothing is forever and some things, like a burning candle, last for a brief time, then vanish in smoke or weeds. This is the way it was with "Father Held's Schools," as they were called. This is what it meant to plant the seed that rotted in the ground, and to let others reap the harvest.[11]

UNIONTOWN AGAIN

Another man much like Held appeared before Held's departure. This was John Faust. In the performance of his first ordination, Bishop O'Dea ordained Faust to the priesthood on December 8, 1896, in St. James Cathedral. The new priest later became well known for his stiff black beard, shaped like a spade, and his ingenious trick for flipping a lighted cigarette when he dove into the water. Unlike many other priests ordained for the Nesqually Diocese, John Faust was around for a long time.[12]

Eventually he replaced Father Nicholas Frei, who was sent back to Uniontown by the bishop when Joehren departed for Wisconsin. After leaving Colfax, Father Nicholas served as pastor of St. Francis Xavier's parish on Cowlitz Prairie, where the elder Blanchet had established his first mission in December of 1838. Father Nicholas had become accustomed to the Cowlitz but his call to serve the people in Uniontown found in his heart a ready response. He knew the people well and enjoyed their love and esteem. Perhaps he could calm the turbulence and ruffled spirits that remained there in the wake of Father Joehren's defection.

He arrived in Uniontown on January 12, 1901. He remained, unfortunately, less than a year. Suffering from asthma, a condition agitated by the dust and chaff of harvest, he decided to return to his monastery to spend the rest of his days in peace. He left Uniontown on December 30, 1901, and embarked on a ship as chaplain with free passage, enroute to Japan. He was returning to Europe via Asia.[13]

From Japan he went to India where he was fatally stricken with the "plague." He died in Calcutta before ever seeing Europe again, and he was buried there by the Jesuits, who "gave him a resting place in their own cemetery."[14]

It was Father Faust, then, who arrived in Uniontown in December, 1901. The Uniontown-Colton feud still simmered beneath the surface. It was not discussed, but everyone was aware of it and, like the Hatfields and McCoys in Tennessee, there were kissing cousins who never spoke to one another. Bishop O'Dea was very much aware of the volatile situation that he had inherited with all the other pleasant things that were happening. But he was more than three hundred miles distant and he seemed to think that it would go away if he appointed a pastor who could understand and speak German.

At this point, Uniontown's new church foundations, began by Joehren, basked in desolation beneath the sun, a ready reminder, if one were needed, that the project required completion. The congregation had grown considerably—these German farmers had large families—so the first task of Father Faust was the building of a church. Well aware of previous financial woes, he favored the execution of Joehren's plans, but many on his building committee disagreed, insisting on a larger and more ornate church than Colton had. There followed another celebrated dispute, this time within the community.

Sister Marie Reilly, a Providence Sister in Seattle, provided some unsolicited remarks about the sequence. She wrote as follows.

> In our living room near the piano, as a child I saw a picture of Leo XIII. I was told that this was a paper from Pope Leo bestowing an apostolic blessing at the hour of death upon my father. It is dated 1903.
>
> This is the way I remember what I heard about our receiving this blessing.
>
> My father had come from Lawler, Iowa, to teach school in Uniontown. We lived with the Taufins [sic] since Mr. Taufin was on the school board and teachers lived there. The Germans needed a church and wanted it big, they had had success with their crops so had some money. The pastor argued with them, that they did not need such a large church, but they insisted. He took their pledges and built. When time came to collect the pledges hard times had come and they had little money. The priest insisted and a dispute broke out. Hard things were said against the priest and a delegation went to the bishop to complain.
>
> My father and some other men wanted the bishop to know the other side of the story, so they went to Vancouver, Washington, to give the other side. The bishop was in Seattle, on business about moving the Cathedral there. My father and that delegation went to Seattle to find the bishop.
>
> Some time after the blessing from Pope Leo XIII came to each [of these men] because they had defended a priest. . . .
>
> Several times [later] my mother remarked on the death of someone there who had died suddenly without a priest. 'So-and-so was one of those who fought against the priest.'[15]

Uniontown today is a sleepy little town, as peaceful and serene as a village in rural Iowa. The "big church" upon the hill looks like a venerable basilica. It is now a mission church, attached to St. Gall's in Colton, but it has a rare and holy distinction: it was dedicated on November 22, 1905 in honor of "St. Boniface and the Mother of God the Immaculate Conception." Five years later, on June 5, 1910, it was solemnly consecrated by Bishop O'Dea. It was the first church in the present Diocese of Spokane to be consecrated. The Germans there had buried the hatchet at least.

THE DEATH OF THE ARCHBISHOP

The archbishop, during these bizarre events, still felt like an outcast in his own diocese because he had destroyed the people's cathedral. There were some of his subjects who continued to complain about what he had done, but most were willing to let bygones be bygones.

The twenty-fifth anniversary of the archbishop's consecration as a bishop was approaching and it was generally agreed that the time had come for Catholics to show him their love and respect. They decided to present him with a new residence, near the cathedral. Land was acquired at Sixteenth and Davis Streets and construction was begun on a modest dwelling that had been designed for the archbishop's exclusive use. A "Catholic Fair" no different from any other fairs except that it was discreetly patronized by more priests and nuns, was conducted in Portland, and this netted $4,274, an impressive amount for hard times and a clear sign of the archbishop's return to popular favor.[16]

When completed, the house cost a total of $10,500. It was formally presented to his Grace on April 26, 1898, the eve of his anniversary. This did much to raise his spirits, but his health was so undermined by this time that perceptive people feared the worst. A month later, his appearance no heartier than before, he patiently consecrated St. Paul's Church at St. Paul, Oregon, which was not only the Northwest's most historic church, it was now the first to be consecrated. Very special conditions for this were required. For example, it must have been built with indestructible materials and must have no debt whatever against it, lest it be reclaimed by others and be put to a less-than-noble use. The ceremony for consecration, unlike that for a formal blessing, was very tedious and long. For Archbishop Gross, it was his last hurrah.[17]

Vancouver Island was still part of the Province of Oregon, in some respects subject to Gross, who became involved in selecting a new bishop when John Lemmens of that see died in Guatamala.[18] Little did Gross realize that he was assisting in the selection of his own successor. Alexander Christie, a priest in the Archdiocese of St. Paul in Minnesota, was chosen eventually for the replacement of Bishop Lemmens, and he was consecrated in St. Paul by Archbishop Ireland on June 29, 1898. Ireland was assisted by Bishop John Brondel of Helena and John Shanley of Fargo, as co-consecrators.[19]

By this time Gross had come to realize the seriousness of his malady. He loved the peace and the serenity of St. Mary's Academy and there "in a quiet corner of his parlor" he frequently prayed and wrote. He was weary and ill and to the sisters he expressed his fears. He had decided to return to Baltimore for medical attention, but he was still anxious about the financial plight of the archdiocese, which was no better or worse than any other diocese after the Great Depression of 1893. He tarried longer in Portland than he intended, trying to put things right. Finally he left in late September, biding his friends goodbye with a heavy heart. Only God knew what lay ahead. In Baltimore his suspicions were confirmed: his sickness was terminal. He gradually grew worse and then, on Monday, November 14, 1898, he died in St. Joseph's Hospital. He was buried in the Most Holy Redeemer Cemetery in his native city.[20]

Back in Portland, his passing was noted with more than regret. There were some who felt, not unreasonably, that their archbishop had been treated shabbily in his declining years. The residence on Sixteenth and Davis now represented something besides a peace offering; it was a cause of comfort for those who had contributed to it.

"The circumstances attending the death of our dear Archbishop," wrote the diarist at St. Mary's Academy in Portland, "are particularly sad for this archdiocese that has passed through so many trials within the last few years. In life our venerated dead ever found the Sisters of the Holy Names obedient, respectful and devoted to him and to the interest of religion."[21]

Their loyalty to the archbishop in his time of trial was now, for the sisters, an occasion of a melancholy peace within themselves.

In retrospect, the accomplishments of Archbishop Gross as the Third Archbishop of Oregon City, were more revealing about the change of the times than about him personally. When his successor arrived, he found sixty-seven churches in the archdiocese, sixty-one priests, and twenty-three parochial schools. If these figures did not compare well with those of Boston or Chicago, they at least indicated how much progress had been made in three generations, during the tenure of only three archbishops, the first of whom had celebrated Mass in a wilderness log church.

More revealing about William Gross the Redemptorist are the cordial relations he fostered with religious orders. In his thirteen years as archbishop, he helped to found the Maria Zell convent, later the Congregation of the Sisters of St. Mary of Oregon. He brought the Christian Brothers to Portland, to take over St. Michael's College in 1886. He encouraged the Benedictines to establish Mount Angel College in 1887, and the Northwest's first seminary in 1889. He founded Mount Calvary cemetery in 1888, and brought from San Jose, California, the first Dominican Sisters of the Congregation of the Queen of the Most Holy Rosary in 1889. In the following year, he brought in the first Redemptorists and in November of 1891, he assisted the Sister Adorers of the Precious Blood in establishing their temporary residence at Gervais, and their permanent monastery in Portland in 1892.[22] He extended the first invitation to the Dominican Fathers to establish a residence in Portland in 1894. He promoted the first candidate for monsignorship on the west coast. He requested the Sisters of Mercy of Carlow, Ireland, to establish a Catholic Young Women's Home in Portland in 1896.[23] He persuaded the Jesuits to take over the Umatilla Mission in 1888 and Pendleton's St. Mary's parish in 1897.[24] And, finally, he invited the Sister Servants of the Immaculate Heart of Mary, from Marywood, Pennsylvania to establish St. Alphonsus Academy in Tillamook, Oregon, in 1897.[25]

Archbishop Gross found his own religious identity in his Redemptorist origins. He did not hesitate to cherish other religious orders, or his own diocesan priests, and it was in and through them that he achieved his own destiny as one of Oregon's great archbishops.

ARCHBISHOP ALEXANDER CHRISTIE

On February 12, 1899, Pope Leo XIII, promoted Bishop Alexander Christie of Vancouver Island to the archiepiscopal see of Oregon City. Christie was formally installed as the fourth archbishop of that see on June 15, 1899.[26] It was the beginning of a reign that lasted for over a quarter of a century.

Alexander Christie was like a king. When he posed for his portrait, he held his head back, like a conquering hero. His heavy locks of hair, greying at the temples, flowed gracefully over and behind him, forming a well-trimmed mane, which gave him a strong, masculine appearance. His deep eyes and patrician nose, sharp as well as prominent, caught one's attention first and held it. As he spoke, even informally, his eyes were as eloquent as his words. One scarcely noticed his lips, pressed with determination, or his sharp chin thrust out stubbornly. As archbishop, he wore his robes majestically, as one born to them. While his predecessor looked learned or holy, Archbishop Christie simply appeared to be magnificently regal, like the Lion of Judah.

A successor, the sixth Archbishop of Portland in Oregon, described Christie's human foibles: "Tall and rangy, impressive and oratund of address, with pawky humor, he was more at ease with his priests taking innocent (or perhaps not so innocent) delight in cheating a bit at poker and purloining any loose cigars that might be around. A man's man. The severance of Baker [Diocese] from his sheepfold doubtlessly caused him tears of anguish."[27]

Despite his height and overpowering personality, Christie was not pompous. He had been born in Vermont in 1848 and was reared in Adams County, Wisconsin, in the simplicity of a rural community.[28] Two of his brothers fought in the Civil War, one of them making the supreme sacrifice of his life at the Battle of Bull Run. Christie was never ashamed of his humble origins, and he held the virtue of humility in high esteem. As archbishop, he strongly promoted higher education, especially for his priests and religious, but he often said, "Sisters, take care that you grow in humble obedience as you develop in intellectual worth."[29]

His Grace would have a splendid opportunity, sooner than he expected, to put his spiritual advice into practice.

O'DEA'S EARLY YEARS

In the Nesqually Diocese, too, the expansion of parishes and recruiting of new priests had occupied most of Bishop O'Dea's time. In June 1898, he persuaded the Jesuits at Seattle College to visit Bremerton regularly and to build a church there.[30] At the same time Father Michael Fanfara completed a new church called Our Lady of Lourdes at Wilkinson, Washington. In August, the bishop requested the Benedictines of St. Martin's to provide Mass at Long Beach and Seaview on the West Coast.[31] Two other churches were completed in the diocese this same summer, one at Republic, built by that roving Frenchman, DeRouge, and another at Hoquiam built by Deichmann of Abderdeen.[32]

In Spokane, Emil Kauten, pastor of Our Lady of Lourdes downtown parish, purchased four lots at Riverside and Madison for $26,000, money he had received for the old church property on Bernard, originally purchased by Cataldo for $400. Kauten had plans for a larger new church, expecting, he hoped, that it would be the cathedral someday.[33] DeRouge, still obsessed with making St. Mary's Mission on Omak Creek the Paraguay Reductions of the Colville Reservation, completed two new buildings, a residence and a church, and the rattlesnakes there fled farther up the valley as he planted orchards and fields of grain.[34]

O'Dea had cast calculating eyes on the surging new giant of the Northwest for his residence. Obviously, Vancouver at the extreme edge of the diocese would not do indefinitely. Seattle was actually located in the center-west, an ideal site if one expected Spokane to become a diocese also. There was, however, a risk in the choice of Seattle: silver-rich Irish Catholics in Spokane insisted that Spokane be selected instead. They correctly argued that Spokane had more Catholics than the coast city. O'Dea knew where his bread was buttered. He needed the help of the wealthy Spokanites to build a new cathedral. Unwilling to offend them, he postponed his decision and waited for the right time.

BEGINNINGS OF THE CATHOLIC NORTHWEST PROGRESS

In March of 1899, a new Catholic monthly appeared. Called *The Progress*, this was published by the Seattle Council of the Young Men's Institute (YMI), a popular Catholic lodge for younger men not unlike the Knights of Columbus, which had already appeared in eastern America. C.E. Summers was editor and one of the people he called upon for assistance was Miss Martina Johnston.

The fare for the reading public of those days included, for example, an account of the visit to Seattle of Monsignor Martinelli, papal delegate, and a rehash of a sermon delivered at the Immaculate Conception church on the "insidious practice of attending balls and other social diversions on Saturday night."

The paper soon attracted O'Dea's attention, but His Lordship was wary. He did not offer it his official endorsement until January 18, 1901. During this same year, T.J. Ivers and A.J. Bookmyer assumed responsibility for the paper, now called *Catholic Progress*. News was submitted by YMI membership throughout the Pacific Northwest. Published items included even social bits, noting visitors to private homes from another city or the arrival of a family to settle in Seattle.

In 1908, the *Catholic Progress* was merged with another paper established earlier, called the *Catholic Northwest*.[35] This had been founded by Martina Johnston, Summer's assistant. The rite of union was briefly affirmed in the new creation, *The Catholic Northwest Progress*, on February 7, 1908:

> The publishers of the *Catholic Progress* and of the *Catholic Northwest*, believing that the interests of the church and its rapidly increasing membership in the State of Washington, can be better served by one strong representative paper than by two, with separate fields of endeavor, have united those publications under the joint name that appears on our title page.[36]

The editorship of that combined publication was given to Miss Johnston, who began her new career by expanding the woman's page

AQUINAS ACADEMY IN TACOMA

On May 22, 1899, O'Dea blessed the cornerstone for the new Aquinas Academy of Tacoma for Mother Thomasina and her Dominicans. This was a girls-only institution, a matter of some regret for most, but Mother Thomasina had plans in her prolific mind for the boys also. In September, she established St. Edward's Hall for Tacoma boys of the first six grades. In the following year she bought the old Lowell Public School and, after remodeling it, moved St. Edward's Hall into it, adding two more grades. This was the kernel from which Marymount Military Academy developed some years later.[37]

At the same time, September 1899, another group of Dominicans arrived in Everett to open Our Lady of Perpetual Help School. Three Sisters of the Congregation of the Holy Cross, while their building was under construction, taught classes in the basement of the church. Their grateful pastor, Father Charles Claessens, assisted the sisters in acquiring nearby a five acre tract of land for their convent, which became their motherhouse.[38]

All this is but a sampling. It demonstrates, I hope, that most history is placid and constructive if a bit dull, and that the most lasting events take place in silent harmony, like the oak tree growing out of the earth, making no noises or disturbance. It is wondrous, but not exciting.

Yet there was excitement even during this decade of tranquility, which might be called the lull before the Battle of Baker City. The historic Immaculate Conception church at Pinkney City, for example, built in 1861 as the first church for whites in the interior, burned to the ground.[39] Another fire destroyed the Cowlitz church, the mother church in the state. Father Van Holderbeke had been in charge for only two days when the fire started, "probably due to the fatigues of a travel-worn priest." A candle had been left burning. The church was soon engulfed in flames, and Van Holderbeke dashed inside to save the records. But he failed and the entire contents of the building went up in smoke. The parishioners found their priest kneeling disconsolately in the snow, his body badly blistered and charred. He was taken to Tacoma where he died.[40]

This was the third St. Francis Xavier church on the Cowlitz. Subsequently, fires destroyed two more churches there, the fourth on August 16, 1916, and the fifth on February 10, 1932. The latter occurred after services on Ash Wednesday, a not inappropriate time for the distribution of the holy ashes, of which there was now quite enough for the whole diocese. The sixth church, which has survived, was made of brick.

These were not the first churches, nor the last to burn up. But many, like the first cathedral in Vancouver and the Redemptorist's church of the Sacred Heart in Seattle, had been torched by arsonists, rapacious people who disliked Catholics. The power of bigotry, far from waning as more Catholics arrived and more churches were built, tended to increase, especially along the coast areas of Washington where the "secret" lodges still flourished.

COLUMBIA UNIVERSITY

One could no longer see the broad sweeping river, nor downtown Portland from most houses in Vancouver, because the buildings in the business district, not to mention the city's shade trees, obscured the view. But across the river, the new archbishop in his residence on Sixteenth and Davis was occupied in the reorganization of his diocese. The disaffection during the later years of Archbishop Gross, occasioned by his decision on the cathedral, the hard times, and his long illness, had left the archdiocese, not in disarray, but in need of immediate attention.

Known by his priests as "the bishop who had the chancery office in his vest pocket," Christie conducted his business in a room upstairs in the cathedral rectory, only technically called "the Chancery."[41] He was uncommonly energetic, especially in his early years when Portland experienced its greatest period of growth.

"Portland grew from a population of some 90,000 to over 200,000 in the first decade of this century," Monsignor George Campbell of the archdiocese stated in a jubilee speech, "The church kept pace with this growth. The years 1904 to 1918 saw the number of east side Portland parishes increase from three to 18."[42]

Christie finally got around to dedicating the huge pro-cathedral at Fifteenth and Davis on December 19, 1899. One would suppose, since it was still unpopular, that he would have done this about two in the morning when everyone was asleep. But that would have been unlike him. He was a direct man, accustomed to taking the bull by the horns, whether the bull kicked or not.

One desire above others seemed to preoccupy him. Like Seghers, he was deeply concerned about Catholic education, though it must be admitted he would not go as far as inviting the Jesuits to build a school. The Jesuits had cast their eyes expectantly on Portland, the cultural center of the Northwest. As yet, they enjoyed little involvement in the archdiocese, a mini mission at Umatilla and a small but vigorous parish at Pendleton, staffed but recently at the earnest request of Archbishop Gross. Anyone with two eyes and less than twenty-twenty vision could see that a boy's prep school, comparable to St. Mary's Academy, was sorely needed in Portland. While the Jesuits complained to the archbishop that they were short of men, having undertaken the Alaska mission and two colleges within the last fourteen years, they were willing to make any sacrifice at all to be in Portland, which would produce enough candidates for the Society to continue the work there.

Apparently that was the rub, because the archbishop, everytime in twenty-five years when the subject of a Jesuit school was discussed, either dissembled or agreed to allow it without providing the required documents. Thus the boys' prep school problem in Portland went unresolved for years.[43]

But Christie did want a Catholic college, and when a local Methodist institution went out of business, he quickly snapped it up and opened it as a diocesan college called Columbia University. Its early history bears telling.

THE METHODIST COLLEGE

The formal beginnings of Portland University, as it was known by its founders, began in 1890 as the result of an extended dispute among faculty and friends of Willamette University in Salem. The latter, one of the over fifty colleges and universities in the United States under Methodist control, was experiencing a temporary slump in enrollment and its highly regarded chancellor, Dr. Charles Stratton, an alumnus of Willamette, conceived the idea of transferring the university to Portland where a greater potential seemed to exist.[44] A division of opinions, not unexpectedly, was held by members of the Board of Trustees. A bitter controversy followed and in its wake a new university was established in Portland. Articles of Incorporation were filed on December 24, 1890, and on January 3, 1891, Dr. Stratton was introduced to the delighted citizens of Portland as the first president of Portland University, a most ostentatious title attached as yet to nothing tangible.

The trustees of the new "university" purchased "a tract of unimproved land on the peninsula between the Willamette and Columbia Rivers. Then adjacent to the city of Portland, the approximate 600 acres of land came to be called University Park, a development scheme formed by the Portland Guarantee Company in conjunction with the newly created Portland University Board of Trustees. Seventy-one acres were given over for the campus which had about a half-mile of frontage on the Willamette, and the remainder was plated with lots of alternate blocks offered for sale.... The plan was that the proceeds from the sale of the land would form a permanent endowment for the University."[45]

It should be noted that bonds were accepted in payment of the land, with expectations that they would be redeemed in full by 1896. This, of course, was the Achilles heel, a weakness so fragile that only a confirmed optimist could hope to succeed.

Designs were drawn for a student residence that never materialized and a classroom structure to be known as West Hall. Ultimately, construction was begun on a multi-purpose building in "Richardsonian-

Romanesque" style, five storied and ponderous, like a Fort Knox vault with rows of impertinent windows, This was not completed for the scheduled commencement of classes, so the trustees rented the old "St. Helen's Hall" on Tenth and Main Streets. On September 14, 1891, these quarters were jammed for "opening day with young people, parents, faculty, ministers, prominent citizens and several board members.... Approximately 100 students matriculated on the first day and within six weeks enrollment had climbed to 160. By January 1892, it reached 210."[46]

It was a sparkling debut in the sunshine of false anticipations about the future. "Is this not an auspicious occasions?" someone had asked, his face doubtlessly radiant with prophecy. But the answer was "No." The villain again was the depression of 1893 when student enrollment dropped, the sale for lots vanished, and Stratton, foreseeing collapse, resigned. Dr. Thomas Van Scoy, the dean, replaced him and due to his superhuman efforts, the university continued to limp along. In 1896, its land was lost by default of payment and two years later, from a desk in a building borrowed from the university's rival Willamette, Van Scoy tendered his resignation. Additional efforts were made to save the university but all was futile.

On April 8, 1900, a notice appeared in the *Oregonian* that simply stated: "After the last of May, the Portland University will cease to exist...."[47] All records were transferred to Willamette and students were given the opportunity to enroll there. Portland alumni were regarded as alumni of Willamette and there the bitter struggle ended.

ENTER THE HOLY CROSS FATHERS

Archbishop Christie had come to Portland during the very month that West Hall was vacated by Portland University. No doubt, thoughts crossed his mind then that he should make an effort to acquire this property for a much needed university in the archdiocese. The idea persisted and, in the course of time, Francis McKenna, agent of the University Land Company, which held the title, and the archbishop, sat down together to discuss terms. An agreement was reached and formalized on July 20, 1901. The land company consented "to deed West Hall and twenty-eight acres of land to the archdiocese for $20,000 on condition that a school be conducted on the site and a major building erected within ten years."[48] Christie accepted the offer, taking also an option on an additional forty-three acres of contiguous land.

Five days later, the *Catholic Sentinel* announced plans for the new school. It would be known as "Columbia University." Father E.P. Murphy, rector of St. Patrick's Church in Portland, formerly a member of the Congregation of Holy Cross, which conducted the University of Notre Dame, would be the first president. Students would be accepted for admission that very autumn.

The archbishop presided over inauguration ceremonies at West Hall, which acquired a new cross on top above the main door, on September 2, 1901. Having blessed the building generously with holy water (which instantly converted it from Methodism to Catholicism), Christie's eyes gazed over the crowd of celebrities before him, and beyond the gliding waters of the Willamette River. "This location," he announced happily, not exercising any powers of infallibility, "is superior to any other on the Pacific Coast."[49] He also added, still quite fallibly, that he believed that in a few years the school "will offer opportunities for higher education unequalled by any Western institution." A collection was then taken, to confirm the pious nature of the occasion. This was the first, but not the last fund drive in the new university's existence. One hundred and thirty dollars were raised, not very much, probably because a large part of the audience was clerical.[50]

It was not likely that Jesuits at Santa Clara, already celebrating its golden jubilee, would agree with the boastful remarks of His Grace. Nor the Jesuits at Gonzaga where recently a second college building, 189 feet in length, had been occupied: "The largest building in the city and with the exception of St. Ignatius College, San Francisco...the largest Catholic college in the West."[51] This was blessed by O'Dea in 1899, when West Hall was still Methodist, but plans were being made already to extend it an additional 255 feet along Boone Avenue. It would be difficult to beat that.

So much for the Jesuits. The Benedictines at Mount Angel and St. Martin's could scarcely agree with the predictions of his Grace. Christie himself had blessed the new cornerstone at Mount Angel shortly after his arrival.[52] He seemed to lack the same enthusiasm for the Benedictines that Archbishop Gross had always felt, though it was sometimes rumored, without evidence to support it, that he had asked them to staff the new Columbia University.[53] St. Martin's now had two buildings and a faculty of nine. According to the Benedictines there, this site was "unexcelled." One must admit that extant photographs of this, taken in 1903, present a rather lugubrious appearance of its landscape. The two buildings look almost naked on top of the hill, with only a few trees standing at some distance to break the empty void around them.[54]

The archbishop, a native of the Midwest, where Notre Dame was believed by some to be the only *Catholic* University worth considering, probably intended to invite Notre Dame's Holy Cross Fathers to take charge of Columbia from the beginning.[55] He lost no time certainly in contacting Father Andrew Morrissey, the president of Notre Dame, and Father John Zahm, the American provincial of the Holy Cross Fathers. Zahm and Morrissey, so it was said, did not get along very well and conferences with Christie about the proposed Holy Cross take over of Columbia often became debates in ideology. Allegedly, at a crucial moment, "Christie in desperation slammed his hand on the arm of his chair and cried, 'Take over Columbia and make it the Notre Dame of the Pacific Northwest!'"[56]

Meanwhile, on September 5, 1901, Columbia opened its doors to fifty-two boys, all but ten from Oregon. The faculty included Father Murphy, the president, another Father James Murphy (not related), as vice president, and Patrick Sullivan, a layman and Notre Dame graduate, as director of students. The teachers included one exiled missionary from China and three seminarians. The story is told that, on opening day, the faculty gathered in the president's office. At about ten in the morning, one of the instructors said to the president, "There are a few boys out there on the campus. Don't you think we ought to start operations?" The president calmly replied, "Oh, I guess we should start. Ring the bell."[57]

Early in 1902, rumors abounded that the Holy Cross Fathers of Notre Dame, which had "practically unlimited financial resources," had purchased Columbia from the archdiocese and planned to make it "the Notre Dame of the West." Events were now moving swiftly. Christie took up the option for the remaining forty-three acres of land and Zahm settled the money claims of the archdiocese. He also appointed a president, "who has a head as well as a heart," a twenty-eight year old English instructor at the University of Notre Dame. This was Father Michael Quinlan who assumed his new duties in May, 1902. In August, two more members of the Holy Cross Congregation arrived, Father Patrick Carroll and Brother Wilfred, the latter for supervising maintenance of the plant. Of the original faculty when the school opened in September 1902, seven were laymen.

Problems quickly appeared, Christie still regarded Columbia as his own and tended to meddle. In other words, he wanted to run the school while someone else paid for it. Zahm, on the other hand, a strong personality like Christie, refused to yield his congregation's jurisdiction. One suspects that Christie soon realized he had bit off more than he could chew. Quinlan was going to run his own show and not even the archbishop was allowed to interfere.

In December, 1902, Zahm visited the university for the first time. He confirmed Christie's growing apprehensions by stating that henceforth, Columbia University would get no additional support from Indiana. Portland would have to provide for its own needs, and that was that.

Fortunately, Morrissey did not agree with this, and when he succeeded Zahm as provincial in August 1906, his Grace celebrated by leaving university matters to the priests in charge. But it was always *his* university and he never allowed people to forget it.

DEATH OF MOTHER JOSEPH

In December of 1900, Mother Joseph first began to discuss her physical sickness. The pain she was experiencing in her face and head was so intense that she was forced to give up her daily habits of toil, but she continued to putter about the convent, usually with several orphan children tagging along.[58] Very rarely had she been seen working in the garden without them. Her peasant sabots, which she had carried from Canada with her almost fifty years before, had been kept on the porch for use on rainy days. Now they mostly amused the children who used them for cracking hazel nuts and took turns shuffling around in them, giggling merrily at one another's clumsiness. On occasion, Mother would gather several older children, take them to the chapel, and lead them in the Way of the Cross, adapting her devotions to their level of thinking.

In the winter of 1901, she had to forego this source of comfort and take to an austere bed in the infirmary, where she kept, beside her, a box of chocolates to reward the children who came to say the rosary with her. her little rice Christians—they truly loved her and, though they could not understand her ever increasing agony, they expressed their concern as children do, by gazing silently upon her, wide-eyed and sad looking.

They could not know that she suffered with a tumor of the brain without modern drugs to alleviate the pain. As time progressed, her malady left her sleepless and her face twitched and distorted, though her eyes retained a kind of peaceful tranquility. When New Year's came in 1902, she knew she was near the end. The last retreat she had made, directed by Father Aloysius Ragaru, a holy Jesuit who later went to Alaska and suffered intensely in the Arctic winters, provided her now with spiritual strength to endure. "With your suffering eye," he wrote to her, "look kindly on Him who allows you to suffer. You gain more merit by suffering than by great action. You have always acted well. Now try to suffer well."[59]

On the eighth of January 1902, her sisters gathered around her bed as Bishop O'Dea administered the last rites. She, Esther Pariseau, Sister Joseph of the Sacred Heart in religion, renewed her vows of poverty, chastity, and obedience, then spoke haltingly of her love for her companions. At last she said to those around her, "Sisters, whatever concerns the poor is always our affair."[60]

Twelve days later, on the eighteenth, her condition became worse. The bishop, summoned by the superior, hurried to her side. But she did not die until the following day, on the feast of the Holy Name of Jesus, seventy-eight in years, but still young in heart. "Oh, if I were young! We would do much good on a mission where there would be misery, and where it would be necessary to make sacrifices. Nowadays we look for too much comfort in this land which offers so much. . . ."[61]

Bishop O'Dea keenly felt the loss of Mother Joseph. She represented something more than a dedicated nun in a convent, or even the foundress of an energetic group of religious. As the most respected woman of her times in the entire Northwest, she gave credibility, in and out of church, to the concept of woman's leadership. Few if any men in the history of the entire nation were more capable than she in her role as administrator of hospitals and schools. In the years to come, she would be recognized as she deserved; but now only a few hundred attended her funeral Mass, conducted by the mournful bishop, and fewer still her burial on the cold hillside, in the simple, almost anonymous grave of a Sister of Providence.[62]

O'DEA'S NEW RESIDENCE IN SEATTLE

O'Dea had other matters to distract him. Rumors that a new diocese was being formed for eastern Washington, with Spokane as its headquarters, had persisted so stubbornly that his Lordship was moved to belie them, both formally and repeatedly.[63] He was at a loss to account for them, he said, and he denied that his diocese was too large for one bishop. It was reported that there were more than 42,000 Catholics in his diocese and forty-two parishes with resident pastors.[64] Was that too many for one bishop? O'Dea did not think so.

Actually the rumors about the proposed new diocese were not entirely without merit. The bishops were discussing two new dioceses, one for eastern Oregon, which made no sense at all, and one for eastern Montana, neither of which had as many Catholics as eastern Washington. The news about Oregon was especially hush-hush. Perhaps someone had started these false reports about Spokane to throw gossiping clerics off the track. It was an open secret that O'Dea was preparing to move from Vancouver. According to a member of the press, "So much pressure has been brought to bear upon Bishop O'Dea by influential members of the diocese that he is seriously considering the advisability of such a step and that, in fact, his presence in Seattle at this time is for the purpose of looking after matters incident to such a change."[65] This was in January 1902, just before Mother Joseph died.

There is no doubt that His Lordship was still intrigued with the idea of moving his residence to Seattle. Spokane, despite the pressures, was out of the question. What mattered now was Rome. O'Dea knew as others did that Archbishop Blanchet had changed his residence twice, setting a precedent that was readily acceptable at the Vatican.[66] Besides, "Nesqually" meant nothing to anyone. Most people did not know even where it was, a post office, little more, southwest of Tacoma, in the parish of old Hylebos, whom the bishop did not particularly understand.

In Seattle, there were now four parishes, including the one in Ballard, St. Alphonsus, which until recently had been staffed by the Redemptorists from Sacred Heart church, the new red brick one with the huge bell tower at Sixth and Bell.[67]

Prefontaine, of the old guard in Seattle, would be a problem like the Jesuits; both had churches that were in the way of the proposed new Cathedral parish. There was nothing to prevent the bishop from making appropriate revisions of the parish limits, but O'Dea was a gentleman and he preferred to avoid an unpleasant confrontation. Strangely, Prefontaine was easily persuaded and there is some reason to suspect that the bishop offered to seek a monsignorship for him if he stepped aside. The fact is, the cathedral property was purchased in 1902, Prefontaine resigned as pastor of Our Lady of Good Help in 1903, and after a discreet interval, was invested with the insignia of a Protonotary Apostolic by Bishop O'Dea himself.[68]

The news regarding the cathedral land did not make the headlines, but it appeared in most northwest papers in an abbreviated form under the dateline of Seattle, January 18, 1902:

> Through the efforts of a few people in Seattle, Bishop O'Dea has secured a site for his cathedral. It is a vacant block known as the Bailey Gatzert property, situated in the paved district, bounded by Ninth and Terry avenues and Marion and Columbia streets. The purchase price is $55,000 and payment has this week been made upon the land and the site thus secured. The bishop has signified his intention as soon as the land is paid for, of moving to Seattle and beginning the construction of a fine cathedral, that when finished will cost a quarter of a million dollars and be one of the handsomest structures in the northwest.[69]

No one, I think, was surprised by this announcement, least of all the Jesuits, who had orders from O'Dea to reestablish their church of the Immaculate Conception "beyond 18th Avenue." Father Adrian Sweere, the gentle, obliging superior of the Seattle Jesuits, purchased land on 18th and Marion, "just beyond the forbidden ground" and built the huge new Immaculate Conception Church which still dominates one of Seattle's skylines. The cornerstone was laid with some pomp and ceremony on May 15, 1904 and dedication solemnities were celebrated on December 4. At this time the church boasted a seating capacity of 950, a far cry from the Kingdome, but then it was the city's largest auditorium or people place. Its debt was equally impressive—$65,000--a lot of cash that forecast an endless round of fund-raising entertainments, card parties, and raffles.[70]

There is no doubt that the Jesuits were proud of this church, but it would never do for the cathedral to be less prestigious. The bishop had been careful to make that clear, and when he announced his plans for actually moving to Seattle, he reminded his readers that the Catholics' new edifice would have no equal in the region.

> Rev. Edward J. O'Dea, Roman Catholic bishop of Nesqually, today announced the removal of the see of his diocese from Vancouver, Wash., where it has been since the diocese was first formed, to its permanent location in Seattle. The change has been contemplated for more than a year, as the rapid growth of the church and the increase in the number of churches has demanded a more central location for the bishop.
>
> The announcement was made this morning from the pulpit of the church of Our Lady of Good Hope which the bishop has decided to use as his pro-cathedral.
>
> In an interview this afternoon the bishop gave his reasons for the change and discussed his plans. He has felt for some time the necessity of being located at some point from which all parts of his diocese could be more readily reached than from Vancouver. He also believes that the see of the bishop should properly be in the largest city of his diocese and among the largest body of his people. The bishop has already purchased a handsome residence on Terry avenue, which is being refitted and refurnished for his use.
>
> 'We have acquired a block of land on Ninth avenue,' said the bishop, 'on which it is intended to build a cathedral that will be a credit to the church, the city and the state. A building such as we have in mind will cost about $250,000. We have not yet the means to begin construction, but expect to have soon. If necessary we can borrow it. Until the cathedral is built the church of Our Lady of Good Hope will be the official church of the bishop. After the transfer from Vancouver to Seattle is completed I will probably make application to Rome to have the name of the diocese changed from Nesqually to the diocese of Seattle.'[71]

About this time, Prefontaine resigned to become chaplain for the sisters at Holy Names Academy. He lived with his niece in old St. Francis Hall, part of which he rented to Catholic clubs like the Hibernians to help pay the fuel and light bills. Not that he needed the money. He seemed to have more friends in City Hall than in the Chancery, for soon after his retirement the City Council bestowed the name "Prefontaine Place" on the site of his first home and chapel in Seattle.[72]

As for Prefontaine's church, O'Dea's "pro-cathedral," a new pastor appeared in the person of Father J.E. O'Brien, who agreed with the bishop that it should be moved. Accordingly, during January and February of 1905, the historic building was "demolished" and its particulars removed and reassembled in part, for a new church of the same name on 5th and Jefferson.[73] The bishop, meanwhile, built a small frame church near the cathedral site. He called it St. Edward's Chapel, for obvious reasons, and this served the Catholics of the cathedral parish until the new St. James was occupied.[74]

THE NEW DIOCESE OF BAKER CITY

It has sometimes been said that no one is a good judge in his own case. What follows here is a classic example of what happens, even in the lives of dedicated priests, when one feels he has been offended and refuses to take the advice of those whose judgments are not influenced by personal involvement.

There are no villains in this sordid affair, there are only victims, perhaps the greatest of whom was the long-suffering archbishop.

The troubles began just one month before the end of the long reign of Leo XIII, when the Apostolic Delegate, Archbishop Diomede Falconio announced the formation of the new diocese of Baker City. The formal disclosure was made on June 19, 1903; Leo died on July 20. In the new diocese, comprising 66,826 square miles, larger in extent than six New England states combined, there were only eleven priests, including three Jesuits at Pendleton and the Umatilla mission.[75] It was commonly believed that in this diocese there were more cows than people. The newly appointed bishop was Charles Joseph O'Reilly, pastor of the Church of the Immaculate Heart of Mary in Portland, an Irish Canadian by birth and an American by adoption.

In clerical circles, at least, the news was sensational, partly because the new diocese numbered only 2,350 Catholics including 450 Indians, fewer than in a large parish in Portland, and less than one for every twenty-two square miles.[76] There seemed to be no explanation for it except that offered by disgruntled priests, who were trapped, so to speak, in a frontier diocese that provided little hope for a decent livelihood and none at all for advancement. The archbishop, some said, had deliberately relegated the discontented priests of Oregon to the eastern half, then cut them off by making a new diocese. There seemed to be no other reason for the change, though the archbishop would not agree.[77]

What is most surprising, perhaps, is that so great a fuss about it followed this division of a diocese. Bishops had proceeded in this manner for centuries and, for nearly as long, the Catholic press had called attention to it and to other actions that today are called "abuses of power." It was only later, when the bishops controlled the Catholic press, for example in the United States, that criticism of the conduct of Catholics in general, including administrators, was not published.[78] It seemed to be appropriate therefore, to call attention to this commonplace, for it keeps in the context of the times the nature of the dissident priests' behavior and lessens their culpability.

The bishop-elect received formal notice of his appointment on July 21, 1903, by telegram from the Apostolic Delegate. "I have forwarded today to the Most Rev. Archbishop of Portland the Brief electing you Bishop of the newly erected Diocese of Baker City. I beg of you to accept my sincere congratulation. . . . "[79]

This is a stale joke among clerics that one offers congratulations or better "condolences" to newly appointed prelates. The latter would have been more appropriate in this case, as the Apostolic Delegate would soon learn. Certainly O'Reilly learned it and it did not take very long.

CONSECRATION OF BISHOP O'REILLY

The new bishop was consecrated in Portland's pro-cathedral on August 25, 1903, by Archbishop Christie, assisted by Bishops O'Dea and Glorieux. This was the first consecration of a bishop in this city, so it attracted more than ordinary attention of the press.[80] Prior Thomas Meienhofer, O.S.B. of Mount Angel read in Latin, and then in English, the papal documents which announced the erection of the diocese of Baker City, its limits and other details, and also the brief which appointed Father O'Reilly as the bishop of the new see. The traditional liturgy was concluded by Bishop O'Reilly pronouncing the oath of allegiance.

The new bishop's vestments during the ceremony hung heavily about him, creating the suggestion of a kind of sacred scarecrow. O'Reilly was forty-one years old, but he looked younger, except for his eyes. These flashed with something more than pious submission.

Six days later, eager to take charge, Bishop O'Reilly arrived by train in Baker City. He was met by the pastor of St. Francis de Sales Church, Father John Heinrich, and by Father L.B. Demarais, neither of whom were Irish. The welcome of the two priests was about as chilling as ice water. One of them carried a gun.[81] Heinrich came to the point: he objected to the bishop's decision to take over the parish house and church, neither of which were actually worth fighting for. There was no room in Baker City, the priests argued. The bishop should "keep going."

Humiliated and shaken with suppressed anger, His Lordship appealed to the sisters at the Academy for lodging. He lived with them for at least nine days and learned how poor they were when they set the table for five people with only four forks.

"My troubles are beginning," he wrote to his sister Theresa in Portland, "the gentleman here refused to obey, and I will be obliged to suspend him if he continues in the same disobedience . . . Rev. D[emarais] claims that *he* is pastor of Baker City—Well, we will see. I ordered him to say the 10 o'Clock Mass on Sunday but he asserts that he will not and insists that he will say the 8 which I announced for myself. His sister is a terror and the people are disgusted."[82]

On September 4, he was still with the sisters, using the expression "when I obtain possession of *my* house." Difficulties he thought, would not deter him in the least, and he ended his letter with expressions of affection. "I think of you all and commend you to Our Lord. My health is fine. Love to all."

The people of Baker City, bewildered by their sudden "good fortune" of having a bishop, remained somewhat aloof and commented sourly that there was not enough money in the city to support him. Their assessment of the situation was more accurate than the archbishop's. The bishop, despite these rumblings, reported that "the people are very kind and delighted that I am here." It seemed, he thought, that he had gained "the good will of all, Catholics and Protestants and Jews, thanks be to God."

Meanwhile, his Lordship was "enthroned" in the rustic shanty church on the day after his arrival. His priests, apparently, shared the event with proper decorum, but their continued obstinance provoked his first formal directive, which bristles with canonical threats:

> The Bishop's Residence, Baker City, Oregon, September 14, 1903
>
>   In order to prevent scandal and consequent harm to religion in the Diocese we hereby inform you that any priest in the Diocese of Baker City, Oregon, who will, at any future time, publish or cause to be published, here or elsewhere, directly or indirectly, any article or letter finding fault with or criticizing the conduct of any ecclesiastic or ecclesiastics, Sister or Sisters, or find fault with or criticize the above named persons in any church, without our written permission, shall *ipso factor* incur the penalty of suspension.
>   Signed Charles J. O'Reilly[83]

That about covered it. It was not taken very seriously, however, because His Lordship was obliged to circulate a second letter containing the same harsh sentiments on November 3, just six weeks later. He was sadly mistaken if he thought threats would scare off those who resented his presence, and their assignment to his diocese even more.

The malcontents were primarily four, but it must be admitted that three of them probably had been drawn into the fracas by the fourth, Father John Schell. Father Bronsgeest of The Dalles, in addition to the two priests at Baker City, made up the rest, a pathetic band of non-Irish pitched in battle against the awesome authority of the archbishop. Bronsgeest, the most respectable of the lot, a veteran of twenty-seven years in Oregon, carried his complaints directly to the archbishop, telling him flatly that he had made a mistake by dividing the diocese. There followed a dispute, not a mild one either, between two strong personalities, concerning the canonical rights of the priest. Despite his anger and frustration, Bronsgeest did not publicly attack the archbishop as alleged, nor Bishop O'Reilly, though evidence is indisputable that he appealed to the Holy See for support of his cause.

MOTHER CABRINI IN SEATTLE

In Seattle, Bishop O'Dea's "handsome residence" was destroyed by fire on October 8, 1903. The newspaper's account of the disaster contains significant details for those who would use some of the early records:

> Valuable records of the Catholic church, which it will be impossible to replace, were destroyed by fire which gutted the residence of Bishop Edward O'Dea at 710 Terry avenue this morning. The fire was caused by a defective flue and had its origin adjacent to the room in which the records were kept.
>
> For some weeks Father J.T. Murphy, secretary to the bishop, has been engaged in transcribing the records of the diocese, and had the fire occurred after this work was completed, duplicate copies of the more indispensable papers and documents would have been filed in another building to guard against a calamity. But as it was, the old and new copies of the important papers were kept in one room, and all of them were either completely destroyed or seriously injured and defaced.
>
> The fire department arrived on the scene promptly and succeeded in confining the flames to the second story and roof of the building, but the entire building was so filled with smoke and water that the furniture and other contents are practically a total loss. The money loss is estimated at $4,000.[84]

A few days later, while the bishop was still pondering his losses, Mother Frances Cabrini arrived in Seattle to found a home for orphans. It was commonly known in the church that Cabrini had been a special favorite of the late Pope, Leo XIII, and that Leo had requested her to send Missionary Sisters of the Sacred Heart (Cabrini Sisters) to the United States. His Holiness picked oranges in the papal gardens to fill her basket and shared with her his anxieties about Italian Catholics who were migrating to America as had the Irish in the potato famine and the Germans in the Bismarck era. One did not ignore a great friend of the

Pope's, not even if the pope was dead. Bishop O'Dea had already welcomed, in March 1903, two of Cabrini's sisters. Now he was pleased to help Cabrini herself find a building.

This was a frame structure on two lots at 1133 Twelfth Avenue South, on Beacon Hill. Cabrini, who was clever at gathering money for orphans, produced the necessary cash and the home, called Mt. Carmel Mission, was officially founded on November 20, 1903. Here Bishop O'Dea offered the first Mass on the feast day of St. Francis Xavier.[85] Meanwhile, Cabrini decided to apply for American citizenship. On November 11, 1903, she made her first application in Superior Court, King County, at Seattle, and six years later, October 13, 1909, Superior Court Judge Edward E. Hardin granted full United States citizenship to become effective after the customary ninety days.[86] Thus it happened that when Mother Cabrini was canonized, she was the first American citizen to receive this honor.[87]

BISHOP BRONDEL'S DEATH

When His Lordship, the Bishop of Helena, celebrated his sixty-first birthday in February 1903, he seemed to be much older. His round face with heavy jowels and hairline that had receded so far back that only a fringe could be seen, gave him a puffy appearance. Unfortunately he was overweight. This, added to his chronic bronchitis, tended to wear him out, but he worked hard, anyhow, traveling throughout the diocese, preaching as often as possible and dedicating buildings with speeches and holy water.

He had a great desire, it was reported, "a mighty cathedral," to replace the present one that had grown too small. For twenty-five years he had hoped to build that cathedral, but he spent his time building small churches on the frontier instead. When he was appointed to Helena, there were only sixteen Catholic churches in Montana. Now there were sixty-three.[88]

Brondel was a realist, perhaps because he lived with *real* people, not caricatures like many people in the soft, sensual climes. He did not expect to build his cathedral. He kept chugging away, preaching and dedicating, despite his difficulties in breathing and the fatigue he often felt. That summer of 1903 he had traveled extensively. When he returned, he admitted to being more tired than usual, and he wheezed and coughed. But he attended meetings and said Mass.

The archbishop in Portland was ailing also. The noisy brouhaha over the division of the diocese, not altogether expected, had left him silent and hurt. In September, he dedicated the new school at Woodburn where he praised the Benedictine Sisters there for their work and restated for the hundredth time the critical need for Catholic education. In early October, he attended the investiture of the pallium for Archbishop Orth in Victoria and he returned to routine work in Portland, uneasy about Baker City and anxious for rest where it was warm and quiet.

He was not prepared for the news from Montana: Bishop Brondel, flushed and breathing heavily, appeared to be very ill. On Thursday, October 29, he had offered his last Mass, and then, at the insistence of his priests, had gone to rest. Two days later, they took him by buggy to St. John's Hospital and there, on November 3, he died peacefully, having edified everyone by his piety and resignation.[89]

On November 6, in the presence of the archbishop, several bishops, many priests, and hundreds of other mourners, John Baptist Brondel, first Bishop of Helena, was buried with great solemnity from the cathedral that was too small. He was praised in eloquent terms, of course, but no one alluded to the fact that in his diocese there was the highest percentage of Catholics in the total population of any diocese in the Northwest.[90] This was due, no doubt, to the heavy concentration of Irish Catholics in the mining settlements like Butte. Of greater significance was the fact that in no state of the West were Catholics held in higher regard than in Montana. Once General Thomas Meagher had wanted to establish it as a Catholic state. He had not succeeded, but Bishop Brondel, who was respected by all, came closer to this than any of his contemporaries. His "mighty cathedral," was realized after all in the hearts of his people, where it would last forever.

Both Christie and O'Dea paused in Spokane to visit Gonzaga College on their journeys home. Christie presented the wildly cheering boys with a holiday and O'Dea entertained a local reporter with comments about the church in eastern Washington. "Gonzaga College," he added, with an eye on domestic consumption, "is the most important Catholic institution in the state."[91] This was true, if only for the present.

MOUNT ANGEL'S NEW ABBOT

At Mount Angel the Benedictine Fathers had completed and occupied their new monastery and college on the day before Christmas, 1903.[92] This was on top of the butte, as they called it, where they had wanted their monastery all along.

The last ten years had been very trying, and misunderstandings had arisen between the mother abbey in Switzerland and Mount Angel. The root of the problem was money. Loss of almost everything they owned in the sudden fire in 1899, and the need to rebuild everything, had put the monks heavily in debt, and the founder-prior, Adelhelm Odermatt, was forced to travel all over the country to raise funds. In his long absences, some matters went unattended and when a new abbot was elected in Engelberg on January 23, 1901, Odermatt found himself and the rest of his monks under painful scrutiny.[93] This was bad enough, but Odermatt was guilty, in the eyes of the new abbot Leodegar Scherer, of an unforgivable gaffe, which triggered the formal investigation of his stewardship.

Odermatt had become accustomed to begging, American style, from anyone he met. It had become a habit. He playfully suggested to Leodegar that Engelberg cancel Mount Angel's debt of $140,000 as if this were "breadcrumbs falling from a rich table."[94] Neither Leodegar nor his community regarded this as humorous, indeed they were all as indignant as slighted monsignors, and Leodegar delegated Abbot Frowin from Conception to conduct a canonical visitation at Mount Angel. Among other things, he was to preside over an *election* of a prior, not necessarily to replace poor old Odermatt, who had been appointed, but at least to give the monks a choice, "as a first step towards eventual independence." This sounded a bit righteous, perhaps ominous as well, for that word "eventual" seemed to imply a longer wait than the monks expected. One suspects, also, that Leodegar was worried about the $140,000 loan, enough money in those days to float a battleship.

Frowin left Conception on June 24, 1901, to make his inspection at Mount Angel. At the same time, the monks at Engelberg began "a solemn Novena" that all would go well. They waited apprehensively for news. To their immense relief, Frowin reported favorably, writing from Mount Angel on July 12, Financially, he said, the priory was not as badly off as presumed. "After considerable balloting and a period of great tension in the community, a new prior was elected July 11, the Rev. Thomas Meienhofer," who had been born in Switzerland, had come to America, and made his profession at Mount Angel in 1890.[95] Frowin considered the selection a wise one.

Prior Thomas wrote to Leodegar, presenting a detailed financial report and reassuring his abbot and the community that he would "honor faithfully the obligation to pay the sum of $1,000 a year until the debt is liquidated...." At this rate it would require only 140 years at one thousand dollars a year, that is, until 2041 A.D. to wipe out the debt.[96] Everyone was happy with this.

But there remained a basic problem that had plagued the foundation from the very beginning. The local superior did not have sufficient authority to make the on the spot decisions often required in a monastery that was at least five thousand miles from the abbot. Meienhofer spoke openly for Leodegar's approval for abbey status for Mount Angel. Leodegar would hear nothing of it and Frowin confirm his views by saying that "matters must not be rushed." It all depended on whose ox was gored.

In 1903, before the monks moved into the new monastery on the butte, Frowin changed his mind. He wrote to Leodegar from Conception telling him that the time had come to raise Mount Angel to the dignity of an independent monastery. On November 9 of that year, Meienhofer, too, wrote to his abbot informing him that "another election of a *prior* would be a sad blow to the young community." A petition was circulated among other abbots of the world, urging the elevation of Mount Angel. Then Leodegar, still somewhat skeptical, caved in. He requested Frowin to preside over the election of an abbot.

On this note, one of hope and jubilation in the new monastery, the year ended. Leodegar wrote in his diary: "On the first of March, I received a letter from Abbot Frowin.... It contains the joyful news that Prior Thomas Meienhofer has been chosen by his community as the person to be presented to the Holy Father."[97] Frowin himself tells how the election took place.

> I arrived in Mount Angel February 1 and was warmly received. February 3 I began the canonical visitation. After its close there was a discussion about the abbacy.... All agreed that the priory should be made an abbey and that an election should be held now to determine the person to be presented.
>
> Today at 11:30 a.m. on the ninth ballot Prior Thomas Meienhofer received the majority of votes required. It was as if a great stone fell from my shoulders.
>
> Difficult as it was to make the choice, once it was made all declared themselves satisfied and promised to sign the petition to the Holy Father. Personally I consider this the best choice under the circumstances and so I take the liberty of congratulating your Reverence and the mother abbey upon the outcome.... I shall now send the Abbot Primate the petition signed by all the capitulars to have the house elevated to the dignity of an abbey, the nomination of Prior Thomas, and the recommendation of the local archbishop.[98]

On March 24, 1904, Pope Pius X raised Mount Angel to the status of an independent monastery and confirmed Prior Thomas as its first abbot. The customary abbatial blessing was scheduled for June 29. Meienhofer, "for urgent business reasons," he says, decided to visit the monastery's Indian missions at Clayoqust on Vancouver Island. On his return journey in a small sailing boat, heavy winds off the ocean capsized the fragile vessel and its occupants lost everything except their lives, even their shoes. A good Samaritan in an Indian canoe rescued them and brought them ashore, but they had to walk barefoot for eighty-five miles on rocky terrain. The ordeal almost killed Mount Angel's first abbot. He lived, however, to attend his own blessing on the date assigned. The ceremony, by common demand, was celebrated in the monastery's new chapel, with standing room only. One of Abbot Thomas' first official acts was to appoint poor old Adelhelm prior of the monastery "to the great satisfaction of all. The Founder [remained] prior until 1916."[99]

MORE BENEDICTINE PROGRESS

Mount Angel's good fortune did not affect St. Martin's, which was subject to the abbot of St. John's in Collegeville. In January of this same year (1904), this monastery received some recognition, at least, by being designated "an independent prior," a canonical privilege that provided for a limited amount of local jurisdiction.[100] Father Demetrius Jueneman of Holy Rosary Parish in Tacoma was elected as its first prior. He undertook the challenges of his new office with fresh vigor by contracting for a major addition to the college building, more than doubling its size, and by securing three Benedictine Sisters from Colton to conduct the most essential department on the campus, the kitchen. These were Mother M. Johanna, still the indestructible Mother Superior, with the sharp eyes and a sharper pen, and Sisters Meinroda and Walburga, good and holy souls, though their names suggested something else.

The sisters arrived on May 30.[101] On July 1 another sister from Colton joined them to take over the care of the sewing room.[102] The departure of four nuns from the motherhouse in Colton shows that the convent, after its many vicissitudes, had begun to prosper. Indeed, Saint Scholastica's had become too small for the burgeoning community and there was lively speculation about the acquisition of another site. Camas Prairie, especially the Cottonwood area, still intrigued the sisters who engaged in "lengthy and serious considerations and debates" regarding the matter, which involved several complex obstacles, like getting the approval of Bishop O'Dea.

There were other compelling reasons. The peripatetic Abbot Frowin in his many comings and goings had finally yielded to his presumably holy aspirations for founding his own daughter monastery. Engelberg had sent out monks. St. John's had sent out monks. Conception, too, would send out monks, and Cottonwood, Frowin decided, was the most attractive place to send them. Bishop Glorieux agreed with him. It was a project dear to the heart of his Lordship, who had appealed more than once to the abbot for a monastery in Idaho.

After Frowin returned to Conception, following the blessing of

Meienhofer at Mount Angel, he submitted his proposal to the General Chapter on September 9. The Chapter approved the plan and on November 7, 1904, Fathers Berthold Jaeggle and Odilo Schieler, and Brother Anthony Kellenberg, entrained for Cottonwood, where they arrived three days later. Glorieux responded joyfully by giving them the care of parishes and missions at Cottonwood, Keuterville, Ferdinand, Grangeville, all on Camas Prairie, and the Salmon River stations below White Bird Pass.[103]

In the following year, on September 29, 1905, Frowin returned to Idaho and purchased a 320 acre farm for a monastery, which was soon built on a small scale. It was dedicated under the patronage of St. Michael. Jaeggle was appointed the first prior, the recitation of the office was inaugurated at once, and Benedictine community life was begun anew in this part of the world, far from Monte Cassino whence the Benedictines had sprung.

The new St. Michael's made a feeble beginning, frought with dangers and unpredictable misfortunes. It finally perished, like Meienhofer's fragile boat in the ocean's storm. It lasted only twenty-one years. In April 1925, a papal rescript was granted for its canonical suppression and the legal corporation of the priory voted its own dissolution, in deference to the wishes of higher superiors at Conception. The monastery as such ceased to exist on July 1, 1925.[104]

Despite appearances, St. Michael's was not a failure. It created a fervent Catholic enclave on the prairie to which the church owes many vocations, and it prepared the way for the final home of the Benedictine Sisters of Sarnen, who discovered its peace at last.

BAKER CITY CONTINUED: THE SCHELL AFFAIR

Archbishop Christie wintered that year in San Francisco.[105] His health improved somewhat, but he was unable to celebrate the pontifical Mass in the pro-cathedral on Easter Sunday. He returned to Oakland May 27, 1904, to enter Providence Hospital where he underwent surgery for a stomach disorder, and it was not until July 5 that he was able to return to Portland.[106]

Conditions prevailing in Oregon then were neither conducive to his recovery nor to his good reputation, which had been cut to shreds in his absence. "Archbishop Is Accused of Nearly Everything," was a headline in the local paper.[107] "Coterie of Disgruntled Priests Is Believed to Be at Bottom of Hysterical Campaign Waged Against the Prelate." There followed an account of a circular dated May 16, 1904 containing numerous charges labeled "Crimes And Acts of Cruelty" and addressed to the Apostolic Delegate. Since none of the charges were true, they are presented in part here to demonstrate the bitterness of the dispute, without damaging the good name of Archbishop Christie.

Archbishop Christie has destroyed priests and sisters, has ruined schools and parishes, has ruined souls and religion, has prostituted his power and dignity in favor of worldly politicians. He has banished from Oregon the priests who have built up Oregon; he has brought with him more than 26 runaway immoral priests, and with them he operates in Oregon. He has deceived your excellency and Rome as well. There are today more runaway or tramp priests in Oregon than are ordained for Oregon. The archbishop flooded Eastern Oregon with these priests, paid them to stay, built churches and pays for them, in order to show to Rome that there are so-and-so many churches with resident priests, yet there are no Catholics. The new diocese has 67,000 square miles and less than 1700 Catholic souls, good and bad, and not one place that ever did or could gave an honest support to a priest.'

The paper then goes on to accuse the apostolic delegate with complicity in the situation. It claims that he knew and had received proofs of the actions of the archbishop of Oregon and had taken no action in the matter. It harps on the division of the Oregon City diocese. . . .

Following this the case of Bishop O'Reilly is taken up, and here the part significant to the authorship of the document creeps in. Bishop O'Reilly is denounced and accused of having knocked Father Desmarais down in his home in Baker City, and having him bound and dragged through the streets of the city to the jail. At the same time very laudatory statements are made regarding Fathers Desmarais, Brongeest and Schell. The good qualities of each of the gentlemen are shown, after which the document closes with the following statement and signature:

'Conditions that can stop this denunciation are as follows:

'1. We want back our good priests, and they must be reinstated according to justice and merits, based on their works for the diocese.

'2. We want that any and all damages be paid to them, which damages they have sustained by the archbishop's cruel and treacherous persecution.

'3. We want that the laws of the Church be proclaimed and kept in Oregon so that the priests, the sisters and the Catholic people are protected and able to know their duties without being forced to lie, to steal, to practice or suffer secret simony.

'4. We want that the expense of this pamphlet—being $650--be refunded in equal parts to the Fathers Heinrich, Desmarais, Schell, and Bronsgeest, the four priests most in need.'[108]

And so forth. A larger pamphlet soon appeared. This contained forty paragraphs of allegations, with the phrase "Proofs on hand" at the end of each. Included in some form or other was criticism of the archbishop by almost everybody whose name would be recognized by Catholics: Bishop

[sic] Orth, the Holy Names Sisters, the Benedictines of Mount Angel, a score of priests, *The Catholic Sentinel*, prominent laymen, The Order of the Foresters, The United Irish League and many more, all of whom became indignantly aroused, protesting their non-involvement and their respect for the archbishop so loudly they could be heard in Rome. They were furious, of course, but they were not sure where they should place the blame, since the pamphlet was anonymous, signed by "The Committee of Action." This sounded to most Catholics like an evil message from the Bolsheviks, who were somehow related to the devil. How did one revile the devil? The pamphlet was a hoax. Its contents were pure fabrication and at least three of the four priests to whom it was attributed had no knowledge or part in this publication. Only Father Joseph Schell, who had been assigned to Sumpter in eastern Oregon can be held accountable, and it is highly unlikely that the text as it appeared came from his pen.

Two other broadsides that are extant were also circulated during this period, one "signed by Bronsgeest," dated Davenport, Iowa, April 26, 1904, addressed to Christie, and another with Schell as the alleged author, dated Baker City, May 16, 1904, addressed to Bishop O'Reilly. Both were put into the mails and delivered "to every person and firm whose name appeared in the City Directory [of Portland]."[109] These, too, prompted many protestations of innocence, including a sworn statement by Bronsgeest: "I solemnly affirm that I have never yet published or given for publication, or allowed or suggested the publication of any letter of circular, fabricated or dictated by myself against any bishop or archbishop, living or dead."

The climax of the storm was reached on June 26, 1904, with publication of a news dispatch from Rome stating that formal charges had been filed against Archbishop Christie. O'Reilly hastened to Portland. *The Catholic Sentinel* bristled with expressions of rage. No words were strong enough for Christie's friends. The Knights of Columbus drew up resolutions vigorously condemning "the unknown author" of the infamous broadsides and his words and his methods. They branded every accusation as "malicious libel" and reaffirmed their confidence in the prelate and his priests.[110]

While others, by the score, rallied to his support, Christie remained silent. Even those with whom he lived "never once heard Archbishop Christie make the slightest reference to the affair."[111]

The Oregonian was impressed.

If the traducers of Archbishop Alexander Christie and the Catholic clergy of Oregon hoped to have the archbishop answer their charges, their hopes and desires have missed fire. At the archbishop's residence yesterday afternoon it was learned that the archbishop, under no circumstances, would answer the attacks made upon him in the circular, which not only was sent to Rome, but scattered broadcast throughout Oregon and Washington.

The archbishop is fully aware who is the originator of the circulars which seek to besmirch his good name, but he is holding himself aloof from criticism of the person himself. His treatment of the charges will be a dignified silence, although it is understood that others will take up the accusations and answer them in due time.[112]

The perpetrator of these "Slanderous Attacks" which continued to appear, was generally believed to be Father Joseph Schell. An unidentified correspondent reported that "Schell's predilection for using virulent language is so well known that he is not taken seriously." There is no doubt that Schell was involved, but the extent of his authorship remains a mystery. It is my opinion that Schell was used, at least in part, by John Doe unknown, for the obvious purpose of damaging the church.

In October, a weary and depressed Bishop O'Reilly dispatched a long, gloomy report to Falconio.

A personal visitation of the greater and best portions of this diocese has demonstrated more forcibly the correctness of every statement made therein, and convinces me of the utter impossibility of maintaining a diocese of this kind.

I am not at all affected by the statement of prominent ecclesiastics, who know our conditions, to the effect that this diocese is a burlesque on the episcopacy, and other expressions of similar character. But after a fair trial of fourteen months, I am compelled to conclude that in my opinion there is no hope of obtaining in this diocese the means necessary for the becoming support of a bishop. I cannot live as a bishop, my poor priests are unable to support me, I have no income from the parish, and but a merely nominal help from a few poor priests on poor missions.

It is therefore impossible to see any reason or necessity for the existence of this diocese. For instead of being a benefit to religion, the Diocese of Baker City has been and will be in the opinion of all directly interested a detriment to Catholic progress in this territory.

In my own name and in the name of my priests, I again ask Your Excellency to assign an adequate remedy.... [113]

The Apostolic Delegate "after discussion with Archbishop Christie," replied on November 9, 1904.

I am convinced that the future of your diocese is not so dark as you seem to think; every new diocese in the beginning finds itself in more or less critical circumstances.

It was like Boise all over again and this time O'Reilly, whose health was being undermined, was repeating the role of Lootens. Lootens had not begun, however, in a cyclone of dissent.

O'Reilly's opinions were confirmed by his priests who prepared reports that got down to brass tacks. First there was the Chancellor's complaint, dated on the same day as O'Reilly's. In brief this appeared as follows:

1) The Parish does not number more than 75 families.

2) These people do not seem to be complimented by having a bishop, on the contrary they object to the expense.

3) They assert that "the poor bishop is to be pitied."

4) The Bishop's appeal on Sunday for a new church, most walked home without attending the meeting.

5) Parishioners say the church will not be built.

6) The people admire the patience of His Lordship.

7) The parish cannot support even one priest.

7) [sic] Bishop gets not one cent of salary, only board.[114]

Other priests added their views, which were similar to the bishop's. "We, as well as most of the Rev. Clergy," they concluded, "contend that the Baker City Diocese was erected on defective information." Great hardship to priests and people and the unfortunate division in the diocese, with grave scandals was the result.[115]

The strain on the bishop began to affect his usually good disposition, for he seems to have quarreled with the archbishop. His Grace had a friend in Rome, a Father W. Haley, who was prodigal with his unsolicited advice. He sounded more like a provacateur. "Your Grace," he wrote. "In your letter telling me of Rt. Rev. Bp. O'Reilly's attack on you, you said you were enclosing the documents and would forward other papers bearing on the matter. Neither one nor the other has reached me.... Bronsgeest is reported to have his lodgings in the Via dei Lucchesi and to have as advisor [sic] or advocate a certain Msgr. Coletti."[116]

So Bronsgeest was in Rome to obtain his "rights." Christie could depend on Haley to keep an eye on him, not that his Grace preferred it that way.

"You did all that human patience could do for Gibney," Haley wrote. "You put DeRoo on his feet... you gave Demarais every place he asked for, you tried in every way to satisfy Fahy, Dielman and Verhaag. You gave every confidence and privilege to old Cestelli, and what has been your reward in every case?"

If one wonders why Haley was so ingratiating, he may find an answer in the last of his letters that survived:

How happy I should be if you were transferred to Boston and take me with you, as Archbishop took his secretary with him to Chicago. You have done your duty to Oregon. You have lifted it out of an impossible chaos to a perfectly workable condition. You have cleared away debt, rejuvenated the clergy, reorganized the religious communities and well equipped the whole territory with schools and churches. And what is the reward or will be the reward you enjoy there? Not even peace of mind. Well indeed then might you shake its dust from off your feet and accept, as I feel sure you could easily obtain a position near your old home in the East, where a higher civilization and culture, and a broader field of labor will serve to alleviate the weariness of the life of the Episcopate. Try for Boston while it is open. . . . [117]

Bronsgeest, meanwhile, embarked for New York. He met Cardinal Satolli there and appealed to him for help. His Eminence was not pleased and he informed the priest that "he is not helping clerical brigands," which indicated quite clearly where Rome stood in the disturbance.[118]

By this time, things were cooling off. There was only one other significant exchange of correspondence, O'Reilly to Christie, which reveals the current status of Schell.

"Today," O'Reilly wrote from Philadelphia, "the [Apostolic] Delegate is the guest of Archbishop Ryan. The Delegate informs me that Schell wrote him that he may publish a book. The Delegate positively forbade him and also says that if he should write, we must sue him for Defamation of Character."[119]

Schell took the dare. His "book" was an enlarged pamphlet with nothing new. By then no one believed Schell any more, and no one except the critics of the church was interested. These had much better printed rubbish for their nefarious purpose.

It has been suggested that Schell was mentally disturbed, an understatement, but true. He seems to have been a good priest in other respects and his death on May 27, 1936, is still recorded with the priests in good standing in the official history of the Diocese of Baker.[120]

Thus ended the Baker City affair, a strange but not unique curiosity in the American church. A similar dispute, mild by comparison, would occur in Spokane. The bishop in that case spoke his piece and even His Honor the judge, in whose court the litigation ended, took careful notice.

THE FIRST COMING OF THE TRAPPISTS

In Europe during this time, a wave of anti-clericalism was sweeping through several so-called Christian countries with governments who were bitterly opposed to religion in any form. Germany, Italy, France, and Switzerland joined North Ireland in attacking priests in particular. In France, Georges Clemenceau, "the Tiger" was conspicuous for his hostility especially toward the contemplative orders whom he regarded as useless drones, consumers of the bread of workmen. The Jesuits were the first to feel the blow of these new Huns, who got around to other orders as time progressed. Among the orders in France, the Cistercians were on the list for expulsion. They were holy men who harmed no one,

St. James Church, Ft. Vancouver, 1851. (National Park Service, Ft. Vancouver.)

Highly imaginative sketch, bearing little resemblance to the original St. Mary's Mission on the Bitteroot, ca. 1845.

Sacred Heart Mission, built 1850-1854. Photo taken about 1920, before the first restoration. (Oregon Province Archives)

St. Paul Church, St. Paul, Oregon, erected as the Northwest's first cathedral in 1846. (St. Paul Mission Historical Society)

Bishop John Baptist Brondel, first bishop of Helena, 1884-1903. (Oregon Province Archives)

Bishop Aegidius Junger, second bishop of Nesqually, 1879-1895. (Oregon Province Archives)

Abbot Adelhelm Odermatt, founder of Mount Angel Abbey in 1884. (Mount Angel Archives)

Archbishop Charles Seghers, second archbishop of Oregon City, 1880-1884. With the pope's approval he resigned to become bishop of Vancouver Island and Alaska, where he was murdered in 1886. (Oregon Province Archives)

Bishop Edward O'Dea, third bishop of Nesqually, 1896-1907, and first bishop of Seattle, 1907-1932. (Oregon Province Archives)

Bishop Mathias Lenihan, first bishop of Great Falls, 1904-1930. (Sisters of Providence Archives, Spokane)

Dr. John McLoughlin, Chief Factor, Hudson's Bay Company, who assisted the first Catholic missionaries. (St. Paul Mission Historical Society.)

Aeneas, or young Ignace, guide for Fr. Peter DeSmet to the Flathead country in the spring of 1840. Drawn by Gustavus Sohon on May 16, 1854.

Fr. Anthony Ravalli, pioneer Jesuit missionary who arrived with DeSmet in 1844. (Oregon Province Archives)

Fr. Casimir Chirouse, O.M.I., ca. 1875. (Archives of Archdiocese of Seattle)

Fr. Charles Pandosy, O.M.I., ca. 1880.

Fr. John Baptist Brouillet, ca. 1870. (Archives of the Archdiocese of Seattle).

Fr. Joseph Joset, S.J., ca. 1880. (Oregon Province Archives)

Mother Joseph of the Sacred Heart. (Providence Archives, Seattle)

Isaac Stevens, first governor of Washington Territory, ca. 1855. (Whitman College Archives)

Fr. Peter J. DeSmet, S.J., with seven Indian chiefs whose tribes were involved in the Indian War of 1858. (Oregon Province Archives)

First faculty and students, St. Michael's College, Portland, 1874. Note the following in the first row: Fr. Alphonsus Glorieux, later Bishop of Boise, Fr. John Fierens, who built the ill-starred cathedral in Portland, and Fr. J. Heinrick, who engaged in a bitter dispute with Christie. Edward O'Dea, future Bishop of Seattle, is in the back row, third from left.

St. John's pro-cathedral in Oregon City. (Seattle Archdiocesan Archives)

St. Mary's Church, first Catholic church in Seattle, ca. 1855. (Oregon Province Archives)

St. James pro-cathedral at Ft. Vancouver on far right, ca. 1850. (Public Archives of Canada)

First St. Mary's convent and academy in Portland, 1859. (Marylhurst Archives)

Holy Angels College, Vancouver, ca. 1866.

Shanty in Baker City, Oregon, rented in 1871 by Fr. L. Dielman for use as first Catholic chapel. (Baker Diocesan Archives)

Artist's sketch of St. Ignatius Mission, Montana, ca. 1860. (Oregon Province Archives)

Our Lady of Good Help Church in Seattle, built by Prefontaine in 1869. Photo taken ca. 1904. (Archives of the Archdiocese of Seattle)

St. Joseph's Academy, Vancouver, built by Mother Joseph. (Providence Archives, Seattle)

Fr. Adrian Croquet, ca. 1890. (Marylhurst Archives)

Fr. Toussaint Mesplie, ca. 1890. (Oregon Province Archives)

Fr. Joseph Giorda, ca. 1870. (Oregon Province Archives)

General Thomas Meagher, ca. 1866. (Oregon Province Archives)

Fr. John Baptist Boulet, founder of the church in the Bellingham area. (Archives of the Archdiocese of Seattle)

Fr. Peter Hylebos, ca. 1890, founder of the church in Tacoma. (Archives of the Archdiocese of Seattle)

Fr. Louis Conrardy, missionary in eastern Oregon, 1875-1888, later a companion of Fr. Damian in Molokai. (Baker Diocesan Archives)

Sr. Bertha Granez, pioneer Sister of Charity of Leavenworth in Helena, 1869. (Archives of the Sisters of Charity of Leavenworth)

Mother Joseph and companion on tour in Indian country, probably eastern Washington, ca. 1885. (Providence Archives, Seattle)

Bishop Charles O'Reilly, first
bishop of Baker City, 1903-1918.
(Oregon Province Archives)

Bishop Augustine Schinner, first
bishop of Spokane, 1914-1925.
(Oregon Province Archives)

Bishop Edwin O'Hara, second
bishop of Great Falls, 1930-1939.
(Sisters of Providence, Spokane)

Bishop Joseph Dougherty, first
bishop of Yakima, 1951-1969.
(Oregon Province Archives)

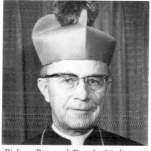

Bishop Bernard Topel, third
bishop of Spokane, 1955-1978.
(Archives of the Diocese of
Spokane)

Bishop Eldon Schuster, fourth
bishop of Great Falls 1967-1977.
(Diocese of Great Falls-Billings)

Providence Sisters at Indian reservation, probably the Flathead reservation in Montana,
ca. 1870. (Providence Archives, Seattle)

First St. Boniface Church in Sublimity, Oregon, (ca. 1887) with
Fr. Wernher Ruttiman standing in the doorway. In the
background is the Convent of Maria Zell, where the Sisters of
St. Mary of Oregon were originally established by Archbishop
Gross in 1886. (Archives of Sisters of St. Mary)

St. Ann's Mission of Fr. Chirouse, near Maryville, Washington, ca. 1870. (Oregon Archives)

Notre Dame Academy in Baker, established by the Sisters of the Holy Names in 1875. (Archives of the Baker Diocese)

Spokane's first church, called St. Joseph's, ca. 1881. It was formerly a carpenter's shop. (Oregon Province Archives)

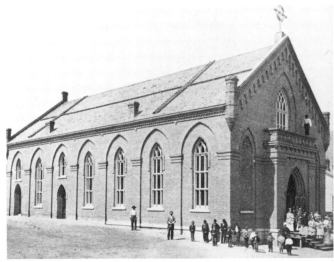

First cathedral in Helena, built by Fr. Lawrence Palladino, S.J., as a parish church in 1876. It was called the Sacred Hearts of Jesus and Mary and became Bishop Brondel's cathedral in 1884. (Oregon Province Archives)

St. Francis Xavier mission on Crow Indian reservation in eastern Montana, ca. 1890. (Oregon Province Archives)

Fort Benton's Immaculate Conception Church and St. Clare's Hospital, founded by the Sisters of Providence in 1885. The church was built in 1878. (Archives of the Great Falls-Billings Diocese)

St. Paul's Mission near Hayes in eastern Montana, founded in 1887. Photo ca. 1910. (Oregon Province Archives)

Bishop Sylvester Treinen, fifth bishop of Boise, 1946-. (Diocese of Boise)

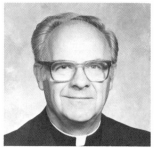

Archbishop Raymond Hunthausen, sixth bishop of Helena 1962-1975, and second archbishop of Seattle, 1975-. (Archives of the Archdiocese of Seattle)

Archbishop Cornelius Power, second bishop of Yakima, 1969-1974, and seventh archbishop of Portland. *(Catholic Sentinel)*

Archbishop Edward Howard, fifth Archbishop of Portland in Oregon, 1926-1966, shown here in retirement, with Sister Mary Andre Campan, S.S.M.O. (Archives of the Archdiocese of Portland)

Bishop Nicholas E. Walsh, third bishop of Yakima, 1974-1976. (Oregon Province Archives)

Bishop Eldon Curtiss, seventh bishop of Helena, 1976-. (Diocese of Helena)

St. Andrew's Convent and Academy in Uniontown (ca.1890), a short time before the famous feud between Uniontown and Colton. On the far right is Fr. Anthony Goehren, who started the feud. Author's mother appears in this photograph in the front row on the far left. (St. Gertrude's Archives, Cottonwood)

Fr. R.W.J. Lindesmith, army chaplain at Fort Keogh, near Miles City, Montana, in 1881. (Oregon Province Archives)

M.M. Cowley, early pioneer and one of the founders of the church in Spokane. (Oregon Province Archives)

Fr. James Frei as an older priest ca. 1918. (St. Gertrude's Archives, Cottonwood)

Fr. Barnabas Held, OSB, ca. 1895. (Mount Angel Archives)

Fr. John Fierens, pastor of cathedral parish in Portland. (Marylhurst Archives)

Stephen J. McCormick, pioneer mayor of Portland and devoted Catholic leader; second editor of the *Catholic Sentinel*. (Marylhurst Archives)

Fr. Joseph Cataldo, superior of the Jesuits in the Northwest for sixteen years, founder of Gonzaga University, and renowned Indian language scholar. (Oregon Province Archives)

Mother Johanna Zumstein, O.S.B., foundress of the Benedictine Sisters' convents in Grand Ronde, Uniontown, Colton, and Cottonwood. (St. Gertrude's Archives, Cottonwood)

Mother Katherine Drexel, foundress of the Sisters of the Blessed Sacrament. (Archives of the Sisters of the Blessed Sacrament)

Fr. Peter Poaps, first pastor of Pomeroy in eastern Washington. Fr. A. Meuwese, first pastor of Sprague in eastern Washington. (Archives of the Archdiocese of Seattle)

Interior of St. Francis Xavier Church in Missoula, Montana, completed in 1892. The frescoes were executed by Brother Joseph Carignano, a noted Jesuit artist who decorated many frontier churches. (Oregon Province Archives)

St. James Cathedral, in Vancouver, Washington, ca. 1890. Chancery building for the diocese of Nesqually is on the left. (Archives of the Archdiocese of Seattle)

St. Francis de Sales church, Baker City, 1903. (Archives of the Diocese of Baker)

Mount Angel ca. 1891. Left to right the buildings are: Benedictine priory, chapel, seminary wing, college. This complex, except the college, was destroyed by fire in 1892. (Mount Angel Archives)

First Gonzaga University campus, ca. 1892. St. Aloysius Church is on the right. (Oregon Province Archives)

Old St. Joseph's Church near Yakima, 1897. (Oregon Province Archives)

St. James Cathedral in Seattle, before the central dome fell in during a snowstorm, 1916. (Oregon Province Archives)

St. Gertrude's first convent and church in Cottonwood, Idaho, ca. 1907. (Archives of St. Gertrude's)

Mount St. Charles College, Helena, ca. 1915, now called Carroll College. (Archives of the Diocese of Helena)

Cathedral of St. Helena in Helena, 1980. (Archives of Diocese of Helena)

Thomas Cruse, wealthy Montana mining magnate who provided funds to build the cathedral, ca. 1910. (Archives of the Diocese of Helena)

James Culligan, distinguished professor for many years at the University of Portland. (University of Portland Archives)

St. Frances Cabrini, who arrived in Seattle in 1903 and became a naturalized American citizen there in 1909. (Archives of the Archdiocese of Seattle)

Judge John P. Kavanaugh, who successfully presented the Catholic position on the Oregon compulsory school bill before the U.S. Supreme Court. (St. Paul Mission Historical Society)

John Goodwin, prominent teacher and later principal of John F. Kennedy High School, Seattle. (Photo from Mrs. John Goodwin)

Henry F. Day, generous benefactor of the Northwest church.

Founders of the Catholic Church Extension Society, ca. 1905. (Extension Society photo)

Chapel Car, "St. Anthony," of the Catholic Church Extension Society, which arrived in the Northwest in 1909. (Extension Society photo)

Bishop William Skylstad, fourth bishop of Yakima, 1977. (Oregon Province Archives)

Bishop Lawrence Welch, fourth bishop of Spokane. (Diocese of Spokane)

Bishop Thomas Murphy, fifth bishop of Great Falls-Billings. (Diocese of Great Falls, Billings)

Bishop Kenneth Steiner, auxiliary bishop of Portland. (Catholic Sentinel)

Bishop Paul E. Waldschmitt, auxiliary bishop of Portland. (Catholic Sentinel)

Bishop Alphonse Glorieux, first bishop of Boise.

Archbishop Alexander Christie, fourth archbishop of Oregon City

Bishop O'Dea in solemn procession, 1925.

Ground breaking for the College of Sister Formation, Providence Heights, Issaquah, 1959. (Sisters of Providence, Seattle)

First St. Elizabeth Hospital and Cathedral in Baker City, ca. 1906. (Archives of Sisters of St. Francis, Palatine Hill, Portland)

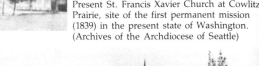

Present St. Francis Xavier Church at Cowlitz Prairie, site of the first permanent mission (1839) in the present state of Washington. (Archives of the Archdiocese of Seattle)

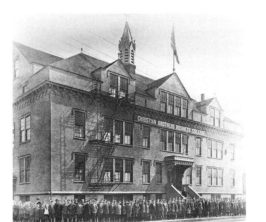

Rectory of the Chiloquin Indian Mission, 1925. The "cellar" for Mass wine is under the innocent looking log in the foreground. (Archdiocese of Baker)

Christian Brothers Business College in Portland, 1908-1922. (Christian Brothers, Moroga, California)

St. Edward's Seminary, Kenmore, WA., opened in 1931. (Archives of the Archdiocese of Seattle)

produced their own food by their labors, and fasted and prayed for sinners, among whom one might include Clemenceau.

The Cistercians, usually called Trappists in this country, were not unaware that in the French Chamber of Deputies Emile Combes and Waldeck-Rosseau had sponsored the bill that had cleared France of the Carthusians, and that the Cistercians were probably next on the list. A meeting of Cistercian Abbots held in Paris on June 28, 1901, ended with a decision to send Dom Jean Baptiste Chautard, Abbot of Sept-Fons, to represent the order in a confrontation with Clemenceau.[121] On the eve of the final vote on the fate of the Cistercians, Chautard was ushered into the presence of the Tiger who promptly greeted him with a tirade "that monks were useless and it was high time they were kicked out of the country." The abbot was not intimidated. He responded with spirit, giving Clemenceau tit for tat, using spiritual arguments rather than political to refute his opponent's unjust diatribe. It is unlikely that the politician understood what Chautard was talking about but he was impressed by the abbot's faith. The interview ended when the Tiger shook hands with the abbot and said, "You are my friend," which was probably as close as he had got to God in a long time.

The entire order could not be saved, for the government had to show its muscle. One or two monasteries had to be sacrificed to save the others. In the end it was Fontgombault that had to go. Its abbot had spent more than a year seeking an asylum in Europe in the event the whole order had to leave. But now Fontgombault was closed down, he could think of nothing better than an abandoned farmhouse near Gethsemani, a well-known Trappist monastery in Kentucky which had been offered to the exiles.

Accordingly in 1903, half of the Fontgombault community sailed to America. Half joined other Trappist monasteries in Europe. Fontgombault was seized by the government and transformed into a reform school.

The Gethsemani farmhouse was only a temporary shelter, a base to reconnoiter for something better. A more suitable location was found near Jordan in Oregon, an old farm that encompassed many favorable features: plenty of timber, a stone quarry, an orchard on the fertile hillside, meadows for raising grain and forage, and a mild climate. The owner of the farm was not indulgent. He wanted "his own price for it," which seems to imply an exorbitant one.

Archbishop Christie was delighted. He had invited the Trappists in the first place "with the rather quixotic idea that they would heal a division that had grown up in [the Jordan] parish of German families."[122] The Germans could not agree on the site for their new church. Half of them who lived on the plateau wanted the church there and the other half wanted it in the valley where they lived. When the church in the valley burned down, it was replaced with another on the plateau, but nothing really changed. Neighbor greeted neighbor with stony stares, yet they sang hymns together in church and heard together Matthew's account of Jesus' Sermon on the Mount.

When the first contingent of the monks arrived to take over the parish on September 24, 1904, they had nothing but debts. As they moved into the presbytery and school, the novelty was expected to make everybody happy. "Certainly all these good Catholic farmers were glad to see the monks among them," wrote the chronicler. "But as far as permanent peace was concerned, the move was a failure."[123]

On October 12, 1904, soon after their arrival, the prior Father Henry Pelletan filed articles of incorporation for the Monastery of Our Lady of Jordan. Other members of the formal corporation were Father George Gaillard and Father Charles Crespan.

> Meanwhile, the handful of Cistercian monks and brothers found themselves cooped up in a parish church to which the farmers and their wives and children came to join lustily in the singing of Mass and Vespers. Some of the monks slept in a small barn, others in the sacristy of the little church, and others still in the classroom of the parochial school. The children still were coming to classes, of course. And when the classes were over in the middle of the day, the schoolroom was hastily transformed into a monastery refectory. There was no farm attached to this property, only a field that was intended for a cemetery. In fact, all that the monks had was a parish church and everything that went with it. It was just what a Cistercian monastery ought not to be.... [124]

It was an impossible situation. Still lacking money, the monks decided to buy the farm. What they got for their borrowed money, an undisclosed amount, was 403 acres, two hundred of which were under cultivation and the balance in pasture and timber.[125] The monks threw their hearts into the farm, determined to show their German critics that they could survive on this harsh frontier.

But alas, nothing went right. The local residents were generous with their time, labor and huge doses of gratuitous advice. The monks slaved at their tasks, handicapped by their unsatisfactory living conditions. They had begun work on a frame monastery, using lumber from their own sawmill, in the winter of 1905. By the following July 4, the building was not ready for occupancy.

The sawmill, assembled on credit, was intended to produce lumber for the market to help support the monastery. The expense of hauling logs, however, ate up the profits. Then the mill burned down before the monks had got around to insuring it. The monks started a dairy, which meant borrowing more money. Interest was high because of the fallout after the Spanish American War, and the monks were unable to pay it. Creditors began to dun them for their debts, an embarrassing situation for which Abbot Fortunatis had no solution. Perhaps most discouraging of all was their failure to attract young Americans to the Order. The monks grew older and more weary, but no younger men joined them to share their burdens.

On July 14, 1907, the archbishop blessed their new chapel.[126] This gave them all new hope of survival. Their luck would change. Their land was beautiful and fertile. But the bills kept coming in and there were threats of lawsuits. If there was among the monks anyone with talent for business, he did not surface during these critical months, so matters went from bad to worse.[127]

When Dom Edward Obrecht came to Jordan in February, 1908, as a canonical visitor delegated by the General Chapter of the Order, he was appalled by what he uncovered. The ruins of the sawmill, the huge debt and almost complete lack of novices or postulants told him all he needed to know of the blunders and mismanagement of the unfortunate foundation. One year later, his report having been duly noted, the General Chapter decreed the suppression of Our Lady of Jordan.[128] The monks were directed to return to France, or to join a monastery of their choice.

The decree was devastating. Some of the monks were so reluctant to accept it that only a threat of ecclesiastical censure persuaded them to give up their labors. In November 1910, the Abbot General himself, Dom Augustin Marre, arrived in person to make certain that the decree was carried out.

The monks moved away, scattered to the four winds. Some went back to France, some passed over to the Benedictines, a few became secular priests in the archdiocese. Abbot Fortunatis spent his last years at St. Gertrude's convent in Cottonwood and there he lies buried.[129] When they departed, the Benedictines of Mount Angel took over the care of the parish.[130] This was most appropriate, for the two orders had come from the same stock. The spirit of the Trappists would linger in Jordan, where fifty years later the remnants of the monastery could still be seen.[131] They would last, weathered and buffeted by the winds, until the second Trappist foundation was made successfully in Oregon.

GREAT FALLS DIOCESE

The struggle over Baker City had left many wounds that never healed. It was not regarded as likely, then, that action would be taken on the formation of another diocese in the immediate future. Eastern Montana, about which rumor had once appeared (before Baker City), was much larger than eastern Oregon. Reportedly it contained some ten thousand Catholics, but there were only fourteen priests and eleven parishes in the entire area, 94,158 square miles. There was an Ursuline Academy at Miles City[132] and a parish school in Lewistown, conducted by the Daughters of Jesus from Three Rivers, Canada.[133] There were also mission schools for Indian children at St. Labre's, St. Xavier's, St. Peter's, and St. Paul's. Despite the heroic efforts to keep this portion of the vineyard active, the record on paper was not very impressive, especially when it was contrasted with the church in eastern Washington.

But Bishop Brondel had long since got it in his bonnet that Montana was simply too big for one bishop. "The immensity of the country, the progress of Catholicism, the growing population which is favorable to our holy religion," he wrote to the Holy See, "the resources in state of development—all makes me believe that for the glory of God and his Church and the welfare of souls, the time has come to beg your Holiness [Leo XIII] to erect here [a new diocese]."[134]

This letter of Brondel was the first of a long correspondence between Helena and Rome regarding the best city for another diocese in Montana. Both Pope Leo XIII and Bishop Brondel died before a decision was made and the matter was left to the new Pope, Pius X, who issued the apostolic letter *Motu Proprio* creating the eastern Montana diocese with Great Falls as the Episcopal See. This was dated in Rome on May 18, 1904.[135] No bishop at that time was assigned to the new diocese.

As the weeks and months dragged by, some began to wonder if Rome was serious about Great Falls. Finally, on August 26, 1904, the formal announcement appeared. The first bishop of Great Falls was Matthias Clement Lenihan, a priest of the diocese of Dubuque. He was in his fifty-first year, having been born on October 6, 1854, the son of Edmond and Mary Donovan Lenihan. He had attended St. Joseph's College in Dubuque and the Grand Seminary in Montreal, and was ordained to the priesthood in Montreal on December 20, 1879, by Bishop Edouard Fabre. He spent the years 1879 to 1904 in pastoral work in the Dubuque diocese, an unusual prologue to the prelacy in an age when bishop's secretaries and college presidents were more likely to be chosen. What this demonstrated, it seems, was the powerful influence in Rome of certain midwestern prelates, such as Ireland in St. Paul and Keane of Dubuque.

Lenihan, sometimes called a "stern man" when he was young, was impatient to occupy his see. He arranged for his consecration for September 21, less than four weeks after his election was made public. He was consecrated by Archbishop John Joseph Keane of Dubuque, who was assisted by Bishop James John Keane of Cheyenne and Bishop Joseph

Cottes of Winona. He was formally installed in his new "cathedral" St. Ann's Church in Great Falls on November 9, 1904. By this time, after long interviews with his few priests, he realized that he was starting almost literally from scratch. Before him was the task of bringing the church out of its clapboard and barrel-stove existence into the age of brick and mortar and stained glass windows, which were the acceptable status symbols of the early twentieth century in Montana.

Quite naturally, the Catholics of the new diocese were eager to see what they had got for a bishop. Though he was of Irish extraction, an almost *prima facie* condition of election with Ireland and Keane, some early photos of him conveyed the impression that he was Italian, an Italian Cardinal, for example. Actually he was more characteristically Irish but ahead of his time by being very tolerant in his attitudes.

Photographs taken on the date of his consecration show him to be a tall man with bright eyes peering intensely at the camera, his head cocked sideways a little bit, like a bird's. the creases on his forehead appear to indicate that he is very anxious to be docile to the cameraman. His small ears, almost covered by a heavy shock of hair, combed back and graying at the temples and his small mouth with a gentle, complacent form, contrasted pleasantly with his large, peasant hands. On his third right finger, highly visible, was his bishop's ring. He wore a purple biretta with a long tassel on one side and a large heavily ornamental pectoral cross with a thick gold chain. He was very serious about becoming a bishop, but also pleased, and eager to win the favor of others.

Years later, photographs present a very different Matthias Lenihan. Time had taken its toll. He had become overweight and when he sat on a chair with his legs sprawled out under his wrinkled cassock, his stomach became the most notable feature of his appearance. One knows he has mellowed. He had new priorities, identified with poverty and simplicity. His close association with the Indian missions and country parishes with down-to-earth people had helped to make him a perceptibly humble bishop, who had come to ignore church politics and to find happiness in prayer and in his people. They dearly loved him, for he was like an indulgent father.

In 1929, he celebrated the diamond jubilee of his birth, the golden jubilee of his priesthood and the silver jubilee of his appointment as a bishop. It was time, he thought, to turn over the diocese to a younger man. At his urgent request the Holy See permitted him to resign. As a mark of honor, he was elevated to the rank of Archbishop and he returned to Dubuque to live out his years in peace.[136] He died there on August 19, 1943, in his ninetieth year.

THE SECOND BISHOP OF HELENA
JOHN PATRICK CARROLL

The Helena diocese, *sede vacante* as they said in Canon law, was directed by Father Victor Day, the "administrator" until the new bishop was appointed. There were doubtlessly some priests in the Northwest who possessed the qualities of "episcopabilis" but for one reason or another they were all passed over, and a second priest from the diocese of Dubuque within a single month, was selected to replace Brondel.[137] Rome's choice, approved by Christie, O'Dea, O'Reilly, and Belgian-born Glorieux, at least collectively, fell upon John Patrick Carroll, a former student and president of St. Joseph's College in Dubuque. Born in the same city, son of Martin and Catherine O'Farrell Carroll, on February 22, 1864, the bishop-elect had attended the Grand Seminary and was ordained there by Bishop Fabre on July 7, 1886. He was ten years younger than Lenihan.

He looked like a college boy of the 1910's. Round shaped and pink complexioned, his faced reminded one of a youthful Al Smith. His black-as-coal hair, parted in the middle like that of many bankers of the time, and his steady eyes staring ahead stonily, tended to create an impression of power and determination and his mouth, set firm, almost grim, was that of a tenacious man who wants and gets his own way. Of all the prelates in the Northwest, he appeared to be the most aristocratic. This was confirmed by his practice of wearing a top hat and black coat with tails even on the streets of Missoula, which was like wearing them at a rodeo.

Two months after Lenihan, Carroll was consecrated in the cathedral in Dubuque on the feast of St. Thomas the Apostle, December 21, 1904. Archbishop John Joseph Keane presided, while Bishop O'Reilly of Baker and Bishop Richard Scannell of Omaha assisted him. When the long ceremony, always referred to in those days as "solemn," was over, Helena could take comfort in having its second bishop, one who would leave two great monuments to his zeal and irresistible determination: Carroll College and St. Helena's, one of the greater cathedrals in the west.

There was one common characteristic of the Northwest's three new Irish-American bishops: they were all especially notable for their opposition "to the drink." All were active Temperance Society organizers. O'Reilly, when pastor of a large parish in Portland, was the most outspoken opponent of the saloons in the whole archdiocese and Lenihan became rather famous as a bishop for demanding sobriety in his priests. Carroll, characteristically, was the most demanding teetotaler of all; he required the children to take "the pledge" before administering the sacrament of confirmation, and if they refused to take it, as sometimes happened, he refused to confirm them.

These were strong men, sometimes dictatorial, but each in his own way won the love and respect of his people.

THE CATHOLIC CHURCH EXTENSION SOCIETY

No history of the Pacific Northwest would be complete without an account of the Catholic Church Extension Society, which was founded at this time in Chicago. The founder and first president of the society was a brilliant young diocesan priest of Lapeer, Michigan, who had taken note of Protestant success in fostering similar organizations. This priest was Francis C. Kelley, later Archbishop of Oklahoma City.

To persuade the American hierarchy of the need for this kind of home mission activity, Kelley gathered data from Protestant sources that indicated among other things, that the unchurched West had been discovered and was rapidly being filled with churches of several denominations, the most successful of which was the Methodist Episcopal.[138] Some of Kelley's findings were as follows:

According to Dr. H.K. Carroll, religion in the United States gained 582,878 communicants in 1904, with 2,310 churches. Catholics gained 241,955 of these communicants, and 226 churches. The Baptists gained only 85,040 communicants, but they built 469 churches. The Methodists gained only 69,244 communicants, but built 178 churches. The Episcopalians gained 25,381 communicants, but built 138 churches. The Congregationalists gained 7,555 communicants, but built 79 churches, while the Universalists gained only 462 communicants, but built 83 churches. There is one church for every 925 Catholics; but there is also one church for every 108 Methodists, for every 65 Universalists, for every 100 Baptists, for every 102 Episcopalians, and for every 118 Congregationalists. When we remember that Doctor Carroll's estimate of our strength is only about 12,000,000 while our estimate is nearer 20,000,000, the figures are still more alarming. On this, the basis of our real strength, we have but one church for every 1,500 people. Since the average church accommodates no more than 400 people, a little further figuring gives abundant food for thought.

There is a reason for this state of things. Let us face it. The Methodists have a regularly organized Extension Board, with a secretary, and assistant secretary, a large community for consultation, both clerical and lay, and many traveling representatives. They have a standing offer of $250 as a gift to aid the building of a Methodist church in any of the frontier states and territories, the only condition being that each church must cost not less than $1,250 above the value of the lot. Over 775 are memorial churches named after the donors. In 1904 the Methodist Extension Board aided 388 churches, and up to the close of 1904 they aided, in all, 13,914. They made loans to poor churches amounting to $11,413.53. They hold annuity funds amounting to $619,734.75. They also received in 1904, for this building work, $270,709.60, and they paid out in actual donations $114,921,15. But the remarkable part of their report is that this Church Extension Board received from all its funds in 1904 the sum of $429,150.81. Add to these figures some $450,000 received by the Home Mission Board annually and you will have an idea of Methodist activity in its pioneer and poor parishes. In a few years Methodists will reach the million mark. This money was raised by conference collections, by personal gifts and by bequests.[139]

It should be noted here that the American Catholic frontier at this time was principally in the deep South and the Pacific Northwest. The latter, it was generally believed, showed greater promise, for the South was old and was handicapped by traditional social crusts and racial discrimination. The Northwest, on the other hand, was still freshly new and, despite the prejudices found in all pioneering society, there was some openness to Catholicism, especially a Catholicism that sheltered the orphan, taught the ignorant, and cared for the sick and the aged.

Kelley's first efforts to sell his concept to the influential archbishops in the wealthy industrial centers met with failure. Six million foreign dollars have been spent to aid in building up the church of America, he told them.[140] And yet, "the Kelleys, Rileys and Murphys in the Protestant ministry were wrenched from us in neglected districts." "The hillsides of Ireland," he wrote,

are dotted with churches built or aided by American Catholic gold. Not only little parishes have asked and have received, but great cathedrals have become beggars. They loom up to meet your eye as you enter the harbors. One ornament from their gilded walls would mean a new church, a reawakened pride and life to the little Western parish. The cost of a certain monstrance I have seen would build three houses for homeless priests, or two churches for dying parishes. The price of a chalice encrusted with gems, given to a curate by a pious friend, would furnish an entire sanctuary or a parish residence in the West or South. Our elaborate memorial chapels would build ten, thirty, fifty better memorials—schools and churches— where they are needed as much as the bread men eat.[141]

The archbishops were impressed but they dismissed Kelley with kind words and no support. Eventually Kelley reached Archbishop Quigley of Chicago. While his Grace smoked peacefully in the twilight of a warm evening, the desperate priest bombarded him with facts and figures of Protestant success, of the crying need for a home mission society, of the plight of priests in the West who had no homes for providing rest after their labors in scattered churchless missions. After twenty minutes, the archbishop spoke. He told Kelley that a similar plan had been lying close to his heart for years. As Kelley reported it:

> He had even done as I had done, and made plans. His plans had been adopted by the then Archbishop of New York, Dr. Corrigan. Each well-to-do ecclesiastical province, by his plan, was to take a missionary province under its protection and supply priests and support for it. As the Eastern dioceses filled up with a proper quota of clergy, each new priest would be ordained to serve a few years in the missions, and be supported partially from home. After these years of service in the missions the young priest would be called back home again, and another and still younger man would be sent to take his place.[142]

And why had the plan failed? "It failed," His Grace responded, "because Archbishop Corrigan died before it was perfected. We waited too long."

On Wednesday, the eighteenth of October, 1905, nineteen men gathered in the home of Archbishop Quigley of Chicago for luncheon and discussion. Two were archbishops, two bishops, eight priests and seven laymen; all were united in their love of the church. Quigley presided. There was much earnest talk. They chose a name: The Catholic Church Extension Society, and before the session ended, they resolved themselves into the first Board of Governors.[143] The second meeting was scheduled for December 28th. Father Kelley was delegated to prepare the By-Laws.

After the newly self-appointed Governors dispersed to their several homes in Philadelphia, Cleveland, Pittsburgh, and elsewhere, the residence of the archbishop was quiet again. But a great and noble plan was already at work. The bishops of the Northwest would soon hear about it and hurry to Chicago to knock at the new Society's door.

14

THE GREAT NEW CATHEDRALS
AND THE CHAPEL CARS

1906–1914

On October 8, 1905, the *Sunday Oregonian* stated for the edification of its Catholic readers that Bishop Charles O'Reilly was in St. Vincent's Hospital as a patient and that he was "a very sick man." He had contracted typhoid, which reached almost epidemic proportions in the Northwest for a brief period from 1904 to 1906.[1] By October 15, no hope was held for the bishop's recovery, and while there were no vigils of prayer beseeching God to spare him, the people in eastern Oregon were genuinely saddened by the news. The bishop was still an outsider and as superfluous to them as an extra church janitor; there were not a few, however, who had come to understand that if they must have a bishop in their mini-city, O'Reilly was the best they could hope for—indeed, he was much too good for them.

His Lordship finally recovered. He was out of danger and on the road to recovery by the end of October, a grace for which Archbishop Christie was more than ordinarily grateful. O'Reilly returned to Baker City, gaunt and chalk colored, like a ghost, and eager to use his pent-up energies. He resumed his duties on January 26, 1906. His people provided a reception for him to express their welcome and make amends.

It was beginning to appear that the apostolic delegate had not made a big mistake after all, for O'Reilly's fledgling diocese had begun to take off, as it were, like a freshly hatched bird from the nest. Even the bishop's obsession with the new cathedral, which God knows Baker City needed desperately, did not turn away his people as it had three years earlier; the project, on the contrary, had brought them closer together. Father Heinrich, too, had caught the spirit, and he was now the bishop's trusted assistant.

O'Reilly was a very determined man. Soon he was visiting the outposts of his diocese, traveling as far as 300 miles in a swaying, bouncing stagecoach to places like Klamath Falls, a journey "longer than from Cincinnati to Chicago... over roads that were mere tracks through the desert or down the side of a steep canyon."[2] He begged money wherever he found it. He had appealed for help in the recently established Knights of Columbus magazine, *Columbia*. At first a little cash trickled in, then more came in larger amounts. O'Reilly finally realized that his diocese, which could not support itself, could be built by generous Catholics in eastern America.

His devout yearnings for his own cathedral were shared by his brother bishops. In Boise, the so-called cathedral, an old frame church, was being moved to a new site so that the old could be excavated for the foundations of a new stone St. John's. Suddenly it brushed a powerline and burst into flames. All the movers had for their trouble was a pile of charred remains.[3] A temporary church, which was really all the people had before, was quickly assembled until services could be conducted in the basement of the proposed new edifice. Thus the holy fire had served its purpose. Not only was the insurance on the old church most gratifying, but sympathy for Bishop Glorieux, who was nearing his silver jubilee as bishop, helped to pry open some of the tighter purses in the diocese. While no one got carried away with generosity, the cathedral fund soon counted something like twenty-one thousand dollars, which was almost astronomical compared to the first church drive thirty-five years earlier, when only $25.00 was raised.[4]

The only diocese in the Northwest that had a cathedral at this time was Helena and plans for replacing it had been under discussion for some time. Bishop Carroll, whose personality radiated all the characteristics of an Irish lord, had determined from the very beginning to abandon the simple spireless temple with the gothic windows and highly ornamental porch built by the Jesuits and converted into a cathedral by Brondel. It looked more like a red brick barn with a cross on it than it did the English or German Medieval cathedrals that Carroll greatly admired. He was determined to have his own neo-Gothic Cologne. This was no pipe dream, because many of the millionaires in his diocese were Irish Catholics who shelled out money freely whenever he needed it.

Bishop O'Dea was also entertaining dreams of grandeur. Like Carroll, he wanted something immortal, a cathedral to last till doomsday, or longer, on a high hill where everyone could see it and say, *"That is the Catholic Cathedral."* There was more than personal vanity in their ambitions. There was the innate pride of the Irishman in his own religious preference. O'Dea eventually got what he demanded, sooner than anyone expected.

The bishops of Great Falls, Baker City, and Boise had more modest goals. They were satisfied with something in stone that would not burn up, large enough for pontifical celebrations, at a cost they could afford. Christie of the archdiocese, who had for his portion a huge wooden crate, as tacky looking as a hand-me-down garment, did not seem to be interested in monumental buildings, at least for the present. His monument for the moment was Columbia University, for which he claimed inordinate credit. He still referred to it as "my university" and he happily supplied campus press productions with his craggy, flint-like profiles in photographs for appropriate recognition. This disaffected no one, for whether you liked Christie or not, you accepted his self-conscious posing as that of an aristocratic prelate, which he certainly was.

The archbishop was still ailing. He did not improve much until he traveled for surgery to Mercy Hospital, Chicago, where Dr. John B. Murphy removed gall stones on November 20, 1907.[5] Meanwhile, his brother bishops were cheerfully occupied with stones of another kind. They were blessing and laying cornerstones for churches, including cathedrals, schools, and hospitals in rapid succession. O'Reilly performed his first ordination when he conferred holy orders on Edward O'Dea Hynes, the first priest ordained for the diocese of Baker City.[6] This was on April 17, 1906. Carroll, on the other hand, buried the most popular priest in his diocese on October 1. Father J.J. Callaghan, pastor of Sacred Heart parish in Butte, died unexpectedly in St. James Hospital on September 25.[7] His obsequies, attended by the two Montana bishops, thirty-five priests, and a multitude of people, was one of the largest in the history of Montana. The funeral cortege of 270 buggies passed to the cemetery through streets lined with thousands of mourners. A stranger might have thought that at least an archbishop was being carried away, but the mourners knew better. Callaghan had been loved by everyone, even the women of the streets, as they called them, then, using delicate terms lest some be offended.

THE CATHEDRAL IN SEATTLE

O'Dea was the first of the bishops to get his building program off dead center. Soon after his arrival in Seattle in 1903, he announced plans for construction, in a hopeful sort of way. Early in the following year, he commissioned Hines and LaFarge of New York, one of the best architecture firms in the United States specializing in churches, to prepare blueprints for a great cathedral on the city's First Hill, a spectacular site said to be worth $75,000 in current value.[8]

Hines and LaFarge designed an edifice "in 14th century Italian Renaissance style with twin towers soaring 175 feet into the sky," flanking the main entrance with its near baroque embellishments. Shaped like a cross, the sanctuary [nave] measured 220 feet in length and 116 feet in width and provided seating for more than 1300 people. Topping the structure was a forty foot dome." The estimated cost of the building was a breathtaking $225,000.

Like O'Reilly, O'Dea was out beating the brush for donations, especially in Spokane, where there were a number of wealthy Irish Catholics, who were flattered with his Lordship's attentions. Most had made their fortunes in the mines of northern Idaho and Montana— instant millionaires, one might say, though they undoubtedly deserved all they had. They were very generous where the church was concerned. In January 1906, one of them, Charles Sweeney, presented O'Dea with a check for $20,000, "to be used in the construction of the new cathedral now under way in Seattle."[9] According to the *Catholic Sentinel*, this was the largest donation the bishop had received, but the amount represented "only a small part of what Mr. Sweeney has contributed to the church in the Northwest."[10]

OUR LADY OF LOURDES IN SPOKANE

Rumors about an eastern Washington diocese persisted, so it was not unreasonable for some Spokanites to suspect that O'Dea was getting money there while he was still its bishop. There were grounds for some uneasiness. Father Emil Kauten, pastor of Our Lady of Lourdes parish in downtown Spokane, was planning his new, elegant church with expectations that it would be a cathedral soon, so he was giving it his best shot. Perhaps he could not compete with St. James in Seattle, which was supported by the whole diocese, but he could, and did, build a cathedral-like edifice for the ambitious Catholics of Spokane, who took themselves too seriously. With appropriate hoopla, construction on this new Our Lady of Lourdes was begun in the spring of 1902.[11] Its estimated cost was $125,000 which Father Kauten's successor had to raise in his own backyard. Designed as "Romanesque," measuring 175 feet in length, 98 feet in width of transepts and 60 feet in ceiling height, it was constructed in red brick, which was readily available in Spokane. Its basement was first occupied for Mass on Christmas in 1903, but construction was far from complete. Because the actual cost was approximately $200,000, delays were inevitable. Our Lady of Lourdes was not dedicated by Bishop O'Dea until Thanksgiving Day, November 26, 1908, almost a year after St. James Cathedral in Seattle.[12] One can be quite sure that the eyes of many Spokane Catholics were ever-watchful on the progress of both churches, and that some gossip, were the bishop to hear it, was at least critical, perhaps even ecclesiastically treasonous.

THE CATHEDRAL IN BAKER CITY

O'Dea's unruffled nerve in making his own beginning of a new cathedral, without Rome's final approval on the change of his diocese from Vancouver to Seattle, gave courage to other prelates in Idaho, Montana, and eastern Oregon. In May 1905, O'Reilly instructed his architect, Mr. M.P. White of Baker, to proceed with construction of both the cathedral and the bishop's rectory, which were designed to complement one another in appearance.

"The style of the cathedral," said Mr. White, "is pure Gothic. The building proper is 144 feet from the front steps to rear of balustrade wall. The front including steps, towers, etc., is 68 feet wide and the nave is 48 feet, two imposing towers rise superbly above the structure to a height of 112 feet from the ground. The entire building will be built of Pleasant Valley local stone.... The basement which will afford splendid accommodations in every respect is 13 feet in the clear. In it is a morning chapel, several meeting rooms and an auditorium 44 by 50. The cathedral proper will be 44 feet high from floor to apex of gothic ceiling...."[13]

Mr. White's complacency with his own creation was unmistakable. The contractor, Mr. Thomas E. Grant, equally satisfied with his own work, began construction on May 24. The project went forward with undiminished energy and the bishop was able to lay the cornerstone on October 1 of the very first year.[14]

THE CATHEDRAL IN BOISE

In Boise, meanwhile, the bishop was plugging away, a plow horse breaking the sod compared to race horses like O'Dea and Carroll. Glorieux did not believe in spending money until he had it. There was a report current in January 1906, when Glorieux decided to excavate a basement, that his Lordship had spent over twelve thousand dollars on the new episcopal residence contiguous to the cathedral site. This report was well founded but no one complained about it because the residence had been paid for already from money received through "the sale of other properties and from savings."[15] So the bishop still had the $21,000 for the cathedral. About this same time, the *Catholic Sentinel* revealed that Carroll in Helena already had $90,000 in *his* war chest, $25,000 of it having been donated by one man.[16] O'Dea had run out of cash but he was able to borrow one hundred thousand dollars from the Knights of Columbus at 4½ percent interest.[17] Not bad. It was not likely the Knights would ever foreclose on their cathedral if the diocese went bankrupt.

Glorieux was not envious. On the eleventh of November, he solemnly blessed the cornerstone, "a memorable day in the Catholic life of Idaho," it was said.[18] Archbishop Christie preached a flowery sermon and three other bishops, besides Glorieux, listened to it with due respect. These were O'Dea, O'Reilly, and Scanlan of Salt Lake. Thus far the foundation of the structure, 100 by 200 feet, represented an outlay of $19,116.64.[19]

"The following year, 1907," says the chronicler of the diocese, "the portion of the building from the water table to the window sills was completed. The construction proceeded slowly, for the Bishop was always a prudent financier and would not incur debt. However, the building fund grew each year; and as sufficient monies accumulated, the Bishop added to the structure. In 1908 he contracted for fourteen feet more of the [stone] walls, in 1909 ten feet more and in the year following he completed the last sixteen feet. In 1912, six years after the cornerstone had been laid, the roof of the cathedral was completed."[20]

This feat had been accomplished without indebtedness, perhaps the first time since the thirteenth century, because the bishop with the advice of his building committee had sold the original cathedral site and a portion of the graveyard for $80,000. Thus by March 1912, when the basement chapel was ready for services, the bishop had received and spent $122,613.72 as a cathedral building fund. More than half of it came from the sale of church property.

GREAT FALLS CATHEDRAL

Bishop Lenihan in eastern Montana, a no-man's-land to most north-westerners, lacked a Monsignor Victor Day to serve as his Boswell, hence his accomplishments have not been recorded in detail. He had no weekly newspaper like Christie and O'Dea, nor hungry press agents like O'Reilly. He built his cathedral out of stone similar to Gothic-piles in Boise, Baker, and many more cities during this decade. Work on this was begun in June 1906, without much fanfare, and after approximately $100,000 had been expended, the bishop was able to dedicate it in honor of St. Ann on December 15, 1907.[21]

The dedication ceremony was something less than "magnificent." A large group of the faithful crowded into the new edifice. They were more devout than curious, for the Catholics of Great Falls, representing about forty percent of the city's population, were as fervent as pilgrims. Bundled up mostly in dark coats and shawls, they looked like a contingent of newly arrived immigrants on Ellis Island. There were only two bishops present to impress them, and not many priests because it was Sunday and their presence was required in their far flung parishes. A new choir under the direction of Mother M. Frances of the Sisters of Humility, who had arrived recently from Ottumwa, Iowa, created a kind of sensation by its renderings, so no one was disappointed.[22]

Lenihan had never sought the acclamation of crowds. He simply did what a bishop had to do in those days. He visited his parishes regularly, preached the true doctrine of the church, blessed their new buildings, and administered the sacrament of confirmation. He was like an old shoe, but his people treasured him and gave him whatever they could spare from their frugal resources.

DEDICATION OF ST. JAMES CATHEDRAL

Bishop O'Dea dedicated his largest of all northwest cathedrals one week later, on December 22, 1907.[23] Four Irish bishops were present for this, O'Dea, O'Reilly, Carroll, and Lenihan. The latter preached the occasional sermon, with customary flourishes no doubt, and O'Dea deeply moved by the significance of his actions, solemnly read the decree of Pope Pius X, changing the title of the diocese from Nesqually to Seattle.[24] Old Father Prefontaine, in the twilight of his years, was present, his hair like snow receding before the rays of the sun, his heavy jaw set like granite and his lips compressed with pride and expectations realized. He had come to terms with the bishop, who treated him gently, like a precious but impractical antique.

Prefontaine was as popular as ever with Seattle's citizens, an advantage not lost on the bishop. For this and other reasons locked in his Lordship's heart, O'Dea requested the Holy See to make him a "Protonotary Apostolic," meaning monsignor,[25] at the ceremony over which O'Dea himself presided. Prefontaine was invested in garments which swirled around his lumpy body like the train of some prelates. When he sat in his robes, he held out his right hand prominently, so that no one could miss seeing his ring on the third finger.

After this he would not live long to enjoy his reward for being the city's pioneer priest. Having made his will, which surprised not a few, he took to his bed for a last time. The bishop administered the last rites, and Father Loiseau, with several Sisters of the Holy Names, prayed at his bedside until the end came at 3:30 in the afternoon of March 4, 1908. His funeral was conducted by the bishop in the Sisters' chapel. When his will was probated, the Sisters were pleased to learn that he had bequested to them his library of eighteen hundred volumes and one thousand dollars.[26] To the City of Seattle he willed five thousand dollars for a fountain to be erected in his memory.[27]

The sisters could have used more money instead of the books. They were being sued by an architect whom they fired for incompetence in designing their new academy.[28] They had recently received state accreditation for conducting two normal schools in Washington, one in Spokane and one in Seattle, after a bitter struggle in Olympia.[29] With

Governor Albert Mead's help, they finally prevailed. The normal school in Seattle opened on September 9, 1907 with Miss M. Armeda Kaiser as the first directress. Four students were enrolled in the first year.[30]

THE RELIGIOUS OF THE SOCIETY OF THE SACRED HEART

Meanwhile, another congregation of teaching sisters arrived in Seattle. At the request of Bishop O'Dea, the Religious of the Society of the Sacred Heart disembarked daintily on March 5, 1907, to found a *convent* school for girls of high school age. Their historian provides details:

> The Religious of the Sacred Heart arrived in Seattle the very year in which it became the residence of Rt. Rev. Edward J. O'Dea, third Bishop of Nesqually and first of the diocese of Seattle. For more than a decade he had been occupied with the spiritual needs of his flock. Education was a matter of special concern for him. In May, 1906, Reverend Mother Charlotte Lewis, Superior Vicar of the West, visited Seattle on the invitation of the Bishop and made preliminary arrangements for the opening of a day school. The foundation was formally begun in March 1907, when Reverend Mother Mary McMenamy arrived with a small band of religious. For five weeks they were given hospitality by the Sisters of Providence, while Reverend Mothers McMenamy and Gorman sought a suitable residence in which to open an academy. After many disappointing searches a small house on North Avenue was purchased, or so the nuns thought, but the protests of a group of bigoted neighbors prevented them from getting actual ownership of the place. They had moved in, however, and there they remained until August, 1909, when they took possession of a handsome new convent erected on Forest Ridge for a boarding and day academy, which was soon enrolling from one hundred and twenty-five to one hundred and forty pupils annually.[31]

BISHOP CARROLL'S NEW CATHEDRAL

At last there was the cathedral in Helena. This has been presented at length because every trifling detail of its planning and construction has been preserved by Monsignor Victor Day in a book that he published for Montana's super patriots.[32] Costing more than twice as much as Seattle's impressive St. James, this ornate architectural triumph was produced in a diocese of few Catholics, in a small city of less than 18,000 people, and in the remote mountains of Montana. St. Helena would be a credit to a large archdiocese like Dubuque, too small, perhaps, but grand enough in concept. In Helena it ought to be regarded as a kind of eighth wonder, achieved by a bishop who possessed an extraordinary charisma for motivating people of all faiths, and extracting money from those who had it.

It would be most improper to say that Carroll toadied to the rich. In Montana no one toadied to anyone else. But his rapport with the aristocracy of America, those with money or those with power, came to him as naturally as blinking his eyes. His secret perhaps was his ability to organize them into groups with power to make decisions and to persuade them to make sacrifices for a lofty ideal. Though his knowledge of history was selective, he did know that medieval cathedral builders were inspired more by the holiness of their objective than by their hope for personal gain. Thus he organized building committees, published project papers and fired up everyone with the hope of an imperishable reward, a cathedral that would last forever.

Every minute detail was first considered and decided by committees. After innumerable consultations, the site was selected on a hill "that was not too steep for old people and others in delicate health." The land, a full block, was carefully acquired for a total of $25,000, which the bishop's friend, Colonel Thomas Cruse, cheerfully provided by check on November 8, 1905, only nine months after Carroll was installed as bishop. Cruse, it might be added, got his money's worth. From his parlor windows and front porch he would enjoy a full view of the new cathedral.[33]

Four months passed, then Carroll received another check for $25,000 on March 29, 1906. This came from Peter Larson, the well known "mining man, lumber king and railroad contractor." The *Montana Daily Record* announced this gift, paying due honor to the donor, then added: "Bishop Carroll said it is expected that other large donations will be forth coming ... at the present time he should not put up a building to cost more than $150,000."[34] This was not only considerably more than his first estimate "of less than $50,000," it was considerably less than the final cost of $645,590.44.

The next major item on the agenda was the selection of an architect. After many harmonious discussions and consultations, Mr. Albert O. Von Herbulis of Washington, D.C. was employed.[35] Carroll had examined some of his buildings in Buffalo, New York and Ottawa and was convinced that Von Herbulis was "a great architect." Meetings with the architect, during which designs for a new college as well as the cathedral were examined, took place in Helena and produced "like instant magic" the final decision to begin both buildings at once. At first the bishop and his committees were impressed with a Romanesque design for the cathedral. Then Von Herbulis presented an alternative, something like medieval Gothic, and everyone was captivated.

On July 26, 1907, Carroll announced that Larson had donated a second $25,000, bringing his total to something like a half-million dollars in today's values.[36] Money from other sources rolled in, $35,000 for the college, $5,000 for scholarships for seminarians in the college, and $5,000 pledged by the Knights of Columbus.[37] By this time the cathedral's cost had advanced "not to exceed $200,000." The "noble Gothic" style had been adopted unanimously on November 5, 1907, and a spirited discussion on the selection of the stone had followed, culminating in the decision to use Bedford Indiana limestone, rather than native granite and Alaskan marble which would have "exceeded our means."

"On April 4, 1908, a meeting of the Building Committee and Advisory Board was called for the special purpose of considering the bids submitted for the construction of the School and Cathedral. At first there was some hesitation to open the bids because they were few in number. After discussion, the motion prevailed to open them. Three bids were offered for the school, but no general bid on the cathedral. The Columbia Construction Company of new York submitted one bid on the school and a second "to furnish labor and material required to construct the foundation walls of the Cathedral, including all necessary excavations for the sum of twenty-two thousand one hundred and sixty dollars."[38] The latter was subject to one condition: that Columbia receive the contract for the construction of the school.

This was not altogether reassuring. The contractors, it seemed, were shying away from work on the cathedral. Not one bid was received on either building from a local firm and none for the superstructure of the cathedral.[39] The committee rejected all bids, then the bishop submitted to its members the following letter:

Helena, Montana,
April 15, 1905.
Most Rev. John P. Carroll, D.D.,
    Helena, Mont.
Most Rev. and Dear Bishop:
    We hereby offer to construct the High School at Helena, Montana, after plans and specifications prepared by A.O. Von Herbulis for the sum of ($107,000.00) One Hundred and Seven Thousand Dollars; and to construct for ($200,000.00) Two Hundred Thousand Dollars at the same place, a Cathedral, two-thirds the size, all the proportions preserved as far as possible, that for which the said A.O. Von Herbulis has already prepared plans and specifications and to construct such Cathedral after plans and specifications as near as may be to plans and specifications for the Cathedral already prepared by the said Architect, except that they shall contemplate

the erection of a building two-thirds the size of the one contemplated in the said plans and specifications already prepared, the proportion, materials, and manner of construction to be preserved as near as may be. The new plans and specifications to be first approved by both parties and signed by them before proceeding with the work.

Very respectfully yours,

COLUMBIA CONSTRUCTION CO.

By D.H. McBride,

President.

P.S.—In case contracts are signed, I agree to furnish a suitable bond for faithful performance of work.

Columbia's offer was accepted. No time was lost. Von Herbulis completed the final blueprints, Carroll organized a systematic fund drive in all the parishes of the diocese, and Columbia Construction hurried its foundation work "to get out of the ground before winter." Progress on the cathedral, noted carefully in many newspapers throughout the country because of Carroll's influence, was so rapid that the foundation was ready for its cornerstone by the end of summer. Ceremonies were scheduled for October 4. The bishop dispatched a letter to all pastors, urging the attendance of everyone in the diocese that could walk. Special trains were chartered. People in churches were harangued, and special invitations were sent to all the V.I.P.'s the bishop could attract. In the end 5,000 people came, "among them high officers of the State, representatives of the National Government, members of the Church from all parts of the diocese and high Church dignitaries from the East and the West. A cablegram of congratulation from Pope Leo and a message of greeting from the President of the United States were among the pleasant incidents in connection with the event."[40]

There was a parade of 2000 Catholics with three brass bands, and enough flags for a regiment, down Helena's muddy streets from Catholic Hill to the Cathedral site. Since this comprised most of the ongoing components of the Helena Diocese, a characteristic inventory of the church in the Northwest at this time, it is presented here in the order of procession:

FIRST DIVISION

Capital City Band.
Priests of the Cathedral parish, headed by Father Day.
Members of the Building Committee.
Children of St. Joseph's Home.
Boys of St. Aloysius' School.
Members of St. Aloysius' Sodality.
Girls of St. Vincent's Academy, St. Mary's and St. Ann's schools.

Members of St. Cyril and Methodius Society of East Helena.
Members of St. Lewis Society of East Helena.
Catholic Knights of America.
Ancient Order of Hibernians.
St. Joseph's Verein.
Knights of Columbus.
Citizens not affiliated with any of the above orders.

SECOND DIVISION

Deer Lodge parish, headed by Father Thomas F. Landy.
Boston & Montana Band.
Butte parishes:
   St. Patrick's parish, headed by Father P. DeSiere.
   St. Lawrence's parish, headed by Father F.X. Batens.
   Sacred Heart parish, headed by Father S.J. Sullivan.
   St. Mary's parish, headed by Father J. English.
   St. Joseph's parish, headed by Father A.D. Leitham.
   Holy Savior parish, headed by Father M. Pirnat.
   Immaculate Conception parish, headed by Father M. O'D. Barry.
Anaconda parishes, headed by the Anaconda Cornet Band:
   St. Peter's parish, headed by Father J.B. Pirnat.
   St. Paul's parish, headed by Father A.R. Coopman.
Missoula parish, headed by Father Albert F. Trivelli, S.J.
Bozeman parish, headed by Father J.B. Thompson.
Kalispell parish, headed by Father F.X. O'Farrell.
Townsend parish, headed by Father H. Aarts.
Boulder parish, headed by Father P. Ryan.
Dillon parish, headed by Father Daniel Foley.
Laurin parish, headed by Father Matthew Lynch.
Whitefish parish, headed by Father Charles McGlynn.
Augusta parish, headed by Father M. McCormack.
Frenchtown parish, headed by Father L. Legris.
Hamilton parish, headed by Father M. Carr.
Plains parish, headed by Father Thomas Phelan.
Marysville parish, headed by Father M. Moran.
Philipsburg parish.

Following the parade and blessing of the stone and walls of the foundation, during which an early season snow fell steadily, the crowd gathered at the city auditorium, where Bishop Carroll read telegrams of praise and made a long speech which included the following:

   The preparation for the event we this day celebrate goes back many years, to the 4th day of October, 1841, when Father De Smet celebrated his first mass at St. Mary's mission, in Western Montana. This is the sixty-seventh anniversary of that event. Twenty-five years later Fathers Kuppens and d'Aste, in 1866, dedicated the first church in Helena. Father Kuppens has written us congratulations and Father d'Aste we have with us today. The third step in the preparation for today's event was that made by Father Palladino when he dedicated the second church and the first cathedral in the diocese.[41]

The mention of Palladino's name produced an outburst of applause which made the rafters ring. Palladino, until this time, was residing in Lewiston, Idaho, at the bottom of the treacherous Lewiston grade. "Do not come to visit me here," he had written rather sarcastically to a friend in Montana, "as it seems to become more dangerous every day of late to travel by rail, you better wait till ballooning comes into use as a common means of travel."[42] Anything to avoid that murderous grade which suddenly dropped almost 2000 feet to the level of the Snake River. Palladino's heart was still in Helena where he and other Montana Jesuits hoped to establish a Jesuit college. The last thing Carroll wanted in his diocese was a "Gesu," which Cardinal Manning had recently called "the worst gossip shop in the world."

BISHOP CARROLL'S INFLUENCE

There is something astonishing about all this manipulated turbulence on the occasion of the blessing. The cathedral, mind you, had not as yet been built, only the basement, yet the bishop's popularity and power to attract were so great that he could command and this unprecedented response would quickly appear. No doubt there were some in his audience that day who expected him to be appointed as archbishop in an important see. He himself, at some point along the way, certainly anticipated a change for the better.[43] It was common knowledge, however, that he was ill-disposed to the presence of male religious in his diocese, especially of exempt orders, over whom his jurisdiction was very limited. This attitude, as noted before, was shared by many Irish prelates and priests, due in part, no doubt, to historical blunders in Ireland

Carroll, however, had another flaw. This was expressed in the presence of Father Julian Loiseau, a French Jesuit serving in his diocese, who was shocked understandably when the bishop manifested an unbecoming chauvinism. "Here after," His Lordship said, "only American born, or Irish born priests could work in this country, *for the glory of God.*"[44] The others could work for something else, maybe, but it appears that if Carroll had his way, the Palladinos, Cataldos, and DeSmets he had just praised could go somewhere else. Kuppens too. Kuppens had built the first Helena church and on this occasion had sent one of the telegrams of felicitations to the cathedral congregation.

Like Bishop Blanchet before him, Carroll underestimated the effect of his attitudes on Rome. He would never be an archbishop, though as a bishop he received, as he deserved, national recognition in other respects. He was appointed, for example, the national chaplain of the Ancient Order of the Hibernians, a vast and powerful Catholic lodge in America at that time, with considerable influence on civic decision making. It was an appropriate position for him because his tongue was tipped with silver and his personality was as magnetic as Daniel O'Connell.

His parting remarks at the blessing concerned the college. The laying of the cornerstone, he announced, would be postponed until spring "when the weather would be less inclement...."[45] The wet snow had continued to fall, dampening the spirits of the seven bishops who had quite enough of speeches and noisy bands for one day.

CURRENT EVENTS

Almost six years would pass before Bishop Carroll's cathedral was completed. There were years of unlimited national optimism, of exploitation, secret treaties, and squandering of Europe's wealth on armaments, a prelude to war. The California earthquake of 1906 had produced a sobering influence on its victims only, and the *Titanic* disaster in 1912 left only a fleeting impression of man's mortality. At a dizzy pace, most Americans were pursuing their goals of riches with unrelenting determination. This was not an unhappy period for Catholics of the Northwest, as their churches and schools made prodigious material progress. But it was not a time of great academic growth compared to what was beginning to appear on the secular scene. There was too much stress on brick and mortar, and too little on teacher accreditation or solid intellectual formation in the seminaries. This could be attributed in part to the nature of an immigrant church with its stress on piety rather than on learning.

There were now three Catholic newspapers in the Northwest. In addition to the *Catholic Sentinel* in Portland and *The Northwest Progress* in Seattle,[47] there was *The Catholic Herald* of Spokane, which enjoyed only a brief existence.[48] The Benedictines of Mount Angel published a family monthly called *Mt. Angel Magazine*.[49] The *Sentinel* was, of course, the most widely circulated paper of all. Unlike the others, it continued to present national and world Catholic news as well as the parochial, with weighty emphasis on Irish politics, especially the struggle for "home rule." The prolonged deluge of immigration from Catholic countries and the awesome proliferation of Catholic buildings had revived the spirit of the A.P.A.'s which manifested itself in local elections, all dutifully reported by the *Sentinel*. Other local news consisted mostly in the activities of the recently established Knights of Columbus, the arrivals of new orders of religious, and blessings of more cornerstones.[50]

A rundown of the more significant Catholic news of this period appeared as follows:

In December 1906, Father DeRouge at St. Mary's Mission near Omak, with the approval of Bishop O'Dea, established his Lady Missionaries of St. Mary's, a society of pious ladies who devoted their lives to teaching Indian children at the mission. The first member of this semi-religious group was Madame La Londe of Tonasket. She was joined by six new members from New York in November 1908. DeRouge composed a book of rules for these Lady Missionaries, who pronounced religious vows, renewing them every six months.[51]

In eastern Montana, the Ursulines, despite Jesuit opposition, had built a huge stone building for a novitiate called Mount Angela. The Jesuits, foreseeing the closure of St. Peter's, had advised the nuns that no priest would be available for Mass in the more immediate future. Later Bishop Brondel berated the Jesuits for leaving the sisters high and dry and it did no good for Van Gorp to explain that the Ursulines had been warned before they built their Mount Angela fifty miles from nowhere.[52] Discussions about this were all very tiresome from everyone's point of view until the Roman mandated reorganization of the Ursuline Order provided for a new "Northern Province" with the motherhouse in New York.[53] Ursulines from Mount Angela, however, continued to go forth to establish parochial schools in Anaconda, Spokane, and Seattle, and prosperous academies in Moscow and Great Falls. The novitiate building was completely destroyed by fire on November 16, 1918, and since then the scattered stone blocks, a haven for rattlesnakes, have baked in the sun or lay buried in snow, melancholy reminders of the distant Ursuline outpost that prepared nuns for their labors in three states.

DECLINE OF THE MISSIONS

The Jesuits had abandoned St. Peter's with reason. As noted above, the reservation boundaries had been shifted north and Holy Family Mission had been established to serve the Blackfeet. This was the golden age for Holy Family, if half-starvation and economic distress can be associated with a golden age. The main point is that it was a peaceful period, at least until the creditors began to besiege the place in the 1930's. That was "The Battle of Holy Family," which remains to be told.

Most of the missions had already taken their long, sad road to decay because of the withdrawal of government subsidies for the support of the children.[54] The Commissioner of Indian Affairs, Robert G. Valentine, who was openly hostile to Catholics, had dispatched a directive forbidding the use of religious garb in schools supported by the government, on the pretext of separation of church and state, a legal nicety that had never bothered any of the bureaucrats when they forced on Catholics Grant's Peace Policy.[55] Valentine's strident blast at the Catholic Missions, more or less staged to placate the obstreperous bigots, disappeared before its echoes could bounce back. President Taft immediately reversed the order.[56]

In 1896, inspired by many protests against growing Catholic influence, Congress decreed as follows: "It is hereby declared to be the settled policy of the government to hereafter make no appropriation whatever for education in any sectarian [Indian] school." Three years later Congress was still protesting its opposition to sectarian schools, "... this being the final appropriation for sectarian [Indian] schools."[57] Funds slowly trickled away until they ceased altogether in 1901. However, Congress continued to provide support for schools like the Hampton Institute, which was technically "government" but openly Protestant.

Catholic mission schools tried desperately to survive, but without government or tribal support for the food and clothing of the children their cause was hopeless. Gradually, over a period of three decades, most of the mission schools ceased to exist. The first to go was the boys' school at St. Francis Regis Mission in Washington. For lack of funds it was closed in September 1908.[58]

JESUITS IN THE ARCHDIOCESE OF OREGON CITY

The missionaries, meanwhile, turned to other more promising activities. The Jesuits, for example, turned to schools. On August 15, 1907, the Jesuit missions of California and the Rocky Mountains had been canonically united under one superior with headquarters in Portland.[59] The first superior was Father George de la Motte who had come from France to serve the Indians but, like Mengarini and Ravalli, had been disenchanted with the Indians' failure to respond. Also like them, he turned to the more cooperative whites.[60]

His first objective was a prep school for boys in Portland. Columbia Prep, an integral part of Columbia University in northwest Portland, was available to a limited portion of Portland's boys. The Christian Brothers' Blanchet Institute, which had succeeded St. Michael's college, had never prospered on its downtown site on Southwest Fifth and Mill, an Italian neighborhood. The archbishop, still very partial to Columbia, was determined to keep the Christian Brothers in Portland, and assisted them in building a new handsome two-story college that occupied a full block at Grand Avenue and Clackamas Street in East Portland. This was dedicated on November 29, 1908, by the archbishop, who encouraged de la Motte to hope for a Jesuit style school on the east side of Portland also.[61]

One has to question the sincerity of the archbishop in this matter. On the one hand, he repeatedly gave verbal approval to the Jesuits for establishing a school, and on the other, he continued to procrastinate in providing the necessary written permission for Rome's final consent. For many years it looked like a game of cat and mouse. Christie was short of priests so at his earnest request de la Motte assigned Jesuit Fathers Joseph Tomkin to take over the little church already functioning at Beaverton, Anthony Villa to serve as pastor of St. Michael's parish in Portland,[62] Charles Mackin to be pastor of Our Lady of the Rosary parish in Ashland,[63] and Augustine Dimier to be missionary in charge of the Siletz Indian reservation formerly attended by Father Adrian Croquet of Grande Ronde.[64]

Most of all the Jesuits wanted a major community in Portland, at that time the Northwest's largest city and located half way between the concentration of Jesuits on the plateau and California's bay area. With this in mind, de la Motte had recommended Portland as the superior's new residence, a hopeful beginning, perhaps, of greater conquests to come—a prep school, for instance. Christie offered a parish instead. Father Francis Dillon, the founder of this parish and one of de la Motte's successors, compiled an account of what followed.

> In the year, 1907, Most Reverend Archbishop Alexander Christie of the Archdiocese of Oregon, under the inspiration of God, called our fathers to the City of Portland. He proposed to them that they take their choice of one of the outlying districts of Portland, preferably Rose City Park or Mount Scott. Moved by Providence, they chose Mt. Scott. After this was settled, Very Reverend Fr. George de la Motte, S.J., Jesuit Superior, and Fr. Francis Dillon S.J., had a meeting with the Archbishop on the second of August in the same year. Together, the three of them examined every part of the proposed area and selected a suitable site for building a church. The Archbishop then established definite boundaries of the parish.
>
> On the seventh of September, 23 acres of land were purchased for $24,000. Later another small piece was bought for $2,000. For the time being—that is, until a school and temporary church could be built—Fr. Dillon rented a hall over a store in Laurel Wood. There, on Nov. 24, 1907, Fr. Dillon celebrated the first Mass in the new St. Ignatius parish in the presence of 60 people. On May 15 of the following year, construction of the church and school was begun. A little later construction of the fathers' residence was also begun. On Sept. 20, 1908, at 3 p.m. and in the presence of

a large throng of priests and the faithful, our Most Reverend Archbishop solemnly blessed the first building which contained both church and school. On the following day, the school was opened for pupils up to the 4th grade. Two Sisters of the Holy Names of Jesus and Mary were the teachers, and they had about 40 children in attendance. During November of that year, the fathers' residence was completed. The cost for the buildings, including land and all furnishings, totaled $55,638.95 and was provided by the Procurator of the Rocky Mountain Mission of the Society of Jesus.[65]

This reveals more than Christie's charm and his customary procedures for the founding of a parish, for it lays bare the Jesuits' ill-founded convictions that their prep school would soon materialize on their "23 acres."[66] As time passed and Christie continue to temporize, the Jesuits sold some of it and built Loyola Retreat House on most of the remainder.[67] The *Sentinel*, meanwhile, added a nice touch. "Archbishop Christie," it reported, "welcomes Sons of St. Ignatius to the Archdiocese."[68] No doubt he meant it. The Jesuits have remained ever since.

MORE HIGH SCHOOLS, ACADEMIES AND HOSPITALS

While the Jesuits were more successful in establishing Missoula's "Loyola College," which was really a boys' high school,[69] Bishop Carroll kept one eye on construction of his cathedral and Mount St. Charles, and the other, momentarily at least, on Butte's Catholics, most of whom were Irish and very loyal, if sometimes critical, of the clergy. Like their bishop, they appreciated the value of their parish schools. High school classes, previously conducted in St. Patrick's, had outgrown their humble beginnings. In the summer of 1908, Carroll appointed Father Stephen Sullivan, who happened to be the first resident of Montana to be ordained to the priesthood,[70] as the principal of the reorganized high school called "Central Catholic."

Central Catholic opened its doors, so to speak, in the old St. Patrick's building on September 8, 1908. New quarters were eventually secured, on a temporary basis, in a building on Granite and North Montana Streets, while a suitable permanent building was planned. The war in 1914, however, postponed developments until 1924.[71]

There was an element of the historic about this school. It was, in a modest manner, the forerunner of others to come, a central Catholic school with girls and boys, staffed by sisters, brothers, priests, and lay people. This first "Central Catholic," relatively small compared to later ones like Blanchet and Kennedy in Seattle, had a faculty consisting of diocesan priests and Sisters of Charity of Leavenworth, along with other elements similar to contemporary public high school.

The concept of a coeducational high school was, of course, one of expedience and something less than the ideal as expressed by Pius XI in his encyclical *Divini Illius Magistri,* which appeared much later.[72] On the other hand, it provided a Catholic enclave for Catholic children during a critical age, and usually higher standards of conduct and learning than their public counterparts.

Academies conducted by the sisters and separate schools for boys and girls of high school age continued to flourish in the pre-war period. The sisters' school, especially, were experiencing their greatest hour, an enormous influence over society at large merely by what they stood for, their recognizable identity, and through their graduates' impact on homes. This was the age when a "convent education" was regarded as the highest possible compliment for a young lady, Catholic or not.

HOLY NAMES SISTERS AND MARYLHURST

Like the bishops building their cathedrals, the sisters were engaged in construction of new buildings everywhere, academies to replace pioneer buildings that had long since outlived their usefulness. The Sisters of the Holy Names, for example, had replaced Seattle's original academy with a magnificent modern one on Capitol Hill in 1908.[73] In the same year they moved St. Mary's Academy from Jacksonville to Medford, and Archbishop Christie dedicated it as a new institution on September 27, 1908.[74] It was during this decade also, that they developed their recently acquired property near Oswego, where they built an orphanage for girls called "Christie Home," then moved their motherhouse from St. Mary's in Portland to the same site. This they called Villa Marie.[75] Later, on September 10, 1912, they opened Marylhurst Normal School there, in part for the convenience of educating their own sisters.

NEW PROVIDENCE HOSPITALS

The Providence Sisters were also busy. Although they dedicated a new St Joseph's Academy in Yakima on December 12, 1909, their more important advances concerned hospitals. Having first arrived in Everett on March 5, 1905, they converted a former hotel called Monte Cristo at 900 Pacific into the first Providence Hospital.[76] In Spokane, they laid the cornerstone for the second Sacred Heart Hospital on Eighth Avenue in a punctilious ritual "attended by Governor Mead, Mayor Moore, many priests and six thousand Catholics."[77] This was on May 26, 1907. Three hectic years later the new six-story building with its 210 rooms for patients was completed, at a cost of $800,000. On March 24, 1910, patients were transferred from the old hospital on Trent Avenue to the new, and proper blessings were performed by Bishop O'Dea, whose schedule for coming and going would kill a mule.[78]

On May 2, 1910, His Lordship presided over another ceremony: he blessed the cornerstone of the new Providence Hospital on the crown of a Seattle hill on Seventeenth and Jefferson. Designed like some mother-houses with a high tower in the center, this was faced with pressed red brick, which tended to look dingy in Seattle's gray weather. On September 24, 1911, the structure was completed and the bishop trotted over in his buggy to help dedicate it. Seven thousand people listened to his brief remarks and were undoubtedly pleased, mostly because the hospital would be there when they needed it.

O'Dea, meanwhile, dedicated a new St. Joseph's Hospital in Vancouver, Washington, on March 19, 1911. On the same day the old St. Joseph's was converted into Blanchet Home for the aged, a kind of model for similar homes established by the sisters in the following years.

Two months later, on May 27, several Sisters of Providence arrived at Medford to take over the Southern Oregon Hospital, which had accommodations for only fourteen patients. Not wasting time on trivialities, the sisters broke ground on June 5 for a new building, called Sacred Heart Hospital, which was completed and dedicated on February 12, 1912.[79]

Yakima was next. A new St. Elizabeth's Hospital on Ninth Avenue was begun in 1913. Its cornerstone was laid on April 13, 1913, and the first patient was admitted by the sisters on New Year's Day, 1914. This was the third St. Elizabeth's, replacing the second, begun in 1892, at Fourth and E Streets.[80]

BENEDICTINE SISTERS MOVE TO COTTONWOOD

It is appropriate, I think, in view of the painful vicissitudes experienced by the Benedictine Sisters at Colton, to present a progress report for them also.

At Colton, they had finally found peace. By 1905, their boarding school was well established with some thirty girls attending it. The few acres around the convent failed to produce enough vegetables, grain, and hay for the convent's needs, so the superior purchased 160 acres of the Leitch farm at a public auction for $20.00 an acre.[81] More land was required but the sisters experienced difficulty in finding it. This was one circumstance that turned their thoughts back to Cottonwood, the Promised Land that never ceased to appeal to them.

In 1905 [according to the Sisters' history], the Reverend Father Berthold Jaeggle, O.S.B., asked for Sister[s] of the Community to conduct a parochial school in his parish at Cottonwood. Three Sisters were sent and the school opened on December 6.

On February 15, 1906 Mother Hildegard Vogler and Mother Johanna Zumstein made a business trip to Cottonwood. They then bought a piece of farmland and good Mr. Uhlenkott donated 100 acres to them, after which they returned to Colton.

In May, Mother Hildegard and Sister M. Gertrude Rickenbach went back, taking with them one of our hired men to plow the ground and the sod. Mr. Hobler also went along to do some of the necessary building. The Sisters roomed for a few days at Mr. Uhlenkott's home nearby. From the very first this good family together with Mr. Ungrund, a son-in-law, did all in their power to help the Sisters along and to make things as convenient and easy as possible.

Seeing that the land they had so far procured did not offer the desired location for the future Convent grounds, Mother Hildegard aided by Mr. Uhlenkott tried to induce Mr. J. Ungrund to sell to them his home place for the purpose. This beautiful tract was far superior to one they had bought and singled out before. The Sisters wished very much to buy it. While at dinner one day in Mr. Ungrund's home to which the Sisters had kindly been invited, they spoke jestingly of buying the place. Soon they began to talk in earnest. No definite answer was given at the time, but enough was said to arouse hopes that the land might eventually be secured....

The Sisters left for Colton the end of June but returned in September when they once more presented their request. The sacrifice was by no means a trifling one on the part of the Ungrund family. However, the thought of having our dear Lord in the Blessed Sacrament so near to their new home which would also make it possible for them to assist daily at Holy Mass prevailed over the truly Catholic hearts of these good people. They made the sacrifice, and the plot of land together with the old home was bought. To this house of three rooms, nestling at the foot of an orchard and a pine covered slope, additions were gradually built. This was the beginning of our first Convent at Cottonwood.

Mr. Hobler began the work of building the first addition. It comprised three rooms, one of which was to be our little chapel. Mr. Ungrund and family moved to Keuterville until their new home nearby would be ready for occupation.

At five o'clock on a bright morning of April 17, 1907, Mother M. Hildegard, Sister M. Gertrude, Sister M. Walburga, and a postulant—now Sister M. Zita, left Colton in a hack with Alois Able, one of our hired men, as driver. It was agreed upon that Mr. Mager and Emil Knecht should start out with household articles, provisions and a little bunch of cattle the day before.[82]

There were only wagon roads at that time, and the distance to the new home was over fifty monotonous miles down the treacherous Lewiston grade, feared by Palladino, across the Clearwater River via unpredictable ferry boat, and up the grade to Camas Prairie, over four thousand feet above sea level. On the prairie the spring weather turned cold. The roads were frozen and the clumsy wagons jolted heavily along. The cattle that accompanied the wagons suffered severely from bleeding hooves. Night lodging had to be begged from homesteaders, who treated the sisters kindly. At 6:00 P.M. on the second day the travelers sighted Cottonwood and three hours later they arrived there. After twenty years and residence in four different convents in two states, the Benedictine Sisters from Sarnen, Switzerland, had come at last to their permanent home in America. They called it St. Gertrude's.

On September 26, 1908, the novitiate was formally transferred from St. Scholastica's in Colton. From this date, with the approbation and blessing of Pius X, and with the consent of Bishop O'Dea in whose diocese St. Scholastica'a was located, St. Gertrude's was canonically established as the motherhouse, a status which it retains to this very day.

This is by no means a complete list of the activities of the sisters, but as a sampling it indicates the extent and growing power of Catholic institutions that would be called upon soon to defend their very existence against hysterical antagonists who would use the polls for their own ends.

CURRENT PROGRESS IN THE COLLEGES

Mount St. Charles would be the fifth Catholic College in the contemporary Northwest. Standing prominently on a knoll, like the cathedral, it was one of the first sights one observed as the train pulled into Helena. Other sights were the rising walls of the cathedral and the railroad station, which looked like a Moslem mosque. These were strange contrasts in a small, congested valley with its twisting narrow streets that looked more like a western tourist trap than a state capitol. Bishop Carroll had stressed the purpose of Mount St. Charles: the new college was for *Montana* students. It would also develop, he explained hopefully, a native clergy for the Helena diocese. His Lordship did not approve of his local youth meandering like inquisitive cattle into other pastures— Gonzaga College, for instance, less than four hundred miles distant, where Father Louis Taelman, a long suffering and garrulous missionary, had become president.

Taelman knew Montana better than Carroll did, having arrived there almost twenty years earlier, and he was not the kind to let anyone forget it. There was a halo of glamour around Taelman's head. An able missionary of his sort enjoyed a privileged status similar to that of "Indian fighters," whose renown cut across state lines and attracted local reporters for interviews, like Hollywood stars in the 1930's.

Seattle College was another no-no for Carroll. It had recently conferred its first degrees, Bachelor of Arts, on three candidates, James C. Ford, John A. Concannon, who entered a Jesuit novitiate and died as a Jesuit after sixty-six edifying years, and Theodore M. Ryan, who entered the diocesan seminary, became a well known monsignor and served as a pastor of Seattle's Immaculate Conception parish for several decades.[83]

Bishop Lenihan, whose diocese in terms of square miles was almost twice the size of Carroll's, was not building a college, nor did he intend to build one. Mount St. Charles would do very well. Lenihan had departed from new York on March 5, 1910, for Rome. He was away four months, during which time he had a personal audience with Pius X, toured Europe as a pilgrim (not as an American seeking a smattering of culture) and visited the Holy Land for the second time in eighteen years. He returned to Great Falls on July 21, a few weeks before the formal dedication of Mount St. Charles on September 10, 1910.

President William Howard Taft himself had attended the Edwardian spectacle of laying the cornerstone, so all subsequent rituals connected with the college were dull by contrast. After the holy water sprinkled generously by the bishop had evaporated, students registered and classes began on September 22.[84] His Lordship's first dream had become a reality: he had a college, named for his patron St. Charles Borromeo, with real, living *Montana* boys inside its massive stone walls (which looked to the critical eye too much like a prison).

MOUNT ANGEL BENEDICTINES

Meanwhile, on August 25, 1910, the *Catholic Sentinel* announced that the monks at Mount Angel would elect a new abbot on the following Tuesday, August 30. Abbot Thomas, the *Sentinel* cautiously reported, threatened with total blindness, had resigned "three months ago." Abbot Frowin would come again from Conception, Missouri, to preside over the election.

In truth, Abbot Thomas had resigned on May 25, not only because he was going blind, but to get married, a shocking revelation that Catholic papers were loathe to print. The secular papers were not so squeamish. Indeed, one suspects that some news reporters then, like many now, enjoyed finding a flaw in the otherwise inspiring lives of the monks.[85] News, like gold, was where you found it, even in the broken or shattered lives of others.

When the monks convened for the election, there was great anxiety, not unlike the day they had chosen Abbot Thomas. But their common sorrow and shame bound them closer together and helped them become better men of God. The election was prayerful, its finale a great relief, as though a dark cloud had passed. Father Placidus Fuerst, the pastor of the parish in Mount Angel, was designated as the monastery's choice on the very first day. Eager to dispel the lingering gloom, the new abbot scheduled his blessing for the following week, October 5, and then closed the door on the past.

While Abbot Placidus had been pastor of St. Mary's, he had begun construction "of a grand parish church, large enough to hold every citizen in the town and many in the surrounding countryside."[86] He was still responsible for this, in a more remote way, so he gave much thought to the appointment of his successor in the parish. There was a Father Waedenschwyler, usually called Father Dominic for obvious reasons, who, like Placidus, was an accomplished musician. It seems there was some difference between the two over the interpretation of plain chant in the liturgy. To avoid conflicts in the abbey, reliable sources state, Placidus appointed Dominic as pastor of St. Mary's.[87]

Father Dominic was equal to the occasion. In a pastorship that lasted nineteen years, he supervised the completion of the "neo-Gothic" church, paying off the debt of $85,000 on it in two years. In 1910, when he arrived at St. Mary's, there were 343 Catholic families; ten years later there were 450. From 1880 to 1920, the parish experienced a fifty-fold growth, from nine families to 450, and by the time Father Dominic retired in 1929, St. Mary's had two thousand parishioners. This kind of growth was characteristic of the period. One should add perhaps that Father Dominic was a characteristic pastor during that incredible era when the church in American had few rivals in the world for growth and generosity.

THE NEW ST. FRANCIS IN PORTLAND

Like the size of the parishes, the size of other new churches increased dramatically. In every major city, huge new structures were being planned and built, at equally impressive costs, in addition to the cathedrals, mind you, for which every parish was assessed. In Portland, for example, there was the new St. Francis Church on the east side. There were now eleven more parishes where St. Francis was originally formed in 1876. The first St. Francis, built that year by Father Louis Verhaag, blew away in a hurricane, an unlikely demise for any building in the Pacific Northwest.[88] The second St. Francis, dedicated by Seghers in 1881, was now much two small, so the pastor, Father James Black, directed the construction of the third. This one occupied one half block, said the *Sentinel* on December 29, 1910, and it could accommodate 1200 people at once, not including the priest and altar boys. Its style, the architect, Mr. A.H. Faber explained, was "classic pointed Gothic" and its two towers extended 226 feet above the street. One new feature was identified with the electric age, something never considered by the inventors of Gothic: the towers had illuminated crosses. This anticipated freeway advertising by a few decades; perhaps one should say it was more like a high class carnival. This latest St. Francis, illuminated crosses and all, was blessed by Archbishop Christie on January 15, 1911. His Grace, no doubt, used the holy water at the appropriate moment, but someone else, the builder or the architect, had failed to do his job. The great building, wonderful to see miles away when the crosses were lighted, was actually defective in design or materials. Condemned about 1937, it was replaced with a fourth St. Francis church, which has survived. [89]

ST. ALOYSIUS IN SPOKANE

St. Aloysius Church in Spokane resembled the above at least in one respect: its two towers, almost identical duplicates of those at St. Francis, were topped by *illuminated crosses*. Which came first? To which should we attribute this wonderful innovation? They were built at the same time, of almost equal size, but it must be admitted, St. Aloysius and its crosses have lasted longer.

The design of St. Aloysius was said to be Romanesque, "the architectural style that had prevailed in Western Europe from the fifth to the twelfth century." An *American* church architecture had not yet been developed, so the architect, Julius Zittel from Germany, used the only style he knew. Ours was still an immigrant church; the parish comprised mostly Irish and Germans of the second generation and Italians of the first. They liked Zittel's work and so did the Jesuits, who commissioned him in the previous decade to design the new Gonzaga.

The church was 195 feet in length (one bay was cut off to save money) and the portico was "buttressed and surmounted by two massive guardian towers 156 feet high...." [90] Its width of 110 feet, added to Gonzaga's length, now presented a frontage of over six hundred feet on Boone Avenue—a formidable brick complex that looked as imposing as an eastern piano factory, fittingly more artistic. Its cost of $176,125.34, leaving the parish $100,000 in debt, dampened the jubilation of the dedication celebration, but Bishop O'Dea's happy smiles were somewhat reassuring.

Dedication was on a brisk, bright October day in 1911.[91] More than two hundred priests attended, including white haired and aging Father Cataldo, who stole the show. As an after-dinner speaker at the banquet for the clergy (an elitist affair in those days), he reviewed the history of the church in Spokane. With his dark Sicilian eyes flashing and old prophet earnestness, he made a plea for the Indians. It was for them, he said, that the Jesuits had come to the Northwest. They were not to be forgotten while the whites celebrated the glories of their new church.

NEW MONSIGNORS

Bishop Carroll was in Rome for his *ad limina* visit to the Pope when St. Aloysius was still under construction. That summer he dispatched two cablegrams from Rome, one to Father Victor Day and one to Father Peter Desiere.[92] These bore the joyful news that both had been designated as monsignors by Pius X. It appears that this was a time not only for building churches, but for creating monsignors. Even old Father Bronsgeest who had dared to cross swords with a bishop and an archbishop to boot, was made a monsignor. Bishop O'Reilly himself had seen to that.

Bronsgeest, with a full beard and bushy head of hair, peered through rimless glasses at his congregation while O'Reilly read the document signed by Cardinal Merry del Val.[93] "Held in high esteem by everybody," the bishop said. My, how times had changed. Father John Heinrich was dead. Having made his peace with the bishop, he had joined his fathers on January 5, 1908. Father Joseph Schell, too, had been reconciled to his bishop, but at this time he was not in residence in the diocese.[94] Christie, no doubt, was as pleased as O'Reilly that the storm over the new diocese had blown itself out.

One of Bishop Carroll's new monsignors, Father Peter Desiere, deserves further comment. He was a Belgian, having been born in Flanders in 1843. Ordained on December 21, 1867, he served as a professor for twelve years, a curate for four, and a pastor in Westende for another four prior to his departure for the missions of America. His proffered services were gladly accepted by Bishop Brondel, and he arrived in Helena in April, 1887, already in middle age but sturdy enough to undertake the hardships of a Rocky Mountain parish. He became the first resident priest in Anaconda in 1888, and there he built the brick church, a residence, and a hospital. "Nor should we omit," says Palladino, "to mention that visiting the Insane Asylum and Penitentiary, two State institutions located in this part of Deer Lodge County, has also been one of his cares."[95]

There is no mystery in Desiere's promotion after twenty-five years of zealous labor in a difficult mission. What surprises us, perhaps, is Carroll's failure to recognize in some formal manner the heroic contribution made by the dean of Montana's diocesan clergy, Father Remigius De Ryckere, the pioneer of forty-six long years. In this world, honors are like afflictions: one can never predict where they will fall.

FATHER PETER HYLEBOS AND ST. LEO'S

When the founder of the church in Seattle, Father Prefontaine, was raised to the lofty state of monsignor, it was quite natural for Peter Hylebos, the founder of the church in Tacoma, to expect the same honors. He received no call to them, however, and deeply chagrined, he made a voyage back to Belgium "to visit his relatives." He had something else on his mind. "He visited Rome," his confidante later noted, "had an audience with the Holy Father [and] saw the Rector of the French or Belgian College at Rome with a view of securing a monsignorship for himself.... The final answer from the Roman correspondent was that nothing could be done except through the Ordinary, Rt. Rev. Bishop O'Dea."[96]

Hylebos had been a close friend and admirer of Archbishop Seghers. He was also much attached to the Jesuits, and it was often said that he wanted the Jesuits to take over St. Leo's parish in Tacoma "because they would develop schools there, perhaps even a college." He and Father George Weibel of Gonzaga were special friends and Weibel had been delegated by him to establish a Jesuit type sodality in the parish.[97]

There was nothing petty about the way Hylebos performed his duties. When William Jennings Bryan presented a major address in Tacoma in 1900, a huge wooden building called "the Wigwam" was thrown together to accommodate the unprecedented crowd. Hylebos bought this Wigwam after the speech, and used its lumber for the third St. Leo's church, adding some brick here and there to eliminate its flimsy appearance. When completed, the new Wigwam, christened St. Leo's, would accommodate 2,200 people for Mass. It was then the largest church in the west.[98]

In Hylebos' absence, Weibel substituted for him at St. Leo's. Weibel was not the acting pastor, however. This office was held temporarily by the parish assistant, Father Van Goethem. Weibel loved Tacoma, but fortunately for him, as matters turned out, he was suddenly recalled to Gonzaga and Father Ignatius Vasta, was sent to replace him[99]

Father Hylebos returned before Christmas 1910. "About two months later," Weibel wrote, "early in 1911, a telegram came to Gonzaga from Rt.

Rev. Bishop O'Dea." Fr. Weibel received the message by phone: "If you want St. Leo's, Tacoma, see me immediately."

What had happened? As Weibel learned later, O'Dea called Hylebos to Seattle. "A stormy scene occurred—it ended with Fr. H. writing out his resignation, at the suggestion of the Bp. [This detail I learned from Bp. O'Dea.)"[100]

Father John Cunningham, the first Jesuit pastor, arrived a few weeks later, determined to justify the faith of Father Hylebos by building a new school. On September 17, 1912, scarcely one year later, the new St. Leo's Grammar and High School was opened for its first students. The seven-hundred student capacity building was dedicated by Bishop O'Dea on November 17.[101] Happily the venerable old founder of the parish was there to see it. He lived now, in humiliating retirement, in a little home near the church he had built, and each morning he offered Mass there on the side altar named for Mary, the Mother of God. He too had reason to be grateful that he was no longer in charge, for at this very time an ugly lawsuit hovered ominously over the church in Tacoma, not excluding St. Leo's. Even his Lordship, the bishop, was involved. He and other prominent Catholics, including Father Van Goethem and the Superior at Visitation Academy, were summoned to court for the alleged abduction and alienation of affection of a seventeen-year-old girl, Marjorie Rieman. The attorney for the plaintiff, Marjorie's twice married mother, hammered the defense mercilessly before a court crowded with avid girls and women with nothing better to do.

A brief account, unlike the sensational reports in Tacoma, appeared in Spokane's morning paper:

> TACOMA. Sept 16.—The Catholic church's great council of Trent in the sixteenth century was made an issue today in the trial of Mrs. Lizzie Magnusson's suit for $40,000 damages for the alleged concealment of her daughter, Marjorie Rieman, in Catholic institutions.
>
> Mrs. Magnusson is suing members and officials of the church. Her counsel sought to show that by a provision of the council of Trent bishops have jurisdiction over religious orders, including sisterhoods, as regards the admission of new members.
>
> Bishop Edward J. O'Dea of Seattle is named a defendant in his capacity as head of the diocese and the plaintiff is trying to show he is responsible to a certain extent for the Academy of Visitation in Tacoma, which, according to the complaint, helped conceal the girl. The Rev. J.J. Cunningham of Tacoma, who was examined as to the council of Trent, had no recollection of any such fixing of responsibility.
>
> Marjorie Rieman disappeared in February, 1911, following her removal from the Tacoma Visitation academy by her mother. She went to the home of the Rev. G.C. Van Goethem, who concealed her in the residence of

Attorney Louis I. Lefebvre. Later she was removed to a Catholic convent in San Francisco. The Rev. G.C. Van Goethem testified he concealed the girl's whereabouts because she told him her mother would place her in an improper environment in Alaska.

Lefebvre disclosed the girl's whereabouts last September as a result of habeas corpus proceedings. She was then restored to the mother, who is now suing Father Van Goethem, the Visitation academy, Attorney Lefebvre and Bishop O'Dea for damages, the bishop made a party to the suit on the ground that he has jurisdiction over the clergy and nuns of the diocese.[102]

The jury believed Marjorie's fancy story, and awarded damages of $23,033 to be paid by the bishop, Van Goethem, Lefebvre, and the Visitation Sisters.[103] On appeal to a higher court, the bishop was completely exonerated. The judge ruled in favor of the church and mama took her darling daughter back to Valdez where, according to witnesses, she conducted a highly profitable "roadhouse bar." Only one person came out of the mess with his reputation unscathed and his dignity unruffled, and that was Bishop O'Dea. Even the seeming prejudices of the jury had left him untouched.

GONZAGA UNIVERSITY AND LAW SCHOOL

Because Archbishop Christie was ailing, he was unable to attend the pompous church inauguration in Spokane. He had predicted some years before that Gonzaga was destined "to become, in the near future, a university of law, medicine and theology, in which students will have all the intellectual and material advantages of any eastern college."[104] This sounded then like a pipe dream, and still does, but the more daring priests at Gonzaga liked what he said. One of these was Father Herman Goller, the new provincial of the California Province, which had replaced the California-Rocky Mountain Mission on September 8, 1909. Goller returned from a high level meeting in San Francisco with grandiose schemes in his over-sized head, but his premature death on November 5, 1910, had left everything in limbo.

Father Taelman fell heir to the predictions of Christie and the schemes of Goller. He, more than any before him, had led Gonzaga out of the immigrant ghetto in which it had been conceived and nurtured. He had come to believe that the time was ripe for Gonzaga to establish a law school and to request a charter from the State of Washington for the status of a university. When he admitted in February 1912 that preliminary steps had been taken, he expressed hope that the college would be declared a university in September. He added that three new schools were under consideration, law, engineering and medicine.

Wheels turned more rapidly than Taelman expected. In May he disclosed that Gonzaga would become formally a university on St. Aloysius day, June 21, 1912. Classes in the new law school would begin in October.[105] Thus on the appointed day, following a triduum of academic fireworks, Taelman, with Archbishop Christie and Governor Hay at his side, exultantly promulgated the university's new charter. This was greeted with tumultuous cheers, partly because it marked the end of the evening's program, which had consisted of eight lengthy speeches, three of them on the dangers of socialism.[106]

THREE MORE GOTHIC CHURCHES AND
A CATHOLIC LIFE INSURANCE COMPANY

Besides the archbishop, Bishops O'Dea, Lenihan, and Glorieux attended these Silver Anniversary proceedings. In O'Dea's backyard, the Dominican fathers had recently established Blessed Sacrament Church.[107] This was in the University district where a more liberal spirit prevailed, not as picturesque as an artists' Bohemia, but wide open enough for any wind to blow through. Father F.P. Driscoll celebrated the first Mass in a temporary chapel, while plans were pieced together for as large a church as the Jesuits' Immaculate Conception on a conspicuous hill to the south. Nothing less would do.

BLESSED SACRAMENT CHURCH IN SEATTLE

The Dominicans, like the Jesuits and the Benedictines at St. Martin's, had much in common. All were engaged in some manner with higher education in a city dominated by the state university. Neither Seattle College nor St. Martin's was setting any records for growth, and the Dominicans as chaplains at the university experienced more lethargic students than fervent ones. At first their headquarters was the parish, but eventually when the Newman Clubs were established across the country, the Dominicans staffed a chapel on the campus.[108]

The new Blessed Sacrament church was neo-Gothic, English style, with one tower that looked like Westminster. Above this soared a steeple 205 above the ground, where it can be seen on Seattle's north skyline for many miles. The first Mass in the church was offered on March 19, 1911, in the nave, over which a temporary wooden roof had been placed. The exterior of the building, including the steeple, was not completed until 1925, and the interior much later. Its capacity was officially designated as 1220, over one hundred above that of St. Aloysius and considerably more than the Benedictines' Holy Rosary church in Tacoma. The latter, however, had a more lofty steeple, five feet higher than Blessed Sacrament. It, too, was Gothic, "considered one of the West's most beautiful examples of early Gothic architecture."[109] Spokane Catholics, it appears, were the only ones who had not succumbed to Gothic fever. Their two largest churches were Romanesque.

FATHER THOMAS PURCELL

In north Idaho, Father Thomas Purcell was pastor. An uncommonly durable priest, he was also an improbable one since he had been kicked out of the Jesuit novitiate at Prairie du Chien because of "delicate" health. That is how much the Jesuits knew about it. Dismayed but determined, Purcell traveled to Spokane, where the Jesuits quickly signed him up for teaching at St. Ignatius Prep School in downtown Spokane. This was a pompous name for an institution that fell slightly short of being a reform school. Purcell's students were teenage "street Arabs" who could not read and write. When Bishop Glorieux visited Gonzaga in 1890, the fathers recommended Purcell for the priesthood. Thus it happened that after a course in theology at Montreal, Purcell was ordained in 1896 for the Diocese of Boise. His Lordship had never got a better bargain. Purcell spent the next twenty-nine years as pastor, during which time he built ten churches for the diocese.[110]

The first was a miniature "Gothic" in red brick, built in Rathdrum, the first church in Idaho to be composed of brick.[111] Purcell called it St. Stanislaus Kostka, after the patron of Jesuit novices, to redeem a vow he had made: if he became a priest, as he ardently hoped, he would build his first church in honor of St. Stanislaus. This was in 1901, when Purcell was pastor of Coeur d'Alene and Rathdrum one of his missions.[112]

Coeur d'Alene claimed only twenty Catholic families at that time, among them Joseph P. Healy of the old fort, an Irish born Catholic of prodigious dedication. Attached to Purcell's church were missions covering some 5600 square miles, all of northern Idaho. In terms of land, it was an empire, larger than some dioceses, and Purcell wanted a prestigious temple of God for the heart of it, a replacement for the humble frame church built in 1890 for $400 by Jesuit Father Robert Smith from Gonzaga.[113] Purcell had to wait many years while his parishioners multiplied in numbers and other priests came to take over some of his missions.

Among Purcell's friends in Spokane was Attorney Edward J. Cannon, one of the founders of the Gonzaga Law School.[114] Cannon, a devout Catholic (not to be confused with John Cannon, against whom Cataldo had filed a landmark lawsuit),[115] proposed the incorporation of a Catholic life insurance company, somewhat similar to the popular lodge insurance organizations, without the cumbersome lodge social obligations. Others, including Purcell, eagerly consented to participate. Thus, on February 25, 1910, The Roman Catholic Life Insurance Company of Spokane filed articles of incorporation at Olympia.[116] The official incorporators were Cannon, Founder and President, Henry Luhn, Edward O'Shea, Thomas Ennis, Thomas Lalley, Edmund Burke, and John Cadigan. Subscribed capital of two million dollars was quickly supplemented with an additional million, which indicates that the concept had more than commendatory support.[117]

In addition to the uniqueness of this combination of the temple in the market place, there are two intriguing consequences. The first is that the initial loan made by the company was $20,000 to Father Purcell to help him build his new church.[118] The second, a disappointment to many in Spokane, was that the company moved its headquarters to Seattle where it prospered fabulously under another name: New World Life Insurance Company.[119]

Purcell's loan, combined with what he had squirreled away, provided enough for the fulfillment of his dream, the new hybrid Gothic-Romanesque-whatever St. Thomas Church in the city by the lake. Designed by F.P. Rooney of Spokane, presumably to incorporate the best of several styles of architecture, this church was constructed by contractor E.M. Krieg for something less than $100,000.[120] It was completed in 1912 and dedicated by Glorieux in his sixty-ninth year, a bishop older in appearance than his age indicated.[121] Beside him were Christie and O'Dea, the latter as robust as a beaver, which he resembled in its tenacious instincts for the performance of duty.

Purcell's cheerful bonhomie and able preaching conspired to make him a celebrity. Though he was born in Wales, he was often called upon to address the Irish on St. Patrick's Day, when he pronounced such outlandish foolishness as this: "The Irish and the Jews are the greatest people in the world because they rule the earth and they have neither a standing army or a navy."

IMMACULATE HEART SISTERS

Among his more solid accomplishments was the sisters' academy. Purcell, as a youth, had worked in Pennsylvania's coal mines and he enjoyed connections in Scranton, where his niece Sister M. Nazarene [Agnes Smith] was a member of the Servants of the Immaculate Heart of Mary. Marywood, near here, was the motherhouse. Purcell journeyed to Marywood and secured four of the sisters for a school in Coeur d'Alene.[122]

Having arrived in Idaho, they lived in the former rectory and taught in a little frame school called St. Cyril's, which Purcell had acquired on the corner of Fourth and Indiana. The first attendance of sixty-three pupils increased so rapidly that these accommodations were inadequate. Purcell purchased the old Fort Sherman Hospital and moved it to a new location. It was then converted into classrooms. At the same time the sisters purchased the old opera house and converted it into a convent and boarding school, giving it a new name, Immaculate Heart Academy.[123]

THE CHAPEL CARS

Purcell's Idaho was like eastern Oregon and eastern Montana, still an abundant wilderness with fewer Catholics than snakes or cows. In rural areas there was a scattering of remote towns here and there, mostly churchless, sometimes occupied by stray Catholics who had not seen a priest in many years. There seemed to be no practical way to reach these strays for most of them cared so little about religion that they never bothered to seek it. Church buildings, sorely needed, would be almost useless without priests and congregations and the hope of bringing all three together seemed to be about as remote as Shangri-la.

At this point, Father Kelley of the Extension Society proposed the use of railroad chapel cars. These, he exclaimed in a moment of inspiration, could provide facilities and a priest for preached "missions" in the remote outposts of America, especially in the deep south and the Pacific Northwest. Because the concept was practical, the first chapel car was built in Chicago in 1907. Called the "St. Anthony," it was designed by Richard Dean, vice-president of the Pullman Company, and paid for by Ambrose Petry, a member of Extension's Board of Governors.[124] It was blessed on the rails at the Lasalle Street Station on June 16 of that year. First sent on an experimental basis to Tennessee, it arrived in Portland in September, 1909.[125]

This first of three cars provided accommodations for fifty people in addition to the altar and quarters for the superintendent, porter, and chaplain. The superintendent was George Hennessey, a warm-hearted, jocular bachelor who could get along with anyone except the devil. In common with many unmarried males, he loved children and dogs. He served for fourteen years until his resignation in October, 1923, when he entered the mortuary business.[126] For his long years of dedicated assistance to priests, Pius XI honored him with the Knighthood of the Holy Sepulchre.[127]

The chaplains of the car were many, often priests in neighboring parishes. They preached the missions, administered the sacraments and gave instructions to countless thousands who often came to the cars out of curiosity. During the years that followed, 268 missions were presented, 108 in the Archdiocese of Portland and 68 in the Diocese of Baker City. After the missions were over, congregations in most places were organized as missions of a parish, and churches were built with money from Extension. In western Oregon alone, Extension helped to build 107 churches. The first was the Good Shepherd Church at Sheridan, recipient of a one thousand dollar gift after Father H.J. McDevitt conducted a mission there in the St. Anthony.[128]

In 1911, the St. Anthony toured eastern Oregon, at Haines on January 9, for example. It brought the first priest there in eight years. Missions were preached in Durkee, Elgin, Heppner, and many other small towns, while Bishop O'Reilly visited Chicago in search of money for churches and health for his chronically sick body. He found both. At Mercy Hospital he suffered the surgeon's knife, but his spirits were quickly restored by news from Oregon.[129] He had submitted a request to the Extension Society for "twenty-five chapels in eastern Oregon." A single donor provided funds for all twenty-five as soon as the need was advertised in Extension's magazine.[130]

Two more chapel cars were put on the line in 1912: the "St. Paul," which was dispatched to the southern states, and the "St. Peter" which came to the Northwest in September of that year.[131] This was a new steel car, forty-three feet long with accommodations for seventy-four persons. It covered all four states in the Northwest for the Extension Society until 1923, when the Catholic Truth Society of Portland took over its operations. It was at Aberdeen, Washington on July 30, 1914; at Fairfield, Idaho for six months, beginning October 31, 1916; at Dietrich, Idaho in 1917, and at Oakridge, Oregon in January 1921.

Meanwhile, the older St. Anthony, constructed in part of wood, was retired from active service. In 1919, it was placed at Wishram, Washington, a desolate looking village below barren cliffs on the north bank of the Columbia, and there it was used for Mass until December 29, 1929. A small chapel called the House of God and the Gate of Heaven, built with Extension funds, replaced it.[132]

Eventually the chapel cars were no longer needed.[133] They had served their purpose. They had been used as the catalyst to get things going. Their influence and the follow-up establishment of mission churches made possible by the Extension Society were so significant in the development of the Northwest church that no one, save God, can calculate them. For three dioceses, at least, they were like exquisite embellishments of a cathedral, without which the cathedral would be forever incomplete.

COMPLETION OF HELENA'S CATHEDRAL

In March of 1912, the *Catholic Sentinel* announced a contest designed to increase subscriptions. The grand prize was a five passenger Paige touring car, the latest in motor car luxury, worth on the street a neat $1,050. At the same time, Woodrow Wilson, the peace candidate, was sworn in as the twenty-eighth president of the United States. The Catholic Church Extension Society, it was also noted, had built ninety-three chapels during the previous year alone, and Bishop O'Reilly of Baker City, in his first ten years as Bishop, had blessed twenty-five new churches, the last one at Wallowa, Oregon.[134]

Bishop O'Reilly was enroute to Rome, to make his report to the Holy Father. He was happy with his report and he hoped the bureaucrats in Rome would be happy also. There were the twenty-five new churches, of course. During his ten year tenure his priests had increased from eleven to twenty-eight. Besides, he now had eight new parishes with resident priests. Not bad for a diocese that began with fewer than three thousand Catholics.

As one might expect, the news from Helena was of a superior kind, not a bit like that from the impoverished dioceses around it. On the first of January, Colonel Thomas Cruse, the local banker, presented $100,000 to the cathedral fund, assuring the completion of the building in 1914.[135] Jim Hill, the railroad magnate, pledged $50,000 toward Mount St. Charles, enough to gladden Carroll's lively ambitions for the school. His Lordship was enthusiastic about his new Catholic colony in the South River Valley where 70,000 acres of land had been purchased with the aid of the Ringling Brothers and the Milwaukee Railroad. Carroll named this village St. Charles. He had other colonies in mind, especially for immigrant Irish men and women, who needed a new start.[136] Carroll had confirmed, he said, "about 1500 people in Butte and Anaconda about 1000."[137] The majority of these were Irish, of course, ardent admirers of his Lordship and militant Catholic Americans who helped to keep bigotry west of the Montana border. It was no accident that Montana had the highest percentage of Catholics of any northwestern state.[138]

As for Helena's cathedral, it was finally completed in time for its first Mass on Christmas Day, 1914. The previous months had been hectic. By July of 1913, the exterior of the building was completed, the spires had been erected and only the tuck pointing and the washing of the walls remained to be done. An "Interior Club" was formed to finance the cost of a lighting system, pews, altars, and doors. The installation of the organ, the fifteen chimes, and the stained glass windows completed the work on Carroll's stupendous achievement. Helena's authentic Gothic cathedral, still bearing the name Sacred Heart,[139] was a solid, three dimension reality, a lasting monument to the people, Catholic and non-Catholic, who built it, and an exquisite prayer in stone. Time, which eats away at most buildings, has only improved it.

15

THE WAR YEARS

1914-1925

The Baker City Diocese had been launched with as much noise as a border war. The creation of Spokane was just the opposite: as peaceful as a parish picnic. Washington Catholics had expected this for so long a time that it was almost ho-hum news when Pius X got around to making a decision. He finalized this, at least, on December 17, 1913, when he signed the appropriate documents for the erection of the diocese.

The decision of His Holiness was a Vatican secret for almost two months. Then the following appeared in the *Catholic Bulletin* of St. Paul.

> The Apostolic Delegation at Washington D.C., has been informed that a new diocese has been created in the eastern part of the state of Washington, with its episcopal see at Spokane.
>
> The new diocese comprises a portion of the territory heretofore belonging to the diocese of Seattle and under the jurisdiction of the Rt. Rev. Edward J. O'Dea, bishop of that see.
>
> For some time it has been known that the establishment of a new diocese in eastern Washington was under consideration by the Holy See. Indeed, it has been a necessity for a long time. Spokane is a populous, enterprising and prosperous city—one of the rapidly growing cities of the west. It has a large Catholic population. There are eight parishes within its confines, equipped with churches, schools, academies and other institutions under the charge of religious. There also is located Gonzaga University, in charge of the Jesuit fathers.
>
> The new diocese of Spokane forms part of the ecclesiastical province of Oregon, of which the Most Rev. Alexander Christie is metropolitan.[1]

The cat, an ancient one as cats go, was now out of the bag, although there still seemed to be lingering doubts about it. A probe by telegraph to St. Paul where the puissant Archbishop Ireland ruled, brought this response from the Associated Press: "Spokane was raised to a bishopric two weeks ago." This information was worth less than a dollar, the cost of the telegram.

In accordance with common procedures, no bishop was appointed immediately, so the northwest clergy was left with a delicious repast of speculation about the forthcoming appointee. In seventy-five years of church establishment in the Northwest, only one native priest, Edward O'Dea, had been selected to be a bishop (he was born in Boston) and only two priests attached to northwest dioceses, O'Dea and O'Reilly, made it to the top. Since this appeared to be disproportionate, it was not unreasonable to expect a priest in Washington or a neighboring diocese to be named. So who was to be the first bishop of Spokane? No one, not even the bishops of the province, who convened to select three possible candidates, knew Rome's final decision.

The newspaper gossips were convinced that the bishops had recommended Father Aloysius Verhagen, the Belgium-born pastor of Our Lady of Lourdes Parish, Spokane's ranking prelate who was vicar general in eastern Washington.[2] His was the only name that surfaced in print, but doubtlessly many others were suggested in clerical conviviality following the solemn conclusions of the Forty Hours ceremonies.

BISHOP AUGUSTINE SCHINNER

Maybe the newspapers were right. Perhaps the bishops did recommend Verhagen. But Pius X and his assistants had other plans, which they kept under their mitres, as it were, for nearly a year. These involved another bishop, a very holy man and dear to the heart of Pius X, the first bishop of Superior in Wisconsin. His name was Augustine Francis Schinner. The Chippewa Indians had another name for him. They called him "Kamiskwanakwad," Red Cloud of the Dawn.[3] He was the pope's choice.

In retrospect, at least, one can find compelling reasons why Schinner was selected. A job description for the first bishop of Spokane would include these three elements in addition to the common requirements: experience in organizing a diocese; concern for and dedication to the Indian apostolate; and a known record for the promotion of abstinence from alcoholic beverages. Augustine Schinner, already recognized as a dedicated, holy prelate, possessed all three and held them with distinction.

As the first bishop of the diocese of Superior in Wisconsin, after serving as the vicar general of the archdiocese of Milwaukee for sixteen years, he certainly enjoyed the experience required for organizing the diocese of Spokane. Superior, when he became bishop, comprised 15,715 square miles, containing a Catholic population of 35,000 whites and 4000 Indians. Much of it, like Spokane, was still a wilderness. Churches had to be built, parishes and schools organized, Indian rights defended. Twice in seven years Schinner had traveled to Washington, D.C. for the sake of his Indians. Once, in the service of his Indians, he had been lost for two days in a blizzard in Wisconsin's subzero weather, barely escaping with his life.

As for the booze, Schinner was no Methodist, but in a gentle, heart-warming manner constantly urged sobriety. There is extant Schinner's quaint little endorsement of "Neal's Three-Day Drink Habit Cure," which read a follows: "The Neal cure is a God-send to any man who is bound by the chains of strong drink." He had persuaded "a splendid man from Superior" to take the cure, and he "was perfectly cured in three days."[4] If true, this had to be a miracle, not Neal's cure, and a miracle was not altogether unlikely.

There was need in Spokane for a bishop with deep aversions "to strong drink." At this time Spokane was one of the naughtiest cities in the west, rated next to San Francisco and Seattle for its wickedness. The demands of wealthy miners had created a cafe society that wined and dined in splendor, using champagne as well as fresh iced oysters by the barrel. Hordes of lumberjacks, too, descended on the city every weekend, seeking refreshments for their thirst and solace for their loneliness. Jimmy Durkin, who owned a bar three hundred feet in length, said to be the longest in the West, bought his supplies by the railroad carload, all for local consumption, and when the state went dry in 1916, he had enough liquor in his warehouse to supply a wild celebration for every alcoholic in Washington.

The dioceses of Superior and Spokane were similar except for one important detail: Spokane's climate was considerably milder, a circumstance that Vatican authorities had not overlooked. When they allowed Bishop Schinner to resign on January 13, 1913, because of ill health, occasioned in part by Superior's severe weather, they "held him in reserve for the new diocese of Spokane."[5]

Meanwhile, speculation about the new bishop persisted. On March 5, 1914, Spokane's morning paper printed a modest report using Schinner's name for the first time, but the editor was so unsure of his source that he resorted to the use of public information that could be found in the *Catholic Directory*. The evening paper in a brief back-page notice simply denied the rumor.[6]

At last, on April 2, 1914, the report was confirmed. On that date Bishop O'Dea received official notice from the apostolic delegate in Washington that Augustine Schinner had been appointed the first Bishop of Spokane, with a diocese that covered all the territory east of the Columbia River in the State of Washington, a spread of 51,922 square miles. There is evidence to believe that Schinner had known this all along, for the previous month he had slipped into Spokane, almost unnoticed, to take a quick look at what Rome had presented him.

The priests especially were much concerned about what they had got for a bishop, so the gossip in rectories continued to flow. This much they soon learned: the new bishop was fifty-one, he had been ordained for the Milwaukee Archdiocese at the precocious age of twenty-three, and consecrated as a bishop when he was only thirty-nine.[7]

Contemporary photographs showed him to be average in height, but slimmer than normal, a gentle, mild person with a narrow, long face and sad eyes. His head, with heavy black hair parted on the side, tilted to the left or to the right, and his small mouth with lips pressed close conveyed the impression that he opened them reluctantly, only when it was necessary. The truth is he was a shy, very sensitive man, unwilling to talk for talk's sake, but fierce and eloquent when duty required it. His almost habitual worried look revealed his distaste for being a bishop, for he much preferred, as he explained to Rome, to be "a simple missionary" for the Indians of South America. On the street he wore a bowler hat with his black suit and though a small bit of purple below his high clerical collar identified him as a prelate, he often kept this covered with a white kerchief around his neck, and tucked inside his coat.

He very much enjoyed the companionship of Jesuits, with whom he felt perfectly at home. There was some consternation then, at Our Lady of Lourdes, designated ad tempus for the pro-cathedral, when he announced that he would remain at Gonzaga after his arrival, pending his formal installation as bishop. As for his permanent residence and choice of cathedral, he kept his own counsel, ignoring with Christian meekness the unauthorized announcements made by Bishop O'Dea regarding these matters.[8]

The date of his installation was set for April 18, 1914. There were, as one would expect in a small city like Spokane, elaborate preparations for the first ceremony of its kind. The schedule went something like this:

    10:30 a.m. Pontifical High Mass celebrated by Bishop Schinner in
            Our Lady of Lourdes Church.
    1:00 p.m. Luncheon at the Hall of Doges [Davenport Hotel] for 75
            prelates and laymen.
    7:30 p.m. Procession of bishops, pastors and laymen through
            downtown streets.
    8:00 p.m. Public Reception at the American Theatre.

All was conducted as planned. In the procession immediately following the ceremony, Spokane's new bishop walked slowly down the street, his head tilted, his face very sad, followed by Archbishop Christie, who towered above him.[9] His Grace gazed about, lord and master of all he surveyed.

ATTACKS ON CATHOLICS

The new bishop's life was not a pleasant one. Rumors of war, confirmed by the German Kaiser's bellicose behavior, brought jitters to Americans, especially those of German descent. Far worse was the new wave of anti-Catholicism that followed in the wake of the flood of immigrants, most of whom came from so-called Catholic countries. The alleged threat to American democracy ticked off a period of hysteria, during which periodicals of virulent hatred, like *The Menace*, covered the land. The A.P.A.'s and the Guardians of Liberty, which included the renowned Indian fighter General Nelson A. Miles (who had conquered Chief Joseph's Nez Perce army), enjoyed great popularity despite their obvious lack of objectivity. They openly attacked respected churchmen like Cardinal Gibbons and Archbishop Ireland, both of whom had been conspicuous for their patriotic spirit. The bogus Knights of Columbus oath was circulated in defiance of court injunctions, the phony Jesuit "oath" long dead and buried was revived, and ignorant people besieged convents and plotted the invasion of church rectories to search for hidden caches of guns and bombs. Attempts were made to blow up St. Patrick's Cathedral in New York, and in Florida three nuns were arrested and paraded through the streets of St. Augustine. "Their crime consisted in teaching in colored schools."[10]

Here in the Northwest, the bishops made every effort to accommodate the Catholic immigrants. As noted above, Archbishop Gross had been deeply concerned about the loss to the faith, of many Germans but the loss had been sharply cut by two happy developments: the first was the Germans' decision to settle on the land in Catholic ghettos like Mount Angel, Uniontown, and Cottonwood; the second was the arrival and activity of the Benedictines whose influence over Germans kept most of them in the fold.

The Irish, who tended to run things anyhow, settled mostly in the cities where there were priests. In the West, unlike those in the deep South, who drifted from the church and provided countless preachers for revivals and hillbilly congregations, the Irish formed the first line of defense for the church and kept things from getting out of hand. The greatest crisis for the church at this time was Italian immigration. To cope with this the northwest bishops established national churches with Italian-speaking priests for the celebration of the liturgy in Latin, Italian style, and pulpit announcements in Italian, especially the notices about parish fund drives.

CHURCHES FOR MINORITY GROUPS

As early as 1894, St. Michael's chapel in Portland was occupied by the Italians, who had taken over the neighborhood previously occupied by the Germans.[11] In Seattle, the Cabrini Sisters acquired an old church on Beacon Hill to provide more room for their orphans at Mt. Carmel Mission. This building was then renovated to serve as a combination church and school. In early September, 1911, Father Joseph De Rop offered the first Mass in the church, which was called Our Lady of Mt. Virgin, the name of the parish in Italy where many Seattle immigrants had their origin. Out of this venture the present Mt. Virgine parish eventually developed. The Cabrini Sisters continued to use the building until 1918 when the property was condemned and purchased by the city for civic use.[12]

In 1912, the Italian colony in northeast Spokane was provided with its own church. Father Aloysius Roccati, attached to Gonzaga, built and dedicated St. Mary's on May 19, with the harmonious assistance of the Gonzaga band. St. Mary's remained a mission of St. Aloysius Church until 1957, when Mary Queen parish was formed for an area that was no longer predominantly Italian.[13]

As the number of Italian-speaking people increased in some of the smaller cities, churches were gradually organized and priests assigned in a desperate attempt to prevent what was becoming a disaster, in terms of loss to the church. On February 6, 1914, Father Anthony Bandizzione arrived in East Pocatello to become pastor of the Italian settlement there. Two months later, St. Anthony's church was completed and dedicated.[14] In the prolific Walla Walla valley, south of Spokane, Italians had tilled orchards and truck gardens for decades. When Father G.R. Balducci finally arrived on September 15, 1914, he found 125 Italian families, some of them second generation. He immediately set about building a new church for them, which was dedicated in honor of St. Francis of Assisi on November 15, 1916 by Bishop Schinner.[15]

By this time, the Italians in Priest River, Idaho, north of Spokane, requested an Italian priest and a church of their own. Roccati offered the first Mass for them on January 31, 1915, in a small chapel called St. Anthony's. Like most Italians, Roccati regarded music as an essential element of any festive occasion, so his choir from Spokane performed for this occasion. Later everyone shared in an elaborate banquet, which Roccati knew how to organize, then the choir returned to Spokane via the Northern Pacific Railroad at a dizzy forty miles an hour, increasing the general hilarity already generated by the good wine.[16]

In Tacoma the Italians belonged to St. Leo's parish where an Italian assistant priest was usually available for their special needs.. This was not adequate, however, for the care of the children, so in July 1917, Father Weibel, who was chaplain of the Catholic Federation of Tacoma, suggested the establishment of a day nursery. Accordingly, a day home was secured at South Thirteenth and M Streets for the Italian children of St. Leo's parish, under the supervision of Mrs. G. Merrutia. Since this, too, was inadequate, an orphanage was opened with the Sisters of St. Francis in charge and a church called St. Rita's was eventually built as a mission of St. Leo's.[17] Father Achilles Bruno, so frail the wind could blow him away, took charge of this, though it must be admitted it was not without risk. Allegedly one of the parishioners bashed in Bruno's head when he refused Christian burial for a wayward member of the colony. Bruno, to the astonishment of all, survived, but he refused to identify his assailant.

Finally, there was Lewiston, Idaho. This was an ancient city by northwest standards, first occupied by miners. But the Italians soon discovered its uncommonly warm climate and fertile lands. On February 29, 1920, Father Vincent Chiappa blessed for them a new church in honor of the Sacred Heart.[18] This was a mission of the Jesuits' St. Stanislaus, with whom, at a later date, Bishop Kelly discovered many differences, not excluding the Italian chapel.

Another substantial Catholic minority in Idaho was the Basques. These had been lured into southern Idaho and eastern Oregon for the care of sheep. On July 11, 1911, Father Bernard Arregui, a Basque priest, arrived at Boise and, with the approval of Bishops O'Reilly and Glorieux, undertook the establishment of a mission in the Jordan Valley, an area straddling the two dioceses of Boise and Baker City. In August, 1914, O'Reilly spent four days in the valley and he was so impressed by its promise that he assigned Father Hugh Marshall as a resident priest and gave him directions to build a church at once. Marshall took charge on August 8, 1915. The new church, named for St. Bernard and constructed in native stone by able parishioners, was dedicated by O'Reilly on Sunday, May 20, 1917.[19]

Gradually many Basques moved into the city of Boise and formed a colony there. Two buildings at the corner of Idaho and Fifth Streets were acquired and re-designed for the use of these Basques. One building was converted into a rectory and the other into a church that was appropriately called the Good Shepherd. Father Arregui became its first pastor, the shepherd of the shepherds.[20]

There were other national churches in the Northwest, especially in cities like Black Eagle, in Montana, and Tacoma, where smelters belched forth black smoke seven days a week. Sturdy Slavic or Polish men were generally employed in these ugly smelters, in substantial numbers, hence churches were provided for them and their families. In the course of time, like the Italian and German national churches, reasons for their existence faded away and the parishes, too, became integrated.[21]

ST. MARTIN'S BECOMES AN ABBEY

Meanwhile, the Benedictines in Washington had been preoccupied with a greater St. Martin's. In November of 1913, they had dedicated the initial unit of this ambitious project, a large new section of their permanent building complex, composed of red brick and fashioned in "collegiate Gothic," which was the rage on American campuses at that time.[22] During the following year, the community's extrovert, Father Sebastian Ruth, a former Jesuit, promoted the college's first publication, anticipating science fiction by calling it *The Martian*. Ruth also established at this time one of the Northwest's first radio stations, known as 7YS. In 1921, this was converted into KGY broadcasting station.[23]

While these accomplishments appeared to be very impressive to their many friends in Olympia and Tacoma, they were mere preliminaries for the main event in St. Martin's current history. Unlike Mount Angel, St. Martin's still lacked the status of an independent abbey. Early in January in 1914, at a meeting of the Capitulars, it was unanimously agreed that the time was ripe for the formation of an abbey. A formal request presented to the Holy See through the normal channels was favorably granted. The required documents arrived at St. Martin's on May 9, 1914, and the date for the election of the first abbot was set for the morning of May 19. Precisely at eight on that Tuesday morning, a solemn Mass was sung by the prior, then the eleven Capitulars retired to the Chapter room to conduct an ancient Benedictine rite, the selection of an abbot. Less than two hours later, the Capitulars emerged with the news. Their choice had fallen upon Father Oswald Baran, pastor of Holy Rosary church in Tacoma.[24]

The documents of confirmation of the election by the Holy See arrived on July 8, and the date of blessing for St. Martin's first abbot was set for September 29. The occasion was a grand one for Holy Rosary parish, because the blessing was celebrated there. Bishop O'Dea presided at Mass and Archbishop Christie preached the occasional sermon. The list of priests in the sanctuary reads like a Who's Who of the Seattle Diocese: the local Redemptorist superior, George Mahoney, was deacon; Hylebos, the assistant priest; Joseph McGrath, soon to be appointed Bishop of Baker City, and Gustave Archtergael, pastor of the church in Ballard, were deacons of honor; the notary was D.A. Hanly, another ex-Jesuit, who achieved some fame as author of the life of a Jesuit saint.[25]

When the ceremony was over, there was much laughter and superficial gaiety, but over it all there hovered the chilling pall of war. "Europe Reverts to Barbarism," the *Catholic Sentinel* had lamented in early August, "Nearly Whole Continent Has Embarked on Campaign of Blood."[26] It was difficult for Belgians like Hylebos to think about anything else. Suddenly the Germans were regarded as villains, a sad situation for the Benedictines, many of whom were German in origin. Bishop Schinner, well known for his identity with German cultural events, was not present for the blessing. He lived in the parish house with Father Verhagen, a Belgian patriot, and people throughout the state gossiped about the strained relations between the two clerics. Schinner's absence at Holy Rosary was noted, but no one criticized it. If anything, people pitied Bishop Schinner for he had already become a lonely, distant man.

His dearest patron was dead. Pope Pius X had expired, prematurely they said, because of grief over the war.[27] Benedict XV was elected only two weeks later on September 3, 1914, but most Catholics, especially those far from Rome, still felt a deep sense of loss.

Despite these gloomy contingencies, the new abbot presented a cheerful countenance for the photographers. Seemingly comfortable in his abbatial robes, with the pectoral cross suspended conspicuously on his chest, he appeared to be a refreshing young prelate, able and willing to undertake a long reign. He would outlive the venerable old archbishop who praised him in the pulpit that day by a scant three years.[28]

MOUNT ST. MICHAEL'S

The Jesuits' west coast scholasticate in the old "Sheds" at Gonzaga gradually evolved into a crowded residence for seminarians pursuing the three-year philosophy course.[29] In the beginning, "The Sheds" had housed a theologate as well, one of only four Jesuit theologates in the United States and Canada. But prosperity had killed this prestigious department at the university. There were so many candidates for the priesthood in the order that the theologians had to go elsewhere and "The Sheds" became the sole inheritance of the philosophers. This situation prevailed for but a brief time because "The Sheds" could accommodate no more than 35 Jesuits, including faculty, and approximately eighty philosophers were expected to occupy it by the year 1915. No one needed a crystal ball to foretell the consequences.

Various locations were proposed for the new scholasticate. In August 1911, a meeting of Jesuit superiors to discuss the matter was held in California. The majority present favored Spokane, which, according to them, enjoyed the best climate for study. The Californians quite naturally disagreed and the final decision was left to Rome. Father Taelman, Gonzaga's rector, produced the decisive arguments for the Jesuit General by listing the merits of the St. Michael's mission property in a letter that sounded more like Pasadena real estate promotion than a description of Spokane country. "There is a natural rock there, a fine place for a graveyard...."[30] The general succumbed to St. Michael's avowed charms, and northwest Jesuits scurried about to gather plans and funds for an appropriate building to stand on a bluff overlooking the city. Father Arthuis, who had supervised the construction of St. Aloysius Church, was placed in charge. On July 29, 1914, the general approved the loan for financing the building and the way was now clear to proceed with construction, which began on August 24. On March 15 of the following year, while two hundred people listened attentively, Bishop Schinner presided over the cornerstone ritual, totally unaware of the subsequent importance of this edifice in his own personal life.

During September, Arthuis' health broke down, despite that wonderful Spokane climate, and he was replaced by Father Dillon who had supervised the construction of Gonzaga's major addition in 1902.[31] When the project was completed at last, the Jesuits had spent over four hundred thousand borrowed dollars on it. Eager scholastics took possession of the place on January 6, 1916, some of them scrambling through the heavy snow, which continued to fall all day, up the lofty heights to their shiny new home.

SEATTLE CATHEDRAL DISASTER

During that same January and the month that followed it, record snowfalls appeared throughout the interior, where snow was not uncommon. The rains on the coast were heavy. Rarely did Seattle experience a snowfall, but the winter of 1916 was unusual. On February 2, Candlemas day, clouds of snow blew into Seattle, first from the south, wet and heavy, then from the east, piling up ominously on both sides of the huge, copper sheaffed dome, which was suspended from curtain walls eighty feet square. No one appeared to be anxious about it, nor did anyone visit the church that afternoon as was customary, because of the deep snow on the walks.

Suddenly at 3:15 in the afternoon, with a roar "like the boom of a gun," the dome with its five great chandeliers, each weighing half a ton, plunged 120 feet to the floor, driving debris many feet into the earth. "Air compression hurled heavy oaken pews to shatter against the back wall." It was a scene of destruction like those "wrought by the cannons in Belgium." Snowflakes whirled through the huge gaping hole in the roof as the bishop's assistants, summoned from the residence next door by the noise, mutely stared at it, shocked into disbelief. Among these was Father W.J. Noonan, pastor of the parish. "Now, William," he said to William O'Connell, recently appointed to the *Northwest Progress*, "not a word of this to the press."

At first the cathedral appeared to be a total loss. Noonan reserved judgment. He said he would await the decision of the diocesan architect, Louis Beezer, who spent days in the ruins before rendering a decision. At last he made his report. The curtain walls which supported the dome were out of plumb, but the structure's side walls were safe. The cathedral could be restored, advisably without the dome, for approximately $75,000.

Bishop O'Dea was satisfied and repairs were begun at once. Mass for the parish was scheduled in the Cathedral Hall. The villainous snow was long gone when workmen began their labors.

More than a year was required to complete the restoration. Finally, in March, 1917, shaped anew at a cost of $150,000, it was opened for divine worship. O'Dea blessed it a second time and Christie preached. "He prefaced his sermon," says the correspondent, "by congratulating and complimenting Bishop O'Dea, the clergy and laity of Seattle for the sacrifice they had all made in restoring St. James' Cathedral to even greater magnificence than had previously characterized it and expressed hope that the day would not be far distant when the new dome would be finally completed...."[32]

Christie's hope, alas, was never realized. The renovated cathedral has presented ever since the appearance of two massive towers with a long gabled roof, as bereft of exterior embellishments as a respectable warehouse.

NEW RELIGIOUS ORDERS

As the number of parishes and schools multiplied, so also did the number of religious orders. Among these two orders of men especially should be noted: the Capuchins who first arrived in the Northwest in 1910 and the Norbertines who came four years later.

The Capuchins, formally designated as the Franciscan Friars of the Capuchin Reform, came from Ireland at the invitation of Bishop O'Reilly.

The first to arrive were Fathers Luke Sheehan and Thomas Dowling, who assumed pastorships at Hermiston and Bend.[33] In 1912, another Irish Capuchin took over the administration of St. Joseph's church in Roseburg, and two years later Capuchins from Bend accepted the care of the Warm Springs Reservation.[34]

On February 5, 1913, Mass was offered for the first time at St. Margaret's church, Cut Bank, Montana, frequently the coldest spot in the lower forty-eight states. Bishop Carroll dedicated this structure on July 5, 1914, then applied to the Norbertine Fathers in Wisconsin for Flemish speaking priests to serve the many Belgians in the Valier-Cut Bank district. Father Pennings, the prior of the Norbertines, sent two priests, Van den Elsan, who was assigned Valier, and Father R.G. Greven, who was assigned to Shelby, Cut Bank, and other missions.[35] These were the first members of their order to come to the Northwest.

THE FRANCISCANS

The Franciscan Fathers had arrived in the Northwest before any other priests, but their popularity in California, where they replaced the Jesuits when the latter were exiled by Charles III of Spain (1767), prevented them from expanding their activities into the Northwest as some of the other large orders had done. By 1906, however, the Franciscans had returned to Oregon. Father Maximilian Klein offered the first Mass in Hood River on September 9 of that year. He built the first church there, called the Immaculate Conception, and Bishop O'Reilly dedicated it on December 8.[36] Father Klein was at Burns, Oregon, in August, 1908, and during the following month Father Ewald Soland became the pastor of St. Francis on the Cowlitz, Washington's mother church. In 1909, a Franciscan from Cowlitz built the church at Kalama, called St. Joseph, and purchased an old Methodist church at Kelso, which was converted into the Immaculate Heart of Mary church.[37] Two years later, a Franciscan from Hood River built St. Patrick's church at Parkdale. Then on April 17, 1916, Father Julius Gliebe arrived from Los Angeles to take charge of the missions of Deer Park, Colbert, and Springdale, all of them in the Spokane Diocese and previously attended by the Jesuits.

Three years earlier, Archbishop Christie had established St. Clare's parish on Capitol Hill in Portland. He invited the Franciscans to administer it, and Father Capistran Damech arrived and supervised the construction of a combination church-school building, which was opened on August 23, 1914. The Franciscans took charge of Ascension parish in Portland in 1915, and at the request of Bishop Schinner, they accepted St. Francis Assisi parish in north Spokane, completing a church-school building there for Christmas of the same year.

In August of 1917, they arrived in Seattle, accepting South Park Mission as their base. They remodeled buildings of the Brothers of Our Lady of Lourdes for a church, using the same name for it that the brothers had bestowed upon it. A year later, they agreed to take over St. George's parish, and arrived there on July 6 to establish a friary, to which the fathers of Our Lady of Lourdes were also attached.[38] The parish was formally transferred to the Franciscans on October 7, 1918.

Within a few brief years, therefore, scarcely more than a decade, the Franciscan fathers returned to the Northwest where their coreligionists had pioneered more than a century before. They came now to undertake a proportionate share of the burden of parochial growth that had become so formidable for the hierarchy that the situation was regarded as desperate.

NEW ORDERS OF SISTERS

The need for priests was but one side of the coin. Sisters, too, were in great demand and for several decades during this era of expansion there was much shuffling around, one order of sisters replacing another when shortages of personnel here or elsewhere required adjustments.

Joining other Dominicans who had come earlier were six Sisters of the Congregation of Catherine of Siena from Ireland. They had been teaching in Portugal until their expulsion by an anti-religious government. They arrived in Baker City at the end of March, 1911 and on April 18 left for Ontario, Oregon where they finally opened Holy Rosary Hospital on April 17, 1912. They also opened a school called St. Catherine's, but for lack of teachers were forced to close it in the following year.[39] With the bishop's warm-hearted approval, they established a novitiate in Ontario, with five postulants for an auspicious beginning. On October 6, 1912, O'Reilly presided over ceremonies as solemn as he could make them for the five aspiring young ladies. Unfortunately, the sisters had second thoughts and moved this novitiate to Kenosha, Wisconsin, eight years later.[40]

The first Sisters of the Society of the Holy Child arrived from Mayfield, Sussex, England, on August 25, 1913.[41] For a time they taught in the recently organized St. Philip Neri school in east Portland, living frugally in a small house nearby. On February 6, 1914, the cornerstone for their new convent school in Rose City Park was laid with holy raptures of song, and construction was begun on the super-structure of the three story English style academy, which would have looked more compatible on the Hudson River than on Sandy Boulevard. Completed some six months later, it was called simply Holy Child Academy. In

September, the sisters registered their first students, girls of high school age, and opened their classrooms for the first time on the fifteenth of the same month.[42]

SISTERS OF THE FRANCISCAN RULE

A very different kind of order appeared in the Northwest when three Poor Clare nuns with their Abbess Mother M. Leopold McNerney occupied a temporary monastery on DeSmet Avenue in Spokane.[43] The Poor Clares are a contemplative order, specializing, with the approval of the church, in prayer and penance. They required a permanent building with cloister, and Mother McNerney, an aggressive, overly-optimistic nun, built a vast brick one with walled gardens, occupying an entire block on Mission Avenue facing "Holy Land," which was the current appellation for St. Aloysius parish. Apparently she expected many vocations to this austere life, but these never materialized. No one could foresee this, not even Bishop Schinner, who dedicated it on July 9, 1916, during the first week of the great battle of the Somme in France, when England lost sixty thousand soldiers in a single day.[44] So the dedication was not altogether a happy one, especially for His Lordship, who anguished over each day's news from the war front.

The Poor Clares observed a strict Franciscan rule. Two other Franciscan orders of sisters ventured into the Northwest during this same period, which could be called appropriately the Franciscan invasion. First, there were the Sisters of St. Francis of Penance and Christian Charity from Stella Niagra, New York. Four of these sisters opened a day and boarding school in St. Mary's Academy at Cowlitz Mission, the ancient convent school that had seen many comings and goings, like certain restaurants that enjoy frequent Grand Openings.[45]

Two months later, on September 29, 1911, these sisters arrived at Havre, Montana and immediately arranged for the construction of the first Sacred Heart Hospital there.[46] They admitted their first patient on December 16 in temporary quarters. Bishop Lenihan, on February 18, 1912, dedicated what was intended to be a permanent hospital, but this was badly damaged by fire two years later. There was no loss of life and the patients were moved to a public school across the street, where they were cared for until August, when the building was repaired. It proved to be inadequate however, so a new Sacred Heart Hospital was constructed in 1916.[47]

The vicissitudes in Havre left the sisters undaunted. They accepted St. Clare's parish school in Portland in 1914.[48] Two years later they arrived at Ascension Parish in Portland to staff the school, and during the same autumn opened parochial schools in St. Francis Parish in Spokane, St. Jude's parish in Havre, and St. Boniface parish in Uniontown.[49]

The second Franciscan contingent, the Franciscan Sisters of Perpetual Adoration, arrived from Lacrosse, Wisconsin on July 17, 1915, to establish St. John's Academy in Colfax. In September of that same year, six sisters opened six classes in both elemental and high school courses in a new two-story brick structure next to the church on the south end of town. St. John's had been made possible by generous benefactions from Mr. and Mrs. John McTierney, for whom it was named, and Mr. Thomas Mostyn.[50]

During this same year, the sisters replaced the Ursulines at St. Francis Xavier's in Spokane. Four years later, in 1919, they opened Holy Rosary school in Bozeman and, in 1920, they took over St. Bernard's school in Blackfoot Idaho.[51]

MOTHER CABRINI AGAIN

Meanwhile, there was Mother Cabrini. She returned to Seattle for the second time, which proves that nuns can gad about, on church business of course, and still be canonized as saints.

Cabrini, still as frail and tiny as a bird, draped heavily in black without patches of white like most nuns, had arrived from Portland to meet with Mr. Michael Heney, a man of wealth. She expected to remain in Seattle for a brief time only, but Heney's proposal, a dazzling one, quickly induced her to change her mind and she hurried off to return her ticket to the railway depot. Heney offered to build a new, safe home for the orphans to replace the temporary buildings on Beacon Hill. Together with Cabrini, he studied a map of Seattle. Finding a large, unplotted tract on Lake Washington, they decided to go for it. Cabrini sent two sisters at once to inspect it, and after receiving a favorable report, she herself took a buggy out to look it over. This was in March, 1913.

Cabrini then approached the owner with an offer to buy the property. The latter replied, rather tartly, that the place was not for sale at any price. A week later, however, he telephoned Cabrini to say that an unexpected situation had arisen and he wanted to sell the property. The lesson here is clear: one should be very cautious when dealing with a saint.

The sisters moved into the house on the property immediately and Father Santo Filippi of Seattle College offered the first Mass there on April 26. Subsequently a costly "fireproof" building, similar in style to Mount St. Michael's in Spokane, was constructed on the site. It was occupied by the sisters and their highly excitable orphans on June 24, 1913.[52]

The forthcoming new orphanage was one thing; Cabrini now wanted something more: a home for the newly born, unwanted babies from Seattle's unwed mothers. She returned to Seattle in June, 1915 and selected the Perry Hotel for her purpose. Locating the owner in New York, she made a deal, paying half the price demanded and agreeing to pay the balance with money acquired by loan. When news of this transaction became public, a storm of opposition blew over the Queen City, like another blizzard. Righteous and godly Christians did not approve of a refuge for unwed mothers in their neighborhood. Seattle banks refused to loan Cabrini the money, but when the cause appeared to be lost, two unknown gentlemen unexpectedly entered the scene and offered to lend Cabrini what she needed. The hotel changed hands and Cabrini converted it into Columbus Hospital, which was dedicated in June, 1916.[53]

Only one year later, on December 22, 1917, Mother Cabrini died from malaria in Chicago's Columbus Hospital, which she also founded. There was a curious sequel. On December 17, 1925, Sister Delfina Grazioli, who helped Cabrini establish the first orphanage on Beacon Hill in Seattle, lay at death's door with an incurable ailment. Mother Cabrini appeared to her and she was instantly cured.[54]

So Cabrini came back to Seattle even after she died. There is no telling at what lengths she would go to provide sisters for her cherished orphans on Lake Washington.

AMERICA AT WAR

Woodrow Wilson, it has sometimes been noted, was not conspicuous for his tolerance of Catholics. Despite this, the Irish Catholic vote helped to elect him to a second term of the presidency on a peace-at-any-cost platform, and he was sworn in as president of the United States for a second time at precisely 12:03 p.m. on Sunday, March 4, 1917. Less than five weeks later, on April 6, he requested Congress to declare war.

The *Catholic Sentinel* in Portland noted these facts with considerable restraint, for its sympathies in Europe lay with the Irish Nationalists who were at odds with the British. It was difficult to be enthusiastically pro-war and allies of the British, who, as Bishop Schinner had pointed out, were guilty of anti-Americanism, too. "Three of our ships were sunk by the English mines, entailing also loss of life, because the warning of England had not been heeded."[55] Most of the Irish in America, nonetheless, supported the war generously after Congress cast our lot with England. Many of them, like Bishop Carroll of Helena, feeling compelled to prove their patriotism, became actively engaged in one way or another. "Me, too," they were saying. Carroll ordered the American flag to be flown from the pinnacle of the Cathedral, a gesture that received hearty applause and enhanced this already prestigious status with populist groups.

For Schinner in Spokane, the issues were not so simplistic. Early in the war he had stated his opinion that most people did not want the war and that the nations involved should conduct a plebiscite. "Our nation should not forget its debt of gratitude owed Germany for past services," he said with anguish in his heart because of hatred for Germany. The *Spokesman-Review,* strongly pro-British, rushed into large print: "Bishop Talks Pacificism," which then was about the most degrading charge the press could make.[56]

In mid-August, 1917, Schinner publicly criticized local officials for twisting the laws to prevent priests from obtaining Mass wine.[57] Most of the Northwest was very "dry," so His Lordship was further alienated from certain godly segments of the population, who already regarded him as a foreigner. He refused to yield to public pressures. When requested to clarify his position on the war, he replied that next to fighting to defend his faith, he would fight to defend his country. This was not enough for his critics, some of whom, preaching my-country-right-or-wrong, expressed virtuous shock that anyone could be so blind as to place their church above the country.[58]

But the bishop's complaint that Wilson's rejection of the pope's peace plan had been a mistake evoked the fiercest response. "Personally," he said, indicating his own opinions modestly, "I think the pope's offer should have been accepted as voicing America's principles. All experts, both of army and navy, declare we face a gigantic task and the misery and suffering will be appalling. The people of all belligerent nations are clamoring for peace. We ourselves are on a volcano, but most of us do not realize the fact. Ugly rumblings are heard on every side and we know not what they portend."[59]

That did it. Even some of his priests joined the chorus of opposition to the bishop, whose prophetic words, expressing still valid truths, merely irritated those whose war spirit had been aroused. The bishop was deeply hurt. Known already as diffident, in spite of his courage in speaking up for peace, he now acquired the image of remoteness or coldness, which drove him further into the arms of his Jesuit friends, especially Father Paul Sauer, whose birthplace, like Schinner's, was Wisconsin. Whenever possible, he took refuge at Mount St. Michael's. Sauer often accompanied him on his excursions for conferring confirmation and the two of them on occasion enjoyed swimming in a remote bay on Loon Lake. It was not likely that his cherished friendship for the Jesuits contributed to the better understanding with the region's Irish bishops and clergy. Indeed, the opposite was noted, which in turn made him even more isolated. In part due to the Jesuits, he survived the dark, terrible years of the war. Far back in his mind, though, was a growing determination to leave Spokane's Jesuits and, when it was feasible, to resign his see in favor of a missionary's humble slot in South America.

DEATH OF BISHOP GLORIEUX

During that same month of August in 1917, when the nation was mobilizing for a war "to make the world safe for democracy," Bishop Alphonse Glorieux, a Belgian like the rector of Spokane's cathedral, lay dying in St. Vincent's Hospital in Portland. His thin, pinched face, like a sainted bishop on some icons, gave evidence of the hard years he had borne as the Bishop of Boise. He had been ordained to the priesthood just fifty years earlier. He had left behind his cherished roses, his cathedral unfinished, and taken to his bed without grumbling.[60]

The diocese was in good hands. Father Remi Keyzer, who had arrived from Louvain in 1891, could serve as an interim administrator, allowing the bishop peace of soul, if there was any while his country was occupied by the enemy. Keyzer had recently established a diocesan newspaper, the *Boise Catholic Monthly*, which was designed to raise funds for the completion of the cathedral.[61] The paper, like Keyzer, served its purpose well; the money poured in, but the holy bishop died before his cathedral could be finished.

Bishop Glorieux passed away peacefully at 7:40 in the morning of August 25, 1917, technically from a kidney failure. Father Arregui, pastor of St. John's Cathedral, who was at his side when he died, telegraphed the news to Boise immediately, and the bell of St. John's tolled the message to the parish and the city. The body was placed in "a gun-metal casket." Accompanied by Archbishop Christie, Bishop O'Dea, and other dignitaries, it was borne from Portland to Boise in the chapel car St. Peter. The Pontifical Mass of Requiem on August 29 was celebrated by the Archbishop. Bishop O'Dea preached the eulogy and the entire city mourned, for Glorieux in his thirty-two years as bishop had endeared himself to the hearts of all.

During that time, the Boise church had changed from a struggling vicariate with seven priests, eleven churches—mostly dilapidated shacks— and thirty-five hundred Catholics to a stable, self-respecting diocese with fifty-three priests, ninety-three churches and approximately sixteen thousand Catholics.[62] More significantly, perhaps, the Catholics no longer felt like outsiders. Though they were heavily outnumbered by the Mormons, who claimed the allegiance of the majority in southern Idaho, they had formed an influential constituency that no longer could be disregarded.

For the interregnum, Keyzer continued to serve as the diocesan administrator. He energetically campaigned for the completion of the cathedral, while the curia in Rome tackled procedures for providing Boise with a new bishop.

The *Catholic Sentinel* announced in September that Bishop Lenihan of Great Falls had scheduled the dedication of twenty churches during the following autumn.[63] Lenihan was also engaged in reforming his diocesan paper, which seems to have lost some of its following. Volume One, Number One of the new weekly called *Great Falls Catholic Review* appeared on November 18, 1917.[64] The *Sentinel* also reported that the Knights of Columbus in Tacoma had opened a pavilion for soldiers at Camp Lewis and that Father Augustine Dinand of St. Leo's parish had offered the first Mass there.[65] Bishop O'Dea in Seattle formally established a new parish called St. John's and Archbishop Christie dedicated a chapel, also called St. John's, at Clatskanie, Oregon.[66]

Although the war effort occupied the attention of most people, Catholic expansion, as the above indicates, had not slowed down. Confirmation, for example, is found in the record of new hospitals, schools, convents and churches that appeared in a two year period prior to the armistice.[67]

BISHOP DANIEL GORMAN

On February 6, 1918, the name of the new Bishop of Boise was finally revealed. He was Monsignor Daniel Mary Gorman, successor to Bishop Carroll as president of Dubuque College in Iowa.[68] In the diplomacy of the American church, Dubuque had lost little of its influence over the northwest dioceses.

But Gorman was an excellent choice for Boise with its Mormon control of the state's political power. His bland, benign appearance completely disarmed anyone of hostile intent. His wide mouth, some said, revealed a generous spirit, which he certainly possessed, and his soft, warm looking eyes, shielded by *prince-nez*, rimless glasses, beckoned to people, especially children, to come to him with confidence. His head, covered with brown wavy hair, brushed back, was held bent forward a little, like father confessor in the tribunal of penance.

Gorman had been born in a sod hut in Wyoming, Iowa, on April 12, 1861, to John and Mary Gorman, nee Rooney, immigrants from Ireland. There was no church in their village; thus John received his First Communion in a railway car. Later he entered Dubuque's college, called St. Joseph's then, to study for the priesthood. He graduated in June, 1887. In September of the same year, he entered St. Francis Seminary,

Milwaukee, where Augustine Schinner had matriculated only one year earlier. He was ordained to the priesthood in the seminary by Bishop John Joseph Zardetti on June 24, 1893, at the age of thirty-two.

His succeeding years prepared him well for Idaho. Teaching children in a rented house, making the rounds of a missionary parish where non-Catholics outnumbered those of his flock, a professorship in college and later administration, directorship of a fund drive, which added $165, 000 to an incipient scholarship endowment, all of these and other recommendations in his *curriculum vitae* were convincing enough for Benedict XV to appoint him to the hierarchy.[69] If anything, he deserved something larger than Boise.

Gorman was consecrated bishop on Wednesday morning, May 1, 1918, in St. Raphael's Cathedral in Dubuque. The consecrating prelate was the Apostolic Delegate, Archbishop John Bonzano, and the assisting consecrators were Lenihan of Great Falls and Bishop Joseph Glass of Salt Lake. Present for the ceremony were the two archbishops, thirteen bishops, four monsignori and over five hundred priests. One must admit that this was an extraordinary outpouring of esteem. Perhaps some pitied poor Gorman, going out to a missionary diocese of fewer Catholics than in the city of Dubuque. But he needed no pity. What he needed was money. Happily, after the solemn installation in his cathedral on May 15, Father Remi Keyzer "approached the throne and with an appropriate speech of presentation handed the Bishop some twenty thousand dollars, a purse from priests and people to be used toward the completion of St. John's Cathedral."[70] This was two hundred times as much as the Boise Catholics had presented to Bishop Glorieux when he arrived, to buy a bishop's throne, though he had no cathedral in which he could place it.

CHANGES AT BAKER CITY

Bishop O'Reilly of Baker had never recovered from his ulcers. In March 1918, he was in Oakland, California, again, seeking medical treatment. Tall and thin, now in his fifty-seventh year, he still walked with lofty dignity, almost solemnity, even in his hospital room. He looked gray, his eyebrows were gray, too, and his kind, warm features bore the marks of the pain he had endured for two decades. He also suffered from diabetes, which no one had yet recognized as one of his physical disabilities. This would kill him later, but for the moment he sought not so much a cure as relief, in order that he might continue to serve his diocese.

He was in Oakland when news of his removal from Baker City was publicized. The pope had transferred him to the diocese of Lincoln, Nebraska, to succeed Bishop John Henry Tihen, who had been transferred to the see of Denver.[71] This action was taken, it was said, to provide for him a less arduous field of labor and a city wherein his health could be more readily attended. The official date of his transfer was March 20, 1918. Clad in his customary frock coat and still walking erect, he departed for Lincoln in August, modestly aware of his record in Baker City. In fifteen years he had built the cathedral the people at first did not want, and thirty-seven churches, and he had remodeled six other buildings for church purposes.

His departure left the see of Baker City vacant. For the interim Monsignor Bronsgeest, who had violently protested the new diocese in 1903, was appointed administrator. Undoubtedly pleased with the recognition, the old Dutchman died before a new bishop was named on December 2, 1918, and Father P.J. O'Rourke replaced him. In Baker City, one of the smaller dioceses, things often have been very complicated.

Meanwhile, an enigmatic notice appeared in the *Catholic Sentinel* for July 25, 1918. "Oregon Bishop Is Appointed," the brief announcement read. "Monsignor Terrence G. Brady of Dubuque, Rector of the Cathedral named for the Baker City Diocese." There is little to say about this except that no correction for it was published. It was six months later that the name of O'Reilly's true successor was revealed. Father Joseph Francis McGrath, whose venture into the Northwest had been purely accidental, "was preconized Bishop of Baker City in the Consistory at Rome, December 21st, 1918. This was also the 23rd anniversary day of his ordination."[72]

Few of our prelates, if any, have experienced the circuitous path to the bishop's throne that Joseph McGrath had taken. Born in County Kilkenny, Ireland on March 1, 1871, one of seven children of James McGrath and Margaret O'Farrell McGrath, young Joseph entered the Grand Seminary at Montreal for the Diocese of Springfield, Massachusetts. After ordination, there was no vacancy in Springfield, so he took temporary duty in parishes in other parts of Massachusetts and Pennsylvania. A vacancy finally appeared in his own diocese, but due to poor health, which had plagued him since seminary days, he was forced to seek a warmer climate. By order of the bishop, he went to Texas. Feeling better after three months, he decided to return home via the West, with a view to visit friends among the clergy. At Seattle he met Bishop O'Dea, who snagged him for the Nesqually diocese, with the approval of the Bishop of Springfield. After an apprenticeship at the pro-cathedral in Seattle, he was appointed pastor of St. Patrick's parish in Tacoma, where he startled everyone with a brilliant record of building and organization.

McGrath, a very handsome man with dark, expressive eyes and the suggestion of a dimple in his chin, looked like the quarterback on Knute Rockne's team, strong and muscular, despite his earlier illness. Well groomed, master of the situation without effort, he embodied the best features of the Irish without gaelic bossiness. Like Gorman, he deserved something better than eastern Oregon in 1919. During a long reign, however, he accomplished wonders, earning for himself an everlasting place in history for his role in promoting the Confraternity of Christian Doctrine (CCD) during its crucial period.

He was consecrated on March 25, 1919, in the restored St. James Cathedral, Seattle, by Bishop O'Dea. The co-consecrators were Lenihan of Great Falls and Carroll of Helena. Archbishop Christie preached the formal sermon. Other prelates in attendance were Gorman of Boise, Timothy Casey, the Archbishop of Vancouver, B.C., and Emil Bunoz, Vicar Apostolic of Prince Ruppert. Conspicuous for his absence was Schinner of Spokane, who still regarded himself, not without reason, as not belonging.

More recently, the ever popular Father Verhagen, pastor of Spokane's Cathedral for twenty-five years, had created a storm of protest that received wide coverage in the press. Schinner, for lack of his own residence, was still living in the cathedral rectory. Tensions had developed between his Lordship and the pastor for various reasons, not excluding Verhagen's Belgian origins, but Schinner, due to "financial conditions," felt he could not move elsewhere.[73] In May, 1918, Verhagen announced that he was leaving the diocese because of "differences" with the bishop. "Much embarrassed, the bishop was forced to plead with Verhagen to remain, all of which was aired in the press in such a manner that Verhagen appeared to have the upper hand. The incident, as petty as most family quarrels, served to confirm the bishop's suspicion about himself: his German ancestry like that of others during this critical time, aroused latent racial prejudices, especially in a provincial city like Spokane. Most administrators could have ignored the problem until it went away, but Schinner was too sensitive and gentle to overlook it or fight back.

END OF THE WAR

During the closing months of the Great War, a "Spanish influenza" epidemic disrupted normal business of the church. At Gonzaga where a prosperous "Students Army Training Corps program (S.A.T.C.) sponsored by the United States Army" competed with war gardens, there were about 350 students, forty more than during the previous school year. The president, Father James Brogan, like Archbishop Christie in Portland, had been uncommonly active in urging the sale of war bonds, while the vice president-treasurer, Schinner's special friend Father Paul Sauer, was trying to hold the lid down on the students' volatile war spirit.[74] It was Sauer who took charge when the epidemic struck in October 1918. One hundred cases of flu in the S.A.T.C. were reported by October 18. In the city itself, the number of cases daily averaged 2,185.[75] Churches, schools and stores were closed.

The first death at Gonzaga was on October 19. It was one of the students. Another student died on the following day and Father John Neander, a tall, strong-as-an-ox Jesuit from Sweden, died on October 21. One of the nurses, pretty Mary O'Brien died on the twenty-third, and the little world of Gonzaga was stunned. Some of the boys wept, others were too sick to weep. There was no time for pity. Another boy died on the twenty-eighth and by this time the epidemic had spread to Mount St. Michael's, where thirty cases were reported in one day. On November 7, the first member of the community died.[77] On the day of his funeral, there were forty-five Jesuits in bed, six with pneumonia.

Oddly, the epidemic arrived in Seattle late and with less violence. Seattle College was spared with no great inconveniences at all, mostly because college classes, for lack of students, were suspended indefinitely on June 12, 1918.[78] High school classes, like those at St. Martin's, convened again in September and were interrupted briefly when the State Board of Health placed a ban on meetings.

The Central Powers in Europe were collapsing and during the flood of peace rumors that followed, few noticed that Congress had passed the Volstead Act, also known as the Prohibition Enforcement Act, over the veto of the president.[79] This was a great victory for a noisy minority, surpassed only by the Allied victory in the war with the unconditional surrender of Germany on November 11.

BEGINNINGS OF FORMAL CATHOLIC ACTION

The end of the war was followed by a wave of strikes and Bolshevik revolutions, which disrupted commerce and agriculture throughout the Northwest. The church found itself under siege from a new kind of enemy—the so-called nihilists, who inaugurated an era of terrorism and opposition to traditional structures, including the historic church. Catholics discovered that now they were isolated more than ever, separated from "Moral Minority" on the prohibition issue, from the neo-humanists on the parochial school issue, from the super-patriots on the immigration issue, from the White House on the peace issue, and now from the poor and the more radical social reformers on the authority or structure issue. There seemed to be no other course but to go it alone, for society had fractionized under the pressures of the great upheaval that followed the war's devastation.

There were few in the northwest church who recognized all this. Bishop Schinner did, I think, as well as Father Edwin O'Hara, pastor of St. Mary's Church in Eugene, about whom we will hear considerably more later. But most clerics and most lay Catholics had not been prepared for it.

But a new spirit was developing to meet the need. New movements among lay men and women were picking up steam, racing rapidly into all parts, even into the hinterlands. Pius XI's call for lay action, "the sleeping giant," had not been made yet, but Catholics in the Northwest were being prepared to accept it, with more enthusiasm perhaps than in other parts of America, because of our isolation and lack of priests.

Some mention has been made already of the Knights of Columbus. While the Knights have sometimes been accused of certain elitism or too much stress on initiations and regalia, there can be no doubt about the significance of their contribution to the Northwest church in the immediate post-war world. The Knights sponsored what has been called "the first Laymen's Retreat" at St. Martin's in July, 1918.[80] The first Laymen's Retreat, actually, was directed by Father John Nobili at Fort Vancouver in June, 1845, when fifty members of the Hudson's Bay Company brigade, mostly Canadians, with some Catholic Indians among them, made the three-day retreat.[81] At later dates, prior to 1918, lay retreats were provided at Mount St. Charles College in Helena in June, 1912, at Forest Ridge Convent in Seattle in February, 1913, and St. Mary's Academy in Portland in June, 1914.[82]

The Knights sponsored a second closed retreat in Spokane, at Gonzaga, August 15 to 18, 1918. This was the beginning of the renowned Laymen's Retreat Association of the Spokane Diocese, which conducted retreats at Mount St. Michael's every year from 1920 until 1959, when Immaculate Heart Retreat House was opened. In the Portland area, eighty-seven Knights of Columbus attended a closed retreat at Mount Angel from June 18 to 20, 1920.[83] Similar retreats for women were begun at Holy Names Academy in Spokane on July 23, 1920, and at Visitation Villa in Tacoma on June 18, 1922.[84]

As early as March 1, 1913, the first unit in the state of Washington of the Daughters of Isabella, Washington Court 196, was established in Spokane. This ladies' auxiliary of the Knights of Columbus later changed its name to Catholic Daughters. In Portland the first court of the Catholic Daughters gathered on February 13, 1916, and in Montana the first, entitled St. Catherine's number 239, was organized on May 24, 1924.

Meanwhile, the Catholic Women's League appeared in Boise on February 28, 1911. This apparently failed to survive, so on October 17, 1920, Bishop Gorman called to order a conference of presidents of local leagues in the episcopal city and organized them state wide. In October, three years later, this group voted to join the National Council of Catholic Women.[85] The Seattle Council of Catholic Women first gathered on May 28, 1919, becoming two years later the Diocesan Council of Catholic Women.[86] Bishop Carroll called together his first meeting of the Helena Diocesan Council of Catholic Women on February 19, 1922.[87] The National Council of Catholic Women, Portland Deanery, was organized in Portland on January 30, 1925.[88]

The formation of councils for men occurred about the same time. For example, on February 14, 1921, Gorman organized the Idaho Council of Men, which affiliated with the National Council, the ninth diocesan council in the United States to affiliate.[89] Several months later, on September 4, delegates from every parish in the Helena Diocese met in Butte to form a Diocesan Council of Catholic Men, affiliated also with the National Council.[90]

These appear to be trifling details, but one must remember that they are the beginnings of some very significant movements. When the crunch on shortage of priests would come, a half century later, there would be second and third generation Catholics ready and willing to share more of the burdens of church management.

MAJOR FIRES

One heavy burden of the church from the very beginning was loss by fire. Mission fires had been common trials for all, due in part to the flimsy construction of buildings. Fire-resistant buildings were simply not affordable during the earlier years and it was not until after the first World War that most Catholic churches and schools consisted of brick and stone rather than wood.

There was a period of approximately nine years, from the end of the war until 1926, when an extraordinary number of major fires destroyed entire blocks of church property, mostly missions in rural areas. These fires occurred with sickening regularity, sometimes with loss of life, almost always with loss of irreplaceable church treasures.

The following examples are merely suggestive of the more important fires. They serve to illustrate the misfortunes of our long-suffering Catholics who were already burdened with debts, oppressed by injustices in law, and badgered by hordes of bigots who popped up everywhere like rodents in the meadow.

The first of these fires was only five days after the Armistice. Mount Angela at St. Peter's Mission in Montana, was completely destroyed. "On a dark morning of November 15 at 2:30, fire was discovered by one of the

mistresses who had been awakened by a girl.[91] The alarm was given, and
the nuns with their forty-two charges, most of them in their night
clothes and bare feet, were hurried out into the snow. Nothing was saved
and the refugees were taken in by the neighbors until later in the day.
Those of the children who were not sent home were taken to Great Falls
or scattered among the other Ursuline houses in the state. The three-
story stone building and its equipment totalled a loss of $75,000.00."[92]

Ten months later, at eight o'clock on a Sunday morning as the
inhabitants of St. Mary's Mission near Omak prepared to go to Mass, a
sudden fire alarm sounded. The pride of the mission, Father de Rouge's
"college," was all ablaze. As the bell tolled and the flames crackled, all of
de Rouge's priceless collections went up in smoke, the famous museum,
the library of two thousand volumes, many of them rare, the school
equipment, and perhaps most valuable of all, de Rouge's correspondence
and the mission diaries. The fire had been set by an Indian boy who had
been reprimanded the previous day by the Superior, Father Celestine
Caldi.[93]

Caldi wrote to Mother Drexel the mission's principal source of
support: "It grieves me immensely to have to notify your maternity [sic],
that our St. Mary's Mission suffered heavy loss by fire, last Sunday
morning, October 5 [1919]. The Indian boy's school, known as the
college, is in ashes today. It was about 300 feet long, some 40 feet
wide. . . . Two dear Sisters and some twenty-five boys have nothing left
except what they wear."[94]

The next sensational fire was St. Leo's Church in Tacoma. This was the
huge wooden structure built by Father Hylebos in 1903 with the
remnants of the famous Wigwam. More than five thousand people
witnessed the conflagration on a Monday afternoon, December 1, 1919.
The loss, it was said, was $75,000. For a "temporary" church, the
basement was provided with a new roof, altars, and pews, and these have
served St. Leo's parish ever since.[95]

A week later, the school, dormitory, and Sisters' convent at St. Ignatius
Mission burned to the ground. "December 9, 1919, a disastrous fire
practically leveled all the buildings that for fifty-five years had harbored
the Indian children of the Mission. The loss was felt by the sisters and
above all by the Indians themselves, more especially when they learned
that the decision of the Administrative Council of the Providence was not
to rebuild the school. Rather it seemed more expedient to center all
interest in the hospital that had been founded in 1914."[96]

On March 6, 1920, St. Andrew's original church and school in Portland
fell victim to the flames. While the remains of the building were
renovated for a temporary church, services were held on the church

ground in a tent, which presented the appearance of a Baptist revival for some months. A new church eventually replaced both, another "French Gothic" creation, one hundred and twenty-feet long, presumably one hundred thousand dollars worth, for that is how much it cost.[97]

Another fire at St. Ignatius Mission on February 19, 1922, took the life of one of the Ursuline nuns. This fire broke out a little before midnight. The sisters and a hundred children had retired for the night, feeling secure because the convent-school's thirty stoves had been replaced recently by a central heating system. The fire was first discovered by one of the Indian girls, lying awake. She sounded the alarm. One of the sisters ordered the children out, in proper order, of course, then awakened the other sisters. By this time the frame building was beyond help. It was two below zero and a wind was blowing. The flames ran along the porches at a rapid rate, making it impossible to save anything at all. The sisters lost everything, even their prayer books and spectacles. As one of them lamented later, "we are poorer now than when we came here. At least we had our trunks."

There were three or four very old sisters in the community. One of them, Sister St. John, a French lady seventy-eight years old, aroused with the others, simply disappeared in the confusion. Her charred remains were found the next day in the smouldering ashes. By then the weather was so cold that the brothers at the mission could not dig a grave. Sister's bones were placed in a coffin and carried to the church belfry for burial after the storm had subsided.

"The Sisters are bravely bearing up under their heavy trial," the superior, Father Ambrose Sullivan, wrote. "They will continue the school."[98]

A year later, another school was gobbled up by the flames, this time in Astoria, Oregon. There was something ironic about this one. Just two months earlier, on December 8, 1922, a vast fire raged out of control in the city, taking with it scores of buildings. St. Mary's Hospital in the path of the fire was vacated. "Throngs of people crowded the streets in the vicinity of the [Holy Names] convent watching the roaring flames as they ate away before their eyes one building after another. By eleven o'clock, all hope of saving the hospital was abandoned and we knew that its destruction meant ours [the convent] also. The fire raged furiously and the direction of the wind made the hospital's doom inevitable.... One was heard to say: "If the hospital stands, I'll believe there is a God.""[99]

At the crucial moment, a heavy rain fell, dousing the roof of the hospital, which had begun to burn, and Star of the Sea Academy as well. "It's remarkable," someone said later that day, "that every building with a cross on it was saved."

Thus the fire of February 18, 1923, which destroyed the academy, was as big a surprise as a tornado would have been. It started in the basement of the convent shortly before seven in the morning. The sisters and pupils were at Mass in the hospital chapel when the janitor gave the alarm. The academy building was a total loss, even though it had a cross on it.[100]

There are three other fires to report, all of them reasonably significant. The first of these, the most tragic, was described in the *Indian Sentinel*.

Six Nez Perce Indian boys gave their lives in an attempt to rescue a baby comrade from death in the fire which destroyed their mission home in the Idaho mountains. On October 3, after their evening meal the boys of St. Joseph's Mission returned to their playground to enjoy the games they loved. At 8 o'clock Sister Mary Angela, the superior of the mission, marched the little fellows to the dormitory for their night's rest. Instead of retiring at the usual time, the Sister remained up to mend some torn clothes of her charges for Sunday morning.

Sister Angela having finished her work, went to put some clothes into a hamper in the bathroom. As she opened the door she was terrified by the scene before her. The night lamp was in a blaze and flames were creeping up the wall. Sister caught up a blanket from a bed and tried to put out the fire. It took her but a few moments to realize that the flames were beyond control. Black smoke was rolling into the sleeping room. The hungry flames were already devouring the paper on the ceiling. Sister Angela rushed from bed to bed dragging the boys still sleeping to their feet. Gathering them about her, she counted the full number, thirty-five. Taking the smallest, a child of five, by the hand, Sister Angela told the others to follow her. All obeyed. Coming to the outside door, Sister let go of the child's hand in order to unlock the door. Panicstricken, the boy darted back into the burning bedroom. Not daring to follow the one and risk the lives of the others, Sister Angela led the thirty-four boys out of the burning building.

Meantime, the other Sisters had awakened the Indian girls in a neighboring building, which was also in danger. The Jesuit Fathers now arrived, coming from their house some distance away. A new count of the boys showed that seven were missing. Six small boys, unobserved, had gone back to save their little pal. No one could now rescue the boys from the fierce fire. Within half an hour after the flames were discovered, the building was burned to the ground. The Fathers searched through the smoking ruins and found the charred bodies of five little heroes close to the lifeless form of their baby comrade. The sixth had found his way out, but was so severely burned that he died a week later in the hospital in Lewiston.[101]

Old Father Cataldo, in his eighty-ninth year, was still at the mission. He had witnessed many heartbreaking tragedies in the lives of the Indians. "This," he said, "is the hardest blow of all." Until the day he died, he mourned his dead little Indians. For ten years he had pleaded for help to build fireproof dormitories for them. In this he had failed them.

The next mission fire was also tragic. At St. Andrew's, the Umatilla Mission, the sister's school caught fire from a kerosene lamp that exploded. Fifty girls and twenty-five small boys were asleep in the building but all were safely evacuated. Sister Lucretia, however, did not escape; she died in the flames. The school and convent were a total loss.[102]

Finally, the biggest fire of them all. For the second time in its history, Mount Angel Abbey and college were entirely wiped out by fire. Father Martin Pollard, the Benedictines' chronicler describes the holocaust and what followed.

> During the night of September 20, 1926, twenty-three years after it was first occupied, the entire abbey and school complex burned to the ground. The fire began in a wooden garage between the carpenter shop and the gymnasium. The night was rainy and windy when the night watchman sounded the alarm at 11:30. The fire soon caused a power outage so that there was no way to pump water to the hilltop. Abbot Bernard retired to the little chapel in the cemetery to pray. The next morning nothing was left standing except the press and the adjoining post office building and these were endangered by sparks from smouldering ruins. A pump truck from Salem kept their roofs wetted down, and they were saved. They became the means by which the now homeless monks would appeal for help to Catholics throughout the country.
>
> The community went to the parish church in Mount Angel to pray the morning office, they would hold community prayers there for the next eighteen months. The monks took up residence in some rented houses and the old parish school. The seminary was moved to two large private houses, but no non-seminary boarders were accepted into college after the fire. Monastic and school life were soon reconstituted on a makeshift basis, but there remained the massive task of rebuilding.[103]

It has been said that two moves are worth one good fire. The monks of Mount Angel survived, instead, two total fires in two decades, and after it all they were more solidly established than before.

PORT TOWNSEND'S ERRANT CHURCH

Bishop O'Dea, content now with his dismembered cathedral, no longer indulged in regrets about the grandiose dome that might have been. Archbishop Christie's junior by nine years, he had mellowed tranquilly, like the gentle grandfather of melodrama, and when adversity struck, as sometimes happened, he took matters in stride, more like Aegidius Junger than Augustine Blanchet.

Some strange situations in his diocese still prevailed despite his efforts at canonical reform. One of the most ridiculous, so bizarre that it first evoked laughter, was the fate of the church at Port Townsend. The bishop had been unable to force its pastor, Father Regis Maniouloux, to transfer the church title from his own name to the diocese. Then cagey old Maniouloux died and his niece was awarded the property by the Court. Thus, St. Mary's Star of the Sea, one of the pioneer churches, regarded yet as one of the finest in the diocese, fell into the grasping hands of an insufferable twit.

The latter, whose name is better forgotten, attempted to sell the church back to the bishop for something over fair market value. Bishop O'Dea refused to cooperate with this nefarious legal skullduggery so the niece sold off the furnishings of the church, vestments, pews, even the altar vessels, to Protestant churches, and converted the building into a theatre. So incensed were the inhabitants of Port Townsend that they boycotted the theatre, and the dollar grasping woman, unable to unload the property, eventually lost it for default on taxes.

Meanwhile, the bishop purchased the Norwegian Lutheran church to replace what had been lost, taking special care to keep the title in the name of the diocese.[104] On October 12, 1919, Father Achilles Vasta of Seattle College offered the first Mass in this new St. Mary's Star of the Sea, a poor substitute for the one that had been lost, but loved by the faithful as an adopted waif.

NEW CAMPUS FOR SEATTLE COLLEGE

There were always compensations for disaster. The diocese had lost one of its best churches. Seattle College, too, had been lost when it was closed because of the war. Although the high school classes had survived on a hope-for-the-better basis, the fate of the Jesuits' school appeared to be doubtful at best. It was still housed in the original Garrand building on the Broadway campus, which was more suggestive of a faded-looking apartment house than a Jesuit college. There were friends of the Jesuits, however, who had faith in its future. One of these was Thomas McHugh, a well-to-do Catholic whose business connections had uncovered a bank's foreclosure on a valuable piece of school property called Adelphia College. Located on Interlaken Boulevard, where Seattle Prep prospers now, this property consisted of two brick veneer buildings valued at $120,000, plus land valued at approximately $100,000 overlooking Lake Union across from the University of Washington. The local Scandinavian Bank had placed it on the market for $75,000 in the process of foreclosure on a $45,000 mortgage.[105]

Strangely, the Bishop of Nesqually had once owned the land. It was the old Holy Cross Cemetery—fourteen acres of mud, "too far out" when it was purchased by Father Demanez in 1884. It was seldom used mostly because it was more like a swamp than a burial ground. In April, 1905, it was evacuated by order of the city. Bishop O'Dea arranged for the removal of the few burials there to Calvary Cemetery and sold the land.[106]

This meant little to McHugh. Having pledged a generous gift to charity, after selling his Deep Sea Cannery, he took the initiative in persuading the Jesuits to buy the property, mostly with his money. The president of Seattle College was Joseph Tomkin, a tall, lean priest whose delicate handwriting revealed a very cautious spirit. His assistant was Francis Burke, a young Jesuit from the nation's capital, who had achieved some modest fame at Gonzaga in Spokane for baseball. Both Jesuits agreed to McHugh's proposal and McHugh, with the approval of his wife, cashed in $48,000 in war bonds and borrowed an additional $3,100 to make a substantial payment on Adelphia College, which had been reduced to a cost of $65,000.[107]

During these edifying procedures, rumors reached the chancery that Tom McHugh was buying Adelphia College for the use of Seattle College and there was great consternation in high places. What followed has been described elsewhere.

> While unnamed members of the chancery were up in arms, and as one Jesuit said, 'by no means friendly,' O'Dea appeared to be opposed, but not hostile. As a compromise he requested the Jesuits to turn over to him St. Joseph's parish, with all its property purchased with Jesuit funds, offering in return a portion of St. Patrick's parish. The pastor of St. Patrick's, Father M.P. O'Dwyer, who admitted later that he had been 'the goat', noisily opposed the presence of the Jesuits in his parish, including any part of it.
>
> Father Dillon [the Jesuit Provincial] during all of this useless and unproductive bickering, remained calm and undisturbed. Insofar as he was concerned, there was no occasion for compromise. The Jesuits had not done, nor intended to do anything wrong. He refused to turn St. Joseph's over to the Chancery and repeated at discreet intervals his request for the bishop's approval for a Jesuit school on the Interlaken Boulevard site.
>
> 'Your Lordship knows of the struggles of Seattle College in the past, and now that some assistance has been offered to the cause of education, we feel confident that our new hopes will not be blasted by a refusal to grant what we have asked, namely, to transfer our education work from the present to the new site.'
>
> The bishop, after sending his vicar general to consult the apostolic delegate, withdrew his objections and finally gave his approval, at first

verbally, then in writing when Dillon pressed for it. Gradually the storm subsided and even Father O'Dwyer accepted the Jesuits, with caution, but eventually with restrained warmth. What appeared to be an insurmountable impasse all during the last half of 1919, soon became instead, the occasion for a renewal of friendship between the bishop and Seattle's Jesuits.[108]

Seattle College now had two separate campuses, but only one high school to occupy them. No time was lost in remodeling one of the new buildings for a residence and by September 3, 1919, the second building was ready for the registration of students. Eleven priests and one hundred and fifteen boys appeared that morning to inaugurate a new era in Seattle Catholic education.

Half-hearted attempts were made to sell the old property on Broadway, but nothing ever came of it. Then the Knights of Columbus requested the use of the old Garrand building as part of a national program the Knights were establishing, free schools for war veterans. The Jesuits gladly shared the use of the building, rent free, and on January 8, 1920, the Knights' evening classes were begun. Eventually these classes prepared the way for reopening Seattle College. On September 5, 1922, the "new" Seattle College made a comeback. Two hundred and ten students registered on that historic Tuesday; only sixteen were enrolled in the first year college course.[109]

COLUMBIA UNIVERSITY

This sounded like small potatoes, and it really was. But one should not be surprised. Similar situations existed elsewhere in the West, particularly in church related schools. Often as noted above, these were called colleges or universities, though most students, knowledgeable in ancient Greek or Latin, were inexperienced in the art of shaving, beardless youths over their heads in conjugations.

Columbia University, like Seattle College, could be classified as one of these. In 1919, in what became known as the beginning of the local reform movement at Columbia, Father Eugene Burke came out from Notre Dame to replace the war-time president, Father John Boland.[110] Burke, apparently, was not happy at first with his new assignment in the boondocks, but he was the proper man for the hour, strong and determined, a man of action. He looked not unlike a hanging judge, except, perhaps, for his youthfulness, which was accented by his thick, wavy black hair. But his eyes peered grimly through rimless glasses that were attached to a black cord dangling symbolically like a gallows rope. His lips pressed firmly together like those of an avenging master and his chin thrust forward belligerently, providing little comfort for student miscreants who, perchance, fell afoul of his good pleasure. He was really harmless enough; only his appearance was stern.

While Columbia was not another Notre Dame, Burke found an adequate campus: the almost monumental brick building acquired from the Methodists still known as West Hall, a gigantic fieldhouse said to be the largest in the Northwest and called the Coloseum, and Christie Hall, "a model dormitory." For the thirteen Sisters of the Presentation, exiles from France, who performed the domestic duties for the school, there was a three-story Colonial-style frame house constructed under the direction of Brother Charles. "There were orchards, fields of produce and pasture land where milk cows or plow horses grazed. . . . The barn, part of the old wooden structure used by the Methodists for a gymnasium, was situated near the present library, and a large water tank stood nearby next to the wall."[111]

General enrollment figures, including all divisions, illustrated steady growth "from fifty-two in 1901 with only periodic dips through the First World War era followed by a major jump over 200 in 1918. The student count for the academic year 1921-1922 was 242."[112] These were mostly students in high school, with some grammar students and a few college men.

The one major obstacle in moving the school toward a full collegiate program was the clash between two priest members of the faculty— Cornelius Hagerty, who favored a return to the traditional Catholic liberal arts college, and Joseph N. Donohue, a recent arrival who demanded greater emphasis on mathematics and the empirical sciences. The in-house battle was a bitter one and though something akin to compromise was finally reached, the liberal arts faction really lost because Hagerty was recalled to Notre Dame in 1925, on the eve of Donohue's appointment as president.

CHRISTIE'S LAST YEARS

Archbishop Christie quite naturally favored Hagerty's position, for he regarded Columbia University as his nursery for candidates to the seminary. He was undoubtedly disappointed at the decision of the Holy Cross Fathers, but he no longer tried to force his will on them. The years were closing in on him. He was seventy-four now and nearing the time of his death. His greatest dilemma, other than the Oregon School Bill, was the proposed cathedral, about which hopes had been expressed for years. A plan designed by Joseph Jacobberger, the most prominent Catholic architect in the state, had been adopted by a building committee as early as September, 1914.[113] This comprised a large school, parish hall, cathedral, and rectory in Romanesque with red brick finish, an ambitious plant that was never fully realized, at least as it came off the board of Jacobberger.

Father Edwin O'Hara was pastor of the cathedral in 1915 when new property was acquired at Seventeenth and Couch. O'Hara gave priority to the school, to replace the old wooden one, "temporary" for many years. The cost of this took all the steam out of the cathedral talk for several years. America was at war, and a great depression followed it, so the years crept by and cathedral plans languished. The archbishop never lost hope. His tendency to vacillate, however, robbed him of the joy of occupying the new edifice, which was completed less than ten months after he died.

FATHER EDWIN O'HARA

On May 29, 1920, Father Edwin O'Hara was appointed pastor of St. Mary's church in Eugene, Oregon.[114] Removed from Portland at his own request to be relocated in a rural parish for promoting the lately established Catholic Rural Life Bureau, O'Hara soon attracted national attention to his social reform legislation and especially to his catechetical program, which developed eventually into the Confraternity of Christian Doctrine (CCD).

O'Hara's own rural beginnings had prepared him well for undertaking his new pastoral duties. Born on September 6, 1881, the youngest of eight children, to Owen O'Hara and his wife Margaret Nugent O'Hara, young Edwin was reared in a great stone house on the family's 320 acre farm near Lanesbora in southern Minnesota. He attended a country school with his older brothers. During some part of the summer he joined neighboring children, most of Norwegian descent, in a vacation Bible school, where he learned Norwegian by reading the Lutheran Bible. In the course of time, Robert, the second oldest of his brothers, became a lawyer and helped to build the frontier town of Hamilton near old St. Mary's Mission in Montana. Robert gave two of his children to the Northwest church: one son, Robert, who became a diocesan priest and one daughter, Sister Edwin Marie of the Sisters of the Holy Names. The oldest sister in the O'Hara family became a Poor Clare nun in Omaha where she served for forty-six years as a member of the community and abbess. One concludes from all of this that Edwin enjoyed the blessings of a devout Catholic family, living among equally devout Lutherans who shared their own spiritual blessings with the O'Haras.

These holy influences prepared him for the priesthood. Having entered the seminary in St. Paul in the autumn of 1900, he was ordained by Archbishop Ireland for the Archdiocese of Oregon City on June 10,

1905.[115] Unfortunately, his father Owen was not present for this great even in the O'Hara family. He had died scarcely ten months before. The other members of the O'Hara family, as firmly united as any Celtic clan, had gathered for the event and later, on the farm, they celebrated cheerfully with their Lutheran neighbors.

When Edwin O'Hara arrived in Portland that summer of 1905, Archbishop Christie made him assistant pastor at the cathedral and editor of the *Catholic Sentinel*. He was soon involved in Catholic activities in many forms. He joined the Knights of Columbus and the ancient Order of Hibernians, where he often heard complaints about labor problems, unemployment, and unjust wages. In 1907, he organized the Catholic Education Association of Portland. In 1911 he completed *The Pioneer Catholic History of Oregon* and was appointed pastor of the cathedral parish. In the following year he was designated Diocesan Superintendent of Schools as well, a prestigious sounding title that had recently come into use.

By this time he had become a familiar speaker on platforms throughout Oregon, especially on subjects related to education and social reform. When a Committee of the Consumer's League of Portland was organized, he was elected to serve as its chairman "to investigate the wages, hours and conditions of work of women employees in the state."[116]

SISTER MIRIAM THERESA

One member of O'Hara's board was Caroline Gleason, an alumna of St. Mary's Academy and the University of Minnesota, a professional social worker who had begun to lobby for a wage law in 1912. O'Hara requested her to survey conditions of working women as a league project. She took a job in a paper box factory in Portland and earned a total of $1.52 by working three ten-hour days. This was only a beginning. Gradually over a five month period, Gleason accumulated shocking details that the League now used for sponsorship of reform legislation on the state level. O'Hara and Gleason worked with Governor Oswald West, State Representative Michael Murnane (the only Catholic in the Oregon legislature) and Representative A.W. Lawrence, a labor-sponsored candidate, to direct the bill through ordinary channels.[117] They met with great opposition even from the labor unions. Employers denounced it as an "outrageous, socialistic measure."[118] Gleason's courage and untiring efforts finally secured passage of America's first effective minimum wage law.[119]

The governor appointed O'Hara to head a three member Industrial Welfare commission to represent the public interests. O'Hara persuaded

Gleason to serve as the commission's executive secretary. Meanwhile, the new law was challenged in the Courts. On March 17, 1914, the Oregon Superior Court upheld the law, and under the title of Stettler vs O'Hara the case went to the Supreme Court. At this point Louis Brandeis of Massachusetts, subsequently an Associate Justice of the Supreme Court, volunteered to defend the Oregon law.[120] Using information from Gleason's survey, Brandeis carried the day. In 1917, the Supreme Court sustained the law, which was regarded as a bench mark in labor history.[121]

Caroline Gleason was not in Court to savor the victory. During the previous year she was able to fulfill a brighter dream she had cherished since childhood. She entered the convent. At the age of thirty, having already achieved national recognition for social reform, she became a Sister of the Holy Names. In religion she was called Sister Miriam Theresa.[122]

ST. MARY'S PARISH, EUGENE

When Father O'Hara arrived, St. Mary's Parish was in its thirty-seventh year, an old one by western standards then, characteristically small-town, struggling for acceptance, and called St. Mary's so that no one could doubt its affiliation. Its first church had been a second-hand one, a discarded Methodist edifice purchased by Father Louis Metayer of Albany in 1886 and moved to "Catholic" property one block distant.[123] It was another year before Eugene had a resident priest, and twenty years before a new St. Mary's appeared.[124] This, too, was only "temporary," but it served its purpose for another twenty years, during which Father O'Hara scattered its fame far and wide.

He had come to Eugene because it was "rural." "Though the city had a population of ten thousand," O'Hara's biographer noted, "the parish was rural enough for anyone. It embraced fifty miles north and south along the Pacific Coast, extending back 175 miles to the Cascade mountains. There were only five other incorporated towns in the whole area plus more than thirty district small communities. The parish church in Eugene served 125 families of which one half were farmers."[125]

So only half the parishioners were farmers and at least three fourths of the parish was heavily forested mountains. But it was "rural" and it would have to do.

One of O'Hara's neighbors was Father Francis Leipzig, pastor of Corvallis, where the state college was located.[126] Leipzig was younger than O'Hara by fourteen years. He had been born in Chilton, Wisconsin, the fourth child of Frank Leipzig and Mary Cordy Leipzig, on June 29,

1895.[127] When his parents moved to Baker, Oregon in 1911, he entered
St. Francis Seminary in Milwaukee. Three years later, when his parents
moved to Portland from Baker, he transferred to Mount Angel Seminary
and later to St. Patrick's in Menlo Park, California. He was ordained by
Archbishop Christie in St. Mary's Cathedral, Portland, on April 14, 1920,
just one month before O'Hara left Portland for Eugene.

From this point on, there is an intriguing relationship between these
two priests, both of whom became bishops in predominantly rural
dioceses. Leipzig's interests and occupations paralleled those of O'Hara,
though it should be acknowledged that O'Hara, who appeared to be more
creative, was the pioneer, the innovator, and Leipzig the faithful disciple
who helped to perpetuate what O'Hara had begun.

There are three areas especially where the two priests collaborated in a
state university or state college town, each reorganized and highly
activated the local Newman clubs; in the early years, each developed
summer catechetical schools for children in rural areas; and each was
identified with the national Catholic campaign to develop parishes in
rural areas, "the Rural Life Movement."

In the summer of 1921, O'Hara arranged to have the Sisters of the
Holy Names conduct summer religion classes for children of the Eugene
area. These classes, taught out-of-doors or in farm homes, included
sacred singing and Bible study. Leipzig organized the first religion
vacation classes in his parish at Corvallis in the summer of 1923. In the
autumn of the same year, both O'Hara and Leipzig attended the first
National Conference on Rural Life, held in St. Louis, Missouri. This
conference had been inspired by O'Hara, who published a widely
circulated bulletin called *St. Isadore's Plow* in which he urged structure and
collective action for a rural life movement on the national level.[128] Leipzig
succeeded O'Hara at St. Mary's in Eugene when the latter joined the
Rural Life Office in Washington, D.C. in 1929.

O'Hara's epitaph many years later, composed by Bishop Mathew F.
Brady of Manchester, New Hampshire, placed the greater stress on his
role as founder of CCD. Brady called him "Father and organizing spirit of
the Conference of Christian Doctrine in this country," to which the
Apostolic Delegate agreed, adding that CCD was "the finest form of
Catholic Action."[129]

O'Hara's biographer summed it all up. "The wisdom of Leo XIII," he
wrote, "guided his thinking on the Minimum Wage Law and the Oregon
School question. The judgement of Pius X inspired his teaching in
Catholic Rural Life and in the Conference of Christian Doctrine."[130]

So reference is made again to "the Oregon School question," which
reached a blood-and-thunder climax when O'Hara was Superintendent

of Diocesan Schools. The time for presenting this has come at last. It was another landmark case, as they say; for Catholics it was a showdown. For the first time in generations, Oregon Catholics joined forces solidly to meet a crisis that threatened the existence of their schools.

The struggle was first carried out in Oregon where allegedly the proportion of American to foreign born in the population was highest in the nation. This sounded ominous and it was, because the appeal to the voters was based on patriotism, not religion. The hypocrisy of the bigot has always concealed itself behind a strategy of this sort, the pretentious virtue of flag waving versus the not-so-subtle implications of treason.

16

LOSSES AND GAINS

1920–1930

Immediately following World War I Japanese nationalists on the West Coast were threatened and harrassed, mostly because of the neo-nativist activities occasioned by disillusionment with the results of the war. In both Oregon and Washington the nativists opposed the presence of all foreigners, except, of course, those of Nordic backgrounds and like themselves, fundamentalist Protestant. Various so-called "patriotic" groups, some in the more structured form of lodges like the Odd Fellows and Knights of Pythias, conducted noisy campaigns to rid the Northwest of immigrants who were not white Protestants, especially blacks, Jews, natives of southern Europe (mostly Catholic), and Orientals like the Japanese and Chinese, some of whom had been in America from the earliest days.

This anti-foreigners movement had become a popular trend before the arrival of the Ku Klux Klan, who later adopted it as an essential in their bid for control with the slogan "100 percent American."

THE ARRIVAL OF MARYKNOLL

It was in this context that Bishop O'Dea invited the Maryknoll Fathers from New York state to Seattle for the care of the Japanese. Father Robert Cairns, the first of the Maryknollers in the Northwest, made his appearance in Seattle on February 3, 1920.[1] Cairns was attached to the Maryknoll Procure in San Francisco. For the present he was content with conferences with the bishop. He returned later in April of the same year, rented a house, secured an option on land, and employed a catechist. On April 7 he was assigned to China and Father Joseph Sweeney replaced him in San Francisco and Seattle. Cairns, however, remained in Seattle during most of May, gathering funds for his mission. On May 30, 1920, two Maryknoll sisters, Teresa and Gemma, opened a kindergarten for Japanese children. They resided with the Providence sisters in Providence Hospital while the Maryknoll priests, when they visited Seattle, used the facilities at the Immaculate Conception rectory, or the rectory in one of the other parishes. Finally on November 13, 1923, Father Charles Walker and Brother Martin took occupancy of a house at 1603 East Jefferson Street in the international section of the city. This became the first Maryknoll residence in the Northwest.

Meanwhile, the Ku Klux Klan had moved vigorously into Oregon with a show of force in their ugly hoods and robes, and their pretentious battle cry, "100 percent American." They had already taken over Portland's City Hall, utility companies, and many churches, and had successfully elected a pro-Klan governor and passed the infamous Compulsory School Law, which was cynically designed to destroy the Catholics' parochial school system. Their leader's mother was a Catholic.

OREGON'S COMPULSORY SCHOOL LAW

Until June of 1921, the Ku Klux Klan was as little known in Oregon as Italy's Carbonieri. It was generally regarded as an exotic group of fanatics in the deep south, committed to the superiority of the white race, only vaguely anti-Catholic and anti-Jewish. Suddenly in Oregon and Washington, it became a spectacular political force.

Anti-Catholicism in the Northwest, as noted already, was nothing new. Catholics had always been regarded as aliens because in fact most of them were foreign born, no less than the ancestors of the sanctimonious "native" sons and daughters who were eager to express their own xenophobic characteristics by persecuting religion.

When the Klan arrived to pursue its infernal business, Oregon claimed 783,389 inhabitants, of whom 258,288 lived in Portland. Normally and ironically, Oregon was Republican by a majority of at least 100,000, "yet time and again the Democrats have carried it by pandering to some transitory fad, faction or fanaticism, upon which party allegiance could be disrupted and diverted." One weakness in the state's political structure, according to the distinguished attorney who organized opposition to the school bill, was the provision for "a fractional percentage of the voting population" that could initiate any kind of law, "however vicious or visionary, and by appealing to the basest passions and vilest prejudices of an ignorant multitude, compel the politicians to support it and delude the people into adopting it...."[2]

Oregon was politically vulnerable, then, but it is unlikely that a consortium of outsiders would have used it for a big-risk test case if other desirable factors had been wanting. As one observer pointed out: "The forces which carried the bill were operating in the state long before the Klan arrived."[3]

Among these forces not already represented were the revelations of so-called ex-nuns and ex-priests, hyped for expectant audiences with spicy sex scandals and horrendous plots. Most were fables and their accounts pure fabrication. But they played their strident tunes to countless thousands who shuddered appreciatively. Anna Lowry was one of the most zealous. "A.P.A.'s Feature 'Escaped Nun,'" the *Catholic Sentinel* lamented. "Former Sister of Charity Appears on Anti-Catholic Platform Bigotry Runs Wild. Protestant Churches Are Placed At the Disposal of Miss Schaffer."[4] Another caption may prove to be interesting: "Ex-Priest Seguin and Wife Routed."[5] While Anna raced to and fro across the Northwest, receiving plaudits as well as honoraria, Seguin for some reason was run out of Harrisburg, Oregon.[6]

Another of these forces preparing the way for the bill was the Oregon Federation of Patriotic Societies, a home-grown monstrosity that made no effort at all to conceal its objectives. This had been organized as early as 1917 with five "secret" directors who subsequently became embroiled in competition with the Klan, not over the school bill, however, for this was the plum they all sought.[7]

Finally, there were the Masons, whose longstanding opposition to parochial schools was common knowledge.[8] Like Klansmen, the Masons made no bones about it. In June 1920, for example, the Grand Lodge of Oregon adopted a resolution requiring compulsory attendance at public schools. Later Wallace McCammant, attorney for the governor, defending the bill, openly stated that he represented the Scottish Rite Masons.[9] Another representative of the Scottish Rite Masons from Washington, D.C., a certain William MacDougal, publicly declared his organization's views in a Portland high school: "Oregon has been chosen as the first state in which to try out the bill because she has no foreign element to contend with, and is, more than any other state, purely and fundamentally American."[10]

Thus, when the Klan invaded Oregon, the state was already set for a tragic drama. Every alert newspaper editor in the country was aware of it, and most knew the basic elements of the conflict. They understood the consequences, but few, if any, expected the Masonic Order and the despised Klan to win the battle, any more than they expected the Klan to present a similar bill in another state. The editors miscalculated on both scores because the Pacific Northwest then, as it still is, was little known to them.[11]

So the Klan finally arrived on the scene. They had been dispatched by the Grand Wizard in Atlanta, a certain W.J. Simmons, "A reverend

Georgia cracker with the quack title of colonel."[12] Their purpose was to organize the Invisible Empire for the struggle ahead. One of the opening sallies in the Portland area was the lecture of R.H. Sawyer "to some six thousand people who were assembled in the Municipal Auditorium on December 22, 1921."[13] Subsequently, Sawyer and two other men were responsible for the phenomenal success of the Portland Klan. These were Fred L. Gifford and Luther Powell. The latter had come to Portland after organizing the Klan in Medford.

Gifford deserves special attention. In a classic article on "The Klan In Oregon," Henry A. Carey, Jr. presents the following:

> By early March 1922, there was wide speculation as to the names of the leaders of the Ku Klux Klan and the Federation of Patriotic Societies in Oregon. March 4, 1922, the *Oregon Voter* announced that the chief of the Ku Klux Klan in Oregon was Frederick L. Gifford, formerly a technical expert in the employ of one of Portland's larger public service corporation,[14] was a fanatic, determined to run Catholics out of public office in Oregon and, incidentally to damage the business and political influence of Jews and aliens. Officially his title was 'Grand Dragon of Oregon and Imperial Representative of the National Order West of the Great Divide.'[15]

Gifford, regarded as an "able" organizer, soon became a virtual dictator in the state. He established Portland as the Klan headquarters and controlled nine thousand Klan members of the state's total of fourteen thousand, including the mayor of Portland, a substantial portion of City Hall's bureaucrats, and the "Portland Police Vigilantes, composed of 100 picked men, all armed and carrying police commissions."[16] For some time Gifford exercised immense influence over the governor himself.

But Gifford's credentials were subject to scrutiny. He was much embarrassed when the Portland *Telegram* in an article entitled "I was a Klansman," revealed that "his own wife is a Catholic, baptized in that Church at St. Paul, July 31, 1881."[17] If this were not bad enough, the *Telegram* also blabbed that he had sent his two daughters, Marcella and Mary, to St. Mary's Academy.

But politics were generous to Gifford. His salary increased from $250 per month to $600, then to the princely stipend of a Grand Dragon, which remained a mystery even to Klansmen.

"ONE FLAG, ONE SCHOOL, ONE LANGUAGE"

The anti-parochial school bill, as it was called generally throughout the nation, was formally submitted to the electorate by fourteen citizens in as many towns and cities of Oregon, on July 6, 1922.[18] The principal terms of it appeared in these words: "Be It Enacted by the People of the State of Oregon: Section I. That Section 5259, Oregon Laws be, and the same is hereby, amended so as to read as follows: Sec. 5259, children Between the Ages of Eight and Sixteen Years. Any parent, guardian or other person in the State of Oregon, having control or charge or custody of a child under the age of sixteen and of the age of eight years or over at the commencement of a term of public school of the district in which the child resides, who shall fail or neglect or refuse to send such child to a public school for a period of time a public school shall be held during the current year in the said district, shall be guilty of a misdemeanor and each day's failure to send such child to a public school shall constitute a separate offense."[19] Certain exceptions to the law were then listed, for example, "Children Physically Unable."

The fat was now in the fire. Catholics hastily assembled in hushed groups throughout the state, first to oppose the bill and second to prepare for a court fight that appeared to be inevitable. Assuming leadership, Archbishop Christie established the Catholic Civic Rights Association of Oregon and, upon the recommendation of others, requested Dudley S. Wooten of Seattle to supervise this organization. "Wooten, a convert prominent in national politics and influential in legal circles, became the executive secretary and opened offices in 316 Morgan Building, Portland."[20]

At first he was not impressed by his fellow Catholics, who could not agree on the strategy to be used. "At the outset," he wrote later,

there was disclosed the weakness of the Church as a political force—the lack of unity in counsel and solidarity in action that characterizes Catholics everywhere, in the United States at least. It is not easy to analyze the reasons for this, but its disastrous effects were felt all through the campaign, although towards the last our people found themselves and worked with harmony and zeal. The outstanding feature of this Caholic short-coming in a political struggle seems to be the inability of the average Catholics to understand and form contact with the non-Catholic public. They think and reason along different lines upon public questions involving religious issues; they occupy an attitude of detachment and isolation towards the outside world, they fail to make themselves an integral factor in the formation and control of public opinion; they appear to be separate and apart from the general movements that engross and direct the interest of their Protestant and non-Catholic fellow-citizens. A few of them engage in political activities and mix freely in the affairs and contests of State and nation and in the pursuits of big business; but just in proportion as they do this they seem to lose identity with the Catholic fellowship, and to undergo a subtle loss of religious loyalty and zeal, which engenders suspicion and resentment among other Catholics not so disposed. It is certain that hereditary Catholics do not realize this trait of their character, and are wholly unconscious of its effects in creating a gulf between them and the world of politics and social agitation.[21]

On the other hand, a small group of the Scottish Rite, closely allied with the Klan, were firmly united and they began to spend huge amounts of money and created an elaborate publicity program to support the bill. But Catholics were not alone. Wooten presented a catalogue of their many friends:

> The Masonic fraternity, however, as a whole did not sponsor the movement, and some of the ablest and most representative Masons in the State publicly opposed it. The Lutherans, the Adventists, the Episcopalians, most of the leading Presbyterians, and the prominent business men and taxpayers were arrayed against it, as also were most of the farmers. The Baptists were divided, some of them being bitterly anti-Catholic, while the Campbellites or Christians were the most vindictive and vicious defamers of the Catholic Church and her institutions. The Methodists were neutral or quiescent, due to the fact that they were conducting a campaign for popular subscriptions to a large endowment fund for Willamette University; but it was understood that their chief representatives were opposed to the bill. With such a medley of discordant and complicated factors entering into the struggle, the result of the election was involved in doubt from the first, and the final adoption of the measure was not a victory to boast of.[22]

With Archbishop Christie and Bishop McGrath of Baker City, Wooten developed a single plan of operations. "The pastor of each of the 130 parishes in Oregon was requested to appoint two executive committees of ten members each, one committee of men and one of women. Each county had its central executive committee. The members of the committees signed a pledge to canvass all of the voters in their area. In this canvas an effort was made to encourage Catholic citizens to register for voting, to entreat active support, as well as to determine the attitudes of non-Catholics on the measure and give them the necessary arguments and literature."[23]

Thus, while America watched with fascination, the sides were drawn up, newspapers declared for or against the bill, church groups agonized over it, and printers worked overtime producing tracts and broadsides that were seldom dull.

Wooten, "standing in the vortex, opposing that hurricane of hate," describes the political hi-jinks prior to the final act:

> In the Republican primaries Governor [Ben W.] Olcott was opposed for the nomination by Mr. [Charles C.] Hall, the avowed champion of the Ku Klux Klan, and he defeated the latter by the small margin of about 600 votes, his success being generally ascribed to his courageous denunciation of the Klan just before election. At once Hall alleged fraud and illegality in the balloting, especially claiming that the Catholics had invaded the Republican primaries by casting Democratic votes for Olcott. He procured an order of court for a recount of the returns, but this had proceeded only a little while

when it was disclosed that the fraud had been perpetrated by Hall's followers and that he would lose votes by a further recount. He dropped the contest and announced himself an independent candidate for Governor, particularly favoring the school bill. Meantime, Mr. Pierce had been nominated by the Democrats, and it was obvious that his chances of success were vastly greater with both Olcott and Hall in the race against him. His views on the school question were not known, but the Ku Klux had become discouraged by Hall's failure in the recount and his want of consistency in bolting the Republican nomination, and they turned to Pierce as a stronger candidate if he could be induced to endorse the school bill. He responded to their overtures by declaring in support of this measure. Hall withdrew in his favor, and thus the issue was squarely drawn between Olcott and Pierce, with the school bill as the critical point of division. Taxation was much discussed, but merely as a 'blind' behind which to conduct a crusade of religious bigotry and State autocracy in education. After the primaries Governor Olcott gave utterance to no opinions on the educational controversy, nor did he renew his attack upon the Ku Klux. If he had received the solid support of his party in the election he ought to have won by 130,000 majority, whereas Pierce beat him by 31,000.[24]

The election took place on November 7, 1922. A total of 333,055 citizens turned out to vote, of these, only 219,191 voted on the school bill: 115,506 for the bill and 103,685 against it.[25] The results showed clearly that the great majority of the Republicans voted for the bill, together with all the nondescript political elements allied with the Ku Klux Klan and "the thick-and-thin" Democratic partisans. The 30,000 Catholics and decent independent non-Catholics to the number of 62,000, voted against it.[26]

I should add, out of concern for justice, that many non-Catholics voted for the bill because they were confused, not because they were opposed to Catholic schools. Wooten explains why.

A potent influence in the election, as it was cunningly contrived it should be, was the false and misleading title given to the bill. It was called on the official ballot a "Compulsory Education Bill," notwithstanding Oregon has had for half a century an adequate and satisfactory system of compulsory education, under which all children between nine and fifteen years of age must attend the public free schools or private schools that maintain the same standards and teach the same studies as the public schools, subject to the inspection and supervision of the State authorities. The effect of this deceptive name misled thousands of others that they refrained from voting at all. Also, it served to put the opponents of the measure in a false light before the general public, by making it appear that they were warring against compulsory education in the free public schools. That cry was the chief weapon of the advocates of the bill, particularly against the Catholics. All through the campaign it was insisted that the opponents of the legislation were the enemies of the great American system of popular instruction, the basis of our civilization and the bulwark of our national safety.[27]

The passage of the bill was only a beginning. Though a considerable portion of Oregon's executive and legislation branches, including of course, His Excellency the Governor, were on the same side as the Klan, the courts were not. Nor was the American press. A hue and cry arose from all parts of the country, accusing Oregon voters of a shameless deed.[28] Support for the legal battle, however, was not as generous. Wooten, in a cynical mood, perhaps, stated categorically that the people of Oregon, mostly Catholics, had to bear the cost of the case all the way to the Supreme Court.[29]

INITIATIVE 49 IN WASHINGTON

While the elated Klansmen shifted their attention to Washington state, their next target, members of the diocesan clergy in Oregon organized The Catholic Truth Society of Oregon and selected Father Charles Smith as the first executive secretary.[30] The state legislature, entirely controlled by Governor Pierce and the Klan, paid little heed to this. As they savored their own victory, they sought other means for satisfying their lusty constituents. They finally seized upon the idea of a "Religious Garb" bill, which they passed on January 31, 1923, with a more than comfortable margin. According to this law, members of religious orders, wearing their customary habits, could no longer teach in public related schools.[31] As a result, Sisters of the Holy Names were barred from teaching in the St. Paul public school, and public schools in Verboort, Sublimity, and Roy, which had been staffed by the Sisters of St. Mary, were returned to the status of secular schools, despite their entirely Catholic membership and tax support.

In Washington, the Klan had already begun its work. On December 4, 1922, "Major" L.J. Powell, King Kleagle of the Ku Klux Klan announced that "the compulsory school law was passed in Oregon" would be "put over in Washington at a very early date...and when we have won in Washington we will move into Idaho, and so on until we have won the entire nation."[32]

True to his word, the King Kleagle returned to Portland, where he claimed to have one hundred Klan lawyers working on the Washington law. Powell promised to announce the wording of the text as soon as it was completed, but he refused to discuss his plans for introducing the law. "A good general," he said complacently, "never tells the enemy of his moves in advance."[33]

But the Catholics had not been idle. During endless conferences, the archbishop and Father O'Hara, as Archdiocesan Superintendent of Schools, formed their own plans for appealing the Oregon law to the United States District Court in Portland. It was determined that the appeal should be presented by the Sisters of the Holy Names, since their legal existence in the state could be traced back to October 24, 1864. The Episcopalian's Hill Military Academy in Portland, which also came under the ban if the school law withstood appeal, joined the Sisters in their court fight.[34] Their attorney was John C. Veatch.

Representing the archdiocese were Judge John P. Cavanaugh and Attorney Dan J. Malarky who presented the oral arguments in court, and two other attorneys who prepared supplemental briefs, Hal S. Lusk and Frank Lonergan. When the case was argued on January 15, 1924, three federal judges occupied the bench: William B. Gilbert, Charles E. Wolverton, and Robert S. Bean. After pondering their decision for many months, the judges declared the bill unconstitutional on March 31, 1924.[35] "It is not too much to say," said the *Oregonian*, "that the action of the court was generally expected."[36]

But the diehards refused to accept this. On April 1, the day following the decision, John A. Jeffrey, Grand Dragon of the Klan, spoke brave words. "The Oregon decision will make no difference in the fight we have started in Washington. Washington has a new, liberal and progressive constitution, while the constitution of Oregon is antediluvian."[37] Adherents of the bill regrouped for the battle, while damaging lies continued to appear. This one was printed in the *Klamath Falls Herald:* "The birth of every male child in a Catholic family is celebrated by burying a gun and ammunition underneath the church, in preparation for the day when the government is to be overthrown on behalf of the pope."[38]

The Klan finally revealed its strategy in Washington. On July 3, 1924, Initiative 49, the Klan's anti-parochial school bill was filed at Olympia. It carried 55,638 signatures. Within the state there was already a storm of opposition to the proposed bill on constitutional grounds. In Seattle, opponents formed the Organization of Friends of Educational Freedom, and sympathetic papers were careful to note that "Officers [are] Non-Catholic."[39]

At this point some of the newspapers published names of those who had signed the initiative, mostly to expose the Klansmen. Exposure produced a panic at the Secretary of State's office, where thousands of people who had signed the initiative demanded that their names be withdrawn. Then the Klan sought an injunction to prevent this, and the court ruled in their favor. *Quod scripsi, scripsi,* said Pilate, as a final act in this almost hilarious scenario. Thousands more protested that they had been deceived in signing the petition and they became at once the Klan's worst enemies.[40]

On November 5, 1924, the citizens of Washington voted on the initiative that had already been declared unconstitutional by a district federal court. Although the proposal lost by 59,000 votes, more than 131,000 people voted in favor of it. If many Americans were shocked by what happened in Oregon, they had reason now to be perplexed as well. How was it possible for more than two out of five voters in Washington to favor a bill that had been unanimously rejected by a federal district court?

TO THE SUPREME COURT

The school bill's failure in Washington took all the wind out of the Klan's sails and members of the Klan who were natives of the Northwest quickly deserted the ship like rats scampering on the wharf.[41] In Oregon, Lem A. Devers, editor of the Klan's paper, *The Western American*, resigned in disgust and published his "Confessions," blowing the whistle, as it were, on Portland's corrupt city hall and Salem's equally corrupt capitol.[42] Only Pierce was left. Stripped of support and shamefully mute, he was stuck with the task of carrying his despised bill to the Supreme Court, an exercise of politics that smelled to Dever's nose something like the sulfur of hell.

When the appeal was finally presented at the Supreme Court on March 17, 1925, Judge Kavanaugh pleaded eloquently for one half hour. William D. Guthrie, a prominent New York attorney who had been invited to enter the case for the Catholic cause, submitted an additional brief to the Court and took the lead in the arguments that followed. Scarcely anyone doubted what the action of the Court would be. On June 1, 1925, the Justices handed down their unanimous decision affirming the decision of the District Court of Oregon and declaring once and for all that the "anti-parochial" or Compulsory School Bill of Oregon was unconstitutional.[43] Justice James C. McReynolds delivered the opinion of the Court: "The fundamental theory of liberty upon which all governments in this Union repose excludes any general power of the state to standardize its children by forcing them to accept instruction from public teachers only. The child is not the mere creature of the state; those who nurture him and direct his destiny have the right coupled with the high duty, to recognize and prepare him for additional obligations."[44]

Dudley Wooten found another bright side in the long struggle, "... the

Catholic Church in Oregon was never so strong as she is today; Catholics were never so united, loyal, vitalized, and awake; never before was there such wide-spread sympathy and understanding towards Catholics by the Protestant and non-Catholic population of the State."[45] The long bitter struggle aptly confirmed the truth of historian James Anthony Froude's benign remarks: "The Catholic Church," said he, "is like a kite, it rises ever against the wind."

FATHER DOMINIC O'CONNOR, O.F.M.CAP.

In Ireland, the winds of violence had been howling for generations. The long struggle for independence had produced bitter fruit locally, but for the church in America it provided some gifts of a better kind. One of these gifts was Dominic O'Connor, a Capuchin who arrived in the Baker City Diocese because Ireland could no longer contain him.[46]

Since the Easter Rebellion of 1916, Celtic blood had flowed freely and many prominent Irish patriots were forced to flee from their native land to live in exile. Others who were imprisoned in England refused to eat, and when the universally popular Terrance MacSwiney, Lord Mayor of Cork, died on October 25, 1920, from starvation after seventy-three days of fast, American Catholics were moved to anger. There were some in both countries who called MacSwiney a martyr.[47] Perhaps he was. The man who knew him best was his chaplain, Dominic O'Connor.

MacSwiney had died in Brixton Prison in England and O'Connor returned to Ireland with the remains. A marked man, he was soon the victim of attempted assassination by the Black and Tans. Later he was arrested in Dublin by British soldiers "and after being first tortured in Dublin Castle by British officers, he was sentenced by a British Court Martial to five years penal servitude for advocating the Independence of Ireland, and was deported to a jail in England."[48] Released in January, 1922, under a general amnesty, he made many efforts to prevent further hostilities and to secure an honorable peace. He was finally exiled in November, 1922 and was assigned to the parish in Bend, Oregon, where he found peace at last among his brother Capuchins.

His arrival was opportune for he was an experienced historian.[49] After serving in parochial work in Bend and Hermiston, he was appointed temporary rector of St. Francis De Sales Cathedral in Baker City, and while there composed his well-known book, *A Brief History of the Diocese of Baker.*[50]

O'Connor's career in the Northwest was relatively short but his influence lasted. He died in Bend on October 17, 1935, at the vigorous age of fifty-two and he was buried, still in exile, in Pilot Butte, eastern

Oregon. As a famous Irish patriot, he deserved better, so his body was removed to County Cork more than two decades later and was interred there with proper honor.[51]

His appearance in the Northwest and his departure in a funeral box characterized the frontier nature of the Baker City diocese. It was still a borderland, staffed for the most part by priests and religious from somewhere else. Like the first bishop of the diocese, they came and they left; they lived briefly and they vanished, like the winter's snow when a Chinook comes from the west.

THE DEATH OF BISHOP O'REILLY

In his Nebraska home, Baker City's first bishop had followed the Oregon School Case with more than ordinary interest. From the Bishop's House, which was also his Chancery, he wrote long, affectionate letters to his family in Portland.[52] His stomach ulcers were never completely healed and his doctor, "a fine Catholic gentleman," kept him in bed for an entire month, though he allowed him an occasional cigar. He admitted to his niece that he was short of money because he had given most of it "to the institutions," meaning the orphanage and the schools. Though he missed Oregon, he liked Lincoln and its people, who kept his hospital room filled with fresh roses, indicating how much they had come to love him. He had an occasional pleasure jaunt in the automobile, he wrote. "Uncle Charles," his niece Mildred added, "never learned to drive."

His life passed in these peaceful pursuits of a bishop. Then quite suddenly he died in a diabetic coma. This was on February 4, 1923, just five days after the Oregon Legislature had passed the infamous Garb Bill.[53]

NEW HIGH SCHOOLS

During these many trials for the church there were comparable achievements that seemed to balance the record. The first of these, happily, were new high schools that began to appear like blossoms in the desert. In the fall of 1921, Marquette in Yakima was inaugurated to provide for boys what St. Joseph's Academy of the Providence Sisters had provided for girls for over forty-five years.[54] Marquette had begun with two laymen on the faculty, but these were replaced by Jesuit scholastics "in the interest of economy," which was reason enough. The scholastics were unsalaried. In the course of time a great storm raged over Marquette. During the early years, however, progress was solid and life serene.[55] One hundred and forty boys were registered for the opening sessions and classes were conducted in the grade school building called "the Rock." The first graduation of seniors occurred in June 1922; on March 7, 1932, Marquette was fully accredited by the State of Washington as a four year high school.[56]

A similar institution, which also had its origins in an elementary school, was O'Dea in Seattle. In September, 1915, the first and second years of high school classes were added to the Cathedral Parish School. This was really the beginning of O'Dea, which formally opened as a four year school on September 4, 1923, with the Christian Brothers of Ireland in charge. Brother Curtis was the first principal.[57]

A new red brick building for O'Dea was finally completed to the immense relief of all, on March 15, 1924. Bishop O'Dea dedicated it on the following day, sprinkling it generously with holy water to make it convincingly Catholic, for it bore the bishop's own name.[58] His Excellency had no illusions. He had gone to an all boys' high school himself. He had seen to it now that everything in the building, including the teachers, who were noted for their iron-like durability, could withstand the ravages of time and the customary roughhouse of most boys. Resembling a fortress, like the Rock at Marquette, but considerably more decorative, O'Dea's first building has survived ever since, an academic oasis in the jumble of hospital buildings and doctors' offices on Pill Hill, Seattle.

In Boise, Bishop Gorman pondered the merits of having his own boys' high school. Why not? And a junior college also. These were prosperous times when some clerics thought religious brothers and sisters were a dime a dozen. While Gorman was not one of these, he cherished hopes for at least a few to fulfill his dream. As early as February, 1921, he appealed to the Christian Brothers at St. Mary's in California to staff a junior college and/or high school, in Boise. The Christian Brothers, taking note of the fact that in and around Boise for one hundred miles in all directions there were only 4500 Catholics of all ages, respectfully declined the invitation.[59]

But Gorman was determined. He thought he had a bone and he would not let go. In 1925, he undertook the construction of a new building, which he called St. Joseph's School. Then he assigned diocesan priests to the faculty for the 130 boys in the entire nine grades. This was scarcely "junior college" even by the sloppy standards of the times. All during that same year he conducted various meetings to discuss "Boise Junior College." Committees were appointed, incorporation formalized, and countless speeches made and letters dispatched.[60] Still no college appeared. By 1927, however, His Excellency had a four-year high school with an enrollment of twenty-eight. Five years later, when sixty-one boys were in attendance, St. Joseph's was combined with St. Teresa's Academy, which then became coeducational.

Bishop Gorman, meanwhile, expressed a desire to have high school classes in Cottonwood, Idaho, where the Benedictine Sisters were now well-established in St. Gertrude's Convent. In April 1923, the sisters had begun to publish a quarterly called *The Echo of St. Gertrude,* which provided another useful medium for the preservation of local Catholic history.[61] Gorman no doubt took note of this gratuitous addition to his diocese and traveled north to exhort the Catholics of Cottonwood, blessed with so many sisters they could publish magazines, to organize that high school. On July 25, 1925, he held a meeting with parishioners who endorsed his proposal, then skillfully passed the buck to the pastor, Father Willibrord Beck, O.S.B. Nothing came of all of this, to the dismay of the bishop. But the sisters themselves eventually resolved the matter. When St. Gertrude's Academy for grade and high school opened in September, 1927, it accepted both boys and girls as day pupils.[62] By this time Bishop Gorman was in his grave.

The Catholic coeducational high school has been discussed before, with reference to Butte's Central Catholic. With reason, then, it should be noted that during this period, in June, 1926, Central Catholic ceased to be a coeducational school. The transition had been made gradually. On September 5, 1924, three Christian Brothers of Ireland arrived in Butte from New York, to take charge of the newly constructed Boys Central High. On September 10, another brother from Vancouver, B.C. arrived to join the original contingent.

In the interim, a parent teachers' meeting was held on September 6, during which it was determined that only freshmen and sophomores would be enrolled in the new school, while the upperclassmen continued their studies in the old central high. Thus on September 8, one hundred and twenty boys presented themselves to the brothers, less than ready for classes and grudgingly obedient to their parents. In two years, Boys' Central, dedicated to St. Gabriel the Passionist, provided classes for all four high school years. The girls, taught by the Sisters of Charity of Leavenworth, remained in the old building.[63]

This new emphasis on high schools raised some embarrassing questions about teacher accreditation. The sisters (God bless them!) were expected to be properly accredited for teaching high school, but it was nearly impossible for them to attend college classes.[64] The northwest's six Catholic universities and colleges accepted men only, though it can be admitted now that occasionally a few women were sneaked in for a class or two, in very discreet circumstances, of course.[65] Nuns in general, were not permitted to attend state institutions or other secular colleges. While the Jesuit general in Rome, Wlodimir Ledochowski, deeply regretted the situation, he protested that the dilemma was a matter for the bishops to resolve. It was unthinkable in Rome then that Jesuits be employed in the

instruction of nuns, although they, like other priests, preached retreats
to them summer after summer.

GONZAGA'S SCHOOL OF EDUCATION

The highest hopes for change rested either with Columbia University
or Gonzaga. Columbia, however, had not moved to the full four-year
college program until 1927, when the prep school and college were
formally separated.[66]

This left Gonzaga University, where other radical improvements were
already occurring. Prodded by the Mothers Superior of various orders of
sisters, Gonzaga's president, Father Walter Fitzgerald, later bishop of
Alaska, established a summer school program beginning in 1924.
Qualified students on all college levels were eligible for admission,
including women. Monday, June 23, was registration day. Classes began
on Wednesday. "Summer School for Sisters began today," says the school
diary for June 25. "All classes except chemistry and physics are held at
H[oly] Names Acad[emy]. The sciences at Gonzaga. There were 58
Sisters, 5 lay people, 6 scholastics and 1 priest—Fr. E. Budde, who arrived
from Tacoma this morning."[67] Twenty-two courses were offered by a
faculty of eight Jesuits and four lay people, one of the latter from
Washington State College.[68]

If this first summer school was not large, at least it was enthusiastic.
For its second session, begun on June 22, 1925, seventy-two sisters were
registered out of a total of 112, and twenty-eight courses were offered,
one of them taught by the president, who decided to take a whirl at
teaching again. The sisters spent some warm, busy summers housekeep-
ing in neighboring residences, studying for their degrees, and praying
quietly at St. Aloysius Church, where the novelty of many Masses held
them for long hours. Children soon became accustomed to the nun's
annual invasion of "the Holy Land" as it was called. They arrived
faithfully every year and for the duration of the summer session they
edified people of the parish with their sweetness and devotion.

As one might expect, the summer school developed rapidly. In 1926,
there were 144 students and in the following year 154, as contrasted with
232 in the College of Arts and Sciences. In this third session, all classes
were conducted on the Gonzaga campus with the guarded approval of
superiors.

In the late summer of 1927, another significant event helped to
accelerate equal opportunities for the sisters. No less a dignitary than the
Apostolic-Delegate of the United States, Most Reverend Pietro Fumasoni-Biondi, arrived for an unannounced visit to the campus, to confer

with the president regarding the status of women in the university. His appeal was made in behalf of the sisters, whose opportunities for higher education were still inadequate especially in view of the expanding parochial school system. Subsequent correspondence with Rome and the delegate's office in Washington produced certain concessions, but an entire generation would pass before Gonzaga University was allowed to become coeducational in all departments.[69] Long before this, in September 1933, Father James McGoldrick, the dauntless Irish dean, had found ways for skirting regulations to permit women students in all courses at Seattle College.[70] Thus Seattle became one of the first Catholic coeducational institutions of higher learning in the United States, anticipating most colleges and universities by twenty long years.

DEATH OF ARCHBISHOP CHRISTIE

The archbishop had always appeared to be imperishable, but alas, he was mortal like the rest of us. Plainly nearing the end, he still had some unfinished business—the new cathedral across town. On Sandy Boulevard, the Servite Fathers, properly called the Servants of Mary, had acquired sixty acres of land near Rocky Butte. Christie had blessed the site on May 29, 1924, in anticipation of a grotto or shrine to Our Lady of Sorrows.[71] The fathers announced a five million dollar drive to develop the shrine, a stupendous amount that seemed to shock no one, despite the archbishop's oft-repeated appeals for the new cathedral fund. His grace had requested a mere two hundred thousand, but even this much was so slow in coming that construction had been delayed indefinitely.

The Servites came from Chicago, where "Catholic" money was plentiful. They had little experience with the Northwest, though two of them for a brief year served in small parishes in eastern Oregon.[72] Both were withdrawn by superiors, but others returned in 1917 to take charge of St. Clement's parish, which they renamed "Assumption of the Blessed Virgin Mary."[73]

The Servites' five million was slow in coming too, in fact, very slow, but the cathedral fund for the two hundred thousand dollar edifice (without furnishings) had grown sufficiently robust for finalizing construction plans. The archbishop, however, was flat on his back in St. Vincent's Hospital, overlooking the city and the cathedral site several miles distant. He had been ill for some months, but this preoccupation with this favored project never waned.

Architect Joseph Jacobberger described the new design that the archbishop had approved. It was an "Early Christian Style," he said. The dominant influence was classical, placing the structure at the end of the neo-classical revival, which came to a climax in the United States at the Chicago World's Fair in 1893.[74] The projected plans provided use for the historic items salvaged from the first cathedral on Third and Stark.[75] These included the large stained glass windows in the transepts, the plaque depicting Our Lady of Perpetual Help over the side altar in the east transept, several statues, the Bishop's throne and two side chairs, the baptismal font, the paschal candle holder and the episcopal cross, which had been given to Archbishop Gross in 1885 by the people of the cathedral parish. The plans also provided for a rectangular tower to accommodate the three bells from the old cathedral. These bells had been cast in Baltimore in 1885 and, in keeping with tradition, had been blessed in honor of the saints. The largest was named "Immaculate Conception," "St. James" was the next largest, and "St. Francis" the smallest.

As one of his last official acts before his death, Christie gave orders for construction to proceed. Then on Monday of Holy Week, April 6, 1925, Alexander Christie, fourth Archbishop of Oregon City, went to his fathers. Because of the Holy Week liturgy, his burial was postponed until April 15, "when amid a large concourse of sorrowing priests and people the funeral rites were held at the pro-cathedral and his body interred at Mount Calvary Cemetery."[76] Bishop Carroll, whose own days were numbered, preached the funeral sermon. "He was the ideal archbishop," Carroll noted. "He ruled by love and not by fear."

Many years later, one of Christie's priests wrote the last word about him. "He was a great man and very close to his priests. He did not have much of a staff in his chancery office which was a room upstairs in the cathedral rectory. He was known by his priests as 'the bishop who had his chancery in his vest pocket'."[77]

THE NEW CATHEDRAL

The contract for the new cathedral had been formally signed in February 1925, by Father George Campbell, pastor of the parish. Ground was broken in that same month, and on June 7, two months after Christie's death, Msgr. Hillebrand presided over the ceremony of laying the cornerstone. Progress on construction proceeded rapidly. The first services in the new building, Lenten devotions consisting of the Way of the Cross and Benediction of the Blessed Sacrament, were conducted on February 19, 1926, at 7:45 in the evening.[78] On the following morning, the dismantling of the old pro-cathedral was begun. At last, the ghost of Archbishop William Gross could be laid to rest. His vision had been vindicated. Many years before this the site of the old cathedral on Third and Stark had deteriorated into an urban slum.

SISTERS OF ST. DOMINIC FROM SPEYER, GERMANY

On December 28, 1923, Bishop Ludwig Sebastian, the rotund ordinary of the ancient diocese of Speyer, delivered a letter personally to the Mother General of the Dominican Sisters in that diocese.[79] The letter from Bishop Carroll of Helena to Mother Aquinata Steinfeltz, expressed an earnest request for sisters who could take charge of domestic affairs at Mount St. Charles College in Helena. Mother Aquinata agreed to send sisters if she could find willing volunteers. When news of Carroll's request became known in the sisters' ninety-four communities in the diocese, so many candidates volunteered that Mother Aquinata found it difficult to make a choice. At length she and her Councilors decided to send the following: two teachers, Mother Bonaventura Groh and Sister Arsenia; two nurses, Sisters Belina and Jucunda; two seamstresses, Sisters Walburgis and Klodia; two kindergarten teachers, Sisters Galena and Mitis; three cooks and housekeepers, Sisters Virginia, Eugenia and Gisela, and one postulant, Hedwig Fiebe.[80]

The time was set for their departure, but complications occasioned by changes in immigration laws in the United States forced the sisters to postpone their journey until the following year. Through Carroll's influence, formalities were finally concluded for the sisters admission to America and on Sunday, July 26, 1925, their departure was celebrated at the motherhouse. On the day following, they left by train for Bremerhaven, where they embarked on the steamer Columbus for New York. On August 9, they boarded the train for Helena, arriving there on August 12 at seven in the evening. A welcoming committee of four priests and a number of ladies of the parish awaited them and brought them by car to their new convent, which had been built by Bishop Carroll during 1924 on the east side of the campus. On the following day, at his residence, they met Bishop Carroll, who manifested toward them such kindness that their long journey and stress from the strange surroundings appeared to be unimportant by contrast. They were very pleased with their new bishop who blessed their convent and offered Mass for them on the Feast of the Assumption.

These were the first sisters of their congregation in America.[81] Only one of them could speak English and the others had to struggle for years to learn it well enough to pass for Americans. Nonetheless, they were immediately successful. Within a brief time, they established eleven communities in Montana and Washington, so that by 1931, they were able to form an independent province with Mother Bonaventura, the guiding force in these accomplishments, as the first Provincial.[82] Draped in Dominican white, with a weighty rosary dangling at her side, she directed her nuns in heavy German gutturals like a captain of the troops, but with maternal kindness and such profound love for each that when two of them died she almost died with them. Until 1939, she wrote all of her letters in a neat German script, using every inch of the page in a spirit of poverty, perhaps, or upon reflection, to provide additional directions. She was the third of her order to die in America, prematurely it was believed, because of immense grief due to the scandalous defection of one of her nuns.[83]

DEATH OF BISHOP CARROLL

When Bishop Carroll welcomed the Dominicans to Montana, there was nothing to indicate that he was failing in health. On the contrary, he had been as alert as always and keenly interested in his two pet accomplishments, his cathedral and his college. Either would have been a smashing monument to any prelate; together they were worthy testimonials for even Carroll's genius.

On September 8, only three weeks after the sisters' arrival, he left Helena to make his *ad limina* visit in Rome. He arrived in Speyer, Germany, on October 28 and remained for a few days in the Dominican's motherhouse. As he traveled through Switzerland, he stopped in Fribourg on October 31. He was very ill. Four days later he died, on November 4, 1925. He was in the sixty-second year of his life.[84] He had been bishop for twenty-one years.

Back in Helena, Father Joseph Willging of the college faculty, was celebrating a solemn high Mass in the chapel to honor St. Charles, the patron of the bishop and the college. Monsignor Victor Day knelt in the sanctuary. At the moment of the "Sanctus," Father James O'Neil came out of the sacristy and handed Day a telegram. Day read it again and again, shaking his head. After Mass, with tears choking his voice, he read the telegram to the congregation. "Our good bishop is dead," he said.[85]

The bishop's body arrived in New York on the ship *De Grosse* on Thanksgiving Day. Two of his closest friends were passengers on the same ship, Archbishop James Keane of Dubuque, who had been instrumental in his elevation to the hierarchy, and Bishop Edmund Heelan of Sioux City. Archbishop Austin Dowling of St. Paul celebrated the pontifical requiem Mass in the cathedral in Helena on December 3, Archbishop Edward J. Hanna of San Francisco preached the eulogy, and a choir of one hundred voices chanted the *Dies Irae* and other parts of the liturgy. Following these melancholy proceedings, the bishop's body was laid to rest in his cathedral.[86] Thus ended the career of Helena's second bishop, whose triumphalistic policies, for better or worse, would live on for three more decades.

RESIGNATION OF BISHOP SCHINNER

So the sees of Oregon and Helena were vacant. Spokane became vacant also. Sometime prior to December 1925, Bishop Schinner submitted his resignation to Pius XI, and on the seventeenth of that month, the pope, having accepted it, gave him the title of Titular Bishop of Sala, and appointed him interim administrator of the diocese. Public notice regarding this was withheld, but in Seattle some clerical wag, who guessed the truth, leaked an indiscreet word and rumors abounded. On January 3, 1926, the *Spokesman-Review* in Spokane brought these rumors to the attention of its readers, quoting to support them a report printed in Archbishop Keane's diocesan paper, *The American Tribune,* that Rome had accepted Schinner's resignation "ten days ago."[87]

A reporter interviewed the hapless bishop. "I prefer to ignore that report," Schinner said. "There is nothing certain about the situation and I have nothing to say."[88] The ambiguity of this left no one in doubt. The bishop, it was said, had resigned "for reasons of health" or because he wanted "to enter the mission field in some foreign country." Those who knew him best questioned the validity of these excuses. Schinner, apparently, had never been happy in Spokane, for reasons not beyond accurate conjecture. He was a deeply spiritual man, generous and zealous, but he did not relish the honors of a bishop, nor did he have the stomach for church politics, nor the thick skin to shield his sensitive feelings from the barbs of some of his own priests. He loved Mount St. Michael's and nothing pleased him more than celebrating Mass there on the feast of St. Michael, when he joined his Jesuit friends behind the protective walls of the cloister. The Mount had been his refuge for years.

On the other hand, he had never given up the idea of going to South America as a missionary. One of his German friends, the Bishop of La Paz in Bolivia, Msgr. Sieffert, had invited him to serve as rector of the La Paz seminary. This appealed to Schinner, largely, I think, because of his felicitous experiences at the Mount.

In September of 1926, the bishop finally announced his departure from Spokane. "I resigned for two reasons," he explained. "I wanted to be relieved of the responsibility of administration and I wished to engage in mission work in some foreign field."[89] It would have been tactless to point out to the bishop that a rectorship in a seminary was also administration.

By this time, the priests of the diocese had come to realize how much they loved their bishop. They sent a collective petition to Rome requesting that Schinner remain in Spokane, but officials there responded "that the petition was too late as other plans were being formulated."[90]

The bishop's departure was a sensation. He was only sixty-two years old, a gifted administrator, and very highly regarded by many prelates in the midwest, especially those of German descent. For him, the ordeal of the last few years had left its mark. He was physically unfit for La Paz. He returned instead to Wisconsin where he "rested" for two years, serving as chaplain of busy St. Joseph's Hospital in Mankato. Finally, in the autumn of 1928, he embarked for Bolivia. Finding peace at last, he assumed the rectorship of the seminary. He was a missionary in a foreign country, where the Spaniards had built a cathedral centuries before Milwaukee had produced a keg of beer.[91]

ARCHBISHOP EDWARD HOWARD

One bishop succeeds another, a diocese loses one and gains a new one. Each is unique, but the church goes on as before with only accidental changes or shifts in priorities. No one, then, was surprised when the new archbishop was announced for Oregon City, though some were very disappointed. The new prelate was another protege of Archbishop James Keane and another product of Dubuque's diocesan college. He was the fourth priest from Dubuque to come to the Northwest as a bishop in the brief span of one generation.[92] He was also of Irish ancestry, and a former colleague in the seminary with Father Edwin O'Hara. His name was Edward Daniel Howard, Titular Bishop of Isaura and auxiliary of the ailing Bishop of Davenport, Iowa. He would be forty-nine years on his next birthday, November 5, 1926.[93] No one suspected then that he would become the oldest bishop in the world.

Howard was born in Iowa, in a rural town called Cresco. He was the younger (by some minutes) of twin boys born that day to Marie Fleming and John R. Howard, who had seen the light of day in Ireland in 1841.[94] His parents operated a small farm where Edward grew up, performing daily chores like splitting kindling and feeding chickens. After completing his early schooling, he entered St. Joseph's College, Dubuque, then, in 1900, St. Paul's seminary in Minnesota where Archbishop Ireland was still as fiercely energetic as a blizzard.[95] Howard was ordained in St. Paul on June 12, 1906.

His archbishop assigned him to teaching at St. Joseph's. For some years, therefore, he lectured in courses of English, Latin, and mathematics, later adding Greek and elocution to his repertoire. He became president of St. Joseph's in 1921. Three years later on April 8, 1924, he was consecrated bishop in St. Raphael's Cathedral, Dubuque, by Archbishop Keane. His appointment to Oregon City followed soon after, on April 30, 1926.[96]

At this time, the new archbishop bore all the classic marks of a doctor of dogmatic theology. Average in height for a male, he looked taller because he was trim, and a trifle older because of a receding hairline. His hair was parted on the left. Mild, steady eyes gazed serenely through his thick glasses with heavy bone rims. A small mouth and broad chin gave his face a round appearance, which never changed. When he dressed for the street he wore his black hat most properly level, like the balancing basket of certain peasants. Beneath his priestly straight coat but visible to all, a heavy gold chain crossed his breast, mysterious looking, one of those ecclesiastical perks that only bishops or monsignors knew about. Unlike Bishop Schinner, who appeared always to be sad or washed out, His Grace looked happy and vigorous, even dapper.

Having got at last their new archbishop, the Catholics of Portland were impatient to see him. But there was some delay in Davenport, due to he condition of Bishop Davis, whose illness persisted into the summer.[97] Since Howard had his own field to plow, he set August 26 as the date for his installation in Portland's new cathedral and invited Archbishop Keane to confer on him the sacred pallium. Enroute west, Howard traveled via Spokane, where Scinner was still in charge. He offered Mass in St. Aloysius Church on a warm summer morning, then proceeded to Portland to take possession of his see.[98] On hand to welcome him was Bishop O'Dea, who made a speech during festivities following the installation. "The Oregon province," O'Dea informed the newcomer from Iowa, "is the largest in the world and second oldest in the United States."[99] If this impressed His Grace, it certainly did not weigh upon him. After all, what could be worse than being a college president in Iowa?

SPOKANE'S NEW BISHOP

Northwest bishops so far had not been conspicuous for speaking out on national social issues. Understandably they were still preoccupied with local and regional problems, which were not by any means secret. Among the bishops, Schinner was probably the best informed on eastern America's industry-labor disputes and similar social conflicts, such as secular politics and poverty, as he had been the most vocal in supporting the Pope's Peace Plan. Sometimes he presented public comments on abuses, taking a forthright stand without fear of the consequences. In this respect his successor was like him.

His successor was Monsignor Charles Daniel White, rector of St. Joseph's Preparatory Seminary in Grand Rapids, Michigan when he was formally appointed Bishop of Spokane on December 20, 1926. The first native son of Grand Rapids to be consecrated a bishop, he was an alumnus of St. Francis seminary in Milwaukee, Bishop Schinner's alma mater. The two bishops had met one another only once, when Schinner directed a retreat in Michigan.[100]

White had been born on January 5, 1879, the son of Patrick and Catherine Bolger White. When he was but three and one-half years old, his father died, leaving his widowed mother to support him. As mother and son during many years of struggle, they became very close to one another, like Monica and Augustine, which is one good reason why Bishop White was so dedicated to his mother later in life. When he was older, he accepted a position with the O and W Thum Company of Grand Rapids, where he remained until he began his studies for the priesthood at the age of twenty-five.

Having completed his collegiate courses at St. Francis, he went to Rome to attend the North American College, and was ordained in St. John Lateran on September 24, 1910, by Pietro Cardinal Respighi, the vicar general to His Holiness Pius X.[101] From 1911 to 1919 Father White was assigned to pastoral work in his home diocese. Then he was appointed rector of the seminary where he was regarded as a very strict disciplinarian.

Following the reception of appropriate documents from Rome, he was consecrated bishop in the cathedral in Grand Rapids on February 24, 1927. The presiding bishop was Gabriel Pinten, who was assisted by Bishops Samuel Stricht of Toledo and Alphonse Smith of Nashville. His enthronement, as it was called in those Renaissance-like years, was scheduled for March 10, 1927, in Our Lady of Lourdes Cathedral. All Spokane was a-twitter. Committees for this and that were formed, menus for receptions were pondered as carefully as a general pondered his battle plans, the cathedral was scrubbed and shined, and collections were taken to provide the new bishop with a purse. The bishop's reputation had preceded him: he was a no-nonsense administrator. No one was taking any chances.

On March 8, in a late winter snowstorm, 125 members of the welcoming committee proceeded via special train to Sandpoint, Idaho, to meet the new bishop and his widowed mother, Catherine, who accompanied him. At Sandpoint the bishop posed self-consciously for photographs. Wearing a black hat almost as large as a cowboy's, he appeared to be too small for a bishop. He smiled wistfully for all, but one gets the impression that he was thinking—let's get this over with. But he was patient and everyone was charmed, and no one talked about the snowstorm.

On Thursday, March 10, the little bishop was "enthroned." It rained all morning, so the umbrellas of onlookers at the procession obscured the view of others, who strained to see. The rain subsided after the long ceremony and photographers could ply their arts on the steps of the cathedral. In one portrait taken that day, Archbishop McNicholas of Cincinnati stole the show: he filled out his robes splendidly, a handsome man with a regal posture. Next to him on the right was Bishop Pinten, also very attractive in his ermine cape draped over his shoulders. And to the left was bishop White, who looked, next to them, like an altar boy in four layers of oversized clothes, with a biretta on his head that also looked three sizes too big. His Excellency's feet were spread outward, causing some to wonder if they had got the notorious disciplinarian after all, or perhaps the office boy.[102]

A banquet that evening was served at the Davenport: an entree "of Breast of Capon with French Mushrooms and Vatican potatoes," whatever these were. The purse of $2,500 was presented probably more than the bishop took as a salary during the next five years. After the speeches had been rendered, White, with his mother, retired to the bishop's modest home at East 238-13th Avenue to reflect on the day's events and to evaluate what he had got for a diocese.

So far the weather had been dreadful, but the city was exceptionally clean looking and, like most isolated small cities, its people of all faiths were spiritually united and hospitable. He learned that eastern Washington had "31,467 Catholics only, with 92 priests, half of whom were religious, 43 churches, 11 of which were in the city, and 56 missions."[103] More missions than parishes. The area's economy was based largely on agricultural and forest products, and the overall population had remained stagnant for several years, despite the population boom in Bishop O'Dea's diocese across the mountains. As dioceses go, it was no jewel, but the new bishop was determined to make the best of it.

When he got around to running the diocese, no one doubted who was boss. An excellent administrator, he was strictly above board and totally fearless, even feisty when aroused. His strong sense of justice and order sometimes brought him into conflict with others, even into court, which never fazed him. The small clique of priests who had made life difficult for Schinner found him more than a match. Unlike the gentle Schinner, White met these critics head on and scattered them like sheep. Strange to say, no objections were raised and peace and harmony reigned, at least most of the time.

BISHOP O'DEA'S NEW MONSIGNORS

In Seattle, Bishop O'Dea's style had never changed. Perhaps he had become too mellow; that was the risk when you made a young priest bishop. After twenty years or so, he trusted too much in God and let sleeping dogs lie. Things got a little out of hand sometimes, then an officious bishop would come in and give orders to everybody to shape up. Recently O'Dea had petitioned the Holy See to bestow the monsignor-ship on six of his priests: the vicar general, Daniel Hanly; the chancellor, Theodore Ryan; Gustave Achtergael, dean of the Seattle district; James Stafford, rector of the cathedral; John Sweens, chaplain at Mount St. Vincent's; and William Noonan, the "Irish pope" in Tacoma.[104] This made O'Dea very popular with the old guard in the diocese.

Recognition of Father Sweens was mostly personal, but the bishop also had a special place in his heart for Mt. St. Vincent. This had been established two years earlier as a Home for the Aged, and for the novitiate and provincial headquarters of the Sisters of Providence.[105] As the title indicated, the home was primarily for the poor, a continuation on the grand scale of the work begun by Mother Joseph in Vancouver.

ST. VINCENT DE PAUL SOCIETIES

O'Dea, like Mother Joseph, was sincerely concerned about the needs of the poor and he never passed up a chance to help them. Very active during this period was an organization of Catholic lay men known as the St. Vincent de Paul Society.[106] More recently affiliated with the national organization, it had taken root in the Northwest many years earlier, first in Portland where Father Fierens served as its first spiritual director in 1869.[107] It appeared in Spokane in December 1889 when Father Charles Mackin gathered a group of twenty-eight members, who elected the pioneer "capitalist" James Monaghan as its first president.[108] Four years later, in November 1893, a group of men calling themselves "Immaculate Conception Association of Charity" was organized in the Immaculate Conception parish in Seattle. This was explicitly recognized as "a society similar to that of St. Vincent de Paul." Officially the first St. Vincent de Paul Society was formed in St. Benedict's parish much later, on January 26, 1920.[109] In Tacoma, the Society sponsored Ozanam Home, a residence for the aged, which Bishop O'Dea dedicated on April 9, 1926.[110]

In the course of time, the Vincentians established "salvage bureaus" like those of the Salvation Army and Volunteers of America. Although these appeared in all of the major cities in the Northwest, two were especially notable.[111] In Seattle, the most famous of all was founded and directed by Peter Emt, a colorful, almost loud personality with the brass of an auctioneer, but heart of wax. For over thirty years Emt ran a perky show that was more like a carnival than a second-hand emporium. In its earlier years, the Seattle bureau salvaged over one half million dollars and gave aid to forty thousand poor people annually.[112]

The other "most successful" bureau was in Portland where in more recent years an annual budget of three million dollars had been supported. Portland's St. Vincent de Paul has promoted programs "for helping the poor help themselves" by funding schools for vocational training and other similar projects.

The overall influence of the Vincentians has been spectacular. Many of us will remember their appearance at the church doors after Mass on Sundays, two at a time, self-effacing men with baskets, collecting money for the poor. They were volunteers with autonomy in their works of charity, but they represented the church officially in the thankless task of providing for poor people of all races and creeds.

THE DEATH OF ONE BISHOP AND THE ARRIVAL OF TWO OTHERS

Bishop Gorman was the next to die. No one should have been surprised, for he was slowly killing himself with work. He never complained. He traveled incessantly about his vast, mostly empty diocese, driving his car patiently over primitive roads to the most remote of missions or the smallest of faraway towns. On May 29, 1927, he administered the sacrament of confirmation for the last time in a small mountain town called Orofino. The same evening he drove to Lewiston, a more than two-hour journey in those days. He arrived at St. Joseph's Hospital to spend the night, intending to drive to Cottonwood on the next day to attend a Knights of Columbus convention. More fatigued than he realized, he retired for the night about nine.[113]

An hour later he summoned a nurse who found him in a critical condition. Doctors and sisters rushed to his aid. Under their care and vigilance he gradually improved. On June 8, he was allowed to sit up in a chair where the sun warmed him. He announced that he would visit the Indians at Lapwai and called his friend Judge George Erb to request the services of a stenographer. On Thursday following, he dictated one letter after another while sitting in bed. The letters were brought to him for signing, and he asked for his glasses. He died that way, with his glasses still in his hand, his letters unsigned.[114] He was only sixty-six. He had given his life for his people and his people were wise enough to realize it. "Bishop Gorman was never one to spare himself," one Boise paper lamented.[115] The whole state mourned his loss. His motto, *Caritas Christi Urget Nos*, was his best epitaph.[116]

BISHOP GEORGE JOSEPH FINNIGAN, C.S.C.

Both Boise and Helena now lacked bishops. Catholics then said they were "widowed," which sounds a bit lugubrious. There was nothing lugubrious, however, about the deep yearnings of the people of Helena for a bishop to occupy their elegant new cathedral.

On May 27, 1927, their yearnings were finally fulfilled. Father George Finnigan, Provincial of the Holy Cross Fathers at Notre Dame, Indiana, was appointed the Third Bishop of Helena. He was the first member of the Holy Cross Congregation to become a bishop in the United States.

Father George looked more like Notre Dame's football coach than its provincial. A tall, portly man with a wide smile on a broad face, and shoulders as heavy as a fullback's, he personified the epitome of health in a strong man. His soft, gentle eyes behind dark rimmed glasses suggested the warmth and appeal of a popular professor on campus—a professor who doubled as a coach.

He had been born at Potsdam in upstate New York, where the Iroquois, who migrated to Montana, once lived. This was on Washington's birthday, February 22, 1885. His parents, John and Louise Canton Finnigan, sent him to Notre Dame when he was old enough, and there at the tender age of seventeen he was admitted to the Congregation of the Holy Cross.[117] Later he studied with the Jesuits at the Gregorian in Rome and was ordained in Rome on June 13, 1915, by Basilio Cardinal Pompilj, the vicar general to His Holiness Pius XI. There followed eleven years of varied activities: missionary work in the United States, chaplain in the American Expeditionary Forces in World War I, and director of the Holy Cross Seminary. In 1926, he was elected provincial.

His consecration on the Notre Dame campus on August 1, 1927, was a family affair. A Holy Cross colleague, Archbishop Peter Hurth, former missionary in Dacca, India, was the principal consecrator. His assistants were old friends, Bishops John Noll of Fort Wayne and Edward Hoban of Rockford. Since the new bishop was only forty-two years old and robust, he was expected to live long enough to make all this expense and fuss worthwhile. Actually, when he died, only five years later, he probably regretted it as much as anyone.

When he was formally installed a bishop, or "enthroned," the clergy and faithful of Helena provided a pageant worthy of their former bishop, the late John Patrick Carroll. On August 18, 1927, notables of the church in the Northwest converged on the Cathedral of Helena. "For two hours," says the chronicler of the medieval-like ceremony, "before the doors of the cathedral were opened to those holding cards, the streets were crowded with people from all walks of life eager to grasp a cherished word or store away a memory of the historic event."

A selection from this same chronicler's description of the procession reveals the quaintness of the spectacle by modern standards:

> In the lead came the Rev. Father Leo Martin, the censer bearer, with acolytes carrying tapers, at his right and left. Then came the Rev. Father Robert O'Dea as cross bearer, wearing his dalmatic of golden cloth lined with Romanic purple. Then followed the diocesan clergy and the visiting clergy.
>
> Following the clergy of the diocese and visitors from all parts of the northwest came the monsignori.
>
> Then came the bishops wearing their golden crosses, golden dalmatics and pontifical garments.
>
> In the processional Bishop Finnigan wore the Cappa Magna the coat of ermine and royal purple equipped with a long train. His two train bearers, Robert McKinnon and James Grainey, marched close behind the bishop with their little hands folded in reverence. He was followed immediately by Archbishop Howard of Oregon City, wearing his official cappa magna, with train fully extended and his train bearers, Custer Baum and Edward Bell, carrying the deep purple garment in reverence.[118]

In the banquet that evening, there were, of course, many flowery speeches extolling the new bishop and predicting the great things to come. All the bishops, including freshman Bishop White, had their say. Charles Lindbergh's recent triumph was alluded to, and the renowned "Con" Kelly of Anaconda Copper Company had some pleasing remarks for all. One statement especially, seems to stand out. This suggestion of Father J.J. Boyle of Notre Dame proved to be prophetic: "The subject assigned to me," he said, "is Mount St. Charles College. I would like to Latinize the name and call it 'Carroll College' for with Carroll's name, the college is inseparably linked with Carroll's memory. Mount St. Charles must live or die."[119]

Five years later, and just two months before his unexpected death, Bishop Finnigan acted on this suggestion. At the twenty-second commencement exercises, on May 29, 1932, the name of Mount St. Charles College was officially changed to Carroll College to honor its founder.[120]

BISHOP EDWARD JOSEPH KELLY

The first bona fide native of the Pacific Northwest to be appointed a bishop was Edward J. Kelly of Boise.[121] His credentials of birth were flawless, indeed, as one's American heritage goes, his blood was as blue as anyone in the Kennedy clan. At the time of his consecration on March 6, 1928, much ado was made of this enviable circumstance, which one finds refreshing. After all, the church had been here for ninety years, time enough to produce at least one bishop.

But even this had not taken place without pressure. In Father Cyprian Bradley's *History of the Diocese of Boise*, the following account, read and approved by Bishop Kelly, revealed the reasons for change.

> In the Autumn of 1927, while the Boise Diocese was vacant after the death of Bishop Gorman, His Excellency Most Reverend Pietro Fumasoni-Biondi, Apostolic Delegate, and on that occasion canonical visitor of the United States for Rome, made his formal visitation in the Baker Diocese. When Bishop McGrath, the Ordinary of Baker City earnestly urged the Delegate to depart from precedent and to appoint western priests to western dioceses, the Delegate, after much consideration, agreed to the proposal of the Bishop of such a candidate for the diocese of Boise. . . . Until 1927 no western priest had ever been appointed to a western diocese. Twenty-one western priests have received episcopal appointments since then [June 1951].[122]

Editors of the *Catholic Sentinel* were delighted with the precedent and printed the new bishop's western pedigree on the front page.

> The Rt. Rev. Bishop Kelly comes of a pioneer Oregon family. His father, when a boy, came with his parents to California in about 1875 and there attended college at Santa Clara. A few years later the family removed to Portland, and desiring to settle on the land, went to eastern Oregon, going as far as Lewiston, Idaho. Owing to Indian outbreaks they were forced to return and finally settled about 20 miles southeast of The Dalles, Ore.
>
> Bishop Kelly's mother, Henrietta Wakefield, was born at Silverton, Oregon, and is a daughter of parents who crossed the plains over the Old Oregon Trail in the covered wagon.
>
> Of the marriage of James L. Kelly and Henrietta Wakefield five boys were born, one of whom died when a child. When the children were of school age the family removed to The Dalles so that the children might have the benefit of better educational facilities.
>
> Bishop Kelly made his early studies at St. Mary's academy in that city. His classical studies were made at Columbia university, Portland and Menlo Park, California. His ecclesiastical training and education were received at the North American college, Rome, and the Propaganda de Fide university, where he made a brilliant course, obtaining the doctorate both in philosophy and in sacred theology. Bishop Kelly was ordained to the priesthood in Rome. Shortly after his return to the diocese of Baker City, he was made chancellor of the diocese and secretary to Bishop McGrath. At the papal consistory, held in Rome, December 16, 1927, his nomination to the bishopric of Boise, Idaho, was announced to the assembled cardinals by Pope Pius XI.[123]

A photograph of the bishop appeared with these punctilious details, revealing a very serious man who could pass for an experienced corporation president announcing bad news to his board. One can see in his shrewd eyes, dark and piercing, and in the firm line of his jaw, that he not only had great executive ability but also the determination to use it. His reign, unlike Bishop Finnigan's, would be a long one, nobody could doubt that. He was only thirty-eight, as lean as a lodge pole, and spiritually tough enough to withstand any hardship.

When Kelly was consecrated in the Cathedral of St. Francis in Baker on March 6, 1928, his parents were present. Also present were his three brothers with their wives and a flock of other Kellys and Wakefields from assorted places in several states. The consecrating prelate was Bishop McGrath, a happy choice, and the co-consecrators were Bishop Mathias Lenihan and Charles White.[124] The procession "included two archbishops [Howard and Hanna], eight bishops, several monsignori and 120 priests," which means that most of the space in the cathedral was occupied by guests and there was precious little left for the parishioners who had never seen a ceremony like it. On this occasion it was performed for the first time in the Diocese of Baker.

THE DEATH OF FATHER CATALDO

Bishop Kelly took possession of his diocese on March 8, 1928. During this same week, the most famous Indian missionary since DeSmet celebrated his seventy-fifth anniversary as a Jesuit. Father Cataldo at this time was resident at St. Joseph's mission, Slickpoo, where the Nez Perce playfully called him *Kaoushin*, "Broken Leg."[125] Though badly crippled from a broken hip incurred several years previously, he consented to appear in Spokane for the anniversary and for his ninety-second birthday. March 11 was the date chosen to bring him to Spokane for the round of ceremonies that were scheduled for the six days following. He arrived on schedule and was met by a contingent of reporters who demanded his opinion on all sorts of irrelevant questions like Governor Alfred Smith, present day opportunities for youth, and so on. His first public appearance for the jubilee was at the Chamber of Commerce luncheon on Tuesday, March 13, where more than five hundred people rose to their feet and cheered when he entered the dining hall. A solemn Mass was offered in St. Aloysius Church, while he sat in a wheelchair in the sanctuary, his head covered with a black beanie, like a bishop's, and his dark Sicilian eyes gazing intently at the celebrant.

During a reception that evening in the American theatre, an extraordinary incident took place. An aged Indian, every bit a chief, strode solemnly to the speaker's rostrum on the stage. It was Joseph La Mousse, the eighty-three year old nephew of the great Ignace La Mousse, who was killed by the Sioux. Joseph spoke to *Kaoushin* in their common tongue, Salish or Flathead. One can only imagine the tenseness of this historic apparition; *Kaoushin*, a frail little relic of the romantic past, sitting rigidly in his wheel chair, his eyes fixed on La Mousse, and seeing beyond him the log cabin missions of Montana, Idaho, and eastern Washington, the missions for which Old Ignace gave his blood. No doubt, as many times before, the words "We are here for the Indians" again crossed his mind, but he said nothing. He had already done what he could. Like Old Ignace, he had given his life, only a little at a time.

"Old Joseph, nephew of Old Ignace, spoke eloquently. When he had finished he performed an Indian dance, a tribal rite that was as sprightly and as graceful as a supple youth would have performed it. Then Father Louis Taelman stepped up. He interpreted the Indian's words, using the same inflection of voice and even the same kind of Indian gestures. *Kaoushin* and Joseph watched him intently, their faces impassive, as though they sensed the drama of their lives would end with the oratory."[126]

Exactly twenty-four days later, *Kaoushin* was dead.

As often happens, Cataldo's death was unexpected, though he had one foot in the grave since he was a boy, for more than seventy-five years. During Holy Week he had labored like a curate. On Holy Saturday the Indians flocked to him, and he was kept busy giving spiritual direction and hearing confessions until ten in the evening. Even on Easter Sunday, after consenting to go to the hospital in Pendleton and on Monday following, he devoted all his time to his Indians. Then about five in the evening on Monday, April 9, 1928, he peacefully breathed his last. He died as he had hoped to die, still in the harness, near an Indian mission, with fresh memories of the Indians' presence that very day.

NEWS ROUNDUP IN THE SENTINEL

Unless he was occupied by more pressing duties, the Archbishop of Oregon City attended every solemn function in the province. This was one of his many attractive virtues. Long before this he had taken firm control of diocesan matters, which did not oppress him. By his own admission he was no worrier. "I never take home problems from the office." Like Bishop White, he slept soundly every night, soon after his head hit the pillow.

He was especially vigilant with the diocesan paper. Its reputation for coverage of major Catholic news events in the Northwest required no endorsement from him, but he gradually came to two decisions regarding it: He wanted it to present wider coverage of Catholic world news, and he wanted to combine its activities with the Catholic Truth Society.

In the weekly issues of 1928, one can find the following:

Announcements regarding the occupation of the new St. Benedict's Monastery and the dedication of the Abbey church.[127]

An advertisement for St. Stephen's Parish High School at East 41st and Salmon Streets in Portland. Accommodations for both boys and girls under the tutelage of the Sisters of St. Mary's of Oregon.[128]

Another ad: "Vote for Governor Alfred E. Smith for President."

The current Catholic population of the four northwest states: Oregon—55,574; Washington—121,249; Idaho—23,143; and Montana—74,224.[129]

Father Edwin O'Hara had visited Mexico to investigate the persecution of the church by President Plutarco Elias Calles. O'Hara's series of articles on this bitter subject was better than anything else that had appeared.[130]

The announcement for new management of the weekly appeared in large print. "Oregon Catholic Truth Society Given Charge of Sentinel."[131] Beginning with this issue of September 6 the broader coverage, which His Grace demanded, considerably altered the old format. Henceforth the front page carried national news mostly and the last page special articles and news in defense of Catholic dogma. Consistent with these were current reports on the Society's "Chapel Cars," the automobiles which had replaced their counterparts on railways.

In September there was notice of a new Jesuit school in Tacoma, called Bellarmine High School, and in October another notice provided details for the opening of Marylhurst College near Portland. Finally on December 6, the news for which all had been waiting, appeared in headlines: "Portland New Title of Archdiocese. Historic Oregon See is Transferred By Recent Papal Brief." The remaining text revealed that this action had been taken at the request of Archbishop Howard and that the brief had been "given at Rome on September 26, 1928."[132] News of the first brief establishing Oregon City in 1843 had required over a year to arrive.

SCHOOLS AND MORE SCHOOLS

The Ku Klux Klan assault had focused attention on parochial schools and its initial success had helped Catholics realize how much they wanted and needed them. Thus it had the opposite effect which the Klan intended. During the post-election period, many new schools were established, among them three distinguished high schools and a sisters' college that became very prominent in the Northwest.

Bellarmine High School in Tacoma, the first of these, was not popular at all. It was like an unwanted waif born out of wedlock. The coeducational high school in the Jesuits' St. Leo's Parish, staffed by Franciscan sisters, was still in debt, and there were many in the parish who opposed any Jesuit expansion until this debt had been liquidated. The Benedictines' high school at St. Martin's, near Olympia, had its own partisans who regarded the proposed new school as a rival. Then there was the Dominicans' Marymount Military Academy some eight miles outside Tacoma, which survived precariously, and though most of its boys were in the elementary grades, a neighboring Jesuit high school was regarded as a threat to its enrollment. Tacoma also had two girls-only high schools, Aquinas of the Dominicans and Visitation Academy conducted by the Visitation nuns.

The pesky question on the minds of some Catholics was how many high schools could they support in the Tacoma area? If Bellarmine were established, it would be the sixth, giving Tacoma as many as Seattle, which was three times as populous.[133] Spokane, larger in population than Tacoma, had only two Catholic high schools, though a third would soon appear.[134]

There were at least two Jesuits who believed that Bellarmine should be established despite the opposition. One was Father Augustine Coudyre, who once expressed the undocumented opinion that "Tacoma is 100% better than Seattle."[135] The other, was Father David McAstocker who wanted nothing less than a *college* like Gonzaga. Without the knowledge and approval of Bishop O'Dea, he purchased twenty acres of land on December 29, 1926, using $8,000 of Jesuit money. Fortunately for all concerned, His Excellency gave his unqualified approval. Opposition melted away and McAstocker built the new school.

On September 4, 1928, the Jesuits opened Bellarmine College, as it was called then. One hundred and thirty-six boys answered the bell for the first class; the first student enrolled was Hugh Boyle. Boyle later became a Jesuit, confirming McAstocker's very vocal contention that the new school would be a prolific source of vocations.[136] On September 23, Bellarmine was solemnly dedicated by Bishop O'Dea. As His Excellency strolled about, throwing holy water here and there, he suddenly saw Mount Rainier in the east, with the sun shining on its snows. "How did you ever find this place?" he said to McAstocker. "It's perfect."[137]

Ever since that day, Bellarmine has prospered, becoming, when times were critical, the city's only Catholic high school with nine hundred teenagers of both sexes.

MARYCLIFF HIGH SCHOOL

Unlike Bellarmine, Marycliff in Spokane was launched with enthusiastic headlines and almost universal approval. It was Bishop White's "free school" for Catholic girls, a church experiment in the great American tradition of free education; *nobody* had to pay for it.

The initiative had been taken by Mrs. Burgess Lee Gordon, a prominent local socialite who had given generously to the church in Spokane. For years Mrs. Gordon, inspired by the age old religious institutions she had seen in Europe, cherished the desire "that her spacious estate and palatial residence might one day be devoted to some religious purpose."[138] Accordingly, in July 1929, she offered her home called "Undercliff" to Bishop White for the purpose of establishing there a school for girls. During the days that followed, the bishop, after prudent consultation with his priests, accepted the offer. Negotiations were hastily completed and the property, valued then at $150,000, was transferred to the Diocese of Spokane.[139]

For teachers, the bishop applied to Mother M. Seraphine, Superior General of the Franciscan Sisters of Perpetual Adoration in LaCrosse, Wisconsin. Mother Seraphine consented to send five sisters for the first year of school, when only the ninth grade would be taught, and to increase the number from year to year until the faculty for a four-year high school was complete. The first superior she appointed was Sister M. Lamberta.[140] Two other teachers were supplied by the bishop, Father William Condon, later Bishop of Great Falls, instructor in religion, and Miss Cecelia Schmidt, teacher of public speaking and physical culture. The sisters moved into their quarters in the servant's addition to the mansion on August 19, 1929.

The dedication ceremony on September 1 attracted more attention than expected, mostly because of the open house following it. Crowds of curious ladies jammed the premises, eager to examine the home of a local aristocrat. Reporters spilled buckets of black ink to inform an eager public about it, and by the time school started on September 9, with fifty-four students, most people knew more about Marycliff than they knew about Gonzaga, which had been there for forty-two years.

"The site and location are exceptionally good," the bishop observed complacently. "The school will be maintained by the 10 Catholic parishes of Spokane. No tuition will be charged pupils residing in the city."[141]

Portland's Archbishop Howard missed nothing that was happening in Spokane. The concept of a "free school" for Portland's Catholic boys had occupied him since he arrived there. In February of this same year, he had presented his views in the pulpit of the cathedral.

> I feel it my duty to place before the Catholics of Portland the very urgent and imperative need of a free Central Catholic high school for boys here in the city. This is a need which I am sure all Catholic parents, who have boys of high school age, have realized for some time.
>
> A little more than a year ago, we sent out a questionnaire to every parish in the City of Portland, in an effort to determine just how many of our boys

and girls who had finished the 8th grade in June in our parish schools are
now attending Catholic high schools. We found out that 188 girls had
finished the 8th grade in the various parish schools of the city and of that
number 112 are now attending Catholic high schools.... Out of 206 boys
who had completed the 8th grade in our parish schools, only 82 are now in
Catholic high schools.[142]

The archbishop's proposal was undoubtedly a noble one, but its timing
was wrong. In the Great Depression, beginning that very year, money
for a free school would be difficult to find.

MARYLHURST

The roots of Marylhurst lie buried in the muddy banks of the
Willamette. You can find the details of how they got there in the Sisters'
Chronicles:

> September 7 [1906] His Grace [Archbishop Christie] came to St. Mary's
> announcing that he had fifty acres of valuable land cleared and a good
> portion under cultivation about one mile and a half from Oswego on the
> west bank of the Willamette River. The land rises from the river and
> overlooks a magnificent landscape on the east bank of the river. The amount
> asked by the owners is twenty thousand dollars but Mr. O'Brien our real
> estate agent, hopes to secure it for fifteen.
> September 8. Mr. O'Brien had secured an option on the Bullock
> Homestead.... The owners are willing to accept fifteen thousand dollars.
> The land will serve for the future college site.
> January 23 [1907]. For some time past we have been considering the
> practibility of the respective location of our Provincial House and of the
> future college buildings. The location of the college buildings seem better
> adapted to the Provincial House and the orphan's home and vice versa.[143]

Just three years later, on May 12, 1910, "the contract for the building of
the Provincial House at Villa Marie is signed by Mr. Edward Killfeather of
Portland.... Work will begin May 17 and it is expected that the building
will be completed and ready for occupancy January 1, 1911."[144]

As usual, more time was required. The provincial administration was
formally transferred to the new quarters "a sail of seven miles up the
river," on June 5, 1911. On the day following, the Novitiate, which had
been established in Portland in 1871, was transferred to Villa Marie also.
In the four decades of its existence at St. Mary's, 228 candidates had
entered this novitiate. "There are now 26 novices who will complete their
probationary period of two years at Villa Marie. There are at present 175
professed religious in the province."[145]

Within a brief time the sisters found themselves in dire financial straits. They had to sell "with deep regret our blocks 151-163, the first property purchased by the Sisters in Oregon," to bail out Holy Names Academy and Normal School in Seattle.[146] Hopes for the college went with the money and the land and the sisters waited patiently for something to happen. Something finally did. On October 21, 1929, just eight days before the ruinous crash of the stock market in the United States, "ground was broken for building the new Marylhurst College at Oswego, Oregon. The solemn event took place on the seventieth anniversary of the arrival of the Sisters of the Holy Names in Oregon." On September 28, 1930, students for the Northwest's first Catholic College for women arrived in numbers so unexpectedly numerous that even the chaplain's quarters had to be converted into another residence hall. When the dust had settled, the Registrar's Office announced "the matriculation for college, one hundred and for Normal, fifty, an excellent showing for the first day."[147]

Several weeks later, on October 21, *The Portland Daily Journal* presented an account of the dedication of Marylhurst. "This article," one of the sisters noted with more optimism than prophecy, "written by a non-Catholic reporter, and appearing in bold type, with large and attractive pictures on the front page of one of the most prominent daily papers, is an encouraging evidence of the decline of bigotry in Oregon."[148]

In retrospect, at least, not everyone would agree with her.

17

DEPRESSION YEARS

1930–1941

The 1930's were characterized by the struggle for survival in the greatest depression in history. For northwest Catholics, most significantly, the depression years coincided with a new isolationism; the church had emerged from the 1920's with a siege mentality. The heartless attack on parochial schools had left its scars, and if the Catholics of the region, outnumbered almost ten to one, had been less than involved in public life, and heretofore uncomfortable with their neighbors, they now withdrew altogether into their own pious ghettos.

In this respect they shared a kind of solidarity with Catholics all over America, where old parish patterns still prevailed despite the social upheaval taking place.[1] Like elsewhere, Catholic men in the Northwest belonged to the Holy Name Society. The St. Vincent de Paul Society "functioned like a Catholic Salvation Army." Women gathered in Altar societies and sponsored card parties as benefits for parish schools. Parish missions replaced building committee meetings and weekend retreats flourished, especially during the summer. In Jesuit parishes, the Novena of Grace captured the hearts of thousands. The Dominicans blessed roses and distributed them on the Feast of the Holy Rosary. A solemn promise to support the National League of Decency, designed to clean up the movies, became a kind of ritual *de rigueur*, like a loyalty oath later, and the repeal of prohibition prompted some bishops to exact the pledge before they administered confirmation or Holy Orders. In Seattle and Portland there were occasional demonstrations of social activism, but most Catholics in the Northwest remained apart, more concerned with the parish debt than the plight of the blacks.

There were two exceptions to this prevailing spirit of remoteness from other American Catholics: the Confraternity of Christian Doctrine and the National Rural Life Bureau, both of which were founded in the

Northwest by Father Edwin O'Hara. O'Hara had resided in Washington, D.C. for ten years, as Director of the Rural Life Bureau of the National Catholic Welfare Council, but he had not lost touch with his associates in Portland and Eugene. He was still attached to the Archdiocese of Portland.

BISHOP O'HARA OF GREAT FALLS

At this point, on January 18, 1930, Bishop Lenihan of Great Falls was permitted by Pope Pius XI to retire. He had been bishop for twenty-six years, and when he departed for residence in Dubuque, as Titular Archbishop of Preslavo, he left his successor a vigorous diocese, including forty-five parishes and eighty-eight missions served by sixty-eight priests.[2] It was the kind of diocese that required a rural oriented bishop like Edwin O'Hara, for it was almost one hundred thousand square miles of farms and ranches with a few sparsely settled cities and towns. No one, then, was astonished when the Vatican made public his appointment as the second Bishop of Great Falls on August 6, 1930.[3]

The new bishop scheduled his consecration for October 28 in Portland. Accordingly on that Tuesday morning, for the first time since Bishop O'Reilly was consecrated in 1903, the elaborate ceremonies were performed in Portland, this time in the new St. Mary's Cathedral which O'Hara had originally planned. Archbishop Howard was the principal consecrator. Co-consecrators were White of Spokane and Crimont of Juneau.[4]

After the ceremony, O'Hara appeared to be more fatigued than usual. His small oval-shaped face showed signs of age, his nose was wrinkled and his eyes squinted warily through his glasses as they met the happy expressions in the eyes of his many friends. Though he was obviously eager to occupy his diocese, which had been "widowed" for ten months, he took time to travel to Eugene to offer his first Pontifical Mass in St. Mary's, where in a sense it had all begun. Only one week later he was installed as bishop in St. Ann's Cathedral. His Grace presided over this, and aging Bishop Lenihan was on hand to preach.[5]

The installation was on November 5. On November 30, the first Sunday of Advent, Bishop O'Hara promulgated his first pastoral letter, in which he outlined the work of the Confraternity of Christian Doctrine, and ordered its establishment in every parish and mission of the diocese. Organizational work for this massive undertaking was begun at once. By the following summer, six thousand five hundred children of the diocese were attending vacation schools in Christian doctrine.[6]

ST. EDWARD'S SEMINARY

In 1928 when the Congregation of Seminaries and Universities issued a reform decree regarding seminaries, there were seven dioceses in the Province of Oregon, but only one seminary for the formation of diocesan priests.[7] This was the Benedictines' Mount Angel Seminary nearing its fiftieth year, but currently without its own quarters, which had been destroyed by fire. Seminary enrollment was increasing and it was becoming obvious that additional quarters would be required soon. The burden of providing these, unfortunately, appeared to be placed on the wrong shoulders. The responsibility for educating priests rested with the bishops, not the Benedictines who were already hard pressed to provide for their own seminarians, and in debt up to their ears because of the recent fire.

Such was the state of affairs on May 22, 1930, when Bishop O'Dea addressed a confidential letter to the clergy of the diocese, announcing the establishment of a new seminary. The letter in part contained the following.

> The founding of the Seminary has been in my mind and heart ever since then, and, in fact, for many years before. Nothing, evidently is more necessary for the welfare and spread of our Holy Religion in the Diocese and Province. Upon its establishment under God, we found our hopes for the future. At a meeting of the Consultors on Monday last, I proposed to them that we begin work this year. Unanimously, they accepted the project and heartily endorsed it. The financial question was considered and a happy solution found. It was decided that a campaign for funds be conducted this Fall, but, as many parishes have great needs it was agreed that the collections made through the parishes be divided equally, half to go to the Seminary and half to the parish. Far from placing a burden on the parishes, the campaign will stimulate our good people to give generously for the training of our future priests and bring financial benefits to the parishes as well as to the Seminary.[8]

His Excellency added at least one compelling detail: Orders for the new seminary had come from the Pope himself. This startling disclosure and other bits of information that demonstrated that O'Dea was dead serious, were communicated to the public on June 5, 1930.[9] He had purchased, O'Dea said, a three hundred acre site between Kenmore and Kirkland with three quarters of a mile of waterfront on Lake Washington. To be known as St. Edward's, in honor of the bishop's patron saint, the first unit for minor seminary and collegiate studies would be under construction by autumn.

In August, Father John Fenlon, the superior o the Sulpician Fathers from Baltimore, who had been selected to staff the new seminary, announced that clearing of the building site had begun, and that Father Thomas Mulligan would be St. Edward's first president. Mulligan, a native of Iowa, had been ordained sixteen years before in Dubuque.[10] He was regarded, like Bishop White, as a firm disciplinarian. Things moved rapidly while Bishop O'Dea, near the end of his rope, scrounged for money to pay the bills. Money was tight, people said, but O'Dea's personal popularity and Catholic traditional devotion to the education of priests produced enough cash to keep the project funded.[11]

On October 13, 1930, the cornerstone was solemnly blessed and laid. A tent was spread above the prelates in attendance to protect them from Seattle's notorious rain while they prayed and puttered with the ceremonial trowel. The Apostolic Delegate from Washington, Archbishop Pietro Fumasoni-Biondi, presided. Bishops from dioceses all over the West were present. Archbishop Howard, unlike the delegate, who presented a ho-hum demeanor, appeared to be as happy-go-lucky as usual. He had taken to coast weather like a water spaniel. O'Dea looked old and weathered, like a tired senior citizen at a rally. Fenlon was there, wearing a long, sad face, and Mulligan, whose bald head with heavy tufts of hair on the sides gave him the appearance of an English butler.[12]

During the ceremony, Archbishop Fumasoni-Biondi used the same silver trowel that Bishop O'Dea used on November 12, 1903, to lay the cornerstone of the cathedral. Contents of the cornerstone were like those in time deposits: copies of the *Catholic Northwest Progress,* medals, documents, coins minted in 1930, two small stones, a pebble from the shores of Lake Galilee and a rock from the streets of Nazareth, a copy of the *New Testament,* the New Code of Canon Law and the *Summa Contra Gentiles* of St. Thomas Aquinas.[13] It was a curious lot, gathered with pious enthusiasm. Undoubtedly the papers and books have rotted long since, but the coins have lost none of their value.

St. Edward's was completed by late summer of the following year, a very handsome four-story brick building exotically placed along the gray-green waters of the lake, surrounded by dark forests and snow-capped mountains, the highest of which had been called "God" by the Indians.[14] The reported cost of the project was $500,000.[15]

On August 30, the first members of the Little Daughters of St. Joseph to reside in the Northwest arrived at St. Edward's to staff the culinary department.[16] They were followed by the arrival of fifty-two seminarians from all over the Northwest and British Columbia, the first of many contingents. They occupied their classrooms on September 19, when formal studies began.[17] On October 13, St. Edward's was blessed by Dennis Cardinal Dougherty with customary eclat, under brilliant sunny skies, which delighted everyone and surprised most. Then the rigid schedule of classes resumed, for some a deadly routine that had to be borne. No one even suspected then that Bishop O'Dea's cherished seminary would die less than five decades after he did, and he already had one foot in the grave.

THE JESUITS AGAIN

One cannot overlook the activities of the Jesuits at this time because they were accounted as the largest single group of clergy in the Northwest.[18] Like the bishops, Jesuit superiors were had-pressed to provide for the formation of their own seminarians. The Jesuit province on the West Coast was called "California" and the Jesuit provincial was Father Joseph Piet, an incurable optimist who frequently exhorted his subjects to perform "with plenty of enthusiasm." In 1927, he had established Manresa Hall in the old Eisenbeis mansion in Port Townsend, where allegedly the former master had shot himself through the head.[19] The Hall was a tertianship or final year of studies for Jesuits.

While this resolved one problem for Piet, two others, much more complex, remained. First, the novitiate at Los Gatos, California could no longer accommodate the ever increasing number of candidates for the Order. Thus a new novitiate in the Northwest was required without further delay. This introduced a second need, the division of the California province.[20] Provincial headquarters at this time were in Portland and it was in the Portland area where Piet sought property for the new novitiate.

Piet had many eccentricities, among which was his conviction that prunes were the best cure-all for young seminarians, especially novices.[21] Hence his search for the new novitiate site focused on land with a prune orchard. He eventually found "Paradise Farm" near Sheridan, about sixty miles southwest of Portland and in spite of the objections of some of his advisors, purchased it for approximately $36,000.[22]

A short time later, on December 25, 1930, the Rocky Mountain Vice-Province was canonically established by Rome. This comprised the four Northwest states and Alaska, approximately one millions square miles, containing less than a million Catholics. The new vice-Provincial was Father Walter Fitzgerald, former president of Gonzaga University, who soon produced a deluge of correspondence with Piet about the lack of money and reasons for building the novitiate elsewhere. But Piet was adamant. He ordered the immediate construction of a temporary building for a novitiate, a flimsy frame structure called "the bungalow," built by Dougan and Reverman of Portland in twenty-two days.[23] This was completed on July 25, 1931, and was occupied by the first six novices four days later. When Archbishop Howard blessed and dedicated the novitiate in honor of St. Francis Xavier on July 31, there were fifteen novices in residence.[24] Twenty-five more arrived in early August, bringing the total to forty who were crammed into all available space like sailors in a submarine.

Plans were already in the making for a permanent building, but the principal obstacle was, as always, money. Bank failures were on all sides and two more mission fires reduced the province's cash resources. The Alaska Mission was on the brink of bankruptcy, and the California province, which had agreed to pay the cost of the new novitiate, was so heavily in debt that it could not pay even its ordinary bills to the northern Jesuits. While Rome mulled over the pros and cons of elevating the status of the vice-province to a province, Fitzgerald, egged on by Piet, who never knew how much money was available, directed Father Nathaniel Purcell to proceed with construction of a concrete barracks.

On December 8, 1931, the Jesuit general signed the required documents for the final erection of the northern province to be called Oregon. These documents, according to custom, were read at dinner on February 2, 1932, at which time they became effective. On February 5, Fitzgerald and his staff formally occupied the provincial's residence in Portland, where they added up the new province's debts of $1,764,855.89.[25] Hence the Northwest's largest religious order could boast also of having the largest debt.

Nonetheless, construction of the new novitiate was scheduled. On April 13, 1932, Father Thomas Meagher, the novice master,"turned over a shovelful of reddish clay and read a number of prayers from the ritual, while the novices sang hymns to St. Joseph: "Bleak sands are all round us, no home can we see." When they finished, workmen who had been standing by curiously, reached for their tools and the project was under way. The first Mass in the new building was celebrated on the Feast of the Sacred Heart, 1933, in a temporary chapel on the third floor.[26] The same day the novices moved in. What the Jesuits had got for their $2.40 per square foot was a damp concrete shell without furnishings, a house that was large enough to serve as a Benedictine Abbey and poor enough to be a Trappist monastery. With a little black tar added to the surface to keep the rain out, it would have to do for thirty-three more years. So there it was crowning an eminence over the Yamhill Valley, a black box like a huge bat roost, surmounted by a cross that was visible to tourists speeding south on Highway 18 West to the Gold Coast of Oregon.

PROGRESS AT PORTLAND

Having expressed his approval, the archbishop had followed closely the recent changes in Jesuit administration. He was uncomfortably aware of the Jesuits' often expressed hope of establishing a boy's high school in the Portland area, but, like his predecessor, who had verbally approved the proposal without providing the required documents, he stalled when the subject was brought up. What Howard desired more than a Jesuit high school was his own Central Catholic, his future nursery for vocations to the priesthood of the archdiocese. Crowded conditions at the Sheridan novitiate were proof enough that the Jesuits were getting their share of candidates, sometimes even from diocesan high schools like those in Butte.[27] His Grace did not envy the Jesuits, at least he did not say so, but he needed his own priests, and he believed that Central Catholic would provide them.

Money for Central, however, was elusive. The Holy Names Society's drive had fallen far short of its goal, and subsequent "benefits" succeeded one another in dreary repetition, adding but little to the school fund, which was more like ten thousand dollars than a hundred thousand.[28] Someone had located an existing school that was a model: Reitz Memorial High School in Evansville, Indiana, and pictures of this appeared regularly in the *Catholic Sentinel*. Donors now had a visual aid to motivate them and a new motto "Ce-Ca-Hi," became a kind of rallying cry for more and better benefits.

This tiresome subject dragged on while another, a vexing matter at best, wasted endless hours of the archbishop's time. This concerned All Saints parish in the affluent Laurelhurst district of Portland, where efforts to establish a parish school had lingered for years. Early in 1930 Archbishop Howard petitioned the City Council for permission to build the one story school, costing an estimated $27,000, on parish property.[29] On April 21, the City Council returned the approved petition subject to the usual proceedings, hearings, and public inspection. No one expected complications. But when the ordinance came up for the final passage, accompanied by a special report from the commissioner of public works, it was rejected by a single vote. The mayor who favored the bill, was miffed.

"The City," he declared in protest, "had granted a permit for the erection of the Christian Science church in the district, and for the erection of the public school there and . . . it grants permits for churches and schools all over the city in residential districts."[30] But not for All Saints.

The Oregon School Bill had been put to rest but the prejudice that fathered it was still alive and well.

The only recourse left was the courts. On April 8, 1932, All Saints and the archdiocese presented their case before Circuit Court Judge H.D. Norton, who decreed that the city's zoning law in this case was unconstitutional.[31] The city appealed to Oregon's Supreme Court on October 18, 1932. The higher court upheld Judge Norton's decision and at long last the way was clear for the school.[32]

The archbishop, meanwhile, acquired a building for a chancery.[33] Assembled for ten thousand pre-war dollars "plus the cost of plumbing and heating," these quarters at 549 Sixth Avenue contained accommodations for diocesan offices, the Catholic Truth Society and the *Catholic Sentinel*. The new building represented more than a unified stage of operations. Since the archbishop was intensely concerned with news of the entire Catholic world, he scheduled, whenever possible, periods of briefing by his assistants, and especially by the editor of the *Sentinel*, who was expected to be well informed on current events everywhere.

NEW CATHOLIC PAPERS

The Pope's encyclical on Catholic Action appeared that summer.[34] This presupposed an enlightened laity and placed new importance on diocesan papers, a contingency not lost on the northwest bishops. O'Hara was the first to respond. By agreement with *The Register* chain of Denver, he established *The Register Eastern Montana Edition*, the first issue of which appeared on November 8, 1931. Father Francis Shevlin was its first editor; seven thousand copies of the first number were printed.[35]

One month later, on December 4, the first issue of Spokane's diocesan weekly appeared. Entitled *The Inland Catholic*, this was independently produced by editor James Emmet Royce who, like the editor of the *Catholic Sentinel*, was very fond of headlines. "Inland Empire's First Catholic Newspaper Is Born," he declared in Volume One, Number One, entirely unaware that his was actually Spokane's second Catholic paper. The first, called the *Catholic Herald*, was published for about two years starting January 10, 1900.[36] Royce's Celtic origins identified the quality of his loyalty to the church and his legal background provided him with a perspective that was uncommonly useful to the bishop. He soon became White's confidante. He possessed enough compassion for the entire staff. "Father Cox's Jobless March on Washington" he announced in an early issue.[37] From the very beginning he was a champion of the oppressed.

Bishop Finnigan in Helena, like O'Hara, opted for a diocesan edition of the *Register*. With Father James Major as its first local editor, the first issue of *The Register Western Montana Edition* made its appearance on March 6, 1932.[38] By this time each diocese in the Northwest, except Baker City, published its own newspaper.[39] All of them appeared weekly except the *Boise Catholic Monthly*.

DEATH OF BISHOP FINNIGAN

The old mission church at Browning, Montana, was like the cave in Bethlehem, primitive and cold.[40] A new church had been anticipated for decades but nothing changed until Monsignor William Flynn of the Marquette League in New York persuaded the Thomas Bradleys of that city to build a new one. The Bradleys, it was said, had built mission churches all over the world, which says something about their zeal and their wealth. Whatever they built was first class, so the second Browning church was composed of the finest stone to withstand the icy chills of Rocky Mountain winters and the slow ravages of time.

Bishop Finnigan of Helena, in whose diocese Browning lay, agreed to provide an especially solemn dedication, because the Bradleys and the monsignor would be present. It was generally understood, also, that the bishops of the Northwest's missionary dioceses would also attend, for obvious reasons. At the request of the donors, the name of the church was changed from St. Michael, an old favorite with the missionaries, to St. Theresa "The Little Flower" whose public cult was very fashionable then.

The dedication took place as scheduled, on May 25, 1932, with Bishop Finnigan in charge. Bishop O'Hara of Great Falls celebrated the Pontifical Mass and Bishop White of Spokane rendered the homily. He was followed by Mountain Chief, the venerable leader of the Catholic Blackfeet, whose wind-burnt face, hollowed with famine and creased with deep wrinkles, spoke almost as eloquently as he did. "You Big Priests," he said, referring to the many bishops present, "I am Mountain Chief. When Mountain Chief is in your church he does what you say. When you are outside the church in my country, you do what Mountain Chief says."[41]

Bishop Finnigan that day provided for his guests with easy charm. There was nothing to suggest that he would not live to celebrate his Silver Jubilee in another twenty years. He had plans for attending the Provincial Council in Portland, the first in four decades.[42] He had scheduled the usual string of summer confirmations in small settlements.

On July 1, Bishop Finnigan confirmed ten men in the state penitentiary at Deer Lodge. All ten were converts as a result of a mission given by the bishop during the previous April. For him it was a last hurrah. In August he suddenly became ill and four days later, on the vigil of the Assumption, he peacefully died.[43] At his own request his body was carried to Notre Dame for burial. Bishop Noll, who had served as one of his co-consecrators just five years earlier, performed the graveside rites on August 23, 1932.[44] The see of Helena was vacant again, and Monsignor Victor Day for the second time became the administrator.

There was a curious sequel to this sad event. The Knights of Columbus had conducted their state convention in Helena during the previous May. In one of its sessions they voted to take out a fifty-thousand dollar life insurance policy on the bishop with Carroll College as the beneficiary. Hence the college received the fifty-thousand, worth a million then, which went a long ways in moderating the president's grief.

THE COLLEGE OF GREAT FALLS

Bishop O'Hara's diocese had no such luck. For some time he had been groping for the means to provide a college for young women in Montana, similar to Carroll College in Helena, which was restricted to male students. Having secured the cooperation of Bishop Finnigan before his death, he pulled together what resources he could spare, or find, and established in temporary quarters the College of Great Falls, which opened to fourteen students on the first day, September 8, 1932.[45] The first president was Father John Rooney of the Helena diocese and the first faculty consisted of Ursulines and Providence Sisters. It was a foolhardy venture, conceived in desperation, and finally realized only because of the genius of its founder.

In September of the year following, a "teacher-training curriculum" was added to the college's program.[46] This was housed in another temporary building on Third Avenue North, suggesting the still unstable existence of the institution. O'Hara, however, was determined, and positive changes appeared each year, bringing credibility to the skeptics and widening the influence of the college over the entire state.

In 1935 Summer Sessions were added to the college.

In 1936 A third year was added to the teacher-training.

In 1937 The college became co-educational.

In 1938 The teacher-training became a four year normal school.

In 1939 This was recognized as a four year college.

In 1940 Evening classes were inaugurated when the college, cooperating with the Civil Aeronautics Association [CAA] provided ground classes to meet the need for civilian pilots.[47]

In 1942 When the Ursulines withdrew from the staff, the teachers-training program was merged with the mother institution.

Long before this, the irrepressible Bishop O'Hara was engaged in a new project, a form of adult education called "study clubs." In the spring of 1933 his parishes and missions had 408 of these study clubs, each with approximately eleven members, earnestly reading and discussing subjects, like the life of Jesus, assigned by the bishops himself. In autumn of the same year, there were five thousand adults, 448 study clubs, and the number gradually increased, because there was nothing his flock would not do for the bishop.[48]

Simply stated, O'Hara was not only creative, but he had a unique flair for motivating others to follow him. These charisms joined to his strong sense of order, made it possible for him to accomplish in his lifetime the achievements of many. O'Hara should be regarded as one of the Northwest's greatest prelates.

BISHOP O'DEA'S DEATH

So should Bishop O'Dea, though for other reasons than the above. O'Hara and O'Dea shared one characteristic in common: dedication to duty. While O'Hara could be likened to a race horse, who was too fast for the track, O'Dea was more like a good family watch dog who loved the children and left nothing to chance. When he was a young man, O'Dea never faltered in labor, but as he grew older he settled back into the role of paternal guardian, permitting younger men to do the leg work while he maintained a benevolent control.

During this autumn of life, the new rector of the seminary, Father Mulligan, resided in his home.

Upon my arrival in Seattle on a Sunday morning in July, 1930, Bishop O'Dea took me into his home, where I lived for over a year, until the Seminary was opened in September, 1931.

The Bishop lived in the dignified residence at 1104 Spring St., only a few blocks from his Chancery Office. Each day about noon the Bishop would return from the Chancery, walking erect, dressed in a long coat, wearing a high hat, and carrying a cane. His step was somewhat slow, and the cane not a mere ornament, for the Bishop must have been in his seventies.

The meals at the Bishop's table were simple, but prepared with care and served with the quiet dignity that marked his household. No one could have been more devoted to the Bishop than his housekeeper, Miss Lucie Frenette, who, with the aid of a fine Filipino boy, Rafael, served the Bishop in the most painstaking manner.

Each evening after supper the Bishop would invite me to come to his study, where he settled himself in a comfortable old chair, lit a cigar, and talked about the old days. When he came across the Isthmus of Panama with his family, enroute from Boston to Portland, Ore., the only things the small boy remembered were the fruit and the birds. Boyhood was happy in the small town of Portland, with memorable escapades on Indian ponies or on log-booms in the river. Even school was happy for a gifted boy, who apparently developed best under the task-masters who taught in the former fire-station converted into a Catholic school for boys. When asked who was the best teacher he ever had, the Bishop did not hesitate to name the strict drill-master who later became Bishop of Boise.

When Edward O'Dea was leaving Portland on his way to the Grand Seminary in Montreal, his pastor gave him a large bag of money, with instructions not to spend any of it this side of the Mississippi, for the bag contained nothing but nickles, which the pastor was trying to put out of circulation in his parish.[49]

Though little was said, O'Dea had been ill for more than a year. He was now seventy-six years old and he had been a bishop for all but forty of them. By Christmas time 1932, his appearance belied his expressions of cheer. He was a dying man. Some of his priests gathered around him on Christmas night, like sons with their dying father, and the old bishop whose kindness was proverbial looked on them fondly. "God bless you all," he whispered, and he quietly died.[50]

We die as we live. O'Dea had blessed all his life; his last act was a blessing. He had also been poor all his life. He left an estate of less than $10,000, all of which he willed to the diocese and the seminary.[51] More significantly, he left the church, entrusted to him thirty-six years before, in the process of amazing growth: the original area of his diocese had increased from one to two dioceses, the number of Catholics from forty thousand to one hundred and thirty thousand. the priests from sixty-nine to three hundred and twenty-four, and the churches from eighty-nine to two hundred and sixty-two.[52]

FATHER WILLIAM CONDON

There were now two Northwest dioceses without bishops, Seattle and Helena. Speculation regarding replacements abounded, and it was wholly unlikely that some of the local clergy thought of themselves as likely candidates. Monsignor Verhagen, once rumored for Spokane, was now too old. He had recently resigned as pastor of the cathedral parish in Spokane because "of poor health."[53] His successor at the cathedral was Father William Condon, Bishop White's secretary, who later succeeded O'Hara as Bishop of Great Falls.

Condon was the son of Patrick and Mary Elizabeth Condon, nee Kavanaugh, minority pioneers among those Germans at Colton, Washington, when the noisy polemics with Uniontown still raged.[55] The Condons favored Father Frei and his friend the Benedictine Barnabas Held. Thus, when they moved to Spokane, they sent William to Held's ill fated Sacred Heart School on Fifth and Bernard. After its closure, they enrolled him with the Holy Names Sisters in the old Our Lady of Lourdes school on Main Avenue. Later, William attended Gonzaga College, graduating with the highly visible class of 1912, which witnessed, during one of its many commencement exercises, Father Taelman's dramatic declaration of Gonzaga's new status as a university.[56] After this, he entered the seminary at Menlo Park in California and was ordained in Spokane by Bishop Schinner on October 14, 1917. Thus he was identified with two of Spokane's first Catholic schools, and the first Catholic College, and was ordained by the first Bishop of Spokane. Only Bishop Kelly of Boise had better frontier credentials.

Though Condon was what contemporary ecclesiastics called "episcopabilis," he was still too young to be promoted, only thirty-seven when O'Dea died, so the Vatican had to look elsewhere. Two eastern priests were selected, for specific reasons, it appears, transcending local church politics.

BISHOP RALPH LEO HAYES FOR HELENA

The first was "The Reverend Dr. Ralph L. Hayes, Pastor of the Church of St. Catherine of Siena, Pittsburgh." Appointed to the vacant see of Helena on June 23, 1933, the bishop-elect looked the part. In his fifty-first year he appeared to be well poised and serene, as bishops are supposed to look, but there was also something bookish about him, his rimless glasses and tired eyes like those of a desk jockey. His wide mouth and broad chin added an illusion of age, but he was in fact vigorous in an unflappable way.[57]

His parents, Patrick Nogle Hayes and Mary O'Donnell Hayes, were residents of Pittsburgh where Ralph attended school and Holy Ghost College.[58] Confirming one's impressions, he was diocesan superintendent of schools after his ordination in Rome on September 18, 1909.[59] In 1925, he was appointed pastor of St. Catherine's and director of the CCD program in the diocese, a tiny circumstance which undoubtedly qualified him for a bishopric in a sparsely settled area like Montana.

BISHOP GERALD SHAUGHNESSY

The Pope's second appointee was for Seattle, "the Rev. Dr. Gerald Shaughnessy S.M., Marist College, Washington, D.C., member of the staff of the apostolic delegation."[60] Catholic papers noted that he "Is [a] Famous Scholar," referring to his celebrated book *Has The Immigrant Kept The Faith?*[61] If Shaughnessy was scholarly, he had come by it honestly. Born on May 19, 1887, in Massachusetts, the commonwealth of high culture, a son of Joseph and Margaret Shaughnessy, nee Colwell, he attended public schools in Boston and Plymouth, graduating from high school in 1904. A year later he won the Cronin four-year scholarship at

Boston College. Later, when his relations with Jesuits ran from cool to frigid, it was playfully alleged that the Jesuits had given him a scholarship and he never forgave them for it.

After matriculating at college, he taught in public schools and the Marists' All Hallows College in Salt Lake City. In 1916 he entered the Marists' Congregation and completed his studies for the priesthood in their college in Washington, D.C., where he was ordained by Giovanni Cardinal Bonzano on June 20, 1920.

Meanwhile, he had become a member of the staff of the apostolic delegate on a part-time basis. He made graduate studies in Europe for a year, earned a doctorate at Catholic University, and lectured at the Marists' College. He also published two other books and served as novice master.[62] Nobody accused him of playing too much golf.

Shaughnessy was a handsome man in a kind of chilling way. He wore a well-trimmed beard that *Time Magazine* mischievously likened to a goat's. This, like his stiff looking hair, had turned gray, increasing rather than diminishing his appearance of serenity. He wore no glasses, unfortunately for his subjects, because without them his eyes glowed darkly, like those of a prefect, intense and penetrating. His thin eyebrows made them look larger than they were. When he appeared in public he often tilted his head forward, as if listening to something confidential, like a father confessor. After his consecration he usually signed his letters and documents, "Gerald Shaughnessy, S.M. by the grace of God and the authority of the Apostolic See Bishop of Seattle." No one could doubt that he took himself seriously.

The two new bishops were consecrated during the same week, Bishop Shaughnessy on September 19, 1934. For the ceremony he chose the crypt of the National Shrine of the Immaculate Conception, which was under construction.[63] Archbishop Ameleto Giovanni Cicognani, Apostolic Delegate, was the principal consecrator and he was assisted by Bishop Michael Keyes of Savannah and Bishop White of Spokane as co-consecrators.[64] The choice of White, a very generous gesture by Shaughnessy, brought him from the relative obscurity of a provincial town into the glamorous limelight of the capital, which really meant little to him. His was a priestly involvement; the rest did not matter.

Hayes was consecrated two days later in St. Paul's Cathedral in Pittsburgh by Bishop Hugh Boyle of that city and co-consecrators Bishop James Griffin of Springfield, Illinois and Bishop Alphonse Smith of Nashville. On October 1, accompanied by Griffin, Hayes departed for Helena, where the customary welcome committees praised and all but buried him with attention.[65] He was installed on October 5, as Helena's fourth bishop, with Archbishop Howard presiding. Bishop Griffin preached for the occasion and the *Catholic Sentinel* presented a brief account of it. "Bishop Griffin said that Catholics are behind President Roosevelt in his heroic fight for social justice." Then a direct quote from the bishop's sermon: "The NRA does not go as far as Pope Pius XI leads in his Encyclicals but the NRA is an effort to do for the American people what the Catholic Guilds did for the people of the Middle Ages."[66]

SHAUGHNESSY'S SEATTLE ADVENT

There was a curious prelude to Shaughnessy's arrival in Seattle. During O'Dea's later years a small faction of older priests, having disapproved of the turn of events in the diocese, formed a kind of informal society of critics, a commonplace occurrence in the course of human events. One of these malcontents, however, carried his criticism beyond the limits of the diocese. He wrote regularly to the papal delegate in Washington, complaining chronically about everything and revealing all the petty foibles of the clergy by verse and chapter. His obnoxious letters were always placed at "the Seattle desk" in the delegate's chambers, to be acknowledged by its clerk in the course of his duties. And who was the clerk at "the Seattle desk?" Father Gerald Shaughnessy!

Thus it happened that when Shaughnessy arrived in Seattle to be installed bishop, there was very little he did not already know about the clerics of the diocese. This was bad enough, at least for the clerics, but this unforeseen blunder was embarrassing to the bishop as well. Presumably, Shaughnessy's appointment to Seattle had been decided long since in the delegate's office. Lacking knowledge of this, Seattle priests, including the Benedictines and Jesuits, signed a petition to the Holy See requesting that Bishop McGrath of Baker City be transferred to Seattle. They wanted him for a bishop. This, too was known to Shaughnessy, and it did not make him feel as welcome as he thought he deserved.

On Tuesday following the installation of Bishop Hayes in Helena, October 10, Archbishop Howard presided again for the installation of Bishop Shaughnessy in Seattle. The ceremony, carried out with meticulous concern, since the new bishop was already recognized as being touchy in such matters, was broadcast to the public on station KOL, another first for Shaughnessy, indicating his willingness to accept innovation. Indeed, were the truth known, there would be many innovations in favor of strict observance of church laws, mostly in technical matters of which the new bishop was exceedingly fond.

All in all, it was not a good beginning for "the goat-bearded bishop of Seattle."

THE BISHOPS' AD LIMINA VISITS

While the nation groaned under the painful burden of unemployment, the year 1933 ended peacefully for the Northwest church. It was a mild winter in the Northwest that year, and record-breaking floods in late December occupied the attentions of many Catholics who were beginning to experience the malaise that had struck eastern America much earlier. Three of our bishops were planning their *ad limina* visits to Rome. Construction on Coulee Dam was begun. The Citizens' Conservation Corps, established by President Roosevelt and administered by Army officers, brought thousands of young men from the East to labor in Northwest forests, making roads and fire trails. Many of these were Catholics, so chaplains were appointed for them and periodically bishops administered the sacrament of confirmation in the remote camps.[67]

In the new year, Archbishop Howard was the first to depart for Rome. He left New York for Havre on January 17 and after his formal visit at the Vatican he sailed for the Holy Land where Bishop O'Hara joined him.[68] Meanwhile, Bishop White left Spokane on Monday, January 22, and was received by Pius XI on February 12, also a Monday.[69]

The third bishop to depart for Rome was McGrath of Baker City. At the end of May he sat with Pius XI who glanced at his formal report on the condition of the Baker Diocese, then said to him: "Tell me, what do you do about the religious education of the children not in Catholic schools, of the children in the isolated, rural districts?"[70]

The bishop was too modest. He admitted "that religious instruction of these children left much to be desired. Pastors and their assistants did what they could, but other pastoral duties frequently crowded out the regular religious instruction of their children...."[71]

The Holy Father offered a suggestion: "Go back and establish the Confraternity of Christian Doctrine in every parish. Enlist the aid of lay people to assist the priests in their work."[72]

The words of Pius XI sounded familiar, perhaps repetitious, but in reality, the Pope had introduced an important, almost new concept that was in keeping with his recent encyclical on Catholic Action. *Enlist the aid of lay people,* he said. For McGrath these words were like a direct revelation from God. Henceforth his diocese became the model for the whole country in its methods for using the laity in CCD. Not only did the lay people fill a great current need, they were being prepared for the future when the lack of priests created innumerable problems, especially in small dioceses like Baker.

GROWTH OF CCD

As previously noted, the roots of CCD were in the "vacation schools" in Eugene, Oregon, whence they spread to all parts of the Northwest. For example, summer vacation schools in western Oregon appeared as follows:

Lebanon in 1924, directed by Father Theodore Bernards.
Harrisburg and Monroe in 1925 directed by Father E.J. Murnane.
Estacada in 1925, directed by Father John Bernards.
Cloverdale in 1925, directed by Father Hildebrand Melchior, O.S.B.
Forest Grove in 1926, directed by Father H.E. Boesch.

In eastern Oregon, the first vacation schools in 1926 were conducted at Baker, La Grande, Pendleton, Condon and Heppner, with 217 children enrolled.

On March 19, 1930, Bishop Kelly of Boise, announced a program of vacation schools for the following summer:

Burke by the Sisters of Providence.
Sandpoint and Priest River by Sisters of the Immaculate Heart of Mary.
Rupert, New Plymouth, Shoshone and Pocatello by the Sisters of the Holy Cross.
Potlatch and Southwick by the Sisters of St. Joseph.
Thorncreek by the Ursulines.
Orofino by the Benedictine Sisters.[73]

Bishop White established the CCD in the Spokane Diocese on April 13, 1932 and classes were scheduled for the following summer.[74] Several years later the archbishop in Portland and the bishop in Seattle did likewise.[75] In these two cities, Portland and Seattle respectively, there were other timely developments that became an essential part of the American church scene. First, there was the Sunday Missal pamphlet published by the Catholic Truth Society. The first issue appeared in October, 1934. This numbered only five thousand copies.[76] Within a few years, however, the monthly editions numbered over one hundred thousand copies and these were distributed all over the world. Marriage and Burial Missals were introduced with similar results.

SERRA INTERNATIONAL

Finally, there was the Serra Club in Seattle. William O'Connell, editor of *The Catholic Northwest Progress*, published an authentic history of this while the founders were still living.

The first Serra Club had its beginnings in Seattle on Wednesday, Dec. 5, 1934, when four men met at luncheon for the purpose of discussing the forming of a service club to be composed exclusively of leading Catholic business and professional men. The four founders were: Harold E. Haberle, Daniel P. Rooney, Leo F. Sharkey and Richard B. Ward. They crystallized their ideas at a series of sessions, and at their fifth meeting, held in the home of Leo F. Sharkey, Jan. 2, 1935, it was determined to proceed with the organization. They decided to select as a major, or primary, purpose of the club one definite objective, representing a distinctive form of important Catholic action, not conflicting with that of any existing organization. For a secondary purpose, the club would promote friendliness and good fellowship among its members. They proposed to seek the approbation of the Bishop of the Diocese and to request the appointment of a chaplain, so that the club activities could be conducted with his spiritual advice.

A distinctly Catholic name of an outstanding historical figure of the church in America was to be chosen for the club. Membership was to be determined on a strictly selective and invitational basis, with prior investigation being made of each prospective member's Catholicity and his general reputation in the community with reference to his business or professional standard of ethics.

Harold E. Haberle was chosen as the first president and Richard B. Ward as the secretary-treasurer. By-laws, which had been prepared by Mr. Ward to implement the club's objectives, were adopted at this fifth meeting.

Four additional men who had been selected as prospective members were invited to attend the next session of the infant club. There were immediately integrated in the organization. This meeting, incidentally, was held in the Stewart Hotel (then the Gowman Hotel) where the Seattle Serra Club, now grown to a membership of 180, meets every Friday.

Selection of the primary objective and the name for the club were considered of such vital importance that much deliberation and discussion were devoted to their choice. The name "Serra" was proposed by John E. Bray at a meeting on March 6, 1935, with 35 members present. Father Junipero Serra (1713-1784), famed missionary of the Pacific Coast, was chosen as patron of the club.

The Serra objective: "fostering of vocations to the priesthood, and assistance in financing the education of seminarians" was unanimously adopted by the club at its meeting July 12, 1935. It was proposed by John I.

Janettee as a result of a suggestion made to him by Father James J. Kortendick, S.S., a member then of St. Edward's Seminary faculty. Full-hearted approval was given to the Serra Club and its objective by the late Most Reverend Gerald Shaughnessy, S.M., Bishop of Seattle, and His Excellency appointed the late Right Reverend Monsignor John F. Gallagher, vicar general, as the first chaplain of the Serra Club.

Enthusiasm of the Serrans for their objective overflowed the boundaries of Seattle and was communicated to Catholic leaders in Spokane, Tacoma, Portland, and San Francisco. Clubs were formed in those cities in the order named, with charters being granted by the Seattle Serra Club. Spread of the Serra movement made a central organization necessary, and representatives of five Pacific clubs met in Seattle July 2, 1938, and organized Serra International. Dr. T.V. Sheehan of Seattle was elected the first president of the international organization, and Father Leo J. Linahen, of the Portland Archdiocese (now at St. Anthony's in Portland), was its first chaplain. Father James V. Hamilton, of the Seattle Archdiocese chaplain of Serra International; and Bishop Shaughnessy himself was the third International chaplain.

The Holy See placed the seal of its approval on the work of Serra Clubs by affiliating them with the Pontifical Work for Priestly Vocations, which the Holy Father had set up in the Sacred Congregation of Seminaries and Universities. Serra is the only organization of laymen affiliated with this pontifical work. The diploma of affiliation was issued by the Holy See in 1951.[77]

FATHER JOSEPH GILMORE

Whenever missionaries from Helena, Montana, visited Bear Gulch, they offered Mass in the home of Mr. and Mr. Christopher Lennen at Bearmouth, which was the entrance of the gulch. On May 5, 1934, the Lennens, having survived the many bears in their backyard, enjoyed the privilege of a Golden Anniversary Mass celebrated by His Excellency Bishop Hayes himself. This was the first time a bishop had visited Bear Gulch, which is not surprising.[78] No mayors or governors had been there either.

The bishop's companion was his chancellor, Father Joseph Gilmore, a man to watch. Gilmore, born in New York on March 23, 1893, was the son of John Joseph and Mary Teresa Gilmore, nee Hanrahn, who moved with their five year-old son to Anaconda, Montana in 1898. The boy attended local parochial schools, then St. Joseph's College in Dubuque. Having expressed his desire to be a priest, he was sent by Bishop Carroll to the Urban College of the Propaganda in Rome. At the precocious age of twenty-two he was ordained to the priesthood by Basilio Cardinal Pompilj on July 25, 1915.[79]

Gilmore's blue eyes, shaggy eyebrows and angular, craggy appearance helped to make him popular with Montana boys at Carroll College where he was assigned to teach English and Latin. Later he was employed in parish work. His very masculine personality asserted itself through leadership and aggressive conduct, which attracted Bishop Finnigan's attention. The bishop made him his chancellor. So there he was when Hayes arrived, running the diocese after Finnigan's premature death. No one then had the vaguest suspicion that Hayes would depart in a few months, and that Gilmore would succeed him.

UNIVERSITY OF PORTLAND

Meanwhile in Portland some significant changes were being made. At Columbia University, after much deliberation, the old name was dropped and another replaced it. To acquire legal permission for the title of "University of Portland," the administration paid off Mark P. Paulson for relinquishing his claim to the name, which he had previously copyrighted.[80] Father Joseph J. Boyle, C.S.C., eighth president of the university (1934-1936) announced the change on February 15, 1935, and released the following press report to expose the university's position.

> Archbishop Christie, the great pioneer and educator who founded the University, chose the name Columbia in honor of the river that figures so prominently in the life and history of Oregon, and while the school was only a college preparatory the name was eminently appropriate. But when the school became a University, an awkward situation was created because of the existence of Columbia University of New York City.... For the last few years a demand on the part of the alumni and friends of the University for a change in the name has become more and more insistent. Multnomah University was suggested, as was, likewise, McLoughlin University, in honor of the pioneer Dr. John McLoughlin. But with the recognition of the school by the accrediting agencies and with the unusual increase of students from Portland, there arose a desire to secure for the school a name which would forever link it with the beautiful City of Roses. It was in consequence of this desire that the name University of Portland was selected.[81]

The university's historian commented favorably on the innovation: "In A real sense it [the change of name] was the beginning of the end of that fixation with the University of Notre Dame so characteristic of the early era; but more importantly, the new name demonstrated that determined effort on the part of the Holy Cross fathers to fasten the University to its city, to make it truly a regional institution of higher learning. In brief, the administrative leadership in that era recognized the challenge: either advance boldly or watch the school wither away. Happily they chose the former."[82]

Archbishop Howard undoubtedly approved the new name. He had revealed his own attitude on name change and identity with the city when he promoted the title "Portland in Oregon" for the archdiocese. There was nothing stuffy about Howard. He not only left the past behind him, he was usually in the vanguard of change.

His determination, then, to have a downtown chapel in Portland surprised no one. Having overcome enough obstacles to reform a state house, he announced at last that the downtown chapel called St. Vincent de Paul would be established at South West Third and Ankeny Street. Adjoining the chapel for the convenience of the down and out men in the Burnside district, there would be a warm reading room, open seven days a week. The archbishop blessed this long sought facility on September 3, 1935.[83] It has flourished ever since.

Two weeks later, Howard was in Spokane to deliver the keynote address at the First Northwest Catholic Action Conference. On October 9, 1935, this conference convened "for the purpose of bringing the hierarchy, the clergy, and the laity together to pool knowledge and experiments on common problems."[84] Seven dioceses were represented and twenty-five hundred leaders from all walks of life participated in its sessions. Pope Pius XI regarded it as sufficiently prestigious that he sent a special message, which Howard read. His was a pleasant manly voice, which carried with it a subliminal message: that he was a tolerant man.

DEPARTURE OF BISHOP HAYES

There are times when some bishops are like birds of passage. They come and go quickly, remaining scarcely long enough to make their nests. Such was the case with Bishop Hayes. On September 11, 1935, in residence for less than three years, he was transferred to a new post in Rome as Titular Bishop of Hieropolis and rector of the North American College.[85] While no one, given the talents of Hayes, could doubt the advisability of the change, the people of Helena were greatly distressed. They had built their magnificent cathedral and since it was completed in 1924 three different bishops had occupied it, while one year out of every four, its bishop's throne had stood idle, as empty as the saddle in a dead general's funeral cortege.

HELENA EARTHQUAKES

Hayes was still in Pittsburgh enroute to Rome on the morning of October 13, 1935. Like other Americans, he was shocked by what he learned that day. Helena was experiencing a series of violent earthquakes that were gradually shaking down its buildings including those of the diocese. Hayes did not wait for a train. He took the first plane flight he could get, a most daring procedure in those dilatory days, and landed in Helena to offer his help while the ground still rumbled and swayed.[86] What he learned was not reassuring. Almost every Catholic institution in the city had been destroyed or seriously damaged.

The quakes continued for weeks. On October 19, the seventh day of the ordeal, papers estimated there had been sixty quakes in six days. On November 1, the *Spokesman-Review* referred to "19 perilous days of shakes" and on November 7 it noted that "Helena [was] jolted for the 877th time." In the downtown area, pedestrians no longer used the sidewalks; because of falling bricks they cautiously walked down the middle of the streets instead.

The Catholics, for all their prayers and holy water, were treated by the gods of earthquakes like everyone else. Two of the walls at Carroll College had collapsed. St. Mary's Church and rectory were badly damaged "in utter ruin," the pastor said. St. Joseph's Orphan Home and St. John's Hospital were declared unsafe. The orphans were moved to the cathedral rectory while the patients were removed by ambulance, with the help of the United States Army, to St. James Hospital in Butte, about eighty miles distant. The House of the Good Shepherd and St. Vincent's Academy had to be abandoned also. Even the cathedral of ponderous stone was severely damaged though it was not beyond saving.

The bishops in other dioceses announced their plans to assist Helena. On December 17, Bishop White dispatched a letter to all pastors in the Spokane Diocese for reading in the pulpits on December 22: "Not one of our eight church institutions in Helena and East Helena escaped without severe damage," he said. "Several of them are total losses. Contractors and engineers have placed the damage to our church properties at a figure approximating $500,000."[87]

THE FIFTH BISHOP OF HELENA

The dreaded quakes eventually subsided and Helena returned to something like normal. Then on December 9, 1935, the apostolic delegate revealed the name of the new bishop: Joseph Michael Gilmore. Many, no doubt, rejoiced. "1st. Montana Priest To Be Bishop," the Catholic papers asserted proudly, down-playing Gilmore's New York birthplace. Whatever else could be said, and it would be, Helena had acquired at last a bishop who would still be around for a few semesters. He was young, tough in spirit and as healthy as a hard rock miner. Had he not accidentally choked to death at the age of sixty-nine, he might have set a record like Archbishop Howard's.

Gilmore was consecrated in Helena Cathedral on February 19, 1936 by

Archbishop Amelato Giovanni Cicognani, apostolic delegate, who was assisted by Bishops Edwin O'Hara and Joseph McGrath.[88] Afterwards, the new bishop took up his duties with gusty vigor and a certain ease. After all, he had practically run the diocese for the last eight years.

TROUBLED TIMES

The next four years for the northwest church were rather dull. Catholic news was dominated by events elsewhere, the continued persecution of the church in Mexico; the Civil War in Spain and the slaughter there of tens of thousands of Catholics; and most of all by Hitler's rise to power and cruel oppression in Europe. Over all was the pall of lugubrious apprehension, unemployment, the "inevitable" war in Europe and an aging pontiff in his struggle with Mussolini and Hitler.

By contrast, our problems were miniscule. Our progress, too, was minimal, and though opposition to the church had been reduced to Judge Rutherford and his Jehovah's Witnesses, there were a few setbacks which, in the context of the times, appeared to be the end of the world.

The Jesuits, for example, had five more devastating fires. The first was St. Stanislaus school in Lewiston, Idaho, which was totally lost on November 3, 1935. A few weeks later, the missionaries' residence at Sacred Heart Mission, DeSmet, burned literally to the ground. Then, on August 4, 1936, St. Francis Regis Mission Church near Kettle Falls, burned down for a second time, while Father George Kugler was away at Inchelium conducting CCD classes.[89] Another disaster was at St. Mary's Mission near Omak, also the second major fire there. The Dominican Sisters were canning fruit on July 31, 1938, when the entire complex of convent, girls' school, kitchen, and dining halls caught fire. The little Indian boys, summoned for help, rushed into the bakery and carried out freshly made sweet rolls, leaving everything else behind, and while the flames roared, they gravely stood guard over the rolls at a safe distance. First things first. The entire complex with most of its contents was lost.

The most disastrous of the fires was again at Sacred Heart Mission, DeSmet on April 4, 1939. While the Indians were devoutly making their annual retreat, the church burst into flames that spread so rapidly that not even the Blessed Sacrament could be saved. More than five hundred rare books and priceless manuscripts in Indian languages were lost. Also lost were the early mission diaries and correspondence of great historical value.[90] This tragedy is still remembered as the greatest in the mission's long history.

Regarding new churches, hospitals and schools, there is little to report. A few new churches were established. Two small hospitals were built and an older one acquired.[91] Cathedral High School in Helena was established by the new bishop, who simply merged the high school department of Carroll College with St. Vincent's Academy, the first school for whites in Montana.[92] For some this maneuver by Gilmore appeared to be ominous. Was he, like his predecessor Bishop Carroll, lukewarm, or worse, toward the religious men and women in his diocese? Time would tell. One facet of the bishop's personality, however, was already recognized: he was exceedingly kind to his own diocesan priests, who responded with loyalty and affection. Whatever the future held, it could not be all bad.

VIGOROUS PROGRESS BY BISHOP SHAUGHNESSY

Most of the action was in Seattle. Bishop Shaughnessy brought with him boundless energy and enough ideas for an encyclopedia. Not all of them were popular, especially with his own priests, most of whom regarded him as a kind of reformer to correct the "excessive" paternalism of his predecessor.

On the surface, at least, most of Shaughnessy's activities involved procedures and social reforms that were sorely needed. There was a Miss Marian Marks, officially the "National Organizer for the Confraternity of Christian Doctrine," who was a kind of pious sensation nationally, like Father Dan Lord in his youth rallies. One of Shaughnessy's first deeds was to invite Miss Marks to Seattle for meetings with the pastors of parishes and he personally introduced her to the first assembly held, making his point as clear as daylight.[93] Then he brought Father William Walsh from Scranton to organize the department of Catholic Charities.

Walsh arrived on January 15, 1936. Like the bishop, he lost no time in making things happen. During the following August, the National Conference of Catholic Charities held its Twenty-Second Annual Meeting in Seattle; two archbishops, twelve bishops and ten thousand priests, religious, and laity assembled in the Civic Auditorium for the opening night. They listened to, or at least heard, Governor Clarence Martin of the state and Mayor Fred Dore of Seattle, describe America's poverty, a subject not entirely foreign to them.[94]

The bishop seemed to be getting up a head of steam. As he reorganized the diocesan archives and shuffled around the pastors, demoting one for an alleged infraction of the marriage regulations, he looked around for other conquests and settled on the idea of street preaching. He acquired from the East a noted convert and lay preacher who initiated the English style of soap-box lectures in public parks. On August 30, 1936, Theodore Dorsey made his debut. In Volunteer Park he began his "open air" polemics, using a car equipped with an amplifier so that no one could overlook him. More than a thousand idle and curious people gathered around to hear about "Christ Who Is He?"[95] Subsequently Dorsey moved to Seattle's Skid Row, where he spoke on street corners, like the Salvation Army without the brass band.

Archbishop Howard was impressed. He appointed a group of priests in Portland to conduct similar lectures in front of the downtown chapel. This form of street preaching on Sunday afternoons proved to be so effective in gathering audiences that it was continued for many years.[96]

But Shaughnessy rose to higher things. He next acquired a "Mother Mission" of his own, a shiny trailer chapel, which was hitched to the bumper of a car. On July 11, 1937, he blessed it under the patronage of St. Paul, and sent it on its way to rural areas under the supervision of Father Joseph Gustafson of St. Edward's Seminary. Assisting him were two seminarians, William and Cornelius Power from Seattle. The first Mass in the Motor Chapel was at Attanum Creek, site of the Oblates' old St. Joseph's Mission, which had been restored by the Knights of Columbus after Father Thomas Sherman, son of the famous general, goaded them into doing it.[97]

Attanum Creek reminded the bishop of the Indians who had been all but forgotten in the long struggle of keeping up with progress. The Jesuits had care of the Yakimas at White Swan. On the West Coast there were something like two thousand Indians of lesser tribes for whom little had been done since Chirouse left them. Shaughnessy requested the Benedictines at St. Martin's to provide them with a missionary. St. Martin's historian tells what followed:

> During a visit of our Rt. Rev. Abbot to the Bureau of Catholic Missions in Washington, D.C., the spiritual care of the two thousand or more Indians on the Quinault, Makah and other reservations in the northwestern part of the State, was discussed. Only occasional visits had been made to the reservations during the past years. As a result, the care of this field of labor was assigned to St. Martin's and the Most Rev. Bishop of the Diocese of Seattle appointed Father Benedict Schweitzer as Indian missionary of Clallam and the western part of Jefferson counties. The new appointee took up his residence at Port Angeles in January 1938, from which place he made weekly trips to his new missionary fields. In September he purchased a house at Forks, where he ministered to the spiritual needs of the natives until his recall to the Monastery in 1944.[98]

So far the only opposition the bishop met came from Catholics, who sometimes saw threats to their own priorities in the great New Order of His Excellency. Then "Judge" Rutherford appeared. On June 5, 1938, the "Judge" delivered a violent attack against all religions in the Civic Auditorium in Seattle, in Shaughnessy's own back yard. More than nine thousand Jehovah's Witnesses cheered him as he railed before a microphone, which carried his voice over an all-coast network of radio stations. Needless to say, there was the devil to pay. All of the churches and newspapers in Seattle hastened to repudiate the charges and to expose the fallacies of the phony prophet. During the fray, Bishop Shaughnessy's letter in defense of Christianity was read in many Protestant pulpits.[99] Not even the Ku Klux Klan had inspired this much cozy fellowship, so the Catholics gained more by the outrage than anyone else.

A month later, taking things in stride, Shaughnessy presided over the Fifth Diocesan Synod in St. James Cathedral.[100] One finds in the report for this synod, called the *"Acta,"* an evaluation for the well organized nature of Seattle's new administration. There were fifty-three pages of Latin, including the names of those priests "invited and present without the privilege of voting." Pages fifty-four to eighty-three contained 181 rules, like those for church music. For example, the only instrument permissible in church was an organ. "Unchurchly compositions are strictly banned." There were three pages of rules concerning the chancery and all of the rules were printed in *English*, making it difficult to violate them with ignorance as an excuse. Pages eighty-nine to ninety-five presented examples of the proper forms to be used including wills in favor of the diocese and the last five pages made explicit the current regulations for the Income Tax.[101]

I suspect that the majority of priests present were somewhat bored with it all, but this was the sort of occupation the bishop was very good at and he enjoyed it immensely. Fortunately the synod lasted only one day.

Finally, there was the chancery building. Shaughnessy believed in prestigious chanceries. In Washington, while he was there, the apostolic delegate had provided an elegant new one, the details of which were published in many newspapers, eliciting, as usual, some criticism not unlike that of Judas. On July 18, 1938, Seattle's old chancery was demolished to permit the construction of a new one on the same site. This was begun on the following Monday, and was completed in January 1939, at which time the offices were occupied.[102]

Like the fires of the Jesuits, these lively exploits, among many others by the bishop of Seattle, gained everyone's attention. Bishop White in Spokane was undoubtedly impressed, but, accepting his own scaled-down status as the bishop of a much smaller diocese, he concerned himself with less momentous undertakings, for example, the restoration of old St. Paul's Mission near Kettle Falls.[103] There was nothing ostentatious about Bishop White. When he bought a car, for example, for his needs as bishop, he bought the cheapest he could find, two

Chevrolets, paying cash to save money, and invited Father Louis Taelman, pastor of the diocesan Indian missions, to turn in his old car and take his choice of the new ones.

BISHOP WALTER FITZGERALD

White collaborated closely with the Jesuit Provincial, Father Walter Fitzgerald, who lived in Portland. There were, in fact, more Jesuits in his diocese than his own diocesan priests. Some accused him of favoritism toward Jesuits, but this criticism could be dispelled as easily as looking at one's watch. White on occasion was severe with Jesuits, but he was also kind to them.[104] He regarded all of his priests with fatherly affection. When it was announced that Fitzgerald had been appointed as coadjutor bishop of Alaska with the right of succession to the venerable Bishop Raphael Crimont, White quickly contacted him to offer the resources of the diocese for his consecration. The new Jesuit provincial, Father William Elliott, was greatly relieved, and in the name of the bishop-elect accepted White's generous offer. It was arranged, then, that the consecration would be celebrated in St. Aloysius Church, Spokane on the feast of St. Matthew, February 24, 1939.

Meanwhile, the Pope died. On February 14, at 5:31 o'clock in the morning, Pius XI, the 260th successor of St. Peter, passed into eternal life, for which he had often prayed. "World in Mourning As Beloved Pontiff Passes," the newspapers said. Eugene Cardinal Pacelli, Secretary of State, was declared *camerlengo* to arrange for the forthcoming election of a new pope.

The church was still in mourning when Fitzgerald was consecrated by Bishop Crimont, assisted by Bishops White and Robert Armstrong of Sacramento. The epic nature of the occasion was not lost on Crimont. He proudly used historic vestments and took care that all details concerning them were widely publicized. The pontifical pectoral cross he used had once been Archbishop Segher's, the crozier Cardinal Farley's, which had been a gift from the Cardinal on his deathbed to Crimont, the bishop-elect's pectoral cross had been presented in 1873 to Archbishop Gross by Savannah's diocesan priests. From Archbishop Gross it had passed down to Archbishop Christie who gave it to Crimont for his consecration in 1917. The crozier Bishop Fitzgerald carried was brand new, a gift to him from Father Felix Geis, a diocesan priest from Lakeview, Oregon.[105] Bishop Fitzgerald had no other more intimate friend than Geis. They had been boys together at Gonzaga, with "Smiling Bob" Armstrong. Though Armstrong had become a bishop before him, Fitzgerald was the first native son of Washington state to be elevated to the episcopacy.[106]

When the photograph of the prelates was being taken after the ceremony, Crimont, already somewhat feeble with age, gazed placidly about, while his new coadjutor, grasping his new crozier as firmly as he would a baseball bat, laughingly greeted his many friends in the crowd, seemingly as carefree as a school boy on graduation day.

At a reception that evening, the principal speaker was Charles P. Moriarity of Seattle. First he praised the new bishop, then he went on to talk about the war brewing in Europe and about men who, more than ever, were looking to the message of the church. Perhaps Moriarity was right. Many were looking to the church but many more could not hear its message because of the noise made by demagogues.

HOLY NAMES COLLEGE, SPOKANE

Three days later, on February 27, 1939, the Sisters of the Holy Names in Spokane announced plans for a new college.[107] This was accomplished without mentioning personal names, of course; the sisters in these enigmatic times often remained anonymous. The papers reported the event with perky approval and produced a long quotation by Bishop White. An excerpt of this demonstrates his bland style.

> Permit me to congratulate the Sisters of the Holy Names of Jesus and Mary for their progress in the work of education . . . because of the crowded conditions of your present building as well as the necessity of separating the college from the high school, the need of a new building is altogether evident. We shall, therefore, be happy to have you plan a campaign to be conducted during a short period in the early part of Lent for the raising of $100,000 needed for the project.[108]

There seemed to be compelling reasons for the college. Marylhurst in Oregon was thriving. Spokane's Gonzaga University accepted women only in extension classes or summer school. There was no local Catholic College for women and a disproportionate number of Catholic girls were attending Washington State College at Pullman. The bishop was hopeful that the new institution would attract some of the girls back into the fold of Catholic education.

During the previous year, the sisters had acquired the stately Stanton Home on Mission and Hamilton for a residence for girls, at a cost of $7,000.[109] An additional investment of $100,000, it was reasoned, would provide two units for classes, dining facilities and gymnasium, for such lady-like pursuits as archery, art, music, and dancing. The fledgling institution would function in the old academy building on Superior Street until the new quarters were ready.[110]

On March 7, specific plans were revealed. The new college buildings would be designed by architect Henry C. Bertelson. Additional land was donated by the Jesuits. The faculty names were published, which was a daring break with tradition: Sister Esther Mary was the new superior and heading the list of instructors was Father John Dunne of Gonzaga. Classes would begin on October 1 and the new quarters would be occupied in the following autumn.

It was an optimistic beginning, like St. Edward Seminary's. But like the latter, it scarcely survived beyond the deaths of its founders. No one then, or for some years to come, could see that the church in America had already changed. The students of Holy Names College like Catholic students everywhere, belonged to that generation that would create the greatest revolution within the church since the sixteenth century.

Meanwhile, the last of the traditional popes was elected. On March 2, 1939, Cardinal Pacelli became Supreme Pontiff, taking the name of Pius XII. It was his successor, John XXII, who, recognizing the temper of the times, opened the windows of the Vatican to let the revolution in.

BISHOP O'HARA TRANSFERRED TO KANSAS CITY

Bishop White was strong on basics like CCD and the Rural Life Program. In 1938, he requested the Rural Life Conference to choose Spokane for its national meeting in 1939. He received a favorable response, and sessions were scheduled for October 15 to 17. White counted heavily on the support of Bishop O'Hara who was near at hand.

Suddenly, on April 15, 1939, White was startled by the Vatican's announcement that O'Hara, in his ninth year as Bishop of Great Falls, had been transferred to Kansas City. The appointment was effective immediately, leaving vacant the see of Great Falls.[111]

It was in a sense, Spokane's turn to provide a bishop. White had shown special interest in William Condon, for whom he had secured a monsignorship just two years earlier.[112] It was quite plain to some that White supported Condon for advancement and local wags were predicting that he would succeed O'Hara. Reasons for these conjectures were not hard to find: Condon, for example, was a native son. He was highly regarded as an administrator, and he had recently been honored by the Jesuits at Gonzaga University who made him an honorary doctor of letters. He looked the part of a bishop. Once slim and willowy, he had become heavier in these middle years, but not stout—a substantial churchman. He possessed a broad face, with just a touch of a sardonic smile on it, and sparkling eyes, indicating, I think, his Gaelic ancestry with its odd mixture of humor and cynicism. Condon was no Irish pope, but occasionally he could be as demanding as one and as arbitrary as some priests' housekeepers. Fortunately he enjoyed more gentle traits also, which balanced off those that were less benevolent.

BISHOP THOMAS ARTHUR CONNOLLY

While rumors abounded about Great Falls, there was another prelate's appointment in San Francisco. On June 10, 1939, Father Thomas A. Connolly of San Francisco, affectionately called "Tac" by his closer associates, was appointed titular bishop of Sila and auxiliary to Archbishop John Mitty of that city. Connolly, less than forty years old, son of Thomas and Catherine Connolly, nee Gilsenan, had been ordained in San Francisco on June 11, 1926, by Archbishop Edward Hanna. He was secretary to Hanna from 1934 to 1935, then to Archbishop John Mitty, who succeeded Hanna. He was consecrated bishop on August 24, 1939, by his archbishop, who was assisted by Bishops Robert Armstrong of Sacramento and Thomas Gorman of Reno.

A betting man would say that this was only the beginning of a distinguished church career. Tall and very handsome, he carried himself in the grand manner of Celtic aristocracy. His head of heavy, dark hair, thin eyebrows and cold, blue eyes shielded by rimless glasses, presented an appearance of the great corporate executive who weighs his words carefully and expects them to be obeyed. In a crowd he would always stand out, a dominating figure whose personality radiated strength rather than warmth. In the years to come he would keep his handsome head of dark, wavy hair. He would become the fifth bishop of Seattle and its first archbishop, a man of stupendous accomplishments, who had left more monuments to his memory than any other person in the history of the Northwest.

SPOKANE'S NATIONAL RURAL LIFE CONFERENCE

When Condon was finally appointed to Great Falls on August 5, 1939, few were surprised or disappointed. He scheduled his consecration for October 18, the day following the conclusion of the Rural Life Conference already in the making, and began preparations for the event with customary interviews with tailors and reporters. There was nothing simple about being a bishop.

There was nothing simple about the conference either. Its sessions, marked with anxiety over the Germans' invasion of Poland on September 2, began with prayer and dismay on October 15 and lasted for three days. The schedule for its many activities appeared on the front page of the

Inland Catholic, which included some extracurricular activities, such as "evening cards" and "turkey dinners." The attendance was not less because of the war, though it was obvious that Spokane's remoteness from eastern interests had discouraged prelates from attending. Three archbishops, however, and a score of bishops joined many thousands of the laity in discussions and meetings. Happily the youth section, conducted at Gonzaga by Father Dan Lord, stirred up so much fervor that older participants caught the spirit and the conference was terminated with unexpected gusto.

Bishop Condon was consecrated on schedule in Our Lady of Lourdes Cathedral by Bishop White. Assisting White were Bishops McGrath of Baker and Kelly of Boise, making the occasion refreshingly spiritual, a local affair completely dominated by three neighboring bishops. Condon had already packed his bags. He left soon for Great Falls where he was installed as its third bishop in St. Ann's Cathedral on October 26. His would be a long reign, not without controversy or personal illness. But compared to the storms about to break upon Helena, his diocese remained as calm as a summer lake.

CATHOLIC CENTRAL IN PORTLAND

Back in 1858, when Portland's Catholic parish was only six years old, land east of the river was purchased for a Catholic cemetery.[114] The first burial there was on October 12, 1858. One Louisa Frederica Koblite, was laid to rest on that day. Until Mount Calvary was opened in 1888, this pioneer burial place served Catholics of the area. The archdiocese retained the property, including the unused portion and here it was that Archbishop Howard planned to build his long cherished Central Catholic High School.

Eighty years after that first burial, on May 1, 1938, His Grace announced plans for construction. The Centenary of the Archdiocese was being celebrated that year; it was his wish that the crowning event would be the completion and dedication of the school.

Father Francis Leipzig, summoned from Eugene, was placed in charge of the Centenary, which was designed to awaken interest in the Catholic-roots in Oregon. An impressive compilation of parish histories was produced by the *Catholic Sentinel* as a centenary edition, liturgical presentations were well attended, and there was a great renewal of faith in the message of the early missionaries.[115] But the climax of it all was the dedication of Central Catholic.

The dedication occurred on May 9, 1939.[116] The apostolic delegate himself, Archbishop Cicognani, traveled from Washington, D.C. to preside, an extraordinary concession, when you think about it, to please another archbishop, who wanted the school so badly he literally begged for it. Studies in the new building did not commence until September 5, when 125 boys in freshman and sophomore grades responded to the first bell. Father Francis Schaefers was the first principal and his faculty consisted of one other priest and five sisters. Ever after, Central Catholic was the apple of Howard's eye and when he died, many long years later, he left for it in his will a carefully hoarded fortune to insure its perpetuity.

In other schools of the Northwest, there was significant progress, indicating a gradually increasing stability of enrollment, of support, and of improvement in methods of teaching. For example, the size of classes were cut down and school libraries were getting more support as America's economy improved.

From St. Edward's Seminary the first twelve graduates were ordained in St. James Cathedral. Among them was Father Cornelius Power, destined to be one of Howard's successors in Portland.[117] Carroll College in Helena was affiliated formally with the Catholic University of America on November 10, 1939. Construction on the new St. Mary's Academy in Portland was begun on August 5, 1940. At Seattle College two new schools were added to the facilities, engineering and nursing, and construction was approved for the new liberal arts building that marked the turning point in the college's history.[118]

Meanwhile, two new hospitals appeared. Providence in East Portland was erected and dedicated on September 8, 1941, as a unit of St. Vincent's Hospital. It was opened on September 15. The second hospital was in Idaho Falls, where privately-owned Spencer Hospital, closed during the previous year, was purchased by the townspeople for $25,000 and presented to the Sisters of St. Francis of Perpetual Adoration.[119] The sisters occupied the building and opened it as Sacred Heart Hospital on November 23, 1941.

From 1940 to 1941, due largely to America's preoccupation with the war in Europe, only six new churches were reported. Three of these, St. Gertrude's at Monse, St. Jude's at Usk, and St. Joseph's at East Omak, were built by the diocese of Spokane for the convenience of Indians.[120] What this suggests is that the church had not given up on Indian missions, despite the prevailing tendency in the country to ignore them. This was the period, especially, when the Indians were swept under the rug. Out of sight on reservations, too poor to support themselves, they starved or barely survived. Since the coming of the missionaries they needed the church more than ever before. In this context, then, one must place what follows, a tragic confrontation with the church, in which the Blackfeet Indians of Montana were caught squarely in the middle.

HOLY FAMILY MISSION CASE

The conflict over Holy Family Mission on the Blackfeet reservation raged for three years, then the Jesuits walked out. They moved out of the mission, lock, stock and barrel in September 1940, because they believed an impossible situation had been created. They had nearly starved with the Indians, or nearly froze to death for fifty-four years. Nothing daunted, they had survived unimaginable hardships like poverty, isolation, disease, misunderstandings and persecutions, but they had remained. Only a bitter controversy with the bishop finally dislodged them.

A detailed account of this appears elsewhere.[121] For the sake of an integral narration, however, some of this is presented here.

Troubles began during the provincialate of Father Walter Fitzgerald. Worrisome financial problems had begun to threaten the very existence of Holy Family, and Fitzgerald dispatched to the scene the province troubleshooter, Father Francis Dillon, to head off bankruptcy. Dillon soon learned that the title to the property had been turned over to the Catholic Indian Bureau in Washington, but the large debt on the mission, incurred with the approval of the bishop, was charged against the Jesuits.[122] Dillon's position was this: the mission, like the parish, had acquired a debt that the bishop had endorsed. The debt, therefore, was identified with the mission or the bishop, not the missionaries. If the Bureau returned the title to the Jesuits, who once owned the land, the Jesuits would pay the debt, otherwise the bishop was responsible.

The controversy, which received wide attention because of its precedence in the relationship of bishop with religious orders, was referred to the apostolic delegate in Washington. Cicognani first ruled that the bishop was responsible, since he had approved the debt, then later reversed his decision, stating that while the Bureau had the *legal* title to the mission, the Jesuits held the *canonical* title, and thus were responsible for the debt. The Jesuits, on the other hand, proposed a compromise. All should share the debt equally, the Jesuits, the bishop, and the Bureau.

At this point, Fitzgerald was appointed coadjutor bishop of Alaska and Father William Elliott became the Jesuit provincial. During his earlier months, Elliott requested a survey of the Indian missions, their histories, debts, and sources of revenue. A committee chaired by Dillon, prepared a devastating report. According to this, only one diocese (Spokane) out of seven in the Northwest, contributed anything at all to the Jesuit Indian missions. "They [the bishops] leave the whole burden to us," the report states, "as though it were not a part of their diocese as well.... They do give something to secular priests engaged in the same work."[123]

The committee was shocked to learn that each of these seven dioceses had received approximately $5,000 in 1938 from the Board of Catholic

Missions and from the Indian and Negro Collections throughout the United States. "Note well," the report continued, these monies are given for the Missionary Bishops and their Dioceses [annually]. We get nothing for the Indian work."[124]

Father Taelman, the dean of Indian missionaries at that time, was requested to submit a report on Jesuit performance. His response was very critical, not only regarding the status of the missions, which had been left in ruin by the complete withdrawal of government support for the Indian children, but also regarding the kind of service some Jesuits were rendering. "The sad fact," he said, "criticized by local Bishops, that for a number of years past, no Jesuit father has been trained or made to learn the Flathead language reveals a lack of proper interest in the spiritual welfare of the old Indians and the right administration of the Sacraments. There seems to be no justification for the sad neglect."[125]

There was more than a grain of truth in Taelman's bristling charges, but it should be noted that Taelman, isolated in western Montana, enjoyed a very narrow vision of the province's activities, and in particular, of its overwhelming financial problems.

The committee's report convinced Father Elliott that he should take a firm stand on Holy Family, so he withdrew the offer of a compromise. The dilemma remained unresolved until the beginning of the school year in 1939, when the Blackfeet Tribal Council offered to allocate $5,000 pending settlement of the crisis. This was less than half enough to provide for the school's current operations, and even this was contingent upon irredeemable conditions. Dillon expected the mission's chattels to be seized by creditors before the end of November, and despite his many appeals, he received no word whatever from the bishop or the Bureau. "So in brief," Elliott wrote, "the school has not opened. The Fathers, of course, are still there." Elliott gave them $150.00 for food.

The closing scene of this sorry imbroglio, presided over by His Eminence Cardinal Dougherty, Chairman of the Bureau's Board, was a very dramatic one. Present were Archbishops Spellman and Curley, Bishop Gilmore, Father John Tennelly of the Bureau, Father Zacheus Maher representing the Jesuits, and major creditors. Though very tense, the meeting was orderly, Maher later reported to Elliott. The bureau was exonerated of any responsibility. After much discussion the blame was placed on Bishop Gilmore, who had given explicit permission for the expenditures, and on Father John Prange, the Jesuit superior when the debts were incurred, "for mismanagement of large sums of money spent by him and his failure to keep accounts."[126] When the dust had settled, it was agreed that after the sale of the mission farm's equipment and animals, the balance of the debt was to be paid equally by the bishop and the Jesuits. The Bureau retained the title to the land.

The Jesuits did not abandon the Blackfeet. High in the Rockies, like a sharp-eyed eagle in his nest, Father Egon Mallman still lived at Heart Butte. Twenty miles south of Browning, isolated by bad roads and unpredictable weather, he lived for forty years in poverty and loneliness, serving 1500 Indians in a parish that spanned as many square miles. "I say Mass at Heart Butte one Sunday, Holy Family the second, Little Badger the third and Old Agency the fourth. But the schedule is upset in winter; last year I was snowed in for 50 days."[127]

Despite this kind of dedication of a faithful member, the Jesuits inherited, not the glory of St. Peter's mission or fifty-four years at Holy Family, but the odium of debt and closure that persisted for many long decades later.

TEXTBOOKS AND BUSES FOR PAROCHIAL SCHOOLS

The so-called anti-parochial school bill in Oregon had backfired, leaving many of Oregon's constituents embarrassed if not ashamed. Some tried to make amends and in Washington others joined them in seeking some forms of aid, not for parochial schools, but for the students who attended them. These efforts began to appear in the 1930's and took the form of proposing textbooks for so-called non-value courses like science, mathematics, and English grammar, or school buses to serve the immediate requirements of many children. Northwest Catholics, having welcomed the proposals, initiated in most cases by others, eagerly joined the lobbyists to secure favorable legislation.

In Washington State, it was a bus law that first gained the attention of Catholics. A bus law had been introduced in 1935, when the state's attorney general announced that it was unconstitutional. In November of the same year, however, this worthy amended his opinion by stating that Catholic students could ride school buses after all.[128] This was a start, but more than two years would elapse before formal legislation was adopted.

In March 1941, the Washington State Legislature passed this school bus law by a vote of one hundred and twelve to seventeen, providing for the transportation in public buses of children attending private and parochial schools. Supporters of the law based their argument on the Fourteenth Amendment of the United States Constitution, which guarantees equal protection.

The 1941 Washington law was immediately challenged by Elmer Allen, president of the Washington State School Director's Association, Bishop S. Arthur Huston of the Episcopal Diocese of Olympia, and the Seventh

Day Adventists.[129] The results of this appear later, for the struggle was long and bitter, not only in Washington, but in other states, including Oregon.

But Oregon's unique dispute, after the Compulsory School Bill, was the Catholics' attempt to gather for themselves, just a few crumbs from the rich man's table. Public education received *all* of the tax money for schools. The Catholics sought merely the use of textbooks which were distributed in public schools. Surely these could not be described as religious propaganda. Surely the loan of a mathematics book could not be construed as an aid to religion. The tug-of-war between Catholics and their opponents over this issue extended over a period of twenty years and, as often happened, the Catholics of Oregon lost the battle.

There will be more about this later. Time was on the side of reform. Sooner or later an educated public would be able to distinguish aid to religion and aid to the child. Until then, there would be no peace for the legislators, the bureaucrats, or the courts.

GONZAGA'S SPECTACULAR FIRE

On the eve of the greatest war in history, Gonzaga was financially stable at last. After ten precarious years, during which it barely survived on its meager income, the vast administration building comprising most of the space on the campus was remodeled, painted, and re-equipped. "God has His arms around us," said the president, Father Leo Robinson. Suddenly, the building was a shambles, a ruin left by a holocaust that swept away most of the improvements and acquisitions the president had laboriously built or gathered.[131]

The fire started during the night of December 10, 1941, just three days after Pearl Harbor. Spokane's fire department responded promptly to the alarm as did most of the neighbors. Hundreds, if not thousands, arrived to witness the free show, which was so spectacular that it could be seen from many parts of the city. Flames sweeping through the upper structure, carrying with them roof slate high into the air, earned countless admiring "oohs" and "ahs" from the excited spectators. This unrehearsed spectacle lasted most of the night, leaving behind damage estimated at $131,461.10, a mind boggling amount in those impecunious times.

The good news is that insurance covered it. While the conflagration elicited gushes of pity and sincere concern for the poor burned-out Jesuits, which did no harm for public relations, the insurance replaced the third and fourth floors of the building with newer and better laboratories and classrooms. It also provided renovations for the rest of the water-soaked structure. These improvements proved to be a godsend when the GI's descended upon the university five years later.

This greatest of Gonzaga's fires has always been associated with the beginning of the war. The one was a blessing not altogether disguised; the other a curse that changed the whole world, including the church in the Northwest.

18

MOSTLY ABOUT BISHOPS

1941–1955

It was no secret during the last days before Pearl Harbor that Bishop White's warm relationship with the editor of the Catholic paper had begun to cool. James Emmett Royce, an ardent defender of anything considered "Catholic," including Ireland's struggle for freedom, had taken very positive editorial positions on many controversial subjects, which irritated some influential Catholics of the diocese and created dignified consternation in the bishop's chancery.[1]

To begin with, Royce was militantly anti-Roosevelt. The American president had conveniently overlooked the persecution of the church in Mexico and despite wide Catholic opposition had pressed for formal recognition of "Red Russia." Roosevelt's cozy partnership with Winston Churchill and England, Ireland's persistent oppressor, and his chilly attitude toward Joseph Kennedy at the court of St. James, aroused Royce's pro-Irish loyalties.[2] He moved into a position of strong vocal opposition to an Anglo-American alliance, which irritated the bishop and evoked some criticism.

Roosevelt's successful efforts to mobilize the country for war, on the side of the English, of course, added injury to insult and pushed Royce, like Kennedy, into an unrelenting campaign for American neutrality. Royce recommended the example of Eire. "Eire Shows Way to American Catholics" he exclaimed in one of his paper's headlines.[3] "No Catholic Can Consent to Aid for Reds" he stated in another.[4] He accused "Hollywood" of making efforts "to increase war fever," and in the following week he printed a long NCWC report: "Assail Roosevelt's Denial That Religion Is Persecuted in Red Russia."[5] Many editorials followed on Harry Bridges, "the Pacific Coast's most vociferous Red," and the consequences of abandoning neutrality, which would occasion "Democracy's End."[6] Monsignor Fulton Sheen, he noted, "Says Church [Is] Crucified Between Two Thieves, Russia and Reich."[7]

No one could doubt where Royce and the *Inland Catholic* stood. Most Catholics, even among those of Irish descent, disagreed with him. Did he represent the views of the bishop? Was the bishop a pacifist? Royce said "yes." He published two excerpts from the bishop's file in a featured front page article, noting that both statements had been made in public.

> There are powerful influences at work to draw us into the present war in Europe. While protesting we do not want to go into it, we doubtless are being secretly impelled by the thought of how grand and glorious a thing it is, worth all the blood and wealth of the land, to save democracy that is being so direly threatened.
>
> And then we go in and discover too late, after spending years in intensifying hate, in slaughtering our brethren, in committing almost suicide ourselves, and in sowing savage seeds of still more gruesome wars, that in starting out to save democracy we end up by going totalitarian ourselves, no longer merely academically, but actually with not one whit left of what is our greatest glory now as American citizens, those God-given rights so correctly enumerated in the second paragraph of the Declaration of Independence."[8]

This appeared in the *Inland Catholic* on September 19, 1941. The second statement appeared one week later:

> I want emphatically to go on record now, nor do I think it too soon to say it, that I am definitely opposed to our entrance into the present war, if alas! we are not already in it.[9]

It would be unjust to judge either the bishop or Royce by what followed. Neither could predict the future. Pearl Harbor, of course, shattered Royce's hopes of neutrality, and deeply humbled, yet forthright, he admitted in his editorial for December 12, 1941, "That Catholic Forces of America [are] Strong in Defense of [the] Nation As War Breaks Out." and that "the war in the Pacific . . . has been forced on the United States."[10] "All that has gone before," he added sadly, "becomes merged in the grim FACT of WAR."[11] Subsequently, he was diligent in supporting the war effort, despite his deep convictions that war, as the bishop predicted, would change America forever.

THE INLAND REGISTER

Royce's *Inland Catholic* did not belong to the diocese, nor was the diocese its legal publisher. Bishop White had given it his blessing, which was a kind of official approbation, but he had never accepted it as his own. During recent months, when Royce's views on politics had clashed with his, he considered a ready alternative: publication of his own paper by the *Catholic Register* of Denver. The *Register* chain of diocesan papers provided for local Catholic news with an additional insert or second section containing national and world news. Twenty-nine American dioceses, mostly the smaller ones, had already teamed up with the *Register* for publishing their papers. White decided to withdraw his support from Royce's *Inland Catholic*. He appointed Father Terrence Tully, who was ordained that year, as his local editor and announced publication of the *Inland Register* as the thirtieth Catholic paper in the Denver chain.[12]

Before this development, Royce had accepted the position of dean of Gonzaga University's Law School and Dan Dirstine, his former assistant, became a carry-over "editor of news." On July 31, 1942, Dirstine publicly announced the termination of the *Inland Catholic* to be effective on August 28, 1942.[13] His carefully chosen words provided ill-concealed resentment toward the bishop's decision.

The Acme Stamp and Printing Company

[Edmund Ripple] will discontinue the publication of the Inland Catholic with the issue of August 28. This discontinuance is happening simply because His Excellency has decided that the Denver Register system can better serve the diocese.

It is not because of any lack of facilities or because of the disability of the management.

The Acme Stamp and Printing Co. will continue its corporate existence as a publisher . . . ."[14]

The new paper made its appearance on schedule, on Friday, September 4, 1942, with the title of *Inland Register*.[15] In his first issue, Father Tully revealed the thrust of the pope's new policy: local news would be given exclusive attention in the first section. His front page presented the following headline: "St. John Bosco Center Gift of Flannery's." This was about as "local" as one could make it.

The St. John Bosco Center was established that month in the so-called [Huetter] mansion at 429 East Sharp, near Gonzaga University. Purchased by the Milo Flannerys, who later endowed the Flannery Chair of Catholic Theology at Gonzaga University, this was converted into a home for twenty-four boys under the direction of three Holy Cross Brothers. Arrangements were made for the boys to attend Gonzaga High School.

CHANGES IN WORLD WAR II

In July of 1942, the War Production Board announced that "it would refuse preference rating for materials to construct church edifices."[17] A major institution, a new provincial house and novitiate for the Sisters of St. Joseph of Newark, had been completed in Bellingham before this military edict was promulgated.[18] Six new churches were also completed during the year despite the hardships created by it.[19] But the consequences were obvious: Catholic building activity would be restricted to only emergency type churches related to the war industry and to emergency hospitals, for the full duration of the war. No one objected. Thus Catholic news for this period concerned itself with "Catholic" war news on all fronts, mostly accounts of heroes and heroines whose destiny was sometimes fatal, but always pious. The war hysteria that swept all parts of the country, including the Northwest, expressed itself in patriotic soirees and bond sales, not to mention innumerable novenas or prayer sessions for the safety of family members. "The Catholic Who Neglects to Pray," said Bishop White, "Is Failing in His Patriotic Duty."[20]

This gratuitous observation on the conduct of the war reflects a change of heart in His Lordship. The American bishops' joint statement on "Victory and Peace" issued in November 1942, presented the United States and its allies as Crusaders in a deadly encounter with evil. We were on God's side. We were engaged in a conflict with nations "united in waging war to bring about a slave world—a world that would deprive man of his divinely conferred dignity, reject human freedom and permit no religious liberty." As one commentator has suggested, "similar examples of religious-patriotic rhetoric issued from Protestant and Jewish sources. Differing traditions had found a common theme."[21]

Major war industries, like the Kaiser Shipyards in Portland and Boeing in Seattle, occasioned massive shifts in populations, bringing into the Northwest large blocks of Catholics and other religious groups, like Baptists from the deep south, who enjoyed no previous exposure to real Catholics. The consequences were mostly favorable to the church, a sharp increase in the Catholic population, and better yet, "the effective beginning of the acceptance of religious pluralism. . . . "[22] While obstacles to peaceful coexistence for Catholics continued to plague them, the overt attacks made in the past vanished forever. Henceforth, opposition to Catholics would have to present itself in ambivalent forms.

CATHOLIC COLLEGES AND UNIVERSITIES AT WAR

The Catholic mens' colleges suffered most from the disruption of the war. Three of the seven in the Northwest held their own against the odds with the aid of government sponsored military programs. Three of the others barely survived and one, practically speaking, was terminated.

Before the war started, both Gonzaga and the University of Portland conducted the Civilian Pilot Training Program at government expense, and in September 1942, the University of Portland announced a "New Reserve Plan Set Up by Services."[23] This was an officers' training program, a kind of watered-down West Point, which attracted many students but ended in confusion.[24] Portland also was selected for the United States Cadet Nurse Corps. This proved to be a popular program, which established the foundations for the university's excellent School of Nursing.

Carroll College in Helena and Gonzaga were awarded contracts by the United States Navy for the V12 Program, a naval officers' course on campus. On July 1, 1943, three hundred apprentice seamen of the navy began their training on the Gonzaga campus. These students came from other colleges of the west, Loyola, Santa Clara, San Francisco, St. Martins, Seattle, Portland, and Mount Angel, to complete their studies in engineering, pre-medicine and so on. To accommodate them, the university established a tri-semester system.[25]

Seattle College, which was *de facto* coeducational, survived, in large part, because of the attendance of girls, and The College of Great Falls remained for the same reasons. The two Benedictine Colleges suffered most. St. Martin's lost many of its students to the armed forces, contributed three of its priests as chaplains and was deprived of its Abbot by death. Abbot Lambert expired suddenly from a heart attack on August 9, 1943.[26] He was replaced with St. Martin's third abbot, Raphael Heider on September 1.

Mount Angel kept its abbot, but lost its college. "By 1944," one of the monks admitted, "the Selective Service Act had begun the final decimation of the College of Mount Angel."[27] As the college declined, the seminary prospered, eventually requiring all of the abbey's resources of housing and classrooms for seminarians who came from all parts of the country. Young men got deferments to study for the priesthood, but they had to attend school year-round. "Consequently the monks shifted teaching loads to the seminary and began offering summer programs for full year study."[28]

Because of the war, Seattle College also presented an accelerated program, adopting the "emergency" quarter system, presumably for the duration. After the war, however, the quarter system was retained. This eliminated, for the most part, opportunities for a teacher-exchange program with Gonzaga University, since the latter kept its semester structure.

A shortage of priests was keenly felt in the colleges, as well as in the parishes. While many priests left their posts to serve as chaplains, others took on additional burdens, like directing Civil Defense units or hospital chaplaincies. Some, like Father Louis Egan at Marquette in Yakima, or Father John Delaunay at the University of Portland, counselled hundreds of service men abroad by mail. They carried heavy loads of sadness that practically killed them both.[29]

COURT ENCOUNTERS OVER BUSING

There was great sadness, too, in Washington State when the Supreme Court of the State finally got around to announcing its decision regarding the legality of the 1941 Mitchell Bill, the School Busing law. In January 1943, while the court still deliberated, the *Inland Register* expressed caution regarding the outcome. "The arguments are now in," Father Tully wrote guardedly. "Meanwhile, in hundreds of rural homes parents are fearful lest their children must soon again trudge the highways to parochial schools on dark winter mornings. Besides the hardships involved, there is grave danger of traffic accidents and of serious injury to children."[30]

The attorney general, Smith Troy, had supported the bill energetically, insisting, as Catholics did, that the buses helped the children, not their religion. The Catholic bishops of Spokane and Seattle, through Joseph Hurley, their attorney in Spokane, filed briefs in support of the law. But the opposition was politically so aggressive that reports about the court's impending decision became more ominous every day. Spokane attorneys representing the opponents were Don F. Kizer, Arthur Davis, and E.J. Barker, who regarded the law "as a dangerous wedge" for the sacrosanct separation of Church and State.

On March 15, 1943, the State Supreme Court in a five to four decision declared the law unconstitutional. Justices Thomas Grady, Bruce Blake, George P. Simpson, William J. Steinert and William J. Millard favored the majority opinion, while Justices John S. Robinson, Walter Beals, C.G. Jeffers, and Joseph A. Mallery dissented. Mallery was especially indignant with the decision of his five colleagues, and the state's assistant attorney general, John Spiller, immediately requested a review of the case, arguing that the majority of the judges themselves "have been unable to agree among themselves upon a precise, definite and tenable ground for such holding."[31] When the justices refused, Tully was quick to point out that in the five to four decision the opinion of one man denied a law passed by elected legislators by a vote of 112 to 17.[32] His Irish wholly aroused now, Tully added fuel to the flames. "In the interests of the State of Washington," he wrote, "children of soldiers in Africa, England, India and Australia, who were giving their lives for their country, could not be protected like other children when they went to school. We are fighting for justice abroad: we shall not desist in our fight for justice at home until all have obtained it."[33]

Prodded by Catholics, the law makers in Olympia passed another busing law two years later.[34] This, like the Mitchell Bill of 1941, made explicit provision for pupils of private and parochial schools. "All children attending school in accordance with the laws relating to compulsory attendance in the State of Washington shall be entitled to use the transportation facilities provided by the school district in which they reside."[35] The wording of this law was as clear as sunshine, but many children in private schools were still denied the use of the buses. On October 24, 1945, Jelte Visser, a farmer in Sumas, and his neighbors, signed a petition for a *Mandamus* writ to force the buses to transport their children to the school of the Christian Reformed Church. When it was reported that the children had been refused transportation because Pearl Wanamaker, State Superintendent of Public Instruction, regarded the 1945 statute as unconstitutional, the state's attorney general publicly reprimanded her, noting that "Constitutionality of all enactments of the legislature is to be presumed, and until a competent court rules otherwise, the law shall be obeyed."[36]

The law was already before the courts, with scant hope of surviving, largely because of the purely secular nature of Washington's state constitution, which had come back to haunt those who had been indifferent when it was enacted in 1889. The hopes of Catholics, however, were enlivened, when the United States Supreme Court in a five to four decision ruled favorably in the Everson case, New Jersey's busing law. "Bus rides," wrote Justice Hugh Black in the majority opinion, "are an aid to children just as police and fire protection, and other welfare services are an aid to the people as a whole."[37]

Soon, however, hopes were dashed again. The Iowa Court disallowed busing for that state, using the absurd argument "that private schools might be in danger of being brought under state control if their students rode in public school buses."[38] As ridiculous as this sounds, the Iowa judges at least recognized the fallacies in the wornout argument about busing being an aid to religion.

Washington's Court finally revealed its ruling in the 1945 bill on June 19, 1949. In a six to two decision it reaffirmed its position in the Mitchell case: the law was unconstitutional "because it conferred benefits on religious schools."[39] The court decided to stick by its previous decision despite the Everson case. Only Justices Beals and Mallery dissented, for the same reasons as the United States Supreme Court, but their opinions were lost in the shouting that followed, especially in the camps of the enemy.

By this time, many fair-minded citizens of the state recognized the source and reasons for the impasse. How could they fail to see it? The public schools and their lobbies like the Washington Educational Association were determined to prevent private or parochial schools from sharing in public funding.[39] The Supreme Court decision in the Oregon School Case was now practically meaningless because of their dog-in-the-manger mentality. Parents were free to choose the education of their children only if they could afford the double taxation. Otherwise they were not free.

In the struggle the name of Pearl Wanamaker had surfaced. It would appear again soon in another attempt to subject the attendance at all schools to the rule of her office. Meanwhile, the school busing laws produced one good result: Catholics had improved perceptibly in political sophistication. They had acquired the ability to discover the activities of their opposition and to use suitable pressures to discredit them.

During these tiresome court proceedings, Bishop Shaughnessy had been silent but not idle. Through diocesan attorneys he waged a vigorous battle, keeping in the background to avoid repercussions in a city that harbored relatively few Catholics. His health, never robust, began to decline alarmingly, as the heavy duties of office consumed his strength.

When he arrived in Seattle he had been deeply disturbed about debts in the diocese and in particular about the crushing rate of interest being paid by the parishes. When he visited Seattle banks to negotiate a diocesan loan at a lower rate of interest, to pay off these debts, the bankers turned him down. With a parting shot, he left them and boarded a train for the East Coast where he got the necessary funds. While this kept the wolves at bay, it was not a final solution, so he planned and completed a major fund drive for two million dollars, half of which was to be placed in a revolving fund to be loaned to the parishes at little or no interest, and half to be equally divided for two projects rated priorities, a chapel at St. Edward's seminary and a "co-instructional" high school in north Seattle.[40]

This decisive, almost despotic manner of acting, sometimes brought Shaughnessy into conflict with other local factions, which did little to improve his image as the successor of Bishop O'Dea. His concern for the poor and the laborer, however, compensated for these less endearing characteristics. He gave staunch support to organized labor, a tricky matter in heavily industrialized Seattle with its growing body of the new rich. He was invited to present an address at the national convention of the A.F. of L., an indication of the high regard in which he was held by some workingmen.

Others found him inscrutable. On Christmas Day, when he preached on the Ten Commandments, he left his congregation baffled and hurt, yet he saw nothing incongruous in what he had done. His clergy soon learned that protests were futile. Their bishop was an angry man, almost blind to his own mistakes but waspish with others, who dared not confront him.

The war had effectively closed down the formation of new parishes and construction. In 1943 only three new Catholic institutions appeared in the entire Northwest: the Sweet Clinic in Centralia, purchased by the Diocese of Seattle, was converted into St. Luke's Infirmary and its management was entrusted to the Carmelite Sisters of the Infirm and the Aged.[41] Several months later in Spokane the former Florence Crittenton Home for unwed mothers, purchased by Bishop White in December 1942, was opened by two Franciscan Sisters as St. Ann's Home for unwanted babies.[42] Finally, on November 29, St. John's Hospital in Longview was opened by the Sisters of St. Joseph of Newark. This was the former Longview Memorial Hospital, which the sisters had purchased several months earlier.[43] All of these institutions, new to Catholics, were acquired as existing facilities. None was created from scratch.

VANPORT AND RICHLAND

In the same year two other Catholic projects were undertaken, with results worthy of comment. The first was in a shipyard housing settlement called Vanport, along the Columbia River between Vancouver, Washington and Portland. Thousands of war production workers settled here and Father Michael Raleigh of Portland started to offer Mass for them in a borrowed building on February 17, 1943. Franciscan sisters came to teach the children catechism and the makings of a permanent parish began to appear. But the entire city, including all of the homes and the temporary church were wiped out in a massive flood of the Columbia River on May 30, 1948. Vanport was never restored.[44]

At Hanford in Washington's desert country west of Spokane, thousands of people were working on a highly classified program called the "Manhattan Project," the atom bomb. The closest church, called Holy Rosary, was a little primitive shack at White Bluffs. Father William Sweeney, missionary priest from Kennewick, exchanged Holy Rosary for a tent at Hanford. This first tent accommodated only 150 people. Later, on October 31, 1943, the government provided another which held fifteen hundred. This was used as a church on Sunday and as a theatre on weekdays.[45]

During this same period the village of Richland, another mission of Kennewick, began to expand rapidly. Sweeney first offered Mass in the school building, then the Grangehall. Because of the quasi-military nature of his congregation, he was able to procure building materials, mostly lumber, with which he built a church large enough to accommodate 750 people. Bishop White blessed this in honor of Christ the King on February 11, 1945.[46]

Only three other churches in the entire Northwest were produced in the last two years of the war: St. John's at Port Orford, Oregon, completed in May, 1944 with Extension funds, the Redemptorists' temporary St. Gerard's Church in Great Falls, first used for Mass on January 1, 1945, and St. Gabriel's temporary church in Port Orchard, Washington, built during May, 1945 by volunteer navy personnel from the huge navy base at Bremerton.[47]

There were a few other isolated happenings. For example, Bishop White purchased the Northwest Business College Building on Howard Street in March 1944 and converted it into Spokane's first official Chancery building.[48] On March 12, 1945, Gonzaga University established a popular labor relations school, which survived for nearly a generation under the name of Industrial Relations Institute.[49] Gonzaga High School, occupying the former Webster School burned down on May 12, 1945, and in Seattle on September 16, just after V-J Day, another fire set by a disgruntled former employee destroyed St. Vincent de Paul's Salvage Bureau and dormitory. Four homeless men in the dormitory burned to death, a shocking tragedy that aroused the whole city. War had rendered people somewhat calloused about death and dying, but this was different. Four unknown and penniless vagrants had been killed in the local sanctuary, so to speak, by another man who had a grudge. War had made human life cheap, but not as cheap as this.

POST WAR PROBLEMS

When news that the war was over burst upon the weary people of Portland, Father Delaunay happened to be downtown.[50] He listened momentarily to the sounds of a noisy peace, then, overwhelmed by relief and grief for the university's sixty-five former students who had been killed, he purchased a ticket at a movie theatre and went inside. He sat down and wept quietly in the darkness. Outside, Broadway was jammed with those who knew how to celebrate victory with singing and dancing and shouting. Only the Delaunays of the city understood that it had been a hollow victory. Youth and treasure on a colossal scale had been sacrificed, but what had been gained? What lay ahead? The bitter struggle for normality after four years of cultural and social deterioration was just beginning.

During these four years the church in the Northwest had been reduced to a me-too kind "of holding on." The big canvas of patriotic triumphalism painted by the Catholic press, concealed a decadent society beneath. As Bishop White had warned, many Americans, including northwest Catholics, had changed. The family had disintegrated when the men went off to war and many of the women worked overtime in war production. There had been too much money in circulation, too much freedom for children, and too much preoccupation with material success. Post-war reports about the great revival in religion were superficial at best. At worst they were downright deceptive as we learned a decade later.

But all this had to be overlooked in the heat of the hour. The disruptions occasioned by the war, especially in the formation of new parishes, were corrected by the inevitable "booms," booms in building, booms in school population, booms in babies, which guaranteed a continuation of higher school attendance for years to come.

BISHOP SHAUGHNESSY'S STROKES

Seattle's fund-raising project, finally completed in 1945, was successful, but the tensions and pressures had taken their toll. In November of that year when Shaughnessy was returning from the bishops' annual meeting in Washington, he suffered a cerebral hemorrhage and had to be taken off the train in Jersey City, where he was hospitalized for several weeks. In early December he was able to complete his journey to Seattle. Refusing to accept his crippled condition, he forced himself into routine activities. In this way he limped along for two more years, suffering minor strokes periodically, always on the ragged edge of collapse, quarrelsome and exhausted by spells, too stubborn to give up. By the end of 1947 he was confined to his residence with nurses around the clock. Yet he considered himself still in charge of the diocese and demanded that all incoming mail be brought to his sick room, where it piled up, unopened and unanswered for an entire year. His laconic and sometimes crusty observations on public events were missed, but the church in Seattle drifted along without him.

ANOTHER ATTEMPT TO CONTROL PAROCHIAL SCHOOLS

This seemed to be a favorable time for legislation to extend the state's control over private schools. Control by the bureaucrats was like a bone stuck in their throats. They could neither leave it alone nor choke it out.

On February 7, 1947, the following was given a prominent place on the front page of the *Inland Register*:

An astonishing piece of proposed legislation, Senate Bill No. 28, introduced in Olympia by Senator Leslie V. Morgan of Yakima and Senator Thomas H. Bienz of Dishman, would, if enacted, forbid any child to attend a Catholic school unless permission were in every case first asked and obtained from the local superintendent of public schools.

On the previous day, the *Spokane Chronicle* had published notice of this bill, but its editors had carefully removed details that were objectionable to Catholics, stating, for example, that the names of children attending private schools would have to be reported only.[51]

The full text of the bill appeared as follows:

SENATE BILL No. 28
By Senators Morgan and Bienz
AN ACT

Relating to education; providing for compulsory school attendance and certain excuses therefrom; amending section 1, subchapter 16, title III, chapter 97, Laws of 1909 (section 5072, Remington's Revised statutes, also Pierce's Perpetual code 870-1).

Be it enacted by the Legislature of the State of Washington:

1   Section 1. Section 1, subchapter 16, title III, chapter
2   97, Laws of 1909 (section 5072 Remington's Revised Statutes,
3   also Pierce's Perpetual Code 870-1), is amended to read as
4   follows:
5   Section 1. All parents, guardians, and other persons
6   in this state having or who may hereafter have immediate custody
7   of any child between eight and * * * * * *eighteen* years of age
8   (being between the eighth and (* * * * * *eighteenth* birthdays)
9   * * * * * shall cause such child to attend the public school
10 of the district in which the child resides, for the full time
11 when such school may be in session * * * * *, unless the super-
12 intendent of the schools of the district in which the child
13 resides, if there be such a superintendent, and in all other
14 cases the county superintendent of * * * * * schools, shall
15 have excused such child from such attendance because the child
16 is physically or mentally unable to attend school or has already
17 attained a reasonable proficiency in the branches required by
18 law to be taught in the first * * * * * *twelve* grades of the
19 public schools of this state as provided by the course of
20 study of such school, *or to attend an approved private school*
21 *for the full time that the public school is in session, or has*
22 *passed his fifteenth birthday and is regularly and lawfully*
23 *engaged in some useful and remunerative occupation, or to assist*
24 *in the relief of labor shortage occasioned by war conditions*
25 *or cannot profitably pursue further school work,* or for some
26 *other sufficient reason: Provided, That the superintendent shall*
27 *excuse any child to attend an approved private school as pro-*
28 *vided in this section when requested so to do by the parent or*
29 *guardian of such child.* Proof of absence from public schools
30 * * * * * *without an excuse herein provided for* shall be prima
31 facie evidence of a violation of this section.[52]

Exposure of this bill and odious comparisons with the Oregon School Bill produced repercussions similar to gangland killings. Suddenly everyone denied knowledge of it or brought forward ironclad alibis to clear themselves. The co-sponsors, caught red-handed, first made promises to remove the objectionable features of the bill, which left nothing new for passage, then openly denied knowledge of its contents. "On February 10, according to reports from Olympia, Bienz and Morgan confessed they had not read the bill and did not know its implications." Morgan sadly admitted, "I didn't even read the bill."[53]

Whence did it come? The *Spokesman Review* traced it to Morgan, who stated that he had received it from Joe Chandler, the Olympia lobbyist for the Washington Education Association.[54] Rumors persisted that the bill had been drafted in Pearl Wanamaker's office. There it was again, the name Wanamaker.

In this manner the comedy of errors performed by the state's leading bureaucrats in education came to an ignominious finale. No one ever proved that Wanamaker had been the villain, but henceforth Catholics examined her school activities with the finesse of a hungry hawk.

LOYOLA RETREAT HOUSE

School problems by this time had all but buried northwest Catholics. New churches appeared, seven in 1947[55] and six more in 1948.[56] But high schools and colleges with swollen enrollments following the war's end taxed existing institutional resources beyond capacity. Portland and Gonzaga University raised new buildings for engineering schools in 1948. In the same year, Gonzaga became co-educational.

What the Jesuits really wanted was a boys' high school in Portland. After forty years of punctilious fencing with the archbishop, they were no closer to their objective than before. What Archbishop Howard requested, instead, was a Jesuit retreat house similar to El Retiro near Los Altos, California.[57] Retreats for lay Catholics had been provided since Blanchet arrived, but as yet there was no institution in the Northwest devoted exclusively to retreat work.

The Jesuit provincial's residence, named Campion Hall, occupied a ten-acre site in southeast Portland adjoining St. Ignatius parish. The provincial, Father Leopold Robinson, before his departure for Rome in 1946, acquired another residence, the Old Mackenzie mansion on Twentieth and Hoyt, so that the building and grounds formally occupied by his staff could be available. Thus it happened that the old brick, three-story structure, erected in 1909, became the Loyola Retreat House. On June 4, 1947, Father Joseph Grady arrived here with his assistant Brother

James Wood. The two sturdy men rolled up their sleeves and began renovations at once. After twenty-three days of Wood's whirlwind operations, on June 27, 1947, Father John McAstocker opened the first closed retreat for twelve expectant men, and Loyola Retreat House has provided scheduled retreats ever since. In the first full year of operations, 1948-1949, twenty retreats were conducted with an average attendance of eight retreatants.[58]

This modest success brought the Jesuits no closer to their long sought school than heretofore. Like his predecessor, Alexander Christie, Howard undoubtedly had reservations about the presence of a Jesuit prep school. Some of his subordinates, it was said, were more openly opposed, so the matter languished and the Jesuits concentrated on their prep schools in Seattle, Tacoma, and Spokane. In Spokane, especially, the situation was critical. The high school students, still housed on the university campus following the Webster fire, like unwanted orphan boys, were moved from pillar to post to make room for the hordes of GI's who had suddenly appeared.[59]

At Columbia Prep in Portland, similar conditions existed. The university campus was bulging at the seams. It was difficult to maintain state accreditation requirements for high school in this crowded situation, which was reason enough for a change. But someone suddenly produced the most respectable argument of all: "The presence of older college students on campus was not conducive to the proper educational and social influence of high school students."[60] So it was agreed that the high school, the backbone of the institution for forty years, "should be separated geographically from the college" meaning the high school should go somewhere else. Enrollment in Columbia Prep had dropped to 159 in 1948 when a new fifty-acre campus on Shattuck Road in southwest Portland's fashionable enclave was acquired for $100,000. Rumors of the school's possible closure in the near future did little to improve enrollment, and as other post-war problems engrossed the Holy Cross fathers at the university, the morale of the faculty and students at Columbia dropped to a new low. This little scenario was not a unique one. On Catholic campuses throughout the country it was repeated many times with happier results.[61]

Columbia Prep was doomed. Finding it impossible to raise needed revenue to sustain and develop the school, the Holy Cross priests decided to close it. The class of 1955 was the last. "And the University of Portland, bereft of its older educational brother, now had to stand alone."[62]

BISHOP FRANCIS GLEESON

Francis Gleeson, the pastor of St. Stanislaus in Lewiston, had survived by five years the periodic purges which Bishop Kelly regarded as useful in conducting his diocese. Transferred then to St. Mary's Mission at Omak, to correct its fiscal adventurism, he soon became accustomed to the insecurity and poverty of life in the missions. He had always been regarded as an uncommonly humble man, very talented, indeed, especially as a cook. When he was rector at the Jesuit novitiate at Sheridan, he often cooked for the entire community of one hundred or more, to spell off the brother who had to cook every day. These times were always memorable because his meals were excellent and he used every pot and kettle in the kitchen to prepare them.

When Bishop Crimont of Juneau died on May 20, 1945, at the venerable age of eighty-eight, he was succeeded by his coadjutor, Bishop Walter Fitzgerald. Fitzgerald, alas, was also a very sick man, too sick to conduct the affairs of the vicariate. While Rome still pondered alternate solutions to this crisis, he died in Seattle on July 19, 1947, and was buried among his brother Jesuits at Mount St. Michael's in Spokane. His death, of course, left the vicariate of Alaska vacant and the customary search was begun for his successor.

Francis Gleeson was selected. As superior of St. Mary's on February 8, 1948, he sent the following telegram to the provincial's office in Portland: "Received telegram from Denver Registrar [sic] congratulating on appointment and asking for biographical data. Is this a joke or should I take it serious. F. Gleeson."[63]

It was no joke. The *Denver Register* had scooped the Apostolic Delegate's office in Washington.

The choice of Gleeson for Alaska was very popular. Like Bishop McGrath, he had lived with poverty. As rector of Bellarmine in Tacoma and the novitiate at Sheridan, he had pioneered, and again at St. Mary's he was poor. The Alaska mission, too, was poor, so its new vicar apostolic began his career by accepting bishop's robes cast off by others. His official portraits were taken by Father Leo Yeats at Gonzaga, at no cost, and his consecration was contrived to be as frugal as possible. This was conducted in St. Aloysius Church, Spokane, on a sunny spring day, April 6, 1948, with dignity and holy prayers, but also with great simplicity. It was the trademark of the new bishop.

ARRIVAL OF BISHOP THOMAS CONNOLLY

Meanwhile at Seattle, Bishop Shaughnessy, still a victim of his stroke in 1945, had been left in a kind of uncertain limbo for nearly two years. A strange silence about him and his condition prevailed throughout the diocese. Little or nothing was said. He lived behind a curtain of mystery, like a nun in a cloistered convent. Bishop White filled in for ordinations when need arose and the vicar general, Monsignor John Gallagher, pastor of the cathedral, conducted the ordinary business of the diocese. An appeal was sent to Rome for a coadjutor as soon as it was known that there was no hope for Shaughnessy's recovery. Thus matters stood on February 28, 1948, when Bishop Thomas Connolly, auxiliary to Archbishop John Mitty in San Francisco, was appointed to Seattle as coadjutor with the right of succession.[64] It was in effect an appointment to the immediate administration of the diocese, since Shaughnessy was generally regarded as beyond help.

Connolly, it was said, had visited Seattle "frequently" and had expressed "fondness for the Northwest." No one had reason to doubt this. On one occasion, at least, he had regaled St. Edward's seminarians with a visit in the company of Monsignor Gallagher, a former classmate at Menlo Park.[65] His elaborate installation as bishop was celebrated in St. James Cathedral on April 21, 1948, with Archbishop Howard presiding. Over twenty-five bishops and abbots attended the ceremony, which ticked off with the precision of a Swiss watch. The public reception that evening in the Civic Auditorium attracted the greatest crowd ever to attend a function in that place, which indicates the kind of joy Seattle Catholics were experiencing with their new shepherd. Bishop Shaughnessy had never been popular. His successor, already the master of the situation, dazzled his people with his lofty manners and regal bearing. He might have been a king at his coronation. It was soon evident that he could snap his fingers and get what he wanted.

SEATTLE UNIVERSITY

During this same spring of 1948, Seattle College acquired the charter and the status of a university. This exalted rank had come almost without anyone noticing it, until it was already there. In 1945, there were only nine hundred full-time students at Seattle College. The ratio was one boy to six girls. Four hundred were freshmen. Then suddenly in 1946, there were twenty-five hundred students, thirteen hundred of them war veterans, and boys greatly out-numbered the girls.[66] With war surplus buildings the school was able to cope with their 108% increase of students in a single year.

Father Harold Small had succeeded Corkery as president, but in the spring of 1948, Small received word that he had been promoted to become provincial of the Jesuits' Oregon Province. Before he departed for Portland, he called his trustees together and drafted "amendatory articles of incorporation which would raise Seattle College to the status of university."[67]

The *Seattle Times*, meanwhile, noted recent progress:

> Many Seattle residents had not suspected that a growing educational institution here has become the largest Catholic center of higher education in the West. Yet this is the attainment of Seattle College in the 50th year of its history. With a student body of 2,500, it has outstripped Gonzaga University in Spokane, the University of San Francisco, Santa Clara, and Loyola University in Los Angeles, the principal Catholic colleges of the western states.[68]

Within a week after the appearance of this editorial the college announced the appointment of the new president, thirty-nine year old Father Albert Lemieux, formerly dean of faculties at Gonzaga University. The installation of the new president took place on May 20, 1948, in an informal ceremony held at the college. Then eight days later, sharing the dais with Bishop Connolly, Lemieux presided over graduation exercises held in the Memorial Gymnasium on the campus. The graduating class of 174 was the largest in history and for the first time graduate degrees were awarded. On this occasion, too, the first honorary doctor of laws degree was awarded, the recipient being Monsignor Theodore Ryan, one of three members of the first graduation class in 1909, and the first native son of Seattle to be ordained to the priesthood. The climax of the evening, however, was the legal declaration of the school's new status. Lemieux, speaking with obvious pride, his warm, resonant voice trembling slightly with deep emotion, addressed the expectant multitude:

> It is my great honor and high privilege, as president of this institution, to make public the document of the State Department of the State of Washington granting to our institution a new charter and a new name. In view of the great growth that has taken place, from a college of liberal arts and sciences, the schools of commerce and finance, of education, of nursing, of engineering and of graduate studies, the State Department has graciously acceded, on this occasion of the golden jubilee of the founding of Seattle College, to the petition of the trustees for the right to the name and charter of Seattle University.[69]

As things turned out, no one in the history of Seattle University had a greater right to speak for it in this, its golden hour.

BISHOP LEO FAHEY FOR BAKER CITY

So much for Seattle. Baker City, too, had an ailing prelate. Joseph Mcgrath had been bishop for twenty-nine years. These years had been good to him but he had grown tired and feeble, a Golden Jubilarian who recognized his limitations. He sometimes sat quietly in the shade of the wide porch of his residence and little children came to greet him, bringing joy to his magnanimous Irish heart. Early in 1948, incapacitated by frequent intervals of sickness, he came to the conclusion that it was time to pass the keys of office to a younger man. His request for a coadjutor was immediately granted on March 13. Father Leo Fahey, pastor of Sacred Heart parish in Hattiesburg, Mississippi, was appointed Titular Bishop of Ipsus and Coadjutor to Bishop McGrath with the right of succession.[70]

Fahey, like Gleeson, belonged to the common man. He had endeared himself to his flock with his warm, easygoing personality. Each year he blessed their fishing boats, which the men loved almost as much as their wives. An obese man with a generous sagging chin, like Pope John, whom he resembled in other ways, he was only forty-eight, but he appeared to be much older.[71] His dark unflinching eyes looked sad or hurt, probably both, because people who love in the way he did get deeply hurt at times.

On May 26, 1948, Fahey was consecrated in the Church of Our Lady of the Gulf in Bay St. Louis, where he was baptized, made his first communion, was confirmed, and was ordained. Richard O. Gerow was the consecrating bishop. He was assisted by Bishop Leo Binz of Winona, later Archbishop of St. Paul, and Bishop Abel Caillouet, auxiliary of New Orleans. Both co-consecrators had been in the seminary with Fahey. The event was regarded as "historic" since Fahey was the first native of Mississippi to be raised to the purple. No one present that day even imagined it possible that soon they would all gather again in the same church to celebrate the new bishop's funeral.

But this was locked in the future. Bishop Fahey was feted and praised and dined, and after it all, he left for Baker, Oregon, arriving there in the crackling dry heat of summer on July 14, 1948. On the following day, he was officially welcomed to the rugged diocese by the Catholics of Baker City. Bishop McGrath was too feeble to attend the long ceremony but Archbishop Howard was there to preach again. And the stalwart priests of the diocese were there, too, very loyal men who had long since proved their love for their bishop and their church.

THE NEW BISHOP'S DEATH

In early June 1949, Bishop Fahey delivered the baccalaureate address at the University of Portland and was awarded an honorary degree of doctor of laws. He planned his first *ad limina* visit to Rome but a confirmation schedule, long delayed, kept him at work until late August.

Other American bishops, including White of Spokane, Armstrong of Sacramento, Gorman of Reno and Condon of Great Falls, scheduled their *ad limina* visits for the same summer, under the aegis of Archbishops Howard and Mitty. They formed a special tour party of 157 members of the hierarchy, priests, and lay people, for a pilgrimage to Rome and Lourdes, combining their episcopal duties with devotions and pleasure. White left Spokane on June 17, 1949, and sailed with the others on the *Queen Mary* from New York on June 22. He returned to Spokane on July 30, with days to spare before the dedication ceremonies of the new St. Francis Xavier Church on Spokane's north side.[72]

Bishop Fahey embarked for Rome later, at the end of August. His companions were Archbishop Joseph Rummell of New Orleans and Bishop Gerow, his old friend. During the journey he became ill and when he returned to the United States he entered a hospital for observation and surgery.[73] Still too ill to perform his duties, he arrived in Baker in January, 1950. For awhile he seemed to improve. In March he was admitted to St. Elizabeth's Hospital for rest in preparation for the long, tedious liturgies of Holy Week. While there March 31, he received a phone call from Bay St. Louis, informing him of the sudden death of his brother Joseph, aged sixty-six. A few moments later he fell back dead, from heart failure it was said. He was only fifty-one years old, though even in death he looked much older.[74]

Officials in Rome, accustomed to almost any kind of crisis, were stunned. McGrath was dying. His coadjutor had died before him.

Cardinal Montissi dispatched a telegram to McGrath: "Holy Father expresses Paternal condolences Demise of Bishop Fahey."[75] They brought the bishop's body to Bay St. Louis for the funeral and burial, and there in Our Lady of the Gulf Church, where he had been consecrated just two years before, Bishop Gerow presided over the obsequies of his friend while many who were present silently pondered the mystery of life.

DEATH OF BISHOP MCGRATH

The funeral of Bishop Fahey was on April 12. On the same day in Baker City, Bishop McGrath was near death. He had often said, "No one but a bishop is sooner forgotten after death than a priest. A priest is forgotten soon; a Bishop sooner."[76] In the excitement of the last few days he had not been forgotten, nor would he be. One of his dearest friends had been at his side. This was Sister Mary Presentina, a Franciscan from Glen Riddle, who had supervised the CCD program in the diocese since 1937. "On his deathbed in 1950," Presentina wrote later, Bishop McGrath said to her, "I die happy. You made it possible for every child to receive instructions in the faith. I would have been ashamed to meet Our Lord if this had not been done. I thank you."[77]

His Lordship passed from this world to the next, quietly and humbly, on April 12, while the funeral procession of Bishop Fahey passed from the church to the cemetery. The vulnerable little diocese in eastern Oregon, which boasted of two bishops just weeks before, was now in mourning for both. Telegrams from all over the United States poured into the chancery to give comfort to the bewildered Catholics. Father Leo Martin, acting provincial for the Jesuits in the absence of Robinson, sent the following, "All the Fathers who have been stationed in the Diocese under Bishop McGrath have been sincere admirers of this priestly and truly pastoral character. His death, coming so soon after the former loss of Bishop Fahey, must be keenly felt."[78]

Joseph McGrath, it was often said, had been generous with the poor. He had loved and cherished his priests. He had been zealous in the care of souls. In thirty-one years as bishop he had taken no salary and he sometimes said that his clothing was the gift of friends. He added six parishes to the diocese, he built twenty-one churches, remodeled three, built fourteen rectories, two schools, and as many hospitals. His diocese, when he died, had only fourteen thousand Catholics, not very many when compared to Boston, but almost twice as many as when he became bishop. More significantly, McGrath in his lonely wilderness, larger than the state of New York, had achieved national acclaim for the quality of his CCD program. As Bishop White observed in his funeral oration on April 18, he blazed "the trail for his brother bishops in a diocese with difficulties similar, but greater than theirs."[79] Bishop O'Hara had founded the CCD. Bishop McGrath had made it work. McGrath's successor would gather the harvest.

RENOVATION OF ST. JAMES CATHEDRAL

During these cheerless vicissitudes, Bishop Shaughnessy still lingered. He had begun to look like an old man whom even death had forgotten. Seattle's vigorous new bishop had begun his long reign like a glorified vice president, with boundless energy. "What struck me in watching him," someone had said, "was his endurance, his amazing capacity for work and his dogged determination to see through to the end whatever he started."[80]

Bishop Connolly had observed at once the tacky appearance of the cathedral interior. He also observed the need for changes in the cathedral rectory, which served as his temporary residence. Placing cathedral renovation high on his list of priorities, he first concentrated on the rectory. He completely re-designed this by adding a third story and other modern facilities, which made it the most spacious residence for parish priests on the West Coast. Begun in 1948, shortly after Connolly's arrival, the project was completed in the following year.[81]

The cathedral of course required more time and money. The proposed observance of the centenary of the Seattle diocese in 1950 presented an opportunity for motivating Catholics to support the concept. Connolly invited Harold Rambusch, one of America's foremost church artists, from New York, and architect John W. Maloney of Seattle, to assist him in what he perceived to be a gigantic undertaking. Changes in design were mapped out and a contractor, J.C. Boespflug, also of Seattle, was engaged. Actual construction work began immediately after Easter in 1950.

A subsequent report contained the details:

> The exterior of the Cathedral was steam cleaned and emerged from the smoke and grime and dirt of nearly 40 years, the structure resumed its former pale gold appearance. It was found necessary to insert steel trusses under the roof of the nave due to the fact that the timbers used in the restoration of the roof after the collapse of the dome in 1916 were found to be badly in need of repair. An entire new ceiling was hung from the newly-placed trusses; complete new heating, ventilating and lighting systems were installed; although several new altars were erected, the main altar block, consecrated by Bishop O'Dea, was left intact. A newly-engraved window was set in the facade of the church and Indiana limestone statutes [statues] were sculptured for the niches. The over-all interior of the Cathedral and Lady Chapel were newly decorated and frescoed under the able direction of Harold Rambusch.
>
> Under the direction of Bishop Connolly a centennial drive for one million dollars was inaugurated. One-third of this fund was to assist in defraying in part the renovation of the Cathedral and two-thirds for parochial projects. The diocese was to undergo a general face-lifting on the occasion of the centenary. The original cost of the Cathedral was in the neighborhood of $250,000; the renovation necessitated an outlay of some $500,000.[82]

BISHOP SHAUGHNESSY'S DEATH

While these grandiose events were taking shape, Bishop Shaughnessy died in the episcopal residence on Spring Street. On May 16, 1950, three days before his sixty-third birthday, he received the last sacraments. He died from heart failure on May 18, at 12:26 P.M., while he was taking his last meal.[83] It was on the feast of the holy Ascension, a good omen, perhaps, but inconvenient, because the cathedral, jammed with scaffolding and the bric-a-brac of construction, was unavailable for a funeral.

The Immaculate Conception church was used instead for two funerals, one on Monday, May 21 for the school children and the sisters, and one on the following day for the clergy and the laity. Both were as elaborate as Bishop Connolly could make them. The front of the church was embellished with huge black and white streamers, the sanctuary likewise, creating an effect of such lugubrious feelings that even the children with an unexpected two-day holiday, became momentarily mournful. On the next day the children were conscripted again, to line up for blocks while the hearse, bearing the bishop's body, passed slowly by.[84]

It was Shaughnessy's last sermon, perhaps more effective than the many harrangues he had delivered in the parishes about obligations and church laws. His was a tragic fate. He had accomplished many wonders for the church, but he had failed to live long enough to become a mellow, understanding shepherd. He will always be remembered as a prickly personality rather than a fatherly one. Even the crusty Blanchets had mellowed. Shaughnessy had only ruled with efficiency.

CENTENNIAL OF SEATTLE DIOCESE

Seattle's cathedral renovations, brilliantly conceived and executed, were completed for the joyful ceremonies of jubilee. Father Andrew Prouty, the editor of the *Northwest Progress,* anticipating this climactic affair on September 14, had assembled a seasoned staff of local pundits, including Father John McCorkle of St. Edward's, Father Vincent Conway of Seattle University, and Mr. William O'Connell, his managing editor. For several hectic months they assisted Prouty in gathering histories of parishes, hospitals, schools, and religious orders. The Centennial edition of the *Progress*—112 slick pages of memorabilia in addition to the bishop's glittering, mostly red, portrait on the front cover, and letters from the Apostolic Delegate and Governor of the State of Washington mingled with bank advertisements and others like them—appeared on September 8, 1950. It was a very useful contribution lacking only a permanent form, like a bound book, to make it a popular regional reference work.

The Centennial Mass was planned with fastidious care, Connolly style, *a la California.* The Apostolic Delegate, Archbishop Ameleto G. Cicognani from Washington D.C., was invited to preside, outranking Archbishop Howard who was almost as ubiquitous as he was ageless. The presence of the delegate assured a good showing of bishops and clergy. One had to be seen on occasions like this if one expected to be advanced in some respect besides age. Thirty-two bishops appeared, forming a glamorous procession into the cathedral not unlike those in longer established cities like Baltimore and Philadelphia. "The celebration," wrote the chronicler of the extravaganza, manifesting some talent for understatement, "was one which will long be remembered by all who were in attendance."[85]

BISHOP FRANCIS LEIPZIG FOR BAKER

On July 18, 1950, Pope Pius XII, while he summered at Castel Gondolfo to escape the oppressive heat of Rome, dispatched the following message "to his beloved sons, the clergy and people of the City and Diocese of Baker."

> On this day, following the advice of our venerable brothers, the Cardinals of the holy Roman Church in charge of the Sacred Consistorial Congregation, We, by our apostolic authority, have appointed our beloved son, Francis P. Leipzig, pastor of the Church of the Blessed Virgin Mary in Eugene, a city of the Archdiocese of Portland in Oregon, to your cathedral church of Baker which is at present without a shepherd and we have placed him in charge of that church as Bishop and Shepherd.[86]

His Holiness approved of two other documents that same day, one directed to the bishop-elect and the other to Archbishop Howard. Each contained announcements for the faithful and instructions for the choice of bishops for the ceremony of consecration. These, too, were dispatched, to be admired, then filed away in the appropriate archives. What remained now was the hullaballoo of newspaper stories and the consecration of the new bishop. There was nothing simple about it all, but it happened almost every day somewhere in the world.

At first glance, one suspects that Francis Leipzig always expected to become a bishop. He appeared to be ambitious; at least he faithfully attended the more solemn events of the archdiocese where he could be seen and heard. St. Paul had said that the desire to become a bishop was good. Perhaps Leipzig entertained this holy desire. If so, it came, I think, from God, for despite appearances, Francis Leipzig was much more zealous than he was ambitious, and as the sequel showed, more given to love of his neighbor than to eagerness to be seen or heard. The greatness of Edwin O'Hara had left its mark on him.

Leipzig was fifty-five years old when he was appointed to Baker. He had been a priest for over thirty years. During those years he was so active in the business of the church and state that one can scarcely keep track of him. Assistant pastor, then pastor, then dean, chairman of committees, member of boards, pioneer in CCD, early promoter of the Newman Clubs, he traveled incessantly all over the state and nation, giving blessings and sermons and receiving countless awards, like an honorary life membership in the International Fire Fighters Association. As a sports enthusiast, he coached local teams in the schools and promoted his own plan for regulating athletics. Designed to establish "B" or "C" leagues for smaller schools, giving them an opportunity for a more fair competition, his plan was first adopted in the state of Oregon in 1934 and became a part of the state's regulations still in effect. Eventually other states adopted it also.

While this appears to be a rather trivial matter, it illustrates the broadness of interest of the new bishop. Almost anything worthy of his interest received his whole-hearted support. Like Bishop Connolly, he possessed an enormous capacity for detail and hard work.

An account of Leipzig's consecration is like most, but it is presented anyhow because it confirms the adage about reaping as one sows.

> St. Mary's Cathedral, Portland, was packed to overflowing on September 12, 1950 (the Feast of the Holy Name of Mary) when Father Leipzig was consecrated third Bishop of Baker City by Most Reverend Edward D. Howard, D.D., Archbishop of Portland, Oregon.
>
> The colorful ceremony of the consecration was witnessed by three Archbishops, twelve Bishops, three Abbots, four Monsignors, two hundred priests, two hundred sisters and hundreds of laity.
>
> Many were unable to gain admission into the Cathedral but were able to follow the ceremonies through the aid of loudspeakers erected around the Cathedral grounds.
>
> The Co-consecrators were Most Rev. Edwin V. O'Hara of Kansas City, Missouri and Most Rev. Edward J. Kelly, Boise, Idaho.[87]

This is dated reporting, to say the least, but one gets the picture, the edifice crowded with priests in surplices, busy reading their breviaries, and with sisters in a dozen different kinds of habits, like different species of birds in an aviary. The sanctuary too, was congested, with so many prelates, whose categories were very respectfully capitalized in print, and a score of altar boys in white cassocks and starched surplices, like pages at court.

In a photograph following the event, Archbishop Howard, shorter than Leipzig, grins happily, almost foolishly, while the new bishop scowls beneath his white mitre, like a prisoner at the bar. This was unlike him. In his official portrait he looks more pleased, like a successful politician. His hair has been cut short, his eyes stare intensely at the camera, his wide mouth is set firmly, German fashion, like a school master. His left hand fingers his pectoral ross affectedly and his right, with his ring exposed for edification, rests on his biretta. The portrait is authentic but it fails to reveal his great sense of compassion, especially for the poor.

The poor were his carefully concealed favorites. "Bishop Leipzig took care of many poor people," replied his secretary Mary Ann Davis, when I questioned her. "All he had he gave to the poor. He begged, borrowed, and stole for the poor. When he attended the national bishop's meeting he had big holes in the bottom of his shoes. He couldn't afford to buy new ones."[88]

Leipzig took possession of his diocese on September 21 with customary pomp and splendor. On the same day he called a meeting with his consultors who realized, without prolonged reflection, that they had got a work horse for a boss. During the same week he went on the road to visit his diocese.

Such was the successor of saintly Bishop McGrath. No one could fault the Pope for appointing him.

SEATTLE BECOMES ARCHDIOCESE

The greater shifts of population in the post-war boom occurred on the west coasts of Washington and Oregon. Portland's and especially Seattle's metropolitan areas experienced unprecedented growth due in part to new industries like electronics and airplanes. Montana and Idaho, on the other hand, gained very little.

Population for the four states as presented by the United States Census in 1940 and 1950 are as follows:

	1940	1950
Washington	1,236,191	2,378,963
Oregon	1,089,684	1,521,340
Montana	559,456	591,024
Idaho	524,873	588,637

Catholic growth was proportionate, but percentages remained as before. Washington State, for example, had 245,000 Catholics in 1950, better than ten percent of the population, but scarcely so many that a new diocese was required.[89] Several new factors, however, deserved consideration, indeed demanded it, lest central Washington's Catholic future be compromised by default. The completion of Coulee Dam in the 1940's and the subsequent development of the vast Columbia Basin into farmlands irrigated by the waters of the Columbia, marked the beginnings of a new migration over one million acres of fertile land. It was common knowledge that a great number of Mormons, who had enjoyed long years of experience with irrigation in Utah, were taking up this land. Protestant church groups, to avoid costly duplication of buildings and services and to forestall a Mormon takeover, made plans for an integrated system of their own.

Catholics had more at stake. Hispanic farm workers from Texas had already begun to move into the Yakima Valley in the same decade. Opportunities then were plentiful and as word got around larger numbers of Hispanics poured in from Mexico. They competed with other migrants, Anglos and American and Canadian Indians, many of whom, like the Hispanics, were at least nominally Catholic. As time passed, it was becoming painfully obvious that a single church unit like a diocese would be required in the basin to meet its special needs.

Central Washington included parts of both dioceses, Spokane and Seattle. Bishop White of Spokane, who was closer to the situation, had followed these fast developing events from the beginning and had done what he could with limited resources to anticipate the arrival of the masses. But this fell far short of the need. No lasting solution was possible without an independent diocese in the threatened area.[90]

The death of Bishop Shaughnessy cleared the way of any possible impasse. The formation of an archdiocese in Seattle, serving a province consisting of all of Washington and Alaska, appeared to be the logical step forward. At the same time, Yakima could be created as a diocese. If a plan like this were adopted, the Archdiocese of Portland would retain all of Oregon, Idaho, and Montana. The latter would count a total of approximately 263,000 Catholics, and the former about 255,000 plus a questionable number in Alaska.

In Rome, the plan appeared to be realistic as well. On June 23, 1951, Pope Pius XII took formal action, but information about this was not released until July 18. On that day, Archbishop Cicognani, the Apostolic Delegate, announced that "the Holy Father has:

> Raised the Diocese of Seattle, Washington, to the rank of archdiocese and made it the Metropolitan See of the new ecclesiastical province.
> Created the new Diocese of Yakima in the State of Washington.
> Created the new Diocese of Juneau in Alaska.
> Named His Excellency the Most Reverend Thomas A. Connolly of Seattle to be the first Archbishop of Seattle.
> Appointed Msgr. Joseph P. Dougherty (Chancellor of the Diocese of Seattle) to be the first Bishop of Yakima.[91]
> Appointed the Rev. Robert Dermot O'Flannagan, pastor of the church of the Holy Family, Anchorage, Alaska, to be the first Bishop of Juneau.[92]

CONSECRATION OF BISHOP DOUGHERTY

These changes, especially as related to the prelates involved, occupied the full attention of Catholics for some weeks to come. Not even another good court fight could have dislodged it as the number one subject in rectories and Gesus, for nothing was more dear as a subject of gossip than bishops, and in this affair there were several of the same for discussion. Editors were quick to note that Connolly was now the youngest archbishop in the country, which was appropriate, since he looked like it. O'Flannagan, scarcely known in the lower forty-eight states, had been a dark horse, but for other reasons a subject of clerical comment. As an ex-Jesuit from Ireland, the probabilities of his being elevated to the hierarchy were almost minimal. It was a long shot, some said, and as time unfolded, it turned out to be an unfortunate choice as well.[93]

Perhaps the same could be said about Bishop Dougherty, for he was forced to resign prematurely because of health problems, occasioned in part by conflicts in his diocese. An excellent priest and capable administrator, as Archbishop Connolly noted when his appointment was announced, Dougherty undoubtedly would have survived in an established diocese like Helena. Unfortunately, another was his vineyard. Yakima, placid on the surface, simmered beneath with ancient loyalties that Dougherty failed to acknowledge. He was a pre-Vatican bishop who was confronted with post-Vatican problems.

Dougherty, born on January 11, 1905, in Kansas City of Patrick and Grace Meehan Dougherty, was brought to Seattle when he was only eight months old. He lived the rest of his life, except for some of his school years, in Seattle, where his father was a streetcar motorman.[94] Thus he never experienced the directness of simplicity of small town people in an agricultural milieu. He attended the University of Portland and St. Patrick's Seminary in Menlo Park and he was ordained in St. James Cathedral in Seattle on June 14, 1930, by Bishop O'Dea. In 1942, Bishop Shaughnessy appointed him chancellor. A few months before his elevation as bishop, he was made a monsignor, an amazing phenomenon in retrospect, since one dignity followed the other so quickly that he lacked an opportunity to show off his monsignor's robes. (One wonders if he were reimbursed for this out-of-date wardrobe.)

Dougherty, like Connolly, believed in hard work. Slightly built, moderately tall in his purple cassock, his small head and chin forward, he moved lightly about, like a bookish, but impetuous professor in an Irish seminary. The broad, wistful smile on his face changed quickly to frowns or a stern reproof when he was crossed. While he was sensitive and gentle by disposition his stubborness could transform him suddenly into an autocrat with unabashed displeasure.

He was aware of new developments in the Columbia Basin. In his long first message to the public he referred to the basin's accelerated growth as a challenge:

The gigantic hydroelectric and atomic energy plants in the Columbia and Yakima Valleys, known the world over, together with the unprecedently great irrigation project under construction in the Columbia Basin now, will be the symbols of the even greater supernatural life and energy which will be brought to the souls of men in Central Washington through the increased channels of grace that will be opened to them by the establishment of their own diocese.[95]

The archbishop's influence over the bishop-elect appeared to be irresistible. Almost immediately Dougherty agreed to be consecrated in St. James Cathedral immediately following Connolly's installation as Archbishop of Seattle. This arrangement bore evidence of the personal solidarity between the two, the one a strong willed elder brother, the other a grateful sibling. "Inspiring Ceremonies Thrill Northwest" the *Progress* headlines blared in red ink after the high drama had been concluded on September 26, 1951. "Archbishop Installed, Bishop Consecrated With Age-Old Rites." Hence the two of them were united forever in one historic happening, the affirmation of the first Archbishop of Seattle and the first Bishop of Yakima.[96]

A vivid account of what has been described as the most solemn event in the history of the northwest church accompanied these eye catching notices:

> Amidst imposing ceremonies, brilliant with beauty and the light of faith, the Most Reverend Thomas A. Connolly was enthroned as Metropolitan of the new ecclesiastical Province of Seattle and the Most Reverend Joseph P. Dougherty was consecrated first Bishop of Yakima, in St. James Cathedral, here Wednesday, Sept. 26.
>
> Participating in the thrillingly-perfect ceremonies, which began with a colorful procession, were 29 archbishops and bishops, their robes glowing in the bright sunshine, a score of monsignori and 300 priests.
>
> Installed by His Excellency, the Most Reverend Edward D. Howard, D.D., Archbishop of Portland in Oregon, on the feast of the American Martyrs, the first official act of Archbishop Connolly was the consecration of Bishop Dougherty as Bishop of Yakima....
>
> The colorful procession of prelates and priests marched at 10:15 a.m. from the rectory into St. James Cathedral over which waved in the sunshine of a beautiful fall morning the Papal flag as well as the Stars and Stripes.
>
> Preceding members of the Hierarchy, in the procession were secular priests of the dioceses and those of several orders including the Sulpicians, the Dominicans, the Jesuits, the Passionists, the Franciscans, the Oblates, and the Redemptorists as well as the Christian Brothers. Two abbots, the bishops and archbishops each with two chaplains, followed the priests.
>
> Then came Bishop-Elect Dougherty with the consecrating prelates and their chaplains and finally His Excellency, the Most Reverend Edward D. Howard, D.D., Archbishop of Portland in Oregon....[97]

The new bishop's own installation followed a few days later. On October 11, traveling by car from Seattle, Dougherty was met at Ellensburg by a caravan of twenty-five cars containing members of the Knights of Columbus and the Catholic War Veterans, and by two jeeps flying the American and Papal flags. Ten more cars joined this welcome caravan before it arrived at St. Paul's, which lately had been designated as the new cathedral. Archbishop Connolly, assisted by Bishop Armstrong who had built St. Paul's in 1914, when he was pastor there, presided over the ceremony of installation, which consisted essentially in the presentation of the bishop's crozier.[98]

Later a Yakima paper commented on Dougherty's energetic beginnings. "Since coming here on October 11, 1951, Bishop Dougherty has driven an average of 1500 miles a month to visit every parish and mission in the 17,000 square miles of the diocese."[99] "It was the development of the Basin," a Seattle paper noted, "which led to the recent establishment of the Catholic Diocese of Yakima. Bishop Dougherty has made his first visit through the Basin and the planning for Catholic churches was begun."[100]

By this time, Dougherty had blue prints in the works for new churches at Moses Lake, Bridgeport, Chelan, and Grandview, as well as schools in Wenatchee and Richland. He had a motor chapel serving the needs of migrant Mexicans and on one occasion he confirmed 513 Mexican children at St. Aloysius Church in Toppenish.[101] These activities coincided with the arrival of water through the west canal, eighty-eight miles long. To celebrate this milestone, Bishops Dougherty and White pontificated at an open air Mass at Soap Lake on May 30, 1952. Five thousand people attended the liturgy of "God's blessing on Soil and Water," which marked "the inauguration of Columbia Basin irrigation with Coulee Reservoir water."[102] The presence of a bishop with the exclusive care of the basin brought immense relief to Bishop White, who no longer worried about a possible disaster for the church there. The time was drawing near when he, too, like Bishop McGrath, would have to render an account to God.

MORE ABOUT SISTERS

At the beginning of 1951, there were 158 bishops in the United States and 44,459 priests. There were also 156,696 sisters, more than three times the number of bishops and priests together. Since all three had different roles to perform in the church, it would be difficult to compare the proportionate influence of any one of them, though it should be stressed that the impact of the sisters on America was beyond human calculation. The sheer numbers alone impressed churchmen, who seemed to think, at that time, that there was an endless supply of them, always available for slave wages, and willing to accept a hidden career in the church solely for the love of God.

Prescinding from a judgment about this, one can recognize the dependence of the northwest church on the presence of the sisters from the very beginning. Without them in 1951 there would have been no parochial schools, no academies, few Catholic high schools or hospitals, and no homes for society's left-overs, the orphans and the aged.

In the 1950's as more and more parochial schools were established, the work of the sisters was greatly expanded in terms of numbers, but more significantly in terms of occupations other than teaching or nursing; in other words, work outside the protective walls of the cloistered school or hospital. Among these new roles was teaching in the diocesan coeducational high school in which sisters of several orders, priests, and lay persons served as a faculty. The sisters' presence in diversity was a notable departure from the past. But they were needed. With the male teachers they provided a pragmatic solution for the high school problem. They also helped to pave the way for the post-Vatican church. There were negative consequences, however. The unaccustomed exposure to more worldly elements in society left many scars and prepared the way for a devastating collapse, which was already in the making by the end of the decade.

Butte Central Catholic, a coeducational response to a need, had been staffed with diocesan priests and Sisters of Charity of Leavenworth as co-teachers. As noted above, the experiment was regarded as a failure. It was replaced with separate schools for boys and girls.[103] Perhaps the timing was wrong. In Helena, in September 1936, after the bishop had closed St. Vincent's Academy in its golden jubilee year, a similar Central Catholic was established, staffed also by diocesan priests and Sisters of Charity of Leavenworth. When the College of Great Falls was organized by Bishop O'Hara the new trend appeared: its faculty consisted of diocesan priests and two orders of sisters, the Ursulines and the Sisters of Providence. Perhaps this was too early also, for the Ursulines eventually dropped out.

In Great Falls in 1952, the modern version of the diocesan Central High finally appeared. Unlike the familiar parish high school, this was the consolidation of three existing institutions, St. Mary's of the Sisters of Humility of Mary, the Ursuline Academy and St. Thomas Orphan Home of the Sisters of Providence.[104] In those days it often happened that bishops and pastors used a heavy hand in dealing with the sisters. It appears in this case that Bishop Condon had done this, though as usual the sisters had to cover their chagrin behind the holy veil of docility.

Be that as it may, Catholic Central in Great Falls was opened in September 1950, with diocesan priests and three orders of sisters. It soon acquired the reputation for being, not the typical Catholic high school *of the future*, but the typical Catholic high school *of the present*, with a young diocesan priest like Father O'Malley in "Going My Way" as principal, a covey of nuns like variously plumed birds from different origins, striving heroically to get along with everybody, a layman as coach, and a lay woman to fill in, such as in conducting Typing One and Typing Two. In such perfect conformity to the ideal was this Central Catholic that it was featured in *Life Magazine* in January 1954.

From the Catholic viewpoint it would be premature, I think, to regard Great Falls Central Catholic as "typical," or in any sense ideal. The encyclical of Pius XI *Divini Redemptoris*, insisting on the separation of the sexes in schools during adolescence, had been promulgated just nineteen years earlier, in 1931. Excusing causes for the neglect of these directives may have been proportionate in smaller cities like Great Falls; one cannot presume the same for similar high schools in the larger cities. But these were, in fact, the wave of the future. What was happening in the Northwest was happening across the nation. The availability of the sisters, meanwhile, made it possible.

Fortunately their contribution was not always ignored. It will be recalled that Sister Miriam Theresa Gleason, who had begun as a lobbyist for Edwin O'Hara's Oregon Consumers' League back in 1912, was largely responsible for the first minimum wage law in Oregon. She was not forgotten. In February 1951, the *Portland Oregonian* listed the names of twenty-five outstanding women in Oregon's last one hundred years. Two of these twenty-five were Sisters of the Holy Names, Sisters Miriam for her part in the wage reform, and Mother M. Flavia who had established the Holy Names' normal schools in Portland, Seattle, and Spokane.[105] Two of these were forerunners of accredited colleges, Portland's Marylhurst and Spokane's Fort Wright College.[106]

While the sisters undoubtedly took great pride in this recognition, since they received so little, others were more impressed by it and the sisters carried on unobtrusively as before. They continued to build hospitals[107] and schools as they studied the trends and prepared themselves for the responsibilities appearing on the horizon. Meanwhile in many parishes the grateful people were building new convents for them, square boxes with modern kitchens, silent, shadowy chapels and little cells for rooms. Most of these would be abandoned after the results of the new order of things were in.

NEW WORKS, NEW ORDERS OF SISTERS

The new order, of course, brought relief from abuse and greater opportunities for the sisters. Bishop McGrath's use of Franciscan Sisters in his CCD program had opened one door. Another was opened when Sister Frederica and three other Sisters of Social Service from Los Angeles arrived in Portland on May 25, 1952. They arranged for an open house in their new center at 3306 N.E. Glisan Street. Three of the sisters were assigned then to parish social work in All Saints, St. Stephen's, and the cathedral parish. When other sisters from Los Angeles arrived to join the first group, they took over additional parishes and CCD work throughout western Oregon.[108]

In the great boom now in progress, seven new orders of sisters came to the Northwest, including some who had arrived much earlier and departed—the Sisters of Notre Dame de Namur and Benedictine Sisters from St. Benedict's Convent, St. Joseph, Minnesota.[109] Because of the flourishing growth of the latter, the Holy See requested its superiors to develop a new motherhouse. Olympia, Washington, was finally selected for one and on July 8, 1952, St. Placid Priory was formally opened in a temporary eight-room house near the city. Mother Placidia Haehn was elected the first prioress and plans were made for a permanent priory and girls school.[110]

The next group of sisters arrived from France. There were four Sisters of Nazareth, the first of their community to come to America. None could speak English, but the superior, Mother Damien, managed to guide the other three to Yakima, where they left their train on December 13, 1952. Bishop Dougherty had invited them to supervise the CCD program in the new diocese.[111]

Like the Benedictines of Minnesota, Franciscan Missionary Sisters of Our Lady of Sorrow from Santa Cruz, California, required a new motherhouse. Thus, on June 13, 1953, Mother M. Leola, O.S.F., with her sturdy band of eleven, arrived at Beaverton to open a convent and novitiate.[112] During this same month, these sisters replaced the Sisters of St. Mary of Oregon on the staff of St. Mary's Home for Boys. The Home, operated by the archdiocese, had two priests, twelve sisters, one caseworker, and about seven lay people on its staff, indicating its size and importance.

Another new foundation was formed by the Sisters of Mercy from Merion, Pennsylvania. Six of these sisters arrived on August 17, 1953, and established St. Alice Convent in Springfield, Oregon.[113]

The next two groups came from California through the efforts of Archbishop Connolly who had admired their work before he came to Seattle. First there were the Sisters of Notre Dame de Namur, the returnees, so to speak, after one hundred and nine years of absence. They were given a rousing welcome on August 28, 1953, and in the following month opened St. Francis of Assisi parish school at Seahurst. Two years later some of these sisters took over another school in Portland, St. Stephen's.[114] By this time they were celebrities featured on television. If Oregon's pride had been injured in 1851 when the sisters departed, then Oregon was enjoying its triumph by the sister's return.

Connolly's second group of proteges were the Sisters of the Presentation of the Blessed Virgin Mary, renowned for their parochial schools in San Francisco. "Presentation Nuns," they were called. Four came to Seattle, Mother Stanislaus their superior, on January 19, 1954. Six days later they opened another parish school, Our Lady of Fatima's, with 155 pupils as a beginning.[115]

In the same year, the first four members of the Congregation of the Sisters of the Holy Cross arrived in Seattle to staff St. Paul's Parochial School.[116] Finally, on August 7, 1955, the new Marian Home at Sublimity, Oregon, was dedicated by Archbishop Howard. This home for the aged was conducted by the Servite Sisters who had come several years earlier from Vienna, Austria.[117]

CHANGE FROM BAKER CITY TO BAKER

There is nothing earthshaking about any of the above events, though one can find in them and others like them, the uncritical euphoria of these fickle times. Almost every issue of the Catholic press contained enthusiastic accounts of the increase in vocations to the priesthood and religious life. Seminaries and novitiates were crowded, anything was possible.

Wiser men knew otherwise and wiser men were cautious. Most of the northwest bishops, I think, understood the risks in what they were forced to do. Pressed, on the one hand, by the overwhelming needs, and conscious, on the other, of the dangers, they did what was required, some more aggressively or with more vision than others.

Archbishop Howard, especially, accepted change with equanimity. He was already over seventy years old when this New Age began in the 1950's. But he met the pressures and later the upheaval with calm determination to make use of both. Archbishop Connolly, almost buried beneath a huge increase in Catholic population, had to take the greatest risks, which he did with courage. Bishop Dougherty, starting almost from scratch, allowed himself to be influenced by others and overreacted to the immediate needs.

The other bishops of the interior had less to fear, either from present demands that appeared to be running wild, like the economy, or the impending changes. Bishop Leipzig, sometimes too fussy even about little things, requested Rome to approve the change of the name of his diocese from Baker City to Baker. This was accomplished by a decree of February 16, 1952, which reached Baker on March 7.[118] It was a milestone that marked more than a change of title. The Baker Diocese, built on the sufferings of O'Reilly and the patience of McGrath, came to new life with the zeal of its third bishop. In Spokane and Boise, bishops were about to pass from the scene. In Great Falls the uncertainties brought illness in their wake.

But on February 14, 1953, all of the bishops with their flocks had reason to rejoice. On that day a seven foot statue of Dr. John McLoughlin was installed in the national capitol, Washington, D.C., as one of Oregon's two representatives. The Reverend Jason Lee, Protestant missionary, was the other Oregonian chosen for the Hall of Fame. The 1921 legislature had selected McLoughlin and Lee as the men to be honored, but this action was not implemented until $29,500 was allocated in 1945 for the completion of the statues by A. Phimister Proctor and Son.[119] So a prominent Protestant and Catholic shared the honors at last, in the new spirit of the times.

His Grace, the Archbishop, regarded this with great personal satisfaction, for his predecessor, "of long memory" now, had benefited enormously through the generosity of Dr. McLoughlin. Howard had other reasons for experiencing a pious complacency. With considerable ingenuity, which was characteristic of him, he had organized St. Elizabeth's parish, which had the distinction of being the only parish in western United States founded specifically for hospital work. Located on Marquam Hill, the medical center at that time for the Pacific Northwest, this new parish was composed largely of hospitals and medical schools. The first pastor was Father Alfred Williams, a former Air Force Chaplain, who collected funds all over the United States for his unique project.[120]

THE NEW GONZAGA PREP

Father Williams did not get his new church until 1958. Meanwhile, scores of other church buildings were popping up all over the Northwest. In one month alone, September, 1954, three new grade schools and three long sought high school buildings were opened to hundreds of students.[121]

The first was that of a sixty-seven year old institution, relocated now on a new campus. This was Gonzaga Prep in Spokane, independent of the university at last and housed in its spanking new million dollar plus building on a twenty-three acre site. Bishop White, as eager as any Jesuit, had urged its construction for years, reminding the Jesuits periodically that his successor might not be as well disposed as he was for a second canonically established Jesuit community in Spokane. But money, or lack of it, not prelates, had been the villain all along. When White's permission was sought for a drive to provide a new retreat house, he quickly refused it, adding that the number one priority in his diocese was the building of a new Gonzaga high school.[122] He urged that land be purchased for this purpose, and with this in mind, Gonzaga's new principal, Father Gordon Toner, arranged to cover the city by air. In early May, 1949, he made his first flight. Two possible sites were noted and during subsequent weeks carefully examined. The Euclid Avenue site appeared to be most promising so steps were taken for its acquisition. On August 15, 1949, two lots on the western extremity of the present Gonzaga Prep campus were purchased at public auction for seventy-five dollars each.[123]

During the next three years, under the determined bishop's inspiration, more land was purchased. A final drive for funds was conducted and plans were drawn by architect John Maloney. Bishop White himself presided over the groundbreaking ceremonies on July 3, 1953. A year later, on September 5, His Excellency presided again over a dedication program which was regarded generally as two decades late. No matter. It was finally over and on the following day 610 students reported for classes. After sixty-seven years, thirteen of them as an orphan, Gonzaga Prep finally had a building and a campus of its own.

BLANCHET HIGH SCHOOL IN SEATTLE

For Seattle's Blanchet High, similar problems, like land and money, had to be overcome, but, it must be admitted, considerably less time was required. There were seven parishes in the area north of the Lake Washington Canal, only one of which, Our Lady of the Lake, had been established in the Shaughnessy years.[124] When Connolly arrived in Seattle he soon realized the shortcomings of previous planning and he set about immediately to acquire property for four new parishes and additional property for the proposed new high school. For over a year following this, Connolly devoted himself to the task of planning the new school and recruiting a faculty to administer it. Construction was begun in February, 1954 on the south wing, which was to be occupied by the first class in September. But unforseen developments, the inability of the contractor to continue on the job, left the project in limbo for some weeks. Scheduled occupation of the building was impossible, so the first class of Blanchet High School, 231 freshmen boys and girls, began their studies in the basement of the Old Blessed Sacrament School at 50th and East Roosevelt on September 6, 1954.[125]

The faculty that year consisted of two diocesan priests, Father John P. Doogan as principal and Father James Mallahan as vice-principal, ten sisters from five different orders, and two lay people.[126] In an official photograph, all appeared to be in their Sunday best, and all except the vice principal presented broad, happy smiles. Doogan, especially, looked gung-ho, like a race horse at the starting gate eager to be off and running.

By this time a new building contractor from San Francisco was employed. Construction proceeded rapidly. The new building was occupied on May 6, 1955. A few months later, during the school's second year, on November 8, 1955, the archbishop dedicated it in honor of the state's first bishop, old Augustin Blanchet, who had died at the age of ninety, many long years before. It was an appropriate title even if twentieth-century students found it almost impossible to relate to the old patriarch. It was the kind of monument that would keep Blanchet's name alive and his deeds utterly forgotten.

BISHOP WHITE'S LAST YEAR

In the late autumn of 1954, Spokane dedicated its new Coliseum. Many events of a triumphal nature were celebrated to acknowledge the historic nature of the accomplishment and even *Life Magazine,* which seldom found anything west of the Rockies worth noting, devoted a feature article to the exuberant Spokanites cavorting in the possession of their cherished new facility.

Bishop White that year was celebrating his twenty-eighth year as bishop of Spokane. He seemed to sense that it was his last and he made no secret of his desire for a mammoth demonstration of loyalty to him, and especially to the Immaculate Conception on the centenary of its definition as a dogma. To commemorate both he requested the use of the Coliseum for an evening Mass in which he hoped that Catholics from all over the diocese could share. City officials, however, alleging that the Coliseum was too large for a religious service, refused the bishop's request. White, not to be put off, set to work to change their minds by organizing Catholic pressures. The city bureaucrats yielded, very reluctantly, and the bishop's Marian Mass, as it was called, was scheduled for 7:15 p.m. on Sunday, December 5, 1954. Determined to teach the bureaucrats a lesson, White dispatched a letter to be read in all the pulpits of the diocese, calling his people to attend the Mass.

The Coliseum seats nine thousand persons. Preparations were made for eight thousand. A choir of fifteen hundred voices, provided by all the parochial schools and Mount St. Michael's, prepared to sing the Mass. A "giant Altar" was built. Thrones for two bishops were installed. Special sections for hundreds of priests and sisters were set apart. Father Tully in his paper, kept up a barrage of publicity. The Catholics, at least, never doubted the results.

Late Sunday afternoon, thousands of cars began to pour into Spokane from all over eastern Washington. The highways were jammed. The greatest traffic jam in Spokane history closed most of the roads leading to the Coliseum. An hour before Mass was to begin, twelve thousand people had already crowded into the Coliseum while another six thousand were still trying to enter.[127] All of Spokane's radio and television stations were preempted by the police to direct traffic out of the city. The Catholics could not fill the Coliseum? When push came to shove, they could do a lot more than that. Even the unflappable Archbishop Connolly, who had been invited to preach the homily, was so astonished by the size and enthusiasm of the crowd that he momentarily departed from his prepared text, a sure sign of his humanness. Only God knows what Bishop White thought. He kept a straight face and said the right things, as serene as always.

After the Mass was over, Bishop White, seemingly small and feeble under his heavy vestments, and clutching his crozier fiercely, stood firmly at the foot of the altar, facing the people, a tiny speck in all that vast crowd. It was a wicked world, he said, in a squeaky nasal voice. What we need is prayer and penance. Gazing intently over the throng, he shouted his message several times."Prayer and Penance. Prayer and Penance." Then he was gone. It was his last legacy to his church, a powerful message that was remembered long after everything else was forgotten.

BISHOP BERNARD TOPEL

Bishop White went to the hospital in April. It was only for a rest, it was said, but few expected him to leave it alive. Weakened with age and worn out with labor, he got worse rather than better. Then he suffered a cerebral hemorrhage and though his doctor reported that he was not critical, his priests knew that it was time to begin proceedings for a new bishop.

On August 9, 1955, Father Bernard Joseph Topel of Carroll College, Helena, was appointed Titular Bishop of Brinda and Coadjutor Bishop *cum jure successionis* of Spokane. He was born on March 31, 1903, the son of Henry and Mary Pauline Hagen Topel of Bozeman, Montana. Henry owned a clothing store. Later Bernard sheepishly admitted that his father regarded himself as a socialist for a period following the first World War when the I.W.W.'s and the Russian Bolsheviks were striking terror in the hearts of many affluent Americans.

Bernard had once applied to enter the Jesuit Order. But the pastor of Holy Rosary parish, citing the needs of the Montana church, persuaded him to enter what was then called Mount St. Charles as a seminarian for the diocese. Later his bishop sent him to the Grand Seminary in Montreal (1923-1924) and to the Sulpician Seminary in Washington, D.C. (1924-1927). He was ordained to the priesthood in Helena on June 7, 1927 by Bishop Mitty of Salt Lake. After earning his master's degree in mathematics at Harvard and a doctorate at Notre Dame, he taught at Carroll College. As director of vocations for the diocese during this same period, he attracted national attention for his success, which seems in retrospect, at least, to be presumptuous. It was a time of record numbers of vocations everywhere. Seminaries and convents were crowded, most of them without the benign influence of a Father Vocation Director. But Topel had labored zealously and partly because of this he was selected to be the third bishop of Spokane.

At this time he appeared to be tall and uncommonly lean. His long face, seemingly longer because of his high forehead, suggested the looks of an ascetic, which was confirmed by his abstract manner, a kind of airy, spaced-out detachment, which sometimes led one to believe his thoughts were on higher, loftier things than the subject at hand. He rolled his head from side to side when he talked. Only his deeply intense eyes and occasional broad smiles reassured one that he was actually present and listening. Bishop White had wanted prayer and penance. In his successor he had got exactly that, for Bernard Topel was above all a man of prayer and penance.

He was consecrated in Helena on September 21, 1955, by Bishop Gilmore, assisted by Bishops Dougherty of Yakima and Joseph Willging of Pueblo. Four days later on September 25, before Bishop Topel was formally received in Spokane, Charles Daniel White breathed his last. Bernard Topel succeeded him on the eve of the stormiest period in the history of the modern church.

19

THE VATICAN COUNCIL YEARS
1955–1966

Down in Oregon, meanwhile, the Trappist monks had made a hopeful comeback. There is a lovely little valley, dotted with ancient twisted and moss-covered oaks and scattered groves of native maple trees, which runs westerly from the village of Lafayette on old highway 99W. Near the end of the valley several miles distant, the land, heavily green with forests of fir, rises abruptly, forming a natural bowl on the right, with flatlands in the foreground and low foothills below the heavier timber, a serene and isolated site only thirty miles southwest of Portland.

Here it was that the Trappists from Pecos, New Mexico found their permanent home. They had been forced out of Pecos for lack of water. Our Lady of Guadalupe Abbey had been established on arid waste land, so dry and cruel that even the Trappists could not produce enough food for their frugal diet. When they decided to move they looked to the lush valleys of western Oregon, selecting at last the prolific hillside near rain-swept Lafayette.

Their abbot was Australian born M Columban Hawkins. "The second foundation of Trappists [in Oregon]" he wrote, "is our own. We arrived here on March 1, 1955, although prior contingents had been at Lafayette preparing the interior furnishings of the house, which was practically finished (by secular contractors) when we arrived. We flew here from our place at Pecos, New Mexico by plane on that day. We were about sixty in number then, and we remain at the same number, but we hope that Our Lady of Guadalupe will obtain God's blessings on this Abbey and make it a stable and permanent part of Catholic life in the Northwest for a long time to come."[1]

Their hopes were justified; they had come to stay. There, below the forested highlands, they plowed the moist fields for gardens, organized a carpenter shop where they assembled pews for the many churches being built in the Northwest, and established a book bindery which has become noted for its excellent craftmanship in the ancient Trappist tradition. Their abbey has become a center for prayer, where visitors come to stay in neat little guest houses, surrounded by flowers and ferns, a stone's throw from the abbey church where the monks chant the praises of God.

AUXILIARY BISHOP THOMAS GILL

The presence of a stable Trappist community in the Northwest could be interpreted as evidence of an adult church. Another sign of this was the appointment of the region's first auxiliary bishop.[2] This was Thomas Edward Gill, a native of Seattle's St. Joseph parish on Capital Hill. Gill was pastor of the Cathedral parish on April 11, 1956, when the apostolic delegate announced that he had been designated Titular Bishop of Lambaesis and Auxiliary to the Archbishop of Seattle.[3]

Gill, the second youngest of ten children, was born on March 18, 1908.[4] His parents were Irish immigrants James J. and Anna Keane Gill, who had come separately to Seattle in their youth and had been married in Our Lady of Good Help Church in 1890. Certainly this, if nothing else, provided the Gills with establishment status in the Seattle church. As a boy, Thomas, known as "the thick haired kid with the strong jaw," served Mass each morning in the convent at Forest Ridge, revealing an early streak of piety, for which he praised his mother "who was wonderfully devout."[5]

No one was surprised then, when he entered the minor seminary at Mountain View, California. He was ordained to the priesthood by Archbishop Hanna in St. Mary's Cathedral, San Francisco, on June 10, 1933. After graduate studies in Washington D.C., he served in the Seattle diocese in various administrative capacities including the directorship of Catholic Charities of the diocese. He became pastor of St. James Cathedral in 1954, "the second busiest man in the archdiocese."

"A princely priest," they had called him. Also "the foster father of the poor." He stood tall in his vestments, straight as a rod. His dark Irish good looks contained an element of gentleness that was easily recognized as "a soft touch." He was deeply and universally loved, the peoples' priest to whom everyone, especially the poor, turned in trouble.

When the news of his appointment as bishop arrived, he was on his way to the chapel to pray. "I continued right onto the chapel," he said. "I never wanted to go into the chapel more than I did right then." Thus he revealed the source of his strength very casually and with characteristic simplicity.

He was consecrated by Archbishop Connolly in St. James Cathedral on May 31, 1956. Co-consecrators were Bishops Donohue of San Francisco and Dougherty of Yakima. More than two thousand relatives and friends witnessed the ceremony in which four archbishops and fifteen bishops participated.[6] At this time Bishop Gill was only thirty-eight years old, in the prime of life and quite possibly the successor to Archbishop Connolly. But this would never happen. Bishop Gill, worn out with labors for the church in Seattle died unexpectedly when he was only in his fifty-sixth year.

BISHOP JAMES BYRNE FOR BOISE

The consecration of Bishop Gill brought the number of bishops in the Northwest to nine. Three weeks later, on April 21, 1956, one of the nine died.

Bishop Kelly was in Boise. It was a Saturday, at six in the morning, and the bishop was preparing to offer Mass. He suffered a heart attack; in a few moments he was gone.[7] His funeral was celebrated in St. John's Cathedral by Archbishop Howard on April 26. Present for the first time in Idaho history was a prince of the church, Francis Cardinal McIntyre. Bishop Gilmore preached the eulogy, and the bishop's coffin with its venerable burden was borne to Morris Hill Cemetery and placed in its grave in the Catholic section called St. John's. Edward Kelly had been bishop of Boise for twenty-eight years, almost three decades during which he had been respected, but not always loved. Some, not without reason, regarded him as an arbitrary, though prayerful man, whose leadership was tainted sometimes with petty squabbles and impulsive, even erratic decisions.

His successor was just the opposite, a gentle relaxed kind of priest who made everyone feel comfortable in his presence. Bishop James J. Bryne, Titular Bishop of Etenna and Auxiliary to the Archbishop of St. Paul, was appointed the fourth Bishop of Boise on June 16, 1956.[8] Like his predecessor, he was as trim as a prisoner of war. His small refined features, topped with graying hairs, and his soft eyes gazing placidly through rimless glasses, produced an impression of calm benigness, like a portrait of Pope Pius XII. He was forty-seven years old. He had been a priest for twenty-three years and a bishop for nine. He was especially known for his love of Mary the Mother of God, and he had chosen for his motto on his coat of arms, the then popular theme *Ad Jesum per Mariam*, which was about as American Catholic as a parish bazaar.[9] Byrne was installed on August 29, 1956, in St. John's Cathedral. Archbishop

Howard presided, as unflappable as ever, and as fresh and alert as an acolyte.

Howard was nearing the age of eighty. At home he walked every day, weather permitting, from his elegant brick residence in northwest Portland to the chancery, nearly two miles of urban pavement.[10] When it rained, as it sometimes did in Portland, he took the bus and entered into conversation with his fellow passengers, presenting homespun philosophy for their edification. This helped to make him a popular local character who was often quoted in the press, always with something clever to say. "I do not take my troubles home with me," he often liked to say, to explain his youthful vigor. "Every night I sleep like a babe."

JESUIT HIGH, PORTLAND

Surrounded in his office by his own staff, some of whom were opposed to the idea of a Jesuit school in Portland, Howard could not bring himself to consider seriously this proposal, which had been a sore one since 1907, when the Jesuits arrived in Portland. They had bailed out Archbishop Christie by taking over several problem parishes, including one in which scandals had occurred, and they were hopeful that His Grace would respond by permitting them to establish their long sought school. Nearly fifty years had passed, and Howard, like his predecessor, dissembled whenever the subject was broached. Since Columbia Prep was closed in June 1955, the Jesuits stepped up their efforts and expressed their willingness to take over the school under the usual Jesuit conditions. Nothing came of this, however, for the archdiocesan director of schools demanded complete jurisdiction over the school. The matter was dropped and the Holy Cross Fathers sold the campus to a real estate developer for subdivision.[11]

But neither the archbishop nor the Jesuit Provincial, Father Henry Schultheis, was satisfied. The former finally admitted that he would encourage the establishment of the school provided that it be located "On the west side, outside city limits," in keeping with conditions recommended by some of his priests. On Saturday, August 4, 1955, Schultheis persuaded the archbishop to accompany him to a site he had uncovered within the perimeters of the conditions imposed. The archbishop expressed his pleasure with this site and gave his consent on the spot, contingent upon one additional condition, that the Jesuits would not establish a collegiate church.

On Tuesday, August 16, both the provincial and the archbishop composed letters. Schultheis wrote as follows: "We will not open a collegiate church or make the chapel available to others than staff and students." Howard wrote that he hereby gave permission for the Jesuits "to open a school in Portland on the site examined last Saturday." He added that he would aid the school substantially by allowing a financial drive and by making a contribution.[12]

Schultheis was elated. He already had an option on the land, which was a fifty-six acre tract on the Bertha-Beaverton highway, fifteen minutes from downtown Portland. The sale price was $165,000 part of which was borrowed by the province and advanced to the new community.[13]

When the formal announcement of the new school, to be called Jesuit High, was made, there were unpleasant repercussions on the part of certain priests, who regarded the Jesuits as rivals. In heart-warming contrast to these was Father Willis Whelan, Principal of Central Catholic, for whom the Jesuits had considerable respect. "Please accept our best wishes," he wrote. "If we can be of assistance, let us know."

Partly due to the opposition, the campaign for funds fell far short of its goal. Undaunted, Father Schultheis appointed the first principal, Father Joseph Perri, and assigned seven more Jesuits to the new faculty. Entrance examinations were administered on April 14, 1956, in the cathedral grade school. By September 10, all was in a more-or-less state of readiness in the new building on the site, and the doors of Jesuit High, forty-third among Jesuit prep schools in the United States, were opened wide for ninety solemn little freshmen, who trooped through into an unfamiliar man's world.

The ninety freshmen advanced in due time to seniors and Jesuit High became a full four-year accredited high school with a faculty of eighteen Jesuits and a half-dozen dedicated lay people. New buildings had arisen, like additions to a home, competitive trophies had been taken, and best of all, the support and esteem of local Catholics, including the clergy, had been earned honestly. When Perri arrived he found an overgrown cow pasture. When he departed ten years later in 1965, he left a well-established prep school with 511 selected students and a developed campus of nearly thirty acres. All beginnings were hard, as old Father Joset used to say. Jesuit High was no exception. But the roots that had been formed in the early dry years eventually supported a resplendent oak tree, which grew firmly and more fair to see as the years passed quickly by.

THE HELENA PROMISES

One of the reasons for opposition to the Jesuits, of course, was their alleged power to attract a disproportionate number of candidates to their order. In a vastly expanding church, the bishops' greatest concern was continuity and growth of the diocesan clergy. Religious orders like the Jesuits did not have the final responsibility for staffing the parishes, the chaplaincies in the hospitals and academies, and the administration of the diocese. When the pressure was on they could come and go, leaving the bishops with vacancies and sometimes in dire straits. One can understand then, why some bishops developed a certain touchiness on the subject of "vocations," that is, potential or real candidates for the priesthood and religious life.

While they were justified in being concerned, perhaps even for being aggressive, it is difficult to acquit them for some aberrations that were entirely unreasonable, not to mention contrary to church law. One recalls the actions of the older Blanchet in trying to prevent the orders from accepting candidates in the area of his jurisdiction. More legitimate was his effort to develop his own vocations by establishing St. Michael's College in Portland. The existence of St. Michael's and other diocesan high schools and colleges were closely identified with this delicate matter. They were intended in part to serve as nurseries for diocesan vocations, as schools like Jesuit High actually served as nurseries for Jesuits.

Thus, Carroll College had been founded primarily as a source of vocations for the Helena diocese. Bishop Gilmore, reigning gloriously in 1956, was so incensed regarding unverified Jesuit "poaching" on his Montana turf that he had promulgated his unilateral directive requiring certain formalities of Jesuits before giving them the faculties of the diocese. In the course of time this had become the celebrated case in Canon Law known as "The Helena Promises."

The "Promises" had actually been imposed on Jesuits in the aftermath of the cold war over Holy Family Mission. The Jesuit Provincial then, Father William Elliott, admitted to his superiors that there had been "unfriendly relations with the Bishop." Sometimes, he explained, members of the Gonzaga faculty in Spokane gave retreats in the Helena Diocese and used these opportunities to seek football players and other students for the university.[14] Gilmore reacted by demanding that hereafter any Jesuit coming into his diocese was required to report to him first in Helena and state his business in the diocese before he could receive faculties. Elliott wrote to the bishop to point out the inconvenience and extra cost of this procedure, but the bishop did not reply. Finally, a Jesuit who was sent to the Jesuit parish in Missoula contacted the chancery in Helena for instructions, and was directed to report to Father Dennis Meade, pastor of the diocesan parish in Missoula. Meade, he was informed, was the head of the deanery. Now all of this was confusing, because prior to this, the pastor of the pioneer St. Francis Xavier parish was the head of the deanery and the Jesuits had never been informed of the change. When the visitor applied to Meade for faculties he was compelled to sign a statement from the bishop, whereby:

(1) he was required to profess the nature of his business in the diocese and the time he was to remain in it;

(2) he was not to solicit students for any Jesuit Colleges;

(3) he was not to solicit [or "rope in"] any members of the Helena Diocese for the Society, and he was to refer anyone who came to him to discuss vocations to his confessor or the Bishop;

(4) failure on his part to live up to the conditions under which the faculties were granted meant *ipso facto* their removal.[15]

This was only the beginning of the tussle about the infamous "Promises." It was also a classic example of the kind of friction that existed between some bishops in the Northwest and the Jesuits throughout this period.

BISHOP TOPEL'S VOCATION WAR

Before coming to Spokane Bishop Topel of Helena had been greatly influenced in favor of Gilmore's position. As vocation director for the diocese, he had become preoccupied with the subject to such an extent that one never thought of him without thinking about vocations. He brought this image of himself to Spokane. On his first visit to Gonzaga Prep, after the students and faculty had regaled him in verse and song, he responded by scolding everyone because *seven* Prep graduates in the previous year had entered the Jesuit novitiate, but none had become diocesan seminarians.[16] His harangue was, in effect, a declaration of war for vocations and Prep's students recognized it for what it was and bitterly resented it.

It was a poor beginning with the subject most cherished by Bishop Topel, but the last word had not been spoken. Gradually "Father Bishop" as he liked to be called, coordinated his resources. He hammered relentlessly "on the vocation crisis" and ordered that every religious event in the diocese was to be concluded with "a Hail Mary for vocations." The number of younger diocesan seminarians increased dramatically, but the Gonzaga Prep boys, in a frank interchange of views with the bishop, accused him of applying undue pressures. "Why is it," they asked, "that every time you come you have a net out for us?" Topel recognized this criticism and responded with vigorous action.

BISHOP WHITE SEMINARY

Topel had occupied his office in the Spokane Chancery building on October 13, 1955. Two weeks later on November 3, he dispatched to all pastors his first directive. He was organizing, he said, "a two pronged campaign to rouse the faithful of the diocese to the need of priestly vocations." Father Robert O'Neil, he added, was the new vocation director. "He will talk to all boys and girls in the diocese on the subject."[17] This was one step. The other was a visit by Topel to seminaries in the East, "in Boston, Canada and Ohio," to induce seminarians there "to go west," at least as far as eastern Washington, to serve as priests in his diocese.

In the Northwest at this time there were seven seminaries, including the recently established Franciscan minor seminary as a department of Serra High School in Salem.[18] The others, all filled beyond advisable capacity were: Mount Angel, where a new minor seminary building called St. Anselm's Hall was dedicated on October 3, 1954;[19] St. Edward's on Lake Washington, which accommodated, willy nilly, all three divisions, minor seminary, philosophy and theology; Carroll College, where on November 4, 1956, Bishop Gilmore broke ground for a new seminary building, dedicated one year later in honor of St. Charles Borromeo; the Jesuits' novitiate at Sheridan, to which several new wings had been added for accommodating additional postulants;[20] Mount St. Michael's with the largest number of scholastics in its four decade history; and finally, St. Martin's for candidates for the Benedictine Order.

To accommodate the windfall he expected, Bishop Topel was determined to have his own seminary. He would start with a minor seminary. First he designated March, 1956 as "Vocation Month" then in July following, announced that his seminary would be opened in September in the St. John Bosco building on Sharp Avenue.[21] He appointed Father William Kelley, a former Jesuit, as the first principal and assigned two young priests to the staff, Robert O'Neil and George Haspedis. Twenty candidates drummed up by O'Neil were accepted and studies began on September 4, 1956 in what was now called Bishop White Seminary. The Spokane diocese at this time had twenty-four other young men studying for the priesthood, nine of them in the major seminary. One of the latter was William Skylstad who later became the third bishop of Yakima.[22]

ST. THOMAS MAJOR SEMINARY

In Seattle, meanwhile, Archbishop Connolly had begun to implement plans for his own grandiose new seminary addition to St. Edward's, a separate complex for philosophy and theology. Unlike Gilmore, Topel, and Dougherty of Yakima, Connolly's cautious relations with the Jesuits did not involve vocations, but rather the threat of a collegiate church like

St. Ignatius in San Francisco, whence he had come.[23] As for seminarians, he had more than enough for his present needs, which was an enviable position, but not one to be neglected.

St. Edward's had been designed for 111 students. In 1956 it had 260 in the twelve-year course, of whom eighteen were graduated in June when they were ordained priests.[24]

On Wednesday, October 17, 1956, St. Edward's celebrated its twenty-fifth anniversary by observing the usually dull formalities by laying a new seminary cornerstone, a Masonic tradition, by the way, which seemed to be more meticulously practiced by the Catholics than anyone else. On this occasion the presence of Cardinal McIntyre bestowed a kind of Vatican perfume over the ceremony, making fragrant the entire project that was most dear to the well-guarded heart of the archbishop.

By December, blueprints by John Maloney's office were completed and on January 16, 1957, contracts totalling $3,418,109.93 were awarded to Henrik Valle Co., Inc. and other contractors.[25] Work was begun on February 4 when the bulldozers roared into action in the muddy clearing a quarter of a mile north of St. Edward's. Completion was expected for autumn of 1958. Accordingly, September 3 was set for the opening day but this had to be postponed until the eleventh. "Thus," says the seminary's chronicler, "August marked the beginning of the Big Drive— the battle of the invasion and occupation of the Seminary of St. Thomas the Apostle."[26] The exodus of the major seminarians, leaving St. Edward's to the minors, was made in the old green dump truck, which rattled over the bumpy roads between the two buildings for an entire week. Then the faculty of Sulpician Fathers was moved. On September 8 the archbishop himself appeared in late afternoon, and this made it official. St. Thomas was a reality.

But months of additional improvements were required before the solemn dedication on April 14, 1959. Cardinal McIntyre returned for the occasion. Archbishop Howard, who could be counted upon to say the right words, delivered the dedication sermon. He laid it on the line: "The work of the seminary," he asserted, "is to produce saints. For the most part the world must be christianized by the laity—that is their function." Yet the laity, he added, will only be as spiritual and only as zealous as their pastors.

> A holy priest—a fervent people
> A fervent priest—a pious people
> A pious priest—a decent people
> A decent priest—godless people.[27]

NEW RETREAT HOUSES

According to this scale it would be inappropriate to judge the Catholic laity of the Northwest. But one indication of their religious vitality was their demand during this period for retreat houses. Another was the successful production of a second Carmelite Convent for contemplatives, similar in lifestyle to the Trappists.[28] This convent was on Greenhill Drive, a few miles outside the City of Eugene. Six Carmelites from Carmel of St. Theresa, Alhambra, California, arrived on November 4, 1957, to occupy an old residence which they called Carmel of Maria Regina. Mass was celebrated for the first time two days later and "Enclosure" was officially established in September 1958.[29]

The four new retreat houses required more time. The first was the Palisades Retreat House located near Mirror Lake, midway between Seattle and Tacoma on the Sound. This was staffed by the Redemptorist Fathers. The first retreat for men, conducted by Father Edward Jennings, began on October 6, 1956 and on the following day Archbishop Connolly dedicated the facility in his customary solemn high manner.[30]

A retreat house specifically for women was opened a year later. Staffed by the Visitation Sisters, it was also located between Seattle and Tacoma. Its first retreat was begun on October 11, 1957.[31]

Perhaps the most noise, with good reason, was made about the Immaculate Heart Retreat House near Spokane. Retreats for laymen had been conducted during the summer months at Mount St. Michael's since 1920. Retreatants there formed a Retreat Association and, encouraged by Bishop White, made plans for a permanent building on the south slope of the Mount. There were some, however, who favored another site on the Little Spokane River, and as the debate dragged on, mostly among the Jesuits. Bishop White died and a new bishop appeared on the scene.

Bishop Topel had other ideas, which prevailed, of course, and the Jesuits discreetly became silent. Topel wanted his own retreat house and he bought a large tract on Moran Prairie overlooking the city from the southeast, instead of from the north. There were certain vocal repercussions from members of the old Retreat Association, but the bishop, a determined man in those earlier years, doggedly named one of his own priests, Father David Rosage, as director of the proposed project, with a mandate to build a first class establishment for the use of women retreatants as well as men. The bishop could not have selected a better director. Rosage soon won the support of all factions and gathered, with the bishop's persistent reminders, something like a half-million dollars, which he spent as carefully as if it were his own. Ground was broken for the new building on April 13, 1958. On January 5, 1959 it was occupied by the domestic staff of Dominican Sisters and six weeks later, February 20-22, under the direction of Bishop Topel, the first closed retreat was presented.[32]

Retreatants in the course of the years came from all parts of the United States. Many were bishops who arrived to make thirty day retreats, a kind of specialty of the house, as it were, conducted with the cooperation of Gonzaga's theology department. Two members of the department in particular should be recognized; Fathers Armand Nigro and Vincent Beuzer. With Rosage, they made a dynamic team whose influence reached into all part of the English-speaking world.[33]

MOUNT ANGEL'S RETREAT HOUSE

The last of the four new retreat houses was at Mount Angel. For forty years some of the Benedictines there had favored lay retreats as a form of monastic employment, but other priorities, occasioned by fires and lack of money, preempted anything like progress toward an on-going program. Nothing is ever simple and by 1958 the activities of the monks had become very complicated. The abbey farm was over 1250 acres of cultivated land. Under the new abbot, Damian Jentges, the number of monks had grown to over one hundred, making Mount Angel one of the largest Benedictine monasteries in North America. Abbot Damian restructured the curriculum and governance of the seminary, giving the secular clergy a greater share in the latter and making it possible for non-Benedictines to become its rector.[34] The seminary, by this time, had become one of the largest in the country.

Damian wanted a year-round retreat program but not all members of his community shared this view. Most, however, recognized the need for improved guest facilities, so a compromise was reached. Construction on a guest-retreat house was begun in 1959. Called Benet Hall, this building when completed in the following year, was designed to accommodate forty overnight guests.[35]

So much for the retreat houses. There were no current controversies about them because there were enough retreatants to go around. But unfortunately, conflicts were occurring elsewhere and an explosive one, which eventually influenced the resignation of the bishop, was in the making in the Yakima Valley. It began with the bishop's determination to have his own central high school.

YAKIMA'S CENTRAL CATHOLIC

Bishop Dougherty had purchased a "palace" in the affluent district of Yakima and a top-of-the-line Chrysler, presumably because he thought of himself as a traditional prince-bishop. Some regarded this as a coverup for an administrator who was not sure of himself. But the truth of the matter was much more simple: Bishop Dougherty took his office seriously and he was trying to represent the diocese as well as other bishops represented theirs. Dougherty was a zealous bishop, eager to please, but an uncertain choice for establishing a new diocese. He recognized his limitations, and though he had been a chancellor himself, with considerable experience in church law, he decided "to borrow" an expert who had been highly recommended, Father Philip Leinfelder of Lacrosse, Wisconsin.

Leinfelder, an alumnus of Loras College, Dubuque, was ordained to the priesthood on December 8, 1939. He was a tall, barrel-chested heavyweight of Germanic origin, built to survive Wisconsin winters and strong-willed enough to resist the blandishments of wealth, women, and wine. He arrived in Yakima, temporarily "on loan" from his diocese, on March 10, 1954. Dougherty appointed him chancellor and vicar general of the diocese, "my assistant in temporal and spiritual cares of the diocese."

Two years later, while vacationing on Vachon Island in Puget Sound, Dougherty suffered a heart attack that was so severe doctors did not expect him to live. For many months following this he was completely isolated from all except Archbishop Connolly, while Leinfelder literally controlled all the business of the diocese. When Dougherty returned, still sickly and weak, he was confronted with a cruel dilemma: either force Leinfelder out, a procedure he was reluctant to pursue because of his chancellor's generosity in the crisis, or accept the fact that Leinfelder's influence in the decisionmaking process would be irresistible. Dougherty despite the archbishop's advice, chose the latter.

What followed, then, is tragic. Bishop Dougherty, tense and overly anxious, and dependent upon another who was determined to rule behind the scenes, acted in his own name, but completely out of character. One thinks of a puppet, but Bishop Dougherty was no puppet, rather he was a victim of his own spirit of gratitude.

The establishment of Yakima's Central Catholic was an example of the consequences. It was not the first incident of its kind, nor the last, but it was the most notorious and the one most deeply resented.[37]

St. Joseph's Academy had been founded by the Sisters of Providence in Yakima in 1875. It was the first school for whites in the Yakima Diocese.

It had been conducted with splendid results for eighty-three years, not as long as Harvard, but long enough to be valued and esteemed by all. Marquette High School had been founded in 1909 by the Jesuits who taught there for over forty years without a salary, with nothing more than their school term expenses. It, too, served with distinction, earning honors of all kinds, especially in debating and college scholarships. Most Catholics, if not all, regarded these two schools, one for girls and one for boys, as the apple of their eyes. They were certainly adequate for the needs of a small city like Yakima.

One can imagine, then, the consternation of Yakima Catholics when His Excellency announced his intention to establish a third high school, a central Catholic involving neither St. Joseph's nor Marquette. Plainly both pioneer schools would have to go if the bishop's proposal were realized. But the bishop vehemently denied this. On August 23, 1957, he published specific details regarding the project. "Yakima's New School Plans Unveiled."[38] Thirty-eight acres of land had been acquired on Teton Drive in west Yakima. A campaign for $704,000 for the first two units would begin soon. Architect T.J. Haugis, Jr., a member of St. Paul's parish, was commissioned to design the campus which would accommodate ultimately, one thousand students, serving the five parishes in the area. Classes for freshmen would start in September in St. Paul's grade school building.

If this were not a declaration of finale for St. Joseph's and Marquette, the Catholics in Yakima did not understand plain English.

Construction on the two new buildings, called "Aquinas Hall" and "Science Hall" was begun on May 4, 1958, and classes on the new campus were first assembled on September 2, 1959. Central's principal, Father Donald McDermott, who was called "the Headmaster" directed a staff composed of priests of the diocese and Dominican Sisters.[39]

Central that year attracted three hundred students while Marquette enrolled 225 boys who had to be content with primitive quarters that reminded one of an impoverished Indian mission in eastern Montana. Attendance at St. Joseph's Academy had dropped drastically, leaving the sisters dismayed.[40] While the question uppermost in the minds of the people was how long could the Academy and Marquette survive, there were others who were more concerned about the future of the church itself. The bishop, they reasoned, would not have made decisions like these without undue pressure and influence from someone close to him in the chancery. Their anxieties were well founded, as the sequel shows. Bishop Dougherty and his chancellor were on the high road to disaster.

JESUITS WITHDRAW FROM MARQUETTE

The new Jesuit provincial was Father Alexander McDonald, a gentle, scholarly priest who never raised his voice or admitted that his degree in English had been granted by Oxford. Whether he liked it or not, he had to come to grips with the Marquette problem. Neither he nor anyone else questioned the right of the bishop to do what he had done. Although the Jesuits staffed Marquette, it was understood by everyone that it was a parish high school. But the Jesuits owned the property and the building, such as it was. The ugly crux of the problem lay elsewhere.[41]

The bishop had taxed all the parishes, including Jesuit administered St. Joseph's, for the support of Central. Marquette, on the other hand, which had a majority of students from parishes other than St. Joseph's, was partly supported with an inadequate tuition fee set by the bishop with deficits made up by the parish and the Jesuits. In other words, St. Joseph's parish had to contribute to Central, located elsewhere, and then pay for the support for non-parish students attending Marquette. The school had survived so far only because the Jesuits had subsidized it.

In January 1960, McDonald made up his mind that Jesuits would have to withdraw from Marquette. He conveyed his decision to the Jesuit General in Rome, Father John B. Janssens, who agreed with him. On February 3 he wrote to Bishop Dougherty.

> My Superiors in Rome have reached a decision which affects the position of Jesuits in Yakima.... In the hope of leaving the field clear for the full development of Yakima Central Catholic, we are to withdraw our Jesuit staff from Marquette High School at the close of the current school year.[42]

The bishop was in California and he did not reply until one month later. "Thanks to the Jesuit Staff," he wrote on March 2, 1960, "Marquette has a rich tradition which must be continued for the good of the Church. Accordingly I have made arrangements to maintain the school with another faculty.... The school will remain in operation."[43]

This was not exactly what McDonald had expected. Nor did it appear reasonable. How on earth could the bishop justify three high schools in Yakima, while Wenatchee and Richland were begging for only one?

McDonald had asked the bishop to publish a statement regarding the Jesuits' departure from Marquette. When this appeared a month later in *Our Times*, the recently established diocesan paper, there was, as the bishop expected, a great blast of protest.[44] A group of lay people wrote to the apostolic delegate, Archbishop Egidio Vagnozzi, who then wrote to McDonald for an explanation. McDonald responded. By this time letters began to arrive in Portland from Yakima, one of them from attorney J.W.

McAndle, who summed it all up. "These people are stunned and shocked, upset beyond belief."[45]

The stormy uproar directed against the bishop only stiffened his resolve to grin and bear it. Standing on rank, he unilaterally assigned a staff of his own priests to Marquette and informed the pastor of St. Joseph's parish that most of them would reside in the Jesuit community there, a precedent that ordinarily would have been negotiated. Those with eyes that could see realized there was worse to come.

OTHER CATHOLIC HIGH SCHOOLS IN PORTLAND AND WALLA WALLA

While these mostly melancholy events were darkening the skies of sunny Yakima, two other diocesan high schools were opened and a third was projected in Seattle for construction in the near future. The first of these was in northeast Portland, opened on September 2, 1958, in a renovated public school, which had been purchased the previous year by the archdiocese.[46] It was called North Catholic. In the first year, freshmen only, both boys and girls, were accepted by the faculty made up of diocesan priests, sisters of several orders, and lay men. Succeeding years were added so that by September 1961 the full four years were in attendance. Sad to relate, this school burned down in 1970, and because of the decrease in numbers of priests and sisters by this time, it was never rebuilt.[47]

More fortunate was DeSales High School in Walla Walla, one of the many items on Bishop Topel's wish list. Topel had talked about it since coming to the diocese and he had approved plans for it before departing with twenty-seven pilgrims for Rome, where he made his first *ad limina* visit to Pius XII on September 18, 1958.[48] He had purchased the land from Whitman College, and raised something like $750,000 for a one-story building designed for three hundred students with potential for expansion to six hundred. All this he did in a hurry, as though the devil were chasing him, and it was only one of several on-going projects.

Topel returned to Spokane on October 2, just one week before the Pope died unexpectedly.[49] He was there when he decided to lend two of his priests to the Guatamala church with an eye to taking a permanent mission there. The two volunteers, Fathers Francis O'Neil and Cornelius Verdoorn spent most of that summer taking first aid courses at Sacred Heart Hospital and gathering supplies and a jeep for the great adventure.[50] They left in a hail of good wishes for the Maryknoll mission at Huehuetenango and the bishop, seeing them go, lamented that the "Increase in Vocations Is Both [a] Blessing and [a] Problem." His seminary fund was running in the red.[51]

SPOKANE'S GUATAMALA MISSION

On February 5, 1960, Topel blessed the new school at Walla Walla in honor of St. Francis DeSales. Two hundred and ten pupils registered on August 31 of the previous year, so His Excellency was pleased with himself when he sprinkled the holy water here and there to drive out the evil spirits A few days later, on February 13, he wrote in his column, "Tonight I leave for Guatamala!"[52] Some of Spokane's old timers sighed and said, "What will this bishop do next?"

They soon learned. When Topel returned two weeks later he gleefully announced that the Spokane Diocese would sponsor a "parish" among the Nahualan Indians in Guatamala and that the two priests there would form the nucleus of the work. "Two full parishes and three missions in Guatamala will comprise a new parish for the Diocese of Spokane."[53] Forty Maryknoll Fathers were already working in the same district. Another volunteer, Father John Rompa, was soon dispatched to join the others and the mission was a sober fact.[54] The bishop's "Padres de Spokane," as they were called in that volatile little country of mountains and revolutions, were there and they intended to remain.

ANOTHER ROUND IN COURT
THE OREGON TEXTBOOK CASE

The church has never lacked critics, some of them, indeed, within the fold. While the latter help to keep it honest, there are others who are like bustling witch hunters, opinionated, dictatorial, and often stupid. Catholic success in any form always brings out the worst in them. Their antics would be hilariously funny if they were not so mischievous and highly costly in terms of time and money. They had not forgotten the drubbing they took in the Oregon School Case and they were delicately attuned to any concession for Catholics that might appear in any one of the forty-eight states. The school busing laws were still a standoff; the dissenters had won some and lost some. Later this would become a national battleground with Oregon on the winning side. The Oregon textbook case was quite another matter. The dissenters needed this one to bolster their sagging egos. They were determined to win it and win it they did by hook and crook. The principal adversaries of the church were three: The American Civil Liberties Union (ACLU), the self-appointed guardians of liberty like the late publishers of *The Menace;* a noisy, rowdy group called Protestants and Others United for Separation of Church and State (PAOU); and, the Scottish Rite of the Masonic Order. For the PAOU the Oregon textbook law was crucial but only an opening match before the main feature. This was the Kennedy Campaign for the presidency two years later.

In February, 1941, Oregon's legislature amended its 1931 free text-book law to include pupils in private schools that met the standards of the state. Governor Charles A. Sprague filed the bill without signing or vetoing it. The measure automatically became law on April 8, 1941 upon expiration of the period required for executive action. It was immediately challenged by the Association Against Public Taxes for Private Schools, but Oregon's Supreme Court upheld the law.[55]

In practice the law meant little at first because private schools, including ours, did not take advantage of it. The long litigation had discouraged most and years passed by before the subject again became widely publicized.

Then, in 1957, Oregon's legislature passed an amendment to the textbook law, S.B. 162, clarifying specific conditions for the use of textbooks by private schools. Governor Robert D. Holmes signed this on May 7, 1957. One month later, Dr. Leo Pfeffer of New York University and Associate General Counsel for the American Jewish Congress, appeared on the Oregon scene. Representing the ACLU, he addressed Portland attorneys on the subject of the textbook law, stating that it was "a violation of the first amendment," and that he opposed this law "as he opposes the teaching of religion in public schools."[56] Essentially, then, the ACLU position was that the provision of textbooks, for example in mathematics and geography, was equated with teaching religion in a public school. This was rubbish, of course, and it revealed the perfidious bias of Pfeffer and his colleagues.

At this time, Father Martin Thielen was superintendent of archdio-cesan schools.[57] Thielen responded to Pfeffer in due time. "The Oregon textbook law, passed at the last legislature, is an application of the child welfare theory. It provides that a child who attends a private school selected by his parents, does not lose the right to the textbooks which were purchased in part by his parents' tax money."[58]

Thielen added a punch or two, which should have brought Pfeffer to his senses: the textbook law, he said, did not allow payment of money to parochial schools. Furthermore, the schools had to provide bond to insure the return of the books in good condition.

Pfeffer was not alone. The POAU, through its garrulous mouthpiece, Paul Blanshard, had been attacking parochial schools all over the nation for years. When he made his appearance at the University of Oregon in 1951, an alert young Benedictine wanted to know if he had been inside a parochial school. Blanshard admitted he had not, and Father

Matt Burger promptly and publicly invited him to visit Mount Angel. Blanshard was more or less forced to accept the invitation. His visit, however, did little to reform his views.[59]

Blanshard published books and articles, which could be refuted, [60] but Glen L. Archer, executive director of PAOU was much more dangerous: he presented his tirades before mass audiences with predisposed minds like his own. He arrived in Portland in April, 1958 and stood before a packed civic auditorium with the Reverend Edward Terry, district president of Portland's Methodist church. Terry attested that the Oregon textbook case could be taken "to the Supreme Court, if necessary," and Archer confirmed this by stating that a court case would be filed "in 60 days," depending upon funds available. He then added that the Portland firm of Ellis and Ellis had been retained already, as well as attorney Walter Wilson of Salem. Regarding the moment as opportune, Terry took up a collection.[61]

Meanwhile, another grandiloquent spokesman for the PAOU was declaiming in New York. This was Bishop G. Bromley Oxnam. His brother bishop, Gerald Kennedy, had stated in Los Angeles that "Catholic schools are doing more damage to the nation than Communism," implying that communism, too, was damaging.[62] But Oxnam, who reportedly belonged to several pro-Communist institutions, for example the National Council of the American-Soviet Friendship, accused the Catholic bishops of being the villains. They were not pro-Communism, but un-American. "Our chief opponent in this struggle has been the hierarchy of the Roman Catholic Church.

While some people trembled over Oxnam's pronouncements, others took their cause to the public school teachers in Oregon. The *Catholic Sentinel* revealed this chicanery:

> A report attacking parochial schools as teaching 'governmental doctrines that are foreign and contrary to the American concepts of government' was mailed last week to more than 2000 public school teachers of Oregon.
>
> The mailing was the report of the education committee of the Supreme Council, 33rd degree, of the Ancient and Accepted Scottish Rite of Freemasonry Southern Jurisdiction.
>
> Leslie M. Scott,[63] a member of the education committee and head of the Scottish Rite affairs in Oregon, told the *Sentinel* the distribution was in connection with a campaign to take from parochial school children books now supplied to them under Oregon law.
>
> 'Members of the Scottish Rite,' he said, 'are working with an organization known as Protestant and Others United for the Separation of Church and State which recently formed a chapter in Oregon.'...[64]

Despite all the hubbub, no direct legal action was taken for a year. Then Stephen Anderson of Salem, an attorney cooperating with the ACLU, filed a suit challenging the constitutionality of the textbook law on behalf of three residents of Clackamas County: William Dickman, Harold E. Salisbury, and Lawrence Smelser.[65] Dr. Judah Bierman of Portland, chairman of Oregon's ACLU, affirmed that his organization "regarded the action as a court test." The state's provision of textbooks for children in St. John's parochial school in Oregon City, "breached the wall of separation of church and state."

The plaintiffs asserted that "the school and not the children benefits by the law," which was nonsense. They retained Pfeffer as an "expert" on the law and assistant to their counsel. Then Ivan B. Carlson, an irate Catholic father of eight children, six of whom attended St. John's, retained attorney Leo Smith of Portland to represent him in the state's defense of the law.[66]

The case was tried before Judge Ralph Holman who frankly admitted to his court that he believed the trial was "only the first round." And so it was. When it ended on February 2, 1960, Holman ruled in favor of the law, saying that he supported the law "reluctantly." He also "registered emphatic dissent" from his own ruling, thereby giving opponents of the law something more than comfort to ease their chagrin.[67]

Catholic rejoicing was short lived. When Holman's decision was appealed, the state supreme court reversed itself, ruling that the bill violated a provision in the state's constitution that banned the use of public money for "the benefit of any religious or theological institution."[68] Because the Supreme Court of the United States refused to review the Oregon decision, the textbook law was as dead as a tombstone and Catholics like Ivan Carlson were forced, once again, to grin and bear their losses, estimated at over one million dollars every five year period.[69]

The PAOU and their allies, however, had other vexing news to mortify them. The Catholic's Pope, John XXIII, was enjoying unprecedented popularity with America's WASPS, and John F. Kennedy's long shadow was cast insidiously over America's most sacred citadel, the White House. For two days in February, 1961, Dr. W. Kenneth, a politicized minister from Portsmouth, Virginia, conducted a rally in Portland, during which he lambasted Catholics for electing Kennedy. Kennedy, he wailed, "had capitalized on the religious issue during the campaign, even though this brought down the wrath of his fellow Catholics." Kenneth did not explain why all those alienated Catholics had voted for Kennedy.[70]

Glen Archer was in Portland, also, with "a sure cure for clericalism." He attacked Catholic hospitals especially and presented two undocumented classics, one film called "Captured" and the other "Boycott." Today both could be regarded as comedies. Later, Archer passed out several "distinguished service awards," including one to Leslie Scott, former state treasurer of the Scottish Rite Masons and "a preserver of a heritage of freedom." Scott was awarded this envious honor for circulating, over his own signature, a letter in which he advised Masons "not to vote for Kennedy because of his Catholic religion."[71] One must admire Scott if only for his persistence.

THE SISTER FORMATION PROGRAM

Thus ended the more rabid of the attacks upon the northwest church from the outside. As once before, after the Oregon School decision by the Supreme Court, the Catholics emerged with new respect from their neighbors. In Portland, for example, they now represented about 20% of the total population.[72] They felt the bouncy optimism of survival after the continued barrage of bitter testing and though they had lost more recently on court issues like "shared time" as well as the textbook law, they felt more confident about the future than ever before. Vocations were at an all time high. Church finances were sound. For some Catholics there was little else to worry about.

In fact, however, in this immediate pre-Vatican II period, the collapse long in the making was about to become manifest. In its earliest form it appeared within the church as open disparagement of its schools, from the much esteemed parochial system to the universities and seminaries. Special criticism was reserved for the teaching sisters, many of whom were teaching without college degrees. They spent their summer, for ten or even twenty years, gathering credits to qualify for the sometimes arbitrary standards of bureaucrats of the ivory-tower persuasion.

This depreciation of Catholic education, coming from Catholics like the president of Notre Dame University, was exactly what Paul Blanshard and the PAOU wanted to hear. Many Americans were already defensive about public schools. There were deep-rooted misgivings about them, reasonably so, during this violent period of integration, when many schools were either resisting integration or were in a state of shock occasioned by the absorption of millions of hitherto deprived students. Compared to these, Catholic schools were actually superior, but the cry of shame, shame, had been leveled at them, and public confidence melted away.

The confidence of many Catholics, too, was undermined. The price they were paying for schools was getting higher each year, not because of increased expenditures by the nuns who lived on forty or fifty dollars a month, but because of the ever-increasing costs of public schools, which they had to support first. Some Catholics asked themselves if all their sacrifices were worth the effort and others openly complained that the church had undertaken a hopeless task by trying to educate, as the Council of Baltimore prescribed, from the kindergarten to college. What the Ku Klux Klan had failed to do, Catholics themselves now began to do. They began to dismantle the system. During the years that followed, there were many other causes related to the decline of the Catholic grade schools of America, but none, it seems to me, had a greater impact than the tragic events of the late 1950's and the early 1960's.

PROVIDENCE HEIGHTS COLLEGE

Meanwhile, the sisters, stung by unjust criticism and charges of unprofessionalism, had meekly begun their own reflections on possible solutions to their problems.[73] From June 1 to August 30, 1956, funded by a grant of fifty thousand dollars from the Fund for the Advancement of Education, fifteen participants, representing religious communities all over the United States, conducted the first national workshop in "Sister Formation," in the Providence School of Nursing, Everett, Washington.[74] In Seattle, the president of Seattle University, Father Albet Lemieux, pledged his full support to assist them. Subsequently, in the fall of 1957, a College of Sister Formation was set up at the university as one of two national demonstration centers for the program, which the participants in the workshop agreed upon.[75]

> Until completion of a separate campus by the Sisters of Providence, at Providence Heights on the east side of Lake Sammamish in 1961, Seattle University will furnish faculty and facilities for the college. The Providence Heights College will become an institutional branch of the university with its own faculty and facilities, but with degrees granted by the university.
>
> The 4 religious orders now participating in the program are: The Sisters of Charity of Providence; the Sisters of St. Joseph of Newark;[76] the Dominican Sisters of the Congregation of St. Thomas Aquinas, Tacoma; and the Dominican Sisters of the Congregation of the Holy Cross, Edmonds.[77]

The dean of the new college was Mother Mary Philothea.[78] The course was designed for five years and the sisters attended four quarters each year, earning between 230 and 240 quarter credits before graduation, at least thirty more than the university required. Specialization was undertaken in the post-graduation years when the sisters returned for master's degrees in their chosen fields.[79]

The Sisters Formation program attracted widespread interest throughout the United States and abroad. Msgr. Frederick Hochwalt, secretary of the National Catholic Educational Association, described it as "the most significant movement in Catholic education today," which it doubtlessly was. In October 1959, a million readers of *The Catholic Digest* learned how the sisters were fighting back.[80] With Seattle university they were facing head-on the greatest challenge to Catholic education since the Oregon School Bill, and they were doing it, not with political lobbies and back-to-the-wall desperation, but with eclat and feminine charm.

On September 12, 1958, the *Northwest Progress* revealed plans for the new campus.[81] Groundbreaking ceremonies with Archbishop Connolly happily presiding, took place on January 21, 1959. The [six] million dollar plant with accommodations in [nine] separate buildings for three hundred sister students and the provincial administration for the Sisters of Charity of Providence, was completed for the summer school session beginning January 19, 1961. Actual registration that summer was 265 sisters from thirty-six different communities. For the dedication on July 27, the apostolic delegate, Archbishop Egidio Vagnozzi presided while eight archbishops and bishops, and countless others applauded. How great were the hopes that day! How sweetly reassuring was this shining new college, set in its wooded hills, an oasis of learning and tranquility! Alas, like St. Thomas the Apostle Seminary, it would be abandoned in a few paltry years.[82]

Had there been no upheaval in the church in the next decade, which no one could predict, Providence Heights College might have succeeded. It was certainly within the stream of continuity in the post-Tridentine church, not unlike the monasteries, convents, select colleges and motherhouses in semi-isolated rural settings, which resembled castles on the Hudson. But times had changed and with them Providence Heights became an anachronism. It had been built in the wrong place for the post-Vatican II church. Eventually it was leased to the state of Washington for a police academy, and then was leased to the Lutheran Church. It is an ill wind that blows no good. For the Lutherans it was an obliging wind, and the rafters of Providence Heights still ring with Luther's "How Mighty Is Our God."

NEW CAMPUS AND COLLEGE BUILDINGS

The fallout of the excitement over Sister Formation included favorable developments on other campuses. The Sisters of the Holy Names, conspicuous for teaching in the Northwest from the beginning, had participated in the Everett Workshop, but had not joined the consortium in the Seattle University college. At this time they had three colleges of their own, Holy Names in Oakland, California; Marylhurst at Lake Oswego, Oregon; and Holy Names in Spokane. The last two, at least, served primarily as Sister Formation programs of their own.

In Spokane, Sister Mary Raphael, president of the college, was engaged in negotiations with the United States Government for the acquisition of surplus land at Fort George Wright. On July 1, 1960, approval was received for a grant of eighty-five acres containing fifty-five buildings, contingent upon the college's occupation of some buildings on the property within eighteen months.[83] Sister Mary Raphael announced that the college would be transferred forthwith and that its curriculum would be expanded. Accordingly on September 24, 1960, the first sisters and forty-seven resident students moved to the new campus. Occupying former officers' quarters, the sisters and the girls commuted to the original college in the Gonzaga district for classes, until the entire institution was gradually moved to Fort Wright.[84]

During this same September in 1960, the College of Great Falls occupied its new 104 acre campus on the southern rim of the city. Eleven new red-brick buildings, designed in almost endless variety but as a single unit, had been constructed in the previous year. Unlike the new Fort Wright College, Great Falls was officially coeducational, with a staff of Sisters of Providence primarily, diocesan priests and lay men and women.

In the following year, 1961, the Benedictine Sisters at Mount Angel dedicated two new buildings, a women's residence hall and a "commons" indicating its hopes for survival after many semesters of capricious enrollments.[85] At Marylhurst, too, the sisters erected a new residence hall and "commons" for something like one and one-quarter million dollars.[86] This indicated, I think, that Marylhurst was riding the crest of optimism in the pre-Vatican II American church, entirely oblivious of the pitfalls ahead. Like Providence Heights, these new buildings would be put to another use within a single decade.

Finally there were the Redemptorists, who established St. Alphonsus College in the former George Nursing Home near Bridal Falls, east of Portland.[87] This first novitiate of the Oakland Province of the Redemptorists was formally opened on August 1, 1961 with an investiture ceremony for twelve novices. On the following day Archbishop Howard presided again. Assisted by the Superior, Father William Fitzgerald, he blessed the old building, now relieved of its "concentration of senectitude" for the more promising use of the young. It was very appropriate for, in America at large, the aged were being discarded and a new cult of youth had already been created.

THE JESUITS GO ABROAD

On November 8, 1960, Father Alexander McDonald notified members of his Jesuit province about its new mission in Africa.

> According to word received from Very Reverend Father General, the Oregon Province has been entrusted with the responsibility of helping the Lusaka Mission in Northern Rhodesia.... It should be remembered, [he added, lest some got carried away with the glamor of Africa], that we are still entrusted with Alaska and the home Indian Missions. Work in these places should be esteemed as no less pleasing to God than work in Africa.[88]

Father Louis Haven, a professor at Gonzaga University, was the first to respond. Having heard about the new mission via one of the province's most productive rumor mills, he had mailed his letter volunteering to leave for Lusaka without further delay.[89] Many others volunteered also, and at the end of 1960 McDonald wrote to the general to say that the number of them "was most gratifying." He wanted Father Joseph Logan, former rector of the novitiate, to scout out the new mission in April following.

The provincial and Logan left Portland on March 27, 1961 for Northern Rhodesia, leaving Father John Monahan in charge of the province. Monahan, the Jesuits' walking encyclopedia, had been consulted about the bugs in Africa. He replied, "The bugs own Africa," and so it was. Besides the tse-tse fly, McDonald found a thriving mission conducted by Polish Jesuits, who could no longer provide new missionaries because of Communist Polish law. When McDonald returned a month later, he brought with him the impression that Lusaka's superiors wanted "a high school, a million dollars and a staff." During the summer they got two Jesuits instead, Haven and Neil McCluskey. Both had shared in formal departure ceremonies, wearing white cassocks, which made them look as glamorous as the White Fathers already in Africa. McCluskey, it turned out, did not think his talents and training would find adequate scope in Northern Rhodesia, so McDonald recalled him to the province and dispatched three young Jesuits to replace him.[90]

Meanwhile, at Gonzaga University, the president, irrepressible Father John Leary, requested McDonald's permission to borrow more money. The new chemistry building under construction, projected at a cost of $700,000, required an additional $128,000 to complete it. Leary, like Father Lemieux at Seattle University, was on a building spree. Their building engines had a full head of steam and appeared, at times, to be out of control. Leary had another brainstorm. He wanted to establish Gonzaga abroad, a Gonzaga-in-Florence, which was the art capitol of Europe. McDonald, cautiously agreeing with him, wrote to the general in

January, 1963.[91] Janssens approved of the new program, which was begun in the following autumn under the direction of Neil McCluskey who had become, by this time, a kind of international celebrity with roots on three continents. Gonzaga-in-Florence developed into a huge success. Among the university-related foreign schools it was rated as one of the best. The fact that it has survived, despite Italy's inflation turmoil, indicates its high level of usefulness and its value in placing Gonzaga University before a world public.

BISHOP ELDON SCHUSTER

The euphoria of 1961 appeared to be justified. Mount Angel Seminary that autumn registered 181 seminarians and turned away another twenty-three who were suitable candidates.[92]

"There is no choice," Bishop Topel said in Spokane. "We must build a minor seminary. We will. As soon as possible."[93] A few weeks later he started another project on skid row, Brother Martin's House of Charity for transients. Catholics in Spokane were not surprised at anything now, and they said again, "What will Bishop Topel do next?"

While Spokane's bishop suffered at least mild symptoms of *workamania*, the bishop in Great Falls, worn out and scarcely able to govern the diocese, was on the sicklist more often than not. On January 18, 1959, a frosty cold day, he had presided over ground-breaking ceremonies at the new College of Great Falls campus. The college was Condon's pet project, and though he had given special attention to the parochial schools of his diocese for over twenty years, he kept a benevolent eye on the college and supported the Providence Sisters there in their superhuman efforts to survive. But his health had worsened after the day's exposure. He had become thin and haggard looking, like a retired judge with too many cares. In an official portrait he frowns sourly and his mouth, a firm straight slash, gives one the impression that ulcers were acting up and he did not care who knew about it. It was time for help. On October 30, 1961, Rome appointed for him an auxiliary bishop, a priest of his diocese who had worked by his side for sixteen years.

The new auxiliary, titular bishop of Amblada, was Monsignor Eldon Bernard Schuster, chancellor of the diocese from 1945 to 1950, currently superintendent of diocesan schools. Though he had been born in Calio, of the Diocese of Fargo, the son of John Francis and Leona Marie Osborn Schuster, whom he resembled in appearance rather than his father, he was a true Montanan. A year after his birth his parents moved to Glentana, in the copper state, where he grew into boyhood, helping with chores on the family farm and in the family store. Having become a favorite of Bishop Lenihan, he was sent by the kindly old prelate to Columbia College, Dubuque,[94] where he graduated *summa cum laude*. Later he attended the Sulpician seminary in Washington, D.C. and Catholic University. He was ordained to the priesthood by Bishop O'Hara in St. Ann's Cathedral on May 27, 1937.[95] He was assigned to studies in Oxford, but his term there was cut short by the war. After attending St. Louis University and Notre Dame, he acquired the deserved reputation as an intellectual, though he looked more like the chancellor of Austria or an Alpine skier. Beneath a head topped with an abundance of naturally curly hair combed back, his bright, steady eyes examined the world placidly through rimless glasses. His broad smile was a warm invitation to companionship that one soon recognized as unaffected and totally without guile. Schuster gave one the feeling of unused power like that of an outdoor man who hunts wild game in the tractless forest.

He was consecrated bishop on December 21, 1961 by Archbishop Egidio Vagnozzi, the apostolic delegate. Co-consecrators were Bishops Condon and Gilmore. Thus he claimed, through Vagnozzi, apostolic succession to four popes, including Pio Nono. He was the first native of the diocese to become a bishop.[96]

MATER CLERI SEMINARY

Bishop Topel had attended Schuster's consecration. He returned to Spokane more determined than ever to build his minor seminary, though grave warnings of change of attitude towards priests were already in the air. At a meeting of vocation directors in January 1962, Bishop Philip Hannan, auxiliary in Washington, D.C., gave reasons for what was becoming a national disaster. "The most dangerous obstacles [to religious vocations today]," he noted soberly, "were the lack of parental authority, causing unsound family life; the critical spirit of our age, [and] materialistic influences." He referred to the position of vocation directors as delicate, even dangerous."[97]   In February of 1962, Topel gave notice that a drive for funds was being organized and that the new seminary, to be called "Mater Cleri," would be built on a 120 acre tract of land recently acquired near Colbert, Washington.[98] "Its doors must be open by September 1963." Accommodations would be provided for 125 students from third year high school to second year college inclusive.[99] Colbert was a country village about fifteen miles northwest of Spokane, almost in the shadow of Mount Spokane and bordering the lake country.

The well organized financial drive was so intense that few slipped through without paying their dues. But the bishop's subjects were enthusiastic. He asked for $600,000 as a goal, and received instead

$825,000 which appears to indicate, by hindsight at least, that Catholics were already becoming apprehensive about the decline in vocations.

On September 23, 1962 "at 4 P.M. on Sunday," ground was broken for the new institution, though blue prints and specifications had not yet been completed. Integral at last, they were submitted to bids, which were opened on November 30, 1962. A local firm was awarded the contract for construction for a total cost of $732,288.

The winter was mild that year, so after construction was begun on December 1, steady progress was made. The architects, Funk, Murray and Johnston of Spokane, predicted a timely completion and classes were scheduled to open on September 8, 1963. The new rector was appointed. This was Father William Van Ommeren, who was also the chancellor of the diocese. About sixty-five seminarians were expected, of whom "fifteen or sixteen" would attend college level classes at Gonzaga University.

As often happens, construction was delayed. The seminarians finally arrived on September 23, 1963, in pouring rain, which lasted all day and transformed the site into a muddy bog. The kitchen was not completed, nor the water supply functioning, so the community lived for some days on sandwiches, which were served on paper plates. "At least," someone observed, "the wall and roof are up."[100]

It was an ominous beginning, but all regarded it as a great adventure, almost a pleasant as the rain-drenched picnics on "Vocation Days" before they decided to become priests.

THE LOSS OF BISHOPS BYRNE AND GILMORE

By this time the bishop's throne in two dioceses in the Northwest had become vacant. On March 7, 1962, the apostolic delegate released news that Bishop Byrne of Boise had been elevated by Pope John XXIII to be Archbishop of Dubuque, replacing Archbishop Leo Binz, who was being transferred to St. Paul.[101] For Catholics in Idaho the news was devastating. Byrne had been uncommonly popular with everyone, especially the clergy. Because of this, in good part, the church made great progress in his brief tenure of only five years. When Byrne left Boise for Dubuque on May 7, 1962, the Catholic population of Idaho had risen to 44,730, an increase of five percent in a single year. The diocese listed twenty-six grade schools, three academies, one Junior College, and nine hospitals. There were three Indian missions: Sacred Heart for the Coeur d'Alenes, St. Joseph for the Nez Perce, and St. Michael's for the Kootenai. It was not an impressive legacy for Byrne's successor, but in a diocese like Boise one did not count souls so much as one weighed them.

Before Byrne's departure, Bishop Gilmore died suddenly at San Francisco on April 2, 1962. He was attending a welcome dinner for Archbishop Joseph McGucken, when he began to choke on his food. Doctors were called. He died in fifteen minutes, tragically gone so quickly from life to death. He had flown that very morning from Helena to San Francisco, in a happy mood, anticipating a brief vacation in the warm, sunny south. Now, his people reflected somberly, the elegant bishop's throne in the cathedral was empty again.

Gilmore had been a good bishop, despite his failure to live in harmony with religious orders. He loved his own priests and he was good to them. They responded with affection and loyalty. His love of predilection for Carroll College brought it into the narrow arena of good western colleges. He was dedicated to his people and he was sorely missed when he was gone.[102]

BISHOP SYLVESTER TREINEN

With seemly dispatch the Vatican provided Idaho with a new bishop during the same month that Byrne left for Dubuque. On May 23, 1962, Archbishop Vagnozzi announced that Father Sylvester Treinen, had been appointed. Born on November 19, 1917, on a farm near Donnelly, Minnesota, he attended a country school near Donnelly, then advanced to high school and college in the Crozier seminary at Onamia, Minnesota. He completed his theology at St. Paul's seminary in St. Paul, and was ordained in Bismarck, North Dakota,, for that diocese by Bishop Vincent Ryan, on June 11, 1946.[103] Later a brother bishop described him as "one of the youngest [bishops] in the world at the time of his appointment, a man of many interests and unrecognized talents, he had but one real love— the church."[104]

Treinen was consecrated as the fifth Bishop of Boise on July 25, 1962 in the Cathedral of the Holy Spirit, Bismarck. The consecrating bishop was Hilary Hecker, who was assisted by bishops Peter Bartholome of St. Cloud and Lambert Hoch of Sioux Falls. Archbishop Leo Binz, looking very pleased with himself (or something else), preached the occasional sermon. Twenty archbishops and bishops were present, which undoubtedly unnerved His Excellency, for he was a most ingenuous person, who easily faded into the background. He liked it that way. On August 3 he was installed in St. John's Cathedral in Boise, which still lacked the church steeples planned by the architects over a half century earlier.[105]

The new bishop was a man of simplicity. All his life he had liked fishing, and he had often accompanied his father on fishing expeditions in Minnesota. Now he recommended this elusive pastime to his priests. In appearance he was small in stature. When he wore his bishop's biretta, which was larger than his head, he looked like someone balancing a large basket up there. Always on his face was a slight smile, shyly maintained, but indicative of a warm, humble personality. He described himself as a "cautious progressive," but there were some who disallowed the adjective because the bishop drove his rundown car over thousands of miles on rugged Idaho roads at all seasons of the year, living dangerously to care for his flock.

BISHOP RAYMOND HUNTHAUSEN

Now that Boise's bishop was in residence, Helena's priests began to speculate more avidly about their own prospects for a liberal bishop. Had they been allowed to vote, most, I think, would have selected the pope's first choice. Monsignor Raymond Gerhardt Hunthausen, president of Carroll College for five years and confidante of two bishops, Gilmore and Topel, seemed to be the favorite of everyone. John XXIII appointed him to Helena on July 8, 1962. Like Gilmore before him, he was home grown; both had come from Anaconda where Hunthausen's grandfather owned the Rocky Mountain Brewery. Hunthausen, the oldest of seven children, was born on August 21, 1921. His parents were Anthony Gerhardt and Edna Marie Tuscherer Hunthausen. After attending Carroll College and St. Edward's Seminary, he was ordained by Bishop Gilmore in St. Paul's Church, Anaconda, on June 1, 1946.[106]

As a student at Carroll, Hunthausen had starred in basketball. He was a student in Father Bernard Topel's mathematics class and one day after Topel noticed him saying long prayers in the chapel he took him under his wing, so to speak, to guide him in spiritual matters. Topel was much impressed by Hunthausen's piety and the latter came to accept the former's direction, becoming in time a faithful spiritual son with high ideals like his mentor.

Hunthausen's consecration in Helena on August 30 was memorable. The apostolic Delegate, Archbishop Vagnozzi, was the principal celebrant, assisted by Bishops Topel and Condon. Archbishop Howard, twice the age of the new bishop, was called upon to preach again.[107] Hearing her son praised was Mrs. Hunthausen who still lived in Anaconda. Also present among the Hunthausen clan was Father John, the bishop's brother, who was on the faculty of Carroll College.

The sixth bishop of Helena looked his age, just forty-one. Photographs of him then remind one of a Bavarian village pastor who had discovered happiness in his own soul. His eyes are soft and gentle. One sees in them the wistful longing of the mystic. His lips are firm but formed with tolerance and his broad chin expresses the blandness of those who seek diplomacy to avoid violence. If anything, the new bishop was a man of peace.

LITURGICAL REFORM

In that summer of 1962, Seattle brazenly, one might say, opened a World's Fair. City fathers had decided to tread where larger cities had not dared to go. The experiment then was touch-and-go.

As a Catholic contribution to the extravaganza, Archbishop Connolly sponsored the forty-seventh annual Liturgical Conference, which convened in Century Twenty-One's vast arena, on August 20. Fifteen archbishops and bishops and five thousand members of the clergy, religious orders, and the laity, gathered for lectures, discussions, and the liturgy itself.[108] There were nearly one hundred distinguished speakers, including Father Daniel Berrigan, regarded then as a poet-theologian, Father Godfrey Diekmann, editor of *Worship*, the foremost journal of liturgical reform, and Father H.A. Rienhold, one of the founders of liturgical reform.

Reinhold was not new to the Northwest. An exile from Nazi Germany, where he had adopted many of Europe's advanced views, he arrived in Seattle in 1938 and two years later was appointed by the bishop to direct the Catholic Seaman's Club.[109] In 1941, apparently in disfavor with Shaughnessy, he was assigned to St. Paul's parish, Yakima, then to Sunnyside from 1944 to 1956. In ill health, he moved to Pittsburgh, where he died unexpectedly on January 26, 1968 from an embolism following surgery.[110]

For these thirty years, Reinhold agitated, sometimes abrasively, by every means possible, for changes in the current rituals.[111] He successfully stirred up national interest in his allegedly wild proposals, making at the same time almost as many enemies as friends, including powerful members of the hierarchy. In truth, he was a prophet, but a joyless one.

These were the times of change. Pius XII had mitigated the rules for the Eucharistic fast, permitting evening Masses, which broke so explosively with tradition that, like a flood after a dam collapses, many other hard and fast customs were swept away. Mass in the vernacular was a major reform objective that was soon allowed. In the years that followed, the format of the Mass, sacred since the Council of Trent, was changed; married laymen were ordained as deacons; the sacrament of penance was altered to the rite of reconciliation; and, a radical new form of church music was introduced. Gone for the most part were the chants of the medieval church; now acceptable, in place of organs, were the ubiquitous guitars and folk music that irritated most elderly Catholics.[112]

THE SECOND VATICAN COUNCIL

The unrest and positive agitation of Catholics like Reinhold, helped to convince Pope John XXIII to call the Council. He finally issued the papal bull, a formal summons for the Second Vatican Council, "given at Rome, St. Peters, December 25, 1961, the fourth year of our pontificate."[113]

Eventually the date for the opening of the Council was set for October 11, 1962 And members of the northwest hierarchy, including auxiliary Bishop Gill and the two recently consecrated bishops, Treinen and Hunthausen, flew off to Rome to participate. Even Archbishop Howard, now eighty-six, attended the first session. After Bishop John Gannon of Eire departed, he was the oldest member of the Council.[114] When Pope John saw him, he exclaimed, "Bravo! You're older than myself!" John wished Howard many more years, which is undoubtedly one reason why Howard lived so long. At the opening session of the Council, Howard joined something like twenty-five hundred bishops in white mitres and copes as they solemnly filed into St. Peter's, while an estimated half-million people gathered in the piazza and strained to see, and goggled at what they saw. If one bishop, enshrined in all of his robes was awesome, two thousand were mind boggling. People love to see pomp and splendor in ritual, as demonstrated by the presence of the half-million. A great irony, then, was the position of the so-called reformers, like Reinhold, whose demands on the pages of *Commonweal* for "less pomp and pageantry" grew more shrill as the Council progressed.[115]

There were four sessions of the Council. Pope John died after the first, on June 3, 1963. Paul VI, John's favorite, was quickly elected and the second session began on schedule on September 29 of the same year. During the last session, which closed with more "pomp and pageantry" on December 8, 1965, Bishop Dougherty suffered a heart attack and was hospitalized at *Salvator Mundi* in Rome until his departure for Yakima.[116] When he arrived home he looked like a gaunt survivor of a concentration camp. His face was thin and pale. His hair, receding rapidly, was white. There were deep shadows beneath his eyes and he presented a twisted smile to those who welcomed him. In a few months he had aged far beyond his years. This was not a good omen for the future.

CHANGES IN PORTLAND

While Rome argued about reform, it was business as usual back in the provinces. A new chancery building for Portland had been purchased in July 1962. This involved the demolition of the old chancery to make way for a ramp on the new freeway. For $150,000 the archbishop purchased the former Rose City Transfer Company on the east side of the river.[117]

Comprising 38,000 square feet, this warehouse-like building, about fifty-two years old but solid, required major alterations for the use of the archdiocese. An architect was employed to provide forty offices, an auditorium, vaults, and complete facilities for the *Catholic Sentinel*. These renovations were partly completed in April, 1963 and the first issue of the *Sentinel* was printed in the new quarters on April 18.

The archbishop and his staff moved into the new chancery quarters on Friday, June 6, 1963. His Grace did not get around to blessing the new building for nearly six months, which suggests the nature of his still-busy schedule. President Kennedy was assassinated just a week earlier so that the beads of holy water were like tears of mourning and shame.[118] Since then, however, in part because of the blessing, the chancery has been a cheerful place, if too small for current needs.

During this same period, the antique-looking original St. Mary's Academy in Portland, as durable as the old Transfer Company, and proudly cherished at the age of one hundred and four years, was razed and hauled away to make room for a new wing on the newer portion of the school. The academy was expanding, too, like the seminaries and the convent-centered colleges built on rivers or in the remote forests. But St. Mary's was in the very heart of the city; all it lacked for instant success were boys. Later it would be sisters, and money also, but for the present the lifestyle of most girls demanded the companionship of boys, even in the classroom. The so-called reformers were already campaigning for girls in the boys' prep schools, stating that it was unnatural for them to be separated during the maturing years.[119] Central Catholic school had become, in fact, coeducational, despite the protests of some bishops, who still distinguished between coinstructional and coeducational.[120] No one can doubt the need for the Central Catholics especially in view of contemporary limitations. Thus new ones continued to appear with startling regularity.

BISHOP KELLY HIGH SCHOOL IN BOISE

Portland's new chancery had cost little by modern standards. As compared to most Episcopal chanceries, it appeared to be drab and merely functional. The archbishop would have explained that it was all the archdiocese could afford, mostly because of the rising cost of schools, not so much of parochial schools but of public education. It was the cost of the latter that was breaking the backs of Catholics, who paid a double tax for the constitutional guarantee of freedom of choice. In 1962, according to published reports, American Catholics saved taxpayers 2.6 billion dollars nationally. In Oregon, Catholics in this year represented only 12.1% of the population, they saved the taxpayer $13,715,776.[121] Thus, while these Catholics were saving huge amounts of money for public education, they had to bear, also, the full costs, which were rising, of their own system.

In Boise, where the sisters' vocation crisis threatened closure of St. Teresa's Academy, established in 1890 by the Sisters of the Holy Cross, Bishop Treinen was seeking ways and means to provide a Central Catholic. Most of Idaho's Catholics lived in Boise and they were as determined as the bishop to keep their children in parochial schools as long as possible. Before leaving for Rome for the Second Vatican Council, on October 6, 1962, Treinen delighted them all by announcing that a Central Catholic, to be called Bishop Kelly High School, would be opened for students by September, 1964.[122]

Treinen returned to Boise on December 10. Among his priorities was the school. A tract of land was acquired at Franklin and Cole, and plans were undertaken for a permanent building estimated to cost $970,000 at $11.50 per square foot. Bids were opened on July 26, 1963, and on August 20, the lowest bid of $872,300 was accepted.[123] Five days later, Treinen blessed the ground and turned over the first spade of dirt, only symbolically, for it was seven in the evening when the builders were drinking beer at home.[124] A month after this, the bishop hurried off to Rome again, no doubt as pleased as Pollyanna that his new school would cost a lot less than the Vatican Council.

For teachers, His Excellency depended still on the Sisters of the Holy Cross. Their number was reduced, of course, so priests of the diocese and lay teachers were recruited for service to complete the faculty. A new home for the sisters near the school was purchased and everything was properly arranged when St. Teresa's Academy hurled its last of fifteen hundred graduates into the hard, cold world, with the strains of "Pomp and Circumstance" fading into the twilight. This was on May 24, 1964. The academy building was formally closed six days later.[125]

Bishop Kelly High School opened its doors on schedule. It was dedicated at 2:30 in the afternoon of August 30, 1964 in the presence of its new faculty of eight priests, seven sisters and five lay persons. Also present were sixteen hundred guests, which indicates more than anything else how highly Boise's Catholics treasured their new school.

On the previous day in Spokane there was another dedication.[126] The Dominican Sisters of Kettle Falls had built a new hospital called Holy Family. Located on Spokane's north side and designed to accommodate 137 patients, it had cost the sisters five million thrifty dollars, mostly borrowed. Bishop Topel, who had encouraged the sisters to build, presided over the formal ceremonies and Bishop Hunthausen of Helena, where the sisters had first come from Germany, offered an invocation. His prayer was for all, but especially the patients the hospital would serve. It was too soon to worry about the debt, but sooner, rather than later, that too would get prayerful attention.

CHURCH AUTHORITY CHALLENGED

Boise's happiness seemed to deepen the melancholy of Catholics elsewhere, when schools, convents, and hospitals began to be closed for lack of sisters.[127] This had become commonplace by the mid-1960's, a cause of grave concern for the bishops, but a very personal misfortune for countless Catholics, whose sons and daughters returned home from seminaries and convents, sometimes after a full decade of service to the church.

"We of the Catholic church," Bishop Topel solemnly observed, "are living in exciting but perilous times."[128] He called 1964 "a year of shame" for the Catholic press because of personal attacks "leveled by a few Catholic magazines and newspapers against bishops."

In a Catholic Press Month pastoral letter read from the pulpits of every church in the Spokane Diocese, the Bishop of Spokane asserted: "The greatest and most serious harm being done is that the teaching authority of the church is presently being undermined by some of the writings that appear in a few of our Catholic publications.... These attacks have been made more personal and bitter than any that have yet appeared in the secular press."[129]

Bishop Hunthausen agreed. Speaking before twelve hundred members of the Knights of Columbus in Denver, he sharply rebuked "populizers and intelligentsia who have passed judgment on Pope Paul VI without waiting for all of the evidence to be in." He added that "this criticism is hasty and unfair."[130]

The continual harsh and irresponsible criticism of the hierarchy and the pope had a devastating affect on the young in Catholic high schools and colleges, the potential pool of most vocations. It helped to shatter the idealism of those already in seminaries and convents, especially after books and articles on "self-fulfillment" began to appear. Topel noted the drop in vocations, "scarcely half of what it was a few years ago." He also called attention to the big gain in the percentage of those leaving seminaries.[131]

"Gonzaga," the Jesuit general Father Janssens had once exclaimed, when the name came up in conversation, "that's the school from which we have received so many vocations." But in 1963 Father Alex McDonald asked, "Why are there no vocations at Gonzaga Prep?"[132]

The Gonzaga Prep experience at this time was characteristic. Its new rector, Father Frank Masterson, was young, liberal and endowed with an uncommonly great gift of common sense. A dynamo of energy, he was trying to build a new residence for the convenience of his community, to replace the old wooden barracks, which leaked like a sieve. He was also trying to cope with the mysterious behavior of a few of the scholastics.

One had rented Spokane's huge new Coliseum for a student party without bothering to inform the principal about it. Some were ridiculing the sacrosanct Epistle on Obedience by St. Ignatius, which was read in the dining room every month. Others were leaving the premises in the evenings without customary permissions. And still others were handing out books allegedly 'great literature' to boys who were unprepared for them. Permissiveness had not yet reached the point where scholastics counseled students that they did not have to attend Mass unless they felt like it, but that would come also, before the authentic reform began.

Masterson was rector at Prep for six full years, during which there was a total of fifty-two scholastics in his community. Of these, twenty-two left the Order before ordination and thirteen left as priests, after ordination. This left seventeen, or one out of three, who survived. Masterson was generally regarded as an excellent superior, if anything a little left of the middle of the road. What was happening at Gonzaga Prep was indicative of what was going on in the province, and in the Church, when the impact of the 1960's was finally recognized.[133]

And what was causing it all? Everyone had a different answer. The spirit of the age. Lack of faith in homes. Contempt for the authority of the church. Existential philosophy that was being taught even in Catholic institutions. Jean Danilou, the great Jesuit theologian, attributed it to "over-emphasis on the social evils of the day."[134] No doubt it was all of these causes and more.

NEW PRESIDENT AT THE UNIVERSITY OF PORTLAND

The Holy Cross Fathers selected Father Howard Kenna, President of the University, for their new provincial. This occasioned two immediate advantages to the university: the new provincial's favor in the assignment of priests, and the appointment of his former assistant to the office of president. Father Paul Waldschmidt became the fifteenth president of the University of Portland in September, 1962.

Waldschmidt was forty-two years old. He had been only thirty-five when he was appointed vice-president by Kenna, in 1955, after he had earned degrees at Notre Dame, Laval University in Quebec, and a doctorate in theology at the Angelicum in Rome.[135] A tall man with long arms and large hands, he looked more formidable than he really was. His black hair combed back, wide eyes framed by bone-rim glasses, his nose of classic shape and his small, firm mouth, gave him the appearance of a busy mayor who has a city to run without money enough to pay the firemen.

When he took office he had reason to project his no-nonsense image. The closure of Columbia Prep had left some friends of the university disenchanted. Termination of football had alienated others. The critical need for a woman's dormitory, negative reports on the establishment of schools of law and engineering, and the invasion of Portland by tax-supported Portland State were only a few of his campus problems.

Actually, with his accession to the highest post, the university was on the threshold of a new age. Waldschmidt's presidency, says the university historian, "witnessed the most productive era in the history of the institution; and by all accounts, he was the architect of the University of Portland in its present form."[136]

Like Leary at Gonzaga and Lemieux at Seattle University, Waldschmit was a builder who was able to attract enough support to bring his institution into academic excellence. In the years following his inauguration, seventy Catholic colleges and universities passed out of existence.[137] The University of Portland was not one of them. Its total assets, recorded at a little over six million dollars in 1962, climbed to nearly eleven million in 1967, "reflecting capital improvements, mostly in the form of new buildings."[138]

Among the will-of-the-wisp buildings projected for the campus was the "University Tower." In the early 1960's, when senior citizen condominiums were coming into vogue, three northwest communities, the Benedictines at Mount Angel, the Dominicans, and the Holy Cross Fathers at the university, announced their sponsorship of ambitious "Towers" as all three called them, for retired Catholics of more than average means. The first of these was Mount Angel Towers, for which full-page advertisements appeared in Catholic papers in June 1962. Benedictine Father Hildebrand Melchior formed an independent corporation for development of a 3.4 million dollar condominium containing 209 apartments, below the monastery in the town of Mount Angel. With government funding the project was already under construction and Father Hildebrand was able to move into his quarters by February, 1963.[139] The Towers were completed and on Sunday, October 3, 1965, they were dedicated "as the only Catholic facility of its kind in the country."[140] This great honor, alas, was shortlived. Only sixty-one of the 209 units were occupied, by a total of eighty people, and the Federal Housing Association (FHA), after granting several forebearances, initiated foreclosure on the mortgage of $2,694,000.[141] On February 7, 1967, Mount Angel Towers was formally turned over to the FHA.

Meanwhile, the Holy Cross Fathers made plans for their twenty-two story University Towers on the Portland campus. Advertisements were placed in Catholic papers on June 21, 1963. The response was less than expected, the projected condominium appeared to be too risky financially, and it was quickly abandoned.[142]

So far the Catholics had fanned out. Only the Dominicans were left. The Dominican Provincial Father Joseph Ayius, believed in miracles, apparently, for he announced the construction of "Rosary Tower" in the heart of Portland, a very elaborate cluster of eight buildings sixteen or more stories high, including a vast hospital. The conglomerate was designed to cover several blocks in east Portland.[143] Perhaps the provincial had an oil well somewhere. If so, it went dry after one apartment complex had been completed. One must agree, however, that this was no mean achievement, a financially solvent condominium, sixteen stories high and containing 273 units. Its name was changed twice, for reasons not advertised, from Rosary to Dominican Towers and thence to Calaroga Terrace, which sounds aristocratic in a high class Italian manner.[144]

MOUNT ANGEL BENEDICTINES IN IDAHO

The Benedictines had nothing to regret. Nearly everyone then was making the same mistake: building condominiums in the suburbs at a time that public transportation was breaking down. Soon the gasoline famine would appear and many people, especially the wealthy, wanted to live in the center of the city, as high above it as the law of gravity permitted.

The Benedictines at Mount Angel, many years before, had established a monastery at Westminster in British Columbia. This had succeeded so well that by 1953 it was raised to an independent abbey.[145] This pleased the Mount Angel monks, naturally, and when requests for two more foundations arrived late in 1964, both were considered favorably. Abbot Damian sent Father Ambrose Zenner and Brother Boniface Arechederra to Cuernavaca, Mexico to establish a mission there, and Father Patrick Meagher to Idaho, initially to establish a seminary in Jerome.[146]

Bishop Treinen had urged the monks to make the Idaho foundation, and on January 15, 1965, in a joint statement with Abbot Damian, he announced that the Boise diocese had purchased five hundred acres of land just outside of Jerome, Idaho, and that this would be occupied by monks from Mount Angel, who would develop an independent priory there.[147] Their first purpose would be the establishment of a *minor seminary*, later a major seminary and retreat house. The demon of false hopes was dying slowly. There would be another seminary out in the country! After appropriate ceremonies, which were as solemn as only Benedictines can make them, Meagher left for Buehl, Idaho, where he remained several weeks before he went to Jerome. On August 3, 1965, Treinen welcomed him at Jerome, at "Ascension Priory" there, where temporary quarters had been acquired.

Treinen had other fish to fry. He was busy with renovations on his "new" chancery, which was the former Good shepherd Church for the Basques in Boise. The steeple was replaced with a mansard roof to make it look Italian Renaissance.[148] While this was gratifying for obvious reasons, the bishop had several unpleasant duties also, like presiding over funeral obsequies for Father Cyprian Bradley who had come to Boise in 1931 and served the diocese well by gathering its history.[149]

About this time, Treinen took up his residence in a duplex, which the diocese purchased.[150] He occupied one section, while his chancellor, Father William Crowley, occupied the other. Each did his own cooking, the bishop sometimes resorting to "Swanson's Boned Chicken." He did his own laundry in a common laundromat with the chancellor and used an exercise machine to keep fit. He worried sometimes about being bishop, imagining himself unsuitable for one reason or another, but when he wrote to Pope Paul VI about it, suggesting that he be replaced, His Holiness replied with tender remarks of comfort and reassurance. What he needed, he finally decided, was more time for fishing.

20

THE POST VATICAN YEARS
A TIME OF TURMOIL
1966–1974

Bishop Treinen was not the only northwest bishop who liked to fish. Archbishop Connolly, when daily routine became boring and his duties burdensome, packed his bait and fishpole and sailed off into the Sound where fish were so plentiful that even book-learned prelates could catch them. His favorite fishing hole, about fifty yards offshore on the northernmost tip of Kitsap Peninsula, was a deep drop-off where the largest of the King Salmons lay. In his tattered green jacket and faded blue denims, holding his rod firmly like reins on a horse, he drifted in his boat over his prey, hoping to catch at least a twenty pounder. He gazed vacantly at the gray skies or the heavy green shoreline, forests of pointed fir, while he pondered his more weighty problems.

On days like this, he liked to be alone. He was a reticent man who found it difficult to express his feelings with just anybody unless he felt indignant about a public matter. He undoubtedly realized that to some people he appeared grumpy. He was really tender-hearted but most of the time he carefully concealed it.

ARCHBISHOP CONNOLLY'S JUBILEE

Unlike Archbishop Howard, he had not been sentimental about jubilees. Howard managed to celebrate something every other year —or oftener. It was hard to keep up with it all, jubilees everywhere in an aging church. Only twice did Connolly consent to celebrate jubilees, once in 1950 for the observance of the Centenary of the Seattle Diocese, and again in 1964, his silver jubilee as a bishop. Whatever his reluctance to accept personal praise and attention, the Catholics of the archdiocese celebrated the latter in a memorable fashion.

There were the customary receptions and banquets and programs all of which were endured with patient acquiescence by His Excellency, a source of heart-warming gratification to those who admired him. What is more remarkable about it, I think, was the production of an elegant monograph containing two essays, a personal appreciation called "Worth Raising" by Father James Gandrau, and a detailed account of his accomplishments, "My Labors Among You..." by Mary Karabaich. [1]

The account is rather shocking, really, in a good sense. Archbishop Connolly had been in Seattle for sixteen years.

> More new parish facilities have been constructed in the half-generation of Archbishop Connolly's episcopacy than had been built in the preceding 100–year history of the Archdiocese. Thirty new parishes have been established in the 16 years the Archbishop has served here and church facilities constructed during that time number a remarkable 298. They include 66 new churches, 33 new elementary schools, 43 new convents, 54 new rectories, 82 parish auditoriums and gymnasiums and 20 new CCD centers. [2]

In addition to these, the archbishop presided over the building of St. Thomas Seminary, dedicated in April, 1959, three new high schools, including Blanchet, a new Seaman's Club in downtown Seattle and a new Holyrood cemetery and mausoleum, costing one million dollars. He sponsored the establishment of two retreat houses and encouraged the Sister Formation Program, a new monastery for the Carmelite Sisters, and new hospitals or major additions in ten cities. One of his major accomplishments was the purchase of the New Washington Hotel at Second and Steward in downtown Seattle for $1,305,948. This fourteen story building, which encompassed 250 rooms, was extensively re-modeled and converted into The Josephinum, a residence for retired men and women. It was dedicated on May 3, 1964. [3]

And how was all of this accomplished?

> It all began with a careful appraisal of the assets of all parishes of the Dioceses of Seattle soon after the Coadjutor Bishop's arrival here. Most of the parishes had savings accounts of some type and Bishop Connolly decided to call in all savings to form a Parochial Revolving Fund. At that time, banks were paying 1½ percent interest; Bishop Connolly paid 2 percent interest on deposits and loaned the money to pastors who undertook construction projects at 2½ percent interest. The many construction starts that resulted attracted the attention of bankers, who wondered where the Bishop was securing funds. (Earlier, a number of banks had been wary about loaning money to the Corporation of the Catholic Bishop of Seattle.)

One bank, Pacific National Bank of Seattle, demonstrated sufficient confidence in the construction program's financing to go along with the Corporation in its ambitious building program. Later, the Bank of California collaborated in underwriting necessary loans.

In recent years, there has been little difficulty in securing loans from banks in all areas of the Archdiocese.[4]

One could add countless details, less tangible than bricks and dollars, but more significant in the course of the church's history. Some of these were as follows: Liturgical reform; the CCD program, 36,000 students in 1964; Catholic Charities, Lay missionaries working in the Far East, Africa and South America; CYO (Catholic Youth Organization), which sponsored four summer camps for children; Interracial Council; Resettlement of 275 Hungarian Freedom Fighters; Archdiocesan Planning Commission; and the Ecumenical program.

"Ecumenism is here to stay," the archbishop told the Lutherans in their own church. "It is not a doctrine, but a movement—a striving for unity. We will do all in our power to eliminate prejudice, bias and ill will. We can disagree without being disagreeable."[5]

It was generally believed that Connolly exercised such great restraint (unlike Archbishop Howard) that no one was sure of what he thought about most matters. If this were ever true, the archbishop was certainly changing. Seattle was in a state of great social upheaval and its archbishop, no doubt inspired by his presence at Vatican II, was taking a firm public stand on major issues, like interracial equality and open housing.[6] An old section of the city, comprising the parishes of the cathedral, Immaculate Conception and St. Joseph's, was gradually being taken over by the blacks because Catholics, among others, had forced them to form their own ghetto there, with devastating results for all. The archbishop did not object to the presence of the blacks, he objected to their being restricted in residential choice, in part because Seattle's Mayor allegedly did not support open housing. Connolly established a Catholic Interracial Council, the first of its kind, in February, 1964, and as the official publisher of the *Catholic Northwest Progress*, he gave public witness to this by presenting a special edition on open housing in March of the same year.[7]

Later, at a Catholic Interracial Banquet, attended by twenty-one hundred persons, Connolly lashed out at the mayor. His Honor, J.D. Brannon, was conspicuous for his absence. "I would counsel our mayor," the archbishop said sarcastically, "not to tremble in his boots... his presence would not be an endorsement of open housing."

Brannon's successor was more concerned, apparently, by the phantom of "population explosion." When Wes Uhlman's staff leaked news of his proposal for a special tax on every third baby in a family, to help pay for abortions, Connolly's paper took up the battle against him, never letting up until Uhlman was defeated at the polls. *The Northwest Progress* "was able to note the inconsistency of the city's chief executive as he announced a search for missing population after the federal government determined the city had lost 40,178 persons since the 1960 census."[9]

The archbishop's commitment to human life was indeed more than editorial or philosophical. Not long after his appointment to Seattle a familiar picture frequently appeared in the press: he was presented each time after he had baptized the twelfth child of a Catholic family. Since 1956, when he had quietly started the practice, he had baptized 114 such "twelfth" children throughout western Washington.[10]

"I am an energizing bishop," he told two hundred of his priests, gathered at St. Thomas Seminary. "That's not just window dressing either. I have drawn up a series of new faculties in an effort to share my authority with you in view of the new decrees on the pastoral office of bishops and the priestly ministry of souls. I am asking for information, advice, and counsel. I am sharing my authority with you."[11] This expressed willingness to promulgate not only the letter, but the spirit of the Council, met with thundering applause.

JOHN F. KENNEDY HIGH SCHOOL

There was one project close to Connolly's heart, the new high school for the thirteen parishes in Seattle's south side, where Boeing's vast industry had brought in tens of thousands of employees. The building of the school had been announced almost a decade before but obstacles had appeared at every turn. Seventeen acres of land had been acquired at 1st Avenue South and 140th Street. Plans had been made for a faculty composed of De La Salle Christian Brothers and Sisters of Providence. These, too, were frustrated by events now taking place within the church.

Returning from the Council in 1963, after John F. Kennedy had been assassinated, the archbishop pondered the problems of the yet-to-be-realized school. It suddenly occurred to him that its name should be Kennedy, "the John F. Kennedy High School," and from that moment he never ceased to promote its completion.[12] He had considerable support in the wake of Kennedy's tragic death. He had found the lodestar for solving his problem.

Foreseeing no alternative, the archbishop decided to form a faculty of sisters and laymen, with Monsignor John Doogan of Blanchet High as the new principal. Contracts for construction of the building were let, but complications arose and both parties ended up in court. Classes were scheduled for September 1966. There was no building, so Father Anthony Palmasani, pastor of St. Thomas parish in Riverton, offered the use of what he had, space for 120 freshmen, both boys and girls. Thus, Kennedy, soon to become a major Catholic high school in the entire west, had its humble origins in borrowed classrooms.

Hopes were expressed for occupation of the new building "after the first of next year," but these, too, proved to be futile. One wing was finally ready in the spring of 1967 and Monsignor Doogan's freshmen moved into that with much chattering and banging of files and expressions of pleasure. Doogan announced that the rest of the school would be ready in September and added that "475-500 students were expected to register."

Kennedy was finally completed by the autumn of 1967. The principal was there when the students arrived. He was sitting at his desk, his worried expression topped with thick, dark hair. There were buttons down his cassock. He looked like an overburdened chancellor of the diocese. Two years later he became one, and by that time Kennedy High School had taken its respected place. "There are no Hippies at Kennedy," the *Progress* declared, Catholic pride scarcely concealed by brevity. "The students are all dynamically aware." It is not likely that many of them knew what this was supposed to mean.

THE ARCHBISHOP AND SEATTLE UNIVERSITY

No one can doubt the brilliance of the archbishop's achievements. Unfortunately a few cracks appeared and one of these seems to have been an "agreeable disagreement" between the archbishop and the Jesuits. Undoubtedly based on the age-old controversy about St. Ignatius Collegiate Church in San Francisco, misunderstandings continued to exist. At least some of the Jesuits thought so. They felt hurt and cheated when, for example, the archbishop referred publicly to the University of Washington, their state-monopoly competitor, as "our university," and directed the rector of the seminary to send seminarians to the University of Washington for classes that were already available at Seattle University.[13] This appeared to be counter-productive for Catholic higher education in the archdiocese, not to mention a humiliation for the Jesuits. More serious, perhaps, was the archbishop's consistent refusal to provide Seattle Jesuits with the required *beneplacitum* for establishing Seattle University as an independent canonical community with its own rector.[14]

The tensions lay deeper, like the archbishop's bigger salmon. These were manifested in other ways that seemed to confirm the view that the archbishop regarded the Jesuits, a substantial portion of his work force, with less than a friendly eye.

The final word on this is more cheerful. Time healed all, or most difficulties. They say that only people who do nothing make no mistakes. No one could accuse the Jesuits at Seattle University or the archbishop of doing nothing. Indeed few churchmen have done as much.

LA SALLE HIGH SCHOOL

Connolly's praiseworthy example in establishing Catholic high schools, using the formula of a mixed faculty of priests and brothers, sisters, and lay persons, was not lost on other bishops nor on members of religious orders, especially the sisters. The latter, in some cases, wise in the stratagems of successful entrepreneurs, quickly discerned that "central Catholics" had two desirable expectations for themselves. First, they relieved the sisters of a particular order or congregation of the financial responsibilities and management of schools—no small gain as costs went up and the availability of personnel went down. Second, these central Catholics gave their sisters greater exposure for attracting candidates to their orders. To take advantage of this they tended to assign the best and more attractive teachers to these posts, often the more *avante garde* who projected a new image of nuns for students.

Archbishop Howard in Portland did not wholly approve of coeducation, and later, when Central Catholic for Boys admitted girls, he was so disappointed, according to reports, that he considered changing his will. But Howard was a realist. If forced to choose a central Catholic or no school, he would quickly accept the former, as he had done when North Catholic had been established. Now, when the southeastern environs of the city were in desperate need of a Catholic high school, bowing to the inevitable, he accepted another central Catholic, this time, however, he invited the Brothers of Christian Schools to co-sponsor the new institution with his favored sisters, the Sisters of St. Mary's of Beaverton.

The brothers had first come to Portland in 1886 at the request of Archbishop Gross. The new contingent arrived in 1966, eighty years later, to staff with the sisters the new La Salle High School in Milwaukie, Oregon, where chain saws were manufactured, a suburb of Portland near Oregon City, the original seat of the archdiocese. There were many references to "the cooperative venture" then, though La Salle was regarded as "the tenth high school of the Christian Brothers on the west coast." Principal of the new school was Brother Emory Leroy, F.S.C., the assistant principal Sister Marietta, S.S.M.O., and the vice-principal

Brother La Salle Bossong, F.S.C. Two other brothers and four other sisters, in addition to four lay persons, completed the roster of the first faculty.[15] The solemn blessing and dedication of an all-new building, artfully designed in western Oregon's woodsy motif, for approximately seven hundred boys and girls, was conducted on May 7, 1967, by Archbishop Howard's successor. But His Grace, of course, was present. As always he was the honored guest who got all the attention.

WASHINGTON PROVINCE OF THE SISTERS OF THE HOLY NAMES

Like the Benedictines at Mount Angel, the Sisters of the Holy Names were expanding. The northwest province was divided into two provinces, Oregon and Washington, on August 6, 1962. Sister Kathleen Clara was appointed to the office of Washington's provincial, effective on the same date.[16] These innovations required further considerations, such as the whereabouts of the new provincialate and provision for retired sisters. For the present the new provincial's office would be located in the Holy Names convent on north Superior in Spokane, while plans for the new motherhouse were discussed.

Eventually a tract of land, seventy-five acres of bull pines on the Spokane River, not distant from the sisters' Fort Wright College, was chosen, and blueprints for the new motherhouse prepared.[17] Bishop Topel presided over the groundbreaking ceremonies for the two-million dollar red brick edifice on October 8, 1966.

Recently Bishop Topel had made a tough decision of his own. The new freeway through downtown Spokane preempted the chancery building of which Bishop White had been so proud. Its loss was really a godsend, but Topel, who had begun by this time to be touchy about being poor, was loath to part with it. The building certainly looked poor enough, even for the bishop. Where would he find another?

Directly across from the cathedral was another building, the Great Northern Life Insurance Company's, which was old enough for any poor man, but it *looked* new, and handsome besides. The price was right, only $300,000, for a structure that had recent improvements costing half that much. Topel was urged to buy it for the new chancery. His scruples about poverty, however, forced him to hesitate, while his business advisors wagged their heads. Fortunately, he finally overcame his reluctance and consented to the acquisition. "Open house," in the new facility, which evoked exclamations of wonder from all who came, was conducted on Saturday, March 12, 1966. Never in the history of the diocese had so much been purchased for so little, but the bishop was still anxious about its elegance. He soon made up for it, though, by selling his residence, a very modest one used by Bishop White for many years. Later he bought another one in a poor neighborhood for four thousand dollars, the tipsy back porch included. There in his shanty-like house he could really be poor.

ARCHBISHOP HOWARD'S DEPARTURE

Archbishop Howard, on the other hand, had no such scruples. He lived simply in his grand brick residence and even as an octogenarian he continued to walk vigorously in the aristocratic neighborhood, wearing on sunny days his old straw hat. Adopting the more liberal views that were current, he appointed four laymen to the Archdiocesan School Board and designated members of a committee to plan for a "Senate of Priests."[18] In April 1965, he blessed St. Alice Church in Springfield.[19] He dedicated the new three million dollar hospital at Eugene in July, as he had dedicated the first Sacred Heart Hospital there twenty-eight years before.[20] In early August he hosted the National Liturgical Conference in Portland's new Memorial Colosseum, and was pleased to learn that his archdiocese was one of the most advanced in the United States in the conduct of the liturgy.[21] In late August he blessed the new Queen of Peace Church, formerly St. Cecelia's in Portland, then St. Matthew's Church in Hillsboro in October, and St. Peter the Fisherman at Arch Cape on the Oregon Coast in December.[22]

This was a typical year. To keep it in perspective, one must remember that the archbishop was in his eighty-ninth year and that he had many additional duties, like administering confirmation in each parish, assigning pastors, and preaching in the cathedral.

In May 1966, he celebrated one of his many jubilees, his sixtieth as a priest and his fortieth as an archbishop.[23] When he came to Portland in 1926, he found 81 parishes and 174 priests in all of western Oregon. Forty years later the archdiocese had 108 parishes and 440 priests, in addition to many new institutions like Central Catholic and Jesuit High.

Autumn was the season for goodbyes. In mid-December, just before the beginning of winter, the papal delegate in Washington dropped a bomb on Portland. It should not have surprised anyone, but it did.

Bishop Robert J. Dwyer of Reno, he said, had been appointed the new Archbishop of Portland in Oregon, succeeding Archbishop Howard. "Howard resigned last August in compliance with a suggestion by Pope Paul that all bishops past 75 retire."[24] Howard was assigned to the titular see of Albule in Mauretania, which by long standing custom he was forbidden to visit.

His Grace as usual made a good face over it. Directed to serve as administrator until the new archbishop was installed, he made arrangements to move to Beaverton, where the Sisters of St. Mary had a comfortable three bedroom home for him. At the end of January he performed what he called "my last official act." There was a special monument at St. Paul on the Willamette, and the graves of three pioneer priests. A violent windstorm had shattered the monument in 1962 and a new one was raised. As his "last official act" His Grace blessed the monument and the three graves, those of Archbishop Blanchet, Father J. DeCraene who died in 1873 at Salem, just four years after ordination, and Monsignor Francis X. Blanchet, the archbishop's nephew who had built up the church in the historic Jacksonville area.[25]

So this was the archbishop's swan song. At the end of January, he moved to Beaverton where the earth was sweet and flat, and suitable for walking. The gentle sisters cared for him there and for his many visitors until the end of his life, still sixteen years away.

ARCHBISHOP ROBERT J. DWYER

The new archbishop was often regarded as a die hard conservative. There were even some who likened him to an ecclesiastical troglodyte, but these were the Catholics who wanted to canonize Martin Luther. By the press he was described as an "educator, historian [and] editor." No doubt he qualified for all three, but the list falls shorts. He was, above all, a Catholic priest of the *Roman* persuasion, a monsignor since 1950, and a bishop since 1952. He took each of these very seriously, especially the latter, though it must be admitted that to his poodle dog (his most cherished possession) he was nothing more than the man who stroked and fed him.

The poodle kept things in perspective, for sometimes one got the impression that the archbishop belonged to a superior race. This was largely due, I think, to certain inner compulsions to correct the world's disorders. A man of great integrity and almost excessive loyalty to the nineteenth-century church, into which he had been born, he regarded it a duty to defend not only its teachings but also its style of life. Thus he really was a prince bishop, with most of the required props and some of the assumed pompousness.

Despite these limitations, which most people saw first and forgot last, Archbishop Dwyer was a brilliant churchman with the deserved reputation of a readable columnist. He had already served the church long and well, not only by his defense of orthodoxy but as an administrator also, which had earned for him a bishop's throne in Reno before he became the sixth archbishop of Portland.

His father, John Charles Dwyer, a physically large man, like a contented farmer, was known as a leader of the Catholic laity in Mormon-dominated Utah. He was a member of the Knights of Columbus, becoming in time a Grand Knight, deeply loyal to the church, which was habitually on the defensive because of the Mormon control of the state's economy and politics. The archbishop's mother, Mabel Maynard Dwyer, a white-haired matron like the grandmother you loved, was a charter member of the Catholic Women's League, which places her in the same category as the bishop's female battalion.[26]

Robert Joseph was born on August 1, 1908 in Salt Lake. He advanced in age and wisdom in a home that was ruled according to traditional Catholicism. He attended public grade schools, then Judge Memorial Catholic High School, where not unexpectedly he decided to become a priest. He attended St. Mary's Manor in South Langhorne, Pennsylvania, and Menlo Park, California and was ordained by Boise's Bishop Kelly on July 11, 1932, at the precocious age of twenty-three. He was the first native of Utah to become a Catholic priest.[27]

His initial assignment was assistant at the cathedral commonly called "The Madeleine." Two years later he was appointed to the editorship of the *Intermountain Catholic*, partly because he had a vocabulary that would choke a bibliomaniac and partly because he could write with a cogent pen. From 1938 to 1941 he attended Catholic University, earning a doctorate in history. He returned to Salt Lake for the war years then became the superintendent of schools for the diocese, and finally the rector of the cathedral. In 1950 he acquired the title and outdated privileges of a monsignor. Two years later he was appointed Bishop of Reno by Pius XII. He was consecrated by Archbishop Mitty, formerly Bishop of Salt Lake, in The Madeleine, on August 5, 1952, four days after his forty-fourth birthday. Co-consecrators were Bishops Thomas Gorman of Dallas and Joseph Federal, an Auxiliary of Mitty in San Francisco.

In fifteen golden years as Bishop of Reno, he built eighty churches, convents, and rectories, a remarkable achievement in a small diocese. He authored many erudite articles for the learned journals, like *America* and *Thought*, read as avidly as some clerics watch Notre Dame football, and preached retreats to anyone who would listen. He was well known throughout the West when Paul VI elevated him to Portland on December 14, 1966. His first official act after his appointment was to notify the editor of the *Catholic Sentinel* that henceforth his column would appear weekly in this Portland paper.[28] When asked what else he had to say he replied, "My purpose is simply to get on with the work."[29] This was probably the shortest statement, using the smallest words, he would make within the next decade. His installation as archbishop took place on Monday, February 6, 1967, at St. Mary's Cathedral, with Archbishop Vagnozzi presiding. Twelve hundred people were present, including nine archbishops, twenty-eight bishops, countless priests and nuns, lay people, and strings of well-scrubbed altar boys, who looked like advertisements for some candle company.

At this time Dwyer was not physically large like his father, but he resembled him almost uncannily in other respects. He wore rimless glasses, through which his small, beady eyes squinted critically, missing nothing. His cheeks puffed out, like cartoons of the northwind blowing, especially when he smiled, which was not often. His chin was sharp and pointed. His tastes ran to the finer things, like original oil paintings, which graced his walls, but his white poodle dog conquered his heart. Often when occupied in his office, listening to the reports of his priests, he fondled the dog in his lap. This became a source of much merriment in the diocese, because priests, if they owned dogs at all, kept big, noisy ones, which became fat from too much food.

DWYER AT WORK

As Dwyer had tartly observed, he was eager to get on with the work. Since his tenure as archbishop was relatively short, only seven years, he had best be about his business. There was a new All Saints Church in Portland, built for something like $600,000, which he dedicated soon after his arrival, on February 26, 1967. This tipped his hand, as it were, so that his uneasy and curious priests knew he meant what he said. Henceforth, the word from the chancery was *cave.* "Take Care."

The priests had a chance to inspect the archbishop more closely when he invited them to organize a Priests' Senate, which was all the rage then, the hoped for cure-all for the infirmities of the archdiocese. Thirteen were elected in March to form the first senate, and the first meeting of these church related statesmen was called to order in the chancery auditorium on May 2, 1967 at 10:00 a.m. Apparently this august body took itself very seriously, for it remained in session for the rest of the day, though it had, as yet, no advisory status or right to vote.[30]

There is no reason to believe the archbishop, like some bishops we have read about, was afraid of his senate or anything else. With amazing virtuosity, he picked up where Howard left off, and despite his reputation and the customary angry look on his face, he was more progressive in making Vatican II reforms than many of his brother bishops.

Normally, the archbishop as metropolitan had no jurisdiction in the dioceses of his suffragans, except when a bishop-ordinary died. Then he had the responsibility to undertake certain formalities involving the appointment of a successor. In Dwyer's first year one of his suffragans gave up the ghost; Bishop William Condon died at the age of seventy-two.

DEATH OF BISHOP CONDON

Bishop Condon had occupied the see of Great Falls for twenty-eight years. Each year, toward the end, he looked much older, not in a natural, progressive way, but like a sickly person who shocks his visitors. In mid-1967 he was advised to undergo major surgery, to which he submitted, and he seemed to be on the road to recovery. Suddenly in his own home, on August 17, 1967, he died. His funeral obsequies were celebrated with becoming respect in St. Ann's Cathedral, with Archbishop Dwyer presiding. Archbishop Howard, summoned from retirement, accepted with alacrity the invitation to preach Condon's eulogy. It was all done properly with dispatch, one might say, for the bishop had been dying for over a decade.

As an auxiliary bishop, rather than a coadjutor, Schuster did not succeed to the see automatically. It was generally believed, however, that he would, and when the consultors of the diocese gathered after the burial to select an administrator, they named Schuster. This did little to encourage other aspirants to the office.

The appointment required several months, not because Rome was hesitant, but because Archbishop Dwyer, in whose hands these formalities lay, was new to the game, and in no special hurry. Finally, on December 2, 1967, Schuster was officially selected as the fourth Bishop of Great Falls. The papal delegate, Archbishop Luigi Raimondi, announced it in Washington on December 6. Since everyone expected it the news created no sensation, but Schuster's many admirers hastened to congratulate him. "Delighted with news of your elevation," Senator Mike Mansfield wired from the nation's capital, "a better choice could not have been made. Am happy for you and the diocese."[31] Howard said, "You are especially qualified in every respect for this position... everyone who knows you is delighted." That made it unanimous. The senator who lived in Washington and the archbishop who lived in Oregon thought everyone in Montana was happy or delighted.

Schuster took it in stride. He altered his coat-of-arms, posed for a new portrait and arranged for his formal installation on January 23, 1968, with Archbishop Raimondi as ranking prelate. Not much else had to be changed, except, perhaps, the chancery letterheads.

RELOCATION OF ST. VINCENT'S HOSPITAL

While Archbishop Dwyer, as metropolitan, had been involved in these proceedings, he had not been in charge. His principal concern, in any case, was doctrinal orthodoxy, which he promoted vigorously in his column. Unfortunately it was a season of restraint for bishops, because some "Catholic" weeklies were picking at everything they said or did. Dwyer's unwillingness to be intimidated by them had cost him the support of the liberals, mostly brash young people, many of them priests and nuns who would soon leave the church. While he regretted this, he realized that he was not the real cause for it and he continued to thunder away at what he regarded as lax doctrine in the church. In time he would tell the pope about it.

Meanwhile there were the customary groundbreakings and dedications, for which his predecessor had observed such punctiliousness. A short time after his installation the Sisters of Providence revealed plans for relocating St. Vincent's Hospital in the green hills west of Portland.[32] Their Providence Hospital in east Portland had been expanding by leaps and bounds since its opening in 1941. It now covered several city blocks. Older St. Vincent's on its second site on the rim of the basin west of Portland was so out of date there was no way to salvage it. Plans for a new building were in preparation and on March 31, 1968, groundbreaking ceremonies were enacted in accordance with tradition and the high cost of the project. The performers in the little production, including Archbishop Dwyer, posed with shovels with huge bows on them. The archbishop was fully vested, in cope and mitre, and an assistant stood by eagerly grasping the crozier. The archbishop's tired smile was for the camera only.[33]

The estimated cost of the building was $7,214,000. This amounted to more than three times the net worth of the Spokane Diocese in 1968. This was Big Time, but another comparison was even more noteworthy: the archbishop's office released a report that the Catholic schools of the archdiocese had saved Oregon taxpayers sixteen million dollars, in addition to an estimated capital investment of forty-six million, which would be required to house twenty-four thousand Catholic students.[34] No one but the Catholics seemed to care, though others benefited most by it.

The archdiocese had recently completed an "Action Drive" during which a total of $6,802,000 was pledged.[35] An unprecedented amount, this proved that Dwyer's methods could pay off. By December 31, 1968, he disclosed that $2,108,006 had been collected. Campaign expenses skimmed off $165,887 from this, leaving a net of $1,942,119. With this the archbishop paid off $561,000 on bank loans and $338,977 on parish debts. He purchased a house of studies for seminarians at Portland State University and gave Newman Clubs at state schools $11,147.[36] He also invested $224,888 in D Notes. Money from pledges that were honored later was put to similar use.

Motivated by the good example of Bishop Topel, who had already released a diocesan financial accounting, Dwyer published a complete statement at the end of his fiscal year in October, 1969.[37] According to this the archdiocese owed a whopping long term debt of $9,200,000. But the archdiocese still owned valuable land, enough to liquidate this debt in the course of time. But critics of the church, please take note: the net value of the Catholic Church in the Northwest has never been high. The endowment of even one major university in the East would exceed it by many hundreds of millions of dollars.[38]

Evidence of the bishops' good will following Vatican II had not been wanting. Vast changes had been made in the liturgy, in shared authority and fiscal accountability, and in greater simplicity of the prelates' lifestyle.

Another decree of the Council was about to be tested. It was called "due process." During the next five years painful experiences involving due process would rack the northwest church. The first of these was the highly publicized strike at Marquette High School in Yakima.

THE STRIKE AT MARQUETTE

One of Bishop Dougherty's most promising young priests was Father Frederick Brenner, formerly one of the priest-teachers at Blanchet High. Brenner had become the superintendent of Yakima's diocesan schools and principal of Marquette, following the departure of the Jesuits. His appointment to Marquette, probably suggested by his chancellor, Father Philip Leinfelder, was a stroke of genius, for Brenner enjoyed the gift of diplomacy. He was an excellent administrator, and a calm, cheerful Pied Piper with the boys. He was respected by the boys' parents and especially by the Jesuits attached to St. Joseph's parish, with whom he resided.

Among the Jesuits were the pastor, Father Paul Weissenberg, who had served patiently as vice-principal at Seattle Prep for almost twenty-five years. He was conscientious to a fault, a diligent priest who chose for himself the most humble tasks of the house and seldom allowed himself the luxury of a day's vacation. Then there was Father Francis Schoenberg, the assistant pastor at St. Joseph's for twenty-eight years, probably the best known clergyman in the Yakima Valley, generally regarded as the local "saint" and selected by the bishop to be his own confessor.

The third Jesuit in the parish was Father Henry Schultheis, provincial of the Oregon Province from 1954 to 1959, a priest of a distinguished record as a rector of Bellarmine in Tacoma, a pastor of St. Ignatius in Portland, and vice-rector at Mount St. Michael's in Spokane.

What is significant here is that all three Jesuits, past middle age and more cautious than adventurous, supported the action of the principal and faculty of the parish's high school.

Besides Brenner, there were six diocesan priests on the Marquette faculty and four lay teachers, making a total of eleven for 207 students.

On Wednesday, September 13, 1967, the principal and faculty of Marquette "walked out," meaning they collectively went on strike, after the bishop refused to meet their requests that the school be improved and that the teachers get a pay hike.[39] The students of Marquette, exhilarated by the excitement and delighted with an unscheduled holiday, went on a strike with them. "Marquette on Strike Students Support Teachers Actions" was the headline that disconsolate Leinfelder read in his evening paper.[40] Brenner, putting his own neck on the block as it were, had assumed leadership of the radical action that was unprecedented in the northwest church. To the press he explained Marquette's dilemma: "[The] money situation [is] very critical and we are short of staff." Marquette in the previous year had a deficit of $30,000 despite efforts of all to gather in every loose dollar in the parish. Brenner himself taught a full schedule of classes, and, because of his duties as principal, he was able to spend less than fifteen minutes a day on his position as superintendent of schools. Marquette, which did not share in diocesan support, was subsidized by St. Joseph parish, which was also assessed for the support of Central Catholic. "[It is] unfair that St. Joseph's has to support both Marquette and Central Catholic." Central had a larger staff, better facilities and diocesan-provided bus service. Marquette did not have any of these advantages, in fact it did not have even a gymnasium. "First no gym, now no school."[41]

When asked for an interview, the bishop replied, "No comment."

St. Joseph's Academy at this time had sixteen teachers, ten sisters and six lay teachers. Sister Ann Maureen was principal. Like Sister Donna Byrne, principal of the parish grade school, she was a Sister of Providence. The grade school had fourteen other teachers, five sisters and nine laywomen. It had 322 students, and the academy 220. They all decided to join the Marquette strike. That evening the boys and girls of all three schools gathered to celebrate and they built a huge bonfire. "Two Schools Join the Strike," said the *Yakima Morning Herald*.

By this time, the spirit of the strike had gripped the inhabitants of the cozy, isolated city in the center of the state. Mrs. Frederick Mercy Jr., a lively and generous activist within the diocese, ordered a sign board with the following inscription: "We Want a Spiritual Leader Not a $ Real Estate Broker $." She demonstrated before the downtown chancery building, boldly waving her sign to get attention. The dollar sign made reference to the elaborate churches and rectories already built or under construction in the diocese on borrowed money. The diocese was already so far in debt that solvency appeared hopeless. It was generally believed that the building tornado had been shaped by Leinfelder, whose affluent tastes far exceeded the ability of the people to pay.

Two spacious ads appeared in the paper. One signed by 177 students read, "We are Proud To Be Marquette Students: We Support Our Faculty." The other signed by 207 academy girls read, "Marquette Faculty, We Think You Are Right." So did the Yakima Valley Federation of Teachers. On Friday, September 15, they announced support for the strike. There were now 42 teachers and 750 children out. The bishop decided to meet the strikers.

Eight members of a "Citizens Committee" presented the complaints at a meeting, which began at 1:30 Friday afternoon. When it was over, they all emerged with long solemn faces. The press reported that they were "tight-lipped" but added that "Progress" was the word. Father Brenner expressed the opinion that the only long range solution was the consolidation of the three Catholic high schools in Yakima "while maintaining the traditions of all three." When asked about this the bishop replied, "The entire matter of consolidation needs further and sympathetic study. Any commitment to consolidate by September 1968 is considered impossible at this time."[43] This sounded more like Leinfelder than the bishop.

All afternoon on Sunday, September 17, the bishop listened to grievances and bartered for time. Leinfelder, he knew, was opposed to all major concessions.[44] Thus the bishop was confronted with two ugly choices: yield to the demands of the faculty, or reject the one to whom, he thought, he owed more than he could repay.

Rumor by this time, asserted that one of the demands of the strikers was the removal of Leinfelder as chancellor. The prospect almost paralyzed Dougherty, but really, what else could he do? Even his best friends urged it, but Dougherty still hesitated.[45]

At last the bishop capitulated. An agreement was reached and on Monday morning a rousing ovation of the student body greeted the Marquette faculty. At a student assembly in the presence of representatives of the press, the following six concessions by the bishop were formally announced by Father Brenner:

1. A 21-member committee would study consolidation of the three high schools. The bishop's decision would be announced by January 1, 1968.

2. The assessment of all parishes would be distributed equitably on a per capita basis.

3. Tuition changes would be uniform. The diocese would set up a salary schedule for all lay teachers.

4. Athletic facilities would be provided at Marquette.

5. Another teacher would be employed to relieve Father Brenner for giving more time to his principal duties.

6. The Superintendent of Schools would have greater authority over the schools of the diocese.

This agreement had been signed Sunday evening at 10:30. It had been a hard day for the bishop.[45]

In the fallout of the strike, one of Marquette's lay faculty members, Alex Deccio, who had also been a member of the Citizens Committee, summarized the meaning of the last five day confrontation. The Marquette situation, he said, "set precedents in the diocese as far as the role of the layman is concerned. The layman's role in the future will be more than just donating money."[46]

If anything, Deccio's prediction was the understatement of the entire ordeal. What was happening at Marquette would soon be happening throughout the nation. The layman's role would be more than just donating money.

EXIT FATHER LEINFELDER

All of these details, really quite scandalous to the timid old ladies of the diocese, were openly reported in the press, including the more conservative *Northwest Progress*, which got around to it a week later. The excitement had subsided by then, but it was quickly revived when Leinfelder resigned. The *Yakima Daily Republic* reported this on September 23: "Father Philip Leinfelder, Vicar General and Chancellor for the past 13 years has asked to be relieved of his duties so that he can return to his home diocese in Wisconsin." Said Bishop Dougherty, "It is with reluctance that I accede to his request. . . . " In the diocesan paper *Our Times,* the bishop presented a letter of praise and gratitude for Leinfelder's services, and a resume of his record before coming to Yakima. It was, in effect, a defense of his chancellor, who left the diocese in a financial shambles.

Leinfelder's departure, an occasion of joyful celebration by some was a portentous prelude to the bishop's own departure less than two years later.

THE LEARY AFFAIR AT GONZAGA

References to the Vietnam War still evoke bitter memories for all, especially for those parents or teachers who were involved in the care of draft-age students. College and university campuses were battlegrounds, sometimes as volatile as those in Asia, with teachers at swords point with other teachers and middle class parents frequently at variance with the schools. On most campuses students were up in arms against administrations who were, it was alleged, withholding their rights. Causes of disruption, present on the American scene since the second World War, were bearing sour fruit.

At Seattle University during this revolutionary period, a bomb or two was thrown into darkened buildings because "student rights" were violated. The university's president, Father Kenneth Baker, was kept hostage in his office by violent blacks because he would not declare a holiday in honor of Martin Luther King. At Gonzaga University in Spokane, students demonstrated against the war and interfered with R.O.T.C. activities. Counseling services for avoiding the draft were provided by the campus ministry. Attempts were made to disrupt graduation exercises.

The situation at Gonzaga was unique. The present, Father John P. Leary and some members of his "cabinet", supported the student partisans in their demands and opposition to most of the faculty, especially the Jesuits. Leary was nobody's fool. Six-footish, balding, with pale blue eyes and an apple blossom complexion that did not tan in the sun, he was second generation Irish and as liberal a Democrat as the party cultivated. He was also a brilliant, original thinker, very innovative, and a speaker who could charm college students into reversing their own stubborn opinions. But he supported them fiercely in their sometimes outrageous expressions of freedom. One should not doubt his sincerity. If he differed with others it was because of is own convictions, which had served not only himself, but Gonzaga and the church remarkably well.

Elements of the final struggle were complex. Some of them gradually surfaced when Bishop Topel decided that the moment of intervention had arrived. He dispatched a letter, bristling with unexpected threats, to President Leary on January 7, 1969, when campus unrest was at its peak

Dear Father Leary:

As you are aware, in the thirteen years I have been Bishop, I have been very careful not to interfere with the internal affairs of Gonzaga University. The time has come, though, when I feel in conscience that as the Bishop of the diocese I must make certain things clear. This letter has been delayed so that it would not be written precipitously. Further, it was good that it not get lost in the Christmas mail or in the other avalanche of mail which I would assume you have received.

Frankly I am deeply concerned with the direction Gonzaga University is taking. In this letter I shall discuss three matters. My concern is that the matters which I will discuss here are leading in the direction of making Gonzaga less and less a Catholic university, perhaps to the point of it even ceasing to be one. It is not my purpose, particularly at this time, to judge whether it is necessary of not for Gonzaga to take this course. At this time, I am only pointing out the direction that Gonzaga in my judgment is taking.

1) The first has to do with the religious program. For too long the liturgy, especially in the student chapel, has been in the minds of many (I believe in the minds of *most*) irreverent. I believe that it has reached the point where the lack of restraint that is used is doing more harm than good. In particular, the almost total disregard for Church authority is in my opinion undermining respect for Church authority. Are you aware that in your theology courses professors have been asked why the Bishop permits things to go on as they are at the university? This disregard for Church authority has been occurring at a time when respect for it needs to be buttressed rather than undermined. Further, to the best of my knowledge, this disrespect is being fostered by some members of the faculty. Very serious too is the fact that the liturgy at Gonzaga is divisive (to the priests as well as to the students) rather than unitive. I am concerned about all the religious practices, those in the student chapel, those in the Jesuit House (which seem to be less objectionable), and those in the halls (apparently the most objectionable of all).

2) The next matter has to do with the Christmas issue of the Gonzaga Bulletin a) because of the blasphemous verse which was featured (something which I considered incredible), and b) because of the objectionable Playboy picture and writeup about it.

3) Finally, there is the matter of parietal hours.[47] I have been told that this is at the present a dead issue. I sincerely hope so. Notwithstanding, what *has happened* has undermined my confidence in the direction Gonzaga University is going. I am very proud of the attitude that almost all the members of the Society took on the issue. I am very proud also of the vote of the parents on the issue. I am proud too of the stand of the faculty senate. On the other hand, I am dismayed and shocked that your administration did approve this experiment. In my opinion, this is flagrantly flouting Catholic standards. That your administration should so totally disregard the almost unanimous attitudes of the Jesuit Fathers and of the parents is incomprehensible to me. Either your administration is living in an ivory tower or it is completely

unconcerned about the almost unanimous judgment of others and apparently felt called upon to lead the way in the Inland Empire in an experiment on parietal hours. Do you realize how much this has shocked certain students, professors, and priests in charge of the Newman Apostolate at nearby state institutions?

Frankly I have come to the conclusion that the words are spoken about Gonzaga aiming to be a Catholic university are often just words, lip service. The Bulletin affair and the parietal hours experiment have in my opinion harmed Gonzaga's reputation as a Catholic university in a very serious way. Unless there is a very clear change of direction, I believe that this harm is irreparable....

It is good for you to realize that the Bishop White Seminary letter of protest was written and mailed before I knew anything about it. Similarly, a statement of protest which you will receive from our Priests Senate was decided entirely independently of me. In neither case was I in the slightest way responsible, even indirectly. This will make you realize, I believe, how disturbed our priests are about what is happening at Gonzaga.

Obviously I hope that Gonzaga remains a truly Catholic institution. I believe it is very important for the Church that it does. I understand something of the difficulties involved in keeping it so. I personally think, though, that standing on Catholic principles will yield greater results than departing from them. I will pray for you and for the university at this difficult time.

Devotedly yours in the service of Our Lady.
+ Bishop Topel
Bernard J. Topel
Bishop of Spokane[48]

The bishop's remarks, intended for Leary and his advisors, were made available to the students, who voluntarily declared Friday, January 11, 1969, "A Day of Affirmation" in support of Leary. A massive rally was conducted, the bishop and university faculty were in effect summoned for discussions, and Don Jensen, president of the student body, an ardent disciple of Leary, read to the assembly what the bishop had written. Topel, when asked to speak, reaffirmed his objections to the changes taking place and added "that if he had to do it over, he would not change the letter, except to encourage Father Leary to discuss the issues with him."[49]

The action of the students, it was said, was precipitated by rumors that Leary had resigned. Members of Leary's staff reported that Leary, who was not present, had not resigned, but he felt that he could not remain without the support of the university's faculty.

Father Leary's was a cruel dilemma. The university had run into huge deficits for several years. At the current rate it was facing bankruptcy eventually. Leary was trying to keep it "Catholic" while he attracted support from secular sources, including the government, which tended to favor "student power." To achieve this he broadened the student base, and leaned toward secularization. To him this appeared to be the only course left for saving the university.

Little of this was revealed, for obvious reasons. Reporters for Spokane's papers, after they had made the bishop's charges appear as sensational as possible, concentrated on student complaints:

> At the close of the discussion Friday, students voiced confusion over their own status in the university....
>
> The students called for 'significant and community-wide decision making to begin immediately on the substantive issues that have been discussed in the past few days.'
>
> The Rev. David M. Clarke, academic vice-president, read a statement that he said was endorsed by the majority of the Jesuit community at Gonzaga.
>
> The statement said the Jesuits feel 'that the governance of the university should involve both lay and Jesuit representation,' and that students should participate in the decision making facets of the university.
>
> The statement continued in saying that there is a general agreement on objectives of the university, but that there 'is a wide variety of attitudes as to the proper and effective mode of implementation of these objectives.'
>
> Jensen said Thursday a small group of Jesuits have called in the Very Rev. John Kelley, provincial general of the Oregon province of the Society of Jesus, to examine the trends at Gonzaga.[50]
>
> Jensen said the Jesuits requested that Father Kelley nullify the lay board of trustees, university policies declaring the rights of students for self-government and to control the persons who have instituted the changes.
>
> Father Kelley was in Spokane Friday, but declined to meet with the students, Clarke said that in conversation with Father Kelley earlier in the day, Father Kelley indicated that his presence would not be helpful to the discussion and that he wished for the problems to be resolved internally.
>
> The students were praised by the administrators and faculty for their actions in discussing the problems openly.
>
> Bishop Topel said he was proud of their actions in these matters. It was a sign of their maturity, he said.[51]

In these proceedings Jensen took himself very seriously. At times he used pejorative expressions like "Old Guard" with reference to the Jesuits, echoing comments previously and frequently made by the president. His leadership kept the "rebellion" in the news all month. At the end of January the following appeared in *The National Register*:

'Student Power' Keeps Fr. Leary at Gonzaga
    When other students around the country are rebelling against their
universities, it's really good to hear our students cheering the administration on.

It was in fact, to "the great student support" that the university's
president, Father John P. Leary, S.J. attributed his decision not to resign.

It has been rumored that Father Leary and several administration
officials had offered their resignations. When the rumor reached the
students, more than 1200 of them abandoned classes to stage a quiet,
orderly "Day of Affirmation" approving the liberal leadership Father
Leary provided.

The students were reportedly also angered by the presence of Father
John Kelley, S.J., provincial of the Jesuits' Oregon province, who was
visiting the campus in response to an SOS from Gonzaga's conservative
Old Guard.

Following the demonstration and an inspection visit by Bishop Bernard
J. Topel of Spokane, Father Leary issued a letter in which he announced
he was not resigning. He also told the student body that with continued
student support they could resolve future problems as they arose.

Student body president Don Jensen said students were upset about
"outside pressure, condemning such progressive education innovations.
. . ."[52]

It should be noted here that Father Kelley was not an intruder as
represented by some of the students. The fact of the matter is that Kelley
was the major superior of the northwest Jesuits, whom Jesuits had taken
a vow to obey. He had come to Gonzaga at the desperate urging of many
Jesuits and he had prudently refrained from direct interference, though
he had a perfect right to do so where Father Leary was concerned. If
anything, Kelley was too patient, as were the vast majority in Jesuit
House, the work horses who had made Gonzaga possible by their
dedicated lives without salary.

When the smoke of battle had cleared, Leary had been forced to
resign.[53] Gonzaga's new board of trustees, part Jesuit and part laymen,
appointed Father Richard Twohy of the faculty as an acting president,
and in the course of the following years, gradually reversed the trend at
Gonzaga by reaffirming its Catholic identity and by placing it on a solid
financial footing.

BISHOP DOUGHERTY'S RESIGNATION

On February 5, 1969, Bishop Dougherty's request for retirement was
granted by the pope. Paul VI himself announced in Rome on this
Wednesday in late winter, that the bishop had resigned because of poor

health and that his withdrawal from office was effective immediately. He would serve as the administrator of the diocese until the new bishop arrived.[54]

In the same press release, the name of the new bishop was revealed. This was Monsignor Cornelius Power, the popular chancellor in Seattle, confidante of Archbishop Connolly and first cousin of his predecessor in Yakima, Bishop Dougherty.

Dougherty, in commenting on this new development in the topsy turvy politics of the Yakima diocese, simply stated that he had made "a difficult decision." He had never really recovered from his heart attack in 1956. The departure of Leinfelder had left him disconsolate. Peace, unfortunately, had not followed in Leinfelder's absence.

More relevant at the moment was another public embroglio with prominent persons of the diocese, occasioned by their attempts to revive Marquette High School under the care of the Jesuits. This startling event had been ticked off by the impending closure of Marquette and St. Joseph's Academy for the consolidation of Yakima's three high schools under a new name.[55] The new Catholic school board had selected the name "Carroll High School" a generous gesture toward the Jesuits because the school's new patron, America's first bishop, had been a Jesuit.[56] To save Carroll from closure also, a desperate drive for a trust fund was currently in progress.[57]

Thus another headline, arranged by a group of Marquette fans "of the good old days" declaring that certain persons had pledged a 2.5 million dollar trust fund to endow Marquette and to bring back the Jesuits, got instant attention in the chancery.[58] Dougherty felt betrayed. He demanded an explanation from the Jesuit provincial, Father Alexander McDonald, an unflappable, experienced administrator who had become accustomed in these hectic times to almost any kind of crisis. McDonald sweetly responded to the implied accusation that the Jesuits had been dealing behind the bishop's back: "At no time would any consideration be given for such a proposal as announced without the approval of the bishop of the diocese. . . . A new high school is simply out of the question."

Mollified, but less secure in his image of authority, Dougherty awkwardly withdrew his hasty conclusions and turned to other business at hand, the consecration of his successor scheduled for May 1 in St. James Cathedral.

BISHOP CORNELIUS POWER

Bishop-elect Power was a native son. He had been born in Seattle on December 18, 1913. His father, William Power, was a devout Catholic who had been born in Ireland seventy-four years ago and had come to

America as a boy. His mother, a sister of Bishop Dougherty's father, Catherine Dougherty Power, had died in 1941. She had left a holy legacy: two sons as priests, Cornelius the bishop-elect, and William, and two daughters as Sisters of the Holy Names, Sister Cecelia Clare and Sister Alice Marie.[59]

Cornelius was ordained to the priesthood on June 3, 1939 two years before she died. Later he attended Catholic University earning his doctorate in canon law in 1943. He served as vice-chancellor from 1943 to 1951 and as chancellor from 1951 to 1969. His consecration during the Mass of St. Joseph the Worker, was like a family affair. Archbishop Connolly presided, Bishops Gill and Dougherty were co-consecrators and Bishop Topel presented the homily.[60] It was noted at this time that three who had been priests in Seattle had become bishops in a relatively brief space of time.[61] This undoubtedly demonstrated the post-Vatican influence of local archbishops, Connolly in particular. Whatever else, it also indicated the termination at long last of Dubuque's appointees in the Northwest. Even Leinfelder had been a graduate of Dubuque. His whereabouts during the consecration is unknown.

Unlike the archbishop in Portland, the new bishop did not take himself too seriously. He was characteristically American-Irish, bearing the priest-look, with heavy dark hair, refined features and eyes that appeared to be gazing far away, with that mysterious Gaelic quality of the dreamer. Like most of the Irish he liked to talk. One suspects that he was sentimental, too, and more than ordinarily compassionate with others. If anything, he was too tolerant, though he was by no means a far-out liberal. In some respects, I think, he was the opposite of Bishop Dougherty, which the diocese needed after thirteen years of sometimes unpleasant turmoil.

After Power was installed in Yakima's Cathedral on May 20, Dougherty left for California to recover from a chronic illness.[62] His health improved considerably, so he was appointed auxiliary to Cardinal McIntyre of Los Angeles and pastor of St. Alphonsus parish. But death was near. While vacationing in the Northwest, a companion of Bishop Gill in a fishing boat off Westport, he died suddenly from a massive heart attack. This was on July 10, 1970. Dougherty was sixty-five years old, the long-sought age for a happy retirement. A funeral Mass was conducted in St. James Cathedral three days later, and he was buried in Calvary cemetery in Yakima, where he still belonged to the people.

Dougherty's successor had some difficult decisions to make, not the least of them being the disposition of Our Times, which Dougherty had cherished in a singular manner. While the diocese no longer teetered on the brink of bankruptcy, its fiscal balance was still too precarious to subsidize the paper. At least Power thought so. The fate of *Our Times*, the northwest's most creative newspaper was doomed "for want of sufficient support" by the people. On October 17, 1969, its zealous editor, Ray Ruppert, announced that its next issue would be the last. It went to its grave with a promise of resurrection. It has never been seen again.

MINISTRY FOR THE HISPANICS

As noted previously, Mexican Americans, now called Hispanics, arrived in the Northwest prior to the 1940's. But it was during the second World War when their labor was required for the gathering of crops that the first surging waves of migrants appeared.

"To resolve the crisis [of labor], the United States government imported agricultural laborers directly from Mexico to the Pacific Northwest between 1944 and 1947," Erasmo Gainboa, lecturer in Mexican studies wrote, reminding us of those "whose labor helped to produce the food for victory."[63]

> During these four years more than 39,000 Mexican males were employed in Idaho, Oregon and Washington. The size alone of this group was important; but more impressive was its labor potential. The men were recruited in Mexico and organized into a regimented work force. Once in the northwest they were on call for employment on a daily basis, including Sundays, and were subject to transfer at a moment's notice to fill labor shortages elsewhere. What is more, employment was limited primarily to agriculture and to jobs demanding hard labor.... On their day off, they did laundry, played games, or gambled. In some localities religious groups tried to reach out to these young men, but with mixed results.

These young men were nominally Catholic. Efforts on the part of the church to fill their needs was complicated by the wartime shortage of priests, and the constant shifting of the men themselves, "whose mail was one step or more behind them." By contract, they were required to return to Mexico.

Following the war, many returned with their families. First they came from Texas, then from Mexico. In the course of the next three decades large numbers settled in the following specific areas which were predominantly agricultural:

Yakima Valley, Washington
Wenatchee Valley, Washington
Columbia Basin, Washington
Hood River, Oregon
Woodburn-Willamette Valley, Oregon

Hermiston-Umatilla, Oregon
Boise area, Idaho
Madras, Oregon
Lyndon area, Washington

The influence of the Hispanics on the church, and the church on them, varied in each place. In the Yakima Valley, where more of them settled than anywhere else, their presence had been noted at Sunnyside by Father Reinhold, who gave them special attention in the ordinary conduct of the parish, despite his great preoccupation with liturgical reform. Bishop Dougherty, after his arrival in 1951, arranged for Mexican priests to come from the old country to preach missions on a temporary basis. There was a varied pattern of priests coming and going, but no lasting organized program was undertaken until 1968, when Dougherty assigned two priests, Jose Ybarra and John O'Shea to full-time work with the Mexican people. This was in August, 1968.[64] Two weeks later Dougherty met in his office with Ybarra and composed the following memorandum regarding the discussion:

> *Spanish Speaking Apostolate,* November 22, 1968
> 1) Job interview
> 2) Budget. Fr. Y's estimate $125.00 per month salary
> 3) Automobile. $1.50 per day plus 4½ a mile
> 4) Phone. Credit card, ok
> 5) Office location—Sunnyside[65]

Ybarra's proposal was not very imaginative. His idea was simply "to bring back Spanish speaking people to the parish by using cursillos and by spending a week in each parish of the diocese." In view of the limitations of his resources, perhaps he could do little more.[66] He started with a survey, which indicated where he should begin:

> *Parishes needing help:*
> Sunnyside 80 families
> Granger 100 families
> Zillah 1 family
> White Swan 3 families
> Wapato 70 families
> Mabton 65 families
> Toppenish ??
> Prosser 40 families
> Grandview 50–100 families
>   15 came to church[67]

The list contains a total of 409 to 459 families plus a large unknown number at Toppenish. The school survey presents a more accurate picture that also reveals "the growing menace" of the Hispanic takeover. These are the percentages of Mexican-American children in the schools in 1968:

Granger 59%
Mabton 63%
Toppenish 36%
Wapato 35%

At the same time Ybarra's survey disclosed that Yakima County had 41% of the state's *migrants*, distributed as follows: 49% Anglos, 41% Latin Americans and 10% American and Canadian Indians.

It must be remembered that none of these statistics can be regarded as fully accurate. because the subjects of the surveys were *migrants,* many of them "illegals," as they were called. They were illegal residents in the United States and very reluctant to be counted or listed in any way that could threaten their positions.

Meanwhile, there were three Jesuits who had become involved in part-time employment with Hispanics. Father Frank Duffy, at his own request, was permitted to go to Mexico in the summer of 1962 to learn Spanish. He was a Latin teacher at Jesuit High in Portland, but he had discovered the plight of the Hispanics in the fields near Hillsboro and Woodburn. While he was still on the Jesuit High staff, he offered Mass in both places, preaching in Spanish when possible, and administering the sacraments, especially baptism, which was in great demand. In the summer months after 1965 he recruited Jesuit scholastics to help him at Woodburn, with dramatic results. While the parish at Woodburn, called St. Luke's remained basically "Anglo," an active Mexican-Catholic community with its own leadership was gradually formed. This was both permanent and identifiable.

Another Jesuit was Father Arnold Beezer, a brilliant student in chemistry, who was also a teacher at Jesuit High. Like Duffy, Beezer became involved in the early years by spending his weekends with the Hispanics, offering Mass when needed, and teaching catechism to the children. He, too, learned Spanish. The third Jesuit knew Spanish from childhood. This was Father Robert Saenz, professor of Spanish at Seattle University. His grandmother was Mexican; his father had married an Irish girl, thus he shared in the benefits of both races. He had the macho image and the endowments of the heart of the Mexicans and the gift-ofgab of the Irish. His involvement with the Hispanics followed his return from Spain where he was ordained. Later he studied for a doctorate in Spanish literature at the University of Washington.[68]

In the city of Yakima the Jesuits controlled St. Joseph's, the pioneer church in the old part of the city, with which the immigrants identified when they came to town. The principal non-Anglo interest here had been American Indian, and members of the Jesuit community had taken care of the mission at White Swan for many years. But during this period, the late 1960's and early 1970's, the Hispanic families began to appear in large numbers and special liturgies in Spanish were conducted for them. Hispanic children formed a substantial portion in the parish school. Thus Yakima was eventually accepted as an appropriate base for Jesuit mission activity in the Valley.

A similar base was required in Oregon, probably at Woodburn, where considerable progress had been made with the approval of the pastor of St. Luke's, Father John Larkin. When Larkin died in the spring of 1968, Father John Kelley, provincial of the Jesuits, suggested to Archbishop Dwyer that the Jesuits take over the administration of the parish and the care of the Hispanics in the valley. Dwyer, no doubt relieved, cheerfully agreed to the proposal. At this time Duffy at Jesuit High was informed that he would be St. Luke's new pastor following the close of the current school year.

There are some misunderstandings about what followed. It was sometimes alleged that the Jesuits had ingratiated themselves with the Hispanics in the valley, with an eye on St. Luke's, that the archbishop was practically forced to turn over the parish to them. There seems to be no evidence to support this theory. There is reason to believe, however, that some of the Anglos in St. Luke's parish deeply resented the arrival of the Jesuits because they expected to be displaced in the parish by the Hispanics. Since this was not the case, misunderstandings were dissipated in time. The bi-cultural nature of the parish has been not only a source of satisfaction but even of pride, to all concerned.

By 1970, then, the Jesuits had two parishes for providing regular services for Hispanics. These were in addition to the Catholic services rendered to Hispanics in other parishes in the Northwest, especially in the Yakima Valley. But everywhere, as the Hispanics continued to flow into the Northwest in an ever-widening stream, there were insurmountable problems, amounting at times to failures, which Father Ybarra in a progress report to the bishop described rather vividly.

SUMMARY REPORT OF THE LAY APOSTOLATE FOR THE SPANISH SPEAKING PEOPLE IN THE DIOCESE OF YAKIMA:

The following report concerns those Spanish-speaking residents living in the Yakima Valley from Prosser to and including Yakima. According to the census taken by the Office of Equal Opportunity, there are approximately 12,000 families of Mexican descent in the above named area. 90% of these Spanish-speaking families are nominal Roman Catholics.

35,000 to 40,000 persons migrate into Washington each year during the agricultural season. This figure is an estimate based on the O.E.O. census and Farm Bureau statistics.

The following information as it relates to individual parishes was given in answer to a questionnaire sent to all pastors in the Fall of 1968.

Sacred Heart Parish, Prosser

There are 120 known Spanish families in residence. The majority of these persons reside in the southwest sector of town which is the area of lower-income people. Also, in the area known as Whitstran. Most of these families rent their homes or live in houses supplied by their employers. Practically all are employed as field hands.

Parish activities for the Spanish-speaking are: Lay Apostolate, formed by Father Ybarra in March, 1969. Its function is to organize the Spanish-speaking parishioners for their own spiritual welfare.

There is no other parochial activity in which the Spanish-speaking are involved.

Blessed Sacrament Parish, Grandview

Inquiry was made of Pastor regarding number of Spanish-speaking in parish. The response was "I don't know." Families are located in the poor section of town, across the tracks.

Parish activities for the Spanish-speaking are: None!

Other than parish activities:

Latin American Club.

Immaculate Conception Parish, Mabton

Because of lack of residential priest, no information was available. My own personal estimate of the number of Spanish-speaking families is 75% of the total population of Mabton and the surrounding rural area.

Parish activities for the Spanish-speaking are: None?

St. Joseph Parish, Sunnyside

Of the 400 families on our parish list, approximately 2/3 are of Mexican descent. These persons, many of which are buying homes, live within the city limits or just outside the city limits. Those ranches providing housing are: Broadview, Sick's Hop Ranch; Newhouse Farms.

Parish activities for the Spanish-speaking are: Lay Apostolate: Cursillistas; Our Lady of Guadalupe Guild, as part of the Women's Club of the parish, Parochial Mass each Sunday in Spanish, Confessions in Spanish; Baptisms in Spanish; Adult inquiry classes in Spanish; Summer CCD centers conducted by two Missionary Sisters of St. Joseph Convent, Sunnyside.

St. Patrick Parish, Granger

There are approximately 120 families of Mexican descent living in and around Granger. The majority of them live in the Crewport Labor Camp.

Parish activities for the Spanish-speaking are: Women's Club; Cursillistas; Mutualistas, a Self-help group.

Other than parish activities:

There is a full-time Spanish-speaking Protestant minister at Crewporot.

St. Aloysius Parish, Toppenish

No report.

Resurrection Parish, Zillah

No report.

St. Peter Claver Parish, Wapato

Of the 250 families in the parish, 100 families are Philipino. There are 200 families residing in the area of Harrah, Brownstown. Pastor does not have information regarding number of Spanish families.

Parish activities for the Spanish-speaking are: None!

SOURCES OF INCOME FOR THE SPANISH-SPEAKING PEOPLE:
1) Seasonal work in agriculture
2) Welfare
3) Anti-poverty programs

Usual employment period begins in the spring and is concluded by October 1st. Peak months in May, June and August. As the harvest indicates, at various times, the people leave their homes to work in the fields on the coast and in Oregon.

THE PROBLEM AS IT EXISTS TODAY
All the priests that I have contacted who have been associated with the Spanish-speaking people have repeatedly confessed that they cannot communicate with or understand the Mexican people. They feel that this is so because they cannot speak the language, and also because they do not understand their customs and way of life. This lack of communication and understanding creates a great deal of friction between the priests and Spanish-speaking which in turn is frustrating to both sides. The priests have confessed that, in order to deal with these people, you have to understand their cultural background and their language. They are the first to admit their lack in these areas. In talking with the Spanish-speaking, they too confess that they are not understood and they cannot communicate with the priest. When they are asked why they do not participate in the Sacramental life of the Church, they say they can't understand the priest and they don't feel at ease. When asked why they don't participate in parish activities, they feel that it is only for the educated and white.

The Mexican people are aware of the lack of concern the Church seemingly has for them. As a result, this has antagonized them against the pastors, and in some cases against the Church. This creates an opportunity for the Evangelical groups to make many converts to their churches. In Sunnyside alone, we have three Spanish-speaking, Mexican ministers who are undermining the work of the Church. They have made a number of converts from nominal Catholics. These converts are made tools by which others can be drawn into their religion. Because of the lack of instruction among our nominal Spanish-speaking Catholics and because of the lack of attention, we cannot blame them for seeking this instruction and attention from some other source. In Mabton, a recreation program is sponsored for the Mexican youth by the Episcopal Church. It is doubtful that this program is solely for recreation. In Wapato, two Baptist Mexican ministers are converting many of our nominal Catholics. In Toppenish, two to three Mexican Protestant ministers are doing the same thing. In Granger, there is a full time minister who works among the Spanish-speaking at Crewport. In Grandview and Prosser, the Episcopalian and Methodist ministers are making great strides among our nominal Catholics by the ministers being

700 A TIME OF TURMOIL

involved in the poverty programs. These English-speaking Protestant ministers are making a great effort to learn the language and the customs of the Mexican people, whereas our pastors who have been working in parishes with majorities of Spanish-speaking can't speak Spanish and have made no effort to learn the language. The area priests have not even expressed a desire to acquaint themselves with the Mexican culture or language. In my opinion, the priests should make an effort to learn at least the fundamentals of the language and the basic cultural differences between the Anglo and Mexican. In Sunnyside, we have bi-lingual nuns who would be willing and eager to teach our priests the fundamentals of the Spanish language.[69]

This report, reflecting the dejected spirits of Ybarra, is one-sided, but it reveals the repetitive nature of immigrant problems for the northwest church, first the Irish, who could speak English, then the Germans who could not, then the Italians. What was happening to the Hispanics had happened before. There was, however, one major difference: the Hispanics represented an entire subculture, which they have brought with them, and to which they cling. As a result they are more collectively demanding. They are also more suddenly numerous, and as many politicians have already learned, they are becoming the most powerful non-Anglo force in America.

"We must make a beginning," said Jose Ybarra at the end of his report, "to restore the confidence of the people in the leadership of the church."

Though some would dispute the fact, a beginning had been made. It was the kind of progress proportionate to the ever-increasing number of Hispanics, which troubled the bishops most.

DUE PROCESS AT ST. THOMAS SEMINARY

There is one more case involving due process, which occurred in the Seattle archdiocese in 1970. It is presented here because it set a precedent in the northwest church, like the Marquette strike. The details of this and what followed were as bland as the ingredients of many family disputes.

The sorry little drama, called a "distasteful incident" by the archbishop, began in late 1969 with a newspaper article, concerning which the *Northwest Progress* had something to say: "An article on the new breed seminarian appeared in the fall of 1969, a preview of one of the issues soon to swirl about the chancery, when a newspaper feature writer stumbled across a St. Thomas Seminarian in a go-go tavern in North Ballard and wrote a story about the patron."[70]

The seminarian was James Pattenaude, a second year theologian, who had visited the tavern to recruit dancers for a charity event, an entertainment planned for the inmates at Washington State Reformatory at Monroe. When the archbishop experienced the shock of discovering the article in the secular press, he suspended Pattenaude for the fall term, stating at the time that the tavern visit tended to "give scandal" constituting conduct unbecoming a candidate for the priesthood.[71] The fat was now in the fire.

Two forms of protests first appeared: The theology student body at the seminary distributed a leaflet stating that Archbishop Connolly had suspended the student "without consulting the faculty at the seminary . . . or Mr. Pattenaude himself." Second, the seminary Theology Senate (comprised of the theology faculty and three students) acknowledged in a letter to the archbishop that it "accepted the suspension as binding, but could not accept the manner in which the decision was made." The Senate invited Connolly to the seminary to discuss the matter.

Connolly visited the seminary on February 12, 1970. He indicated that his suspension was appropriate and that "because of violation of canon law in the case," he could not modify his original decision. On the next day forty seminarians appeared at the chancery to seek an interview with the archbishop. They were informed that he was "out of the city." On the same day classes at the seminary were called off, for obvious reasons. The seminarians then dispatched a telegram to Connolly, who responded by agreeing to meet formally with them at the seminary on February 16. True to his word, the archbishop met behind closed doors with the theologians and faculty. He agreed to appoint an inquiry board of six members, Father Ibar Lynch, chairman, Fathers Thomas Pitsch, William Gallagher and William Lane, members of the priests' grievance committee, Jesuit Father Joseph Perri, archdiocesan personnel director, and Father Michael J. Ryan, secretary, member of the Priests' Senate.[72]

For ten days the inquiry board met to investigate not only the facts in the Pattenaude Case, but also "the underlying causes that precipitated unrest at St. Thomas the Apostle Major Seminary. . . ."[73] Attending these sessions were Monsignor John Doogan, now chancellor, and two Sulpician fathers, the seminary rector Eugene Nicolaus and Paul Caringella, professor of moral theology. By this time the affair had received wide-spread attention and the board's decision was awaited with some apprehension by seminarians elsewhere. On March 5, 1970, the board submitted its nine-page report to the archbishop, who refused at this time to comment on it—standard procedure in view of its support for Pattenaude.[74] It is to the archbishop's lasting credit that he accepted his board's recommendations and reinstated Pattenaude who was ordained two years later.

There is one bizarre ending to the case: at some point after ordination, Pattenaude left the priesthood and was laicized, for reasons entirely unrelated to the strike. In retrospect, at least, there is considerably more data available regarding the "new breed" than the board of inquiry had at its disposal in March 1970, yet the phenomenon is as enigmatic as it ever was. The Pattenaude incident occurred during that decade of confusion, when, for many complex reasons, the attitudes of young Catholics had changed dramatically toward, for example, authority, parents, social standards, sex, drugs, almost everything. The consequences of World War II had finally caught up with us with a vengeance.

In the years ahead many of Pattenaude's peers in seminaries across the country would freely accept ordination with its commitments and then, like him, request laicization within a relatively brief time. The "new breed" have never been fully understood. Fifteen years after Pattenaude they are still discussed with countless explanations for what happened. All agree on one point at least: the world had changed, the Church had changed; the one much more radically than the other.

RECENT EVENTS IN THE PORTLAND AREA

In the Portland chancery the events at St. Thomas Seminary received more than ordinary attention. One of the three seminarians on the Senate was Bill Thomas of Portland, so the archbishop watched developments from hour to hour, like a stockbroker on Black Friday, prepared for the worst. No one had to tell him what was really happening. Like an Old Testament prophet he had been complaining at the city gates for years.

His parochial schools were beginning to close. Last June it was Cottage Grove, this June it would be Corvallis. The Sisters of the Holy Names at St. Mary's Academy had decided to sell their old convent, built in 1890, for $705,000.[75] They would have to live in makeshift lodgings, "small communities," which was the latest craze. The buyer of the sisters' convent and the block of land on which it stood, was Colon De Silva, who planned a commercial development there. That was the way nowadays, one moved out God's business to provide room for man's. Thirty-seven sisters had lived in the old convent. They would have to go elsewhere by August 31. In late July they conducted an auction. The old furnishings, memorabilia, objects of art or sentimental value, treasured by the older sisters, disappeared under the auctioneer's hammer. "We have not here a lasting city." Older nuns everywhere were being dispossessed in the name of holy progress.

At Mount Angel, too, changes in the church had involved the tranquility of the monastery. For some the upheaval was too much. "A number of priests and brothers left the community." For all who loved the sacred traditions of the Order, it was a painful period. The Latin liturgy with its familiar chants was changed to English and the order of the psalms in the divine office, almost unchanged since St. Benedict's day, was redone. The cherished liturgical books were replaced by leaflets and mimeographed breviaries. The community found itself with no composers and almost no organists. The distinction between lay brothers and solemnly professed choir monks was abolished. Few candidates for the Order presented themselves; still fewer persevered.[76]

Since 1959, the monks had run Mt. Angel High School in town but in 1964 this was made coeducational by merging it with Mt. Angel Academy of the sisters. The college preparatory department of the seminary, however, continued to function as a unit of the college. In the reorganization period of 1967–1968 the liberal arts college was separated from the secondary school, which was finally discontinued.[77] In 1969–1970 the college began to offer a master's program in theology apart from the seminary program leading to ordination. Even more radical was the decision to allow nuns to study at the seminary. On December 18, 1970, the *Catholic Sentinel* reported that "Sisters were to be admitted to graduate programs of theology and undergraduate programs of philosophy and theology, starting with the new term next month." The historic change, it was said, had been approved by the board of regents on December 8 and by the monastic chapter on December 14.

The abbey's foundation in Idaho had not prospered. The original site at Jerome had been left behind for later development and the two monks assigned there had taken up residence at Twin Falls where they established a student center and priory near the college of Southern Idaho. Father Patrick Meagher, the prior, supervised construction of a chapel and social center, costing $125,000.[78] It was a gallant gesture, with scant hope of success, mostly because the area had a high percentage of Mormons who were cooly aloof to the Benedictines' advances.

More encouraging news concerned moving day for the sisters and staff of St. Vincent's Hospital. January 31, 1971 was the day scheduled for the exodus. In the old hospital there were three hundred and seventy beds, but with careful planning the number of patients to be moved was reduced to two hundred.[79] Two thousand people were briefed and on the job when the ambulances began to transfer the patients and their pills exactly 4.5 miles to the new facility of four hundred beds, all completed in a day without a single hitch. It was nice to know that there were still some activities in the church that the current turmoil had not touched.

It was obvious, also, that some hospitals could take care of themselves. But now was the time for some painful soul-searching about the fate of the schools. Basically the problem was one of discrimination in the use of public funds, which were contributed by Catholics as well as others. In the 1969–1970 school year alone, parochial schools in the northwest states saved taxpayers the following amounts based on costs per student in public schools.

Washington	$743 per student cost	$30,636,862
Oregon	$831 per student cost	$20,902,974
Montana	$740 per student cost	$ 9,938,940
Idaho	$602 per student cost	$ 3,444,042

For the entire United States the saving was $3,990,709,846.[80] It was becoming obvious, as the number of religious teachers declined, that Catholics would have to shift the greater portion of this amount onto other shoulders, where it belonged, either by getting some tax support, or by closing their schools.

THE NEW BISHOP OF BAKER

The time had come for Bishop Leipzig to retire. He had reached the magic age of seventy-five, old and weary, his most recent years spent begging in the service of the church. Like Bishop Schuster of Great Falls, he had been spared the anguish of school closures, or the demonstration of the very pious who oppose the new liturgy. Although his Baker Diocese was still one of the smallest in the nation, in terms of Catholic population, he had reason for pride in his long tenure. With the help of his flock and the Catholic Church Extension Society, every parish and mission now had a church and decent rectory. No longer was it necessary for his priests to live in hovels that were unfit for animals.

The name of his successor was revealed on May 4, 1971.[81] This was Father Thomas J. Connolly, pastor of Carson City, Nevada, in horse country like that found in eastern Oregon, exactly 485 miles from Baker. The antecedent details of Connolly's appointment may be of interest, because they illustrate the customary formalities in the post-Vatican Church.[82]

Connolly was in his rectory at Carson City in April, 1971. His phone rang. Bishop Joseph Green of Reno was calling. "Is anybody else where you are? Go to another room. Anyone else on the phone?"

"What's this all about?" Connolly asked.

"Ready for a shock? The Holy Father wants you to be Bishop of Baker."

"I've never been to Baker in my life. Will the Holy Father put this in writing?"

"Yes."

"Is the Holy Father *asking* if I *want* to be Bishop of Baker?"

"Yes." A long pause.

"Send the correspondence. How many days do I have?"

"You can talk with only one person. On the tenth day I will be in Vegas. I want your answer so that I can notify the apostolic delegate."

"I will talk it over with Father [Charles] Shallo."

Within ten days Connolly sent his notice of acceptance. He was then informed that current protocol required consecrations, now called "ordinations" to be celebrated in the cathedral where the bishop-elect would serve and that the ceremony of installation should take place on the same day.[83] The date was set: June 30, 1971.

Connolly was forty-eight years old at this time. He had been born at Tonapah, a glamorous ghost town in central Nevada on July 18, 1922. He was ordained at St. Patrick's church there on April 8, 1947, by Bishop Thomas Gorman of Reno. For two years following ordination he studied at Catholic University in Washington, then spent a final year at the Pontifical Institute of St. John Lateran in Rome, where he was awarded a doctorate in canon law. When he returned to the Reno diocese his bishop was Robert Dwyer, who undoubtedly recommended Connolly for Baker, a suffragan see when Dwyer was Archbishop of Portland.

Connolly, who was unruffled as a Vatican monsignor, liked horses and owned several, one of which he usually rode in the Reno rodeo parade. Costumed in his cowboy outfit, reminiscent of his happy youth, he presented a handsome sight on his horse, his trim boyish figure belieing his age, and his smiling eyes glancing right and left in friendly recognition of many who knew him as a popular priest of the diocese. Connolly was always a happy man, whether on a horse or not, and his far west casualness put everyone at ease.

He planned his departure by car from Carson City on June 28, two days before his consecration. After working hard all that day, loading a U-Haul truck, he dispatched his nephew in the driver's seat and hitched to his own car his horse trailer with his favorite horse. He left two hours later, about five in the evening. At first nothing occurred to distract his godly reflections, then, as he rattled along Interstate 40, enroute to Winnemuca, he noted a patrol car with red and blue lights flashing. When he stopped the officer said, "Would you be Bishop Connolly? We have an urgent message. Call Bishop Green in Reno."

Green was flustered. He was worried about the Hughes Air West plane they had chartered to bring Nevada friends to the consecration. "That plane has just crashed in California. Frank Sinatra's mother was on it. Hughes says they cannot supply our plane."

"Well now," said Connolly, as calm as a Mandarin, "let's see what we can do. We paid for that flight. They have to get us another plane."

And Air West did. Seventy-six passengers took that flight from Reno to Baker on June 30.

The bishop-elect reached Baker at seven in the morning on June 29, after driving all night in a heavy rainstorm, getting into the ditch and chasing his horse, which had bolted into the darkness when a big truck roared by. He was covered with mud from head to toe. There were some at hand who began to wonder about the kind of bishop Pope Paul VI had sent them.

But Connolly's consecration, scheduled for four-thirty in the afternoon, was only three minutes late. Archbishop Dwyer served as the principal consecrator. He was assisted by Bishops Thomas Gorman and Joseph Green, all of whom were bishops of Reno at one time or another. After the two hour ceremony (on the dot) old Bishop Gorman, who did not like the new terminology, snapped to a reporter, "You can say he was *ordained*, I *consecrated* him."

At the banquet that evening in the Elk's Building, there were 508 guests, including Bishop Leipzig. "I am in retirement," he replied when called upon to speak. And so he was. He was honored at a farewell party on January 16, 1972, but, reluctant to leave Baker after all, he did not move into Portland until May.[84] Then he occupied an apartment in Calaroga Terrace, and an office in the chancery, where he was regarded as the official church historian of Oregon, an honor in which he basked with almost shameless felicity.[85]

THE LEAP FROM FOREST RIDGE TO SOMERSET HILL

More than three generations had passed since the Religious of the Sacred Heart established Forest Ridge Convent school for the upper-class young ladies in Seattle.[86] School life in cloistered serenity had occupied the sisters and their students so intensely that the world outside had passed them by. But the turbulence of the 1960's, reaching a shrill climax with Vatican II, awakened the occupants of Forest Ridge and forced them, like those in other Catholic institutions, to produce changes, which were gratuitously called "reforms." Many old traditions were swept away in this partly secular renaissance, leaving the old nuns numb with incomprehension and the girls in a tizzy of pleasurable excitement. There is nothing more eagerly sought by youth than innovation and innovation in 1965 was the very air they all breathed.

At Forest Ridge, the many changes in religious life occurred simultaneously with a search for a new site for the school. "On April 18, 1963," wrote the schools' historian, "Mother de Valon [Superior General] visited Forest Ridge for three days.... To her the buildings were dark, cold, dank and crowded, unsuitable for the education of young girls. She had just come from the sun-washed California schools, and much of the time she spent in Seattle it rained, but her desire to have the school moved was not based on whim."[87]

Several compelling reasons for the acquisition of a site and new buildings had been brought forward. The present site, occupied in 1910, was too limited in size for expansion, and too dark and gloomy because of the heavily wooded portions, which could not be altered.[88] The buildings, designed in an era of simplicity and frugality, were inadequate as well as fire traps, and Seattle's vigilant Fire Department had issued notice that the two upper floors of the principal structure would have to be vacated. The department also ordered the sisters to install costly fire protection devices and to make changes in stairways and halls for the protection of the children. Finally, and this was not the least of motives for moving, the present campus, located on the north bank of Capitol Hill, was contiguous to the "central area," which was rapidly declining. The upper middle class families had fled to suburbs like Bellevue. The school, some of the sisters asserted, ought to be where the majority of their students resided.

Mother de Valon agreed. Shortly after her visit in Seattle, she formally approved of a change. Sister Virginia McMonagle, formerly a student at Forest Ridge, was summoned from California to take charge. On a wintry morning in 1965, accompanied by a real estate agent, Robert Smith by name, she inspected a muddy tract of land in Bellevue, high on Somerset Hill. This was as yet an undeveloped area, and the site was thickly forested with fir trees, over one hundred acres of them. The price was $3,500 per acre. Tradition relates that when Brigham Young first saw the valley west of the Wasatch Mountains, he exclaimed, "This is the place," and that is where the Mormans settled in Utah. Before leaving Somerset Hill, Sister McMonagle told herself "This is the place." She needed to see no more. "It is the will of God," she stubbornly insisted, "that Forest Ridge be built on that mountain."[89]

The inevitable drive for funds was begun. Through the efforts of the Forest Ridge Academy Building Fund Committee, chaired by the local Catholic philanthropist, Mr. Charles Pigott, $1,200,000 was raised toward the cost of construction. A new five-building complex was designed for the site and bids were awarded in 1970 for construction. These totalled a whopping $2,600,000 which was about $8,250 per student for the first student body in the new quarters.[90] The sisters had to borrow over a million dollars to meet the cost. At eight on the summer evening of June 3, 1970, the ground was broken with many people in attendance, and construction was begun on the morrow. Fifteen months later 315 girls, with their faculty, occupied the new Forest Ridge, and the old building on Capitol Hill was sold to a Jewish educational corporation.

"Today," says the school historian, "the school remains one of the most modern, efficient, and aesthetically appealing educational institutions in the Pacific Northwest."[91] Without doubt this is true. But something piously familiar had changed with the location. "At Forest Ridge in the late 1950's, out of a faculty of approximately twenty-five, at least twenty were religious; in 1973, out of a faculty of twenty-nine, there were but five."[92] The so-called "reforms" had helped to create the difference.

THE HOSPITAL CRISIS

Presuming good management, Catholic hospitals, unlike the schools, paid for themselves, especially when they were adequately staffed by unsalaried sisters. The crisis for the hospital, then, did not involve money so much as sisters. As the supply of the latter dwindled away, management problems appeared from three unrelated sources: the reduced ability to control policy and practice within the hospitals, the enormous proliferation of an exotic medical technology, and the more liberal court decisions related to ethical principles and patient care.

Soon it was a question of survival. Smaller hospitals had to be closed or converted into community hospitals, sometimes with sisters on the staff. St. John's Hospital in Helena, Montana's first hospital, opened in 1870 by the Sisters of charity of Leavenworth, became a community hospital in the summer of 1973.[93] If this in the greenwood, what in the dry?

For the larger hospitals that survived, it was often necessary to expand or risk annihilation. A case in point was Sacred Heart Hospital in Spokane. When, like St. Vincent's in Portland, Sacred Heart's facilities fell behind current standards elsewhere, a very solemn decision had to be faced—build a better and larger hospital, despite the loss of many sisters to staff it, or face the greater loss of leadership in the medical community, and possibly eventual conversion to something else. Sacred Heart's top administrator, Sister Peter Claver, knew the options well. She chose the risks of bigger and better. Without government grants, she succeeded in the construction and efficient management of the largest private hospital in the Northwest, a fourteen story building that cost $34,765,100, probably more than the resources of the entire northwest church. Begun in 1968, this new Sacred Heart Medical Center, as it was called, was finally completed in 1971. It was dedicated at 2:30 in the afternoon on a bitterly cold October 29 of that year. The ceremony outside was brief, so that Sister Frederic Marie, who had given more than fifty years of service to the institution, could cut the ribbon and allow the spectators to gather inside where it was warm.

The splendid courage of Sister Peter Claver and the Sisters of Providence to persevere in their ministry, in spite of the sinister action of the courts, can best be appreciated when placed in contrast with the ongoing campaign for abortion on demand. As one Catholic paper noted, "[The] Court Abolishes Rights of the Unborn."[94] The abortion decision was labelled "The Top News of 1973"—regrettable but true. Throughout the entire period, the Catholic press was preoccupied with the defense of Christian principles concerning the unborn.[95] In Oregon a bill was introduced in the state legislature that would require Catholic hospitals in Oregon to permit abortion when requested.[96] This proposal was thrown out, but in Billings, Montana, a federal judge ruled that St. Vincent's Hospital there, was obliged by law, to allow tubal ligation to prevent birth when certain conditions were present.

THE BILLINGS CASE

Details of this case as presented by the press were as follows:

U.S. District Court Judge James F. Battin ordered St. Vincent's to perform the operation based on a suit brought by two Billings residents, Mr. and Mrs. James Michael Taylor. In their action the Taylors demanded that Mrs. Taylor be sterilized after delivery of her child because her diabetic condition dictated she bear no other children.

The Taylors also noted that they were forced to go to St. Vincent's because it was the only hospital in the area with maternity care facilities. Last June St. Vincent's and Deaconess Hospital, a non-Catholic institution, merged their facilities and centered them in St. Vincent's.

St. Vincent's hospital complied with the order, which may have been the first federal court decision in this country requiring a Catholic medical facility to perform such an operation.

Several days after he issued his original order, which seemed to open the hospital doors to all women seeking a sterilization operation after giving birth, Judge Battin said his decision 'only applies to women who will undergo a Caesarean and want a tubal ligation at the same time....

In a related development, a federal judge earlier this month denied a court suit that tried to force the Miles City, Mont., Holy Rosary Hospital to perform a sterilization operation. The suit contended Holy Rosary was the only area facility where a sterilization could be performed.

U.S. District Court Judge Russell E. Smith, ruling in Missoula, denied the petition because he said the case was not a proper matter for a federal court.

An attorney for Claudia Ann Kransky and Richard William Kransky, who brought the suit, said he would go to the state courts in another attempt to make the hospital perform the operation.

The lawyer is Robert L. Stephens Jr. of the American Civil Liberties Union, who also filed the suit brought by the Taylors in Billings.[97]

The Catholic position, prescinding from the moral implications of Judge Battin's decision, was that it violated religious liberty in matters involving conscience. Countless others agreed with this. As a result of the court's action, for example, Senator Frank Church [D-Idaho] introduced an amendment to allow hospitals and individuals to refuse to perform sterilization and abortions on the basis of religious belief or moral conviction. Congress passed this resolution by an overwhelming majority, after which Battin reversed himself and decided in favor of St. Vincent's. His ruling was upheld by the Ninth Circuit Court in San Francisco. Taylor's challenge to this ruling was appealed to the Supreme Court, which refused to review it, thus allowing the decision of the Circuit Court to stand.[98]

Meanwhile, Bishop Schuster had not been asleep. He assembled a panel of five doctors to study the Taylor case on its medical merits. In November 1972, he revealed their conclusions. Three of the doctors, opposed by two, voted against the medical need for tubal ligation in this case. "If the Civil Courts," Schuster added, "can enjoin a Catholic hospital to permit sterilizing procedures in the absence of serious pathological conditions, may it not also force them to permit abortion and euthanasia . . . ?[99]

The Billings case was buried at last, but not the hatchet with it. Bitterness and suspicions lingered on. How could one be sure when the judge in the case changed his own verdict two times in as many years?

ARCHBISHOP DWYER RESIGNS

In November 1973, when Bishop Gill died suddenly in Washington, D.C., the Archbishop of Portland in Oregon was quietly preparing for his own departure.[100] He had requested permission from the Holy Father to resign "for reasons of health." In terms of age he, like Gill, was sixty-five, but unlike the auxiliary bishop of Seattle, he felt time-worn and discouraged. He seemed to think, not without reason, that the northwest church was going to hell in style. He pined for the peace of solitude with his books and the more pliable tools of authorship.

His unexpected contention with one of his priests in September of the previous year had left him humiliated and depressed, a situation that no one foresaw or intended. His authority had been challenged and he had been forced to back down. When Father Emmett Harrington, the archdiocesan director of education had issued books that Dwyer regarded as violating "Vatican norms," he dismissed him from the office. [101] But representatives of the education board and priests' senate insisted on a meeting, during which the archbishop was persuaded to reinstate Harrington and make a little speech about his innocence of wrongdoing. The board, on the other hand, agreed to withdraw the objectionable books and to submit teaching materials to the archbishop "for judgment."

It was a storm in a teacup, as they say, but the archbishop was sincerely concerned about Catholic doctrine in the schools. In March, 1972, before the Harrington fuss, Bishop Connolly of Baker had addressed a meeting of prelates, priests, religious, and lay leaders. He had this to say.

> We have recently conducted a tour of the Diocese of Baker to analyze where we are and to determine what needs to be done in the adult, the high school and the grammar school level. Everywhere the same problem cropped up—that by the time the children had advanced to the sixth grade, it became very apparent they lacked clarity and substantial content in their faith. [102]

Public surveys revealed a trend. Mass attendance was down. The sacrament of Penance, now called "the rite of reconciliation," was everywhere neglected. Vocations were down fifty-five percent. Divorce rates for Catholics were no better than for others, and, proportionately, as many Catholic as non-Catholic women practiced illicit birth control or consented to abortions. How, Dwyer asked, did one square all this with the cavalier, pollyanna mentality of the new breed? He did not think he should be archbishop any longer. His health was failing, and he hoped that the pope would let him retire.

Paul VI agreed. On January 22, 1974, Dwyer's resignation was officially approved and the name of his successor was announced. Bishop Cornelius Power of Yakima was the new Archbishop of Portland in Oregon. [103] Dwyer was appointed administrator until his successor was formally installed.

As administrator, Dwyer felt free to express his anxieties to the pope. In a letter bristling with resentment toward the innovators, he said:

> Papal authority and the teaching of the magisterium of the church are being challenged: The U.S. Catholic Conference and the National Conference of Catholic Bishops are a 'superhierarchy' separating bishops from the Pope; modernistic ideas are being introduced in education at all levels; distortions in English translations have diluted the meaning of the Mass; biblical scholars are depriving Scripture of its supernatural character; the Pentecostal movement is separating the Holy Spirit from Christ and 'is one of the most dangerous movements in the Church in America today'; there is schism in beliefs in the church. [104]

Many, perhaps most, bishops would have said that these remarks were too reactionary. But for Dwyer and countless others like him, his perception of the church in 1973 appeared to be accurate. The lauded pluralism of the American church, they believed, was destroying it.

Their opponents, on the other hand, believed that the monolithic Church of the Middle Ages, perpetuated by the Council of Trent, was already dead. Only time and God's Providence would resolve the differences that separated the archbishop from those who embraced this view.

Fortunately, Dwyer's sense of humor had not vanished with his confidence in the future. On April 8, 1974, when Archbishop Howard, still referred to as "His Grace" celebrated another anniversary, Dwyer was called upon to speak. He provided a witty "roast" of Howard, which proved to be highly amusing.

"Not," he said, "that we are here to canonize him; he made his mistakes in life, perhaps the greatest of them being his choice of birthplace, for, deplorable, he saw the light in Cresco, Iowa, the very heart of the intellectual Sahara of the United States, on November 5, 1877. He has compounded this error ever since by taking a morbid pleasure in the fact, even boasting about it publicly! St. Paul was his seminary, in the brave days of 'the consecrated blizzard of the North,' Archbishop Ireland, and he returned to his diocese of Dubuque to begin a career of teaching. . . ."[105]

This was nine days before Archbishop Power was installed. It was also Dwyer's last public appearance in Portland. He left for retirement in his own home in Piedmont, a suburb of Oakland, California. When urged by the owner of the *National Catholic Register*, Patrick Hawley of Schick Industries, to become its publisher-editor, he consented. But his time was running out. On February 17, 1976, he entered the hospital for exploratory surgery. About one month later, on March 24, he quietly passed away, a victim of cancer of the pancreas.

He was sixty-seven years old, an old man in terms of disenchantment with the world. His funeral Mass was celebrated in St. Mary's Cathedral in Portland, and he was buried on the outskirts of the city.

INSTALLATION OF ARCHBISHOP POWER

Before the new archbishop was installed on April 17, 1974, he met with the archdiocesan consultors and presented to them the papal bull of appointment. At that moment he was officially the archbishop. In the photograph taken for the occasion, his consultors, one of them with a fashionable beard, appear to be very solemn but, Archbishop Powers laughs heartily, like someone telling a good joke and reflecting on the end of it. His hairline is receding, his dark rimmed glasses lend an air of professorship, but his obvious merriment transcends it all, even the mirthless gravity of the consultors.[106] Perhaps they knew something about the archbishop that he did not.

During the rite of installation that followed, Archbishop Jadot, the papal delegate, presided, but Bishop Treinen of Boise, in the absence of Dwyer, co-starred with him in the installation formalities. His Grace, Archbishop Howard, was also present. He had slowed down a little, but no one present was more alert. When it was all over, and the dining and laughter were done with, the new archbishop had to look at his spiritual domain. It could have been worse. The number of his priests was down, from 193 to 185. More alarming was school enrollment, down from 26,000 to 16,000. The university was thriving as never before. Under the presidency of Father Paul Waldschmidt, enrollment had steadily advanced to 2024 in 1973. In the post-Watergate world, student radicalism had subsided almost totally, and campus priorities had returned to normal.

The worst news concerned Marylhurst College. On March 27 its board of trustees had voted "to discontinue the college program," explaining to its many alumnae and friends that it was simply "a casualty of the financial crunch."[107] The last graduation would be observed on May 11, 1974. In its eighty-one years of existence, Marylhurst had awarded 2516 degrees. It would all come to a disconsolate end on August 31, upon the completion of summer school.

This left some questions unanswered. How would the campus debt be liquidated? What would be the future use of the campus, which was one of the most attractive in the Northwest? More basic, perhaps, was the future of the Holy Names Sisters who had provided leadership in Catholic education in the Northwest since 1859. Someone had irreverently referred to Marylhurst as the "nun factory." Where would the church obtain nuns if the factory was closed?

It was a new ball game and no one realized it better on the seventeenth of April, nineteen hundred and seventy-four, than the seventh archbishop of Portland in Oregon.

21

THE END OF AN ERA: THE OLDEST
ARCHBISHOP DIES
1974–1983

Bishop Topel, by this time, had attracted widespread attention for the eccentric change in his lifestyle and for the peculiar kind of decisions he was making in the conduct of the diocese. His actions were undoubtedly rooted in Vatican II, but this personal, conciliar transformation, if you can call it that, did not appear until several years later. He had always been regarded as a conventional bishop. Then almost overnight he abruptly decided that his fears about the erosion of authority in the church were foolish. Authority, he came to think, "would survive if exercised more by example than proclamation."[1] He was now, he said, "a liberated man."

With renewed interest in the poor, whatever their aberrations, he aided two complete strangers in escaping the toils of "an unjust law" and was immediately catapulted into national prominence as a prelate with an oversized heart. In a self-deprecating manner, he related how it happened.

"Just before Christmas of 1970, I went bail for two young men. Hippies! They were in jail in Clarkston because of drug charges. One of the two was never brought to trial. The charge, however, could not be proved. Had I not gone bail for these two they would have been in jail on Christmas . . . and several months afterwards. In jail, though, nothing could be proved against them."[2]

The enthusiastic response of the media left him humbled. He had once scolded the Jesuits at Gonzaga Prep because too few of their graduates entered the diocesan seminary. He regretted this now. " . . . In past years," he wrote in his weekly column, "there was opposition, and even hostility [towards the Jesuits]." But now he "had reversed" his thoughts and he was glad that the Jesuits "had a big jump in the number of young men entering the novitiate last fall."[3] Like gold, vocations were where you found them and Topel was suddenly indifferent about their source or destiny as long as God provided them.

But he expected seminarians to pray. Many clerical eyebrows were raised when he dispatched the following to each of his own seminarians: "If it appears that you are not likely to practice daily mental prayer in the priesthood, I ask that you cease studying for the priesthood."[4]

This was, according to some, bad timing, because the number of candidates for the altar had dropped off sharply. Topel, too, recognized the obvious, but he preferred to be short on priests than long on priests who did not pray. "I knew and admired Bishop [James] Shannon," he once said, "and I am sorry that he has left the priesthood. But you know, I can't remember seeing him pray."[5]

The fact is, Bishop Topel was experiencing a profound change in his life. It was odd that this new life reminded him of his earlier resentment toward the Jesuits. For many years he had shown no sign of it. Indeed, he had the best of relations with all the religious orders. Whatever he once felt, that was all over. He had entered a new phase of the spirit. He was, as he often explained, on his "poverty binge."

When he bailed out the two "hippies," it had cost him two thousand dollars of his personal money. This was returned to him and he used it, plus another two thousand, to buy the small, drab, four-room, shanty-like house at 1908 East 14th Avenue in a low income neighborhood in southeast Spokane. Reporters, having heard about this, had to see it for themselves. Topel proudly showed it off.

At first sight, the house looked "more expensive" than four thousand dollars. The bishop agreed. "I was astonished to see how nice it is ... the modern appliances. It's a real bargain."[6] On further investigation, however, one had doubts. Paint was peeling on the outside, the back porch listed and sagged heavily when walked upon, and the linoleum in the kitchen was badly cracked. An oil heater stood in the corner with a primitive painting above it, a gift presented by a grateful felon who was executed for murder. The other furnishings were old and unsteady, and even the chapel, arranged in the former dining room, showed signs of bleak privation. On the back porch were the bishop's wash tub and board on which he scrubbed his clothes. Beyond was the clothes line and the garden where he raised most of his food. As bishop he had never taken a salary. He lived on what people gave him. Now he lived on his social security check, ninety-seven dollars a month, and some of that he saved for the poor.

He was photographed in his garden clothes, an old straw hat, shirt and trousers from the mission barrel. He looked scrawny and weatherbeaten, like scarecrow with glasses on.[7] The photo was used extensively throughout the nation and one magazine printed it, unwittingly, to illustrate an article on farming. "We wanted a real farmer looking farmer," the editor explained anxiously, when he learned that his subject was the Catholic Bishop of Spokane.

Reporters came from Lewiston, Idaho, and he offered them lunch. "The Church must become a visible sign to and for the poor," he lectured them, "and while we should be concerned about the materially poor, we must not forget the spiritually and emotionally poor."

"It is too clear—as many youths point out—that we profess Christianity, but do not live it. We should question current economic and social standards. I reject them."[8] That last remark, of course, was superfluous.

While he sliced cucumbers over his kitchen sink he discussed the menu. Fish head soup, he said, was nourishing and cheap. He could use the fish heads later for fertilizer in his garden. His guests did not prefer fish head soup for lunch? The bishop smiled sweetly and instead served noodles, which he bought for 24 cents, and chicken necks, which cost 15 cents a pound. "It's the cheapest meat on the market," he explained.

The bishop said he had grown in his concern for the poor. "I want to be one of them. I want to live with them." He did not expect everyone to live like him. "But I do think it is the best style for me."[9]

Not everyone agreed. Some wanted a bishop with style, not one who always looked as though he had slept in his clothes. There were others who were embarrassed. "He looks and acts as though we neglect to take care of him," they complained. "What do non-Catholics think when they read that the bishop keeps his house at forty degrees in cold weather?" Some wag suggested, sarcastically, that he might sell the shack and live in his car, a 1964 Chevy, which rattled so much that it was bound to fall apart at any moment.

The bishop enjoyed the sally. When he wrote in his column one day that "Black is Beautiful," giving three reasons why he would like to be black himself, an irritated parishioner dropped off a box of black shoe polish. The bishop laughed. No doubt he joyfully used the polish on his best shoes, two sizes too large, which he had inherited from one of his dead priests.

But Topel's brother bishops praised him as did many priests. "Bishop

Topel," said Father Alfred McBride at the National Catholic Education Association meeting in Harrisburg, Pennsylvania, "is a great moral leader ranking with Caesar Chavez and Dorothy Day. Spokane's prelate is persuading the rest of us to think about a simplicity of life."[10]

It is comforting to know that at least one cleric compared favorably with two of the church's respected laity, but the affinity opened a Pandora's box of less-than-pleasant speculation. At best an articulate minority praised all three. Most Catholics, if polled, would have no definite opinion about anyone of them.

BISHOP WALSH FOR YAKIMA

The elevation of Bishop Power to Portland left Yakima vacant. On September 10, 1974 Yakima's chancery released the following bulletin.

Father Nicolas E.[ugene] Walsh, Pastor of St. Mary Parish in Caldwell, Idaho, has been appointed Bishop of Yakima by His Holiness, Pope Paul VI. Bishop-designate Walsh was born in Burnsville, Minnesota, October 20, 1916, the son of Patrick J. and Julia McDermott Walsh He completed his philosophical and theological studies at St. Paul Seminary, St. Paul, Minnesota, and was awarded a Master of Education degree at Catholic University, Washington, D.C....

He was ordained a priest for the Diocese of Boise, Idaho on June 6, 1942, at St. Paul Cathedral, St. Paul, Minnesota, by Archbishop John G. Murray. Bishop-designate Walsh's first assignment was as an Assistant Pastor at St. Mary Parish, Boise, Idaho.[11]

In addition to being excessively formal, this news release fails to mention that Walsh was one of eleven children. His parents' busy farmhouse, crowded with his brothers and sisters, provided many richly human experiences that influenced him so deeply that in his adult years he could never live or work comfortably without people around him. In other ways his big-family boyhood shaped him. He was never shy. With down-to-earth, easy manners, he was able to share himself with everyone he met.

These qualities served him and his diocese well. Nicolas Walsh labored as pastor, chancellor, director of CCD, vocation director and superintendent of schools. Back in 1958 he was the founding editor of the *Idaho Catholic Register*, which first appeared that year on April 4. No one doubted then, or later, I think, that some day he would be a bishop. He looked like a bishop and he acted like the kind of bishop people expected—fatherly, in a simple loving way, prayerful even on the street, dignified without being stuffy. He looked Irish, too, and he expressed the highest prerogatives of Ireland's patriots: he was consistently liberal in his demands for freedom and justice.

MISSION VOLUNTEER GROUPS

In 1966, Bishop Treinen appointed Walsh to undertake an assignment that changed his life and ultimately brought him to Yakima. He was named as director of Boise's new mission in conjunction with the Papal Volunteers of Latin America, PAVLA, in Bogata, South America. [12] It will be remembered, especially by church watchers in the United States, that Cardinal Cushing of Boston, at the request of Pope John XXIII, had established PAVLA as a high priority in his own archdiocese. Other American dioceses became involved immediately. For example on September 21, 1961, Archbishop Connolly of Seattle announced that his archdiocese would sponsor a PAVLA mission "in the near future." Walsh had organized volunteers in Boise in this same year, and in the following year he presented mission crosses to four lay volunteers and two sisters in departure ceremonies in St. John's Cathedral. [13]

Meanwhile, another significant group of mission volunteers had developed under the direction of the Jesuits. This was called Jesuit Volunteer Corps, JVC. A brief account of this has been provided by Michael F. Radding, a former volunteer.

> The J.V.C. had begun in 1956 when Sister George Edmund, S.S.A., brought five women from Regis College in Weston, Mass., to work at Copper Valley School, near Glenallen, Alaska. Looking back, Sister George recalled her 'great admiration for these girls who accepted very primitive lodging, limited food and lack of comfort at all levels.' In 1957, Jack Morris, S.J., arrived at Copper Valley to develop what became the Alaska Lay Volunteers and eventually the Jesuit Volunteer Corps. From around the country, he recruited volunteers, established headquarters in Portland, Ore., and expanded the J.V.C. throughout the Pacific Northwest, where by 1970 it boasted 175 volunteers. Through the 1970's the corps grew to encompass the entire country with independent offices in the Midwest (1974), East (1975), Southwest (1977) and South (1980). There are approximately 350 volunteers nationwide, including Alaska, where the J.V.C. is still very active. By providing volunteers at low cost for church programs, social agencies and schools, the J.V.C. saves the organizations over $2 million each year. [14]

Under Father Morris, spiritual motivation was heavily stressed. Patriotism or humanism found in the Peace Corps was a kind of appeal not to be despised, but mission work undertaken with and for God was a different category, more lofty and noble. This was not overlooked by members of the JVC, which probably accounts for its growth and popularity.

PAVLA, too, was regarded as a Christian apostolic experience, the spreading of the Gospel. Unlike JVC, which accepted only lay men and women, its membership included priests and religious. At Bishop Treinen's suggestion, Father Walsh became an active member of PAVLA. Having left Boise in 1966, he arrived on January 25, 1967, at Cali, Bogata, where he established a mission called San Juan Battista.[15] In that same year, 1967, Father David Kundtz of the Boise diocese joined him and, in the year following, Father William Weigand, also of the Boise diocese and later Bishop of Salt Lake, joined the other two.

Walsh remained in Bogata for six years, during which he learned to speak Spanish fluently. He was visiting professor in the seminary there, and he took considerable pains to study Latin American politics, which continued to baffle most *Norte Americanos*. When he returned to Boise in 1973, the bishop appointed him as his vicar for Mexican-born Catholics in Idaho.[16]

Then the see of Yakima became vacant. Walsh appeared to be the most logical and promising candidate to fill it. He was well prepared for meeting the needs of Mexican Americans in the valley, who now represented almost half of the Catholics in the diocese.

In the papal documents of his appointment to Yakima, four reasons were given for Walsh's selection: his pastoral experience, his work with Hispanics, his experience in Christian education, and his activities as a spiritual director. This covered about everything except his ability to write [he had been a columnist for nineteen years], so he was episcopabilis by the strictest standards, even by the pope's.[17]

Walsh was ordained bishop on October 28, 1974, in St. John's Cathedral in Boise. Bishop Treinen was the ordaining prelate. Co-consecrators were Archbishop John Byrne, formerly of Boise, and Bishop Albert Uribe of Bogata. Archbishop Jadot, the papal delegate, presided placidly over the age-old ceremony. Two days later Archbishop Connolly of Seattle presided, more relieved than jubilant, over the installation formalities in Yakima.

There is an interesting sequel, characteristic of Bishop Walsh. He arranged for a civic reception in Holy Family Church, Yakima's largest. There he captivated all who came. His thick, wavy hair, the teasing gleam in his eyes, and his slightly sardonic smile conveyed the image of an almost playful prelate, like Pope John XXIII—much leaner, of course, but equally lovable. Later the bishop held a special reception for his priests, at a minor seminary at Cowiche, where they were requested to appear in informal attire. This was a giveaway on the kind of bishop he would be for those closest to him, his priests.[18]

When the hoopla was all over almost everyone agreed that Yakima had been presented the best bishop possible. It was too perfect to last. The see of Yakima would be vacant again within a brief time: indeed, even before the bishop had time to enjoy a second fruit harvest in the valley.

THE RESIGNATION OF BISHOP WALSH

In December following his ordination, Bishop Walsh joined other bishops in what was now called Region XII for a meeting to discuss mutual interests. The Holy Year had been announced by Pope Paul. Walsh made a pious proposal that the bishops fast two days a week during the Holy Year to identify with the poor. The proposal was adopted, which speaks eloquently about our bishops.[19] Although this was not the most important item on the agenda, it revealed Walsh's priorities (a world vision of Christianity) and his determination to live them.

It revealed something else, though it did not yet appear. This was Walsh's readiness to forego his lofty position as bishop of a diocese for the greater good of the church. With his qualities and at the vigorous age of fifty-seven, he was an ideal bishop. And yet there was an insuperable problem: his health rapidly declined. He suffered from degenerative arthritis. With this he could cope. But something more mysterious affected him so profoundly that his activities had to be curtailed. He consulted doctors in various cities without relief, and finally entered the Mayo Clinic in Rochester, Minnesota. A report prepared by fourteen doctors of the clinic was sent to Pope Paul, who personally studied it and gave his permission for Bishop Walsh to resign his see.

This report was released in general terms on August 10, 1976, when Archbishop Jadot announced that Bishop Walsh had been transferred to Seattle to serve as an auxiliary bishop to Archbishop Connolly. In part it read as follows.

> Bishop Walsh released part of a combined report of the 14 doctors at the Mayo Clinic in Rochester who examined him. According to the physicians' report, the bishop's 'general health is unusually good. But in order to preserve it, the bishop should be in a position in which he can better use his pastorally-oriented experience and where the burdens of administrative work will be lighter.

The reports indicated that it was the doctors' hope that Bishop Walsh have 'non-tension activities which for him seem to be giving retreats, making parish visitations, working with the Spanish-speaking and, in general, being with people.'[20]

After only twenty-two months as bishop, Walsh left Yakima with the title "Former Bishop of Yakima" and with "a new lease on life" in a very real sense, as he noted with some embarrassment. For the second time Yakima had been widowed by the resignation of an ailing bishop. One suspects that at least one cause in both cases was the legacy of Father Philip Leinfelder: the gargantuan debt of the diocese.

THE BUSY BISHOP OF BOISE

Bishop Treinen quite naturally was aware of his former chancellor's crisis in Yakima. He, too, had undergone a period of illness when some of his priests had become so alarmed they wrote to Archbishop Dwyer about it.[21] There had been trouble also in the Wallace area; first the sisters closed the academy, then the hospital, and finally the bishop himself had to close the church at Burke.[22] St. Joseph's Children's Home, the last remnant of the old mission for the Nez Perce, which Father Cataldo had built after the tragic fire, had to be closed also. Like the old mission church, it was sold to a neighboring farmer.[23]

There were other closures as well. In Cottonwood, St. Gertrude's Academy was forced by money problems to consolidate with the public high school,[24] and in Post Falls the historic church, built by Father Tom Purcell and called St. George, was sold to the state to make room for the new freeway. While some of the older people grumbled and felt like weeping at the last service, most of the younger Catholics rejoiced in the acquisition of a new church on a more convenient site, partly at the expense of the state.[25]

Treinen was getting a reputation similar to that of Helena's Bishop Hunthausen, who stepped on some delicate toes by terminating certain schools and consolidating other parishes. According to their critics they were leading the church into ruin by dismantling what others had sacrificed to build. Then, as now, there was considerable controversy about where the church should expend its resources—on elementary schools? on high schools? or on CCD? Hunthausen seemed to prefer the latter, and Carroll College, too, where he had been president.

Treinen could not afford preferences. He had gone to Rome with Archbishop Connolly and Bishop Hunthausen in August 1974, for a

month-long theology refresher course, but he returned on time for
festivities related to the ordination of Bishop Walsh.[26] Then he looked at
his problems with new interest. There were always chronic problems
such as an unexpected illness or an alcoholic priest in a small town where
everyone knew about it. But now he could prioritize his more perplexing
obstacles. He took them one at a time.

First there was the shortage of priests. He placed the following notice
in the *National Catholic Reporter:*

> Priests wishing to return to the active ministry contact Bishop Sylvester
> Treinen Box 769, Boise, Idaho 83701. Telephone (208) 342-1311. Guideline:
> 'Impose no burden beyond what is indispensable.' (Vat. II. on Ecumenism,
> No. 18).[27]

The bishop's second concern involved the Mexican Americans. Sister
Elisa Maria Martine, working among them, provided an up-to-date
report.

> Today an estimated 30,000 people of Mexican descent reside in Idaho year
> round. They are employed in all types of occupations, including plumbing,
> carpentry, interior decorating, trailer manufacturing and agriculture. They
> own trucking companies, tortilla factories, restaurants and barber shops.[28]

This failed to reveal how many were going to church on Sundays, but
Treinen knew at least that his Hispanics were making progress in finding
employment.

His next concern was resolved by appointing a committee. There were
some in northern Idaho who were very vocal in demanding a new diocese.
Idaho was like two states: the northern part, the panhandle, was
mountainous, more WASP than Catholic, and rich in mines; the southern
half, connected only by a long crooked highway, was mostly open desert
or agricultural land, based on irrigation. It was also Mormon territory.
From the bishop's residence in Boise it was over four hundred miles of
narrow roads to his northernmost mission. Should the northern
panhandle be made into a new diocese? After months of in-depth study,
Treinen's task force recommended a negative response. "There are
approximately 20,000 Catholics up north," the bishop said, "and 40,000
down here. More than 1000 of 1200 Catholics polled favored the diocese
as is."[29]

RESTORATION OF THE OLD MISSION CHURCH

More complex for all involved was the painful uproar over the Coeur
d'Alene mission near Cataldo, Idaho. The old Sacred Heart Mission

Church, designed by Father Ravalli and built by Jesuit brothers with the help of the Indians, had deteriorated to such an extent that its survival was in danger. Certain pressures had been placed on Father Wilfred Schoenberg, of the Pacific Northwest Indian Center in Spokane, to undertake the cost of restoration.[30] Initial estimates revealed that this cost would exceed $500,000, far beyond the resources of the Center, which was heavily in debt at the time. Schoenberg recommended that the State of Idaho undertake the restoration as a bicentennial project for 1976, with the aid of federal and state funding. Dr. Roderick Sprague of the University of Idaho carried this proposal to higher officials in the state, who contacted Bishop Treinen. "In 1972," Treinen later wrote, "a representative of the bicentennial commission requested permission from me to have the old mission designated as a bicentennial site; he also asked approval to have the building undergo a process of preservation and restoration. He assured me the money would be provided by state and federal funds to be matched in part by private donations. There were to be no strings attached."[31]

The project was approved. Mr. Geoffrey W. Fairfax, a renowned restoration architect from Honolulu, was consulted. His estimate of cost was $746,350. Mr. Henry Day of Wallace, whose parents had been married in the old mission, accepted the chairmanship of a committee to raise funds not supplied by government grants, and Fairfax was ordered to proceed with the work.[32] At the same time Dr. Sprague and his volunteer archeology students, without cost to the Coeur d'Alene tribe or diocese, conducted professional excavations throughout the premises and turned over to the tribe all of the artifacts that were salvaged.

As the stately old temple took on a new beauty in the process of restoration, members of the tribe suddenly expressed a demand for tribal ownership of the building and property. This placed Treinen squarely in the middle between the state, which expected title after the improvements were completed, and the tribe. Many discussions to settle the dispute, which became more intense as the work progressed, did not produce a decision that was agreeable to all. At length Treinen offered a compromise, which the state accepted. "Governor Cecil Andrews," Treinen reported, "and his advisors were most kind and cooperative." Some members of the tribe opposed it, but the bishop, who still held title to the land, announced his decision anyway.[33] The following news release appeared in many of Idaho's papers.

Cataldo, Idaho—After months of negotiations, the Roman Catholic Diocese of Boise, the State of Idaho and the Coeur d'Alene Indian Tribe have agreed to a plan whereby the Coeur d'Alene Tribe will become owners of the historic Old Mission of the Sacred Heart and the State Parks and Recreation Department will lease the property to care for it and insure that it will be open to visitors.

In a statement made public Nov. 7, announcing the decision of the Diocese, Bishop Sylvester Treinen said that it was made because the Diocese is financially unable to bear the financial cost of the upkeep of the Old Mission and also because the Church wishes 'to at least partially redress the injustices done to the Coeur d'Alene Indians when they were forced to the reservation and away from their home near the Old Mission.'[34]

The text of Bishop Treinen's statement follows:

The Old Mission of the Sacred Heart near Cataldo, Idaho, has been the center of much attention lately. It is said to be the oldest standing building of any kind in the state. Because of this it was singled out by the Bicentennial Commission in 1972 as a site for restoration and of special significance during the bicentennial observance.

In the meantime, some $300,000 has been spent on the preservation and restoration of the Old Mission. This money came from private donations especially through the efforts of Henry L. Day of Wallace, from state and federal bicentennial allocations. While there is great value in preserving historic sites, and while I recognize that value, I have personal difficulty seeing so much spent like this, when so many people wonder how they are to be fed and clothed. At the same time, I am confident that the entire renovation project was performed with the highest competence and the utmost integrity.

The future disposition of the Old Mission has been of deep concern to me during the past two years. The Catholic Church is not financially able to provide the high grade care the Old Mission will need from now on, given its restoration and the national attention focused on it.

The Coeur d'Alene Indian Tribe desires ownership of the Old Mission. Their ancestors built the Old Mission between 1848–50.[35] They lived there and worshiped there constantly for 27 years. They would undoubtedly still live there and use the old church regularly, if the U.S. Government had not in 1877 forced them to the reservation in the DeSmet area.[36]

The State of Idaho has an enormous monetary investment in the Old Mission now that the restoration has been completed. The legislature last spring appropriated funds to care for the Old Mission, conditioned upon some kind of legal title to the property.

The Old Mission has been a Catholic Church from the beginning. No one questions the title of the Church to the property.

Now after months of negotiations with the Tribe and the State, an arrangement acceptable to all three parties has been agreed upon.[37]

1. The Catholic church is to lease the Old Mission to the State Department of Parks and Recreation which will be completely responsible for the care of

the Mission and will make it available to the use and view of all responsible parties. This lease is for 40 years.

2. After the signing of the lease, the Catholic Church is to deed the site to the United States Government in Trust to the Coeur d'Alene Tribe, subject to the lease agreement. The Tribe by agreement is to resolve to care adequately for the Old Mission by everyone after the lease to the State expires.

3. The Catholic Church takes these steps for the following reasons:

a. To at least partially redress the injustices done to the Coeur d'Alene Indians when they were forced to the reservation and away from their homes near the Old Mission.

b. To recognize the financial investment of private citizens, the State of Idaho and the Federal Bicentennial Commission.

c. To assure the adequate care of the Old Mission and free access to the building and grounds by visitors and all religious denominations for religious purposes.

As Catholic Bishop of Idaho, I do this to assure myself that there is no racism in my own heart and perhaps to help others to do the same.[38]

The Old Mission restoration was completed in August 1975.[39] Since then the Idaho State Parks have established a permanent museum on the broad sweep of the slope below it. Ravalli's masterpiece crowns the top of the hill, "Joset's knoll," which can be seen for many miles in three directions. At the bottom of the hill in the restored cemetery lie the bones of the first Christians in this vast mountain-locked empire. These Christians are at rest; their beloved "house of prayer" stands firm, while the winds and the rain batter it, as they did long, long ago.

SCHISMATIC CHURCHES IN IDAHO

Compared to the forgotten embroglio over the Old Mission, the presence of two schismatic churches in Treinen's diocese was like two warts on his hand, more of a nuisance than painful. They never went away. These two groups of dissidents popped up unexpectedly in the confusion following Vatican II. Both were in northern Idaho, about as far from a Catholic bishop as anybody could get in this country, one in Rathdrum and the other in Post Falls. Both claimed to be more "Catholic" than the pope, and both denounced Vatican II as an invalid, ecumenical council. There the similarities ended.

Schismatic churches were not new to the Northwest. A small group of Polish "Old Catholics," reactionaries who refused to accept Vatican I in 1870, settled in Pe Ell, Washington, south of Olympia, and established a church there.[40] Their hopes never flowered and eventually the remnants of the flock joined the Anglican Church, with which the Old Catholics held "inter-Communion."

THE TRIDENTINE RITE CHURCH

In north Idaho, the Coeur d'Alene church that called itself the "Roman Catholic Church of the Tridentine rite" was aggressive and well organized under its eccentric founder, Bishop Francis K. Schuckardt. Schuckardt had been a model student at Seattle University, a prefect of the Sodality of Mary there, and director of the altar boys in affluent Sacred Heart parish in Bellevue. He had become involved in the Blue Army of Our Lady of Fatima and was a frequent lecturer at Catholic meetings throughout the country, especially in the Toledo, Ohio, and Spokane areas. For a time he was the international secretary for this Blue Army.[41] He first broke with Rome over the Mass, insisting on the retention of the Tridentine form. In 1971, when he was thirty-three years of age, he obtained ordination from an Old Catholic bishop, Daniel O. Brown, whose credentials as a validly ordained bishop were sometimes regarded as shaky. Brown ordained Schuckardt first in priestly then in episcopal orders, in a Chicago hotel room.[42]

Schuckardt subsequently established Christ the King Priory near Coeur d'Alene which claimed in 1974 to have "three priests, 39 clerics, deacons, sub-deacons and seminarians and 50 novices and professed sisters."[43]

The Tridentine community, according to contemporary records, believed "in corporal punishment for children at the community's school [in Rathdrum] and severe modesty in dress, with ankle-length dresses and long sleeves for women. . . . Schuckardt has claimed that there are as many as 3,000 Tridentine Catholics in the Toledo area alone, and many, many more across the country."

One of Schuckardt's churches was St. Joseph's in Coeur d'Alene. Clerics ordained by him and allegedly in residence there traveled into other dioceses posing as "Roman Catholic priests." They persuaded pastors of other parishes to permit them to preach in their pulpits on "The Third Fatima Secret." In July 1974, Treinen found it necessary to send warnings to all bishops in the United States that these volunteer preachers from his diocese belonged to a dissident sect that "has effectively cut itself off from the church . . . [and] which is acting contrary to Catholic Church policies."[44]

Despite its bad press, which seemed to be shamelessly one-sided, the Schuckardt problem did not go away. The Tridentine stress on traditional Catholic practice, especially on devotion to Mary, the Mother of God, confused many Catholics who were tricked into joining the church without knowing the consequences. Thus the church did expand, and with expansion its needs and financial resources increased proportionately. At this point the Jesuits' Mount St. Michael's in Spokane, no longer used as a seminary, attracted Schuckardt's attention.[45] With its 735 acres of good land it was for sale at the bargain price of 1.5 million dollars.

When the sale of the Mount was finalized on December 30, 1977, it was reported that the Pillar Investment Company had purchased it "for investment purposes only."[46] The president of Pillar was Thomas Drahmen, a member of the Tridentine church. Drahmen admitted to the press that Schuckardt had signed a lease on the buildings, but an investigation by Father Brad Reynolds, editor of the Jesuit in-house paper, revealed that the Pillar Investment Company "has definite ties to the Tridentine Latin Rite Church."[47] A flurry of complaints about "a phony front" for Schuckardt followed, during which another surprise surfaced: Archbishop Marcel Lefebvre of the Traditionalist schismatic church also was interested in buying the Jesuit property.[48] Schuckardt had beat him to it.

This was all news to the Jesuits, who were embarrassed to hear that Bishop Topel was disturbed because Treinen's problem was now in his own backyard. In fact, when the Tridentines occupied the Mount in early February 1978, Schuckardt moved his own residence from Coeur d'Alene to Spokane, where he took possession of the palatial Larson estate on Altamont Boulevard, just ten city blocks from Topel's current domicile on East 14th Avenue.

Lefebvre, who also had his eye on the Mount for use as a seminary, was, in a way, an international celebrity. As a validly ordained archbishop in the Catholic Church, he had come to grief over Vatican II's decrees, which he denounced. He organized his own church, usually referred to as the Traditionalists, with headquarters in Econe, Switzerland. His presence in the diocese of Boise and Spokane requires some explaining.

THE TRADITIONALISTS AT POST FALLS

The second schismatic church in Treinen's diocese slowly evolved, innocently at first, through the pious intentions of a retired Canadian priest. Father Edward De Busschere had spent many difficult years as pastor in rural Alberta before he moved into a large residence in the milder Spokane valley. When the liturgy in the vernacular was approved, he continued to offer Mass in his "rumpus room" in the Tridentine Latin. Other Catholics who shared his aversion to the changes, "sometimes as many as sixty," attended his Mass. When St. George's Church in Post Falls was purchased by the state highway department in 1971, and sold at auction, De Busschere and his associates purchased it for $1400 and moved it to a new site south of the freeway. He renamed it the Immaculate Conception church and conducted services twice on each Sunday and holy day. "The 9 a.m. Mass is always full," he said, "and the 11 a.m. normally fills about three-fourths of the 130 seating capacity."[49]

DeBusschere was now in violation of church law in two respects: first, Post Falls was in Idaho, and he had no faculties to preach or administer the sacraments in Idaho; and second, the Tridentine Mass in Latin had been specifically and repeatedly forbidden. In other words, DeBusschere was contumacious. He turned to Lefebvre for legitimacy and assistance. On May 13, 1976, Lefebvre, who had recently incurred ecclesiastical penalties for the unauthorized ordination of thirteen priests, confirmed eighty-five persons in DeBusshere's Post Falls church.[50] This certainly identified DeBusschere's church with the Traditionalists.

While DeBusschere's Immaculate Conception Church enjoyed a tranquil existence, without significant growth, Schuckardt's was constantly in the eye of a storm. Newspaper accounts of lawsuits, counter suits and appeals to higher courts appeared with boring regularity. No one could predict how it would all end. One could be sure, however, that turmoil of these early years would be regarded as minor events, when death, or the civil courts, removed the Tridentine's charismatic leader.[51]

ARCHBISHOP CONNOLLY RETIRES
AN ASSESSMENT

In Seattle, the time had come for Archbishop Connolly's retirement. He had been a bishop for thirty-six years and the local ordinary in Seattle for twenty-seven years, more than three times the average term of the state's governors. Though he was still vigorous and capable of many more semesters of service, he quietly submitted his resignation to Paul VI "for reasons of age."

Connolly had begun his Seattle episcopate on a dead run. His predecessor, Bishop Shaughnessy, during his seventeen years had erected only two buildings, though the diocese had grown faster than most. Connolly's construction projects totalled in cost more than ninety-one million dollars. The "most meaningful event" in his history, he himself said, was the dedication of the major seminary that bore the name of his patron saint.[52] He believed this would be the source of priests needed for decades to come.

More important than construction and more significant than his seminary, as things turned out, was his stand on public issues.

> At first, in the late 1940's and the early 1950's the topics were expectable from a Catholic prelate of the time.
>
> He railed against communism; he excoriated shopping on Sunday; he banned Catholic attendance at the motion picture 'Baby Doll.'
>
> The agenda changed in the late 1950's and 1960's. The civil-rights movement was taking root.... [53]

Then he supported open housing. He endorsed a boycott of public schools because of discrimination. In every construction project he included a clause forbidding discrimination in hiring workers. He initiated Project Equality, committing diocesan institutions to buy its goods from firms pledging Affirmative Action. He strongly endorsed ecumenism and actively participated in the Church Council of Greater Seattle.

The early years, he admitted, were the golden ones, when he could lay his head on his pillow at night "and fall asleep." "However, during the past few years...the situation had changed. I do not recall having a problem I could not resolve until six or seven years ago, when the problems became personnel problems—the defection of priests and nuns, the disappearance of teaching sisters from our classrooms. These indeed were great, great disappointments."[54]

When he said this he knew not that the greatest disappointment of all lay hidden in the immediate future. He was thinking of death instead: "Bishop O'Dea died in this house. So did Bishop Shaughnessy. I hope I will."

ARCHBISHOP HUNTHAUSEN OF SEATTLE

When Archbishop Jadot in Washington formally announced Connolly's retirement, he also presented the name of his successor, Seattle's sixth bishop: Raymond Hunthausen of Helena, a prelate as different from Connolly as Connolly had differed from his predecessor, Gerald Shaughnessy.[55] Until then Hunthausen's reputation for liberal views had little impact on Seattle's Catholics, but he was a popular choice with those who knew him. Like Bishop Topel of Spokane, his spiritual director, he had adopted a simplicity of style, an openness to change, and most notable of all, a pacifist mentality that earned for him the populist sobriquet of "Patron Saint of Peace."[56]

His installation in Seattle's Civic Center was scheduled for May 22, 1975. Some weeks before this, on March 16, he administered the sacrament of confirmation at the Little Flower Mission Church at Browning, Montana. Following this ritual, another was performed, during which Chief Tom Many Grass presided. Hunthausen was adopted into the Blackfeet Tribe with the title of "Ne-no-Na-two-Wap-Poo-wa-ka," meaning "Chief Holy Travelers."[57] He had traveled indeed, since the neighbor kids called him "Dutch" when he was only six. He thanked the Blackfeet for the honor now, and he requested their prayers as he traveled again to Seattle, to become the "Chief Bishop" there.

At the installation, Jadot, as usual, presided. Cardinal Timothy Manning of Los Angeles was present, as were many other prelates, priests, and religious, and five thousand members of the laity. Hunthausen carried a wooden crozier, with a sharp hook on it, in appearance like a six-foot cane, which he grasped in the middle with one hand, his other hand over his heart. Monsignor John Doogan, wearing his cassock and surplice, read the papal brief. Appropriate remarks were offered and the five thousand applauded.[58]

For some the applause was premature. The new archbishop, they soon learned, had very firm views on the instruments of war, some of which were produced in his very own archdiocese by Catholics in good standing. A confrontation was inevitable. By the time it came, many of his opponents had been disarmed by his honest-to-goodness humility and his great compassion for all. He lived in a third floor room in the cathedral rectory, traveled by foot when he could, and hitchhiked when he could not. Like Bishop Topel, he gave what he had to the poor. What he was doing in Seattle, whether you liked it or not, had larger implications for the American church itself, indeed for all Christians.

CLOSING OF THE SEMINARIES

Hunthausen's noisy pacifism was one thing, the closing of St. Edward's Minor Seminary was quite another. This was in May 1976, and the news was like a nail in Archbishop Connolly's coffin. When Hunthausen announced it, he presented only one reason for his decision: lack of candidates. Although this was reason enough, many Catholics growled openly and some took their complaints to Hunthausen's predecessor, who kept his peace and bore his "disappointment" patiently.

Father Michael Ryan, chairman of a committee studying Seattle's vocation problem, explained that the move was aimed at promoting "healthy adolescent growth" and realistic decisions about the priesthood independent of a "somewhat isolated boarding school setting."[59] High school seminarians, he said, would be placed in a House of Formation near Kennedy High School and attend classes with other students. Not all would agree with this. The Pope himself had ordered Bishop O'Dea to build St. Edward's. But that was fifty years ago. Vatican II, some said, had changed all that.

The soot of bitterness had scarcely settled when, in February 1977, repeating his performance of the previous year, Hunthausen announced another closure; this time it was sacrosanct St. Thomas Seminary "the most meaningful accomplishment" of the Connolly years. This was a second nail in Connolly's coffin. there were only forty seminarians, Hunthausen explained. Next year these would be fewer than twenty-five. The Sulpician Fathers before their departure would negotiate transfers to other seminaries and Bishop Walsh would serve as chairman of a *task force* to redesign the entire seminary program.[60]

Father Ryan's *committee* was still at work. There were two groups in St. Thomas, the College students, or philosophers, and the theologians. Only the theologians were being transferred to other seminaries. The philosophers, like the high school seminarians, would live in college dormitories or residences of their choice, and attend classes "in local colleges and universities." This would implement a priestly formation program with closer ties to the community. Father Ryan offered further comment.

> OUR STUDY committee found that experience at a traditional college seminary today can be unduly restrictive in terms of exposure to a universe of people, ideas, lifestyles and experience.
>
> The social setting of the seminary can contribute to a lopsided process of socialization since the population of the seminary is all male, racially homogeneous and comprised of those intending to devote themselves to a life of celibacy.
>
> It seems important to enrich the mix during these important years by giving greater opportunities for ongoing dialogue with other young people who are trying to discover the implications of their faith in terms of service.[61]

This was heavy stuff. Who could dispute it?

HELENA'S BISHOP ELDEN CURTISS

After the departure of Bishop Hunthausen, Helena's diocesan consultors met to choose an interim administrator of the diocese. They elected a close personal friend of the former bishop, Father Joseph Oblinger. No one expected a long wait before the new bishop would be appointed, since the matter had been under consideration at Rome for some months before Connolly's resignation. But the days and weeks dragged by, and the bishop's throne in the cathedral remained empty for the fifth time.

At last, the good news arrived. On March 4, 1976, Archbishop Jadot revealed that Helena's seventh bishop was Father Elden F. Curtiss of the Baker diocese, currently president and rector of the seminary at Mount Angel, Oregon. The news release included the customary details. Curtiss had been born on June 16, 1932, in Baker, Oregon. He had attended St. Francis Academy there, then St. Edward's and St. Thomas Seminary near Seattle. He had been ordained in 1958, and later attended Fordham University, the University of Portland, and Notre Dame for graduate studies. He had been vocation director in Baker and more lately, active in Region XII in promoting vocations to the priesthood. In 1970, he was assigned to the Mount Angel Seminary staff as a counselor. He became the seminary president and rector in the following year when he was only forty years old.[62]

A reporter questioned him regarding his personal feelings at this time. "The furthest thought from my mind," he replied, "on August 30, 1962, as I stood in the beautiful gothic cathedral in Helena for the consecration of your sixth bishop Raymond Hunthausen, was that I would be his successor some day."[63]

Curtiss sought information on his new diocese and the *Catholic Sentinel* provided it.

> There are nearly 67,000 Catholics in Western Montana (24 percent of the total population) served by 158 priests, 121 Sisters and 10 Brothers as well as several thousand lay volunteer teachers and workers. Carroll College in Helena (with 1250 students) is operated by the Diocese as are three high schools and six grade schools. An additional 9000 public school students are enrolled in diocesan sponsored programs.[64]

The new bishop was ordained on April 28, 1976, at 7:30 P.M. in the Carroll College Center. Archbishop Power was the principal consecrator and he was assisted by Bishops Connolly and Leipzig, both from Oregon. After ordination and the reading of the Gospel, Archbishop Jadot, who had become as ubiquitous as Howard used to be, conducted Curtiss to the episcopal throne, signifying his installation as Helena's seventh bishop.[65]

Curtiss appeared to be younger than his given age. Smaller than average, trim as a jockey, and crowned with dark brown hair that looked bushy under his mitre, he presented the just-scrubbed countenance of a first year seminarian. Beneath his dark eyes, sparkling with Boy Scout eagerness, he proffered a wide, toothy smile, which reminded one of the vivacious young man next door. He was known as "a man of unity" a middle-of-the-roader, a dangerous place to be, when many of "the People of God" had taken positions on the far right or the far left. As things turned out, he was an able match for the best of them.

MORE NEWS GOOD AND BAD

The bicentennial year was a smashing success for most Americans, but in the northwest church, as usually happens, there were as many downs as ups during all the patriotic gymnastics. In Boise, the Sisters of the Holy Cross lost their tenderly guarded hospital, St. Alphonsus, which was demolished and hauled away to make room for a government building. This was the result sometimes, when you built too close to the turf of the bureaucrats. Though a new hospital was provided, one wondered whether it was worth the effort.[66]

Most of the bad news came from Oregon. The Sisters of the Holy Child had closed their Portland Academy.[67] Then the Jesuits admitted to the sale of their Sheridan Novitiate. The provincial, Father Kenneth Galbraith, informed his subjects by letter.

> On January 2nd [1974] negotiations were concluded with the Delphian Foundation, a branch of the Church of Scientology, for the sale of our novitiate at Sheridan, Oregon. Ownership will become effective February 1st.
>
> As for the novitiate program, it has already been relocated to the site of the former Holy Child Academy in Portland. In place of purchase, which at this time seems unwise for a number of reasons, the province has chosen to lease the site. Novices will now carry out their collegiate experiment at either Mt. Hood Community College or Portland State University."[68]

Gone were the cows and goats and the messy ducks of Sheridan. Gone, too, Piet's prune orchard. The "fresh air" of Pope John and the world's nervous breakdown, had provided some strange consequences.

At Mount Angel the cows were sent away also, because of a new tax. The Benedictine brothers were sorely distressed when they were forced to close down their farm. They had cultivated this fertile earth, sprinkled it with their own sweat, and prayed over it for ninety-four years, mostly for the benefit of students, whose costs were less because of the food brought to the abbey's tables. With the coming of Advent in 1976, they could till the land no longer. A new law imposed corporate taxes on all "non-related" income of churches and religious institutions, such as abbeys.[69] The law, alas, passed in 1969 and effective on January 1, 1976, had been supported by Protestant and Catholic groups, mostly to protect other exemptions. With all the bicentennial hoopla about great American traditions, "In God We Trust," the government had really become secular officially, and godly persons had to make concessions to it that other rights be saved.

While the brothers mourned the loss of their farm, neighboring Benedictine Sisters at Queen of Angels Priory were performing a ritual with few precedents in modern Oregon. The prioress pronounced her blessing, as fervently as she knew how, over four of her subjects who were ready to depart for Deer Lodge, Montana. Kneeling before her in humble contemplation were Sisters Lioba Hoffer, Carmel Wiser and Regina Mary Kust, and one postulant, Luella Kay. Bishop Curtiss had requested their services for his diocese. He had a convent in Deer Lodge that had been vacant for seven years. The Benedictines agreed to staff it and when they arrived there on November 30, 1976, they were welcomed like royalty.[70]

There were elements of the historic in their arrival. All around them convents were closing. Opening this one was like the liberation of a besieged city for the Catholics of Deer Lodge, who dared to think that the famine in religious vocations had come to an end.

THE UNCHURCHED

There was sanctimonious talk now about America's return to God, and sometimes on paper it looked that way.[71] In Oregon for example, in 1976, there was a total population of 2,435,572 of which nearly 300,000 were nominal Catholics, 260,241 in the Portland archdiocese and 24,103 in the Baker diocese. This reflected a growth of 7,500 over the previous twelve months, no cause for boasting at best.

But how many of the 300,000 Catholics went to church regularly? Unscientific guesswork indicated then that two out of three Catholics in Oregon did *not* attend Mass regularly. Like Washington state, Oregon was generally regarded as having more "unchurched people than the average."[72]

About Archbishop Hunthausen of Seattle it was said, "He lives in the least Catholic American City outside the south...."[73] A carefully conducted study, a once-every-decade compilation called "Churches and Church Membership in the United States," revealed that Washington State was forty-eighth among the fifty states in religious *adherence.*[74] "Washington showed an *adherence* percentage of 31 percent while Idaho edged over the one-half mark with 50.1 percent. Montana came in under 50 percent with 44.4 percent." Oregon with 36.1 was nothing to crow about.

It should be noted that these are not *attendance* records. They merely indicate how people regarded themselves as members of a church, any church. If, for example, one out of three of Washington's nominal 9.2 percent of Catholics went to church regularly, as in neighboring Oregon, only three out of one hundred were actively practicing Catholics. Presumably other religious groups rated no better. This would indicate that in Washington State, ninety people out of every hundred did not go to church *regularly.*

The subject of "Why?" keeps coming up. Why is the Pacific Northwest singled out as the principal unchurched area of America? An "Unchurched Survey" conducted by J. Russell Hale of an Oregon Lutheran Seminary provided "the leading list of reasons for not going to church."[75]

I Do Not Go to Church Because:

1. The church is populated by Pharisees, hypocrites, phonies and fakes. "Inside the church a member thinks he is Jesus Christ. Outside you can't tell him from anybody else."

2. The smallest group, the atheists, Agnostics, Deists, Humanists and Secularists. "I would like someone to convince me that there really is a God."

3. The anti-intellectuals. "I don't feel that a man has to go to church to lead a Christian life."

4. Boxed-in-feeling. "No church, no priest is going to possess me.... The church isn't going to tell me how to vote, how many children I should have."

5. Some are burned out; active then left. "They had done their bit."

6. Outside activities. "I spent my Sunday mornings surfing. the churches can't compete with that."

7. Locked out, the rejected, over-looked, disregarded.

8. The Pilgrims. "I need to acquire more wisdom before I can say what I believe." or "All the different churches turn me off."

9. "I don't know why I don't go to church."

These views were expressed by a select group including only those who did not go to church, something less than ninety percent of us. Some were Catholics. The reasons given are only excuses, symptomatic of something deeper: in many cases the passive acceptance of a secular philosophy. After all, is not the religion of the state school system secularism in its most simple form?

One hesitates to suggest why secular thinking is more general in the Northwest than elsewhere in the nation. However, I offer the following reasons for further consideration.

1. The majority of those who came here in the first place were unchurched. Frontiers attracted the reckless, the non-committed, the failures, the wild spirits who wanted to be free—meaning unattached.

2. The area was largely churchless when people entered it. Over one generation went by before churches were readily available.

3. Lodges filled in the vacuum. In the early years many, perhaps most marriages were conducted in civil ceremonies, and most funerals in fraternal lodges.

4. Many who came had experienced church problems where they had lived formerly, like some of the Lutherans in Minnesota. This applied to other religious groups who had become disillusioned. Thus alienated they reared their children without formal religious affiliations. This was especially true on the West Coast.

5. Many who came, e.g., the German Catholics, like the Hispanics today, faced unpleasant obstacles in the practice of their faith. As Archbishop Gross lamented, the heavy saturation of Irish priests and bishops, who spoke no German and failed to give special attention to German demands, cost the church countless members, who remained unchurched and stubborn.

6. Other obstacles to religion, peer pressures or laws unfavorable to religious freedom; for example, the opposition to religious schools by double taxation, which does not provide freedom of choice for those who cannot pay double.

7. The pragmatic outlook and education of most northwesterners, who learn to prioritize practically in developing a frontier. Northwest institutions of higher learning tend to be more pragmatic than humanistic or theology centered. Newman's *Idea of A University* could not be recognized here.

8. The effects of the prodigious progress of science on people when they are young. Science becomes for them the immediate and last cause.

9. Bad example, especially as projected constantly on television.[76]

These last two suggested causes are not exclusive to the Northwest, but they have helped to produce the final results in the late 1970's, namely an area called Christian, with an overall average of less than ten percent Catholic, an area in which ninety percent of the population do not attend church often, if at all.[77] This has not changed much in one hundred years.

If these reflections are depressing, there are others to give us joy. One of these is the great victory of an old friend, Mother Joseph.

MOTHER JOSEPH'S STATUE IN THE NATIONAL CAPITOL

On August 12, 1974, the Vancouver Historical Society's six hundred members formally nominated Mother Joseph for the honor of representing the State of Washington in the Hall of Fame in the National Capitol. This was the beginning of a bitter struggle during which the members of the Historical Society could not be bullied. The preliminary skirmishes, as described by the press were push-overs.

> Mother Joseph of the Sacred Heart must have had a big heart—and a strong one, too. She arrived in Vancouver, Wash. in 1856 when she was 33 and broke the wilderness ground to build no less than 11 hospitals, seven academies, five Indian schools and two orphanages in the state before her death 46 years later.
>
> Acclaimed the first Pacific Northwest architect by the American Institute of Architects in 1953, Mother Joseph designed or supervised construction of numerous buildings.... [78]
>
> A state-wide campaign has been launched to place a statue of Mother Joseph in the Hall of Statues in the Capitol Rotunda in Washington, D.C. Each state is allowed two statues in the Statuary Hall. Marcus Whitman occupies one of Washington State's spots. The other is vacant.
>
> In October of last year the board of Washington State's Pioneer Assn. voted on behalf of its 4,200 members to submit Mother Joseph's name to the state legislature to fill the vacant niche in Statuary Hall.[79]

This article ended on a sour note. "The Pioneer Assn. recommendation was passed on to the state Bicentennial Commission. The Commission has not made a move on the proposal." Nor would it. This was in fact almost the end of the bicentennial year.[80]

Undaunted, Mother Joseph's many admirers took the cause to the state legislature where politics were less bureaucratic and more democratic. Legislation to place Mother Joseph's statue in Washington, D.C. was introduced in the state senate by Daniel Marsh, a Democrat from Vancouver. By a vote of 32 to 13, March eventually won approval. In the house the bill was proposed by the Reverend Al Bauer, also a Vancouver

Democrat. It was passed by a vote of 79 to 13. The director of the State Historical Society in Tacoma was outraged. Mr. Bruce LeRoy threw his tart remarks into the pot, already boiling with dissent. "Mother Joseph's 'cause' was railroaded through the legislature," he snapped. "Her reputation did not get beyond Vancouver [Washington]. A small determined group has been able to push this to a vote while the State Historical Society wasn't aware of the action."[81]

One could easily refute LeRoy's assertion that Mother Joseph's influence was restricted to a small corner of the state. But emotions were aroused in a highly sensitive matter. There was still time to block the bill until the governor signed it.

"There are two dozen other candidates worthier of immortalization in the Capitol," LeRoy asserted, without identifying any of them. "Mother Joseph had a profound influence on Vancouver, but others had influence throughout the nation."[82]

Only one hurdle remained. Would the governor sign the bill? The governor, a woman like Mother Joseph, made a determined effort to justify her verdict. Dixie Lee Ray had been a scientist of world renown, and chairperson of the national committee on atomic energy. She made the customary inquiries. The Eastern Washington Historical Society in Spokane, not especially noted for a pro-Catholic bias, cheerfully endorsed the bill, as did many others who gallantly rose to defend the honor of Mother Joseph.[83] Governor Ray finally signed it and someone recalled the last words of Mother Joseph: "Remember whatever concerns the poor is our affair."[84] Reminiscent of the words of Mother Teresa of Calcutta, these became a kind of motto, which was frequently quoted and which gradually discredited all opposition.

The way was now clear for gathering the required funds and for choosing the sculptor. Felix de Wildon, renowned for his Iwo Jima memorial in Arlington, Virginia, was finally selected to design the bronze.[85] DeWildon, a Catholic, was delighted. He would place "the Old Mother," as Mother Joseph was called, on her knees in ecstatic prayer. Two life-sized pieces would be cast, one for the state capitol in Olympia and one for the National Statuary Hall. They would be ready by spring of 1980.

On May 1, 1980, "the Old Mother" was dedicated in the Hall. Present for the ceremony was "born again" President Jimmy Carter; Washington's governor Dixie Lee Ray; and Washington's Senators Warren Magnuson and Henry Jackson; Congressman Tom Foley, an alumnus of Gonzaga; fifty archbishops and bishops, including Jadot and Hunthausen; and best of all, two hundred Sisters of Providence.[86]

Mother Joseph was the 92nd person to be honored in the Hall, the first of an estimated 500,000 sisters in the United States during the last two and one-half centuries. She was the fifth woman[87] and the fifth member of Catholic religious orders, the other four having been priests.[88]

There is some strange irony in all of this. Washington, the state of the unchurched, had selected two missionaries for its representation in the Hall, Mother Joseph and Marcus Whitman, who wanted to smear his own blood on a Catholic Ladder. Was this recognition of religious leadership by many people who did not go to church, or compensation, perhaps, for the lack of spiritual experiences in the lives of many of its people?

YAKIMA'S NEW BISHOP: WILLIAM SKYLSTAD

On February 22, 1977, the papal delegate in Washington informed the press that the see of Yakima, vacant since the resignation of Bishop Walsh, had been provided with a new bishop. His name was William Skylstad, Chancellor of the Spokane diocese and pastor of the Assumption parish in northwest Spokane.[89] Skylstad was Spokane's third contribution to the hierarchy, not as many as Dubuque's but one more than prolific Anaconda.[90]

Skylstad was born at Omak, Washington on March 2, 1934, moments after his twin brother, who died in birth. He was the oldest of six living children of Stephen and Reneldes Danzl Skylstad, who produced some of Washington's finest apples in the Methow Valley, a lovely, mountain-surrounded portion of the Wenatchee region. Stephen Skylstad was not a Catholic then, but he faithfully drove his devout wife and children to church every Sunday and knelt beside them when they prayed at Mass.[91] When the oldest son, William, wanted to be a priest, his father encouraged him. Bishop White sent him to the Josephinum in Worthington, Ohio, where he studied for twelve years, from high school until ordination in the seminary on May 21, 1960.[92] Later he attended Washington State University and Gonzaga for graduate studies.

His ordination as bishop took place in Yakima's Holy Family parish church "because of the larger space," on May 12, 1977. Archbishop Hunthausen was the principal celebrant, and he was assisted by co-consecrators Topel of Spokane and Bernard Law of Springfield, Cape Girardeau, Missouri, Skylstad's classmate at the Josephinum. After the ceremony the prelates and priests, beaming with pleasure that it was over, emerged into the valley's bright sun and submitted to the customary ritual of photographing.

What had Central Washington got for its fourth bishop? The old ladies in the crowd peered sharply at him, and doubtlessly decided to keep him, for he looked young enough to be their grandsons. He was rather short, not much larger than one of his altar boys, and his features were as refined as one of noble birth. His high forehead and gray-white hair tended to make his face look round, like Charlie Brown's, but his eyes behind rimless glasses had a happy, dreamy look, like a monk at prayer. Below was a generous mouth and a dimple in his chin, indicating according to some, that "mischief was within." He kept fit by jogging, not with a pained expression, like most joggers, but smiling broadly. He smiled all the time, even when correcting someone.

Most of his people were Hispanic. He would learn to speak their language, he said on that eventful day, and he kept his promise. Years later he still jogged, but he listened at the same time to the sounds of a portable cassette, the New Testament in Spanish. He learned to preach in Spanish, but for the sake of hearers, he did not experiment much, nor get carried away with weeping or shouting as many Spanish preachers were wont to do. He was, and still is, a man of great simplicity, who cooks his own dinners and drives the cheapest car he can buy.

Bishop Topel lived in a four thousand dollar house. Archbishop Hunthausen lived on the third floor in a parish rectory. The state's third bishop lived as frugally, in one of those smoky black stone, ancient forts, commonly seen in the Yakima Valley and nowhere else, a former seminary building at Cowiche, which might have been more useful for storing atom bombs. But then the archbishop would not have liked that. Nor would the new bishop of Yakima who lived there rent free.

A NEW SPIRIT IN THE CHURCH

The editors of Catholic newspapers, for some enigmatic reason, decided that the top news of 1977 was the American bishops' decision to allow Holy Communion in the hand. The decision was rendered in the November meeting of the bishops in Washington, D.C., probably in record time. One ought to agree with the editors, of course, for they gather more news than we do. But I would like to suggest that at least one alternative, "The Return to Sanity" had greater weight.

One had to admit that surveys like those on the unchurched were sobering. But America's aberrations, I think, had bottomed out; there was a sacred healing of the American people in the Bicentennial year, the Vietnam War was finally put behind us. In the year that followed, there was a sacred healing among Catholics also, even for many who no longer regarded themselves as members of the church. Peace had descended and in this new comforting peace there was renewed hope for all.

Vatican II had adjourned with a rousing *Te Deum* more than one decade earlier. Its fruits, like those in orchards, required time to mature. They appeared now in the church's leadership, the bishops, no longer princes preoccupied with canon law, but priestly men who had eased gracefully into pastoral activities. Problems still abounded, for them and the laity, but Catholics were finally communicating with one another on all levels.

It was appropriate that in this prevailing spirit, Archbishop Howard, who had seen it all, should celebrate his one hundredth birthday. On November 5, 1977, his living successor wrote to him:

> Today you will be one hundred years old. You are the first American Archbishop—or Bishop for that matter—who in almost five hundred years had attained the age of one hundred years.[93] You were ordained a priest seventy-one years ago. You were consecrated a Bishop fifty-three years ago. You are the only American Archbishop who has ever celebrated the golden jubilee of his appointment as Archbishop. You are the oldest Archbishop in the world. You actively and competently governed the affairs of this archdiocese until you were eighty-nine years of age.[94]

This was like some of our prayers, in which we tell God all about Himself; but readers gobbled it up like caviar and poured into the vast civic auditorium for a public reception. Howard, in full liturgical regalia, walked in briskly with laughter on his lips and something like impudence in his eyes, brearing his crozier in one hand and a cane in the other. Later he departed for a public banquet in a golf cart, sitting aboard like a farmer in the back of a truck, still clinging to his crozier and cane.

The effect was stimulating. What Oregon needed was more bishops. Portland had two archbishops: now it received two additional bishops at the request of Archbishop Power, who never felt threatened, as some did, by other ranking members of the establishment.

PORTLAND'S AUXILIARY BISHOPS
KENNETH STEINER AND PAUL WALDSCHMIDT

The appointment of two auxiliary bishops for Portland was announced the day after Howard's birthday festivities.[95] It was not, however, an overnight decision. For two years Archbishop Power had conducted a search within his own territory and he had finally recommended two priests, both of whom were more than ordinarily popular, but as different as a peach and a pear. Father Paul Waldschmidt was fifty-seven years old, a large, robust man.[96] He held his head high and he walked with nervous haste, a creative person with the administrative ability of a corporation chairman and the energy of a high school football hero. As president for sixteen years, he had put the University of Portland on the nation's map, confirming the view of many that it was as solid as Notre Dame without Notre Dame's dowry.[97]

He had wanted to be a doctor. But his undergraduate years at Notre Dame influenced him to enter the Holy Cross order instead. After ordination to the priesthood on June 24, 1946, he earned a doctorate at the Angelicum in Rome. His was life in academia, but not far from the busy streets where he raised funds to build the modern university.

Unlike him, Father Kenneth Steiner had always served in parishes.[98] He was forty-one when he was appointed bishop, having been born on Thanksgiving Day in 1936 on a farm near David City, Nebraska.[99] Thus his predilection for the bucolic was well-founded. He attended Mount Angel Seminary and was ordained at St. Thomas Seminary in 1962. Tall and lean like a lodgepole pine, he had dark hair and dark eyes with sadness in them. His mother, an immigrant from Belgium, was especially dear to him. Together they enjoyed skiing on the snows of Mt. Hood, more like brother and sister than a son with his mother.

The two priests were made bishops in the same hour. Papal delegate Jadot presided in Portland's Civic Auditorium on May 2, 1978, when Archbishop Power, assisted by Bishop Curtiss and Bishop Alfred E. Mendez, retired bishop of Arecibo, Puerto Rico, administered the holy sacrament.[100] In the photograph taken afterwards, Power is dwarfed by Waldschmidt and Steiner is taller than either. Power, as usual, presents a happy appearance, but it is Waldschmidt who is providing the humor. Archbishop Howard was there, in his second century, as curious about people as he was in his first.

THE RESIGNATION OF BISHOPS SCHUSTER AND TOPEL

The Northwest now had four archbishops, two of them retired, and nine bishops, which set a record of sorts for this distant and all but forgotten portion of God's vineyard. The record survived, though Archbishop Jadot, again, announced the resignation of Bishop Schuster of Great Falls "for reasons of health," only three weeks later.[101]

Schuster was scarcely sixty-six years old. "I will remain in the diocese," he explained when the news was public, "I hope to serve in some pastoral role."[102] Two days later the diocesan consultors met to choose an interim administrator. They elected Bishop Schuster, who was back on the job before he had an opportunity to get away.

Nothing, I am sure, surprises the bishop-makers in the Vatican. Some things they know before they happen; others they simply expect. No one there has lived two thousand years but that is the amount of their cumulative experience. This beats the Standard Oil Company, General Motors, and a lot of other corporations combined. Despite all this, the year 1978, which was about to begin, was a freakish year—not even the Pope's favorite cardinal could predict its shocking revelations.

Bishop Topel's resignation was expected. He would be seventy-five on May 31, 1978, and he had dispatched to Rome the proper papers for telling church officials what they already knew. Seemingly in a hurry, these officials acted upon Topel's formal request before his time was up. In April, Topel himself revealed that "Pope Paul VI has accepted my resignation for reasons of age." He was requested to serve as "apostolic administrator" until his successor arrived. 103

Pope Paul himself was near the end of his life, so one suspects that a privileged subordinate handled the matter, which was routine at best. For Bishop Topel, it was the end of the road. A reporter from *Time* magazine sought him out. "These days" Jane Estes wrote later,

> when the bishop brings home a guest, he tends to grin and confess. 'Lost the front door key. We'll have to go round the back.' Then he leads the way to an entrance that has been patched with plywood since thieves broke in to steal last spring. They only got $1.00 the bishop happily reports, and were lucky at that. Normally there is nothing of value in the house. The $1.00 had been put aside to buy seeds for the large, ragged vegetable garden that provides most of his food. 'Funny thing,' says Bishop Topel, 'I've only bought one packet of seeds in ten years I've lived here.' That first packet apparently gave him a flying start on the rows of beans, peas, carrots, squash, turnips, potatoes, Jerusalem artichokes and comfrey, an herb he mainly uses for tea, that now fill his garden. Neighbors often help with staples. 'I like certain things,' admits the bishop, 'and the word gets around. But it is literally correct that I have not paid one penny for food for my house for the past four or five years.'
>
> It follows that the bishop does not favor rich viands even for an occasional guest. 104

No more of those delicious chicken necks at fifteen cents a pound.

Topel had once wanted to become a Trappist, but he liked to talk. He had found, at last, the perfect life for him: he lived like a Trappist, but he could talk with his neighbor over the back fence.

BISHOP THOMAS MURPHY

Once again the two sees of Great Falls and Spokane were vacant and as forlorn as a cold cathedral. Discussion about either was overshadowed by events in Rome: Paul VI, whose reign had been torn by controversy and even the contempt of those who should have supported him, was reported to be declining rapidly. When he made public appearances, he was assisted by two clerics, one on each side, holding him up. Bishops in the Northwest were alarmed. The time scheduled for *ad limina* visits of the American bishops this year ran from April 20 to November 9, and most bishops from the Northwest expected to be in Rome before the end of summer, that is, before their annual grind of confirmation appointments began anew. Would Pope Paul be there to see them?

As matters turned out, he was not. He died on Wednesday, August 9, 1978. One of the last bishops he appointed was Thomas Joseph Murphy to Great Falls.[105] Father Murphy, Doctor of Sacred Theology and rector of Mundelein Seminary near Chicago, had been born in Chicago, educated there and ordained there, a true son of the Windy City with roots in its deeply Catholic traditions, in the largest archdiocese in America and one of the largest archdioceses in the world. A move to Great Falls was like a move to a dude ranch, but, judging from his own words, one concludes that he was not altogether unhappy with the assignment. For this motto he adopted the theme of the Second Vatican Council: *Gaudium et Spes*, "In Christ Joy and Hope." He brought both when he came.

Like Bishop O'Reilly of Baker, he was uncommonly attractive in appearance, with the fine features of the photogenic Irish. His thick, dark hair, longer than that of most bishops, and parted neatly on the left, gave him a contemporary, youthful look, like a junior executive on the rise. All he needed was a pin-stripe suit and a briefcase to take his seat on Wall Street. Endowed with boundless energy, he seemed to be in perpetual motion, activated by an invisible computer that guided him flawlessly through every crisis. This, of course, singled him out, but one other feature of his personality seemed to dominate the others: his ability to speak out with daring bluntness, like another Archbishop Ireland, the blizzard of the north.

His ordination as bishop occurred on August 21, 1978, five days before the election of Pope John Paul I. Thirty-five members of the hierarchy were present in the McLaughlin Memorial Center on the College of Great Falls campus. Archbishop Power was the ordaining prelate and retired Bishop Schuster and Auxiliary Bishop Alfred Abramawicz assisted him as co-consecrators.[106] The long ceremony finally spent,

Schuster rose to speak. "He welcomed Bishop Murphy in the name of the diocese," a reporter noted. "He said the new bishop who may feel at first he has come to the end of the world, will soon discover the rich treasure in Montana, particularly its people."[107] An enthusiastic crowd gave Schuster a standing ovation.

Then Bishop Murphy spoke. Standing there, an impish glint in his eyes, he tried to be solemn. According to the reporter he said that "people also should know what kind of bishop he hoped to be. He said he would like to be pastor, brother and friend to the priests of the diocese. He said he hopes to be able to recognize and support the ministry of all people. . . . In conclusion, he quoted from a prayer recently given him by a friend: May your Crozier be as lean as the prophet's staff and may your ring fit the finger of everyone."[108]

THE NORTHWEST BISHOPS WITH POPE JOHN PAUL I

In September 1978, fifty American bishops met collectively with the new pope. Among them were the following: Archbishop Power from Portland, Archbishop Hunthausen from Seattle, and Bishops Curtiss from Helena, Connolly from Baker, Skylstad from Yakima, Treinen from Boise, Whelan from Fairbanks [Alaska], and Auxiliary Bishops Walsh from Seattle and Waldschmidt from Portland. As senior metropolitan from Region XII, the archbishop from Portland spoke for all, and the new pope, who seemed to float endlessly in an ecstasy of joy, responded in Italian.[109] Later the northwest bishops enjoyed private audiences and made their customary reports on their dioceses.

For some, like Bishop Curtiss, it was a first experience. Curtiss was very orderly, one could see that even in the way he dressed. His report to the Holy Father, covering the years 1974–1977, was a model of its own kind. It was not a flattering account because it showed more losses than gains, but bishops were not expected to gloss over the truth.

There were 64,000 Catholics in the Helena diocese, the report stated, out of a total population of 376,000. This represented a loss of 12,000, not counting another 30,000 who were believed to be "inactive."[110] The diocese had 57 parishes and 49 resident priests. The number of seminarians had dropped from 28 to 13, the number of sisters from 121 to 86. Just nine years earlier the diocese had 254 sisters, and if one questioned reasons for the closures of hospitals and schools, this alone provided the answer.

Like everyone else in Rome during these fateful days, the northwest bishops were completely captivated by the new pope. They posed with

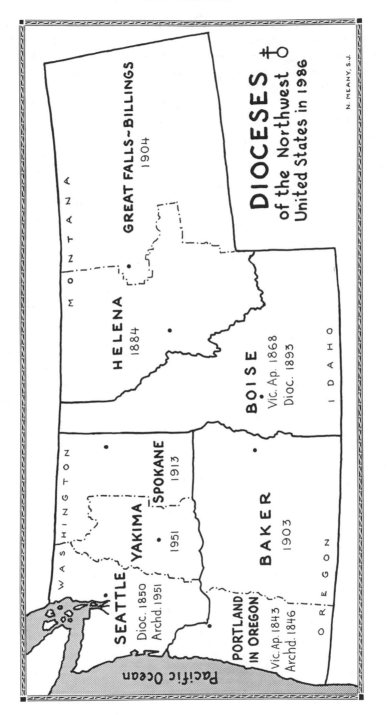

DIOCESES ✝
of the Northwest
United States in 1986

N. MEANY, S.J.

GREAT FALLS~BILLINGS
1904

MONTANA

HELENA
1884

BOISE
Vic. Ap. 1868
Dioc. 1893

IDAHO

WASHINGTON

SPOKANE
1913

YAKIMA
1951

BAKER
1903

SEATTLE
Dioc. 1850
Archd. 1951

PORTLAND
IN OREGON
Vic. Ap. 1843
Archd. 1846

OREGON

Pacific Ocean

him for photographs, most of them as solemn as kings at another king's funeral. Without realizing it, they were sharing the last hours of the 263rd Pope whose reign was only thirty-three days.[111] Pope John Paul I was found dead in his bed on the morning of September 29, 1978. He had died of heart failure.

THE NEW BISHOP OF SPOKANE: LAWRENCE HAROLD WELSH

One of the last appointments of the deceased pontiff was the new bishop of Spokane. Father Lawrence Welsh, Chancellor of the diocese of Grand Rapids in South Dakota and two other priests, were named bishops on September 28, but due to the death of the pope before the candidates had expressed their acceptance, the appointments were ineffective. When the new pope, John Paul II, was elected, he confirmed at once the action of his predecessor. On November 7, 1978, Welsh, one of the few bishops in all history appointed by two popes, became the bishop-elect of Spokane.[112]

Welsh was forty-two years old. His father, also Lawrence Welsh, one of a family of eleven, grandson of William who had migrated from Ireland, started to work at the age of seventeen to help support his family. He was a coal miner for forty-seven years and eventually died of the miner's special disease, black lung.[113] The new bishop's mother, Mary Theresa Fornengo Welsh, had been born in northern Italy, in Torino, whence many of the early Jesuit missionaries had come. Lawrence Junior, born on February 1, 1935, one of four children, grew up in mining camps, "down under, in Rock Springs—not the end of the world, but you can see it from there."[114] As a boy he took up the saxophone, which emitted mournful sounds in deadly contrast with the dispositions of its performer. In contemporary portraits, he was the innocent altar boy with a never ending smile on his features.

Rock Springs boasted of a parochial school, which he attended. After matriculation at the local high school, he entered the seminary at St. John's, Collegeville "for all eight years." While there he spent some of his vacations in the Red River Valley in North Dakota, teaching catechism to the Hispanics, who were migrants working in the sugar beet fields. From them he learned to speak Spanish. One suspects that this was an important factor later in his selection as bishop of Spokane, where many Hispanics have gathered in the agricultural Tri-City area.

Welsh was ordained at Collegeville for the diocese of Rapid City on May 26, 1962, by Redemptorist Bishop William McCarty. "Why Rapid City?" he was asked. "Wyoming," he replied, "had a lot of priests then. It was still under the Propagation of the Faith. South Dakota had very few."

His rector at St. John's was a diocesan priest, Harold Dimmerling, who became bishop of Rapid City in 1969. Dimmerling's fondness for his former student was exceeded only by the student's admiration for his former rector and current bishop. Thus Welsh chose Dimmerling for one of his co-consecrators. As metropolitan, Archbishop Hunthausen would serve as principal consecrator, and, of course, Bishop Topel, his predecessor, should be the other co-consecrator. Reflections on this gave him "the jitters." He had been reminded frequently, especially after news of his appointment got around, about Bishop Topel's lifestyle. "I did not know what to expect." He had never seen Spokane before, but he flew there as soon as possible to make plans for the ordination. In the *Inland Register*, which appeared on the day of his arrival, he read the following with some little amusement. "Chancery officials noted that the ordination-installation would definitely take place at Our Lady of Lourdes Cathedral."[115]

But this was not possible. Ordinations of bishops nowadays were attended by thousands, and for some times past they had been performed in civic auditoriums. Did Spokane have a civic auditorium? The Coloseum. The Coloseum was rented for December 14, 1978, and that was that.

For the ceremony that day, "seven to eight thousand people" many of them from Rapid City, as well as the bishop elect's mother and father, and other members of the family and friends, poured into the Coloseum. The procession of the clergy filed in, with Archbishop Jadot, his bland, Gallican-like features displaying his frequently publicized smile, bringing up the rear. The bishop-elect was smiling, too, in his gentle manner. A little taller than average, he looked lean as a young pin oak, not a sapling, straight and rigid. His dark eyes glistened behind metal-rimmed glasses as they sought out familiar faces in the crowd. When he spoke his voice crackled softly, a voice easy to remember. After he was ordained, he promised to extend "an unprotected hand into the coldness of society."[116]

Archbishop Jadot spoke also. He praised Bishop Topel for his twenty-three years of devoted service. Then Bishop Welsh tenderly embraced Topel, a stirring moment while the appreciative thousands jumped to their feet and applauded thunderously.

It was a warm beginning, but cooler winds would soon start to blow. The first crisis was Marycliff High School. Gonzaga Prep, like Central Catholic in Portland several years later, had become coeducational and Marycliff's enrollment had dropped abruptly.[117] The bishop's final word on its closure on May 29, 1979, sparked a storm of protest that soon became so heated that a few noisy matrons neglected their genteel manners and threatened to sue the diocese. Though the young bishop was deeply hurt and perplexed, he stood his ground and the bloody battle was on.

THE MARYCLIFF AFFAIR

Whenever a school, Catholic or public, is closed, there is the devil to pay. Mothers, usually, get excited and bandy words about carelessly and write letters to the editor and call meetings together for hearing one another's indignant speeches. Sometimes they visit the offices of the most vocal of local barristers. This is what happened in Spokane in 1979.

Bishop Welsh had fallen heir to a vexing predicament: the diocese owned a costly campus of nine buildings near downtown Spokane that was used exclusively for a handful of girls, mostly at diocesan expense. This meant it was subsidized by parishes, which lacked funds to maintain their own parochial schools.[118] Welsh learned that Marycliff had its own school board. The president of this board was James Mansfield, Director of Admissions of Gonzaga University. In view of the projected Marycliff enrollment of 87 students for the following year, rumors abounded that the school would be closed.[119]

This was the situation on May 17, 1979, when Welsh addressed "a gymnasium full of people at the school . . . to hear parents' opinions and to get more people involved."[120] Inaccurate reports, subsequently circulated, accused the bishop of stating categorically that Marycliff would *not* be closed.[121] Five days later on May 22, a vote regarding closure was taken by members of the board. The seven members present voted unanimously to terminate the school. Mansfield reported that "declining enrollment was the key factor. . . . The board wanted to put it to rest with dignity, rather than let it fizzle, so that people would remember it as the great school it was for 50 years."[122]

Having accepted this decision, Welsh ordered the school's closure and made his own reasons known as quickly and as tactfully as possible.

> With only 87 students expected for next fall, the Most Rev. Lawrence H. Welsh, Bishop of Spokane, announced the closure of the school last Tuesday.
>
> In a news release he stated:
>
> 'For 50 years the Catholic community of Spokane has been committed to providing education to young women at Marycliff High School.
>
> 'Marycliff has been for a number of years now the only single-sex Catholic school in the Diocese of Spokane. It was provided quality education in this unique mode for those young women in Spokane who have availed themselves of this service.

'We are proud of the contributions which it has made.

'Times have changed; social attitudes toward a single-sex school have evolved rather rapidly in the past few years.

'The enrollment of Marycliff has reflected that changing attitude. Because of this significant change in attitude and enrollment, it is quite clear that the service rendered by Marycliff is no longer a necessary or viable alternative for the Catholic community to provide.'[123]

The bishop simply did what any good manager would have done, but for a few angry mothers it was not good enough. "If Marycliff failed, it was the church that failed," One of them protested without respect for logic. "Where was the church leadership encouraging the pastors to encourage attendance at the only diocesan school?"

A lawyer was consulted "to check church and school by-laws and the agreements made...." An inflammatory broadside was dispatched to Archbishop Jadot, who had recently bestowed on Welsh his own holy blessing. This was not the first letter of its kind that the papal delegate had received, nor the last. Schools were shutting down all over the country, "for economic reasons," a spokesman in Washington, D.C. explained, when contacted by the press. There had been "some distress in some of those areas."[124] The bishop's critics might have saved their breath; there was no sensible way in which he could reverse his decision. The last student passed through Marycliff's doors on June 5, 1979.[125]

Her departure became the occasion for an up-to-date survey of Catholic high schools for girls in the state.

The era of the all-girl Roman Catholic high school is not over in the state of Washington although Marycliff High School is closing its doors in Spokane at noon Tuesday.

Four all-girl schools in the Archdiocese of Seattle plan to remain open in the 1979-1980 school year, The Spokesman-Review learned Saturday.

One—Holy Names Academy in Seattle's Capitol Hill District—will celebrate its centennial year beginning in November, a spokesperson said.

However, student tuition will rise from $750 to $950. An additional registration fee will raise the cost to the student to $1,000.

With 414 students, Holy Names was the largest all-girl school in the state in the 1978-79 school year. Ninety-four of them graduated in the 99th class last week.

Enrollment in the school was at 700 several years ago. After it fell there was talk of closing the academy, but strong fund raising campaigns and support of the Catholic community kept it alive.

One person interviewed said the school's financial position appeared to be solid.

Forest Ridge Secondary/High School in Bellevue has 278 students in grades six through 12 and charges $2,500 tuition, according to figures supplied by the Seattle Archdiocese office of education.

Immaculate High School in Seattle is subsidized by the archdiocese. It has 112 students and has a $650 tuition fee.

The fourth all-girl school is St. Placid High in Olympia with 80 students.

The archdiocese also has two co-educational high schools in Seattle— Blanchet and Kennedy.

According to figures in the 1969–70 Washington Education Directory, Seattle's Holy Names Academy then had 707 students while Spokane's two all-girl high schools enrolled 1,033--Marycliff 578 and Holy Names Academy (which closed in 1975) 455.

By September 1977, Marycliff enrolled only 147 students. Last fall only 118 were counted. [126]

Only two other Catholic high schools for girls have survived in the Northwest, both in Oregon. St. Mary's in Portland, like a flagship sailing serenely on familiar waters, still provided an inspiring precedence after one hundred and twenty years. Another St. Mary's has also survived, St. Mary's of the Valley at Beaverton, which is the only resident convent school in the Northwest. As Bishop Welsh had observed, times had changed. What had changed most of all was the availability of sisters, whose numbers had been reduced drastically by the bright New Order of things.

A FINAL NEWS ROUNDUP

A faithful disciple of the Catholic press in 1980, or in the two following years, would find the usual tidbits of local copy about their bishop's travels, for confirmation or jubilees, the deaths of priests and nuns and sometimes of elderly parishioners, the dedications of church buildings, never a convent or a school anymore, only rarely a church, but more often a CCD building or "a parish center," and sympathetic accounts of the activities of pro-life groups or the neighboring war on pornography. Sometimes secular news crept in, if it concerned the church even remotely.

The most untimely tidings of this sort was the eruption of Mount St. Helen's on May 18, 1980. It was like the death of Kennedy, a watershed event; everyone could remember what he was doing when it happened and one's memory tended to date other eventualities by it; before and after. The skies of the Northwest became as black as doom that day and all activities east of the Cascades were terminated suddenly because of the falling ash, which measured as deep as six inches in some parts. Churches were closed, hospitals placed on an emergency basis only, and parish rectories became havens for immobilized travelers. [127] Jesuits from all over the world, including the Father General, Pedro Arrupe from Rome, had started to arrive for a week's meeting at Gonzaga's Waikiki

Retreat House. Some never made it. "Ash Monday," Montanans called the fallout, and like citizens of other states, when the ash had settled, they acquired paper face masks dispensed by Catholic hospitals, and pitched in to clean up the mess.[128]

There was no comparable eruption of Catholic volcanoes and though the murderous mountain had the name of a saint, the Catholics did not claim it. Knowing the practice of some editors, one should regard this as a wonder in itself. Other topics, tame by contrast and as rare as rainbows, occupied the clergy in their gatherings at the deaneries, along with the usual sobering reports about priests going over the hill. The more significant of this tittle tattle was as follows.

In June 1980, when the diocese of Great Falls observed its seventy-fifth jubilee, Bishop Murphy promulgated its new official name: Great Falls-Billings. This was a concession to the people of God in Billings, who had looked forward expectantly to having their own bishop. This was wishful thinking, since the whole diocese claimed only 66,000 Catholics including those who went fishing on weekends, instead of attending Mass. Bishop Murphy's Confirmation schedule could kill an army mule, but he was able and willing; hence the Vatican was satisfied with a change of name rather than a division of the diocese.

This was called progress. There was some more progress, long in coming, in the Boise diocese: the Benedictines' priory at Jerome was finally occupied and dedicated. One should not find fault with the Benedictines for the delay. This was Mormon country, with few Catholics. The Benedictines' student center at the college in Twin Falls had faced many obstacles, the Jerome priory even more. "After ten years in Twin Falls," Father Pollard wrote, "the Ascension Priory Community, under the supervision of Father Stephen Hofmann, began to work on a new monastery complex on their farm near Jerome, Idaho. Designed for twelve monks, the new building looks out over the panorama of the Magic Valley. It was blessed by Bishop Nicolas Walsh, long a friend and benefactor of the priory, on August 3, 1980. Bishop Treinen celebrated Mass for the occasion. Shortly before, Father Simeon Van de Voord was appointed prior."[129]

There was also cause for happiness when Bishop Treinen blessed the residence for the first Carmelite fathers in Idaho on March 19, 1981. The three Carmelites, Fathers Peter Bourne and Matthias Montgomery and Brother Maurice Mansfield, had arrived in the diocese on June 15, 1979. On August 21, enroute to Leadore from Salmon River, the mountainous terrain described by Archbishop Seghers a century before, they followed "a short cut," usually a disastrous procedure in the mountains, but this time providential. They passed a small ranch house with five acres of land with a "For Sale" sign conspicuously displayed. They liked it so well they bought it. Here they established their hermitage, which they called St. Joseph's.

Bishop Treinen was unrelenting in his efforts to attract priests and sisters to his diocese. His pleas with religious superiors were so persistent and compelling that he received at least part of what he sought. His success can be measured by comparing numbers with another northwest diocese of the same size.

Boise had 116 priests, including 25 religious, 198 sisters, 4 brothers, 18 permanent deacons.

The Helena diocese had 135 priests, including 15 religious, 80 sisters, 6 brothers and 7 permanent deacons.

Treinen's latest appeal produced three Sisters of St. Mary at Beaverton, the first of their order to reside in Idaho. [130] They arrived on June 16, 1981 to staff the domestic department of Nazareth Retreat House, which Treinen had built several years earlier.

In Helena, it was a new chancery building that attracted comment. In this acquisition there is some antiquarian interest that should not be passed over. The "new" chancery was the former Emanu-el synagogue, the first in Montana, it was asserted, built in 1891, and sold to the state during the depression years. In the spring of 1980, the diocese of Helena purchased it at auction for the lone bid of $83,000. After extensive renovations, Bishop Curtiss sprinkled Christian holy water over it and then in the words of Good Pope John, "The Old Testament before the New," it was put into immediate service in February 1981. [131]

PROPOSED NEW DIOCESE IN OREGON

In the Archdiocese of Portland in 1981, the principal excitement— thank God there was no worse—was the proposal to establish a new diocese in southern Oregon, with a bishop's residence in Eugene. In a poll the priests of the area in question voted heavily in favor of it, some of them, perhaps, with an eye on their own prospects for being elevated to the throne. The plan was submitted to the parishes, also, with facts and figures about numbers of priests and sisters, and costs, especially those concerning retirement. No timetable was included with the dollar signs, and it all sounded to some like speculation from the Land of Oz.

In Eugene, the pastor of St. Mary's was Father Emil Kies, whose predecessors included two bishops and one monsignor. [132] Like the monsignor, Kies had plumped fervently in favor of the new diocese, despite probabilities that St. Mary's would become the pro-cathedral and that he would lose his position as pastor. He had nothing to gain and much to lose. But his strong feelings in this seemingly simple matter focused attention on the growing conviction of many priests that there should be more bishops. The dioceses in the Northwest, some argued, should be divided into smaller units.

There were some, on the other hand, who said the timing was bad. Duplication of chanceries when priest shortages were imminent did not seem to be a good idea. The extra costs when dioceses were already hard pressed to maintain their schools appeared to be foolish, if not irresponsible.

And so the case was debated, the pros balancing the cons, and when that happens the *status quo* is almost always sustained. Thus the proposal for the new diocese of Eugene, like the proposals for Coeur d'Alene and Billings, was dropped. Kies departed for a sabbatical in the following year, but the subtle perturbation about a new diocese in Oregon remained. It was an issue that would not go away.

THE PILGRIMAGE OF MICHAEL McHUGH AND HIS GANG

There is a charming little sketch for these annals, which illustrates the spontaneity of Catholics in the Northwest during this time. Pope John Paul II, while visiting the slums of the poor on his Brazilian visit, suddenly presented his pontifical ring to alleviate some of their poverty. This act of compassion did not go unnoticed. In Seattle, restaurant proprietor Michael McHugh, whose grandparents had donated the campus for Seattle Prep, mustered an assemblage friends, Catholics, Protestants, and Jews, to scrape together a purse of $100,000. With his support, Judy Thel, a local artist, designed a new ring for the pope, using funds provided by her parents. Then McHugh's gang of twenty, filled with the wine of happy expectancy, flew off to Rome with Bishop Nicolas Walsh as their noble guardian. Walsh arranged for a private audience with the pope, and when they met the pope they presented him with a new ring and a heavy purse for the poor. They received, each one in turn, some remarks from His Holiness that, like an heirloom, they will pass on to their children. They left Rome with more than they brought; it was something they could not describe, but they knew they had it.[133]

CLOSURE OF FORT WRIGHT COLLEGE

This was the good news. The bad was another closing. "December 19, 1982, marked the end of an era at Fort Wright College—the last commencement. As was customary, faculty and administration gathered in the Common Lounge to lead applicants for degrees to their places...."

As they settled themselves, more than one tear escaped from eyes loathe to look upon the definitive closing of something that through the years had become dear."[134]

For the Sisters of the Holy Names this was a bitter finale, less palatable because they attributed its causes in part to Gonzaga University's success in coeducation. Gonzaga, they said, had failed to keep its agreement regarding the admission and instruction of the nice, young ladies, most of whom were attending Washington State College anyhow.[135] Thus the sisters' college was deprived of potential scholars. "The Jesuits," one sister noted, "are taking the bread off our table." It was like Marycliff High School all over again, on the college level. Those rascal Jesuits had done it again!

But the Jesuit Rascals did not accept the sisters' reasoning. Their version regarding agreements failed to coincide with the sisters' version, which should not surprise anyone, because it all happened forty years ago.[136] What is perhaps more revealing in determining causes for the untimely termination of the college is the closure of Marylhurst at Oswego, Oregon, some time prior to this. Despite its long, distinguished traditions and vast resources, Marylhurst, too, was required to close for lack of students. The fact is, times really had changed. No one, not even the bishop or the sisters, could turn the clock back. Small colleges, especially those established for women, were being phased out all over the nation. Coeducation, forsooth, was here to stay.

DEATH OF ARCHBISHOP HOWARD

For the oldest archbishop in the world, time finally ran out. On Sunday, January 2, 1983, Edward Daniel Howard, fifth archbishop of Portland in Oregon, died peacefully in the Maryville Nursing Home in suburban Beaverton. He was 105 years old. With his passing, the church in the Northwest reached another milestone—the last of the old bishops was gone, the bishops before and after the first World War, the bishops before the Great Depression, the bishops who laid the foundations of the church in this part of the world. When Howard was born, the Indian Wars were still in the news. There was only one city in the Northwest then. That was Portland. The other larger settlements were merely towns. Spokane was a frontier village. There was no railroad connecting the Northwest with the rest of the nation. There were no Catholic colleges in the modern sense. There were no cathedrals.[137] There were no chanceries, no abbeys, no motherhouses in the usual sense, no monsignors, no Knights of Columbus.

Bishops at Mass wore robes so long that little pages carried their trains, and in public the bishops dressed in long frock coats and top hats, any color they preferred as long as they were black. Priests rode horses to and from their missions, though some few pastors had buggies. The sisters remained in convents and were not allowed to eat with other people, not even with their own families.

Mass was in Latin, in the same form since the sixteenth century. All "adult" Catholics fasted, even from water, from the previous midnight before receiving the Eucharist.[138] Lent was a time of great penance. Benediction of the Blessed Sacrament and novenas were common, as were May devotions in honor of Mary. On Corpus Christi parishioners proudly formed long public processions to honor the Eucharist. Parish entertainment consisted mostly of slide lectures or singing hymns. Dancing was strictly forbidden.

THE FUNERAL

In the life time of Archbishop Howard, all this had changed and he had contributed significantly to these changes. Unlike some of his contemporaries, long since gone, he had been able to move with the church in the hectic years following Vatican II. Called "a liberal and a progressive," he had not been a radical reformer. Mostly, he had allowed his subordinates to exercise their creativity. He had been open to suggestion. He had provided his authority and high level of respectability to those who required it to lead the church in catechetics, in social justice, in street preaching, or in church music and liturgical reform.

His funeral, like his life, during which he attended every episcopal ordination and jubilee in the territory, was highly festive. Two days of formal mourning preceded it and thousands of friends passed by the remains placed in the cathedral like a head of state, awesome in appearance, not like ordinary corpses with painted faces and hands crossed with a rosary in them. The archbishop was clothed in his robes of office, with the mitre on his head, more like a dead pope than the kid from Cresco, Iowa.

On Friday, January 7, 1983, at six in the evening, the two-hour Christian burial ceremony, already planned for two years, began with a mournful dirge and clicking television cameras. Fourteen bishops with solemn faces and more than one hundred and fifty grim looking priests, hundreds of bereaved sisters and the laity, including the governor and the long-faced mayor, jammed the cathedral, while Archbishop Power went through the proper motions, as imperturbable as ever. The bishops concelebrated the Mass with him, the choir of one hundred and twenty, mustered by Sister Jeanne Frolick, sang like birds, sometimes with joyful raptures, and the student body president of Central Catholic made an ingenuous speech that evoked peals of laughter. There were other eulogists, too. The celebration ended as it had begun, with a long procession into the dark, cold night. Howard would have loved every minute of it and it was a pity he was not alive to enjoy it.

On the following day his body was laid to rest in Mount Calvary Cemetery in the plot reserved for priests. On one of those many days when he was reflecting on death, His Grace had expressed his desire to be buried "with my priests." It was his last expression of solidarity with those who had shared the *magisterium* with him.

And there this pioneer era ended, on January 8, 1983, on the winter-green grass of the Oregon hills, below the lofty stone canopy for an altar on which is written: *In Sacerdotium Memoriam*, "In Memory of Priests."

Priests are forgotten after death, Bishop McGrath had said, but bishops are forgotten sooner. With due respect for the learned prelate, I totally disagree. The copious remarks made in the pages above demonstrate that not only are the bishops remembered, but their deeds, both good and bad, are never erased from the minds of God and man.

EPILOGUE

Catholic priests have been in residence in the Pacific Northwest for one hundred and forty-six years, since 1838, a time span roughly comparable to the founding of Maryland and the Declaration of Independence. A bishop has been resident for the same number of years less six. By any institutional standard neither of these periods is regarded as a very long time. Contrasted with its presence in most American cities the northwest church is still in its childhood.

Yet, in a sense, it is as "old" as it will ever be. It has reached the age of agelessness, like the church in many American states, a condition of being much the same with foreseeable innovations occasioned by another wave of immigrants or a cutback in the number of priests and religious, altering, mostly, its schools and hospitals. Always the same and always changing, it has borne witness to the Spirit: beginnings in the wilderness, immigration, opposition from without, buildings and debts, crisis in authority, and back to immigration again.

One imagines, sometimes, that the present is more precarious than the past. Upon reflection, however, one realizes that every stage of history is precarious, some perhaps more than others, all of them proof of the church's other-world mission, its inability to coexist peacefully with mammon. If there is a lesson in all of this it is so simple we often miss it: history repeats itself. There is nothing new in the long history of the church.

A final overview of the northwest church in 1984 can be reassuring: There are two archdioceses and six dioceses in the four states. In administration there are two active archbishops, six active bishops, two auxiliary bishops, one retired archbishop and two retired bishops. There are 1598 priests in good standing, 128 religious brothers and 2576 sisters. There are 589 parishes and 249 missions. The total number of Catholics is 957,187. Most of these live in cities, only two of which are "large" by eastern comparisons, Seattle and Portland. There are visitors who still regard us as primitive, "the church of the uncouth," and there are prelates elsewhere who have said "NCWC," Nothing Counts West of Chicago. One of our bishops rides his horse in a rodeo, most of them cook their own meals. Our priests are quite informal, and there is still a very personal relationship among the people in the parish. In some respects we are still the American frontier. Most of our past history is known by eyewitness. I have personally met, or seen as a boy, most of our bishops since the beginning. The lives of my contemporaries overlap many of the founders of the northwest church, like Father Cataldo. Though we have matured, the people of God here regard themselves as members of a young church and a church that has always tolerated, more graciously than not, those of other faiths.

And how do we see our future? Having survived the various vicissitudes common to Christian collectivities elsewhere, and having experienced the blessings of an adequate clergy and a fairly complete parochial school system, we are most concerned now by cutbacks in both respects.

Our first anxiety is the lack of vocations to the priesthood and religious life, which means that we place a high value on both. Retrenchment in parish services or activities has already occurred, especially in the less populated areas, where priests are required to offer Mass on Sundays in as many as four different churches, each thirty miles distant from another. Recent developments, such as the new permanent deacon program and the new role of the laity, are expected to relieve this problem. but there is no substitute for the priest in certain matters like consecrating the Eucharist. Unless a turnabout in vocations to the priesthood occurs soon, the northwest church, like the church in other parts of the world, will have to make critical adjustments.

The second area of crisis is the parochial school. Without adequate numbers of sisters and brothers, dependence on lay teachers has become commonplace, but the higher costs involved have driven away many who need the schools most, such as minority pupils and children of poorer families. While the consolidation of schools has been resorted to, partly because of dropping enrollments and partly to cut costs, more significant values have been lost, for example, the intimate relationship between the parents and the parish school. The presence of the school as a parish responsibility has, in the past, served as a rallying point for more than classroom activities. While the church was the soul of the parish, the school was its heart. Today, more than ever, because of the breakdown of family unity and the diverse nature of family activities, the parishes desperately need the identity that the school gives it, the common need, the common interest, the common goal, which in part often served to bring families together and sometimes back to the church.

The last of the foreseeable crises concerns the mass migration into the Northwest of Hispanics, many of them only nominally Catholic. These people of a different language and culture require special care that cannot be provided without a sizable increase in the number of priests and religious. The language barriers alone are overwhelming. The northwest church has never experienced anything comparable to this Mexican migration, either in size or in complexity. If in the past almost insurmountable problems were encountered with the German and Italian immigrants, even greater challenges lie in the future, and greater losses to the church will occur than, for example, in the case of the Italians or the Germans.

These are the principal obstacles to complacency. Bishop Welsh expressed them and Bishop Treinen, having considered them, declared himself to be an optimist despite them. He preferred to regard them as "priorities" rather than "concerns." He manifested the mood of the frontier by seeking new crusaders rather than by weeping over lost victories. In the world of vast changes, most of which we cannot change anyhow, we have but one recourse, trust in divine providence. We follow the Spirit as it leads us. As Pedro Arrupe so aptly expressed it, "We must make our paths by walking on them." The church in the Northwest has never experienced any other way.

Notes

Chapter 1. EARLY CATHOLIC INFLUENCES

1. These are as follows: Portland in Oregon and Seattle, archdioceses. Baker, Yakima, Spokane, Boise, Helena and Great Falls, dioceses.

2. The church in the City of Spokane is a notable exception. While Catholics represent 13% of the population in the Diocese of Spokane, they represent 30% of the population in the city. Thus Spokane is the most "Catholic" city in the Northwest. The most "Catholic" state is Montana, which is 18.2% of the population.

3. It should be noted that the Indians of the interior lacked horses until after the Spanish conquest. Horses were acquired by northwest Indians in the early part of the eighteenth century. Until then Indians used dogs to help them carry their baggage as they moved about.

4. The number of Indians in the four northwestern states cannot be exactly determined until a much later date. Lewis and Clark estimated the number of Indians in the Columbia Valley at 40,000 in 1806. Thirty years later the estimate had become 30,000. George W. Fuller, *The Inland Empire of the Pacific Northwest A History*, 4 vols., (Spokane, 1928), I: 44. This figure does not include Indians of the plains in Montana or southern Idaho. A rough estimate of these tribes in *The Report of the Commissioner of Indian Affairs for 1842*, (Washington, 1843), p. 389, would total something like twenty-five thousand. It is difficult to estimate the Blackfeet because many of these people lived north of the 49th parallel, that is, in Canada.

5. For example, in the writings of many missionaries, like the Blanchets, DeSmet, Mengarini, Point, Grassi, and others, there are detailed accounts of a variety of primitive religious beliefs, various forms of shamanism, animism, even agnosticism. There are occasional reports of monism, belief in one Supreme Being.

6. Coquard left the expedition at Michillimakinac according to this source. A.G. Morice, O.M.I., *History of the Catholic Church in Western Canada from Lake Superior to the Pacific (1659-1895)*. 2 vols., (Toronto, 1910), I:37.

7. Charles E. De Land in "The Verendrye Explorations and Discoveries" in *South Dakota Historical Collections*, VII, (1914) p. 197 seq., identifies the "shining mountains" as the Black Hills of South Dakota, a position not held by all other authors.

8. A.G. Morice, O.M.I., *History of the Catholic Church in Western Canada*, I:37.

9. Reuben Gold Thwaites, ed., *The Jesuit Relations and Allied Documents; Travels and Explorations of the Jesuit Missionaries in New France 1610-1791*, 73 vols., (Cleveland, 1896-1901), 68:334.

10. Sister Providencia Tolan, S.P., *A Shining From the Mountains*, (Montreal, 1980), p. 9.

11. His full name was Antonio Maria Bucareli y Ursua.

12. The present California-Oregon border, southern boundary of the Pacific Northwest as it is known today, is the 42° latitude. The Oregon-Washington border, mid-stream of the Columbia River for the most part, is north of the 45° and south of the 46°. The northern boundary of most of Washington and Idaho and Montana is the 49° latitude.

13. Zephyrin Englehardt, O.F.M., *The Missions and Missionaries of California,* 2 vols., (San Francisco, 1912), II:146–147.

14. *Ibid.,* p. 147.

15. *Ibid.*

16. This was July 10, 1774.

17. Edward Eberstadt and Sons, *The Northwest Coast A Century of Personal Narratives of Discovery, Conquest and Explorations From Bering's Landfall to Wilkes' Surveys 1741–1841,* (New York, [1941]), p. 33.

18. Englehardt, *Missions and Missionaries,* II:154.

19. Edward Eberstadt and Sons, *The Northwest Coast,* p. 34.

20. Englehardt, *Missions and Missionaries,* II:157.

21. This was called the Strait of Anian, which appeared on various maps after 1577. It was purely imaginary. A Greek by the Spanish name of Juan de Fuca made the claim that he had seen it, thus the name given the Straits of Juan de Fuca between Washington State and Vancouver Island. George W. Fuller, *A History of The Pacific Northwest,* (New York, 1931), p. 46.

22. *Ibid.,* p. 42.

23. Edward Eberstadt and Sons, *The Northwest Coast,* p. 34.

24. *Ibid.*

25. Allegedly, Catholic bureaucrats attached to the Bourbon kings promoted the destruction of the Jesuits for their own political ends. They succeeded brilliantly. First the Jesuits were expelled from Spanish dominions in 1767. This ultimately cost Spain the entire west of the United States. The bureaucrats finally succeeded in forcing Franciscan Pope Clement XIV to suppress the whole Society of Jesus in 1773.

26. This point, rarely if ever acknowledged, is a significant one. The Jesuit missions in California were listed by Archbishop Francis Norbert Blanchet in 1880 in an unidentified clipping in *Oregon Missions etc.* Since they are difficult to find, I have listed them here:

> At the time of their suppression, the Jesuits had sixteen prosperous missions, viz: The Mission of Our Lady of Loretto, founded in 1697; population 400. St. Francis Xavier, founded in 1699; population 480. Our Lady of Dolores, founded in 1699; population 450. St. Louis de Gonzaga, population 310. St. Rose of Mulege, founded in 1705; population 300. St. Joseph of Comandu, founded in 1708; population 310. Immaculate Conception founded in 1718; population 330. Our Lady of Guadalupe, founded in 1721; population 530. St. Ignatius, founded in 1728; population 650. Our Lady of Dolores of the North, population 548. St. Mary Magdalen; population not given. St. James' villages—three; population 350. All Saints, founded about 1737, population 90. St. Francis Borgia, population 1,500. St. Gertrude, population 1,000. St. Mary, population 330. Total number of missions—16. Total number of Christians in all the missions—7,628.

> Such was the state of affairs when the Viceroy of Mexico, armed with the royal Decree of April 2nd, 1767, came on the 25th of June in the same year, in the name of his Sovereign Charles III., and signified to the missionary Fathers that, their society having ceased to exist in the Spanish realm, they had to quit the country, and commit to other hands the glorious work they had pursued during a remarkably successful career of seventy years. Portland. July 26, 1880 F[rancis] N.[orbert] B.[lanchet]

Englehardt in *Missions and Missionaries,* I, Section II, pp. 80–321 contains "The Jesuit Period" in California, the most complete available account of a little known history.

27. The use of citrus fruits and potatoes, especially, prevented scurvy.

28. The full name of the one was *"Nuestra Senora del Rosario"* or *La Princesa.* Cuadra was captain of the *Favorita.* Englehardt, *Missionas and Missionaries,* II:321.

29. Eberstadt, *The Northwest Coast,* p. 36.

30. Riobo kept a journal that has appeared in print: "Alaska in 1779" a narrative of a voyage in Alaska by Father John Riobo, O.S.F., translated into English by Walter Thornton, S.J. English version published in *United States Catholic Historical Society: Records and Studies,* 12(June 1918):222–229. The original manuscript is in the University of Santa Clara archives.

31. Englehardt, *Missions and Missionaries,* II:324.

32. Edward Eberstadt and Sons, *The Northwest Coast,* p. 37.

33. This was Captain James Cook who had embarked on his third voyage in 1776. On this voyage he discovered the Sandwich Islands [Hawaii].

34. These ships left San Blas on February 3, 1790. Hubert Howe Bancroft, *History of The Northwest Coast,* 2 vols. (San Francisco, 1884), I:239 seq. and Englehardt, *Missions and Missionaries,* II:438.

35. Bancroft, *History of the Northwest Coast,* I:240.

36. Henry R. Wagner, *Spanish Exploration in the Strait of Juan de Fuca,* (Santa Ana, 1933), p. 15.

37. Wagner, *Spanish Exploration,* 126. Manual Nunez was a Spanish naval officer.

38. The complete document appears in Wagner, *Spanish Exploration,* p. 132–134. It also appears in another form in Charles E. Hoonan, *Neah Bay, Washington A Brief Historical Sketch* (Crown Zellerbach Corporation, 1964), p. 8 seq.

39. Wagner, *Spanish Exploration,* p. 126.

40. He arrived in Monterey on September 2, 1790. Bancroft, *History of the Northwest Coast,* I:243.

41. Wagner, *Spanish Exploration,* p. 63.

42. Fuller, *A History of the Pacific Northwest,* p. 53.

43. Boits' log is contained in Frederic W. Horvay, ed. *Voyages of the "Columbia" to the Northwest Coast 1787–1790 and 1790–1793,* (Boston, 1941), p. 416.

44. Fuller, *A History of the Pacific Northwest,* p. 51 seq. Gray destroyed an Indian village of two hundred "houses."

45. Neah Bay was abandoned in September 1792.

46. Bancroft notes that Elwood Evans, one of Washington State's earliest historians, found the ruins at Neah Bay almost a century later. Confer Bancroft, *History of the Northwest Coast,* I:283.

47. Bancroft, *History of the Northwest Coast,* I:300 seq.

48. The Lewis and Clark expedition left the Mandan Village on the Upper Missouri on April 7, 1805. The journals of the Lewis and Clark expedition have been edited at least twice as follows: Elliott Coues, ed. *History of the Expedition Under the Command of Lewis and Clark,* 3 vols. (New York, 1965), and Reuben Gold Thwaites, ed. *Original Journals of the Lewis and Clark Expedition, 1804–1806; Printed from the Original Manuscripts, etc.,* (New York, 1904–1905), 8 vols.

49. Obviously Charbonneau did not have three legitimate wives. He had acquired Sacajawea in a game of gambling.

50. Fuller, *A History of the Pacific Northwest,* p. 62.

51. The Honorable Hudson's Bay Company was chartered by King Charles II.

52. In the Archives of the Archdiocese of Portland, Blanchet Folio IV, 1863–1881. Gilbert J. Garraghan, S.J., *The Jesuits of the Middle United States,* 3 vols. (New York, 1938), II:238, gives 1816 as the date of the Iroquois arrival in Montana. Another authority, John C. Ewers in his article "Iroquois Indians in the Far West," *Montana the Magazine of Western History,* 13 (April 1963), 4, places six Iroquois with David Thompson at Salish House [Montana] in February 1810.

53. John P. O'Hara, "A Letter From The Columbia in 1821," [broadside], Portland, 1943. Copy in Oregon Province Archives. This is a complete account of the incident with copies of the Association De La Propagation De La Foi. Nouvelles Recues Des Missions. No. 11. (Lyons and Paris, 1823), pp. 52-53.

54. "Early in that year [1820], as if Providence had intervened on behalf of the unionists, Alexander Mackenzie and Lord Selkirk died within a few weeks of each other." Richard G. Montgomery, *The White-Headed Eagle, John McLoughlin,* (New York, 1934), p. 39.

55. The Treaty of Joint Occupancy of 1818 provided for a ten-year period. After this, negotiations permitted the treaty to stand with the proviso that either nation could terminate it by giving one year's notice. Joint Occupancy ended in 1846, the division of the territory on the 49th parallel.

56. La Riviere du Loup is situated on the south bank of the St. Lawrence River about 120 miles below Quebec. This was only a few miles from Tadoussac downriver on the north bank of the St. Lawrence.

57. Robert C. Johnson, *John McLoughlin Father of Oregon.* (Portland, 1935), p. 26.

58. *Ibid.*

59. McKay's widow was Marguerite Wadin. This "marriage" known as "a fur trade marriage" was an occasion of dispute later on. The tragic destruction of the Tonquin is described in detail in Washington Irving, *Astoria, Or Anecdotes of an Enterprise Beyond the Rocky Mountains,* (Norman, 1964), p. 108-114.

60. In 1839, McLoughlin moved the trading post again, about one mile downriver, where the City of Vancouver, Washington is today.

61. Edwin V. O'Hara, *Pioneer Catholic History of Oregon,* (Portland, 1911), p. 7.

62. *Ibid.,* p. 13-14.

63. E.E. Rich, [ed], *Peter Skene Ogden's Snake Country Journals, 1824-25 and 1825-26.* (London, 1950), xlii seq.

64. There were really four Astor employees who became early settlers in the Willamette Valley. Besides those named here was Michel Laframboise.

65. O'Hara, *Pioneer Catholic History,* p. 37. *Campement de Sable* means "The Camp of the Sands," or sandy beach. This was the same site as "Champoeg" a name taken from both French and Calapooya Indian origin: "Champooick" meaning "fields of roots." It was one of the few openings in the forest for access to the river, a sandy beach and field of roots.

66. *Ibid.,* p. 26.

67. A vicar general or prefect apostolic is a priest with jurisdiction in mission territory. A vicar apostolic is a bishop with jurisdiction in mission territory.

68. The Bishop of Upper and Lower Louisiana had his residence in St. Louis from January 6, 1818. On July 18, 1826, the Diocese of Louisiana was divided and the sees of St. Louis and New Orleans were canonically erected.

69. Kenneth L. Holmes. "Pierre Chrysologne Pambrun," in *The Mountain Men and the Fur Trade of the Far West.* 10 vols (Glendale, 1966), III:244.

70. *Ibid.,* p. 243.

71. If true this should confirm the Catholics' contention that the delegation sought Blackrobes, not "the white man's Book of Heaven" since Pambrun taught Catholic doctrine.

72. The date 1831 is the first *known* journey. There is reason to believe that others were made at an earlier date.

73. L.B. Palladino, S.J., *Indian and White in the Northwest.* (Lancaster, 1922), p. 9. Palladino, who had first hand information regarding the composition of the delegation stated: "It is well to note here that two of these were partly Nez Perces and partly Flat Heads, being the former by blood, and the latter by choice, since they lived with the Flat Heads as actual members of the tribe."

The Protestant version, originally proposed by the Reverend Henry Spalding, noted especially for his hatred of "Romanist priests," was as follows: "The Flatheads and Nez Perce had determined to send four of their number 'to the Rising Sun' for that Book from Heaven. They had got word of the Bible and a Savior in some way from the Iroquois.... They fell into the hands of General Clark. He was a Romanist and took them to his church." Senate Executive Document No. 37, 41st Congress, 3rd Session, p. 8. This is also presented in O'Hara, *Pioneer Catholic History*. 70. Note that Clark was not a Catholic as Spalding asserted. He was a charter member of two Masonic lodges and helped organize Christ Church (Protestant Episcopal) in St. Louis. Fuller, *A History of the Pacific Northwest*, p. 360.

74. Palladino, *Indian and White*, p. 10.

75. Francis D. Haines, "The Nez Perce Delegation," *Pacific Historical Review*, 6(March 1937), p. 71-78.

76. Palladino, *Indian and White*, p. 11.

77. Palladino, *Indian and White*, p. 20-21.

78. O'Hara, *Pioneer Catholic History*, p. 10.

79. Jason Lee calls it "the east bank." An account of the founding of the mission appears in H.K. Hines, D.D., *Missionary History of the Pacific Northwest Containing the Wonderful Story of Jason Lee*. (Portland, 1899), p. 97 seq.

80. Fuller, *A History of the Pacific Northwest*, p. 126-127.

81. Edward J. Kowrach [ed], *Historical Sketches of the Catholic Church in Oregon by Most Rev. Francis Norbert Blanchet*. (Fairfield [Washington], 1983), p. 38. There are several editions of Blanchet's *Historical Sketches*. This is the latest and by far the best.

82. This was a highly technical matter involving validity of the marriages insofar as Catholics were concerned. In Canon Law the Church recognized the validity of marriages of Catholics *without* the "authorized priest" when the "extraordinary form" was permitted under certain conditions.

83. These appear in Kowrach, *Blanchet Historical Sketches*, p. 43 et seq.

84. Harriet Duncan Munnick, *Catholic Church Records of the Pacific Northwest: St. Paul, Oregon 1839-1898*. (Portland, 1979), p. xvii. The letter was dated March 22, 1836.

85. Faculties carried by Fathers Francis Norbert Blanchet and Modeste Demers contained these directives. Confer: *Claim of the Missionary Station of St. James*, p. 8. and *Claim of the Missionary Station of St. James at Vancouver, Washington Territory to 640 Acres of Land, Statement of Facts*, [Printed by W.H. Moore, 1860 (?)] in Elwood Evans "Scrapbooks" Vol III,"Roman Catholic" in Oregon Province Archives.

86. The Green River Rendezvous was about one hundred miles south and east of an area later known as Jackson Hole, Wyoming. Gilbert J. Garraghan, S.J., *The Jesuits of the Middle United States*, 3 vols. (New York, 1938), II:246.

87. Clifford Merrill Drury, *Marcus Whitman, M.D. Pioneer and Martyr*, (Caldwell, 1937), p. 100 seq.

88. Palladino, *Indian and White*, p. 22.

89. These Indians had been taught, very probably, by Pambrun. The incident is described in Hiram Martin Chittenden and Alfred Talbot Richardson, *Life, Letters and Travels of Father Pierre-Jean DeSmet, S.J. 1801-1873*. (New York, 1905), p. 380. DeSmet's text refers to Rev. Samuel Parker, A.M., *Journal of an Exploring Tour Beyond the Rocky Mountains, Under The Direction of the A.B.C.F.M. Performed in the Years 1835, '36, and '37*, (New York, 1838).

90. Thomas E. Jessett, S.T.D., ed., *Reports and Letters of Herbert Beaver 1836-1838*, (San Francisco, 1959), p. xix seq.

91. *Ibid.*, p. xxi.

92. *Ibid.*

93. Old Ignace had brought his sons Charles and Francis to St. Louis for solemn baptism in a church. There is a touching account of the event in Garraghan, *Jesuits in the Middle United States*, II:247.

94. Palladino, *Indian and White*, p. 26. Also W.H. Gray, *History of Oregon 1792-1849*, drawn from *Personal Observations and Authentic Information* (San Francisco, 1870), p. 173. Gray lived to return to the Northwest where his family prospered and where, in his old age, he wrote this classic of biased history. No scholar takes this widely circulated book seriously.

95. Palladino, *Indian and White*, p. 26-27. Palladino notes that the details he presents were provided by Father DeSmet, "who had them from the Sioux themselves." Gray has presented his own version of the tragedy in Donald R. Johnson, ed., *William H. Gray Journal of His Journey East, 1836-1837*, (Fairfield, 1980), p. 67 et seq. He gives the date, Monday, August 7. The editor of Gray's account provides additional data that seems to confirm Palladino's account. *Ibid.*, p. 83.

96. The church was originally built in 1836. This and other details about the early church in St. Paul can be found in Harvey J. McKay, *St. Paul, Oregon 1830-1890*, (Portland, 1980), p. 11 et seq.

97. Champoeg was regarded as "a quasi-capital" of the Willamette settlements. When the settlers met to organize a provisional government in 1843, they chose Champoeg on the Willamette for their sessions.

Chapter 2. FIRST RESIDENT MISSIONARIES

1. Bishop Joseph Signay of Quebec even looked like a *French* prelate. Balding with white hair parted in the middle and flowing on either side, he resembled a pious George Washington wearing a French embroidered collar and vest. [Mother M. Antoinette F.C.S.P.] *The Institute of Providence: History of the Daughters of Charity Servants of the Poor Known as the Sisters of Providence*, 5 vols., (Montreal, 1937-1949), V:10.

2. Edward J. Kowrach, ed., *Historical Sketches of the Catholic Church In Oregon by Most Rev. Francis Norbert Blanchet*, (Fairfield, 1983), p. 72.

3. *Ibid.*

4. *Ibid.*

5. *Ibid.*, p. 45.

6. *Ibid.*

7. There is a considerable amount of material available on Francis Norbert Blanchet, the founder of the church in the Northwest. The archives of the Archdiocese of Portland in Oregon contain many Blanchet manuscripts, some of them unpublished. The definitive biography of Blanchet remains to be written but two published works are useful: Sister Letitia Mary Lyons, M.A., *Francis Norbert Blanchet and the Founding of the Oregon Missions (1838-1848)*, (Washington, 1940), and M. Leona Nichols, *The Mantle of Elias*, (Portland, 1941).

8. Kowrach *Blanchet Historical Sketches*, p. 46.

9. For example, Signay directed the missionaries to erect high crosses "in all places remarkable either for their position or the passage of *voyageurs*." One would suppose that matters like this would have been left to the judgment of the vicar general. The longer form of instruction appears in Lyons, *Francis Norbert Blanchet*, p. 23 seq.

10. Kowrach, *Blanchet Historical Sketches*, p. 46.

11. George W. Fuller, *A History of The Pacific Northwest*, (New York, 1931), p. 90.

12. *Ibid.*

13. Kowrach, *Blanchet Historical Sketches*, p. 47.

14. The slow, lumbering ox teams on the Oregon Trail scarcely even averaged fourteen miles a day. The fur trade canoes, on the other hand, sometimes averaged over sixty miles per day.

15. Events at Red River and a description of the missionaries' departure appear in Lyons, *Francis Norbert Blanchet*, p. 10 seq.

16. Two biographies of Spokane Garry have appeared: William S. Lewis, *The Case For Spokane Garry*, (Spokane, 1917) and Thomas E. Jessett, *Chief Spokane Garry*, (Minneapolis, 1960). Garry was born in 1811.

17. Jessett in *Chief Spokane Garry*, p. 73 seq. states that Garry taught a simple form of Anglicanism. This is specifically contradicted by Father Joseph Cataldo, who knew Garry well enough to witness his pledge for sobriety. Cataldo, a trained and brilliant theologian, states: "It is good for posterity to know that poor old Garry never pretended to be an Episcopalian when he came back from the East...he passed for a Presbyterian." Oregon Province Archives, Cataldo Papers, Notes on Spokane Garry. Confer also *Gonzagan*, III(1911–1912), p. 114.

18. A detailed account of Marcel Bernier appeared in *Catholic Sentinel*, January 2, 1890. Bernier died on December 27, 1899.

19. Bernier was also a companion to Father Jean Baptiste Bolduc on his highly publicized trip to Puget Sound in 1844. Bernier directed the Indians when they built the first church there.

20. According to Blanchet, the two priests wore their cassocks at all times during the journey and he added: "This practice he will continue to observe, at home and abroad." Kowrach, *Blanchet Historical Sketches*, p. 62.

21. Mass was begun before daybreak, because it had to be completed before the brigade began its early start. Not even the priests or their devotions could delay the schedules of the caravan.

22. Kowrach, *Blanchet Historical Sketches*, p. 48.

23. *Ibid.*, p. 47.

24. *Ibid.*, p. 48.

25. In the mountain passage over smaller rivers and high meadow lakes, small canoes were used. When the brigade reached the upper Columbia, they exchanged the canoes for much larger wooden boats.

26. Kowrach, *Blanchet Historical Sketches*, p. 48. Both priests could not say Mass together. Concelebration, except at ordination, did not become permissible in the modern church until the Second Vatical Council.

27. As noted, after 1846, British Columbia was no longer "Oregon." Because of the probability of Mass having been said by Spanish priests along the coast prior to this, one would have to qualify Blanchet's statement further, for example by describing the Mass as "the first in the interior of the Oregon country."

28. Kowrach, *Blanchet Historical Sketches*, p. 49.

29. *Ibid.* Blanchet describes the particulars of the accident which occurred at the place everybody dreaded, "The Dalles of the Dead," on the upper Columbia. The final cause of the disaster, after the boat had struck a rock, and matters were in hand again, was a Mr. Wallace, an English botanist, who leaped up at a critical point, pulled off his coat and jumped overboard with his young wife. The boat lost its balance and upset. The list of dead was given by James Douglas in a letter to headquarters of the Hudson's Bay Company in London as follows:

```
Mr. & Mrs. Wallace          Botanists
Mr. Banks
Mr. Leblanc and his three children
Keneth [sic] McDonald                           in the
Fabien Vital                                    Comps
J. Bte. Laliberte                               Service
Two Children of Andre Chalifoux
```

This was dated November 7, 1838. No first names were given. Confer E.E. Rich, ed. *The Letters of John McLoughlin From Fort Vancouver To The Governor and Committee, First Series 1825-1838,* (London, 1941), p. 293.

30. Kowrach, *Blanchet Historical Sketches,* p. 50.

31. This historic ceremony took place near Kettle Falls, about ninety miles northwest of Spokane.

32. Kowrach, *Blanchet Historical Sketches,* p. 51.

33. *Ibid.,* p. 60. Blanchet is in error in calling Whitman a minister. Whitman was a medical doctor attached to the mission, which he directed.

34. *Ibid.,* p. 63. Their apartment had been vacated by the Reverend Beaver and his wife only three weeks earlier.

35. More will appear later about the foundation and names of these churches.

36. Lieutenant George Wilkes, U.S.N., Commander of an American expedition that explored the Northwest Coast in 1841. Edward Eberstadt and Sons, *The Northwest Coast,* (New York, 1941), p. 43.

37. Kowrach, *Blanchet Historical Sketches,* p. 63 seq.

38. The mission lasted from November 24 to April 15, 1839. Kowrach, *Blanchet Historical Sketches,* p. 73. Usually "missions" preached in parish churches, a kind of parish renewal, lasted for about one week or eight days.

39. *Ibid.,* p. 72.

40. *Ibid.,* p. 74.

41. *Ibid.,* p. 68. This appears in Demers's letter to Cazeau in Quebec, March 1, 1839. This same passage contains an excellent account of the Chinooks and a good description of their language and the Chinook jargon.

42. Blanchet and others used this number of four families. However, within a short time Blanchet referred to other families in the service of the H.B.C. He described Cowlitz as follows:

> The Cowlitz settlement has been five years in existence. It is on the west side of the river, in a prairie six miles long and two miles wide, bounded on the east by the river, on the west by a large quantity of timber. It is a very fine location for a colony. Its soil is rich and fertile; grass, fishing and game are in abundance. The situation is beautiful; in the northwest appears Mount Rainier, and Mount St. Helen on the east, whose high peak is always covered with snow. The Hudson Bay Co. has a farm there on which a large number of men are employed in farming on a large scale. The young colony was then composed of only four Canadian farmers, whom Dr. McLaughlin had discharged from further long services. The Cowlitz river runs from north to south and empties into the Columbia; it is very tortuous and full of snags, which renders its navigation difficult and dangerous, especially for small crafts, and by reason of its numerous rapids of dangerous ascent.

Kowrach, *Blanchet Historical Sketches,* p. 78.

43. This was Louis Henriette Peletier. Confer: Mikell DeLores Wormell Warner and Harriet Duncan Munnick, *Catholic Church Records of The Pacific Northwest Vancouver Volumes I and II and Stellamaris Mission,* (St. Paul [Oregon], 1972), A-66.

44. Francois Fagnant, Failland, and Faillant appear to be the same person who often served as godfather for baptisms in the region of Cowlitz Mission.

45. Kowrach, *Blanchet Historical Sketches,* p. 77.

46. *Ibid.,* p. 80.

47. *Ibid.*

48. One was an old Indian man, the other an Indian girl. *Ibid.,* 66. The "new cemetery" referred to here is not the present St. Paul Cemetery.

49. *Ibid.,* p. 81.

50. *Ibid.*, p. 84.

51. *Ibid.*, p. 83. Many versions of ladders are listed and describe in Philip M. Hanley, Doctoral dissertation, "The Catholic Ladder And Missionary Activity In The Pacific Northwest," University of Ottawa, 1965, Copy in Oregon Province Archives.

52. Nellie B. Pipes, "The Protestant Ladder," in the *Oregon Historical Quarterly*, XXXVII (1936) 237–240. In describing it to the Mission board, Spalding said, "Pope a sword in one hand and torch or fagot in the other, a king burning one foot and a bishop the other."

53. The Reverend D. Leslie succeeded in acquiring land in Nisqually and later departed leaving "Brother Wilson there to build a house for the mission. Wilson, a former sailor, was over his head in his competition with the priests.

54. Kowrach, *Blanchet Historical Sketches*, p. 84.

55. A biography, containing this Simpson comment, appears as follows: LeRoy R. Hafer, *The Mountain Men and The Far West*, 10 vols., Glendale, 1972, IX: 245–250. For Kitson [or Kittson] cf also: Warner and Munnich, *Catholic Church Records*, A-42-43. For Finan McDonald, Helene Kitson's father, cf the same, A-53.

56. Kowrach, *Blanchet Historical Sketches*, p. 86.

57. *Ibid.*, p. 87. The obscene book referred to here was Maria Monk's *Awful Disclosures of the Hotel Dieu Nunnery in Montreal*, 1836.

58. This brigade was from the Snake River country. The Montreal brigade arrived in late fall. The brigade of the South, from southern Oregon, arrived, usually, in mid-June. The priests were free to accompany any of them to serve the scattered Indian tribes.

59. Warner and Munnick, *Catholic Church Records*, A-55. Cuthbert Lambert, dit Robillard had been born in 1808. Later in 1846 he settled on French Prairie in Oregon.

60. Kowrach, *Blanchet Historical Sketches*, p. 89.

61. L.B. Palladino, S.J., *Indian and White In The Northwest A History of Catholicity in Montana, 1831 to 1891*, (Lancaster, 1922), p. 27.

62. *Ibid.*, p. 31.

63. The "long knives" were fur traders, only one of many terms with reference to them. Most fur traders had splendid knives coveted by the Indians.

64. Kowrach, *Blanchet Historical Sketches*, p. 91.

65. This is now Oregon City, a short distance southwest of Portland.

66. Edwin V. O'Hara, *Pioneer Catholic History of Oregon*, (Portland, 1911), p. 111.

Chapter 3. DESMET AND THE JESUITS

1. Blanchet became an American citizen. Demers, who was assigned to Canadian territory, retained his citizenship in that country.

2. DeSmet wrote many books that confirm this description. The two most important books explicitly about him are: E. Laveille, S.J., *The Life of Father DeSmet, S.J.*, authorized translation [from French] by Marian Lindsay, (New York, 1915); and Hiram Martin Chittenden and Alfred Talbot Richardson, *Life, Letters and Travels of Father Pierre-Jean DeSmet, S.J. 1801–1873*, 4 vols., (New York, 1905).

3. Photographs of him also indicate that on occasion he allowed his beard to grow. This was scruffy looking like General Grant's.

4. DeSmet returned to Europe to find his father's chair empty. Though no longer a Jesuit, DeSmet spent several years seeking support for the Indian missions. He finally returned to America and was readmitted to the Society on November 29, 1837. He remained a Jesuit until his death.

5. Laveille, *The Life of Father DeSmet, S.J.*, p. 105.

6. *Ibid.*, p. 107. Laveille states: "July 3d was a Sunday." This is incorrect. July 5th that year was a Friday. DeSmet offered Mass on Sunday.

7. Gilbert J. Garraghan, S.J., *The Jesuits of the Middle United States*, 3 vols, (New York, 1938), II:254 seq. Translated this is "Saint Ignatius Patron of the Mountains, on the 23rd of July, 1840."

8. L.B. Palladino, S.J., *Indian and White In The Northwest A History of Catholicity in Montana 1831 to 1891*, (Lancaster, 1922), p. 33. This poem in French is translated as follows:

Ye Rockies hail! Majestic Mounts
of future bliss the favored shrine
For You God's Heart Divine
Opens this day its precious founts.

9. *Ibid.*, p. 34.

10. *Ibid.*, p. 34. This letter appears in its entirety in Edward J. Kowrach, ed., *Historical Sketches of The Catholic Church In Oregon By Most Rev. Francis Norbert Blanchet*, (Fairfield, 1983), p. 41 seq.

11. Palladino, *Indian and White*, p. 98.

12. Garraghan, *Jesuits in the Middle United States*, II:255.

13. Kowrach, *Blanchet Historical Sketches*, p. 100.

14. *Ibid.*

15. *Ibid.*

16. *Ibid.*, p. 98. "Sokwamish" usually spelled Suquamish. This was Chief Seattle, of course.

17. *Ibid.* The Wilkes expedition was the first American naval expedition to the northwest coast. Charles Wilkes, U.S.N., *Narrative of the United States Exploring Expedition. During the Years 1838, 1839, 1840, 1841, 1842.* 5 vols., (Philadelphia, 1844).

18. *Ibid.*, p. 99.

19. Garraghan, *The Jesuits in the Middle United States*, II:274.

20. Sister Letitia Mary Lyons, M.A., *Francis Norbert Blanchet and The Founding of the Oregon Missions (1838-1848)*, (Washington, 1940), p. 50.

21. Garraghan, *The Jesuits in the Middle United States*, II:273. Blanchet specifically stated that the Reverend Beaver had blocked Company help to Catholic missionaries. He said he learned this from Simpson himself. Kowrach, *Blanchet Historical Sketches*, p. 110.

22. Garraghan, *The Jesuits of the Middle United States*, II:273 seq.

23. The Church in America, including its Jesuits, was not merely "different" from that in Europe, it was "revolutionary." A committee of Catholic priests wrote to Rome in 1783: "in these United States, our Religious system has undergone a revolution, if possible, more extraordinary, than our political one." Quoted in James Hennessey, S.J., *American Catholics A History of the Roman Catholic Community in the United States*, New York, 1981, 68. Complete religious freedom, unknown in Europe, was a difference that created disputes among Catholics for decades.

24. Joseph P. Donnelly, S.J., ed. *Wilderness Kingdom Indian Life in the Rocky Mountains: 1840-1847 The Journals and Painting of Nicolas Point, S.J.*, (New York, 1967), p. 6.

25. Fitzpatrick had been a fur trader and trapper for some years. He acquired his Indian name by losing a finger when a gun exploded.

26. Gilbert J. Garraghan, S.J., *Chapters in Frontier History*, (Milwaukee, 1934), p. 139-140. There are many accounts of this journey, including Gregory Mengarini's "Memories of the Rocky Mountain Mission" found in manuscript in the Oregon Province Archives.

27. Bidwell's group had selected California as their destiny. They parted from the Jesuits at Soda Springs, Idaho, and passed through the deserts of Utah and Nevada into northern California. Confer John Bidwell, "The First Immigrant Train to California," *The Century Illustrated Monthly Magazine*, XLI (Nov. 1890), p. 103-106.

28. Laveille, *The Life of Father DeSmet, S.J.*, p. 126 seq.

29. For example: Mengarini's Flathead grammar: Gregory Mengarini, S.J., *A Salish or Flathead Grammar*, (New York, 1861), and Gloria Ricci Lathrop, ed., *Recollections of the Flathead Mission Containing Brief Observations both Ancient and Contemporary Concerning This Particular Nation by Fr. Gregory Mengarini, S.J.*, (Glendale, 1977).

30. The usual route from St. Mary's to Fort Colville was as follows: north through the Bitteroot Valley to present Missoula, then up the Evaro grade northwest of Missoula to the valley into present Ravalli, west along the Clark Fork River to Lake Pend Oreille river to present Usk, across the Flowery Trail from Usk to present Chewelah, then up the Colville Valley to Kettle Falls on the Columbia, where Fort Colville was located.

31. Laveille, *The Life of Father DeSmet, S.J.*, p. 140.

32. *Ibid.*, p. 130. DeSmet's letter to Verhaegen on December 30, 1841, was somewhat pretentious. God's name had been made known by the Christian Iroquois at least twenty years earlier.

33. Kowrach, *Blanchet Historical Sketches*, p. 105. Blanchet called the Protestant Ladder the Evangelical Ladder.

34. Pambrun died on May 15, 1841. He left his widow Kitty, five sons and four daughters, all of whom moved to Vancouver after the tragedy.

35. Kitson was about forty-eight years old, but he had been ill for over a year. He died "of a long and painful malady," of which there is no specific diagnosis extant.

36. DeSmet's estimate of the population in the Northwest included Vancouver Island and other parts of Canada, where there were far more Indians than in the four (later) northwestern states. Sister Letitia Mary Lyons, *Blanchet Historical Sketches*, p. 102 seq., presents estimates of numbers by various travelers.

37. The letter was dated September 28, 1841. Confer: P.J. DeSmet, S.J., *Letters and Sketches with a Narrative of a Year's Residence Among the Indian Tribes of the Rocky Mountains*, (Philadelphia, 1843), p. 229 seq.

38. Chittenden and Richardson, *Life, Letters and Travels*, IV·1555.

39. Edwin V. O'Hara, *Pioneer Catholic History of Oregon*, (Portland, 1911), p. 97.

40. Laveille, *The Life of Father DeSmet*, p. 135.

41. Blanchet's new home at St. Paul was 62 feet by 25 feet. The Cowlitz Church was still unfinished in August 1842 when Blanchet was there. Kowrach, *Blanchet Historical Sketches*, p. 110.

42. Laveille, *The Life of Father DeSmet*, p. 142.

43. *Ibid.*, p. 144.

44. *Ibid.*, p. 145.

45. Kowrach, *Blanchet Historical Sketches*, p. 109.

46. *Ibid.*

47. Blanchet's bills had been accumulating and McLoughlin, despite his great friendliness and service to the church, professed "company policy" and charged six per cent interest for unpaid bills.

48. Garraghan, *The Jesuits in the Middle United States*, II:277.

49. *Ibid.*, p. 353 footnotes.

50. DeSmet traveled over land through Blackfeet and Crow territory to Fort Union on the Missouri River, thence by boat to St. Louis.

51. Kowrach, *Blanchet Historical Sketches*, p. 110.

52. Antoine Langlois was born in 1812 and was ordained in Quebec in 1838. He remained in Oregon until 1854 when he went to California. He returned to Canada in 1859.

53. John Baptist Bolduc was born in 1818 and was ordained in 1841. He returned to Canada in 1850.

54. Kowrach, *Blanchet Historical Sketches*, p. 110. Blanchet, I'm sure, intended no pejorative difference between the "ladies" of the fort and the "women" of the village.

55. *Ibid.*, p. 75.

56. Felix Hathaway was an employee of the Methodist Mission. Bancroft, *History of Oregon,* I:204 seq. Bancroft presents a detailed account of the land case.

57. O'Hara, *Pioneer Catholic History of Oregon,* p. 112.

58. *Ibid.*, p. 113.

59. Fuller, p. 132. The missions to be closed were Waiilatpu and Lapwai. Only Tshimakain of the Spokanes was to be retained.

60. Many books have been written in support of the "Whitman Saved Oregon" story. All of them, without exception, have been completely discredited. The classic work on the subject is William I. Marshall's *Acquisition of Oregon and the Long Suppressed Evidence about Marcus Whitman,* 2 vols. (Seattle, 1911). Marshall's work is like a sledge hammer used to kill mosquitoes.

61. Not only was the Santa Fe Trail longer, but it passed through high altitude country with deep winter snow.

62. He arrived in St. Louis in October.

63. His first book: P.J. DeSmet, S.J., *Letters and Sketches with a Narrative of a Year's Residence Among The Indian Tribes of The Rocky Mountains,* (Philadelphia, 1843).

64. Garraghan, *The Jesuits of the Middle United States,* II:290.

65. *Ibid.*, II:291.

66. *Ibid.*, II:291.

67. O'Hara, *The Pioneer Catholic History of Oregon,* p. 79.

68. A lengthy history of this missions' beginnings appears in Wilfred P. Schoenberg, S.J., *Jesuit Mission Presses,* (Portland, 1957), p. 49 seq.

69. For a brief time, 1843–1849 (as noted in the text later) the Coeur d'Alene Mission on the river was called "St. Joseph."

70. This was on the St. Joe River site. A photograph, allegedly related to this first mission, has appeared in publication. For example: [George W. Weibel, S.J.], *Gonzaga's Silver Jubilee a Memoir,* (Spokane, 1912), p. 23. This first mission was never photographed, not even in the state of ruin.

71. The Indian camp was located where the Spokane River flows out of Lake Coeur d'Alene, presently the campus of the College of North Idaho.

72. For example Blanchet lists "four missions at the Rocky Mountains" in 1843. Among these the Coeur d'Alene mission was listed as "St. Joseph." Kowrach *Blanchet Historical Sketches,* p. 122.

73. *Ibid.*, p. 112.

74. *Ibid.*

75. *Ibid.*

76. *Ibid.*, p. 113.

77. *Ibid.*, p. 114.

78. It was about this time, on September 25, 1843, that Bishop Rosati died in Rome.

Chapter 4. AN ARCHBISHOP FOR OREGON

1. Gilbert J. Garraghan, S.J., *The Jesuits in The Middle United States,* 3 vols., (New York, 1938), II:278.

2. Sister Letitia Mary Lyons, S.H.N., *Francis Norbert Blanchet and The Founding of The Oregon Missions (1848–1948),* (Washington, 1940), p. 141.

3. *Ibid.*, p. 131.

4. *Ibid.*, p. 141. Letter of Signay to Blanchet, April 17, 1841. The correct name is Bishop Stephen Rouchouze Nicopolis.

5. *Ibid.*, p. 141.

6. *Ibid.*

7. *Ibid.*

8. Peter Kenrick at this time, Coadjutor to Rosati, was Titular Bishop of Drasa. On Rosati's death in 1843, Kenrick became Bishop of St. Louis and his title of Drasa became vacant. The Council referred to here was the Second Plenary Council of Baltimore.

9. Garraghan, *The Jesuits in The Middle United States,* II:279.

10. *Ibid.*

11. *Ibid.*, I:519-524. Archbishop Kenrick eventually became a most coridal friend of the Jesuits.

12. Garraghan, *Blanchet Historical Sketches,* II:280.

13. *Ibid.*

14. Lyons, *Francis Norbert Blanchet,* 146, footnote.

15. DeSmet had 120,000 francs in cash.

16. The ship DeSmet chartered has been called the *Infatigable* and the *Indefatigable*. Most historians like Laveille and Garraghan use the former, which is the English form. Bancroft uses the latter, the French form, which undoubtedly appeared on the ship.

17. Garraghan, *The Jesuits in The Middle United States,* II:281.

18. Lyons, *Francis Norbert Blanchet,* p. 147.

19. *Ibid.*, p. 149.

20. Garraghan, *The Jesuits in The Middle United States,* II:283.

21. E. Laveille, S.J., *The Life of Father DeSmet, S.J., (1801-1873),* (New York, 1915), p. 158.

22. Clarence B. Bagley, ed., *Early Catholic Missions in Old Oregon, Volume Two Containing Sketch of the Territory of Oregon and Its Missions followed by Several Letters of the Sisters of Notre Dame Established at St. Paul on the Willamette,* (Seattle, 1932). An excellent account of these sisters and their voyage is [A Sister of Notre Dame] *In Harvest Fields By Sunset Shores, The Work of The Sisters of Notre Dame on The Pacific Coast,* (San Francisco, 1926).

23. A photograph of Birnie appears in Michell DeLores Wormell Warner and Harriet Duncan Munnick, *Catholic Church Records of the Pacific Northwest Vancouver Volumes I and II and Stellamaris Mission,* (Portland, 1972), I-5. A brief biography appears on A-8.

24. Lyons, *Francis Norbert Blanchet,* p. 151.

25. Edward J. Kowrach, ed., *Historical Sketches of the Catholic Church In Oregon by Most Rev. Francis Norbert Blanchet,* (Fairfield [Washington], 1983), p. 117.

26. Garraghan, *The Jesuits in The Middle United States,* II:296.

27. Kowrach, *Blanchet Historical Sketches,* p. 117.

28. Hubert Howe Bancroft, *The Works of Hubert H. Bancroft,* 29 vols., *History of Oregon,* (San Francisco, 1886), I:224.

29. Garraghan, *The Jesuits in The Middle United States,* II:297.

30. *Ibid.*

31. There is some dispute about the exact day on which DeSmet left the Willamette. Garraghan, *The Jesuits in The Middle United States,* II:298, gives October 3. Blanchet says he left on October 6, which was Holy Rosary Sunday, an unlikely time. Kowrach, *Blanchet Historical Sketches,* p. 118.

32. The buhrstones, used in the erection of the flour mill, had been presented to Ravalli by a Mr. McCoy in Antwerp. L.B. Palladino, S.J., *Indian and White In The Northwest,* (Lancaster, 1922), p. 59.

33. Soderini had remained behind. Later he came west, applied to Blanchet for incardination into the Oregon Mission and was rejected. He later left the Jesuit Order in Rome.

34. Garraghan, *The Jesuits in The Middle United States,* II:295.

35. Zerbinatti drowned on September 15, 1845. Magri died at Lewiston, Idaho on June 18, 1869. Palladino has an interesting account of an Indian many miles distant seeing Magri going to heaven in a chariot. Palladino, *Indian and White In The Northwest*, p. 181 seq. Joset died, where he wanted to die, at the Coeur d'Alene mission on June 19, 1900.

36. Lyons, *Francis Norbert Blanchet*, 150. Blanchet was only 44 years old.

37. *Ibid.*, p. 151.

38. Kowrach, *Blanchet Historical Sketches*, p. 118. Though Blanchet was first appointed Titular Bishop of Philadelphia, Rome changed it to Drasa when possible confusion with the Pennsylvania diocese was pointed out. It should be noted that the titular see of Drasa was held by Bishop Peter Kenrick until Rosati's death in 1843, thus Drasa was opened for Blanchet.

39. Father Reginald Yzendoorn, SS.CC., *History of the Catholic Mission in the Hawaiian Islands*, (Honolulu, 1927), p. 153. Yzendoorn presents a quaint little epilogue worthy of the best tradition in the Martyrology.

> The last time anything was heard from the vessel was from the Island of St. Catherine, off the Brazilian coast, under date of February 11, 1843. There the party landed to bury one of the sisters and the young native.
>
> Recently it has been stated that on the Marshall Islands a tradition exists concerning the arrival of a French vessel having on board a bishop, priests and sisters. The passengers would have come ashore and approached the natives with various demonstrations of friendship, which were met with a rain of arrows. The captain wanted to repell the attack by a fusillade but the Bishop forbade him, saying: 'We would kill them uselessly; this were not fitting for missionaries who come to bring these people a message of peace.' They then knelt down in prayer and were massacred, the captain and his sailors escaping, it is thought in a boat.

40. This is given in Lyons, *Francis Norbert Blanchet*, p. 155seq.

41. Blanchet states that Demers was appointed vicar general and administrator of the vicariate by letters of November 25. But in his pastoral letter found above, he explicitly names DeVos as administrator. This conflict is readily resolved. DeVos was first appointed. Before Blanchet departed, however DeVos pointed out that Jesuits were excluded by rule from ecclesiastical offices. Blanchet accepted his resignation and appointed Demers. *Ibid.*, p. 156.

42. "Christian" for Blanchet meant Catholic. His statistics did not include Protestants, who were also Christians.

43. Kowrach, *Blanchet Historical Sketches*, p. 122.

44. Hiram Martin Chittenden and Albert Talbot Richardson, *Life, Letters and Travels of Pierre-Jean DeSmet, S.J.*, 4 vols., (New York, 1938), II:482.

45. This first St. Michael's was on the Pend Oreille River. It was never completed.

46. Laveille, *The Life of Father DeSmet, S.J.*, p. 164. The exact location of this site is one of the mysteries of mission history. There is further discussion on the various sites of the Kalispel mission in Wilfred P. Schoenberg, S.J., *Paths To The Northwest*, (Chicago, 1982), p. 36.

47. Near present Newport, Washington.

48. Chittenden and Richardson, *Life, Letters and Travels*, II:468.

49. *Ibid.*, II:474.

50. Maria Laach Benedictine Monastery in Germany was an influential center of learning and culture for centuries.

51. Garraghan, *The Jesuits in The Middle United States*, II:286.

52. Lyons, *Francis Norbert Blanchet*, p. 157.

53. *Ibid.*

54. St. Louis Archdiocese with Peter Kenrick as its first archbishop was established in 1847. Kenrick's official title was Titular Archbishop of Marionapolis.

55. Kowrach, *Blanchet Historical Sketches*, p. 126.

56. *Ibid.*, p. 123.

57. *Ibid.*

58. This famous case will be presented later.

59. An extract of the most interesting parts of the *Memoriale* appears in Carl Landholm, ed., *Notices and Voyages of the Famed Quebec Mission to the Pacific Northwest*, (Portland, 1956), p. 212 seq.

60. Garraghan, *The Jesuits in The Middle United States*, II:287.

61. George W. Fuller, *A History of The Pacific Northwest*, (New York, 1931), p. 176 seq.

62. Lyons, *Francis Norbert Blanchet*, p. 163.

63. *Ibid.*, p. 164.

64. The orders were, in a sense, the right arm of Rome, a counter balance in the event a local ordinary opposed Rome's authority.

65. Kowrach, *Blanchet Historical Sketches*, p. 122.

66. Lyons, *Francis Norbert Blanchet*, p. 183.

67. *Ibid.*

68. Blanchet and Demers had unlimited credit at the Hudson's Bay Company. By this time their indebtedness had reached about $50,000 in current gold.

69. This site was just north of the present Chewelah, Washington.

70. Chittenden and Richardson, *Life, Letters and Travels*, II:483.

71. Details appear in Wilfred P. Schoenberg, S.J., *Jesuit Mission Presses*, 1957, p. 52 seq.

72. Present Old Mission or Cataldo Mission near Cataldo, Idaho. This is now an Idaho State Park.

73. Garraghan, *The Jesuits in The Middle United States*, II:307.

74. Palladino, *Indian and White*, p. 59 seq. The grist mill was in operation by May 1845.

75. Garraghan, *The Jesuits in The Middle United States*, II:270.

76. Prior to this, wheat was boiled or baked before it was used. Flour for hosts had to be imported from Fort Vancouver.

77. Laveille, *The Life of Father DeSmet, S.J.*, p. 197.

78. Joseph P. Donnelly, S.J., ed. *Wilderness Kingdom Indian Life In The Rocky Mountains 1840–1847 The Journal and Paintings of Nicolas Point, S.J.*, (New York, 1867), p. 8 seq. These baptismal records were sent to the general's archives in Rome.

79. In a sense this ship was not "chartered." Blanchet paid the freight costs and the passage money for himself, the sisters, the secular priests, and the seminarians. The six Jesuits paid for their own passage, 1600 francs per person. Lyons, *Francis Norbert Blanchet*, p. 169.

80. *Ibid.*, 128.

81. The names of the sisters were as follows: Sisters Lawrence, Mary Bernard, Renilde, Odelie, Aldegonde, and Francesa. The names of the Jesuit brothers, which Blanchet omitted, were: Natalis Savio, Aloysius Bellomo and Marcarius Marchetti.

82. Kowrach, *Blanchet Historical Sketches*, p. 128.

83. Two of the Jesuit brothers left the Order after their arrival in Oregon, Aloysius Bellomo and Macarius Marchetti. After their departure from the Order, they disappeared from the scene. Blanchet's contingent of diocesan priests and seminarians also fared badly. Several left the Northwest and two, despite Blanchet's noisy objections, joined religious orders, Veyret the Jesuits and Jayol the Oblates.

84. "Bishop-elect" was Blanchet's expression. *Ibid.*

Chapter 5. STORM CLOUDS OVER OREGON

1. He was born on August 23, 1797.

2. This was Bishop Charles Joseph Eugene de Mazenod, founder of the Oblates. An account of de Mazenod and the Oregon Missions appears in Msgr. Jean Leflon, *Eugene de Mazenod, Eveque de Marseille Fondateur des Missionaries Oblats de Marie Immaculee 1728–1861,* ([N.P.], 1965), p. 175 et seq.

3. The Oblates actually embarked from Le Havre on February 4, 1847, on the *Zuric.* Rev. Father George M. Waggett, "The Oblates of Mary Immaculate in the Pacific Northwest of U.S.A. 1847–1878," *Etudes Oblates,* 6(1947), p. 20.

4. Sister Letitia Mary Lyons, SNJM, *Francis Norbert Blanchet and the Founding of The Oregon Missions 1838–1848,* (Washington, 1940), p. 180. A louis was a French gold coin worth 20 francs, $3.80 in current pre-Civil War money.

5. The two students were Louis Rousseau, a deacon, and William Leclair.

6. Edward Kowrach, ed., *Rt. Rev. A.M.A. Blanchet, Journal of A Catholic Bishop On The Oregon Trail The Overland Crossing of The Rt. Rev. A.M.A. Blanchet, Bishop of Walla Walla, From Montreal to Oregon Territory, March 23, 1847 to January 23, 1851,* (Fairfield, 1978).

7. Kowrach, *Blanchet Journal,* p. 24.

8. *Ibid.,* p. 26.

9. That is, sitting on deck chairs. *Ibid.,* p. 28.

10. *Ibid.,* p. 29. It should be noted perhaps that the Bishop of Pittsburgh, referred to here, was Bishop Michael J. O'Connor, who resigned his see in 1860 and entered the Jesuit Order, in which he served for twelve years. He died at Woodstock, Maryland on October 18, 1872.

11. *Ibid.,* p. 31.

12. Kay Cronin, *Cross in The Wilderness,* (Vancouver, B.C., 1960), p. 5.

13. Kowrach, *Blanchet Journal,* p. 35.

14. *Ibid.,* p. 41.

15. *Ibid.,* p. 50.

16. Jansenism, named for Cornelius Otto Jansen, usually seen in the Latin form Jansenius, was a system of theology involving divine grace and human freedom. It presented a harsh image of God, and tended to create stern, unforgiving Catholics, like the New England Puritans of the 17th century. Jansenism appeared in France, the Low Countries, and Italy in the 17th and 18th centuries and in Ireland later, because many Irish priests were educated in these countries.

17. According to Blanchet, the oxen traveled about two miles per hour.

18. McBean, like Pambrun, deserves to be remembered for his assistance to the missionaries and his zeal in teaching catechism.

19. Lyons, *Francis Norbert Blanchet,* p. 180 et seq.

20. Clarence B. Bagley, ed., *Early Catholic Missions in Old Oregon,* Volume One containing *The Very Rev. J.B.A. Brouillet, Authentic Account of The Murder of Dr. Whitman By The Cayuse Indians of Oregon, In 1847, and the causes which led to that horrible catastrophe,* (Seattle, 1932), p. 188.

21. According to Archbishop Blanchet, 197 Indians died that winter. Edward J. Kowrach, ed., *Historical Sketches Of The Catholic Church In Oregon By the Most Rev. Francis Norbert Blanchet,* (Fairfield, 1983), p. 132.

22. "Yellow Chief" was designated as "Chief of the Yakimas," though other chiefs had followings. Waggett, "The Oblates of Mary Immaculate," p. 21.

23. Ricard's letter of May 4, 1848, to Joset, in The Society of Jesus Archives, Rome, *Montes Saxosi,* 2-II-11a.

24. Kowrach, *Blanchet Historical Sketches,* p. 76.

25. *Ibid.,* p. 139 et seq.

26. For some inexplicable reason, A.M.A. Blanchet did not realize the necessity of his presence at St. Paul on November 30. He was determined to organize Walla Walla. Had he attended Demers' consecration, he would have missed some of the blame for what happened, following the Whitman Massacre.

27. Waggett, "The Oblates of Mary Immaculate," p. 21.

28. *Ibid.*, p. 22.

29. This has been referred to above. There are many editions most of them in the Oregon Province Archives.

30. This letter was dated Fort Walla Walla, March 2, 1848. It is presented in full in William I. Marshall, *The Acquisition of Oregon and The Long Suppressed Evidence About Marcus Whitman,* 2 vols., (Seattle, 1911), II:212 et seq.

31. The Lapwai Mission site is on the Clearwater River, twelve miles east of present Lewiston, Idaho. Spalding's grave is in the mission cemetery now part of the Nez Perce National Park.

32. Marshall, *The Acquisition of Oregon,* II:217.

33. *Ibid.*, II:216 et seq.

34. This Council was on December 23, 1847.

35. George W. Fuller, *History of The Pacific Northwest,* (New York, 1931), p. 153.

36. Armed forces left Vancouver shortly after Ogden's departure. They remained at The Dalles to protect the Protestant mission there. *Ibid.*, p. 153.

37. Waggett, "The Oblates of Mary Immaculate," p. 25.

38. The number of prisoners at Waiilatpu was 51. Those at Lapwai were 11. Kowrach, *Blanchet Historical Sketches,* p. 134.

39. Fuller, *History of The Pacific Northwest,* p. 154.

40. *Ibid.*

41. Clifford Merrill Drury, *Henry Harmon Spalding,* (Caldwell, 1936), . 358 et seq.

42. Marshall, *Acquisition of Oregon,* II:210.

43. The sruggle has been very bitter, and as late as 1917 when the following, very biased account was published: Eliza Spalding Warren, *Memoirs of The West The Spaldings,* (Portland, [1917]).

44. Edwin V. O'Hara gives a detailed account of the causes of the massacre in *Pioneer Catholic History of Oregon,* (Portland, 1911), p. 145 et seq.

45. Waren, *Memoirs of The West,* p. 129 et seq.

46. Kowrach, *Blanchet Historical Sketches,* p. 136.

47. Waggett, "Oblates of Mary Immaculate," p. 24–25.

48. Kowrach, *Blanchet Historical Sketches,* p. 135.

49. They arrived at St. Paul on January 15, 1848.

50. General of The Society of Jesus Archives in Rome, Ricard's letter to Joset, May 4, 1848. *Montes Saxosi,* 2–II–11a. The bishops insisted that money received by the Oblates and not used in the missions should be turned over to them. This does not appear to be unreasonable.

51. Bishop Blanchet arrived at St. Paul on January 15, 1848.

52. Kowrach, *Blanchet Historical Sketches,* p. 130.

53. *Ibid.*, p. 139.

54. *Decreta Concilii Provincialis Oregoniensis I. Sancti Pauli Habiti, Diebus 28–29 Februarii et 1 Martii 1848. Necnon et Kalendariun Romanum cum Officiis Provinciae Oregonensis a Sancta Sede Concessis,* (Portland, 1855), p. 3. Copy in the Oregon Province Archives.

55. *Ibid.*, p. 5.

56. John P. Marschall, "Diocesan and Religious Clergy: The History of a Relationship," in John Tracy Ellis, ed., *The Catholic Priest in The United States.* (Collegeville, 1974), p. 401.

57. Noted above, footnote number 54.

58. Waggett, "Oblates of Mary Immaculate," p. 29.

59. Later it was known as "St. Joseph of Olympia."

60. Archives of the Archdiocese of Portland, Blanchet correspondence. Book I, p. 116.

61. This is in accordance with F.X.N. Blanchet's account (Kowrach, *Blanchet Historical Sketches*, p. 139). Actually, it is an over-simplification. Father Rosseau had preceded the arrival of Bishop Blanchet at The Dalles by several weeks, having arrived, to live there, on May 16, 1848. When Blanchet came, there was a log church and rectory.

62. The ship went down on May 8, 1848. Hubert Howe Bancroft, *History of Oregon*, 2 vols., (San Francisco, 1886), II:23.

63. Waggett, "Oblates of Mary Immaculate," p. 29.

64. [George F. Weibel, S.J.], "Fifty Years of Peaceful Conquest," in *Gonzaga* (1913–1914), p. 127.

65. Gilbert J. Garraghan, S.J., *The Jesuits of the Middle United States*, 3 vols., (New York, 1938), II:346.

66. Fuller, *History of The Pacific Northwest*, p. 364, note 20, provides Gilliam's background.

67. Kowrach, *Blanchet Historical Sketches*, p. 137.

68. [Aegidius Junger], *Claim of The Mission of St. James, Vancouver, Washington Territory, to 460 Acres of Land*, ([N.P., N.D.]), p. 1.

69. Father Honore Lempfrit left for Victoria on March 2, 1849. Note that Blanchet calls him "Father Lampfrit, O.M.I." Kowrach, *Blanchet Historical Sketches*, p. 139. Lempfrit, who left the Oblates, became a kind of non-person in the history of the church in Victoria. Mention only appears in P.P. Morice, O.M.I., *Historie De L'Eglise Catholique Dans L'Ouert Canadien Du Lac Superieur au Pacific (1659–1915)*, 4 vols., (Montreal, 1923), IV:207.

70. This dictionary was acquired by the Smithsonian Institution in Washington. It was published in 1853. Mikell De Lores Wormell Warner and Harriet Duncan Munnick, *Catholic Church Records of The Pacific Northwest Vancouver Volumes I and II and Stellamaris Mission*, (St. Paul [Oregon], 1972), p. A-49.

71. Kowrach, *Blanchet Historical Sketches*, p. 139.

72. Joseph W. Riordan, S.J., *The First Half Century of St. Ignatius Church and College*, (San Francisco, 1905), p. 18.

73. *Ibid.*, p. 19.

74. Kowrach, *Blanchet Historical Sketches*, p. 140.

75. An article by John Bernard McGloin, S.J., presents details of Nobili's New Caledonia years: "John Nobili, S.J., Founder of California's Santa Clara College: The New Caledonia Years, 1845–1848," in *British Columbia Historical Quarterly*, 17(1953), p. 253 et seq.

76. Oregon Province Archives, Joset Papers, Mss. "Joset."

77. DeVos lasted only four years. Burned out at the age of fifty-three, he was sent to California to recover in 1851.

78. Named Lake Roothaan by DeSmet, this lake was called Blackrobe Lake by the Indians who could not pronounce "Roothaan." Later railroad schedules influenced another name change by listing Blackrobe River, which came out of the lake, as Priest River. The lake is now known as Priest Lake, one of the most beautiful in America.

79. Garraghan, *The Jesuits in The Middle United States*, II:375 et seq.

80. The Jesuit debt was $6,000.

81. Accolti learned of his appointment accidentally in San Francisco in March 1850. He returned to Oregon in July.

82. Nobili died on March 4, 1856 from the effects of his hardship in New Caledonia.

83. Eventually the archbishop replaced Accolti on the Mission of the Yamhill with Father Patrick McCormick, a secular priest from Dublin.

84. Bishop Demers complained to Rome that "... he [Accolti] has such dislike for Oregon in general that he cannot refrain from expressing it on every occasion." Wilfred P. Schoenberg, *Paths To The Northwest, A Jesuit History of The Oregon Province*, (Chicago, 1982), p. 56.

85. John P. Marschall, "Diocesan and Religious Clergy," p. 402.

86. *Ibid.*

87. Spalding requested to see these Indians, but they refused to meet him or pray with him. Kowrach, *Blanchet Historical Sketches*, p. 140.

88. *Ibid.*, p. 141. The use of Nesqually, rather than Nisqually, the original spelling of the word, had been adopted by the missionaries and was retained in the documents from Rome.

89. The Walla Walla diocese was suppressed by a papal brief on July 29, 1853.

90. Thus the Nesqually Diocese, later changed to Seattle, covered approximately the same territory as the present archdiocese of Seattle, western Washington.

91. Bishop Miege was consecrated on March 25, 1851. He resigned from the vicariate on November 8, 1874 and retired to Woodstock College in Maryland, to serve as a counselor for young Jesuits. He died on July 21, 1884.

92. Garraghan, *The Jesuits in The Middle United States*, II:385.

93. *Ibid.*, p. 379. Nobili had visited the mission before leaving for California.

94. Father Nicholas Congiato, who succeeded Accolti as superior of the Jesuits in the Northwest, attributed closure of St. Mary's to Jesuit failings. "From the lack of zeal and love of the Indians and of tact on the part of Ours resulted the fall of the famous mission of the Flatheads." *Ibid.*, II.386. Congiato, having the advantage of being on the scene, wrote this in 1851. In my opinion, this is not an objective judgment, for the Jesuits at St. Mary's, whatever their faults, were like saints. Congiato as superior, lived in California, rarely visited an Indian mission and never lived in one.

95. O'Hara, *Pioneer Catholic History*, p. 113. A classic work on this subject is Frederick V. Holman, *Dr. John McLoughlin The Father of Oregon*, (Cleveland, 1907).

96. O'Hara, *Pioneer Catholic History*, p. 114.

97. Many testimonies to McLoughlin's nobility appear in Holman, *Dr. John McLoughlin*, p. 159 et seq.

98. O'Hara, *Pioneer Catholic History*, p. 118.

99. *Ibid.*, p. 118.

100. This was taken in 1856. He died one year later. In Holman, *Dr. John McLoughlin*, frontispiece, there appears an excellent reproduction of a daguerreotype made in 1856.

101. O'Hara, *Pioneer Catholic History*, p. 118.

Chapter 6. SISTERS COME TO STAY

1. The classic work on the subject of Fort Vancouver is John Hussey, *The History of Fort Vancouver and Its Physical Structure*, (Tacoma, 1957), p. 180. This excellent volume presents many photographs, sketches, and maps.

2. Henry G. Alsberg, ed., *The American Guide A Source Book and Complete Travel Guide for the United States*, (New York, 1949), p. 1236.

3. Bishop A.M.A. wrote in his diary for March 17, 1849: "It has been reported these last days that almost all Canadians at Fort Vancouver had departed for California." Edward J. Kowrach, ed., *Journal of a Catholic Bishop On The Oregon Trail, The Overland Crossing of the Rt. Rev. A.M.A. Blanchet, Bishop of Walla Walla from Montreal to Oregon Territory, March 23, 1847 to January 23, 1851*, (Fairfield, 1978), p. 107.

4. Kowrach, *Journal*, p. 116.

5. Hussey, *The History of Fort Vancouver*, p. 179.

6. *Ibid.*, p. 179.

7. *Ibid.*, p. 209.

8. Hussey noted that the fence had not been built, meaning I assume, when the church was completed. The fence was installed later.

9. This refers to a small vestry that had been constructed about the same time as the church. This vestry was rarely occupied until 1851.

10. Hussey, *The History of Fort Vancouver*, p. 209 et seq. M. Leona Nichols, *The Mantle of Elias The Story of Fathers Blanchet and Demers in Early Oregon*, (Portland, 1941), p. 280. This gives May 30, 1846 as the date for the dedication. Hussey corrects this.

11. Hussey, *The History of Fort Vancouver*, p. 181. Louis Rossi gives a most unflattering description of Bishop Blanchet's house: W. Victor Wortley, ed., *Six Years on the West Coast of America 1856–1862*, (Fairfield, 1983), p. 81.

12. Kowrach, *Journal*, p. 116.

13. Brouillet, it will be recalled, belonged to Augustine Blanchet's diocese. There is some mystery here. It was undoubtedly the archbishop who recalled him and appointed him vicar general of the Oregon City archdiocese.

14. Kowrach, *Journal*, p. 144.

15. The attitude of easterners has been expressed very aptly by Archbishop John Hughes of New York, when he returned from Europe in 1862: "There is no love for the United States on the other side of the water. Generally speaking on the other side of the Atlantic, the United States are ignored, if not despised—treated in conversation in the same contemptuous language as we might employ towards the inhabitants of the Sandwich Islands, or the Washington Territory, or Vancouvers Island or the settlement of the Red River or of the Hudson's Bay Company Territory." Quoted in: James Hennessey, S.J., *American Catholics A History of the Roman Catholic Community in The United States*, (New York, 1981), p. 150.

16. The Jesuits had orders from Rome to *sell* the Willamette property in 1854. This was very difficult to do in an area where thousands of acres of free land were still available. However, Father Urban Grassi sold the property on September 26, 1868, for six thousand dollars. The buyers were the three Niebler brothers and Michael Schultheis, about whom much will be said later.

17. Sister M. Dominica McNamee S.N.D. de N., *Willamette Interlude*, (Palo Alto, 1959), p. 254.

18. Edwin V. O'Hara, *Pioneer Catholic History of Oregon*, (Portland, 1911), p. 130.

19. Sister Mary of the Blessed Sacrament McCrosson, *The Bell and The River*, (Palo Alto, 1957), p. 79.

20. Mother M. Antoinette, F.C.S.P., *The Institute of Providence: History of The Daughters of Charity Servants of the Poor Known as The Sisters of Providence*, 6 vols. (Montreal, 1937–1949), III:22 et seq.

21. *Ibid.*, III:77.

22. O'Hara, *Pioneer Catholic History*, p. 162.

23. At this time, Sacred Heart Mission was located on Joset's Knoll, on the Coeur d'Alene River. It was moved again twice, in February 1877 to *Nilgo—Alko* [Hole in the Woods], and again in 1878 to the present site at DeSmet, Idaho. Wilfred P. Schoenberg, S.J., *Jesuit Mission Presses in The Pacific Northwest: A History and a Bibliography of Imprints 1876–1899*, (Portland, 1957), p. 54 et seq.

24. Later called St. Mary's.

25. When St. Joseph's on Attanum Creek was established, the St. Joseph Mission at Aleskecas was abandoned.

26. George M. Waggett. O.M.I., "The Oblates of Mary Immaculate in The Pacific Northwest of U.S.A. 1847–1878," in *Etudes Oblates*, 6(1947), p. 27.

27. *Ibid.*

28. *Ibid.*, p. 31.

29. Father James Croke arrived in autumn 1851.

30. The Jesuits in San Francisco regarded Croke as the leader of the opposition to them. Croke's comments about Jesuits, it must be admitted, were less than flattering. The Marschall presentation of this and other similar disputes appears to me to be very one sided. John P. Marschall, "Diocesan and Religious Clergy: The History of a Relationship 1789-1969," in John Tracy Ellis, *The Catholic Priest in The United States*, (Collegeville, 1971), p. 392.

31. *Ibid.*, p. 393.

32. *Ibid.*, p. 394. It should be noted that during this period in American church history, the pre-Vatican I period, many bishops, and even some pastors, conducted themselves rather arbitrarily and resented the presence of exempt religious who were identified with papal jurisdiction within the dioceses. On the other hand, the ever present question before the bishops was: "Who has control in this diocese?" *Ibid.*, p. 400.

33. *Ibid.*

34. *Ibid.*

35. Theoretically, Veyret was sent to Santa Clara to complete his novitiate. Confer Bryan J. Clinch, "The Jesuits in American California" in *Records of The American Catholic Historical Society of Philadelphia*, XVII(1906), p. 454. None of these three Jesuits returned to the Northwest.

36. Marschall, "Diocesan and Religious Clergy," p. 394.

37. George W. Fuller, *A History of The Pacific Northwest*, (New York, 1931), p. 206.

38. Archives of the Archdiocese of Portland in Oregon. Blanchet Correspondence Book I:268.

39. O'Hara, *Pioneer Catholic History*, p. 166.

40. He was succeeded at Astoria by Father Patrick McCormick. Cyril Van der Donckt, "The Founders of the Church in Idaho," *The Ecclesiastical Review*, XXXII(1905), p. 1.

41. O'Hara, *Pioneer Catholic History*, p. 176.

42. William McLeod, comp. *Souvenir 1858-1958*, (Jacksonville, 1958), p. 1.

43. This subject has been presented at length in: Wilfred P. Schoenberg, S.J., *Paths To The Northwest, A Jesuit History of The Oregon Province*, (Chicago, 1982), p. 59 et seq.

44. Nobili died at Santa Clara on March 4, 1856. Unlike Accolti, he had been greatly disturbed by their journey to California without the general's approval.

45. This was on August 1, 1854. Gilbert J. Garraghan, S.J., *The Jesuits in The Middle United States*, 3 vols., (New York, 1938), II:436.

46. All three groups were bands of the mighty Blackfeet. Fuller, *History of The Pacific Northwest*, p. 207.

47. Lawrence Kip, "The Indian Council at Walla Walla," in *Sources of The History of Oregon*, I(1897), pp. 1-28.

48. Robert Ignatius Burns, S.J., *The Jesuits And The Indian Wars of The Northwest*, (New Haven, 1966), p. 96 et seq.

49. The fire occurred on February 26, 1855. Archives of the Archdiocese of Portland in Oregon, Blanchet Folio I-II:43.

50. Waggett, "The Oblates of Mary Immaculate," p. 35.

51. Fuller, *History of The Pacific Northwest*, p. 223.

52. Bolen's horse, too, was killed and burned. *Ibid.*

53. Waggett, "The Oblates of Mary Immaculate," p. 34.

54. Ricard to Bishop de Mazenod, October 2, 1855. *Ibid.*, p. 35.

55. Van der Donckt, "The Founders of the Church," p. 2.

56. Independent witnesses affirmed this in defense of the Oblates. Waggett, "The Oblates of Mary Immaculate," p. 37.

57. Ibid.

58. Kay Cronin, Cross In The Wilderness, (Vancouver [B.C.], 1960), p. 40.

59. Waggett, "The Oblates of Mary Immaculate," p. 38.

60. Ibid., p. 40.

61. Ibid.

62. Cronin, Cross In The Wilderness, p. 48.

63. Ibid., p. 44.

64. O'Hara, Pioneer Catholic History, p. 161.

65. No copy of this pamphlet has been known to surface, but its publication is indisputable.

66. D'Herbomez was appointed superior in 1858.

67. Ricard was in the last stage of "consumption" or tuberculosis. He wanted to die in the mission, but de Mazenod, who had a great attachment to him, wanted to make his last months as comfortable as possible, in France.

68. Waggett, "The Oblates of Mary Immaculate," p. 47.

69. Ibid., p. 48.

70. The three Oblates built a log house which served as a church, school and residence. Chirouse remained at this mission for many years. Indian Sentinel, I(1918), p. 9.

71. Waggett, "The Oblates of Mary Immaculate," p. 48 et seq.

75. This was Father Charles Grandidier, a new arrival from Europe.

76. Archives of the Archdiocese of Seattle, Journal de Eveque de Nesqualy.

77. L.B. Palladino, S.J., Indian and White In The Northwest A History of Catholicity in Montana 1831 to 1891, (Lancaster, 1922), p. 96.

78. Ibid., p. 96.

79. It will be recalled that Father Nicolas Point conducted a one room "school" at Fort Lewis in 1846-1847. This was not a formal school as such. It's principal subject of instruction was catechism.

80. Palladino, Indian and White, p. 97.

81. Ibid.

82. The three tribes were Flatheads, Kalispels, and Kootenai.

83. Palladino, Indian and White, p. 97.

84. McCrosson, The Bell and The River, p. 12 et seq.

85. Ibid., p. 40.

86. Ibid., p. 42.

87. This admirable man died in Montreal on August 23, 1857, less than one year after his daughter departed for Oregon.

88. Mother Gamelin died from cholera on September 22, 1851. Ibid., p. 76.

89. Rossi's original name was Abramo DeRossi, Born on June 14, 1817 in Ferrara, Italy of Jewish parents, he converted to Catholicism on November 19, 1846. At that time he took the name Luigi Angelo Maria Rossi. He entered the Passionist order twice, first in 1838 at Paliono, second at Monte Argentario during the later part of the same year. He was ordained in Rome in April 1843. Ten years later he left Italy with other Passionists to found a new community at Bordeaux in France. There, after initial success, he was accused of scheming against a local superior and was asked by higher superiors to resign his position. He left the Passionists altogether in October, 1855. Wortley, Six Years On The West Coast, p. 10 et seq.

90. Ibid., p. 30.

91. McCrosson, The Bell and The River, p. 81.

92. Ibid., p. 5.

93. *Ibid.*, p. 82.

94. Election Day was November 4, 1856. Rossi describes the hysteria and violence that accompanied it. Wortley, *Six Years On The West Coast*, p. 43 et seq.

95. Aspinwall was called Colon at a later date.

96. Rossi presents a vivid description of the storm and the dangers crossing the Bar of the Columbia River. Wortley, *Six Years On The West Coast*, p. 77 et seq. Missionaries traveling in the *Brother Jonathan* had reason to be afraid. The *Brother Jonathan* went down at the mouth of the Columbia in 1865 with all on board, including Colonel George Wright and his wife.

97. *Ibid.*, p. 81.

98. Brouillet wanted the Sisters to build their orphanage and hospital at Olympia where the territorial capital was located. Thus he had not provided for one in Vancouver.

99. The annals, using the date February 22, were in error. Ash Wednesday in 1857 was on February 25. McCrosson, *The Bell and The River*, p. 119.

100. This was on March 16, 1857.

101. In Oregon, the two schools of the Sisters of Notre Dame de Namur, at St. Paul and Oregon City, were earlier by at least a decade of years.

102. From the army's point of view, the best known book on this subject is: B.F. Manring, *The Conquest of The Coeur d'Alenes, Spokanes and Palouses*, (Spokane, 1912). However, the best work is Father Burn's: *The Jesuits and The Indian Wars*. The details in the text are from this account.

103. William N. Bischoff, S.J., *The Jesuits in Old Oregon*, (Caldwell, 1943), p. 134.

104. Fuller, *The History of The Pacific Northwest*, p. 251.

105 Oregon Province Archives, Joset Papers, Letter of Colonel George Wright to Joset.

106. E. Laveille, S.J., *The Life of Father DeSmet, S.J., 1801-1873*, (New York, 1915), p. 276.

107. A notable portrait of DeSmet with the nine chiefs was taken at Fort Vancouver 1859. A copy of this from the Oregon Province Archives appears in Burns, *The Jesuits and The Indian Wars*, photograph section.

108. *Ibid.*, p. 343.

109. *Ibid.*

110. McLeod, *Souvenir 1858-1958*, pp. 15 and 35.

111. Vercryusse remained at St. Ignatius Mission until 1863 when he was transferred to California. Within several years he returned to Belgium where he died in 1867. Palladino, *Indian and White*, p. 463.

112. [Sisters of St. Anne], *The Sisters of St. Anne in British Columbia, Yukon and Alaska, 1858-1958*, (Victoria, 1958), p. 17.

113. The sisters were assigned on August 13, 1859. [Sister Mary Flavia, S.N.J.M.], *Gleanings of Fifty Years, The Sisters of the Holy Names of Jesus and Mary In The Northwest 1859-1909*, (Portland, 1909), p. 60. The family names are presented here, also.

114. [Sisters of The Holy Names], *Excerpts from Oregon Chronicles 1859-1959*, (Marylhurst, 1958), pp. 2-12.

115. Father Andre Poulin became one of the pioneer priests in the Vicariate of Idaho, 1863-1877. Rt. Rev. Cyprian Bradley, O.S.B. and Most Rev. Edward Kelly, D.D., Ph.D., *History of The Diocese of Boise 1863-1952*, (Boise, 1953), p. 119 et seq.

116. Sister M. Flavia, *Gleanings*, p. 76.

Chapter 7. DECADE OF EXPANSION

1. James Stevens, "Introduction" in Sister Mary of the Blessed Sacrament McCrosson, *The Bell and The River*, (Palo Alto, 1956), p. ix et seq.

2. Oregon acquired statehood in 1859.

3. George W. Fuller, *A History of the Pacific Northwest*, (New York, 1931), p. 316.

4. A detailed account of these missions appears as follows: Wilfred P. Schoenberg, S.J., "Historic St. Peter's Mission," in *Montana, The Magazine of Western History*, Vol. 11 (1961), p. 63 et seq.

5. The teacher was probably Mr. Kinsela, who had arrived during the same year.

6. W. Victor Wortley, ed., *Louis Rossi, Six Years on The West Coast of America 1856-1862*, (Fairfield, 1983), p. 90.

7. *Ibid.*, p. 99 et seq.

8. These divisions present an inaccurate picture. The Oblates in fact were still in the Yakima area, the Jesuits farther east.

9. *Ibid.*, p. 111.

10. *Ibid.*

11. *Ibid.*, p. 125.

12. *Ibid.*, p. 140, footnote No. 2.

13. *Ibid.*, p. 132.

14. Rossi's ailment was probably stomach ulcers.

15. George W. Fuller, *A History of the Pacific Northwest*, p. 237.

16. Robert Ignatius Burns, S.J., *The Jesuits and the Indian Wars of The Northwest*, (New Haven, 1966), p. 125.

17. Leschi died at the hands of civil officials. He had murdered no one. His "crime" was really misguided patriotism. Ezra Meeker, *Pioneer Reminiscences of Puget Sound; The Tragedy of Leschi; an Account of the Coming of the First Americans, Their Institutions, etc.*, (Seattle, 1905).

18. Wortley, *Six Years on the West Coast*, p. 142.

19. In Mary Ann Conklin's hotel, however, he preached a long sermon to a packed house; not one of his listeners was a Catholic. Wortley, *Six Years on The West Coast*, p. 149. Mary Ann, called "Mother Damnable" because of her picturesque vocabulary, weighed between three and four hundred pounds and was sometimes seen, with three vicious dogs, pelting her adversaries with rocks.

20. *Ibid.*, p. 177.

21. *Ibid.* Rossi's account differs from other sources that state that the building was completed on November 28, 1860 [after Rossi had departed] and was dedicated in honor of St. Anthony. *Journal de l'Eveque de Nesqualy* in The Archives of the Archdiocese of Seattle. Also the Peter Halpin Manuscript on Port Townsend in the Oregon Province Archives.

22. Wortley, *Six Years on The West Coast*, p. 130 et seq.

23. Rev. J. Van Der Heyden, "Monsignor Adrian J. Croquet, Indian Missionary 1818-1902," in *Records of The American Catholic Historical Society of Philadelphia*. Vol. XVI (1905) p. 120.

24. *Ibid.*, p. 123.

25. *Ibid.*, p. 124.

26. The reservations were Umatilla, Warm Springs, and Klamath in addition to the two near the coast, the Grand Ronde and the Siletz Reservations.

27. Mother Joseph established St. Vincent's Orphanage for boys and St. Genevieve's Orphanage for girls in Vancouver in October, 1860. In 1873 a handsome new building was erected to house the orphanage and this flourished for fifty years under the Sisters of Providence.

28. The Modocs. The Shoshone Indians were also called "the Snakes."

29. Van Der Heyden, "Croquet," p. 131 et seq.

30. This was St. Patrick's in Muddy Valley where a colony of Irish settlers had farms.

31. The Siletz Reservation.

32. Van Der Heyden, "Croquet," p. 152.

33. *Ibid.*, p. 143.

34. *Ibid.,* p. 144. The writer was Father Peter De Roo, also a very learned and pious priest in Oregon.

35. *Ibid.,* p. 149.

36. Junger was attached to the Diocese of Nesqually. He was consecrated second Bishop of Nesqually on October 28, 1879.

37. Vermeersch was succeeded by Orth in 1873. The latter remained only two years before becoming Bishop of Vancouver Island, succeeding Charles Seghers on April 19, 1900.

38. *Reminiscences and Current Topics of The Ecclesiastical Province of Oregon* [Baker], No. 3 (1897), p. 58 et seq.

39. [Sister Mary Flavia, S.N.J.M.], *Gleanings of Fifty Years; The Sisters of The Holy Names of Jesus and Mary in The Northwest 1859–1909,* (Portland, 1909), p. 81.

40. *Ibid.,* p. 89.

41. Archives of the Archdiocese of Portland in Oregon, Blanchet Correspondence, Book I, p. 394.

42. Mother M. Antoinette, F.C.S.P., *The Institute of Providence: History of the Daughters of Charity Servants of the Poor Known as the Sisters of Providence,* 6 vols. (Montreal, 1937–1949), Vol. 5, p. 375.

43. *Ibid.,* V:126.

44. *Ibid.,* V:123 et seq.

45. Wortley, *Six Years on The West Coast,* p. 173.

46. Note this was in 1858 before St. Joseph's was closed. Tulalip was not formally designated as a reservation until 1859.

47. *Indian Sentinel,* I, No. 7 (1918), p. 14.

48. George M. Waggett, O.M.I., "The Oblates of Mary Immaculate in The Pacific Northwest of U.S.A.," *Etudes Oblates,* 6 (1947), p. 53.

49. *Ibid.* Chirouse held this position until September 1861, when Samuel D. Howe was named as the first regular sub-agent.

50. *Ibid.,* p. 55.

51. The Sisters of Charity of Providence.

52. Waggett, "The Oblates," p. 57.

53. *Ibid.,* p. 58.

54. *Ibid.,* p. 59.

55. This was near present Marietta, Washington. This log cabin church was replaced eight years later with a frame structure that was dedicated by Bishop Blanchet on June 27, 1869. *Journal de l'Eveque de Nesqualy* in the Archives of the Archdiocese of Seattle.

56. Chief Seattle died on June 7, 1866 at the probable age of 80 years. His funeral was conducted in the Suquamish mission church and he was buried in the nearby church cemetery.

57. In 1877 Chirouse enlarged this church and Bishop Blanchet blessed it in honor of St. Paul the Apostle on July 10, 1877. *Journal de l'Eveque de Nesqualy* in the Archives of the Archdiocese of Seattle.

58. The first church for whites in LaConnor, called Sacred Heart church was built by Prefontaine, who did most of the carpentry work himself. It was dedicated by Bishop Blanchet on July 8, 1873. *Catholic Sentinel,* November 2, 1872 and July 28, 1898.

59. Wagget, "The Oblates," p. 51.

60. The other two Jesuits were Father Camillus Imoda and Brother Francis De Kock. They arrived at Fort Benton on October 25, 1861. L.B. Palladino, S.J., *Indian and White In The Northwest,* (Lancaster, 1922), p. 193.

61. *Ibid.,* p. 194.

62. *Ibid.,* p. 195.

63. Palladino provides details regarding one of Giorda's excursions to the Milk River. Opposed by the chiefs and influential men at first, Giorda prayed for their change of heart. Soon all opposition disappeared. Giorda offered the first Mass in that area and baptized 134 children on the same day. *Ibid.,* p. 196.

64. This was by the Apostolic Brief *Per Similes Nos ras,* July 29, 1853.

65. Edwin V. O'Hara, *Pioneer Catholic History of Oregon,* (Portland, 1911), p. 197.

66. Archives of the Archdiocese of Portland in Oregon, Blanchet's Folio I-II, 111.

67. At this time (1853–1868), southern Idaho, south of the 46th parallel, was under the jurisdiction of Oregon City. Northern Idaho, north of this to the 49th parallel from the Pacific Ocean to the Rocky Mountains, was under Nesqually. A comprehensive account of the early jurisdiction of Idaho is presented by Rt. Rev. Cyprian Bradley, O.S.B., and Most Rev. Edward J. Kelly, D.D., Ph.D., *History of the Diocese of Boise 1863–1952,* (Boise, 1953), p. 35 et seq.

68. *Ibid.,* p. 89.

69. *Ibid.* The name of the settlement was eventually changed to Pioneerville.

70. Mesplie was administrator of St. Patrick's from 1859– 1862.

71. Bradley and Kelly, *History of Boise,* p. 89.

72. *Ibid.,* p. 90 et seq.

73. *Ibid.,* p. 93.

74. Gilbert J. Garraghan, S.J., *The Jesuits in The Middle United States,* (New York, 1938), II:128.

75. Hiram Martin-Chittenden and Alfred Talbot Richardson, *Life Letters and Travels of Father Pierre-Jean DeSmet, S.J. 1801– 1873,* 4 vols., (New York, 1905), 4:1526.

76. This had been begun by Ravalli in 1858. Catholic Soldiers completed it in October 1861, using lumber provided by the government mill. [George F. Weibel, S.J.], "Fifty Years of Peaceful Conquest," in *Gonzaga Magazine,* Vol. V (1911–1912), p. 299.

77. Palladino, *Indian and White,* p. 138.

78. The Coeur d'Alene River.

79. Palladino, *Indian and White,* p. 297.

80. *Catholic Sentinel,* January 8, 1875.

81. This was at Longueil. A brief biography of Prefontaine has appeared: Rev. W.J. Metz, *Life Sketch of Monsignor F.X. Prefontaine,* (Seattle, 1908).

82. Edward J. Kowrach, ed., *Victor Garrand, S.J., Augustine Loure, S.J. Missionary To The Yakimas,* (Fairfield, 1977), p. 15.

83. *Sadler's Catholic Directory, Almanac and Ordo,* 1833 to 1896, preceded *The Official Catholic Directory* published annually by P.J. Kenedy and Sons, New York. It will be noted that this directory places Prefontaine at Fort Steilacoom for the year 1865, when in fact he was appointed to reside in Port Townsend in May 1864. Most clerical catalogues and directories then were a year behind in their classifications because of the problems of communication. The wonder is that they produced data like this at all.

84. Oregon Province Archives, fragment of an unidentified thesis on Prefontaine, Appendix 1.

85. Prefontaine did not visit Seattle until 1867.

86. Arthur A. Denny, *Pioneer Days On Puget Sound,* (Fairfield, 1965), p. 51. Also, [anon], *St. James Cathedral 1907– 1957,* (Seattle, 1957), [p. 9].

87. Metz, *Life Sketch,* p. 10.

88. *Ibid.,* p. 11 et seq.

89. *Journal de l'Eveque de Nesqualy* in the Archives of the Archdiocese of Seattle.

90. Oregon Province Archives, Mss. Walla Walla.

91. Fuller, *History of the Pacific Northwest,* p. 292.

92. Most immigrants in this period came from Catholic countries like Ireland. Confer: James Hennessey, S.J., *American Catholics A History of The Roman Catholic Community in The United states*, (New York, 1981), Chapter X. "Immigrants Become the Church."

93. Thomas Francis Meagher, Irish patriot, was born in Waterford, Ireland on August 3, 1823. He was condemned to die by the British for his opposition to their occupation of Ireland, but his sentence was commuted to deportation to Tasmania as a life felon. He escaped and entered the United States in 1852. He died near Fort Benton, mysteriously, on July 1, 1867.

94. Letter of Archbishop John Ireland to Lawrence Palladino, S.J., St. Paul, January 10, 1912. Quoted in full in Palladino, *Indian and White*, p. 501 et seq.

95. The Vicariate of Montana established in 1868 included only that part of Montana that was east of the Rockies.

96. Bishop Lootens, a Belgian, had been ordained by Bishop Demers in Paris on June 14, 1851, for the Diocese of Vancouver Island.

97. Palladino, *Indian and White*, p. 502.

98. W.F. Lyons, *Brigadier-General Thomas Francis Meagher*, (New York, 1886), p. 204.

99. Palladino, *Indian and White*, p. 308.

100. Montana's first Territorial Legislature convened on March 5, 1866. Giorda was elected chaplain in the second session on March 7.

101. Easter in 1866 was on April 1.

102. The Squawman was John B. Morgan who had been involved in the treacherous murder of at least four Indians, whose bodies had been dumped, through holes in the ice, into the Missouri River. Palladino, *Indian and White*, p. 205 et seq.

103. *Ibid.*, p. 209 et seq.

104. Thomas Moran told Palladino that when Giorda polled the Jesuits, all four favored closing the mission. Their premonitions were correct. Kuppens later stated that the Mullan Road had become unsafe to travel and Palladino estimated that "in one summer alone, fifty-six whites were killed either from ambush or in the open along that road by Indian war parties." *Ibid.*, p. 204.

105. Owens described the dedications in Seymour Dunbar and Paul C. Phillips, eds., *The Journals and Letters of Major John Owen Pioneer of The Northwest 1850–1871*, 2 vols., (New York, 1927) II:31 et seq.

106. Palladino, *Indian and White*, p. 320.

107. Palladino states that Imoda, between 1866 and 1874, when St. Peter's was occupied again, visited the mission once a year and remained there "for several months" on each occasion. *Ibid.*, p. 211.

108. DeRyckere, it will be remembered, was not the first diocesan priest in Montana. Father John Raverdy from Denver visited Virginia City in the fall of 1864 and remained there for over a month. DeRyckere arrived at Deer Lodge in July, 1866.

109. March 19, 1864. Palladino, *Indian and White*, p. 339.

110. *Ibid.*, p. 341.

111. *Ibid.*, p. 343.

112. A brief authentic biography is George W. Weibel, S.J., *Rev. Joseph M. Cataldo, S.J. A Short Sketch of a Wonderful Career*, (Spokane, 1928).

113. *Ibid.*, p. 9.

114. This first St. Michael's Mission for the Spokanes was located on a sloping hillside facing north, above Peone Prairie. The Treaty Tree, still standing, grows some three to four hundred yards to the northeast.

115. Weibel, *Cataldo*, p. 12.

116. Lane, before he died, returned to the Masons to take advantage of Masonic insurance to benefit his family.

117. There were no "old buildings" in Roseburg at this time, for the town was yet a new one. The record doubtlessly refers to the state or condition of the building, an almost forsaken one.

118. The title of the church was changed to St. Joseph in 1880.

119. The other girl's name was Irene Smith.

120. Joseph Lane became a monsignor in 1920. St. Paul's first native born priest was Father Leo Kaufman, S.J., ordained in San Francisco on June 15, 1951.

121. Mother M. Antoinette, *Institute of Providence*, V:197.

122. Oregon Province Archives, Boulet Mss. on Yakima Mission.

123. *Ibid.*

124. On June 7, 1866. Eva Greenslit Anderson, *Chief Seattle*, (Caldwell, 1943), p. 321.

125. Metz, *Life Sketch*, p. 13.

126. This is at variance with Rossi's report and subsequent notations regarding the Rossi purchase of two lots in 1858.

127. Metz, *Life Sketch*, p. 15.

128. *Ibid.*, p. 15.

129. Mother M. Antoinette, *Institute of Providence*, V:389. After his novitiate, Vary served as a missionary in Canada for nine busy years. He was found dead in his room at Port Arthur, Ontario on April 12, 1878.

130. Weibel, *Short Sketch*, 13. This states that Cataldo arrived in Lewiston "about the beginning of November." Father Bradley appears to be more accurate in stating that Cataldo arrived in Lewiston in October 1867. Bradley and Kelly, *History of Boise*, p. 148.

131. Bradley notes that Richards, acting for Bishop Blanchet, "made a thorough survey of the Clearwater Country" in 1864. *Ibid.*

132. *The Bookmark*, [University of Idaho], Volume 19 (June, 1967), p. 190.

133. The second St. Stanislaus, built by Father Alexander Diomedi, was not opened for services until 1866. OPA, Mss. Lewiston; Post 1.

134. There is a remarkable account of Magri's death in Palladino, *Indian and White*, p. 181 et seq. According to this, an Indian over 200 miles distant saw Magri going to heaven in a chariot at the time of his death.

135. This second St. Michael's Mission was built in March 1868.

136. Weibel, "Fifty Years," p. 300 et seq.

137. Father Tosi offered the first Mass in this third St. Francis Regis Mission on April 13, 1873.

138. Bradley and Kelly, *History of Boise*, p. 181 et seq.

139. The Petaluma Church was called St. Vincent's.

140. Father Killian Coll and Father A. Perret.

141. Bradley and Kelly, *History of Boise*, p. 185. It should be noted that it was John Farrell who gave a block of property for the first church in Boise. Confer: Cyril Van der Donckt, "The Founders of The Church in Idaho," in *The Ecclesiastical Review*, XXXII (1905), p. 9.

142. *Ibid.*, p. 189.

143. *Ibid.*, p. 183.

Chapter 8. LAST OF THE BLANCHET YEARS

1. Edwin V. O'Hara, *Pioneer Catholic History of Oregon*, (Portland, 1911), p. 213.

2. *Ibid.*, p. 214. The Union Pacific Railroad had just been completed to the West Coast.

3. Augustin Blanchet's malaria has been seldom recognized as a factor in his administration of the diocese. Fortunately, he was home with malaria when he took legal action to prevent the United States Army from occupying the church's Vancouver land.

4. *Catholic Sentinel*, October 1, 1870.

5. This pastoral was so long that the *Catholic Sentinel*, which frequently published long articles in one issue, had to publish it in two installments, on November 5 and November 12, 1870.

6. *Catholic Sentinel*, October 29, 1870.

7. The *California* enroute from Portland to Sitka, ran onto rocks 28 miles above Nanaimo, B.C. on June 13, 1872. It was a total loss. *Catholic Sentinel*, June 23, 1872.

8. At this time, Eastern Montana was still under the jurisdiction of the Vicariate of Nebraska, Bishop James O'Gorman, O.C.S.O. O'Gorman, consecrated on May 8, 1859, died on July 4, 1874. He was succeeded in 1876 by Bishop James O'Connor.

9. *Catholic Sentinel*, February 12, 1870. In subsequent issues of the *Sentinel*, the Catholic population figure varied. For example, on February 25, 1871, the *Sentinel*, quoting the *Catholic Directory*, gave 23,000 as the total number of Catholics. A year later, April 13, 1872, the *Sentinel* gave "about 50,000 Catholics, including upwards of 20,000 Indians."

10. O'Hara, *Pioneer Catholic History*, p. 217. The one hospital was in Vancouver. St. Vincent's in Portland would be opened on July 19, 1875.

11. Demers died on July 28, 1871.

12. *Catholic Sentinel*, February 5, 1870. The partnership of the two men was dissolved on February 17, 1872, and for some time Herman was the sole owner of the paper. He was also the editor.

13. *Catholic Sentinel*, February 3, 1870.

14. J.B.A. Brouillet, *Authentic Account of the Murder of Dr. Whitman and Other Missionaries by the Cayuse Indians of Oregon in 1847, And the Causes Which Led to That Horrible Catastrophe*, (Portland, 1869). This second edition of the work by Brouillet, published by McCormick, is regarded as the classic edition. A copy may be found in the Oregon Province Archives.

15. L.B. Palladino, S.J., *Indian and White in The Northwest*, (Lancaster, 1922), p. 328.

16. *Ibid.*, p. 329.

17. The names of the parishioners were given as follows: Mrs. Brown, Mr. and Mrs. L.F. LaCroix and Mr. and Mrs. H. Galen.

18. *Ibid.*, p. 330.

19. There is a photograph of the tree in Palladino, *Indian and White*, opposite p. 332.

20. *Ibid.*, p. 333.

21. In 1884, a new hospital was finally provided for the sisters in Helena. This lasted until the earthquake of 1935. Since it was rendered useless, a new St. John's was built to replace it.

22. [Sisters of Charity of Leavenworth], *History of The Sisters of Charity of Leavenworth, Kansas*, (Kansas City, 1898), p. 474.

23. This St. Mary's was closed in 1879. *Ibid.*, p. 475.

24. The terms of the treaty protected all rights of the Company until 1859.

25. *Claim of The Missionary Station of St. James, at Vancouver, Washington Territory to 640 Acres of Land*, The Statement of Facts, Part I (n.d., n.p.). This was probably published in Olympia in 1859. A complete copy of all of the reports at this period are in the Oregon Province Archives.

26. This transaction, according to Thomas M. Anderson, later commandant of the Vancouver Barracks, and defendant in the case, was conducted by a Major Hathaway, who had come to the old Hudson's Bay Company post in 1849, requesting the use of a building. "When he applied to Mr. [Peter Skene] Ogden, then Chief Factor for a room in which to store some articles, he offered to rent him the church. Major Hathaway did not want the church but his Quartermaster did rent and occupy for a time the little log house." Thomas M. Anderson, "The Vancouver Reservation Case," in *The Quarterly of the Oregon Historical Society*, VIII (1907), p. 220. In my opinion, Anderson, as a defendant in the case, was a biased

witness. Further evidence of this appears later. Witnesses, when a trial was finally conducted, testified that a company *clerk* rented the log house to the army but this "clerk" was never produced.

27. John A. Hussey, *This History of Fort Vancouver and Its Physical Structure*, (Tacoma, 1957), p. 211.

28. [Mother Mary Antoinette, F.C.S.P.], *The Institute of Providence*, 5 vols. *The Sisters of Providence in Oregon 1856*, (Montreal, 1949), V:377.

29. In *Catholic Sentinel*, March 12, 1870.

30. Mother Mary Antoinette, *The Institute of Providence*, V:61. The bishop had given Mother Joseph $5,000 in 1857. She used at least some of this for buying land.

31. *Ibid.*, V:379.

32. *Ibid.*

33. [George F. Weibel, S.J.], "Fifty Years of Peaceful Conquest," in *Gonzaga Magazine*, V (1913), p. 179 et seq. and 232 et seq.

34. This new mission of St. Joseph on Attanum Creek, on the same site as the old, was a short distance outside the Yakima reservation line.

35. St. Onge died November 26, 1901. Oregon Province Archives, "St. Onge file."

36. One of the most important works on Grant's Peace Policy is Peter J. Rahill, *The Catholic Indian Missions and Grant's Peace Policy 1870-1884*, (Washington, 1953).

37. *Ibid.*, p. 22.

38. Palladino, *Indian and White*, p. 173. Palladino gives specific examples; for instance, St. Ignatius Mission received four bolts of cloth from the agent and three years later, learned that the agent charged the government $1,600.66 "by domestics" meaning the four bolts of cloth.

39. Rahill, *Grant's Peace Policy*, p. 24.

40. *Ibid.*, p. 27.

41. *Ibid.*

42. *Ibid.*

43. *Ibid.*, p. 42.

44. Laveille gives the Catholics eight *agencies*, Tulalip and Colville in Washington, Grande Ronde and Umatilla in Oregon, Flatheads in Montana, Papagos in Arizona and the Sioux of Grand River and Devil's Lake in Dakota. E. Laveille, S.J., *The Life of Father DeSmet, S.J. (1801-1873)*, (New York, 1915), p. 363. Rahill states that seven *reservations* were given to Catholics. Neither list includes the Coeur d'Alenes, who were attached to Colville and regarded as Catholic. Rahill, *Grant's Peace Policy*, p. 105.

45. *The Catholic Review* for November 1, 1873, listed Indians by tribes and agencies, arriving at a total of 106,911 Catholics. For approximately 15,000 Protestant Indians, sixty-six agencies were allotted, while the Catholics received seven, with a total Indian population of about 17,000. Rahill, *Grant's Peace Policy*, p. 105.

46. Laveille, *Father DeSmet*, p. 366. On April 30, 1871, about five hundred Apaches were shot near Camp Grant in Arizona. This is only one example.

47. *New York Freeman's Journal*, December 14, 1872.

48. The Secretary of the Interior was Columbus Delano. Laveille, *Father DeSmet*, p. 365.

49. Red Cloud, too, the great Chief of the Sioux, has suffered the same fate. DeSmet, Red Cloud, and many others, who realized that the Indians' only hope was cooperation with whites, have been condemned for not resisting the vastly superior forces.

50. It was customary then for Methodists to address their ministers as Brother, but because of the high esteem in which Wilbur was held, he was ordinarily addressed as "Father."

51. Maurice Kendall, *There Were Giants, The Life of James W. Wilbur*, (Yakima, 1980), Chapter 14.

52. *Ibid.*, p. 80.

53. *Ibid.*, p. 80–81.

54. *Ibid.*, p. 112.

55. *Ibid.*, p. 113.

56. *Ibid.*

57. *Catholic Sentinel,* February 25, 1871.

58. Probably Father Wilbur.

59. Letter of Grassi in *Catholic Missions,* (1873), p. 15.

60. *Catholic Sentinel,* July 29, 1871.

61. There is abundant material on the life of Seghers. The most complete of these are two: Gerard George Steckler [S.J.], "Charles John Seghers Missionary Bishop In The American Northwest 1839-1886," unpublished thesis submitted in partial fulfillment of the requirements of the degree of Doctor of Philosophy, University of Washington, 1963. Copy in Oregon Province Archives. A published work: Sister Mary Mildred, S.S.A., *The Apostle of Alaska Life of the Most Reverend Charles John Seghers,* (Paterson, 1943).

62. The church was dedicated on December 25, 1870. Rt. Rev. Cyprian Bradley, O.S.B. and Most Rev. Edward J. Kelly, D.D., Ph.D., *History of The Diocese of Boise 1863–1952,* (Boise, 1953), p. 32.

63. This second Boise church was called St. John, name of the present cathedral. It was dedicated in December 1876.

64. *Catholic Sentinel,* February 25, 1871.

65. Father Dominic O'Connor, *A Brief History of the Diocese of Baker City,* (Baker, 1930), p. 32.

66. This St. Peter's was dedicated by Bishop Blanchet on August 18, 1871. The Cherokee's name has survived only as "Mr. Temple." George M. Waggett, O.M.I., "The Oblates of Mary Immaculate in the Pacific Northwest of U.S.A. 1847-1878," in *Etudes Oblates,* 6 (1947), p. 55. Confer also *Catholic Sentinel,* September 16, 1871.

67. *Catholic Sentinel,* November 11, 1871.

68. This is the probable time. This first Grassi church was the model for the replica constructed in 1959 as part of a frontier museum project. Weibel, "Fifty Years," p. 184 et seq.

69. *Catholic Sentinel,* September 28, 1872 and October 24, 1873.

70. Prefontaine started construction on this edifice on October 16, 1872. Rev. W.J. Metz, *Life Sketch of Monsignor F.X. Prefontaine,* (Seattle, 1908), p. 16.

71. William N. Bischoff, S.J., *The Jesuits in Old Oregon,* (Caldwell, 1945), p. 146.

72. *Catholic Sentinel,* October 2, 1874.

73. *Ibid.,* May 1, 1874.

74. The Deer Lodge church was blessed on March 19, 1875. Palladino, *Indian and White,* p. 342. The Helena church was built by Palladino. *Ibid.,* p. 402 et seq.

75. *Catholic Sentinel,* June 17, 1875.

76. *Ibid.,* May 1, 1874 and September 9, 1875.

77. Robert S. Neugebauer, *Diamond Jubilee Visitation-Church Verboort, Oregon, 1875-1950,* (N.P., 1950), p. 4 et seq.

78. Oregon Province Archives, Mss. "Yakima Mission."

79. *Catholic Sentinel,* June 29, 1876 and October 18, 1906.

80. *Ibid.,* July 13, 1876 and October 5, 1876.

81. A set of these rare periodicals may be found in the Oregon Province Archives.

82. Charles M. Smith, ed., *Centenary of Cathedral Parish,* (Portland, 1951), p. 57. Also, *Catholic Sentinel,* September 28, 1876 and May 6, 1880.

83. [Stephen J. Sullivan], *The Golden Jubilee of St. Joseph's Church Canton, Montana, October 24, 1926,* (N.P., 1926), p. 12.

84. Father Mesplie estimated that in the United States, in this period, there were 30,000 soldiers, of whom 20,000 were Catholic, mostly of Irish and German extraction.

85. Colin Brummitt Goodykoontz, *Home Missions on The American Frontier*, (Caldwell, 1939), p. 362. It should be noted that the author's remarks concerning the "West" bear direct reference to the west of an earlier period, therefore of mid-America. In context, they are applicable, however, to the same situation in the far west twenty years later.

86. It survived the opening of Gonzaga by twenty-four years. Holy Angels College, unfortunately, suffered from poor management. The Diocese of Nesqually was simply too short-handed to staff it. When the Christian Brothers were called in to take it over in July 1897, it was too late to change its parochial image.

87. *Catholic Sentinel*, August 16, 1871.

88. O'Hara, *Pioneer Catholic History*, p. 216.

89. [John J. Callanan], *Centennial Souvenir of The Catholic Church in Walla Walla Valley 1847-1947*, (N.P., 1947), p. 88.

90. Mother Mary Antoinette, *The Institute of Providence*, V:338.

91. Palladino, *Indian and White*, p. 362 et seq. This presents a detailed account of the academy's early history.

92. There is some confusion on the exact date of arrival. The accurate account can be found in [Sisters of the Holy Names], *Excerpts from Oregon Chronicles 1859-1959*, (Marylhurst, 1958), p. 159 et seq. This includes a long excerpt from the *Catholic Sentinel*, April 24, 1874.

93. Archives of the Sisters of the Holy Names at Marylhurst, Mss. "Three Sisters of Holy Names at Grand Ronde," p. 3 et seq.

94. The sisters estimated that there were 700 Indians on the reservation, 250 of the children of school age.

95. *Catholic Sentinel*, September 4, 1874.

96. The Holy Names Sisters arrived in Astoria in May 1896, and opened their new school on September 14. The first sisters in Astoria were, of curse, the six Sisters of Notre Dame du Namur, July 31, 1844.

97. Sisters of the Holy Names, *Excerpts*, p. 172 et seq. The train finally reached Baker City in 1884, an event of much rejoicing.

98. Maria Monk again. As noted above, this had been circulated before, this time, in the lower Columbia.

99. Sister Dorothy Lentz, S.P., *The Way It Was in Providence Schools, Stories of Seven Providence Schools in The West Founded Between 1856-1920*, (Montreal, 1978), p. 68 et seq.

100. *Prairie Life*, VIII (1930), p. 14 et seq.

101. Mother Mary Antoinette, *The Institute of Providence*, V:231 et seq. Mother Caron arrived at Vancouver on May 20, 1873.

102. *Ibid.*, p. 232 et seq.

103. *Ibid.*, pp. 245-249.

104. The sisters still had a debt of twenty thousand dollars, so they were unable to complete and occupy the chapel until January 25, 1883. *Ibid.*, p. 250.

105. *Ibid.*

106. Oregon Province Archives, Mss. "Sisters of Providence."

107. St. Vincent's expanded rapidly. In four years a wing was added, then three years later another wing. It was the forerunner of Portland's present two vast hospitals conducted by the Sisters of Providence, one on the east end called Providence Hospital the other in the western suburb, called St. Vincent's. *Catholic Sentinel*, July 22, 1875. Also, Mother Mary Antoinette, *The Institute of Providence*, V:258 et seq.

108. Metz, *Life Sketch*, p. 16.

109. *Ibid.*, p. 16.

110. *Ibid.* The site is presently called Georgetown.

111. Oregon Province Archives, Mss. "Sisters of Providence."

112. Metz, *Life Sketch,* p. 16.

113. *Catholic Sentinel,* November 6, 1874.

114. Bradley and Kelly, *History of Boise,* p. 197 et seq.

115. Thomas Donaldson, *Idaho of Yesterday,* (Caldwell, 1941), pp. 59–60.

116. Bradley and Kelly, *History of Boise,* p. 110.

117. *Ibid.*

118. *Ibid.,* p. 113.

119. *Ibid.,* p. 198.

120. *Ibid.,* p. 199.

121. He died of a stroke on January 12, 1898, at the age of seventy, forty-six years a priest, and about thirty years a bishop.

122. Sadler's *Catholic Directory* for 1875.

123. The debt was still there on March 10, 1874, when Lootens wrote to say that he could find no one to underwrite it. Since things got worse before Looten's departure, it is unlikely that he was able to pay it. Bradley and Kelly, *History of Boise,* p. 198.

124. Archives of the Archdiocese of Portland in Oregon, Box XII, Folder 2.

125. *Ibid.*

126. Bradley and Kelly, *History of Boise,* p. 137.

127. *Ibid.*

128. Archambault spent two years in Portland, then returned in broken health to Canada, where he died on January 25, 1811.

129. Rahill, *Grant's Peace Policy,* p. 72.

130. *Ibid.*

131. *Ibid.,* p. 73. Emphasis mine. What became a permanent assignment for Brouillet was originally intended as a temporary one by the bishops.

132. Brouillet was not the first director of the incipient *bureau.* This honor was reserved for a layman, General Charles Ewing, an attorney from a well-known American family. Rahill, *Grant's Peace Policy,* p. 118.

133. *Catholic Sentinel,* September 19, 1873. DeCraene, born on February 12, 1843, came to Portland on October 10, 1869.

134. *Ibid.,* March 16, 1876.

135. *Ibid.,* December 23, 1875.

136. Waggett, "The Oblates of Mary Immaculate," p. 66. To be fair to Grant, this is what he preferred, control of the reservations by the army, but Congress had refused to yield to him on this point.

137. *Ibid.,* p. 67.

138. *Annals of The Catholic Indian Missions of America,* I(1877), p. 52. Copy in Oregon Province Archives.

139. Waggett, "The Oblates of Mary Immaculate," p. 71.

140. *Ibid.,* p. 76.

141. *Ibid.,* p. 77.

142. *Ibid.,* p. 82. Chirouse died at New Westminster, British Columbia on May 28, 1892.

143. *Ibid.,* p. 76.

144. Raiberti was only forty-five years old then, but he looked over seventy. He had been a Jesuit only eleven years. He died in Yakima on September 1, 1899 at the age of 69.

145. This church required three years to build. It burned to the ground a few years later, on Christmas Eve, 1888.

146. Wilfred P. Schoenberg, S.J., *Jesuit Mission Presses In The Pacific Northwest A History and a Bibliography of Imprints 1876–1899,* (Portland, 1957).

147. *Ibid.,* p. 12.

148. *Ibid.,* p. 18.

149. The Oregon Province Archives contains the Jesuit Indian language collection, one of the greatest in the world.

150. Prior to the publication of the *Reports of The Bureau of American Ethnology* at the expense of the Smithsonian Institution, The United States Government began a series of similar reports with tax money. A Mengarini manuscript was published in the second volume of this series: Gregory Mengarini S.J., "Vocabulary of the Shwoyelpi, S'chitzui and Salish Proper" in *Contributions to North American Ethnology,* John Wesley Powell, ed., (Washington, 1877), pp. 267–282.

151. The Colville boundaries were changed by the executive order of President Grant on July 2, 1872. It should be stated that in the case of the Coeur d'Alenes, the missionaries agreed with the government's proposal to move the reservation to better land for agriculture, over thirty miles south.

152. This was February, 1877. On the eleventh the Indians had agreed to move. They accompanied Diomedi to *Nilgo-Alko* or "Hole in the Woods" where Diomedi began work on the new mission. But the Indians returned to the Old Mission. Diomedi then resorted to the stratagem of removing the statues. *Nilgo-Alko* was only a temporary site. In the following year, the mission was moved to its permanent site near DeSmet, Idaho.

153. Morvillo with Brother Carfagno, arrived at St. Joseph's Mission, Slickpoo, on November 2, 1875. They were the first resident Catholic missionaries among the Nez Perce.

154. Father Mesplie, who had worked with the Cayuse, cancelled a trip to Europe to return to Oregon for meetings with the Cayuse and Umatilla. He was partly instrumental in their remaining neutral.

155. Conrardy arrived in Umatilla in late January 1875. He found Orth in charge. Vermeersch had been transferred to the St. Louis church on French Prairie.

156. This was finally established. On November 22, 1878, three Sisters of Providence arrived at DeSmet to open the school. They occupied their convent of Mary Immaculate on December 1, 1878, and started instructions for girls before the building was completed.

157. It will be recalled that in the war of 1858, Joset had been caught in the middle. This Nez Perce War is covered at length in Robert Ignatius Burns, S.J., *The Jesuits And The Indian Wars of The Northwest,* (New Haven, 1966).

158. Before leaving Omaha, the bishop had ordered a three day period of prayer for the extermination of the grasshoppers. *Catholic Sentinel,* May 24, 1877.

159. Palladino, *Indian and White,* p. 410.

160. Quoted in the *Catholic Sentinel,* September 20, 1877.

161. Palladino, *Indian and White,* p. 410.

162. This took place on August 15, 1878. *Catholic Sentinel,* August 22, 1878.

163. The pastoral appeared on May 8, 1879.

164. *Catholic Sentinel,* July 3, 1879.

165. *Ibid.,* September 11, 1879.

166. *Ibid.,* October 30, 1879.

Chapter 9. MONTANA'S FIRST BISHOP

1. Seghers not only *made* these voyages, he wrote extensively about them, reporting all his adventures faithfully for the readers of the *Catholic Sentinel.* Thus it is in the *Sentinel* one can find his accounts for these years of journeys that rivaled those of St. Paul.

2. Gerard George Steckler [S.J.], "Charles John Seghers Missionary Bishop In The American Northwest 1839–1886," a thesis submitted in partial fulfillment of the requirements for the degree of Doctor of Philosophy, University of Washington, 1963, p. 166.

3. *Catholic Sentinel*, September 4, 1879.

4. The Jesuits were Giorda, Van Gorp, Joseph Bandini, Parodi, Lattanzi, and Tosi.

5. Missoula's first church dedicated to St. Francis Xavier on December 11, 1881 was a small frame building that served the parish only eleven years. It was replaced with the present brick structure in 1892. L. B. Palladino, S.J., *Indian and White In The Northwest A History of Catholicity In Montana 1831 to 1891*, (Lancaster, 1922), p. 376.

6. He had but seven brief years to live.

7. Quoted in Sister Mary Mildred S.S.A., *The Apostle of Alaska,-Life of The Most Reverend Charles John Seghers*, (Paterson, 1943), p. 169.

8. There were an estimated 3,000 white Catholics in Idaho and Western Montana in 1879. The number of Indian Catholics was about 2,650.

9. Palladino refers to this subject in *Indian and White*, p. 422.

10. Palladino gives August 1, 1879 as the date for the dedication of St. Patrick's Church. *Ibid.*, p. 345. Gerard Steckler, however, gives the date as August 31, which appears to be correct. Steckler, "Charles John Seghers," p. 179.

11. Steckler, "Charles John Seghers," p. 179.

12. *Catholic Sentinel*,; November 6, 1879.

13. Sister Mary Mildred, *The Apostle of Alaska*, p. 163.

14. *Catholic Sentinel*, November 6, 1879.

15. Sister Mary Mildred, *The Apostle of Alaska*, p. 164.

16. *Ibid.*, p. 165.

17. *Catholic Sentinel*, January 23, 1879.

18. They arrived in September, 1883.

19. Apparently one of these brothers left, for there were only five at Baker City, three working on the farm and two teaching in the college.

20. *Catholic Sentinel*, December 11, 1879.

21. [Anon.], *The Right Reverend John B. Brondel Bishop of Helena A Memorial*, (Helena, 1904). The author of this tribute was probably Lawrence B. Palladino, S.J.

22. Brondel's ordination by Cardinal Stercks was on December 17, 1864. Palladino, *Indian and White*, p. 425.

23. [Anon.], *The Right Reverend John B. Brondel*, p. 7.

24. William J. Metz, "History of the Catholic Church in the State of Washington" in the *Inland Empire Catholic Messenger*, I,xii (1919), p. 36.

25. Oregon Province Archives, Mss. "Bender." For Uniontown Confer: *Catholic Sentinel*, March 21, 1878. The Uniontown church was not completed until later. According to the *Catholic Sentinel*, November 20, 1879, Father Thomas Duffy of Walla Walla, who succeeded Brondel, offered the first Mass in St. Boniface Church on September 12, 1879. At that time there were 140 Catholics in the vicinity.

26. *Catholic Sentinel*, December 18, 1879.

27. Palladino, *Indian and White*, p. 475.

28. Cataldo saved the day by jumping on the horses and gradually gaining control.

29. *Catholic Sentinel*, April 15, 1880.

30. He was provided with blankets often, but gave them all to the Indians. Later Archbishp Gross gave him blankets "on loan" so that he could not give them away.

31. Rev. J. Van Der Heyden, "Monsignor Adrian J. Croquet, Indian Missionary," in *Records of the American Catholic Historical Society of Philadelphia*, 17(1906), p. 280.

32. *Ibid.*, p. 221.

33. Seghers arrived at French Prairie on April 17, 1880. The new church cost $2,137. *Catholic Sentinel*, April 22, 1880.

34. This journey was described in detail in the *Catholic Sentinel*, July 22, 1880.

35. Additional information on Wheeler may be found in Steckler, "Charles John Seghers," p. 218.

36. Klamath Catholic Monthly, (N.P., N.D.), cited in Father Dominic O'Connor [O.F.M. Cap.], *A Brief History of The Diocese of Baker City*, (Baker, 1930), p. 112.

37. *Catholic Sentinel*, July 29, 1880.

39. The Oregon School Bill of 1922 should have surprised no one. Catholic opposition to public schools for four decades had united others in their opposition to parochial schools.

39. The only church Seghers failed to visit was "the Yamhill church," that is, St. Patrick's in Muddy Valley near McMinnville.

40. Sister Mary Mildred, *The Apostle of Alaska*, p. 174.

41. *Catholic Sentinel*, March 3, 1881. The Pastoral was dated February 27, 1881.

42. Benedictine Archives in St. John's Abbey. Collegeville, Minnesota, letter of Conrardy from Molokai to Abbot Edelbrock, November 29, 1888, in which Conrardy admits that he intended to leave Umatilla as early as 1876.

43. Mother Scholastica visited the Umatilla Reservation in May and June, when the weather was unseasonably warm.

44. Conrardy, who later abandoned Umatilla for Molokai, praised eastern Oregon rather intemperately. "I can affirm," he said, "[that] I like Eastern Oregon better than the climate of Belgium, France, East Indies, Africa [,] a thousand times more than that of the Willamette Valley." Gerard G. Steckler [S.J.], "The Founding of Mount Angel Abbey," in *The Oregon Historical Quarterly*, 7(1969), p. 323.

45. The Washington constitutional convention was held in 1889.

46. Hylebos Creek, Hylebos Waterway, and so forth, in or near Tacoma have been named for Peter Hylebos, founder of the Church in Tacoma. He died on November 28, 1918.

47. *Catholic Sentinel*, January 22, 1880.

48. Mother M. Antoinnette, *The Institute of Providence History of the Daughters of Charity, Servants of the Poor Known As The Sisters of Providence*, 6 vols. (Montreal, 1949), V:211.

49. Father Duffy died in San Francisco on February 15, 1885.

50. *Catholic Sentinel*, May 6, 1880.

51. *Ibid.*, June 3, 1880. As early as 1865, farmers of the Catholic Italian colony in Walla Walla shipped onions to Portland. These were not the renowned "Walla Walla sweets." The latter appeared about the turn of the century. Joe J. Locati, *The Horticultural Heritage of Walla Walla County 1818-1977*, (Walla Walla, 1977), p. 34 and p. 207 et seq. This contains considerable material regarding the Catholic families forming the Walla Walla church.

52. Joseph W. Gaffney,*A History of Sprague 1880-1962*, (Spokane, 1962), p. 3.

53. A full account of this appears in Wilfred P. Schoenberg, S.J., *Gonzaga University Seventy-five Years 1887-1962*, (Spokane, 1963), p. 32 et seq.

54. It will be recalled that the Sisters of Providence had opened a girls school at St. Francis Regis five years earlier.

55. The Treaty Tree near the original site of the first St. Michael's Mission on Peone Prairie northeast of Spokane. It was called Treaty Tree because of alleged meetings between Indians and whites beneath the tree. It still stands.

56. Thus this was the first Catholic school for whites in the Spokane area.

57. The Northern Pacific was not completed until 1883, but tracks reached Spokane from the west in 1881. By Act of Congress, the railroad was granted a ten mile strip along its line in alternate one mile blocks allowing the government to grant homesteads in the remaining blocks along the railroad. Cataldo favored a homestead site, but was too late to get one.

58. Schoenberg, *Gonzaga University*, p. 33.

59. The school was transfered in 1885, but Wilkinson was removed from the program three years earlier.

60. Grant's Peace Policy was formally put to rest by a letter dated Aug. 5, 1882, from Henry M. Teller, Secretary of the Interior.

61. Judge Lewis of Cheney represented the railroad. He wrote the contract for the sale on October 13, 1881. There were subsequent obstacles to the final receipt of the deed, but eventually the proper documents were received by the Jesuits.

62. These lots were purchased on August 8, 1881. On December 5, Cataldo bought two more lots from Glover. Eventually these five lots were sold and the money from the sale was used to buy the present site of Spokane's Cathedral.

63. What follows has been taken from Steckler., "The Founding of Mount Angel," p. 312 et seq.

64. [Martin Pollard, O.S.B.], *Mount of Communion: Mt. Angel Abbey 1882 1982*, (St. Benedict [Oregon], 1982), p. 2. A recent book covers this period: Lawrence J. McCrank, *Mt. Angel Abbey A Centennial History of the Benedictine Community and its Library, 1882–1982*, (Wilmington, 1983), p. 17 et seq.

65. Note that these were not the first Benedictines to arrive in the Northwest. According to the *Catholic Sentinel*, Father Otto Kopf arrived in Portland on the steamer *Elder* during October, 1876. Kopf, it was reported, came to study prospects of placing a colony of German immigrants in Oregon, Washington, or Idaho. What he decided was never revealed. Kopf left as he had come, clothed in mystery. He was never heard from again.

66. A former parishioner of the Benedictines in Conception had urged Odermatt to found their New Engelberg in southwest Oregon.

67. *Catholic Sentinel*, September 15, 1881.

68. Fillmore was also called "Roy station." Names of small towns along the railroad, mostly milk stops, were changed frequently at the whim of railroad bureaucrats.

69. Seghers' subsequent suggestion for the Benedictines to fill in at Fillmore for the weekend implies that he had something like this in mind. The butte itself was said to be an ancient Indian site called *Tap-a-lam-a-bo*, meaning "Mount of Communion." Whites called it Lone Butte Hill or Groves Butte. McCrank, *Mount Angel Abbey*, p. 24.

70. The two monks were at Fillmore on the weekend of October 2, 1881. High Mass was sung by Frei, the sermon preached by Odermatt [Benedictine Fathers], *The Souvenir of Dedication St. Mary's Church, Mt. Angel, Oregon*, (Mt. Angel, 1912), p. 66.

71. Steckler, "Founding of Mount Angel," p. 313.

72. *Ibid.*, p. 319. White's comments were plainly in error. St. Paul Church on the Willamette, a brick church, had been built in 1846.

73. White was wrong again. There were, of course, many schools in the Northwest, some of them like St. Mary's in Portland in flourishing condition.

74. Steckler, "Founding of Mount Angel," p. 320.

75. *Ibid.*, p. 321.

76. *Ibid.*, p. 320.

77. *Ibid.*, p. 324.

78. *Ibid.*, p. 327.

79. There were Archbishop Joseph Alemany and Francis Mora.

80. Steckler, "Founding of Mount Angel," p. 329.

81. *Ibid.*, p. 330.

82. Pollard, *Mount of Communion*, p. 3.

83. Sister M. Ildephonse Nuxoll, O.S.B., *Idaho-Benedictine*, (Cottonwood, 1982), p. 9.

84. *Ibid.*, p. 7.

85. *Ibid.*, p. 9.

86. Van Der Heyden, "Monsignor Adrian J. Croquet," p. 287.

87. Cataldo, having selected this site, almost forgot to purchase it. Suddenly in April, 1882, he recalled the matter and hastily concluded the transaction on April 8. Oregon Province Archives, Cataldo Papers, Mss. "Spokane Mission."

88. The first St. Michael's site was near the Treaty Tree. The Upper Spokanes occupied what is known as Hillyard today. The site of the new mission of 1882 is now marked with a monument, near which is the Indian cemetery. The latter has a large headstone with the name Schoenberg on it, to commemorate my grandmother, uncle, and other relatives buried there in the 1880's.

89. While the vicariate of Idaho lacked its own bishop, it still had its Vatican-appointed administrator, the Archbishop of Oregon City.

90. Brondel in his first *ad-limina* visit to Rome in 1882, brought with him the northwest's bishops' petition for the erection of Montana into a diocese.]Anon.], *The Right Rev. John B. Brondel.*

91. Cyril Van Der Dockt, "The Founders of the Church in Idaho," in *American Ecclesiastical Review*, XXXII(1905), pp. 289- 290.

92. Letter of Lootens to Mesplie, June 21, 1882, in *The American Ecclesiastical Review*, XXXII(1905), p. 280.

93. Rt. Rev. Cyprian Bradley, O.S.B. and Most Rev. Edward J. Kelly, D.D., Ph.D., *History of The Diocese of Boise 1863 1952*, (Boise, 1953), p. 113.

94. On April 26, 1952, Bishop Edward Kelly, third Bishop of Boise, filed a petition to the United States Army to rescind the court martial against Father Mesplie without success.

95. Mesplie died on November 21, 1895. Bishop Edward Kelly of Boise placed a monument over his grave in 1950.

96. As Simeoni no doubt realized, this would have been a disaster. Jesuits at this time covered all of eastern Washington except Walla Walla, and all of northern Idaho. Gonzaga College in Spokane Falls would never have been realized. So great would the consequences be, that I very much doubt that Beckx would have actually followed through with his threat if Cataldo had been appointed.

97. Giorda's death was attributed to heart failure. He died on August 4, 1882. *Catholic Sentinel*, August 24, 1882.

98. The Sisters had arrived about one month earlier. *Catholic Sentinel*, December 7, 1882

99. Pollard, *Mount of Communion*, p. 3

100. The name was changed in this same year 1883. McCrank, *Mount Angel Abbey*, p. 54.

101. By another decree, March 11, 1883, Eastern Montana was detached from the Ecclesiastical Province of St. Louis and joined to that of Oregon, "On April 7 of the same year, a decree bestowed on Montana a resident administrator in the person of the Rt. Rev. John B. Brondel, Bishop of Vancouver Island . . . one year later, March 7, 1884, the Vicariate of Montana became the Diocese of Helena." Palladino, *Indian and White*, p. 293.

102. *Ibid.*, p. 425. The text reads: "Mary went with haste into the hill country [Montana]," (Luke 1:39).

103. "The administrator of Montana went with haste into the hill country."

104. *Ibid.*, p. 430.

105. *Ibid.*, p. 431.

106. One of Brondel's successors, Bishop Charles Carroll, took exception to any future commitments made to the Jesuits in Missoula.

107. *Catholic Sentinel,'* October 30, 1884.

108. Barcelo had made his novitiate at Santa Clara where his Novice Master, Father Ravalli, had inspired him to work with the northwest Indians. Barcelo was so penitential, even when on difficult missions, that Palladino reported him to the superior for what he regarded as excessive penance.

109. Palladino, *Indian and White*, p. 255.

110. The first Mass in this church was celebrated on Christmas Day 1881.

111. St. Joseph Labre, known as the "Beggar of Rome," and the "Saint of the Forty Hours Devotions," was born in France, March 25, 1748. Unable to live in conventional monasteries because of his eccentricities, he became a beggar and shared all he had with other beggars. He died in a home for the poor on April 16, 1783 and was immediately proclaimed a saint by the populace.

112. The first Diocesan Synod in the Nesqually Diocese convened on October 23, 1883. The first in Helena began on June 24, 1884.

113. *Catholic Sentinel*, July 26, 1883 and March 13, 1884.

114. This was on November 19, 1883.

115. This and the following details are found in the *Catholic Sentinel*, July 21, 1887.

116. The other four are Portland, Baker, Juneau, and Vancouver Island.

117. Bradley and Kelly, History of Boise, p. 204.

118. *Ibid.*, p. 205.

119. Ravalli died at St. Mary's on October 2, 1884, on the feast of the Holy Angels.

120. Anderledy became vicar general on September 24, 1883, and became general when Peter Beckx died on March 4, 1887.

121. Bradley and Kelly, *History of Boise*, p. 204.

122. Sister Mary Mildred, *The Apostle of Alaska*, p.201.

123. The acts of the Council were published as follows: *Acta-Et Decreta Concilii Plenarii Baltimorensis Tertii*, (Baltimore, 1886), p. LV.

124. One of the signers was Father Fierens, pastor of the Cathedral in Portland. It is quite possible, though unlikely, that the forged signatures represented priests, who, in the judgment of DeRoo, would have signed the petition if he had requested it. In other words, DeRoo may have *presumed* their acquiescence.

125. [Holy Names Sisters], *Excerpts from Oregon Chronicles*, (Portland, 1958), p. 182.

126. *Ibid.*, p. 183.

127. *Catholic Sentinel*, April 2, 1895. Seghers took possession of the See of Vancouver Island on April 1, 1885. A year later, in May 1886, he received the pallium, reserved for archbishops, for the second time, because Leo XIII insisted that he retain his status as archbishop. Father Conrardy brought the pallium from Rome. *Catholic Sentinel*, May 30, 1907.

128. The Redemptorists first came to the United States in 1832, but failed to find a permanent foundation until 1839, when they became established in Pittsburgh. Answering the appeal of the bishops they undertook the care of German immigrants.

129. *Catholic Sentinel*, March 5, 1885.

130. The Battle of Gettysburg took place July 1 to July 3, 1863.

Chapter 10. NEW CHURCHES AND SCHOOLS

1. Riel taught at St. Peter's Mission in 1884. Later he composed a poem in honor of Father Joseph Damiani, the mission's superior.

2. Riel was hanged by the Canadian government on November 18, 1885.

3. This event took place shortly after Barcelo's arrival in September, 1884, but news of it reached Portland much later. L. B. Palladino, S.J., *Indian and White In the Northwest A History of Catholicity In Montana 1831 to 1891*, (Lancaster, 1922), p. 245.

4. Sister M. Ildephonse Nuxoll, O.S.B., *Idaho Benedictine*, (Cottonwood, 1976), p. 10.

5. Msgr. John P. Kleinz, Ph.D., *A Short History of St. Boniface Parish, Uniontown, Washington*, (Moscow [Idaho], 1960), p. 25.

6.Mother M. Johanna has described all of these details in her journal. Sister M. Ildephonse Nuxoll, O.S.B., *Idaho Benedictine*, p. 12 et seq.

7. Three years later a new pastor, Father Anton Joehren, disapproved of Sister Rosalia's position in the district school, and agitated with Catholics until she left it. This and other troublesome doings of Joehren finally forced the sisters to leave Uniontown.

8. Martin Pollard, O.S.B.,*Mount of Communion: Mt Angel Abbey 1882-1892*, (St. Benedict, 1982), p. 4. The monks occupied this building in the summer of 1884.

9. *Catholic Sentinel*, February 26, 1885.

10. Rt. Rev. Cyprian Bradley, O.S.B. and Most Rev. Edward J. Kelly, D.D., Ph.D., *History of The Diocese of Boise 1863-1952*, (Boise, 1953), p. 205.

11. It should be noted that Gibbons was not yet a cardinal. The classic biography of him recorded the consecration of Glorieux in a simple sentence: "On April 19, 1885, Gibbons consecrated his fourth bishop in the person of Alphonsus [sic] Glorieux, Vicar Apostolic of Idaho." John Tracy Ellis, *The Life of James Cardinal Gibbons Archbishop of Baltimore, 1834- 1921*, 2 vols., (Milwaukee, 1952) II, 288.

12. These and the following details are taken from the *Catholic Sentinel*, May 28, 1885.

13. Bradley and Kelly, *History of Boise*, p.207.

14. *Ibid.*, p. 208.

15. *Ibid.*, p. 212.

16. These were the remarks of Father Van der Heyden, one of Glorieux' first recruits. *Ibid.*, p. 260 et seq.

17. *Ibid.*, p. 211.

18. The terminology used here is as follows: A *parish* is where the priest is resident, a *mission* is where there is a church, but no resident priest. A mission is attached to a specific parish. A *station* is a settlement or town where there is neither a church nor a resident priest. A priest visited his stations at regular intervals saying Mass and administering the sacraments in an available room, for example in a home, or hotel lobby.

19. Like most church directories on the frontier, this one was in error. Gazzoli, for example, had been dead for three years.

20. There were five nuns at DeSmet and three in Lewiston, Idaho. There were also two Jesuit scholastics and two brothers at DeSmet.

21. In 1870, however, the population of Idaho was about ten thousand less.

22. Emmanuel Nattini born in Genoa, Italy, October 22, 1826, entered the Jesuit Order when he was twenty years of age. He left the Jesuits of the California Mission in 1880 and volunteered for the Vicariate of Idaho, where he served until 1887. He died in Genoa with the reputation of a holy priest in 1910.

23. Bradley and Kelly, *History of Boise*, p. 214.

24. *Ibid.*, p. 216.

25. This second St. Stanislaus Church was completed some time in the last part of 1884. Oregon Province Archives, Lewiston Papers, Mss. on "St. Stanislaus Church."

26. William G. Elliott, S.J., *1867 Lewiston Catholic Centennial 1967*, (Lewiston, 1967).

27. Bradley and Kelly, *History of Boise*, p. 209. These sisters were succeeded by Sisters of the Third Order of St. Francis from Glen Riddle, Pennsylvania, who conducted the school from August 28, 1888 to June, 1893. They in turn were succeeded by Jesuit scholastics.

28. *Ibid.*, p. 210. Bishop Glorieux reported the Indian Catholic population as follows: Coeur d'Alenes 500, Nez Perce 300, and Kootenai 100.

29. In 1889 after the great fire, the residents dropped the word Falls from the name of the city.

30. The dedication ceremonies were described in the *Catholic Sentinel*, August 20, 1885.

31. *Ibid.*

32. *Ibid.*, November 5, 1885.

33. Bishop Blanchet lived during retirement in the Sisters' hospital in Vancouver.

34. Actual cost was $25,000. Gerard George Steckler [S.J.], *Charles John Seghers Missionary Bishop In The American Northwest 1839-1886*, A thesis submitted in partial fulfillment of the requirements for the degree of Doctor of Philosophy, University Washington, 1963, p. 427.

35. *Ibid.*, p. 431.

36. Sister Mary Barnaba, O.S.F., M.A., *A Diamond Crown for Christ the Kind A Story of the First Franciscan Foundations In Our Country 1855-1930*, (Glen Riddle, 1930), p. 206.

37. Gerard George Steckler [S.J.], "The Case of Frank Fuller The Killer of Alaska Missionary Charles Seghers," in *Pacific Northwest Quarterly*, 59(October 1968), p. 190.

38. [George W. Weibel, S.J.], *Gonzaga's Silver Jubilee A Memoir*, (Spokane, 1912), p. 27.

39. Ruellan died at St. Francis Regis Mission on January 7, 1885.

40. Wilbur was succeeded as agent for the Yakimas by General R. H. Milroy on August 15, 1882.

41. [George W. Weibel, S.J.], "Fifty Years of Peaceful Conquest," in *Gonzaga Magazine*, V(1913-1914), pp. 463 and 522.

42. Oregon Province Archives, Mss. "Yakima."

43. *Catholic Sentinel*, July 22, 1886, *The Chewelah Independent*, June 11, 1953.

44. *Catholic Sentinel*, December 2, 1886. Robert Monaghan, son of James and later hero of Samoa, was baptized in this church. H. L. McCulloch, S.J., *Life of John Robert Monaghan The Hero of Samoa*, (Spokane, 1906).

45. Oregon Province Archives, Mss. "Parodi."

46. Aloysius Parodi was institutionalized, but recovered sufficiently to undertake parish work. He died in the odor of sanctity at Detroit on April 15, 1928.

47. Palladino, *Indian and White*, p. 353. See also: *Indian Sentinel* I(1917), p. 37 et seq.

48. Sister Maria Ilma Raufer, O.P., *Blackrobes and Indians On The Last Frontier A Story of Heroism*, (Milwaukee, 1963), p. 174 et seq.

49. Mother Angela Clotilda, O.S.U., *Ursulines of the West 1535-1935: 1880-1935*, (Everett, 1936), p. 38.

50. *Catholic Sentinel*, August 6, 1885. A correspondent known only as "C. F." Father Charles Follett, a later companion of the bishop, did not arrive in Helena until 1887.

51. *Catholic Sentinel*, January 28, 1886.

52. Brother Angelus Gabriel, F.S.C., *The Christian Brothers in The United States 1848-1948; A Century of Catholic Education*, (New York, 1948), p. 390.

53. The parish of the Holy Rosary in Pomeroy was formally organized in the spring of 1878. The first church in Sprague was built by Father Joset in the spring of 1882.

54. [Joseph Sondergeld], *Holy Rosary Parish 1878-1928*, (Pomeroy, 1928), p.9.

55. Nuxoll, *Idaho Benedictine*, p. 15.

56. *Catholic Sentinel*, February 25, 1886 and March 4, 1886.

57. Appendix "Difficulties of Father Prefontaine," from unpublished thesis: Sister Mary Oliver Borky, O.S.F., "Msgr. Francis Xavier Prefontaine," Seattle University, p. 194.

58. *Ibid.*

59. *Ibid.* Junger decided to sell this cemetery land while Prefontaine was in Europe in 1888-1889.

60. The academy was opened on January 10, 1881, with twenty-one students registered on the first day. Prefontaine spent his last years as chaplain there.

61. The Jesuits did not arrive in Seattle to found a school until 1891.

62. Dittonhall was in England, where he was ordained. More complete details for this period can be found in Wilfred P. Schoenberg, S.J., *Gonzaga University The First Seventy-five Years*, (Spokane, 1963), p. 67 et seq.

63. Frank Gully, alias Fuller, liked to be called Brother Fuller. He had been a postulant in the Jesuit Order, but was dismissed as unsuitable. The best published source on Fuller and this period of Seghers' life is: Steckler, "The Case for Frank Fuller," p. 190 et seq.

64. This was the customary route followed by many gold seekers during the rush to the Klondike in 1898.

65. *Catholic Sentinel*, June 24, 1886. Imoda died on May 12, 1902. Later, when his body was disinterred for removal to Mount St. Michael's cemetery in Spokane, the coffin was opened and Imoda's body was found to be incorrupt.

66. Father J. P. Halton of Livingston rented this frame building in Billings for $50.00 a year on August 31, 1885. The new church was erected in 1886. This was Billings' first Catholic church. It was dedicated on August 21, 1887 by Bishop Brondel.

67. Guidi had built this chapel three years earlier. It was located a few miles down the Jefferson River at a place called Old Town. Palladino, *Indian and White*, p. 441.

68. *Ibid.*, p. 160.

69. Pauwelyn, a Belgian deacon, had accompanied Brondel on his return to America in 1885. He spent many productive years as a priest in Montana,then returned to Belgium where he died at Cortrai on April 20, 1940.

70. *Catholic Sentinel*, September 2, 1886.

73. In the *Catholic Sentinel* for May 27, 1886, there is a touching entry: "The soldier boys at Fort Walla Walla donated $57.75 to the Sisters of Mercy on pay day, Troop F leading with $21.25."

74. The Franciscan Sisters were in the Northwest to stay. They soon conducted schools in Lewiston (1888), Tacoma (1888), Spokane (1890), Tekoa (1893), La Grande (1894).

75 This long letter appeared in the *Catholic Sentinel*, December 23, 1886.

76. Steckler, "The Case for Frank Fuller," p. 192.

77. Both Jesuits objected to the archbishop's plan. They were particularly concerned about the danger that the presence of Fuller indicated.

78. Harper's Place, a trading post called Forty Mile at the headwaters of the Yukon, where the Stewart River flows into the Yukon.

79. These two volumes, salvaged by the Indians who had removed Seghers' body, were eventually brought to Holy Cross Mission, whence I retrieved them for the Oregon Province Archives in 1957. They are found now among the Seghers papers there.

80. Tosi wrote "Mouth of the Stewart River, 24 Novembre 1886" and Robaut "Mouth of the Stewart River, November 28, 1886." These long narratives are in the Oregon Province Archives.

81. Sister Mary Mildred, SS.A. *The Apostle of Alaska, Life of the Most Reverend Charles John Seghers*, (Paterson, 1943), p. 245.

82. Steckler, *Charles John Seghers Missionary Bishop*, p. 501 et seq.

83. Fuller's trial was held in Sitka in November 1887. Due to a lack of preparation by the government, the trial was a farce. Fuller was convicted of manslaughter and was sentenced "to ten years at hard labor and a thousand dollar fine." A strange sequel: After his release from the penitentiary at McNeil Island, Fuller was shot and killed by a neighbor, *in self defense.* Steckler, "The Case for Frank Fuller," p. 200.

84. Of the five, Provost had disappeared, Seghers was murdered, Fuller the murderer was in custody. Tosi had gone to the States for instructions, only Robaut was left in Alaska.

85. Sister Mary Mildred, *The Apostle of Alaska*, p. 248. On September 11, 1888, the mortal remains of Archbishp Seghers were exhumed and brought aboard the *Thetis*, which arrived on Thursday, November 15, 1888, at the port of Esquimalt, British Columbia. Bishop Lemmens, Seghers' successor, and Bishop Brondel, with members of the clergy, received the body and transported it for burial in the Cathedral at Victoria.

86. *Atsimoikhani*. Wilfred P. Schoenberg, S.J., *Jesuit Mission Presses in the Pacific Northwest A History and Bibliography of Imprints 1876-1899*, (Portland, 1957), p. 22.

87. Oregon Province Archives, Prando Papers, Mss. "St. Xavier Mission."

88. Palladino, *Indian and White*, p. 258.

89. Rappagliosi died on February 7, 1878. There is some evidence but not conclusive, that he was poisoned. *Ibid.*, p. 218.

90. McLoughlin died in 1857 and Petrain in 1878.

91. Barclay died in 1873.

92. Brouillet had been caught in a blizzard while touring the missions in the Dakotas. He suffered snow blindness and paralysis which caused his death on February 5, 1884.

93. McBean died in 1872; Peter Skene Ogden in 1854.

94. DeSmet died in 1873, Accolti five years later.

95. Nobili died in 1856 and DeVos in 1859.

96. Mengarini in 1886, Spechts in 1884, and Magri in 1869.

97. Ravalli in 1884, Giorda in 1882, Gazzoli in 1882, and Brother Huybrechts in 1872.

98. Claessens died in Santa Clara on October 11, 1891. Hoecken died in Milwaukee on April 19, 1897.

99. This was Louise Henriette Pelletier, Plamondon's third wife.

100. Bermier died on December 27, 1889.

101. *Catholic Sentinel*, April 21, 1887.

102. This was Lieutenant Anderson who welcomed Cardinal Gibbons to Vancouver by releasing prisoners in his honor. The Anderson article appeared as follows: Thomas M. Anderson, "The Vancouver Reservation Case. A Legal Romance" in *The Quarterly of the Oregon Historical Society*, VII(1907), p. 219 et seq.

103. *Ibid.*

104. Schoenberg, *Gonzaga University*, p. 44.

105. [Benedictine Fathers], *Silver Jubilee 1887–1912*, (Mount Angel, 1912), p. 14.

106. Pollard, *Mount of Communion*, p. 4.

107. These and other particulars are found in Wilfred P. Schoenberg, S.J., *Paths To The Northwest A Jesuit History of The Oregon Province*, (Chicago, 1982), p. 154 et seq.

108. *Passing Events In The Life of Cardinal Gibbons*, N.P., N.D., [Rare fragment in the Archives of the Archdiocese of Baltimore], p. 315 et seq.

109. *Catholic Sentinel*, September 13, 1974.

110. The Cardinal conferred the pallium on Gross on Sunday, October 9, 1887.

111. Several students were in attendance in Mount Angel College with a view to entering the priesthood. These were the nucleus of the first seminary. [Fathers of St. Benedict], *Mount Angel Seminary 1889–1964*, (St. Benedict, [Oregon], 1964), [2].

112. *Ibid.* [1].

113. *Ibid.* [2].

114. *Catholic Sentinel*, August 25, 1887.

115. *Ibid.* September 23, 1875 and October 9, 1890.

116. This was St. Joackim's, which was replaced in 1908 with a new, larger church called St. Patrick's. *Ibid.*, September 1, 1887.

117. St. Peter's Hospital in Olympia was opened on June 18, 1887.

118. He had begun to correspond with Father Damien DeVeuster the famous Apostle of the Lepers in 1877. One of the best published sources on Conrardy is Patricia Dayton, "In Oregon and In China He Fed God's Lambs, The Story of Father Louis Lambert Conrardy . . . 'China's Father Damien'," in *St. Joseph Magazine* reprint, *Catholic Contributions to Oregon History*, (Mount Angel, 1959), p. 2 et seq.

119. *Ibid.*, p. 3.

120. Conrardy had been born in Liege, Belgium, in 1841.

121. *Ibid.*, p. 2.

122. Conrardy was a non-conformist, like Damien, and he was unable to remain in Molokai after Damien's death. After earning a medical degree, and many other vicissitudes, he established his own leper colony at Sheklung, China. He died in Hong Kong clutching a crucifix in one hand and a Chinese dictionary in the other. He was buried according to his wish, rolled up in a mat between two lepers.

123. Born November 25, 1830, at Girola in the Province of Voghera, Italy, Grassi entered the Society of Jesus on December 5, 1850. Three years later he came to America.

124. William J. Metz, "History of The Catholic Church in the State of Washington," in *The Inland Catholic Messenger*, II,4(May, 1920), p. 32.

125. Schoenberg, *Gonzaga University*, p. 41.

126. *Reminiscences and Current Topics of the Ecclesiastical Province of Oregon*, II, 2(February, 1898), p. 23.

127. *Ibid*.

128. The mission of St. George struggled along, barely surviving with the help of Mother Drexel, until 1938.

129. In 1890, the total Indian population, exclusive of Alaska, was 243,534. U.S. Government, *Forty-Ninth Annual Report of the Commissioner of Indian Affairs to the Secretary of the Interior, 1890*, (Washington, 1890), p. 464. Note also that the Indian population in 1983 has been estimated at 1,400,000. *America*, Vol. 148(May 28, 1983), p. 416.

130. This church called "Assumption" after 1895, was built "a short time after April 29, 1888" when the first Mass was offered in Napavine by Father Frei. Thus the exact date is not certain.

Chapter 11. SISTERS OF ST. MARY

1. Not all of the following has been published heretofore out of respect for living persons. Some particulars appear in the following: Mark Schmid, O.S.B., *Sublimity, the Story of an Oregon Countryside 1850–1950*, (Mount Angel, 1951), p. 87 et seq. The early history of Albrecht's Colony is presented in detail in Sister M. Grace McDonald, O.S.B., *With Lamps Burning*, (St. Joseph [Missouri] 1957), p. 113 et seq. Additional material has been provided in an interview and in writing by Sister Frances Zenner, S.S.M.O., historian for the Sisters of St. Mary of Oregon. Finally a jubilee publication has appeared: Sisters of St. Mary of Oregon, *Souvenir of Golden Jubilee 1886–1936*, (N.P., 1936). This contains a photograph of five of the heroic foundresses on page 20.

2. Albrecht, formerly a mayor in a town of Germany, felt a call to a higher life. He and his wife agreed to separate and enter a religious order. He chose the Society of the Precious Blood, He came to the United States, was ordained in Cleveland in 1849 and was pastor of Himelsgarten in Mercer County, Ohio for ten years. McDonald, *With Lamps Burning*, p. 113.

3. *Ibid*, p. 114.

4. Interview July 18, 1983 with Sister Francis Zenner.

5. McDonald, *With Lamps Burning*, p. 115.

6. Not only was the leader dead, his despotism had allowed no one else to become a leader. So the colony drifted.

7. This was Emma Bliley, aged 26 at the time. Sister Frances Zenner interview, July 18, 1983. The following details were provided by Sister Zenner.

8. *Catholic Sentinel*, June 29, 1961.

9. The Benedictine priest, Father Ruttiman, did not have much time to enjoy his triumph. He died of tuberculosis during the night of December 31, 1886. On New Year's morning, one of the sisters discovered his body and tolled the old bell to mourn his passing.

10. Among these students were the two Prange boys, Frank and John. Both became Jesuits. Frank became the superior of the Jesuits in Alaska, John superior at Holy Family Mission, Montana. Frank died at Beaverton, in the Maryville Nursing Home conducted by the Sisters of St. Mary of Oregon, at the age of 82. John, though younger, had died of cancer many years before in 1958.

11. *Catholic Sentinel*, February 14, 1889.

12. *Ibid.*, June 30, 1889.

13. Oregon Province Archives, Mss. "Sisters of St. Mary of Oregon."

14. Some of the sisters, however, remained at Sublimity to staff the parochial school. *Ibid.*

15. *Ibid.* This was on August 12, 1905. Prior to this the sisters' collective title was "Congregation of the Precious Blood."

16. *Ibid.* The status of Pontifical Institute permitted the sisters to establish residences in other dioceses.

17. There were as follows:

Congregation of St. Thomas Aquinas (1888)
Congregation of the Queen of the Most Holy Rosary (1889)
Congregation of the Holy Cross (1890)
Congregation of the Perpetual Rosary (1907)
Congregation of St. Catherine of Siena (1911)
Congregation of the Immaculate Heart of Mary (1922)
Congregation of the Sacred Heart (1922)

18. Sister Mary Rita Flanagan, O.P., *The Work of the Sisters of St. Dominic of the Congregation of St. Thomas Aquinas in the Diocese of Seattle 1888-1951*, (Seattle, 1951), p. 14.

19. *Ibid.*, p. 21 et seq.

20. *Ibid.*, p. 36.

21. *Ibid.*, p. 21 et seq.

22. Sister Mary of St. Teresita, R.G.S., *The Social Work of the Sisters of the Good Shepherd*, (Cleveland, 1938), p. 239.

23. [Sisters of the Good Shepherd], *Fifty Golden Years*, (Portland, 1952), p. 6.

24. The sisters arrived on September 20, 1905. Oregon Province Archives, Mss. "Sisters of the Good Shepherd."

25. *Ibid.* Michael Patrick O'Shea was a colorful Irish layman who "had emigrated from England as a young man, an emigration encouraged by the British authorities because of his Irish political activisim." Later he moved his family from Salem, Massachusetts to Spokane Falls in 1887, where he became a colorful, sometimes contentious member of St. Aloysius parish. All four sons went to Gonzaga; three of them went off to Harvard Medical College and became illustrious doctors. Son, Dr. John O'Shea, practiced in Spokane. He was "house doctor" for the Jesuits, who called him affectionately "Jack the Ripper" because he removed the appendix of many a scholastic. Confer: the letter of Edward Patrick Lenahan to Schoenberg, New York, August 3, 1983, in Oregon Province Archives.

26. There were, of course, mission schools at Sacred Heart Mission and at Slickpoo.

27. Rt. Rev. Cyprian Bradley, O.S.B. and Most Rev. Edward J. Kelly, D.D., Ph.D., *History of the Diocese of Boise 1863-1952*, (Boise, 1953), p. 256.

28. *Ibid.* After being released from the hospital, Glorieux repaired to Astoria, Oregon, where the sea breezes soon restored him to health. He returned to Boise on October 4, 1889.

29. *Ibid.*, p. 257.

30. *Catholic Sentinel*, November 25, 1897.

31. Bradley and Kelly, *History of Boise*, p. 257.

32. *Catholic Sentinel,* May 30, 1907, [page 20].

33. Rev. J. Van Der Heyden, "Monsignor Adrian J. Croquet Indian Missionary," in the *Records of the American Catholic Historical Society of Philadelphia,* XVII (1906), p. 224.

34. Croquet returned to his mission in October, 1889.

35. DeRoo had engaged in research in the Vatican Archives for a history of Alexander VI. He uncovered other documents of interest, related to pre-Columbian America and produced the two volumes as a consequence. They were published in Philadelphia and London in 1900.

36. *Catholic Sentinel,* June 27, 1889. *Vancouver Independent,* June 26, 1889.

37. DeRouge was absent from the mission to undertake his last year of Jesuit studies, from May, 1888 to April, 1889. Sister Maria Ilma Raufer, O.P., *Black Robes and Indians on the Last Frontier,* (Milwaukee, 1963), p. 190.

38. Oregon Province Archives, Aloysius Parodi, S.J., Mss. "Reminiscences."

39. *Ibid.*

40. This was Christmas 1888, when DeRouge was away.

41. Raufer, *Black Robes and Indians,* p. 191.

42. Construction of a new church was begun immediately.

43. George Washington was born on February 22, 1732, according to the Gregorian calendar.

44. Edmond S. Meany, M.L., *History of the State of Washington,* (New York, 1946), p. 281.

45. Idaho was finally admitted as a state on July 3, 1890, when its population was estimated to be 88,548.

46. Meany, *History of the State,* p. 282.

47. Mary W. Avery, *History and Government of the State of Washington,* (Seattle, 1961), p. 317.

48. We have no listings of the delegates' religious preferences, but since the Catholic population of Washington at this time was less than ten percent, it is most unlikely that more than two or three Catholic delegates were elected. Many voters in the more populous centers had demonstrated against the Yakima Oblates at the time of the Yakima Indian War.

49. The names of all seventy-five delegates appear in Lancaster Pollard, *A History of the State of Washington,* 4 vols. (New York, 1937), I:413–414.

50. Arguments for the passage of the Oregon School Bill in 1923 included this one.

51. For example, Father Edward McGlynn and Richard Burtsell of New York, "They opposed parochial schools...." James Hennessey, S.J., *American Catholics, A History of the Roman Catholic Community in the United States,* (New York, 1981), p. 166. Hennessey, p. 172 et seq., presents a detailed account of the struggle within the church hierarchy on the school issue.

52. The Germans comprised the largest percentage of Catholic immigrants to the United States in the 1880's. Unlike many of the Irish, they settled on land in western states, forming colonies like Uniontown and Colton in eastern Washington.

53. Oregon Province Archives, Mss. "History of Colfax Parish," by Rev. W.B. Bender.

54. A Sister of St. Benedict, *History of the American Swiss Congregation of the Order of St. Benedict,* (Cottonwood, 1929), p. 56.

55. Sister M. Idelphonse Nuxoll, O.S.B., *Idaho Benedictines,* (Cottonwood, 1976).

56. *Ibid.,* p. 15.

57. *Ibid.,* p. 16.

58. *Ibid.* Frei was a diocesan priest, under Bishop A. Egger in Switzerland. He had befriended the Benedictines at Mount Angel. Also, the anti-religious laws of Switzerland drove him, like the Benedictines, from his native home.

59. *Ibid.,* p. 17.

60. *Ibid.*

61. *Washington Post* [Uniontown], June 8, 1888.

62. Nuxoll, *Idaho Benedictines,* p. 18.

63. The laymen signers were George Bauer, Ernest Becker, Michael Reisenauer, M. Thee, Joseph Semler, Jr., and Carl Seng. County Courthouse Records, Colfax, Washington, Henry Michels, Treasurer of the Catholic Church at Uniontown, Washington, Plaintiff, etc.

64. In December 1892, Colton residents sent a delegation to Uniontown to offer the sisters twenty acres of land near town, the selection of the site being left to the sisters. They decided to accept the invitation and chose twenty acres just north of Colton "part of Mr. E. Becker's property."

65. Nuxoll, *Idaho Benedictines,* p. 18.

66. The road was narrow and buggies in passing were very close to one another.

67. E.S. Barnett [attorney] Plaintiff vs. Rev. A. Joehren, Case No. 4840, July 27, 1874, in Whitman County, Colfax.

68. Mrs. Viola Weis, local historian, has identified these foundations, which still exist beneath the larger church, built at a later date.

69. The year 1893 was the first and only crop failure in Palouse Country.

70. Notice of the Sheriff's sale has been attached to the Court documents in the case. This notice was published August 31, 1894 and September 28, 1894.

71. Nuxoll, *Idaho Benedictines,* p. 18.

72. *Ibid.,* p. 19.

73. Father Frencker did not stay long. *Ibid.,* p. 20.

74. *Ibid.*

75. Henry Nichels [Treasurer of Uniontown Church] Plaintiff vs J. Frei et alii, Case No. 4813 in Superior Court, Whitman County Courthouse, Colfax.

76. The case dragged on for many months. It was finally dropped when Bishop O'Dea, Junger's successor, ordered both sides of the dispute to end it.

77. Nuxoll, *Idaho Benedictines,* p. 20.

78. Before he left for Wisconsin, Joehren went about and made peace with his antagonists, shaking their hands and acknowledging his mistakes.

79. Mackin's hair had been black until the night of March 19, 1890. During the previous day one of Gonzaga College's best students, only son of a wealthy, influential Seattle businessman, had been killed in a dreadful accident. [George W. Weibel, S.J.], *Gonzaga Silver Jubilee A Memoir,* (Spokane, 1912), p. 99.

80. This was May 4, 1888.

81. At this time, 1890, the Umatilla Mission was called St. Joseph's. Its name was changed to St. Andrew's in 1893 to honor the director of the Catholic Indian Bureau. However, St. Joseph remained the patron of the church.

82. The Monaghan mansion still stands. It is the present Music Building on the Gonzaga University campus.

83. This was Father Rebmann, who became president of the college after Mackin.

84. Dwyer's parents were Denis Dwyer and Mary Mulcahy Dwyer, who were married in Tipperary County, Ireland, September 4, 1796. William was born in New York State on July 2, 1840, the first of his parents' middle age. Rev. Edward Kowrach, *How Silently A History of the Catholic Church of the Big Bend Mission and St. Anne Church, Medical Lake,* (Medical Lake, 1963), p. 27.

85. Dwyer was ordained on May 22, 1865.

86. The only other priests in northern Idaho were the Jesuits at the Coeur d'Alene mission, or Jesuits from Gonzaga College who attended places like Bonners Ferry on weekends.

87. Kowrach, *How Silently*, p. 25. These "communities of any size" consisted of only several hundred people, of whom only a score or two were Catholics.

88. This church, measuring only thirty by twenty feet, cost a total of $1,200. It was replaced in 1928 by Father Gerald Feirst. *Catholic Sentinel*, September 22, 1881.

89. This first St. Anne's was replaced in 1931 with a new church, by Father William Condon, later bishop of Great Falls. In 1957 St. Anne's was made an independent parish with Father Edward Kowrach as first pastor.

90. Father William Dwyer should be regarded as the Founder of the Big Bend Missions, which have developed into several independent parishes like St. Ann's.

Chapter 12. THE IRISH ARE COMING

1. The Seattle fire occurred on June 6, 1889.

2. In 1891, for example, when Seattle had two parishes, Our Lady of Good Help and the Sacred Heart, Spokane had four. Proportionate to population, Spokane has always had more parishes and more Catholics.

3. Mackin, Jesuit pastor of the parish was also president of the college. He could not do both and Cataldo had no one to replace him.

4. Mentioned elsewhere as the founder of many churches in northern Idaho.

5. It was a common custom in the good old days for visiting prelates or celebrities to grant holidays. Junger carefully observed the custom and earned in return his popularity with the boys. This was one reason why he was so attached to Gonzaga College.

6. Oregon Province Archives, Gonzaga Diaries.

7. Later this congregation was called Sisters of St. Joseph of Newark, then Sisters of St. Joseph of Peace.

8. Le R.P.A.G. Morice, O.M.I., *Dictionnaire Historique Des Canadiens Et des Metis francais De L'Ouest*, (Quebec, 1908), p. 41.

9. Chirouse left Tulalip on August 15, 1878.

10. *Catholic Sentinel*, July 17, 1890.

11. Junger dedicated this St. Mary's on June 26, 1890. *Ibid.*, July 27, 1890.

12. William J. Metz, "History of the Catholic Church in the State of Washington," in *The Inland Empire Catholic Messenger*, II 5(June 1920), p. XV.

13. [Thomas Pitsch], *Assumption Church Golden Jubilee Year Book 1889-1939*, (Bellingham, 1939), p. 13.

14. *Catholic Sentinel*, October 11, 1900.

15. Some copies are in the Oregon Province Archives.

15. At first these Dominicans were known as the Province of St. Rose, attached to Newburgh. In June 1923, however, the province became a separate Congregation called Holy Cross. Oregon Province Archives, Mss. "Sisters of St. Dominic Congregation of the Holy Cross."

17. *Catholic Sentinel*, February 2, 1888.

18. The bishop's first name was Aegidius. Further details, *Ibid.*, October 18, 1888.

19. [H.B. Conrad, O.M.I.] *Silver Jubilee of Holy Rosary School Moxee City, Washington 1915-1914*, (N.P., 1940), p. 43.

20. Oregon Province Archives, Mss. "Sisters of Charity of Providence."

21. Mother M. Antoinette, F.C.S.P., *The Institute of Providence: History of the Daughters of Charity Servants of the Poor Know As the Sisters of Providence*, 6 vols. (Montreal, 1937=1958), V:337.

22. *Ibid.*

23. *Ibid.*

24. *Great Falls Catholic Review*, III(January 1920), pp. 25- 26.

25. Oregon Province Archives, Mss. "Historical Sketch of St. Ignatius Hospital, Colfax."

26. New units were added to this St. Vincent's in 1910, 1924, and 1957. In 1941, Providence Hospital east of the river was established as a dependent unit of St. Vincent's, but it outlived its dependency status in three years. In 1944 it became a separate hospital. Oregon Province Archives, Mss. "Sisters of Charity of Providence."

27. These journals are all extant and are securely kept in the Archives of the Sisters of the Holy Names at Marylhurst, Oregon. A compilation of selections was translated from the French [all early journals are in French], and a very limited number of mineographed copies were produced under the title: *Excerpts from Oregon Chronicles 1859-1959.* Copies may be found in the Marylhurst Archives and in the Oregon Province Archives.

28. [Sisters of the Holy Names], *Excerpts From Oregon Chronicles 1859-1959,* (Marylhurst, 1959), p. 52.

29. *Ibid.,* p. 53.

30. *Ibid.,* p. 83.

31. *Ibid.,* p. 53.

32. *Ibid.,* p. 194.

33. *Ibid.,* p. 220. This academy was opened at the request of the Jesuits in Spokane "who donated a tract of four acres in Sinto Addition for that purpose." [Sister M. Flavia], *Gleanings of Fifty Years,* (Portland, 1909), p. 159.

34. [Sisters of the Holy Names], *Excertps from Oregon Chronicles,* p. 122.

35. *Ibid.,* p. 150. The Jacksonville Academy was closed on September 8, 1908. The sisters moved to Medford and opened St. Mary's Academy there on September 14, 1908. On the first day they had twenty-six students, six of whom were resident. *Ibid.,* p. 154.

36. Joseph Bernard Code, *Dictionary of the American Hierarchy (1789-1964),* (New York, 1964), p. 224.

37. Edward John O'Dea was born on November 23, 1856.

38. Father Dominic O'Connor, *A Brief History of the Diocese of Baker,* (Baker, 1930), p. 4.

39. O'Reilly was editor of the *Catholic Sentinel* from 1900-1903.

40. They were ordained at Walla Walla on January 2, 1848.

41. Kay Cronin, *Cross in the Wilderness,* (Vancouver, 1960), p. 157.

42. *Catholic Sentinel,* August 20, 1891. Bishop Francis Leipzig published an appropriate eulogy of McCormick in the *Catholic Sentinel, September 9, 1977.*

43. The Horse Plains (now called Plains) Church, called St. James, was dedicated by Bishop Brondel on October 6, 1889. L.B. Palladino, S.J., *Indian and White in the Northwest A History of Catholicity in Montana 1831-1891,* (Lancaster, 1922), p. 389.

44. The church was completed for St. Ignatius Day, July 31, 1893. More details can be found in the Oregon Province Archives, Crosby Library, St. Ignatius Mission Diaries. Confer also: Wilfred P. Schoenberg, S.J., *Paths to the Northwest,* (Chicago, 1982), pp. 171-172.

45. *Ibid.,* p. 145.

46. Timothy F. Cronin, S.J., "Seattle University: 1891-1966." A dissertation presented in partial fulfillment of the requirements for the degree of Doctor of Education, Seattle University, 1982, p. 6.

47. This is known as the Garrand Building. It serves the biology department.

48. Schoenberg, *Paths to the Northwest,* p. 179.

49. Gross came from a family of Alsatians, whose country Germany dominated before World War I.

50. The first Redemptorists in the Northwest were Fathers J.A. McLoughlin, Charles Kern, Henry Meuer and William Shea, all from St. Louis. They gave a series of missions throughout the Northwest in 1887. *Catholic Sentinel,* May 19, 1887. The four Redemptorists who established the parish in Portland on July 5, 1890, were as follows: Fathers Edward Cantwell, Augustine Guendling, and James Moye, and Brother Francis. There is some

evidence to believe that they left Portland for Seattle because Archbishop Gross, also a Redemptorist, interfered too much in the parish.

51. The Redemptorists returned to Portland on August 13, 1906, and established Holy Redeemer Parish.

52. The Sacred Heart Church, at Sixth and Bell, constructed by Father Charles Sigl as the second parish church in Seattle, was destroyed by fire in March 1899.

53. A permanent brick church replaced this temporary Our Lady of Perpetual Help church in 1925. Built by Father Anthony Fischer, this was dedicated on September 6, 1925, *Northwest Progress*, September 4, 1925.

54. This was the first St. Michael's Church in downtown Portland.

55. *Catholic Sentinel*, March 17, 1887, March 24, 1887, and August 25, 1887.

56. Apparently this had been built recently as a mission church of St. Leo's. Demetrius Jueneman, O.S.B. and Sebastian Ruth, O.S.B., *Between the Years 1895–1945, St. Martin's College, Lacey*, (N.P., 1945), [pp. 10–11.]

57. *The Builder*, [Gonzaga Preparatory School], May 12, 1945.

58. [Martin Pollard, O.S.B.] *Mount of Communion Mt. Angel Abbey 1882–1982*, (St. Benedict, 1982), p. 5.

59. Jueneman and Ruth, 1891. *Between the Years*, [p. 12].

60. This was in June, 1891. *Ibid.*, [p. 11].

61. They generously agreed to allow the Benedictines to retain the Dryad property.

62. A.P.A. stood for the "American Protective Association," which was founded by Henry F. Bowers in 1887 at Clinton, Iowa. "Members promised never to vote for a Catholic, never to hire one when a Protestant was available, and never to join Catholics in a strike." James Hennessey, S.J., *American Catholics A History of the Roman Catholic Community in the United States*, (New York, 1981), p. 182.

63. Jueneman and Ruth, *Between the Years*, [p. 12].

64. *Ibid.*, [p. 15].

65. *Ibid.*, [p. 16].

66. *Catholic Sentinel*, March 28, 1975.

67. These lots were on Third and Clackamas Streets.

68. This was on February 15, 1909. After 1935, Holy Rosary was no longer a priory. Oregon Province Archives, Mss. "Holy Rosary Church, Portland."

69. The *Oregonian* in April 1893 reported that the archbishop's residence would be moved from Third and Oak streets to Stark Street. The *Catholic Sentinel* for January 10, 1875, quotes this item and provides additional history of the Bishop's House.

70. Its present address is 218 Stark Street.

71. This was in 1970. *Catholic Sentinel*, April 17, 1970. The Bishop's House later became a Chinese Tong, a speakeasy, then quarters for the Aero Club. When the old section of downtown Portland was undergoing renewal, William Rogers restored it (1965). At present, the building contains a restaurant and law offices.

72. The cathedral had been dedicated on August 15, 1885.

73. The *Oregonian*, November 1, 1891.

74. Rt. Rev. Cyprian Bradley, O.S.B. and Most Rev. Edward J. Kelly, D.D., Ph.D., *History of the Diocese of Boise, 1863–1952*, p. 267.

75. Gross concluded his moving on Janaury 10, 1894. Previously six rooms had been added to the rectory at St. Joseph's to accommodate the archbishop and his staff.

76. J. Van der Heyden, "Monsignor Adrian J. Croquet, Indian Missionary", in *The Records of the American Catholic Historical Society*, XVII(1906), pp. 227–228.

77. *Ibid.*, p. 229.

78. Including three future bishops, Fathers Orth, O'Dea and O'Reilly.

79. *Ibid.*, p. 239.

80. Adrian Croquet, failing in health and too feeble to work longer, received permission from the archbishop to return to Belgium in 1898. He died there piously in the Lord on August 8, 1902.

81. This Magdalen Home was completed and dedicated by the Archbishop on August 29, 1897. *Catholic Sentinel*, September 2, 1897.

82. *Catholic Sentinel*, August 8, 1895. Lane was made a Protonotary Apostolic with the title of monsignor by Benedict XV in 1920. He died in Portland on November 3, 1941.

83. The Christian Brothers came with the college and lived in miserable confinement above the church. Conditions there soon became very crowded. Among other uses, space there was allocated to the Archdiocesan Archives or records, which were jammed into one cubbyhole and later discarded in part to make room for other purposes.

84. Brother Angelus Gabriel, F.S.C., *The Christian Brothers in the United States 1848–1948; A Century of Catholic Education*, (New York, 1948), p. 390.

85. St. Aloysius School for Select Boys was founded in Helena as a development of St. Aloysius Institute, which began in 1870. In September 1910, St. Charles High School Department was opened to take its place.

86. In 1911, the Sisters of Providence took over Holy Angels College and converted it into a parochial School. Gabriel, *The Christian Brothers*, p. 390.

87. Archives of the Diocese of Helena Scrapbooks, II:25; also, [Sisters of Charity of Leavenworth], *History of the Sisters of Charity of Leavenworth, Kansas*, (Kansas City, 1898), p. 441 et seq.

88. Interestingly, both The University of Portland and Loyola-Marymount in Los Angeles, in large urban areas, experienced problems similar to the University of San Francisco's troubled beginnings.

89. *Catholic Sentinel*, May 9, 1895. For documentation confer: *U.S. Supreme Court Reports, 158, U.S. 155.*

90. [Sisters of the Holy Names], *Excerpts from Oregon Chronicles*, p. 296.

91. Sister Mary of the Blessed Sacrament McCrosson, *The Bell and the River*, (Palo Alto, 1956), p. 253.

92. [Sisters of the Holy Names], *Excerpts from Oregon Chronicles*, p. 196.

93. *Ibid.*, p. 197.

Chapter 13. GROWING PAINS

1. Oregon Province Archives, Bishop of Nesqually correspondence Schram circular letter, January 22, 1896.

2. Peter C. Yorke (1864–1925) was also a strong advocate of temperance societies, in itself a great recommendation for advancement. Joseph S. Brusher, S.J., *Consecrated Thunderbolt Father Yorke of San Francisco*, (Hawthorne [New Jersey], 1973).

3. Oregon Province Archives, Bishop of Nesqually correspondence Schram circular letter, July 23, 1896.

4. Sister Mary of the Blessed Sacrament McCrosson, *The Bell and the River*, (Palo Alto, 1956), p. 256.

5. "By reference to the Dalles Mission case, it will be seen there were some circumstances showing that the Mission was not *absolutely* in occupancy on the 14th Aug., 1848, in consequence of the hostilities of the Indians, it being shortly after the massacre of the late Dr. Whitman. Besides, a transfer had been made in 1847 from the Methodist Mission to the American Board. The Station was re-transferred to the Methodist Mission in February, 1849. Broken as was this possession and occupancy, the *grant* was considered absolute and a

vested interest in the Mission and the land intruded upon by the military authorities at the Dalles, cost the Government $20,000." *Report and Decision of the Surveyor General of Washington Territory in the Matter of the Cntent of the Claims to Lands At and near the City of Vancouver, in the Territory of Washington, etc.,* No. V of *Claim of the Mission of St. James, Vancouver, Washington Territory to 640 Acres of Land,* (N.P., N.D.), p. 16.

6. *Catholic Sentinel,* April 6, 1905.

7. Archives of the Diocese of Spokane, Correspondence previous to 1914, Van de Ven to O'Dea.

8. *Catholic Sentinel,* October 21, 1897.

9. Later the title was changed to *Reminiscences and Current Topics of the Ecclesiastical Province of Oregon.* This monthly lasted only a year and three months. Verhaag was requested by the archbishop to discontinue publication, because *Reminiscences* was in competition with the *Catholic Sentinel.*

10. *Reminiscences and Current Topics of the Ecclesiastical Province of Oregon,* I(November 1897), p. 204.

11. My father attended Father Held's school and always spoke affectionately about it. It was the only formal education he received.

12. Father Faust was first assigned to establish a parish for German settlers in a place called "the California Settlement" northwest of Almira, Washington. He built St. John's Church there, completing it in December 1901, just before leaving for Uniontown. On the same day he dedicated the first Sacred Heart Church in Wilbur. *The Inland Empire Catholic Messenger,* XI, 4(January, 1929), p. 66.

13. Father Nicholas carried with him the large choir books which the monastery in Engelberg had loaned Mount Angel. After his death the captain of the ship refused to release the choir books until Father Nicholas' passage had been paid, because the priest had not completed the journey as chaplain.

14. Sister M. Ildephonse Nuxoll, Q.S.B., *Idaho Benedictine,* (Cottonwood, 1976), p. 23.

15. Letter of Sister Maria Reilly, F.C.S.P., to Rev. Wilfred P. Schoenberg, S.J., Seattle, May 12, 1983.

16. *Reminiscences and Current Topics of the Ecclesiastical Province of Oregon,* 2(January, 1898), p. 16.

17. The last formal dedication by Archbishop Gross was at Huntington, Oregon, where he blessed St. Joachim's Church on August 22, 1898. Father Verhaag was the pastor. *Catholic Sentinel,* September 2, 1898.

18. Bishop Lemmons died at Coban, Guatamala on August 10, 1897, while begging for money to pay off the debt on his cathedral.

19. *Catholic Sentinel,* July 14, 1898.

20. *Ibid.,* November 17, 1898 and November 24, 1898.

21. [Sisters of the Holy Names], *Excerpts from Oregon Chonicles 1859–1959,* (Marylhurst, 1959), p. 57.

22. *The Centenary 100 Years of the Catholic Church in the Oregon Country,* supplement to the *Catholic Sentinel,* May 4, 1939, p. 61.

23. *Ibid.,* p. 52.

24. Oregon Province Archives, Cataldo Mss. Chronology of St. Andrew's Mission.

25. *Catholic Sentinel,* October 7, 1897.

26. *Ibid.,* June 22, 1899.

27. Archbishop Robert Dwyer's remarks appeared in the *Catholic Sentinel,* April 19, 1974.

28. *Ibid.,* April 19, 1974.

29. [Sister M. Flavia, S.N.J.M.], *Gleanings of Fifty Years the Sisters of the Holy Names of Jesus and Mary in the Northwest 1859–1909,* (Portland, 1909), p. 181.

30. In the early years, Father Boulet offered Mass in the Bremerton area in a little church he had built for the Indians east of Chico. In June 1898, Father Albert Trivelli, S.J. from Seattle College visited Bremerton regularly. The first church, Our Lady Star of the Sea, was built by Father Henry Woods, S.J. in 1902. *Catholic Sentinel,* October 9, 1902.

31. *Ibid.,* July 27, 1899.

32. *Ibid.,* September 1, 1898, September 22, 1898, and November 3, 1898.

33. *The Spokesman-Review,* November 22, 1908.

34. Oregon Province Archives, DeRouge Papers, correspondence of DeRouge regarding St. Mary's Mission.

35. This was begun in 1897 under the title of *The Washington Catholic.*

36. *Northwest Progress,* 75th Anniversary Edition. October 20, 1972, p. 1.

37. Sister Mary Rita Flanagan, O.P., *The Work of the Sisters St. Dominic of the Congregation of St. Thomas Aquinas in the diocese of Seattle 1888–1951,* (Seattle, 1951), p. 73 et seq.

38. *Northwest Progress,* September 11, 1925.

39. This was on April 1, 1900. *Colville Examiner,* April 5, 1930.

40. This was on January 18, 1901. *Catholic Progress,* January 25, 1901.

41. Archives of the Archdiocese of Portland, letter of Father J. Bernards to Father Leo Remington, March 11, 1977, from Mt. Angel Towers.

42. *Catholic Sentinel,* January 19, 1961.

43. Columbia Preparatory School served a very small percentage of Portland's Catholic boys and Central Catholic founded by Archbishop Howard, did not open until September 5, 1939.

44. These and other details regarding the history of the University of Portland have been taken from James T. Covert, *A Point of Pride: The University of Portland Story,* (Portland, 1976).

45. *Ibid.,* p. 11.

46. *Ibid.,* p. 13.

47. *Ibid.,* p. 21.

48. *Ibid.,* p. 33.

49. *Ibid.,* p. 34.

50. Priests, even bishops then, were notoriously underpaid. They had scarcely enough to buy decent clothes.

51. The present Administration building at Gonzaga University. Wilfred P. Schoenberg, S.J., *Gonzaga University Seventy-five Years,* (Spokane, 1963), p. 137.

52. This was on June 21, 1899.

53. Covert, *A Point of Pride,* p. 33.

54. [Demetrius Jueneman, O.S.B. and Sebastian Ruth, O.S.B.], *Between the Years 1895–1945 St. Martin's College, Lacey,* (N.P., 1945), [p. 21].

55. Covert, *A Point of Pride,* p. 35.

56. *Ibid.*

57. *Ibid.,* p. 34.

58. McCrosson, *The Bell and the River,* p. 264.

59. *Ibid.,* p. 265.

60. *Ibid.,* p. 266.

61. *Ibid.,* p. 260.

62. Mother Joseph died on January 19, 1902. The funeral Mass was celebrated in the cathedral on January 23. Burial in the Vancouver Catholic cemetery followed.

63. *The Spokesman-Review,* October 15, 1902.

64. *The Catholic Northwest Progress,* Special Edition, September 8, 1950, p. 105. This figure is given for 1900, at which time there were forty diocesan priests and twenty-nine religious priests in the diocese.

65. *The Spokesman-Review,* January 6, 1902.

66. Archbishop Blanchet changed his residence from St. Paul to Oregon City, to Portland. At this time and until 1928, the name of the Archdiocese was Oregon City.

67. The first Sacred Heart Church, destroyed by an arsonist after several attempts in March 1899, was replaced by a second, which was dedicated on July 9, 1900. In 1928, in the Denny Regrade Project, this second church was razed and replaced with a third. The latter was dedicated on May 20, 1928.

68. This was on September 24, 1908. The long delay in the appointment of Prefontaine as a monsignor could be explained by the death of Pope Leo XIII in July 1903, and the election of his successor. O'Dea made his *ad limina* visit to Rome in May 1905.

69. *The Spokesman-Review,* January 20, 1902.

70. Wilfred P. Schoenberg, S.J., *Paths to the Northwest A Jesuit History of the Oregon Province,* (Chicago, 1982), p. 243. 71. *The Spokesman-Review,* February 19, 1903.

72. *Catholic Progress,* March 25, 1904.

73. Oregon Province Archives, Mss. of Father J.E. O'Brien in Our Lady of Good Help Church.

74. *Catholic Progress,* November 18, 1904.

75. This compares very unfavorably with eastern Washington, which according to Bishop O'Dea, at this very time had "about 75 priests east of the mountains in Washington and 13 Catholic institutions. *The Spokesman-Review,* November 11, 1903.

76. *Catholic Sentinel,* February 3, 1967. Baker City had only 6000 people in 1903.

77. The Archbishop's reasons for the division appear to me to be window dressing. He had convinced the Apostolic Delegate that his diocese was so broad in extent that the development of the church in eastern Oregon had to be neglected for other priorities, and that the appointment of a bishop for that distant area would help to advance more surely and rapidly the development of the church there. The fact is, O'Dea's diocese was in similar straits, though Oregon is larger than Washington. Seghers covered the area, and Idaho, too, by *horse.* In 1903 Christie had the use of railroads over vast parts of eastern Oregon.

78. Witness innumerable examples in the early chapters of James Hennessey, S.J., *American Catholics A History of The Roman Catholic Community In The United States,* (New York, 1981).

79. Archives of the Diocese of Baker, telegram of D. Falconio, Apostolic Delegate to Charles O'Reilly, Bishop Elect of Baker City.

80. *Catholic Sentinel,* August 27, 1903.

81. There has been a long standing rumor among priests in eastern Oregon concerning "the gun" when Bishop O'Reilly arrived. No reference is made to it in O'Reilly's diary, which contains other data. However, the incident has been confirmed by O'Reilly's niece, who knew of it from the bishop himself.

82. Oregon Province Archives, Letter of O'Reilly to his sister Theresa, September 4, 1903.

83. Archives of the Diocese of Baker, Bishop Charles O'Reilly's circular letters.

84. *The Spokesman-Review,* October 8, 1903.

85. This was on December 3, 1903. [Missionary Sisters of the Sacred Heart], *In Memoria della Rev. ma Madre Francesa Saverio Cabrini,* (Rome, 1918), p. 384.

86. *Northwest Progress,* December 24, 1948.

87. Cabrini was canonized on July 7, 1946 by Pope Pius XII.

88. *The Right Reverend John B. Brondel Bishop of Helena A Memorial,* (Helena, 1904), p. 13.

89. *Ibid.,* p. 16.

90. When Brondel died, there were approximately 50,000 Catholics in Montana. This represented about 23% of the total poulation of 228,000. *Ibid.,* p. 18.

91. *The Spokesman-Review,* November 11, 1903.

92. Martin Pollard, O.S.B., "Abbey Chronicle" in *Mount Angel Newsletter,* XXXIV, 4(1982), p. 5.

93. The old abbot, Anselm Villiger, had died on January 14, 1901. Martin Pollard, O.S.B., "Abbey Chronicle" in *Mount Angel Letter,* XXXIV, 3(1982), p. 6.

94. *Ibid.,* p. 7. Odermatt's finances are discussed in depth in Lawrence J. McCrank, *Mt. Angel Abbey A Centennial History of the Benedictine Community and its Library 1882–1932,* (Wilmington, 1983), p. 33 et seq.

95. Pollard, "Abbey Chronicle," p. 7.

96. *Ibid.*

97. *Ibid.,* p. 6.

98. *Ibid.,* p. 7.

99. *Ibid.*

100. Jueneman and Ruth, *Between the Years,* [p. 22].

101. *Ibid.* Mother Johanna died at the age of 76 on July 31, 1926.

102. *Ibid.* This was Sister M. Xavier Wieber.

103. Rt. Rev. Cyprian Bradley, O.S.B., and Most Rev. Edward J. Kelly, D.D., Ph.D., *History of the Diocese of Boise 1863–1952,* (Boise, 1953, p. 274.

104. Oregon Province Archives, Mss. St. Michael's Monastery, Cottonwood.

105. *Catholic Sentinel,* March 24, 1904.

106. *Ibid.,* June 2, 1904.

107. *The Oregonian,* probably May 17, 1904. This is taken from an undated clipping in the Archives of the Diocese of Baker. The newspaper report was a condensation of the much longer pamphlet, which bore the date of May 16, 1904. A copy of this is in the Archives of the Diocese of Baker.

108. *Ibid.*

109. Archives of the Diocese of Baker, Bishop O'Reilly papers related to the Schell affair.

110. *The Catholic Sentinel,* July 21, 1904.

111. This statement was made by Father Edwin O'Hara, the archbishop's secretary then, later bishop and archbishop. Archives of the Archdiocese of Portland in Oregon, unpublished Mss. on Archbishop Christie by Sister Miriam Margaret O'Donnell, S.N.J.M., "In Faith and Kindness The Life of the Most Reverent Alexander Christie, D.D., Fourth Archbishop of Portland in Oregon," Masters Thesis, University of Portland, 1945, p. 58.

112. *The Oregonian,* July 18, 1904.

113. Archives of the Diocese of Baker, O'Reilly to Falconio, October 6, 1904.

114. Archives of the Diocese of Baker, Chancellor's request to Apostolic Delegate, October 6, 1904.

115. *Ibid.*

116. Archives of the Archdiocese of Portland in Oregon, W. Haley to Christie, March 1, 1905.

117. *Ibid.*

118. Archives of the Archdiocese of Portland in Oregon, unidentified letter to Christie, May 14, 1905.

119. Archives of the Archdiocese of Portland in Oregon, O'Reilly to Christie, June 20, 1906.

120. Father Patrick J. Gaire, Volume II *A Brief History of the Diocese of Baker 1928–1966,* (St. Benedict [Oregon], 1966), p. 317.

121. These and some of the following details are taken from Thomas Merton [O.C.S.O.], *Waters of Siloe,* (New York, 1949), p. 173 et seq.

122. It will be recalled that some of these Germans had come from Rush Lake, Minnesota in 1884.

123. Merton, *Waters of Siloe*, p. 175.

124. Archives of the Archdiocese of Portland in Oregon, Papers related to Our Lady of Jordan Monastery.

125. Merton, *Waters of Siloe*, p. 175.

126. *Catholic Sentinel*, July 25, 1907.

127. The bills against the monastry totalled at this time $27,000. Presumably this does not include the mortgage on the land. Archives of the Archdiocese of Portland in Oregon, Papers related to Our Lady of Jordan Monastery.

128. Merton, *Waters of Siloe*, p. 176.

129. Mark Schmid, O.S.B., *Sublimity, The Story of an American Countryside 1850-1950*, (St. Benedict [Mount Angel], 1951), p. 84.

130. The prior, Father Henry Pelletan, remained as pastor of Jordan for three years after the departure of the other monks. The Benedictines replaced him in 1914. *Ibid.*, p. 85.

131. *Ibid.*, p. 84.

132. L.B. Palladino, S.J., *Indian and White In the Northwest A History of Catholicity In Montana 1831-1891*, (Lancaster, 1922), p. 238.

133. *Eastern Montana Catholic Register*, special number, *50 Years of Growth 1904-1954*, December 3, 1954, p. 41.

134. *Ibid.*, p. 14.

135. *Ibid.*

136. Lenihan retired in 1930 and returned to Dubuque to live out his years as Titular Archbishop of Preslavus.

137. Carroll was appointed on September 12, 1904.

138. Now simply called the Methodist Church.

139. The Right Rev. Francis C. Kelley, D.D., L.L.D., *The Story of Extension*, (Chicago, 1922), p. 32 et seq.

140. This was Kelley's estimate based on *The Annals of the Propogation of the Faith*.

141. *Ibid.*, p. 37.

142. *Ibid.*, p. 44.

143. Present were Archbishops Quigley and Peter Bourgade of Santa Fe, Bishops John J. Hennessey of Wichita and Peter J. Muldoon, auxiliary bishop of Chicago, Gilbert Jennings, Joseph Roche, B.X. O'Reilly, E.P. Graham, F.A. O'Brien, Edward Kelly, F.J. Van Antwerp and P.L. Duffy, all priests, and the following laymen: A.A. Hirst, S.A. Baldus, C.A. Plamondon, M.A. Fanning, A.V.D. Watterson, William P. Breen and Joseph Roe.

Chapter 14. CATHEDRALS AND CHAPEL CARS

1. At Gonzaga College, for example, typhoid caused the greatest crisis in its early history when an epidemic broke out on campus. Six students died. Goller Hall, on campus, was erected as an infirmary to prevent a repetition of the tragedy.

2. Father Dominic O'Connor [O.F.M. Cap], *A Brief History of the Diocese of Baker*, (Baker, 1930), p. 11.

3. This was on August 23, 1905. *Catholic Sentinel*, September 7, 1905.

4. This was 1870. The exact amount of money was $21,559.20, of which Catholics in Boise had contributed $12,045.70. Rt. Rev. Cyprian Bradley, O.S.B. and Most Rev. Edward J. Kelly, D.D., Ph.D., *History of the Diocese of Boise 1863-1952*, (Boise, 1953), p. 289.

5.*Catholic Sentinel*, November 28, 1907.

6. O'Connor, *A Brief History*, p. 38.

7. *Anaconda Standard*, September 26, 1906.

8. *Landmark*, II(Fall, 1982), p. 13.

9. *Catholic Sentinel*, January 11, 1906. The next largest donor, John B. Agen of Seattle, gave the bishop $3,000.

10. *Ibid.*

11. *Spokesman Review*, November 22, 1908.

12. *Ibid.*, November 27, 1908. St. James Cathedral had been dedicated on December 22, 1907.

13. *The Morning Democrat*, [Baker], November 30, 1905.

14. O'Connor, *A Brief History*, p. 34.

15. Bradley and Kelly, *History of Boise*, p. 291.

16. *Catholic Sentinel*, April 5, 1906.

17. *Ibid.*, May 24, 1906.

18. Bradley and Kelly, *History of Boise*, p. 291.

19. *Ibid.*

20. *Ibid.*

21. *Catholic Sentinel*, December 26, 1907.

22. *Eastern Montana Catholic Register*, Special Edition. *50 Years of Growth 1904 to 1954*, (December 3, 1954), p. 24.

23. [James Gordon Stafford], *Silver Jubilee St. James Cathedral Parish*, (Seattle, 1920), p. 27. *The Catholic Progress* published a special *Cathedral Dedication Number* on December 14, 1906.

24. *Catholic Sentinel*, December 26, 1907.

25. *Ibid.*, October 1, 1908.

26. [Holy Names Sisters], *Excerpts from Oregon Chronicles 1859–1959*, (Marylhurst, 1959), p. 209.

27. *Catholic Sentinel*, March 4, 1909 and March 18, 1909.

28. Holy Names Sisters, *Excerpts*, p. 204. The matter was settled out of court to the advantage of the sisters.

29. *Ibid.*, p. 203. This school was discontinued in 1930.

30. *Ibid.*

31. [Mother] Louise Callan, R.S.C.J. *The Society of the Sacred Heart in North America*, (New York, 1937), p. 702.

32. Rt. Rev. Victor Day, V.G., *The Cathedral of St. Helena*, (Helena, 1938).

33. *Ibid.*, p. 8.

34. *The Montana Daily Record*, April 2, 1906.

35. Day, *The Cathedral*, p. 15.

36. *Ibid.*, p. 13.

37. The $35,000 was from an anonymous non-resident of Montana.

38. Day, *The Cathedral*, p. 31.

39. The four bidders were Columbia Construction Company of New York, Newman and Smith of Washington, D.C., Nelson and Patterson of Butte, and Gagnon and Company of Billings.

40. *Anaconda Standard*, October 5, 1908. President Theodore Roosevelt sent the telegram from the White House. It read as follows: "I wish I could be present. But as I cannot, I send greetings and congratulations. I hail the event as marking the extraordinary advance of Christianity in the northwest, beginning with De Smet in 1841, down to the present." Day, *The Cathedral*, p. 39.

41. *Ibid.*

42. Oregon Province Archives, Palladino Papers. Letter of Palladino to Miss May Summer of Clyde Park, Montana, August 20, 1907. Palladino left Lewiston for Yakima during the later summer of 1908.

43. When Carroll made his *ad limina* visit to Rome just before his death on November 4, 1925, it was commonly rumored that he expected to be named Archbishop Christie's successor. Christie had died on April 6, 1925, and his successor was not announced until April 30, 1926.

44. Oregon Province Archives, D'Aste Papers, D'Aste to de la Motte from St. Ignatius Mission, August 30, 1908.

45. Day, *The Cathedral*, p. 44.

46. Father James Hennessey, S.J., in his *American Catholics A History of the Roman Catholic Community in the United States* (New York, 1981), provides data regarding this in Chapter XV, "Growing Pains in the Catholic Community."

47. *The Progress*, which first appeared in 1899, became the *Northwest Catholic* in 1908. On May 26, 1911, it was reorganized as *The Northwest Progress*.

48. *The Catholic Herald*, a weekly edited by Frank Butler, first appeared on January 10, 1901. Since no complete file is known to exist, there is no record of its demise. Some original copies are in the Oregon Province Archives.

49. This first appeared in October, 1900. Subsequently it developed into the national monthly called *St. Joseph Magazine*.

50. The Knights of Columbus were first organized in Oregon on June 15, 1902, in Washington on June 22, 1902, in Montana on July 9, 1902 and in Idaho on May 13, 1904. Their subsequent influence, especially in the Oregon School Bill struggle, is incalculable.

51. In 1934, eighteen years after DeRouge's death, only four members of the Lady Missionaries remained. Three of threse entered the Dominican Sisters when the latter took over St. Mary's Mission school in 1938.

52. Wilfred P. Schoenberg, S.J., *Paths to the Northwest A Jesuit History of the Oregon Province*, (Chicago, 1982), p. 203.

53. [Mother Angela Clotilda, O.S.U.], *Ursulines of the West, 1535–1935: 1880–1935*, (Everett, 1936), p. 44.

54. The nature of these subsidies should be noted. They were provided for food, lodging, and clothing for the Indian children, "wards of the government."

55. There were only 55 teachers in all sectarian schools wearing religious garb. This was out of a total of 2000 teachers receiving government support. *Catholic Sentinel*, September 26, 1912.

56. *Ibid.*, March 12, 1912. Taft, a Republican President, was openly favorable to Catholics and their missions, though most Catholics belonged to the Democratic party.

57. A complete account appears in the *Catholic Sentinel*, Ibid.

58. Oregon Province Archives, St. Francis Regis Mission Diaries.

59. *Catholic Sentinel*, August 29, 1907 and September 16, 1909.

60. Oregon Province Archives, De La Motte papers. Note passing comments in his diaries.

61. An architectural rendering of the new college appears in the *Catholic Sentinel*, April 23, 1908. This college prospered from the beginning. When it opened in December 1908, it had 70 students. In the year 1911–1912, it had 214 students from ninth grade up.

62. *Oregon-Jesuit*, XXII, 4(April, 1953), p. 1.

63. Mackin kept a meticulous diary that provides an amusing history. Oregon Province Archives, Mackin Papers.

64. The first church on the Siletz Reservation of Oregon, built by Father Felix Bucher, S.D.S., was dedicated by Gross on August 1, 1897. A year later, Bucher became the reservation's first resident priest. In 1909, Dimier took over the care of Siletz and Newport on the Oregon Coast. *Catholic Sentinel*, June 20, 1957.

65. Oregon Province Archives, St. Ignatius Parish, Portland, Mss. account by Father Francis Dillon, S.J.

66. De la Motte in a letter to the Jesuit general, Father Francis Wernz, states that "20 acres" were purchased. Dillon's estimate is more correct.

67. Loyola Retreat House was opened on June 27, 1947, when Father John McAstocker, S.J. directed the first retreat of twelve laymen.

68. *Catholic Sentinel*, September 24, 1908.

69. Loyola College in Missoula opened in September 1908. Though it was called a college, it was an elementary school until the new Loyola High School was opened on September 7, 1911. Loyola was accredited as a high school on July 1, 1915.

70. Father Stephan J. Sullivan, born in Pennsylvania, came to Butte with his parents when he was three years old. He attended Gonzaga College and was ordained for the Helena diocese on May 20, 1900 in Rome. He died in Seattle on September 16, 1941, while on vacation from his parish in Montana.

71. *The Register* [Western Montana], *Souvenir Centenary Edition*, August 10, 1941, II:18.

72. *Divini Illius Magistri* appeared in 1931.

73. The cornerstone for this was laid on May 19, 1907. Classes began on September 8, 1908 and formal dedication was celebrated one month later.

74. *Catholic Sentinel*, October 1, 1908.

75. [Holy Names Sisters], *Excerpts*, pp. 67–68.

76. This was replaced in 1923 with a new Providence Hospital. Oregon Province Archives, Mss. Sisters of Providence.

77. *Spokesman-Review*, May 27, 1907.

78. *Catholic Sentinel*, March 31, 1910. Our attention is called to the fact that Sacred Heart Hospital, between April 30, 1886 and March 24, 1910, had cared for 29,000 patients. In 1909 alone there were 2056 patients. The sisters had fed 100 poor people each day.

79. Oregon Province Archives, Mss. Sisters of Providence.

80. The first in a rented building was opened on August 2, 1891. *Northwest Progress*, February 13, 1914.

81. This was on July 6, 1901. Sister M. Ildephonse Nuxoll, O.S.B., *Idaho Benedictine*, (Cottonwood, 1976), p. 23.

82. *Ibid.*, p. 28.

83. This was on June 23, 1909, in the college's eighteenth year. In the early years, Bishop Carroll had nothing to fear from Seattle College's attraction for Montana students. The City of Seattle then was too large and complex for most Montana boys. They favored smaller and closer Spokane.

84. *The Register* [Western Montana], *Souvenir Centenary Edition*, August 3, 1941, II:16. Note: this edition has different dates for separate sections.

85. [Martin Pollard, O.S.B.], *Mount of Communion Mt. Angel Abbey 1882–1982*, (St. Benedict, 1982), p. 19.

86. Albert Bauman, O.S.B., *"The Monk-Musician Becomes a Pastor"* in *Mount Angel Letter*, 34(August 1982), p. 3. This church was 180 feet long, it was designed with only one tower 180 feet high.

87. *Ibid.*

88. The Pacific Northwest rarely experienced hurricanes or tornadoes.

89. *Catholic Sentinel*, January 19, 1911. The new St. Francis church was dedicated on November 20, 1938.

90. *Gonzaga*, III(October, 1911), p. 61.

91. October 12, 1911. *Gonzaga*, III(November, 1911), p. 54 et seq.

92. *Catholic Sentinel*, June 29, 1911.

93. This ceremony occurred at The Dalles on April 5, 1910. *Ibid.*, April 14, 1910.

94. Schell spent the years following the dispute with O'Reilly until 1918, on leave of absence in the archdiocese of Milwaukee. He died in Pendleton on May 27, 1936.

95. L.B. Palladino, S.J., *Indian and White In the Northwest A History of Catholicity In Montana 1821–1891*, (Lancaster, 1922), p. 347.

96. Oregon Province Archives, St. Leo's Parish papers, Memorandum on St. Leo's by Father George Weibel, S.J.

97. Oregon Province Archives, St. Leo's Parish papers, Weibel correspondence.

98. This was dedicated on August 30, 1903. *Catholic Progress*, September 4, 1903.

99. Weibel arrived in Tacoma on August 13, 1910. Vesta replaced him on October 13, 1910. The alleged kidnapping or abduction of Marjorie Reiman occurred on February 7, 1911.

100. Oregon Province Archives, St. Leo's Parish papers, Memorandum on St. Leo's by Father George Weibel, S.J.

101. *Northwest Progress*, November 22, 1912.

102. *Spokesman-Review*, September 17, 1912.

103. *Spokane Chronicle*, October 4, 1913.

104. Wilfred P. Schoenberg, S.J., *Gonzaga University Seventy-five Years 1887–1962*, (Spokane, 1963), p. 214.

105. Law classes began on October 1, 1912, as scheduled. This is the first and only Catholic law school in the Northwest.

106. Schoenberg, *Gonzaga University*, p. 219.

107. *The Catholic Northwest Progress Centennial of the Diocese of Seattle 1850–1950*, September 8, 1950, p. 61.

108. Newman House for Catholic students at the University of Washington was opened on October 7, 1926 at 4555 15th N.E. The Diocesan Council of Catholic Women assisted the Dominican fathers in providing it. *Northwest Progress*, October 1, 1926.

109. Completed in 1921, after nine years of planning and construction, Holy Rosary had a capacity of 750 people. *Northwest Progress*, November 25, 1921.

110. Thomas Purcell died on September 3, 1925, at the age of sixty-five. *Spokesman-Review*, September 4, 1925.

111. *Catholic Sentinel*, June 6, 1912.

112. Purcell became pastor of St. Thomas in Coeur d'Alene on May 1, 1897.

113. Bradley and Kelly, *History of Boise*, p. 253. Healy died in Spokane on September 1, 1929.

114. The other founders were ex-Senator George Turner and J. Stanley Webster, a distinguished judge for many years. All of them taught in the first law school.

115. This concerned the right of ownership of land under nonnavigable rivers. Schoenberg, *Gonzaga University*, p. 55.

116. *Spokane Daily Chronicle*, February 25, 1910.

117. *Catholic Sentinel*, Special Edition, July 14, 1910, p. 10.

118. *Ibid.*, July 28, 1910.

119. New World Life Insurance Company, in 1951, merged with Farmer's Life, of Farmer's Underwriters Association of Los Angeles.

120. Cost estimates ran from $68,500 to $100,000.

121. Dedication was on May 30, 1912. *Catholic Sentinel*, June 6, 1912.

122. This was in 1903. The sisters arrived in Coeur d'Alene on September 15, 1903. It should be noted that members of this congregation of sisters had come to the Northwest prior to their arrival in Coeur d'Alene. There were Servants of the Immaculate Heart at Tillamook from 1897 to 1903; at St. Lawrence parish in Portland from 1903 for a brief period; at St. Joseph parish in Spokane from 1905 until 1921; and St. Andrew's in Portland from 1908–1921. Oregon Province Archives, Mss. Servants of the Immaculate Heart of Mary.

123. The new academy was opened on September 18, 1905. *Catholic Sentinel*, September 22, 1905. Another new academy replaced this one in 1957. The sisters were withdrawn from Coeur d'Alene in 1973.

124. The Right Rev. Francis C. Kelley, D.D., L.L.D., *The Story of Extension*, (Chicago, 1922), p. 71.

125. *Catholic Sentinel*, Special Edition, October 6, 1960, III:23.

126. *Ibid.*, June 28, 1974.

127. This was in St. Mary's Cathedral, Chicago, on February 23, 1933.

128. This gift was made on December 12, 1909.

129. *Catholic Sentinel*, January 19, 1911.

130. *Ibid.*, March 16, 1911.

131. The St. Paul served the southern states until 1936, when it was parked at Gardiner, Montana to be used as a church. In 1954, Bishop Gilmore of the Helena Diocese acquired it for a temporary chapel at the east entrance of Glacier Park. *Catholic Sentinel*, Special Edition, October 6, 1960, III:23.

132. *Ibid.*, January 9, 1930.

133. They were replaced with "motor chapels." The first of these called "St Peter," was built for use in Texas. Photographs and further details appear in the *Catholic Sentinel*, Special Edition, April 24, 1913, p. 14.

134. *Ibid.*, May 15, 1913.

135. Cruse had contributed already a considerable sum of money at an earlier date Day, *The Cathedral*, p. 7.

136. *Catholic Sentinel*, May 15, 1913.

137. Msgr. Victor Day also started a colony of Belgian Catholics at Williams, Montana. This was in March 1913. *Helena Independent*, July 4, 1914.

138. Montana still does. Even today Montana has more Catholics than members of any other religion.

139. Bishop Carroll received Rome's approval to change the name from Sacred Heart to St. Helena. This was announced on January 18, 1916. *Catholic Sentinel*, June 20, 1916.

Chapter 15. THE WAR YEARS

1. *The Catholic Bulletin*, February 7, 1914, quoted in the *Spokane Daily Chronicle*, February 11, 1914.

2. *Spokane Daily Chronicle*, April 16, 1914.

3. *Ibid.*

4. *Catholic Sentinel*, February 2, 1911.

5. *Spokane Daily Chronicle*, April 16, 1914.

6. *Spokesman Review*, March 5, 1914.

7. Agustine Francis Schinner was born in Milwaukee, son of Michael and Mary Schinner, devout German Catholics. He attended St. Francis College, where he later taught as a young priest, was ordained to the priesthood on March 7, 1886. His consecration by Archbishop Michael Heiss took place in Milwaukee on July 25, 1905.

8. O'Dea had informed the press that Our Lady of Lourdes church was the new cathedral and that the Lourdes rectory was the new bishop's residence. Schinner had other ideas, but matters turned out as O'Dea had predicted.

9. *Spokesman Review*, June 19, 1914.

10. James Hennessey, S.J. covers several periods of anti-Catholicism including this one in *American Catholics, A History of the Roman Catholic Community In the United States*, (New York, 1981), p. 182 and p. 221 et seq.

11. Oregon Province Archives, Mss. St. Michael's church, Portland.

12. *Northwest Progress,* October 27, 1911 and December 29, 1911.

13. Oregon Province Archives, Gonzaga College Diaries for May 19, 1912.

14. Archives, Diocese of Boise, Bradley notebooks, Parishes; *Catholic Sentinel,* July 23, 1914.

15. Oregon Province Archives, Mss. St. Francis Parish, Walla Walla.

16. Oregon Province Archives, Mss. Priest River Parish; *Northwest Progress,* February 12, 1915.

17. Oregon Province Archives, Mss. St. Ann's Children's Home in Tacoma; *Northwest Progress,* July 15, 1921 and April 25, 1924.

18. Oregon Province Archives, St. Stanislaus Church, Lewiston, Diaries for February 29, 1920.

19. Dominic O'Connor, O.F.M. Cap., *A Brief History of the Diocese of Baker City,* (Baker, 1930), p. 99. and Rt. Rev. Cyprian Bradley, O.S.B., and Most Rev. Edward J. Kelly, D.D., Ph.D., *History of the Diocese of Boise 1863–1952,* (Boise, 1953), p. 307.

20. Bradley and Kelly, *History,* pp. 307 and 340.

21. For example, there was Blessed Sacrament Church at Black Eagle near Great Falls in Montana, built in 1923, Holy Cross Church in Tacoma, dedicated on January 2, 1915, and Sts. Peter and Paul church in Tacoma, dedicated on January 6, 1924.

22. [Demetrius Jueneman, O.S.B., and Sebastian Ruth, O.S.B.], *Between the Years 1895–1945, St. Martin's College, Lacey,* (N.P., 1945), p. 30.

23. *Ibid.,* p. 32.

24. *Ibid.*

25. *Ibid.,* p. 33. The life of the Jesuit saint was as follows: D.A. Hanly, *Blessed Joseph Pignatelli,* (New York, 1937). Pignatelli was canonized by Pius XII in 1954.

26. *Catholic Sentinel,* August 6, 1914.

27. Grief over the war hastened the death of Pius X on August 23, 1914. *Catholic Sentinel,* August 27, 1914.

28. Abbot Oswald died on August 1, 1928.

29. The "Old Sheds" was the nickname for the original Gonzaga College building, which had been converted into the scholasticate in 1899. A detailed history appears in Wilfred P. Schoenberg, S.J., *Gonzaga University Seventy-Five Years 1887–1962,* (Spokane, 1963), p. 146 et seq.

30. *Ibid.,* p. 151.

31. This was Father Francis Dillon, S.J., Provincial of the Jesuit's western province from 1918 to 1924. He died in Spokane on October 5, 1947.

32. *Catholic Sentinel,* March 22, 1917.

33. O'Connor,, *Brief History,* p. 87.

34. *Catholic Sentinel,* January 25, 1912.

35. *Helena Independent,* July 4, 1914.

36. O'Connor, *Brief History,* p. 96.

37. *Catholic Sentinel,* September 30, 1909.

38. *Northwest Progress,* August 17, 1917; October 12, 1917.

39. O'Connor, *Brief History,* p. 198.

40. *Ibid.,* p. 199.

41. This order had been founded by an American, Mrs. Cornelia Connelly.

42. *Catholic Sentinel,* September 17, 1914.

43. The Poor Clare nuns established their temporary monastery on July 22, 1914. *Northwest Progress,* July 14, 1916.

44. This large monastery proved to be more than the nuns required, so they built a smaller one on north Hawthorne Street in 1925. The Sisters of Providence then converted the old monastery into St. Joseph's Home for the aged. This was opened on June 16, 1925.

45. This was August 24, 1911. Eleven boarders and forty day students occupied St. Mary's on the opening day. *Prairie Life,* VIII, 2(1939), p. 17.

46. [Joseph H. Gerharz], *50 Years of Growth Golden Jubilee, Diocese of Great Falls 1904 to 1954, The Eastern Montana Catholic Register,* XXX, 49, Section Three (December 3, 1954), p. 72.

47. This was also replaced with another hospital built in 1929 and dedicated by Bishop Lenihan on March 17, 1931. *Ibid.*

48. In 1921, the Sisters of Charity, B.V.M. of Dubuque, Iowa, assumed direction of this school. [Charles M. Smith], *The Centenary, 100 Years of the Catholic Church in the Oregon Country, Supplement to the Catholic Sentinel,* (May 4, 1939), p. 51.

49. These sisters were withdrawn from both Spokane schools in 1932. Oregon Province Archives, Mss. Sisters of St. Francis of Penance and Christian Charity.

50. St. John's High School was discontinued in 1927. *Northwest Progress,* October 8, 1915 and October 15, 1915.

51. Sister M. Milata Ludwig, F.S.P.A., *A Chapter of Franciscan History; the Sisters of the Third Order of St. Francis of Perpetual Adoration 1849 1949,* (New York, 1950), p. 441.

52. The new orphanage was dedicated on May 30, 1924.

53. Projected first as an infants' home, Columbus became a hospital instead. The name was changed to St Francis Xavier Cabrini Hospital in 1957. St. Paul's Home, a nursery and boys' home was established on the Lake Washington site in August 1927. [Andrew Prouty, ed.], *1850—Centennial of the Diocese of Seattle—1950; The Catholic Northwest Progress,* LIII, 36, Second Section, (September 8, 1950), Seattle, 1950, p. 16.

54. Mother Cabrini was canonized by Pius XII on July 7, 1946. One of the required miracles presented in the process was the instant cure of Sister Delfina. *Ibid.*

55. *Spokesman Review,* April 3, 1917. It should be noted that Catholic sympathies throughout the nation were generally with the Central Powers during the early part of the war. In part this was due to anti-British feeling. Hennessey, *American Catholics,* p. 223.

56. *Ibid.*

57. Washington had adopted local option prohibition laws in 1916.

58. *Spokesman Review,* September 15, 1917.

59. *Spokane Chronicle,* August 31, 1917.

60. Bishop Glorieux first occupied a room in St. Alphonsus Hospital Boise, but was moved to Portland for care by heart specialists there. Bradley and Kelly, *History,* p. 323.

61. The first issue appeared in September 1916.

62. Bradley and Kelly, *History,* p. 328.

63. *Catholic Sentinel,* September 20, 1917.

64. This replaced *The New Northwest,* which Bishop Lenihan established shortly after his arrival in Great Falls.

65. *Northwest Passage,* October 12, 1917.

66. Prouty, *Centennial,* p. 67.

67. Examples of new hospitals in small towns are as follows:
St. Anthony Hospital, Wenatchee, June 1, 1916
Our Lady of Lourdes Hospital, Pasco, September 24, 1916
Hotel Dieu Hospital, Polson, Novmber 6, 1916
Nampa General Hospital, called Mercy Hospital later, Nampa, May 30, 1917
St. Charles Hospital, Bend, January 1, 1918
St. Anthony's Mercy Hospital, Pocatello, January 20, 1918
La Merced Hospital, Twin Falls, September 24, 1920
St. Valentine's Hospital, Wendell, May 27, 1923

68. Bradley and Kelly, *History,* p. 333.

69. *Ibid.*

70. *Ibid.,* p. 335.

71. *Catholic Sentinel*, March 21, 1918. Bishop Tiben was transferred to Denver on September 21, 1917. He died in Wichita on January 14, 1940.

72. O'Connor, *Brief History*, p. 17.

73. According to the *Spokane Chronicle*, May 21, 1918, Bishop Schinner owned a home at East 242 Manito Place, but the bishop stated that this had been leased and that "Financial conditions at the present time absolutely prohibit [his moving into the residence.]"

74. Archbishop Christie dispatched an official notice in the *Catholic Sentinel*, September 12, 1918, urging all people to support the Fourth Liberty Loan.

75. Schoenberg, *Gonzaga University*, p. 255.

76. The student's name was James Clinton.

77. This was Edward Peacock, a scholastic from the Missouri Province.

78. [Seattle University], *Seattle University, Fifty Golden Years 1898-1948*, (Seattle, 1948), p. 7.

79. This was on October 28, 1918.

80. Jueneman and Ruth, *Between the Years*, p. 35.

81. Gilbert J. Garraghan, S.J., *The Jesuits of the Middle United States*, 3 vols., (New York, 1938), II, 326.

82. The St. Mary's Academy retreat, for example, was presented from June 23 to June 26 by Father George Butler. *Catholic Sentinel*, June 11, 1914.

83. *Ibid.*, June 24, 1920. The first laymen's retreat in the Baker Diocese was not held until June 21, 1923. O'Connor, *Brief History*, p. 46.

84. The retreats at Holy Names Academy in Spokane were discontinued in 1950.

85. Bradley and Kelly, *History*, p. 355.

86. *Northwest Progress*, May 30, 1919.

87. *The Register Western Montana Edition*, April 19, 1959, p. 73.

88. *Catholic Sentinel*, February 5, 1925.

89. Bradley and Kelly, *History*, p. 357.

90. *Helena Independent*, September 4, 1921.

91. The date for this is usually given as November 16, because the fire occurred very early in the morning of that day.

92. [Mother Angela Clotilda, O.S.U.], *Ursulines of the West, 1535-1935: 1880-1935*, (Everett, 1936), p. 45. Note that this was one of the very few stone buildings in the missions.

93. Sister Mary Ilma Raufer, O.P., *Black Robes and Indians on The Last Frontier, A Story of Heroism*, (Milwaukee, 1963), p. 391.

94. *Ibid.*, p. 392.

95. *Tacoma Daily Ledger*, December 2, 1919.

96. [Augustine Ferretti, S.J.], *100 Years In The Flathead Valley*, (St. Ignatius, [Montana], 1954), p. 41.

97. Smith, *Centenary*, p. 65. The impressive new stone St. Andrew's church was built in 1928. Details and photographs of this appear in *Catholic Sentinel*, June 28, 1928.

98. *Indian Sentinel*, II, 10 (April, 1922), p. 461.

99. [Mother M. Flavia, S.N.J.M.], *Excerpts from Oregon Chronicles 1859-1959*, (Marylhurst, [1959]), p. 242.

100. *Ibid.*, p. 243.

101. This was on October 4, 1925. *Indian Sentinel*, VI (1925), p. 5.

102. This was on April 1, 1926. [James P. Hurley, S.J.], *St. Andrew's Mission Jubilee Centennial 1839-1956*, (Pendleton, 1956), p. 7.

103. [Martin Pollard, O.S.B.], *Mount of Communion Mt. Angel Abbey 1882-1982*, (St. Benedict [Oregon], 1982), p. 32.

104. This was Port Townsend's third church. The present church, in solid red brick, was dedicated on February 18, 1951. *Northwest Progress*, October 16, 1951.

105. Wilfred P. Schoenberg, S.J., *Paths to the Northwest A Jesuit History of the Oregon Province*, (Chicago, 1982), p. 322.

106. Archives of the Archdiocese of Seattle, Correspondence related to Holy Cross Cemetery, memorandum by Hayes [sic].

107. Schoenberg, *Paths to the Northwest*, p. 323.

108. *Ibid.*

109. *Ibid.*, p. 327. Gonzaga University had nothing to crow about. In the 1920–1921 school year there were only 144 students registered in the entire university, including the law school.

110. James T. Covert, *A Point of Pride: The University of Portland Story*, (Portland, 1976), p. 43.

111. *Ibid.*, p. 40.

112. *Ibid.*, p. 42.

113. An illustration of this appears in the *Catholic Sentinel* for September 17, 1914. Note the more elaborate design of the cathedral.

114. This and other details regarding O'Hara appear in a biography about him: J.B. Shaw, *Edwin Vincent O'Hara American Prelate*, (New York, 1957).

115. One of O'Hara's seminary friends, Father George Thompson, had opted for the Archdiocese of Oregon City because of the greater need for priests. O'Hara chose to do likewise.

116. *Catholic Sentinel*, March 19, 1914.

117. Michael Murnane was the father of Monsignor Edmund Murnane of the archdiocese.

118. *Catholic Sentinel*, March 25, 1983.

119. It should be noted that Massachusetts had passed a minimum wage law before this but it lacked enforcement powers.

120. Justice Brandeis served on the Court from 1916 to 1939.

121. *Catholic Sentinel*, April 12, 1917.

122. *Ibid.*, March 25, 1983.

123. *Ibid.*, May 27, 1886 and January 31, 1889

124. *Ibid.*, March 28, 1907 and October 6, 1927.

125. Shaw, *Edwin Vicent O'Hara*, p. 72.

126. Leipzig did not arrive at Corvallis until March 1922. Very Rev. Patrick J. Gaire, *A Brief History of the Diocese of Baker*, Vol. II, (St. Benedict, [Oregon], 1966), p. 174.

127. *Ibid.*, p. 173.

128. The first issue of *St. Isadore's Plow* appeared in October, 1922. St. Isadore (1070–1130) is the patron of farmers.

129. Shaw, *Edwin Vincent O'Hara*, p. vi.

130. *Ibid.*, p. vii.

Chapter 16. LOSSES AND GAINS

1. Oregon Province Archives, Seattle, papers related to the Maryknoll Fathers.

2. Dudley G. Wooten, *Remember Oregon*, (Denver, [1923]), p. 5.

3. *The Catholic Standard and Times*, Philadelphia, November 15, 1922.

4. *Catholic Sentinel*, June 8, 1916.

5. *Ibid.* February 15, 1917.

6. Lowry did not succeed as well in the East. For example, in Albion, New York, all churches refused her the use of their pulpits.

7. Lem A. Dever, *Confessions of An Imperial Klansman*, (Portland, 1924), p. 42.

8. Edwin V. O'Hara, *Pioneer Catholic History of Oregon*, *Centennial Edition*, (Paterson [New Jersey], 1939), p. 210.

9. A.B. Cain, ed., *The Oregon School Fight A True and Complete History*, (Portland, 1924), p. 45.

10. Henry A. Carey, Jr., "The Klan in Oregon," in *Catholic Contributions to Oregon History*, reprinted from *St. Joseph Magazine*, May, 1959, p. 14.

11. This refers to the Klan's subsequent attempt to pass a similar law in Washington through Initiative 49.

12. Dever, *Confessions*, p. 29.

13. Lawrence J. Saalfeld,"Forces of Prejudice In Oregon 1920-1925," unpublished dissertation, Catholic University of America, 1950. Copy in Archives of the Archdiocese of Portland, 31. Sawyer was the former pastor of Portland's East Side Christian Church.

14. According to Dever, this was the Northwestern Electric Company, a subsidiary of Fleishacker's in San Francisco. Dever, *Confessions*, p. 23.

15. Carey, "The Klan In Oregon," p. 14.

16. Dever, *Confessions*, p. 22.

17. Carey, "The Klan In Oregon," p. 14.

18. The fourteen citizens who initiated the bill are listed in Cain, *The Oregon School Fight*, [p. 5].

19. *Ibid.*

20. Wooten, *Remember Oregon*, p. 10.

21. *Ibid.*, p. 11.

22. *Ibid.*, p. 7. The Lutherans, never doubting that the bill would win with the electorate, wisely saved their money for the court fight.

23. Saalfeld, "Forces of Prejudice," p. 140.

24. Wooten, *Remember Oregon*, p. 5.

25. Cain, *The Oregon School Fight*, [p. 4].

26. Wooten, *Remember Oregon*, p. 6.

27. *Ibid.*, p. 7.

28. Many adverse reports from all over the country were published in: National Catholic Welfare Council, *Public Opinion and the Oregon School Law*, Education bulletins, No. 4 (February 1923).

29. There seems to be some difference of opinion regarding the financial support for the court case. O'Hara, *Pioneer Catholic History*, p. 212, states that "the financing of the case was assumed by the National Catholic Welfare Conference." Vergil C. Dechant of the Knights of Columbus states: "It was in 1922 that the Knights of Columbus funded a court case in Oregon which tested the constitutionality of the so-called Oregon School Law...." "A Tradition of Devotions—A Century of Service The Report of The Supreme Knight To The 100th Annual Meeting of The Supreme Council," in *Columbia*, LXII, 10 (October 1982), p. 37. My own recollections of the case are germane. As a second grader in St. Aloysius School, Spokane, taught by the Holy Names Sisters, I assisted my teacher in collecting pennies and nickels from my classmates to help pay the court costs of the sisters. This was my first lesson in the cost of politics.

30. *Catholic Sentinel*, September 6, 1928.

31. [Mother M. Flavia, SNJM], *Excerpts From Oregon Chronicles, 1859-1959*, (Marylhusrt, 1959), p. 88.

32. *Spokane Chronicle*, December 4, 1922.

33. *Ibid.*, December 7, 1922.

34. The Hill Military Academy was conducted by the Hill family, who classified it as "Episcopalian" until the Oregon School Bill was proposed. Subsequently they changed this to "private" with expectations to avoid loss in the event the bill was passed.

35. The text for the court's decision may be found in Cain, *The Oregon School Fight*, p. 132 et seq.

36. *The Oregonian*, April 3, 1924.

37. Cain, *The Oregon School Fight*, p. 152.

38. *Klamath Falls Herald*, December 5, 1923.

39. *Spokesman Review*, May 11, 1924.

40. *Northwest Progress*, July 4, 1924; August 1, 1924; and November 7, 1924.

41. According to the *Washington Post* at this time (1925), there were 150,000 members of the Ku Klux Klan in Oregon. This dropped to 86 by 1930. In 1925, there were 8,904,871 members in the United States. By 1930 this dropped to 34,694. *Catholic Sentinel*, November 6, 1930.

42. Dever, *Confessions*, especially p. 14 et seq.

43. *Catholic Sentinel*, June 4, 1925.

44. Carey, "The Klan In Oregon," p. 16.

45. Wooten, *Remember Oregon*, p. 15.

46. A short biography of O'Connor appears in Very Rev. Patrick Gaire, *Volume II A Brief History of the Diocese of Baker, 1928-1966*, (St. Benedict, [Oregon], 1966), p. 343.

47. In the Catholic press at this time, there was considerable discussion regarding the morality and merit of MacSwiney's fast. Some, including Americans, justified MacSwiney's conduct though he failed to use the required ordinary means to presrve his life. *Catholic Sentinel*, October 28, 1920.

48. Gaire, Volume II of a *Brief History*, p. 343.

49. O'Connor had conducted considerable historical research in Ireland, France, and Belgium for the Papal Commission on the Beatification of the Irish martyrs of the 16th and 17th centuries.

50. Father Dominic O'Connor, *A Brief History of the Diocese of Baker*, (Baker, 1930). Note that this was reprinted with Volume II authored by Very Rev. Patrick Gaire, (St. Benedict, [Oregon], 1966).

51. Gaire, *Volume II A Brief History*, p. 343.

52. These letters have been in the possession of his niece in Portland.

53. O'Connor, *A Brief History*, p. 14. Bishop O'Reilly was buried in Lincoln, Nebraska.

54. *Northwest Progress*, September 23, 1921. St. Joseph's Academy had been founded in 1875.

55. Details regarding Marquette's controversial closure will appear later.

56. Seattle College High School and Gonzaga High School were both accredited in 1921 during the first year of accreditation of the state university.

57. O'Dea was the second foundation of the brothers in the Seattle diocese. Prior to this, on September 14, 1914, they had taken over the direction of Briscoe Memorial, a resident school for orphan boys endowed by Edwin Briscoe and others. *Northwest Progress*, August 31, 1923.

58. *Ibid.*, March 14, 1924; March 21, 1924.

59. Rt. Rev. Cyprian Bradley, O.S.B., and Most Rev. Edward J. Kelly, D.D., Ph.D., *History of the Diocese of Boise, 1863-1952*, (Boise, 1953), p. 348.

60. *Ibid.*, p. 349.

61. Volume I, No. 1 *The Echo of St. Gertrude's* appeared in April 1923. Copies at St. Gertrude's and in the Oregon Province Archives.

62. Oregon Province Archives, Mss. History of St. Gertrude's by Sister M. Alfreda Elsensohn, O.S.B.

63. A new girls' Central Catholic was built in 1951.

64. The Sisters of The Holy Names conducted three Normal Schools: St. Mary's in Portland, Holy Names in Seattle, and Holy Names in Spokane. These schools could not grant degrees.

65. The six Catholic colleges or universities were Mount Angel College, Gonzaga University, Columbia University, St. Martin's College, Seattle College and Carroll College. Significantly, Catholic University in Washington, D.C. admitted women students as early as 1911. Catholic University, however, was principally a graduate school.

66. James T. Covert, *A Point of Pride: The University of Portland Story*, (Portland, 1976), p. 95. Columbia's first college graduation occurred in 1929, when six candidates were granted degrees.

67. Oregon Province Archives, Gonzaga University Diaries, June 25, 1924.

68. This was Joseph Graham.

69. Gonzaga University became coeducational in all departments in 1948.

70. Oregon Province Archives, Seattle College Diaries for September 25, 1933. For a complete account see Wilfred P. Schoenberg, S.J., *Paths To the Northwest A Jesuit History of the Oregon Province*, (Chicago, 1982), p. 411 et seq.

71. *Catholic Sentinel*, June 5, 1924.

72. In August 1909, two Servite fathers from Chicago arrived in Hermiston, Oregon. Father Hyacinth remained in Hermiston and Father Simon was assigned to Joseph, Oregon in the Wallowa Valley. They remained until January 1910 when they were withdrawn by superiors.

73. Charles M. Smith, ed., *Centenary of Cathedral Parish*, (Portland, 1951), p. 67.

74. Oregon Province Archives, Mss. "Background of St. Mary's Cathedral."

75. These had been incorporated in the pro-cathedral and were moved for the second time to the present cathedral.

76. O'Hara, *Pioneer Catholic History*, Centennial Edition, p. 209.

77. Archives of the Archdiocese of Portland, letter of Father J. Bernards to Father [Leo] Remington, March 11, 1977.

78. An organ recital by Charles Courbain, noted Belgian organist, had taken place in the church some days before, on February 8. This recital, sponsored by the Altar Society, was designed to dedicate the new $7,000 organ made by Kimball of Chicago. *Catholic Sentinel*, January 21, 1926.

79. Sister Birgetta Mott, O.P., "Carroll College and The Dominican Sisters," typescript reprint of article in the *Montana Catholic Register*, August, 1971, p. 1 et seq.

80. Hedwig, after one year, returned to Speyer and received the habit of the order as Sister Theresita. Subsequently she was murdered by the Nazis in an extermination camp.

81. Cecelia M. Hatfield, *The Story of Our Lady of the Valley Convent Near Meyers Falls, Washington*, (n.p., 1936), p. 11 et seq.

82. These Dominicans established schools at Shelby and Cut Bank in Montana, at St. Mary's Mission, Omak, at Oroville and Spokane in Washington. They operated five hospitals; in Conrad, Montana, and in Chewelah, Tonasket, Colville, and Spokane in Washington.

83. Mother Bonaventura died on September 23, 1942.

84. Bishop Carroll was born during the Civil War, on February 22, 1864.

85. Sister Birgetta Mott, "Carroll College," p. 2.

86. *San Francisco Monitor*, December 5, 1925.

87. *Spokesman Review*, January 3, 1926.

88. *Ibid.*

89. *Ibid.*, September 16, 1926.

90. *Ibid.*

91. *Catholic Sentinel*, September 6, 1928. Bishop Schinner died of pneumonia in Milwaukee on February 7, 1937. An obituary appears in the *Spokesman Review*, February 8, 1937.

92. The three others were Carroll, Lenihan and Gorman.

93. Howard was born on November 5, 1877, the year of Chief Joseph's War.

94. The other twin died in infancy. An excellent biography of Marie Howard appeared at the time of her death in the *Catholic Sentinel*, January 5, 1933.

95. Howard spent only three years at St. Joseph's College, then one year at St. Mary's in Kansas.

96. One of the best published sources for Howard's personal history is Edward O'Meara's account in *The Oregonian*, January 3, 1983. Note that a press dispatch from Rome on April 22, 1926, stated that Howard had been appointed to Oregon City "this morning." *Catholic Sentinel*, April 22, 1926.

97. Bishop James Davis died on December 2, 1926.

98. Howard arrived in Spokane on the morning of August 25, 1926. The Gonzaga University Diaries for that day has the following comment. "Brogan met the Archbishop-elect at the depot. The new archbishop went to see Mount St. Michael's. Fr. Minister saw him off in the evening. The Jesuits were the only priests who saw the archbishop in Spokane." As an eleven year old altar boy, I served the archbishop's Mass that morning.

99. *Catholic Sentinel*, August 26, 1926.

100. Interview. Father Edward Kowrach, archivist for the Diocese of Spokane, December 10, 1983. Father Kowrach was a seminarian in Grand Rapids.

101. Thus Bishop White was the first of the Roman trained priests to become a bishop in the Northwest. All members of his class became bishops, except one, Father Leo Martin, who became a Jesuit despite Bishop Carroll's continued opposition

102. *Spokane Chronicle*, March 10, 1927.

103. *Catholic Sentinel*, December 23, 1926.

104. O'Dea announced the recipients of the honor on January 1, 1926. Investiture for all six monsignors took place in the Cathedral of St. James on March 15, 1926.

105. *Northwest Progress*, January 25, 1924.

106. The Society was named for St. Vincent de Paul (1581-1660) patron for those who work with the poor.

107. *Catholic Sentinel*, October 6, 1960, III, 24. It will be remembered that the St. Vincent de Paul Society presented the Sisters of Providence the property for their new hospital in Portland on July 19, 1874. The Vincentians also gave the Sisters one thousand dollars toward building the new St. Vincent Hospital.

108. *Ibid.*, December 12, 1889.

109. [Andrew Prouty, ed.], *1850—Centennial of the Diocese of Seattle—1950, The Catholic Northwest Progress*, LIII, 36, Second Section (September 8, 1950), Seattle, 1950, p. 45.

110. *Northwest Progress*, April 16, 1926.

111. Salvage bureaus were established also in Spokane, Walla Walla, Pasco, Clarkston, Missoula, Tacoma, and Yakima; later in Boise, and Coeur d'Alene. A salvage bureau was opened in Great Falls in August 1940.

112. The Seattle Salvage Bureau was organized by Emt on March 1, 1926. Portland's bureau was begun in 1930.

113. Bradley and Kelly, *History of the Diocese of Boise*, p. 372 et seq.

114. These letters were mailed, unsigned, with a note of explanation.

115. *Ibid.*, p. 379.

116. "The love of Christ impels us," from St. Paul, II Corinthians, 5:14.

117. Finnigan entered the Congregation of the Holy Cross on August 28, 1902.

118. *Helena Catholic Monthly*, XI(1927)iii.

119. *Ibid.*, p. xix. *Carolus* is the Latin form for Charles.

120. *Register Eastern Montana Edition*, May 29, 1932.

121. Bishop O'Dea was born in Boston.

122. Bradley and Kelly, *History of the Diocese of Boise*, p. 387. Bradley's name is used as author because of his remark to me at Keuterville in July 1961, when he said, "I did all of the writing [of the history] and each morning Bishop Kelly used a red pencil to cut out what was not edifying. He believed that history was intended to edify." Bishop Gerald Shaughnessy of Seattle agreed also with this view.

123. *Catholic Sentinel*, March 8, 1928. Bishop Kelly was born on February 26, 1890, on a farm eighteen miles east of The Dalles.

124. *Ibid.*, March 15, 1928. The bishop's father died in November of the following year.

125. Details regarding Cataldo's broken bones appear in Wilred P. Schoenberg, S.J., *Gonzaga University Seventy-Five Years, 1887–1962*, Spokane, 1963, p. 21.

126. Schoenberg, *Paths To The Northwest*, p. 358.

127. *Catholic Sentinel*, March 22, 1928.

128. *Ibid.*, July 25, 1928.

129. *Ibid.*, August 9, 1928.

130. *Ibid.*, beginning with August 16, 1928.

131. *Ibid.*, September 6, 1928.

132. *Ibid.*, December 6, 1928.

133. Seattle's Catholic high schools were: Forest Ridge, Holy Angels, Holy Names, Holy Rosary, O'Dea, and Seattle Prep.

134. Spokane's Catholic high schools were Holy Names and Gonzaga High. Marycliff would appear in the following year.

135. Gregory C. Rathbone, [S.J.], *A Heritage on Bellarmine Hill*, Tacoma, 1983, p. 3.

136. Hugh Boyle was ordained a priest in 1946 and is currently (1983) pastor of Harlem, Montana.

137. Wilfred P. Schoenberg, S.J., *Father Dave*, (Milwaukee, 1959).

138. Oregon Province Archives, Mss. History of Marycliff High School. The Gordons had purchased this home in 1909 for $125,000 from F. Lewis Clark, who had built it "about 1896."

139. *Spokesman Review*, August 2, 1929.

140. The other sisters were: Sister M. Francesca, music department, Sister M. Avita, household duties, Sister M. Antonia and Sister M. Valentina, teachers.

141. *Spokesman Review*, August 2, 1929. Non-Catholic students were charged twenty-five dollars per semester "in advance."

142. *Catholic Sentinel*, February 21, 1929.

143. Mother M. Flavia, *Chronicles*, p. 62.

144. *Ibid.*, p. 67.

145. *Ibid.*, p. 68.

146. This was on November 30, 1911.

147. Mother M. Flavia, *Chronicles*, p. 282.

148. *Ibid.*

Chapter 17. DEPRESSION YEARS

1. James Hennessey, S.J., *American Catholics A History of the Roman Catholic Community in the United States*, (New York, 1981), p. 265.

2. Bishop Lenihan died in Dubuque on August 19, 1943.

3. *Catholic Sentinel*, August 7, 1930.

4. Bishop Finnigan was scheduled to serve as a co-consecrator but he became ill suddenly and Bishop Crimont substituted for him. *Ibid.*, October 30, 1930.

5. *Ibid.*, November 13, 1930.

6. J.G. Shaw, *Edwin Vincent O'Hara American Prelate,* (New York, 1957), p. 128.

7. By October 1930, Mount Angel's new seminary quarters were occupied by the seminarians. Lawrence J. McCrank, *Mt. Angel Abbey A Centennial History of the Benedictine Community and Its Library 1882–1982,* (Wilmington, 1983), p. 66.

8. Letter of Edward O'Dea, May 22, 1930 to the clergy of the Seattle Diocese, copy in Oregon Province Archives.

9. *Catholic Sentinel,* June 5, 1930.

10. Very Rev. Thomas C. Mulligan, S.S., "A Rector Reminisces," in *The Harvester,* XVIII, 3 (October 1956), p. 30 seq.

11. *Catholic Sentinel,* October 16, 1930.

12. For example, Mrs. Mary Condon, a widow, provided $12,000 for the seminary in her will at a critical time. *Ibid.,* March 5, 1931.

13. *The Harvester,* XVIII (October 1956), p. 21.

14. Mount Rainier, called Mount Tahoma, "the mountain that was God." Construction had been started in the first week of March. *Catholic Sentinel,* March 19, 1931.

15. *Ibid.,* September 3, 1931.

16. The names of the sisters were as follows: Sister M. Theophane, Sister M. Victoria, Sister M. Emmanuel, Sister M. Jean d'Avila, Sister M. Rose de Lima, Sister M. Madelain. *The Harvester,* XVIII (October 1956), p. 33.

17. The first student roster appears in the *Catholic Sentinel,* September 24, 1931.

18. At this time, the Portland archdiocese had about 90 priests, the Seattle diocese about 120. There were 396 Jesuits in the Northwest, including some scholastics who were ordained clerics.

19. Manresa Hall was opened on September 8, 1927. Wilfred P. Schoenberg, S.J., *Paths To The Northwest A Jesuit History of The Oregon Province,* (Chicago, 1982), p. 347.

20. The Pacific Northwest, including Alaska, had ten more Jesuits than California in 1930 when the northern vice-province was established.

21. Schoenberg, *Paths To The Northwest,* p. 373.

22. The land, totalling 891 acres, was purchased on October 30, 1930.

23. Schoenberg, *Paths To The Northwest,* p. 377.

24. *Catholic Sentinel,* August 13, 1931.

25. Schoenberg, *Paths To The Northwest,* p. 385.

26. Diaries St. Francis Xavier Novitiate in Oregon Province Archives.

27. When six graduates of Central Catholic in Butte entered the Jesuit Order in 1931, a great storm erupted in the bishop's office in Helena.

28. *Catholic Sentinel,* November 6, 1930.

29. Edward F. O'Meara, *Continue To Prosper—The History of the First Half Century of All Saints Parish Portland, Oregon,* [Portland, 1970], p. 16.

30. *Ibid.,* p. 17.

31. *Ibid.*

32. *Ibid.*

33. Ground was broken for this new two-story chancery on August 9, 1931. *Catholic Sentinel,* August 13, 1931.

34. The encyclical on Catholic Action [*Azione Catholica*] was signed on June 29, 131 under the title *Non Abbiomo Bisogno.*

35. Archives of the Diocese of Great Falls, original copies.

36. Frank Butler was the first editor, James Stewart Associate Editor. Original copies in Oregon Province Archives. An article about this paper appeared in the *Spokane Chronicle,* December 28, 1960.

37. This was Father James Cox of Pittsburgh. *Inland Catholic,* January 22, 1932.

38. Archives Diocese of Helena, original copies.

39. Baker diocesan news was included in the *Catholic Sentinel*.

40. This had been built in 1905 for $1500 by Father J.B. Carroll, S.J. on Willow Creek South of Browning. It was moved into town in 1910.

41. *The Calumet*, July, 1932.

42. This Fourth Provincial Council was held in Portland, October 8-10, 1932.

43. *The Register Western Montana Edition*, August 21, 1932 and October 9, 1932.

44. *Catholic Sentinel*, August 26, 1932.

45. *The Register Eastern Montana Edition*, September 18, 1932.

46. Mss. "College of Great Falls" in Oregon Province Archives.

47. *Ibid.*

48. *Catholic Sentinel*, January 4, 1934.

49. Mulligan, "A Rector Reminisces," p. 30 et seq.

50. *Northwest Progress*, December 30, 1932.

51. *Catholic Sentinel*, January 5, 1933.

52. *Northwest Progress*, December 30, 1932.

53. *Inland Catholic*, August 5, 1932.

54. *Ibid.*, August 19, 1932.

55. William Condon was born at Colton on April 7, 1895.

56. Schoenberg, *Paths To The Northwest*, p. 295.

57. *Catholic Sentinel*, June 29, 1933.

58. The name of this was later changed to Duquesne University.

59. Hayes attended Holy Ghost College 1898-1905, and the North American College in Rome till 1910. He was diocesan superintendent of schools from 1917-1925. *Catholic Sentinel*, July 6, 1933.

60. *Ibid.*, July 13, 1933.

61. Gerald Shaughnessy, S.M., *Has the Immigrant Kept the Faith?* (New York, 1925). This was Shaughnessy's dissertation for his doctoral degree in theology at Catholic University.

62. The two books were: *To Die With Jesus* and *With Jesus To The Priesthood*.

63. This was the first consecration of a bishop in the National Shrine. *Inland Catholic*, September 22, 1933.

64. Both of Shaughnessy's parents were present for the Mass.

65. Hayes arrived in Helena on October 4 with Griffin.

66. N.R.A. was Roosevelt's "National Recovery Act." *Catholic Sentinel*, October 5, 1933.

67. For example, on September 16, 1934, one hundred and forty CCC boys were confirmed by Bishop Kelly in the presence of a great crowd at Pierce, Idaho. The event gained national attention. Rt. Rev. Cyprian Bradley, O.S.B., and Most Rev. Edward J. Kelly, D.D., Ph.D., *History of the Diocese of Boise 1863-1952*, (Boise, 1953), p. 434.

68. Howard returned to Portland in April via Manila. *Catholic Sentinel*, April 26, 1934.

69. White sailed on the *Vulcan* to Naples, arriving there on February 9. *Inland Catholic*, February 16, 1934.

70. Very Rev. Patrick J. Gaire, *A Brief History of the Diocese of Baker 1928-1966*, Volume II, (St. Benedict [Oregon], 1966), p. 162.

71. *Ibid.* McGrath had already addressed a letter to the clergy and laity of his diocese formally establishing the CCD in every parish and mission. This was on February 11, 1934.

72. *Ibid.*

73. Bradley and Kelly, *History of the Diocese of Boise*, p. 412.

74. *Inland Catholic*, April 29, 1932.

75. CCD was established in Portland in June 1936, and in Seattle sometime in 1938.

76. Interview with Mrs. Rose Gilles of the Catholic Truth Society on June 14, 1961.

77. Mr. William P. O'Connell, "Patrons of the Priesthood," in *The Harvester*, XVIII (October 1956), p. 37 et seq.

78. [Patrick Casey, ed.], *1841–1941 A Century of Catholicity in Montana: Souvenir Centenary Edition The Register Diocese of Helena*, XVII, August 27, 1941, III, p. 12.

79. For this a dispensation was obtained since church law required candidates for the priesthood to be 25 years of age or more.

80. James T. Covert, *A Point of Pride: The University of Portland Story*, Portland, 1976, p. 87.

81. *Ibid.*

82. *Ibid.*, p. 94.

83. *Catholic Sentinel*, September 5, 1935. Later this devotion chapel was traded for another building across Burnside to make room for a new multi-storied bank building. As part of the trade, the new acquisition was completely remodeled. It was occupied on February 23, 1973.

84. *Inland Catholic*, October 4, 1935 and October 11, 1935.

85. Hayes remained in Rome until November 16, 1944, when he was appointed Bishop of Davenport. He died on July 4, 1970.

86. *Inland Catholic*, November 8, 1935.

87. *Ibid.*, December 20, 1935.

88. *Catholic Sentinel*, February 20, 1936.

89. *Jesuit Seminary News*, V (September 1936), p. 1.

90. Diaries Sacred Heart Mission in Oregon Province Archives.

91. At Tonasket, Washington, St. Martin of Tours Hospital built by the Dominican Sisters was blessed by Bishop White on August 25, 1930, and at La Grande, Oregon, the Sisters of St. Francis dedicated St. Joseph's Hospital on October 4, 1938. At Eugene, Oregon, the Sisters of St. Joseph of Newark acquired the Pacific Christian Hospital and converted it into Sacred Heart Hospital.

92. St. Vincent's had been founded in 1869, thus it was demolished in its sixty-seventh year.

93. *Northwest Progress*, March 15, 1935.

94. *Ibid.*, June 19, 1936 and *Catholic Sentinel* August 6, 1936.

95. *Northwest Progress*, August 28, 1936.

96. [Charles M. Smith, ed.], *The Centenary, 100 Years of the Catholic Church in the Oregon Country, Supplement to the Catholic Sentinel*, (May 4, 1939), Portland, 1939, p. 79.

97. Father Thomas Sherman, S.J., addressed the Knights of Columbus in Yakima and urged them to restore the old mission. The Knights responded and the restoration was dedicated on July 13, 1919. *Northwest Progress*, July 18, 1919.

98. [Demetrius Jueneman, O.S.B. and Sebastian Ruth, O.S.B.], *Between the Years 1895–1945 St. Martin's College, Lacey*, [n.p.], 1945, [p. 61].

99. *Northwest Progress*, June 17, 1938.

100. This was on June 1, 1938.

101. The acts of the synod were published as follows: *Statuta Diocesis Seattlensis Lata ac Promulgata ab Excellentissimo ac Reverendissimo Geraldo Shaughnessy, S.M. Episcopo Seattlensi in Synodo Dioecessana Seattlensi Quinta*, Seattle, [1938].

102. Open house was celebrated on January 15, 1939. *Northwest Progress*, January 13, 1939.

103. On May 30, 1938, White conducted a memorial Mass on this site where the first Mass in the interior of the Northwest was offered by Demers in 1838. Bishop O'Hara spoke at this memorial which was attended by 3000 people. White suggested then that the old mission built by Ravalli be restored.

104. For example, White removed Father Michael O'Malley, S.J. as pastor of St. Aloysius Church, Spokane, because of a disagreement over money. Timothy J. O'Leary, S.J., ed., *Flocks That I Watched Memoirs of Fr. Michael M. O'Malley, S.J., (1875–1970)*, (Spokane, 1971), p. 76.

105. *Inland Catholic,* February 24, 1939.

106. Walter Fitzgerald was born at Peola, Washington Territory on November 17, 1883. A long biography of him appeared as follows: Wilfred P. Schoenberg, S.J., "Beggar Bishop" in *Woodstock Letters,* 81 (1952), p. 204 et seq.

107. *Spokesman Review,* February 28, 1939.

108. *Ibid.*

109. An account of this pioneer hall, called Durocher, appeared in the magazine section of the *Spokesman Review,* September 16, 1956.

110. In other words, the high school department shared its building with the new college.

111. O'Hara subsequently received the personal title of archbishop on June 29, 1954. His title was changed to "Bishop of Kansas City and St. Joseph" on July 2, 1956. He died in Milan, Italy on September 11, 1956. He was buried in Kansas City.

112. Condon became a monsignor in May 1937 and at the end of the same month received the honorary doctorate from Gonzaga University.

113. *Catholic Sentinel,* October 13, 1939.

114. This land had been purchased from Timothy Sullivan.

115. This publication was edited by Father Charles Smith as noted above: *The Centenary, 100 Years of the Catholic Church in the Oregon Country.*

116. *Ibid.,* p. 34.

117. *The Harvester,* I(June 1939), pgs. 4–5.

118. This new building was designed to accommodate 1100 students. *Seattle Times,* June 22, 1941.

119. This was replaced with a new building in 1949. Sister M. Mileta Ludwig, F.S.P.A., *A Chapter of Franciscan History; The Sisters of the Third Order of St. Francis of Perpetual Adoration 1849–1949,* (New York, 1950), p. 275.

120. The churches for others were: St. Thomas More in Portland, dedicated on September 29, 1940; St. John Vianney in Darrington [Washington] opened in July 1941; and St. Catherine's, later called St. Richard, in Big Fork [Montana], begun in December, 1941.

121. Schoenberg, *Paths to the Northwest,* p. 405 et seq.

122. The debt was $57,682.40, not including interest.

123. Schoenberg, *Paths to the Northwest,* p. 407.

124. *Ibid.* The committee also reported that sometimes Jesuits were at fault because they did not appeal to the bishops for funds.

125. *Ibid.,* p. 408.

126. The latter appears to be an unfair indictment, partly because the bishop did not have all the facts. Prange kept good accounts, but in the initial stages of the dispute he concealed them when the bishop's assistants attempted to confiscate them, presumably, for their own use.

127. *Ibid.,* p. 409.

128. *Inland Catholic,* November 8, 1935.

129. *Inland Register,* March 26, 1943.

130. *Inland Catholic,* April 18, 1941.

131. A full account of the fire appears in Wilfred P. Schoenberg, S.J., *Gonzaga University Seventy-Five Years 1887–1962,* (Spokane, 1963), p. 406 et seq.

Chapter 18. MOSTLY ABOUT BISHOPS

1. James Emmett Royce, born in Chicago in 1888, moved to Spokane after his marriage in 1911. Two of his five children became Jesuits, Thomas and James. The elder Royce died on October 30, 1951.

2. Kennedy had earned Roosevelt's frigid response by suggesting that Germany would be victorious in its war with England.

3. *Inland Catholic*, September 26, 1941.

4. *Ibid.*

5. *Ibid.*, October 3, 1941.

6. Harry [Alfred Renton] Bridges, Australian born (1900) was involved as a labor organizer in the United States Maritime industry.

7. Sheen, later Archbishop and Bishop of Rochester, presented the European conflict as a spiritual one. He had great influence over American Catholics who came to accept his position.

8. Bishop White had made this statement publicly on September 21, 1940. Royce published it in the *Inland Catholic* on September 19, 1941.

9. White reflected current Catholic views in both of these statements. On October 24, 1941, Royce noted in the paper that "Catholic Priests of America Vote Nine to One Against War and Giving Aid to Red Russia." Not only England's tyrannical behavior toward Ireland influenced this vote, but Russia's persecution of religion made America's clergy implacable enemies of the communists who became allies of the British.

10. *Inland Catholic*, December 12, 1941.

11. *Ibid.*

12. The bishop actually announced the termination of the *Inland Catholic* on July 3, 1942.

13. The *Inland Catholic* ceased publication on this date. It was replaced by the *Inland Register* one week later. Editor Royce's personal bound copies of the *Inland Catholic* were presented to the Oregon Province Archives by Mrs. Royce.

14. *Inland Catholic*, July 31, 1942.

15. Tully, a local seminarian, was informed by Bishop White prior to his ordination in 1942, that his first assignment would be editor of *"The Spokane Register."* Following ordination and a brief vacation, he was sent to Denver for a thirty-day speed course under the *Register's* editor, Monsignor Matthew Smith.

16. The three brothers names were Octavius the superior, Cleophas, and Marion.

17. *Inland Catholic*, July 17, 1942.

18. Oregon Province Archives, Mss. "Sisters of St. Joseph of Newark," The name of this congregation has been changed to Sisters of St. Joseph of Peace.

19. These churches were St. Margaret's at Cut Bank, St. Joseph's at Choteau, and St. John's at Cooke City, all in Montana, St. Martin of Tours in Fife, Sacred Heart at Wellpinit and St. Brendan in Bothell, all in Washington.

20. *Inland Register*, September 25, 1942.

21. James Hennessey, S.J., *American Catholics A History of the Roman Catholic Community in the United States*, (New York, 1981), p. 280.

22. *Ibid.*

23. James T. Covert, *A Point of Pride: The University of Portland Story*, (Portland, 1976), p. 116.

24. The university assured its students in the program that they would be allowed to graduate, but the army, allowing a few exceptions, called them to active duty on March 5, 1943. *Ibid.*

25. Gonzaga had two other programs prior to this, the V-1 and the V-7. Both were merged into the V-12. Wilfred P. Schoenberg, S.J., *Gonzaga University Seventy-Five Years 1887-1962*, (Spokane, 1963), p. 414 et seq.

26. [Demetrius Jueneman, O.S.B., and Sebastian Ruth, O.S.B.] *Between the Years 1895-1945 St. Martin's College, Lacey*, (N.P., 1945), [p. 69].

27. Lawrence J. McCrank, *Mt. Angel Abbey A Centennial History of the Benedictine Community and its Library*, 1882-1982, (Wilmington, 1983), p. 69.

28. *Ibid.*

29. Louis Egan died on September 14, 1945, leaving behind cartons of letters received from GI's all over the world. John Delaunay, one of the most popular teachers in the history of the University of Portland, died in 1953.

30. *Inland Register,* January 22, 1943.

31. *Ibid.,* April 16, 1943. Troy had gone into the army and Spiller was acting attorney general.

32. *Inland Register,* June 4, 1943.

33. *Ibid.*

34. *Ibid.,* March 13, 1945. This report contains the list of the 69 representatives who voted for the bill and the 28 who voted against it, as well as the 27 senators who voted for it and the 18 who voted against it.

35. *Ibid.*

36. *Ibid.,* November 2, 1945. This warning came from Troy who had returned to civilian life.

37. *Ibid.,* February 21, 1947.

38. *Ibid.,* October 31, 1947.

39. "Public Educators Approve All Forms of Tax Aid to Parochial Schools" is a forthright article in which the injustices of the system are exposed. *Ibid.,* March 10, 1950.

40. The north side coeducational high school referred to here was Blanchet, which was not occupied until 1955.

41. These sisters withdrew on July 31, 1945 and the Sisters of Providence replaced them.

42. Archives of the Diocese of Spokane, Record Book of Dedications, p. 62. Mr. and Mrs. John Collins provided the money for this purchase.

43. *Northwest Progress,* December 3, 1943.

44. This church was located at 2701 N. Victory Boulevard. *Catholic Sentinel,* March 11, 1943.

45. *Inland Register,* December 17, 1948.

46. *Ibid.,* March 23, 1945.

47. For Port Orford see *Catholic Sentinel,* May 11, 1944. For Great Falls, *Register Eastern Montana Edition,* December 17, 1944. For Port Orchard, Oregon Province Archives, Mss. "Port Orchard." John Day, Oregon's first church called St. Charles, was opened this year, 1946, in a renovated two-cabin makeshift provided by the Hines Lumber Company. Archives, Diocese of Baker, Leipzig manuscript.

48. *Inland Register,* February 23, 1945, Spokane's present chancery, formerly headquarters for an insurance company, was acquired by Bishop Topel who regarded it as too affluent looking, but the cost was so low he could not pass it up. Besides it was across the street from the cathedral.

49. This was founded by James Linden, S.J., but was directed for many years by Clifford Carroll, S.J. head of the university's economics department.

50. Covert, *A Point of Pride,* p. 119.

51. *Spokane Chronicle,* February 6, 1947.

52. Changes in the existing bill were noted as follows:

> In line 5 of Senate Bill No. 28 the following words contained in the present law have been omitted—'fifteen years of age.' and the amendatory word on line 6 increases the age limit to 'eighteen' years of age. In line 9, after the word 'session,' the following words have been deleted 'or to attend a private school for the same time.' In line 11, after the word 'of' the word 'common' has been deleted. In line 14, the word 'eight' has been deleted and the word 'twelve' has been inserted to amend. Beginning with the word 'or' in line 15, all the underlined words have been inserted to amend. In line 22, the deleted words after the word 'schools' are 'or approved private schools.'

53. *Inland Register*, February 21, 1947.

54. *Ibid.*

55. In 1947 new churches were opened in Eden, Riggins and Boise in Idaho, in Silverton and Springfield in Oregon and in Spokane and Preston in Washington.

56. In 1948 there were new churches in Hagerman and Kamiah in Idaho, in Connell and Glenwood, Washington, in Nyssa, Oregon and Neihart, Montana.

57. El Retiro, founded in 1925 and conducted by California Jesuits, was the first retreat house in western America.

58. Wilfred P. Schoenberg, S.J., *Jesuits in Oregon 1844-1959*, (Portland, 1959), p. 54.

59. Lacking other facilities, one high school class was conducted on a stairway and was frequently interrupted by college students who were on a different class schedule. I was the teacher.

60. Covert, *A Point of Pride*, p. 149.

61. For example at the University of Santa Clara, Gonzaga University, University of San Francisco and others.

62. Covert, *A Point of Pride*, p. 150.

63. Wilfred P. Schoenberg, S.J., *Paths to the Northwest A Jesuit History of the Oregon Province*, Chicago, 1982, p. 449.

64. *Northwest Progress*, March 5, 1948.

65. *The Harvester*, X(May 1948), p. 7 et seq. Connolly visited St. Edward's Seminary on November 3, 1943.

66. Timothy F. Cronin, S.J., unpublished dissertation, "Seattle University: 1891-1966" Seattle University, 1982, p. 242.

67. *Ibid.*, p. 263.

68. *Ibid.*, p. 264.

69. *Ibid.*, p. 266.

70. *Catholic Sentinel*, June 3, 1948.

71. Father Dominic O'Connor and Very Rev. Patrick J. Gaire, *A Brief History of the Diocese of Baker*, (St. Benedict [Oregon], 1966), p. 168.

72. *Inland Register*, August 5, 1949.

73. O'Connor and Gaire, *A Brief History*, p. 169.

74. *Catholic Sentinel*, April 6, 1950.

75. Archives Diocese of Baker, telegram Martin to McGrath, April 4, 1950.

76. Sister Mary Presentina, *And Away We Go*, (New York, 1975), p. 181.

77. *Ibid.*, p. 180.

78. Archives Diocese of Baker, telegram Martin to Baker City Diocese.

79. O'Connor and Gaire, *A Brief History*, p. 165.

80. Rev. James H. Gandrau, *'Worth Raising' Solemn Observance of the Silver Jubilee of the Most Reverend Thomas Arthur Connolly, D.D., J.C.D., Fifth Bishop of Seattle, Washington, August 26, 1964.* [Seattle, 1964], p. 17.

81. [Most Rev. Thomas Gill, D.D.], *Commemorating the Golden Jubilee of the Cathedral of St. James*, [Seattle, 1957], [p. 21].

82. *Ibid.* The commentator is in error regarding the initial cost of the cathedral. Its estimated cost was $250,000. Its actual cost was $500,000.

83. *Northwest Progress*, May 19, 1950. Shaughnessy's housekeeper, Marguerite MacDonald was present when he died.

84. *Ibid.*, May 26, 1950.

85. Gill, *Commemorating the Golden Jubilee*, [p. 23].

86. O'Connor and Gaire, *A Brief History*, p. 173.

87. *Ibid.*, p. 175 et seq.

88. Interview with Mary Ann Davis, Baker, April 22, 1983.

89. Percentages of Catholic dioceses for 1950 were as follows: Baker City 6%, Boise 5%, Helena 25%, Great Falls 17%, Seattle 10%, Portland 11% and Spokane 11%. The City of Spokane, as noted before, was the most Catholic of northwest cities with a Catholic population greater in percentage than twice that of the diocese.

90. *Seattle Post Intelligencer*, May 1, 1952.

91. Dougherty was appointed on July 9, 1951.

92. *Northwest Progress*, July 20, 1951. Juneau, hitherto the residence of the Vicar Apostolic of Alaska, Bishop Francis Gleeson, was cut off from the vicariate and Bishop Gleeson moved his headquarters to Fairbanks. Bishop O'Flannagan was consecrated on October 3, 1950 in Juneau.

93. Regarded as an active pastor in Anchorage, Bishop O'Flannagan seemed to retire within a shell after becoming a bishop. His flock seldom saw him.

94. Patrick Dougherty died in 1952. *Seattle Times*, February 15, 1952.

95. *Northwest Progress*, July 18, 1951.

96. *Ibid*. Archbishop Connolly did not receive the pallium until March 14, 1953.

97. *Ibid.*, September 28, 1951. Co-consecrators for Dougherty were Bishop White and Hugh Donahoe, auxiliary in San Francisco.

98. *Ibid.*, October 12, 1951.

99. *Yakima Herald*, October 4, 1952.

100. *Seattle Post Intelligencer*, May 1, 1952.

101. *Northwest Progress*, July 25, 1952.

102. *Ibid.*, June 6, 1952.

103. In the 1982–1983 school year, Butte's two schools, North Central Catholic and South Central Catholic, were merged into one Central Catholic School which was coeducational.

104. St. Mary's was founded in 1906, St. Thomas in 1910 and the Ursuline Academy in 1911.

105. On July 29, 1959, the *Congressional Record* printed laudatory remarks about Sister Miriam by Senator Wayne Morse. The *Catholic Sentinel*, March 25, 1983, summarizes some of the honor bestowed on her.

106. These normal schools were established at St. Mary's, Portland and Holy Names Academy in Seattle and Spokane.

107. Benedictine Sisters from Cottonwood established St. Benedict's Hospital in Jerome, Idaho in 1952. The Dominican Sisters built a new Mount Carmel Hospital in Colville during the same year.

108. *Catholic Sentinel*, October 6, 1960, Section 3, p. 27.

109. Sisters of Notre Dame de Namur had come with DeSmet in 1844 but left Oregon during the California Gold Rush. The Benedictine sisters from Minnesota spent a brief period with Father Croquet at St. Michael's Mission, Grand Ronde in 1881.

110. Oregon Province Archives, Mss. Benedictine Sisters, Olympia.

111. *Northwest Progress*, February 27, 1953.

112. Oregon Province Archives, Mss. "Franciscan Missionary Sisters, Beaverton."

113. Oregon Province Archives, Mss. "Sisters of Mercy, Springfield."

114. *Northwest Progress*, September 4, 1953.

115. *Ibid.*, January 22, 1954.

116. *Ibid.*, August 13, 1954.

117. *Catholic Sentinel*, August 4, 1955.

118. Archives Diocese of Baker, original decree.

119. *Inland Register*, February 13, 1953.

120. [Alfred A. Williams], *Dedication of St. Elizabeth Catholic Church,* (Portland, 1958), p. 19 et seq.

121. The three grade schools were at Richland and Puyallup, Washington, and Coos Bay, Oregon. The high schools were Gonzaga in Spokane, Blanchet in Seattle and Serra, a Franciscan high school in Salem, which survived only a few years.

122. Wilfred P. Schoenberg, S.J., *A Chronicle of the Catholic History of the Pacific Northwest 1743–1960,* (Portland, 1962). The Introduction contains a detailed history of Gonzaga Prep.

123. The accumulated cost of the seventeen acre campus was $27,000, additional land was acquired later.

124. This was originally St. Ignatius Church, a mission served from Seattle College begun in November 1929. In 1940, Father Hugh Gallagher of the diocesan clergy became pastor of the newly established parish called Our Lady of the Lake.

125. Oregon Province Archives, correspondence of (Rev.) John P. Doogan with Wilfred P. Schoenberg, S.J., May 17, 1960.

126. Names of the first faculty appear in [John P. Doogan] *We Dedicate To God and Country Blanchet High School,* [Seattle], 1955, p. 10.

127. *Inland Register,* December 10, 1954.

Chapter 19. VATICAN COUNCIL YEARS

1. Oregon Province Archives, Letter of Hawkins to Schoenberg. Trappists at Lafayette, in the *Catholic Sentinel* for August 20, 1973, there is a detailed history of the Pecos foundation.

2. An auxiliary bishop is an assistant bishop with no canonical jurisdiction of his own and no right of succession.

3. *Northwest Progress,* April 13, 1956.

4. Oregon Province Archives, Mss. "Thomas Edward Gill Auxiliary Bishop of Seattle 1956 to 1973," by Denise Gill, 1976.

5. Forest Ridge was a convent of the Religious of the Sacred Heart.

6. *Northwest Progress,* June 7, 1956.

7. *The Harvester,* XVIII, 2 (May 1956), p. 40 et seq.

8. Bishop Byrne was installed as the fourth bishop of Boise on August 29, 1956. *Ibid.,* 4 (December 1956), p. 77.

9. The translation is "To Jesus through Mary."

10. Howard's residence was the old Mills home at Northwest 20th and Johnson. Howard himself recorded how he acquired it. Christie had purchased a residence in Portland Heights at 16th and Myrtle. Howard lived there when he succeeded Christie but sought a residence within walking distance from the chancery. When the Mills' heirs offered their home, they expressed willingness to trade it for the archbishop's for an extra $15,000. Howard stalled. The heirs finally agreed to an even trade. Thus Howard acquired not only a residence but charming quarters for his famous ladies' teas, which raised large amounts of money for the archdiocese. *Catholic Sentinel,* November 5, 1977.

11. Wilfred P. Schoenberg, S.J., *Paths To the Northwest, A Jesuit History of the Oregon Province,* (Chicago, 1982), p. 480. What follows appears here in some detail.

12. Archbishop Howard contributed $5,000 to the drive.

13. Jesuit High was established as an independent corporation responsible for its own indebtedness. The province advanced the $35,000 down payment, which was later returned. *Ibid.,* p. 481.

14. *Ibid.,* p. 405 et seq.

15. Jesuit Provincial Archives in Portland. Letter of Elliott to Zacheus Maher, March 2, 1940. This was the first form of the so-called promises. Later they were revised and made

more simple, though their meaning remained the same. They were not abrogated until the death of Bishop Gilmore on April 2, 1962.

16. The writer was present for this event, during which Bishop Topel noted that he had applied to enter the Jesuit Order, but changed his mind when his pastor in Bozeman convinced him that he had an obligation to become a priest for the diocese.

17. *Inland Register*, November 11, 1955.

18. This seminary department was moved to Troutdale, east of Portland, in June 1958. Its name was changed to St. Francis Seminary.

19. This minor seminary for boys of high school age was the fourth unit completed at Mount Angel since 1927; the abbey in 1927, the major seminary in 1931, the Abbey Church in 1952, St. Anselm's Hall in 1954.

20. The novitiate and juniorate, comprising four years at Sheridan, had been inadequately housed until the completion of the entire building with three new wings in 1956. The number of novices entering the novitiate for each year was as follows: 35 in 1955; 27 in 1956; 35 in 1957, 24 in 1958, 21 in 1959; and, 28 in 1960. It must be remembered that these were candidates for a province that covered three archdioceses and eight dioceses, a million square miles.

21. This was the Huetter mansion, which had originally been used as a boys' home dedicated to St. John Bosco.

22. In the following year, the Spokane diocese had 85 seminarians from first year high school to fourth year theology, a period of twelve years. All, of course, would not be ordained. If only half made it to the altar there would have been a surplus of priests for the current needs.

23. Uneasiness of western bishops, especially, regarding San Francisco's St. Ignatius collegiate church was not altogether unreasonable, though northwest Jesuits tried for years to convince the bishops that this mistake would not be repeated. Even after Vatican II, the impasse created by St. Ignatius church did not vanish.

24. Not all of thse seminarians belonged to the Seattle archdiocese, although the greater number did.

25. *The Harvester*, XIX, 1(April 1957), p. 16.

26. *Ibid.*, XXI, 1(Autumn 1958), p. 16.

27. *Ibid.*, XXI, 3(Spring 1959), p. 77.

28. This was Oregon's first Carmelite monastery. The first in the Northwest was St. Joseph's in Seattle, founded on December 8, 1908.

29. Oregon Province Archives, Mss. regarding Carmelites at Eugene. A new monastery at Eugene was built in 1962.

30. Oregon Province Archives, Mss. regarding Palisades Retreat House.

31. Oregon Province Archives, Mss. regarding Visitation Nuns.

32. *Inland Register*, February 27, 1959.

33. Father Armand Nigro was unique. Besides lecturing in theology, giving spiritual guidance to hundreds of religious and directing retreats at the Immaculate Retreat House, he buzzed all over the western hemisphere, giving retreats on weekends and during vacation periods. More than others he made the Spokane retreat house famous all over the world.

34. Lawrence J. McCrank, *Mt. Angel Abbey A Centennial History of the Benedictine Community and its Library 1882-1982*, (Wilmington, 1983), p. 71.

35. *Catholic Sentinel*, March 17, 1960.

36. The name of this school was changed, following a great crisis in Yakima in 1968, to Carroll High School.

37. Another conflict, for example, occurred when Yakima Jesuits met with promoters of a new stadium for Marquette without the bishop's approval. The bishop angrily withdrew their faculties, indicating that they could no longer serve as priests in his diocese, and all had to be replaced by the Jesuit provincial at a moment's notice.

38. *Northwest Progress,* August 23, 1957.

39. *Our Times,* May 15, 1959 and August 21, 1959.

40. When Central graduated its first class in June 1963, the number compared unfavorable with the two pioneer schools: Central, 72 graduates, mostly girls; Marquette, 43; St. Joseph's, 41. In the following year, Central graduated only 64, mostly girls; Marquette, 42 and St. Joseph's 66. It was not *numbers* only that affected the two schools, it was the lack of money to operate.

41. Schoenberg, *Paths to the Northwest,* p. 500 et seq., presents a documented account of this unhappy embroglio.

42. *Ibid.,* p. 501.

43. *Ibid.*

44. *Our Times* first appeared on February 6, 1959. Its first issue on that date consisted of 16 pages, mostly advertisements. But, under the direction of the capable and experienced editor, layman Ray Ruppert, it soon became a sprightly weekly that was a credit to the diocese. On January 29, 1960, in the first anniversary edition, Ruppert presents a personalized account of the history of the paper's founding.

45. Schoenberg, *Paths to the Northwest,* p. 502.

46. The purchased school had been called Peninsular School before the archdiocese acquired it. *Catholic Sentinel,* October 9, 1958.

47. *Ibid.,* August 7, 1970.

48. Bishop Topel and his pilgrimage party, including Father Terrance Tully and Bernard Schiller, left New York on August 20, 1958.

49. Pope Pius XII died on October 9, 1958.

50. *Inland Register,* June 12, 1959.

51. *Ibid.,* September 25, 1959.

52. *Ibid.,* February 26, 1960.

53. *Ibid.,* March 11, 1960.

54. Rompa left Spokane in August 1960.

55. *Inland Catholic,* April 18, 1941. This textbook "law" was an amendment to sections 111–2015, 111–2016, 111–2020, and 111–2025, Senate Bill 259, 1941. It was proposed by Senator Leo Smith, prominent Catholic attorney who later defended it in court for the archdiocese. There were only 10 Catholics in the sixty-member House, but the bill passed with only one dissenting vote. The Masons lobbied against the bill but 39 Masons voted for it. Interview with Leo Smith, June 12, 1984.

56. *Oregon Journal,* February 16, 1959.

57. Thielan was superintendent of archdiocesan schools from 1956 to 1964.

58. *Catholic Sentinel,* March 5, 1958.

59. At this time Father Matt Burger of Mount Angel was teaching at St. Mary's High School, Eugene. *Inland Register,* December 7, 1951.

60. Blanshard's best known book was: Paul Blanshard, *American Freedom and Catholic Power,* (Boston, 1952). An earlier version appeared in 1948.

61. *Catholic Sentinel,* April 24, 1958.

62. This was at the ninth National Conference of PAOU on Church and State, in the First Baptist Church, Los Angeles. *Inland Register,* February 15, 1957.

63. Leslie Scott was a member of the well known Harvey Scott family, publishers of *The Oregonian.*

64. *Catholic Sentinel,* March 6, 1958.

65. *Our Times,* March 6, 1959.

66. *Ibid.,* March 27, 1959. During this year, according to Thielan, parochial schools saved the state $9,473,000 in taxes. Estimated cost of the textbooks used in all private schools was about $400,000 per year.

67. Holman based his decision on the New Jersey busing case. *Inland Register,* February 12, 1960.

68. *Catholic Sentinel,* November 16, 1961.

69. *Ibid.*

70. *Ibid.,* February 16, 1961.

71. *Ibid.*

72. Catholics in the state, however, represented about 12% of the total population.

73. The Sister Formation movement had been working toward a better education of the sisters since 1952. It had grown out of the efforts of a few sisters in the College and University departments of the NCEA. These sisters sponsored annual local conferences for four years prior to 1956.

74. A detailed report of the conference was published as follows: Sister Mary Emil, I.H.M., Director of Project and Editor of Report, *Report of Everett Curriculum Workshop,* (Seattle, 1956).

75. The second center was the College of St. Teresa in Winona, Wisconsin.

76. Later called Sisters of St. Joseph of Peace.

77. *The Oregon Jesuit,* 28:2(February, 1959), p. 5.

78. Sister Genevieve Gorman, known for many years as Mother Mary Philothea, was a Sister of Providence for fifty-four years. She died on September 9, 1983, at Seattle.

79. The first two graduates of the program were Sisters of Providence from Spokane, Sister Celeste Malerich and Sister Jeanine Gilmartin.

80. Paul Doyle, "College for Nuns," in *The Catholic Digest,* October, 1959.

81. Seattle University president Father Albert Lemieux and Jesuit superior, Father John Kelley, strongly urged that the new College be built contiguous to the university, between the latter and Providence Hospital. Public announcement of the Issaquah site was made without the university's knowledge.

82. Providence Heights as a Sister Formation College was closed June 1, 1969. *Our Times,* April 18, 1969.

83. *Inland Register,* July 8, 1960. Technically the college purchased the land for one dollar.

84. *Ibid.,* October 21, 1960.

85. These buildings were dedicated on January 28, 1961. *Catholic Sentinel,* January 26, 1961. Mount Angel College became Cesar Chavez College for Mexican Americans. This, too, failed to survive.

86. These were dedicated by Howard on December 9, 1961.

87. *Ibid.,* July 27, 1961.

88. Oregon Province Archives, Provincial Papers, McDonald letter to the Province, November 8, 1960.

89. These and other details of the African Mission can be found in Schoenberg, *Paths to the Northwest,* p. 505 et seq.

90. These were John O'Leary, later superior of the mission, Patrick Bonner and John Leonard. The two latter left the Jesuit Order later.

91. *Ibid.,* p. 509.

92. These twenty-three candidates were sent to the Benedictine seminary in British Columbia.

93. *Inland Register,* August 18, 1961.

94. The college of many names, presently Loras College.

95. *Ibid.*, November 10, 1961.

96. Supplement to the *Eastern Montana Register*, January 24, 1968. The four popes were Leo XIII, Benedict XIV, Pius VIII and Pius IX.

97. *Catholic Sentinel*, January 11, 1962. Hannan was later Archbishop of New Orleans.

98. *Inland Register*, February 23, 1962.

99. Bishop White Seminary, as intended, would continue to accommodate first and second year high school.

100. *Inland Catholic Register*, October 6, 1963. Note change of title of the *Inland Register*. On April 7, 1963, *The Inland Register* was replaced by the *Inland Catholic Register*, which included copy from *Our Sunday Visitor*.

101. *Idaho Register*, May 4, 1962.

102. Bishop Gilmore's funeral was celebrated on April 11, 1962.

103. *Ibid.*, May 25, 1962.

104. *Ibid.*, April 9, 1976. Bishop Nicolas Walsh mistakenly refers to him as the first native born western bishop. Bishop Kelly of Boise was the first.

105. Bishop Sylvester Treinen in an interview on May 5, 1983, said. "Father [James] Grady left a stipulation in his will for St. John's to complete the steeples, but it would cost close to a million dollars to complete them."

106. Bishop Hunthausen was the first graduate of St. Edward's Seminary to become a bishop. *Inland Register*, July 20, 1962.

107. Hunthausen, then, was the youngest bishop of a diocese. Archbishop Howard was almost eighty-five.

108. *Northwest Progress*, August 24, 1962.

109. The Catholic Seamen's Club in Seattle was one of Bishop Shaughnessy's pet projects. In April 1940, it was opened in its own quarters at 905½ Third Avenue, with Reinhold as its first chaplain. *Northwest Progress*, September 20, 1940.

110. Archives of the Diocese of Yakima, papers regarding H.A. Reinhold.

111. *Ibid.* Reinhold's autobiography appeared as follows: Hans Ansgar Reinhold, *H.A.R. The Autobiography of Father Reinhold*, (New York, 1968).

112. Major liturgical changes began about 1965.

113. *Catholic Sentinel*, January 4, 1962.

114. *Ibid.*, November 8, 1962.

115. James Hennessey, S.J., *American Catholics A History of the Roman Catholic Community in the United States*, (New York, 1981), p. 310 et seq. presents a brief account of American Catholics and the Council. References to *Commonweal* appear on p. 311.

116. Bishop Dougherty suffered his heart attack on November 9, *Catholic Sentinel*, November 12, 1965. Even before his departure for Rome Dougherty appeared to be a very sick man. Note the photograph in *Our Times*, October 8, 1965.

117. *Catholic Sentinel*, February 14, 1963.

118. Kennedy was assasinated on November 22, 1963. The chancery was blessed on December 1.

119. Bellarmine Prep in Tacoma was the first of Jesuit northwest schools to become coeducational. Efforts were made to achieve this in 1967, on the basis of need, but it was seven years later when superiors in Rome yielded on the point and gave permission for it. Schoenberg, *Paths to the Northwest*, p. 525.

120. Bishop Topel, with some concern for papal directives, carefully nursed the distinction. *Inland Register*, August 26, 1960.

121. Catholic percentages in other states in 1961 were as follows: Washington, 12.4%; Montana, 22.2%; and Idaho, 6.7%. The United States average is 23.7%, the world at large 18%. *Catholic Sentinel*, October 4, 1962 and February 7, 1963.

122. *Idaho Register,* October 5, 1962.

123. *Ibid.,* August 30, 1963.

124. *Ibid.,* September 6, 1963.

125. *Ibid.,* May 15, 1964.

126. Holy Family Hospital was completed one year before schedule. *Inland Catholic Register,* August 30, 1964.

127. "Enrollment in Catholic elementary and secondary schools fell from 5.6 million in 1965 to less than 3.2 million in 1980. In 1965, there were 10,879 grade schools, against 8,149 in 1980. High schools in the same period dropped from 2,413 to 1,527." Hennessey, *American Catholics,* p. 323.

128. *Inland Catholic Register,* Mary 24, 1964.

129. *Catholic Sentinel,* March 5, 1965.

130. *Ibid.,* April 16, 1965.

131. *Inland Catholic Register,* May 24, 1964.

132. Schoenberg, *Paths to the Northwest,* p. 508.

133. *Ibid.*

134. *Inland Catholic Register,* May 23, 1965.

135. Born in Evansville, Indiana, Waldschmidt entered Notre Dame as an underclassman. He was ordained there later, on June 24, 1946. *Catholic Sentinel,* September 13, 1962.

136. James T. Covert, *A Point of Pride: The University of Portland Story,* (Portland, 1976), p. 174.

137. The number of Catholic colleges and universities peaked in 1965 at 309. In 1980 there were 239.

138. *Ibid.,* p. 180.

139. *Catholic Sentinel,* February 21, 1963.

140. *Ibid.,* October 1, 1965.

141. *Ibid.,* March 24, 1967.

142. Covert, *A Point of Pride,* p. 185.

143. *Our Times,* April 24, 1964.

144. Calaroga, Italy, was the birthplace of St. Dominic.

145. [Martin Pollard, O.S.B.], *Mount of Communion: Mount Angel Abbey 1882–1982,* (St. Benedict [Oregon], 1982), p. 50.

146. *Ibid.,* p. 57. Both foundations were intended to establish seminaries. This was never realized in either place.

147. *Our Times,* January 15, 1965.

148. *Idaho Register,* September 24, 1965.

149. Bradley, former Abbot of Holy Cross Abbey in Colorado (1926–1931), died on May 9, 1965. *Ibid.,* May 21, 1965.

150. Prior to this, Bishop Treinen lived in an old house that had to be removed for the chancery parking lot.

Chapter 20. A TIME OF TURMOIL

1. These appear in the following: *Solemn Observance of the Silver Episcopal Jubilee of the Most Reverend Thomas Arthur Connolly, D.D., J.C.D., Fifth Bishop of Seattle St. James Cathedral, Seattle, Washington, August 26, 1964.* [Seattle, 1964].

2. *Ibid.,* p. 29.

3. The Washington Hotel had been built in 1907 by Adolph Schmidt of the Olympia Brewery to replace the hotel of the same name at the top of Denny Hill. *Northwest Progress,* September 13, 1963.

4. *Solemn Observance,* p. 31.

5. *Ibid.*

6. "Open housing" means the unrestrained right of people to buy homes without restrictions of race or religion.

7. The special edition of the *Progress* appeared on March 6, 1964.

8. *Catholic Sentinel*, February 16, 1968.

9. *Northwest Progress*, October 20, 1972, p. 15. This is the *Progress'* 75th anniversary special edition.

10. *Ibid.*

11. *Ibid.*, September 2, 1966.

12. *Ibid.*, December 13, 1963.

13. The seminarians did not attend the University of Washington because the university did not accept certain credits for courses taught at St. Thomas. Thus arrangements were made for attendance at Seattle University where the Jesuits graciously accommodated them without the slightest suggestion of resentment. Father James McGuigan was especially helpful.

14. A *beneplacitum* is the bishop's formal, written approval for the establishment of an independent Jesuit community in his diocese. Seattle University for many years was dependent upon Seattle Prep, which enjoyed canonical approval.

15. The two brothers were Edward Barrientos and John Achin. The four sisters were Margaret, Augusta Marie, Agnes Therese, and Rose Imelda. The lay persons were Mrs. B. Parish, librarian; Sandra Behles, counselor; William Bauer, athletic director; and, Mrs. Lillian Anderson, director of the cafeteria. *Aide Memoire of the Solemn Blessing and Dedication of LaSalle High School*, (Milwaukee, 1967).

16. *Inland Catholic Register*, June 29, 1962.

17. *Ibid.*, August 22, 1965.

18. Lay members of the school board were: Dr. David Willis, E. S. Ritter, Hon. Edward Leavy, and Carl Brophy. *Catholic Sentinel*, January 22, 1965

19. St. Alice Church was blessed on May 12, 1965. *Ibid.*, April 16, 1965.

20. Sacred Heart Hospital in Eugene was dedicated on July 17, 1965. This replaced the hospital that Howard dedicated on March 19, 1937. *Ibid.*, July 23, 1965.

21. The Liturgical Conference met in Portland on August 16- 19, 1965. *Ibid.*, August 20, 1965.

22. *Ibid.*, August 20, 1965, October 22, 1965 and December 31, 1965.

23. *Ibid.*, May 20, 1966. This provides an excellent biography of Archbishop Howard.

24. *Ibid.*, December 16, 1966.

25. Monsignor Blanchet died in 1903.

26. John Charles Dwyer died on April 12, 1942, and Mabel Dwyer died on January 11, 1950. Thus neither lived to see Robert raised to the hierarchy.

27. *Ibid.*, December 16, 1966.

28. *Ibid.*, December 23, 1966.

29. *Inland Catholic Register*, February 19, 1967.

30. The right to vote was granted in the meeting of January 23, 1969. *Catholic Sentinel*, January 31, 1969.

31. Supplement to the *East Montana Register*, January 24, 1968.

32. The new site was at Southwest Barnes Road near the Cedar Mills interchange. *Catholic Sentinel*, April 7, 1967.

33. *Ibid.*, March 29, 1968 and April 5, 1968.

34. The capital investment of $46,000,000 was based on a required $2,000 per student for 24,000 students in Catholic elementary and high schools. *Ibid.*, March 21, 1969.

35. By July 1, 1969, the total collected had become $2.9 million. An additional report appears in *Ibid.*, July 4, 1969.

36. Newman Clubs received considerably more money later.

37. This appeared in *Ibid.*, October 17, 1969.

38. For example, on June 30, 1983, the endowment of Harvard University was $2,451,290,000. *The Chronicle of Higher Education*, (May 9, 1984), p. 16.

39. *National Catholic Reporter*, September 20, 1967.

40. *Yakima Daily Republic*, September 13, 1967.

41. Marquette students used St. Joseph's grade school gymnasium.

42. *Yakima Morning Herald*, September 15, 1967.

43. *Yakima Daily Republic*, September 16, 1967.

44. *Yakima Sunday Herald*, September 24, 1967.

45. *Our Times*, September 22, 1967.

46. *Yakima Daily Republic*, September 18, 1967.

47. "Parietal Hours," the battle-cry of freedom on the campuses, means permission for boys and girls to visit one another's rooms in dormitories during specified times.

48. Oregon Province Archives, Topel Papers, Letter to John P. Leary, S.J., January 7, 1969.

49. It is not clear who leaked the letter to the students in the first place.

50. Jensen's comment is inaccurate. A *large* group of Jesuits, almost the entire Jesuit Community, sought Kelley's intervention.

51. *Spokesman-Review*, January 11, 1969.

52. *The National Register*, January 26, 1969.

53. Subsequently Leary spent some months on the East Coast, then accepted a position at the University of Utah.

54. *Seattle Times*, February 5, 1969.

55. Bishop Dougherty accepted the board's proposal for a consolidated school. Chairman of the Board Len Cockrill announced this on January 5, 1968. *Our Times*, January 5, 1968. The last graduation for the two pioneer school was conducted in June 1969.

56. Bishop John Carroll, Bishop, later Archbishop of Baltimore (b. 1735-d.1815) 1789-1815.

57. Bishop Dougherty as administrator was conducting the drive.

58. *Yakima Herald Republic*, April 3, 1969.

59. *Northwest Progress*, August 15, 1952.

60. *Seattle Times*, May 2, 1969.

61. These were Bishops Gill, Dougherty, and Power.

62. Dougherty was titular bishop of Altino, a town in northern Italy near Venice on the Adriatic Sea. It was suppressed in 1818.

63. Erasmo Gamboa, "Mexican Labor in the Pacific Northwest A Photographic Essay," *The Pacific Northwest Quarterly*, 73:4(October 1982), p. 175 et seq.

64. *Our Times*, August 9, 1968.

65. Archives of the Diocese of Yakima. Papers related to the Spanish Speaking Apostolate.

66. *Ibid.* Ybarra was directed to reside at St. Joseph's Parish Sunnyside, which he did almost the same month. The assistant pastor was transferred, so Ybarra was required to serve as assistant, besides being full-time Director of the Spanish Speaking Apostolate. As he observed, he could not do justice to either job.

67. These and following details are found in the Archives of the Diocese of Yakima, papers related to the Spanish Speaking Apostolate.

68. Interview with Robert Saenz, September 15, 1983.

69. This report was dated July 23, 1969 when Dougherty was still administrator. It may be found in the Archives of the Diocese of Yakima, papers related to the Spanish Speaking Apostolate.

70. *Northwest Progress, 75th Anniversary Edition,* October 20, 1972, p. 14.

71. *Catholic Sentinel,* February 20, 1970.

72. *Northwest Progress,* March 6, 1970.

73. *Ibid.*

74. *Ibid.* The report was published in full in this issue.

75. *Catholic Sentinel,* April 10, 1970. Property sold was one square block bounded by 4th to 5th Avenue and Market to Mill Street.

76. [Martin Pollard, O.S.B.], *Mount of Communion,* (St. Benedict, [Oregon], 1982), p. 57.

77. Lawrence J. McCrank, *Mt. Angel Abbey A Centennial History of the Benedictine Community and its Library 1882-1982,* (Wilmington, 1983), p. 73.

78. The College of Southern Idaho had 1500 students, very few of whom were Catholic. Twin Falls was located in the heart of Mormon Country. Details regarding the priory may be found in *Catholic Sentinel,* January 19, 1969.

79. *Catholic Sentinel,* January 8, 1971.

80. *Idaho Register,* August 14, 1970.

81. *Catholic Sentinel,* May 7, 1971.

82. Interview with Bishop Thomas Connolly, April 22, 1983.

83. Prior to this it was common for a bishop to be ordained in his native diocese where his friends and associates lived. More recent procedures, however, favor the ordination in the cathedral of his assigned diocese with installation ceremonies taking place at the same service.

84. *Catholic Sentinel,* May 19, 1971.

85. Bishop Leipzig died on January 17, 1971.

86. The first convent school was opened in 1907. Three years later the Forest Ridge site on Capitol Hill was occupied.

87. David M. Buerge, *Children of the Sacred Heart A History of Forest Ridge,* (Bellevue, 1982), p. 65.

88. Neighborhood environmentalists opposed any change in the wooded areas.

89. *Ibid.,* p. 68.

90. *Ibid.,* p. 69.

91. *Ibid.,* p. 71.

92. *Ibid.,* p. 65. This, of course, greatly influenced costs. Between the years 1971 to 1981 tuition costs increased from $1,100 to $3,000 per year.

93. *Westmont Word,* June 14, 1973.

94. *Ibid,* June 25, 1973.

95. *Catholic Sentinel,* January 4, 1974.

96. *Westmont Word,* March 15, 1973.

97. *Inland Register,* December 21, 1972. Note change in title of Spokane's Catholic paper.

98. *Westmont Word,* March 11, 1976

99. *Inland Register,* December 21, 1972.

100. Bishop Gill died suddenly of a heart attack in Washington, D.C., just after arriving for the meeting of bishops. His funeral was in St. James Cathedral in Seattle on November 17, 1973.

101. *Westmont Word,* October 5, 1972.

102. *Ibid.,* March 23, 1972.

103. *Catholic Sentinel,* January 15, 1974.

104. This letter was written to Pope Paul VI in 1974. It was released to the public on April 1, 1977. *Catholic Sentinel*, April 1, 1977.

105. *Ibid.*, April 19, 1974.

106. *Ibid.*

107. *Ibid.*, April 5, 1974.

Chapter 21. END OF AN ERA

1. *Inland Register*, special supplement, November 30, 1978, p. 31.

2. *Ibid.*, June 24, 1976.

3. *Ibid.*, September 7, 1972.

4. Letter sent to seminarians in 1972. *Catholic Sentinel*, April 14, 1978.

5. James Shannon, Auxiliary Bishop of St. Paul, created a sensation in 1969 by leaving the priesthood to marry. *Inland Register*, June 6, 1969.

6. *Ibid.*, June 24, 1976.

7. *Spokesman Review*, Sunday Magazine, November 12, 1972, p. 9 et seq.

8. *Lewiston Morning Tribune*, Sunday, November 28, 1971, Section 4, p. 29.

9. *Ibid.*

10. *Inland Register*, October 23, 1975.

11. Yakima Diocesan Archives, News Release, September 10, 1974, Bishop Nicolas Walsh file.

12. *Idaho Register*, August 5, 1966.

13. Cardinal Cushing established PAVLA in Boston in 1960 and Walsh organized it in Boise in early 1961.

14. *America*, May 26, 1984, p. 399. During the early years students from Gonzaga University and Regis College formed the majority membership of the corps. The "orientation week" was held at Gonzaga. In recent years the Franciscans have established a similar volunteer corps.

15. In August 1966, Treinen requested Walsh to supervise work in Bogota. Thus Walsh resigned other positions in the diocese and left Boise. There is some obscurity about the time. The *Idaho Register*, February 10, 1967, states that he departed in January 1967. In a personal interview Bishop Walsh stated to me that he left "in 1966." Currently engaged in writing his memoirs, among other tasks, Bishop Walsh would not likely be in error.

16. Walsh returned to Boise in January 1973. He was appointed vicar in May. *Ibid.*, June 1, 1973.

17. These details and others were provided by Bishop Walsh in an interview on July 17, 1984.

18. The priests' reception was held on November 3, 1974.

19. *Westmont Word*, December 12, 1974.

20. *Ibid.*, August 12, 1976.

21. In 1973, Bishop Treinen, who had problems of hypoglycemia, got the flu while visiting Tuscon, Arizona. While convalescing, he picked up another type of flu that "punched him out." This left him in an alarming state of weakness that worried his priests. Interview with Bishop Treinen on May 5, 1983.

22. The Wallace Hospital was closed on November 13, 1967. *Idaho Register*, November 10, 1967. It was sold at auction to Bill Morrow on January 20, 1968, for his bid of $32,000. For this Morrow received eight acres of land, the hospital, five other buildings and water rights. *Ibid.*, February 7, 1968.

23. St. Joseph's Children's Home was closed at the end of the school year in 1968. At this time it had only 59 students of whom 15 were in residence. *Ibid.*, October 31, 1969.

24. *Ibid.*, April 3, 1970.

25. *Ibid.*, July 10, 1970.

26. The bishop arrived in Rome on August 31, 1974.

27. *Ibid.*, September 19, 1975.

28. *Ibid.*, May 14, 1976.

29. *Ibid.*, May 27, 1977.

30. Father Neil Byrne, S.J., missionary with the Coeur d'Alene Indians, had got it into his head that the Pacific Northwest Indian Center should restore the mission. He insisted, despite my protests that this involved large amounts of money. He expected me to raise these funds, mostly because he was not a practical man. He died Oct. 2, 1983 in the odor of great holiness.

31. *Ibid.*, November 14, 1975

32. *Ibid.*, April 20, 1973.

33. The bishop's formal title to the land had been presented to him by the Jesuits who received it, with the approval of the Indians, from the government on May 17, 1889. In return, the bishop of Boise agreed at that time (1919) to maintain the site as a religious shrine. During the controversy, Treinen admitted that he himself had suggested to the state that the deed of ownership be transferred from the diocese to the state. *Ibid.*, November 14, 1974.

34. This statement overlooks the *reasons* why the Jesuits used persuasion and even legitimate strategy to move the Indians from the Cataldo site to the DeSmet site. In the Cataldo area, the land was poor, marginal for agriculture. Farther south in the DeSmet area, the land was rich and very valuable. Hence the Jesuits first battled the government to get this land for a reservation, then used every form of argument to persuade the old Indians to move there. This Jesuit maneuver has been vindicated without a shadow of a doubt. All that the Indians left behind was the church.

35. This is misleading. Actually the Indians *helped* to build the church. They provided some of the labor. Jesuit brothers, I think, contributed more to its construction than the Indians. Confer Wilfred P. Schoenberg, S.J., *Jesuit Mission Presses*, (Portland, 1957), p. 54 et seq.

36. As noted above, the U.S. government did not force the Indians to move.

37. The three parties in the dispute were the diocese, the state, and the tribe. There is reason to believe that the latter accepted the decision with reluctance, in part, I think, because of misconceptions regarding the role of the tribe in the construction of the old church.

38. *Idaho Register*, November 14, 1975.

39. The old mission was rededicated by Bishop Treinen on Sunday, June 14, 1976, with the assistance of Boy Scouts from Pineville, Idaho. *Ibid.*, June 25, 1976. "The actual dedication," Treinen said, "was done by Henry L. Day, Chief fund raiser, whose parents were married at the mission in August 1900." Interview with Bishop Treinen on May 5, 1983.

40. An article regarding Old Catholics appears in the *New Catholic Encyclopedia*, (New York, 1966), Volume 10, p. 672c.

41. Schuckardt was dismissed from the Blue Army because of his extreme views in ecclesiology. *Catholic Sentinel*, July 31, 1981.

42. Brown's credentials as a validly consecrated bishop are based on the valid consecration of an English bishop who was consecrated by the old Catholic Archbishop of Utrecht.

43. *Inland Register*, January 12, 1978 and January 16, 1978.

44. *Westmont Word*, July 25, 1974.

45. The Jesuits, because of Vatican II changes, moved their scholasticate to Gonzaga University on September 12, 1970. It is now called St. Michael's Institute on the campus.

46. *Inland Register*, January 12, 1978.

47. *Northwest and Alaska Exchange*, March 2, 1978.

48. *Inland Register*, March 2, 1978.

49. *Westmont Word*, July 29, 1976.

50. These people who were confirmed came from Spokane, Coeur d'Alene, Sandpoint, and Bonners Ferry in Idaho. A brief time following this ceremony, Lefebvre attracted world attention for ordaining a group of priests at Econe, Switzerland in defiance of a papal threat of ecommunication. This was on June 29, 1976.

51. In May and June 1984, a violent schism split the Tridentine Church. Schuckardt, with a small group, the records, and a large amount of cash, took flight. *Inland Register*, June 20, 1984.

52. Ray Ruppert in the *Seattle Times Magazine*, May 18, 1975, p. 8-9.

53. *Ibid.*

54. *Ibid.*

55. Hunthausen was transferred to Seattle on February 25, 1975.

56. Hunthausen took a strong stand against taxation for what he regarded as unreasonable defense expenditures and withheld part of his taxes. He became, for many, a great hero for defying the Internal Revenue Service, the notorious tax collectors.

57. *Westmont Word*, March 20, 1975.

58. *Ibid.*, May 22, 1975.

59. Father Ryan's remarks were directed against a long-standing policy of "hot-house" protection of teen-age seminarians, a policy that had been under critical scrutiny for nearly a century.

60. *Catholic Sentinel*, April 29, 1977.

61. *Ibid.*, February 4, 1977. Father Theodore Bradley of the Spokane Diocese was the last seminarian of St. Thomas to be ordained to the priesthood.

62. *Ibid.*, November 19, 1971. Father James Ribble of the Spokane Diocese succeeded Curtiss as the Rector-President of the seminary.

63. *Westmont Word*, March 18, 1976.

64. *Catholic Sentinel*, March 12, 1976.

65. *Ibid.*, May 7, 1976.

66. The new hospital called St. Alphonsus Regional Medical Center, was located at 1055 North Curtiss Road in Boise.

67. The Sisters of the Holy Child heretofore had three provinces in the United States. There were reduced to one with 480 sisters in all. *Ibid.*, August 13, 1976.

68. Wilfred P. Schoenberg, S.J. *Paths to the Northwest*, (Chicago, 1982), p. 551.

69. *Catholic Sentinel*, March 5, 1970.

70. *Westmont Word*, December 2, 1976.

71. For example, Benedictine Father Colman Barry of Catholic University in an address was reported to have said, "[The] primary sign of our times is an unprecedented spiritual renewal begun and promoted in large part by Catholics." *Catholic Sentinel*, January 7, 1977.

72. Bishop Kenneth Steiner made a careful study, including a church attendance survey by parishes in 1982 and 1983. This eight page census was distributed to the parishes in 1983. Copy in Oregon Province Archives.

73. *The Weekly, Seattle's Magazine*, December 21, 1983, p. 24. Neighboring Spokane in Washington is about thirty percent Catholic.

74. This study was made for 1980. Only Nevada and Alaska were below Washington. Rhode Island, mostly Catholic, was highest in church adherence. Utah, mostly Mormon, was second. *Spokesman Review*, October 9, 1982, p. 9.

75. This appeared in the *Catholic Sentinel*, September 9, 1977.

76. Indifference to formal religion is reflected in conduct, e.g., human abortions, which Catholics regard as immoral. In 1980, the number of *reported* abortions for the four

northwest states was as follows: Washington, 87,000; Oregon, 17,700; Idaho, 2,700; Montana, 3,700. Survey by Allan Guttmacher Institute, *Westmont Word*, March 10, 1982.

77. While the average percentage of Catholics in the four states is 11.7, based on the sum total of state averages, the figure is much smaller based on population averages. Washington with two-fifths more population than the other three states combined, was 9.2% in 1980. Idaho was 7.5%, Oregon 12.2%, and Montana 17.8%.

78. This, as noted above, is in error. Father Anthony Ravalli was the first archtect in the Northwest. Unlike Mother Joseph, he was professionally trained.

79. *Inland Register*, November 25, 1976.

80. One suspects that both the Commission and the State Historical Society in Olympia were waiting for the proposal to die and blow away.

81. *Catholic Sentinel*, April 15, 1977. Olympia, where the vote was argued, was in LeRoy's back yard, only thirty miles distant.

82. *Ibid.* One can think of others who had greater influence natinally, as Le Roy stated. Father Cataldo, for example, probably had much greater influence than Mother Joseph. But Mother Joseph, I think, was a more suitable candidate for reasons that could not be excluded; for instance, the fewness of women represented in the hall.

83. Through Mr. Joseph F. McKinnon, the governor's assistant, I had the pleasure of recommending the governor's signature on the bill, a small part, I hope, in the final disposition of the matter.

84. *Ibid.*, May 13, 1977.

85. DeWildon had designed 120 public bronzes, 32 of them in Washington, D.C. *Westmont Word*, May 7, 1980.

86. *Ibid.*, May 7, 1980.

87. The other four women were Frances Willard, temperance leader in Illinois; Maria Sanford, professor from Missouri; Dr. Florin Sabin, a scientist from Colorado; and, Esther Norris, Wyoming's first justice of the peace.

88. The four priests were Damian de Veuster of Hawaii, Junipero Serra of California, James Marquette of Wisconsin, and Eusebins Kino of Arizona.

89. *Inland Register*, February 24, 1977. The report that Skylstad was Spokane's second bishop, William Condon being the first, is in error. The first was Walter Fitzgerald, a Jesuit.

90. Anaconda's two bishops were Gilmore and Hunthausen.

91. Mr. Stephen Skylstad entered the church two days before his seventieth birthday, after the death of his wife in 1966 and after the ordination of his son as bishop of Yakima.

92. These and other details are taken from a personal interview with Bishop Skylstad on May 4, 1984.

93. Howard was not the oldest bishop in the world then, as sometimes appears. Bishop Antonio Tentonica in Saint' Elia Pianisi, Italy, was 103.

94. Open letter of Archbishop Power to Archbishop Howard. *Ibid.*, November 5, 1977.

95. *Ibid.*, December 9, 1977.

96. Waldschmidt was born in Evansville, Indiana, on January 7, 1920. His parents were Edward B. and Olga Marie Moers Waldschmidt.

97. Waldschmidt was at the University of Portland for a total of twenty-two years. When appointed bishop, he offered his resignation as president. *Inland Register*, December 8, 1977.

98. Steiner was pastor of St. Francis Assisi Parish at Roy.

99. Kenneth was the second oldest of five children. His parents were Lawrence and Florine Preters Steiner.

100. An ordination issue of the *Catholic Sentinel* appeared on March 2, 1978. Details of the ordination appeared *Ibid.*, March 10, 1978.

101. Jadot released this news on December 27, 1977. Schuster's physician had advised him to resign because of failing health.

102. *Ibid.*, December 30, 1977.

103. *Inland Register*, April 13, 1978.

104. *Time*, November 13, 1978, p. 6.

105. According to the *Catholic Directory*, Murphy was appointed bishop on July 5, 1978. The *Westmont Word* on August 30, 1978, states that Jadot announced his appointment on July 2, 1978.

106. Cardinal Cody had been called to the papal conclave for electing a new pope.

197. *Westmont Word*, August 30, 1978.

108. *Ibid.*

109. *Catholic Sentinel*, September 29, 1978. The text of Power's address appears in the *Westmont Word*, October 11, 1978.

110. The full report appears in *Westmont Word*, September 27, 1978.

111. This is given variously as 33 or 34 days depending upon the time of the pope's death before or after midnight.

112. Interview with Bishop Welsh on April 26, 1984.

113. The bishop's father was born in Mineral, Kansas in 1908. He moved to Rock Springs when he was 16. He died in January 1980. *Inland Register*, January 17, 1980.

114. Rock Springs in Wyoming.

115. *Ibid.*, November 9, 1978.

116. *Catholic Sentinel*, December 29, 1978.

117. Central Catholic became coeducational in August 1979. *Ibid.*, August 31, 1979.

118. The annual cost of operating the school then was $183,000. Students paid $675 in tuition. The diocese provided $58,000 in 1978-1979. However, as the enrollment dropped, diocesan subsidies tended to increase enormously because costs remained practically the same.

119. Only fourteen freshmen were enrolled for the following year. *Inland Register*, May 31, 1979.

120. *Spokesman Review*, May 18, 1979.

121. What the bishop said was that at the present time no plans for closure were being considered.

122. *Spokane Chronicle*, June 8, 1979.

123. *Spokesman Review*, June 20, 1979.

124. *Spokane Chronicle*, June 22, 1979.

125. It should be noted that the bishop pledged the use of Marycliff property for Catholic education. When the property was finally sold in June 1984, for approximately 1.5 million dollars, this money was placed in trust for endowing Spokane's parochial schools.

126. *Spokesman Review*, June 3, 1979. It has since been announced that St. Placid in Olympia will close in the late spring of 1985. Immaculate in Seattle was closed, leaving only four girls' schools, two in the Seattle area, Holy Names and Forest Ridge, and two in the Portland are, St. Mary's and St. Mary's of the Valley.

127. Father Theodore Bradley at St. Agnes church in Ritzville, Washington, for example, hosted in his small rectory fifty-four strangers including a nine-day old baby, who were stranded there for four days.

128. The ash fallout reached Helena, 600 miles distant on Monday, the day following the eruption. "We had to cancel everything," said Father Robert O'Donnell, executive editor of the *Westmont Word*. "Nobody could go anywhere. It was eerie."

129. Martin Pollard, O.S.B., *Mount of Communion: Mt. Angel Abbey 1882-1982*, (St. Benedict, 1982), p. 74.

130. The three sisters' names were: Sister Beverly Greger, Sister Rebecca Mary Bonnell, and Sister Rose Therese Smith.

131. The old chancery in Helena was the Carriage House of the Power Family, behind the T.C. Power mansion. The new chancery was located at 515 Ewing Street, behind the Cathedral.

132. The bishops were John O'Hara and Francis Leipzig; the monsignor was Edmund Murnane.

133. *Idaho Register,* January 30, 1981.

134. Letitia Mary Lyons, S.N.J.M., *A Chronicle of Fort Wright College of the Holy Names, 1960–1982 Normal School 1907– 1938 College 1938–1960,* (Spokane, 1984), p. 1.

135. *Ibid.,* p. 13.

136. The long standing tradition among the sisters, as presented by Sister Letitia Mary Lyons, does not agree with records at Gonzaga University and the testimony of contemporary witnesses. Two points germane to the disagreement should be presented. First, Gonzaga became coeducational at the insistence of Bishop White. Confer Wilfred P. Schoenberg, S.J., *Gonzaga University Seventy-five Years 1887–1962,* (Spokane, 1963), p. 477. Second, as noted *Ibid.,* p. 478, footnote #4, the enrollment of Holy Names College, only four blocks distant then on land donated by the Jesuits, did not decrease after Gonzaga became coeducational; on the other hand, it increased.

137. Portland's first cathedral was dedicated August 15, 1885, eight years after Howard's birth. The cathedral in Vancouver, Washington was dedicated in the same year. The catehdral in Boise was dedicated in 1894. Montana's first cathedral, built as a parish church in Helena, was designated as Brondel's cathedral in 1884.

138. Small children were not allowed to receive Communion until 1910. Viaticum, the Eucharist for the dying, could be received without fasting.

INDEX